Guide to EU and UK Pharmaceutical Regulatory Law

Guide to EU and UK Pharmaceutical Regulatory Law

Eighth Edition

Edited by

Sally Shorthose

Published by:
Kluwer Law International B.V.
PO Box 316
2400 AH Alphen aan den Rijn
The Netherlands
E-mail: lrs-sales@wolterskluwer.com
Website: www.wolterskluwer.com/en/solutions/kluwerlawinternational

Sold and distributed by:
Wolters Kluwer Legal & Regulatory U.S.
920 Links Avenue
Landisville, PA 17538
United States of America
E-mail: customer.service@wolterskluwer.com

Printed on acid-free paper.

ISBN 978-94-035-3025-3

e-Book: ISBN 978-94-035-3023-9
web-PDF: ISBN 978-94-035-3024-6

© 2023 Kluwer Law International BV, The Netherlands

All rights reserved. No part of this publication may be reproduced, stored in a retrieval system, or transmitted in any form or by any means, electronic, mechanical, photocopying, recording, or otherwise, without written permission from the publisher.

Permission to use this content must be obtained from the copyright owner. More information can be found at: www.wolterskluwer.com/en/solutions/legal-regulatory/permissions-reprints-and-licensing

Printed in the Netherlands.

About the Editor and Authors

Editor

Sally Shorthose

Sally joined Bird & Bird in September 2006 as a partner in the Intellectual Property (IP) Group based in London; she is also joint head of the International Life Sciences Regulatory Group.

She trained at Herbert Smith and qualified in 1988, and after a period as a solicitor at that firm, Sally spent eleven years working in-house, first as senior legal advisor at ICI/Zeneca and later as legal director of Novartis, United Kingdom (UK), where she was responsible for all legal matters for the Novartis Group within the UK with particular responsibility for IP protection, regulatory compliance, and competition law compliance. She was head of IP and life sciences at another international firm before joining Bird & Bird.

As a transactional IP lawyer, Sally has been involved in providing advice in relation to the protection and exploitation of a full range of intellectual property rights (IPRs), from design rights to patents, trademarks, copyright, and confidentiality across a range of jurisdictions, both in stand-alone transactions and in conjunction with her corporate colleagues as part of an acquisition, divestment, or investment activity. She provides a full range of IP commercial advice and support to her clients, including licensing, partnering joint ventures, exploitation agreements, research, development, and marketing collaborations. She also frequently advises clients on 'freedom to operate' matters and manages significant due diligence matters.

The other part of her practice relates to providing regulatory advice to all types of life sciences companies. This advice can cover strategic guidance in bringing products to market, assessing hybrid products and classifications, and advertising and promotional matters, as well as supporting colleagues with regulatory litigation matters.

She led the Bird & Bird teams providing advice on the impact of Brexit and is joint head of the newly opened Irish office.

Sally is a regular speaker at conferences and seminars on a range of IP-related subjects, particularly in relation to regulatory, licensing, and exploitation matters.

About the Editor and Authors

BIRD & BIRD LLP
12 New Fetter Lane
London EC4A 1JP
United Kingdom
Tel: +44 (0) 207 415 6000
E-mail: sally.shorthose@twobirds.com

Authors

Edzard Boonen

Edzard is an associate at Bird & Bird in the Dutch IP Group based in The Hague.

Edzard specialises in a broad range of intellectual property rights (IPRs), including trademarks, patents, and copyright, assisting clients both on advisory work and in litigation. Edzard has a special interest in life sciences and food regulatory, advising clients on both the national and European aspects of this complex and ever-evolving field.

He attended Leiden University for his Bachelor of Laws and Master of Laws, in which he specialised in IP Law and was a student tutor at his university.

BIRD & BIRD (NETHERLANDS) LLP
Zuid-Hollandplein 22
2596 AW Den Haag
The Netherlands
Tel: +31 (0)70 353 8800
E-mail: edzard.boonen@twobirds.com

Hester Borgers

Hester is an associate at Bird & Bird in the Dutch IP Group based in Amsterdam.

Hester specialises in regulatory matters (both advisory work and litigation) as well as patent litigation, focused on both the healthcare and life sciences industries. In her regulatory practice, Hester has advised on both a national and European level on topics, including pharmaceuticals, medical devices, (novel) foods, market access, advertising, and packaging matters, clinical trials, price and reimbursement issues, and telemedicine. She is also a board member of the Dutch Pharma & Law Association (in Dutch: *Vereniging Farma & Recht*).

She attended Amsterdam University for her Bachelor of Laws, including a semester at the University of Copenhagen. She further holds a degree from Tilburg University for an LLM in Law & Technology (*cum laude*).

BIRD & BIRD (NETHERLANDS) LLP
SOM1, Gustav Mahlerlaan 42
1082 MC Amsterdam
Netherlands
Tel: +31 (0)20 301 2319
E-mail: hester.borgers@twobirds.com

About the Editor and Authors

Alexander Brøchner

Alexander joined Bird & Bird in 2020 as an associate in the Competition & European Union (EU) group based in Copenhagen.

Alexander advises on all aspects of competition & EU law, including merger control, state aid, anti-competitive agreements, and abuse of dominance. Moreover, Alexander has extensive experience in both contentious and non-contentious competition law matters in the pharma sector and other highly regulated sectors.

After studying law at Aarhus University (2016), Alexander completed his training and qualified in 2020.

BIRD & BIRD ADVOKATPARTNERSELSKAB
Sundkrogsgade 21
2100 Copenhagen
Denmark
Tel: + 45 72 24 12 12
E-mail: alexander.brochner@twobirds.com

Nicolas Carbonnelle

Nicolas is a partner in the Bird & Bird Regulatory and Administrative Practice Group based in Brussels. He is also a member of the International Life Sciences and Food & Beverage Sector Groups.

Nicolas advises on market access, pricing and reimbursement issues, and marketing policies at both the EU and domestic levels. He notably focuses on regulations on the use of biological material for therapeutic applications and scientific research activities, including biobanking. Nicolas also assists clients with issues relating to REACH, CLP, and related regulations on safety and environmental requirements applicable to chemical products and on regulatory law relevant to the conduct of business in the field of Food & Beverage.

Across the spectrum of these sectors, Nicolas assists on borderline product classification and on regulatory path definition and compliance strategies.

Nicolas holds a Law Degree from the Free University of Brussels (ULB, 2007) and a university certificate in Chemical Risk Management (ULB, 2014).

BIRD & BIRD LLP
The Platinum Building
Avenue Louise 235 box 1
1050 Brussels
Belgium
Tel: + 32 2 282 6000
E-mail: nicolas.carbonnelle@twobirds.com

Clara Clark Nevola

Clara works in the Technology Policy team at the Information Commissioner's Office, as a principal policy adviser. She was previously an associate in Data Protection team at Bird & Bird and worked in both London and Paris. She has also spent time as a

About the Editor and Authors

secondee in the Information Commissioner's Office Policy Legal team and as the European legal counsel at an international pharmaceutical company.

Clara has a particular interest in investigating the privacy impact of new technologies and healthcare research. As a lawyer, she has assisted pharmaceutical, biotechnology and medical device companies, healthcare organisations and research institutions, advising on the data protection aspects of complex, often multijurisdictional, projects. At the ICO, she continues to be involved in these industries from the policy development side and focuses particularly on anonymisation, reuse of data for research and biometric technologies. Clara holds a BSc in Biology from Imperial College London and is qualified as a Solicitor in England and Wales.

E-mail: clara.clarknevola@gmail.com

Fenna Douwenga

Fenna was a senior associate in Bird & Bird's IP Group based in The Hague.

Emma Drake

Emma is a Legal Director in Bird & Bird's Privacy and Data Protection Group based in London.

Emma's work covers all aspects of data protection law, including advice on privacy notices, policies, and procedures, data processing and data sharing agreements, data protection impact assessments and data subject rights. She has assisted numerous clients with personal data breaches and knows the importance of prompt pragmatic advice when handling security incidents. She also helps clients with e-privacy compliance.

Emma works with a variety of healthcare and life science clients, from traditional pharmaceutical companies to health informatics providers to new entrants handling patient or healthcare professional data in the context of wellness apps or new technology. She has helped clients with sector-specific issues, including application of research exemptions, anonymisation, assessing the compliance of new medical technologies, and the processing of data for pharmaceutical regulation such as pharmacovigilance.

Over recent years, she has also gained considerable regulatory affairs experience, having worked with organisations seeking amendments to the draft of the General Data Protection Regulation (GDPR) and the UK's data protection framework.

During her time at Bird & Bird, Emma has completed two secondments with clients in the consumer retail and pharmaceutical sectors. She also acts as a data protection officer (DPO) for clients, including a sports governing body. Emma is CIPP/E certified by the International Association of Privacy Professionals and has presented at the IAPP Europe Data Protection Congress.

Emma holds an LLB in European Law from the University of Warwick and has been admitted as a Solicitor since 2012.

About the Editor and Authors

BIRD & BIRD LLP
12 New Fetter Lane
London EC4A 1JP
United Kingdom
Tel: +44 (0) 207 415 6000
E-mail: emma.drake@twobirds.com

Jonathan Edwards

Jonathan was an associate in Bird & Bird's IP Group based in London.

He advises clients across the spectrum of IP rights, with a particular focus on patents and IP enforcement.

Jonathan studied Pharmacology at the University of Manchester at undergraduate level and, upon graduating, spent some time working in the pharmaceutical industry. He completed a Master's in the Management of IP at the Queen Mary University of London before converting to a career in law. He qualified as a solicitor in the IP department at Bird & Bird LLP in 2020, where he completed his training contract. Since qualifying, Jon has been involved in a number of high-profile SEP litigation cases, including Mitsubishi & Anr *v.* Oppo & Ors, Nokia & Anr *v.* Oppo & Ors, and InterDigital & Ors *v.* Oppo & Ors. He also advises a US pharmaceutical company with ongoing patent clearance and infringement advice. Jonathan recently completed his postgraduate diploma in IP at the University of Oxford.

Pieter Erasmus

Pieter is a senior associate in Bird & Bird's IP Group based in London.

Having a keen interest in all things life sciences and healthcare, he specialises primarily in providing regulatory and commercial advice in relation to a broad range of matters in these sectors. His experience includes advising on the regulation of pharmaceuticals, medical devices, general healthcare, clinical trials, marketing and advertising of health products, borderline products, food and beverages (including food supplements and novel foods), cosmetic products, and legislative drafting in the healthcare context.

As a member of the firm's Product Compliance and Liability Group, he further advises on various product compliance matters relating to a broad range of manufactured products being placed on the UK and EU markets, including CE/UKCA marking, RoHS, WEEE, EMC, REACH, and various other product compliance regulations. The implications of Brexit on the regulatory regimes applicable to an extensive range of product compliance regulations (including those applicable to health products) have been a recent focus.

Pieter's practice further includes commercial work, including supporting corporate transactional work and the drafting of a wide range of general and bespoke commercial agreements in the life sciences and healthcare sectors, including transactional IP work.

Before joining Bird & Bird in 2019, Pieter spent more than six years at the Johannesburg offices of Africa's largest law firm. He obtained BComm LLB degrees

About the Editor and Authors

from Stellenbosch University in 2011 and LLM (Biotechnology, Ethics and Law) (with distinction) degree from the University of Cape Town in 2012. He was admitted as an attorney of the High Court of South Africa in 2015 and completed, on a part-time basis, a Master's in Bioethics and Law (with distinction) from the University of Barcelona in 2018.

BIRD & BIRD LLP
12 New Fetter Lane
London EC4A 1JP
United Kingdom
Tel: +44 20 7415 6000
E-mail: pieter.erasmus@twobirds.com

Wolfgang Ernst

Wolfgang was an associate in Bird & Bird's IP Group based in Munich.

Wolfgang's areas of practice include trademark, design, and unfair competition law, but his particular specialisation is in advising clients from heavily regulated industries, most notably from the life sciences sector, but also from related sectors, such as food, beverages, and cosmetics.

Wolfgang is experienced in contentious and non-contentious matters at the interface between IP – in particular, unfair competition – and regulatory law, such as in matters relating to the labelling, distribution and advertising of pharmaceuticals, medical devices, food supplements, and other food products.

Sarah Faircliffe

Sarah Faircliffe is a legal director in the IP Department of Bird & Bird's London office.

She first joined the firm in 1992 by qualifying as a solicitor and specialised in pharmaceutical industry-related IP matters, including litigation and regulatory advice. In 1997, she moved on to work as a legal adviser at the European Medicines Agency (EMA), where she advised on a wide range of issues, including orphan drugs, paediatric medicines, generics of centrally authorised products, advanced therapy products, biosimilars, and various other procedures related to the grant of marketing authorisations. She also worked closely with the European Commission on various litigious matters in the European Courts, which involved the EMA, on the drafting of legislation and guidelines and on the programme to assist the ten new Member States joining the EU in 2004 with bringing their pharmaceutical legislation and procedures in line with EU requirements.

In 2011, Sarah returned to Bird & Bird and now specialises in regulatory law and practice, with a particular emphasis on medicinal products. She advises clients on a wide range of questions relating to the regulation of medicines, medical devices, and other borderline products such as novel foods, and assists them with various regulatory procedures such as applications for authorisation, scientific advice, orphan designation, applications for Paediatric Investigation Plans, approval of invented names, and transfers of authorisation (in particular where the EMA is involved). Sarah also speaks and publishes on a range of pharmaceutical regulatory topics.

About the Editor and Authors

Sarah obtained an honours degree in biochemistry from the University of Oxford (1988) and then went on to The College of Law to study before qualifying as a Solicitor in 1992. She also has an LLM in European and International Law from the European University Institute in Florence, Italy (1995).

BIRD & BIRD LLP
12 New Fetter Lane
London EC4A 1JP
United Kingdom
Tel: +44 (0) 207 415 6000
E-mail: sarah.faircliffe@twobirds.com

Johanna Harelimana

Johanna is an associate in Bird & Bird's Healthcare and Life Sciences group based in Paris.

Her experience includes advising clients on regulatory matters across several sectors, especially in life sciences, food and beverages, and environmental sectors. She advises on product qualification, clinical trials, market access, price and reimbursement, anti-gift regulation, advertising and promotion, e-health (including telemedicine), as well as drafting contracts (distribution, professional services, clinical trial agreements, etc.). She also provides regulatory advice on other products, such as cosmetics, biocides, phytopharmaceuticals, and novel food.

Prior to joining Bird & Bird, Johanna gained professional experience working for a renowned pharmaceutical company which enhanced her understanding of the complex regulatory frameworks pharmaceutical, biotech, and medical devices companies face. She also worked for the French National Agency for the Safety of Medicines and Health Products (ANSM), during which time she gained valuable practical experience in the context of the authorisation, manufacture, and distribution of medicines in the EU.

Johanna holds a Master's in Pharmaceutical Law from the Paris V Descartes University (2017) and is admitted to the Paris Bar (2022).

BIRD & BIRD AARPI
2 rue de la Chaussée d'Antin
Paris 75009
France
Tel: +33(0)1 42 68 6000
E-mail: johanna.harelimana@twobirds.com

Anna Koster

Anna is an associate at Bird & Bird in the Dutch IP Group based in Amsterdam.

Anna specialises in intellectual property law in a broad sense, including patents, trademarks, and copyright. She attended Leiden University for her Master of Laws, with a special focus on IP. During her studies she was an external law clerk at the Court of Appeal in The Hague, where she mainly focused on IP disputes.

About the Editor and Authors

BIRD & BIRD (NETHERLANDS) LLP
SOM1, Gustav Mahlerlaan 42
1082 MC Amsterdam
Netherlands
Tel: +31 (0)70 353 8800
E-mail: anna.koster@twobirds.com

Christian Lindenthal

Christian is a partner in Bird & Bird's IP Department based in Munich.

Having an IP background, Christian specialises in advising clients from heavily regulated industries, most notably from the life sciences sector, but also from related sectors such as food and beverages, and cosmetics. His clients range from global players to innovative start-ups.

Christian is experienced in contentious and non-contentious matters relating to the commercialisation of the products and services offered by clients from these sectors. This includes, in particular, the distribution, labelling, and advertising of pharmaceuticals, medical devices, as well as the provision of healthcare services. He represents clients in substantial and complex litigation – mostly with competitors – as well as advising them on the regulatory and general legal framework for marketing their products in Germany. He further supports clients in contractual matters with creative advice and assists foreign companies in entering the EU market.

Christian completed his legal studies at the University of Hanover and holds a Master's in IP Law from the universities of Dresden and Seattle. He is admitted to the German Bar (2011).

BIRD & BIRD LLP
Maximiliansplatz 22
80333 Munich
Germany
Tel: +49 (0)89 3581 6000
E-mail: christian.lindenthal@twobirds.com

Kevin Munungu

Kevin is a senior associate in Bird & Bird's Regulatory, Public and Administrative Law Department based in Brussels.

Kevin advises both Belgian and international clients on both contentious and non-contentious advice across several regulated sectors, especially in the life sciences and the energy sectors. His areas of expertise include European public procurement and related litigation.

Prior to joining Bird & Bird in 2019, he worked at a Belgian law firm for four years, where he was involved in all areas where authorities interface with businesses, particularly in public procurement, budgetary law (in light of the rules adopted by EUROSTAT) and aviation law.

Kevin is an assistant professor at the Faculty of Law and Criminology at the *Université libre de Bruxelles*, and he regularly speaks at events and publishes reports on Administrative Law and public procurement.

Kevin holds a Master's in Law as well as a PhD in Legal Sciences, both from the *Université Libre de Bruxelles*. He is admitted to the French Association of the Brussels Bar (2015).

BIRD & BIRD LLP
The Platinum Building
Avenue Louise 235 box 1
1050 Brussels
Belgium
Tel: +32 2 282 6000
E-mail: kevin.munungu@twobirds.com

Marc Martens

Marc is the co-head of Bird & Bird's International Life Sciences Group as well as Head of the Regulatory, Public, and Administrative Law Group in Brussels.

Specialising in life sciences, he provides strategic advice (contentious and non-contentious) to Belgian and international pharmaceutical, biotech, and medical devices companies, as well as (national and European) industry associations facing complex regulatory frameworks. Marc's areas of expertise cover issues relating to life-cycle management, clinical trials and data, data exclusivity, marketing, price and reimbursement authorisations, e-health, as well as to distribution and advertising issues. He advises numerous biotech companies and deals with a wide range of issues regarding Advanced Therapy Medicinal Products as well as legal and bioethical issues relating to research and/or the use of human cells and tissues.

His expertise also covers a full range of public procurement, environmental law, REACH, RoHS, WEEE, and other Belgian and EU regulatory issues. He advises companies, public bodies, and industry associations on related matters.

Marc holds a Master's in Law from the Vrije Universiteit Brussel (VUB), where he also worked for four years as a research assistant. He also holds Master's in Public and Administrative Law from the University of Brussels (ULB). Prior to working at Bird & Bird, Marc worked for three years as an expert for the Vice-Prime Minister of Belgium.

Marc regularly publishes and speaks on life sciences regulatory topics and provides an introduction to Biotech Law at the VUB. He is also a member of the Board of the Belgian Biotech sector organisation BIO.BE.

BIRD & BIRD LLP
The Platinum Building
Avenue Louise 235 bte1
1050 Brussels
Belgium
Tel: +32 2 282 6000
E-mail: marc.martens@twobirds.com

About the Editor and Authors

Benedicte Mourisse

Benedicte is an associate in Bird & Bird's Regulatory, Public and Administrative Law Department based in Brussels.

Benedicte advises clients in a wide range of regulated sectors, including life sciences, food, and beverages. She also advises on public and administrative law matters, such as public procurement, in addition to issues relating to environmental law in its broad meaning.

After graduating from the University of Ghent in 2017, Benedicte completed an additional year of study at the Erasmus University of Rotterdam to obtain a Master's in International Trade Law. She was admitted to the Antwerp Bar in 2018 and to the Brussels Bar in 2020.

BIRD & BIRD LLP
The Platinum Building
Avenue Louise 235 box 1
1050 Brussels
Belgium
Tel: +32 2 282 6000
E-mail: benedicte.mourisse@twobirds.com

Morten Nissen

Morten is a partner and co-head of Bird & Bird's International Competition & EU Group based in Copenhagen. He also leads the Competition & EU team in Denmark.

Morten has a particular focus on applying competition & EU law as a tool to achieve specific and measurable business objectives for his clients. His primary focus is on state aid, competition-restricting agreements, and abuse of dominance. His sector experience is particularly strong in the pharmaceutical, copyright, media, IT, telecoms, passenger transport, and international payment systems sectors. Over the years, he has represented clients in a large number of legal procedures before the EU Court of Justice in Luxembourg.

Until 2012, Morten was a partner in Bird & Bird's Brussels office. He left Bird & Bird to start a pharmaceutical business and other start-ups. After this, he was Of Counsel at a leading Danish firm before returning to Bird & Bird in 2018.

Morten is a member of the World Competition and Law and Economics Journals Advisory Board (Kluwer). He holds LLB and LLM, both from the University of Copenhagen, and furthered his law studies at the *Université libre de Bruxelles, Institut d'Études Européenes*. He is admitted to the Danish Bar & Law Society (1998).

BIRD & BIRD ADVOKATPARTNERSELSKAB
Sundkrogsgade 21
2100 Copenhagen
Denmark
Tel: +45 72 24 12 12
E-mail: morten.nissen@twobirds.com

Phillipus Putter

Phillipus is an associate in Bird & Bird's IP Group in London, with a particular interest in life sciences and healthcare.

After studying biomaterials science and tissue engineering at Sheffield University, he completed his DPhil at the University of Oxford, with a research focus on regenerative medicine and neurobiology. After obtaining a Graduate Diploma in Law from City University, Phillipus was called to the Bar of England and Wales in 2021 and qualified as a solicitor in 2022.

Phillipus is involved in a broad range of contentious and non-contentious matters for various healthcare clients, in addition to companies with an interest in the healthcare sector. He advises clients on a wide range of regulatory issues, including medicinal products, medical devices, and borderline products such as novel foods. His experience extends to patent litigation, where he has been instructed in complex multi-jurisdictional disputes before the English courts.

BIRD & BIRD LLP
12 New Fetter Lane
London EC4A 1JP
United Kingdom
Tel: +44 20 7850 7113
E-mail: phillipus.putter@twobirds.com

Nour Saab

Nour joined Bird & Bird's Healthcare and Life Sciences Paris group in January 2022.

After following a double degree in law and history, Nour completed a Master's degree in business law. Having acquired a solid legal foundation, she specialised in medical liability and pharmaceutical law by obtaining a diploma in "Medical Risks and Liability" from the Sorbonne University.

Prior to joining Bird & Bird, she gained professional experience working at a law firm specialised in litigation involving healthcare industries. Her experience allowed her to gain great knowledge of the French healthcare system and the regulatory obligations regarding pharmaceutical products from the start of their lifecycle.

Nour's current position at Bird & Bird includes the provision of legal advice on regulatory issues encountered by Life Sciences companies. She gained regulatory expertise advising clients on matters regarding clinical trials, product classification, market access and CE marking, advertising and promotional activities as well as transparency obligations in relationships with healthcare professionals.

BIRD & BIRD AARPI
2 rue de la Chaussée d'Antin
Paris 75009
France
Tel: +33(0)1 42 68 6019
E-mail: nour.saab@twobirds.com

About the Editor and Authors

Marta Sznajder

Marta was a senior associate in Bird & Bird's IP Group based in Warsaw.

Sophie Vo

Sophie Vo is an associate in the Bird & Bird IP Group in London with a particular focus on the life sciences and healthcare sectors.

Sophie joined Bird & Bird from an Australian law firm, having obtained an honours degree in pharmacology, in conjunction with a law degree, from The University of Sydney. Sophie qualified in Australia with the Supreme Court of NSW in 2019.

Sophie is experienced in a broad range of both contentious and non-contentious matters for pharmaceutical, medical device, and healthcare clients. She has worked with pharmaceutical and medical device suppliers and distributors, hospitals, aged care and disability service providers, private health insurers, and software providers, among a variety of other companies that operate in the life sciences and healthcare space.

Sophie's experience consists of interpreting and advising on complex regulatory frameworks, including medicines and medical devices, aged care, health insurance, and data privacy. She has notably assisted clients with issues regarding software as medical device, advertising compliance, and commercialisation through supply, distribution, and licensing arrangements.

In addition to non-contentious work, Sophie's specialisation extends to patent litigation, having assisted with cases heard before the Federal Court of Australia and now assisting with patent cases before the English courts.

BIRD & BIRD LLP
12 New Fetter Lane
London EC4A 1JP
United Kingdom
Tel: +44 20 3017 6984
E-mail: sophie.vo@twobirds.com

Alexandre Vuchot

Alexandre is a partner in Bird & Bird's International Commercial Group based in Paris. He has been a co-managing partner of the firm's Paris and Lyon offices since 2016.

He offers comprehensive advice on all aspects of general business law and assists on commercial contracts covering distribution, franchise, sales, agency, cooperation and procurement arrangements, acting for suppliers and customers, particularly in the life sciences, retail, technology & communications, as well as gaming, entertainment, and sports sectors.

Alexandre has specific expertise in the field of online business-to-consumer (B2C) matters and advises clients on all aspects of trading practices and marketing with a particular focus on advertising and sales promotion schemes.

About the Editor and Authors

Complementing his commercial expertise, Alexandre leads Bird & Bird's initiatives to support entrepreneurs in the corporate social responsibility (CSR) sector, using this experience to assist clients in the implementation of their CSR initiatives.

Alexandre obtained the DEA, *Droit des affaires* and *Maitrise, Droit des affaires et fiscalité* from the *Université Panthéon Sorbonne (Paris I)* and *Université Panthéon Assas (Paris II)*, respectively. He further holds an LLM in Commercial and Business Law from King's College London. He is admitted to Paris Bar (1997).

BIRD & BIRD AARPI
2 rue de la Chaussée d'Antin
Paris 75009
France
Tel: +33(0)1 42 68 6000
E-mail: alexandre.vuchot@twobirds.com

Peter Willis

Peter Willis is a Partner in Bird & Bird's Competition and EU law practice group based in London. His practice covers all areas of competition law (both EU and UK) and includes advising on investigations by competition authorities and regulators, cartel leniency applications, sector enquiries, complaints, and merger filings.

He brings an in-depth understanding of the interaction between competition rules and the complex technical, commercial, and regulatory arrangements governing the operation of range of technology- and knowledge-based industry sectors, particularly the technology, pharma, energy, and communications sectors.

Peter's work also involves advising on disputes between businesses in which competition and regulatory issues arise, including competition follow-on damages claims. As well as authoring books and articles on EU and UK competition law, Peter is a regular contributor to competition and regulatory issues in the media and at conferences around Europe.

BIRD & BIRD LLP
12 New Fetter Lane
London EC4A 1JP
United Kingdom
Tel: +44 (0) 207 415 6000
E-mail: peter.willis@twobirds.com

Authors of National Variations (Where Not Mentioned Above)

ITALY

Mauro Turrini

Mauro joined Bird & Bird in April 2008 as an associate in the IP and Life Sciences Groups.

After studying law at Bologna University, he completed his training and qualified in 2005. He also completed with merit a specialisation course on IP Law in 2006.

About the Editor and Authors

He has spent a number of years working in both the IP and the life sciences field.

Mauro has been involved in providing advice in relation to the protection and exploitation of a full range of IPRs, from design rights to patents, trademarks, copyright, and confidentiality.

In addition, he worked for both the Italian Medicines Agency (AIFA) and the EMA, where, *inter alia*, he was responsible for all legal matters relating to IP protection and innovation development.

Mauro's current position at Bird & Bird includes the provision of legal advice in several areas relating to the life sciences sector and alike, including pharmaceuticals, medical devices, food additives, and cosmetics, at both national and community levels.

He regularly speaks and writes on IP law and life sciences matters.

STUDIO LEGALE BIRD & BIRD
Via Flaminia n. 133
00196 – Rome
Italy
Tel: +39 06 69 66 7000
E-mail: mauro.turrini@twobirds.com

SPAIN

Ana María Sánchez-Valdepeñas López

Ana María joined Bird & Bird in 2020 as an associate in the Administrative Law Department of Bird & Bird's Madrid office. She is also a member of the International Life Sciences and Food & Beverage Sector Groups.

She specialised in Pharmaceutical Law in 2020, when she started to provide legal advice in multiple matters related to the health and pharmaceutical sectors, such as contracting for the development of clinical studies, the authorisation regime of medicines and medical devices, advertising of medicines and medical devices, labelling of medical devices and medicines, liability for adverse effects of medicines, proceedings before the Spanish Agency for Medicines and Medical Devices (AEMPS), the introduction in the market of medical devices, computer applications, and software for medical purposes, the Spanish regulation of the cultivation and importation of cannabis for medical and research purposes, authorisations for the operation of health centres and clinical laboratories, among other issues.

Her legal services range from preliminary legal advice to legal defence in administrative proceedings before Spanish and European authorities and in contentious-administrative proceedings before national and European Courts.

In addition, she is specialised in public procurement, as well as in regulated economic sectors (including the health sector) following the completion of the Postgraduate title of 'Specialist in Public Procurement' (Deusto University, Spain) and Master in 'Law of Regulated Economic Sectors' (School of Legal Practice, Complutense University of Madrid, Spain).

BIRD & BIRD LLP
Paseo de la Castellana, 7, 7th floor
28046, Madrid
Spain
Tel: + 34 91 790 6000
E-mail: anamaria.sanchezvaldepenas@twobirds.com

Coral Yáñez

Coral is a partner in Bird & Bird's Administrative Law Department based in Madrid and is managing partner of the Madrid office.

She specialised in Pharmaceutical Law in 2002, when she was seconded to Merck Sharp & Dohme España for twelve months. She acquired a deep knowledge of the pharmaceutical business from inside one of the biggest multinationals in the sector. Since then, she has focused on the development of the Life Sciences area of the law firms she has worked on. Before joining Bird &Bird in 2011, Coral worked at Eversheds and at Hogan Lovells.

During her more than twenty years of legal practice, Coral has offered legal advice to pharmaceutical companies settled in Spain and international companies on regulatory issues and administrative proceedings, re-clinical trials, non-interventional studies, marketing authorisations, branded and generic pharmaceutical products, medical devices, price fixing, GMP, parallel trade, etc. She is also an expert litigator acting before the Spanish administrative Courts of Justice.

Coral has been ranked in Chambers since 2016.

BIRD & BIRD LLP
Paseo de la Castellana, 7, 7th floor
28046, Madrid
Spain
Tel: + 34 91 790 6000
E-mail: coral.yanez@twobirds.com

SWEDEN

Gunnar Hjalt

Gunnar is a senior counsel in Bird & Bird's IP Department based in Stockholm.

Gunnar has more than twenty-five years of experience in advising and representing small- and medium-sized clients with valuable IP portfolios, advising when building up and maintaining adequate and balanced IP portfolios while assessing risks, and representing in negotiations and conflicts. He is involved in sectors including life sciences, energy, tech, retail, automotive and sports. He further provides strategic advice in relation to all stages of the product life cycle, from design through to manufacturing, distribution, marketing, and retailing.

Gunnar holds an LLM from Uppsala University and is admitted to the Swedish Patent Attorneys Board and is registered with the EUIPO.

About the Editor and Authors

BIRD & BIRD ADVOKAT KB
Norrlandsgatan 15
Stockholm, SE-103 95
Sweden
Tel: + 46 8 506 320 00
E-mail: gunnar.hjalt@twobirds.com

Gabriel Lidman

Gabriel Lidman is a partner and head of Bird & Bird's IP Group in Stockholm and the Nordics. Gabriel has extensive experience with contentious and non-contentious IP as well as commercial work in the fields of life sciences, technology, and media. Gabriel is also an experienced litigator, regularly advising and representing clients in court disputes and arbitrations.

BIRD & BIRD ADVOKAT KB
Norrlandsgatan 15
Stockholm, SE-103 95
Sweden
Tel: + 46 8 506 320 00
E-mail: gabriel.lidman@twobirds.com

Summary of Contents

About the Editor and Authors	v
List of Abbreviations	lv
Preface	lxi

CHAPTER 1
Brexit
Sally Shorthose — 1

CHAPTER 2
Overview of European Pharmaceutical Regulatory Requirements
Sally Shorthose — 11

CHAPTER 3
Overview of Intellectual Property Rights
Sally Shorthose, Marta Sznajder & Jonathan Edwards — 41

CHAPTER 4
Clinical Trials
Sally Shorthose, Pieter Erasmus, Hester Borgers, Edzard Boonen & Anna Koster — 79

CHAPTER 5
Obtaining a Marketing Authorisation
Sally Shorthose, Sarah Faircliffe & Phillipus Putter — 147

CHAPTER 6
Conditional Marketing Authorisations
Sally Shorthose & Jonathan Edwards — 183

Summary of Contents

CHAPTER 7
Supplementary Protection Certificates
Marta Sznajder & Jonathan Edwards — 201

CHAPTER 8
Paediatrics
Sally Shorthose, Sarah Faircliffe & Pieter Erasmus — 247

CHAPTER 9
Advertising Medicinal Products for Human Use
Hester Borgers & Edzard Boonen (main chapter, the Netherlands); Marc Martens & Benedicte Mourisse (Belgium); Alexandre Vuchot, Johanna Harelimana & Nour Saab (France); Christian Lindenthal & Wolfgang Ernst (Germany); Mauro Turrini (Italy); Coral Yáñez & Ana María Sánchez-Valdepeñas López (Spain); Gabriel Lidman & Gunnar Hjalt (Sweden); and Sally Shorthose, Sarah Faircliffe & Pieter Erasmus (United Kingdom) — 279

CHAPTER 10
Pharmacovigilance
Sally Shorthose, Alexandre Vuchot, Pieter Erasmus, Johanna Harelimana & Nour Saab — 363

CHAPTER 11
Variations to Marketing Authorisations
Alexandre Vuchot, Johanna Harelimana, Nour Saab & Phillipus Putter — 421

CHAPTER 12
Combination Products
Sarah Faircliffe — 447

CHAPTER 13
Abridged Procedure
Pieter Erasmus — 461

CHAPTER 14
Orphan Medicinal Products
Sarah Faircliffe & Pieter Erasmus — 491

CHAPTER 15
Biopharmaceuticals
Marc Martens, Benedicte Mourisse & Sophie Vo — 535

Summary of Contents

CHAPTER 16
Homeopathic, Herbal, and Traditional Herbal Medicinal Products and
Cannabis-Based Medicinal Products
Pieter Erasmus   559

CHAPTER 17
Advanced Therapy Medicinal Products
Marc Martens, Benedicte Mourisse & Sophie Vo   585

CHAPTER 18
Vaccines
Marc Martens & Phillipus Putter   603

CHAPTER 19
Medical Devices
Kevin Munungu & Sophie Vo   631

CHAPTER 20
Parallel Trade
Christian Lindenthal, Pieter Erasmus & Jonathan Edwards   657

CHAPTER 21
Competition Law in the Pharmaceutical Sector
Morten Nissen, Peter Willis & Alexander Brøchner   685

CHAPTER 22
Pandemics and Epidemics
Hester Borgers, Fenna Douwenga, Edzard Boonen & Phillipus Putter   729

CHAPTER 23
Data Protection in the Pharmaceutical Sector
Clara Clark Nevola & Emma Drake   745

Appendix Guidelines and Publications	789
Table of Cases	803
EU Directives	823
Other Legislation	829
EU Regulations	835
Index	839

Table of Contents

About the Editor and Authors	v
List of Abbreviations	lv
Preface	lxi

CHAPTER 1
Brexit
Sally Shorthose 1
§1.01	Introduction		1
	[A]	Legislation	2
	[B]	Medicinal Products and the TCA	2
	[C]	Research	3
	[D]	Clinical Trials	4
	[E]	Marketing Authorisations	4
	[F]	Quality Assurance and Product Safety	5
	[G]	Pharmacovigilance	6
	[H]	Regulatory Authorities	6
	[I]	Parallel Importation	6
§1.02	Specific Impacts on IPR		7
	[A]	Unitary Patent System	7
	[B]	SPCs	7
	[C]	Trademarks and Registered Community Designs	8

CHAPTER 2
Overview of European Pharmaceutical Regulatory Requirements
Sally Shorthose 11
§2.01	Introduction		11
	[A]	History of Pharmaceutical Regulation	11
	[B]	The European Union	13

Table of Contents

	[C]	Major EU Pharmaceutical Legislation	14
	[D]	Key EU Pharmaceutical Reform Legislation	15
	[E]	National Law and Interface with EU Directives	15
§2.02		Definitions	16
	[A]	Medicinal Product	16
	[B]	Generic Medicinal Products	16
	[C]	Paediatric Medicines	16
	[D]	Orphan Drugs	17
	[E]	Biotechnology-Derived Medicinal Products	18
	[F]	Homeopathic Medicinal Products	18
	[G]	Herbal Medicinal Products	18
	[H]	Traditional Herbal Medicinal Products	19
	[I]	Radiopharmaceuticals	20
	[J]	Non-prescription Medicines	20
	[K]	Immunological Medicinal Products	21
	[L]	In-vitro Diagnostic Devices	21
	[M]	Medical Devices	22
§2.03		The Regulatory Agencies	23
	[A]	The European Commission	23
		[1] DG Health and Consumers (Commonly Known as 'SANTE')	23
		[2] The EMA	25
	[B]	Committees of the EMA	26
		[1] CHMP	26
		[2] CVMP	28
		[3] COMP	28
		[4] HMPC	29
		[5] PDCO	29
		[6] CAT	30
		[7] PRAC	31
	[C]	The Heads of Medicines Agencies	32
	[D]	NCAs of European Member States	32
	[E]	CMDh	33
	[F]	European Directorate for the Quality of Medicines	34
	[G]	International Conference on Harmonisation of Technical Requirements for Registration of Pharmaceuticals for Human Use	34
§2.04		Applicable EU Legislation, Including Regulations and Guidance	35
	[A]	EU Treaties	35
	[B]	Directives	36
	[C]	Regulations	36

		[D]	The Official Journal of the European Communities	37
		[E]	Guidelines	37
§2.05			Guidelines/Publications	39

CHAPTER 3
Overview of Intellectual Property Rights
Sally Shorthose, Marta Sznajder & Jonathan Edwards   41

§3.01					Introduction	41
	[A]				The Importance of IPRs	42
	[B]				Ownership	43
§3.02					Patents	43
	[A]				European Patents	44
		[1]			Patentability and Scope of Protection	45
			[a]		Requirements	45
			[b]		Novelty and Inventive Step	46
			[c]		Scope of Protection	47
		[2]			Prosecution and Enforcement	48
			[a]		EPO Opposition Proceedings	48
			[b]		National Courts	49
		[3]			Duration	49
	[B]				Specific Issues Relating to Pharmaceutical Patents	50
		[1]			Product by Process	50
		[2]			Products Obtained Directly by a Patented Process	50
		[3]			New Chemical Entities (NCEs)	51
		[4]			Composition and Formulation Claims	51
		[5]			Methods of Treatment	51
		[6]			Medical Use	52
		[7]			Biotechnological Inventions	54
	[C]				Infringement and Defences	56
		[1]			Bolar Exemption	56
		[2]			Experimental Use Defence	57
	[D]				Unitary Patent System	57
		[1]			The Legislative Framework	59
			[a]		Legislative Instruments	59
			[b]		Ratification	60
		[2]			Unitary Patent	60
		[3]			UPC	61
		[4]			Practical Considerations	62
			[a]		Cost	62
			[b]		Divisional Applications	62
			[c]		Opting Out	62
			[d]		Licences and Technology Transfer Agreements	62
§3.03					SPCs	63
§3.04					Trademarks	63

Table of Contents

		[A]	Registration of Trademarks	64
			[1] Routes to Registration	64
			[2] Criteria for Registration	65
			[a] Absolute Grounds	65
			[b] Relative Grounds	66
			[3] Duration	67
		[B]	Regulatory Issues with Pharmaceutical Names	68
			[1] International Nonproprietary Names	68
			[2] Public Health Concerns and Patient Safety	70
			[a] Purely National, Mutual Recognition and Decentralised Procedures	70
			[b] Centralised Procedure	71
		[C]	Trademark Infringement	72
			[1] Criteria for Establishing Infringement	72
			[2] Parallel Imports	74
	§3.05	Copyright, Database Rights, & Design Rights		74
		[A]	Copyright	74
		[B]	Database Rights	74
		[C]	Design Rights	75
	§3.06	Confidential Information		76

CHAPTER 4
Clinical Trials
Sally Shorthose, Pieter Erasmus, Hester Borgers, Edzard Boonen & Anna Koster   79

§4.01	Introduction		79
§4.02	Regulation (EU) No. 536/2014: CTR		81
	[A] Introduction to the CTR		81
	[B] When the CTR Applies		81
	[C] Implementation of the CTR		82
	[D] Aims of the CTR		82
§4.03	Authorisation Procedure for a Clinical Trial		83
	[A] Introduction to the Authorisation of a Clinical Trial		83
	[B] CTIS		84
	[C] Authorisation Procedure for a Clinical Trial		85
	[D] Ethical Committee Approval		90
		[1] Introduction	90
		[2] Ethical Committee Approval Process	91
	[E] Informed Consent		93
§4.04	The Substantial Modification of a Clinical Trial		96
§4.05	Start, End, Halt, and Early Termination		97
	[A] Start		98
	[B] End		98
	[C] Halt		99
	[D] Early Termination		100

Table of Contents

§4.06	Conduct of the Clinical Trial		100
	[A] Introduction to the Conduct of Clinical Trials		100
	[B] GCP Standards		101
	[C] Good Manufacturing Practice		103
§4.07	Clinical Trial Oversight/Role of the sponsor and Investigator		104
	[A] Introduction to Clinical Trial Oversight		104
	[B] Monitoring		105
	[C] GCP Inspection		107
	[D] Sponsor and Investigator as the Same Entity		108
	[E] Pharmacovigilance		109
§4.08	Trial Data		112
	[A] Introduction to Trial Data		112
	[B] Public Access to Trial Data		112
	[C] The Trial Master File: Essential Documents		113
	[D] Archiving of the Trial Master File		114
	[E] Collection of Data		114
	[F] Protection of Data and Storage Requirements		116
§4.09	FIM Studies Following the TGN1412 Case ('TeGenero')		118
	[A] Background		118
	[B] Revised CHMP Guidelines as a Result of the TeGenero Case		120
§4.10	Clinical Trials and Patent Legislation: The Bolar and Research Exceptions		121
§4.11	Introduction to Clinical Trials in the UK		122
	[A] Introduction		122
	[B] When the UK Regulations Apply		122
	[C] Consultation for Legislative Change (2022)		123
§4.12	Preparing to Apply for CTIMP Authorisation in the UK		125
	[A] Introduction		125
	[B] The Sponsor and Overview of Sponsor Duties		125
	[1] The Sponsor		125
	[2] Overview of Sponsor Duties		125
	[C] The Investigator, Chief Investigator, and Principal Investigator		127
	[D] Registration and Preparing the CTIMP Authorisation Application		127
	[E] Requests for MHRA Scientific Advice		129
§4.13	Approval to Commence a CTIMP in the UK		130
	[A] Introduction to the CTIMP Authorisation Process in the UK		130
	[B] MHRA CTIMP Authorisation		130
	[C] REC Approval		131
	[D] HRA Approval		133
§4.14	Conduct of CTIMPs in the UK		133
§4.15	UK CTIMP Oversight		134
	[A] Introduction to CTIMP Oversight		134
	[B] Monitoring		134

Table of Contents

		[C]	MHRA GCP Inspections	135
		[D]	Internal Audit	136
		[E]	Urgent Safety Measures	136
		[F]	Pharmacovigilance	137
§4.16	Amendments, Suspension, and Termination of CTIMPs in the UK			138
		[A]	Introduction	138
		[B]	Amendments by the REC or the MHRA	138
		[C]	Substantial Amendments by the Sponsor	138
		[D]	Temporary Suspension of CTIMPs	140
		[E]	Early Termination of CTIMPs	140
		[F]	End of CTIMPs	140
		[G]	CTIMP Summary Results	141
§4.17	CTIMP Data in the UK			141
		[A]	Introduction	141
		[B]	Dissemination of CTIMP Results	141
		[C]	Storage of Trial Master File	143
		[D]	Access to NHS Electronic Health Records	144
§4.18	Guidelines/Publications			145

CHAPTER 5
Obtaining a Marketing Authorisation
Sally Shorthose, Sarah Faircliffe & Phillipus Putter   147

§5.01	Approval of Medicines for Human Use: Securing a Marketing Authorisation				147
		[A]	Introduction and Overview of the Processes		147
		[B]	Goals of the Approval Process: Demonstration of Quality, Safety, and Efficacy		148
		[C]	Legislative Background		148
		[D]	Overview of the Application Dossier		150
		[E]	Overview of the MA Procedures		150
§5.02	Requirements of the Application Dossier				151
		[A]	Required Contents of an Application Dossier		152
			[1]	Manufacturing Authorisations	153
			[2]	Assurance of Quality of All Constituents	154
			[3]	New Active Substances	154
			[4]	Certification of Suitability (CEP)	155
			[5]	Orphan Drugs	155
			[6]	Naming the Product	155
			[7]	Required Product Information	156
			[8]	SmPC	156
			[9]	Environmental Risks	157
			[10]	Pharmacovigilance Systems	157
			[11]	Submission of Test Results	157
		[B]	Presentation of the Dossier: CTDoc		158

§5.03	The CP			159
	[A]	Scope		159
		[1]	Optional Scope	160
		[2]	Mandatory Scope	160
	[B]	Submission to the EMA		161
	[C]	Application and Approval Procedure: An Overview		162
		[1]	The CHMP	163
		[2]	Rapporteur of the CHMP	163
		[3]	CHMP Assessment	164
		[4]	Commission Decision	165
		[5]	Withdrawal	165
		[6]	Publication	166
	[D]	Marketing a Medicine		166
	[E]	Special Procedures		167
		[1]	Compassionate Use	167
		[2]	Conditional/Exceptional Circumstances Authorisations	167
	[F]	Timing of the Process		168
	[G]	Alternatives to the CP		168
§5.04	MRP			168
	[A]	Introduction		168
	[B]	Application Process		169
	[C]	Dispute Procedure		170
	[D]	Timing of the Process		171
§5.05	DCP			171
	[A]	Introduction		171
	[B]	Application Process		172
	[C]	Dispute Procedure		172
	[D]	Timing of the Procedure		172
§5.06	The National Procedure			173
	[A]	Introduction		173
	[B]	Application Process		173
§5.07	Summary and Comparison of the Four Procedures			173
	[A]	The CP		173
	[B]	MRP		175
	[C]	The DCP		175
	[D]	The National Procedure		176
§5.08	Continuing Validity, Renewal, and Termination of MAs			177
§5.09	Obtaining MA in the UK			178
	[A]	Introduction		178
	[B]	Overview of the MA Procedures in the UK		178
	[C]	Summary		180
§5.10	Guidelines/Publications			181

Table of Contents

CHAPTER 6
Conditional Marketing Authorisations
Sally Shorthose & Jonathan Edwards — 183

§6.01	Introduction			183
§6.02	Criteria for a CMA			184
	[A]	New MAAs		184
	[B]	Justification That the Medicinal Product Falls Within the Scope of a CMA		185
		[1]	Seriously Debilitating Diseases or Life-Threatening Diseases	185
		[2]	Medicinal Products to Be Used in Emergency Situations	187
			[a] Influenza Pandemic	187
			[b] Bioterrorism	187
			[c] COVID-19 Pandemic	188
		[3]	Orphan Medicinal Products	189
	[C]	Requirements for a CMA		190
		[1]	The Risk/Benefit Balance of the Product Is a Positive	190
		[2]	It Is Likely That the Applicant Will Be Able to Provide Comprehensive Data	190
		[3]	Fulfilment of Unmet Medical Needs	191
		[4]	The Benefits to Public Health of Immediate Availability Outweigh the Risks Inherent in the Fact That Additional Data Are Still Required	192
	[D]	Specific Obligations		192
	[E]	Timeframe		193
	[F]	Amendment to Full MA		193
§6.03	Procedure			193
	[A]	Prior to Submission of a CMA		193
	[B]	Timing of the Submission and Documentation to Be Supplied		193
		[1]	Documents to Be Submitted	194
			[a] General Requirements	194
			[b] Requirements for the Interim Report on the Specific Obligations	195
			[c] CHMP Assessment and Opinion	196
	[C]	CHMP Assessment of a Request for a CMA		196
	[D]	Information Included in the Summary of Product Characteristics and Package Leaflet		197
	[E]	EMA Timetable		197
§6.04	MA Granted in Exceptional Circumstances			197
§6.05	United Kingdom			198
§6.06	Guidelines/Publications			199

CHAPTER 7
Supplementary Protection Certificates
Marta Sznajder & Jonathan Edwards — 201

§7.01	Introduction		201
§7.02	The Legislation		202
§7.03	Duration and Scope		204
	[A]	Duration	204
		[1] Basic Term	204
		[2] Paediatric Extensions for Medicinal Product SPCs	205
	[B]	Scope	206
		[1] What Is a 'Product'?	207
		[2] The Distinction Between a 'Product' and a 'Medicinal Product'	209
§7.04	The Procedure for Seeking SPC Protection		210
	[A]	Time Limit	210
	[B]	Content of the Application	211
	[C]	Conditions for Obtaining an SPC	212
	[D]	Entitlement	212
	[E]	Third-Party Oppositions and Observations	213
§7.05	Infringement and Invalidation		213
§7.06	Transitional Provisions		214
§7.07	Issues in Relation to SPCs		217
	[A]	When Is a Product 'Protected by a Basic Patent in Force'?	218
		[1] Construction of Patent Claims	218
		[2] Combination Products	219
		[3] Amendments to the Basic Patent	224
		[4] Functional Specifications	225
		[5] Multiple SPCs Based upon a Single Patent	226
	[B]	The Product Has Not Already Been the Subject of a Certificate	227
	[C]	First Authorisation to Place the Product on the Market as a Medicinal Product	228
		[1] 'First Authorisation'	228
		[2] Date of First Authorisation	231
	[D]	What Happens When the Basic Patent and MA Have Different Holders?	231
	[E]	What Form Can an SPC 'Claim' Take and What Effect Does It Have on the Scope of Protection Conferred?	232
§7.08	Legislative Changes and Reforms		233
	[A]	SPC Manufacturing Waiver	233
	[B]	The Unitary Patent System and SPCs	234
		[1] European SPC	235
		[2] Unitary SPCs	236
		[a] Grant Authority	236
		[b] Scope	236

Table of Contents

		[c]	Brexit		237
		[d]	Reform		237
	[C]	Medical Devices			237
		[1]	Does the Scope of the SPC Regulation Extend to Medical Devices?		238
		[2]	European Decisions Concerning Class III Medical Devices		239
		[3]	Active Implantable Medical Devices		242
		[4]	Borderline Products		242
		[5]	Reform		243
§7.09	UK				243
	[A]	Procedure for Seeking SPC Protection Post-Brexit			244
	[B]	Duration			245
	[C]	Paediatric Extensions			245
	[D]	SPC Manufacturing Waiver			246
	[E]	CJEU Interpretation			246

CHAPTER 8
Paediatrics
Sally Shorthose, Sarah Faircliffe & Pieter Erasmus   247

§8.01	Introduction				247
§8.02	European Regulations Relating to Paediatric Studies				248
	[A]	Overview of the EU Paediatric Regulation			248
	[B]	PDCO			249
	[C]	PIPs			250
		[1]	PIP Approval Procedures		252
		[2]	PIP Compliance Check		254
		[3]	Issues Concerning PIPs		255
	[D]	PIP Exemptions, Waivers, and Deferrals			257
		[1]	Exemptions		257
		[2]	Waivers		257
		[3]	Deferrals		258
§8.03	Rewards for PIP Completion				258
	[A]	The SPC Extension Reward			258
		[1]	Zero and Negative-Term SPCs		260
	[B]	Rewards for Orphan Medicinal Products That Comply with Regulation (EC) No. 1901/2006			261
	[C]	Free Scientific Advice from EMA			263
§8.04	Paediatric Use Marketing Authorisation (PUMA)				263
§8.05	Post-Approval Obligations				265
	[A]	Duty to Place Product on Market			265
	[B]	Pharmacovigilance			265
	[C]	Product Discontinuation			265
	[D]	The Paediatric Symbol			266
§8.06	Penalties				266

§8.07	Transparency	267
§8.08	Paediatric Research	267
§8.09	Developments	269
§8.10	UK	271
	[A] Introduction	271
	[B] PIP Submissions	272
	[C] PIP Modifications	273
	[D] PIP Waivers	274
	[E] Compliance Checks	274
	[F] Completed Paediatric Studies	275
§8.11	Guidelines/Publications	275

CHAPTER 9
Advertising Medicinal Products for Human Use
Hester Borgers & Edzard Boonen (main chapter, the Netherlands); Marc Martens & Benedicte Mourisse (Belgium); Alexandre Vuchot, Johanna Harelimana & Nour Saab (France); Christian Lindenthal & Wolfgang Ernst (Germany); Mauro Turrini (Italy); Coral Yáñez & Ana María Sánchez-Valdepeñas López (Spain); Gabriel Lidman & Gunnar Hjalt (Sweden); and Sally Shorthose, Sarah Faircliffe & Pieter Erasmus (United Kingdom) 279

§9.01	Introduction	279
§9.02	Legislative Basis	282
	[A] The General Principles	282
	[B] Promotion of OTC Medicines	283
	[C] What Is Advertising?	285
	[D] Internet Advertising	285
	[E] Television Advertising	286
	[F] European Case Law on Advertising of Medicinal Products	286
§9.03	Self-Regulation in Europe	289
	[A] Advertising of Prescription-Only Products	289
	[1] The EFPIA HCP Code	289
	[2] Applicability of the EFPIA Code	290
	[3] EFPIA Code and Principles for the Use of Digital Channels	290
	[B] Advertising of OTC Products	290
§9.04	Implementation in Belgium	291
	[A] Legal Basis	291
	[B] Sanctions	291
	[C] Role of the National Competent Authority	291
	[D] Self-Regulation	292
	[E] Cases	293
	[F] General Advertising Rules	293
§9.05	Implementation in France	293
	[A] Legal Bases	293

Table of Contents

		[1]	Binding Rules		293
		[2]	Non-binding Rules		294
	[B]	Scope of Application			295
	[C]	French Legal Requirements			296
		[1]	Medicinal Products Advertising		296
			[a]	Medicinal Products Advertising Directed at Healthcare Professionals	297
			[b]	Medicinal Products Advertising Directed at the Public	297
		[2]	Medical Devices Advertising		297
	[D]	Specific Forms of Advertising			298
		[1]	Meetings and Congresses		298
		[2]	Advantages and Gifts		298
		[3]	Samples of Medicinal Products		300
	[E]	Sanctions			301
		[1]	Administrative Sanctions		301
			[a]	Administrative Authorities	301
			[b]	Control of Advertising Directed at the Public	301
			[c]	Control of Advertising Directed at Healthcare Professionals	302
		[2]	Criminal Sanctions		302
§9.06	Implementation in Germany				303
	[A]	Legal Basis			303
	[B]	Scope of the Advertising of Medicinal Products Act			303
	[C]	National Sanctions			304
	[D]	Role of the National Competent Authority			305
	[E]	National Implementation Beyond Requirements of Directive 2001/83/EC			305
		[1]	Testimonials		305
		[2]	Internet Presentations		306
		[3]	Advertising for Telemedicinal Services		307
		[4]	Further Requirements		307
	[F]	Self-regulation			308
§9.07	Implementation in Italy				308
	[A]	Legal Basis			308
	[B]	Scope of the Decree			308
	[C]	Role of the National Competent Authority			309
	[D]	Self-Regulation for Promotion of Prescription-Only Products			310
	[E]	Self-Regulation for Promotion of OTC Products			310
	[F]	General Advertising Rules			310
	[G]	Regional Control			311
	[H]	National Sanctions			311
	[I]	Online Sales of Medicinal Products on the Internet			311
§9.08	Implementation in The Netherlands				312

	[A]	Legal Basis			312
		[1]	The Dutch Medicines Act		312
			[a]	Enforcement	313
			[b]	Sanctions	313
			[c]	Inspections	314
			[d]	Cooperation with Other Regulating Institutes	315
	[B]	Civil Law			315
	[C]	Criminal Law			316
	[D]	Self-regulation			316
		[1]	Enforcement		316
		[2]	Sanctions		317
		[3]	Code of Conduct Pharmaceutical Advertising		317
			[a]	Information	318
			[b]	Comparative Advertising	319
			[c]	Samples	319
			[d]	Internet Advertising	319
		[4]	OTC Advertising Code		320
		[5]	Inducement		320
			[a]	Gifts	321
			[b]	Hospitality	321
			[c]	Sponsoring and Grants	322
			[d]	Services	322
	[E]	Medical Devices			323
	[F]	Healthcare Products			323
§9.09	Implementation in Spain				324
	[A]	Regulatory Aspects			324
		[1]	Legal Basis		324
		[2]	The General Principles as Interpreted by Spanish Authorities		325
		[3]	Advertising Aimed at Persons Qualified to Prescribe or Supply Medicinal Products		325
			[a]	Advertising Using the Internet	326
		[4]	Advertising Aimed at the General Public		327
	[B]	Infringements and Remedies under the Law			328
	[C]	Self-regulation			332
		[1]	Spanish Code of Good Practice for the Pharmaceutical Industry		332
			[a]	Promotion of Medicines and Interaction with Healthcare Professionals	332
			[b]	Relationships Between the Pharmaceutical Industry and Patient Organisations	334
		[2]	Spanish Code of Good Practices for the Promotion and Advertising of Non-Prescription Medicinal Products		335
	[D]	Infringements and Remedies under the Farmaindustria Code			335

Table of Contents

§9.10	Implementation in Sweden			336
	[A]	Legal Basis		336
	[B]	Scope of the Regulations		338
	[C]	Role of the MPA: The National Competent Authority		338
		[1]	Complaints to the MPA	338
		[2]	Sanctions	339
	[D]	Self-Regulation		339
		[1]	The LIF	340
		[2]	The Ethical Rules	340
		[3]	The IGN and the NBL	341
		[4]	The IGN	341
		[5]	The NBL	342
		[6]	Agreements on Forms of Collaboration with the Healthcare Sector	343
		[7]	Other Applicable Rules	344
§9.11	Implementation in the UK			344
	[A]	Legal Basis		344
	[B]	Scope of the Regulations		346
	[C]	Regulation by the MHRA		347
		[1]	The Blue Guide	347
		[2]	Advertising Using the Internet	347
		[3]	Complaints to the MHRA	349
	[D]	Sanctions		350
	[E]	Self-Regulation		351
		[1]	The Association of the British Pharmaceutical Industry (ABPI) and PMCPA	352
		[2]	PAGB	354
			[a] The PAGB Consumer Code	355
			[b] The PAGB Professional Code	355
	[F]	ASA		356
	[G]	Association of British Healthcare Industries (ABHI)		357
Annex: Case Histories				358

Chapter 10
Pharmacovigilance
Sally Shorthose, Alexandre Vuchot, Pieter Erasmus, Johanna Harelimana & Nour Saab   363

§10.01	Introduction and Background			363
§10.02	Pre-authorisation Pharmacovigilance			367
	[A]	Legislative Framework		368
	[B]	First-in-Man Trials		370
		[1]	Case Study 1	371
	[C]	Clinical Trials in Patients		371
	[D]	The Investigator Brochure		372

xxxviii

	[E]	Reporting SUSARs	372
§10.03		The Marketing Authorisation Application	372
	[A]	Legislative Framework	373
	[B]	The Requirements Set Out in Directive 2001/83/EC	375
	[C]	The Reporting of Adverse Reactions	377
		[1] Reports to the MAH	377
		[2] Reports from Patients/Consumers	378
		[3] Reports with Name of Active Substance Only	379
		[4] Literature Reports	379
		[5] Reports from Non-Medical Sources	380
		[6] Timescales for Expedited Reporting	380
		[7] MedDRA	381
		[8] Electronic Reporting	381
		[9] Pregnancy Registries	382
		[10] Lack of Efficacy	382
		[11] Abuse, Misuse, or Overdose	382
		[12] Public Health Emergency	382
§10.04		PSURs	383
	[A]	Introduction	383
	[B]	Contents of the PSUR	383
	[C]	Periodicity of Submission of PSUR	384
	[D]	PSUR Work-Sharing Initiative	385
§10.05		The Pharmacovigilance Activities of the Key Parties	386
	[A]	The EMA	386
	[B]	Pharmacovigilance Working Party	387
	[C]	Competent Authorities of the Member States	387
§10.06		Risk Management and EU-RMP	390
	[A]	Introduction	390
	[B]	Content of the EU-RMP	391
	[C]	Monitoring of the Risk/Benefit Balance and Identification of Safety Signals	392
	[D]	Risk Management at the MAH's Initiative	392
	[E]	Risk Management at the EMA's Initiative	393
		[1] Case Study 2: Cerivastatin (Lipobay) Withdrawal	394
	[F]	Risk Management at National Competent Authorities' Initiative	395
		[1] Case Study 3: Bupropion	396
§10.07		Compliance with Pharmacovigilance Obligations	396
	[A]	Legal Basis for Pharmacovigilance Inspections	397
	[B]	Composition of the Inspection Team	398
	[C]	Timing of Inspections	399
	[D]	Conduct of Pharmacovigilance Inspections	400
	[E]	Common Findings of Inspections	401
	[F]	Sanctions	403
§10.08		Summary of Recent Changes	405

Table of Contents

	[A]	Pharmacovigilance System Master File	405
	[B]	Coordination and Inspection: PRAC	406
	[C]	PASS and PAES	408
	[D]	Specific Conditions Relating to PhV affecting EMA	409
		[1] PSUR Requirements	409
		[2] Set-Up of Interconnected Web Portals	410
		[3] GVP Guidelines	410
§10.09	UK		410
	[A]	Introduction	410
	[B]	Submission and Receipt of ICSRs	412
	[C]	Signal Detection	413
	[D]	Risk Management Plans (RMPs)	413
	[E]	Periodic Safety Update Reports (PSURs)	414
	[F]	Post Authorisation Safety Studies (PASS)	415
	[G]	Safety Referrals	416
	[H]	Major Safety Reviews	417
	[I]	Post-authorisation Measures (PAMs)	417
	[J]	Implementation of Outcomes of EU Referrals and Procedures Concerning PSURs, PASS, Signal Assessments and PAMs	418
	[K]	Requirements for MAs Granted via the Unfettered Access route	418
	[L]	Submitting ICSRS	418
	[M]	Provision of Other Pharmacovigilance Data	418
§10.10	Guidelines/Publications		418

CHAPTER 11
Variations to Marketing Authorisations
Alexandre Vuchot, Johanna Harelimana, Nour Saab & Phillipus Putter 421

§11.01	Reason for Variations			421
	[A]	Changes Not Requiring a Variation		422
	[B]	Variation Legislation		422
§11.02	Classification of Changes			423
	[A]	Types IA and IB		423
		[1] Type IA		423
		[2] Type IB		425
		[3] Re-classification of Type IA and Type IB Variations		425
	[B]	Type II		425
		[1] Definition		425
		[2] Type II Categories		425
		[3] The International Council on Harmonisation (ICH) Design Space Concept		426
			[a] Introduction	426
			[b] Process Analytical Technology (PAT)	427
			[c] Quality Risk Management	427
	[C]	Extensions		427

xl

		[1]	Changes in Pharmaceutical Form	428
		[2]	Changes in Strength	428
	[D]		Classification of Unforeseen Variations	429
§11.03			Substantive Requirements of the Variation Application	429
	[A]		Variation Applications for Biological Medicinal Products	430
		[1]	Issues Arising in Relation to Biologicals	430
		[2]	Regulatory Guidelines	430
		[a]	Quality Guidelines	431
		[b]	Safety and Efficacy Requirements	431
§11.04			Variation Application Procedure	432
	[A]		Forms and Format	432
	[B]		Grouping of Applications	433
		[1]	Grouping of Variations Granted under the Mutual Recognition, Decentralised and Centralised Procedures	433
		[2]	Grouping of Variations to Purely National MAs	434
	[C]		Work-Sharing Procedure	434
	[D]		Products Authorised Through Mutual Recognition	436
		[1]	Type IA	436
		[2]	Type IB	437
		[3]	Type II	438
	[E]		Centrally Authorised Products	439
		[1]	Advance Notice	439
		[2]	Type IA and IB Variations	439
		[3]	Type II Variations	439
	[F]		Purely National Procedure	441
		[1]	Type IA Variations	441
		[2]	Type IB Variations	441
		[3]	Type II Variations	441
	[G]		Urgent Safety Restrictions	442
	[H]		Human Influenza Vaccines	443
	[I]		Human Coronavirus Vaccines	443
§11.05			Variations to MAs in the UK	443
	[A]		Introduction	443
	[B]		Variation Procedure in the UK	444
	[C]		Northern Ireland	446
	[D]		Summary	446

CHAPTER 12
Combination Products
Sarah Faircliffe 447

§12.01		Introduction	447
	[A]	Combination Products	447
	[B]	Combination Products: Requirement for a MA and Regulatory Data Protection	448

Table of Contents

§12.02	Requirements for Marketing Approval of Fixed-Combination Medicinal Products		450
	[A]	The Application Dossier	450
	[B]	The Application Procedure	450
	[C]	Scientific References, Non-Clinical Tests, and Clinical Trials	451
	[D]	Necessity for Non-Clinical Tests and Clinical Trials	452
		[1] Situations Where Additional Studies Are Necessary	452
		[2] Situations Where Fewer Studies Are Necessary	453
		[a] Combinations Already in Widespread Use as Free Combination Therapy	453
		[b] Combination of Components Already Approved as a Fixed-Combination Product	455
§12.03	Criteria for Approval of Fixed-Combination Products		455
	[A]	The Risk/Benefit Ratio	455
	[B]	Relevance of Each Active Substance of the Combination	457
	[C]	Relevance of the Specific Dosage Regime	457
§12.04	UK		457
§12.05	Guidelines/Publications		458

CHAPTER 13
Abridged Procedure
Pieter Erasmus   461

§13.01	Introduction		461
§13.02	Three Types of Abridged Procedures		462
	[A]	Abridged Procedure Based on Cross-Reference to Data with Holder's Consent	463
	[B]	Abridged Procedure Based on Bibliographic Application for Well-Established Use	464
		[1] Well-Established Medicinal Use	464
		[2] Ten Years of Use	465
§13.03	Abridged Procedure for Generic Products		466
	[A]	Data Protection of a Registration File for Six or Ten Years	466
	[B]	Data Protection and Marketing Exclusivity, 8 + 2 Years	469
	[C]	Data Protection Rules Applicable Within the EU until 30 October 2015	469
	[D]	European Reference Medicinal Product	470
		[1] Global MA	472
		[2] Reference to Products Authorised in the Member States: Cyprus, Lithuania, Malta, Poland, and Slovenia	473
		[3] Similar Biological Medicinal Products	474
	[E]	Essential Similarity and Generic Medicinal Product	474
		[1] Development of 'Essentially Similar' and Scope of Abridged Procedure for Generic Medicinal Products up to October/November 2005	474

xlii

		[a]	Meaning of 'Essential Similarity'	475
		[b]	Scope of Application of the Hybrid Abridged Procedure	476
		[c]	Essential Similarity and Line Extensions	478
		[d]	Differences in Active Substance	478
		[e]	Safety and Efficacy	479
	[F]	Abridged Procedures for Generic Medicinal Products after October 2005		480
		[1]	Definition of 'Generic Product' (Instead of 'Essentially Similar')	480
			[a] Same Qualitative and Quantitative Composition	481
			[b] Same Pharmaceutical Form	481
			[c] Bioequivalence Demonstrated by Studies	481
			[d] Salts, Esters, Ethers, Isomers, Mixtures, Complexes, or Derivations	482
			[e] The Hybrid Procedure	482
			[f] New Active Substance	483
	[G]	Additional Terms for Protection of Line Extensions		484
		[1]	Extension for New Therapeutic Indication	485
			[a] Justification of New 'Therapeutic Indication'	486
			[b] Justification of 'Significant Clinical Benefit'	486
		[2]	Extension for New Indications for Well-Established Substances	487
		[3]	Change of Supply Status	488
§13.04	UK			489

CHAPTER 14
Orphan Medicinal Products
Sarah Faircliffe & Pieter Erasmus 491

§14.01	Introduction			491
§14.02	The EU Orphan Medicinal Product Regulation			492
§14.03	Applications for Orphan Designation			493
	[A]	Pre-application Meeting		493
	[B]	Application Contents and Format		494
	[C]	COMP		495
	[D]	Criteria for Orphan Designation		495
		[1]	Medicinal Product	495
		[2]	Article 3(1) Requirements	495
		[3]	Article 3(1)(a) Requirements	496
			[a] The Prevalence Criterion	496
			[b] The Insufficient Return on Investment Criterion	499
			[c] Medical Plausibility	501
		[4]	Article 3(1)(b) Requirements	501
			[a] Existing Satisfactory Method	502

Table of Contents

		[b] Significant Benefit	503
	[E]	Clinical Data at the Designation Stage	506
	[F]	Timing of Designation Applications	506
	[G]	Designation Application Review Procedure and Appeal Process	507
	[H]	Annual Reports	508
	[I]	Amendment of a Designation	508
§14.04	Orphan Medicinal Product MA		509
	[A]	The Centralised Procedure	509
	[B]	Review and Confirmation of Orphan Designation Criteria at the Time of MA ('maintenance review')	510
§14.05	Market Exclusivity and Other Incentives		511
	[A]	Protocol Assistance and Fee Reductions	511
	[B]	Market Exclusivity	512
		[1] Meaning of 'Similar Medicinal Product'	513
		[2] 'Breaking' Market Exclusivity	514
		[3] Procedure for Assessing Similarity and Derogations	515
		[4] Impact of a Second Orphan Authorisation Granted under the Derogation Provisions	517
		[5] Interpretation of the Market Exclusivity Provisions: European Court Judgments	517
		[a] Case T-140/12, Teva v. EMA	517
		[b] Case T-452/14 Laboratoires CTRS v. European Commission	519
		[c] CaseT-583/13 Shire Pharmaceutical Contracts v. European Commission	520
	[C]	Market Exclusivity Review: Possible Reduction of Term	522
§14.06	Transfer of Orphan Designation		523
§14.07	Transparency		524
§14.08	Research		524
§14.09	Future Developments		525
§14.10	UK		528
	[A]	Introduction	528
	[B]	Application for Orphan Designation in Great Britain	529
	[C]	Market Exclusivity	529
	[D]	SMEs	530
	[E]	MA Variation Applications	530
	[F]	Orphan Register	530
§14.11	Guidelines/Publications		531

CHAPTER 15
Biopharmaceuticals
Marc Martens, Benedicte Mourisse & Sophie Vo   535
§15.01   Introduction   535
§15.02   Specific Nature of Biopharmaceuticals and Consequences   536

	[A]	Biological Starting Materials	536
	[B]	Product Complexity and Variability	536
	[C]	Possible Immunogenicity	537
§15.03	Market Access for Innovative Biologicals		537
	[A]	MAA Routes	537
§15.04	MA Dossier		538
	[A]	General Requirements Applicable to All Biological Medicinal Products	538
	[B]	Information Concerning the Active Substance	538
	[C]	Manufacturing Process of the Active Substance	539
	[D]	Description and Composition of the Finished Medicinal Product	539
	[E]	Non-clinical Aspects	540
§15.05	Clinical Trials		541
§15.06	Product-Specific Requirements		541
	[A]	Plasma-Derived Medicinal Products	541
§15.07	ATMPs		543
§15.08	Vaccines		543
§15.09	Specific Market Surveillance Measures Applicable to Biological Medicinal Products		543
	[A]	Pharmacovigilance Requirements	543
	[B]	Changes to the Manufacturing Process	543
§15.10	Regulatory Data Protection		544
§15.11	The EMA's Biologics Working Party		545
§15.12	Biosimilars		545
	[A]	Concept of 'Biosimilar'	545
	[B]	Generics Versus Biosimilars	546
§15.13	'Me-Betters'		548
§15.14	MAA Route		548
§15.15	MAA Dossier Requirements		549
§15.16	Strategic Issues and Next Steps		550
§15.17	UK		556

CHAPTER 16
Homeopathic, Herbal, and Traditional Herbal Medicinal Products and Cannabis-Based Medicinal Products
Pieter Erasmus 559

§16.01	Introduction		559
§16.02	Homeopathic Medicinal Products		562
	[A]	Introduction to Homeopathic Medicinal Products	562
	[B]	Legal History of Homeopathic Medicinal Products	562
	[C]	Current Legislative Framework for Homeopathic Medicinal Products	563
	[D]	Definition of Homeopathic Medicinal Product	564
	[E]	Homeopathic Simplified Registration Procedure	565

Table of Contents

	[F]	Application Procedure for Homeopathic Simplified Registration	565
	[G]	Article 16 Authorisation Procedure	567
	[H]	Applicability of Other Provisions of the Directive to Homeopathic Medicinal Products	567
§16.03	Herbal and Traditional Herbal Medicinal Products		568
	[A]	Introduction to Herbal and Traditional Herbal Medicinal Products	568
	[B]	Herbal Medicinal Products	569
		[1] Definition of Herbal Medicinal Products	569
		[2] General MA Procedure for Herbal Medicinal Products	570
	[C]	Traditional Herbal Medicinal Products	570
		[1] Current Legislative Framework for Traditional Herbal Medicinal Products	570
		[2] Definition of Traditional Herbal Medicinal Products	571
		[3] Traditional Use Registration	571
		[4] Application Procedure for Traditional Use Registration	572
		[5] Labelling, Package Leaflet, and Advertising of Traditional Herbal Medicinal Products	574
		[6] Other Applicable Provisions for Traditional Use Registration	575
	[D]	Safety and Efficacy of Herbal and Traditional Herbal Medicinal Products	575
	[E]	Manufacturing and Quality of Herbal and Traditional Herbal Medicinal Products	576
	[F]	HMPC	576
	[G]	EU Herbal Monograph	577
	[H]	EU List	578
§16.04	Cannabis-Based Medicinal Products		579
§16.05	UK		582

CHAPTER 17
Advanced Therapy Medicinal Products
Marc Martens, Benedicte Mourisse & Sophie Vo   585

§17.01	Introduction		585
	[A]	History	585
	[B]	Definitions	587
		[1] Gene Therapy Medicinal Products (Section 2.1, Part IV, Annex I to Directive 2001/83/EC)	587
		[2] Somatic Cell Therapy Medicinal Products (Section 2.2, Part IV, Annex I to Directive 2001/83/EC)	587
		[3] Tissue-Engineered Products (Article 2(b) of the ATMP Regulation)	588
	[C]	Combined ATMPs and the Classification Rules	589
		[1] Combined ATMPs	589

Table of Contents

		[2]	Classification Rules		590
§17.02	Relationship Between the ATMP Regulation and Other European Legislation				591
§17.03	The Market Access for ATMPS				593
	[A]	Ordinary Regime			593
		[1]	The Procedure		593
		[2]	The CAT		593
			[a]	Role and Responsibilities	594
			[b]	Composition	594
	[B]	Exemptions			595
§17.04	MAA Dossier				597
	[A]	Specific Requirements Set Out in Part IV of Annex I to Directive 2001/83/EC			597
	[B]	Other Requirements Applicable to ATMPs			598
		[1]	Summary of Product Characteristics, Labelling, and Package Leaflet		598
		[2]	GMPs		598
		[3]	Post-Authorisation Requirements		599
			[a]	Follow-Up of Efficacy and Risk Management	599
			[b]	Traceability	599
§17.05	Incentives for SMEs				600
§17.06	Transitional Period				601
§17.07	UK				601
§17.08	Conclusion				601

CHAPTER 18
Vaccines
Marc Martens & Phillipus Putter 603

§18.01	Introduction			603
	[A]	General Overview		603
	[B]	Vaccines Working Party		604
	[C]	The EU Vaccines Strategy		605
§18.02	Development of Vaccines			605
	[A]	Non-clinical Aspects		606
		[1]	Basic Science Phase	606
		[2]	Preclinical Testing	607
	[B]	Clinical Trials		608
		[1]	Pharmacokinetic/Pharmacodynamic Studies	610
		[2]	Efficacy and Effectiveness	611
		[3]	Special Considerations for Vaccine Development	612
		[4]	Revision of the Guideline of Clinical Evaluation	612
§18.03	MAA			613
	[A]	The MA Procedures		613
		[1]	Centralised	613

xlvii

Table of Contents

		[2]	National		613
		[3]	Decentralised and Mutual Recognition		614
	[B]	MAAs			614
		[1]	Module 1		614
		[2]	Module 2		615
		[3]	Module 3		615
		[4]	Module 4		616
		[5]	Module 5		616
	[C]	Conditional MA in Emergency Situations			617
§18.04	The Official Control Authority Batch Release				617
§18.05	Post-marketing Surveillance: Pharmacovigilance				620
	[A]	Some Institutions That Ensure Post-Authorisation Safety of Vaccines			621
	[B]	GVP Module for Vaccines			622
	[C]	Post-Marketing Authorisation Approval Requirements			624
		[1]	RMP		624
		[2]	Variation of the Original VAMF Certificate		624
		[3]	License Renewals		625
§18.06	Vaccines in the UK				625
	[A]	Introduction			625
	[B]	Development of Vaccines in the UK			625
	[C]	Pre-approval and MA			626
	[D]	Post-marketing Pharmacovigilance			627
	[E]	Summary			628
§18.07	Guidelines/Publications				628

CHAPTER 19
Medical Devices
Kevin Munungu & Sophie Vo 631

§19.01	Introduction					631
§19.02	Medical Devices					633
	[A]	Notion of Medical Device				633
		[1]	Regulatory Definition of a Medical Device			633
		[2]	Classification of Medical Devices			634
			[a]	General Principles		634
			[b]	Classification Rules		635
	[B]	Placing a Medical Device on the Market in the EU				636
		[1]	General Safety and Performance Requirements for Marketing of Medical Devices			636
			[a]	General Requirements Regarding the Design and Manufacture of the Medical Device		637
			[b]	General Requirements Regarding the Information to Be Supplied with the Device		637
		[2]	Conformity Assessment Procedures			638

		[a]	Role of Notified Bodies	638
		[b]	Supporting Evidence	639
		[c]	CE Marking	640
		[d]	CE Labelling	641
		[e]	Registration	642
		[3]	The Responsibilities of Manufacturers of Medical Devices	642
	[C]	Post-Market Surveillance, Vigilance, and Market Surveillance		643
	[D]	Surveillance Role of Member States and Competent Authorities		644
§19.03	In Vitro Diagnostic Medical Devices			644
	[A]	Notion of in Vitro Diagnostic Medical Device		645
		[1]	Regulatory Definition of In Vitro Diagnostic Medical Device	645
		[2]	Classification of In Vitro Diagnostic Medical Devices	646
	[B]	Placing an In Vitro Diagnostic Medical Device on the Market		647
		[1]	General Safety and Performance Requirements for Marketing In Vitro Diagnostic Medical Devices	647
		[2]	Conformity Assessment Procedures	647
§19.04	How to Advertise Medical Devices			649
§19.05	UK			650
	[A]	Definition of Medical Device		651
	[B]	Borderline Products		651
	[C]	Classification of Medical Devices		652
	[D]	In Vitro Diagnostic Medical Devices		652
	[E]	Software as Medical Devices		653
	[F]	Placing Medical Devices on the UK Market		654
		[1]	Registration	654
		[2]	Conformity Assessment Procedures	655
		[3]	UKCA Marking	655
		[4]	Post-Market Surveillance, Vigilance, and Market Surveillance	656
§19.06	How to Advertise Medical Devices			656

CHAPTER 20
Parallel Trade
Christian Lindenthal, Pieter Erasmus & Jonathan Edwards 657

§20.01	Introduction to Parallel Trade			657
§20.02	Parallel Distribution Law			658
	[A]	EMA Notice		658
	[B]	Necessary Licences for Parallel Distributors		659
	[C]	Other Requirements		660
		[1]	Changes in the Package or Label	660
		[2]	Notice to Local Authorities	661
		[3]	MA Updates	662
		[4]	Maintenance Notice	662

Table of Contents

	[5]	Quality Control	662
	[6]	Falsified Medicines	663
§20.03	Parallel Importation		664
	[A]	Parallel Importation Law	664
	[B]	The Simplified Procedure	665
	[C]	General Requirements for the Simplified Procedure	667
§20.04	Intellectual Property Law		668
	[A]	Introduction	668
	[B]	Patent Rights and Parallel Trade	668
		[1] Exhaustion of Patent Rights	669
		[2] Specific Mechanism	670
	[C]	Trademark Law and Parallel Trade	673
		[1] The Repackaging Does Not Affect the Product	674
		[2] The Repackaging Is Not Likely to Damage Reputation	675
		[3] Indication of the Original Manufacturer and the Repackager	676
		[4] Notice to the Trademark Owner	676
		[5] The Repackaging Is 'Necessary'	677
		[6] Burden of Proof	678
		[7] Rebranding	678
§20.05	Competition Law		679
§20.06	UK		679
	[A]	Brexit and Exhaustion of IP Rights	679
	[B]	Implementation in the UK	680
	[C]	UK Procedure	681
	[D]	Product Repackaging and Potential Trademark Infringement	682
	[E]	Notification of Patent Holders	683

CHAPTER 21
Competition Law in the Pharmaceutical Sector
Morten Nissen, Peter Willis & Alexander Brøchner   685

§21.01	Introduction		685
§21.02	Market Definition in the Pharmaceutical Sector		685
	[A]	Approved Medicines	686
	[B]	Active Substances	687
	[C]	Pipeline Products	687
§21.03	Article 101 TFEU		688
	[A]	The Application of Article 101(1) TFEU	688
		[1] The Definition of an Undertaking	688
		[2] Definition of Agreements, Concerted Practices, and Decisions of Associations	689
		[a] Agreements	689
		[b] Concerted Practices	690
		[c] Decisions by Association of Undertakings	690

		[3]	A Restriction of Competition by Object and/or Effect	691

          [3] A Restriction of Competition by Object and/or Effect 691
          [4] An Appreciable Restriction of Competition: *de Minimis* 691
          [5] An Appreciable Effect on Trade Between Member States 692
    [B] The Application of Article 101(3) TFEU 692
          [1] Individual Exemptions 693
          [2] Block Exemptions 693
                [a] The TTBER 694
                [b] The R&D Block Exemption 695
                [c] The Damages Directive 696
    [C] Selection of Cases/The Pharmaceutical Sector Inquiry 697
          [1] Agreements Between Originators and Generics 697
                [a] Reverse Payment Patent Settlements 697
                [b] Other Agreements Having the Effect of Delaying Generic Market Entry 699
                [c] Other Anti-Competitive Agreements 699
§21.04 Article 102 TFEU 700
    [A] Establishing Dominance under Article 102 TFEU 701
    [B] Abuse of a Dominant Position 702
          [1] Non-price-Based Exclusionary Conduct 703
                [a] Misuse of IP Rights 703
                [b] Refusal to Supply 704
                [c] Other Non-price-Based Exclusionary Abuses 705
          [2] Price-based Exclusionary Conduct 706
                [a] Fidelity Rebates and Exclusive Purchase Obligations 706
                [b] Excessive Pricing 707
§21.05 Parallel Trade 707
§21.06 The EU Merger Control Regulation 709
    [A] Merger Control Procedure 710
    [B] Referral of Concentrations That Do Not Meet the Thresholds 711
    [C] Substantive Assessment 711
          [1] Horizontal Mergers 712
          [2] Non-horizontal Mergers 712
    [D] Selection of Cases 713
          [1] GlaxoWellcome/Smithkline Beecham 713
          [2] Novartis/Hexal 714
§21.07 State Aid 714
    [A] Definition of State Aid under the Treaty 714
    [B] Exemptions 715
§21.08 UK 718
    [A] Introduction 718
    [B] Merger Control 720
    [C] Anti-competitive Behaviour 721

Table of Contents

		[1]	UK Competition Act 1998 Chapter I: Restrictive Agreements	721
			[a] Reverse Payment Agreements (Pay-For-Delay)	721
			[b] Recent and Ongoing CMA Chapter I Investigations	722
			[c] UK Competition Act 1998 Chapter II: Abuse of Dominance	723
			[d] Market Definition in Abuse Cases	725
	§21.09	Guidelines/Publications		726

CHAPTER 22
Pandemics and Epidemics
Hester Borgers, Fenna Douwenga, Edzard Boonen & Phillipus Putter 729

§22.01	Introduction	729
§22.02	Definitions of Pandemic and Epidemic	730
§22.03	The COVID-19 EMA Task Force and Steering Group	731
	[A] ETF	731
	[B] The EMA COVID-19 Steering Group	732
§22.04	The Commission's Coronavirus Response Team	732
§22.05	Availability and Market Access of Medicines	733
	[A] EMA Executive Steering Group on Shortages and Safety of Medicinal Products	733
	[B] EMA Additional Temporary Measures	734
	[C] Guidelines and Guidance from the EC on Avoiding Medicines Shortages	735
	[D] Recommendation from the EC on Conformity Assessment and Market Surveillance Procedures	735
	[E] Compassionate Use	736
§22.06	Clinical Trials Effected by A Pandemic or Epidemic	737
	[A] Guidance from the EC and EMA	737
§22.07	Postponement of Regulations (EU) 2017/745 and 2017/746 On Medical Devices	738
§22.08	Vaccine Strategy	738
	[A] The EU Vaccine Strategy	738
	[B] Advance Purchase Agreements	739
	[C] Inclusive Vaccine Alliance	739
§22.09	Healthcare Personnel	740
	[A] Exceptions to Work as Healthcare Personnel	740
	[B] Cross-Border Migration of Healthcare Personnel	741
§22.10	Pandemics and Epidemics in the UK	741
	[A] Vaccine Task Force	742
	[B] Clinical Trials and MA	742
	[C] Vaccine Development and Strategy	743

CHAPTER 23
Data Protection in the Pharmaceutical Sector
Clara Clark Nevola & Emma Drake 745
§23.01 Introduction 745
§23.02 Legal Framework and Penalties 745
    [A] Applicable Laws 745
    [B] Territorial Scope and Establishment 746
    [C] Material Scope of the GDPR 747
    [D] Supervision, Enforcement, and Penalties 749
§23.03 The Definition of Personal Data 749
    [A] Identifiable 750
    [B] Relating 750
    [C] Deceased Individuals 751
    [D] Special Category Personal Data 751
        [1] Generally 751
        [2] Data Concerning Health 752
    [E] Criminal Convictions and Offence Data 753
    [F] Pseudonymised Data 753
    [G] Anonymised Data 754
§23.04 Controllers and Processors 756
    [A] Assessing the Roles of the Parties 756
    [B] Joint or Separate Control 758
    [C] Data Protection Roles in Clinical Trials 759
        [1] Site as a Processor 760
        [2] Site as a Controller 760
        [3] Role of the CRO 761
        [4] Other Parties and Data Subjects 761
    [D] Controllers and Processors in Contract 762
        [1] Processing Agreements 762
        [2] Joint Controllers 762
§23.05 Data Protection Principles 763
§23.06 Lawfulness 763
    [A] Legitimate Interests 765
        [1] Identifying a Legitimate Interest 765
        [2] Necessity 766
        [3] Balancing These Interests Against the Individual's Rights and Freedoms 766
    [B] Consent 767
        [1] Freely Given 768
        [2] Specific 768
        [3] Informed 768
    [C] Confidentiality and Consent 768
    [D] Consent in Clinical Trials 769
    [E] Withdrawing Consent 770

Table of Contents

	[F]	Quality and Safety Monitoring	771
	[G]	Research	772
§23.07	Further Processing		772
	[A]	Compatible Purposes: Research	772
	[B]	Compatible Purposes: Anonymisation	773
§23.08	Fairness and Transparency		774
§23.09	Data Minimisation, Accuracy, and Storage Limitation		776
§23.10	Security and Breach Reporting		778
§23.11	Accountability		779
§23.12	Data Subject Rights		780
	[A]	Access and Portability	781
	[B]	Right of Rectification	782
	[C]	Objection	782
	[D]	Erasure and Restriction	783
	[E]	Significant Automated Decisions	784
§23.13	Data Transfers		784
§23.14	Marketing to Healthcare Professionals		786
	[A]	B2B Marketing and B2C Marketing	786
	[B]	Consent	787
	[C]	Soft Opt-In	787

Appendix Guidelines and Publications	789
Table of Cases	803
EU Directives	823
Other Legislation	829
EU Regulations	835
Index	839

List of Abbreviations

ABPI	Association of the British Pharmaceutical Industry
ADR	Adverse Drug Reaction
AE	Adverse event
AEMPS	Spanish Agency of Medicines and Medical Devices
AFSSAPS	The French Health Products Safety Agency – Previous French authority (*L'Agence française de sécurité sanitaire des produits de santé*)
AIFA	Agenzia Italiana del Farmaco
ANSM	The French National Agency for the Safety of Medicines and Health Products (*L'Agence nationale de sécurité du medicament et des produits de santé*)
ARS	French Regional Health Authority (*Agence régionale de santé*)
ASA	Advertising Standards Authority
ASMF	Active Substance Master File
ATC	Anatomical Therapeutic Classification
ATMP	Advanced Therapy Medicinal Product
AxMP	Auxiliary Medicinal Product
BfArM	The Federal Institute for Drugs and Medical Devices
BMPWP	Biosimilar Medicinal Products Working Party
BPCA	Best Pharmaceuticals for Children Act of 2002
BWP	Biologics Working Party
CA	Competent Authority
CAT	Committee for Advanced Therapies
CBER	Center for Biologic Evaluation and Research
CBD	Cannabidiol

List of Abbreviations

CBG	Dutch Medicines Board (*College ter boordeling van geneesmiddelen*)
CDER	Center for Drug Evaluation and Research
CE	*Communauté européenne*
CEP	Certificate of Suitability
CEPS	French Economic Committee for Health Products (*Comité économique des produits de santé*)
CF	Consent form
CFI	Court of First Instance
CFR	Code of Federal Regulations
CG	Collaborative group
CHMP	Committee for Medicinal Products for Human Use
CI	Chief investigator
CIOMS	Council for International Organisation of Medical Sciences
CMD (h)	Co-Ordination Group for Mutual Recognition and Decentralised Procedures: Human
CMS	Concerned Member State
COMP	Committee for Orphan Medicinal Products
COREC	Central Office for Research Ethics Committee
CP	Centralised Procedure
CPMP	Committee for Proprietary Medicinal Products (now the CHMP)
CRF	Clinical record form/case report form
CRO	Contract research organisation
CTA	Clinical Trial Authorisation
CTAG	Clinical Trials Coordination and Advisory Group
CTC	Clinical Trial Certificate
CTD	Clinical Trials Directive
CTDoc	Common Technical Document
CTIMP	Clinical Trials of Investigational Medicinal Products
CTIS	Clinical Trials Information System
CTR	Clinical Trials Regulation
CVMP	Committee for Medicinal Products for Veterinary Use
DCD	Developmental Co-ordination Disorder
DCP	Decentralised Procedure
DG	Directorate General
DGCBF	Directorate General of Basic Services of the National Health System and Pharmacy

List of Abbreviations

DGCCRF	French General Directorate for Competition, Consumption and Fraud Enforcement (*Direction générale de la concurrence, de la consommation et de la répression des fraudes*)
DHSC	Department of Health and Social Care (UK)
DMC	Data Monitoring Committee
DMEC	Data Monitoring and Ethics Committee
DPIA	Data Protection Impact Assessments
DTC	Direct to Customers
EAMS	Early Access to Medicines Scheme
EC	European Commission
ECJ	European Court of Justice
ECMR	EC Merger Control Regulation
eCTDoc	Electronic Common Technical Documents
EDMA	European Diagnostic Manufacturers Association
EDPB	European Data Protection Board
EDQM	European Directorate for the Quality of Medicines
EEA	European Economic Area
EFPIA	European Federation of Pharmaceutical Industries & Associations
EFTA	Norway, Iceland and Lichtenstein
EMA	European Medicines Agency
EMRN	European Medicines Regulatory Network
ENCePP	European Network of Centres for Pharmacoepidemiology and Pharmacovigilance
EPAR	European Public Assessment Report
EPC	European Patent Convention
EPO	European Patent Office
ETF	Emergency Task Force
EU	European Union
EUDAMED	European Data Base on Medical Devices
EudraCT	European Clinical Trials Database
EudraVigilance	European Database for Pharmacovigilance
EUMR	EU Merger Control Regulation
EU-RMP	EU Risk Management Plan
FAMHP	Federal Agency for Medicines and Health Products (Belgium)
FDA	Food and Drug Administration
FENIN	Association of Manufacturers of Medical Devices
GCP	Good Clinical Practice

List of Abbreviations

GDPR	General Data Protection Regulation (EU)
GLP	Good Laboratory Practice
GMO	Genetically modified organisms
GMP	Good Manufacturing Practice
GPRD	General Practice Research Database
GSL	General Sales List
GTAC	Gene Therapy Advisory Committee
GVP	Good Pharmacovigilance Practice
HERA	Health Emergency preparedness and Response Authority
HMA	Heads of Medicine Agencies
HMA-h	Heads of Agencies for Human Medicines
HMA-v	Heads of Agencies for Veterinary Medicines
HMPC	Committee for Herbal Medicinal Products
HRA	Health Research Authority (UK)
IB	Investigator's Brochure
ICH	International Convention on Harmonisation
ICO	Information Commissioner's Office (UK)
ICSRs	Individual Case Safety Reports
IEC	Independent Ethics Committee
IFPMA	International Federation of Pharmaceutical Manufacturers and Associations
IMP	Investigational medicinal product
IMPD	Investigational medicinal product dossier
IND	Investigational New Drug
INN	International non-proprietary name [for a drug]
IPRs	Intellectual Property Rights
ISPAD	International Society of Paediatric and Adolescent Diabetes
ISRCTN	International Standard Randomised Controlled Trial Number
JCVI	Joint Committee on Vaccines and Immunisation (UK)
LEEM	French Pharmaceutical Companies Association (*Les entreprises du médicament*)
LR	Legal representative
MA	Marketing Authorisation
MAAs	Marketing Authorisation Applications
MABEL	Minimal anticipated biological effect
MAH	Marketing Authorisation holder
MEDDEV	Commission Guideline relating to Medical Device Directions
MedDRA	Medical Dictionary for Regulatory Authorities

List of Abbreviations

MHRA	Medicines and Healthcare products Regulatory Agency (UK)
MPA	The Medical Products Agency (*Läkemedelsverket*)
MREC	Multi-centre Research Ethics Committee
MRP	Mutual Recognition Procedure
MSSG	Executive Steering Group on Shortages and Safety of Medicinal Products
MSSO	Maintenance and Support Services Organisation
NANDO	New Approach Notified and Designated Organisations
NHS	National Health Service
NOAL	No observable adverse effect level
NOEL	No observable effect level
NTA	Notice to Applicants
ODR	Orphan Drug Regulations
OTC	Over the counter
P	Pharmacy (product, may be supplied under the supervision of a pharmacist)
PAES	Post Authorisation Efficacy Studies
PASS	Post-Authorisation Safety Studies
PAGB	Proprietary Association of Great Britain
PAT	Process Analytical Technology
PDCO	Paediatric Committee
PHC	French Public Health Code
PhV	Pharmacovigilance
PhV IWG	Ad Hoc Pharmacovigilance inspections Working Group
PI	Principal investigator
PIAG	Pharmacovigilance Inspection Action Group
PIP	Paediatric Investigation Plan
PMCPA	Prescription Medicines Code of Practice Authority
PPE	Personal Protective Equipment
PRAC	Pharmacovigilance Risk Assessment Committee
PREA	Paediatric Research Equity Act of 2003
PSMF	Pharmacovigilance system master file
PSURs	Periodic Safety Update Reports
PUMA	Paediatric Use Marketing Authorisation
QA	Quality assurance
QbD	Quality by design
QP	Qualified Person
RCT	Randomised controlled trial

List of Abbreviations

RD	Royal Decree
REC	Research Ethics Committee
RMS	Reference Member State
SAE	Serious adverse event
SANCO	Directorate General – Health and Consumers
SAR	Serious adverse reaction
SAWP	Scientific Advice Working Party
SCC	Standard Contractual Clauses
SDV	Source document verification
SMEs	Small and medium-sized enterprises
SmPC	Summary of Product Characteristics
SMQ	Standardised MedDRA Queries
SOC	System Organ Class
SOPs	Standard Operating Procedures
SPC	Supplementary Protection Certificate
SPOC	Single Point of Contact
SPS	Summary of Pharmacovigilance Systems
SSA	Site-specific assessment
SUSAR	Suspected unexpected serious adverse reaction
TCA	EU-UK Trade and Cooperation Agreement
TFEU	Treaty on the Functioning of the EU
TMG	Trial management group
TSC	Trial steering committee
TSE	Transmissible Spongiform Encephalopathy
TTBER	Block Exemption Regulation on Technology Transfer
UPC	Unified Patent Court
USR	Urgent Safety Restriction
VABEO	Vertical Agreements Block Exemption Order (UK)
VAMF	Vaccine Antigen Master File
VBER	Vertical Block Exemption Regulation (EU)
VTF	Vaccine Task Force
WHO	World Health Organisation
WIPO	World Intellectual Property Organization
WSMI	World Self-Medication Industry

Preface

Welcome to the eighth edition of the EU (and the UK) Guide to Pharmaceutical Regulatory Law; there has been a bit of a hiatus in publication as we waited for the fallout from Brexit to settle. There have been a number of changes resulting from the UK's departure from the EU, and rather than excluding this jurisdiction, we added to most chapters a UK-specific section to demonstrate what remains the same and what may yet change. There is also an introduction to Brexit in a separate chapter. This year, we have included a couple of totally new chapters dealing with pandemics – this was seen as somewhat more topical, even more so than when we first thought it should be covered! – and a chapter on data protection which, of course, is so relevant to regulatory pharmaceutical law. Given the time that has elapsed since the seventh edition, significant redrafting has been undertaken throughout the chapters. For example, the Clinical Trials Regulation finally came into effect, as did the Medical Devices Regulation. There have also been developments in the area of orphan drugs, too.

Over the last few decades, there have been innumerable legislative actions relating to the development and sale of pharmaceuticals throughout the world, not least through the management of the International Council on Harmonisation of Technical Requirements for Registration of Pharmaceuticals for Human Use (ICH). At the same time, the EU has since 1957 increased in size (from six to twenty-seven Member States), and, as a result, ever-increasing numbers of Directives and Regulations have been passed to stimulate and regulate the establishment of a single market. The key pieces of EU pharmaceutical regulation have been enacted to streamline the process of introducing a pharmaceutical product or medical device, and then to apply harmonised standards relating to the sale and use of that product or device, at all times, ensuring that consistent standards of safety, quality, and efficacy are maintained throughout the EU. An immensely complicated system has evolved as a result of the need to balance the constitutional requirements of the EU and its constituent Member States; the EU legislation needs to be reflected in national laws and can at times be at odds with local standards and cultural differences. Where relevant, this publication

Preface

also deals with the relationship with countries within the European Economic Area (EEA).

The aim of this book is to provide up-to-date information on the processes, legislation, cases, and customs that apply to the introduction, marketing, and sale of a medicinal product (or a medical device) in Europe and to provide some clarity concerning the aforementioned complicated systems. It is written by and for lawyers, both in-house and in private practice, who find themselves having to advise a client or clients on this ever-changing area of law, perhaps on the steps needed to bring a product to market, including any supplementary obligations (such as the need to conduct a clinical trial of the product for paediatric use), or perhaps when advising on clinical trial agreements, what 'normal' rights and obligations of parties should be included in the agreement governing the trials. We hope the book will also be of interest and assistance to regulatory advisers as well as non-regulatory pharmaceutical/healthcare industry scientists and managers.

Each chapter presents a particular process or subject from an EU and UK-wide perspective. The chapters take the reader through the life of a medicinal product or medical device, from development to clinical trials to product launch and afterwards, and we provide guidance in matters where regulatory law is used as an instrument of lifecycle management.

The book could be viewed as comprising four main sections. The first section (Chapters 2–3) comprises an introduction to the regulatory setup and a chapter offering an overview of relevant intellectual property rights (IPRs). The second section (Chapters 4–8) deals with the 'mainstream' medicinal products from cradle to grave. The third section (Chapters 9–18) deals with a number of specific regimes which do not readily fall within that arrangement. The final section includes five very important, related, but stand-alone subjects – Medical Devices, Parallel Imports, Competition Law, Pandemics, and Data Protection. Further detail is set out below.

Chapter 1 provides an overview of the Brexit process and its impact on the pharmaceutical sector. Chapter 2 provides an introduction to the types of products dealt with within the book, to the regulatory framework, and to the relevant committees and agencies. Chapter 3 provides an overview of IPRs, which are relevant to the pharmaceutical and medical devices industries. Chapter 4 deals with clinical trials and considers in depth the Clinical Trials Regulation and stages and standards that must be undertaken in collating the information for a product dossier. Chapter 5 outlines the requirements and various routes for obtaining a Marketing Authorisation and provides a comparison between the various procedures whilst demonstrating the degree of harmonisation that has already been achieved. Reporting and collating adverse events centrally, thereby increasing the industry and practitioners' knowledge of a product, are important tenets of the EU legislation. Conditional Marketing Authorisations are available in certain emergency situations. Chapter 6 explains the criteria for a Conditional Marketing Authorisation and how this can or should be converted to a full Marketing Authorisation in due course. Supplementary Protection Certificates are peculiar to the Pharmaceutical (Agrochemical and Veterinary) industry, and we have

Preface

added a chapter providing some background to their importance and an update on the recent and interesting case law (Chapter 7).

The rectification of the unmet needs of the paediatric population (most medicines prescribed for them for serious illness have historically been untested in children) has been a high-profile aim of the EU. The United States (US) introduced, with some success, legislation to ensure that new drugs would be tested for safe use in children, and similar and enhanced legislation has been introduced recently in the EU, covering not only new medicines but also existing medicines that are off-patent. Chapter 8 provides some background to the legislation relating to paediatric use of medicinal products or devices and to the rewards and potential penalties for pharmaceutical companies arising out of that legislation.

Moving now to the third section of the book: Chapter 9 discusses the advertising of medicinal products or devices and covers in detail the body of both European and local legislation and regulation that affects and governs the sale of pharmaceutical products in the EU and the UK. The EU regime is less liberal than the US advertising regime, and this chapter explains how and why this is.

Chapter 10 deals with pharmacovigilance, how it applies throughout the life of a pharmaceutical product and provides guidance to the reporting procedures that must be undertaken in relation to the notification of adverse events. Before a product can be considered for sale, its safety, efficacy, and quality must be proven through the conduct of closely-monitored clinical trials. Again, this legislation has been updated recently.

Variations to existing Marketing Authorisations, and the steps that need to be undertaken to permit the sale of various types of variations to a product, are considered in Chapter 11.

Certain combinations of existing products or active ingredients may be brought to market with fewer clinical trials having been undertaken than would be required for a completely new product or active ingredient; Chapter 12 explains the criteria and the process for obtaining a Marketing Authorisation for a combination product.

Some procedures vary from those set out in Chapter 4. Chapter 13 provides guidance on how and when the abridged Marketing Authorisation procedure can be used – that is, where there is already a body of knowledge and evidence regarding the profile of an existing product that can serve as the basis for the approval of the Marketing Authorisation so that the full procedure need not be undertaken. Generic products and essential similarities are considered in this chapter.

Chapter 14 deals with another area of otherwise unmet medical need – that of orphan drugs. The chapter provides an overview of the criteria for consideration and the standards that must be maintained by the holder of a Marketing Authorisation of an orphan drug.

Biological products are becoming increasingly prevalent, particularly for new medicines; they make up an increasingly larger proportion of medicinal products, as traditional small-molecule drugs are no longer able to achieve the same novel results. Legislation relating to the testing and marketing of biologicals has therefore been introduced, as well as the introduction of 'biosimilars' and the analogous process to the abridged applications. Chapter 15 provides guidance to this legislation and explains the steps to be undertaken in introducing a biological medicinal product.

The sale and use of homeopathic and herbal medicines are subject to increased regulation and scrutiny to prevent the sale of potentially dangerous or toxic products whilst also ensuring that unrealistic or simply false and unsubstantiated claims about such products are not made. Chapter 16 covers this area of the legislation.

Moving on to another relatively new and fast-moving area, we have included a chapter on advanced therapy medicinal products (ATMP). Chapter 17 provides guidance on the regulation of gene therapies and somatic cell therapies and tissue-engineered products.

We have introduced a new chapter on vaccines as this is an area of increasing focus, and we find that we are dealing with a large number of queries on this subject (Chapter 18).

Finally, the fourth section, with five stand-alone chapters. There is often an overlap between regulation of medical devices and pharmaceutical products, and on the basis that the relevant Regulations will have to be considered in a pharmaceutical arena, we thought it would be helpful to include, in Chapter 19, an overview of what a medical device is, and what steps need to be taken before the sale of that product will be authorised. We also provide an overview of the vigilance procedures for medical devices.

A subject that has been a cause of much litigation and interest is that of parallel imports – what is permitted and what is not. In Chapter 20, we give an overview of parallel trade, including which transactions are lawful or unlawful.

Competition law has always been of crucial importance to the pharmaceutical sector since the industry is both highly competitive and involves so many IPRs. With the recent Pharmaceutical Sector Inquiry, it has again been in the news. Chapter 21 covers competition law in the pharmaceutical sector. Finally, as mentioned, we have chapters dealing with the changes introduced to deal with pandemics and with the Data Protection regime (Chapters 22–23).

With the exception of the advertising chapter, this book deals primarily with the European level of legislation. Where there are significant national deviations or differences in interpretation, we have been able to take advantage of the breadth of Bird & Bird experience in a number of major jurisdictions (namely the UK, France, Germany, Spain, Belgium, the Netherlands, Italy, and Sweden) to create national variations tables that appear at the end of certain chapters. These tables provide information on how the subject matter of the chapter is implemented in those seven major Member States plus the UK, and they also serve to illustrate how implementation of the EU regulations varies between Member States. We have only included relevant or significant information, so the length of these charts varies, and for some subjects, such as paediatrics, the legislation is so new and pan-European that we decided that no local variation needed to be included.

In addition, at the end of each chapter, we have included a list of guidelines/publications that will direct the readers to sources of additional information. European legislation is peppered with acronyms. For help keeping them all straight, we included a list of the most commonly used ones in the pharmaceutical area, in addition to those that appear in each chapter.

Rather than double the size of this publication by including all relevant legislation, we have included links to the major Directives to help the reader find these. Certain other relevant material, such as examples of forms, is included in the appendices.

Finally, it is important to note that whilst EU pharmaceutical regulation extends to products intended for use in animals; I have restricted the discussion in the present volume to the requirements for testing and marketing products for human use. However, in Chapter 2, I have included the names of the EU agencies and regulations that oversee veterinary products as part of our general description of the regulatory framework.

Despite the improvements and advancements that have resulted from EU pharmaceutical regulation, the inherent complexity of the system makes this publication a 'work in progress'; there is a continual discovery of new areas where the legislation needs to be strengthened, streamlined, or harmonised. Where such developments are on the near horizon, we have discussed them under the heading 'Future Developments', and we have been producing, and will continue to produce, with Kluwer Law International, regular updates to this book.

Production of this book has been a real team effort. I have drawn on the expertise of colleagues in Bird & Bird across Europe, who were invaluable in contributing chapters in their specialist subjects as well as on national variations. They have all helped to make this the comprehensive book we hoped for, and I cannot thank them enough for their assistance; it has been such a busy year for all of us and to find the extra time necessary to research and write the chapters is hugely appreciated. A special mention must be made to our Senior Associate, Pieter Erasmus, who has undertaken Herculean efforts to bring this new edition to fruition, and Phillipus Putter, who has carried out so much proofreading.

CHAPTER 1
Brexit

Sally Shorthose

§1.01 INTRODUCTION

In June 2016, the United Kingdom (UK) public voted to leave the European Union (EU); and thethen Prime Minister Theresa May wrote to the European Council President Donald Tusk to notify of the UK's intention to leave the EU, thereby triggering Article 50 of the Treaty on the EU.

After three and a half years of negotiation, extension of the notice period, and then final agreement on the EU-UK Withdrawal Agreement and Political Declaration, the UK exited the EU on 31 January 2020. The EU-UK Withdrawal Agreement came into force and gave effect to a transition period until 31 December 2020, during which time EU law continued to apply in and in relation to the UK, and the UK continues to be part of the EU Single Market and Customs Union. Following its exit from the EU, the UK is now treated as a third country, and neither can it participate in the EU's decision-making processes nor is it represented in the EU institutions. The Withdrawal Agreement has been implemented into UK law by the European Union (Withdrawal Agreement) Act 2020 which amended the European Union (Withdrawal) Act 2018. Under the amended 2018 Act, direct EU legislation continued to apply in UK domestic law after the end of the transition period unless and until it is amended or revoked by UK regulations made under that amended Act. At the time of writing, a 'bonfire' of the EU laws is in the parliamentary process whereby all grandfathered EU laws will be deleted from the UK's statute books unless specifically retained by the relevant government minister.

During 2020, the UK and the EU negotiated a trade agreement which came into force at the end of the transition period; the negotiations were extremely fraught and caused significant upheaval in the UK, causing Theresa May to resign as prime minister and be succeeded by Boris Johnson. The transition period was intended to give businesses time to prepare for the changes that would occur when the UK ceased to be part of the EU Single Market and Customs Union. In the event, the EU-UK Trade and Cooperation Agreement (TCA) was signed only on 30 December 2020, meaning that businesses had little time to review the TCA or its implications for trading with the EU, and were unable to assess the impact of the increased requirement for documentation and of restrictions on free movement of people and vehicles.

I have set out below, briefly, the considerations and anticipated how UK's withdrawal from the EU has and will continue to impact the pharmaceutical industry. The effects of Brexit on the pharmaceutical and medical devices sector are substantial. This is because, as a third country to the EU, the UK no longer has access to many of the benefits of the EU system, such as the centralised procedure for market authorisations (MAs), the EU portal for clinical trials, and the Pharmacovigilance database.

[A] Legislation

The pharmaceuticals sector is one of the most highly regulated and globally harmonised industry sectors, especially in terms of the development of pharmaceutical products. A large amount of the regulation originates from membership of the EU in the form of directives or regulations. In the case of directives (e.g., Directive 2001/83/EC governing medicinal products), these have been implemented into national law and will therefore remain in place *pro tem* (subject to amendment). Regulations, in contrast, were directly applicable in the UK without the need for national implementation, but as mentioned, in the short term, at least from the end of the transition period, much was reflected in UK law. It was hoped that the EU Withdrawal Act would be effective in buffering the effect of a lapse in applicability of regulations; if the Act serves as a way of incorporating existing regulations (subject to amendments) into UK law, then the effect should be to fill the vacuum left if a regulation were to just cease to apply. The EU legislation that was retained in UK law is set out in sections 3 and 20(1) and Schedule 6[1] to the European Union (Withdrawal) Act 2018 (c. 16).

If, however, as seems increasingly likely, the UK government decides to no longer align itself closely with European law, the administrative burden of pharmaceuticals companies could increase significantly because regulatory requirements, for example, clinical trial authorisations and marketing authorisation applications (MAAs) may need to be obtained under a new and different legal framework.

[B] Medicinal Products and the TCA

Medicinal Products are covered in Annex TBT-2 in the TCA (the Medicinal Products Annex (MPA)), which applies to all medicinal products listed in its Annex C, including human and veterinary products and Advanced Therapy Medicinal Products (ATMPs).

The TCA provides that any changes to either the UK or the EU's regulation regime should be on sixty days' notice and be subject to discussion.

---

1. https://www.legislation.gov.uk/eu-legislation-and-uk-law.

There are provisions which will affect the medicinal products industry included in the IP section (Title V) of the TCA. They include:

- the treatment of regulatory data protection:
  - a requirement to ensure that commercially confidential information submitted to obtain an MA is protected against disclosure to third parties in the absence of an overriding public interest and that steps are taken to ensure the data is protected from unfair commercial use;
  - that regulatory protections will be 'for a limited period of time to be determined by domestic law' so that each of the UK and the EU may determine the length of such regulatory exclusivities under their own regulatory regimes; and
  - Supplementary Protection Certificates (SPCs) – as set out below.

[C] Research

There was some good news for research and development activities in the UK – the TCA provides that as long as the UK continues to make financial contributions, the UK will continue participating in EU programmes, including the EU's research and innovation funding programme, Horizon Europe, and, perhaps in light of the COVID-19 pandemic, there is express provision for UK/EU cooperation on 'serious cross-border threat[s] to health'. In practice, the level of cooperation has not been as effective as hoped, and British universities lament their exclusion from many international projects.

The EU has nonetheless provided funding and coordinates research collaborations through funding programmes such as the Innovative Medicines Initiative and Horizon 2020; UK-based researchers were among the largest beneficiaries of those programmes.

In accordance with the terms of the TCA, UK researchers will remain eligible for European research funding. In exchange for a contribution to the EU budget, they will join the forthcoming Horizon Europe research program, which will spend EUR 85 billion over the next seven years. While at first sight, this is good news, the UK will have no influence over how that money is spent. Furthermore, since the contributions are calculated on the basis of gross domestic product (GDP), there is a fear that in due course this involvement may be deemed too costly.

It has been feared that UK-based research facilities would see the loss of talented researchers to research facilities in the EU, and this has indeed happened to some extent. The UK remains nonetheless an attractive centre for research with its excellent universities and science parks. The UK government has undertaken to replace lost funding and perhaps to seek to establish bilateral agreements with other nations in order to access other funding/collaboration options.

[D] Clinical Trials

The new Clinical Trials Regulation 536/2014 was adopted on 16 June 2014, and it was finally implemented in 2021, following confirmation of full functionality of a Clinical Trials Information System through an independent audit. The UK did not become part of the new system as following Brexit; the Regulation did not automatically continue to apply.

If the UK adopts significantly different national legislation to Regulation 536/2014, this is likely to make the clinical trials procedure increasingly complex with greater administrative burden and cost for companies wishing to conduct multicentre clinical trials in the EU and the UK. In particular, UK companies will not have access to the single portal for applications for clinical trials, or if they do, there may be a substantial fee, and separate centralised and national clinical trial authorisation procedures will need to be followed. Furthermore, companies will have to ensure that sponsors of a clinical trial have legal representation established in the EU, but, for large life science companies at least, this is unlikely to pose a significant administrative issue.

Additional questions will also arise in relation to data protection (in particular, clinical trial data and personal data) currently falling under the EU Data Protection Directive which should be borne in mind. Data protection is considered in more detail in Chapter 23.

[E] Marketing Authorisations

The majority of marketing authorisations (MAs) in the EU are applied for under the decentralised procedure (national) or the centralised procedure[2] (EU-wide); each application process is determined by Directive 2001/83/EC. Following the end of the transition period, a system for independent MA approval had to be adopted in the UK.

MAs granted by the UK were unaffected, and MAs granted in the EU under the centralised procedure prior to the exit were to be recognised by the UK. However, centralised MAs covering the EU held by UK companies had to be transferred to companies established in EU countries as no mutual recognition agreements are put in place, and it remains unlikely that such agreements will be agreed.

A Working Group on Medicinal Products was established to facilitate mutual consultation so that the EU and the UK can work together to implement agreed international guidelines, monitor and review implementation of the MPA, and check how it is operating. Disputes arising out of the MPA will, however, fall outside of the TCA's disputes mechanism; it is hoped that the structure of the Working Group will suffice for dealing with disputes or blips arising out of the implementation of the MPA and the development of the parties' relationship post-Brexit. The TCA provides that any changes to either the UK or the EU's regulation regime should be on sixty days' notice and be subject to discussion.

---

2. *See* Chapter 5 – Obtaining a Marketing Authorisation.

If nothing else, having to apply for MA in the UK as well as the EU has added to the regulatory burden, increased barriers to the market, and costs for the pharmaceutical industry. As mentioned below, the Medicines and Healthcare Products Regulatory Agency (MHRA) has found that its workload has increased commensurately as the centralised procedures are dismantled whilst also dealing with the regulatory implications of the COVID-19 pandemic.

[F]   Quality Assurance and Product Safety

Quality assurance processes have to have been transferred from the UK (or at least replicated in the EU) in line with current EU good manufacturing practices in order to ensure that products can be sold in the EU. All European Economic Area (EEA) located manufacturers and importers of medicines need to hold a manufacturing authorisation; the European Medicines Agency (EMA) determined that all MA holders must have had by 1 January 2020 batch-testing facilities in the EEA and completed all necessary regulatory submissions.

Even with the UK not being part of the EEA after Brexit, UK manufacturers can continue to export products to the EEA, although the cost of importing into the EU has increased as the EU imposes additional requirements and inspections on non-EU imports. While mutual recognition of regulatory approvals has not been agreed, in light of the stated aim of the MPA to 'facilitate availability of medicines, promote public health and protect high levels of consumer and environmental protection in respect of medicinal products', the Annex provides for:

- the mutual recognition of Good Manufacturing Practice (GMP) inspections and certificates, meaning that manufacturing facilities do not need to undergo separate UK and EU inspections;
- the individual inspection, on notice, by the EU or UK of each other's facilities; and
- the suspension of the mutual recognition arrangements.

Furthermore, uniform product safety laws, as applied currently across the EU (e.g., the General Product Safety Directive (2001/95/EC)), are likely (but not a given, as the UK government can publish their own national standards) to continue post-Brexit in common with those of the EU and globally so as to maintain the competitiveness of UK goods and suppliers. If a product is subject to a specific provision in retained EU law, then these will continue to apply to that product. The Product Safety and Metrology etc. (Amendment etc.) (EU Exit) Regulations 2019 came into force on exit day and amended the General Product Safety Regulations 2005. Please note that there is divergence in the rules for uniform product safety laws in Northern Ireland.

[G] Pharmacovigilance[3]

The EU pharmacovigilance system is coordinated by the EMA, which, as discussed below, had to be relocated following Brexit. UK companies will therefore need to revise their pharmacovigilance reporting system as a single person cannot perform the pharmacovigilance function for the EU, and the UK as the appropriately qualified person, should reside and operate in the EU.

[H] Regulatory Authorities

As the UK chose not to become part of the EEA, the EMA and MHRA will both be significantly affected. The EMA had to relocate to Amsterdam, and the MHRA had to increase employee numbers to carry out the regulatory work, which would have previously been handled by EMA. In addition, where previously the EMA cooperated with the International Convention on Harmonisation (ICH), Food and Drug Administration (FDA), Japanese Pharmaceuticals and Medical Devices Agency (PDMA), and other competent authorities, the MHRA will now need to negotiate its own cooperation agreements to replace those agreed by the EMA.

There will be further, hopefully, more minor, impacts made to other UK agencies (e.g., NICE) that are beyond the scope of this chapter.

[I] Parallel Importation[4]

As far as exhaustion of intellectual property rights (IPR) is concerned, the UK government has, in The Intellectual Property (Exhaustion of Rights) (EU Exit) Regulations 2019[5] (the SI), proposed an asymmetric regional exhaustion.

The SI provides that the present system of EEA-wide exhaustion will be retained to the extent possible. Following the end of the transition period, rights in goods put on the market in the EEA are exhausted in the UK but absent any agreement with the EU, there will be no such reciprocity for goods put on the market in the UK; putting the goods on the market in the UK will not exhaust the IPR in the EEA.

Therefore, although owners of UK IPR will not be able to prevent parallel imports from the EEA, as the UK will no longer be a Member State, owners of rights in the EEA will be able to prevent parallel imports from the UK. The Intellectual Property Office's (IPO's) guidelines on exhaustion and parallel trade post-Brexit, therefore, stress the need for parallel importers to review whether they will need the EEA-based IPR holder's permission to export goods to the EEA.

EU exhaustion of rights rules will cease, and it is unclear what the UK government will replace them with; there has been a consultation, but no conclusions have been reached so far. As the UK has left the single market, pharmaceutical companies may be

---

3. *See* Chapter 10 – Pharmacovigilance.
4. *See* Chapter 20 – Parallel Trade.
5. the Intellectual Property (Exhaustion of Rights) (EU Exit) Regulations 2019.

able to assert their IPR to stop parallel importation into the UK (in addition to other existing defences), which may be seen as a benefit of Brexit by the Pharmaceuticals sector.

§1.02 SPECIFIC IMPACTS ON IPR

[A] Unitary Patent System[6]

The new EU patent regime was intended to provide patentees with the option to apply for a single pan-EU Unitary Patent (UP) covering most of the EU. It would also create the Unified Patent Court (UPC) to hear and determine patent disputes on an EU-wide basis.

The introduction of the new regime, whose future was already uncertain after the Brexit vote in June 2016, was further delayed and complicated by the challenges to the regime going through the German courts, but now it will proceed without the UK, whose ratification of the UPC Agreement in April 2018 became of questionable relevance given the UK's non-inclusion in the regime. In addition, the planned Unitary Patent Court Central Division (which was to be based in London) will have to be relocated (likely candidates were Milan and The Hague, but the Netherlands now appears to have given up its claim) following Brexit.

[B] SPCs[7]

The additional protection afforded to patentees by SPCs is part of UK law by virtue of two EU Regulations. These extensions to patent protection of up to five years are very valuable, and similar extensions are available in many countries around the world (e.g., the US and Japan). The Patents (Amendment) (EU Exit) Regulations (the Patents Regulations) came into effect after the transition period to preserve as far as possible any SPCs that have been previously applied for under the regulations by incorporating those regulations into UK law. The Patents Regulations bring current EU legislation into UK law as far as possible to maintain current systems and processes, but there are clear anomalies since the existing SPC system relies on EMA MAs, and the ultimate arbiter is the European Court of Justice. For a new post-Brexit UK SPC, a UK patent and an MA granted by the MHRA will be required. During the transition period, the UK's SPC regime was unaffected, so UK SPCs granted before the transition period expired will remain valid on the same term. Furthermore, in accordance with the Withdrawal Agreement, all pending SPC applications filed in the UK before 31st December 2020 will continue in the same way regardless of Brexit, and it will provide the same rights once granted.

The position has changed now that the transition period has ended; while the UK's SPC regime remains largely unchanged, and many of the processes for applying

---

6. *See also* Chapter 3 for an analysis of the UPC.
7. *See* Chapter 7 – Supplementary Protection Certificates.

for an SPC will remain the same, applicants for new SPC applications filed from 1st January 2021 will require (as before), a UK patent granted by the EPO or the UKIPO, and an MA valid in the UK. New SPC applications filed from 1st January 2021 can therefore be based on either:

- existing EMA authorisations, if the product has already been authorised by the EMA before 2021 and that EMA MA has become a UK MA by virtue of the grandfathering which was introduced to ensure that authorised products remained on the UK market; or
- MAs granted by the UK's MHRA.

From the end of the transition period, since Northern Ireland is continuing to be aligned with the EU in relation to medicinal products post-Brexit, UK MAs may have one or two of three different territorial scopes. This means there will be three types of MAs that apply within the UK:

- MAs for Northern Ireland (NI) granted as part of the EMA's centralised procedure;
- MAs for England, Scotland, and Wales (Great Britain or GB), granted by the MHRA; or
- UK Mas valid across the whole UK (where based on grandfathered EMA MAs).

It may be that applicants end up with multiple MAs – a Great Britain MA and a NI MA. New legislation has had to be introduced (Supplementary Protection Certificates (Amendment) (EU Exit) Regulations 2020) to replicate, as far as possible, a regime as familiar as possible to the previous regime. It is intended that an SPC may be granted if there is an MA which allows the product to be sold anywhere within the UK, but such an MA must fulfil the same requirements as in the current system – i.e., it must be valid for placing the product on the market and must be the first such authorisation for its particular territory.

[C] **Trademarks and Registered Community Designs**

After the transition period, EU Trademarks (EUTMs) and Registered and Unregistered Community Designs no longer have effect in the UK. The UK government provided that at the end of the transition period, a comparable UK trademark was created for every registered EUTM at no charge. The same will be applied for Registered Community Designs (RCDs) but not to pending EUTM applications, so companies with pending applications need to register a comparable UK trademark in the nine months after exit day to benefit from the same filing date as the related EUTM application.

Therefore, there was no need for companies with existing EUTM and RCD registrations to refile for equivalent registrations in the UK, as comparable UK registrations arose automatically. However, for new filings, companies need dual-file in the EU and UK; this was advised even during the transition period. This was because

EUTM applications pending at the end of the transition period needed to be refiled in the UK anyway. Rights owners should also review the following:

- Whether they have any pending oppositions/cancellation actions at the EU IPO: actions which are only based on UK rights will fall away; parallel actions against the new comparable UK trademark will need to be brought.
- Whether their existing EUTM legal representatives will remain entitled to represent them before the EU IPO after Brexit. Bird & Bird will be able to represent clients before both the UK and the EU IPOs.
- Their broader enforcement strategy: a new pan-EU injunction will not cover the UK and will not be available in the UK, meaning both EU and UK proceedings will need to be brought to cover all of Europe.
- Whether they have an EU customs notice ('Application for Action') in place which was filed via UK Customs: these will fall away and need to be renewed/refiled via one of the remaining EU countries. A UK filing will also be needed.
- Whether they have hardware businesses affected by parallel imports between the UK and continental Europe: the ability for trademark owners to prevent imports from one territory to the other will differ depending on which way the goods are going.
- References to the EU in brand licence agreements will need to be considered.

CHAPTER 2
Overview of European Pharmaceutical Regulatory Requirements

Sally Shorthose

§2.01 INTRODUCTION

This second chapter provides an introduction to the relevant regulatory agencies, legislation, and many of the terms that are used throughout the book.

[A] History of Pharmaceutical Regulation

In its earliest days, the pharmaceutical industry was essentially an unregulated market in which products were developed and marketed in a haphazard and inconsistent way.

The introduction of schemes in different jurisdictions to independently evaluate medicinal products before they could be put on the market did not happen simultaneously; various triggers gave rise to the implementation of such schemes at different times, and the United States (US) led the way, from the Pure Food and Drug Act of 1906, establishing the US Food and Drug Administration (FDA), through to the Food, Drug and Cosmetics Act of 1938 which was passed after a mistake in the formulation of the medicinal product elixir of sulphanilamide resulted in the deaths of 107 people, many of whom were children, to the Kefauver-Harris Amendment in 1962 gave the FDA even greater control over prescription drugs, new drugs, and experimental drugs, as well as oversight of prescription drug advertising. For the first time, drug manufacturers were required to prove to the FDA that their products were effective.

The FDA continues to authorise and monitor medicinal products in the US, but there are significant differences between the US and the European positions, especially in relation to the promotion of medicines: in the US, physicians are permitted to advertise their services, and drug manufacturers may advertise and promote their products directly to consumers. These practices are not permitted in Europe.[1]

In Japan, government regulations requiring all medicinal products to be registered for sale were first introduced in the 1950s.

Throughout Europe and other countries, there was a significant increase in legislation in the 1960s and 1970s following the thalidomide tragedy. Thalidomide is a sedative-hypnotic and multiple-myeloma medication and was widely believed at the time to be an effective treatment for insomnia, coughs, colds, and headaches, as well as being an antiemetic. The drug was prescribed to hundreds of thousands of pregnant women all over the world between 1957 and 1961, mainly to treat morning sickness. It was withdrawn from the market in 1961 after it was found to have caused severe birth defects in between 10,000 and 20,000 infants.[2] Hitherto, the safety of medicines used by pregnant women had not been questioned because it was believed that substances could not pass from the mother to the baby through the placenta.[3] However, the thalidomide tragedy made it abundantly clear that this presumption was incorrect. It was now apparent that the new-generation synthetic drugs, which were revolutionising medicine at the time, needed far stricter regulation before they were made available to the public.

In the wake of the thalidomide tragedy, many countries introduced new legislation, regulations, and guidelines that required far stricter and more rigorous testing of medicinal products prior to their being placed on the market and also mandated the monitoring of medicinal products after they had been put on the market.

However, even as the pharmaceutical industry was becoming international, national laws still governed the registration and approval of medicines. Despite the fact that the various regulatory systems were designed to ensure a consistent standard of efficacy, safety, and quality, there were technical and procedural differences among countries, which meant that pharmaceutical innovators wanting to market their products internationally had to repeat expensive, time-consuming processes, and tests to meet each country's requirements.

This entailed higher costs for the pharmaceutical companies, and together with the higher costs being borne by national health authorities, this resulted in elevated healthcare costs for consumers. Harmonisation was needed to reduce costs; at the same time, there was public pressure to have new drugs on the market as quickly but as safely as possible.

Pharmaceutical rules and regulations are designed to satisfy quality, safety, and efficacy criteria at all stages of a medicinal product's life, including research and development, clinical trials, and authorisation for sale and post-marketing pharmacovigilance obligations. The International Conference on Harmonisation (ICH) of the

---

1. *See* Chapter 9.
2. Since that tragedy, thalidomide has been found to be a valuable treatment for a number of medical conditions, including leprosy and tuberculosis, and in 1998, it began to be prescribed again in a number of countries, on a very limited basis (a named-patient basis in the UK, for example).
3. C.A. Heaton, *The Chemical Industry* (Springer, 1994), 40.

Technical Requirements for Registration of Pharmaceuticals for Human Use[4] initiates most of the efforts to harmonise the manner in which those criteria are satisfied. However, even now, a company seeking to bring a new product to market in several territories must undertake many time-consuming and expensive procedures in order to demonstrate compliance with the relevant national procedures. The company must also take into account cultural and linguistic differences. The attempts to streamline the authorisation process move slowly and full harmonisation will take a long time to achieve. It is estimated that it costs between USD 1.3 billion[5] and USD 2.6 billion[6] to fulfil all the requirements of bringing a new product to market, including research and development (R&D) costs, the costs associated with abandoned compounds, and the cost of producing several marketing authorisation applications (MAAs) dossiers.

[B]   **The European Union**

The European Union (EU), originally established in the 1950s, currently comprises twenty-seven European states (the Member States) – the United Kingdom (UK) left the EU on 31 January 2020. The EU now acts in a wide range of policy areas – economic, social, regulatory, and financial – providing the institutions through which new policies may be legislated, implemented, and policed.

The EU provides legislation for social affairs, agricultural and environmental policies and encourages innovation. The basic purpose of the EU was to create a *single market* that facilitates the free movement of people and goods among the Member States and to promote the limitation or elimination of restrictions between Member States on trade and free competition, with the aim of increasing the standard of living for the inhabitants of those Member States. The single market is differentiated from a *single economic area*, which has not been achieved, as some sectors, such as the public services, remain subject to national laws, and the Member States are still broadly responsible for their own taxation and social welfare regimes. In the Commission Communication on the Single Market in Pharmaceuticals,[7] the European Commission (the Commission) sets out its conclusions on how the single market was being implemented in the European pharmaceutical industry, having initially, in 1994,[8] expressed concern at the lack of progress in this area. It was stated that the purpose of the single market for pharmaceuticals was not simply to provide a favourable environment for research, development, and innovation but also to increase consumer choice

---

4. The concept of ICH was first conceived at the European Federation of Pharmaceutical Industries & Associations (EFPIA) in 1990, and the first meeting of members was held in Tokyo in October of the same year. The six founder members were the European Commission; the EFPIA; the Japanese Ministry of Health, Labour and Welfare; the Japan Pharmaceutical Manufacturers Association; the FDA Health Organisation; and the Pharmaceutical Research and Manufacturers of America. This group works closely with the World Health Organization, the European Free Trade Area (EFTA), and Canada.
5. O.J. Wouters, M. McKee, & J. Luyten. Estimated research and development investment needed to bring a new medicine to market, 2009–2018. *JAMA*. DOI: 10.1001/jama.2020.1166.
6. https://doi.org/10.1016/j.jhealeco.2016.01.012.
7. COM (98) 588.
8. COM (93) 718.

while, as ever, maintaining the harmonised standards in quality, efficacy, and safety at an affordable cost. Affordability would be achieved by improving cost-effectiveness, by improving efficiency, and by maintaining consistent quality standards. The tension among the interest of patients, prescribers, and social security institutions as third-party payers was recognised, as well as those of the research-based industry. While medical care remained a national responsibility (there are regional variations in disease prevalence as well as in economic strength) and the concept of subsidiarity would remain, there were clear benefits in seeking consistency in standards. Since that time, there has been ever-increasing harmonisation of rules and regulations covering the development and sales of pharmaceutical and medical devices products.

[C] Major EU Pharmaceutical Legislation

Council Directive 65/65/EEC of 26 January 1965 on the 'approximation of provisions laid down by Law, Regulation or Administrative Action relating to proprietary medicinal products' was the first European Community pharmaceutical Directive, that is, a Directive that would have to be applied in all of the then Member States of the European Community. It was the first step towards harmonising different national regulatory regimes.

Directives 75/318/EEC and 75/319/EEC of 20 May 1975 followed a decade later. These introduced a procedure for the mutual recognition of Marketing Authorisations (MAs) across the EU Member States. After the harmonisation of the different regimes in the European Community, the next step was for Member States to acknowledge such equality of safety standards. If a medicine was authorised in one Member State under the mutual recognition procedure (MRP), the other Member States would be obliged (with a few exceptions; *see* §5.04 to permit the product to be marketed in each Member State.

Directive 75/319/EEC of 20 May 1975 established the Committee for Proprietary Medicinal Products (CPMP), now called the Committee for Medicinal Products for Human Use (CHMP), which assessed whether candidate products complied with Directive 65/65/EEC.

Council Regulation (EEC) 2309/93 of 23 July 93 introduced the centralised procedure in 1995, which was at that stage mandatory for biotechnology products and optional for new chemical entity medicines.

The Codification Directive 2001/83/EC of 6 November 2001 brought the eleven Directives on human medicinal products into one legislative text. These were Directives 65/65/EEC, 75/318/EEC, 75/319/EEC, 89/342/EEC, 89/343/EEC, 89/381/EEC, 92/25/EEC, 92/26/EEC, 92/27/EEC, 92/28/EEC, and 92/73/EEC. This codification was an important step in the reform of the EU pharmaceutical legislation. Directive 2002/83/EC has been amended by twelve further Directives between 2003 and 2012 and was amended by a Corrigendum in 2007.

[D] Key EU Pharmaceutical Reform Legislation

Article 71 of Regulation 2309/93 required the Commission to report on the operation of the two authorisation procedures – the *centralised procedure* (CP) and the *mutual recognition procedure* (MRP) – within six years after the date of entry into force of the Regulation. In addition, Article 15c Directive 75/319/EEC required that the Commission publish a detailed review and propose any amendments to the procedures by 1 January 2001.

In order to fulfil these obligations, the Commission hired the firms CMS Cameron McKenna and Andersen Consulting to write 'Evaluation of the Operation of Community Procedures for the Authorisation of Medicinal Products'. The report led to the Pharma Review 2001, which was aimed at securing a high level of public health protection throughout Europe, promoting the internal market for pharmaceuticals, meeting the new challenges arising from EU enlargement, and simplifying the European medicines authorisation system. The review proposed changes in the law that were subject to the 'co-decision' procedure requiring the formal agreement of both the European Parliament and the Council of Ministers. The Commission proposed a new Regulation to replace Regulation 2309/93 and changes to the newly codified Directives: Directive 2001/83/EC (Human Medicinal Products) and Directive 2001/82/EC (Veterinary Medicinal Products).

The Commission's main changes to Regulation 2309/93, which governed the CP, included expanding the list of products for which the CP is mandatory and making optional the use of the CP for generic medicinal products of centrally authorised medicines or other products where the applicant can show that the product constitutes a significant innovation or that there is EU interest for patients or animals. Although the CP would effectively stay the same under the changes enacted, provisions were added to accelerate assessment by shortening some steps and allowing the possibility of fast-tracking the assessment of products of major interest in terms of public health and therapeutic innovation.

The major change to the Directives was to introduce a new procedure called the *decentralised procedure* (DCP). The national route to authorisation and MRP remains in place.

[E] National Law and Interface with EU Directives

EU law is implemented at a national level by different mechanisms, depending upon the type of legislation involved. A treaty must be ratified by a referendum or an act of parliament. An EU Regulation has general application, and Member States do not have to legislate at a national level in order for an EU Regulation to be directly effective. However, a Directive does not automatically become national law; it must be implemented by domestic legislation. The Directive itself sets out the Member State's obligations; however, a Member State is free to determine the manner in which it implements these obligations.

Together, the Commission and the Court of Justice of the European Union (CJEU) ensure that the obligations of the Member States under EU legislation are fulfilled. If the Commission suspects an infringement of EU law, it may refer the matter to the CJEU to investigate and rule on the matter. If the Court then rules that the Member State has not fulfilled its obligations, the Court will order the Member State to cease the infringement immediately or face financial penalties.

§2.02 DEFINITIONS

[A] Medicinal Product

A *medicinal product* is defined in Directive 2001/83/EC (as amended) as:

(a) 'Any substance or combination of substances presented as having properties for treating or preventing disease in human beings or
(b) any substance or combination of substances which may be used in or administered to human beings either with a view to restoring, correcting or modifying physiological functions by exerting a pharmacological, immunological or metabolic action, or to making a medical diagnosis'.

Substance is defined as any human, animal, vegetable, or chemical matter, irrespective of origin. This broad definition therefore covers substances ranging from insulin to nicotine patches.

[B] Generic Medicinal Products

A *generic medicinal product* is defined under Article 10 2(b) of Directive 2001/83/EC (as amended) as:

> A medicinal product which has the same qualitative and quantitative composition in active substances and the same pharmaceutical form as the reference medicinal product, and whose bioequivalence with the reference medicinal product has been demonstrated by appropriate bioavailability studies. The different salts, esters, ethers, isomers, mixture of isomers, complexes or derivatives of an active substance shall be considered to be the same active substance, unless they differ significantly in properties with regard to safety and/or efficacy ...The various immediate-release oral pharmaceutical forms shall be considered to be one and the same pharmaceutical form.

Common examples of a generic medicinal products include paracetamol, ibuprofen, and amoxicillin.

[C] Paediatric Medicines

Paediatric medicines are medicines used to treat children and babies.

Regulation (EC) 1901/2006 (the Paediatric Regulation), amending Regulation (EC) 1902/2006, entered into force on 26 January 2007. Following years of unlicensed and off-label use of medicinal products in children, the Paediatric Regulation required pharmaceutical companies to perform studies on any medicinal products intended for use in the paediatric population. The groundwork for this had been laid by the implementation in Europe of an ICH guideline, 'Note for guidance on clinical investigation of medicinal products in the paediatric population' (ICH Topic E11), which has been in force since July 2002, and the Clinical Trials Directive (Directive 2001/20/EC), which lays down criteria for the protection of children in clinical trials.

The Paediatric Regulation provides incentives for companies to develop products and formulations for the paediatric population. Incentives include a six-month extension of the Supplementary Protection Certificate (SPC), if still in force, or, for off-patent products, a ten-year period of market protection for the paediatric formulation. In order to obtain these benefits, strict criteria must be met. The process is considered in depth in Chapter 7. The process is managed by the Paediatric Committee (PDCO) within the European Medicines Agency (EMA), which met for the first time in July 2007.

[D] Orphan Drugs

Orphan medicinal products, or 'orphan drugs', are medicines used to treat rare diseases. They are intended for either:

(a) the diagnosis, prevention, or treatment of life-threatening or chronically debilitating conditions that affect no more than five in 10,000 people in the EU; or
(b) are medicines that, for economic reasons, would be unlikely to be developed without incentives.

The medicines that have been designated as orphan products have generally increased year on year since 2000, although there were 148 new orphan drug designations given in 2012 and 136 in 2013. Around 8% of these designations have successfully gone through the MAA process to the grant of an MA, such that there are now more than sixty orphan medicines authorised. These cover a wide variety of rare diseases, including genetic diseases and rare cancers. Previously, there were limited or unsatisfactory treatments for these conditions.

In order to treat unmet needs and to try to ensure that patients who suffer from rare diseases have access to the same quality of treatment as patients with more 'mainstream' diseases and conditions, the EU established a legislative framework[9] designed to stimulate research and development of medicinal products for rare

---

9. The legislative framework (Regulation [EC] No. 141/2000 adopted on 16 Dec. 1999 [OJ No. L 19, 22 Jan. 2000] and Commission Regulation [EC] No. 847/2000 of 27 Apr. 2000 [OJ No. L103/5, 28 Apr. 2000]) introducing an EU public health policy on orphan medicinal products came into effect in the EU in April 2000.

diseases by providing incentives to the pharmaceutical industry. Through this legislation, the Committee for Orphan Medicinal Products (COMP) was established. The COMP assesses whether for orphan drug status should be granted.

[E]   Biotechnology-Derived Medicinal Products

Biotechnology-derived medicinal products are listed in the Annex of Regulation 726/2004. The Regulation itself sets out the medicinal products to be authorised by the EU (products for which an application using the CP is mandatory). Biotechnology-derived medicinal products are developed by means of one of the following biotechnological processes: recombinant DNA technology, controlled expression of genes coding for biologically active proteins in prokaryotes and eukaryotes, including transformed mammalian cells, or hybridoma and monoclonal antibody methods. This includes any product intended for gene therapy or as a vaccine from strains developed by means of recombinant DNA technology. An example of a biotechnology-derived product is ATryn (Genzyme Europe BV), which contains antithrombin alfa, a recombinant DNA anti-clotting blood protein.

[F]   Homeopathic Medicinal Products

A *homeopathic medicinal product* is defined in Directive 2001/83/EC (as amended) as:

> Any medicinal product prepared from substances called homeopathic stocks in accordance with a homeopathic manufacturing procedure described by the European Pharmacopoeia or, in the absence thereof, by the pharmacopoeias currently used officially in the Member States. A homeopathic medicinal product may contain a number of principles.

Homeopathic products are derived from raw materials that are diluted numerous times, so that the eventual product is extremely diluted. Homeopathic products can be derived from either natural or synthetic stock. Raw materials of botanical, animal, or human origin may be in either fresh or dried form, whereas fresh plant material is macerated in ethanol to produce the 'mother' (original) tincture.

Examples of natural raw materials include the following:

- Botanical: *Calendula officinalis* (marigold).
- Animal: *Apis mellifera* (honeybee).
- Chemical: Natrium chloridium (NaCl, table salt).
- Mineral: Quartz.

[G]   Herbal Medicinal Products

Directive 2001/83/EC (as amended) defines a *herbal medicinal product* as 'any medicinal product, exclusively containing as active ingredients one or more herbal substances or one or more herbal preparations, or one or more such herbal substances in combination with one or more such herbal preparations'.

Herbal substances are defined as all 'mainly whole, fragmented or cut plants, plant parts, algae, fungi, lichen in an unprocessed usually dried from, but sometimes fresh'. Certain exudates that have not been subjected to a specific treatment are also considered to be herbal substances. Herbal substances are precisely defined by the plant part used and the botanical name according to the binomial system (genus, species, variety, and author).

Herbal preparations are defined also by Directive 2001/83/EC (as amended) as 'preparations obtained by subjecting herbal substances to treatments such as extraction, distillation, expression, fractionation, purification, concentration or fermentation'. These include comminuted or powdered herbal substances, tinctures, extracts, essential oils, expressed juices, and processed exudates.

Aniseed is an example of a herbal medicinal product for which both the seeds and oil are used for the treatment of expectorant coughs.

[H]   Traditional Herbal Medicinal Products

A *traditional herbal medicinal product* is defined as a herbal medicinal product that fulfils the conditions in Article 16(a)(1) of Directive 2001/83/EC (as amended). This article describes a simplified registration procedure – 'traditional use registration' – for such products, where:

- the herbal medicinal products have indications exclusively appropriate to traditional herbal medicinal products, which are designed for use without the supervision of a medical practitioner for diagnostic purposes or for prescription or monitoring of treatment;
- they are exclusively for administration in accordance with a specified strength and dosage;
- they are an oral, external, and/or inhalation preparation;
- the period of traditional use has elapsed (a period of at least thirty years preceding the date of application, including at least fifteen years within the EU);
- the data on traditional use of the medicinal product are sufficient, particularly that the product proves not to be harmful in the specified conditions of use, and the pharmacological effects or efficacy of the medicinal product are plausible on the basis of long-standing use and experience.

An example of a traditional herbal medicinal product is devil's claw root, which has long been used for the relief of backache, rheumatic or muscular pain, and general aches and pains in the muscles and joints.

[I] Radiopharmaceuticals

A *radiopharmaceutical* is defined in Directive 2001/83/EC (as amended) as any medicinal product that, when ready for use, contains one or more radionuclides (radioactive isotopes) included for a medicinal purpose.

[J] Non-prescription Medicines

Title VI, Articles 70–75 of Directive 2001/83/EC (as amended) deals with the classification of medicinal products. When an MA is granted, the Competent Authorities specify whether the medicinal product is classified as a medicinal product subject to prescription or a medicinal product not subject to prescription. A change in classification of a medicinal product can occur when new facts are brought to the attention of the Competent Authorities (Article 74) or when applied for by an applicant. Article 71 states:

> Medicinal products shall be subject to medical *prescription* where they:
> - are likely to present a danger either directly or indirectly, even when used correctly, if utilised without medical supervision; or
> - are frequently and to a very wide extent used incorrectly, and as a result, are likely to present a direct or indirect danger to human health; or
> - contain substances or preparations thereof, the activity and/or adverse reactions of which require further investigation; or
> - are normally prescribed by a doctor to be administered parenterally.

A Member State must also take account of the following factors when determining whether a medicinal product should be classified as a prescription-only medicine:

- the medicinal product contains, in a non-exempt quantity, a substance classified as a narcotic or a psychotropic substance within the meaning of the international conventions in force, such as the United Nations Conventions of 1961 and 1971;
- the medicinal product is likely, if incorrectly used, to present a substantial risk of medicinal abuse, to lead to addiction or be misused for illegal purposes;
- the medicinal product contains a substance which, by reason of its novelty or properties, could be considered as belonging to the group envisaged in the second indent as a precautionary measure;
- the medicinal product, because of its pharmaceutical characteristics or novelty or in the interests of public health, is reserved for treatments which can only be followed in a hospital environment;
- the medicinal product is used in the treatment of conditions which must be diagnosed in a hospital environment or in institutions with adequate diagnostic facilities, although administration and follow-up may be carried out elsewhere; or

- the medicinal product is intended for outpatients, but its use may produce very serious adverse reactions requiring a prescription drawn up as required by a specialist and special supervision throughout the treatment.

It is, however, possible for a Competent Authority to waive all of the above criteria if it has regard to the maximum single or daily doses, the strength, the pharmaceutical form, the packaging, and/or any other circumstances the Competent Authority specifies.

A medicinal product that does not require a prescription is defined under Article 72 as any medicinal product that does not fulfil any of the requirements of Article 71, as outlined above.

Under Article 74a, a one-year period of data exclusivity is granted for the results of pre-clinical tests or clinical trials (if the results are significant) that are submitted by an applicant to change the classification. A change in category (such as from prescription-only to over-the-counter or 'pharmacy sale only') may be appropriate after several years of use of a medicinal product as a prescription-only medicine when an applicant can show that the medicinal product can be used safely for self-medication, within defined parameters. Depending on the Member State, the non-prescription use may be under the supervision of a pharmacist (P), or for some medicines, without supervision at all (e.g., sold in pharmacies without supervision, or supermarkets) (general sales list (GSL)).

[K] Immunological Medicinal Products

An *immunological medicinal product* is defined in Directive 2001/83/EC, as amended, as 'any medicinal product consisting of vaccines, toxins, serums or allergen products'. Directive 2001/83/EC further states that:

> vaccines, toxins and serums shall cover in particular:
> (i) agents used to produce active immunity such as cholera vaccine, BCG, polio vaccines, smallpox vaccine;
> (ii) agents used to diagnose the state of immunity, including in particular tuberculin, PPD, toxins for the Shick and Dick tests, Brucellin;
> (iii) agents used to produce passive immunity, such as diphtheria antitoxin, anti-smallpox globulin, antilymphocyte globulin;

'allergen product' shall mean any medicinal product which is intended to identify or induce a specific acquired alteration in the immunological response to an allergising agent.

[L] In-vitro Diagnostic Devices

An *in-vitro diagnostic device* is defined in the Regulation on In-Vitro Diagnostic Devices (EU) 2017/746 (IVDR) as:

any medical device which is a reagent, reagent product, calibrator, control material, kit, instrument, apparatus, piece of equipment, software or system, whether used alone or in combination, intended by the manufacturer to be used in vitro for the examination of specimens, including blood and tissue donations, derived from the human body, solely or principally for the purpose of providing information on one or more of the following:

- concerning a physiological or pathological process or state;
- concerning congenital physical or mental impairments;
- concerning the predisposition to a medical condition or a disease;
- to determine the safety and compatibility with potential recipients;
- to predict treatment response or reactions;
- to define or monitor therapeutic measures.
- Specimen receptacles shall also be deemed to be *in vitro* diagnostic medical devices;

The IVDR places specific obligations on manufacturers, authorised representatives, distributors, importers, and healthcare institutions throughout the supply chain.

[M] Medical Devices

A *medical device* is defined by the Regulation on Medical Devices Regulation (EU) 2017/745 as:

any instrument, apparatus, appliance, software, implant, reagent, material or other article intended by the manufacturer to be used, alone or in combination, for human beings for one or more of the following specific medical purposes:

- diagnosis, prevention, monitoring, prediction, prognosis, treatment or alleviation of disease;
- diagnosis, monitoring, treatment, alleviation of, or compensation for, an injury or disability;
- investigation, replacement or modification of the anatomy or of a
- physiological or pathological process or state; or
- providing information by means of in vitro examination of specimens derived from the human body, including organ, blood and tissue donations,

and which does not achieve its principal intended action by pharmacological, immunological or metabolic means, in or on the human body, but which may be assisted in its function by such means.

This broad definition encompasses a wide range of instruments, from X-ray machines to cardiac pacemakers. The EU strives to promote innovation and competition in the sector, while maintaining high standards of public safety through the regulation of market access to medical devices and international trade relations.

Medical devices are regulated by the Medical Devices Regulation (EU) 2017/745 (MDR) which now governs the production and distribution of medical devices in the European Economic Area (EEA) and replaced the three Directives which used to govern this area. An update was needed to bring the legislation in line with new products and technologies (especially software) and to introduce a whole product life-cycle approach to medical device regulation rather than just focusing on pre-approval regulation. Medical device manufacturers now have systems in place to ensure the medical devices are traceable with the use of unique device identifiers. The European database on medical devices (EUDAMED) was also introduced to provide and hold information on clinical investigation, product registration, and post-market surveillance. The Active Implantable Medical Devices Directive (AIMDD) has also been incorporated, again to reflect the more sophisticated technology comprised in medical devices than was anticipated in previous legislation.

§2.03 THE REGULATORY AGENCIES

[A] The European Commission

The European Commission (the Commission), formerly called the Commission of the European Communities, is the executive arm of the EU, and it is responsible for proposing legislation, implementing decisions of the European Parliament and the Council, upholding the EU's treaties, and conducting the general day-to-day running of the EU. Each Member State is allowed to appoint one commissioner; the twenty-seven commissioners act together as a form of cabinet, also known as the 'college of commissioners'. Individual commissioners are bound to represent the interests of the EU as a whole rather than those of their home countries.

The term 'the Commission' can refer to the twenty-seven-member cabinet or to the larger administrative body of about 32,000 European civil servants. Based in Brussels, the Commission comprises a number of Directorates General and governmental departments, each of which is responsible for a particular policy area. The Pharmaceuticals Unit sits within Directorate General for Health and Consumer Protection of the Commission – DG SANTE (formerly DG SANCO), the Commission department responsible for EU policy on food safety and health and for monitoring the implementation of related laws.

[1] DG Health and Consumers (Commonly Known as 'SANTE')

The DG Health and Consumers stated vision is 'We intend to make Europe a healthier and safer place. Our mission is to protect the citizens' *health* and monitor their *food* making sure it is safe'.

The Directorate-General is made up of seven Directorates (as of December 2021):

- Directorate A: Resource management and better regulation
- Directorate B: Health systems, medical products, and innovation
- Directorate C: Public Health
- Directorate D: Food sustainability, international relations
- Directorate E: Food and feed safety, innovation

- Directorate F: Health and food audits and analysis
- Directorate G: Crisis preparedness in food, animals, and plants.

Directorates A, B, D, E, and G are based in Brussels, Directorate C is based in Luxembourg, and Directorate F in Grange.

The common goal of these units is to enable EU citizens to be able to live safe, healthy, and full lives, with an aim to build a strong European Health Union[10] to protect and improve public health.[11] Within Directorate B (Health Systems, Medical Products & Innovation) are specialist groups:

- B.1 Performance of National Systems
- B.2 Cross Border Healthcare & Tobacco Control
- B.3 Digital Health, European Reference Networks
- B.4 Medical Products, Quality, Safety, Innovation
- B.5 Medicines Policy, Authorisation and Monitoring
- B.6 Medical Devices, Health Technology Assessment.

The groups will reflect and develop the Pharmaceutical Strategy for Europe[12] which has the aim creation of a future-proof regulatory framework while supporting industry in promoting patient-oriented research and technologies in order to fulfil patients' therapeutic needs while addressing market failures. The experience of the COVID-19 pandemic will be taken into account, and lessons learned will be applied in order to strengthen the system.

The new strategy will be based on four pillars, as follows:

- Ensuring access to affordable medicines[13] for patients and addressing unmet medical needs (in the areas of antimicrobial resistance and rare diseases, for example).
- Supporting competitiveness, innovation, and sustainability of the EU's pharmaceutical industry and the development of high-quality, safe, effective, and greener medicines.
- Enhancing crisis preparedness and response mechanisms, diversified and secure supply chains[14] while addressing medicines shortages.
- Ensuring a strong EU voice in the world by promoting a high level of quality, efficacy, and safety standards.

---

10. https://ec.europa.eu/info/strategy/priorities-2019-2024/promoting-our-european-way-life/european-health-union_en.
11. https://health.ec.europa.eu/index_en.
12. https://health.ec.europa.eu/system/files/2021-02/pharma-strategy_report_en_0.pdf
13. Making medicines more affordable (europa.eu)
14. https://health.ec.europa.eu/medicinal-products/pharmaceutical-strategy-europe/structured-dialogue-security-medicines-supply_en.

This initiative is in line with the new Industrial Strategy for Europe[15] and the priorities set out in the European Green Deal,[16] the Breast Cancer Beating Plan,[17] and the European Digital Strategy.[18]

[2] The EMA

Established in 1995, the EMA is a decentralised body of the EU with headquarters in The Hague, having previously been established in London before Brexit. Its main responsibility is the protection and promotion of public (and animal) health through the evaluation and supervision of medicines for human and veterinary use. The EMA initially managed the implementation of the two new procedures for obtaining MAs in Europe, the community or CP[19] and the MRP.[20] Its responsibilities included the evaluation, supervision, and pharmacovigilance of medicinal products marketed within the EU.

While the EMA is still involved in referral procedures relating to medicinal products that are approved or under consideration by Member States in non-centralised authorisation procedures, its main tasks today are to conduct scientific assessments of medicinal products and to coordinate the scientific evaluation of the safety, efficacy, and quality of the medicinal products that are evaluated by CP, MRP, and the DCP.[21]

The EMA constantly monitors the safety of medicines through a pharmacovigilance network. The information reported about adverse drug reactions is stored in a central database so that the EMA can keep a record of trends. If adverse drug reaction reports suggest changes to the benefit-risk balance of a medicinal product, the EMA can take action, including revoking or suspending the MA.

The EMA provides Member States and EU institutions with scientific advice. The EMA may charge a fee, but in certain areas, such as advice on paediatric products and advice on questions about the safety, quality, and efficacy of medicinal products for humans (on which it provides guidelines), it may provide free advice. The EMA also offers protocol assistance to companies that are developing new medicinal products.

It has established a pool of multinational expert scientists from over forty National Competent Authorities (NCAs) in the thirty EU and EEA/European Free Trade Area (EFTA) countries, creating a network of over 3,600 European experts. The EMA contributes to the EU's international activities through its work with international organisations and initiatives, such as the European Pharmacopoeia, the World Health

---

15. https://ec.europa.eu/info/strategy/priorities-2019-2024/europe-fit-digital-age/european-industrial-strategy_en.
16. https://ec.europa.eu/info/publications/communication-european-green-deal_en.
17. https://ec.europa.eu/info/law/better-regulation/have-your-say/initiatives/12154-Europes-Beating-Cancer-Plan_en.
18. https://digital-strategy.ec.europa.eu/en.
19. *See* Chapter 5, Section 3.
20. *See* Chapter 5, Section 4.
21. These procedures are set out in detail in Chapter 5.

Organization (WHO), and the ICH and VICH trilateral (EU, Japan, and the US) conferences on harmonisation.

There are seven scientific committees in the EMA comprising members of all EU and EEA/EFTA states and some patient and doctor representatives. The committees that conduct the main scientific work of the EMA are: the CHMP; the Committee for Medicinal Products for Veterinary Use (CVMP); the COMP; the Committee on Herbal Medicinal Products (HMPC); the PDCO; and the Committee for Advanced Therapies (CAT); and the Pharmacovigilance Risk Assessment Committee (PRAC) which was established as a result to the revised pharmacovigilance legislation. It reports to both the CHMP and the Coordination Group for Mutual Recognition and Decentralised Procedures – human (CMDh). The first meeting of PRAC took place in July 2012, and it now meets once a month at the EMA unless the meeting is replaced by a written procedure, for instance, during holidays.

The EMA is also charged with stimulating innovation and research in the pharmaceutical sector. To this end, in 2005, the EMA established a dedicated group, the SME Office, to provide special assistance to small- and medium-sized enterprises (SMEs). Such assistance includes reduction of fees for scientific advice and inspections, fee deferral, or exemption for MAAs.

The EMA is headed by an executive director who is under the supervision of an internal management board. The executive director has a secretariat of nearly 900 staff members. The management board is the supervisory body of the EMA, responsible, in particular, for budgetary and planning matters. It consists of two representatives of the Commission, two representatives from the European Parliament, one representative from each Member State (e.g., the heads of the NCAs), and the *civil society representatives*: two representatives from patient organisations and one representative from each of a doctor and veterinarian organisations. In addition, there are observers from each of the EEA/EFTA Member States.[22] Each member is appointed by the Member State or institution that he or she represents, and the civil society representatives are appointed by the Council of the EU.

[B] Committees of the EMA

[1] CHMP

The CHMP is responsible for preparing the EMA's opinions on all questions concerning medicinal products for human use in accordance with Regulation (EC) No. 726/2004. The CHMP and its working parties also provide assistance to companies researching and developing new medicines, prepare scientific and regulatory guidelines for the pharmaceutical industry, and cooperate with international partners on the harmonisation of regulatory requirements for medicines.

---

22. The EEA comprises the EU plus the EFTA. The EFTA comprises Iceland, Liechtenstein, and Norway.

The CHMP plays a vital role in the marketing procedures for medicines in the EU. In the CP, the CHMP conducts the initial assessment of medicinal products for which an EU-wide MA is sought. The CHMP is also responsible for several post-authorisation and maintenance activities, including the assessment of any modifications or extensions, that is, 'variations' to the existing MA. It takes into account the opinions and recommendations of the PRAC regarding the safety of medicines on the market and, when necessary, will make recommendations to the Commission regarding changes to a medicine's MA or its suspension or withdrawal from the market.

In the MRP and DCP, the CHMP arbitrates in cases where there is a disagreement between Member States concerning the MA of a particular medicinal product. Disagreements about whether a medicinal product causes potential serious risks to public health may arise in the DCP and are passed to the CHMP if no agreement can be found by the CMDh. The CHMP also acts in referral cases initiated when there are concerns relating to the protection of public health or where other EU interests are at stake (the 'Community referral procedure'). Such referrals can be made by the Commission or by Member States.

Assessments conducted by the CHMP are based on purely scientific criteria. They determine whether or not the products concerned meet the necessary quality, safety, and efficacy requirements in accordance with EU legislation, particularly Directive 2001/83/EC. These assessments ensure that medicinal products have a positive risk/benefit balance for consumers once they reach the marketplace.

The CHMP publishes a European Public Assessment Report (EPAR) for every centrally authorised product, setting out the scientific grounds for the committee's opinion in favour or not of granting the authorisation and, if granted, a summary of product characteristics (SmPC), labelling and packaging requirements for the product, and details of the procedural steps taken during the assessment process. EPARs are published on the EMA website. A more patient-friendly document called the EPAR Summary for the Public was introduced in 2006. Members of the EMA medical information team, which is part of the post-authorisation unit, have written such public summaries for existing medical products.

CHMP members and alternates are nominated by the Member States in consultation with the EMA Management Board and are chosen on the strength of their qualifications and expertise with regard to the evaluation of medicinal products. They serve on the committee for a renewable period of three years.

The CHMP comprises:

- a chair and a vice-chair, elected by serving CHMP members;
- one member (and an alternate) nominated by each of the twenty-seven EU Member States;
- one member (and an alternate) nominated by each of the EEA/EFTA states; and
- up to five co-opted members, chosen from experts nominated by Member States or the EMA and recruited, when necessary, to gain additional expertise in a particular scientific area.

[2] CVMP

The CVMP prepares the EMA opinions on all questions concerning veterinary medicinal products in accordance with Regulation (EC) No. 726/2004.

The CVMP performs activities that are similar to those of the CHMP, except the CVMP activities are all with regard to veterinary medicinal products. Veterinary medicinal products can be approved through the CP, DCP, or MRP.

The CVMP assesses veterinary medicinal products on purely scientific criteria, and it determines whether or not the products meet the quality, safety, and efficacy requirements in accordance with EU legislation, particularly Directive 2001/82/EC.

The EU's network of national veterinary medicines agencies, in close cooperation with veterinary professionals and the pharmaceutical companies themselves, conducts subsequent monitoring of the safety of authorised products. The CVMP plays an important role in this EU-wide pharmacovigilance activity by closely monitoring potential safety concerns and, when necessary, making recommendations to the Commission regarding changes to a product's MA or the product's suspension/withdrawal from the market.

The CVMP establishes the maximum residue limits (MRLs) of veterinary medicinal products permissible in food produced by or from animals for human consumption, including dairy products, meat, and honey. The CVMP establishes these limits for all pharmacologically active substances contained in a medicinal product before an MA can be granted.

The CVMP and its working parties also assist companies in researching and developing new veterinary medicines to prepare scientific and regulatory guidelines for the veterinary pharmaceutical industry and cooperate with international partners on the harmonisation of regulatory requirements for veterinary medicines.

The members of the CVMP are chosen in a similar way to those of the CHMP, with representatives nominated from each Member State, Iceland, and Norway, plus up to five co-opted members with expertise in the veterinary medicine field or selected to provide experience. In some Member States, the veterinary agencies are completely separate from the human medicines' agencies, and in others, they are within the same agency.

No advice or guidance is given in this book on products for use in the treatment of animals.

[3] COMP

The COMP is responsible for reviewing applications from persons or companies seeking orphan medicinal product designation for products that they intend to develop for the diagnosis, prevention, or treatment of orphan conditions, defined in the EU as life-threatening or very serious conditions that affect not more than five in 10,000 persons. Parliament and Council Regulation (EC) No. 141/2000 of 16 December 1999 provides an EU procedure for the designation of medicinal products as orphan medicinal products, provides incentives for the research, and establishes the COMP.

The COMP also advises the Commission on the establishment and development of a policy on orphan medicinal products in the EU. It assists the Commission in drafting guidelines, and it acts as a liaison for international matters relating to orphan medicinal products. See Chapter 14 for a complete discussion of the approval process for orphan medicinal products. COMP members and alternates are nominated by the Member States in consultation with the EMA Management Board, and they are chosen on the strength of their qualifications in science and medicine and their expertise with regard to the evaluation of medicinal products. They serve on the committee for a renewable three-year period.

The COMP comprises:

- a chair who is elected by serving COMP members;
- one member appointed by each of the twenty-seven EU Member States; three representatives of patients' organisations appointed by the Commission; three members appointed by the Commission on the EMA's recommendation, and one member appointed by each of Iceland and Norway.

[4] HMPC

The HMPC was established in September 2004, replacing the CPMP Working Party on Herbal Medicinal Products. The committee was established in accordance with Regulation (EC) No. 726/2004 and Directive 2004/24/EC, which introduced a simplified registration procedure for traditional herbal medicinal products in the EU Member States.

The HMPC assists with standardisation and harmonisation of procedures and provisions concerning herbal medicinal products in the EU Member States. The HMPC also works to integrate herbal medicinal products into the European regulatory framework.

The HMPC provides the EU Member States and European institutions its scientific opinion on questions relating to herbal medicinal products. It also establishes a draft EU list of herbal substances, preparations, and combinations thereof for use in traditional herbal medicinal products and establishes EU herbal monographs.

The committee consists of one member appointed by each of the EU Member States and also includes one member appointed by Iceland and Norway for a term of three years, which may be renewed. The committee may also co-opt up to five additional members based on specific scientific expertise for a non-renewable period of three years. The representatives have been drawn from NCAs or universities.

[5] PDCO

The PDCO is required by Regulation (EC) No. 1901/2006, as amended.

The main responsibilities of the PDCO are to assess the content of paediatric investigation plans and to adopt opinions on them in accordance with Regulation (EC) No. 1901/2006, as amended. This includes the assessment of applications for full or partial waivers and deferrals. More generally, it supports the development of such medicines in the EU by providing scientific expertise and defining paediatric needs.

The PDCO also analyses data generated in accordance with agreed paediatric investigation plans, and it adopts opinions on the quality, safety, or efficacy of any medicine for use in the paediatric population. The PDCO renders opinions at the request of the CHMP or when requested by a Competent Authority. It advises Member States on the content and format of data to be collected for a survey of all existing uses of medicinal products in the paediatric population; advises and supports the EMA on the creation of a European network of persons and bodies with specific expertise in the performance of studies in the paediatric population; and provides advice on any question relating to paediatric medicines, at the request of the EMA Executive Director or the Commission. Finally, the PDCO maintains an inventory of paediatric medicinal product needs and advises the EMA and the Commission on the communication of arrangements available for conducting research into paediatric medicines.

The PDCO does not grant MAs for medicinal products for paediatric use. The CHMP and the committee have sole authority over MAAs. However, the CHMP or any other Competent Authority may request the PDCO to prepare an opinion on the quality, safety, and efficacy of a medicinal product for use in the paediatric population, if these data have been generated in accordance with an agreed paediatric investigation plan.

The PDCO is composed of five CHMP members with their alternates, appointed by the CHMP itself; one member and one alternate appointed by each Member State (except Member States already represented through the members appointed by the CHMP); three members and alternates representing healthcare professionals; and three members and alternates representing patients' associations. Members of the PDCO are appointed for a renewable period of three years. The members of the PDCO elect the chair.

The basis for decision-making by the PDCO has recently been considered by the CJEU.[23] In the judgment handed down on 14 December 2011, the court held that the PDCO was correct in not taking into account the indication proposed by the applicant (who applied for a waiver). The PDCO must base its opinion on the scientific and objective evidence.

[6]   CAT

The CAT is the committee at the EMA that is responsible for assessing the quality, safety, and efficacy of advanced therapy medicinal products (ATMPs) and following scientific developments in the field. It is a multidisciplinary committee gathering together some of the best available experts in Europe. It was established in accordance with Regulation (EC) No. 1394/2007 on ATMPs. Further detail is provided in Chapter 17.

The main responsibility of the CAT is to prepare a draft opinion on each ATMP application submitted to the EMA before the CHMP adopts a final opinion on the

---

23. Case T52/09 *Nycomed v. EMA*.

granting, variation, suspension, or revocation of an MA for the medicine concerned. At the request of the EMA executive director or of the Commission, an opinion is also drawn up on any scientific matter relating to ATMPs.

The members of the CAT are appointed for a renewable period of three years. The chair and vice-chair are elected from its members for a term of three years, which may be renewed once.

The CAT is composed of the following:

- five members or co-opted members of the CHMP with their alternates. These members are appointed by the CHMP itself;
- one member and one alternate appointed by each EU Member State that is not represented by the members and alternates appointed by the CHMP;
- two members and two alternates appointed by the commission to represent clinicians; and
- two members and two alternates appointed by the Commission to represent patient associations.

[7] PRAC

The PRAC is the committee at the EMA responsible for assessing and monitoring safety issues for human medicines; it was established in line with the pharmacovigilance legislation, which came into effect in 2012. Its responsibilities include the detection, assessment, minimisation, and communication relating to the risk of adverse reactions while taking the therapeutic effect of the medicine into account. It also has reasonability for the design and evaluation of post-authorisation safety studies and pharmacovigilance audits.

The main responsibility of the PRAC is to prepare recommendations on any questions relating to pharmacovigilance activities related to a medicine for human use and on risk-management systems, including the monitoring of the effectiveness of those risk-management systems.

The PRAC's recommendations are considered by the CHMP when it adopts opinions for centrally authorised medicines and referral procedures and by the CMDh when it provides a recommendation on the use of a medicine in Member States. It can also provide recommendations on pharmacovigilance and risk-management systems to the EMA Secretariat, the Agency's Management Board, and the Commission.

The members and alternates of the PRAC are nominated by the EU Member States in consultation with the Agency's Management Board. They are chosen on the strength of their qualifications and expertise with regard to pharmacovigilance matters and risk assessments of medicines for human use.

To represent healthcare professionals and patient organisations, the Commission appoints two members and two alternates following consultation with the European Parliament. The Commission also appoints six independent scientific experts.

All serve on the committee for a period of three years which is renewable once.

The PRAC comprises:

- a chair and a vice-chair, elected by serving PRAC members;
- one member and an alternate nominated by each of the twenty-seven Member States;
- one member and an alternate nominated by Iceland and by Norway;
- six independent scientific experts nominated by the Commission, appointed to ensure that the relevant expertise is available within the PRAC, including clinical pharmacology and pharmacoepidemiology, on the basis of a public call for expressions of interest;
- one member and an alternate nominated by the Commission after consultation with the European Parliament to represent healthcare professionals; and
- one member and one alternate nominated by the Commission after consultation with the European Parliament to represent patients' organisations.

[C] The Heads of Medicines Agencies

The Heads of Medicines Agencies (HMA) is a network of the heads of each of the NCAs, i.e., the organisations responsible for the regulation of medicinal and veterinary products in the EEA.

The HMA is coordinated and supervised by a management group and is supported by several focused working groups, as well as by a permanent secretariat. The members meet regularly to assess key strategic issues, exchange information, information technology (IT) developments, and share best practices throughout the EU. In particular, they provide support to the network of European medicines' agencies through the provision of professional and scientific resources, including research laboratories, population health databases, and external experts from academia or practice.

The HMA is not mandated by law, but it has a key role in formulating a balanced view on the operation of the European procedures and their resource implications for the Member State agencies, including the development, coordination, and consistency of the European medicines regulatory system. This is achieved through the provision of a mechanism for communicating the views of Member State Competent Authorities to the Commission and to the EMA in order to ensure the most effective and efficient use of resources across the network. This includes developing and overseeing arrangements for work-sharing.

The HMA can therefore devise and deliver prompt and practical solutions to problems that affect Member States. It also provides leadership and an oversight of the DCP and MRP procedures within the European system.

[D] NCAs of European Member States

All assessment of MAAs in the EU is carried out by assessors employed by the NCAs, irrespective of whether the applicant chooses the CP, DCP, MRP, or a national procedure.

All inspections – for instance, Good Clinical Practice (GCP), Good Manufacturing Practice (GMP), and pharmacovigilance inspections – of companies and sites relevant to MAs and MAAs are carried out by inspectors employed by the NCAs.

In each Member State, one or more Competent Authorities are responsible for human and veterinary medicinal products. Some of these agencies may also be responsible for medical devices. All MAs granted through DCP, MRP, or national procedures are national and therefore under the supervision of the NCAs.

[E] CMDh

The CMDh was set up in 2005. It replaced the informal Mutual Recognition Facilitation Group.

The CMDh examines questions relating to the MA of human medicines in two or more (EU) Member States in accordance with the MRP or the DCP, and questions concerning variations of these MAs.

If there is disagreement between Member States during the assessment of the submitted data based on the grounds of a potential serious risk to public health, the CMDh considers the matter and strives to reach an agreement within sixty days. If this is not possible, the Member State responsible for the product brings the case to the attention of the CHMP for arbitration.

The CMDh examines questions concerning the safety of non-centrally authorised medicines marketed in the EU, where centrally authorised products are not affected. This includes adopting a CMDh position on safety-related EU referral procedures, taking account of the recommendations of the PRAC.

Each year the CMDh identifies a list of medicines for which harmonised product information should be drawn up to promote the harmonisation of MAs across the EU.

The CMDh is made up of representatives from each Member State plus one representative from each of Norway, Iceland, and Liechtenstein. They may each appoint an alternate, and observers from the Commission and EU accession countries also participate in meetings. The EMA provides the secretariat. Each group meets monthly at the EMA offices for three days and provides a forum where procedural issues can be discussed and problems regarding individual applications can be resolved. The specific Reference Member State (the RMS) organises and chairs scientific discussions related to individual applications. If an application is referred to the CMD for resolution, the decision will involve only the RMS and the Concerned Member States (CMSs). If the issue cannot be resolved by the CMD, the issue is referred to the CHMP, HMPC, or CVMP for arbitration. The CHMP generally renders a decision six months after referral by the CMDh.

The CMDh considers points of disagreement raised by Member States during MRP or DCP procedures on the grounds of potential serious risk to public health only and makes every effort to resolve issues to avoid referral to the CHMP or HMPC.

[F] European Directorate for the Quality of Medicines

The European Directorate for the Quality of Medicines (EDQM) was created in 1996, and it is a Directorate of the Council of Europe. It is an organisation that protects public health by enabling the development, supporting the implementation, and monitoring the application of quality standards for medicines and their safe use. The EDQM is based in Strasbourg, France, the seat of the Council of Europe, to which it belongs.

The EDQM is responsible for the Technical Secretariat of the European Pharmacopoeia Commission, which was set up in 1964 by the European Pharmacopoeia Convention. The European Pharmacopoeia Commission prepares and publishes adopted texts and distributes the European Pharmacopoeia. The European Pharmacopoeia contains both general monographs and monographs that define the specifications for active drug substances.

The EDQM is also responsible for organising activities related to the procedure for assessment and approval of the certificates of suitability of European Pharmacopoeia Monographs. Directive 2003/63/EC requires that applications for MAs in Europe refer to the specific and general monographs of the European Pharmacopoeia, which provides a legal and scientific reference for the quality control of medicines.

The EDQM also develops guidance and standards in areas, such as blood transfusion, organ transplantation, and consumer health issues.

Finally, the EDQM is involved in the surveillance of medicinal products distributed in Europe. It coordinates a European network of official medicines control laboratories. The EDQM also sets standards used in the quality control testing of medicinal products.

[G] International Conference on Harmonisation of Technical Requirements for Registration of Pharmaceuticals for Human Use

The ICH brings together the regulatory authorities of Europe, Japan, and the US, and experts from the pharmaceutical industry in the three regions, to discuss scientific and technical aspects of product registration.

Harmonisation of regulatory requirements was pioneered by the EU in the 1980s as the European Community (now the EU) moved towards the development of a single market for pharmaceuticals. The success achieved in Europe demonstrated that harmonisation was feasible. At the same time, Europe, Japan, and the US discussed possibilities for harmonisation. It was, however, at the 1989 WHO International Conference of Drug Regulatory Authorities (ICDRA), in Paris, that specific plans for action began to materialise.

In April 1990, representatives of the regulatory agencies and industry associations of Europe, Japan, and the US met in Brussels, primarily to plan an International Conference. The meeting also discussed the wider implications and terms of reference of the ICH. The ICH Steering Committee was established at that meeting, and the committee has since met at least twice a year. The meeting location rotates between the three regions.

The purpose of the ICH is to make recommendations on ways to achieve greater harmonisation in the interpretation and application of technical guidelines and requirements for product registration in order to reduce or obviate the need to duplicate the testing carried out during the research and development of new medicines.

The objective of such harmonisation is a more economical use of human, animal, and material resources and the elimination of unnecessary delay in the global development and availability of new medicines while maintaining safeguards on quality, safety, and efficacy, and regulatory obligations to protect public health.

§2.04 APPLICABLE EU LEGISLATION, INCLUDING REGULATIONS AND GUIDANCE

[A] EU Treaties

EU treaties, which are arrived at after negotiation between the governments of all Member States, make up the EU's 'primary legislation'; in other words, they are equivalent to constitutional law at the national level. They set out the most fundamental features of the *raison d'etre* and operation of the EU. Although unanimity was previously a prerequisite to the adoption of a treaty, this is no longer the case. Once a treaty has been adopted, *Member States are obliged to ratify the contents of the treaty by referendum or act of Parliament and to adopt its measures into national law*. The most notable treaties include:

- Treaty of Paris (1951). The treaty that was signed on 18 April 1951 between Belgium, Luxembourg, the Netherlands, France, Italy, and West Germany established the European Coal and Steel Community (ECSC).
- Treaty of Rome (1957) that led to the creation of the European Economic Community (EEC). The aim of the EEC was to increase economic integration between the signatory states.
- Merger Treaty (1965). The treaty was signed between the founding states of the ECSC and EEC on 8 April 1965 and resulted in the creation of the first joint institutions.
- Schengen Agreement (1985). The treaty that was signed on 14 June 1985 resulted in abolition of the border checks between the members of the EU. The so-called Schengen Area, however, was created only in 1995.
- Single European Act (1986). This treaty, which was signed between twelve members of the EEC, revised the Treaty of Rome and provided the basis for foundation of a single market.
- Maastricht Treaty (1992). It is one of the most important EU treaties not only because it formally created the EU but also because it laid the foundation for formation of the Eurozone.
- Amsterdam Treaty (1997). The Treaty of Amsterdam defined EU citizenship and individual's rights in terms of justice, freedom, and security.

– Treaty of Lisbon (2007). The treaty was signed by all EU member states on 13 December 2007 with an aim to complete the reform process started by the Amsterdam Treaty.

[B] Directives

EU law requires that all Directives be implemented into national law by the Member States within a predetermined timeframe. The Directives contain certain endpoints and aims that are required to be incorporated into national law, but each Member State can adapt the Directives to its specific requirements. This provision for localisation accounts for variations in implementation among Member States.

The most important Directive relating to medicinal products for human use is Directive 2001/83/EC, as amended by Directive 2004/27/EC. This Directive of the European Parliament and Council sets out all the general principles for bringing a medicinal product to market, whether in accordance with a national procedure, the CP, DCP, and/or MRP,[24] and it determines the requirements that are common to all procedures in relation to the SmPC, package labelling, patient information leaflets, and pharmacovigilance.[25]

> Numerous other Directives are relevant to medicinal products, for example, those dealing with GMP provisions for medicinal products for human use and investigational medicinal drugs for human use;[26] and
> Provision for a legal framework for managing the risk of falsified medicines[27] entering the legal supply chain.[28]

[C] Regulations

Regulations are the most direct forms of European law. They become binding national law in every Member State as soon as they are passed; no further action is needed to implement them.

Regulation (EU) No. 726/2004, dated 31 March 2004, details EU procedures for the authorisation and supervision of medicinal products for human and veterinary use, and it established the EMA. This regulation replaced Regulation 2309/93.

Other relevant regulations, which are considered elsewhere in this book, include:

– Regulations (EU) No. 1084/2003 and (EU) No. 1085/2003, which specify the variations in national and centrally authorised MAs.

---

24. Each of these procedures is explained in depth in Chapter 5.
25. Pharmacovigilance is considered in detail in Chapter 10.
26. Directive 2003/94/EC of 8 Oct. 2003.
27. https://www.ema.europa.eu/en/glossary/falsified-medicine.
28. Directive 2011/62/EU of the European Parliament and of the Council of 8 June 2011 amending Directive 2001/83/EC on the Community code relating to medicinal products for human use, as regards the prevention of the entry into the legal supply chain of falsified medicinal products: https://eur-lex.europa.eu/LexUriServ/LexUriServ.do?uri=OJ:L:2011:174:0074:0087:EN:PDF

- Regulations (EU) No. 141/2000 and (EU) No. 847/2000, which are relevant to orphan drugs, applications for which must now be via the CP. These regulations describe what constitutes an orphan drug and how it shall be treated.
- Regulation (EC) No. 1902/2006, the Paediatric Regulation, which introduced the testing requirement for new paediatric medicines and provided incentives to encourage the introduction of paediatric indications for existing products.
- Regulation (EC) No. 507/2006 relating to conditional MAs, where a product can be permitted for sale even though the full set of clinical trials has not been completed.
- Regulation (EC) No. 540/95, which relates to the procedures for reporting suspected unexpected adverse reactions which are not serious to centrally authorised medicinal products.
- Regulation (EC) No. 1394/2007, which relates to the regulation of advanced therapy medicinal products.
- Regulation (EU) No. 1235/2010 and Regulation (EU) No. 1027/2012 amending, as regards pharmacovigilance, Regulation (EC) No. 726/200

[D] The Official Journal of the European Communities

The Official Journal, which is published both in hard copy and in pdf format on the website Eur-Lex, contains the Regulations, Directives, and Decisions. There are between 700 and 800 editions published each year. It also publishes references to questions from national courts to be determined by the CJEU. The Official Journal is available in different official languages of the EU.

[E] Guidelines

The pharmaceutical legislation is supplemented by an extensive body of guidelines. The most important collection is the Notice to Applicants (NTA). The NTA is published on the Commission website under Eudralex, and it has been prepared by the Commission in consultation with the Competent Authorities of the Member States and the EMA. The NTA has no legal force, and it does not necessarily represent the final views of the Commission.

The NTA was first published in 1986, and it is regularly updated.

Volume 1 of the NTA contains a listing of and links to all the pharmaceutical legislation relevant to medicinal products for human use. It includes a consolidated version of Directive 2001/83/EC in English only.

Volume 2A is divided into seven chapters: 'Marketing Authorisation', 'Mutual Recognition', 'Union Referral Procedures', 'Centralised Procedure (deleted in July 2015)', 'Variations', 'Community Marketing Authorisation', and 'General Information.' The different chapters are updated at different times, as they are kept up-to-date by a dynamic process.

Volume 2B deals with presentation and content of the dossier and incorporates the common technical document (CTDoc). The CTDoc is the internationally accepted format for applications for MAs. The intention is to have a common format across Europe, the US, and Japan, although there are local sections and requirements. Volume 2B includes the application forms, questions-and-answers (Q&A) documents, and details on the now compulsory electronic common technical document (eCTDoc).

Volume 2C includes guidelines on processing renewals; fast-track procedures for human influenza vaccines; the SmPC; dossier requirements for Type 1a and 1b variations; the application form for variations; packaging information; information on changing the legal classification of human medicinal products (e.g., from prescription to non-prescription); package-label and leaflet readability information; a requirement to consult with target patient groups on the package leaflet; the definition of the 'potential serious risk to public health'; and guidance on the Vaccine Antigen Master File/Plasma Master File.

Volume 3 relates to the scientific guidelines that refer to the quality, biotechnology, non-clinical, clinical safety and efficacy, and multidisciplinary guidelines, which are held on the EMA website.

Volume 4 covers GMP for human and veterinary medicinal products.

The guidance for veterinary products is included in Volume 5. It contains a listing of all relevant legislation. The notice of applicants is in Volume 6, and guidelines are in Volume 7. Volume 8 concerns the MRLs for residues of veterinary medicinal products in foodstuffs of animal origin.

Volume 9A of NTA sets out the guidelines on pharmacovigilance for medicinal products for human use but has been replaced by the Good Pharmaceutical Practice Guidelines (GVP), which is still relevant for cross-referencing purposes.

Volume 9A is presented in four parts: (i) guidelines for MA holders, (ii) guidelines for Competent Authorities and the agency, (iii) guidelines on electronic exchange of pharmacovigilance in the EU, and (iv) guidelines on pharmacovigilance communication.

Volume 9B sets out the guidelines on pharmacovigilance for medicinal products for veterinary use.

Volume 10 covers guidance for clinical trials, and it is divided into six chapters. Chapter I concerns the application and application form, and it gives detailed guidance for the request to Competent Authorities in the EU for authorisation of a clinical trial on a medicinal product for human use. It also gives guidance on the European database of clinical trials (EudraCT). Chapter II deals with safety reporting and gives detailed guidance on the collection, verification, and presentation of adverse reaction reports arising from clinical trials and on the European database of suspected unexpected serious adverse reactions (SUSARs). Chapter III covers information on the quality of investigational medicinal products (IMPs), including GMPs. Chapter IV concerns inspections, specifically the qualification of inspectors and recommendations on inspection procedures. Chapter V contains additional information, archiving, Q&A documents, and guidance on GCP. Finally, Chapter VI lists the relevant legislation.

§2.05 GUIDELINES/PUBLICATIONS

- 'Evaluation of the Operation of Community Procedures for the Authorisation of Medicinal Products.' Report published by CMS Cameron McKenna and Andersen Consulting. Pharma Review 2001.
- Heaton, C.A. *The Chemical Industry*. Springer, 1994, 40. ISBN 0751400181.

CHAPTER 3
Overview of Intellectual Property Rights

Sally Shorthose, Marta Sznajder & Jonathan Edwards[*]

§3.01 INTRODUCTION

The term 'intellectual property' covers a diverse range of transferable territorial rights that are not easily defined. These 'intangible' rights can be extremely valuable and typically include (among other rights) patents, trademarks, design rights, copyright, database rights, and rights in confidential information. Although there is a degree of overlap between these rights, intellectual property rights (IPRs) generally seek to protect three broad concepts:

- ideas and inventions (e.g., patents and designs);
- information and data (e.g., rights in confidential information, copyright and database rights); and
- brand and trade names (e.g., trademarks).

The value of these rights is not necessarily ownership of them per se but the ability to exploit them to generate revenue (e.g., through licensing or assignment) and to enforce them against third parties. Registered rights (e.g., patents, registered trademarks, and registered designs) are generally perceived to be the 'strongest' rights. One of the reasons behind this is related to the fact that these rights provide exclusive protection against all third parties which is not dependent on a fault. Another reason pertains to a presumption as to validity. However, irrespective of the scrutiny of relevant intellectual property office during prosecution of the registrable right, the final

---

[*] The authors wish to acknowledge *Tasmina Goraya*, an author of the earlier edition of this Chapter.

word on validity generally falls within the domain of the courts or respective administrative offices. Registered rights also provide information to, and put on notice, third parties as regards ownership.

[A] The Importance of IPRs

The investment made in developing novel medicines greatly outweighs their cost of manufacture and distribution. There will normally be many 'also rans' that fell by the wayside during the research and development process. In order to drive innovation, pharmaceutical companies require a period of exclusivity during which they can maintain high profit margins on the sale of their products. The patent system therefore aims to 'reward' innovation by providing a time-limited monopoly. However, the expiration or indeed cancellation or narrowing of a patent can mean a substantial reduction in the value of a company – this is particularly the case when the patent protects a 'blockbuster' product or one of company's key products. Competitors may have been developing competing products to be launched on the expiry of the patent, and the launch of these products will generally depress the price of the innovator product. In these circumstances, the innovator company may be able to rely on its trademark rights, design rights, or copyright if the competitor attempts to capitalise on the innovator's brand names or packaging.

Marketing authorisations (MAs) can take a considerable amount of time to obtain, and this delay erodes the term of patent protection. As patent applications are generally filed at the discovery stage, companies often find that there are only a few years of patent protection to run when the product is eventually launched. The legislators have therefore devised supplementary protection certificates (SPCs) to compensate companies for the term of patent protection they lost on account of obtaining patent protection. SPCs are discussed in Chapter 7.

The protection of trademarks is also an important consideration for any business but is vital in the pharmaceutical sector. The industry is built on reputation and market confidence, so it is important for a company to protect its business name. In addition, companies must select the brand name for their medicines before an application for an MA is sought.

It is also imperative that a company ensures that its confidential information is kept confidential. Disclosure of the subject matter of a patent application prior to the filing date (or priority date, as the case might be) can be potentially fatal for the validity of a patent. Further, manufacturing processes, protocols, and material know-how may also be confidential, and their disclosure to a competitor might have very serious negative consequences and a reduction in competitive advantage. It is therefore essential that companies have appropriate confidentiality procedures in place.

It is clear that there is an overlap between the different IPRs which can collectively act to create a significant hurdle for competitors to take a similar product to market.

[B] Ownership

Who owns an intellectual property right will depend on the right in question and the law of the country where it is created or registered.

Issues of ownership of IPRs often arise in collaboration agreements, particularly in the context of research and development. Often, parties agree that IPRs owned by the respective parties prior to the start of the agreement (i.e., background IPRs) will remain vested in the party which owned it at the effective date. At the time the agreement is drafted, the parties are generally considering entering into a collaborative venture using each other's IPRs to develop innovative technologies or research. Matters of who owns, and has rights to exploit, the IPRs in the resulting technology (commonly referred to as 'foreground intellectual property rights') throughout the collaboration, and especially when the relationship comes to an end or if there is a dispute are not considered as often as they should be.

Commonly, collaboration agreements provide for joint ownership of foreground IPRs. This solution, however, creates uncertainties as to who owns the IPRs and what they can do with it; and the rights of the co-owner vary in different jurisdictions. For example, the law that determines first ownership of IPRs depends not only on the right in question but also the country in which it was created. The ownership of biological material also poses its own problems, e.g., the creation of a human cell line may require consent from the original donor. At present, there is no international harmonisation on the ownership of biological material, so issues of ownership will generally be considered by national courts.

The remainder of this Chapter provides a brief summary of the main IPRs relevant to the pharmaceutical industry.

§3.02 PATENTS

There are currently two ways by which patents may be prosecuted within the EU:

(1) the national route through the patent office of the relevant country; and
(2) centrally through a single application filed at the European Patent Office (EPO).

A new, third route (which is not yet operational but which is expected to commence in early 2023) is through the Unitary Patent System, which is discussed in more detail in §3.02[D] below.

The international patent system established by the Patent Cooperation Treaty (PCT) provides a further means whereby patent protection may be obtained in a number of countries whilst minimising cost. The PCT application does not give any rights per se, but it is converted into a number of national or regional patent applications (at the time of writing, the PCT has 155 Contracting States).[1] Further

---

1. *See* http://www.wipo.int/pct/en/pct_contracting_states.html.

details of the PCT system can be found on the website of the World Intellectual Property Organization (WIPO).²

A number of EU Member States (Austria, Bulgaria, Croatia, Czech Republic, Denmark, Estonia, Finland, France, Germany, Greece, Hungary, Ireland, Italy, Poland, Portugal, Romania, Slovakia, Slovenia, and Spain)³ also provide the option of protecting inventions through utility models, which are also referred to as 'petty patents'. The requirements for the registration of utility modesl are less onerous than for patents – there is generally no requirement for an inventive step, and there is a significantly lower threshold of inventiveness than for patents. The procedure for obtaining a utility model is also generally quicker than patents, as novelty and inventive steps are not usually examined.

National routes to patent protection are not discussed in this Chapter. However, a list of national intellectual property offices is available on WIPO's website, and the processes can be reviewed on the relevant intellectual property office's website.⁴

[A]   European Patents

Sitting outside the legislative framework of the European Union (EU), the European Patent Convention (EPC)⁵ provides the main basis for patent law in Europe.

After more than twenty years of negotiations, the EPC was finally signed by sixteen countries on 5 October 1973 in Munich. The EPC entered into force on 7 October 1977 with the accession of seven countries: Belgium, France, Germany⁶, Luxembourg, the Netherlands, Switzerland, and the United Kingdom (UK). Revisions to the EPC in 2000 came into effect sometime later on 13 December 2007. The current seventeenth Edition of the EPC was published in November 2020.

Since coming into force, the number of contracting states has grown to thirty-eight countries, including all twenty-seven current Member States of the EU and some countries outside the EU (e.g., Albania, Norway, Iceland, Liechtenstein, Monaco, Former Yugoslav Republic of Macedonia, San Marino, Switzerland, Serbia, UK, and Turkey). There are also two extension states (Bosnia and Herzegovina and Montenegro)⁷,⁸ and four validation states (Morocco, the Republic of Moldova, Tunisia, and Cambodia).⁹

---

2. See http://www.wipo.int/pct/en/.
3. See https://www.wipo.int/patents/en/topics/utility_models.html.
4. See http://www.wipo.int/directory/en/urls.jsp.
5. A copy if the EPC and related legal text can be found on the EPO's website: https://www.epo.org/law-practice/legal-texts/html/epc/2016/e/index.html.
6. The Federal Republic of Germany.
7. The UK's departure from the EU will not affect its membership of the EPC.
8. Extension agreements are bilateral agreements with European states that are not a party to the EPC. They allow European patents and applications to be extended to the extension states where they have the same effect as national patents and applications, and patents have the benefit of substantially the same protection as patents granted by the EPO. For further information, see https://www.epo.org/law-practice/legal-texts/html/natlaw/en/a/index.htm.
9. e Validation agreements are bilateral agreements with non-EPC countries and are not limited to European countries. Under the validation system, patent applicants can validate their European

Chapter 3: Overview of Intellectual Property Rights §3.02[A]

Most notably, the EPC established a system where a patent could be prosecuted and granted centrally through the EPO, which has its headquarters located in Munich, a branch in The Hague, and offices in Berlin, Vienna, and Brussels. Once granted, the 'European Patent' gives rise to a bundle of national patents. Given the scope of the EPC and European Patents, it is not surprising that its provisions have been mirrored in the national law of EPC contracting states.

[1] Patentability and Scope of Protection

European Patents may be obtained for products or processes (e.g., manufacturing processes). Pharmaceutical patents under the EPC may relate to a new compound or new class of compound, an enantiomer for which the racemate is known, and to known compounds where the invention lies in the process, combination, or medical uses. Patents relevant to the pharmaceutical industry may also relate to biological medicinal products, manufacturing processes, and devices for the administration of medicinal products.

[a] Requirements

A European Patent must satisfy the requirements of Article 52(1) of the EPC. Article 52(1) of the EPC states (emphasis added):

> European patents shall be granted for any inventions, in all fields of technology, provided that they are *new, involve an inventive step and are susceptible of industrial application.*

Certain inventions are, however, excluded from being patentable under the EPC. Those that are relevant pharmaceutical patent applications are:

- discoveries;[10]
- inventions, the commercial exploitation of which would be contrary to *'ordre public'* or morality; such exploitation shall not be deemed to be so contrary merely because it is prohibited by law or regulation in some or all of the Contracting States;[11]
- plant or animal varieties or essentially biological processes for the production of plants or animals (this provision does not apply to microbiological processes or the products thereof);[12] and

---

patents and applications in the validation states after which they will confer essentially the same protection as patents granted by the EPO. The status of the validation agreements are as follows: Morocco (as from 1 March 2015); Republic of Moldova (signed on 16 October 2013 and came into force on 1 November 2015); Tunisia (as from 1 December 2017); and Cambodia (as from 1 March 2018).
10. EPC, Article 52(2).
11. EPC, Article 53(a).
12. EPC, Article 53(b).

– methods for treatment of the human or animal body by surgery or therapy and diagnostic methods practised on the human or animal body; this provision shall not apply to products, in particular substances or compositions, for use in any of these methods.[13]

Patent applications must also comply with the 'unity of invention' concept, i.e., they must only relate to one invention or to a group of inventions which form a single general inventive concept.[14] Further, a patent application must disclose the invention in a manner that is sufficiently clear and complete for it to be carried out by the person skilled in the art[15] and must not add matter.[16]

[b]   Novelty and Inventive Step

Novelty is generally a strict test which is assessed at the filing date (or priority date[17] if there is one) of the patent application. The invention claimed in the patent is considered to be new if it does not form part of the 'state of the art' (also known as 'prior art').[18] The state of the art is everything made available to the public by means of a written or oral description, by use, or in any other way, before the date of filing (or the priority date as the case may be) of the European patent application.[19] This does not include information disclosed under a duty of confidentiality. However, it will include information disclosed to the public by the inventor and/or applicant, e.g., descriptions of the claimed invention in scientific publications or conferences.

An invention is considered as involving an inventive step, if it is not obvious to a person skilled in the art in light of the state of the art.[20] The 'person skilled in the art' is a notional character that may be given particular qualities by the national courts. However, the skilled person in the art is described in the following terms in the EPO's Guidelines for Examination:[21]

> The 'person skilled in the art' should be presumed to be a skilled practitioner in the relevant field of technology, who is possessed of average knowledge and ability (average skilled person). The person skilled in the art is aware of what was common general knowledge in the art at the relevant date .... The skilled person is also presumed to have had access to everything in the 'state of the art', in particular the documents cited in the search report, and to have been in possession of the means and capacity for routine work and experimentation which are normal

---

13. EPC, Article 53(c).
14. EPC, Article 82.
15. EPC, Article 83 and Article 100(b).
16. EPC, Article 138(1)(d) EPC.
17. The priority date is the filing date of the first patent application for a specific invention. The subsequent patent application must be filed within twelve months of the filing date of the first application in order to claim priority. The filing date of the first application has priority over applications filed after that date, including those filed before the filing date of the subsequent patent application that claims priority.
18. EPC, Article 54(1).
19. EPC, Article 54(2).
20. EPC, Article 56.
21. http://www.epo.org/law-practice/legal-texts/html/guidelines/e/g_vii_3.htm.

for the field of technology in question. If the problem prompts the person skilled in the art to seek its solution in another technical field, the specialist in that field is the person qualified to solve the problem. The skilled person is involved in constant development in the relevant technical field.... The skilled person may be expected to look for suggestions in neighbouring and general technical fields...or even in remote technical fields, if prompted to do so... Assessment of whether the solution involves an inventive step must therefore be based on that specialist's knowledge and ability.... There may be instances where it is more appropriate to think in terms of a group of persons, e.g. a research or production team, rather than a single person... It is to be borne in mind that the skilled person has the same level of skill for assessing inventive step and sufficient disclosure.

Third parties seeking to invalidate a patent after grant will often advance arguments based on lack of both novelty and inventive step. Novelty is more difficult to establish, given its strict application.

[c] Scope of Protection

The extent of protection conferred by a European Patent is determined by its claims pursuant to Article 69 of the EPC, which provides:

> The extent of the protection conferred by a European patent or a European patent application shall be determined by the claims. Nevertheless, the description and drawings shall be used to interpret the claims.

However, the Protocol on the Interpretation of Article 69 EPC specifies:

Article 1

General Principles

Article 69 should not be interpreted as meaning that the extent of the protection conferred by a European patent is to be understood as that defined by the strict, literal meaning of the wording used in the claims, the description and drawings being employed only for the purpose of resolving an ambiguity found in the claims. Nor should it be taken to mean that the claims serve only as a guideline and that the actual protection conferred may extend to what, from a consideration of the description and drawings by a person skilled in the art, the patent proprietor has contemplated. On the contrary, it is to be interpreted as defining a position between these extremes which combines a fair protection for the patent proprietor with a reasonable degree of legal certainty for third parties.

Article 2

Equivalents

For the purpose of determining the extent of protection conferred by a European patent, due account shall be taken of any element which is equivalent to an element specified in the claims.

The construction of patent claims is often a key battleground in infringement and validity actions brought in national courts. However, European national courts adopt different approaches to patent construction, and the Protocol on Interpretation seeks to provide some means of a common approach to the construction of European Patent claims.

[2] Prosecution and Enforcement

European Patents are prosecuted centrally and undergo a single examination procedure at the EPO. Applications can be made under the EPC or the PCT and consist of:

- a request for grant;
- a description of the invention;
- claims;
- drawings if there are any; and
- an abstract summarising the claimed invention.

An application can be filed in any language, but if it is not an official EPO language (English, French, or German), a translation in one of these languages must also be filed.

Patent applications first undergo a formalities examination to check whether all the required information and documents have been filed.[22] A European search report is then prepared listing all documents available to the EPO which it considers relevant to the issues of novelty and inventive step. This is sent to the applicant together with an initial opinion on whether the application meets the requirements of the EPC.

The application is published (usually with the search report) eighteen months after the date of filing, or the priority date if priority is claimed. Applicants then have six months to decide whether to continue with the application by requesting a substantive examination by the Examination Division. The applicant has the opportunity to submit amendments to the patent application in order to overcome any objections.

Once granted, the European Patent effectively becomes a collection of national patent rights, subject to validation.

[a] EPO Opposition Proceedings

The validity of European Patents may be challenged by third parties centrally at the EPO by way of opposition proceedings during a window of nine months after the grant of the patent. This window is known as the 'opposition period'.

Opponents are generally competitors of the patentee who may request revocation or limitation of the European patent. Oppositions begin with the Opposition Division which normally comprises three examiners. Opposition proceedings at the EPO are slow, and a final decision can take years to obtain if all rights of appeal are exhausted.

If an opposition is filed at the EPO, the patentee will be given the opportunity to respond in writing. Invalidity arguments are further considered at oral hearings.

---

22. The claims can be filed within two months of filing the request of grant.

Patentees are permitted to amend their patents to overcome adverse decisions of the Opposition Division.

The Technical Board of Appeal (TBA) hears appeals against a decision of the Opposition Division. The TBA consists of three members, two of which will be technically rather than legally qualified. The Enlarged Board of Appeal considers appeals from the TBA, but only on a point of law. Neither decisions of the EPO Boards of Appeal nor decisions of other courts are binding on national courts.

If the European Patent is amended centrally during opposition proceedings at the EPO, the amendments will carry through to the national patents arising from the European Patent.

[b] National Courts

The validity of a European Patent may be challenged in a national court or a competent administrative office by way of revocation proceedings. Circumstances sometimes arise where there may be parallel proceedings before the national courts or offices and the EPO. For example, where opposition proceedings have commenced during the opposition period and the patentee subsequently commences infringement proceedings in a national court or office.[23] Depending on applicable national law, the defendant may seek to invalidate the patent in suit by way of a counterclaim or must file a separate action with a relevant administrative office (in case of a 'bifurcated' system). Revocation proceedings may also be brought in national courts or offices in their own right after the opposition period has ended.[24]

Issues of infringement and validity are heard by national courts at the same time in all EPC countries except Germany, Austria, and Poland. The German and Austrian courts operate a 'bifurcated' system where issues of infringement and validity are heard separately. In Poland, validity issues are recognised by the Polish Patent Office which has exclusive competence in that regard, while patent infringement matters are heard exclusively by the Regional Court in Warsaw (22nd division).

[3] Duration

Article 33 of the Agreement on Trade-Related Aspects of Intellectual Property Rights (TRIPS Agreement) requires that World Trade Organisation members must provide a minimum term of protection of twenty years for patents from the filing date of the application. Prior to the TRIPS Agreement, patent terms varied from jurisdiction to jurisdiction.

The twenty-year duration of European Patents is reflected in Article 63(1) of the EPC.

---

23. Revocation proceedings.
24. It is possible to bring proceedings to revoke a European Patent in the UK, while opposition proceedings are pending before the EPO. However, the courts may stay the proceedings pending the outcome of the opposition.

[B] Specific Issues Relating to Pharmaceutical Patents

[1] Product by Process

Product claims are sometimes drafted so that they claim a product obtained by a particular process. These types of claims are often known as 'product by process claims'. These claims should be construed as a claim to the product as such. The technical content of the invention lies not in the process per se but rather in the technical properties imparted to the product by the process.[25]

According to the EPO's Guidelines for Examination,[26] claims defined in terms of a process of manufacture are only permitted if the products as such meet the requirements for patentability (including novelty and inventive step). A product will not be considered novel 'merely by the fact that it is produced by means of a new process'. The EPO Guidelines stress that a 'product by process claim' may take the form 'Product X obtainable by process Y'. The claim must make clear that it is directed to the product per se regardless of whether the terms 'obtainable', 'obtained', 'directly obtained', or an equivalent wording is used. Accordingly, a claim to a product obtained or produced by a new process will not be novel, if the product per se has been disclosed in the prior art, irrespective of how it was made.

[2] Products Obtained Directly by a Patented Process

The provisions described in the TRIPS Agreement that offer protection against products that are the result of patented processes require that the product be 'obtained directly' from the process claimed in the patent. The protection conferred by a claim directed at a process for preparing a product covers that process. Indeed, this position is reflected in Article 64(2), which states, 'if the subject-matter of the European patent is a process, the protection conferred by the patent shall extend to the products directly obtained by such process'.

The definition of what 'directly' means in this context is therefore important (and this definition is subject to variations in national law). To give an example of how this requirement has been interpreted under national law, the English Courts have held that 'obtained directly' means 'without intermediary', i.e., products that were the direct and immediate result at the end of applying the patented process.[27] It does not necessarily matter that the product undergoes further processing provided the further processing does not cause the product to lose its identity, i.e., it retains its essential characteristics, notwithstanding the processing.

---

25. *See* https://www.epo.org/law-practice/legal-texts/html/guidelines/e/f_iv_4_12.htm.
26. *Ibid.*
27. *Pioneer Electronics Capital Inc v. Warner Music Manufacturing Europe GmbH* [1997] R.P.C. 757.

[3] New Chemical Entities (NCEs)

Generally, the first person who finds a use for an NCE will seek a patent claim that will protect the chemical per se. Such claims may be characterised as a chemical formula. However, if the formula is not known, the compound may alternatively be characterised in terms of a process of manufacture or by reference to parameters.

The patentee is also likely to claim structurally similar compounds that may also have some therapeutic effect. Such claims may take the form of a 'Markush' claim.[28] These claims are generally achieved through the use of 'R groups' in the structure to represent a range of groups in a molecule attached to the position indicated by the particular R group giving rise to a potentially large number of possible compounds.

The EPO Guidelines for Examination specify that 'if it can be shown that at least one Markush alternative is not novel, unity of invention should be reconsidered. In particular, if the structure of at least one of the compounds covered by a Markush claim is known, together with the property or technical effect under consideration, this is an indication of lack of unity of the remaining compounds (alternatives).'[29]

[4] Composition and Formulation Claims

Patents claiming formulations of pharmaceuticals are largely found to be invalid for lack of an inventive step principally because the methods of formulating medicinal products are generally well-known. However, there are a few exceptions that have survived invalidity attacks. For example, in *Novartis AG v. IVAX Pharm UK Ltd*, the English High Court held the following claim to be valid:

> A pharmaceutical composition comprising cyclosporine as an active ingredient, (1) a hydrophilic phase, (2) a lipophilic phase and (3) a surfactant, which composition is an 'oil-in-water micro emulsion pre-concentrate'.

The patent was not held to lack an inventive step because, although micro emulsions were known, they were not previously used in the field and did not form part of the common general knowledge of the skilled person in the art. Composition or formulation claims can rely on a synergistic effect, which 'must be possessed by everything covered by the claim, and it must be described in the specification. No effect is described in the present specification that is not the natural prediction from the properties of the two components of the combination'.[30]

[5] Methods of Treatment

Article 53(c) EPC prohibits the grant of a patent in respect of:

---

28. Markush claims are named after Eugene Markush, the named inventor for US patent, US1506316, which was one of the earliest patent applications to include such claims.
29. See http://www.epo.org/law-practice/legal-texts/html/guidelines/e/f_v_5.htm.
30. *Glaxo Group's Patent* [2004] EWHC 477; [2004] RPC 43.

methods for treatment of the human or animal body by surgery or therapy and diagnostic methods practised on the human or animal body; this provision shall not apply to products, in particular substances or compositions, for use in any of these methods.

This exclusion is principally a public policy measure to provide a safeguard to medical and veterinary practitioners from the threat of patent infringement when exercising and providing treatment to their patients. However, what amounts to a 'treatment' or 'therapy' has given rise to a considerable amount of EPO case law.

In *DUPHAR/Pigs I*,[31] a liquid to control ectoparasites on pigs was construed as a therapeutic treatment, even though the product was applied ectopically and could be used by farmers (i.e., non-veterinary qualified persons). In *RORER/Dysmenorrhoea*,[32] a treatment for dysmenorrhoea was considered to be a 'treatment' even though it relieved symptoms by reducing discomfort experienced by patients during menstruation rather than the cause.

A requirement of the term 'therapy' appears to be related to whether the treatment is considered cosmetic or therapeutic (i.e., has a medical purpose). Cosmetic treatments will generally not fall within this exception; however, in *ICI/Cleaning Plaque*,[33] a treatment for dental plaque was considered to be a therapy notwithstanding its cosmetic use.

The Boards of Appeal will generally construe diagnostic methods more narrowly than surgical and therapeutic methods.[34]

As explained in EPO Guidelines, the exclusion does not extend to new products (substances, compositions, or other) for use in these methods of treatment or diagnosis.[35]

[6] Medical Use

As discussed above, one of the key requirements for patentability is that the invention should be novel over the prior art. However, first, second, and subsequent medical use may be considered patentable if the requirements of Articles 54(4) and 54(5) of the EPC are satisfied:

(1) An invention shall be considered to be new if it does not form part of the state of the art.
(2) The state of the art shall be held to comprise everything made available to the public by means of a written or oral description, by use, or in any other way, before the date of filing of the European patent application.
(3) Additionally, the content of European patent applications as filed, the dates of filing of which are prior to the date referred to in paragraph 2 and which were published on or after that date, shall be considered as comprised in the state of the art.

---

31. Case T-0116/85.
32. Case T-0081/84.
33. Case T-0144/83.
34. Case T- 81/84 DU PONT/Appetite suppressant and G01/04 *Diagnostic Methods*.
35. *See* https://www.epo.org/law-practice/legal-texts/html/guidelines/e/g_ii_4_2.htm.

(4) Paragraphs 2 and 3 shall not exclude the patentability of any substance or composition, comprised in the state of the art, for use in a method referred to in Article 53(c), provided that its use for any such method is not comprised in the state of the art.
(5) Paragraphs 2 and 3 shall also not exclude the patentability of any substance or composition referred to in paragraph 4 for any specific use in a method referred to in Article 53(c), provided that such use is not comprised in the state of the art.

Articles 54(1), (2) and (3) identify when an invention is considered to be new and what constitutes the state of the art for the purpose of determining novelty.

Article 54(4) therefore provides that a first medical use may be patentable if the method does not form part of the state of the art. In other words, if a known chemical has a medical use that was not previously known, it is potentially patentable. That is to say, if a known substance or composition not previously used in surgery, therapy, or diagnosis is found to be useful in treating, say, a human disease, or to obtain a specific 'therapeutic' effect (e.g., analgesic or antibiotic), a patent for the substance or composition for use in therapy (unspecified) may be obtained, i.e., the claim need not be limited to the specific therapeutic effect; additional claims directed towards more than one specific therapeutic effect may be allowed in the same patent application, provided of course that they are supported by the description.

Second and subsequent medical use is permitted under Article 54(5), which was introduced by with the EPC 2000 amendments. Second and subsequent medical use claims were previously worded in what often referred to as 'Swiss' type claims in the form: 'the use of substance X for the manufacture of a medicament for a specified new and inventive therapeutic application'. However, the Enlarged Board of Appeal's decision in G 02/08 *ABBOTT RESPIRATORY/Dosing Regime* made clear that applicants could no longer claim second medical use in the form of Swiss-type claims. Swiss-type claims had previously been accepted as a means of filling a gap provided by EPC 1973.[36] Following the decision in G02/08, the UK Intellectual Property Office (UKIPO) issued a Practice Note on 26 May 2010 informing applicants that Swiss-type claims in new and pending patent applications would be objected to on the grounds of clarity and provided guidance that such claims should be either deleted or replaced in the format: 'substance X for use in the treatment of disease Y'. According to the German Federal Court of Justice, Swiss-type and EPC-type claims are both construed as purpose-related product claims (*Pemetrexed*, BGH X ZR 29/15).

Patents for second or subsequent medical use have been obtained for use in certain patient populations,[37] new pharmaceutical forms,[38] new modes of administration,[39] and treatment regimes.[40]

---

36. G 05/83 EISAI/Second medical indication.
37. T-0893/90 Queen's University Kingston/Controlling bleeding.
38. T-0051/93 SERONO/HCG.
39. T-0143/94 MAI/Trigonelline.
40. T-0570/92 BAYER/Nifedipine.

Enlarged Board of Appeal's decision in *ABBOTT RESPIRATORY/Dosing Regime* also made clear that an invention that differed from the prior art only by virtue of a dosing regime is potentially patentable.

[7] Biotechnological Inventions

Although the EPC sits outside of the EU legislative framework, there are further exceptions to patentability provided under Directive 98/44/EC[41] (the Biotech Directive), which takes into account ethical considerations concerning the grant of patents for biotechnological inventions.

In particular, the Biotechnology Directive prohibits the grant of patents for:

- plant and animal varieties (unless the technical feasibility of the invention is not confined to a particular plant or animal variety)[42] and essentially biological processes for the production of plant or animals[43]
- the human body, at the various stages of its formation and development, and the simple discovery of one of its elements, including the sequence or partial sequence of a gene, cannot constitute patentable inventions[44]
- inventions where their commercial exploitation would be contrary to ordre public or morality,[45] including:
  (a) processes for cloning human beings;
  (b) processes for modifying the germ line genetic identity of human beings;
  (c) uses of human embryos for industrial or commercial purposes;
  (d) processes for modifying the genetic identity of animals which are likely to cause them suffering without any substantial medical benefit to man or animal, and also animals resulting from such processes.

An element isolated from the human body or otherwise produced by means of a technical process, including the sequence or partial sequence of a gene, may constitute a patentable invention, even if the structure of that element is identical to that of a natural element. However, the industrial application of a sequence or a partial sequence of a gene must be disclosed in the patent application.[46]

The Biotech Directive has also been implemented in the form of the Implementing Regulations to the Convention on the Grant of European Patents (Implementing Regulations).[47] Rule 26(1) of the Implementing Regulations states:

---

41. Directive 98/44/EC of the European Parliament and of the Council of 6 July 1998 on the legal protection of biotechnological inventions (OJ L 213, 30.7.1998, p.13).
42. Articles 4(1)(a) and 4(2) of the Biotech Directive.
43. Article 4(1)(b) of the Biotech Directive. Pursuant to Article 4(3), a prohibition on essentially biological processes for the production of plants or animals (Art. 4(1)(b)) shall be without prejudice to the patentability of inventions which concern a microbiological or other technical process, or a product obtained by means of such a process.
44. Article 5(1) of the Biotech Directive.
45. Biotech Directive, Article 6.
46. Biotech Directive, Articles 5(2) and 5(3).
47. http://www.epo.org/law-practice/legal-texts/html/epc/2013/e/ma2.html

Chapter 3: Overview of Intellectual Property Rights §3.02[B]

> For European patent applications and patents concerning biotechnological inventions, the relevant provisions of the Convention shall be applied and interpreted in accordance with the provisions of this Chapter. Directive 98/44/EC of 6 July 1998 on the legal protection of biotechnological inventions shall be used as a supplementary means of interpretation.

'Biotechnological inventions' are inventions which concern a product consisting of or containing biological material or a process by means of which biological material is produced, processed or used.[48] 'Biological material' means any material containing genetic information and capable of reproducing itself or being reproduced in a biological system.[49]

The remainder of chapter 5 of the Implementing Regulations further echoes the prohibitions provided in the Biotech Directive. Rule 27 of the Implementing Regulation does however provide that biotechnological inventions are patentable if they concern:

(a) biological material which is isolated from its natural environment or produced by means of a technical process even if it previously occurred in nature;
(b) plants or animals if the technical feasibility of the invention is not confined to a particular plant or animal variety;
(c) a microbiological or other technical process,[50] or a product obtained by means of such a process other than a plant or animal variety.

Patent claims concerning human embryonic stem cells have been particularly contentious. Human totipotent cells have the potential to develop into an entire human being. Further, there have been ethical issues relating to the use and destruction of human embryos. In November 2008, the EPO Enlarged Board of Appeal decided in *WARF/Use of embryos*,[51] a case relating to human embryonic stem cell cultures, that it was not possible to grant a patent for an invention that involves the use and destruction of human embryos.

Article 6(2)(c) of the Biotech Directive provides that use of human embryos for industrial or commercial purposes is prohibited on the grounds that it is contrary to '*ordre public* or morality'. However, the CJEU in *Oliver Brüstle v. Greenpeace*[52] held that Article 6(2)(c) must be interpreted as meaning that term 'human embryo' includes 'any human ovum after fertilisation, any non-fertilised human ovum into which the cell nucleus from a mature human cell has been transplanted, and any non-fertilised human ovum whose division and further development have been stimulated by parthenogenesis'. The exclusion from patentability under Article 6(2)(c) also covers the use of human embryos for the purposes of scientific research only, use for therapeutic or diagnostic purposes which is applied to the human embryo and is useful to it being patentable. Further, subject matter that requires the prior destruction of human embryos or their use as base material is not patentable irrespective of the stage

---

48. Implementing Regulations, Rule 26(2).
49. Implementing Regulations, Rule 26(3).
50. 'Microbiological process' means any process involving or performed upon or resulting in microbiological material (Rule 26(6) of the Implementing Regulations).
51. Case G 2/06 Use of embryos/WARF.
52. Case C-34/10 *Oliver Brüstle v. Greenpeace eV* of 18 October 2011.

at which that takes place and even if the description of the technical teaching claimed does not refer to the use of human embryos.

[C] Infringement and Defences

Infringement of a European patent is a matter of national law. Article 64 of the EPC provides:

> A European patent shall, subject to the provisions of paragraph 2, confer on its proprietor from the date on which the mention of its grant is published in the European Patent Bulletin, in each Contracting State in respect of which it is granted, the same rights as would be conferred by a national patent granted in that State.
> If the subject-matter of the European patent is a process, the protection conferred by the patent shall extend to the products directly obtained by such process.
> Any infringement of a European patent shall be dealt with by national law.

However, there are two notable exceptions to patent infringement that are particularly relevant to the pharmaceutical sector: the 'Bolar Exemption' and the 'Experimental Use Exception'.

[1] Bolar Exemption

The so-called Bolar exemption to patent infringement is governed by Directive 2001/83/EC[53] (as amended by Directive 2004/27/EC). Article 10(6) provides:

> Conducting the necessary studies and trials with a view to the application of paragraphs 1, 2, 3 and 4 and the consequential practical requirements shall not be regarded as contrary to patent rights or to supplementary protection certificates for medicinal products.

Paragraphs 1 to 4 relate to abridged applications for generic/biosimilar medicinal products. However, Article 10(6) does not prevent national legislatures from granting more extensive defences than those it mandates. For example, the exemption will apply in some countries to cover clinical trials directed to securing MAs for generic products and/or abroad.[54]

The application of the Bolar Exemption in the UK was revised on 1 October 2014, and the Bolar exemption now applies in respect of certain clinical trials in certain circumstances. It permits the carrying out of necessary trials and health technology assessments in the UK for all medicines (novel as well as generic) and all applications for marketing approval (national, European, as well as non-European), which would otherwise infringe a patent.

---

53. Directive 2001/83/EC on the Community Code relating to medicinal products for human use.
54. For example, France, Germany, Italy, Spain, and, since 1 October 2014, the UK.

[2] Experimental Use Defence

The origin of the experimental use exemption in Europe is the Community Patent Convention 1975[55] (CPC), which attempted to give unitary and autonomous effect to European patents granted under the EPC and to establish a Community patent system. Article 31 of the CPC provided that the rights conferred by a Community patent would not extend to (among other things):

(a) acts done privately and for non-commercial purposes;
(b) acts done for experimental purposes relating to the subject-matter of the patented invention

Most European countries have since adopted this exemption in their national law by using wording that is almost identical to that which appears in the CPC. For example, section 60 of the UK Patents Act 1977 provides:

(5) An act which, apart from this subsection, would constitute an infringement of a patent for an invention shall not do so if –
  (a) it is done privately and for purposes which are not commercial;
  (b) it is done for experimental purposes relating to the subject-matter of the invention

The exemption is therefore a two-limb test: (i) the acts must be done for experimental purposes; and (ii) they must relate to the subject matter claimed in the patent. The application of this test to the facts of a particular case is a matter of national law, but the exemption has undergone considerable scrutiny by two of the most experienced patents courts in Europe: the courts of England & Wales[56] and Germany.[57] Although decisions of these national courts are not binding on courts of other countries, the decisions may be persuasive.

[D] Unitary Patent System

Despite the events of Brexit, and constitutional challenges in Germany, the opening of the Unified Patent Court (UPC), while delayed, is expected in early 2023.

Despite the UK ratifying the UPC Agreement in 2018, following Brexit, it withdrew from participation in the Unitary Patent System. It deposited its notification

---

55. Convention for the European Patent for the Common Market 76/76/EC (OJ L17, 26 January 1976, p.1 (see http://eur-lex.europa.eu/LexUriServ/LexUriServ.do?uri=CELEX:41975A3490:EN:HTML).
56. See, for example, *Monsanto Co v. Stauffer Chemical Co and Another* [1985] RPC 515 (English Court of Appeal), *Corevalve Inc v. Edwards Lifesciences AG and Another* [2009] EWHC 6, *Smith Kline & French Laboratories v. Evans Medical Ltd* [1989] FSR 513 (Patents Court), and *Auchinloss and anr v. Agricultural and Veterinary Supplies Limited and ors* [1997] RPC 649 (Patents Court); [1999] RPC 397 (English Court of Appeal).
57. *Klinische Versuche (Clinical trials) I* [1997] RPC 623 (German Federal Supreme Court). and *Klinische Versuche (Clinical Trials) II* [1998] RPC 423 (German Federal Supreme Court).

of withdrawal of ratification on 20 July 2020. Despite the UPC being an international initiative and not strictly a product of the EU, the UK government decided nonetheless to withdraw to maintain sovereignty of UK law. As the CJEU is the ultimate court in the UPC system, participating in the UPC would inevitably mean being bound by EU law. The UK was not a mandatory signatory to the UPC system, so despite the UK's withdrawal, the UPC system was still able to go ahead.

The constitutional challenges brought before the German Constitutional Court (*Bundesverfassungsgericht*) culminated in a ruling that the German ratification act for the UPC Agreement was void because an insufficient number of members of parliament was present for the vote. According to the Court, this is crucial because the UPC Act forms a material change to the German Constitution, which requires a majority of two-thirds of the members of parliament. The act was unanimously adopted by the 35 members of parliament present for the vote, but the parliament has 709 seats. There were other complaints made to the German court, but these were declared inadmissible. The German government introduced a new bill to ratify the agreement, with the required two-thirds majority, to parliament in June 2020. On 23 June 2021, the German Federal Constitutional Court passed an Order which cleared the way for Germany to participate in the UPC Agreement and Protocol on the Provisional Application of the UPCA (the PAP-Protocol). The German Federal President signed the German ratification bill on 7 August 2021 and was promulgated on 12 August 2021. On 27 September 2021, Germany finally ratified the Protocol on the Provisional Application of the UPCA.

The subsequent ratifications of the PAP-Protocol by Slovenia (on 15 October 2021) and Austria (on 19 January 2022) resulted in the threshold of thirteen Member States to participate in the provisional application of the UPC Agreement. The Austrian ratification triggered the entry into force of the PAP. The PAP is the final phase of the setup of the UPC. The coming into force of the PAP-Protocol established the legal capacity and organisational capability of the UPC. The remaining preparatory work to be completed is mostly administrative and includes assembly of the governing bodies, preparation of secondary legislation, finalisation of budget and the IT systems, and recruitment and training of UPC judges. Once this final preparatory work is sufficiently progressed, the UPC and the last outstanding instrument of ratification of the UPC Agreement is deposited by Germany; the UPC Agreement will then enter into force on the first day of the fourth month following the deposit of this instrument. Once entered into force, the UPC will start its work and be available to the users of the European patent system. The German deposition will also mark the start of the sunrise period during which it will be possible to opt out of existing European patents from the jurisdiction of the Court. The Unitary Patent System represents the most significant change to patent law in Europe since the EPC came into force around forty years ago. The Unitary Patent System will introduce a new, single patent right (the Unitary Patent) that will be centrally granted by the EPO and effective in twenty-four Member States[58] of the EU as a single territory.

---

58. All Member States of the EU except Poland, Croatia, and Spain.

The European Patent system conceived through the EPC has faced criticisms that it is expensive and is applied inconsistently across Europe. As discussed above, the grant of a European Patent gives rise to a bundle of national patents. Renewal fees for each of these national patents are paid in each of the relevant countries. Further, patent proceedings are commenced in the national courts of the country where the infringement took place.

In addition to having a central register, the holder of the Unitary Patent would only have to pay a single annual fee following grant as opposed to various fees payable to national patent offices. A single Court (the Unitary Patent Court) will enforce the new Unitary Patents and, unless opted out of the system during the transitional period, European Patents.

The Unitary Patent System therefore adds a further option in the patent landscape that exists in Europe and does not replace the existing systems that are in place. The Unitary Patent System also impacts on SPCs as discussed in Chapter 7.

[1]   The Legislative Framework

[a]   Legislative Instruments

In 2011, the Council of the EU (Council) adopted a decision[59] that authorised enhanced cooperation with a view to creating a Unitary Patent between twenty-five Member States of the EU (including the UK at the time, but with Spain and Italy refusing to participate). In December 2012, the Council and the European Parliament agreed on two EU Regulations (Regulation (EU) 1257/2012[60] and Regulation (EU) 1260/2012)[61] and the Agreement on a Unified Patent Court was signed on February 2013 (UPC Agreement).[62]

However, proposed Unified Patents System has been fraught with legal challenges, in particular from Spain. In 2011, Spain and Italy challenged the legality of the 'enhanced cooperation mechanism' before the CJEU by seeking annulment of Council Decision 2011/167/EU. Spain principally contended that the Council Decision was vitiated by misuse of powers and the failure to have due regard for the judicial system of the EU (among other arguments). Italy contested the Council Decision on several grounds, including that the Council had no competence to establish enhanced cooperation in

---

59. Council Decision 2011/167/EU of 10 March 2011 authorising enhanced cooperation in the area of the creation of unitary patent protection (OJ L 76, 22.3.2011, p.53).
60. Council Regulation (EU) No. 1257/2012 of 17 December 2012 implementing enhanced cooperation in the area of the creation of unitary patent protection (OJ L361, 31.12.2012, p.1).
61. Council Regulation (EU) No. 1260/2012 of 17 December 2012 implementing enhanced cooperation in the area of the creation of unitary patent protection with regard to the applicable translation arrangements (OJ L361, 31.12.2012, p.89).
62. https://ec.europa.eu/commission/presscorner/detail/en/PRES_13_61

order to create protection by a unitary patent.[63] The CJEU rejected the arguments in its decision of 16 April 2013.[64]

In May 2013, Spain appealed, challenging the validity of the two Regulations and raising number of different pleas. In respect of the Translation Regulation (Regulation (EU) 1260/2012), Spain also pleaded infringement of the principle of non-discrimination on the ground of language (applications for Unitary Patents would be translated into the three official languages of the EPO: English, French, and German). On 5 May 2015, the CJEU dismissed Spain's appeal against the Unitary Patent System[65] removing the legal obstacle for full implementation.

Shortly after the CJEU's judgment, the Italian Ministry of Economic Development announced on 13 May 2015 that becoming part of the Unitary Patent System was in line with the country's interests. On 3 July 2015, the Vice Secretary of the Italian Government (European Policies)[66] notified European Commissioner for the Internal Market, Industry, Entrepreneurship, and small- and medium-sized enterprises (SMEs) and the EU Presidency, announcing Italy's decision to adhere to the unitary patent.

[b]   Ratification

The Unitary Patent will become available once thirteen Member States (including France and Germany, and it is assumed Italy as a replacement for the UK) have ratified the UPC Agreement. At the time of writing, sixteen Member States have ratified the UPC Agreement: Austria, Belgium, Bulgaria, Denmark, Estonia, Finland, France, Italy, Latvia, Lithuania, Luxembourg, Malta, The Netherlands, Portugal, Slovenia, and Sweden.[67] As at the date of writing, Germany is yet to ratify formally the UPC Agreement. The UK had stated that it would ratify, thereby enabling the system to move to the next level, but as mentioned, it withdrew this intention in March 2020.

The UPC Agreement was signed by twenty-five Member States of the EU: Spain, Poland, and Croatia are yet to do so. Poland has declared that its economic analysis of the package will not benefit Poland and has not signed the UPC Agreement. Croatia acceded to the EU on 1 July 2013 and has not yet signed the UPC Agreement.

[2]   Unitary Patent

The Unitary Patent builds on the existing framework provided by the EPC. Therefore, there will be no change to the current system for European Patents in the pre-grant phase.

---

63. Italy had signed the UPC Agreement but opted out of the enhanced cooperation procedure that led to the adoption of the two EU Regulations.
64. Joined Cases C-274/11 and C-295/11 *Kingdom of Spain and Italian Republic v. Council of the European Union.*
65. Case-146/13 *Kingdom of Spain v. European Parliament and Council of the European Union*, 5 May 2015 and Case C-147/13 *Kingdom of Spain v. Council of the European Union*, 5 May 2015.
66. *See* http://www.politicheeuropee.it/sottosegretario/19382/brevetto-ue-ladesione-italiana.
67. http://www.consilium.europa.eu/en/documents-publications/agreements-conventions/agreement/?aid=2013001.

The Unitary Patent is created by applying for unitary effect within one month of the grant of a European Patent (i.e., the patentee 'opts in'). However, only European Patents with the same set of claims in respect of all the participating Member States may benefit from unitary effect.[68] Therefore, withdrawal of designated Member States or amending claims for particular territories should be avoided as this will negate unitary effect. The Unitary Patent extends to Member States of the EU that have ratified the UPC Agreement as of the date of the registration.

The patentee may have the option of validating the patent as a traditional European Patent in non-participating countries and those who have not yet acceded to the UPC Agreement. Patentees may also validate the patent in the other eleven European Convention countries, which are not EU Member States.

[3]   UPC

The UPC will comprise a Court of First Instance, a Court of Appeal, and a Registry. The Court of First Instance will be a single court with several divisions:[69]

(1) The *Central Division* – This will have its seat in Paris with sections in Munich and another city to replace London. London was due to deal with cases concerning chemistry (including pharmaceuticals), metallurgy, and human necessities. Munich will hear cases concerning mechanical engineering, lighting, heating, weapons, and blasting. The remainder (including cases concerning physics and electricity) will be heard in Paris.
(2) Local Divisions in individual countries (at the time of writing, thirteen locations have been proposed for local divisions of the UPC).
(3) Regional Divisions in two or more countries (at the time of writing, one regional division of the UPC has been proposed for Estonia, Latvia, Lithuania, and Sweden, located in Stockholm).

The Central Division will have exclusive jurisdiction over declarations of non-infringement and revocation actions (other than counterclaims).[70] If a revocation action is pending in the Central Decision, the patentee may bring an infringement action there too. Infringement actions and counterclaims for revocation will be heard in the Local and Regional Divisions. The Court of Appeal will be seated in Luxembourg.

The patentee may bring infringement claims in the local or regional division where the infringement is or has been occurring or where the defendant has residence or place of business. Proceedings against a non-EU defendant are brought in the Central Division. A judgment of the UPC will, based on the current status, extend to twenty-four contracting Member States of the EU.

Traditional European Patents and SPCs will also be subject to the exclusive jurisdiction of the UPC unless the proprietor 'opts out' (*see* §3.02[D][4] below).

---

68. Regulation (EU) 1257/2012, Article 3(1).
69. UPC Agreement, Article 7.
70. UPC Agreement, Article 32(5) and (6).

[4] Practical Considerations

The Unitary Patent System therefore adds a further option in the patent landscape that exists in Europe and does not replace the existing systems that are in place. However, the choice between the traditional European Patent and the new Unitary Patent will need to take into consideration a number of aspects.

[a] Cost

Although centrally prosecuted, a patentee of a European Patent will face the additional cost of validation and renewal fees in the relevant countries in which patent protection is desired. There are no validation costs for a Unitary Patent, save for one translation that is required to be filed during the transitional period. Further, a single renewal fee will be payable in respect of a Unitary Patent.

[b] Divisional Applications

As of 1 April 2014, it is possible to file divisional applications for European Patents at any time up to grant. Filing divisional applications would allow patentees to pursue a Unitary Patent and a traditional European Patent for essentially the same technology.

[c] Opting Out

Unitary Patents and future and existing European Patents will fall within the exclusive jurisdiction of the UPC. However, transitional rules allow a European Patent to be opted out from the exclusive competence of the UPC,[71] so that it can only be challenged through national courts.

In order to opt-out, the European Patent holder will need to notify their opt-out to the Unified Patent Registry no later than one month before the expiry of the transitional period at the latest.[72] The transitional period is seven years from the entry into force of the Agreement at the first instance, but it is likely that this period will be extended by a further seven years.

[d] Licences and Technology Transfer Agreements

As the legal framework for the Unitary Patent System is relatively new, many existing licences, development, and technology transfer agreements are unlikely to have provided for its impact.

The UPC Agreement provides that the decision to opt-out is that of the proprietor of the European Patent. This can, for example, create tensions between the rights of an

---

71. UPC Agreement, Article 83.
72. UPC Agreement, Article 87.

exclusive licensee and that of a proprietor. In most cases, an exclusive licensee will have more to lose than the proprietor if the validity of the patent is challenged. Such agreements should therefore be reviewed to set out a process whereby the parties can agree as to whether there is a need for opting out.

The UPC Agreement also provides that exclusive licensees will obtain the authority to enforce a patent without the prior consent of the patentee unless otherwise provided in the licence. Article 47(2) of the UPC Agreement states that 'unless the licensing agreement provides otherwise, the holder of an exclusive licence in respect of a [European Patent and/or a Unitary Patent] shall be entitled to bring actions before the Court under the same circumstances as the patent proprietor, provided that the patent proprietor is given prior notice'. This provision is less stringent than the national law of most European countries.

The position with exclusive licensees could give rise to the patentee facing a bifurcation of proceedings in Europe: the exclusive licensee to commence infringement proceedings in a local or regional court, but the patentee might face a revocation action in the Central Division.

§3.03 SPCs

SPCs are sui generis rights which operate at the interface of regulatory law and patent law.

For a limited period of generally no more than five years after the expiry of the basic patent, the SPC protects the active ingredient of a pharmaceutical (or active substance of an agrochemical as the case may be) for which an MA was granted by conferring the same rights on its holder as were conferred by the patent. As an SPC protects the active ingredient (or active substance), its scope will typically be narrower than the basic patent (which can protect a range of compounds). SPCs are discussed in detail in Chapter 7.

§3.04 TRADEMARKS

Although patents are generally considered to be the most valuable intellectual property owned by pharmaceutical companies, trademarks are also a material consideration in bringing a medicinal product to market.

Pharmaceutical companies are required to determine a brand name under which a particular medicinal product is to be marketed before an application for MA is made. This is because the identity of the medicinal product forms part of the MA, and the proposed name will be evaluated as part of the approval process. Indeed, a major factor in the criteria applied by regulatory bodies when considering the acceptability of a proposed name for a medicinal product is the risk of confusion.

Confusing one medicinal product with another could have potentially serious consequences for patients. Although choosing invented names that have no relation to the medicinal product in question may reduce this risk, this does not eliminate the risk.

The regulatory authorities, such as the European Medicines Agency (EMA), have therefore issued guidelines to assist applicants.

The risks of an application to register a trademark being opposed or a registered trademark being invalidated by third parties are also material considerations in choosing a trademark. Both of these considerations may adversely affect the MA. Trademarks may also be enforced against third parties long after the patent or SPC has expired.

[A] Registration of Trademarks

Trademarks are generally distinctive signs that are capable of distinguishing goods or services of one undertaking from those of other undertakings. Trademarks are not limited to words or logos but may also comprise colours,[73] packaging and 'get-up' of the products, shapes, sounds and, in some limited cases, smells.

[1] Routes to Registration

Within the EU, a trademark may be registered through several different routes:

- A national trademark prosecuted at a national intellectual property office. The national intellectual property offices and national courts where the right has been registered are subject to national laws which also implement Directive (EU) 2015/2436[74] (Trademark Directive), which seeks to harmonise trademark law across the EU. In Belgium, the Netherlands, and Luxembourg, the Benelux trademark replaces national trademarks.
- A unitary EU trademark (EUTM) prosecuted centrally through the European Union Intellectual Property Office (EUIPO),[75] which is enforceable in all twenty-seven Member States of the EU, and governed by Regulation (EU) 2017/1001 (EUTM Regulation).[76]
- An international trademark designating national, regional offices, or EUIPO. These are obtained through WIPO in accordance with the Madrid System.[77]

---

73. Application for trademarks in Europe must be with reference to an internationally recognised identification system such as Pantone.
74. Directive (EU) 2015/2436 of the European Parliament and of the Council of 16 December 2015 to approximate the laws of Member States relating to trademarks (OJ L 366/1, 23.12.2015, p.1).
75. The EUIPO was formerly known as the Office of the Harmonization of the Internal Market (OHIM). The name change officially took effect on 23 March 2016 pursuant to the Regulation (EU) No. 2015/2424.
76. Regulation (EU) No. 2017/1001 of the European Parliament and of the Council of 14 June 2017 on the EU trademark (OJ L 154, 16.6.2017, pp.1–99).
77. The Madrid System allows applicants to file a single application (based on a national registered trademark or application) in one language and pay one set of fees. The international trademark can give rise to national trademarks in up to ninety-seven countries or regions. *See* http://www.wipo.int/madrid/en/.

Chapter 3: Overview of Intellectual Property Rights   §3.04[A]

In addition to registered trademarks, unregistered trademarks may be asserted in some countries under national laws of unfair competition (e.g., Germany) or 'passing-off' (UK and Republic of Ireland). However, these rights are generally more difficult to assert than registered rights. In the case of 'passing off', the trademark owner will have to establish goodwill in the mark, reputation, and damage. For the purpose of clarity, the procedural aspects set out in this section are limited to EUTMs.

Following the end of the Brexit transition period, as of 1 January 2021, EUTMs are no longer protected trademarks within the UK. For EUTMs existing on 1 January 2021, under the terms of the Withdrawal Agreement, a comparable UK trademark was automatically created for all right holders. There were no changes to UK-registered national trademarks as a result of the UK leaving the EU.

[2]   Criteria for Registration

The registration of a trademark application can be refused on two bases: absolute grounds and relative grounds. Absolute grounds relate to the inherent qualities of the sign whereas relative grounds relate to potential conflicts with earlier trademarks.

EUIPO will not refuse a trademark application on its own motion on relative grounds; it is, however, open to third parties to challenge the registration of the mark based on their earlier rights. Both absolute and relative grounds (among others) may also be raised by third parties seeking to revoke a registered trademark.

[a]   Absolute Grounds

The absolute grounds for refusing an EUTM application (or challenging the validity of a registered trademark) are provided in Article 7(1) of the EUTM Regulation,[78] which include:.

(a) signs which do not conform to the requirements of Article 4;
(b) trademarks which are devoid of any distinctive character;
(c) trademarks which consist exclusively of signs or indications which may serve, in trade, to designate the kind, quality, quantity, intended purpose, value, geographical origin or the time of production of the goods or of rendering of the service, or other characteristics of the goods or service;
(d) trademarks which consist exclusively of signs or indications which have become customary in the current language or in the bona fide and established practices of the trade;
(e) signs which consist exclusively of:
  (i) the shape, or another characteristic, which results from the nature of the goods themselves;

---

78. Similar provisions appear in Article 3(1) of the Trade Mark Directive.

(ii) the shape, or another characteristic, of goods which is necessary to obtain a technical result;

(iii) the shape, or another characteristic, which gives substantial value to the goods;

(f) trademarks which are contrary to public policy or to accepted principles of morality;

(g) trademarks which are of such a nature as to deceive the public, for instance as to the nature, quality or geographical origin of the goods or service;

(h) trademarks which have not been authorised by the competent authorities and are to be refused pursuant to Article 6ter of the Paris Convention for the Protection of Industrial Property ('Paris Convention');

(i) trademarks which include badges, emblems or escutcheons other than those covered by Article 6ter of the Paris Convention and which are of particular public interest, unless the consent of the competent authority to their registration has been given;

(j) trademarks which are excluded from registration, pursuant to Union legislation or national law or to international agreements to which the Union or the Member State concerned is party, providing for protection of designations of origin and geographical indications;

(k) trademarks which are excluded from registration pursuant to Union legislation or international agreements to which the Union is party, providing for protection of traditional terms for wine;

(l) trademarks which are excluded from registration pursuant to Union legislation or international agreements to which the Union is party, providing for protection of traditional specialities guaranteed;

(m) trademarks which consist of, or reproduce in their essential elements, an earlier plant variety denomination registered in accordance with Union legislation or national law, or international agreements to which the Union or the Member State concerned is a party, providing for protection of plant variety rights, and which are in respect of plant varieties of the same or closely related species.

Trademark applicants may overcome objections on the basis of Article 7(1)(b) and (c) if they can show acquired distinctiveness.

[b]   Relative Grounds

Relative grounds are those that are dependent on an earlier trademark right that existed prior to the filing date of the later trademark. These grounds are set out in Article 8(1) of the EUTM Regulation. Specifically, a trademark shall not be registered or, if registered, shall be liable to be declared invalid:

(a) if it is identical with the earlier trademark and the goods or services for which registration is applied for are identical with the goods or services for which the earlier trademark is protected; or
(b) if because of its identity with, or similarity to, the earlier trademark and the identity or similarity of the goods or services covered by the trademarks there exists a likelihood of confusion on the part of the public in the territory in which the earlier trademark is protected; the likelihood of confusion includes the likelihood of association with the earlier trademark.

The 'earlier trade mark' means:

- registrations or applications – with a date of application for registration which is earlier than the date of application for registration of the EUTM, taking account, where appropriate, of the priorities claimed in respect thereof – for EUTMs, national trademarks (or in the case of Belgium, the Netherlands, or Luxembourg, a Benelux trademark), an international trademark under the Madrid System having effect in a Member State of the EU or EUIPO; and
- trademarks which on the date of application for registration of the EUTM, or where appropriate, of the priority claimed in respect of the EUTM application, are well known in a Member State in the sense in which the words 'well known' are used in Article 6bis of the Paris Convention.[79]

[3] Duration

The initial duration of protection for an EUTM is ten years from the filing date; the trademark can, however, be renewed indefinitely if the requisite renewal fees are paid. National trademarks in Member States of the EU have the same duration.

---

79. Article 6bis of the Paris Convention provides:

    (1) The countries of the Union undertake, ex officio if their legislation so permits, or at the request of an interested party, to refuse or to cancel the registration, and to prohibit the use, of a trademark which constitutes a reproduction, an imitation, or a translation, liable to create confusion, of a mark considered by the competent authority of the country of registration or use to be well known in that country as being already the mark of a person entitled to the benefits of this Convention and used for identical or similar goods. These provisions shall also apply when the essential part of the mark constitutes a reproduction of any such well-known mark or an imitation liable to create confusion therewith.
    (2) A period of at least five years from the date of registration shall be allowed for requesting the cancellation of such a mark. The countries of the Union may provide for a period within which the prohibition of use must be requested.
    (3) No time limit shall be fixed for requesting the cancellation or the prohibition of the use of marks registered or used in bad faith.
    Reference to 'Union' is not a reference to the EU. Article 1 of the Paris Convention states '[t]he countries to which this Convention applies constitute a Union for the protection of industrial property.'

[B] Regulatory Issues with Pharmaceutical Names

[1] International Nonproprietary Names

An International Nonproprietary Name (INN) is a unique name for a pharmaceutical substance or active pharmaceutical ingredient that is internationally recognised and is public property. It is the generic name of a product, e.g., propranolol.

Initiated in 1950 by a World Health Assembly resolution WHA3.11, the INN system began operating in 1953. Over 7,000 names have been designated since that time, with the number increasing at a rate of 120–150 new INNs each year.[80] The aim of the INN system is to provide healthcare professionals with a unique and universally available designated name to identify each pharmaceutical substance, allowing clear identification, safe prescription and dispensing medicines to patients, and communications and exchanges of information among health professionals and scientists worldwide. All INNs are published by the World Health Organization (WHO) in a cumulative list which includes INNs in Latin, English, French, Spanish, Arabic, Chinese, and Russian.[81]

Under the INN system, pharmacologically active substances of the same class are given the same common 'stem' to indicate their relationship to each other. This facilitates the recognition by medical professionals of medicinal products that belong to a group of substances with the same pharmacological effect. For example, all beta adrenoceptor antagonists have the suffix '-olol' (such as propranolol and atenolol). A full list of stems used in the selection of INNs is published by the WHO.[82]

Some countries operate their own systems, such as the United States Accepted Names (USAN) or Japanese Accepted Names (JAN), which are generally identical to the INN.

Trademarks should not be derived from or based on INNs. The need to maintain the integrity of the system was highlighted in the Fifth Report of the WHO Expert Committee on the Use of Essential Drugs which met in November 1991:

> The procedure for selecting INNs allows manufacturers to contest names that are either identical or similar to their licensed trade-marks. In contrast, trade-mark applications are disallowed, in accordance with the present procedure, only when they are identical to an INN. A case for increased protection of INNs is now apparent as a result of competitive promotion of products no longer protected by patents. Rather than marketing these products under generic name, many companies apply for a trade-mark derived from an INN and, in particular, including the INN common stem. This practice endangers the principle that INNs are public property; it can frustrate the rational selection of further INNs for related substances, and it will ultimately compromise the safety of patients by promoting confusion in drug nomenclature.

---

80. *See* https://www.who.int/teams/health-product-and-policy-standards/inn/guidance-on-inn.
81. *See* https://www.who.int/teams/health-product-and-policy-standards/inn/guidance-on-inn.
82. *See* https://www.who.int/teams/health-product-and-policy-standards/inn/inn-lists.

Chapter 3: Overview of Intellectual Property Rights §3.04[B]

According to the WHO's website,[83] these concerns were debated during the sixth International Conference of Drug Regulatory Authorities in October 1991. Based on recommendations made by the WHO Expert Committee on the use of Essential Drugs, resolution WHA46.19[84] on non-proprietary names for pharmaceutical substances was adopted by the Forty-sixth World Health Assembly in 1993, requesting Member States to:

- enact rules or regulations, as necessary, to ensure that international non-proprietary names (or the equivalent nationally approved generic names) used in the labelling and advertising of pharmaceutical products are always displayed prominently;
- encourage manufacturers to rely on their corporate name and the international non-proprietary names, rather than on trade-marks, to promote and market multisource products introduced after the expiry of a patent;
- develop policy guidelines on the use and protection of international non-proprietary names, and to discourage the use of names derived from them, and particularly names including established stems, as trade-marks."

Guidelines on the Use of International Nonproprietary Names (INNs) for Pharmaceutical Substances are also available on the WHO's website.[85]

The EUIPO trademark examination guidelines that entered into force on 31 March 2022 specify that the criteria for assessing descriptiveness of trademarks for pharmaceuticals are no different from those applicable to other categories of trademarks.[86] In particular, 'EMA's assessment is based on public health concerns and takes into account the WHO World Health Assembly resolution (WHA46.19) on protection of INNs/INN stems to prevent any potential risk of confusion. The [EUIPO's] assessment of the registrability of pharmaceutical trade marks, however, has no specific legal basis for taking such health-related concerns into consideration'. These guidelines go on to state that objections should be raised by the examiner where:

- the EUTM is an INN (also considering the general rules on misspellings);
- an INN appears within an EUTM and other elements of the EUTM are descriptive/non-distinctive too (e.g., 'bio', 'pharma', 'cardio', 'med', 'derma'); or
- the EUTM consists only of a stem.

The EUIPO may accept figurative trademarks containing INNs or stems after applying the same criteria that apply to other figurative trademark applications containing descriptive word elements. Objections may also be raised under Article 7(1)(g) of the EUTM Regulation where the list of goods in class 5 refers to a different medicinal product than is covered by the relevant INN.

---

83. *See* http://apps.who.int/medicinedocs/en/d/Jh1806e/4.html.
84. The full text of the resolution WHA46.19 can be found on the WHO's website at http://apps.who.int/medicinedocs/en/d/Jh1806e/11.html.
85. *See* https://www.who.int/teams/health-product-and-policy-standards/inn/guidance-on-inn.
86. EUIPO Guidelines (https://guidelines.euipo.europa.eu/1935303/2044527/trade-mark guidelines/2-13-inn-codes).

[2] Public Health Concerns and Patient Safety

As discussed in detail in Chapter 5, an MA of a medicinal product may be granted through several routes: national authorisations (which can be purely national authorisations or can be granted following the mutual recognition procedure or a decentralised procedure) or EU authorisations which are granted centrally through the centralised procedure. The legislation covering the national procedure, mutual recognition procedure, and the decentralised procedure is set out in Directive 2001/83/EC (Medicinal Products Directive).[87] Regulation (EC) No. 726/2004[88] sets out the requirements for the centralised procedure. Provisions in the national laws of the Member States determine implementation of Medicinal Products Directive and local variations in the various national procedures, so implementation of certain aspects can, to some extent, vary between Member States.

Invented names that have no connection with medicinal product generally form the strongest type of trademark from a validity and enforcement perspective. However, given the nature of the goods that are protected by the trademark and the potentially serious consequences of confusing two different pharmaceuticals, it is vital that the chosen trademark is sufficiently different from other medicinal products available on the market and from INNs.

[a] Purely National, Mutual Recognition and Decentralised Procedures

Article 8 the Medicinal Products Directive requires that an application to obtain MA must be accompanied by certain information set out in Annex I, including (among other things):

- the name of the medicinal product; and
- qualitative and quantitative particulars of all constituents of the medicinal product, including the reference to its INN, where an INN for the medicinal product exists, or a reference to the relevant chemical name.

Article 1(20) of Directive 2001/83/EC defines 'name of the medicinal product' as 'the name, which may be either an invented name not liable to confusion with the common name, or a common or scientific name accompanied by a trade mark or the name of the marketing authorisation holder'. The 'common name' is the INN or, if one does not exist, it is the usual common name.

---

87. Directive 2001/83/EC of the European Parliament and of the Council of 6 November 2001 on the Community code relating to medicinal products for human use (OJ L 311, 28.11.2001, p.67).
88. Regulation (EC) No. 726/2004 of the European Parliament and of the Council of 31 March 2004 laying down Community procedures for the authorisation and supervision of medicinal products for human and veterinary use and establishing a European Medicines Agency (OJ L 136, 30.04.2004, p.1).

The name of the medicinal product must appear in the summary of product characteristics[89] and on the outer packaging (or where there is no outer packaging, the immediate packaging) of the medicinal products.[90] Where the name of the medicinal product appears on packaging, it must be followed by its strength and its pharmaceutical form and if appropriate, whether it is intended for babies, children, or adults. Where the product contains up to three active substances, the INN must be used or, if one does not exist, the common name.

[b] Centralised Procedure

Article 6 of Regulation (EC) No. 726/2004 requires that 'each application for the authorisation of a medicinal product..., otherwise than in exceptional cases relating to the application of the law on trade marks, shall include the use of a single name for the medicinal product'. Accordingly, the centralised route requires a single, invented name for the medicinal product to be authorised. However, the Regulation recognises that a proposed trademark might be cancelled, opposed, or objected to under trademark law. In this case, the marketing authorisation holder (MAH) must obtain derogation in writing from the Commission and provide evidence of its failed efforts to secure the trademark in question.

EMA published a draft Guideline on acceptability of names for human medicinal products processed through the centralised procedure, which will replace the guideline EMA/CHMP/287710/2014, Revision 6 (end of consultation occurred on 16 March 2022).[91] The Guideline provides details on the criteria applied by the EMA when considering proposed invented names and the procedure for approval.

According to these Guidelines, the EMA will not take into consideration aspects of IPRs or trademark registration within its review of acceptability of a proposed invented name for a medicinal product. The EMA's role is restricted to evaluating the safety of the medicinal products within the authorisation procedure as the proposed invented name could pose public health concerns or potential safety risks. Although 'likelihood of confusion' may be an important aspect in registrability, validity, or infringement of a trademark, these considerations will not affect the EMA's consideration of new proposed invented names. The material consideration will be public health concerns and potential safety risk.

The (Invented) Name Review Group (NRG) will evaluate proposed names to ensure the requirements of Article 6 of Regulation (EC) No. 726/2004 and Article 1(20) of Medicinal Products Directive are met. The Guidelines set out a non-exhaustive list of criteria the NRG will apply when evaluating proposed invented names. With respect to addressing general safety concerns and other public health concerns, the invented name of the medicinal product should not (among other things):

---

89. Medicinal Products Directive, Article 11.
90. Medicinal Products Directive, Article 54 and Article 55.
91. EMA/CHMP/287710/2014 – Rev 7 dated 6 December 2021: https://www.ema.europa.eu/en/documents/scientific-guideline/draft-guideline-acceptability-names-human-medicinal-products-processed-through-centralised-procedure_en.pdf.

- be liable to cause confusion in print, handwriting, or speech with the invented name of another medicinal product;
- covey misleading therapeutic and/or pharmaceutical connotations;
- be misleading with respect to the composition of the product;
- convey a promotional message with respect to the therapeutic and/or pharmacological characteristics and/or the composition of the medicinal product; or
- be offensive or have inappropriate connotation in any of the official EU languages.

Consideration should also be given to the phonetics and the potential difficulties a proposed (invented) name may create in terms of pronunciation in different official EU languages. The NRG will also consider elements such as the labelling and pack design.

The Guideline also advises applicants of MAs and MAHs to take into consideration WHO resolution WHA46.19 (where appropriate), i.e., 'It would therefore be appreciated if invented names were not derived from international non-proprietary names (INNs) and if INN stems were not used in invented names'.

[C] Trademark Infringement

[1] Criteria for Establishing Infringement

Under Article 9 EUTM Regulation, the proprietor of a registered EUTM is entitled to prevent third parties from using the following signs in the course of trade, in relation to goods or services, without the proprietor's consent. Specifically, Article 9(2) of the EUTM Regulation provides:

> 2. Without prejudice to the rights of proprietors acquired before the filing date or the priority date of the EU trademark, the proprietor of that EU trademark shall be entitled to prevent all third parties not having his consent from using in the course of trade, in relation to goods or services, any sign where:
>
> (a) the sign is identical with the EU trade mark and is used in relation to goods or services which are identical with those for which the EU trade mark is registered;
>
> (b) the sign is identical with, or similar to, the EU trade mark and is used in relation to goods or services which are identical with, or similar to, the goods or services for which the EU trade mark is registered, if there exists a likelihood of confusion on the part of the public; the likelihood of confusion includes the likelihood of association between the sign and the trade mark;
>
> (c) the sign is identical with, or similar to, the EU trade mark irrespective of whether it is used in relation to goods or services which are identical with, similar to or not similar to those for which the EU trade mark is registered, where the latter has a reputation in the Union and where use of that sign without due cause takes unfair advantage of, or is detrimental to, the distinctive character or the repute of the EU trade mark.

The following, in particular, may be prohibited under paragraph 2:

(a) affixing the sign to the goods or to the packaging of those goods;
(b) offering the goods, putting them on the market, or stocking them for those purposes under the sign, or offering or supplying services thereunder;
(c) importing or exporting the goods under the sign;
(d) using the sign as a trade or company name or part of a trade or company name;
(e) using the sign on business papers and in advertising;
(f) using the sign in comparative advertising in a manner that is contrary to Directive 2006/114/EC of the European Parliament and of the Council.[92]

Furthermore, Article 9(4) sets out the provisions relating to goods in transit:

Without prejudice to the rights of proprietors acquired before the filing date or the priority date of the EU trademark, the proprietor of that EU trademark shall also be entitled to prevent all third parties from bringing goods, in the course of trade, into the Union without being released for free circulation there, where such goods, including packaging, come from third countries and bear without authorisation a trademark which is identical with the EU trademark registered in respect of such goods, or which cannot be distinguished in its essential aspects from that trademark.

The entitlement of the proprietor of an EU trademark pursuant to the first subparagraph shall lapse if, during the proceedings to determine whether the EU trademark has been infringed, initiated in accordance with Regulation (EU) No. 608/2013 of the European Parliament and of the Council[93] concerning customs enforcement of intellectual property rights, evidence is provided by the declarant or the holder of the goods that the proprietor of the EU trademark is not entitled to prohibit the placing of the goods on the market in the country of final destination.

Article 10 further provides that where the risk exists that the packaging, labels, tags, security, or authenticity features or devices or any other means to which the mark is affixed could be used in relation to goods or services and such use would constitute an infringement of the rights of the proprietor of an EUTM mark under Article 9(2) and (3), the proprietor of that trademark shall have the right to prohibit the following acts if carried out in the course of trade:

(a) affixing a sign identical with, or similar to, the EU trademark on packaging, labels, tags, security or authenticity features or devices or any other means to which the mark may be affixed; and
(b) offering or placing on the market, or stocking for those purposes, or importing or exporting, packaging, labels, tags, security or authenticity features or devices or any other means to which the mark is affixed.

---

92. Directive 2006/114/EC of the European Parliament and of the Council of 12 December 2006 concerning misleading and comparative advertising (OJ L 376, 27.12.2006, p.21 https://eur-lex.europa.eu/legal-content/EN/TXT/?uri = OJ%3AL%3A2006%3A376%3ATOC).
93. Regulation (EU) No. 608/2013 of the European Parliament and of the Council of 12 June 2013 concerning customs enforcement of IPRs and repealing Council Regulation (EC) No. 1383/2003 (OJ L 181, 29.6.2013, p.15).

[2] Parallel Imports

A large proportion of trademark infringement cases in the pharmaceutical sector concerns parallel trade. Parallel trade of pharmaceuticals is a particularly litigious area giving rise to a large body of European case law. This is not surprising given that the parallel trader may purchase medicinal products that are marketed in one Member State of the EU at a low price and sells them in another Member State where the same products are marketed at higher prices.

The extent to which the manufacturer can enforce their IPRs (including trademark rights) against a parallel trader is discussed in Chapter 20.

§3.05 COPYRIGHT, DATABASE RIGHTS, & DESIGN RIGHTS

[A] Copyright

Copyright arises automatically when a copyright work is created and generally does not require registration or any pro-active steps to protect it. This, however, can give rise to issues of ownership as it may be difficult to establish when a work was created and by whom.

Copyright protects original works against copying. In the context of the pharmaceutical industry, copyright can provide some protection against copying of literary or artistic works such as data sheets, patient information leaflets, packaging, and advertising materials among other recorded works.

In 2001, Directive 2001/29/EC[94] on copyright in the information society was adopted, which harmonised (to an extent) the rights of reproduction, distribution, communication to the public, the legal protection of anti-copying devices, and rights management systems in light of growing use of the Internet. Presently, the EU copyright law consists of eleven directives and two regulations, harmonising the essential rights of authors, performers, producers, and broadcasters.

[B] Database Rights

The use of databases or collections of information is widespread within the pharmaceutical industry, from the collection and presentation of data to the results of gene sequencing and screening.

The Database Directive (Directive 96/9/EC)[95] introduced the sui generis database right, which protects collection of information (which are not protected by copyright) against extraction and reutilisation. However, prior to the implementation of the Database Directive, compilations of data may have been protected under national

---

94. Directive 2001/29/EC of the European Parliament and of the Council of 22 May 2001 on the harmonisation of certain aspects of copyright and related rights in the information society (OJ L 167, 22.6.2001, p.10).
95. Directive 96/9EC of the European Parliament and of the Council of 11 March 1996 on the legal protection of databases (OJ L 77, 27.3.1996, p.20).

copyright law as literary works on the condition that they were recorded on some medium and 'original'.

A 'database' for the purpose of the Database Directive is defined as 'collection of independent works, data or other materials arranged in a systematic or methodical way and individually accessible by electronic or other means.'[96]

The sui generis right is an automatic right that comes into existence when the database is created. The Database Directive describes the right granted to the 'maker' of the database a 'right for the maker of a database which shows that there has been qualitatively and/or quantitatively a substantial investment in either the obtaining, verification or presentation of the contents to prevent extraction and/or re-utilization of the whole or of a substantial part, evaluated qualitatively and/or quantitatively, of the contents of that database.'[97] In other words, the right will subsist if there has been substantial investment in obtaining, verifying, or presenting the contents of the database. The term 'extraction' means the permanent or temporary transfer of all or a substantial part of the contents of a database to another medium by any means or in any form. Reutilisation means any form of making available to the public all or a substantial part of the contents of a database by the distribution of copies, by renting, by online or other forms of transmission.

The duration of sui generis database rights is fifteen calendar years from the date of completion of the database, expiring on the first of January. In the case of a database which is made available to the public in whatever manner before expiry of the fifteen-year period, the term of protection by that right shall expire fifteen years from the first of January of the year following the date when the database was first made available to the public.

[C]   **Design Rights**

Design rights may apply to the appearance of the whole or part of a product subject to certain exceptions. In the pharmaceutical sector, design rights might apply to packaging, containers, the design of medical devices (such as inhalers), tablets, and capsules. In general terms, registration of design rights is simpler than the procedure required for the registration of trademarks.

At an EU-wide level, design rights may exist as unregistered 'Community design' rights and registered 'Community design' rights, which have unitary effect and are governed by Regulation (EC) 6/2002. Registered design rights also exist at a national level and are largely harmonised through Directive 98/71/EC.

The duration of design rights depends on whether they are registered or unregistered. Registered design rights have a duration of five years and can be renewed up to a maximum of twenty-five years. Unregistered Community design rights last for a

---

96. Article 1(2) of the Database Directive.
97. Article 7.

period of three years from the date the design was first made available to the public within the EU.[98]

National unregistered designs may also be protected in some Member States by unfair competition laws or national unregistered design right law (such as in the UK).

§3.06 CONFIDENTIAL INFORMATION

Various types of commercial and technical information may be regarded as confidential information. These will include (among other things) formulae of investigational or pipeline products, methods and protocols, business and financial information, and inventions where a patent application is yet to be filed. As the name suggests, rights in confidential information depend on keeping the information confidential.

The protection of confidential information is mandated by the TRIPS Agreement. Article 39(2) of the TRIPS Agreement states:

> Natural and legal persons shall have the possibility of preventing information lawfully within their control from being disclosed to, acquired by, or used by others without their consent in a manner contrary to honest commercial practices so long as such information:
>
> (a) is secret in the sense that it is not, as a body or in the precise configuration and assembly of its components, generally known among or readily accessible to persons within the circles that normally deal with the kind of information in question;
> (b) has commercial value because it is secret; and
> (c) has been subject to reasonable steps under the circumstances, by the person lawfully in control of the information, to keep it secret.

Article 39(3) of the TRIPS Agreement provides further safeguards stating that:

> Members, when requiring, as a condition of approving the marketing of pharmaceutical or of agricultural chemical products which utilize new chemical entities, the submission of undisclosed test or other data, the origination of which involves a considerable effort, shall protect such data against unfair commercial use. In addition, Members shall protect such data against disclosure, except where necessary to protect the public or unless steps are taken to ensure that the data are protected against unfair commercial use.

Accordingly, Article 39(3) of the TRIPS Agreement requires countries to provide a limited period of 'data exclusivity' so as to protect the investment in order to be the first to take the regulated product to market. In other words, it protects the investment made in demonstrating to the regulatory authorities that the product is safe and

---

98. Article 11 of Regulation (EC) 6/2002 provides 'a design shall be deemed to have been made available to the public within the Community if it has been published, exhibited, used in trade or otherwise disclosed in such a way that, in the normal course of business, these events could reasonably have become known to the circles specialised in the sector concerned, operating within the Community. The design shall not, however, be deemed to have been made available to the public for the sole reason that it has been disclosed to a third person under explicit or explicit conditions of confidentiality.'

efficacious by preventing regulatory authorities from relying on that data when reviewing MAAs from third parties.

To a certain extent, the protection of confidential information has been harmonised across the EU by virtue of the Directive (EU) 2016/943 of the European Parliament and of the Council of 8 June 2016 on the protection of undisclosed know-how and business information (trade secrets) against their unlawful acquisition, use, and disclosure. The Directive lays down rules on the protection against the unlawful acquisition, use, and disclosure of trade secrets. Pursuant to Article 4(1) of the Directive (EU) 2016/943, Member States shall ensure that trade secret holders are entitled to apply for the measures, procedures, and remedies provided for in this Directive in order to prevent, or obtain redress for, the unlawful acquisition, use, or disclosure of their trade secret. Article 4(3) stipulates that the use or disclosure of a trade secret shall be considered unlawful whenever carried out, without the consent of the trade secret holder, by a person who is found to meet any of the following conditions:

(a) having acquired the trade secret unlawfully;
(b) being in breach of a confidentiality agreement or any other duty not to disclose the trade secret; or
(c) being in breach of a contractual or any other duty to limit the use of the trade secret.

The acquisition, use, or disclosure of a trade secret shall also be considered unlawful whenever a person, at the time of the acquisition, use, or disclosure, knew or ought, under the circumstances, to have known that the trade secret had been obtained directly or indirectly from another person who was using or disclosing the trade secret unlawfully (Article 4(4)). In addition to that, the production, offering, or placing on the market of infringing goods, or the importation, export, or storage of infringing goods for those purposes, shall also be considered an unlawful use of a trade secret where the person carrying out such activities knew, or ought, under the circumstances, to have known that the trade secret was used unlawfully (Article 4(5)).

In some countries, confidential information is protected through the law of unfair competition. In others (such as the UK), the right to protect confidential information falls within the scope of the law of confidence.

In the UK, the law of confidence will protect information if two key criteria are met: (i) the information has the necessary quality of confidence, and (ii) it is disclosed to the recipient in circumstances importing an obligation of confidence. The rights in confidential information will, however, cease if information enters the public domain (irrespective of the manner it was disclosed). It is therefore very important that disclosure of any confidential information should be documented and subject to a non-disclosure agreement.

CHAPTER 4
Clinical Trials

Sally Shorthose, Pieter Erasmus, Hester Borgers, Edzard Boonen & Anna Koster

§4.01 INTRODUCTION

A clinical trial is a rigorously controlled test of a new medicine or a new invasive medical device (an 'investigational agent') on human subjects that is intended to determine the clinical pharmacological, pharmacokinetic,[1] and/or other pharmacodynamic[2] effects of that investigational agent and/or to identify any adverse reactions to that investigational agent. Clinical trials are required in order to assess the safety and efficacy of the investigational agent before it is authorised for release to the public.

Clinical trials take place before the launch of a new medicinal product, and they may also be carried out in order to obtain further data on a medicine or device that is already accessible to the public. For example, a manufacturer might undertake a trial to demonstrate the efficacy of its products compared to its competitors' products or to placebo products. Either way, the conduct of clinical trials is strictly regulated. The European regulatory landscape has changed drastically for clinical trials, as on 31 January 2022, the Clinical Trials Regulation (EU) No. 536/2014 (CTR) entered into application, repealing the Clinical Trials Directive (EU) No. 2001/20/EU (CTD). The main aim of this new CTR is to harmonise the processes for assessment and supervision of (multinational) clinical trials throughout the European Union (EU).

Before a clinical trial commences, approval must be obtained. Under the CTR, it is now possible to submit one single online application for approval for commencing a clinical trial in several European countries. The new online system, the so-called Clinical Trials Information System (CTIS), makes it more efficient for all Member States

---

1. Pharmacokinetics is the branch of pharmacology concerned with the rate at which drugs are absorbed, distributed, metabolised, and eliminated by the body.
2. Pharmacodynamics is the branch of pharmacology that studies the effects and modes of action of drugs upon the body.

to evaluate the incoming applications and authorise them. In the future, the aim of the CTR and CTIS is to ensure that, in a more efficient way, larger clinical trials can be conducted across the EU Member States and the European Economic Area (EEA) countries. Both the new legislation and the application process are discussed in more detail below.

Generally, the first clinical trials of a medicine or device involve a small number of healthy volunteers. One of the main purposes of a first-in-man (FIM) trial is to assess human tolerance to a medicine rather than to determine its therapeutic benefit, so it has traditionally been considered irrelevant whether the subject is a patient or a healthy volunteer. However, the Committee for Medicinal Products for Human Use (CHMP) has advised[3] that the choice of the study population (i.e., healthy volunteers or patients) should be determined on a case-by-case basis for high-risk medicinal products,[4] having consideration for the risks inherent in the type of medicinal product, its molecular target, immediate and potential long-term toxicity, the presence of the target in healthy subjects or in patients only, and the possible variability in patients. In the case of patients, consideration also must be given to other medications the patient is taking concurrently in combination with the trial medication to determine whether that other medication will either cause adverse reactions or result in confusing clinical data. If the efficacy and safety data from the FIM pilot trial justify a larger-scale trial, the number of trial participants will be increased in order to build up the body of knowledge on the investigational agent. Clinical trials may vary in size from a single centre in one country to multicentre trials in a number of countries.

Clinical trials are set up, run, and monitored by a sponsor, who may be the pharmaceutical or biotechnology company that developed the medicine or device being studied. Alternatively, the sponsor may be a distributor or co-marketer who wishes to obtain approval to launch its product in a new territory. Furthermore, universities or research centres can act as a (co-)sponsors of the clinical trial. The sponsor may not have the capacity, experience, or geographic reach to carry out (the practicalities of the) clinical trials, and the conduct of trials is frequently outsourced to a partner such as a contract research organisation (CRO).

This chapter discusses the quite recently introduced CTR. The CTR established rules and guidelines for the approval, conduct, and management of clinical trials in the EU. We begin with a general description of the new regulation. Beginning in §4.03, there is a detailed discussion of the steps and requirements of the clinical trial process from pre-trial authorisation via CTIS through commencing and ending the trial, safety reporting, and the conduct of the trial. There is also a discussion of the changes brought about following the 2006 TeGenero case, in which six volunteers were seriously injured (§4.10), as are discussed investigational medicinal products and auxiliary medicinal

---

3. CHMP Guideline on requirements for FIM clinical trials for potential high-risk medicinal products, EMEA/CHMP/SWP/28367/2007.
4. High-risk IMPs are defined when there are concerns that serious adverse reactions in FIM clinical trials may occur. These concerns may be derived from particular knowledge or uncertainties on (1) the mode of action, and/or (2) the nature of the target, and/or (3) the relevance of animal models.

products (AxMP), the role of the sponsor and investigator, and further guidance on clinical trials.

§4.02 REGULATION (EU) NO. 536/2014: CTR

[A] Introduction to the CTR

The CTR plays a considerable role in further harmonising the rules of carrying out clinical trials. To be expected in this regard, the goal of the CTR is to harmonise the rules for submission, assessment, and supervision of clinical trials throughout the EU on a supranational level. Other main goals are the introduction of an EU portal, CTIS, for the submission of clinical trials, as well as certain transparency requirements. Also, the protection of subjects participating in a clinical trial is still paramount. The CTR also requires monitoring of adverse reactions that occur during clinical trials and reporting to the European Medicines Agency (EMA).[5] This section describes the types of trials that are governed by the CTR and offers a general guide to the rules provided by the CTR against the background of specific aims of the CTR.

The International Conference on Harmonisation (ICH) of Technical Requirements for the Registration of Pharmaceuticals for Human Use have created a detailed set of guidelines on good clinical practice which sets the international standard for clinical trials (ICH-GCP), finding its origin in the World's Medical Association's Declaration of Helsinki. The ICH guidelines provide an internationally recognised set of GCP guidelines governing the conduct of clinical trials. Whilst applying the set of rules as laid down in the CTR, the ICH guidelines should always be taken into account.[6] The ICH-GCP is discussed in more detail later in this chapter.

[B] When the CTR Applies

The CTR applies to the broader concept of clinical studies, of which a clinical trial is a category. The CTR applies to all clinical trials in the EU, other than non-interventional clinical trials.[7]

For the purposes of the CTR, a clinical study is broadly defined as:

any investigation in relation to humans intended:

a) to discover or verify the clinical, pharmacological or other pharmacodynamic effects of one or more medicinal products;
b) to identify any adverse reactions to one or more medicinal products; or
c) to study the absorption, distribution, metabolism and excretion of one or more medicinal products; with the objective of ascertaining the safety and/or efficacy of those medicinal product.'[8]

---

5. Articles 41–42 Regulation (EU) No. 536/2014.
6. Recital 43, Regulation (EU) No. 536/2014.
7. Article 1 Regulation (EU) No. 536/2014.
8. Article 2(1) Regulation (EU) No. 536/2014.

Forming a category within the definition of a clinical study, a clinical trial is defined by the CTR as follows: 'Clinical trial means a clinical study which fulfils any of the following conditions: a) the assignment of the subject to a particular therapeutic strategy is decided in advance and does not fall within normal clinical practice of the Member State concerned; b) the decision to prescribe the investigational medicinal products is taken together with the decision to include the subject in the clinical study; or c) diagnostic or monitoring procedures in addition to normal clinical practice are applied to the subjects."[9] The CTR applies to clinical trials from both commercial and non-commercial Sponsors. The CTR also encourages Member States to take measures in order to help facilitate clinical trials that are conducted by non-commercial sponsors. The contribution of this type of sponsor should be maximised and stimulated without compromising the quality of clinical trials.[10]

[C] Implementation of the CTR

In accordance with the constitutional laws of the EU, the CTR, as a Regulation, did not have to be adopted into national laws of the Member States and ensures that the rules for clinical trials are identical throughout the whole of the EU. As mentioned, the CTR entered into application on 31 January 2022. However, there is a transition period in place of three years. In the first year, that is, from 31 January 2022 until 31 January 2023, sponsors can choose between submitting an application via the old CTD-system or by using the new CTR-governed CTIS system. From 31 January 2023 onwards, the use of CTIS for submitting initial applications becomes mandatory, and as of 31 January 2025, all clinical trials will be governed by the CTR and transitioned to CTIS.

[D] Aims of the CTR

As mentioned, the goal of the CTR is to harmonise the rules for submission, assessment, and supervision of clinical trials throughout the EU. The most important step in this harmonisation process is the introduction of the online EU portal that enables sponsors to file a single application to run a clinical trial in several European countries. The so-called Expert Group on Clinical Trials, consisting of representatives of all EU Member States and EEA contracting parties and chaired by the European Commission (Commission), published an extensive Q&A regarding the CTR. According to this document, the main characteristics of the CTR include:

- a streamlined application procedure via a single-entry point – an EU portal and database, for all clinical trials conducted in EEA;
- a single set of documents to be prepared and submitted for the application;

---

9. Article 2(2) Regulation (EU) No. 536/2014.
10. Recital 81 Regulation (EU) No. 536/2014.

- a single authorisation procedure for all clinical trials, allowing a faster and thorough assessment of an application by all Member States concerned, and ensuring one single assessment outcome and authorisation per Member State;
- a harmonised procedure for the assessment of applications for clinical trials;
- strictly defined deadlines for the assessment of clinical trial application;
- the involvement of the ethics committees in the assessment procedure in accordance with the national law of the Member state concerned but within the overall timelines defined by the CTR;
- simplified reporting procedures which will spare sponsors from submitting broadly identical information separately to various bodies and different Member States;
- clinical trials conducted outside the EU, but referred to in a clinical trial application within the EU, will have to comply with regulatory requirements that are at least equivalent to those applicable in the EU:
- strengthened transparency for clinical trials data;
- a coordination and advisory committee that will serve as a forum for exchanging best practices between Member States;
- EU controls in Member states and third countries to ensure that clinical trials rules are being properly supervised and enforced.[11]

§4.03 AUTHORISATION PROCEDURE FOR A CLINICAL TRIAL

[A] Introduction to the Authorisation of a Clinical Trial

In advance of the commencement of a clinical trial, a number of steps must be undertaken in compliance with the CTR. In this section, we set out the process to authorisation, all the formalities for the submission of an application for a clinical trial, the contents of the application dossier, as well as the task of the reporting Member State in respect of the application dossier, which is described in Chapter II of the CTR. This section also describes the possibilities for a modification of the clinical trial and the requirements that must be met in that regard, which are laid down in Chapter III of the CTR.

Prior to the implementation of the CTR (Reg. (EU) No. 536/2014), that entered into application on 31 January 2022, this approval had to be obtained from the competent authority and ethics committee in the country where the trial was taking place. As mentioned, implementing the CTR, however, also resulted in the advent of an online platform known as the CTIS. This new platform enables all sponsors to submit only one application for clinical trial authorisations in all EU Member States and EEA countries. Approval will only be granted if satisfactory information has been provided,

---

11. Question 1.1 of the CTR (EU) No. 536/2014 Questions & Answers version 6.1, Expert Group on Clinical Trials, May 2022.

together with an application dossier, including, among others, a protocol that details the manner in which the trial will be carried out.

In order to submit an application to the Member States concerned, a scientific and ethical review must be exercised in accordance with the CTR. Ethical reviews are performed by national ethics committees and in accordance with the law of said Member States. The Member States are also responsible for the coordination of the timelines of both the national ethics committees and the timelines provided in the CTR. The purpose of prior authorisation is to allow for an independent check of whether the rights, safety, dignity, and well-being of participants of clinical trials are protected and carried out properly.

[B] CTIS

The CTIS, the information system to be used for the information flow between clinical trial sponsors, EU Member States, EEA countries, and the Commission, was set up in accordance with Chapter XIV of the CTR. This chapter covers the information and technology (IT) infrastructure regarding the EU portal and the database and its functionality. As mentioned before, the CTR aims to harmonise assessment and supervision of clinical trials, more specifically through the CTIS. The system oversees information about clinical trials in the EU and EEA.

As briefly mentioned, on the basis of Article 5 CTR, sponsors are able to submit their application for authorisation in up to thirty countries (EU and EEA), using the CTIS as a single submission point. The sponsor proposes one Member State as a reporting Member State. In case this Member State does not wish to be the reporting Member State or another Member State concerned is willing to be the reporting Member State, this will be reported through the CTIS. In the event more than one or none of the Member States concerned is willing to be the reporting Member State, the Member States concerned select the reporting Member State by agreement.[12] If no agreement is reached, the proposed reporting Member State will be the reporting Member State. The reporting Member State notifies the sponsor and other Member States within six days.[13]

An important part of the online authorisation process is the submission of the application dossier, which consists of Part I and Part II. This application dossier is dealt with in detail in the next subchapter §4.03[C]; however, with regard to CTIS, the following applies. The reporting Member State is also in charge of drawing and submitting Part I of the application dossier through the CTIS.[14] In case the reporting Member State concludes that Part I of the application dossier with regard to the conduct of the clinical trial is acceptable, this conclusion is deemed to be the conclusion of all the Member States concerned. If the conclusion of the reporting Member State is that, regarding Part I of the application dossier, the clinical trial is not acceptable, this

---

12. Article 5(1) Regulation (EU) No. 536/2014.
13. *Ibid.*
14. Article 6(2) Regulation (EU) No. 536/2014.

conclusion is deemed to be the conclusion of all the Member States concerned.[15] Disagreement with the conclusion of the reporting Member State is only possible on the grounds of Article 8(2), second subparagraph CTR and should be communicated through the CTIS. Part II of the application dossier is drafted by each Member State concerned and submitted through the CTIS within forty-five days from the validation date.[16] The aspects covered by Part I of the application dossier are listed in Article 7(1) CTR. All additional information needed for both Part I and Part II can be requested and submitted through the CTIS. Decisions on the clinical trial are also communicated through the system.[17] The CTIS can also be used to expand clinical trials to other EU/EEA countries.

Through the publicly accessible website, the CTIS aims to enable transparency and access to information. The website is, as stated above, used by clinical trial sponsors to apply for authorisation and to submit clinical trial results. National regulators use the platform to assess the application, ask questions about the application, and collaboratively process, authorise, or refuse and, in case of authorisation, oversee the clinical trial. Anyone with interest in clinical trials in the EU/EEA can access all information in the database.[18] The only exceptions to this public access are laid down in Article 81(4) CTR and include protection grounds for: (a) personal data, (b) commercially confidential information, (c) communication between Member States relating to the application dossier, and (d) data which ensures effective supervision by Member States of the conduct of the clinical trial.

The CTIS and the publicly accessible website went live on 31 January 2022 after being postponed in 2015 due to technical difficulties. As of this date, the system was ready for use. However, clinical trial sponsors are not obliged to use the system until 31 January 2023. As of then, all new clinical trials in the EU/EEA have to be submitted through CTIS. The transition period will end on 31 January 2025, when all ongoing clinical trials should be transferred to CTIS. In November 2021, the EMA published a so-called CTIS sponsor Handbook aiming to provide sponsors with the information they might need to use the CTIS.[19]

[C] Authorisation Procedure for a Clinical Trial

As mentioned above, the application dossier for a clinical trial is submitted by the sponsor via CTIS. In short, the following applies regarding the process. The sponsor shall propose one of the Member States as reporting Member State. In case the Member State is not willing to be the reporting Member State, or another Member State wishes to be the reporting Member State, this will be notified in the CTIS within three days

---

15. Article 8(5) Regulation (EU) No. 536/2014.
16. Article 7(2) Regulation (EU) No. 536/2014.
17. Article 8 Regulation (EU) No. 536/2014.
18. Article 81(4) Regulation (EU) No. 536/2014.
19. Clinical Trials Information System – sponsor Handbook, EMA (30 November 2021), EMA/299895/2021 – v. 2.00.

after application of the dossier.[20] Upon agreement but at last, within six days from submission, the reporting Member State shall notify the sponsor and other Member States of its role.[21] Within ten days from the submission of the application dossier, the reporting Member State shall validate the application and notify the sponsor, considering that the clinical trial falls within the scope of the CTR and the application dossier is complete.[22]

The application dossier is built up of two parts; a central part (Part I) and a national part (Part II). The assessment of both parts depends on the type of clinical trial, whether it has a multinational or a national character. For multinational clinical trials, Part I is jointly assessed by all Member States concerned, whilst Part II follows a national assessment. For clinical trials with a national character, both parts are assessed by the one Member State concerned, as no other Member States are involved in a national clinical trial.[23]

Annex I of the CTR contains all the documents and information that should be included in the application dossier for the initial application. The application dossier consists of the following documents:

(a) The Sponsor's signature and reference to any previous applications;
(b) A cover letter;
(c) EU application form;
(d) The protocol;
(e) The investigator's brochure (IB);
(f) Documentation relating to compliance with good manufacturing practice (GMP);
(g) Investigational medicinal product dossier (IMPD);
(h) AxMP dossier;
(i) Scientific advice and paediatric investigation plan (PIP);
(j) Content of the labelling of the investigational medicinal products;
(k) Recruitment arrangements;
(l) Subject information on informed consent;
(m) Suitability of the investigator;
(n) Suitability of the facilities;
(o) Proof of insurance cover or indemnification;
(p) Financial arrangements;
(q) Proof of payment of fee;
(r) Proof that data will be processed in compliance with Union law.

Part I of the application dossier consists of: the cover letter, the proof of payment of fee, the proof of compliance with Union data protection law, the protocol, the IB,

---

20. Article 5(1) Regulation (EU) No. 536/2014.
21. *Ibid.*
22. Article 5(3) Regulation (EU) No. 536/2014.
23. Articles 6(5) and 7(1) Regulation (EU) No. 536/2014. As follows from Article 7, each Member State shall assess the application for its own territory, whilst the assessment of Part I in Article 6 follows a Communautaire approach.

GMP compliance, the IMPD, the AxMP dossier, the PIP, and the content of the labelling.[24]

Part II consists of: recruitment arrangements, subject information on informed consent, the suitability of the investigator, the suitability of the facilities, the proof of insurance cover or indemnification, financial arrangements, compliance with national requirements on data protection, and compliance with use of biological samples.[25]

After submission of the application dossier, the reporting Member State has ten days to validate the dossier.[26] During the validation process, other Member States concerned can express any considerations they might have.[27] In the event that the application is incomplete, the sponsor is notified thereof via the EU portal, at which moment a ten-day recovery period starts.[28] During that time, the sponsor has the opportunity to comment on the application or to complete its submission. No further message from the reporting Member State means good news, and that the clinical trial applied for shall be deemed to fall within the scope of the CTR and that the dossier shall be considered complete.[29]

Sponsor's signature

The signature holds a confirmation from the sponsor that the application is complete and accurate and in compliance with the CTR.[30]

Cover letter

The cover letter specifies the EU trial number and the universal trial number, as well as certain features that are particular to the clinical trial. If, however, this information is already mentioned in the application, it is not necessary to recount that information again in the cover letter. Note that exceptions do apply.[31] Other important elements of the cover letter are the indication of where to find information on adverse reactions and safety information.[32]

EU application form

The application form can be found online and is to identify the sponsor and applicant, as well as to provide general information on the clinical trial.[33]

Protocol

A protocol is defined in the CTR as a document that describes the objectives, design, methodology, statistical considerations, and organisation of a clinical trial. The term

---

24. Article 6 Regulation (EU) No. 536/2014.
25. Article 7 Regulation (EU) No. 536/2014.
26. Article 5(3) Regulation (EU) No. 536/2014.
27. Ibid.
28. Article 5(5) Regulation (EU) No. 536/2014.
29. Article 5(4) Regulation (EU) No. 536/2014.
30. Annex I under A Regulation (EU) No. 536/2014.
31. Annex I, B and under 7 Regulation (EU) No. 536/2014.
32. Annex I, B Regulation (EU) No. 536/2014.
33. Annex I, C Regulation (EU) No. 536/2014.

'protocol' encompasses successive versions of the protocol and protocol modifications.[34] The protocol provides a more in-depth view of the clinical trial. It should describe the objective, design methodology, statistical considerations, purpose, and organisation of the trial.[35] Furthermore, the protocol gives the clinical trial a title, and it mentions the EU trial number for identification.[36]

IB

An IB is defined in the CTR as a compilation of the clinical and non-clinical data on the investigational medicinal product or products which are relevant to the study of the product or products in humans.[37] The IB holds clinical and non-clinical data that is relevant to the study of the investigational product(s). The purpose of the IB is to provide the investigators and others involved in the clinical trial with information to facilitate their understanding of the rationale for, and their compliance with, key features of the protocol, including matters such as dose, dose frequency/interval, methods of administration, and safety monitoring procedures.[38] Chapter 7 of the Good Clinical Practice guideline describes the requirements for the content of an IB.[39]

Documentation relating to compliance with GMP

This part of the application is only necessary in the case the investigational product has not been authorised yet. This means that if the product is authorised and not modified, no documentation is needed. This applies even if the product is manufactured outside of the EU.

Products without EU authorisation, nor an authorisation form a country that is a third party to the International Conference on Harmonisation of Technical Requirements for Registration of Pharmaceuticals for Human Use (ICH), and that are manufactured in the EU, need an import authorisation ex Article 61 CTR, together with a declaration from a Qualified Person (QP) that the manufacturing complies with GMP.[40]

IMPD

An Investigational Medicinal Product (IMP) is defined in the CTR as a medicinal product which is being tested or used as a reference, including as a placebo, in a clinical trial. An Investigational Medicinal Product Dossier (IMPD) contains information on the quality, manufacturing, and control of the researched product, combined with data from non-clinical studies and clinical use of the product. The IMPD is built up of two parts: on the one hand, a quality section and, on the other hand, a safety and efficacy section, with regard to which a reference to the IB can be sufficient. Reference can also be made to the Summary of Product Characteristics (SmPC).[41]

---

34. Article 2(22) Regulation (EU) No. 536/2014.
35. Annex I, D and under 17 Regulation (EU) No. 536/2014.
36. Annex I, D Regulation (EU) No. 536/2014.
37. Article 2(23) Regulation (EU) No. 536/2014.
38. Annex I, E Regulation (EU) No. 536/2014.
39. CHMP/ICH135/95, Chapter 7 (p.52 and further).
40. Annex I, F Regulation (EU) No. 536/2014.
41. Annex I, G Regulation (EU) No. 536/2014.

AxMP dossier

An AxMP is defined in the CTR as means of a medicinal product used for the needs of a clinical trial as described in the protocol but not as an investigational medicinal. AxMP is thus used for the clinical trial, but it is not the product that is being researched. The documentation requirements described under F and G also apply to AxMPs, unless the AxMP is authorised in the Member State concerned.[42]

PIP

If the clinical trial is part of a PIP, as meant in Title II, chapter 3 of Regulation (EC) No. 1901/2006, the summary of scientific advice given by the EMA or any Member State, or third country, regarding the clinical trial, must be submitted with the application.[43]

Content of the labelling of the investigational medicinal products

Reference is made to Chapter X and Annex VI of the CTR. The content of the labelling of the medicinal product being researched must be provided in accordance with the guidance set out in Chapter X and Annex VI.[44]

Recruitment arrangements

If recruiting subjects is done through advertisements, copies of the advertising material must be submitted with the application. Only if it is not already disclosed in the protocol, a separate document is needed to describe advertising procedures. This document must also provide an indication of what the first act of recruitment is.[45]

Subject information on informed consent

All information accessed by subjects of the clinical trial before their decision to either participate or not must be submitted with the application. Accompanying this documentation is a form for written informed consent. Different forms of consent are in place for minors.[46]

Suitability of the investigator

The clinical trial sites, as well as names and positions of principal investigators, are submitted with the application. In addition, a current CV of investigators and other information that can be of relevance are also submitted. This includes economic interests and affiliations.[47]

Suitability of the facilities

The site of the clinical trial must be suited for the nature and use of the investigational medicinal product(s). Proof thereof must be written in a statement that includes a

---

42. Annex I, H Regulation (EU) No. 536/2014.
43. Annex I, I Regulation (EU) No. 536/2014.
44. Annex I, J Regulation (EU) No. 536/2014.
45. Annex I, K Regulation (EU) No. 536/2014.
46. Annex I, L Regulation (EU) No. 536/2014.
47. Annex I, M Regulation (EU) No. 536/2014.

description of the facilities, equipment, and human resources. All in accordance with the system with the Member State concerned.[48]

Proof of insurance cover or indemnification

If applicable, proof of insurance is submitted.[49]

Financial arrangements

A description of the financing of the clinical trial is submitted with the application as well. This description contains compensation for subjects and investigators. Any other financial agreement between the sponsor and the site should also be submitted.[50]

Proof of payment of fee

A proof that the fee for the site is being paid is submitted as well. Additional rules per Member State apply.[51]

Data protection proof

There must be a statement by the sponsor that all clinical trial and subject's data will be collected and processed in accordance with the General Data Protection Regulation (GDPR).[52]

[D] Ethical Committee Approval

[1] Introduction

Before commencing a clinical trial, the sponsor must apply for ethical approval from the ethics committee within the Member State in the reporting Member State,[53] which will normally be the Member State which was proposed by the Sponsor. The CTR provides that the concerned Member State should be able to determine which appropriate body or bodies should be involved in the assessment of the application to conduct a clinical trial and to organise the involvement of ethics committees in a manner that will ensure compliance with the timelines for the authorisation of that clinical trial. Member States have to ensure that appropriate laypersons, in particular, patients or patients' organisations, are involved in ethics committees and also that necessary mix of experience and expertise is made available. The recipient and assessor of the application must be independent of the sponsor, the clinical trial site, and the investigators involved, and moreover, free from any other undue influence.

Each Member State shall have established an ethics committee in each Member State. An ethics committee, as defined in the CTR, is:

---

48. Annex I, N Regulation (EU) No. 536/2014.
49. Annex I, O Regulation (EU) No. 536/2014.
50. Annex I, P Regulation (EU) No. 536/2014.
51. Annex I, Q Regulation (EU) No. 536/2014.
52. Annex R, C Regulation (EU) No. 536/2014.
53. Article 5(1) Regulation (EU) No. 536/2014.

An independent body established in a Member State in accordance with the law of that Member State and empowered to give opinions for the purposes of this Regulation, taking into account the views of laypersons, in particular patients or patients' organisation.[54]

[2] Ethical Committee Approval Process

In determining whether to approve the trial, the ethics committee will assess compliance with the application dossier with Part I of the Assessment Report.[55] The ethics committee considers the following:

(a) Whether the clinical trial is a low-intervention clinical trial; if this is claimed by the sponsor and as such, whether lighter review will be entailed;
(b) Ensuring the protection of subjects and compliance with the informed consent requirements as follows:
- The anticipated therapeutic and public health benefits taking account of all of the following:
  - the characteristics of and knowledge about the investigational medicinal products;
  - the relevance of the clinical trial, including whether the groups of subjects participating in the clinical trial represent the population to be treated, or if not, the explanation and justification provided in accordance with point (y) of paragraph 17 of Annex I to CTR; the current state of scientific knowledge; whether the clinical trial has been recommended or imposed by regulatory authorities in charge of the assessment and authorisation of the placing on the market of medicinal products; and, where applicable, any opinion formulated by the Paediatric Committee on a paediatric investigation plan in accordance with Regulation (EC) No. 1901/2006 of the European Parliament and of the Council (12);
  - the reliability and robustness of the data generated in the clinical trial, taking account of statistical approaches, design of the clinical trial and methodology, including sample size and randomisation, comparator and endpoints;
- the risks and inconveniences for the subject, taking account of all of the following:
  - the characteristics of and knowledge about the investigational medicinal products and the auxiliary medicinal products;
  - the characteristics of the intervention compared to normal clinical practice;
  - the safety measures, including provisions for risk minimisation measures, monitoring, safety reporting, and the safety plan;

---

54. Article 2(11) Regulation (EU) No. 536/2014.
55. Article 4 Regulation (EU) No. 536/2014.

- the risk to subject health posed by the medical condition for which the investigational medicinal product is being investigated;
(c) compliance with the requirements concerning the manufacturing and import of investigational medicinal products and auxiliary medicinal products set out in Chapter IX (Manufacturing and import of investigational medicinal products and auxiliary medicinal products);
(d) compliance with the labelling requirements set out in Chapter X (Labelling); and
(e) the completeness and adequateness of the IB.

The reporting Member State writes up an assessment report which will comprise the Part I assessment report (to be submitted through the EU Portal no later than forty-five days from the validation date) and will set out one of the following conclusions:

(a) the conduct of the clinical trial is acceptable in view of the requirements set out in this Regulation;
(b) the conduct of the clinical trial is acceptable in view of the requirements set out in this Regulation, but subject to compliance with specific conditions which shall be specifically listed in that conclusion; or
(c) the conduct of the clinical trial is not acceptable in view of the requirements set out in the CTR.

For clinical trials involving more than one Member State, the assessment process shall include three phases:

(a) an *initial assessment* phase performed by the reporting Member State within twenty-six days from the validation date;
(b) a *coordinated review* phase performed within twelve days from the end of the initial assessment phase involving all Member States concerned;
(c) a *consolidation phase* performed by the reporting Member State within seven days from the end of coordinated review phase.

During the initial assessment phase, the reporting Member State develops a draft Part I of the assessment report and circulates it to all other concerned Member States.

During the coordinated review phase, all concerned Member States jointly review the application based on the draft Part I of the assessment report and shall share any considerations relevant to the application.

During the consolidation phase, the reporting Member State shall take due account of the considerations of the other Member States concerned when finalising Part I of the assessment report and shall record how all such considerations have been dealt with. The reporting Member State submits the final Part I of the assessment report to the sponsor and all other concerned Member States within the requisite time periods. The reporting Member State is entitled to extend the time period by a further fifty days for clinical trials involving an advanced therapy investigational medicinal product or a medicinal product as defined in point 1 of the Annex to Regulation (EC) No. 726/2004, for the purpose of consulting with experts. As a result, all other reporting periods shall be equivalently extended.

The reporting Member State (but only the reporting Member State) may request additional information from the sponsor to abate concerns noted in each of the initial assessment, the coordinated review, and the consolidation phases and re-response time periods shall be extended by not more than thirty-one days.

The sponsor must submit the requested additional information within the period set by the reporting Member State which shall not exceed twelve days from the receipt of the request.

Any further information submitted by the sponsor shall be reviewed, within a maximum of twelve days of the receipt of the additional information, jointly by all of the concerned Member States, together with the original application, and a consolidated review completed within seven days of the end of the coordinated review. The reporting Member State must reflect the views of all concerned Member States.

The application shall be deemed to have lapsed in all Member States concerned if the sponsor fails to supply the requisite additional information.

[E] Informed Consent

The ethics committee must determine whether clinical trial participants have given informed consent to participate in the trials. The CTR defines *informed consent* as:

> a subject's free and voluntary expression of his or her willingness to participate in a particular clinical trial, after having been informed of all aspects of the clinical trial that are relevant to the subject's decision to participate or, in case of minors and of incapacitated subjects, an authorisation or agreement from their legally designated representative to include them in the clinical trial

Chapter 5 of the CTR sets out in detail rules to apply to the conduct of clinical trials in terms of protecting subjects and securing informed consent,[56] with Article 28(1) setting out the conditions that must be met in order for a clinical trial to be conducted.

The CTR details a process for obtaining informed consent from incapacitated adults,[57] children,[58] and a less-complex process for obtaining consent from a conscious, cognisant adult.[59] However, local custom and practice may affect how the term 'informed consent' is interpreted. In some cultures, for example, a man traditionally speaks for his wife; a mother often speaks for her child. The investigator must reconcile CTR-informed consent requirements with local interpretation.

---

56. L_2014158EN.01000101.xml (europa.eu).
57. Article 31 Regulation (EU) No. 536/2014.
58. Article 32 Regulation (EU) No. 536/2014.
59. Article 29 Regulation (EU) No. 536/2014.

General rules

The Informed Consent must be written, dated, and signed by the interviewing member of the investigation team together with the subject, unless the subject is not able to give informed consent, when the legally designated representative will sign, following due briefing. There are prescribed processes set out in case the subject cannot write.[60]

The subject (or their legal representative, if applicable) must be given full information about the purpose and conduct of the clinical trial and of their rights,[61] including the following:

- the nature, objectives, benefits, implications, risks, and inconveniences of the clinical trial;
- the subject's rights and guarantees regarding his or her protection, in particular, his or her right to refuse to participate and the right to withdraw from the clinical trial at any time without any resulting detriment and without having to provide any justification;
- the conditions under which the clinical trial is to be conducted, including the expected duration of the subject's participation in the clinical trial; and
- the possible treatment alternatives, including the follow-up measures if the participation of the subject in the clinical trial is discontinued.

The information must be presented in a full form, comprehensible to a layperson, and provided by a suitably qualified member of the investigation team. The subject must have information relating to compensation claims. The form must include the EU trial number and information about the availability of the clinical trial results.

Informed consent in cluster trials

Where the clinical trial is to be carried out in only one Member State, that Member State may secure the Informed Consent in a slightly modified and simplified form.

Clinical trials on incapacitated subjects

The CTR is subject to any national law which requires that the incapacitated person signed the informed consent form.[62]

If an incapacitated adult is not able to give consent or has refused consent, a clinical trial may only proceed if further conditions are met:

- The informed consent of their legally designated representative has been obtained;
- The incapacitated subjects have received the relevant information in a way that will facilitate their understanding of that information.
- The explicit wish of an incapacitated subject is respected by the investigator.

---

60. Article 29(1) Regulation (EU) No. 536/2014.
61. Article 19(2) Regulation (EU) No. 536/2014.
62. Article 29(7) Regulation (EU) No. 536/2014.

- No financial incentives are provided other than expenses relating to the conduct of the clinical trial.
- The clinical trial is essential to the incapacitated subject and there is no alternative route to achieving the desired outcome; it related to a medical condition from which the subject suffers and there are scientific grounds for encouraging participation.
- The direct benefit of going ahead with the trial will outweigh the risks and burdens involved.
- The clinical trial relates directly to a medical condition from which the subject suffers, or there is a likely benefit for the population represented by the incapacitated subject if the trial relates to a life-threatening or debilitating condition suffered by the subject, and the risk benefit analysis has been carried out (although national rules may supersede such a point).

The subject must as far as possible take part in the informed consent procedure.

Clinical trials on minors

These provisions are without prejudice to any national law which requires that, in a minor who is capable of forming an opinion and assessing the information given to him or her, must be able to assent to their taking part in a clinical trial, in addition to their legal representative.

A clinical trial may only proceed with the involvement if further conditions are met:

- The informed consent of their legally designated representative has been obtained;
- the minors have been provided with the relevant information in a way that is adapted to their age and maturity, by a member of the investigating team who is trained in dealing with minors.
- – If the minor is capable of forming an opinion and assessing the information, their explicit wish to refuse participation, or to withdraw from participation, must be respected by the investigator.
- No financial incentives are provided other than expenses relating to the conduct of the clinical trial and loss of earnings for legal representative.
- The clinical trial is related to a medical condition from which the subject suffers or is of such a nature that it can only be carried out with minors.
- The scientific evidence that the direct benefit of going ahead with the trial will outweigh the risks and burdens involved or, there will be some benefit for the population represented by the minor, and the clinical trial will pose only a minimal burden on the minor when compared to the potential upsides.
- If the minor reaches the age of legal competence according to the concerned Member State, their express consent to participation must be obtained.

Clinical trials for pregnant or breast-feeding women

Article 33 sets out additional conditions for clinical trials involving pregnant breast-feeding women, such that the interests of the embryo or the breast-fed child shall be taken into account.

Clinical trials in emergency situations.

Article 35 sets out certain derogations from the general rules which are permitted in emergency situations. These derogations can take place as long as the decision to proceed with a clinical trial, even though all steps towards obtaining informed consent have not been achieved, is taken at the time of the first intervention on the subject, in accordance with the protocol for that clinical trial.

These derogations may take place in life-threatening situations where there is no alternative and no informed consent or all prior information can be obtained, but the intervention can be justified on scientific grounds, notwithstanding the absence of full information. Any derogation would be negated by any known expression of an objection to participate by the subject. A risk/benefit balance shall be carried out.

Informed consent should be sought as soon as possible to permit continued participation in the clinical trial

§4.04 THE SUBSTANTIAL MODIFICATION OF A CLINICAL TRIAL

Modifications in a clinical trial are either classified as a substantial modification, a change relevant to the supervision of the trial, or a non-substantial modification.[63] A substantial modification means, according to the CTR, any change to any aspect of the clinical trial which is made after notification of a decision referred to in Articles 8, 14, 19, 20, or 23 of the CTR and which is likely to have a substantial impact on the safety or rights of the subjects or on the reliability and robustness of the data generated in the clinical trial.[64]

Modification is always substantial when it has a significant impact on either the safety or rights of the subjects or on the reliability and robustness of the data generated in the clinical trial. A non-exhaustive list of significant modifications is given in Annex IV of the Regulation (EU) No. 536/2014 Questions & Answers May 2022 document. Examples include a change of sponsor entity, a change of legal representative, and changes in the full title of the clinical trial which modify the meaning. When assessing whether the modification should be classified as a substantial modification, the sponsor should keep in mind that the changes might also lead to the clinical trial having to be considered a completely new clinical trial.[65]

Substantial modifications can only be implemented if they are authorised in accordance with the procedure in Chapter III CTR, which covers the authorisation

---

63. CTR (EU) No. 536/2014 Questions & Answers version 6.1, Expert Group on Clinical Trials, May 2022, p.36.
64. Article 2(13) Regulation (EU) No. 536/2014.
65. CTR (EU), *Supra* n. 63, p.36.

procedure for a substantial modification of a clinical trial. The sponsor has to submit their application dossier to all the Member States concerned through the CTIS,[66] after which the reporting Member State (which is the same Member State as the reporting Member State during the initial authorisation procedure) has to validate the application within six days.[67]

According to Article 17(2) CTR, the reporting Member States communicate through the CTIS whether the substantial modification concerns an aspect covered by Part I of the assessment report and whether the application dossier is complete in accordance with Annex II. If the reporting Member State fails to make this deadline, the substantial modification shall be deemed to meet these two criteria.[68] The reporting Member State shall assess and draw up an assessment report of the application of a substantial modification regarding Part I of the assessment report, in line with Article 18 CTR. In clinical trials that involve multiple Member States, the reporting Member State has the responsibility to draw up a draft assessment report and communicate this report with the other Member States concerned.[69] As laid down in Article 19 (1) CTR, each Member State concerned communicates its conclusion as to whether the substantial modification is authorised through the CTIS.

With regard to substantial modifications of an aspect covered by Part II of the assessment report, the Member State concerned communicates through the CTIS whether the substantial modification concerns an aspect covered by Part II of the assessment report and whether the application dossier is complete in accordance with Annex II.[70] In line with the procedure for substantial modifications in Part I, the substantial modification shall be deemed to meet these two criteria, if the Member State concerned fails to make this deadline.[71]

Article 21 CTR applies in case the substantial modification regards aspects covered in both Parts I and II of the assessment report. Article 21(1) CTR declares the procedure in Article 17 CTR applicable for validation in cases where the substantial modification application regards both parts of the assessment report. According to Article 21(2) CTR, the assessment of the reports shall be in accordance with respectively Article 18 CTR for part I and Article 22 for part II.

§4.05   START, END, HALT, AND EARLY TERMINATION

Chapter VI CTR covers the start, end, temporary halt, and the early termination of a clinical trial. These dates defined and reported to allow patients to assess possibilities to participate and to allow effective supervision by the Member State concerned.[72]

---

66. Article 16 Regulation (EU) No. 536/2014.
67. Article 17(2) Regulation (EU) No. 536/2014 with regard to aspects covered by Part I of the assessment report, Article 20(1) Regulation (EU) No. 536/2014 with regard to aspects covered by Part II of the assessment report.
68. Article 18 Regulation (EU) No. 536/2014.
69. Article 18(4) Regulation (EU) No. 536/2014.
70. Article 20(1) Regulation (EU) No. 536/2014.
71. Article 20(2) Regulation (EU) No. 536/2014.
72. Recital 37 Regulation (EU) No. 536/2014.

[A] Start

Article 36 CTR concerns the notification of the start of a clinical trial. Each Member State concerned should be notified of the start of the clinical trial by the sponsor,[73] the first visit of the first subject,[74] and the end of the recruitment of subjects.[75] These notifications shall be reported through the CTIS, within fifteen days of the start of the clinical trial, the first visit of the first subject, and the end of the recruitment of subjects, respectively.

The start of the clinical trial is defined as the first act of recruitment of a potential subject for a specific clinical trial, unless defined differently in the protocol in the CTR.[76] The Expert Group on Clinical Trials Q&A document provides examples of 'first acts of recruitment'.[77] These examples are, among others, the date of initiation of the clinical trial in the first site, the date when the first study-specific advertisement is published.[78] Ultimately, this date is to be identified by the sponsor in the recruitment strategy[79] and is always in between the authorisation date and the date of the first visit of the first subject.[80]

The first visit of the first subject is the date that the subject or their legal representative signs their first informed consent to participate in the clinical trial.[81]

[B] End

The end of the clinical trial is defined as the last visit of the last subject, or at a later point in time as defined in the protocol in the CTR.[82]

In line with Article 37(1) CTR, the sponsor had to notify Member States of multiple end dates:

(1) In line with Article 37(1) CTR: notify each Member State concerned of the ending of the clinical trial in relation to that Member State.
(2) In line with Article 37(2) CTR: notify each Member State concerned of the ending of the clinical trial in all Member States.
(3) In line with Article 37(3) CTR: notify each Member State concerned of the ending of the clinical trial in all Member States concerned and in all third countries in which the clinical trial has been conducted.

---

73. Article 36(1) Regulation (EU) No. 536/2014.
74. Article 36(2) Regulation (EU) No. 536/2014.
75. Article 36(3) Regulation (EU) No. 536/2014.
76. Article 2(25) Regulation (EU) No. 536/2014.
77. CTR (EU) No. 536/2014 Questions & Answers version 6.1, Expert Group on Clinical Trials, May 2022.
78. *Ibid.*, 99.
79. Point K.49 Annex I Regulation (EU) No. 536/2014.
80. CTR (EU), *Supra* n. 63, p.99.
81. *Ibid.*
82. Article 2(26) Regulation (EU) No. 536/2014.

These notifications shall be made through the CTIS no later than fifteen days from the respective end dates.[83]

Within one year after the end of a clinical trial in all Member States concerned, the sponsor has to submit a summary of the results of the clinical trial through CTIS.[84] In the case that this is not possible, the summary should be summitted as soon as it is available.

[C] Halt

The temporary halt of a clinical trial is defined as an interruption not provided in the protocol of the conduct of a clinical trial by the sponsor with the intention of the sponsor to resume it in the CTR.[85] The halt of recruitment due to a potential change in subject safety should be considered a temporary halt in terms of Article 38 CTR and is subject to the rules for these kinds of temporary halts as mentioned below.[86] If the halt of recruitment is due to 'problems of reaching potential subjects for participation in the clinical trial', the halt should be notified through the CTIS as the end of recruitment.

According to Article 37(5) CTR, each Member State concerned should be informed through the CTIS of the temporary halt, including the reasoning for this action, if the clinical trial is ended for reasons which do not affect the benefit-risk balance within fifteen days. This term is the same for communicating the restart of a clinical trial.[87] If the clinical trial has not restarted within two years of the temporary halt, the end date will be either the expiry date of this period or the date of the decision of the sponsor not to resume, depending on which of these dates is the earliest.[88]

The temporary halt can also be part of urgent safety measures, as defined in Article 54 CTR.[89] In case of a temporary halt which concerns subject safety, the procedure differs from the previously mentioned situation. According to Article 38(1) CTR, the sponsor has to notify each Member State concerned through the CTIS within fifteen days of the date of the temporary halt, including the reasoning for this action whilst also specifying the follow-up measures. Subjects in the clinical trial have to be monitored and the temporary halt should be used to assess the issues of concern and possibly change the clinical trial, after which the sponsor can decide to either end or resume the clinical trial.[90] In case of resumption, the sponsor has to submit a substantial modification and therefore subject to the authorisation procedure in Chapter III of the CTR.[91] This substantial modification has to be submitted within the aforementioned two-year period for restarting the clinical trial, but the clinical trial is,

---

83. Article 37(1)(2)(3) Regulation (EU) No. 536/2014.
84. Article 37(4) Regulation (EU) No. 536/2014.
85. Article 2(28) Regulation (EU) No. 536/2014.
86. CTR (EU, *Supra* n. 63, p.101.
87. Article 37(6) Regulation (EU) No. 536/2014.
88. Article 37(7) Regulation (EU) No. 536/2014.
89. CTR (EU), *Supra* n. 63, p.100.
90. *Ibid.*
91. Article 38(2) Regulation (EU) No. 536/2014.

only in this case, allowed to be resumed after the two-year period.[92] Sponsors are encouraged to notify Member States concerned about follow-ups regarding the clinical trial before the two-year expiry date.[93]

[D]   Early Termination

The early termination of a clinical trial is defined as the premature end of a clinical trial due to any reason before the conditions specified in the protocol are complied with in the CTR.[94] According to Article 37(7) CTR, the date of early termination is deemed to be the date of the end of the trial.

If the early termination is due to reasons which do not affect the benefit-risk balance, the sponsor will notify Member States concerned through the CTIS about the reasons for early termination and, if appropriate, the follow-up measures for subjects.[95]

If the early termination is due to reasons which do affect the subject safety, according to Article 38 CTR, the same regime applies to early termination as for the temporary halt. Therefore, early termination of a clinical trial, for reasons of a change in the benefit-risk balance, has to be notified through the CTIS, including the reasons for early termination and the follow-up measures.

In all clinical trials which are terminated early, a summary of relevant information should be given, including data from the post-study follow-up, if applicable. The only exception is for clinical trials in which no subject was included.[96]

§4.06   CONDUCT OF THE CLINICAL TRIAL

[A]   Introduction to the Conduct of Clinical Trials

Once the ethical approval and trial authorisation have been obtained, the trial(s) can commence. The CTR requires that all trials are carried out in accordance with the protocol and GCP standards.[97] The GCP standards are based on preceding law and the ICH guidelines set out in the Declaration of Helsinki, and they follow the principles set out in that declaration. Furthermore, the CTR provides that manufacture, labelling, and storage of IMPs must comply with GMP. This section discusses the CTR guidelines with respect to the application of GCP standards (Table 4.1) and the Principles of the Declaration of Helsinki (Table 4.2). It also discusses the requirements of GMP as they are set forth in the Helsinki Declaration and the CTR, including the appointment of a QP to ensure that the product being tested meets GMP standards.

---

92. CTR (EU), *Supra* n. 63, p.101.
93. *Ibid.*
94. Article 2(27) Regulation (EU) No. 536/2014.
95. Article 37(7) Regulation (EU) No. 536/2014.
96. CTR (EU), *Supra* n. 63, p.102.
97. Article 47 Regulation (EU) No. 536/2014.

[B] GCP Standards

GCP is an international ethical and scientific quality standard for designing, recording, and reporting trials that involve the participation of human subjects. Compliance with the GCP standard provides public assurance that the rights, safety, and well-being of trial subjects are protected, consistent with the principles that have their origin in the Declaration of Helsinki (set out later in this section). [98]

The CTR governs conduct of trials for IMPs. Specifically, the Regulation applies the principles of GCP to clinical trials on human subjects involving and requires that systems with procedures that assure the quality of every aspect of the trial should be implemented. The principles of GCP are set out in Table 4.1.

Table 4.1   The Principles of Good Clinical Practice[99]

- Clinical trials should be conducted in accordance with the ethical principles that have their origin in the Declaration of Helsinki, and that are consistent with GCP and the applicable regulatory requirement(s).
- Before a trial is initiated, foreseeable risks and inconveniences should be weighed against the anticipated benefit for the individual trial subject.
- The rights, safety, and well-being of the trial subjects are the most important considerations and should prevail over the interests of science and society.
- The available non-clinical and clinical information on an investigational product should be adequate to support the trial.
- Clinical trials should be scientifically sound, and described in a clear, detailed Protocol.
- A trial should be conducted in compliance with the Protocol that has received a favourable IEC opinion.
- The medical care given to, and medical decisions made on behalf of, subjects should always be the responsibility of a qualified physician.
- Each individual involved in conducting a trial should be qualified by education, training, and experience to perform his or her respective task.
- Freely given informed consent should be obtained from every subject prior to clinical trial preparation.
- All clinical trial information should be recorded, handled, and stored in a way that allows its accurate reporting, interpretation, and verification.
- The confidentiality of records that could identify subjects should be protected, respecting the privacy and confidentiality rules.

The CTR sets forth the requirements for authorising the manufacture or importation of IMPs,[100] and it provides detailed guidelines on documentation relating to clinical trials, archiving, qualifications of inspectors, and inspection procedures.

---

98. Article 1(2) Directive 2001/120/EC.
99. Set out in ICH Harmonised Tripartite Guideline: Guideline for Good Clinical Practice, 4 September 1996 and the 'GCP Directive' (Directive 2005/28/EC as far as IMPs are concerned).
100. L_2014158EN.01000101.xml (europa.eu)

The preface to the CTR notes that in its preparation, regard has been given to the 1996 paper ICH E6[101] that sets out, in more detail, the guidelines for GCP in the pharmaceutical industry. The CTR expands the detail of the ICH but does not override the principles contained therein. The objectives of the ICH-GCP guidance are to guarantee that data resulting from clinical trials are credible and accurate and to protect the integrity, safety, and confidentiality of the trial subjects. The ICH provides a unified standard for the EU, Japan, and the United States (US) to facilitate the exchange of clinical data; since the CTR does not conflict with these principles, design of multinational protocols is made easier than if the CTR had comprised a completely new set of guidelines. The guidance applies to the production of all clinical trial data that are intended to be submitted to regulatory authorities. The ICH follows the principles established in the Declaration of Helsinki, which are listed in Table 4.2.

Table 4.2   Principles of the Declaration of Helsinki

(1) Before a trial is initiated, foreseeable risks and inconveniences should be weighed against the anticipated benefit for the individual trial subjects and society. A trial should be initiated and continued only if the anticipated benefits justify the risks.

(2) The rights, safety, and well-being of the trial subjects are the most important considerations and should prevail over the interests of science and society.

(3) The available non-clinical and clinical information on an investigational product should be adequate to support the proposed clinical trial.

(4) Clinical trials should be scientifically sound, and described in a clear, detailed Protocol.

(5) A trial should be conducted in compliance with the Protocol that has received prior IRB/IEC approval.

(6) The medical care given to, and medical decisions made on behalf of, subjects should always be the responsibility of a qualified physician or, when appropriate, or a qualified dentist.

(7) Each individual involved in conducting a trial should be qualified by education, training, and experience to perform his or her respective task(s).

(8) Freely given informed consent should be obtained from every subject prior to clinical trial participation.

(9) All clinical trial information should be recorded, handled, and stored in a way that allows its accurate reporting, interpretation, and verification.

---

101. An FDA document, available on ICH website < www.ich.org >.

> (10) The confidentiality of records that could identify subjects should be protected, respecting the privacy and confidentiality rules in accordance with the applicable regulatory requirement(s).
> (11) Investigational products should be manufactured, handled, and stored in accordance with applicable GMP. They should be used in accordance with approved Protocol.
> (12) Systems with procedures that assure the quality of every aspect of the trial should be implemented.

[C] Good Manufacturing Practice

Principle 11 of the Helsinki Declaration requires that IMPs shall be manufactured, handled, and stored in accordance with GMP. The GMP Directive 2003/94/EC replaced Directive 91/356/EC, and it was enhanced by provisions in CTR[102] and now provides the standards for the manufacture, import, quality management (including documentation), and labelling of IMPs. For example, a sample of the label for the IMP must accompany the clinical application. The sample must show that the text, its format, and the size of the print provide clear and unequivocal instructions. In a trial of a marketed product dispensed by a retail chemist, the normal label used on that product is acceptable.[103] All IMPs for human use must be manufactured in accordance with GMP[104] to make sure that there is batch consistency in IMPs, ensure that the results of clinical trials are unaffected by unsafe or faulty IMP manufacturing, and, most important, ensure that clinical trial subjects are not placed at risk.

The manufacturer or importer of IMPs must designate a QP,[105] whose role is to verify that the product meets the GMP standards of quality throughout the establishment and conduct of a clinical trial. The QP's responsibilities are to guarantee the following:[106]

- That each batch of IMP has been manufactured and checked in compliance with all GMP requirements. Prior to the release of the IMP, the QP must declare, in the prescribed form, that the batch has been manufactured in accordance with GMP, that it complies with the product specification file,[107] and that there is a valid request for authorisation for commencement of a trial.
- That an IMP with an MA from outside the EU has been manufactured in accordance with standards equivalent to GMP, and that the batch has been

---

102. Article 63 Regulation (EU) No. 536/2014.
103. Annex 13 of vol. 4 of Rules Governing Medicinal Products in the EU: Good Manufacturing Practices.
104. Article 9 Directive 2005/28/EC.
105. As defined in Directive 2001/83/EC Article 13, and in Directive 75/319/EEC Article 23.
106. Directive 2001/83/EC Article 13.3.
107. The reference file containing, or referring to files containing, all the information necessary to draft the detailed written instructions on processing, packaging, quality control testing, batch release, and shipping an IMP.

checked to confirm its compliance with its product specification and the information contained in the authorisation request. If the QP cannot demonstrate that the IMP has been manufactured in accordance with standards equivalent to GMP, then the QP must confirm that the batch has been subjected to all relevant analyses, tests, and checks necessary to confirm its quality as contained in the authorisation request.
- That contractual responsibility for GMP compliance is clarified in signed technical agreements.
- That GMP standards are applied to the purchase, import, and manufacture of bulk ingredients, packaging (of bulk ingredients, intermediary products, and finished products), quality control throughout the manufacture and supply processes, the quality of information to be collected for the clinical trial authorisation and product specification file, release for sale of products, and regulatory compliance.
- That destroyed or unused IMP supplies are returned to the manufacturer, or disposed of in accordance with the legislation of the Member State concerned.

The QP may delegate responsibility for GMP implementation, operation, and compliance. The GMP Directive provides that the manufacturer must have the requisite number of qualified personnel to achieve the pharmaceutical quality assurance objective.[108] The hierarchy of responsibility must be clearly set out in an organogram, that is, in an organisation chart including individuals' names instead of simply job titles. All personnel must have a clear job description and sufficient responsibility to be able to carry out their designated tasks.

Member States are obliged[109] to take all appropriate measures (here it is assumed that 'measure' means making compliance with these rules compulsory) to ensure that the manufacture or importation of IMPs is in accordance with GMP, and each therefore has implemented, through its local laws, inspection systems to monitor compliance with GMP. More particularly, Member States must take all appropriate measures to ensure that manufacturers and importers have secured authorisation by complying with the requisite GMP measures and to ensure that such authorised persons always have at their disposal a QP, who is responsible for the matters set out above in this paragraph.

§4.07 CLINICAL TRIAL OVERSIGHT/ROLE OF THE SPONSOR AND INVESTIGATOR

[A] Introduction to Clinical Trial Oversight

The sponsor of the clinical trial must provide, either itself or, more likely, through qualified delegates, ongoing monitoring of the trial. In addition, the investigator and

---

108. Article 7.1 Directive 2002/94.
109. Article 13 Directive 2001/83 EC.

the institution where the trial takes place must allow the sponsor to audit the trial and allow the appropriate regulatory authorities to inspect the trial. In this section, we outline the role and responsibilities of the trial monitor, from pre-commencement site-assessment to periodic on-site assessments and other types of checks, the measured factors of compliance, and reporting protocols. We also discuss the GCP Inspection, internal (voluntary) audits, the objectivity standards, and when to bring in a third-party inspector to ensure that objectivity is attained. If the monitoring or auditing identifies serious or persistent non-compliance with the terms of the CTR on the part of the investigator or the institution, the sponsor must terminate its participation in the trial. When the participation of an investigator or institution is terminated because of non-compliance, the sponsor should promptly notify the appropriate regulatory authorities (CHMP).

[B] Monitoring

Monitoring is the act of overseeing the progress of a clinical trial to verify that the rights and well-being of human subjects are protected and that the reported trial data are accurate, complete, and verifiable from source documents; The CTR has introduced less stringent rules regarding monitoring and the requirements for the contents of the drug master file and the traceability for IMPs. Monitoring is still designed however to ensure that the trial is conducted in accordance with the approved Protocol (as amended if applicable), Standard Operating Procedures (SOPs), GCP guidelines, and applicable regulatory requirements.

The sponsor is responsible for overseeing the clinical trial's progress to ensure subject safety, taking into account the characteristics of the clinical trial and respect for fundamental rights of subjects.[110] When establishing the extent of monitoring, the characteristics of the clinical trial should be taken into account.[111] Those involved in monitoring must be suitably qualified and trained in GCP guidelines and the regulatory requirements governing conduct of clinical trials and more generally in patient care. The sponsor must ensure that the investigating team must also have sufficient scientific and/or clinical knowledge to supervise the trial and ensure compliance with all aspects of the Protocol.

It is the Sponsor's responsibility to ensure that each clinical trial is adequately monitored. 'Adequately' means that the monitoring is carried out with sufficient regularity and intensity to ensure that all elements of the Protocol are complied with. In determining the level of monitoring required, the sponsor must take into account the objective purpose of the trial, its design, complexity, blinding, size, and end points. A complex trial involving many subjects and a product whose pharmacology is unusual or novel will require more scrutiny than a small trial involving a well-known molecule whose pharmacology is familiar to the sponsor, the investigator, the monitor, and the competent authorities. Furthermore, the experience of Investigators and their staff will

---

110. Article 47 Regulation (EU) No. 536/2014.
111. Article 44 Regulation (EU) No. 536/2014.

affect the frequency of monitoring. The monitoring process can be simplified by the use of statistically selected sample data and subjects.

The Sponsor of the trial usually undertakes an in-person site-assessment before the trial starts; they may well sub-contract this responsibility, and a formal agreement is drawn up between the sponsor and the monitor that will provide information about what is expected of the investigator during the monitoring process. The monitoring usually entails site visits by the monitors, together with other desk-based checks; however, the on-site review is particularly important.[112] For a small trial involving a well-known product and an experienced and knowledgeable investigator, the monitor can carry out off-site monitoring in conjunction with confirmation of the level of the Investigator's training and meetings off-site rather than at the trial site, and with extensive written guidance, telephone calls, and desk reviews of the documentation.

The monitor's principal responsibility is to verify on behalf of the sponsor that trial procedures comply with the ICH Harmonised Tripartite Guideline for GCP, and other relevant guidelines and the CTR.[113] The monitor verifies the following:

- the investigator has adequate facilities and personnel available to undertake the study at all times, and the investigator and his or her team do not delegate tasks to unauthorised individuals;
- the IMP storage times and transport conditions are adequate;
- IMP supplies are sufficient, and IMPs are supplied only to correct subjects at the doses specified in the Protocol;
- subjects are given proper instructions in relation to the use, handling, storage, and return of the IMP, and the use, return, and disposal of the IMP is sufficiently controlled, monitored, and documented;
- the investigator follows the approved Protocol and any approved amendment(s);
- the investigator only recruits eligible subjects, and written informed consent has been obtained from all trial subjects prior to commencement of the trial;
- the investigator receives the current IB and other necessary documents so that the investigator and his or her team are fully informed about the trial;
- source documents and other trial records, reports, notifications, applications, and submissions are accurate, complete, kept up-to-date, and properly maintained; they accurately identify the trial; and the investigator maintains the essential documents (see ICH E6[M] Essential Documents for the Conduct of a Clinical Trial) during the course of the trial;
- the case report form (CRF) entries accurately and completely report and explain dose and/or therapy modifications, adverse events, failed or missed tests, and all withdrawals and dropouts of enrolled subjects from the trial; and
- adverse events are reported in accordance with regulatory requirements, GCP, the Protocol, the IRB/IEC, and the Sponsor.

---

112. See ICH Guidance E6(R1) Good Clinical Practice: Consolidated Guideline, paragraph 5.18.4.
113. Paragraph 5.18.4 E6(R1).

A monitor acts as the main line of communication between the sponsor and the investigator and has certain reporting duties. They must prepare a written report for the sponsor after each site visit. The report will include the data site, name of the monitor, names of the investigator and other individuals contacted, the recruitment rate, a summary of what was reviewed, and a list of concerns and deviations of significant findings (i.e., a finding that might affect the safety or well-being of subjects, or the conduct of the trial either at a site that has been visited or elsewhere). The Sponsor's designated representative reviews the report and works with the monitor to address any concerns or recommended actions. The monitor will report to the investigator deviations from the Protocol, SOPs, GCP, and the applicable regulatory requirements, as well as any CRF entry error, omission, or illegibility, and take appropriate action to prevent recurrence of the detected deviations.

[C]   **GCP Inspection**

The EU has set out guidelines for how to apply GCP[114] to the conduct of clinical trials, and the EMA has sought to harmonise and coordinate the processes and standards applied during GCP inspections and to ensure that the sponsor and investigator comply with the guidelines. In order to ensure compliance with the CTR, Member States should be able to conduct inspections and should have adequate inspection capacities as many responsibilities are delegated to them; they are required to appoint inspectors to supervise compliance. The inspectors must be adequately qualified and trained.[115]

'Inspection' is defined in the CTR as:[116]

> the act by a competent authority of conducting an official review of documents, facilities, records, quality assurance arrangements, and any other resources that are deemed by the competent authority to be related to the clinical trial and that may be located at the clinical trial site, at the Sponsor's and/or contract research organisation's facilities, or at other establishments which the competent authority sees fit to inspect.

Compliance with GCP is checked by inspectors who are tasked by CHMP with carrying out inspections to:

- determine whether a trial is conducted in accordance with all relevant regulatory requirements, regulations, and ethical standards;
- provide answers to the assessment process where the CHMP have determined that these would best be answered through inspection; and
- determine whether the data submitted in the dossier are credible and accurate.

GCP inspections are conducted by inspectors appointed by the relevant Member State; there may be more than one inspector, if there are a number of sites to visit. One of these inspectors will be designated as the reporting inspector who will coordinate the

---

114. Directive 2005/28/EC.
115. Article 78 Regulation (EU) No. 536/2014.
116. Introduction (31) Regulation (EU) No. 536/2014.

preparation of the inspection, the conduct of the inspection, the activities of the inspectors, and the writing and co-signing of the integrated inspection report (the composite report of all separate site reports) together with all the lead inspectors, as well as being the main route of communication with EMA Inspection Sector. A lead inspector will be responsible for the inspection of at least one inspection site; he or she will be responsible for the conduct of the inspection at that site(s) and will prepare the inspection report for that site(s).

Inspections may be routine, as part of the EMA surveillance of GCP compliance, or may be triggered for a number of reasons, for example, to verify the GCP compliance statement, or to undertake further examination when the circumstances of the trial give rise to concerns. These concerns can be where:

- the MA application is particularly important;
- there are ethical concerns such as recruitment of subjects from a vulnerable group; or
- there are concerns regarding the efficacy and credibility of the data – for instance, if the trial site has a history of non-compliance with GCP, if the data are inconsistent with those obtained from analogous trials, if results vary dramatically from site to site, or if recruitment patterns are unusual and give rise to suspicion.

Notice of the inspection is usually given two or three months in advance, and the inspectors identify which representatives of the sponsor company will be asked to participate in the inspection. Inspections may be requested and coordinated by the EMA within the scope of Regulation (EC) No. 726/2004 of the European Parliament and of the Council, especially in connection with clinical trials relating to applications that will use the Centralised Procedure.[117] The lead inspector will prepare a report of his or her visit to the EMA Inspection Sector and his or her findings will be added to the European Clinical Trials Database (EudraCT). An inspection report will be prepared for each site visited and should be written in English unless local regulations provide instead that it should be written in the local language, in which case a translation into English is also arranged by the lead inspector. An integrated inspection report must be prepared in respect of each request for inspection made by the CHMP. This report summarises the findings from each of the site inspections and includes copies of those reports.

[D] Sponsor and Investigator as the Same Entity

The sponsor and the investigator may be the same entity. Where a CRO has not been appointed, and the sponsor has the capacity to also act as investigator, the sponsor will fulfil both roles. However, when the sponsor is also the investigator, objective oversight of the clinical trial can be rather difficult, if not impossible. It is good practice to involve an experienced third party in some role, not only to facilitate the monitoring

---

117. Article 15(1) and (2) Directive 2005/28/EC and *see* Chapter 2.

but also to demonstrate that steps were taken to introduce an objective arbiter. In these circumstances, the Sponsor/investigator must be able to show that patient safety has not been compromised, and that the integrity of the data is protected by appropriate safeguards and contractual arrangements.

[E] Pharmacovigilance[118]

Pharmacovigilance is the pharmacological science relating to the detection, assessment, understanding, and prevention of adverse effects, particularly long-term and short-term side effects of medicines.[119] Pharmacovigilance is achieved through the collection, monitoring, assessment, and evaluation of data on the adverse effects of medical products. Data are gathered from healthcare providers (whether companies or practitioners) and patients. The data are then evaluated in order to understand the effects of such products on humans and to prevent harm to humans.

Pharmacovigilance relates to the monitoring of adverse drug reactions (ADRs), which are described as: 'A response to a drug which is noxious and unintended, and which occurs at doses normally used ... for the prophylaxis, diagnosis or therapy of disease, or for the modification of physiological function.'[120]

Pharmacovigilance is of particular importance in clinical trials that test the safety and efficacy of an IMP on subjects before the IMP is introduced to the market because these can involve several thousand patients on whom the safety and efficacy of an IMP is being tested prior to its launch. However, some side effects may not become apparent during the course of a small trial. For this reason, post-marketing pharmacovigilance to reveal any patterns in ADRs is extremely important and is legally required – the safety of all medicines is monitored throughout their use in healthcare practice. New regulations were introduced after GlaxoSmithKline was sued after allegedly suppressing negative data regarding the use of paroxetine (Seroxat, Paxil) in the paediatric population.

During a clinical trial, the sponsor and the investigator must exercise pharmacovigilance, and monitor the safety of the clinical trial subjects. The responsibilities of the sponsor and investigator as regards safety reporting for clinical trials in the EU are set out in the CTR. In complying with the CTR, the detailed guidance on pharmacovigilance rules released by the EC in June 2011 should be complied with,[121] as well as the detailed requirements set out in the CTR, which provides for the use of the European Union Drug Regulating Authorities Clinical Trials Database (Eudravigilance).[122] It addresses the collection, verification, and reporting of adverse events and adverse

---

118. *See* background and definition in Chapter 10
119. 'The Importance of Pharmacovigilance', WHO 2002.
120. WHO Technical Report No. 498 (1972).
121. Communication from the Commission – Detailed guidance on the collection, verification, and presentation of adverse event/reaction reports arising from clinical trials on medicinal products for human use ('CT-3'), 2011/C 172/01.
122. Chapter VII Regulation (EU) No. 536/2014.

reactions that occur in a clinical trial and replaces several previous guidance documents.[123]

Under the CTR:

- An *adverse event*[124] is defined as any untoward medical occurrence in a patient or clinical trial subject administered a medicinal product that does not necessarily have a causal relationship with this treatment.
- An *adverse reaction*[125] is defined as all untoward and unintended responses to an investigational product related to any dose administered.
- A *serious adverse event or serious adverse reaction*[126] means any untoward medical occurrence that at any dose requires inpatient hospitalisation or prolongation of existing hospitalisation, results in persistent or significant disability or incapacity, results in a congenital anomaly or birth defect, is life-threatening, or results in death.
- An *unexpected adverse reaction*[127] means a serious adverse reaction, the nature, severity, or outcome of which is not consistent with the reference safety information.

The Investigator's responsibilities are:[128]

- reporting of serious events to the sponsor, without delay if these have even a suspected causal relationship with the IMP prior to a clinical trial;
- reporting of certain non-serious adverse events and/or laboratory abnormalities to the sponsor, except as otherwise provided for in the protocol.

The Sponsor's responsibilities are[129]

- recording of adverse events;
- reporting of suspected unexpected serious adverse reactions (SUSARs), whether it occurred in the EU or at another site;

(in each case using the Eudravigilance database):

- informing the Investigators; and
- annual safety reporting to the appropriate competent authority and the ethics committee.[130]

---

123. 'Detailed guidance on the European database of Suspected Unexpected Serious Adverse Reactions (Eudravigilance – Clinical Trial Module)', 'Questions & Answers specific to adverse reaction reporting in clinical trials', and 'Revision 2 of the Detailed guidance on the collection, verification and presentation of event/reaction reports arising from clinical trials on medicinal products for human use (CT-3)'.
124. Article 2(32) Regulation (EU) No. 536/2014.
125. Article 2(n) Directive 2001/20/EC.
126. Article 2(34) Regulation (EU) No. 536/2014.
127. Article 9(34) Regulation (EU) No. 536/2014.
128. Article 41 Regulation (EU) No. 536/2014.
129. Article 42 Regulation (EU) No. 536/2014.
130. Article 43 Regulation (EU) No. 536/2014.

The investigator must immediately (within a maximum of twenty-four hours) report to the sponsor any serious adverse event (except those which the Protocol or the IB identifies as not requiring immediate reporting), and the investigator must then follow-up with a detailed, written report.[131] The reporting requirement is intended to minimise unanticipated risks to other trial participants and allows the sponsor to take appropriate measures to address potential new risks. The stringency of the reporting requirement reflects the nature of the IMP. For example, for a novel product, swelling or shortness of breath could indicate another problem, and the ADR should be treated as a serious adverse event and reported. If the trial involves a well-known product, and a trial subject exhibits a mild but well-known ADR, then immediate reporting is not required. The investigator does not need to actively monitor trial participants after the trial has ended, unless otherwise provided in the Protocol, but shall nonetheless report any serious adverse event without delay to the Sponsor.[132]

If the reaction is fatal or life-threatening, the sponsor must report the SUSARs to the ethics committees and competent authorities in all the Member States concerned as soon as possible, and in any event, within seven days after the sponsor becomes aware of the SUSARs. Relevant follow-up information (e.g., if the initial report is incomplete), must be provided within an additional eight days. All other SUSARs must be reported within fifteen days.[133] The time limits are stringent and are designed to catch problems before they become widespread or more serious. It is for this reason that a SUSAR must be reported even if it is 'suspected' but not definitely proven. In addition to reporting to the competent authorities and ethics committees, all SUSARs must be entered in the EudraVigilance database[134] (EudraVigilance Clinical Trials Module) as an individual case safety report (ICSR). Guidance on completing the report can be found in the 'ICH E2B guideline on Clinical Safety Data Management: Data Elements for Transmission of ICSRs' and the 'Note for guidance EudraVigilance Human – Processing of safety messages and ICSRs'.[135] As mentioned, the EMA has launched a new version of the EudraCT, which marks the final step of a process through which summary clinical trial results will be made publicly available through the EU Clinical Trials Register (EU CTR). Sponsors' representatives are now recommended to register with EudraCT in order to become results users before they can log into EudraCT.

Furthermore, reporting of SUSARs to competent authorities can be done directly through the database. In addition, the sponsor must provide the Member States in whose territory the clinical trial is being conducted and the ethics committee(s) with an annual listing of all SUSARs that have occurred during the preceding year. *See* Chapter 10, 'Pharmacovigilance', for the complete discussion of pharmacovigilance, including post-authorisation requirements and procedures.

---

131. Article 41(2) Regulation (EU) No. 536/2014.
132. Article 41(4) Regulation (EU) No. 536/2014.
133. Article 42(2) Regulation (EU) No. 536/2014.
134. Article 17(3)(a) Directive 2001/20/EC and *see* description of database at Chapter 10.05[C].
135. < www.ich.org/products /guidelines/efficacy/article/efficacy-guidelines.html > , and Doc Ref EMA/H/20665/04/Final Revision 2 of 15 October 2010 at < www.ema.europa.eu/docs/en_GB /document_library/Regulatory_and_procedural_guideline/2009/11/WC500015697.pdf > .

§4.08 TRIAL DATA

[A] Introduction to Trial Data

The data and other information, such as the details of patients, collected during the clinical trial must be presented, maintained, and stored in accordance with strict rules and guidelines in order to both comply with GCP and protect the interests of the subjects and patients. In this section, we discuss the trial master file, which contains all the documents related to the trial and is held by the sponsor and investigator. These documents track the conduct of the trial from start to finish and must be updated after the trial ends. We also discuss the collection of data, particularly the requirements of the trial master file. Because the data will also be used to support Marketing Authorisation applications (MAAs), we also discuss Marketing Authorisation (MA) dossier requirements. Finally, we discuss data protection and storage, data-retention, and archiving requirements specified in the CTR.[136] Because data must be held securely and in such a way that the data can be accessed accurately and comprehensively, the EU has developed systems and databases to promote transparency of data, such as EudraCT and EudraVigilance, and launched an online database making certain clinical trial data available to the public.

[B] Public Access to Trial Data

In March 2011, the EU Register of Clinical Trials (RCT) was launched online to enable EU citizens to access information held in the EudraCT database for the first time.[137] As a further step towards the EMA's flagship policy of publication of clinical data, as of October 2016, it has published clinical data submitted by pharmaceutical companies to support their regulatory applications for human medicines under the CP. By making such information freely available, the EMA aims to: avoid duplication of clinical trials, foster innovation and encourage development of new medicines, build public trust and confidence in EMA's scientific and decision-making processes, and enable academics and researchers to re-assess clinical data. This level of transparency has not wholeheartedly been welcomed by all participants, who see the conduct of and results arising out of clinical trials as being commercially sensitive. The EMA has issued guidance to the industry[138] to enable compliance.

As of 5 December 2018, and still at the date of writing, the EMA has suspended the publication of clinical data as a result of the EMA's business continuity plan[139]

---

136. Article 58 Regulation (EU) No. 536/2014.
137. Europa press release IP/11/339, 22 March 2011.
138. Support for industry on clinical data publication | European Medicines Agency (europa.eu).
139. *Ibid. See also* Brexit: the United Kingdom's withdrawal from the European Union | European Medicines Agency (europa.eu) and External guidance on the implementation of the European Medicines Agency policy on the publication of clinical data for medicinal products for human use | European Medicines Agency (europa.eu).

caused by Brexit, it is no longer sending letters of invitation and only COVID-19-related clinical trial data has been published.

When the system is operable, the scope of the information available includes clinical data submitted by pharmaceutical companies to support their request for MA, and which are assessed by the CHMP and will normally include the documents comprising modules 2.5, 2.7, and 5.3 of the Common Technical Document:

- the clinical overview, including a critical analysis of the clinical data in the submission package, including the conclusions and implications of the clinical data;
- the clinical summary, which provides a detailed factual summarisation of all the clinical information submitted;
- the study reports on the individual clinical studies; and
- three appendices to the clinical study reports, namely the study protocol, the sample case report form used to record information on an individual patient, and documentation of the statistical methods used to analyse the data.

Certain data do not need to be published, including:

- those relating to an MA application prior to 1 January 2015 or as part of new indication or line extension applications submitted before 1 July 2015;
- CP products not held by EMA;
- that submitted to the Agency for non-centrally authorised products;
- pharmacovigilance data based on individual case safety reports (ICSRs);
- components of an application that do not fall under the definition of 'clinical data', with the exception of the anonymisation report.

The data must be anonymised to comply with European data protection legislation. Some data may be redacted following suitable justification for such redaction from companies in the prescribed form.

[C] **The Trial Master File: Essential Documents**

The trial master file contains the essential documents, the full set of documents required to be compiled by or on behalf of the sponsor prior to commencement of the clinical phase of the clinical trial, during the clinical conduct of the trial, and after completion or termination of the trial. The essential documents individually and collectively permit the evaluation and verification of the conduct of the clinical trial and the quality of the data produced.[140] taking into account all characteristics of the clinical trial, including, in particular, whether the clinical trial is a low-intervention clinical trial. The Trial Master File must be made freely available and directly accessible upon request to the Member States. Different copies of the Trial Master File may have

---

140. CPMP/ICH/135/95 – Note for Guidance on Good Clinical Practice and Article 57 Regulation (EU) No. 536/2014.

different content, if justified by the different nature of the responsibilities of those parties.

[D] Archiving of the Trial Master File[141]

The sponsor and the investigator are required to archive the content of the clinical trial master file for at least twenty-five years after the end of the clinical trial, although the medical files of subjects shall be archived in accordance with applicable national law. The contents need to be kept in a way that ensures ready and easy access to competent authorities. If the ownership of the clinical trial master file changes, the change must be documented, and the new owner becomes responsible for the maintenance of the file. The sponsor must appoint responsible individuals who will manage the archives, which shall only be available to those individuals.

The files need to be retained on media that will remain legible throughout the retention period, and any alteration must be traceable.

[E] Collection of Data

One of the essential documents used to collect data is the CRF. It is defined in the ICH-GCP as 'a printed or electrical document designed to record all the Protocol required information to be reported to the Sponsor on each trial subject'. The CRF can vary in length, complexity, and presentation, depending on the number of sites and subjects involved in the trial and the nature of the IMP being investigated, for example, its novelty (or otherwise) to the pharmaceutical community; clearly, medical staff dealing with an IMP with a predictable action will require less guidance as to its use than an unusual biological product whose action is less certain. An example of a CRF with guidance on how to complete this form is found on the EMA website.[142]

Since the CRF is the principal mechanism for clinical trial data collection and its contents can directly affect the success or veracity of a clinical trial, the design and timely completion of the form is crucial. The investigator should ensure the accuracy, completeness, legibility, and timeliness of the data reported to the sponsor in the CRF and make sure that the CRF is signed and dated as necessary. An accurate and complete CRF is required by the GCP and the EMA. Before an MA can be granted, the CRF must be verified by source documentation, and any discrepancies between the source documentation and the CRF must be explained. Any amendments to the CRF must be initialled, dated, and explained to make sure that no unofficial amendments are made. Changes or corrections to a CRF should not obscure the original entry. Sponsors should provide guidance to Investigators on making such changes.

The sponsor or investigator is likely to use the CRF to record trial-specific requirements, such as:

---

141. Article 58 Regulation (EU) No. 536/2014.
142. < www.emea.europa.eu >.

Chapter 4: Clinical Trials §4.08[E]

- demography of subjects;
- inclusion/exclusion criteria;
- screening pages (blood and other tests, concomitant medication);
- reports of visits by the monitor;
- early termination or withdrawal of participants;
- end-of-study conclusions, with reasons for any early termination.

Clinical trials are usually precursors to an application for an MA, and therefore the data collection standards for clinical trials should reflect the requirements for preparing an MA application. The EU (together with the US and Japan though the ICH) has been trying to harmonise the data requirements for MAs.

Annex I to Directive 2001/83/EC (as replaced by Annex to Directive 2003/63/EC) sets out the detailed scientific and technical requirements for the presentation and content of the MA application dossier for human medicinal products with the aim of simplifying completion of the Common Technical Dossier (CTDoc).[143] The standardised MA dossier requirements should be applicable to any type of medicinal product for human use and to any procedure for granting the MA (national, decentralised, or centralised procedure). However, since medicinal products have such specific features, not all requirements can be fulfilled, or specific requirements are necessary. The updated Directive provides guidance and sets out 'analytical, pharmacotoxicological and clinical standards and Protocols in respect of testing of medicinal products'. Since some medicinal products have such specific features that not all requirements set out in Annex 1 can be fulfilled or specific requirements are necessary, the updated Annex 1 is divided into four different parts:

(1) Part I: Standardised Marketing Authorisation Dossier Requirements
(1) Part I describes presentation requirements for *standard applications* and is adapted to the format and terminology of the harmonised CTDoc (Modules 1–5):
  - Module 1: Administrative and prescribing information.
  - Module 2: Overview and summaries of modules 1–5.
  - Module 3: Quality documentation – chemical, pharmaceutical, and biological information for medicinal products containing chemical and/or biological active substances.
  - Module 4: Safety (toxicology studies).
  - Module 5: Efficacy (clinical study reports).
(1) Note: There are some anomalies in terminology between Annex I and the CTD. For example, 'Drug Substance' as mentioned in the CTD is called 'Active Substance' in Annex I; 'Drug Product' as mentioned in the CTD is called 'Finished Medicinal Product' in Annex I.

---

143. 'Common Technical Dossier' is a set of specifications for the application dossier for the registration of medicines and designed to be used across Europe, Japan, and the United States'. *See* §4.02[B].

(1) Parts II, III, and IV refer to those medicinal products that require simplified or specific dossier presentations.
(2) Part II: Specific Marketing Authorisation Dossiers and Requirements
(2) Part II describes simplified dossier presentations for 'specific applications', for example, for medicinal products that contain drug substances of well-established medicinal use.
(3) Part III: Particular Medicinal Products
(3) Part III deals with particular requirements for biological medicinal products, such as plasma-derived medicinal products, vaccines, radio-pharmaceuticals, homeopathic medicinal products, herbal medicinal products, and orphan drugs.
(4) Part IV: Advanced Therapy Medicinal Products
(4) Part IV describes special dossier presentations for advanced therapy medicinal products, such as gene therapy products and somatic cell therapy medicinal products.
(4) Annex I provides in each case:
- examples of forms to be completed;
- guidance on preparation of summaries;
- the level of chemical, pharmaceutical, and biological information for medicinal products containing chemical and/or biologically active substances;
- non-chemical report requirements;
- clinical study report requirements;
- specific MA and dossier requirements;
- special treatment of certain categories of products; and
- treatment of advance therapy medicinal products.

[F] Protection of Data and Storage Requirements

The investigator is responsible for protecting and storing the essential documents either at its own premises or those of the sponsor (specific requirements are set out in paragraph 8 of ICH E6 [R1] – Guideline for Good Clinical Practice). The essential documents have to be updated, monitored, and stored according to the CTR; during the transition period, both local and central storage can take place. In addition, documents should be filed in an organised way in order to facilitate management of the clinical trial, audit, and inspection. The filing system should include a systematic description of the documents in a filing index and log, so that documents can be easily found and extracted. The monitor, auditor, ethics committee, and regulatory authorities may all request the investigator to provide them with access to the trial master file. Thus, the sponsor must ensure the filing system is routinely updated by the sponsor him- or herself, the investigator, or any CRO so that all elements of the trial master file are entered into the archive (i.e., closed files) and are readily accessible.

Records can be kept on electronic, magnetic, optical, or other non-indelible media, if suitable controls are implemented to maintain the security and accuracy of the files. Files must be protected from deletion (by way of back-up), and the investigator must ensure that the records cannot be altered without proper authorisation and the creation of an audit trail. When original records are transferred to another media, the accuracy and completeness of the transfer of data must be validated by someone with appropriate authority (such as a trial manager). Regardless of the media on which the records are held, the requisite mechanism for rendering them into a readable format must be readily available.

The GDPR[144] imposes obligations on those controlling and processing both personal data (which relate to a living individual who can be identified from that data) and sensitive personal data (which include personal data relating to the physical or mental health or condition of an individual). Of course, clinical trial data if not anonymised are sensitive personal data and must be protected in compliance with the GDPR.[145] True anonymisation of data means that the subject itself cannot recognise him- or herself in a presentation of the data; more often than not, this will not be the case because key identifiers need to be included, and therefore the majority of clinical trial data will comprise sensitive personal data. Sensitive personal data are kept by the investigator to allow urgent medical intervention, and as a controller of that data, the investigator must comply with the provisions of the GDPR and maintain data security and confidentiality. If the aggregation of data renders the subject identifiable (e.g., with rare diseases where the population is small, a combination of age, gender, and location could disclose the identity of the subject), then the sponsor must provide additional security to prevent such identification. Pursuant to the GDPR, personal data must not be transferred outside the EU, unless the country that data is being transferred to ensures an adequate level of protection for the personal data.

In accordance with GDPR, the trial subject must be informed about who will collect and process the personal and sensitive data, and for what purpose that data will be used. Informed consent forms[146] must expressly deal with these issues, before explicit consent to the same is given by the data subject. It is possible (and often advisable in order to obtain the greatest value from the trial data) to secure informed consent from the subject for use of the data for secondary purposes outside of the trial to which he or she is subject.

The GDPR protects the privacy of trial subjects by separating personal data from sensitive data. Data that are 'non-aggregated data for statistics'[147] are normally analysed in clinical trials, together with the aggregated data. To create non-aggregated

---

144. Directive (EU) 2016/680 of the European Parliament and of the Council of 27 April 2016 on the protection of natural persons with regard to the processing of personal data by competent authorities for the purposes of the prevention, investigation, detection, or prosecution of criminal offences or the execution of criminal penalties, and on the free movement of such data, and repealing Council Framework Decision 2008/977/JHA.
145. For a fuller analysis of the GDPR see Chapter 23.
146. See §4.03[E] for more on informed consent.
147. That is, data which have not been mixed with others and can therefore be analysed individually.

data for statistics, subjects are allocated a code, and thereafter all information related to that subject is linked to that code; data from that subject are not mixed in with data from other subjects immediately but only later, on aggregation. The system has been introduced to try to maintain the anonymity of the subject whilst providing sufficient information to the statisticians and physicians to allow them to analyse the clinical data arising out of the trial. For the purposes of gathering and analysing data, the sponsor is only concerned with the information and the code, but not the key to the code, which would provide access to the subject's personal sensitive data.

§4.09 FIM STUDIES FOLLOWING THE TGN1412 CASE ('TeGenero')

[A] Background

In March 2006, an FIM trial of an 'immuno-modulator' compound (TGN1412), a novel monoclonal antibody developed to treat autoimmune/inflammatory diseases and hemato-oncological malignancies, resulted in unprecedented and unexpected toxicity that seriously injured six healthy volunteers. The results triggered a widely publicised scientific debate, as well as a controversy in the lay community over the principles of design and content of a clinical trial, as well as the use of FIM studies. Prior to this, FIM trials had a good safety record; the adverse reaction suffered by the recipients of TGN1412 was unprecedented. Following the TeGenero case, it was seen that with novel medicines, further consideration should be given to the conduct of FIM trials. In this section, we discuss the recommendations made by the agencies responsible for reviewing the case as well as the new CHMP guidelines that resulted from it.

Initially, the impact of this tragedy was felt mostly in the UK. A joint taskforce of the BioIndustry Association (BIA) and the Association of the British Pharmaceutical Industry (ABPI) prepared a report[148] in which it was determined that the incident was not a result of any errors made in the manufacture of TGN1412, its formulation, dilution, or administration to trial participants, and, whilst there were GCP discrepancies, the incident was caused as a result of an unexpected biological effect. In light of this, it proposed that:

- dosing for monoclonal antibodies that are agonists should take into account the drug's biological effect;
- test doses should be staggered to ensure that if there is an unfortunate side effect, not all subjects would be exposed to it simultaneously;
- new mechanisms to share information on safety issues for drug testing should be introduced;
- patients should be used in more cases instead of healthy volunteers, since the action of a biologic is likely to vary significantly from a patient suffering the disease to a healthy volunteer; and

---

148. May be found at <www.abpi.org.uk/information/pdfs/Expert-trials-Consultation14Sep06.pdf>.

- specialised hospitals and suitable training of staff should be introduced.

Thereafter, the UK Secretary of State for Health appointed an Expert Scientific Group that was tasked with considering what may be necessary in the transition from pre-clinical to FIM Phase 1 studies, and in the design of these trials, with specific reference to:

- biological molecules with novel mechanisms of action;
- new agents with a highly species-specific action;
- new drugs directed to immune system targets.

The 600-page 'Expert Scientific Group, Phase One Clinical Trials Final Report'[149] was published on 7 December 2006; it made twenty-two recommendations, building on those produced by the ABPI, including:

- *Recommendation 1*: Decisions on the strategy for pre-clinical development of a new medicine and the experimental approaches used to assemble information relevant to the safety of FIM studies must be science-based, made and justified case-by-case by individuals with appropriate training.
- *Recommendation 5*: More communication should be encouraged between developers and the regulator at an earlier stage before an application is filed, especially for higher-risk agents, to ensure that there is time for an appropriate consideration of any safety concerns without introducing undue delay to product development. Ways to increase communication between the regulator and research Ethics Committees should also be considered.
- *Recommendation 6*: For appraisal of applications for trials of higher-risk agents, as defined by the nature of the agent, its degree of novelty, its intended pharmacological target, and its intended recipient, the regulator should have access to additional opinions from independent, specialist experts with research knowledge of their fields.
- *Recommendation 9*: Special consideration should be given to agents for which the primary pharmacological action for the proposed therapeutic effect cannot be demonstrated in an animal model.
- *Recommendation 10*: Reconsider whether dose calculation, beyond reliance on 'No Observable Effect Level' (NOEL) or 'No Observable Adverse Effect Level' (NOAL) in animal studies, should be taken.
- *Recommendation 13*: Careful consideration should be given to the route and the rate of administration of the first dose in FIM trials, with careful monitoring for an exaggerated response.
- *Recommendation 15*: New agents in FIM trials should be administered sequentially to subjects with an appropriate period of observation between dosing. The interval of observation between sequential dosing of the subjects should

---

149. < www.dh.gov.uk/prod_consum_dh/groups/dh_digitalassets/@dh/@en/documents/digital asset/dh_073165.pdf > .

be related to the kind of adverse reactions that might be anticipated based on the nature of the agent, its target, and the recipient.
- *Recommendation 16*: A similar period of monitoring should occur between sequential dosing of subjects during dose escalation.
- *Recommendation 20*: FIM studies of higher-risk medicines should always be conducted in an appropriate clinical environment supervised by staff with appropriate levels of training and expertise, with immediate access to facilities for the treatment and stabilisation of individuals in an acute emergency, and with pre-arranged contingency availability of intensive treatment units in reasonable proximity.

[B]   Revised CHMP Guidelines as a Result of the TeGenero Case

The debate resulted in the production of a revised set of guidelines from CHMP – 'Guideline on Strategies to Identify and Mitigate Risks for FIM Clinical Trials with IMPs.'[150] These draw heavily on the Expert Scientific Group recommendations. They were updated in 2017[151] to emphasise the requirement that the safety and well-being of trial participants are of the utmost priority and emphasise the responsibility on the sponsor to determine risks arising from uncertainty.

The original Guidelines provided criteria for the classification of new IMPs as potentially high-risk products and gave guidance on quality aspects, non-clinical testing strategies, and designs for FIM clinical trials for high-risk medicinal products. In particular, and in addition to the Expert Scientific Group recommendations, it gave guidance as to calculation of the initial dose to be used in humans, the subsequent dose escalation and management of risk, as well as giving considerable detail on the other aspects highlighted earlier. The revision reflects the increasingly complex nature of clinical trial protocols in the past ten years since the first guidelines were published. It was noted that clinical trial protocols now often include different parts within a single clinical trial protocol aimed at assessing, for example, single and multiple ascending doses, food interactions, or different age groups.

The strategies to mitigate and manage risks for trial participants described in the original guideline referred specifically to the calculation of the starting dose to be used in humans, the subsequent dose escalations, and the criteria for maximum dose. Guidance is also provided on criteria to stop a study, the rolling review of emerging data with special reference to safety information for trial participants, and the handling of adverse events in relation to stopping rules and rules guiding progress to the next dosing level.

The original guidelines introduced a new concept – when calculating the first-dose-in-man doses for high-risk medicinal products, an additional approach

---

150. Available on EMA website – < www.emea.europa.eu >.
151. Revised guideline on first-in-human clinical trials | European Medicines Agency (europa.eu).

Chapter 4: Clinical Trials §4.10

should be taken: minimal anticipated biological effect level (MABEL). This comprises the anticipated dose level leading to a minimal biological effect level in humans; safety factors are usually applied for the calculation of the first-dose-in-man from MABEL. To determine MABEL, all *in vivo* and *in vitro* data and information, derived from pharmacokinetic/pharmacodynamic (PK/PD) data should be utilised and included in a PK/PD modelling approach. Other safety factors should be applied in the calculation of MABEL:

- novelty of the active substance;
- its biological potency and mode of action;
- degree of species specificity;
- shape of the dose/response curve.

When both NOEL and MABEL have been calculated, the lower dose should be administered.

Other aspects of the applicability of the guidelines are reflected in the body of the chapter.

§4.10 CLINICAL TRIALS AND PATENT LEGISLATION: THE BOLAR AND RESEARCH EXCEPTIONS

A patent is a monopoly over an invention that gives the owner the right to prevent third parties from making, using, selling, or importing their invention for up to twenty years. If a third party does any of the above acts without the consent of the owner, the third party has infringed the patent, and the owner can take legal action against the infringer.

While patents encourage investment and innovation by guaranteeing the right for the owner to exploit any resulting invention in the pharmaceutical industry, it also has the potential to stifle new research if scientists risk infringing a drug patent when conducting clinical trials. In order to encourage and facilitate the development of the pharmaceutical industry, and in particular, the development of generics (which account for a major part of the drug market), two EU Directives (2004/27/EC for human medicines, 2004/28/EC for veterinary medicines[152]) introduced a 'safe harbour' from patent (and supplementary protection certificate) infringement research activities performed to obtain regulatory approval for generic medicines. Such research activities include clinical trials and other studies. This exemption became known as the 'Bolar' exception, deriving from the US case of *Roche Products v. Bolar Pharmaceutical*[153] which prompted Congress to pass US legislation exempting generic companies from patent infringement when performing bioequivalence studies.

In relation to the research activities of innovator companies using patented inventions to develop new therapies, Member States have differing legislative regimes.

---

152. Directives have been in force from 30 April 2004, implemented by Member States by 30 October 2005.
153. 733 F.2d 858 (Fed. Cir. 1984).

In most countries, there is an experimental use exception (the 'Research exception'), which permits the use of a patented invention for experimental purposes without infringing the rights of the patent owner. This exception was originally introduced to harmonise national laws with the Community Patent Convention, which never actually came into force as it was not ratified by enough countries. The exception is more favourable in some countries than in others. For example, in France and Germany, clinical trials conducted to obtain regulatory approval are not infringing, regardless of whether the approval is for a generic or new drug. However, in the UK, the scope of the patent infringement exception for new drugs is much narrower, and it applies only to acts done for experimental purposes relating to the 'subject-matter' of the invention.[154] Therefore, while clinical trials conducted to investigate a new use for a patented product would fall under the exception, trials to obtain regulatory approval for a follow-on drug may not. Other countries, such as Spain and the Netherlands, do not have Research exceptions and only cover clinical trials conducted for generics under the Bolar exception.

§4.11 INTRODUCTION TO CLINICAL TRIALS IN THE UK

[A] Introduction

Insofar as the implementation of the (EU) CTR took effect after the Brexit transition period, the CTR has not been retained in UK law. While the CTD has since been repealed in the EU by the CTR, in the UK, the Medicines for Human Use (Clinical Trials) Regulations 2004, as amended (UK Regulations), continue to implement into UK law the EU Directive 2001/20/EC: The Clinical Trials Directive (as at 31 December 2020) (EU CTD). For the time being, the UK regulatory regime applicable to clinical trials therefore remains based on the EU CTD.

As seen in paragraph [C] below, the Medicines and Healthcare Products Regulatory Agency (MHRA) is in the process of revisiting the UK Regulations, and significant amendments to the UK Regulations, especially in the context of IMPs, may be seen in the near future. Since this area is in flux, it is not the intention to provide a very detailed description of the UK regime in this Chapter, but rather a practical overview of the main elements of the current UK regulatory framework and guidance applicable to clinical trials of investigational medicinal products (CTIMPs).

[B] When the UK Regulations Apply

The UK Regulations apply to all clinical trials in the UK, other than non-interventional clinical trials. A 'clinical trial' for the purposes of the UK Regulations is broadly defined as:

---

154. Patents Act 1977, s. 60(5)(b).

any investigation in human subjects, other than a non-interventional trial, intended:

(a) to discover or verify the clinical, pharmacological or other pharmacodynamic effects of one or more medicinal products,
(b) to identify any adverse reactions to one or more such products, or
(c) to study absorption, distribution, metabolism and excretion of one or more such products,
(d) with the object of ascertaining the safety or efficacy of those products.[155]

The above definition encompasses a broad range of research activities in respect of a medicinal product. For purposes of assisting with the assessment as to whether or not a study will constitute a 'clinical trial' for purposes of the UK Regulations (i.e., a CTIMP), the MHRA have put together an online algorithm[156] that assists with the assessment as to whether or not a study constitutes a CTIMP and accordingly requires MHRA authorisation.

The MHRA authorisation for CTIMPs must be distinguished from applications made in respect of studies involving the National Health Service (NHS), which are common in the UK context. Practically, the various application processes may overlap to a certain extent (including applications for research ethics committee (REC) approval), but conceptually they should be distinguished from one another. To the extent that a study involves the NHS and amounts to 'research',[157] further applications must be made with the applicable authority (for example, in the case of research conducted in England, the applicable authority is the Health Research Authority (HRA)).

[C] Consultation for Legislative Change (2022)

During the period from 17 January 2022 to 14 March 2022, the MHRA facilitated a public consulate process during which a number of proposals were made to amend the UK Regulations so as to provide for a more streamlined and flexible regulatory regime, whilst continuing to protect the interests of patients and trial participants. These proposals were made under the auspices of the Medicines and Medical Devices Act 2021, which provides the powers to update the regulatory framework in respect of, *inter alia*, clinical trials. As of the date of writing, there have been no published outcomes of the aforesaid public consultations, but significant legislative change is anticipated in the short- to medium-term.

---

155. Regulation 2 of the UK Regulations.
156. Accessible at https://www.gov.uk/guidance/clinical-trials-for-medicines-apply-for-authorisation-in-the-uk#when-a-clinical-trial-authorisation-cta-is-needed.
157. *See*, for example, the HRA decision tool accessible at http://www.hra-decisiontools.org.uk/research/.

The policy objectives, as set out in the consultation document[158] and as jointly developed by the MHRA and HRA, include updating and strengthening the UK Regulations to:

(a) promote public health and ensure protection of participants remains at the heart of legislation;
(b) remove obstacles to innovation, whilst maintaining robust oversight of the safety of trials;
(c) streamline the regulation of clinical trials and reduce unnecessary burden to those running trials by embedding risk proportionality into the framework;
(d) facilitate the evaluation and development of new or better medicines to reduce the burden of disease on patients and society;
(e) ensure the legislation builds international interoperability so that the UK remains a preferred site to conduct multinational trials.

Various proposals were made, including in the following key areas:

(a) ensuring that the protection of participants remains the main aim of legislation, but introducing a requirement to work in partnership with people and communities (including patients and carers who have experience of living with the relevant condition) in the design, management, conduct, and dissemination of a clinical trial;
(b) improving research transparency by introducing a requirement to register a clinical trial in a World Health Organization (WHO) compliant public register prior to its start and to publish summary of results within twelve months of the end of the trial. A further requirement envisaged is the sharing of clinical trial findings with participants in a suitable format within twelve months of the end of the clinical trial;
(c) various proposed amendments to existing clinical trial approval processes to promote a more streamlined approach (for example, allowing sponsors to make a combined MHRA/research ethics application submitted through a single UK portal);
(d) relation to research ethics review, an update in the requirements for the composition of RECs and the ability to improve agility in decision-making;
(e) with regard to informed consent, streamline requirements by introducing a simplified manner of obtaining participant consent for certain low-intervention clinical trials (such as co-called cluster trials);
(f) certain updates to the existing safety reporting requirements;
(g) introducing a more proportional approach to compliance with good clinical practice, based on the risk profile of the clinical trial in question; and
(h) certain updates in the context of manufacture and assembly of IMPs, including, as is the case in the EU CTR, the introduction of the concept of AxMPs.

---

158. Accessible at https://www.gov.uk/government/consultations/consultation-on-proposals-for-legislative-changes-for-clinical-trials/proposals-for-legislative-changes-for-clinical-trials.

§4.12 PREPARING TO APPLY FOR CTIMP AUTHORISATION IN THE UK

[A] Introduction

Prior to the commencement of a clinical trial in the UK, a number of steps must be undertaken to ensure compliance with the UK Regulations.[159] Many of these steps continue to be broadly aligned with those required to be taken in the EU. Accordingly, the UK section in this Chapter does not repeat what has been stated above in respect of the EU where the position remains largely similar. Instead, the UK-specific practical nuances are highlighted. In this section, we set out an overview of the role and responsibilities of the sponsor, including when the appointment of a legal representative is required. We also describe some of the current UK-specific administrative processes related to the preparation of an application for CTIMP authorisation.

[B] The Sponsor and Overview of Sponsor Duties

[1] The Sponsor

As is the case in the EU under the CTR, all clinical trials governed by the UK Regulations require a sponsor or co-sponsors. A sponsor is defined in the UK Regulations as 'in relation to a clinical trial, the person who takes responsibility for the initiation, management and financing (or arranging the financing) of that trial'.[160] Clinical trials may be sponsored by two or more persons or organisations; this scenario is referred to as joint or co-sponsorship. A sponsor of a clinical trial conducted in the UK must be established in the UK or a country on an approved country list (as published on the MHRA website);[161] post-Brexit, such countries currently include EU and EEA countries. If this is not the case, then the sponsor must appoint a UK-based legal representative.

The sponsor may of course sub-contract some or even all of its obligations to a third party such as a CRO. However, the ultimate responsibility always rests upon the sponsor. Such CRO is also able to act as the sponsor's legal representative if the sponsor is not based in the UK.

[2] Overview of Sponsor Duties

As is the case in the EU context, overall, the sponsor must ensure that the clinical trial is properly conducted and that the data collected are reliable. Prior to starting a clinical

---

159. *See* helpful *Routemap* guidance compiled by the National Institute for Health and Care Research (NIHR) that sets out the various stages (including legal and good practice requirements) applicable to conducting CTIMPs in the UK, at: https://www.ct-toolkit.ac.uk/routemap/.
160. Regulation 3(1) of the UK Regulations. *See* Regulation 3 of the UK Regulations generally for provisions relating to sponsors and their responsibilities.
161. https://www.gov.uk/government/publications/importing-investigational-medicinal-products-into-great-britain-from-approved-countries.

trial, the sponsor defines, establishes, and allocates all trial-related duties and functions. During the design of the trial, and throughout the whole trial, the sponsor is required to use qualified individuals, such as biostatisticians, clinical pharmacologists, and physicians to set up and conduct the clinical trial, design the Trial Protocol[162] and shared access file systems, plan the analysis of the trial data, and prepare the interim and final clinical trial/study reports. The sponsor also designates qualified medical personnel who will be readily available to advise on trial-related medical questions or problems. The sponsor will consider the timeframe for carrying out the trials, including the anticipated recruitment of suitable subjects and manufacture of the IMP. If a sponsor of a CTIMP is a commercial or other non-NHS body, a copy of an insurance or indemnity certificate should normally be included with the REC application as evidence of the cover in place for the potential liability of the Sponsor.

In particular, further categories of sponsor responsibilities include ensuring that:[163]

(a) research proposals and protocols take into account systematic reviews of relevant existing research evidence and other relevant research in progress, make appropriate use of patient, service user, and public involvement, and are scientifically sound;
(b) the investigators, research team, and research sites are appointed and are suitable;
(c) roles and responsibilities of the parties involved in the clinical trials and any delegation by the sponsor of its tasks are agreed and documented;
(d) appropriate arrangements are made for making information about the clinical trial publicly available before it commences and agreeing to appropriate arrangements for making data and tissue accessible, with adequate consent and privacy safeguards, in a timely manner after the clinical trial has finished;
(e) the IB for the clinical trial, and any update of that brochure, is drawn up and presents the information it contains in a concise, simple, objective, balanced. and non-promotional form that enables a clinician or potential investigator to understand it and make an unbiased risk-benefit assessment of the appropriateness of the proposed clinical trial. Such IB must further be validated and updated at least once a year, unless circumstances give rise to an immediate update;[164]
(f) arrangements for information about the findings of the clinical trial to be made available, including, where appropriate, to participants;
(g) where expected or required, the clinical trial has approval from a REC and any other relevant approval bodies before the clinical trial begins;

---

162. *See* further guidance regarding the development of the Protocol in the NIHR's *Routemap* guidance, at: https://www.ct-toolkit.ac.uk/routemap/protocol-development/. Further guidance regarding the finalisation of the Protocol may be found at: https://www.ct-toolkit.ac.uk/routemap/final-protocol/.
163. *See* further *UK Policy Framework for Health and Social Care Research* (updated April 2022).
164. Regulation 3A of the UK Regulations.

(h) regulatory and practical arrangements are in place before permitting the clinical trial to begin in a safe and timely manner;
(i) arrangements for adequate finance and management of the research project, including its competent risk management and data management, are put in place and maintained;
(j) effective procedures and arrangements are kept in place and adhered to for reporting and for monitoring the clinical trial, including its conduct and the ongoing suitability of the approved proposal or protocol in light of adverse events or other developments.

[C]   The Investigator, Chief Investigator, and Principal Investigator

All clinical trials require an Investigator. The UK Regulations define an investigator as 'in relation to a clinical trial, the authorised health professional responsible for the conduct of that trial at a trial site, and if the trial is conducted by a team of authorised health professionals at a trial site, the investigator is the leader responsible for that team'.[165]

The investigator should be thoroughly familiar with the appropriate use of the investigational product(s) as described in the Protocol, the current IB, the product information, and other information sources provided by the sponsor.

The investigator must demonstrate an ability to recruit the required number of suitable subjects within the agreed recruitment period, and the investigator must have qualified staff and adequate facilities to conduct the trial safely. The investigator must inform persons assisting with the trial about the Protocol, the investigational product(s), and their trial-related duties and functions.

The 'Chief Investigator'[166] is the overall lead researcher for a research project. In addition to their responsibilities,[167] if they are members of a research team, chief investigators are responsible for the overall conduct of a research project. The 'Principal Investigator' (PI), by contrast, is an individual responsible for the conduct of the clinical trial at a research site. There should be one PI for each research site. In the case of a single-site study, the chief investigator and the PI will normally be the same person.

[D]   Registration and Preparing the CTIMP Authorisation Application

Each CTIMP must be allocated a unique trial number and be registered on a publicly accessible database. Such registration assists researchers fulfil research transparency and result dissemination requirements and is a condition of favourable ethics opinion (unless a deferral of registration has been granted). In respect of UK-only CTIMPs,

---

165. Regulation 2 of the UK Regulations.
166. As defined in Regulation 2 of the UK Regulations for purposes of CTIMPs.
167. *See* further *UK Policy Framework for Health and Social Care Research* (updated April 2022).

established international registers such as ISRCTN[168] registry, or ClinicalTrials.gov may be used. Based on MHRA guidance,[169] from 1 January 2022, the HRA will, in relation to CTIMPs, automatically register clinical trials with ISRCTN registry as one of the steps to ensure research transparency. From a practical application process perspective, from 1 January 2022, all new CTIMP approval applications must be prepared, submitted, and reviewed via the combined review service in the new section of the Integrated Research Application System (IRAS) online platform.[170] This facilitates a single application route and coordinated review by the MHRA and REC, leading to a single UK decision.

Please note that it is still a standard condition of a REC favourable opinion for clinical trials to be registered on a publicly accessible database, and as such, this requirement has not changed. For any submissions submitted up to 31 December 2021 (either via new IRAS or old IRAS), applicants should register their CTIMPs on an established international register such as ISRCTN registry or ClinicalTrials.gov.

As a matter of good practice, prior to submitting the application for CTIMP approval, depending on the nature of the CTIMP, the following key documents/information should be on hand:[171]

- Sponsor(s) identified and agreements for allocation/delegation of responsibilities (if necessary) are in place
- Arrangements for appropriate patient and public involvement
- Input from a statistician secured
- Peer review complete
- Arrangements for a data monitoring committee, steering group, and/or management group in place (with consent from members)
- Trial risk assessment carried out, trial management systems, and monitoring plan/arrangements in place
- Funding secured
- Unique trial number (including a EudraCT number for trials with EU sites)
- R&D and local NHS support departments (e.g., pharmacy, labs, radiology etc.) consulted and capacity available, if applicable

---

168. While the scope of this register has widened to include not only randomised controlled trials but any study designed to assess the efficacy of health interventions in a human population (including observational and interventional trials), ISRCTN stands for 'International Standard Randomised Controlled Trial Number'.
169. See https://www.gov.uk/guidance/clinical-trials-for-medicines-apply-for-authorisation-in-the-uk.
170. See further guidance regarding obtaining the IRAS ID at https://www.myresearchproject.org.uk/help/hlpirasid.aspx. See further guidance regarding the combined process at https://www.hra.nhs.uk/planning-and-improving-research/policies-standards-legislation/clinical-trials-investigational-medicinal-products-ctimps/combined-ways-working-pilot/step-step-guide-using-iras-combined-ways-working-cwow/.
171. See the NIHR's Routemap guidance at: https://www.ct-toolkit.ac.uk/routemap/ci-checklist-before-seeking-approval/. See further MHRA guidance applicable to CTIMPs at: https://www.gov.uk/guidance/clinical-trials-for-medicines-apply-for-authorisation-in-the-uk#documents-to-send-with-your-application.

- Contracts and agreements in place including third-party agreements where outsourcing of any trial-specific test/services is required
- Insurance and indemnity arrangements in place (non-NHS)
- CVs of investigators (signed and dated)
- Arrangements for trial supplies in place
- Arrangements for pharmacovigilance considered
- Systems in place to ensure trial will be conducted to the principles of GCP and UK Regulations
- Trial Master File established
- Protocol and associated documents, including: the unique trial number(s) on all documentation, where applicable; end of trial defined; safety reporting section of the Protocol outlining definitions and reporting requirements; all written information provided to be reviewed by participants (for example, participant information sheets, consent forms, patient diaries, recruitment advertisements); and all other relevant trial documentation (such as questionnaires, case report forms, trial-specific SOPs, IB, or SmPC).

[E] Requests for MHRA Scientific Advice

At any stage of the initial development of a medicine, including before the commencement of a clinical trial, the sponsor may elect to request advice from the MHRA[172] in respect of a specific medicinal product,[173] which offers various categories of scientific advice, including quality, non-clinical and clinical aspects related to the conducting of CTIMPs. Advice may also be sought in respect of pharmacovigilance plans and post-authorisation safety study protocols, the advertising of a medicinal product, etc. A joint scientific advice meeting with the MHRA and National Institute for Healthcare and Excellence (NICE)[174] may also be requested. During these meetings, the clinical study design may be discussed so as to ensure compliance with both regulatory and NICE requirements.

After a meeting during which any questions are discussed, the MHRA endeavours to respond to such questions within thirty working days of the meeting. The advice provided by the MHRA is without prejudice to applicable legislation relating to particulars and documents which should be submitted in support of any MA (or other)

---

172. *See* MHRA guidance at: https://www.gov.uk/guidance/medicines-get-scientific-advice-from-mhra. This guidance includes information on the practical requirements (including fees) in respect of requesting scientific advice form the MHRA.
173. Broader scope meetings that are not product specific may also be requested, which include discussions relating to general approaches to product development, overall product development plans, complex issues of drug/device combination products, practical issues of study design, management and analysis, etc.
174. Briefly, NICE's role is to improve outcomes for users of the NHS and other public health and social care services by: publishing evidence-based guidance and advice for health, public health and social care practitioners; developing quality standards and performance metrics for those providing and commissioning health, public health and social care services; and providing a range of information services for commissioners, practitioners and managers across health and social care. *See* further at: https://www.nice.org.uk/.

application; it is also without prejudice to any intellectual property rights to third parties. Moreover, scientific advice provided by MHRA is not legally binding in respect of any future application of the product discussed.

Advice from the MHRA (and NICE, if applicable) is valuable as it may have access to relevant information or expertise that will enable it to give particularly valuable advice and guidance that would not otherwise have been available.

§4.13 APPROVAL TO COMMENCE A CTIMP IN THE UK

[A] Introduction to the CTIMP Authorisation Process in the UK

Before commencing a new CTIMP in the UK, from 1 January 2022, the sponsor must apply for approval via the 'new' IRAS portal, as briefly set out above. Practically, while one combined CTIMP authorisation application is made for approval via IRAS, once obtained, such approval comprises of the following sub-approvals: (i) the MHRA's CTIMP approval; (ii) REC approval; and (iii) the HRA approval (if the CTIMP involves the NHS). We deal with each of these processes briefly in this section.

[B] MHRA CTIMP Authorisation

The MHRA will process the application based on the type of the trial (Type A, B, or C, with Type A being the lowest risk and Type C the highest) in accordance with the MHRA guidance document *Risk Adapted Approaches to the Management of Clinical Trials of Investigational Medicinal Products*.[175]

Once the combined application is successfully submitted, the initial combined review assessment will be completed within thirty days of being submitted via IRAS.[176] Applications for healthy volunteer trials and Sponsor-determined phase I CTIMPs in non-oncology patients may qualify for a shortened assessment time, and MHRA will work with the REC to endeavour to expedite these applications. Applicants should state on the covering letter accompanying the application if the CTIMP is eligible for such expedited route.[177]

The outcome of the combined review of the application will be communicated and the result may be: (i) acceptance of the request for CTIMP authorisation; (ii) acceptance of the request for CTIMP authorisation subject to conditions; or (iii) grounds for non-acceptance of the request for CTIMP authorisation, in which case the

---

175. Available at https://assets.publishing.service.gov.uk/government/uploads/system/uploads/attachment_data/file/343677/Risk-adapted_approaches_to_the_management_of_clinical_trials_of_investigational_medicinal_products.pdf.
176. In the case of CTIMPs involving gene therapy, somatic cell therapy (including xenogenic cell therapy) product, tissue engineered products, or products containing genetically modified organisms, decisions are communicated to the applicant within ninety days of receipt of the original application, unless otherwise indicated.
177. *See* at https://www.gov.uk/guidance/clinical-trials-for-medicines-apply-for-authorisation-in-the-uk#assessment-of-your-submission.

Chapter 4: Clinical Trials §4.13[C]

applicant may respond, usually within fourteen days (which may be extended on request).[178]

[C] REC Approval

Based on the CTD, the UK Regulations continue to provide for the establishment of the United Kingdom Ethics Committees Authority.[179] Regulation 12(3)(a) of the UK Regulations makes it compulsory for a favourable REC opinion to be obtained prior to commencing with a CTIMP, including any recruitment (or advertising intended recruitment) of participants.[180] An application for REC approval in relation to a CTIMP must be made by the chief investigator for that trial to a REC established under the UK Regulations.[181] Such application must be in writing, signed by the chief investigator making the application, and accompanied by the various particulars and documents specified in Part 1 of Schedule 3 of the UK Regulations. Note that where the CTIMP involves the NHS, the application for REC approval is slightly different.[182]

In reaching an opinion, the REC will consider elements such as the following:[183]

(a) in relation to trial design, a summary of the CTIMP, including justification and relevance, and the methodology to be used; the primary, and any secondary, research hypothesis; statistical analysis and justification for the numbers of subjects to be recruited for the trial; and details of the process for peer review of the scientific value of the trial;

(b) brief details of any plans to conduct the trial outside the UK and any authorisation given in relation to the trial by a competent authority of an EEA State;

(c) details relating to the sponsor, including details of any arrangements under which the sponsor has delegated any of their responsibilities in relation to the proposed CTIMP;

(d) as regards financial arrangements for the CTIMP, details regarding sources of funding for the CTIMP and information on financial or other relevant interests of the applicant; arrangements for remuneration of, or reimbursement of expenses incurred by, subjects; any provision for compensation in the event of injury or death attributable to the CTIMP; details of any

---

178. *Ibid.* Confirmation of the MHRA and REC decisions following receipt of such responses are usually sent within sixty days of receipt of the original valid application. If an extension to the response date has been agreed, this will impact the final decision timeline.
179. Part 2, read with Schedule 2, of the UK Regulations.
180. Regulation 12 of the UK Regulations.
181. Regulations 14(1) and (3) of the UK Regulations. Note that an application for a REC opinion in relation to a CTIMP involving medicinal products for gene therapy, must generally be made to the Gene Therapy Advisory Committee (*see* Regulation 14(5) of the UK Regulations).
182. *See* at http://www.hra-decisiontools.org.uk/ethics/ if the CTIMP involving the NHS requires NHS REC review.
183. *See* Part 1 of Schedule 3 to the UK Regulations.

insurance or indemnity to cover the liability of the sponsor and investigator; and summary details of any financial arrangements between the sponsor or person funding the trial and the investigator on the one hand, and the sponsor or person funding the trial and the owner or occupier of the trial site on the other;

(e) arrangements for the recruitment of subjects, including the materials to be used;

(f) the criteria for inclusion and exclusion of patients, including justification for recruiting from vulnerable groups;

(g) in the case of Phase I trials, methods for recording and verifying health status of healthy volunteers;

(h) procedures for checking simultaneous or recent involvement of potential subjects in other trials;

(i) details of any relationship between subject and investigator which may be relevant for the purposes of an ethical opinion;

(j) details of any proposed additional investigational procedures or other interventions over and above those required for normal clinical care; any aspect of normal clinical care to be withheld or other deviation from normal treatment; and the plan for treatment or care of subjects once their participation in the trial has ended;

(k) the procedures for providing information to potential subjects, including a contact point where additional information can be obtained about the trial and the rights of trial subjects; providing subjects with updated information during and (where relevant) after the CTIMP; and obtaining informed consent;

(l) details of the arrangements for access to confidential data about the subjects and the arrangements to protect subjects' privacy;

(m) the rules for terminating or concluding the trial before the date for the conclusion of the trial specified in the protocol, or the event specified in the protocol as the event which indicates that the end of the trial has occurred;

(n) any agreement on the access by the investigator or their team to the data produced by the trial, and the policy for publication of that data;

(o) an assessment of the ethical issues relating to the trial, including the importance of the trial and of the new knowledge to be gained; an assessment of the potential benefits; and an assessment of the possible risks for the subjects;

(p) details relating to the chief investigator and each investigator, including experience in conducting research, and any potential conflicts of interest; and

(q) details of any proposed trial site and its suitability for conducting the trial.

As mentioned above, the REC must determine whether clinical trial participants have given informed consent to participate in the trials. The UK Regulations expand on the various elements of *informed consent* in Schedule 1 to the UK Regulations.

Essentially,[184] a person gives informed consent to take part, or that a subject is to take part, in a clinical trial only if their decision is given freely after that person is informed of the nature, significance, implications, and risks of the trial. The UK Regulations detail a process for obtaining informed consent from children and incapacitated adults and a less-complex process for obtaining consent from a conscious, cognisant adult.[185]

[D] HRA Approval

CTIMPs conducted on the premises of an NHS organisation, with NHS patients or with NHS staff, require permission from the local NHS R&D office. Coordinated systems for NHS R&D review are in place across the UK. The system available will depend on where the lead NHS R&D office is based (the part of the UK where the chief investigator is located). For example, *HRA and Health and Care Research Wales (HCRW) Approval* is the process for applying for approvals for all project-based research in the NHS taking place in England or Wales.[186] Comments made above in respect of the combined CTIMP authorisation application via the 'new part' of IRAS apply in this context, too.[187]

§4.14 CONDUCT OF CTIMPs IN THE UK

Once the ethical approval and trial authorisation have been obtained, the trial(s) can commence. Generally, as is the case in the EU, the UK Regulations require that all trials are carried out in accordance with GCP standards. The GCP standards are based on preceding law and the ICH guidelines set out in the Declaration of Helsinki, and they follow the principles set out in that declaration. Furthermore, the UK Regulations provide that manufacture, labelling, and storage of IMPs must comply with GMP (*see* further §4.06[C] above). In the UK context, the MHRA have published detailed guidance[188] regarding the adherence to GCP during the course of conducting CTIMPs, including provision for the conduct of inspections by the MHRA, as discussed in further detail below. Regulation 29A of the UK Regulations require the sponsor (or a person legally authorised by the sponsor to perform this function) to notify the MHRA GCP Inspectorate of any 'serious breach' of GCP or the trial protocol.[189]

---

184. Schedule 1 to the UK Regulations.
185. Schedule 1 to the UK Regulations. *See* further guidance at https://www.ct-toolkit.ac.uk/routemap/informed-consent/ and https://www.myresearchproject.org.uk/help/hlpethical review.aspx.
186. *See* further guidance at https://www.hra.nhs.uk/approvals-amendments/what-approvals-do-i-need/hra-approval/. Researchers wishing to conduct research in the NHS in Scotland (or Health and Social Care (HSC) in Northern Ireland) must obtain 'NHS (or HSC) management permission' for each NHS/HSC research site.
187. *See* further guidance at https://www.myresearchproject.org.uk/help/hlphraapproval.aspx and https://www.hra.nhs.uk/planning-and-improving-research/policies-standards-legislati on/clinical-trials-investigational-medicinal-products-ctimps/combined-ways-working-pilot/st ep-step-guide-using-iras-combined-ways-working-cwow/.
188. *See* https://www.gov.uk/guidance/good-clinical-practice-for-clinical-trials.
189. *See* further guidance at https://assets.publishing.service.gov.uk/government/uploads/system /uploads/attachment_data/file/905577/Guidance_for_the_Notification_of_Serious_Breaches _of_GCP_or_the_Trial_Protocol_Version_6__08_Jul_2020.pdf.

§4.15 UK CTIMP OVERSIGHT

[A] Introduction to CTIMP Oversight

This area of the regulation of CTIMPs in the UK has remained largely in alignment with the EU post-Brexit. Please refer to §4.07 above for general comments regarding monitoring, GCP inspections, audits and pharmacovigilance in the CTIMP context. In this section, we focus on UK-specific guidance regarding these matters.[190]

[B] Monitoring

As is the case in the EU, monitoring is one of the key mechanisms whereby the sponsor can be assured that the CTIMP remains compliant with applicable legislation and the trial protocol/procedures. Effective monitoring may also provide an opportunity for feedback to the sponsor for process improvement. Traditionally, 'monitoring' has tended to focus on monitors visiting sites as part of quality control, and this approach has been extensively used by commercial sponsors consisting of regular on-site visits covering the activities outlined in ICH-GCP guidance. Non-commercial trials have primarily taken a more centralised approach to monitoring activities with less reliance on on-site visits.[191]

The MHRA has provided guidance regarding CTIMP monitoring, which is based on a risk-based approach.[192] While monitoring may aim to assess compliance with every detail of the protocol and trial procedures and conduct checks of every data point for consistency with source documents and validity, such an approach is resource intensive. The key aim of monitoring is to ensure the rights, safety, and well-being of the trial participants are protected and that the final results of the trial are reliable. The MHRA recommends that a proportionate approach to the management and monitoring of the CTIMP is undertaken based on the trial-risk assessment that identifies the areas that matter to achieving the above key aim, i.e., those activities/data that, if incorrect, would have a negative impact on participant safety and trial results. A thorough risk assessment of the trial should be conducted to identify the risks and then determine the strategies and procedures to mitigate them. This risk-based approach is consistent with ICH-GCP where the 'Sponsor should determine the extent and nature of the monitoring'.[193]

---

190. *See* https://www.ct-toolkit.ac.uk/routemap/ongoing-management-and-monitoring/ for overarching guidance relating to CTIMP oversight.
191. *See* https://www.gov.uk/government/publications/oversight-and-monitoring-of-investigational-medical-product-trials.
192. *Ibid. See also* Appendix 2 of *The Risk-adapted Approaches to the Management of Clinical Trials of Investigational Medicinal Products* (October 2011), available at https://assets.publishing.service.gov.uk/government/uploads/system/uploads/attachment_data/file/343677/Risk-adapted_approaches_to_the_management_of_clinical_trials_of_investigational_medicinal_products.pdf.
193. *See* further https://www.gov.uk/government/publications/oversight-and-monitoring-of-investigational-medical-product-trials/oversight-and-monitoring-activities.

The risk assessment should document the necessary oversight/monitoring actions put in place to mitigate risks and further documentation to implement these would usually be prepared. How this is done is decided by the sponsor. This may be contained in one document, for example, the protocol, an SOP, or a monitoring plan which clearly outlines for a particular trial how the trial would be overseen, managed, and monitored to ensure compliance with the regulations. There is no requirement to send additional documentation outlining the oversight and monitoring strategy to the MHRA or the REC as part of the approval process, as there is no requirement for this to be approved by the MHRA or REC, and there are currently no plans for this to be introduced in the future. The protocol must, however, according to the principles of GCP that must be adhered to, contain the monitoring policy though this may not contain the level of detail that other sponsor documentation contains.

Evidence of the activities outlined in the monitoring strategy should be documented to provide evidence to support compliance. Whilst site visit reports are well-established monitoring evidence and take a similar format across organisations, activity reports from central and statistical monitoring are not established in the same way, so all the documentation and checks undertaken to demonstrate the planned central monitoring activities must be retained. It is of particular importance that documentation shows that any non-compliance issues were effectively dealt with in a timely manner, including documentation of any escalation actions.[194]

[C] MHRA GCP Inspections

The majority of MHRA GCP inspections are carried out under the risk-based compliance programme, which can be either systems-based or trial-specific. MHRA GCP systems inspections examine the systems used by the sponsor to conduct the CTIMP. The MHRA inspectors usually select a number of the sponsor's CTIMPs to examine how the sponsor's trial procedures are applied. One or two investigator sites involved in the selected trials may also be inspected. Trial-specific GCP inspections assess clinical trials that have been completed and reported.

The risk-based inspection programme uses information available to the MHRA to determine risk. This information includes internal information about previous inspection history, organisational changes, as well as intelligence from external sources. Each sponsor/organisation is risk assessed, and inspections are prioritised for those considered to be the highest risk. This being said, a small number of organisations in the medium- and low-risk categories are usually randomly selected for routine risk-based inspections. Routine MHRA GCP inspections are conducted in accordance with the MHRA flowchart,[195] which includes the following steps:

- notification of MHRA GCP inspection under the routine risk-based inspection programme, including request for information in the form of a GCP inspection

---

194. *Ibid.*
195. *See* https://assets.publishing.service.gov.uk/government/uploads/system/uploads/attachment_data/file/420781/GCP-flowchart.pdf.

dossier and a clinical trials spreadsheet, which must be furnished to the MHRA within thirty days. The MHRA may also request the complete trial master file for review;[196]
- inspection date agreed and information provided inspection team and the practical logistical aspects of the inspection;
- the inspection plan is developed in consultation with the sponsor, and finalised;
- the actual inspection takes place,[197] which includes interviews with relevant staff and a review of documentation, such as the trial master file. The inspectors may visit data management units, archives, pharmacy, laboratories, etc.;
- inspection findings are made and the inspection report provided to the sponsor. At the end of the inspection the inspector usually provides a verbal summary of the inspection findings and allows the sponsor the opportunity to correct any misunderstandings;
- if there are critical findings identified these are referred to the GCP Inspection Action Group (IAG). This is a cross-agency group that oversees all critical findings and decides on the actions to be taken; and
- an infringement notice may be issued when instances of serious or serious and persistent non-compliance with GCP requirements have been identified.

[D]   Internal Audit

As is the case in the EU, the internal audit or a sponsor's audit is a voluntary audit, independent and separate from routine monitoring or quality control functions. Audit activities are sample-based and may occur during or after the CTIMP is completed, or for cause in response to issues detected by monitoring activities. The auditor also assesses the effectiveness of the monitoring activities and compliance with the processes outlined in the protocol/monitoring plan/SOPs.[198]

[E]   Urgent Safety Measures

Regulation 30 of the UK Regulations makes provision for urgent safety measures (USMs). The sponsor or the chief investigator, or the local principal investigator at a trial site, may take appropriate USMs in order to protect the trial participants against any immediate hazard to their health or safety. The UK Regulations require that the

---

196. *See* further detail and requirements at https://www.gov.uk/guidance/good-clinical-practice-for-clinical-trials#pre-inspection-documentation.
197. *See* further https://www.gov.uk/government/statistics/good-clinical-practice-inspection-metrics-2007-to-present for an indication of the metrics produced by the MHRA in respect of GCP inspections.
198. *See* https://www.gov.uk/government/publications/oversight-and-monitoring-of-investigatio nal-medical-product-trials/oversight-and-monitoring-activities.

REC and the MHRA must be notified within three days that such measures have been taken, the reasons why, and the plan for further action.

From a practical perspective,[199] the MHRA's Clinical Trials Unit must be contacted telephonically to discuss the issue with a medical assessor, ideally within twenty-four hours of measures being taken, but no later than three days from the date the measures are taken. After discussing the USM with the MHRA assessor telephonically, written notification of the measures taken and discussed with the medical assessor must be provided within three days from the date the measures were taken.

[F] Pharmacovigilance[200]

As remains the case post-Brexit, pharmacovigilance (PV) is achieved through the collection, monitoring, assessment, and evaluation of data on the adverse effects of medical products. Systems should therefore be put in place to enable the identification, recording, reporting, and analysis of safety information so that any safety signals that arise during a trial are quickly identified and acted upon. In the UK CTIMP context, the sponsor's responsibilities for PV are outlined in Part 5 of the UK Regulations. The terminology associated with PV is based on the assessment of seriousness, causality, and expectedness of an adverse event.[201]

Under Part 5 of the UK Regulations:[202]

- Suspected Unexpected Serious Adverse Reactions (SUSARs) occurring during CTIMPs in the UK must be notified to the REC and MHRA without delay. A SUSAR which is fatal or life-threatening must be reported as soon as possible and in any event within 7 days after the sponsor became aware of the event. Any additional relevant information must be reported within 8 days of sending the first report. A SUSAR which is not fatal or life-threatening must be reported as soon as possible and in any event within 15 days after the sponsor first became aware of the event;
- there is no requirement to notify SUSARs occurring in the CTIMP outside the UK or in other trials of the IMP;
- there is no requirement to notify serious adverse events occurring in the CTIMP, other than SUSARs;
- for each IMP being tested in the CTIMP, the UK Regulations require the sponsor to provide the REC and the MHRA with an annual safety report of the safety of the subjects in CTIMP for which it is the sponsor (whether in the UK

---

199. *See* MHRA guidance at https://www.gov.uk/guidance/clinical-trials-for-medicines-manage-your-authorisation-report-safety-issues#urgent-safety-measures.
200. *See* general discussion, including post-Brexit comments, in Chapter 10.
201. *See* https://www.ct-toolkit.ac.uk/routemap/pharmacovigilance/. *See also* the *Adverse Event flowchart* referenced in the aforesaid text to provide an overview of the assessments required.
202. *See* https://www.gov.uk/guidance/clinical-trials-for-medicines-manage-your-authorisation-report-safety-issues#suspected-unexpected-serious-adverse-reactions-susars. *See also* https://www.hra.nhs.uk/approvals-amendments/what-approvals-do-i-need/research-ethics-committee-review/applying-research-ethics-committee/ctimps-sl-ar1/#pharmacovigilance.

or elsewhere). The report should be provided in the required format for Development Safety Update Reports (DSURs).[203] The DSUR should include an aggregated global listing of all Suspected Serious Adverse Reactions (SSARs) occurring in the relevant trials in the reporting period; and
- in the case of double blind trials, un-blinding should take place before reporting adverse reactions.

Practically, from 1 October 2022,[204] SUSARs should be reported to the MHRA via the *Individual Case Safety Report (ICSR) Submissions* portal.[205] If relevant, the dual reporting of UK-relevant SUSARs may be required to the EMA's *Eudravigilance* Clinical Trial Module (EVCTM), as well as to other National Competent Authorities, using the European submission routes.

§4.16 AMENDMENTS, SUSPENSION, AND TERMINATION OF CTIMPs IN THE UK

[A] Introduction

As is the case in the EU, adherence to the Protocol is a fundamental part of the conduct of a CTIMP, but sometimes the Protocol must be amended. In this section, we discuss how amendments must be made and approved in the UK context, as well as how, and why, a trial can be terminated. Both events will affect the contents of the Protocol.

[B] Amendments by the REC or the MHRA

The sponsor must notify all concerned Investigator(s), the REC(s), and the MHRA of findings that could adversely affect the health of subjects, impact the conduct of the clinical trial, or alter the MHRA's authorisation to continue the trial in accordance with the UK Regulations. On the basis of this notification, the REC or MHRA may call for a change to the Protocol. In exceptional situations, if the finding is particularly serious, the trial may be suspended or terminated.

[C] Substantial Amendments by the Sponsor

After commencement of the CTIMP, the sponsor may amend the Protocol. If the amendments are substantial, the sponsor must inform the MHRA in accordance with

---

203. *See* further https://www.gov.uk/guidance/clinical-trials-for-medicines-manage-your-authorisation-report-safety-issues#development-safety-update-reports-dsurs.
204. *See* https://www.gov.uk/guidance/clinical-trials-for-medicines-manage-your-authorisation-report-safety-issues#suspected-unexpected-serious-adverse-reactions-susars. The MHRA eSUSAR website/portal was decommissioned on 30 September 2022.
205. *See* further https://www.gov.uk/guidance/register-to-make-submissions-to-the-mhra#registering-to-use-the-vigilance-systems-mhra-gateway-and-icsr-submissions.

relevant guidance.[206] Amendments are 'substantial' if it is likely to affect to a significant degree: the safety or physical or mental integrity of the subjects of the trial; the scientific value of the trial; the conduct or management of the trial; or the quality or safety of any investigational medicinal product used in the trial.[207]

From a practical perspective, the process for requesting amendments depends on whether or not the CTIMP was authorised via the combined review process. For CTIMPs authorised via the combined review process, the amendment application must be prepared and submitted via the new part of IRAS, as referenced above. For CTIMPs not approved or yet transitioned over to the combined review process, submissions should continue to be submitted via the *MHRA Submission* portal. The following documents must be furnished to the MHRA when submitting an application for a substantial amendment:

- *covering letter* detailing the CTIMP reference numbers (IRAS ID, CTA number, EudraCT, etc.) along with Purchase Order Number, outlining the substantial changes (if there have been any non-substantial changes, these should be described separately);
- a PDF copy of the completed and locked *Amendment tool*.[208] It should be ensured that this document contains a clear description of the substantial amendment and reasons for the proposed changes;
- a PDF file of the *Clinical Trial Authorisation application form* generated in IRAS with changes highlighted, if the amendment affects the information previously submitted; and
- *list of the proposed changes to the protocol or any other documents* compared to the current MHRA-approved document, showing previous and new wording where applicable and a rationale to justify each substantial change. If applicable, the following should also be provided: summaries of data; updated overall risk benefit assessment; possible consequences for subjects already in the trial; and possible consequences for the evaluation of results.

The MHRA will assess the application, usually within thirty-five days. If the trial requires an expedited assessment (for example, patient safety reasons), this should be stated in the covering letter along with the rationale for the expedited assessment request.

---

206. *See* https://www.gov.uk/guidance/clinical-trials-for-medicines-manage-your-authorisation-report-safety-issues#amending-your-trial-protocol-or-other-documentation.
207. For a change in contact details, refer to practical guidance at https://www.gov.uk/guidance/clinical-trials-for-medicines-manage-your-authorisation-report-safety-issues#change-your-contact-details.
208. Accessible from https://www.myresearchproject.org.uk/help/hlpamendments.aspx#Amendment-Tool.

[D] Temporary Suspension of CTIMPs

The temporary suspension by a sponsor of a CTIMP must be notified to the MHRA.[209] Such notification should be made as a substantial amendment using the above-referenced *Amendment tool*, clearly explaining what has been stopped and the reasons for the suspension. Substantial amendments relating to temporary suspension must be submitted using *MHRA Submissions*. For applications that have gone through the Combined Review process (via IRAS), relevant guidance on the HRA website should be followed.[210] To resume a trial that has been temporarily suspended, a request to do so must also be submitted as a substantial amendment (as described above), providing evidence that it is safe to resume such trial.

[E] Early Termination of CTIMPs

The sponsor may also terminate the CTIMP early for a number of reasons and must also notify the MHRA of this.[211] The sponsor must complete and submit the prescribed *end of trial declaration form* and include a brief explanation of the reasons for ending the trial early. Such notification must be sent within fifteen days of the global early termination of the trial. This form must be submitted using *MHRA Submissions* portal, and for CTIMP applications that were processed through the combined review process via IRAS, relevant guidance on the HRA website should be followed.[212]

[F] End of CTIMPs

The sponsor must also communicate the end of a clinical trial to the MHRA.[213] The sponsor must complete the prescribed *end of trial declaration form* and submit, along with a covering letter, within ninety days of the global end of the clinical trial.

Legislation only requires the global end of trial to be submitted; however, a facility to inform the MHRA of the local (UK) end of trial via the *end of trial notification form* also exists.[214] If sponsors wish to request an exemption to this requirement, this

---

209. See further https://www.gov.uk/guidance/clinical-trials-for-medicines-manage-your-authorisation-report-safety-issues#suspend-or-terminate-a-trial.
210. See https://www.hra.nhs.uk/planning-and-improving-research/policies-standards-legislation/clinical-trials-investigational-medicinal-products-ctimps/combined-ways-working-pilot/step-step-guide-using-iras-combined-ways-working-cwow/#amendment.
211. https://www.gov.uk/guidance/clinical-trials-for-medicines-manage-your-authorisation-report-safety-issues#suspend-or-terminate-a-trial.
212. See https://www.hra.nhs.uk/planning-and-improving-research/policies-standards-legislation/clinical-trials-investigational-medicinal-products-ctimps/combined-ways-working-pilot/step-step-guide-using-iras-combined-ways-working-cwow/#reporting.
213. See guidance at https://www.gov.uk/guidance/clinical-trials-for-medicines-manage-your-authorisation-report-safety-issues#end-of-trial.
214. Local end of trial notifications will not be acknowledged, and the *MHRA Submissions* automatic e-mail confirmation should be considered evidence of submission. If a local end of trial is submitted, the MHRA would still expect to receive relevant safety updates and substantial amendments for the ongoing trial until the global end of trial notification is received.

must be done via a substantial amendment for approval, as discussed above. Such amendment must clearly state to what documents the proposal relates and provide rationale for such request. In this regard, all safety documentation must be submitted unless there are no other ongoing trials with the same IMP in the UK.

As mentioned above, sponsors are required to submit the *end of trial declaration forms* using the MHRA Submissions portal, and for CTIMP applications that were processed through the combined review process via IRAS, relevant guidance on the HRA website should be followed.[215]

[G] CTIMP Summary Results

The time frame for publishing the summary of results of the CTIMP is within one year of the end of trial. Sponsors must publish such summary results within this timeframe on the public register(s)[216] upon which such CTIMP was originally registered.[217]

§4.17 CTIMP DATA IN THE UK

[A] Introduction

As is the case in the EU, the data and other information, such as the details of patients, collected during the clinical trial must be presented, maintained, and stored in accordance with strict rules and guidelines in order to both comply with legislation, GCP, and to protect the interests of the subjects and patients. This section provides a brief overview of the requirements relating to the dissemination of CTIMP results, the storage of the trial master file, and the general management of personal data processed in relation to research. Please note that Chapter 23 provides a more general discussion of privacy and data protection considerations, which is also applicable to CTIMPs. Accordingly, general privacy and data protection aspects of CTIMPs are not included in this chapter.

[B] Dissemination of CTIMP Results

Other than early phase trials, sponsors of CTIMPs should publish a research summary of their findings within one year of the CTIMP's completion. As mentioned above,

---

215. *See* https://www.hra.nhs.uk/planning-and-improving-research/policies-standards-legislation/clinical-trials-investigational-medicinal-products-ctimps/combined-ways-working-pilot/step-step-guide-using-iras-combined-ways-working-cwow/#reporting.
216. Sponsors are not required to submit clinical trial summary reports to the MHRA. However, Sponsors must send a short e-mail to CT.Submission@mhra.gov.uk, including the information set out in the MHRA guidance.
217. *See* guidance at https://www.gov.uk/guidance/clinical-trials-for-medicines-manage-your-authorisation-report-safety-issues#end-of-trial.

summary results should be published in the public register(s) where such CTIMPs have been registered.[218]

Where the main findings are also to be submitted for publication in a journal, this should also be done within one year of study completion to be published through an open-access mechanism in a peer-reviewed journal.[219] Information concerning the dissemination or publication of CTIMP results should be included in the Protocol; funders will likely ensure such provisions are in place. The REC application form also requires the applicant to confirm how they intend to report and disseminate their results.[220] CONSORT (Consolidated Standards of Reporting Trials) is an initiative that was developed to improve the reporting of randomised controlled trials, enabling readers to understand a trial's design, conduct, analysis, and interpretation and to assess the validity of its results. In the UK context, especially in relation to non-commercial trials, it is strongly recommended that the CONSORT guidelines are followed when preparing final study reports.[221]

The sharing of data produced during CTIMPs has the potential to provide benefits to patients and the scientific community. In the UK context, the *Guidance on the Good Practice Principles for Sharing Individual Participant Data from Publicly Funded Clinical Trials*[222] has been produced for publicly-funded clinical trials. This guidance summarises the good clinical practice principles to follow when sharing individual participant data using a controlled access system.[223]

Informing trial participants of results acknowledges their contribution, and it is good practice to determine if a participant would want to be informed of trial results, or whether they would prefer to obtain the results independently.[224] Information about the publication and dissemination arrangements should be included in the participant information sheet.[225] Information about research findings should therefore be available to those who took part in the CTIMP (as well as interested groups or communities and the general public) in a format that is accessible and easy to understand. As part of the HRA's transparency strategy,[226] sponsors are requested to include a plain language summary of the CTIMP findings in their final report to be published on the HRA website alongside the CTIMP summaries.[227]

---

218. *See* https://www.hra.nhs.uk/planning-and-improving-research/best-practice/publication-and-dissemination-research-findings/.
219. *Ibid.*
220. *See* https://www.ct-toolkit.ac.uk/routemap/dissemination-of-results/.
221. *Ibid. See also* http://www.consort-statement.org/consort-2010.
222. *See* http://www.methodologyhubs.mrc.ac.uk/files/7114/3682/3831/Datasharingguidance2015.pdf.
223. *See* https://www.ct-toolkit.ac.uk/routemap/dissemination-of-results/.
224. *Ibid.*
225. *See* https://www.hra.nhs.uk/planning-and-improving-research/best-practice/publication-and-dissemination-research-findings/.
226. *See* https://www.hra.nhs.uk/planning-and-improving-research/policies-standards-legislation/research-transparency/.
227. *See* https://www.hra.nhs.uk/planning-and-improving-research/best-practice/publication-and-dissemination-research-findings/.

[C] Storage of Trial Master File

Regulation 31A of the UK Regulations define the archiving requirements for CTIMPs. All essential documents (i.e., mainly the trial master file)[228] should be archived and this includes essential records held by investigators, sponsors, and others involved in the conduct of a CTIMP (including services departments such as pharmacy, laboratories, and radiology).[229] Essential records should be maintained in a legible condition and ready access must be possible. The storage of the sponsor's documentation may be transferred to a sub-contractor, but the ultimate responsibility for the quality, integrity, confidentiality, and retrievability of the documents remains with the sponsor. Access to archives should further be restricted to authorised personnel. Please note that any

---

228. Essentially, the trial master file comprises of the following records:

(1) Before the Clinical Phase of the Trial Commences:
   - Investigator's Brochure.
   - Protocol and amendments, with sample CRF.
   - Information given to subjects (including informed consent form) and other relevant written information given to subjects.
   - Advertisement for subjects (if any).
   - Financial aspects of the trial (including budgets, costs of staff and facilities, payments to subjects, if applicable, and insurance provisions).
   - Favourable opinion of the Ethics Committee, dated prior to the trial commencement, and verification that the Ethics Committee has been constituted in accordance with GCP.
   - Signed agreements between involved parties (such as the Sponsor, the Investigator, the institution, and professional staff) setting out their respective roles and responsibilities.
   - Regulatory notification and approval of Protocol by the Competent Authority.
   - Details of the trial site(s), staff, and processes for dealing with the IMP.
   - Decoding procedures for blinded trials.

(2) During the Clinical Conduct of the Trial:
   - Updates on all of the above.
   - Certificates of analysis for the IMP.
   - Signed consent forms.
   - Monitoring visit reports.
   - Source documents to demonstrate the integrity of trial data.
   - Signed and dated CRFs, including corrections.
   - SUSAR and ADR reports.
   - Reports to Ethics Committees.
   - Details of subject enrolment and logging of their details.
   - Record of retained body fluids/tissue samples.

(3) After Completion or Termination of the Trial:
   - Confirmation that the IMP has been used in accordance with the Protocol.
   - Proof of IMP destruction, or return and disposal as agreed with the manufacturer of the IMP.
   - Completed subject identity code list.
   - Audit certificate.
   - Final trial close-out monitoring report.
   - Final report to Ethics Committee.
   - Clinical study report.

229. See https://www.ct-toolkit.ac.uk/routemap/archiving/.

storage of personal data is subject to applicable elements of data protection legislation (as more fully described in Chapter 23).[230]

As regards the duration of the storage of the trial master file, it is important to determine if the CTIMP results will or may be included in a MAA and should take the necessary steps to ensure appropriate retention of such essential documents. Where the results of CTIMPs are not going to be used in regulatory submissions, such records must be retained for *at least five years* after completion of the trial, unless other applicable regulatory requirement(s), the sponsor or the funder of the trial requires a longer storage period.

Where the results of CTIMPs are indeed going to be used in regulatory submissions in the UK, the sponsor should retain all sponsor-specific essential documents in conformance with the applicable UK regulatory requirement(s). In this regard, such documents should be retained until *at least two years* after the last approval of an MAA in the UK.[231] These documents should, however, be retained for a longer period if required by the applicable regulatory requirement(s) or if needed by the sponsor.[232] In the UK context, to the extent that the NHS is in any way involved in CTIMPs, the NHS *Records Management Code of Practice*[233] shall apply, which imposes further documentation retention requirements. For example, certain records (such as the master file relating to advanced medical therapy research) attract a *twenty-year* retention period.

The above storage requirements also apply to original source documents retained at trial sites. Should a site wish to replace paper medical records with scanned copies, there must be a process to ensure authentic copies are produced prior to any destruction of original source documents. The *MHRA Position Statement and Guidance: Electronic Health Records*[234] provides further guidance in this regard.

[D] Access to NHS Electronic Health Records

The MHRA has, in consultation with the HRA and the UK Information Commissioners Office (ICO), published guidance[235] intended for sponsors, CROs, and investigator sites regarding the management of personal data processed in relation to research, including access to participants' (existing) electronic health records (EHRs) held by the NHS. Such guidance should be read alongside the HRA/MHRA joint advice on *Data Protection Impact Assessments*.[236]

---

230. *See* https://www.ct-toolkit.ac.uk/documents/archiving/27153.
231. Or at least two years since: the formal discontinuation of clinical development of the IMP; or there are no pending or contemplated MAAs.
232. *See* https://www.ct-toolkit.ac.uk/documents/archiving/27153.
233. Available at https://transform.england.nhs.uk/information-governance/guidance/records-management-code/. *See* in particular, Appendix II (*Retention Schedule*).
234. *See* https://assets.publishing.service.gov.uk/government/uploads/system/uploads/attachment_data/file/470228/Electronic_Health_Records_MHRA_Position_Statement.pdf.
235. *See* https://www.gov.uk/guidance/on-site-access-to-electronic-health-records-by-sponsor-representatives-in-clinical-trials.
236. Available at https://www.hra.nhs.uk/planning-and-improving-research/policies-standards-legislation/data-protection-and-information-governance/gdpr-guidance/what-law-says/data-privacy-impact-assessments/.

Increasingly, medical records are now in electronic form, which presents certain challenges. One of these is ensuring that access to such EHRs is restricted to only those participants in the trial and ensuring that records of patients not in the trial, but maintained on the same system, are not accessed by trial staff. The trial participants must of course consent in writing (as part of the consent to take part in the clinical trial) to the access by trial staff of their EHRs.[237] *See* further Chapter 23 in this regard.

§4.18 GUIDELINES/PUBLICATIONS

Clinical Trials Information System (CTIS): online modular training programme | European Medicines Agency (europa.eu)

EudraLex – Volume 10 (europa.eu)

Microsoft Word – CTR QnA v6.1 27-05-2022 (europa.eu)

https://www.ema.europa.eu/en/documents/other/clinical-trial-information-system-ctis-Sponsor-handbook_.pdf

Revised guideline on first-in-human clinical trials | European Medicines Agency (europa.eu)

---

237. *See* https://www.gov.uk/guidance/on-site-access-to-electronic-health-records-by-sponsor-representatives-in-clinical-trials.

CHAPTER 5
Obtaining a Marketing Authorisation

Sally Shorthose, Sarah Faircliffe & Phillipus Putter

§5.01 APPROVAL OF MEDICINES FOR HUMAN USE: SECURING A MARKETING AUTHORISATION

[A] Introduction and Overview of the Processes

Before a medicine can be sold or prescribed in the EU, a *Marketing Authorisation* (MA) must usually be obtained. The MA stipulates the condition(s) (indications), patient population(s) and dosage etc. for which the medicine is authorised, together with any conditions imposed on its use or on the Marketing Authorisation holder (MAH) in terms of post-authorisation commitments. Authorisation is granted following an assessment of the safety, efficacy, and quality of that medicine based on data provided by the applicant.

A full application dossier contains manufacturing information, results of pharmaceutical and pre-clinical tests as well as the results of clinical trials (which themselves are regulated – *see* Chapter 4 for the complete discussion) and other supporting data such as a summary of the pharmacovigilance system, the risk-management plan, and an evaluation of the potential environmental risks posed by the medicine. Applications must be submitted in a standardised format, as discussed in §5.02. The applicant must demonstrate that the medicine is suitable for marketing in terms of its safety, efficacy, and quality profile. Economic issues are not considered at this time – those are a matter for the local health authorities, which may or may not choose to reimburse the cost of a particular medicine. Either the European Medicines Agency (EMA) or a national 'Competent Authority' (regulatory authority) considers the dossier submitted by the applicant and delivers an opinion on whether or not an MA should be granted and whether any specific conditions should be imposed.

There are a number of different types of application, depending on the nature of the medicinal product's active ingredient (e.g., whether it is new or whether it has been marketed previously), all of which are discussed in this book. Furthermore, MAs may be amended or renewed, and again, these processes are dealt with elsewhere in this book.

This Chapter examines the four different MA application procedures and provides an overview of the advantages and disadvantages of the various procedures as well as of the information required to support an application for an MA.

[B] Goals of the Approval Process: Demonstration of Quality, Safety, and Efficacy

The main objective of the European pharmaceutical legislation is to safeguard public health. MAs are granted after a thorough assessment of the MA application by the competent authority or authorities,[1] which collectively are responsible for authorising the sale and marketing to the public of safe and effective medicinal products. Applicants must prove the quality, safety, and efficacy of the medicinal product by submitting particulars and documents relating to the results of pharmaceutical (physico-chemical, biological, or microbiological) tests, as well as pre-clinical (pharmacological and toxicological) tests and clinical trials carried out on the medicinal product to be placed on the market.[2] Ongoing pharmacovigilance is also recognised as an important way of gathering safety and efficacy data, so information on proposed pharmacovigilance systems and risk-management plans is assessed as part of the dossier (see Chapter 10).

At the same time, conducting repetitive tests on humans or animals is to be avoided as much as possible for ethical reasons. Therefore, Directive 2001/83/EC stipulates certain cases in which the results of toxicological and pharmacological tests or clinical trials do not have to be provided in order to obtain an MA.[3]

Unless there are 'serious grounds for supposing that authorisation of the medicinal product concerned may present a risk to public health',[4] an MA granted by the competent authority of one Member State should be recognised by the competent authority of another Member State (see §5.04 and §5.05 below). In the event of a dispute, the matter can be referred to the EMA for resolution (as described below).

[C] Legislative Background

Since the implementation of the original harmonising Directive 65/65/EEC[5] in 1965, the EU Member States have gradually developed and established a comprehensive

---

1. The competent authority or authorities are that or those that the Member States designate as responsible for performing the duties arising from a Directive (European Directive 97/11/EC).
2. Article 8(3)(i) Directive 2001/83/EC.
3. Articles 10, 10a, 10b, 10c Directive 2001/83/EC.
4. Article 12 Directive 2001/83/EC.
5. Council Directive 65/65/EEC of 26 January 1965 on the approximation of provisions in law, regulation, or administrative action relating to medicinal products (OJ L No. 22 of 9 February 1965, 369).

Chapter 5: Obtaining a Marketing Authorisation §5.01[C]

harmonised legislative framework for medicinal products. The legislation is designed both to ensure a high level of public health protection and to remove some obstacles to the internal market. One such obstacle results from the differences in application procedures in the various Member States, which could make the bringing to market of a new medicine in multiple Member States both time-consuming and inconsistent. This would act as a disincentive to the free movement of goods, in this case, medicines, throughout the internal market and could damage the competitiveness of the European pharmaceutical industry.

The 2001 Directive 2001/83/EC[6] codified and consolidated in a single text all the previous Directives[7] and many years of legislation and case law on medicinal products for human use, in the interest of clarity and rationalisation. National procedures and the mutual recognition procedure (MRP) relating to medicines for human use are governed by this Directive. Directive 2001/83/EC has itself been amended several times by subsequent Directives relating to, for example, advanced therapy medicinal products and pharmacovigilance.

Fundamentally, the Directive provides that no medicinal product may be placed on the market of a Member State unless an MA has been granted by the competent authority of that Member State for its own territory,[8] or an MA has been granted by the Commission for the entire EU.[9] It sets out in detail all the processes that must be undertaken in order to bring a medicinal product to market, including the form of the application for an MA and the review process whereby the application is assessed. It also contains sections on supervision and sanctions, homeopathic and traditional herbal products, product information and advertising, pharmacovigilance, classification of products, manufacturing and importation, amongst other things.

Alongside Directive 2001/83/EC, Regulation No. (EC) 726/2004 is the text by which the activities of the EMA and the 'centralised procedure' (CP) for the grant of MAs (*see* §5.03) are governed.

Various specific aspects of the authorisation procedures, such as paediatric studies and the orphan drugs framework (*see* Chapters 8 and 14) are governed by separate legislation, and in addition to the basic legal framework, there are numerous pieces of implementing legislation and guidelines which must be considered alongside

---

6. European Parliament and Council Directive of 6 November 2001 on the Community code relating medicinal products for human use.
7. The first relevant was Directive 65/65/EEC, thereafter the European Community adopted a number of Directives dealing with various aspects of the law on medicinal products. There were, for example, Directives specifically dealing with radiopharmaceuticals, homeopathic medicinal products, immunological medicinal products, and so on, and different legal aspects of medicinal products such as classification, labelling, and promotion were subject to separate Directives. Over time each of these different Directives – due to scientific, technical, and judicial progress – underwent several revisions and amendments. As a result, the implementation and application of EU legislation within the Member States had become particularly complex.
8. Article 6 Directive 2001/83/EC; Article 5 of the same Directive provides for the possibility that certain products may be excluded from this requirement in specific circumstances, and certain products are outside the scope of the Directive – *see* Article 3.
9. Article 3 Regulation (EC) 726/2004 of the Regulation laying down Union procedures for the authorisation and supervision of medicinal products for human use and establishing a EMA, as amended.

the legislation, such as the 'Notice to Applicants' guidance ('soft law') published by the European Commission (Commission).

[D]   Overview of the Application Dossier

Article 8(3) of Directive 2001/83/EC contains the basic requirements for an application for an MA (regardless of the procedure to be followed). The application and accompanying documents must be presented in accordance with Annex I of Directive 2001/83/EC and must follow the guidance published by the Commission in the Notice to Applicants, Volume 2B, Common Technical Document (CTDoc). Further detail is provided in subsequent sections of this Chapter.

Articles 10, 10a, 10b, and 10c of Directive 2001/83/EC cover specific types of applications where the dossier requirements may not be as extensive as that of a 'full application' as specified in Article 8(3), or (in the case of Article 10a) where the data required may be provided by way of reference to published scientific studies.

[E]   Overview of the MA Procedures

Regardless of whether the MA is to be obtained at the EU level or a national level, there are many common features and requirements to be followed, and the application processes are similar. All four MA procedures (as listed below) require submission of comprehensive safety and efficacy data (unless cross-referral to such data by way of an abridged application is permitted). Article 8 of Directive 2001/83/EC provides an outline of the contents of each application for an innovative product authorisation, which will include the results of pre-clinical and clinical trials, in a CTDoc, which is now an internationally recognised format, a proposed summary of product characteristics (SmPC) and other information relevant to the MA application. For some types of products, such as radionuclide generators, further information will be required. Article 10 of the Directive provides a simplified 'abridged' procedure for certain generic products.[10]

A first step in bringing a medicinal product to the market is the consideration of which MA procedure to adopt. For some products, the route is compulsory while for others there is a choice. Any decision as to which procedure to use depends in part on whether the applicant wishes to market the medicinal product in one or more Member States or throughout the whole EU.

There are four different routes to obtaining MA within the EU (further details are set out in §5.03–§5.06 below):

(1) *CP*: the Commission grants the MA, which is automatically valid in all Member States. The CP is compulsory for certain types of products and orphan drugs, and it is optional for certain other products, as described in detail under the section on the CP below.

---

10. *See* Chapter 12 for a detailed analysis of this and associated procedures.

(2) *MRP*: national MAs are granted in Member States chosen by the applicant. The MAs are issued following an initial assessment by the Reference Member State (RMS) which prepares a report for the Concerned Member State(s) (CMS). The CMS authorisations are based on 'mutual recognition' of the RMS assessment.

(3) *Decentralised procedure (DCP):* this is available *before* an MA is issued by a Member State, but in other respects, it is procedurally similar to the MRP.

(4) *National procedure:* this is now only used in very limited circumstances and, as its title suggests, is carried out at Member State level.

Where a choice of procedure is possible, each one offers various advantages (*see* the discussion in §5.07 below). For example, the CP is used most often by the larger pharmaceutical companies that wish to market products on an EU-wide basis. The national procedure may still be preferred by small- and medium-sized enterprises (SMEs) if they only wish to market the product in their own (or a limited number of) Member State(s). It should be noted that although there are differences in the process among the four procedures, the requirements regarding quality, safety, and efficacy of the medicinal product and the procedures to bring the product to market are the same.

The legislation covering the national procedure, MRP, and the DCP is set out in Directive 2001/83/EC. Regulation (EC) No. 726/2004 sets out the requirements for the CP. Provisions in the national laws of the Member States determine implementation of Directive 2001/83/EC and local variations in the various national procedures, so implementation of certain aspects can, to some extent, vary between Member States.

§5.02 REQUIREMENTS OF THE APPLICATION DOSSIER

The CTDoc is a uniform set of specifications for an application dossier. The CTDoc has been adopted by the EU, the United States (US), Japan, and elsewhere, and it is maintained by the International Conference on Harmonisation (ICH) of Technical Requirements for the Registration of Pharmaceuticals for Human Use (*see* Chapter 2 for the definition and history of the ICH). The CTDoc comprises five modules:

(1) administrative and prescribing information;
(2) overview and summary of modules 3–5;
(3) quality (pharmaceutical documentation);
(4) safety (toxicology documentation); and
(5) efficacy (clinical studies).

All regulatory authorities have adopted the specific language of the CTDoc as the standard; however, there are subtle differences in interpretation and implementation.

[A] Required Contents of an Application Dossier

All information that is relevant to the evaluation of the medicinal product, whether favourable or unfavourable, must be included in the application.[11] For example, the details and information prescribed in Article 8(3) must be provided for any incomplete or abandoned pharmaco-toxicological clinical trial or test relating to the medicinal product, and/or completed trials concerning therapeutic indications not covered by the application.

Article 8(3) and Annex I of Directive 2001/83/EC contain the legal requirements for submitting an MA application; they include the following:

(a) name of the applicant, address of the applicant, name of the manufacturer, address of the manufacturer, sites involved in the different stages of the manufacture (including the manufacturer of the finished product and the manufacturer(s) of the active substance(s)), and name and address of the importer;

(b) name of the medicinal product, name of the active substance, strength of the medicinal product, final presentation – including packaging, identification of the type of application, indication of what samples (if any) are provided, and copies of Manufacturing Authorisations;

(c) qualitative particulars of all the constituents of the medicinal product, quantitative particulars of all the constituents of the medicinal product, reference to the international non-proprietary name (INN),[12] or a reference to the relevant chemical name of the medicinal product;

(d) description of the manufacturing method;

(e) therapeutic indications, contra-indications, and adverse reactions;

(f) dose, pharmaceutical form, method of administration, route of administration, and expected shelf life;

(g) reasons for any precautionary and safety measures to be taken for the storage of the medicinal product, its administration to patients, and for the disposal of waste products, together with an indication of any potential risks presented by the medicinal product to the environment (if the medicinal product constitutes a genetically modified organism (GMO), further information must be provided);[13]

(h) description of the control methods employed by the manufacturer;

(i) results of pharmaceutical (physico-chemical, biological, or microbiological) tests, results of pre-clinical (pharmacological and toxicological) tests, and results of clinical trials;

---

11. Annex I, paragraph 3 of Introduction, Directive 2001/83/EC.
12. INN is the official non-proprietary, or generic, name given to a pharmaceutical substance, as designated by the WHO.
13. Refer to Notice to Applicants, vol. 2B, Medicinal products for human use, presentation and format of the dossier, CTDoc, Module 1 paragraph 1.6.2, edn May 2008.

(j) the SmPC (*see* the requirements of the SmPC at §5.02[A][8] below), one or more mock-ups of the outer packaging, primary packaging, and the package leaflet.

Applications for an MA are to be accompanied by the name or corporate name and permanent address of the applicant for the MA (and, if applicable, the manufacturer). The MAH may be a natural or legal person and must be established (with a permanent place of business or home) in the European Community (Community), including the European Economic Area (EEA).

[1]   Manufacturing Authorisations

As a pre-requisite for obtaining an MA, the manufacturer of the product must hold a manufacturing authorisation. Manufacturing authorisation holders are obliged to guarantee the consistent quality of the product by complying with the Good Manufacturing Practice (GMP) for medicinal products[14] and to use as starting materials only active substances that have been manufactured in accordance with the detailed guidelines on GMP for starting materials.[15] The principles and guidelines for GMP for medicinal products for human use are stated in Directive 2003/94/EC. Compliance with these principles and guidelines is mandatory within the EEA, and guidance to interpret these requirements is available.[16]

Where the manufacturer is not the MAH (or applicant), both the MAH and manufacturer must sign a written agreement to guarantee that the manufacturer's operations comply with the rules (namely GMP and any local requirements) in force and with the manufacturing conditions described in the dossier. This is usually in the form of a technical agreement between the parties.

The MA application includes a description of the manufacturing method. This describes the techniques and equipment used, the amounts of ingredients for the batch size, the order in which the ingredients are mixed, and timings and conditions. The control methods used by the manufacturer in manufacturing the medicinal product are described, including in-process controls (e.g., to check the active ingredient is evenly distributed in the granule) and quality control methods for the finished product.

For a manufacturing site to be allowed to manufacture medicinal products, it must have a valid GMP certificate issued by a competent authority, and it must agree to undergo periodic inspections at the request of the competent authorities. A GMP certificate is issued within ninety days following a GMP inspection of the manufacturing site. The competent authority responsible for carrying out the inspection issues the

---

14. Title IV, Directive 2001/83/EC, as amended.
15. Article 46(f) Directive 2001/83/EC, as amended; *see also* Part II of Eurdralex, Vol. 4 'GMP – Basic requirements for active substances used as starting materials'; https://health.ec.europa.eu/medicinal-products/eudralex/eudralex-volume-4_en.
16. Part I 'Basic requirements for medicinal products' of the EU Guidelines for Good Manufacturing Practice, published in vol. 4 of Eudralex; https://health.ec.europa.eu/medicinal-products/eudralex/eudralex-volume-4_en.

certificate to confirm the GMP compliance status of the inspected site. GMP certificates are site-specific and can be restricted to particular activities (e.g., manufacturing activities related to a specific product).

If the site of manufacture of the medicinal product is outside the EU, the Qualified Person[17] must ensure that each imported batch has undergone, in the importing country, the testing specified in paragraph 1 (b) of Article 51, Directive 2001/83/EC. For medicinal products manufactured within the EU, a Qualified Person must ensure that each batch has been produced and tested/checked in accordance with the Directives and the MA.

A document showing that the manufacturer is authorised in its own country to produce medicinal products is appended to the application. This is usually a certificate of compliance with GMP issued by a competent authority. Mutual Recognition Agreements are in place for GMP inspections of manufacturing sites for human and veterinary medicinal products in countries such as Australia, Canada, and Switzerland.

[2] Assurance of Quality of All Constituents

Full qualitative and quantitative particulars of all the constituents of the medicinal product – that is, the active substance(s) and the excipients[18] – are required as part of the application dossier to ensure that the quality, safety, and efficacy of all the components can be assessed by the competent authority and to ensure consistency of quality of the end product. The applicant will therefore have to include data relating not only to the active ingredient but also to all other constituents to be included in the final product and must also include a description of the composition of the product expressed in terms of biological activity.

[3] New Active Substances

If the medicinal product contains a new active substance, the contents of the application dossier may differ somewhat from the dossier that is required for an active ingredient that is not a new active substance. A new active substance is defined in Annex I of Chapter 1, Volume 2A of the European Commission's Notice to Applicants[19] guidance as follows:

- a chemical, biological, or radiopharmaceutical substance not previously authorised as a medicinal product for human use in the EU;
- an isomer, a mixture of isomers, a complex, or a derivative or salt of a chemical substance previously authorised as a medicinal product for human use in the EU but differing significantly in properties with regard to safety and/or efficacy from that chemical substance previously authorised;

---

17. The duties of the Qualified Person(s) are fully described in Article 51 of Directive 2001/83/EC.
18. CHMP Guideline on excipients in the dossier for application for marketing authorisation of a medicinal product Ref. EMA/CHMP/QWP/396951/2006, Rev 2.
19. Latest version Revision 11, July 2019.

- a biological substance previously authorised in a medicinal product for human use in the EU but differing significantly in properties with regard to safety and/or efficacy which is due to differences in one or a combination of the following: in molecular structure, nature of the source material, or manufacturing process; or
- a radiopharmaceutical substance that is a radionuclide, or a ligand not previously authorised as a medicinal product for human use in the EU, or the coupling mechanism to link the molecule and radionuclide has not been authorised previously in the EU.

However, the question of what constitutes a 'new active substance' is not always straightforward, and it is discussed in more detail in §13.03.[F][1][f].

[4] Certification of Suitability (CEP)

For active substances, CEPs may be issued. CEPs are certificates issued by the European Directorate for the Quality of Medicines (EDQM) to confirm that a certain active substance is produced according to the requirements of the relevant monograph of the European Pharmacopoeia or of the monograph on transmissible spongiform encephalopathy (TSE). CEPs can be used by companies to replace much of the documentation required for the active substance in the MA dossier. The physical site where the active substance is manufactured must also comply with GMP. In the context of the CEP certification scheme, the EDQM may request GMP site inspections of active substance manufacturers.

Inactive ingredients may have a CEP to show compliance with the monograph on TSE.

[5] Orphan Drugs

There are specific application requirements depending on the product applied for – for example, applications for orphan drugs need to include a copy of any designation of the medicinal product as an orphan medicinal product under Regulation (EC) No. 141/2000 of the European Parliament and of the Council of 16 December 1999 on orphan medicinal products, accompanied by a copy of the relevant agency opinion.

[6] Naming the Product

Choosing an appropriate and acceptable product name is an important precursor to the application process.

The active substance is named according to the INN designated by the World Health Organization (WHO) or using the relevant chemical name. During clinical trials, the manufacturer applies to the WHO for an INN if the active substance does not already have one. The application form allows the applicant to suggest three names in order of preference (the WHO provides general principles for guidance in devising

INNs based on the use of stems). A consultation committee considers the selected names, and the one accepted name is published.

The name of the medicinal product itself may either be a single, 'invented' name (trade name) or a common or scientific name, usually the INN of the active substance(s), accompanied by a trade mark or the name of the MAH. For applications using the CP, guidance on invented names and the procedure for submitting them for acceptance is available on the EMA website.[20]

[7] Required Product Information

The language of the pharmaceutical form(s) and route of administration of the medicinal product should conform to the List of Standard Terms published online by the EDQM. This list covers dosage forms, routes of administration, and containers used for medicines for human and veterinary use. It gives the approved equivalents (if not exact translations) of several hundred terms in thirty-one languages, including the official languages of the EU.

The applicant also has to provide proposed packaging details, which include the expected shelf life of the medicinal product. For some products, such as liquid preparations (e.g., eye drops or oral suspensions), an 'in-use' shelf life for the product after it has been first opened is also suggested. The shelf life and storage conditions are finalised according to the results of stability testing, which may be ongoing at the time of the application. The applicant makes a commitment in its application to continue stability testing and conduct new stability tests on production batches.

Other documents that must be submitted include a summary of the product characteristics in accordance with Article 11 of Directive 2001/83/EC, a mock-up of the outer packaging containing the details provided for in Article 54 and of the immediate packaging of the medicinal product containing the details provided for in Article 55, together with a package leaflet in accordance with Article 59. Articles 59(3) and 61(1) require that the package leaflet reflects the results of consultations with target patient groups to ensure that it is legible, clear, and easy to use. This testing is more commonly called 'user testing'; or 'readability testing', and guidance is available to explain how testing should be performed.[21] Article 56a requires that the product name must also be expressed in Braille format on the packaging.

[8] SmPC

The proposed SmPC must also be included in the application dossier. The SmPC contains a description of the medicinal product's properties, and the conditions

---

20. Guideline on the acceptability of names for human medicinal products processed through the CP (EMA/CHMP/287710/2014 – Rev.6).
21. Guideline on the readability of the labelling and package leaflet of medicinal product for human use, revision 1 (12 January 2009) and Operational procedure on Handling of 'Consultation with target patient groups' on Package Leaflets (PL) for Centrally Authorised Products for Human Use Doc. Ref. EMEA/277378/2005, 20 October 2005.

attached to its use, as agreed between the applicant and the assessor(s) of the medicinal product; it is finalised during the application process. It forms the basis of the information that will be provided to healthcare professionals, and its contents are reflected in packaging and patient information leaflets. While the SmPC does not provide general advice regarding the treatment of particular medical conditions, specific aspects of treatment insofar as it relates to the particular medicinal product are mentioned, as well as other details of the product and how, and to whom, it should be administered (including side effects).[22]

[9] Environmental Risks

The applicant must include the reasons for any precautionary and safety measures required in the storage, administration, and disposal of the medicinal product, together with an indication of any potential environmental risks presented by the medicinal product. Handling precautions are relevant for medicines, such as cytotoxic drugs and radionuclides. All applicants and MAHs need to take into account the Committee for Medicinal Products for Human Use (CHMP) note for Guidance on Environmental Risk.[23]

[10] Pharmacovigilance Systems[24]

The applicant must include a description of the pharmacovigilance systems in place, which must include a risk-management system. Also required is proof that the applicant has the services of a qualified person responsible for pharmacovigilance and has the necessary means for the notification of any adverse reaction suspected of occurring either in the Community or in a third country.

[11] Submission of Test Results

A full application dossier must include the results of pharmaceutical (physico-chemical, biological, or microbiological) tests, pre-clinical (toxicological and pharma-cological) tests, and clinical trials. Proposed therapeutic indication(s), contra-indication(s), and adverse reactions, and the recommended dosing regimen or posology must also be included.[25]

The documents and information concerning the results of the pharmaceutical and pre-clinical tests and the clinical trials must be accompanied by detailed summaries in

---

22. An example of an SmPC is provided at Appendix 2.
23. CHMP Guideline on the environmental risk assessment of medicinal products for human use (EMA/CHMP/SWP/4447/00) – Corr 2, January 2015; *see also* Questions and answers on CHMP Guideline on the Environmental Risk Assessment of Medicinal Products for Human Use (EMA/CHMP/SWP/44609/2010), Rev. 1 June 2016.
24. *See* Title IX, Directive 2001/83/EC.
25. Article 8(3) of Directive 2001/83/EC.

accordance with Article 12 of Directive 2001/83/EC. Specifically, the summaries must be supported by the relevant scientific literature and approved by an expert.

According to Article 10(1) of Directive 2001/83/EC, the applicant is not required to provide the results of pre-clinical and clinical tests for applications for generic products, where the data exclusivity period of the reference product has expired (for a detailed explanation *see* Chapter 13 (Abridged Procedure)). Article 10(4) provides that where a biological medicinal product is similar to a reference biological product, results of appropriate tests and trials (as required by the Annex to Directive 2001/83/EC and related detailed guidelines) must be included in the application dossier. The CHMP has issued guidance for the requirements for similar biological medicinal products.[26]

[B] Presentation of the Dossier: CTDoc

Volume 2B of the Notice to Applicants is solely concerned with the presentation of the application dossier.

The CTDoc is an internationally agreed format for the preparation and presentation of MA applications submitted to regulatory authorities in the ICH territories (Europe, Japan, the US) and other non-ICH territories including Australia, Canada, and Switzerland. It was first published as a separate document in 1998; the final CTDoc was completed in November 2000. Annex I of Directive 2001/83/EC sets forth all the scientific, technical, and legal requirements for implementation of the CTDoc format,[27] and in July 2003, CTDoc requirements became mandatory for MA applications in all ICH territories. The CTDoc is intended to save time and resources and to facilitate regulatory review and communication, and to this end, in November 2005, the ICH steering committee adopted a new modification for ICH Guidelines to ensure that the numbering systems are consistent, logical, and clear in order to facilitate ease of cross-referencing.

The CTDoc is applicable to all types of MA applications, irrespective of the procedure, type of application, or type of medicinal product (e.g., stand-alone or generic products). The type of medicinal product for which the application is submitted determines the level of detail in the application. The amount of detail varies based on whether the product is:

- standard;
- specific (e.g., for a medicinal product containing drug substances of well-established medicinal use);
- biological product;
- advanced therapy medicinal product.

---

26. Guideline on similar biological medicinal products (CHMP/437/04) Rev 1, October 2014 and other related, more specific, guidelines. *See also* Chapter 15 (biopharmaceuticals).
27. Notice to Applicants, vol. 2B, Medicinal products for human use, presentation and format of the dossier, CTDoc, edn May 2008.

The CTDoc does not give information about the content of a dossier, and it does not indicate which studies and data are required for successful approval.

The CTDoc requirements are divided into five modules as follows:

(1) Module 1: Specific administrative and prescribing information (such as the application form, SmPC, labelling and package leaflet, information about experts, environmental risk assessment, information relating to pharmacovigilance, clinical trials, and paediatrics).
(2) Module 2: Quality overall summary, non-clinical and clinical overviews, and summaries.
(3) Module 3: Chemical, pharmaceutical, and biological information (quality).
(4) Module 4: Non-clinical study reports (toxicology studies).
(5) Module 5: Clinical study reports.

Detailed subheadings for each module are specified for all jurisdictions. The contents of Module 1 and certain subheadings of other modules will differ based on national requirements. Following adoption by the US,[28] the EU,[29] and Japan,[30] several other countries, including Canada and Switzerland, adopted the CTDoc. The electronic version (the e-CTD) allows electronic submission of the CTDoc from applicant to regulator. It has a study report structure, guidance on lifecycle management presentation, and standardised style sheets for a uniform table of contents across the ICH countries.

As of July 2015, it became mandatory for companies submitting CP applications to use an electronic application form, with all information submitted via the agency's own electronic submission channel. From January 2016, only the latest version of the electronic application form will be used for all EU procedures, including CP, MRP/DCP, and national procedures.

§5.03   THE CP

[A]   Scope

The CP leads to a European MA that allows the MAH to market its medicinal product throughout the EU. The CP is governed by Regulation (EC) No. 726/2004 and is mandatory for medicinal products that are specified in Annex I to that Regulation.[31] For some medicinal products, use of the CP is optional.[32]

---

28. By the FDA November 2003.
29. The re-edited version was adopted by the CPMP, November 2003: CPMP/ICH/2887/99 rev. 2 Organisation CTDoc.
30. By the Japanese Ministry of Health, Labour and Welfare on 25 May 2004, PFSB/ELD Notification No. 0525003.
31. Article 3(1) Regulation (EC) No. 726/2004.
32. Articles 3(2) and 3(3) Regulation (EC) No. 726/2004.

It is an efficient system in that one SmPC text can be used across the EU (after translation into the various official languages of the Member States) and an MAH can (and indeed, usually must) use a single name for a medicinal product marketed throughout the EU.[33] Applicants should identify at an early stage an invented name that is valid and acceptable throughout the whole EU. In exceptional cases, the Commission may authorise the use of a different invented name in a Member State or States where the invented name has been cancelled, opposed, or objected to on the grounds of trademark law.[34]

One potential disadvantage of the CP is that the fees payable to the EMA to obtain an MA through this procedure are high (unless the intention is to market the product in all EU Member States, the applicant would otherwise only need to pay fees in relation to selected Member States).

[1] Optional Scope

The use of the CP is optional (i.e., applicants can choose whether or not to use it) for:

- medicinal products that contain a new active substance that was not authorised in the Community before 20 May 2004,[35] and that do not fall under the mandatory scope of the Regulation;
- medicinal products that constitute a significant therapeutic, scientific, or technical innovation;
- products for which the granting of an MA through the CP is in the interests of patients' health at EU level;[36] and
- generic medicinal products referring to centrally authorised products.

[2] Mandatory Scope

The CP for obtaining an MA must be used for:

(i) Medicinal products developed by means of one of the following biotechnological processes:
- recombinant DNA technology;
- controlled expression of genes coding for biologically active proteins in prokaryotes and eukaryotes, including transformed mammalian cells;
- hybridoma and monoclonal antibody methods.

(ii) Advanced therapy medicinal products.

(iii) Medicinal products for human use containing a new active substance for which the therapeutic indication is the treatment of:

---

33. Article 6(1) Regulation (EC) No. 726/2004.
34. Notice to Applicants, vol. 2A, Chapter 1, Marketing Authorisation, July 2019, Rev. 11
35. *See* Article 3(2)a Regulation (EC) No. 726/2004.
36. Article 3(2)b Regulation (EC) No. 726/2004.

- acquired immune deficiency syndrome (HIV/AIDs);
- cancer;
- neurodegenerative disorders;
- diabetes;
- auto-immune diseases and other immune dysfunctions;
- viral diseases.

(iv) Medicinal products that are designated as orphan medicinal products.

[B] Submission to the EMA

Applications for the CP are submitted to the EMA in e-CTD format (*see* §5.02[B]) via the e-Submission gateway or web client. Confirmation of the product's eligibility for assessment under the CP must be requested by the applicant prior to submission (providing any necessary justification).

The application is first validated to check that all necessary elements required for scientific evaluation are present. If all is in order, the EMA's main scientific committee for evaluation of human medicines (CHMP) conducts the scientific assessment, and upon receiving the EMA/CHMP's scientific opinion, the Commission considers whether or not to adopt a decision granting an MA (which will cover the entire EU).[37] When the EMA issues a positive opinion in favour of granting an MA, then the Commission will usually accept this and proceed to grant an authorisation, but it has the power to – and occasionally will – refuse the application. The role of the CHMP is described in more detail in the sections below.

Regulation (EC) No. 2309/93 introduced the CP in 1995. Through experience acquired over time, changes to the legislation were necessary and Regulation (EC) No. 726/2004 was subsequently adopted. Regulation (EC) No. 726/2004 repealed Regulation (EC) No. 2309/93 and amended the CP to (a) update and improve the procedure for placing medicinal products on the market within the EU; (b) adapt the procedure to take account of the development of science and technology; (c) adapt the procedure to take into account the future enlargement of the EU; (d) change the name of the European Agency for the Evaluation of Medicinal Products to the EMA; (e) broaden the scope of the CP; (f) clarify changes to the system since the first Regulation came into force; and (g) amend some administrative procedures of the EMA. In addition to its role in managing CP applications, pursuant to Regulation (EC) No. 726/2004, the EMA is responsible for coordinating the scientific resources put at its disposal by the competent authorities of the Member States for the evaluation, supervision, and pharmacovigilance of medicinal products.[38] Within the EMA, the CHMP is responsible for preparing the opinion of the EMA on any question relating to the evaluation of medicinal products for human use.[39] Strict timetables have been established to ensure that the aims of speed and efficiency of assessment are achieved.

---

37. Article 13(1) Regulation (EC) No. 726/2004.
38. Article 55 Regulation (EC) No. 726/2004.
39. Article 56(1)(a) Regulation (EC) No. 726/2004.

[C] Application and Approval Procedure: An Overview

Applicants should give the EMA prior warning of their intent to submit an MA application by filing a pre-submission request form and requesting appointment of a rapporteur. The form should be filed at least seven months prior to the intended submission date of the MA application.

Applications for a centralised MA must be submitted to the EMA.[40] The application must contain specific information and documents.[41] The documents must include a statement that any clinical trials carried out outside the EU meet the ethical requirements of Directive 2001/20/EC. The application must designate a single name for the medicinal product.[42] To market the product under more than one invented name in different Member States, duplicate applications can be made with different names, but there are restrictions in place concerning this practice.[43] The application must also include the fee payable to the Agency for the examination of the application.

In the event that the medicinal product contains or consists of GMOs,[44] the application must be accompanied by certain further particulars, including a copy of the written consent to the deliberate release into the environment of the GMO and an environmental risk assessment.[45] Where the CHMP evaluates an MA application for medicinal products that contain GMOs, it must consult with the relevant GMO competent authorities in applicable Member States set up under Directive 2001/18/EC.[46]

Based on the data contained in the application dossier, the CHMP will assess both the benefit of the product in the proposed indication(s)/patient population(s) and the likely side effects of such treatment, in order to determine the risk/benefit profile of the medicinal product. The CHMP has a maximum of 210 days to reach a final decision.[47] This period may be interrupted (by so-called clock stops) if the CHMP requests supplementary information or gives the applicant the opportunity to answer questions.[48] In addition, both the CHMP and the applicant have the opportunity to request that the applicant provide a verbal explanation of the submitted data at an oral hearing. If the CHMP concludes that the overall benefit/risk profile of the product is positive and that the quality data is robust and satisfactory, it will issue a position opinion in favour of granting an MA. Various sorts of conditions may be imposed on the granted

---

40. Article 4 Regulation (EC) No. 726/2004.
41. Details of the particulars and documents required are contained in Directive 2001/83/EC.
42. Article 6(1) Regulation (EC) No. 726/2004.
43. Article 82(1) Regulation (EC) No. 726/2004; Commission Notice – Handling of duplicate marketing authorisation applications of pharmaceutical products under Article 82(1) of Regulation (EC) No. 726/2004 (2021/C 76/01) 1.
44. GMOs within the meaning of Article 2 of Directive 2001/18/EC.
45. Article 6(2) Regulation (EC) No. 726/2004.
46. Directive on the deliberate release into the environment of GMOs and repealing Council Directive 90/220/EC.
47. Article 6(3) Regulation (EC) No. 726/2004: 150 days if the CHMP accepts a request for an accelerated assessment procedure in respect of a medicinal product of major interest to public health or that is a therapeutic innovation (Article 14(9) Regulation (EC) No. 726/2004).
48. Article 7(c) Regulation (EC) No. 726/2004.

Chapter 5: Obtaining a Marketing Authorisation §5.03[C]

authorisation (as recommended in the CHMP opinion). The final opinion of the CHMP is sent to the Commission for a definitive decision.[49] Usually, the Commission accepts the opinion of the CHMP in its entirety. In the case of a positive opinion, the SmPC and the package leaflet are annexed to it. The issuance of the European MA is recorded in the European Register for medicinal products. The packaging of a medicinal product authorised using the CP must state the European registration number, which commences with 'EU'.[50]

[1]   The CHMP

The CHMP is one of the seven scientific committees of the EMA.[51]
The CHMP is composed of:

- a chairperson, elected by serving CHMP members;
- one member (and an alternate) nominated by each of the twenty-seven EU Member States;[52]
- one member (and an alternate) nominated by each of the EEA- European Free Trade Association (EFTA) states; and
- up to five co-opted members, chosen among experts nominated by Member States or the EMA and recruited, when necessary, to gain additional expertise in a particular scientific area.

The members of the CHMP are responsible for the assessment procedure. They make use of the expertise that is available within their own national regulatory organisations for the preparation of the assessment reports.

[2]   Rapporteur of the CHMP

Where the CHMP is required to scientifically evaluate a medicinal product, it appoints one of its members (or alternate members) to act as 'rapporteur'.[53] The rapporteur is supported by an assessment team and coordinates the work of the EMA, the national competent authorities, and the consultative bodies concerned with the MA. A second CHMP Member is usually appointed as 'co-rapporteur'.

Although an applicant must request the appointment of co-rapporteurs by submitting a pre-submission request form, no consideration is given to any proposals/preferences indicated by the applicant. The appointment of the rapporteur(s) is linked to one of the main tenets of the CHMP, that is, to provide Member States and institutions within the EU with the best possible scientific advice. The CHMP uses objective criteria to determine which rapporteur will be best placed to make any

---

49. Article 9(3) Regulation (EC) No. 726/2004.
50. Article 13(1) Regulation (EC) No. 726/2004.
51. Article 56(1) Regulation (EC) No. 726/2004.
52. Article 61(1) Regulation (EC) No. 726/2004.
53. Article 62(1) Regulation (EC) No. 726/2004.

necessary scientific evaluation and to give the best possible scientific advice. The rapporteur then assembles an assessment team of experts, selected from the EMA-prescribed experts list. The CHMP will notify the applicant of its choice of rapporteurs after the CHMP meeting at which they are appointed.

[3]   CHMP Assessment

CHMP ensures that an assessment opinion on whether or not an MA should be granted is drawn up within 210 days after receipt of a valid application (*see* §5.03[F] for a timetable).[54] To prepare its opinion, the CHMP:

- verifies that the submitted application complies with all requirements;[55]
- examines whether the conditions specified for the granting of an MA have been satisfied;
- may request that an Official Medicines Control Laboratory, or a laboratory that a Member State has designated, test the medicinal product, its starting materials, its intermediate products, and/or other constituents' materials to ensure that the control methods employed by the manufacturer and described in the application are satisfactory;[56]
- may request that an applicant supplement the particulars accompanying the application;[57]
- may request that a Member State forward information to the CHMP showing that a manufacturer or an importer from a third country is able to manufacturer the medicinal product and/or carry out any necessary control tests; and
- may require an applicant to undergo a specific inspection of the manufacturing site of the medicinal product (announced or unannounced).[58]

The assessment timetable is normally punctuated by one or two 'clock-stop' periods to allow the applicant to prepare answers to questions raised by the CHMP (clock-stop periods are agreed by the CHMP, but the first typically lasts from three to six months and the second lasts from one to two months).

The balance between the benefits and risks of a medicine is the key principle guiding a medicine's assessment. A medicine can only be authorised if its benefits outweigh the risks. The final CHMP recommendation is reached by a formal vote, and it is usually adopted by consensus. If a consensus opinion cannot be reached, the CHMP's final recommendation will represent the majority view, with divergent opinions reflected in the assessment report.

---

54. Article 6(3) Regulation (EC) No. 726/2004: 150 days if the CHMP accepts a request for an accelerated assessment procedure in respect of a medicinal product of major interest to public health or that is a therapeutic innovation (Article 14(9) Regulation (EC) No. 726/2004).
55. Article 7(a) Regulation (EC) No. 726/2004.
56. Article 7(b) Regulation (EC) No. 726/2004.
57. Article 7(c) Regulation (EC) No. 726/2004.
58. Article 8(2) Regulation (EC) No. 726/2004.

If the CHMP concludes that an application does not satisfy the criteria for authorisation, the EMA must immediately inform the applicant.[59] An MA must be refused if it appears that, after the submission and consideration of the application dossier, the applicant has not properly or sufficiently demonstrated the quality, safety, or efficacy of a medicinal product.[60] The applicant may (within fifteen days of receipt of the opinion) request that any negative opinion is reconsidered (by the CHMP) in a 're-examination' procedure.[61] The EMA must grant public access to information about refusals and the reasons for them.[62]

[4] Commission Decision

Within fifteen days of the receipt of the opinion (positive or negative) from the CHMP, the Commission prepares a draft of the decision regarding the application.[63] If the draft decision is not in accordance with the opinion, the Commission must annex a detailed explanation of the reasons for the differences.[64] The Commission sends the draft decision to the Standing Committee on Medicinal Products for Human Use, allowing for its scrutiny by EU countries. They have fifteen days to return their linguistic comments and twenty-two days for substantial ones. Once a favourable opinion is reached, the draft decision is adopted via an empowerment procedure. The adoption of the decision should take place within sixty-seven days of the EMA's opinion.[65] The Commission sends the final decision to the EMA.

[5] Withdrawal

When an applicant withdraws its application for an MA before an opinion has been given on the application, the applicant must communicate its reasons for doing so to the EMA. The EMA must make this information publicly accessible, and it must publish the assessment report, if available, after deletion of all commercially confidential information.[66] An applicant may decide to withdraw from the procedure when it receives a strong indication that the opinion to be adopted is likely to be negative.

However, withdrawal can impact the applicant's ability to challenge the outcome of the assessment procedure. Sepracor Pharmaceuticals, unusually, withdrew its application for Lunivia (containing the active ingredient eszopiclone) after obtaining a positive opinion from the CHMP. The reason for the withdrawal before the

---

59. Article 9(1)(a) Regulation (EC) No. 726/2004.
60. Article 12(1) Regulation (EC) No. 726/2004.
61. Article 9(2) Regulation (EC) No. 726/2004; for details see CHMP procedural advice on the re-examination of CHMP opinions (EMEA/CHMP/50745/2005 Rev.1), February 2009.
62. Article 12(3) Regulation (EC) No. 726/2004.
63. Article 10(1) Regulation (EC) No. 726/2004.
64. Ibid.
65. Articles 10(2) and 87(3) Regulation (EC) No. 726/2004.
66. Article 11 Regulation (EC) No. 726/2004.

Commission decision to grant the MA was that the CHMP had also recommended that eszopiclone should not be awarded 'new active substance' status. Without this status (which Sepracor believed it was entitled to) and the consequent period of regulatory data protection from which Lunivia would benefit, Sepracor considered that the commercial viability of launching the product in Europe was compromised. After the withdrawal of the MA application, Sepracor brought an action against the Commission before the General Court to annul the opinion regarding (lack of) new active substance status.[67] This application was held inadmissible for procedural reasons because there was no final, binding decision which could be challenged. Sepracor appealed this decision, but the appeal was dismissed.[68]

[6]   Publication

MAs granted via the CP are published in the Official Journal of the EU. The publication contains:

- the date of authorisation of the MA;
- the registration number under which the MA is registered in the Community Register;
- the INN of the active substance of the medicinal product that is the subject of the MA;
- the pharmaceutical form of the medicinal product;
- any Anatomical Therapeutic Classification (ATC) code given to the medicinal product.[69]

The EMA must publish the CHMP's assessment report on the medicinal product and the reasons for any positive opinion, after deletion of all commercially confidential information.[70] This information is published in the European Public Assessment Report (EPAR) along with a summary written in a manner that is understandable to the public. All such reports and summaries are available on the EMA website.

[D]   Marketing a Medicine

After the Commission has granted an MA under the CP, the MA is valid in all EU Member States. This grant confers the same rights and obligations in each Member State as an MA granted in accordance with the Directive 2001/83/EC procedures.[71] The product may be placed on the market in each of the Member States, subject to any local requirements such as negotiation of a reimbursement price/conditions.

---

67. Sepracor Pharmaceuticals (Ireland) Ltd v. European Commission Case T-275/09.
68. Order of the Court of 14 May 2012 Sepracor Pharmaceuticals (Ireland) Ltd v. European Commission Case C-477/11 P (2012/C 303/10).
69. Article 13(2) Regulation (EC) No. 726/2004.
70. Article 13(3) Regulation (EC) No. 726/2004.
71. Article 13(1) Regulation (EC) No. 726/2004.

Chapter 5: Obtaining a Marketing Authorisation §5.03[E]

The grant of an MA does not necessarily mean that the MAH will place the medicinal product on the market. However, the MAH must take account of the 'sunset clause' provisions, as described in §5.08. The MAH is responsible for the marketing of the product, even if the actual marketing is done via one or more other persons designated to that effect.[72]

The holder of an MA must inform the EMA of any dates of actual marketing of the medicinal product in any of the Member States. The holder of an MA must also inform the EMA two months before any planned interruption to the marketing of the medicinal product in any Member State (whether temporary or permanent).[73]

[E] Special Procedures

[1] Compassionate Use

The CHMP may provide 'compassionate use' opinions regarding the conditions for distribution and use and the groups of patients for which compassionate use of a product (that would otherwise be eligible under the CP but that is currently unauthorised) is permitted.[74] Compassionate use applies to medicinal products that are made available for compassionate reasons for the treatment of patients with a 'chronically or seriously debilitating disease, or whose disease is considered to be life threatening and who cannot be treated satisfactorily by an authorised medicinal product'. The medicinal product must be the subject of either an MA application under the CP or undergoing clinical trials.

[2] Conditional/Exceptional Circumstances Authorisations

It is possible to obtain a conditional authorisation, valid for one year on a renewable basis.[75] The conditional authorisation may be granted subject to conditions, such as an applicant being required to introduce specific procedures, such as safety procedures, or to notify competent authorities of any incident relating to use of the medicinal product. A conditional authorisation of this nature may be granted only for objective reasons.[76] See Chapter 6 for a full explanation, together with details of the requirements and procedure for the grant of MAs under exceptional circumstances, where continuation of the authorisation is likewise linked to annual reassessment of conditions requiring the applicant to fulfil particular measures.

---

72. Article 2 Regulation (EC) No. 726/2004.
73. Article 13(4) Regulation (EC) No. 726/2004.
74. Article 83 Regulation (EC) No. 726/2004.
75. Article 14(7) Regulation (EC) No. 726/2004.
76. Article 14(8) Regulation (EC) No. 726/2004.

[F] Timing of the Process

The basic timetable of 210 days is broken down into stages; the EMA website shows an outline of these.[77] Where a product is of major public interest (particularly in relation to therapeutic innovation), the applicant can request an accelerated assessment procedure[78] by justifying that the medicinal product promotes the interests of major public health through therapeutic innovation. If the CHMP accepts the request, the timetable for assessment is reduced to 150 days. It should be noted that there is no definition of what constitutes major public health interest, but these requests are reviewed on a case-by-case basis. The prevailing medical concerns will be taken into account. For example, a treatment for HIV/AIDS is of major public health interest and in 2009, swine flu was of major public health interest. Applicants must demonstrate that the medicinal product introduces new methods of therapy or improves on existing methods.

[G] Alternatives to the CP

If the applicant is not obliged and does not wish to use the CP (because, for example, MAs are not required in every Member State), the DCP or MRP can be used to gain approval to market a medicinal product in more than one Member State. Both the MRP and DCP are based on the principle of mutual recognition whereby one Member State recognises the MA granted by (or approves the assessment of the medicinal product prepared by) another Member State.

§5.04 MRP

[A] Introduction

The MRP is used when one Member State, the RMS, has already assessed and granted an MA to the applicant.[79] The other Member States involved in the procedure are referred to as CMSs.

This procedure may be used to 'roll-out' a national MA granted in just one Member State to additional countries or, for example, when new Member States join the EU. For instance, when the DCP has been used for authorisation of a product in a selection of Member States, a subsequent MRP can be used to obtain further MAs for the same product in additional Member States. The MRP may be used on multiple occasions to obtain MAs in additional Member States.

---

77. Pre-authorisation guidance | European Medicines Agency (europa.eu)
78. Article 14(a) of Regulation (EC) 726/2004; Guidelines relating to the same are on the EMA website.
79. Article 28(2) Directive 2001/83/EC.

Chapter 5: Obtaining a Marketing Authorisation §5.04[B]

The Coordination group for Mutual Recognition and Decentralised Procedures – Human (CMDh)[80] examines questions relating to MAs of medicinal products in two or more Member States under the MRP or DCP. The RMS is responsible for preparing the initial assessment report, and a CMS is permitted to raise objections to the MA of a medicinal product on the grounds that it poses a 'potential serious risk to public health'. A Commission guideline[81] clarifies the threshold for what may constitute a 'potential serious risk to public health', namely:

- where there is no sound scientific justification to support the claims for efficacy;
- where there is not enough evidence to show that all potential safety issues have been appropriately and adequately addressed;
- where production and quality control mechanisms may be inadequate;
- where the potential risks of the product outweigh the intended benefits of the product (risk/benefit balance);
- where product information is misleading.

A CMS raising objections based on the above conditions must provide an explanation for its refusal to the RMS, other Member States concerned, and the applicant. Objections need to be scientifically justified, taking all factors into account, such as the degree and magnitude of the risks and the potential benefits for the target patient population.

[B] Application Process

The RMS will have already prepared an assessment report prior to issuance of an MA through the national procedure.[82] The assessment report (including SmPC, labelling, and package leaflet) on the medicinal product of the RMS forms the basis for requesting the other CMS(s) to mutually recognise and acknowledge the MA.[83] Once the assessment report has been updated, the applicant submits separate copies of the application and accompanying report to the CMS(s). The consolidated file takes into account updates in the assessment report since the MA was issued under the initial procedure. Unless any CMS has objections on the grounds of a potential serious risk to public health, a CMS must approve the assessment report and authorise the medicinal product for its territory.[84] Once a CMS has received the application and assessment report, it must validate the application within fourteen days in order to verify that it has all the necessary documentation and that fees have been paid. Following validation, the ninety-day MRP procedure starts, and the CMS can raise questions, which the applicant has to answer within the ninety-day procedure period. If agreement is reached within

---

80. See Chapter 2 for an explanation of the role of the CMDh.
81. Guideline on the definition of a potential serious risk to public health in the context of Articles 29(1) and 29(2) of Directive 2001/83/EC – March 2006 (2006/C133/05).
82. Article 28(1) Directive 2001/83/EC.
83. Article 28(4) Directive 2001/83/EC.
84. Articles 28(4) and 29(1) Directive 2001/83/EC.

the ninety-day period, the application procedure is completed, and the applicant submits the local-language SmPC, labelling, and leaflet to each CMS, these documents all being part of the MRP agreement.

Once these are accepted, an MA is issued for the medicinal product in each CMS.[85]

[C]   Dispute Procedure

The MRP often gives rise to disagreements between CMSs that lead to delays in the procedure. All of the CMSs must use their best endeavours to reach an agreement.[86]

However, if the CMSs have not reached an agreement within ninety days of receiving an application and the RMS assessment report, there is a detailed dispute procedure that must be followed.[87]

The contested issues are referred to the CMDh, which coordinates a meeting with all Member States and breakout sessions to discuss the outstanding questions. The applicant may be required to attend these meetings. If consensus is not reached at the level of the CMDh, the RMS refers the matter to the CHMP for arbitration.

The CHMP is provided with a detailed statement of the matters on which the CMSs have been unable to reach an agreement and the reasons for their disagreement.[88] The CHMP formulates an opinion concerning the evaluation of the product.[89] The CHMP should produce an opinion within sixty days, but this period may be extended for an additional ninety days if two or more applications have been made in relation to a particular medicinal product, or if there are particular Community-wide interests involved.

If the CHMP opinion is unfavourable, for example, because the application does not satisfy the criteria for authorisation, or the SmPCs need to be amended, or if it is made subject to conditions, or if an MA is to be revoked, an applicant has a right of appeal based on submission of a written request for re-examination. The request must be submitted to the EMA within fifteen days of receipt of the opinion.[90]

The Commission usually adopts the opinion of the CHMP and makes a final decision on the appeal within sixty days of the request for re-examination. The Member States typically grant the MA, if the Commission decides that the MA should be granted. However, there is still a further right to appeal the decision of the Committee at a plenary meeting of the Standing Committee. If new facts are raised, the Standing Committee can take additional time to consider the new facts and deliver an opinion.[91] This iterative process can continue for some time, which is a disadvantage of this procedure.

---

85. Article 28(4) Directive 2001/83/EC.
86. Article 29(2) Directive 2001/83/EC.
87. Refer to Article 32 Directive 2001/83/EC.
88. Article 29(3) Directive 2001/83/EC.
89. Article 32(1) Directive 2001/83/EC.
90. Article 32(4) Directive 2001/83/EC; CHMP procedural advice on the re-examination of CHMP opinions (EMEA/CHMP/50745/2005 Rev.1), February 2009.
91. Article 34 Directive 2001/83/EC.

[D] Timing of the Process

A flowchart showing the stages of the MRP process can be found on the Heads of Medicines Agencies website.[92]

§5.05 DCP

[A] Introduction

When the applicant has not yet received an MA for its medicinal product in any Member State and wishes to apply for authorisations in two or more territories from the outset, the DCP is used[93] (unless the CP is a compulsory or a chosen option).

The DCP aims to avoid delays resulting from the very slow national phase in some Member States by engaging each of the Member States in which an MA is being sought at the same time, so that the launch of a product is not determined by the lowest common denominator – that is, the slowest Member State. This procedure is therefore available for medicinal products that have not yet received an MA in any Member State at the time of application. As with the MRP,[94] the applicant asks one Member State to act as the RMS. The other Member States in which an application is pending are referred to as the CMSs. The procedure differs slightly depending on whether a Member State or the applicant initiates the DCP, but in all cases, an identical application for MA is submitted simultaneously to the competent authorities of the RMS and of the CMSs. At the end of the procedure, the draft assessment report, SmPC, labelling, and package leaflet, as proposed by the RMS, are approved, if acceptable to all Member States involved.

The CMSs generally adopt the assessment of the RMS and grant the MA for their territory. The MA is only valid in the territories of the CMSs that issue the MA. However, a CMS can object to the authorisation if they have important reasons based on the grounds of a potential serious risk to public health.[95] In such cases, further discussions are held in the CMDh.[96]

In the event that a Member State asserts a 'potential serious risk to public health', all Member States involved in the procedure will, within the CMDh, use their best endeavours to reach agreement on the action to be taken. The applicant is allowed to express a view. If within sixty days from the date that they are notified of the objection, the Member States reach agreement, then the RMS closes the procedure based on that agreement.

---

92. CMDh_081_2007_Rev.3_2020_02_clean.pdf (hma.eu)
93. Articles 28(4) and 29(1) Directive 2001/83/EC.
94. Article 28 Directive 2001/83/EC.
95. Article 29 Directive 2001/83/EC; Guideline on the definition of a potential serious risk to public health in the context of Articles 29(1) and 29(2) of Directive 2001/83/EC – March 2006 (2006/C133/05).
96. Established pursuant to Directive 2004/27/EC, amending Directive 2001/83/EC, and replacing the Mutual Recognition Facilitation Group. *See also* Chapter 2 for background on the CMDh.

[B] Application Process

The applicant usually initiates the procedure by obtaining the agreement of a national competent authority to act as the RMS. There is a 'slot' booking procedure in most Member States, with submission dates being allocated by the competent authority agreeing to act as RMS; these dates may be re-allocated in the event of cancellations or on appeal. On the allocated date, the applicant submits the application to the RMS and the selected CMSs simultaneously. The RMS and CMS validate the application. The RMS assesses the application and prepares a draft assessment report that is submitted to the other CMSs for their consideration and approval.[97] In allowing the other Member States access to the application in this early stage, any potential issues and concerns of Member States can, in theory, be addressed quickly and efficiently.

The SmPC, package leaflet, and product labelling are all part of the DCP agreement.

[C] Dispute Procedure

In the event of disagreements, the DCP has a dispute resolution procedure similar to that of the MRP. If the RMS and CMSs reach divergent opinions, the RMS will refer the disputed issues to the CMDh, and the CMDh representatives of the CMSs will try to resolve the differences. The resolution may require the applicant to make post-procedure commitments, such as additional pharmacovigilance undertakings.

If an agreement still cannot be reached, the issues are referred to the CHMP.[98] The CHMP issues an opinion about whether to grant the MA, and the EMA forwards the opinion to the RMS, CMSs, the MA applicant, and the Commission.[99] The Commission usually adopts the opinion of the CHMP and makes a final decision on the application. The CMSs must grant the MA if the Commission approves the application.[100] The applicant is responsible for submitting high-quality translations of product information to the CMSs within five days following the closure of the procedure. MAs are granted under the national procedure when (and if) the translations are accepted.

[D] Timing of the Procedure

The timeframe for obtaining an MA under the DCP depends on the level of consensus reached among the RMS, CMSs and the applicant, the quality of the application, and the degree of harmonisation among the product characteristics, the dossier, and the assessment report.

---

97. Article 18 Directive 2001/83/EC.
98. Article 30 Directive 2001/83/EC.
99. Article 32(4) Directive 2001/83/EC.
100. Article 34 Directive 2001/83/EC.

§5.06 THE NATIONAL PROCEDURE

[A] Introduction

The national procedure is used for medicinal products that are intended for use only in one Member State and that do not fall under the mandatory scope of the CP. In addition, the national procedure was used previously in the initial phase of the MRP; however, an applicant wishing to obtain MAs in more than one Member State will now use the DCP.

[B] Application Process

Although specific procedures and timescales are different in each Member State, the basic application process consists of the following:

- submission of an MA dossier to the national competent authority;
- a risk/benefit and quality assessment by the competent authority, which must be completed within 210 days from the receipt of the application (this period may be suspended, if deficiency questions are sent to the applicant);
- determination of SmPC, package leaflet, and label text (including layout);
- the grant of the MA;
- the recording of the decision in the register of medicinal products;
- assignment of a product MA number that must be included in the packaging.

Although the requirements governing the MA dossiers to be submitted in the context of applications under national procedures vary slightly among the Member States, the basic principles remain consistent, based on the provisions of Directive 2001/83/EC.

§5.07 SUMMARY AND COMPARISON OF THE FOUR PROCEDURES

[A] The CP

The CP is a quicker, more efficient procedure for obtaining an MA throughout the EU. The time from submission of an MA to granting of an MA is only 210 days, or 150 days if the accelerated procedure is requested and accepted (not including 'clock-stops').[101] The procedural steps are the giving of notice to the EMA, pre-submission meeting, dossier validation, preliminary CHMP assessment report, further questions, oral explanation, final CHMP assessment report, and final Commission decision. In addition, the appeal process by which an applicant can request a re-examination in the

---

101. Articles 6(3) and 14(9) Regulation (EU) No. 726/2004.

event of an unfavourable CHMP opinion occurs within fifteen days of receipt of the opinion.[102]

Another efficiency is that a single SmPC can be used across the EU. The MAH must normally also use a single name for a medicinal product marketed throughout the EU.[103] Applicants identify an invented name that is valid throughout the whole EU at an early stage. In exceptional cases, the Commission may authorise the use of a second, different invented name in a Member State where the invented name has been cancelled, opposed, or objected to on the grounds of trademark law.[104]

The EMA offers a dedicated office to support micro, small- and medium-sized enterprises (MSMEs); this support is open to all companies and enterprises that have SME-status assigned by the EMA. There are also special schemes which provide assistance with the authorisation of particular products. The PRIME scheme for priority medicines aims to enhance support for the development of medicines that target an unmet medical need. It provides enhanced interaction and early dialogue with developers of promising medicines. This proactive support facilitates the generation of robust data on a medicine's benefits and risks, allowing for accelerated assessment of authorisation applications. The focus is on medicines that may offer a major therapeutic advantage over existing treatments or benefit patients without treatment options. To be accepted for the scheme, a medicine has to show its potential to benefit patients with unmet medical needs based on early clinical data.

The EMA also offers an 'adaptive pathways' approach in an effort to improve timely access for patients to new medicines. The adaptive pathways route adopts a scientific concept for medicine development and data generation which allows for early and progressive patient access to a medicine. The approach makes use of the existing EU regulatory framework and is based on three principles:

- iterative development, which either means approval in stages, beginning with a restricted patient population then expanding to wider patient populations, or confirming the benefit-risk balance of a product, following a conditional approval based on early data (using surrogate endpoints) considered predictive of important clinical outcomes;
- gathering evidence through real-life use to supplement clinical trial data; and
- early involvement of patients and health-technology-assessment bodies in discussions on a medicine's development.

This concept applies primarily to treatments in areas of high medical need where it is difficult to collect data via traditional routes and where large clinical trials would unnecessarily expose patients who are unlikely to benefit from the medicine. Medicine

---

102. Article 9(2) Regulation (EU) No. 726/2004; CHMP procedural advice on the re-examination of CHMP opinions (EMEA/CHMP/50745/2005 Rev.1), February 2009
103. Article 6(1) Regulation (EU) No. 726/2004.
104. Notice to Applicants, vol. 2A, Chapter 1, Marketing Authorisation, July 2019, Rev.11, paragraph 2.5; *ibid.*

developers interested in the adaptive pathways approach may submit a proposal to the EMA, following EMA guidance.[105]

National regulatory agencies are also developing their own similar initiatives to support early access to new, innovative medicines for patients, reflecting a fundamental shift in the approach to regulatory decision-making in order to allow patients to benefit from medical and technological advances at the earliest opportunity.

[B]   MRP

The CMS(s) must recognise the MA granted by the RMS within ninety days of receipt of the application and assessment report, unless the CMS(s) find that the medicinal product may present a serious risk to public health.[106,107] The assessment of 'risk to public health' is determined on a case-by-case basis, taking into account the prevailing medical concerns. The MRP timescale is relatively short, though one disadvantage of the MRP is that disagreements between Member States can lead to a delay in the procedure. However, there is a ninety-day appeal process by which an applicant can request a re-examination in the event that the CMSs are unable to reach agreement to grant an MA.[108]

Furthermore, since the applications made pursuant to the MRP are made sequentially, rather than simultaneously, post-marketing data acquired by the applicant can be produced to allay the concerns of the CMS. A disadvantage is that the 'piecemeal' launch of a new medicinal product means that brand recognition across Europe can be difficult to manage or develop, unlike a simultaneous launch as per the CP or DCP, where all marketing efforts, costs, and product awareness can be funnelled into a single campaign. Since the competent authority for any particular Member State can only have capacity and jurisdiction in that Member State, an MA issued by a national authority is only valid in the territory of the Member State that issued the MA.

[C]   The DCP

The DCP can have a commercial advantage over the MRP, since the aim is that the applicant receives MAs for its medicinal product in all the CMSs at approximately the same time and so can launch a new product on the market in several different EU countries simultaneously, subject to national procedures post-grant to obtain reimbursement prices from national health authorities. This can reduce the associated launch costs, and the initial marketing can help to create a strong brand identity and market presence for the product throughout the EU.

---

105. Guidance for companies considering the adaptive pathways approach EMA/527726/2016, 1 August 2016
106. Guideline on the definition of a potential serious risk to public health in the context of Articles 29(1) and 29(2) of Directive 2001/83/EC – March 2006 (2006/C133/05).
107. Article 18 Directive 2001/83/EC.
108. Article 32(4) Directive 2001/83/EC.

One disadvantage is that the RMS is obliged to deal with all CMS objections simultaneously, which may delay the final grant of MA.

Because identical MAs will be issued for the medicinal product concurrently, in theory, this should lead to a significant reduction in the regulatory hurdles for the applicant to first obtain the MA. In addition, the administrative burden on the MAH has been reduced with regard to the variations, extensions, and renewals of the MAs in each Member State.

[D]   The National Procedure

The MA granted as a result of a national procedure is not recognised in any other Member State, and so this procedure is intended only for situations where the product will (initially) be marketed in a single Member State; the relevant medicinal product may not be sold outside the Member State issuing the MA. However, a national procedure can be used in conjunction with a subsequent MRP to obtain an MA in other Member States:

	Advantages	*Disadvantages*
Centralised procedure	– Covers all Member States simultaneously – Rapporteur and co-rapporteur level process; other Member States can comment – 210 days process (accelerated procedure available in certain cases) – Fees can be cost-effective if MAs required in all Member States – Coordination in EMA at one point – Additional regulatory support may be available from the EMA (although some national regulatory agencies have various schemes as well)	– Can be cumbersome and lengthy process if the CHMP raises objections – Cannot 'cherry pick' Member States – that is, select only those Member States where the applicant wishes to market – Translations of SmPC, labelling, and package leaflet required in all community languages – If invented name required, can be difficult to get first choice 'approved' by the EMA; single EU-wide invented name is usually required – Withdrawn applications are published on the EMA website
Mutual Recognition Procedure	– Can select countries, reducing financial and administrative burden – Used for 'repeat use' applications when applicant wishes to add new Member State	– Procedure may vary between territories – Long process (needs national MA, and assessment report from the RMS, before MRP can start) – Can be delays of six months or more if referral made to the CMDh and then, if necessary, arbitration by the CHMP

Chapter 5: Obtaining a Marketing Authorisation §5.08

	Advantages	Disadvantages
Decentralised procedure	– Decision on MA at same time in all applicable Member States – Quicker than MRP – 210 days	
National procedure	– Cheaper option for single Member State application (good for small firms) – No need to translate dossier/product information – Familiar application forms/regulatory agency	– lp;&-2qMA is for one Member State only

§5.08 CONTINUING VALIDITY, RENEWAL, AND TERMINATION OF MAS

Pursuant to the 'sunset clause', an MA ceases to be valid if the medicinal product is not placed on the Community market within three years after authorisation (*see* the next paragraph for details of how this date is interpreted), or if a product previously placed on the market is no longer actually present for three consecutive years.[109] The MA will not invoke the sunset clause, and it will remain valid if at least one presentation of the product is placed on the market ('placed on the community market' means that the medicinal product is marketed in at least one Member State of the Community), and if at least one pack-size of the existing pack-sizes for that presentation is marketed.[110] For the purposes of the sunset clause, a product is 'placed on the market' at the date of release into the distribution chain. This is the date when the product comes out of the control of the MAH.

The three-year period within which the product must be marketed starts on the date that the product can legally be marketed by the MAH, taking into account, for example, the market exclusivity and other protection rules.[111] In exceptional circumstances and on the grounds of public health, the Commission may grant exemptions.[112] 'Exceptional circumstances' are outside the control of the applicant, and exemptions must be 'duly justified'.

An MA is valid for five years from the date of grant.[113] It may be renewed after five years if, when the regulatory authority re-evaluates the product, it finds that the

---

109. Articles 14(4) and 14(5) Regulation (EC) No. 726/2004; Articles 24(4) and 24(5) Directive 2001/83/EC; *see also* 'Sunset Clause Monitoring - Questions and Answers' on http://www.ema.europa.eu.
110. Notice to Applicants, vol. 2A, Chapter 1, Marketing Authorisation, July 2019, Rev.11, paragraph 2.4.2.
111. *See* 'Sunset Clause Monitoring - Questions and Answers' on http://www.ema.europa.eu
112. Article 14(6) Regulation (EC) No. 726/2004; Article 24(6) Directive 2001/83/EC.
113. Article 14(1) Regulation (EC) No. 726/2004; Article 24(1) Directive 2001/83/EC.

benefits still outweigh the risks.[114] After an initial renewal, the MA is valid for an unlimited period, unless the regulatory authority decides that it should be subject to one additional five-year renewal (such decision to be based on justified grounds relating to pharmacovigilance).[115]

§5.09 OBTAINING MA IN THE UK

[A] Introduction

The UK left the EU on 31 January 2020. Although EU law continued to apply after Brexit, the UK Government is steadily sculpting its own regulatory landscape. In the UK, pharmaceutical products are governed primarily by The Human Medicines Regulations 2012, as amended[116] (the 2012 Regulations). The 2012 Regulations retain Directive 2001/83/EC.[117]

As outlined in §5.01[C], under Directive 2001/83/EC, medicinal products can only be placed on the market of a Member State if an MA has been granted by a competent authority of that Member State. The competent authority in the UK is the Medicines and Healthcare products Regulatory Agency (MHRA), which is an executive agency of the Department of Health and Social Care. The end of the post-Brexit transition period also witnessed the end of the EMA's power in the UK, although much of the MHRA's regulatory procedures are built on well-established principles developed by the EMA.

Fundamentally, the retained Directive 2001/83/EC still applies to the MA of medicinal products in the UK, with some minor differences. In this section, we provide an overview of the MA procedure in the UK in so far as it diverges from retained EU law.

[B] Overview of the MA Procedures in the UK

Following the end of the Brexit transition period, centrally authorised products were automatically 'converted' from EU to UK MAs as if the authorisation had been granted on the date of the corresponding EU MA.[118] The conversion process required that MAHs submit essential baseline data to the MHRA using e-CTDoc[119], in addition to other related information, however the time limit for submission expired on 31 December

---

114. Article 14(2) Regulation (EC) No. 726/2004; Article 24(2) Directive 2001/83/EC.
115. Article 14(3) Regulation (EC) No. 726/2004; Article 24(3) Directive 2001/83/EC.
116. The Human Medicines Regulations 2012 (SI 2012/1916), as amended.
117. Directive 2001/83/EC of the European Parliament and of the Council of 6 November 2001 on the Community code relating to medicinal products for human use, as amended.
118. Pursuant to the Human Medicines Regulations (Amendment etc.) (EU Exit) Regulations 2019. Note, however, that this provision only applies to Great Britain (i.e., England, Wales, and Scotland).
119. See §5.02[B] for further information on the presentation of the application dossier, including the CTDoc. The current version of the e-CTDoc can be accessed here: https://esubmission.ema.europa.eu/ectd/.

Chapter 5: Obtaining a Marketing Authorisation §5.09[B]

2021. Following the implementation of the Northern Ireland Protocol, existing EU MAs will remain valid for any product marketed for sale in Northern Ireland. The MHRA issued a guidance note in relation to the conversion of centrally authorised products, 'grandfathering' and managing lifecycle changes.[120]

Notwithstanding the conversion procedure discussed above, with effect from 1 January 2021, all new applications for MA must be submitted to the MHRA through its *Submissions Portal*. These rules apply to any new medicinal product that is to be placed on the UK market, including innovative products, biological medicines, generics, or biosimilar products. The MHRA has the power to make decisions on applications, in addition to managing renewals and variations to existing applications. The application for MA is largely identical to that of the EMA, including the submission of an application dossier,[121] which must now be submitted as an e-CTDoc. The MHRA encourages the use of its pre-submission checklist to ensure that all formalities have been complied with,[122] and it provides a template cover letter to accompany the application. Fees for MA applications vary based on the type of product and the application route.[123]

There are several routes to MA in the UK, differentiated by the intended market and the type of application being made:

(1) *Decentralised and mutual recognition reliance procedure* – applications submitted through this route may rely on MAs granted in EU Member States, however it is not available where authorisation was granted only through national procedures. Applications are submitted via the e-CTDoc accompanied by a cover letter and fee. Successful applications are usually granted within forty-two days (if no concerns are raised) or sixty-seven days (if, for example, further information was requested by the MHRA).

(2) *Unfettered access procedure for MAs approved in Northern Ireland* – applications are submitted via the e-CTDoc and must be submitted as approved for marketing in Northern Ireland. Applications must be accompanied by a cover letter and fee and should be granted within forty-two days (if no concerns are raised) or sixty-seven days (if further information was requested).

(3) *European Commission decisions reliance*[124] – this procedure is only available to applicants with MA approved through the CP, and until 31st December 2023. It allows the MHRA to rely on a decision taken by the Commission. Applications should be submitted upon receipt of a positive opinion from the CHMP, although applications can be submitted at any time after grant of the

---

120. For detailed MHRA guidance on the conversion of EU to UK Marketing Authorisation *see* here: https://www.gov.uk/guidance/converting-centrally-authorised-products-caps-to-uk-marketing-authorisations-mas-grandfathering-and-managing-lifecycle-changes.
121. For a detailed overview of the application dossier *see* §5.02.
122. https://assets.publishing.service.gov.uk/government/uploads/system/uploads/attachment_data/file/368314/Pre-submission_checklist.pdf
123. https://www.gov.uk/government/publications/mhra-fees.
124. The Commission decisions reliance procedure is only available when determining an application for a Great Britain Marketing Authorisation (i.e., England, Scotland, and Wales).

EU MA. Applications are usually granted within forty-two days (if no concerns are raised) or sixty-seven days (if further information was requested).

(4) *The 150-day assessment for national applications for medicines* – high-quality applications for MA can rely on this procedure, and it is available for new active substances, biosimilar products, or existing active substances.[125] The assessment process runs in two phases totalling 150 days, aimed at accelerating the availability of authorised medicinal products in the UK.

(5) *Rolling review* – this is a new route whereby an applicant submits modules of the e-CTDoc incrementally for pre-assessment by the MHRA (as opposed to submitting the whole dossier at once). The purpose of the rolling review is to streamline research and development of novel medicinal products and is available for all new active substances in the UK, Great Britain, and Northern Ireland. Authorisation is usually granted within one hundred days once the final phase of assessment has begun.

(6) *Project Orbis* – oncology products can be submitted concurrently for review and approval by the United Stated Food and Drug Administration (FDA) and several international partners including the MHRA.[126] The aim of Project Orbis is to accelerate patient access to innovative treatments where there may be a benefit over existing medicinal products.

Applications for authorisation can be fast-tracked; however, there must be compelling evidence of public benefit (for example, health emergencies), or where there are shortages of supply as verified by the Department of Health and Social Care. Applications must be made in writing, with a description of the clinical properties of the product, evidence supporting the claims for the proposed indications, and a justification for fast-tracking. No additional fees are applicable for fast-tracked applications.

[C]   Summary

The MHRA is now a stand-alone medicines regulator and is steadily establishing its own MA procedures for various types of medicinal products. The MHRA can, in certain circumstances, rely on or refer to the decisions of other competent authorities. Some applications can be fast-tracked, but there must be a compelling reason and evidence of a public benefit (for example, the COVID-19 pandemic). Time will tell how far the MHRA, and the UK's legislation, will diverge from EU law, and further changes to the MA framework in the UK should be expected.

---

125. There are different application processes for: (i) existing active substances; and (ii) new active substances and biosimilar products. For further guidance *see* https://www.gov.uk/guidance/guidance-on-150-day-assessment-for-national-applications-for-medicines.
126. Other international partners include Australia (through the Therapeutic Goods Administration), Canada (through Health Canada), Singapore (through the Health Sciences Authority), Switzerland (through Swissmedic), and Brazil (through Agência Nacional de Vigilância Sanitária).

§5.10 GUIDELINES/PUBLICATIONS

- Vol. 2A of the Rules Governing Medicinal Products in the European Community, Notice to Applicants (Chapter 1, Rev. 11, July 2019).
- Marketing Authorisation, Notice to Applicants. Volume 2B. Common Technical Document (CTDoc). Edition May 2008.
- Guide to GMP, published in volume 4 of Eudralex; https://health.ec.europa.eu/medicinal-products/eudralex/eudralex-volume-4_en.
- CHMP Guideline on excipients in the dossier for application for marketing authorisation of a medicinal product Ref. EMA/CHMP/QWP/396951/2006, Rev. 2.
- CHMP Guideline on the Environmental Risk Assessment of Medicinal Products for Human Use, EMEA/CHMP/SWP/4447/00 – Corr 2, January 2015.
- Questions and answers on CHMP Guideline on the Environmental Risk Assessment of Medicinal Products for Human Use (EMA/CHMP/SWP/44609/2010), Rev. 1, June 2016
- Guideline on Similar Biological Medicinal Products, CHMP/437/04, Rev 1 October 2014.
- Guideline on the Acceptability of Names for Human Medicinal Products Processed Through the Centralised Procedure, EMA/CHMP/287710/2014– Rev. 6.
- Guideline on the Definition of a Potential Serious Risk to Public Health in the Context of Articles 29(1) and 29(2) of Directive 2001/83/EC – March 2006 (2006/C133/05).
- List of Standard Terms, published online by the EDQM.
- Procedural advice on publication of information on negative opinions and refusal of Marketing Authorisation Applications for Human Medicinal Products EMA/599941/2012, May 2013.
- Guideline on the readability of the labelling and package leaflet of medicinal product for human use, revision 1 (12 January 2009).
- Operational procedure on Handling of 'Consultation with target patient groups' on Package Leaflets (PL) for Centrally Authorised Products for Human Use Doc. Ref. EMEA/277378/2005, 20 October 2005.
- Commission Notice Handling of duplicate marketing authorisation applications of pharmaceutical products under Article 82(1) of Regulation (EC) No. 726/2004 (2021/C 76/01).
- CHMP procedural advice on the re-examination of CHMP opinions (EMEA/CHMP/50745/2005 Rev.1), February 2009.
- Guidance for companies considering the adaptive pathways approach EMA/527726/2016, 1 August 2016.
- MHRA Guidance: Converting Centrally Authorised Products (CAPs) to UK Marketing Authorisations (MAs), 'grandfathering' and managing lifecycle changes.
- Statutory Guidance: MHRA Fees.
- MHRA Guidance: 150-day assessment for national applications for medicines.

- Sepracor Pharmaceuticals (Ireland) Ltd *v.* European Commission Case T-275/09.
- Sepracor Pharmaceuticals (Ireland) Ltd *v.* European Commission Case C-477/11 P (2012/C 303/10).

CHAPTER 6
Conditional Marketing Authorisations

Sally Shorthose & Jonathan Edwards

§6.01 INTRODUCTION

The European Commission (Commission) allows early authorisation for emergency medicines when applications are submitted via the centralised procedure (CP).[1] Conditional Marketing Authorisations (CMAs) were introduced to deal with the length of time it normally takes to bring a product to market, as they may be granted on the basis of less complete data than is normally required. The usual timelines for the development of a medicine are considered too long (on average, ten years) for patients suffering from life-threatening diseases. It was also recognised that new medicines may also be needed at short notice to respond to emergencies, such as bioterrorist attacks or a pandemic.[2] In addition, the CMA procedure is often used in tandem with the procedure for orphan products (medicines for rare diseases).[3]

To address these three perceived needs, alongside Article 14-a of Regulation (EC) No. 726/2004, the Commission proposed Regulation (EC) No. 507/2006. This introduced a new type of Marketing Authorisation (MA) available via the CP, and it was applied immediately to all applications pending at the time of entry into force (29 March 2006), as well as future applications. The Commission has stressed that a balance needs to be drawn between the need to maintain high safety standards while

---

1. *See* Chapter 5, §5.03 for guidance on the Centralised Procedure. *See also* the updated *European Medicines Agency pre-authorisation procedural advice for users of the centralised procedure* (EMA/821278/2015, dated 20 June 2022), which also addresses conditional marketing authorisations (CMAs), available at https://www.ema.europa.eu/en/human-regulatory/marketing-authorisation/pre-authorisation-guidance.
2. During the COVID-19 pandemic, the CMA procedure was used to expedite the approval of safe and effective COVID-19 treatments and vaccines in the EU. *See* further §6.02[C][2] and Chapter 22 (Pandemics and Epidemics).
3. Guidance on the procedure for introducing orphan products is given in Chapter 14.

allowing patients with unmet medical needs to receive treatment earlier during product development. Under Regulation (EC) No. 507/2006, CMAs will be valid for one year (which can be extended) and will legally bind companies to complete studies to confirm the new medicine's safety and effectiveness.[4]

In 2021, the European Medicines Agency (EMA) granted a recommendation for a CMA in respect of thirteen medicines, which secured early access by patients to these new medicines.[5]

§6.02 CRITERIA FOR A CMA

A CMA may be requested by the applicant or proposed by the Committee for Medicinal Products for Human Use (CHMP). Regardless of the source of the request, the applicant will have to present the EMA with a 'letter of intent' setting out its request for a CMA in advance of the MA application (MAA) submission.

The applicant may alternatively present a request for a CMA at the time of the application for an MA. The request will include:

- justification that the medicinal product falls within the scope of the CMA regulation;[6]
- confirmation that the requirements for CMAs are fulfilled;[7] and
- the applicant's proposal for completion of ongoing or new studies or the collection of pharmacovigilance data.

The request may cross-refer to specific parts of the application to support the assertion that it justifies the grant of a CMA. When the EMA has received a request for a CMA, it will inform the Commission, which will review the submitted data and application.[8]

[A] New MAAs

CMAs are only available in relation to new MAAs; they cannot apply to new indications when a normal/full MA has already been granted, whether submitted as part of a variation or extension procedure. Although at first sight this procedure may seem similar to that for the grant of a MA in exceptional circumstances, there are significant differences between those procedures: once an MA is granted as either 'marketing authorisation not subject to specific obligations' or as a 'marketing authorisation under exceptional circumstances', it cannot then be transformed into a CMA. A CMA, however, is a temporary measure designed to give the applicant time to provide

---

4. Further detail may be found here http://www.ema.europa.eu/ema/index.jsp?curl=pages/regulation/q_and_a/q_and_a_detail_000133.jsp&mid=WC0b01ac058066e978
5. *See* EMA 2021 Annual Report at https://www.ema.europa.eu/en/about-us/annual-reports-work-programmes.
6. Article 2 Regulation (EC) No. 507/2006.
7. Article 4 Regulation (EC) No. 507/2006.
8. Article 3 Regulation (EC) No. 507/2006.

Chapter 6: Conditional Marketing Authorisations §6.02[B]

missing data and is intended to be replaced by a full MA once those data are provided. In contrast, neither it is expected, nor it is normally possible to put together a full dossier in respect of an MA granted in exceptional circumstances.

[B] Justification That the Medicinal Product Falls Within the Scope of a CMA

The applicant must demonstrate that the medicinal product will fall within the scope of the criteria set out in the CMA Regulation. The applicant must demonstrate that the medicinal product is for human use, falling under Article 3(1) and (2) of Regulation (EC) No. 726/2004, and also that it belongs to one or more of the following three categories.

[1] Seriously Debilitating Diseases or Life-Threatening Diseases

The applicant must support an assertion that the medicinal product is for treatment of a 'seriously debilitating or life-threatening disease' with objective and quantifiable medical or epidemiological information. 'Life threatening' can be demonstrated on the basis of number of deaths, but demonstrating that a disease is 'seriously debilitating' is a more subjective exercise involving an analysis of patients' day-to-day functioning. Although there are subjective elements to this analysis, as far as possible, these criteria should be set out in objective terms.

To satisfy inclusion into this category, the CHMP must be convinced that debilitation, or a fatal outcome, will be a likely consequence of the disease for which the medicinal product is intended.

The procedure has already been used on occasions for the early authorisation of medicinal products to treat rare diseases:

- Sutent® (sunitinib) was approved for the treatment of renal cell cancer (cytokine-refractory mRCC), where a high proportion of patients have an advanced stage of the disease at diagnosis and clinical symptoms are infrequent, with about 25% to 40% of cases being discovered incidentally. Cancer causes over 100,000 deaths per year, with a five-year survival rate from 0% to 13%. The CMA was based on data from two Phase 2 open-label studies involving 169 advanced kidney cancer patients for whom standard therapies had failed. Sutent-treated patients experienced an objective response rate of 38% in the confirmatory study and 36.5% in the supportive study. Moreover, Sutent's side effects were generally moderate. In clinical trials, the most common treatment-related side effects (experienced by at least 20% of patients) included fatigue; gastrointestinal disorders such as diarrhoea, nausea, stomatitis, dyspepsia, and vomiting; skin discolouration; loss of taste; and anorexia. The MA was switched from conditional to full approval on 11 January 2007 after the results of further clinical trials and clinical experience became available.

- Diacomit® (stiripentol) was approved for the adjunctive therapy for refractory generalised tonic-clonic seizures in patients with severe myoclonic epilepsy in infancy. This is a very rare type of epilepsy, which is also known as Dravet's syndrome. This was approved conditionally as it was superior to a placebo in controlling seizures, and the safety profile was considered acceptable. The clinical study was in sixty-five children aged between three and eighteen years of age, as well as additional data regarding a total of 200 patients having taken the medicinal product. In 2014, CHMP concluded that Diacomit had shown its effectiveness in severe myoclonic epilepsy in infancy (SMEI), albeit in studies limited and did not last as long as the Committee expected. It decided that Diacomit's benefits were greater than its risks and recommended that it be given an MA. As the company has supplied the additional information necessary, the authorisation has been switched from conditional to full approval.
- In 2014, a CMA for BOSULIF® (bosutinib) was granted for the treatment of adult patients with chronic phase (CP), accelerated phase (AP), and blast phase (BP) Philadelphia chromosome positive chronic myelogenous leukaemia (Ph+ CML) previously treated with one or more tyrosine kinase inhibitor(s) (TKIs) and for whom imatinib, nilotinib, and dasatinib are not considered appropriate treatment options. The Commission decision was based on data from Study 200, a global, single-arm, open-label, multi-cohort, Phase 1/2 study of BOSULIF in more than 500 patients with Ph+ CML who had previously been treated with at least one TKI. The study included separate cohorts for patients with chronic, accelerated, and blast phase disease. Data on fifty-two patients were considered as main evidence for the CMAs, as these patients were identified as having an unmet medical need because other TKIs were not considered appropriate treatment options for them due to disease resistance or the risk of severe side effects. The supply of further additional information is required before authorisation will be switched from conditional to full approval.

More recently in 2021, CMAs were granted for among others:

- Abecma® (idecabtagene vicleucel) for the treatment of adults with multiple myeloma when the cancer has relapsed and has not responded to treatment. It is used in adults who have received at least three prior therapies, including an immunomodulatory agent, a proteasome inhibitor, and an anti-CD38 antibody and whose disease has worsened since the last treatment. Abecma® is a type gene therapy. Multiple myeloma is rare, and Abecma® was designated an orphan medicine on 20 April 2017;
- Nexpovio® (Selinexor) for the treatment of adults with multiple myeloma and who have received at least four previous treatments and whose disease has worsened since the last treatment. Nexpovio® is used together with another medicine, dexamethasone; and

– Pemazyre® (pemigatinib) for the treatment of adults with cholangiocarcinoma (biliary tract cancer or cancer of the bile ducts) when the cancer cells have an abnormal form of a receptor (target) called FGFR2 on their surface. Pemazyre® is used when the cancer has spread to other parts of the body or cannot be removed by surgery and has worsened after previous treatment with at least one cancer medicine. Cholangiocarcinoma is rare, and Pemazyre® was designated an orphan medicine on 24 August 2018.

[2]   Medicinal Products to Be Used in Emergency Situations

If the applicant is relying on this justification, it must show that the medicinal product is intended for use in an emergency situation that has been recognised by the World Health Organization (WHO) and/or the EU.[9] The applicant must refer within its application to the duly recognised emergency situation by the relevant WHO Resolution or Decision or to the measures adopted by the Commission in the framework of Council and Parliament decisions.

[a]   Influenza Pandemic

An influenza pandemic occurs when a radical change in the influenza virus takes place. There have been three influenza pandemics in the last century. The change is so radical that those affected have no immunity against this new virus. Given the increased mobility of people, as well as conditions of overcrowding, epidemics caused by a newly emerging influenza virus are likely to spread quickly across the globe and risk becoming a pandemic. The Commission has been working with the Health Security Committee and European vaccine manufacturers to ensure that an adequate supply of influenza vaccines in the European Union (EU) can be provided in the shortest possible time in the event of a pandemic. Part of this provision is the ability to obtain conditional approval for vaccines rapidly.

For example, in January 2010, the EMA carried out an assessment on Humenza (pandemic influenza vaccine (h1n1) (split virion, inactivated, adjuvanted)[10] for use as prophylaxis of influenza in an officially-declared pandemic situation. Based on the CHMP review of data on quality, safety, and efficacy, the CHMP considered by majority decision that the risk/benefit balance of Humenza in that situation was favourable and therefore recommended the granting of the CMA.

[b]   Bioterrorism

The terrorist attacks in the United States on 11 September 2001 and, more specifically, the subsequent 'anthrax' scare, brought to the world's attention the threat of deliberate

---

9. Decision of the European Parliament and of the Council No. 1082/2013/EU on serious cross-border threats to health Repealing Decision no. 2119/98/EC.
10. Procedure No. EMEA/H/C/001202.

attacks through the use of biological, chemical, or nuclear agents. The threat of deliberate attacks with the use of biological agents is called bioterrorism. The EU has taken a proactive approach to the issue and reviewed existing systems of protection to minimise the health threats to its citizens. Protective measures need to be taken, notably for the coordination of public health emergency planning throughout the EU, preparedness, and the availability of the appropriate treatments. The EU has been particularly keen to improve coordination between Member States in the evaluation of risks, early warning and intervention, prevention of major accidents involving dangerous substances, and limiting consequences by approaching such occurrences in a consistent manner. International cooperation has been established with partner countries and the WHO to ensure optimal coordination of worldwide preparedness, response, and crisis management strategies regarding potential threats to public health from international biological, chemical, and radio-nuclear terrorism.

The Council of Europe and the Commission have developed a programme laying out the measures to be taken to establish a health expert consultation mechanism; strategies on availability and stocks of serums, vaccines, and antibiotics; and a European network of experts for evaluating, managing, and communicating risks.[11] One of the key actions in the programme was the preparation and dissemination of clinical EU guidelines on biological agents likely to be used in terrorist attacks or threats. Since 2003, this task force has been part of the Commission's Health Threat Unit.

In cooperation with the European pharmaceutical industry, DG Health and Consumer Protection and DG Enterprise have looked into the availability and development of effective vaccines to combat infectious diseases, which might be caused by a deliberate attack. The EMA has developed guidelines for the treatment and prophylaxis of diseases identified as having a major public health impact in the case of an attack.

[c]   COVID-19 Pandemic

On 30 January 2020, the WHO declared the outbreak of COVID-19 a public health emergency of international concern; and on 11 March 2020, it characterized the outbreak as a pandemic. Crucial to combatting the spread of COVID-19, the CMA procedure played an important role in expediting the development and availability of effective medicines and vaccines. In line with EU legislation which foresees the use of CMAs as the fast-track authorisation procedure during public health emergencies, regulators looked to grant CMA as soon as sufficient data became available, with robust safeguards and controls in place post-authorisation.

---

11. *EMA/CHMP Guidance document on use of medicinal products for treatment and prophylaxis of biological agents that might be used as weapons of bioterrorism* (CPMP/4048/01, rev. 6, dated 18 November 2014), available at https://www.ema.europa.eu/en/human-regulatory/overview/public-health-threats/biological-chemical-threats.

The CHMP held medications under a rolling review, meaning clinical trial data was evaluated as soon as it became available. This approach allowed the CHMP to propose developers apply for MA as soon as there was enough evidence.

The EMA assessed all applications for COVID-19 treatments and vaccines in accordance with its usual standards for quality, safety, and efficacy to allow a thorough evaluation of a medicine's benefits and risks but under the minimum timeframe necessary. It granted CMAs for various COVID-19 treatments and vaccines in the interests of public health, and because these medicines addressed unmet medical needs, the benefit of immediate availability of which outweighed the risk of having less comprehensive data available than normally required.

COVID-19 treatments for which the EMA granted CMAs included:

- PAXLOVID™ (PF-07321332 / ritonavir) (CMA granted: 28/01/2022)
- VEKLURY® (remdesivir) (CMA granted: 03/07/2020)

COVID-19 vaccines for which the EMA granted CMAs for included:

- COMIRNATY® (Tozinameran / COVID-19 mRNA Vaccine (nucleoside-modified)) (CMA issued: 21/12/2020)
- Jcovden® (previously COVID-19 Vaccine Janssen) (COVID-19 Vaccine (Ad26.COV2-S [recombinant])) (CMA issued: 11/03/2021)
- NUVAXOVID® (COVID-19 Vaccine (recombinant, adjuvanted)) (CMA issued: 20/12/2021)
- SPIKEVAX® (previously COVID-19 Vaccine Moderna) (elasomeran/COVID-19 mRNA vaccine (nucleoside-modified)) (CMA issued: 06/01/2021)
- VAXZEVRIA™ (previously COVID-19 Vaccine AstraZeneca) (COVID-19 Vaccine (ChAdOx1-S [recombinant])) (CMA issued: 29/01/2021)

See further Chapter 22 (Pandemics and Epidemics) for more on the COVID-19 pandemic.

[3]   Orphan Medicinal Products

CMAs can also be submitted with orphan medical product MAAs, provided that there is a Commission decision on the designation as an orphan medical product. A copy of the relevant decision must be submitted with the request for a CMA.

Sutent, mentioned earlier, was granted orphan drug designation in the EU for both advanced kidney cancer and GIST, two rare types of cancer that affect less than 0.5% of the European population. Whilst the CMA for Sutent to treat cytokine-refractory mRCC was based on data from two Phase 2 open-label studies, the orphan status for GIST was based on data from a Phase 3 study involving 312 patients with imatinib-resistant or intolerant metastatic GIST. The median time to tumour progression was significantly prolonged to 28.9 weeks for Sutent-treated patients versus 5.1 weeks for patients who received a placebo. *See* further the examples of Abecma® and Pemazyre®, as briefly mentioned above at §6.02[B][1].

[C] Requirements for a CMA

Article 4 of Regulation (EC) No. 507/2006 sets out the requirements that the applicant must satisfy for a CMA. In a request for a CMA, the applicant must set out its justification for why and how it has satisfied these criteria. There are four criteria (two negative and two positive):

(1) the risk/benefit balance of the medicinal product must be positive;
(2) it is likely that the applicant will be in a position to provide the comprehensive data set;
(3) unmet clinical needs will be fulfilled; and
(4) the benefit to public health by the availability of a medicinal product outweighs the risks caused by the missing data.

[1] The Risk/Benefit Balance of the Product Is a Positive

The CHMP must satisfy itself that, notwithstanding that comprehensive clinical data relating to the safety and efficacy of the medicinal product have not been supplied, the risk/benefit balance of the product is positive. The risk/benefit balance is defined in Article 1(28a) of Directive 2001/83/EC. The starting point for demonstrating a positive risk/benefit balance would normally be based on comprehensive scientific evidence derived from therapeutic confirmatory trials.[12] The design of clinical studies will be closely controlled to avoid bias with methods of randomisation and blinding. In principle, the same requirements are applicable for products granted CMAs. Therefore, the design and choice of control of the clinical studies used in support of the application could be justified as adequate.

[2] It Is Likely That the Applicant Will Be Able to Provide Comprehensive Data

If it appears that the risk/benefit balance is positive but is based on incomplete or less-than-comprehensive clinical data, then a CMA would be justified. It is expected that comprehensive data will be provided in due course and that ongoing or new studies will be ultimately completed.

The allowance relating to the lack of comprehensive clinical data in a CMA means that all other parts of the application must be significantly free of uncertainty. So, for

---

12. See further *Guideline on the scientific application and the practical arrangements necessary to implement Commission Regulation (EC) No. 507/2006 on the conditional marketing authorisation for medicinal products for human use falling within the scope of Regulation (EC) No 726/2004* (EMA/CHMP/509951/2006, Rev.1, dated 25 February 2016), available at https://www.ema.europa.eu/en/guideline-scientific-application-practical-arrangements-necessary-implement-regulation-ec-no-5072006.

example, comprehensive non-clinical and pharmaceutical data should be available.[13] The applicant must be able, using clinical, non-clinical, and pharmaceutical data, to define adequately and appropriately the safety profile of the medicinal product, thereby justifying a positive risk/benefit analysis.

The Commission Guideline on the Scientific Application and Practical Arrangements Necessary to Implement Commission Regulation (EC) No. 507/2006 on the CMA for Medicinal Products for Human Use Falling within the Scope of Regulation (EC) No. 726/2004 (the Guidelines) suggests that for each ongoing and new study produced by the applicant as part of the CMA application or ongoing application for a full MA, the applicant must provide a short description/study synopsis. The style and quantity of information will depend on the type of study undertaken but is likely to include:

- a title;
- an introduction (rationale for the study);
- treatments (specific drugs, doses, and procedures);
- patient population and the number of patients to be included;
- level and method of blinding/masking;
- type of controls (e.g., placebo, no treatment, active drug, dose response) and study configuration;
- method of assignment to treatment (randomisation, stratification);
- sequence and duration of all study periods, including pre-randomisation and post-treatment periods, therapy withdrawal periods, and single and double-lined treatment periods;
- primary and secondary efficacy and safety variables;
- description of main methods for interim and final analysis of efficacy or safety;
- timing and description of important milestones for the study to start, conduct, analysis, and reporting (including contents of interim reports); and, finally
- a discussion about the rationale and feasibility of the study.

[3] Fulfilment of Unmet Medical Needs

Article 4(1)(c) provides that unmet medical needs will need to be fulfilled as a result of the grant of the CMA. Article 4(2) defines 'unmet medical needs' as:

> A condition for which there exists no satisfactory method of diagnosis, prevention or treatment authorised in the Community, or even if such a treatment method exists, in relation to which the medicinal product concerned would be of major therapeutic advantage to those affected.

The interpretation in determining unmet medical needs is taken on a case-by-case basis and, as with the determination of 'seriously debilitating', to the greatest extent possible justifications should be supported by quantifiable medical or epidemiological data.

---

13. Article 4.1 Regulation (EC) No. 507/2002.

Generally, justification will be supported by demonstrating a meaningful improvement of efficacy or clinical safety, thereby reducing the likelihood of onset and the duration of the condition or reducing the number of deaths caused by the disease. The applicant must show that the new product methods are likely to be more successful than anything currently used. Where possible, data secured from well-conducted randomised controlled trials should support this criterion. The aforesaid EMA guidelines provide that the applicant will be expected to provide:

- a critical view of available methods of prevention, medical diagnosis, and treatment highlighting an unmet medical need;
- quantification of the unmet medical need taking into account technical argumentation (e.g., quantifiable medical or epidemiological data); and
- the justification of the extent to which the medicinal product addresses the unmet medical need.

[4]   *The Benefits to Public Health of Immediate Availability Outweigh the Risks Inherent in the Fact That Additional Data Are Still Required*

Article 4(1)(d) provides that the applicant will have to provide a justification to support its claim that the benefits to public health by *immediate* availability of the medicinal product outweigh the risks of launching a product without comprehensive data. As far as possible, this justification must be supported by subjective and quantifiable epidemiological information rather than just clinical data. Any assessment of the risks involved in waiting for the additional data should be quantified as far as possible on objective and quantifiable terms.

The Guidelines provide more specifically that the applicant should include a justification in conjunction with the following issues:

- benefit to public health with immediate availability on the market;
- risks inherent in the fact that additional data are required; and
- how the benefits to the public health in the context of immediate availability outweigh the risks (also taking into account the remaining questions).

[D]   **Specific Obligations**

Article 5 of Regulation (EC) No. 507/2006 provides that the holder of a CMA will complete ongoing studies or conduct new studies in order to support the justification of the final requirements set out in Article 4. These obligations will sometimes involve the collection of additional pharmacovigilance data post-launch of the medicinal product. These obligations will be clearly set out in the CMA and must be complied within an agreed timeframe. These further obligations and the timeframe will be publicly available.

[E] Timeframe

A CMA is initially granted for one year, and it may be renewed annually. If the applicant hopes to renew the CMA, an application for a renewal should be submitted to the EMA not less than six months before the expiry of the current CMA, together with an interim report demonstrating that the holder of this CMA has fulfilled its specific obligations or is at least on track to do so.

The CHMP assesses the application for renewal using the same criteria as it did in determining whether the CMA should be granted initially. It will give its opinion within ninety days following the application, consisting of an initial sixty-day assessment procedure, and, if necessary, an additional thirty-day procedure for the assessment of responses to any outstanding issues.

[F] Amendment to Full MA

Once the holder has the opinion of the CHMP and has satisfied the specific obligations that are set out in Article 5 regarding the carrying out of further studies and the collection of pharmacovigilance data, the CHMP may at any time (not necessarily at the end of the period of grant) give an opinion in favour of granting a full MA in accordance with Article 14(1) of Regulation (EC) No. 726/2004.

§6.03 PROCEDURE

Applicants must use the CP.

[A] Prior to Submission of a CMA

Applicants for a potential CMA may request CHMP scientific advice or protocol assistance, as applicable, on whether a specific medicinal product being developed for a specific therapeutic indication falls within one of the categories set out in Article 2 and fulfils the requirement laid down in Article 4(1)(c) ('unmet medical needs will be fulfilled') of Regulation (EC) No. 507/2006. In addition, the intention to request a CMA and any practical or procedural issues with regard to a potential request for a CMA should be addressed at the pre-submission meeting.

[B] Timing of the Submission and Documentation to Be Supplied

At least seven months before submission, applicants should notify the EMA of their intention to submit an application and include a statement on the intention to request a CMA in accordance with Article 14(7) of the Regulation.

The applicant may present a request for a CMA at the time of the application for MA by indicating so in the appropriate place on the application form and including a justification in module 1.5.5. Such justification should show that the medicinal product falls within the scope of the CMA Regulation (Article 2) and that the requirements for a CMA are fulfilled (Article 4), together with the applicant's proposal for completion of ongoing or new studies or the collection of pharmacovigilance data.

[1] Documents to Be Submitted

[a] General Requirements

The following provides a minimum amount of information to be included:

(a) A chronological list of follow-up measures and specific obligations, submitted grant of MA indicating scope, status, date of submission, and date when issue has been resolved (where applicable).
(b) Summary of product characteristics, Annex II, labelling, and package leaflet (one relevant example).
(c) An interim report on the fulfilment of the specific obligations, including details for each specific obligation. The aim of this report is to inform about the status of the data that is the subject of a specific obligation to provide interim data as appropriate and agreed and to inform about the likelihood that the applicant will be able to provide the data (*see also* §5.02).
(d) A clinical expert statement addressing the current benefit/risk of the product on the basis of periodic safety update report data and safety or efficacy data accumulated since the granting of the MA. In exceptional cases, a non-clinical or quality expert statement may also be required.
(e) Data related to a specific obligation and/or periodic safety update report, where the due date for submission of such data coincides with the renewal application.

Practical details on the presentation of renewal applications are given in the EMA post-authorisation guidance document on the EMA website.[14]

On the occasion of a possible fifth annual renewal of the CMA, Marketing Authorisation holders (MAH) should provide all of the information listed in Annex 2 of the Notice to Applicants 'Guideline on the processing of renewals in the centralised procedure', together with the interim report on the fulfilment of the specific obligations.

---

14. *See European Medicines Agency post-authorisation procedural advice for users of the centralised procedure* (EMEA-H-19984/03, Rev.99, dated 20 June 2022), available at: https://www.ema.europa.eu/en/documents/regulatory-procedural-guideline/european-medicines-agency-post-authorisation-procedural-advice-users-centralised-procedure_en.pdf.

[b] Requirements for the Interim Report on the Specific Obligations

One report should be submitted for the product including all specific obligations. The structure and contents of the interim report will vary depending on the type of study and available data. The purpose of the information to be submitted for each study is to allow an assessment of the fulfilment of the specific obligations, and it should provide sufficient information to allow an assessment of whether such obligations and their timeframes should be retained or modified. In the typical situation where the specific obligations refer to data collected from clinical trials, the following general structure is suggested for interim reporting. It is understood that even for clinical studies, depending, for example, on the design and blinding of the trial, one or more subheadings may not be applicable and other data may be required. Agreement on the key elements of the interim reports should be sought during the assessment procedure. MAHs may seek additional guidance from the rapporteurs about the optimal format of submitting an interim report.

Within the interim report for a product, for each specific obligation consisting of a clinical study, it is recommended to provide the following items:

(a) Title page and synopsis. For each of the ongoing or new studies that is part of a specific obligation, a short description (limited to one page or less) should be provided. The description should address the expected overall study plan and design.
(b) Introduction. Describe the status of development of the study, any issues that are still outstanding or that have a significant impact on the feasibility of the study, expected delays, and so forth.
(c) Accrual. Describe enrolment; accrual over time; accrual by centre, country, and region; accrual by treatment group; information on data availability and follow-up status; and duration of follow-up. Include analyses of issues such as assumptions about accrual, event rates, implications for study power, evaluation of changes in characteristics of enrolled patients over time, conditional power calculations, and implications for timing of final analysis.
(d) Baseline Characteristics. Display baseline variables by treatment group, eligibility. Describe any issues with screening criteria, impact of exclusion criteria, and issues of generalisability.
(e) Adverse Events. Describe adverse events by treatment and severity, at the body system level and at the level of preferred term, and describe the occurrence of serious adverse events.
(f) Study Endpoint Analysis. Describe the expected timing and, to the extent that this can be published based on the protocol and operating procedures, the outcome of interim analyses or of final analyses, or other available data, as appropriate.
(g) Study Conduct and Compliance. Describe treatment compliance, compliance with efficacy and safety assessments, significant changes in the conduct of the

study or planned analyses, important protocol deviations, dropout and missing data, and critical quality assurance and quality control findings.

Final reporting of clinical trials should follow the conventional format of study reports (see ICH Topic E3 Note for guidance on structure and content of clinical study reports, CHMP/ICH/137/95).

[c]   CHMP Assessment and Opinion

The CHMP will assess the renewal application, in order to confirm the benefit/risk balance of the medicinal product and whether the specific obligations or their timeframes need to be retained or modified (as detailed in Annex II).

In order to ensure that medicinal products are not removed from the market except for reasons related to public health, the CMA will remain valid until the Commission reaches a decision based on the renewal assessment procedure. Therefore, following adoption of a positive opinion, the renewal decision will refer to the expiry date of the preceding MA so that the renewed authorisation will be valid for one year from the date of the previous expiry.

Upon receipt of a valid application containing a request for a CMA, the EMA will inform the Commission.

Guidance on the criteria for CMAs is given in Guideline EMA/509951/2006, entitled 'Guideline on the scientific application and practical arrangements necessary to implement Commission Regulation (EC) No. 507/2006 on the conditional marketing authorisation for medicinal products for human use falling within the scope of Regulation (EC) 726/2004' (as referenced above at footnote 11).

[C]   **CHMP Assessment of a Request for a CMA**

The rapporteur, co-rapporteur, and the other CHMP members will assess the justification/data submitted for a CMA as part of the overall assessment of the benefit/risk of the application. The assessment of the justification will be reflected in the relevant assessment reports and in the final CHMP assessment report.

A CMA may be requested by the applicant, as described earlier, or proposed by the CHMP. Therefore, during the scientific assessment, after having consulted with the applicant, the CHMP may also propose a CMA. Normally, the proposal and explanatory reasons will be given to the applicant in the Day 120 list of questions or, exceptionally, later, in the Day 150 joint assessment report and Day 180 list of outstanding issues. The reasons for proposing a CMA will also be detailed in the relevant assessment reports and in the CHMP assessment report.

Upon granting of a CMA, the specific obligations and the timeframe for their completion will be clearly specified in the CMA (Annex II.C to the Commission Decision) and will be made publicly available by the EMA as part of the EPAR, which is published on the EMA website.

[D] Information Included in the Summary of Product Characteristics and Package Leaflet

In order to provide clear information to patients and healthcare professionals on the conditional nature of the authorisations, the summary of the product characteristics and package leaflet will mention that a CMA has been granted subject to certain specific obligations to be reviewed annually.

CMAs are distinct from MAs granted in exceptional circumstances in accordance with Article 14(8) of Regulation (EC) No. 726/2004 (as amended by Regulation (EU) No. 1235/2010). In the case of the CMA, an authorisation is granted before all data are available. The authorisation is not intended, however, to remain conditional indefinitely. Rather, once the missing data are provided, it should be possible to replace it with an MA that is not conditional, that is to say, that is not subject to specific obligations. In contrast, it will normally never be possible to assemble a full dossier in respect of an MA granted in exceptional circumstances.

[E] EMA Timetable

The following timetable will apply:

Day 1	Start of evaluation.
Day 40	Rapporteur's assessment sent to co-rapporteur.
Day 50	Joint rapporteur and co-rapporteur assessment report.
Day 60	First discussion at CHMP: Day 60.→ If no outstanding issues: adoption of CHMP opinion.→ If outstanding issues: adoption of list of outstanding issues + decision on possible oral explanation by the Marketing Authorisation holder.
Day 70	Answers from the Marketing Authorisation holder on outstanding issues.
Day 80	Revised rapporteur and co-rapporteur assessment report.
Day 90	Oral explanation by the Marketing Authorisation holder (if applicable). Adoption of CHMP opinion.

§6.04 MA GRANTED IN EXCEPTIONAL CIRCUMSTANCES

Article 14(8) of Regulation (EC) No. 726/2004 (as amended by Regulation (EU) No. 1235/2010) states that:

> In exceptional circumstances and following consultation with the applicant, the marketing authorisation may be granted subject to certain conditions, in particular concerning the safety of the medicinal product, notification to the competent authorities of any incident relating to its use, and action to be taken. The marketing authorisation may be granted only when the applicant can show that he is unable to provide comprehensive data on the efficacy and safety of the medicinal product

under normal conditions of use, for objective, verifiable reasons and must be based on one of the grounds set out in Annex I to Directive 2001/83/EC, as amended. Continuation of the marketing authorisation shall be linked to the annual reassessment of these conditions.

Directive 2001/83/EC, as amended, Annex I, Part II, on documentation for applications in exceptional circumstances, states that when, as provided for in Article 22, the applicant can show that he or she is unable to provide comprehensive data on the efficacy and safety under normal conditions of use because:

- the indications for which the product in question is intended are encountered so rarely that the applicant cannot reasonably be expected to provide comprehensive evidence; or
- in the present state of scientific knowledge, comprehensive information cannot be provided; or
- it would be contrary to generally accepted principles of medical ethics to collect such information.

An MA may be granted subject to certain specific obligations. The type of obligation is that the applicant shall complete an identified programme of studies within a time period specified by the competent authority, the results of which shall form the basis of a reassessment of the benefit/risk profile. It may be a requirement that the medicinal product in question may be supplied by medical prescription only. In certain cases, it may be administered only under strict medical supervision, possibly in a hospital, and in the case of a radio-pharmaceutical, by an authorised person, and the package leaflet and any medical information shall draw the attention of the medical practitioner to the fact that the particulars available concerning the medicinal product in question are as yet inadequate in certain specified respects.

Document EMA/357981/2005 entitled 'Guideline on procedures for granting of a marketing authorisation under exceptional circumstances pursuant to Article 14(8) of Regulation (EC) No. 726/2004'[15] describes the procedure and gives guidance for the scientific assessment of the grounds and conditions for the granting of an MA under exceptional circumstances. The procedure is applicable to MAAs for medicinal products for human use falling within the scope of Articles 3(1) and 3(2) of Regulation (EC) No. 726/2004. Therefore, such applications must be made using the CP.

§6.05 UNITED KINGDOM

Following the UK's withdrawal from the EU, applicants seeking a CMA are required to submit their applications via a separate and parallel scheme with respect to Great

---

15. Available at https://www.ema.europa.eu/en/documents/regulatory-procedural-guideline/guideline-procedures-granting-marketing-authorisation-under-exceptional-circumstances-pursuant/2004_en.pdf.

Britain.[16] The MHRA has introduced a national CMA procedure for new medicinal products in Great Britain effective from 1 January 2021, and applications via that procedure will cover England, Wales, and Scotland. CMA applications via the CP to the EMA will no longer cover Great Britain but will still cover Northern Ireland.

The new scheme covering Great Britain has the same eligibility criteria as the EU scheme, and it is intended to be a parallel, mirrored procedure. Applicants wishing to submit an application for a CMA should do so to the MHRA. Applications should still contain the same information as if applying to the EMA, including adequate evidence of safety and efficacy.

There is no specific application route when applying to the MHRA for a CMA. Applicants should submit their applications seeking full MA. The MHRA will then determine upon assessment of any applications, whether to approve the application and grant a CMA or whether the risk-benefit ratio is negative and reject the application.

The designation of a product as being eligible for a CMA by the EMA or another jurisdiction may be taken into account by the MHRA, but the final decision on eligibility of the product for the Great Britain scheme will rest with MHRA. CMAs will be valid for one year and will be renewable annually.

With regard to applying for MAs under exceptional circumstances in Great Britain, the MHRA's existing scheme for applications under exceptional circumstances will continue to be available[17] for medicines where comprehensive data cannot be provided because the condition to be treated is rare or because collection of full information is not possible or is unethical. Applications for MAs under exceptional circumstances in Northern Ireland must still be submitted to the EMA. The scheme has the same eligibility criteria as the EU scheme. Approvals will only be granted under this scheme where there are exceptional circumstances and where the applicant can demonstrate that it is not possible to provide comprehensive data on the efficacy and safety under normal conditions of use. The designation of a product as being eligible for an exceptional circumstances scheme by the EMA or another jurisdiction may be taken into account by the MHRA, but the final decision on eligibility of the product for the purposes of Great Britain remains the prerogative of the MHRA.

See Chapter 1 for more on Brexit.

§6.06 GUIDELINES/PUBLICATIONS

- EMA, Guideline on the scientific application and practical arrangements necessary to implement Commission Regulation (EC) No. 507/2006 on conditional Marketing Authorisation for medicinal products for human use falling within the scope of Regulation (EC) No. 726/2004, EMEA/509951/2006.

---

16. See MHRA guidance at https://www.gov.uk/guidance/conditional-marketing-authorisations-exceptional-circumstances-marketing-authorisations-and-national-scientific-advice.
17. The legal basis for this process is Regulation 60 of the Human Medicines Regulations 2012, as amended.

- EMA, Guideline on procedures for granting of a Marketing Authorisation under exceptional circumstances pursuant to Article 14(8) of Regulation (EC) No. 726/2004, EMEA/357981/2005.
- ICH Topic E3, Note for guidance on structure and content of clinical study reports, CHMP/ICH/137/9.
- Further advice http://www.ema.europa.eu/ema/index.jsp?curl = pages/regulation/q_and_a/q_and_a_detail_000133.jsp&mid = WC0b01ac058066e978
- http://www.ema.europa.eu/docs/en_GB/document_library/Scientific_guideline/2016/03/WC500202774.pdf
- https://www.gov.uk/guidance/conditional-marketing-authorisations-exceptional-circumstances-marketing-authorisations-and-national-scientific-advice

CHAPTER 7
Supplementary Protection Certificates
Marta Sznajder & Jonathan Edwards[*]

§7.01 INTRODUCTION

Bringing a new pharmaceutical to market is a time-consuming and costly process. Traditionally, the pharmaceutical industry has looked to patent protection to recover the investment made in research and development. However, the increasing regulation of medicinal products has brought delays in the commercial exploitation of such products. Further, these regulatory hurdles have left insufficient patent protection to compensate for the investment made in developing and bringing that product to market.

Accordingly, after years of pressure from those who bring new pharmaceuticals to market, many countries introduced measures extending the effective term of patent protection for pharmaceuticals. Such measures are in place in the United States (US), Japan, most of Europe and other jurisdictions, such as China, where the patent term extension has been available since June 2021. India currently does not allow the extension of patent terms.

In the European Union (EU), Norway, and Iceland, these 'extension' measures have been achieved through the means of a Supplementary Protection Certificate (SPC) which was introduced through two European Regulations in the 1990s. At the time, some countries within Europe had their own extension measures, and the Regulations sought to provide a degree of harmonisation. Furthermore, the use of Regulations was adopted because the legislative institutions of the EU had no competence over the European Patent Office (EPO), the latter being separate from the EU. Moreover, any extension of the standard twenty-year term provided by Article 63(1) of the European

---

[*] The authors wish to acknowledge *Tasmina Goraya*, the author of the earlier editions of this Chapter.

Patent Convention (EPC) would not have been readily, or sufficiently rapidly, ratified by the members of the EPO to give effect to the SPC regime.

SPCs are neither patent rights nor extensions of patent rights. They are sui generis rights that lie at the interface between the patent and regulatory approval systems. For a limited period of time of generally no more than five years after the expiry of the patent, the SPC protects the active ingredient of a pharmaceutical (or an agrochemical) for which a marketing authorisation (MA) has been granted by conferring the same rights on its holder as those conferred by the patent. As the SPC applies to the active ingredient,[1] it will typically be narrower in scope than the basic patent, which can protect a range of compounds. As explained by the Court of Justice of the European Union (CJEU)[2] in recent case law, the EU legislature intended, in establishing the SPC regime, to protect not all pharmaceutical research giving rise to the grant of a patent and the marketing of a new medicinal product, but to protect research leading to the first placing on the market of an active ingredient or a combination of active ingredients as a medicinal product.[3]

SPCs are currently national rights based on either a national patent or a European Patent designating a particular country[4] and are granted and maintained by the relevant national intellectual property offices that granted the patent. However, the SPC framework in the EU will be amended with the introduction of the Unitary Patent. The implications of the Unitary Patent and the Unified Patent Court (UPC) are discussed further in §7.08.

§7.02 THE LEGISLATION

Two separate types of SPC exist: one for medicinal products and the other for plant protection products.

Regulation (EEC) No. 1768/92 concerning the creation of an SPC for medicinal products (Medicinal Products SPC Regulation)[5] came into force in the European Community (as it was then)[6] on 2 January 1993 and applied in most of the European

---

1. Active substance in the case of agrochemicals.
2. The European Court of Justice (ECJ) was replaced by the Court of Justice of the European Union (CJEU) under the Treaty of Lisbon. Decisions of the ECJ and the CJEU are referred to in this Chapter.
3. Case C-443/17 *Abraxis Bioscience* of 21 March 2019.
4. European patents applications are prosecuted and granted by the EPO. However, Article 2 of the EPC provides that a European patent shall, in each of the contracting states for which it is granted, have the effect of and be subject to the same conditions as a national patent granted by that state, unless otherwise provided in the EPC.
5. Regulation (EEC) No. 1768/92 of 18 June 1992 concerning the creation of an SPC for medicinal products (OJ No. L 182, 2.7.1992, p. 1), as amended by the 1994 Act of Accession (OJ C 241, 29.8.1994, p. 21; OJ No. L 1, 1.1.1995, p. 175), the 2003 Act of Accession (OJ No. L 236, 23.9.2003, p. 33), the 2005 Act of Accession (OJ No. L 157, 21.6.2005, p. 203) and Regulation (EC) No. 1901/2006 of 12 December 2006 on medicinal products for paediatric use (OJ No. L 378, 27.12.2006. p. 1).
6. The European Union (abbreviated to the 'EU') replaced and succeeded the European Community pursuant to the Treaty of Lisbon (OJ C 306, 17.12.2007, p. 1) with effect from 1 January 2009. As European legislation pre-dating the Treaty of Lisbon generally refers to the European

Economic Area (EEA) from 1 July 1994.[7] Liechtenstein became a member of the EEA on 1 May 1995 but did not adopt either the Medicinal Products SPC Regulation or the Plant Protection Products SPC Regulation.[8]

The Plant Protection Products SPC Regulation[9] came into force on 8 February 1997. Although one would not expect this later Regulation to have any bearing on medicinal products, the later measure sought to clarify certain issues relating to interpretation of Medicinal Products SPC Regulation. Recital 17 of the Plant Protection Products SPC Regulation provides:

> Whereas the detailed rules in recitals 12, 13 and 14 and in Articles 3(2), 4, 8(1)(c) and 17(2) of this Regulation are also valid, mutatis mutandis, for the interpretation in particular of recital 9 and Articles 3, 4, 8(1)(c) and 17 of Council Regulation (EEC) No 1768/92.

The Medicinal Products SPC Regulation was amended several times and was eventually repealed and replaced with a codified version, Regulation (EC) No. 469/2009 (SPC Regulation).[10] However, pursuant to Article 22 of the SPC Regulation, references to the Medicinal Products SPC Regulation are to be construed as references to the SPC Regulation and read in accordance with the correction table in Annex II of the later Regulation. Accordingly, the reference to Recital 9 of the Medicinal Products SPC Regulation in Recital 17 of the Plant Protection Products SPC Regulation is now to be read as a reference to Recital 10 of the SPC Regulation.

Recitals 13 and 14 of the Plant Protection SPC Regulation also have direct significance to the scope and validity of an SPC. These provide:

> (12) Whereas all the interests at stake in a sector as complex and sensitive as plant protection must nevertheless be taken into account; whereas, for this purpose, the certificate cannot be granted for a period exceeding five years;
> (13) Whereas the certificate confers the same rights as those conferred by the basic patent; whereas, consequently, where the basic patent covers an active substance and its various derivatives (salts and esters), the certificate confers the same protection;
> (14) Whereas the issue of a certificate for a product consisting of an active substance does not prejudice the issue of other certificates for derivatives

---

Community, references to 'Community' in legislative instruments and case law cited in this Chapter have been left unchanged.

7. On 2 May 1992, Austria, Finland, Iceland, Norway, and Sweden (members of the European Free Trade Association (EFTA) signed an agreement on the EEA with the twelve Member States of the European Community at the time. This agreement entered into force on 1 January 1994 and amended the Medicinal Products SPC Regulation so that it applied to those States. Austria, Finland, and Sweden have since become members of the EU.
8. Liechtenstein has a patent union with Switzerland and is subject to an equivalent patent extension regime but under Swiss law, which is based on the first MA in Switzerland, rather than that in the EU or EEA.
9. Regulation (EC) No. 1610/96 of 23 July 1996 concerning the creation of an SPC for plant protection products (OJ No. L 198, 8.8.96, p. 30) as amended by the 2003 Act of Accession (OJ No. L 236, 23.9.2003, p. 33), the 2005 Act of Accession (OJ No. L 157, 21.6.2005, p. 203).
10. OJ No. L 152/1 of 16 June 2009. The SPC Regulation was amended following the accession of Croatia to the EU on 1 July 2013 (OJ No. L 112/10 of 24 April 2012).

(salts and esters) of the substance, provided that the derivatives are the subject of patents specifically covering them;

An SPC must satisfy the four conditions set out in Article 3 of the SPC Regulation, namely:

> A certificate shall be granted if, in the Member State in which the application referred to in Article 7 is submitted and at the date of that application:
>
> (a) the product is protected by a basic patent in force;
> (b) a valid authorisation to place the product on the market as a medicinal product has been granted in accordance with Directive 2001/83/EC or Directive 2001/82/EC, as appropriate;
> (c) the product has not already been the subject of a certificate;[11]
> (d) the authorisation referred to in (b) is the first authorisation to place the product on the market as a medicinal product.

The interpretation and effect of these requirements are discussed in the remainder of this Chapter.

§7.03 DURATION AND SCOPE

[A] Duration

[1] Basic Term

An SPC cannot be granted for a product unless there is both an MA for that product and a basic patent in force in the Member State in which the SPC is sought.[12] The duration of the SPC is therefore determined by the dates of grant of the MA[13] and filing of the patent.

Article 13 of the SPC Regulation imposes a maximum term on an SPC by reference to the first MA for an active ingredient or combination of active ingredients in the EEA:[14]

> 13(1) The certificate shall take effect at the end of the lawful term of the basic patent for a period equal to the period which elapsed between the date on which the application for a basic patent was lodged and the date of the first authorisation to place the product on the market in the Community, reduced by a period of five years.
>
> 13(2) Notwithstanding paragraph 1, the duration of the certificate may not exceed five years from the date on which it takes effect.

As the basic patent term is generally twenty years from the filing date, Article 13 effectively prescribes that the maximum term of an SPC is the lesser of either: (1) fifteen

---

11. A previous SPC (Article 1(d) of the SPC Regulation).
12. SPC Regulation, Article 3.
13. See §7.07[C][2] for further discussion on what is meant by the date of first authorisation.
14. What is meant by 'first authorisation' is discussed in further detail in §7.07[C][1].

years from the date of first authorisation to place the product in the EU (or EEA) or (2) five years from the date it takes effect (i.e., patent expiry). It also follows from Article 13 that an SPC would have no effective duration where the date of the first MA for the active ingredient in the EU is less than five years after the filing date of the basic patent and so, on its face, there would be no purpose served by granting it. However, the regime allowing extension of SPCs where paediatric trials are carried out has changed this position by allowing the duration of an SPC to be extended by a further six months as discussed below.

Subject to any paediatric extension, the operation of Article 13 of the SPC Regulation also means that, irrespective of the basic patent that is chosen in each Member State and its expiry date, the SPC for that active ingredient has a single last potential expiry date throughout the EU (or EEA as the case may be).[15] However, in practice, different SPCs for the same active ingredient may have shorter expiry dates depending upon the filing date of the basic patents chosen in each Member State.

The expiry of the basic term for an SPC is set out in Article 14 of the SPC Regulation, which provides that an SPC will lapse:

- at the end of the period provided for in Article 13;
- if the SPC holder surrenders it;
- if the relevant annual fee is not paid on time; or
- if and as long as the product covered by the SPC may no longer be placed on the market following the withdrawal of the appropriate authorisation or authorisations to place on the market in accordance with Directive 2001/83/EC or Directive 2001/82/EC. The granting authority can decide on the lapse of the SPC in this situation either of its own motion or at the request of a third party.

[2]   Paediatric Extensions for Medicinal Product SPCs

The Medicinal Products for Paediatric Use Regulation[16] introduced the potential for extending the duration of an SPC by a single six-month period in the cases set out in Article 36 of that Regulation. This is now reflected in Article 13(3) of the SPC Regulation itself.

To obtain such an 'extension of the duration' of an SPC, or an application for one, the applicant must first agree with the competent authority for a paediatric investigation plan (PIP) and then, when applying for the extension, submit the results of all studies conducted in accordance with the plan. It does not matter whether the result is that the product is or is not suitable for paediatric use.[17] Many future SPCs are likely to have the benefit of the paediatric extension since no application for MA for a previously unauthorised medicinal product, or new indication, pharmaceutical form of route of administration for a previously authorised medicinal product is now valid unless such

---

15. Case C-127/00 *Hässle AB v Ratiopharm GmbH*, 11 December 2003
16. Regulation (EC) No. 1901/2006 of 12 December 2006 on medicinal products for paediatric use.
17. Medicinal Products for Paediatric Use Regulation, Article 36(1).

studies are filed with it, unless a general waiver applies or a specific waiver or a deferral has been agreed.

For products not authorised by the centralised procedure, the extension is only available if the product has an MA in all Member States.[18] Moreover, the extension is not permitted where product has been designated as an orphan medicinal product[19] or where applicant is the beneficiary of a one-year extension of the period of regulatory data marketing protection attributable to a new indication where this is a paediatric one.[20]

Since an application for a paediatric extension of the duration of a medicinal product SPC may be filed not only with the application for a product's SPC but also subsequently it can, surprisingly, make sense to apply for an SPC with a zero term or a negative term of less than six months which could subsequently be rendered positive by such an extension of duration. Indeed, the CJEU has confirmed that an SPC can be granted on this basis.[21]

The impact of the paediatric extension on 'negative term' SPCs is discussed further in Chapter 8, §8.03[A][1].

[B]   Scope

SPCs are territorial rights and have effect only in the Member State in which they are granted. The protection conferred by an SPC attaches only to the 'product' as set out in Article 2 of the SPC Regulation:

> Any product protected by a patent in the territory of a Member State and subject, prior to being placed on the market as a medicinal product, to an administrative authorisation procedure as laid down in Directive 2001/83/EC...or Directive 2001/82/EC... may, under the terms and conditions provided for in this Regulation, be subject of a certificate.

The 'product' is defined in Article 1(b) of the SPC Regulation as meaning 'the active ingredient or combination of active ingredients of a medicinal product' and should not be confused with the product specified in the MA. The SPC is granted with respect to the active ingredient or combination of active ingredients in the medicinal product for which MA has been obtained and not to other compounds that fall within the scope of the basic patent. The SPC will apply only to a single product, but it will not extend to a product that has been placed on the market as a medicinal product for human use before obtaining MA in accordance with Directive (EC) 2001/83.[22]

Article 4 of the SPC Regulation specifies that protection extends to the active ingredient and to any use of the active ingredient as a medicinal product which is

---

18. Regulation (EC) 1901/2006, Article 36(3).
19. Regulation (EC) 1901/2006, Article 36(4).
20. Regulation (EC) 1901/2006, Article 36(5).
21. Case C-125/10 Merck Sharp & Dohme Corp v. Deutsche Patent und Markenamt of 8 December 2011.
22. Case C-195/09 *Synthon BV v. Merz Pharma GmbH & Co. KGaA* of 28 July 2011 and Case C-427/09 *Generics (UK) Ltd v. Synaptech Inc* of 28 July 2011.

Chapter 7: Supplementary Protection Certificates   §7.03[B]

authorised before the expiry of the SPC, so protection could extend to an authorisation for a new indication of that active ingredient or a combination of it with other active ingredients.[23]

Whether scope of the SPC Regulation extends to medical devices is addressed in §7.08.

[1]   What Is a 'Product'?

What amounts to a 'product' within the meaning of the SPC Regulation is of critical importance not only to the scope of protection afforded by an SPC but also to its validity. Given the commercial importance of SPCs, it is therefore not surprising that the meaning of 'product' has given rise to a large body of case law over recent years.

In general terms, only one SPC can be granted for one 'product'; however, minor changes to the product such as a new dose or use of a different salt or ester will be protected within the scope of an SPC, unless the changes would give rise to a new active ingredient.[24, 25]

However, the European Court of Justice (ECJ) made clear in *Massachusetts Institute of Technology v. Deutsches Patentamt*[26] that the concept of a 'product' as defined in Article 1(b) must be strictly interpreted to mean 'active substance' or 'active ingredient'. The ECJ stated that in the absence of a definition of 'active ingredient' in Regulation 1768/92 (the SPC Regulation's predecessor), the meaning and scope of the term must be determined by considering the general context in which the term is used and its meaning in everyday language. The term 'active ingredient' was generally accepted in pharmacology not to include substances forming part of a medicinal product that do not have an effect on their own on the human or animal body.

The applicant in *Massachusetts Institute of Technology* had attempted to argue that an earlier authorisation for a particular formulation of the active ingredient was not for the same product because its reformulated version was instead a new product being a 'combination of active ingredients of a medicinal product' in which the other element of the combination was an excipient. The ECJ disagreed, holding that:

> Article 1(b) of [the Regulation] must be interpreted so as not to include in the concept of 'combination of active ingredients of a medicinal product' a combination of two substances, only one of which has therapeutic effects of its own for a specific indication, the other rendering possible a pharmaceutical form of the medicinal product, which is necessary for the first substance for that indication.

---

23. Cases C-31/03 *Pharmacia Italia* of 19 October 2004 and C-442/11 *Novartis AG v. Actavis UK Ltd* of 9 February 2013.
24. *Draco AB's SPC Application* [1996] RPC 417.
25. Explanatory Memorandum of 11 April 1990 to the Proposal for a Council Regulation (EEC) concerning the creation of a supplemental protection certificate for medicinal products (COM(90) 101 final – SYN 225).
26. Case C-431/04 *Massachusetts Institute of Technology v. Deutsches Patentamt* of 4 May 2006.

This reasoning applied even where the new excipient (which did not have therapeutic activity) had improved the toxicological profile of the product to such an extent that it could be authorised for a particular indication for the first time.

This narrow view 'product' was unsuccessfully challenged in *Yissum*[27] by the owner of a patent for a second medical use where the active ingredient, the subject of the basic patent, had already long been authorised for a different use. The ECJ held that where a second medical use is claimed in the basic patent, that use will not form part of the definition of the product. This is hardly surprising as an active ingredient remains the same active ingredient irrespective of the particular indication as an authorised medicinal product for which it is responsible. Similarly, where an authorisation is granted for an impure active ingredient and then granted for a purer version of the same active ingredient, these are treated as the same product since the two products differ only in the proportion of impurity they contain.[28]

Whether adjuvants can be 'active ingredients' or a 'combination of active ingredients of a medicinal product' was considered by the CJEU in *GlaxoSmithKline Biologicals SA*.[29] The CJEU confirmed the decision in *Massachusetts Institute of Technology* that the term 'product' should be interpreted narrowly and held that the term 'active ingredient' did not apply to substances that had no therapeutic effect on their own. The combination of such a substance with an active ingredient did not make the combination a 'combination of active ingredients'. Although an adjuvant enhanced the therapeutic effects, it had no therapeutic effect on its own and cannot be considered as an 'active ingredient' or 'combination of active ingredients'.

The CJEU has considered the scope of Article 1(b) in *Arne Forsgren v. Österreichisches Patentamt*.[30] In this case, the Austrian Supreme Patent and Trade Mark Adjudication Tribunal asked the CJEU to consider whether an SPC could be granted for an active ingredient that was protected by the basic patent (in this case, a protein) where it was covalently bound with other active ingredients in a medicinal product but nonetheless retained its own activity.

The CJEU held that the answer as to whether a substance which was part of a medicinal product is an active ingredient within the meaning of Article 1(b) depended on whether the substance 'has a pharmacological, immunological or metabolic action of its own, independently of any covalent binding with other active ingredients'. Articles 1(b) and 3(a) of the SPC Regulation did not preclude the grant of an SPC where the active ingredient was covalently bound to other active ingredients in a medicinal product. However, the pharmacological, immunological, or metabolic action of the covalently bound substance must be covered by the therapeutic indications of the MA, which appears to be consistent with the ruling in *GlaxoSmithKline Biologicals SA*.

---

27. Case C-202/05 *Yissum Research & Development Company of the Hebrew University of Jerusalem v. Comptroller-General of Patents* of 17 April 2007.
28. Case C-258/99 *BASF v. Bureau voor de Industriele Eigendom* ECJ 10 May 2001, [2002] RPC 9. The reference was under the Plant Protection Products SPC Regulation, but the principle is identical.
29. Case C-210/13 *GlaxoSmithKline Biologicals SA & Another v. Comptroller-General of Patents, Designs and Trade Marks* of 14 November 2013.
30. Case C-631/13 *Arne Forsgren v. Österreichisches Patentamt.of 15 January 2015*.

This view was confirmed in the *Abraxis* case, in which Abraxis applied for an SPC on the basis of the basic patent and the MA granted for nab-paclitaxel, being a combination of nanoparticles of paclitaxel coated with albumin, where the albumin and the paclitaxel are closely linked in such a way that they pass the cell membrane as a single entity. Nab-paclitaxel thus demonstrates greater efficacy than earlier formulations of paclitaxel for the treatment of certain cancerous tumours. Albumin acts as a carrier for paclitaxel and does not have any therapeutic effects of its own. In the CJEU's view, even the alliance of such a carrier with another substance which does have therapeutic effects of its own cannot give rise to a combination of active ingredients within the meaning of Article 1(b) of the SPC Regulation.

The CJEU has provided a judgment on when a product will be protected by a basic patent within the meaning of the SPC Regulation when it is composed of several active ingredients with a combined effect, and where the claims of the basic patent in force specifically relate to that combination, even if the combination of active ingredients composing the medicinal product is not expressly disclosed in the basic patent's claims.[31] In such circumstances, the combination of active ingredients must, in the eyes of the skilled person and in consideration of the prior art as at the priority date of the basic patent, determine that the invention is covered by the scope of the basic patent, and that each of the active ingredients is specifically identifiable in light of all the information disclosed by the basic patent.

Recently the CJEU interpreted Article 1(b) of SPC Regulation in the content of potential use limitations and held that the fact that an active ingredient, or a combination of active ingredients, is used for the purposes of a new therapeutic application does not confer on it the status of a distinct product where the same active ingredient, or the same combination of active ingredients, has been used for the purposes of a different, already known, therapeutic application.[32]

In summary, the CJEU takes a narrow approach to the meaning of the term 'product', which is applied strictly. This has an immediate impact on how pharmaceutical patent claims are drafted, which is discussed in more detail below, and the scope of protection that is conferred by an SPC.

[2] The Distinction Between a 'Product' and a 'Medicinal Product'

The SPC Regulation deliberately distinguishes between a 'medicinal product' and a 'product'. A 'medicinal product' is defined in Article 1(a) of the SPC Regulation as:

> any substance or combination of substances presented for treating or preventing disease in human beings or animals and any substance or combination of substances which may be administered to human beings or animals with a view to making a medical diagnosis or to restoring, correcting or modifying physiological functions in humans or in animals.

---

31. Case C-121/17 *Teva UK Ltd & Ors v. Gilead Sciences*.
32. Case C-673/18 *Santen SAS v. Directeur général de l'Institut national de la propriété industrielle* of 9 July 2020.

In broad terms, the product referred to in the MA granted to the applicant of an SPC will equate with the 'medicinal product' as defined in Article 1(a). The 'product' within the SPC Regulation will be the active ingredient or combination of active ingredients which are part of the medicinal product, provided they are covered by a basic patent.

Numerous unsuccessful attempts (such as those discussed in §7.03[B][1]) have been made to try to avoid the fundamental constraint that this imposes on the availability or duration of an SPC where there has been an earlier MA somewhere in the EU (or EEA or Switzerland)[33] for the same active ingredient or product. Such attempts have all sought to present the earlier authorised version of the 'product' as being different in some way from the 'product' for which an SPC is being sought, despite the active ingredient being the same.

§7.04   THE PROCEDURE FOR SEEKING SPC PROTECTION

[A]   Time Limit

An application for an SPC must be lodged with the patent office of the Member State which granted the basic patent and the MA, unless the Member State designates another authority for the purpose of granting the latter,[34] either:

- within six months of the grant of the first MA effective in a Member State to place the product on the market as a medicinal product; or
- where the authorisation effective in a Member State is granted before the basic patent is granted in such Member State, within six months of grant of the patent.[35]

Thus in order to seek an SPC a patentee must choose in each Member State in which an MA for a medicinal product is granted (a centralised MA having automatic effect in all Member States), a suitable local patent that is in force and that protects the active ingredient of the authorised medicinal product. This patent becomes the 'basic patent'. The active ingredient (or combination of active ingredients) is referred to in the SPC Regulation as the 'product', which is important to distinguish in the terminology of the SPC Regulation from the term 'medicinal product'.

In *Abbot Laboratories' SPC Application*,[36] the UK Intellectual Property Office (UKIPO) held that the six-month period begins on the date of authorisation and not the date on which the authorisation is published. However, the six-month period in respect of MAs granted under the centralised procedure may now start with the date when the applicant was notified of the grant in at least some European countries, such as the UK. The CJEU has ruled on the meaning of date of first authorisation in Article 13(1) of the

---

33. Switzerland is not part of the EU or EEA but has a number of agreements that allow it to be part of the EU's single market.
34. SPC Regulation, Article 9(1).
35. SPC Regulation, Article 7.
36. *Abbot Laboratories' SPC Application* [2004] RPC 20.

SPC Regulation (*see* §7.07[C]). An authorisation to conduct a clinical trial is not an MA.[37]

Pursuant to Article 7(3) and (4) of the SPC Regulation, the application for an extension of the duration may be made when lodging the application for a certificate or when the application for the certificate is pending and the appropriate requirements of Article 8(1)(d) or Article 8(2), respectively, are fulfilled.[38] The application for an extension of the duration of a certificate already granted shall be lodged not later than two years before the expiry of the certificate.

Specific relaxations of the deadline for applying for an SPC have been introduced for each round of enlargement of the EU, by Article 20, to provide for the fact that no SPC application may have been possible in the acceding states within the Article 7 deadline.

The various requirements and constraints set out in Article 3 relate only to the particular Member State in which the application is made. Accordingly, the requirement that the active ingredient is not already the subject of an SPC under Article 3(c) means only that there must not already be an SPC *in that Member State* – it does not matter whether it has been the subject of an SPC in another Member State.

[B] Content of the Application

An applicant for an SPC must provide documents relating to the MA in the Member State giving rise to the right to apply for the SPC as well as the earliest authorisation for the active ingredient in the EU and details of the basic patent.[39] An application for an SPC must contain:

- the name and address of the applicant and the name and address of his/her appointed representative (if one has been appointed);
- the number of the basic patent and the title of the invention;
- the number and date of the local authorisation;
- a copy of the local authorisation in which the product is identified and the summary of the product characteristics; and
- if the market authorisation provided is not the first authorisation for placing the product on the market as a medicinal product: (i) information regarding the identity of the product which was the subject of the first authorisation in the Community, (ii) the legal provision under which that authorisation took place, and (iii) a copy of the notice publishing the authorisation in the appropriate official publication.

It is not necessary to provide a copy of the first MA itself if the patent holder applying for the SPC is not the holder of the local MA and cannot provide a copy. It is

---

37. *British Technology Group Ltd's SPC Application* [1987] RPC 118.
38. Cf. §7.03[A][2].
39. SPC Regulation, Article 8(1).

also not a basis for refusing an SPC as the national authority granting the SPC can obtain a copy from the national authority which granted the MA.[40]

An application for an SPC will be published by the relevant national patent office,[41] and the application will be examined to ensure it meets the requirements of the SPC Regulation.[42] If the application is rejected, the applicant is asked to rectify the irregularity within a specified time, and if these irregularities are not remedied, the application will be rejected. The grant of the SPC is also published.

An SPC can only be applied for once an MA has been secured, after all the investment associated with getting to this stage. It is also apparent from the case law that, unless it has been granted an MA as a medicinal product, a patented product may not give rise to the grant of an SPC.[43] It therefore makes sense, even where the prospects of success are not great, to challenge any refusal to grant one in those national jurisdictions such as Germany, the Netherlands, and the UK, where the national patent offices examine applications for SPCs carefully before deciding whether or not to grant them.

[C]   Conditions for Obtaining an SPC

An SPC can only be granted if, at the date of the application, the following conditions are satisfied:[44]

- the product is protected by a basic patent in force;
- a valid authorisation to place the product on the market as a medicinal product has been granted in accordance with Directive 2001/83/EC or Directive 2001/82/EC, as appropriate. This authorisation must be the first authorisation to place the product on the market as a medicinal product; and
- the product has not already been the subject of a certificate.

The first two conditions are discussed in further detail in §7.07. An SPC cannot be granted to the holder of an SPC for the same product. However, SPCs for the same product may be granted to a different patent holder for a product that is already protected by an SPC.

[D]   Entitlement

The SPC Regulation is silent on who can apply for an SPC. However, an SPC can only be granted to the holder of the basic patent or his/her successor in title.[45] Situations

---

40. Case C-181/95 *Biogen v. SmithKline Beecham Biologicals SA* of 23 January 1997.
41. SPC Regulation, Article 9(2).
42. SPC Regulation, Article 10.
43. Case C-631/13 *Arne Forsgren* of 15 January 2015, paragraph 34.
44. SPC Regulation, Article 3.
45. SPC Regulation, Article 6.

may also arise where the relevant MA holder and the holder of the basic patent are not the same. This situation is discussed further in §7.07[D].

[E] Third-Party Oppositions and Observations

The procedural aspects of prosecuting and granting and SPC application are fairly minimal in the SPC Regulation, but Article 19 specifies:

1. In the absence of procedural provisions in this Regulation, the procedural provisions applicable under national law to the corresponding basic patent shall apply to the certificate, unless the national law lays down special procedural provisions for certificates.
2. Notwithstanding paragraph 1, the procedure for opposition to the granting of a certificate shall be excluded.

The SPC Regulation expressly excludes third parties from opposing the grant of an SPC. However, some Member States allow observations to be made by third parties before granting an SPC.

§7.05 INFRINGEMENT AND INVALIDATION

Provided the product is the active ingredient that falls within the scope of Article 1(b), SPCs provide recourse against infringement in much the same way as the basic patent would.[46] Indeed, Article 5 of the SPC Regulation provides that the SPC confers the same rights as the basic patent, and it is subject to the same limitations and obligations.

Therefore, whether an SPC has been infringed would be determined according to principles that would govern infringement of the basic patent under the national law of the relevant Member State; however, noting that the term 'product' is generally narrowly construed. However, the issue of infringement of SPCs granted for a single product by third parties using combination products was addressed by CJEU in *Novartis AG v. Actavis UK Ltd*,[47] where it was held that:

> Articles 4 and 5 of Regulation No 469/2009 must be interpreted as meaning, where a 'product' consisting of an active ingredient was protected by a basic patent and the holder of that patent was able to rely on the protection conferred by that patent for that 'product' in order to oppose the marketing of a medicinal product containing that active ingredient in combination with one or more other active ingredients, an SPC granted for that 'product' allows its holder, after the basic

---

46. Case C-322/10 *Medeva BV v. Comptroller General of Patents, Designs and Trade Marks* of 24 November 2011; Case C-422/10 *Georgetown University and Others v. Comptroller General of Patents, Designs and Trade Marks* of 24 November 2011; Case C-630/10 *University of Queensland and CSL Ltd v. Comptroller General of Patents, Designs and Trade Marks* of 25 November 2011; Case C-6/11 *Daiichi Sankyo Company v. Comptroller General of Patents, Designs and Trade Marks* of 25 November 2011.
47. Case C-442/11 *Novartis AG v. Actavis UK Ltd*, 9 February 2012.

patent has expired, to oppose the marketing by a third party of a medicinal product containing that product for a use of the 'product', as a medicinal product, which was authorised before that certificate expired.

In other words, the SPC holder has the benefit of enforcing an SPC that covers active ingredient A only against a third party using a 'product' comprising active ingredient A (e.g., a combination product comprising 'A + B', 'A + B + C', 'A + B + C + D' etc.).

The validity of the SPC can be challenged on the same grounds as could be used against the basic patent as well as on the basis that it should not have been granted. Article 15(1) of the SPC Regulation provides that an SPC will be invalid if:

(a) It was granted contrary to Article 3;
(b) The basic patent has lapsed before its lawful term expires; and
(c) the basic patent is revoked or limited to the extent that the product for which the [SPC] was granted would no longer be protected by the claims of the basic patent or, after the basic patent has expired, grounds for revocation exist which would have justified such revocation or limitation.

However, the list of grounds of invalidity in Article 15(1) of the SPC Regulation may not be exhaustive.[48] A third party may also submit an application or bring an action for a declaration of invalidity of an SPC before anybody responsible under national law for the revocation of the basic patent.[49]

§7.06 TRANSITIONAL PROVISIONS

The Medicinal Products SPC Regulation was, on its entry into force in 1993, subject to a wide variety of transitional provisions which differed between Member States for medicinal products that were already on the market. This resulted in SPCs being available to extend protection for already authorised products in some countries but not in others, occasioning significant scope for differences in the effective term of protection for pharmaceuticals between Member States. This problem has now worked its way through the system, even though along the way, it occasioned a considerable body of case law of more general application, notably as to what constituted a 'marketing authorisation for a product' for the purposes of the Regulation.

The accession of Austria, Sweden, and Finland to the EU in 1995 and of further new Member States to the EU in May 2004, January 2007, and July 2013 also entailed the introduction of a range of differing transitional provisions applying to such new Member States. As a result, medicinal products and plant protection products that were already authorised and were the subject of granted patents could, under certain circumstances, provide a basis for SPCs to be secured in such Member States despite applications for such SPCs not complying with the usual time limits set by the SPC Regulation. The first wave of the most recent accessions took place on 1 May 2004, and

---

48. Case C-127/00 *Hässle AB v. Ratiopharm GmbH*, 11 December 2003.
49. SPC Regulation, Article 15(2).

Chapter 7: Supplementary Protection Certificates §7.06

the Act of Accession inserted a new Article 19a in the Medicinal Products SPC Regulation making such provision.[50] Further Amendments to the SPC Regulations followed the accession of Croatia to the EU in 2013.[51] In so far as the transitional provisions had not already been spent before accession (because, for example, they provided for SPCs to be applied for before accession), they can be summarised as follows:

New Member State	Transitional SPC Provisions under Accession Treaty for Medicinal Products or Plant Protection Products Authorised before Accession on 1 May 2004
Cyprus	First authorisation before 1 May 2004; application lodged within six months of first market authorisation unless precedes grant of basic patent, when application lodged within six months of date of patent grant.
Czech Republic	First authorisation after 1 November 2003; application lodged within six months of first market authorisation. Other transitional provisions spent before accession.
Estonia	First authorisation before 1 May 2004; application lodged within six months of first market authorisation.
Hungary	First authorisation after 1 January 2000; application lodged within six months of 1 May 2004.
Latvia	First authorisation before 1 May 2004; application lodged within six months of 1 May 2004.
Lithuania	First authorisation before 1 May 2004 and basic patent applied for after 1 January 1994; application lodged within six months of 1 May 2004.
Malta	First authorisation before 1 May 2004; application lodged within six months of 1 May 2004.
Poland	First authorisation after 1 January 2000; application lodged within six months of 1 May 2004.
Slovakia	First authorisation after 1 January 2000; application lodged within six months of 1 July 2002. (Transitional provisions spent before accession)
Slovenia	First authorisation before 1 May 2004, application lodged within six months of 1 May 2004.

---

50. Act concerning the conditions of accession of the Czech Republic, the Republic of Estonia, the Republic of Cyprus, the Republic of Latvia, the Republic of Lithuania, the Republic of Hungary, the Republic of Malta, the Republic of Poland, the Republic of Slovenia and the Slovak Republic, and the adjustment to the Treaties on which the EU is founded (OJ L 236, 23.9.2003, p. 33).
51. Treaty of Accession of Croatia (2012) (OJ L 112, 24.4.2012, p. 10).

The variations between these provisions meant that a product authorised in several new Member States before 1 May 2004 could be eligible for an SPC in one such Member State but not in another.

A similar issue arose on the accession of Bulgaria and Romania, which took place on 1 January 2007, with the following transitional provisions:[52]

New Member State	Transitional SPC Provisions under Accession Treaty for Medicinal Products or Plant Protection Products Authorised before Accession on 1 January 2007
Bulgaria	First authorisation after 1 January 2000; application lodged within six months of date of accession.
Romania	First authorisation after 1 January 2000; application lodged within six months of date of accession. In cases where the period provided for by Article 7(1) has expired, the possibility of applying for a certificate shall be open for six months after date of accession.

The latest round of amendments followed the accession of Croatia to the EU on 1 July 2013:

New Member State	Transitional SPC Provisions in the SPC Regulation following the Treaty of Accession of Croatia (2012)
Croatia	First authorisation after 1 January 2003; application lodged within six months from date of accession.

These provisions are now incorporated in Articles 20 and 21 of the SPC Regulation. However, in November 2015, the Riigikohus (Supreme Court of Estonia) lodged a reference to the CJEU[53] asking two questions:

> Must Article 21(2) of the [SPC Regulation][54] be interpreted as shortening the duration of a supplementary protection certificate issued in a Member State which was issued under national law before the accession of the State in question to the European Union and whose duration in relation to an active substance, as stated in the supplementary protection certificate, would be longer than 15 years from the time when the first marketing authorisation in the Union was granted for a medicinal product consisting of the active substance or containing it?

---

52. Act of Accession of Bulgaria and Romania (OJ No. L 157, 21.6.2005, p. 203) – *see* the list referred to in Article 19 of the Act of Accession: adaptations to acts adopted by the institutions, Part (1)(II)(1)(a) and (2)(a).
53. Case C-572/15 *F. Hoffmann-La Roche AG v Accord Healthcare OÜ*.
54. Article 21(2) states: 'This Regulation shall apply to supplementary protection certificates granted in accordance with the national legislation of the Czech Republic, Estonia, Cyprus, Latvia, Lithuania, Malta, Poland, Slovenia and Slovakia prior to 1 May 2004 and the national legislation of Romania prior to 1 January 2007.'

If the answer to the first question is in the affirmative, is Article 21(2) of the [SPC Regulation] compatible with EU law, in particular the general principles of EU law on the protection of acquired rights, the principle of the prohibition of retroactive effect of law, and the Charter of Fundamental Rights of the European Union?

The outcome of the reference addressed interesting issues relating to the validity of the SPC Regulation under EU law. The CJEU answered the second of these two questions first, holding that it did not have jurisdiction to rule on the validity of Article 21(2) of the SPC Regulation. The CJEU noted at the outset that Article 267 Treaty on the Functioning of the European Union (TFEU) confers jurisdiction on the CJEU to give preliminary rulings on the interpretation of acts of the institutions, bodies, offices, or agencies of the EU and the validity of those acts. Provisions resulting directly from an Act of Accession, such as article 20(2) of Regulation No. 1768/92,[55] do not constitute acts of institutions and are not therefore open to review. The CJEU held that adjustments, as set out in an Act of Accession, are to be the subject of agreement between the Member States and the applicant State. They do not constitute an act of an institution but are provisions of primary law which may not be suspended, amended, or repealed otherwise than by means of the procedures laid down for the revision of the original Treaties. The CJEU held that any differences in treatment therefore are not arbitrary but rather the consequence of the respective procedures chosen by Member States for the purpose of adoption.

With respect to the first question, the CJEU held that Article 21(2) of the SPC Regulation, as amended, should be interpreted as meaning that it applies to an SPC, relating to a given medicinal product, granted by a Member State prior to its accession to the EU. To the extent that that medicinal product was the subject, within the EEA, of an MA before that granted in the Member State concerned, and, as the case may be, before its accession to the EU, only the first MA must be taken into account for the purposes of determining the duration of validity of the SPC.

§7.07 ISSUES IN RELATION TO SPCs

In recent years, there has been a spate of referrals to the CJEU on the interpretation of the SPC Regulation, and in particular, the conditions required for the grant of an SPC under Article 3. The number of cases is not only an illustration of the commercial value of SPCs but the drafting of the SPC Regulation. A summary of the issues is provided below.

---

55. Which was inserted into the Medicinal Products SPC Regulation by the Act concerning the conditions of accession of the Czech Republic, the Republic of Estonia, the Republic of Cyprus, the Republic of Latvia, the Republic of Lithuania, the Republic of Hungary, the Republic of Malta, the Republic of Poland, the Republic of Slovenia and the Slovak Republic and the adjustments to the Treaties on which the EU is founded. Regulation No 469/2009 consolidated Regulation No 1768/92, so that Article 20(2) became Article 21(2) of the SPC Regulation.

[A] When Is a Product 'Protected by a Basic Patent in Force'?

One of the pre-conditions to the grant of an SPC under Article 3 of the SPC Regulation is that the product must be protected by a 'basic patent'. The term 'basic patent' is defined in Article 1(c) of the SPC Regulation as being 'a patent which protects a product as such, a process to obtain a product or an application of a product, and which is designated by its holder for the purpose of the procedure for the grant of a certificate'. The basic patent must therefore cover at least one of the following: (i) the product as such, (ii) a process manufacturing the product, or (iii) a use of the product. A product is an active ingredient or combination of active ingredients of the medicinal product. Further, where the basic patent only covers a manufacturing process, the SPC will extend only to the 'product' obtained by that process (if products by process are permitted under the relevant national law).

[1] Construction of Patent Claims

The construction of patent claims is governed by non-EU rules, such as Article 69 of the EPC, Article 1 of the Protocol on the Interpretation of Article 69, and relevant national laws. Article 69 of the EPC specifies that the extent of protection conferred by a European patent extends to the claims only:

(1) The extent of the protection conferred by a European patent or a European patent application shall be determined by the claims. Nevertheless, the description and drawings shall be used to interpret the claims.
(2) For the period up to grant of the European patent, the extent of the protection conferred by the European patent application shall be determined by the claims contained in the application as published. However, the European patent as granted or as amended in opposition, limitation or revocation proceedings shall determine retroactively the protection conferred by the application, in so far as such protection is not thereby extended.

Article 1 of the Protocol on the Interpretation of Article 69 EPC (Protocol on Interpretation) explains that patent protection is determined solely by the claims in light of the description and drawings:

Article 69 should not be interpreted as meaning that the extent of the protection conferred by a European patent is to be understood as that defined by the strict, literal meaning of the wording used in the claims, the description and drawings being employed only for the purpose of resolving an ambiguity found in the claims. Nor should it be taken to mean that the claims serve only as a guideline and that the actual protection conferred may extend to what, from a consideration of the description and drawings by a person skilled in the art, the patent proprietor has contemplated. On the contrary, it is to be interpreted as defining a position between these extremes which combines a fair protection for the patent proprietor with a reasonable degree of legal certainty for third parties.

However, Recital 7 of the SPC Regulation specifies that one of the objectives of the legislation is to 'prevent the heterogeneous development of national laws leading to further disparities which would be likely to create obstacles to the free movement of medicinal products within the Community'. This disparity was recognised by the ECJ in *Farmitalia*,[56] but the ECJ provided a circular answer stating that in the absence of EU harmonisation, the extent of patent protection could only be determined on the basis of non-EU rules. As there were no harmonising laws on the construction of patents in the EU, the question of the scope of patent claims was left to national law. This can clearly give rise to differences in the interpretation of patent claims in different Member States. Indeed, the English Court of Appeal in *Medeva*[57] commented that the test formulated in *Farmitalia* was insufficiently clear in jurisdictions that admitted more than one answer, as in the UK.

[2]   Combination Products

In the UK, a patent for a combination of active ingredients has been held not to qualify as a basic patent where the product to be protected by SPC was one component only of the combination, and the medicinal product was formulated as a single version of the single component product, even though this was commonly administered along with other components of the patented combination.[58]

However, it is important to note that a patent will not necessarily 'protect' the active ingredient, the subject of the MA, in the sense required by the SPC Regulation just because dealings in that active ingredient might infringe the basic patent on some basis (the 'infringement test'). In *Medeva*[59] and *Georgetown University*,[60] the CJEU dismissed the 'infringement test' (i.e., the product would be protected if it infringed the claims of the basic patent), ruling that a 'product is protected by a basic patent in force', as required by Article 3(a) of the SPC Regulation, when the product is 'specified in the wording of the claims of the basic patent' in the claims of that patent. In applying the CJEU's decision in *Medeva*, the English Court of Appeal[61] recognised that the ambit of 'specified' may range from 'expressly naming, through description, necessary implication to reasonable interpretation'. However, the Court concluded that CJEU's decision required some wording indicating that the active ingredients are included in the claims. Otherwise, the CJEU would be imposing the infringement test, which was not the case. The English Court also examined whether including the traditional term 'comprising' could satisfy the CJEU's test and concluded that it would not amount to specifying any other active ingredients in the claim.

---

56. Case C-392/97 *Farmitalia Carlo Erba's SPC Application* of 16 September 1999.
57. *Medeva BV v. Comptroller-General of Patents, Designs and Trade Marks* [2012] R.P.C. 26.
58. *Takeda Chemical Industries Ltd's Applications* [2004] RPC 3.
59. Case C-322/10 *Medeva BV v. The Comptroller General of Patents*.
60. Case C-422/10 *Georgetown University, University of Rochester, Loyola University of Chicago v. Comptroller-General of Patents, Designs and Trade Marks*.
61. *Medeva BV v. The Comptroller General of Patents* [2012] EWCA Civ 523.

Following its decision in *Medeva*, the CJEU also held in *Yeda*[62] that if a patent claims a product comprising two active ingredients but does not make any claim in relation to one of those active ingredients individually, the grant of an SPC will be precluded. In other words, Article 3(a) precludes the grant of an SPC where the active ingredient specified in the SPC application, even though identified in the wording of the claims of the basic patent as an active ingredient forming part of a combination in conjunction with another active ingredient, is not the subject of any claim relating to that active ingredient alone.

However, in *University of Queensland*[63] and *Daiichi Sankyo Company*,[64] the Court considered its ruling in *Medeva* concluded that Article 3(a) of the SPC Regulation precludes the grant of an SPC unless the active ingredients are 'identified in the wording of the claims of the basic patent relied on in support of the SPC application'.

This issue was further addressed by the English High Court in *Novartis Pharmaceuticals UK Limited v. Medimmune Limited and Medical Research Council*.[65] Novartis contended that ranibizumab was not protected by the basic patent within the meaning of Article 3(a) of the SPC Regulation as it was neither specified nor identified in the wording of the claims of the basic patent as the product deriving from the claimed process.

Having considered *Medeva* and the related case law, the English High Court held that ranibizumab was not 'identified' within the wording of the relevant claim as required by the ruling in *University of Queensland*. In its judgment, the Court considered that *University of Queensland* decision laid down a narrower rule in respect of process claims than *Medeva* and that the test 'requires the product to be identified in the wording of the claim as the product deriving from the process in question. Furthermore, [the CJEU in University of Queensland] says that it is irrelevant whether or not it was possible to obtain the product directly by means of that product, which points away from an infringement-type test'. The claim in question identified the product of the method as 'a molecule with binding specificity for a particular target', which could cover potentially millions of different molecules of various kinds.

Although not specifically addressing the English High Court's question relating to the criteria to be applied when deciding whether a product is protected by a basic patent in force under Article 3(a) of the SPC Regulation the CJEU in *Actavis Group PTC EHF and Actavis UK Ltd v. Sanofi*[66] considered that the 'basic objective of [the SPC Regulation] is to compensate for the delay to the marketing of what constitutes the *core inventive advance* that is the subject of the basic patent' (emphasis added).

---

62. Case *C-Yeda Research and Development Company Ltd and Aventis Holding Inc v. Comptroller General of Patents*, decision of the CJEU 9 December 2011.
63. Case C-630/10 *University of Queensland, CSL Ltd v. Comptroller-General of Patents, Designs and Trade Marks*.
64. Case C-6/11 *Daiichi Sankyo v. Comptroller General of Patents. Designs and Trade Marks*.
65. *Novartis Pharmaceuticals UK Limited v. Medimmune Limited and Medical Research Council* [2012] EWHC 181 (Pat), 3 February 2012.
66. Case C-443/12 *Actavis Group PTC EHF and Actavis UK Ltd v. Sanofi* of 13 December 2013.

Chapter 7: Supplementary Protection Certificates §7.07[A]

CJEU's alternate use of 'specified' and 'identified' has led to some uncertainty and the national courts and have sought further clarity on this issue in respect of functional specifications (*see Functional Specifications* below).

With respect to Article 3(b), the SPC is intended to protect the 'product', as specified in the claims of the basic patent and not the medicinal product. It follows that an SPC can be granted for a product, specified in the claims of the basic patent, where the MA contains not only that combination of active ingredients but also other ingredients.

Therefore, an SPC to product 'A + B' can be granted when the basic patent specifies in the claims 'A + B', and the first MA relied upon for the application may encompass any product containing product 'A + B', be it 'A + B + C', 'A + B + C + D', etc. It does not follow, however, that a patent claim to 'A' alone can found an application for an SPC where the MA is to 'A + B'.[67]

The High Court of England and Wales referred questions to the CJEU in 2018 once more in relation to combination products and the interpretation of Article 3(a).[68] The product concerned was an antiretroviral product indicated for HIV marketed by Gilead under the name TRUVADA. TRUVADA contained two active ingredients: tenofovir disoproxil and emtricitabine, which have a combined therapeutic effect. The High Court referred the following question to the CJEU: 'What are the criteria for deciding whether 'the product is protected by a basic patent in force' in Article 3(a) of Regulation No 469/2009?' Referring to its previous judgment in *Eli Lilly and Company v. Human Genome Sciences Inc*,[69] the CJEU confirmed 'that the rules for determining what is "protected by a basic patent in force" within the meaning of Article 3(a) are those relating to the extent of the invention covered by such a patent, just as is provided, in the case before the Court, in Article 69 of the EPC and the Protocol on the interpretation of that provision, to which section 125 of the UK Patents Act 1977 gives effect in the United Kingdom'.

The CJEU held that a combination product will fall within the scope of Article 3(a) when 'from the point of view of a person skilled in the art and on the basis of the prior art at the filing date or priority date of the basic patent:

- the combination of those active ingredients must necessarily, in the light of the description and drawings of that patent, fall under the invention covered by that patent, and
- each of those active ingredients must be specifically identifiable, in the light of all the information disclosed by that patent'.

This test was subsequently affirmed by the CJEU in 2020,[70] which further ruled that the functional definition of the product in the basic patent did not meet the

---

67. C-518/10 *Yeda Research and Development Company Ltd and Aventis Holdings Inc v. Comptroller General of Patents* decision of the CJEU 9 December 2011.
68. Case C-121/17 *Teva UK Ltd & Ors v. Gilead Sciences Inc*.
69. Case C-493/12.
70. Case C-650/17 *Royalty Pharma Collection Trust v. Deutsches Patent- und Markenamt*.

requirements of Article 3(a) if the approved product was 'developed after the filing or priority date of the basic patent, following an independent inventive step'.

More recently, the Irish Supreme Court referred two questions to the CJEU regarding the eligibility of combination medicinal products for SPC protection, seeking resolution of the uncertainty of the interpretation of Article 3(a):[71]

> (a) For the purpose of the grant of a supplementary protection certificate, and for the validity of that SPC in law, under Article 3(a) of Regulation (EC) No 469/20091 concerning the supplementary protection certificate for medicinal products, does it suffice that the product for which the SPC is granted is expressly identified in the patent claims, and covered by it; or is it necessary for the grant of an SPC that the patent holder, who has been granted a marketing authorisation, also demonstrate novelty or inventiveness or that the product falls within a narrower concept described as the invention covered by the patent?
> (b) If the latter, the invention covered by the patent, what must be established by the patent holder and marketing authorisation holder to obtain a valid SPC?

Where, as in this case, the patent is for a particular drug, ezetimibe, and the claims in the patent teach that the application in human medicine may be for the use of that drug alone or in combination with another drug, here, simvastatin, a drug in the public domain, can an SPC be granted under Article 3(a) of the Regulation only for a product comprising ezetimibe, a monotherapy, or can an SPC also be granted for any or all of the combination products identified in the claims in the patent?

Where a monotherapy, drug A, in this case ezetimibe, is granted an SPC, or any combination therapy is first granted an SPC for drugs A and B as a combination therapy, which are part of the claims in the patent, though only drug A is itself novel and thus patented, with other drugs being already known or in the public domain; is the grant of an SPC limited to the first marketing of either that monotherapy of drug A or that first combination therapy granted an SPC, A + B, so that, following that first grant, there cannot be a second or third grant of an SPC for the monotherapy or any combination therapy apart from that first combination granted an SPC?

If the claims of a patent cover both a single novel molecule and a combination of that molecule with an existing and known drug, perhaps in the public domain, or several such claims for a combination, does Article 3(c) of the Regulation limit the grant of an SPC;

> only to the single molecule if marketed as a product;
> the first marketing of a product covered by the patent whether this is the monotherapy of the drug covered by the basic patent in force or the first combination therapy, or

---

71. Case C-149/22 *Merck Sharp & Dohme Corp v. Clonmel Healthcare Limited.*

either (a) or (b) at the election of the patentee irrespective of the date of market authorisation?

And if any of the above, why?

It is hoped that the CJEU's answers will provide definite and resolute guidance on how Article 3(a) should be interpreted and SPC eligibility for combination medicinal products. It is worth noting that the UK, following Brexit, will not be bound by the CJEU's judgment (*see* section §7.09 below for more on Brexit and SPCs); however, it is likely the UK Courts will consider any ruling given its importance and current level of uncertainty.

The Finnish court has recently referred a question to the CJEU concerning combination products.[72] Specifically, whether a second certificate can be granted for a combination product, where the first SPC granted covers one of the active ingredients within that combination, both products being covered by the same basic patent. The questions referred by the Finnish court are as follows, judgment for which is awaited: What criteria must be applied to determine when a product has not already been granted a supplementary protection certificate within the meaning of Article 3(c) of Regulation (EC) No 469/2009 1 of the European Parliament and of the Council of 6 May 2009 concerning the supplementary protection certificate for medicinal products ('SPC Regulation')?

Must the assessment of the condition set out in Article 3(c) of the SPC Regulation be regarded as being different from the assessment of the condition set out in Article 3(a) of that regulation, and if so, in what way?

Must the statements on the interpretation of Article 3(a) of the SPC Regulation in the judgments of the Court in Case C-121/17 1 and Case C-650/17 2 be regarded as relevant to the assessment of the condition in Article 3(c) of the SPC Regulation and, if so, in what way? In that connection, particular attention should be paid to the statements made in those judgments regarding Article 3(a) of the SPC Regulation, specifically:

> the essential meaning of patent claims; and
> the assessment of the case from the point of view of a person skilled in the art and in the light of the prior art at the filing date or priority date of the basic patent.

Are the concepts 'core inventive advance', 'central inventive step' and/or 'subject matter of the invention' of the basic patent relevant to the interpretation of Article 3(c) of the SPC Regulation and, if any or all of those concepts are relevant, how are they to be understood for purposes of interpreting Article 3(c) of the SPC Regulation? For the purposes of applying those concepts, does it make any difference whether the product in question consists of a single active ingredient ('mono-product') or a combination of active ingredients ('combination product') and, if so, in what way? How is the latter question to be assessed in a case in which the basic patent contains, on the one hand, a patent claim for a mono-product and, on the other hand, a patent

---

72. Case C-119/22 *Teva B.V. and Teva Finland Oy v. Merck Sharp & Dohme Corp.*

claim for a combination product, the latter patent claim relating to a combination of active ingredients consisting of the active ingredient of the mono-product plus one or more active ingredients from the known prior art?

[3] Amendments to the Basic Patent

Actavis Group PTC EHF & Actavis UK Ltd v. Boehringer Ingelheim Pharma GmbH & Co KG[73] was the first case before CJEU to consider post-grant amendments to the basic patent.

Boehringer filed an application for a European patent entitled 'Benzimidazol derivatives, medicaments containing them and process for their preparation' in 1992, which disclosed and claimed numerous molecules, including telmisartan. Claims 5 and 8 of the patent are related to telmisartan alone and to one of its salts. Boehringer subsequently obtained an SPC from the UKIPO based on the European patent and an MA granted in 1998. The product description for the telmisartan SPC was '[t]elmisartan, optionally in the form of a pharmaceutically acceptable salt'. The telmisartan SPC expired in December 2013. The medicinal product was used to treat cardiac disease and was sold under the brand name Micardis.

In April 2002, one of Boehringer's group companies was granted an MA for telmisartan and hydrochlorothiazide (the latter acts as a diuretic and was known to exist since 1958). The medicinal product was sold under the brand name, MicardisPlus. Boehringer later applied to the UKIPO for an SPC for the combination of telmisartan and hydrochlorothiazide ('combination SPC'). The UKIPO wrote to Boehringer stating that the combination of active ingredients must be clearly claimed in the basic patent in order for it to be regarded as requiring protection as such and suggested that Boehringer should apply to amend the basic patent to insert a claim to the combination of telmisartan and hydrochlorothiazide. Following the amendment (insertion of new claim 12), the combination SPC was granted. Actavis sought to invalidate the combination SPC on the grounds that at the time of the application, the basic patent did not contain claim 12. The English High Court referred the question of post-grant amendments to the CJEU. Specifically, if a patent does not on grant contain a claim that explicitly identifies two active ingredients in combination, but the patent is subsequently amended, can the amended patent be relied on as the basic patent in force for a product comprising those active ingredients in combination pursuant to Article 3(a) of the SPC Regulation?

The CJEU's decision appears to be largely driven by the fact that it was common ground between the parties that in combination, telmisartan was the sole subject matter of the invention claimed in the basic patent. Accordingly, the CJEU ruled that 'Article 3(a) and (c)…must be interpreted as meaning that, where a basic patent includes a claim to a product comprising an active ingredient which constitutes the sole subject-matter of the invention, for which the holder of that patent has already obtained a supplementary protection certificate, as well as a subsequent claim to a

---

73. Case C-577/13.

product comprising a combination of that active ingredient and another substance, that provision precludes the holding from a second supplementary protection certificate for that combination'.

Post-grant amendments to patents are commonly used as a means to comply with Article 3(a) in respect of combination products following the ruling in Medeva and subsequent judgments. However, rather than providing much-needed guidance on post-grant amendments to patents, the CJEU failed to address the issue. The issue of whether post-grant amendments are permitted is likely to require a further reference to the CJEU, but SPC holders in the meantime are left in a position of uncertainty as to whether post-grant amendments to the basic patent are permissible.

As an alternative to amendment of the patent, the applicant may consider filing divisional applications in respect of a European patent in an attempt to get around the issues posed by Article 3. From 1 April 2014, the previous time limit for filing divisional applications with respect to European patents (being twenty-four months of the first examination report) has been repealed, and any pending European patent application may be divided, giving rise to separate patents.[74] Thus, the patentee may be able to separate out a combination of active ingredients into a separate patent application.

[4] Functional Specifications

In *Eli Lily and Company v. Human Genome Sciences Inc*[75] the patent, owned by Human Genome Sciences, claimed 'an isolated antibody or portion thereof that binds specifically to (a) the full length Neutrokine-α polypeptide ... or (b) the extracellular domain of the Neutrokine-α polypeptide'. Nowhere in the specification was any information given as to the structure or sequence of any antibody which might have such binding properties. The questions which the CJEU was asked to consider concerned the use of the active ingredient in a combination product and not the functional nature of the claim. Accordingly, the English Court asked for a preliminary ruling as to whether an antibody which would infringe such a claim, since it did have the claimed binding properties, could properly be described as 'specified' within the claim in the sense required by the SPC Regulation. The CJEU ruled that it was 'not necessary for the active ingredient to be identified in the claims of a patent by a structural formula'. Where a functional formula was used in the claims, this did not preclude the grant of an SPC for that active ingredient unless it was not possible to reach a conclusion on the basis of those claims 'interpreted inter alia in the light of the description of the invention, as required by Article 69 of the EPC and the Protocol on Interpretation, that the claims relate, *implicitly but necessarily and specifically*, to the active ingredient in question, which is a matter to be determined by the referring court.' (emphasis added).

The task of interpreting the CJEU's decision fell on the English Court in the summer of 2014.[76] The English Court observed that the CJEU's decision did not give the

---

74. See http://www.epo.org/news-issues/news/2013/20131018.html.
75. Case C-493/12.
76. *Eli Lilly and Company v. Human Genome Sciences Inc* [2014] EWHC 2404 (Pat).

clear guidance that the reference was designed to obtain. Indeed, both parties could find support for their respective positions in the CJEU decision. However, the English Court concluded that:

> the CJEU decision did give a clear answer as to whether a functional definition, in principle, be sufficient to bring an active ingredient within the protection of a patent. The answer was that they could, provided the 'claims relate implicitly but necessarily and specifically to the active ingredient'; and the words 'relate, implicitly but necessarily and specifically to the active ingredient in question' demands an application of Article 69 of the EPC (or section 125 of the Patents Act 1977)[77] to ascertain the extent of the invention and what the claims relate to. If the active ingredient in question is covered by the claims, it would be protected for the purpose of Article 3(a) subject to a proviso which was necessary to reflect the approach in *Medeva* relating to products which were combinations of active ingredients.[78]

What is meant by 'protected by the basic patent' requires further clarification from the CJEU, but it is clear that patents with broad claims are unlikely to be sufficient to form the basis for valid SPCs.

[5] Multiple SPCs Based upon a Single Patent

The Dutch and English courts both requested rulings from the CJEU in related cases as to whether a second SPC can validly be obtained where the SPC to a particular active ingredient has expired, but the active ingredient is also claimed, in the same basic patent, and is the subject of a MA as part of a combination product.[79] The question can be summarised as whether or not multiple SPCs may be granted based upon one and the same basic patent, since this was not addressed by the CJEU's answer in *Medeva*.

In *Actavis Group PTC*,[80] the basic patent covered a family of compounds which included the antihypertensive active ingredient, irbesartan. On the basis of this basic

---

77. The Patents Act 1977 applies in the UK.
78. The proviso is set out in paragraph 66 of the Judgment:

> The proviso relates to products which are combinations of active ingredients and is necessary to reflect the Medeva approach where the claims contain some general word or words extending their extent beyond the principal scope of the claims, typically by the use of a word such as 'comprises'. In the absence of such an extending word, the claims have a focused scope and the question is simply whether the product falls within the scope of the claims. In the language of Medeva, the question is whether the product (i.e. the combination of active ingredients) is 'specified' in the claims, a question which is answered by a close examination of the claims. If general words are included, the position is different. The product does not fall within the focus of the claims and is not within its scope apart from the general words. In such a case, the product is not 'specified' any more than it is 'specified' where the general words are absent.

79. Case C-484/12 *Georgetown University v. Octrooicentrum Nederland*; *Actavis Group and Actavis UK v. Sanofi and Sanofi Pharma BMS SNC*.
80. Case C-443/12 *Actavis Group PTC EHF and Actavis UK Ltd v. Sanofi* of 13 December 2013.

patent and MA, in respect of a medicinal product which contained ibesartan as its single active ingredient, Sanofi was granted an SPC for ibesartan. MAs were subsequently granted in respect of another medicinal product which comprised a combination of ibesartan and a diuretic, hydrochlorothiazide, which was used to treat primary hypertension. Sanofi was granted a second SPC relating to the ibesartan-hydrochlorothiazide combination. In broad terms, Sanofi was granted two SPCs on the basis of the same basic patent. The CJEU held that, in circumstances where the holder of a patent has already obtained an SPC on the basis of a patent protecting an active ingredient that entitles the holder to oppose the use of that active ingredient either alone or in combination with other active ingredients, Article 3(c) will preclude the patentee from obtaining a second SPC relating to a combination on the basis of the same patent but not a subsequent MA for a different medicinal product containing that active ingredient in conjunction with another which is not protected by the patent. In other words, the patentee cannot obtain a second SPC because the second active ingredient was not protected by the basic patent.

In *Georgetown*,[81] the CJEU recognised that 'in principle, on the basis of a patent which protects several different 'products', it is possible to obtain several SPCs in relation to each of those different products, provided, inter alia, that each of those products is 'protected' as such by that 'basic patent' within the meaning of Article 3(a) ...in conjunction with Article 1(b) and (c) of that regulation and is contained in a medicinal product with an MA'. However, it went on to conclude that on the facts of the case where, on the basis of a basic patent and an MA for a medicinal product consisting of a combination of several active ingredients and the patentee has already obtained an SPC for that combination protected by the basic patent, Article 3(c) of the SPC Regulation precluded the patentee from obtaining a subsequent SPC for one of those active ingredients, which individually, is also protected by that patent.

[B]   The Product Has Not Already Been the Subject of a Certificate

Article 3(c) provides that an SPC cannot be granted where the product is already subject to an SPC in the concerned Member State.

A point clarified in the *Biogen*[82] case was that different proprietors of different basic patents can each secure separate SPCs in respect of the same product. Such SPCs may have different expiry dates as a result of the different basic patents expiring at different dates, but they are all subject to the same constraint that they must also expire not more than fifteen years after first MA for the product. However, a single entity cannot hold more than one SPC for the same product; the different basic patents must be in separate legal ownership,[83] although there appears to be no reason why separate companies within a group could not each hold a basic patent. There is also no bar to the holder of a basic patent over a product applying for an SPC even though an earlier

---

81. Case C-484/12 *Georgetown University v. Octrooicentrum Nederland*.
82. Case C-181/95 *Biogen v. SmithKline Beecham Biologicals SA*.
83. Article 3(2) of the Plant Protection Products SPC Regulation, which by Recital 17 is expressed also to apply to the Medicinal Products SPC Regulation.

applicant (holding a different basic patent over the same medicinal product) has already been granted one.[84]

[C] First Authorisation to Place the Product on the Market as a Medicinal Product

[1] 'First Authorisation'

In addition to Article 3(d), the issue of 'first authorisation' also arises in an EU context, either as 'the first authorisation to place the product on the market in the Community' under Article 13(1) of the SPC Regulation affecting its maximum duration or to the transitional provisions under Article 20 of the SPC Regulation, which relate to the availability of an SPC for a product that had already been authorised when the SPC Regulation came into force under the transitional provisions. Thus, for example, (disregarding any transitional provisions), where the MA in respect of which an SPC is secured is not the first in the Member State in issue, or elsewhere in the EU, then an SPC based on such MA either has reduced or zero duration under Article 13 of the relevant Regulation (where the earlier authorisation was elsewhere in the EU), or is in addition invalid as contrary to Article 3(d) of the SPC Regulation (where the earlier authorisation was in the same Member State).

The CJEU has confirmed that for medicinal products, no distinction is made between an authorisation granted under the regulatory regime for veterinary medicinal products and one granted under that for human medicinal products.[85] Thus where a product has been authorised for veterinary use as well as for human use, it is the earlier of those two authorisations that is to be regarded as the first MA of the product as a medicinal product for the purposes of the SPC Regulation. However, in the controversial *Neurim* judgment, the ECJ held that if the later MA relates to a different medical use, then a later SPC's duration can be calculated from the date of the later MA.[86] The CJEU later explained that the exception to the narrow interpretation of Article 3(d) of SPC Regulation, as held in the *Neurim* judgment, does not, in any event, refer to cases of a new formulation of the product at issue. That exception cannot, therefore, in any

---

84. Case C-482/07 *AHP Manufacturing BV*, 3 September 2009.
85. Case C-31/03 *Pharmacia Italia v. Deutsches Patentamt* [2005] RPC 640.
86. Case C-130/11 *Neurim Pharmaceuticals (1991) Ltd v. Comptroller-General of Patents* of 19 July 2012. The CJEU held that Articles 3 and 4 of the SPC Regulation must be interpreted as meaning that: 'the mere existence of an earlier MA obtained for a veterinary medicinal product does not preclude the grant of a supplementary protection certificate for a different application of the same product for which a MA has been granted, provided that the application is within the limits of the protection conferred by the basic patent relied upon for the purposes of the application for the supplementary protection certificate.' The CJEU further held that the position would not be different 'where the same active ingredient is present in two medicinal products having obtained successive MAs, the second MA required a full application in accordance with Article 8(3) of Directive 2001/83/EC of the European Parliament and of the Council of 6 November 2001 on the Community code relating to medicinal products for human use, or if the product covered by the first MA of the corresponding medicinal product is within the scope of protection of a different patent which belongs to a different registered proprietor from the SPC applicant.'

event, be relied on in the case of an MA granted for a new formulation of an active ingredient which has already been the subject of an MA, even if the MA for that new formulation was the first to come within the scope of the basic patent relied on in support of the SPC application for that new formulation.[87]

The question of whether Article 3(d) of SPC Regulation, read in conjunction with Article 1(b) of that regulation, must be interpreted as meaning that the MA referred to in Article 3(b) of that regulation, relied on in support of an application for an SPC concerning a new formulation of an old active ingredient, may be regarded as being the first MA for the product concerned as a medicinal product, when that active ingredient has already been granted an MA as an active ingredient, was repeated in later judgments. In the *Abraxis* case, the CJEU considered the situation in which Abraxis applied for an SPC on the basis of the basic patent and the MA granted a new formulation of an old active ingredient, nab-paclitaxel which consisted of the active ingredient paclitaxel (which had been marketed in another form by other companies under previous MAs) and a carrier which had no therapeutic effect on its own linked together in the form of nanoparticles. By decision of 26 August 2016, the Comptroller General of Patents turned down that application on the ground that it did not comply with Article 3(d) of SPC Regulation. It held that although that provision permits the grant of an SPC for a new and inventive therapeutic use of an old active ingredient, its scope does not extend to a new and inventive formulation of an old active ingredient. The CJEU considered that the MA issued for nab-paclitaxel, i.e., new formulation of an old active ingredient, cannot be regarded as being the first MA for the product concerned as a medicinal product in the case where that active ingredient has already been the subject of an MA as an active ingredient.

The understanding of the notion of 'first authorisation' has been considered again by the CJEU in the recent *Santen* case, in which it was decided that Article 3(d) of SPC Regulation must be interpreted as meaning that an MA cannot be considered to be the first MA, for the purpose of that provision, where it covers a new therapeutic application of an active ingredient, or of a combination of active ingredients, and that active ingredient or combination has already been the subject of an MA for a different therapeutic application.[88]

The ECJ has also held that an MA for a medicinal product granted by the French authorities, which was, from a practical point of view, ineffective because it did not of itself allow the medicinal product so authorised to be marketed (because before doing so, a price had to be agreed with the authorities), had still to be treated as the first one in the Community for the product, thereby rendering a German SPC invalid as it did not meet the requirements of Article 19 of the Medicinal Products SPC Regulation.[89]

A different issue was considered by CJEU in the case *Merck Sharp & Dohme Corporation*, where it has been decided that an end-of-procedure notice issued by the

---

87. C-443/17 *Abraxis Bioscience LLC v. Comptroller General of Patents* of 21 March 2019, paragraph 43.
88. Case C-673/18 *Santen SAS v. Directeur général de l'Institut national de la propriété industrielle* of 9 July 2020.
89. Case C-127/00 *Hässle AB v. Ratiopharm GmbH* of 11 December 2003.

reference Member State in accordance with Article 28(4) of Directive 2001/83/EC of the European Parliament and of the Council of 6 November 2001 on the Community code relating to medicinal products for human use, as amended, as regards pharmacovigilance, by Directive 2010/84/EU of the European Parliament and the Council of 15 December 2010, before the expiry of the basic patent, as defined in Article 1(c) of Regulation No. 469/2009, may not be treated as equivalent to an MA within the meaning of Article 3(b) of that regulation, with the result that an SPC may not be obtained on the basis of such a notice. This is because the adoption of the end-of-procedure notice under Article 28(4) of Directive 2001/83 represents an intermediate stage in the decentralised procedure so that the notice does not have the same legal effects as a 'valid' MA, since such a notice does not authorise the applicant to place the medicinal product on a particular market.

Thus, under Article 10(3) of the SPC Regulation the fact that no MA has been granted by the Member State concerned at the time the SPC application is lodged in that Member State does not constitute an irregularity that can be cured under that provision.[90]

The CJEU has also held that, even though Switzerland is not a member of the EEA, a Swiss MA could also count as the earliest one in the Community for the purposes of the Medicinal Products SPC Regulation because Swiss MAs for medicinal products had (at the time) automatic effect in Liechtenstein, which is a member of the EEA.[91] Further, it is immaterial that the Swiss authorisation is suspended and later reinstated.[92]

The status under the Medicinal Products SPC Regulation of early 'authorisations' that were not granted, in the words of Article 3(1)(b), 'in accordance with Directive 65/65 (or its replacement Directive 2001/83/EC)' has also been a matter of controversy, culminating in the CJEU ruling that medicinal products placed on the market within the Community prior to having obtained an MA in accordance with Council Directive 65/65/EEC and, in particular, without undergoing safety and efficacy testing, are not within the scope of the SPC Regulation and may not, therefore, be the subject of an SPC.[93] The Court considered that the objective of the SPC Regulation, apparent from its recitals, is to compensate the patentee for loss of effective protection as a result of the time required to acquire the authorisation to place the product on the market. It would be contrary to that objective of offsetting the time taken to obtain an MA – which requires long and demanding testing of the safety and efficacy of the medicinal product concerned – if an SPC, which amounts to an extension of exclusivity, could be granted for a product which has already been sold on the Community market as a medicinal

---

90. Case C-567/16 *Merck Sharp & Dohme Corporation v. Comptroller General of Patents, Designs and Trade Marks* of 7 December 2017.
91. Joined cases Case C-207/03 *Novartis AG, University College London and Institute of Microbiology and Epidemiology v. Comptroller General of Patents, Designs and Trade Marks* and Case C-252/03 *Ministre de l'Economie v. Millennium Pharmaceuticals* of 21 April 2005.
92. Case C-617/12 *Astrazeneca AB v. Comptroller General of Patents, Designs and Trade Marks* of 17 January 2014.
93. Case C-195/09 *Synthon BV v. Merz Pharma GmbH & Co. KGaA* of 28 July 2011 and Case and Case C-427/09 *Generics (UK) Ltd v. Synaptech Inc* of 28 July 2011.

product before being subject to any administrative authorisation procedure as laid down in Directive 65/65/EEC, including safety and efficacy testing.

[2] Date of First Authorisation

Since November 2013, the UKIPO has adopted the approach that where the MA is granted under the centralised procedure, the date of first authorisation is the date the applicant is notified of the decision as recorded in the Official Journal of the EU.[94] The notification date may be a few days later than the date of grant of the MA. This change in procedure also affects the dates of related paediatric extensions but extends only to the duration of SPCs granted in the UK where the first authorisation is granted by the European Commission (Commission).

A difference of a few days can have a significant financial value for the pharmaceutical industry; however, there is a clear disparity in the practices adopted across Europe. Several other European countries (such as Portugal) have adopted a similar approach to the UK, but the majority of countries rely on the date of grant.

This issue was recently brought before the CJEU in *Seattle Genetics*.[95] The Austrian Court referred two questions to the CJEU, specifically: (1) was the date of first authorisation referred to in Article 13(1) of the SPC Regulation to be determined under EU law or the date on which the authorisation takes place under the national law of the relevant Member State, and (2) if the date is determined by Community law, which date is taken into account – the date of first authorisation or the date of notification. The CJEU held that Article 13(1) of the SPC Regulation must be interpreted as meaning the 'date of first authorisation of the product on the market in the EU' determined by EU law. This meant that the SPC would commence on the date on which notification of the decision granting MA was given to the addressee of the decision.

[D] What Happens When the Basic Patent and MA Have Different Holders?

The holder of a potential basic patent and the holder of the MA for the medicinal product protected by that patent will not always be the same, and their interests may not always coincide. For instance, a licensee may be responsible for getting the pharmaceutical to market and so has access to the MA. The licensor, however, lacking access to the MA, may have real difficulty in complying with the requirement to provide a copy of the MA as required by Article 8(1)(b) of the SPC Regulation when applying for an SPC. If the licensee also has its own patent coverage, it would prefer to secure its own rights to the product by choosing one of its own patents as the 'basic' patent and securing an SPC in relation to that. Then unless it can itself secure an SPC, the licensor has no benefit of any royalties during the SPC term and indeed may itself,

---

94. *See* https://www.gov.uk/government/uploads/system/uploads/attachment_data/file/327280/2014-6502-special.pdf.
95. Case C-471/14 *Seattle Genetics Inc v. Österreichisches Patentamt*.

subject to the terms of the licence, even be prevented from commercialising the product after expiry of its own patent. Alternatively, the holder of a potential basic patent may be in dispute with the MA holder as to whether or not the latter requires a patent licence from the former in the first place – indeed there may already be patent infringement proceedings between them.

This problem was referred to the ECJ in *Biogen v. SmithKline Beecham Biologicals SA*.[96] In this case, SmithKline Beecham was the holder of the MAs and had licences from two separate companies (Biogen and Institut Pasteur) under two separate patents. As the Medicinal Products SPC Regulation appeared to only permit one SPC to be granted in relation to one product, there was a concern that an application by the first licensor would preclude an SPC from being granted to the other licensor. Biogen sought a declaration that SmithKline Beecham, in refusing to provide them with a copy of their Belgian MA so that they could obtain an SPC in Belgium but providing such a copy to Institut Pasteur had discriminated against Biogen and committed an act of unfair competition contrary to honest commercial practices under Belgian law, and sought an order compelling SmithKline Beecham to provide the authorisation.

The ECJ found broadly in favour of Biogen, holding that a patent holder which does not hold or have access to an MA for the medicinal product protected by its patent may nevertheless secure an SPC. Thus it held that where the owner of the basic patent and the holder of the MA were different persons and the owner of the basic patent was unable to provide a copy of the authorisation in accordance with Article 8(1)(b) of the Medicinal Products SPC Regulation, the application for the SPC could not be refused on that ground alone. The national authority granting the SPC could obtain a copy of the MA from the national authority which issued it. Thus not only is there no requirement that the holder of the basic patent and applicant for SPC be the same, or that the holder of the MA for the medicinal product which gives rise to the right to apply for an SPC, consents to the application, but it is also not possible for the holder of such MA to prevent the grant of an SPC by withholding a copy of the MA required by Article 8(1)(b).

[E] What Form Can an SPC 'Claim' Take and What Effect Does It Have on the Scope of Protection Conferred?

Article 4 of the SPC Regulation reads:

> 'Within the limits of the protection conferred by the basic patent, the protection conferred by a certificate shall extend only to the product covered by the authorisation to place the corresponding medicinal product on the market and for any use of the product as a medicinal product that has been authorised before the expiry of the certificate.'

Patent claims are drafted as broadly as possible, subject only to constraints as to novelty, inventive step, and sufficiency. However, as discussed above, the emerging

---

96. Case 181/95 *Biogen Inc v. SmithKline Beecham Biologicals* [1997] ECR I-357; [1997] RPC 833.

case law indicates that widely-drafted patent claims are unlikely to be sufficient for an SPC. By contrast, clearly identifying the active ingredient in the claims, such as through use of the chemical formula, might suffice.

Recitals 13 and 14 of the Plant Protection Products SPC Regulation, which apply to the SPC Regulation (*see* §7.02), suggest that an apparently narrow SPC 'claim' that does not refer to salts and esters generally should not *for that reason* be treated as excluding from protection such as salts and esters. These provisions were explored by the ECJ in *Farmitalia*,[97] which held that:

> '21 ... where an active ingredient in the form of a salt is referred to in the ... authorisation concerned and is protected by a basic patent in force, the [SPC] is capable of covering the active ingredient as such and also its various derived forms such as salts and esters, as medicinal products, in so far as they are covered by the protection of the basic patent.
> 22 ... where a product in the form referred to in the marketing authorisation is protected by a basic patent in force, the certificate is capable of covering that product, as a medicinal product, in any of the forms enjoying the protection of the basic patent.
> 23 ... in order to determine ... whether a product is protected by a basic patent, reference must be made to the rules which govern that patent.'

Accordingly, the various degrees of liberality with which a patent claim may be interpreted by the national courts of the Member States will also affect the breadth of interpretation of SPC claims.

§7.08 LEGISLATIVE CHANGES AND REFORMS

[A] SPC Manufacturing Waiver

Regulation (EU) 2019/933 of the European Parliament and of the Council of 20 May 2019 amending the SPC Regulation entitles EU-based companies to manufacture a generic or biosimilar version of an SPC-protected medicine during the term of the certificate, if done either for the purpose of exporting to a non-EU market, or for stockpiling during the final six months of an SPC ahead of entry into the EU market (SPC Manufacturing Waiver). It entered into force on 1 July 2019.

The Commission's rationale for an SPC Manufacturing Waiver[98] is that manufacturers of generic and biosimilar medicines based in non-EU countries where SPC protection does not currently exist (e.g., Brazil, Russia, India, and China) enter markets in which patent protection expired up to five years earlier than EU-based manufacturers. This is because SPCs granted in certain EU countries may cause the launch of

---

97. Case C-392/97 *Farmitalia Carlo Erba's SPC Application* [2000] RPC 580, [2000] 2 CMLR 253.
98. Upgrading the Single Market: More opportunities for people and business (COM(2015) 550 final), https://ec.europa.eu/transparency/regdoc/rep/1/2015/EN/1-2015-550-EN-F1-1.PDF; and Commission staff working document – A Single Market Strategy for Europe – Analysis and Evidence – Accompanying the document Upgrading the Single Market: More opportunities for people and business (SWD (2015) 202 final).

generic and biosimilar medicines. Consequently, this may give an unintended lead-time advantage to non-EU-based manufacturers to enter the EU market (or part of it) on expiry of the SPC. An additional consequence may be that EU manufacturers move their production outside the EU to remain competitive. An SPC Manufacturing Waiver for export purposes to non-EU countries with no SPC protection could allow EU-based generic and biosimilar companies to remain competitive. The view was supported by the European Parliament's Committee on the Internal Market and Consumer Protection, which urged the Commission's view to introduce and implement an SPC manufacturing waiver before 2019.

Thus, the aim of this regulation is to remove a major competitive disadvantage of EU-based manufacturers compared to manufacturers based in non-EU countries (where SPC-type protection is not available or not enforceable) and ensure a better deal for patients. The revision constitutes an adjustment to the current regime striking a balance between ensuring the attractiveness of Europe for innovative pharmaceutical companies and allowing EU-based generics and biosimilars to compete on the global market.[99]

[B] The Unitary Patent System and SPCs

SPCs are currently granted and enforced at a national level, which can give rise to a lack of harmonisation. For example, an SPC application for the same product may be granted in one Member State and refused by another. Equally, there may be divergent court decisions on the validity and infringement of SPCs. The concept of a 'unitary' SPC that is centrally granted and centrally enforced within the EU may present an attractive alternative for companies seeking SPCs for the same product in more than one EU Member State.

As explained in the summary of the *Evaluation of EU Regulations 469/2009 and 1610/96 on supplementary protection certificates for medicinal and plant protection products* (25 November 2020), the fact that SPCs are nationally administered and managed undermines the effectiveness and efficiency of the SPC system is the system's main shortcoming. It creates legal uncertainty, red tape, and extra costs for businesses, especially small- and medium-sized enterprises (SMEs). Purely national examination and grant procedures also entail extra costs and administrative burden for national administrations.[100]

The Unitary Patent System is briefly discussed in Chapter 2. Although the Unitary Patent System (including the UPC) is not yet operational, this new system will have important consequences for the SPC holders and applicants. Under the new regime, all SPCs issued in respect of products protected by Unitary Patents (Unitary SPCs) and in some cases *existing and future* European Patents (European SPCs) will be the subject of the exclusive competence of the UPC. Article 32 of the Agreement on the UPC (the

---

99. https://ec.europa.eu/growth/industry/strategy/intellectual-property/patent-protection-eu/supplementary-protection-certificates-pharmaceutical-and-plant-protection-products_en.
100. *See* https://ec.europa.eu/docsroom/documents/43847/attachments/3/translations/en/renditions/native.

Agreement) provides that the following types of actions concerning European SPCs (or Unitary SPCs) among others will fall within the exclusive competence of the UPC:

- actual or threatened infringements and related defences;
- declarations of non-infringement;
- provisional and protective measures and injunctions;
- declarations of invalidity; and
- counterclaims for declaration of invalidity.

The new system does not affect SPCs where the basic patent has been granted by a national patent office – these will still be granted and enforced in the relevant Member State.

[1] European SPC

At present, European SPCs are currently matters for the national law of the country in which the basic patent was granted, but this position will change under the Unitary Patent System.

However, there is a transitional regime that allows the holder of a European SPC to opt out from the exclusive competence of the UPC.[101] In order to opt out, the European SPC holder will need to notify their opt-out to the Unified Patent Registry one month before the expiry of the transitional period at the latest.[102] The transitional period is seven years from the entry into force of the Agreement at the first instance, but this may be extended by a further seven years.

The mechanism for opting out is currently provided by Rule 5 of the draft Rules of Procedure of the UPC (Draft Rules).[103] An application to out a European Patent or application pursuant or an application to withdraw an opt-out under Rule 5 extends to any SPCs based on that patent.[104] This means that there will be an automatic opt-out where the SPC is granted after the opt-out of the European Patent. However, where the SPC has already been granted at the date of the application to the opt-out, the holder of the SPC and the proprietor of the patent (if different) will need to lodge the application together. The 'proprietor' of the patent is the person shown on the register of the EPO as the proprietor.[105] This clearly may create problems where the basic patent has expired and registered owner has changed or is no longer in existence.

Litigation for infringement or for a declaration of invalidity of a European SPC may still be brought before national courts during the transitional period[106] unless an action has already been brought before the UPC before the holder has opted out.

---

101. Article 83 of the Agreement.
102. Article 87 of the Agreement.
103. Eighteenth Draft Rules of Procedure of 19 October 2015. *See* https://www.unified-patent-court .org/news/draft-rules-procedure-updated-march-2017.
104. Rule 5.2 of the Draft Rules.
105. Rule 8.4 of the Draft Rules.
106. Article 83(1) of the Agreement.

[2] Unitary SPCs

Although the Agreement sets out the competency of the UPC in respect of European and Unitary SPCs, there are no provisions as to how a Unitary SPC can be obtained or which body will grant them. Issues also arise as to the scope of Unitary SPCs.

[a] Grant Authority

Article 9(1) of the SPC Regulation specifies that 'an application for an [SPC] shall be lodged with the competent industrial property office of the Member State which granted the basic patent or on whose behalf it was granted and in which the authorisation referred to in Article 3(b) to place the product on the market was obtained, unless the Member State designates another authority for the purpose'. Similar provisions exist in the Plant Protection Product SPC Regulation. The current regime therefore allows Member States to designate another authority to issue SPCs. This indicates that there is a mechanism in the existing SPC legislation that would allow the EPO or an EU institution to issue Unitary SPCs. Given its experience, the EPO is likely to be chosen as the grant authority.

Choosing the EPO poses interesting questions of international law. Decisions of national intellectual property offices concerning SPCs may be challenged through the national courts, which are permitted to make references to the CJEU concerning the interpretation of EU legislation. However, the EPO is an organisation that sits outside the EU and is governed principally by the EPC and its decisions are subject to its own appeal procedures and cannot be challenged by national courts[107] or the CJEU.

If the EPO is to be the granting authority for Unitary SPCs, it is likely that the EPC would have to be amended to allow its decisions, with respect to its interpretation of the two SPC Regulations, to be subject to judicial review by the CJEU. An alternative would be that appeals from the EPO in respect of Unitary SPCs would fall within the competence of the UPC (which would in turn be permitted to make references to the CJEU on points of EU law if required).

[b] Scope

Unitary SPCs will confer the same rights as conferred by the Unitary Patent and shall be subject to the same limitations and the same obligations.[108] By their nature, Unitary SPCs will be based on a Unitary Patent and, should at least in theory, have effect in all Member States participating in the cooperation on the unitary patent protection (currently, all Member States of the EU except Spain, Poland, and Croatia).[109] This could potentially be the case if the SPC was based on a Unitary Patent and an MA

---

107. Although legal arguments have been raised in some Member States as to whether this is indeed the case.
108. Article 30 of the Agreement.
109. Poland and Croatia were not part of the EU when the Agreement was signed.

procured through the centralised procedure. The centralised MA procedure under Regulation (EC) No. 726/2006 results in a single MA that is valid in all EU Member States and EEA countries (provided the MA has not been suspended or revoked). However, Article 3(b) of the SPC Regulation refers to MAs granted in accordance with Directive 2001/83/EC[110] or Directive 2001/82/EC,[111] i.e., those granted pursuant to national, decentralised, or mutual recognition procedures.

[c]   Brexit

The future of the UPC was uncertain in light of Brexit at that time and how, or if, the UK would continue to participate in the system despite its withdrawal from the EU. On 20 July 2020, however, the UK deposited notification of the withdrawal of its ratification of the UPC Agreement, confirming its withdrawal from the UPC. The UPC will continue without the participation of the UK.

[d]   Reform

There is currently a disconnect between the Unitary Patent System and the MA procedures as it is currently unclear on which MA a Unitary SPC can be based. There are also concerns over the identity of the grant authority and interim measures that would be needed to be put in place before the implementation of an EU-wide SPC. Such concerns have been raised in the joint position paper by the European Crop Protection Association, European Federation of Pharmaceutical Industries and Associations, and International Federation for Animal Health Europe published in July 2015 (Joint Position Paper).[112]

Both the Joint Position Paper and the Call for Tender suggest that SPC users wishing to use the future Unitary Patent System will have to rely on national SPCs under the current EU legislation as an interim measure.

[C]   Medical Devices

Medical devices in the EEA were governed by three EU Directives: Directive 90/385/EEC (concerning active implantable medical devices; AIMDD), Directive 98/79/EC (concerning in vitro diagnostic medical devices; IVDD), and Directive 93/42/EEC (other medical devices; MDD). New regulations governing medical devices came into force in 2021 (Medical Devices Regulation (Regulation (EU) 2017/745)) and in 2022 (In-Vitro Diagnostic Devices (Regulation (EU) 2017/746)) which changed the

---

110. Directive 2001/83/EC of the European Parliament and of the Council of 6 November 2001 on the Community code relating to medicinal products for human use.
111. Directive 2001/82/EC of the European Parliament and of the Council of 6 November 2001 on the Community code relating to veterinary medicinal products.
112. See https://www.efpia.eu/media/15414/ecpa-efpia-and-ifah-europe-joint-position-paper-proposal-for-a-unitary-spc-july-2015.pdf.

European legal framework and introduced new responsibilities for the European Medicines Agency (EMA) and for competent national authorities.[113]

Whether SPCs can be granted for medical devices has been an issue of concern for the medtech sector, as highlighted in the Call For Tender. There have been a number of divergent decisions in Member States over the years; and CJEU case law so far has only touched upon medical devices which incorporate an active pharmaceutical ingredient as part of its activity (*see* below).

[1] Does the Scope of the SPC Regulation Extend to Medical Devices?

The Recitals to the SPC Regulation appear to refer clearly to its application to medicinal products. Indeed, Recitals 2 to 4 explain the need for an SPC regime to effectively compensate for the erosion of patent protection due to the time taken to obtain MA to place the 'medicinal product' on the market.

The SPC Regulation defines 'medicinal product' as follows:[114]

> 'medicinal product' means any substance or combination of substances presented for treating or preventing disease in human beings or animals and any substance or combination of substances which may be administered to human beings or animals with a view to making a medical diagnosis or to restoring, correcting or modifying physiological functions in humans or in animals.

This is distinct from the term 'product', which means 'the active ingredient or combination of active ingredients of a medicinal product'[115] as discussed in §7.03.

By Article 2 of the SPC Regulation, SPCs attach to the 'product' protected by the basic patent (emphasis added):

> Any product protected by a patent in the territory of a Member State and subject, prior to being placed on the market as a medicinal product, to *an administrative authorisation procedure as laid down in [Directive 2001/83/EC (the Medicinal Products Directive) or Directive 2001/82/EC (the Veterinary Medicinal Products Directive)]*, may, under the terms and conditions provided for in this Regulation, be the subject of a certificate.

It would seem that Article 2 is quite restrictive – SPCs can only be granted to medicinal products for human or veterinary use. However, Article 3 (which governs the conditions for obtaining an SPC) is less clear: one of the conditions for granting an SPC is that a valid MA has to be granted '*in accordance*' with the Medicinal Products Directive or the Veterinary Medicinal Products Directive, as appropriate.[116]

The ambiguity appears to be dispelled by Article 8(1), which provides that the content of the application for an SPC must include (among other things):

---

113. The regulation of medical devices, including classification, is discussed in further detail in Chapter 19.
114. Article 1(a), SPC Regulation.
115. Article 1(b), SPC Regulation.
116. Article 3(b), SPC Regulation.

a copy of the authorisation to place the product on the market, as referred to in Article 3(b), in which the product is identified, containing in particular the number and date of the authorisation *and the summary of product characteristics listed in Article 11 the [Medicinal Products Directive] or Article 14 of the Veterinary Medicinal Products Directive.*

Taken together, it would seem that the answer to whether SPCs can be granted for medical devices is clear – no. However, some ambiguity may arise with borderline products, which might include active implantable devices and Class III medical devices. The classification and regulation of medical devices is discussed in Chapter 19.

[2] European Decisions Concerning Class III Medical Devices

Pre-market evaluation of the medical devices is risk-based, so Class III devices (which have the highest risk profiles) undergo stringent pre- and post-market control as discussed in Chapter 19. Class III medical devices (as defined in Article 9 and Annex IX of the MDD) are devices that incorporate a substance as an integral part, which if used separately, may be considered to be a medicinal product which acts upon the body with an action ancillary to the device. As such, Class III devices require the safety, quality and usefulness of the substance to be assessed, in an analogous way to authorisation under the Medicinal Products Directive.

In 1998, the UKIPO granted two SPCs to Genzyme Biosurgery Corporation for products relating to Hylan A and Hylan B on the basis of an authorisation under the MDD.[117] However, the same products were also litigated in the Netherlands[118] and Germany with different outcomes – the Dutch Court held that an approval under the MDD was in accordance with the Medicinal Product Directive whereas the German Court took the opposite view. The District Court of The Hague held that the mere fact that Article 2 of Medicinal Products SPC Regulation made no reference to the MDD did not necessarily prohibit the application of the Medicinal Products SPC Regulation, but the scope of Article 2 could not be extended to medical devices, in general, but only to those where the procedure under paragraph 7.4 of Annex I to the MDD applies.

A series of decisions during 2014–2016 suggest it is increasingly unlikely to be able to obtain SPCs for Class III medical devices in at least the UK and Germany: *Cerus Corporation*,[119] *Leibniz*[120, 121] and *Angiotech Pharmaceuticals Inc. and University of British Columbia*.[122]

---

117. SPC/GB96/012 for an SPC in respect of 'Hylan A (rooster comb hyaluronan cross-linked with formaldehyde) and Hylan B (Hylan A further crossed-linked with divinyl sulfone)' and SPC/GB96/013 for an SPC in respect of 'Hylan B (rooster comb hyaluronan sequentially crossed-linked with formaldehyde then divinyl sulfone)'.
118. *Genzyme Biosurgery Corp v. Bureau voor de Industriele Elgendom*, BIE 70 (2002) 360–362 (Netherlands) DC (the Hague).
119. UK IPO Decision BL O/141/14 Cerus Corporation, 31 March 2014.
120. UK IPO Decision BL O/328/14 Leibniz-Institut für Neue Materialien Gemeinnützige GmbH, 29 July 2014.
121. Leibniz-Institut für Neue Materialien gemeinnützige GmbH (14 W (pat) 45/12.
122. BL O/466/15 Angiotech Pharmaceuticals Inc. and University of British Columbia, 6 October 2015.

In March 2014, the UKIPO considered two SPC applications filed by Cerus Corporation for its INTERCEPT product: SPC/GB/07/043 for 'Platelet preparation obtainable by addition, and subsequent photoactivation, of amotasalen or its salt to a suspension of platelets in plasma' and SPC/GB/07/044 for a similar product. The MAs in support of the applications were EC design examination certificates issued by a notified body in accordance with the MDD. During examination, the UKIPO considered that the applications did not meet the requirements of Medicinal Products SPC Regulation (which was in force at the relevant time). Cerus Corporation submitted that an EC declaration of conformity for a Class III medical device was equivalent to an authorisation to place a medicinal product on the market under the Medicinal Products Directive. The UKIPO disagreed and decided that EC design examination certificates could not form a valid authorisation to put the product on the market under Article 3(b) of the Regulation (EEC)1768/92 (the same provision in the SPC Regulation) and consequently was not eligible to be subject to an SPC. However, an SPC application made by Cerus Corporation for the same product was granted in Italy.[123]

In July 2014, an SPC application made by *Leibniz-Institut für Neue Materialien Gemeinnützige GmbH* to protect a product that was described as 'aqueous dispersion of iron oxide nanoparticles' was also refused by the UKIPO.[124] The iron aminosilane-coated iron oxide nanoparticles are magnetic particles which were inserted into or placed near cancerous tissue. When subjected to an alternating magnetic field, the nanoparticles either heated up, causing irreparable cancer cell damage or sensitised the cells to further treatment by chemotherapy or radiotherapy. The aminosilane coating allows the nanoparticles to be targeted to tumour cells.

The UKIPO[125] followed its decision in *Cerus Corporation* again ruling that an EC design examination certificate for Class III medical devices granted under Directive 93/42/EEC did not meet the requirements of Article 3(b) of the SPC Regulation. The applicant had tried to argue (among other things) that Article 3(b) of the SPC Regulation (as an EU legislative text) should be interpreted teleologically. However, the hearing officer considered that this principle did not mean that individual words could be exchanged for synonyms (e.g., synonyms for 'in accordance with').

The German Federal Court also upheld the German Patent and Trade Mark Office's decision to refuse the corresponding German SPC for similar reasons in December 2015.[126] However, the applicant did find some sympathy from the Court. In its judgment, the German Federal Court remarked that the term of patent protection for medical devices may not be sufficient in light of the pre-clinical and clinical studies that may be required during the authorisation procedure (e.g., as is required for Class III devices), but this was a matter for the legislators to consider.

---

123. SPC number C-UB2007CCP983.
124. SPC/GB/10/051.
125. UK IPO Decision BL O/328/14 *Leibniz-Institut für Neue Materialien Gemeinnützige GmbH*, 29 July 2014.
126. *Leibniz-Institut für Neue Materialien gemeinnützige GmbH* (14 W (pat) 45/12.

In October 2015, the UKIPO confirmed again in *Angiotech Pharmaceuticals Inc. and University of British Columbia* [127] that an EC design examination certificate relating to a medical device is not sufficient to satisfy the requirements for the grant of an SPC. The decision is not surprising in light of the UKIPO's earlier decisions in *Cerus Corporation* and *Leibniz*. The two applications concerned SPC/GB14/0030 for Taxol®[128] and SPC/GB14/031 for 'Taxol®-eluting stent'. Both applications concerned the use of Taxol® for treating or preventing restenosis of blood vessels. The applicants lodged a Notice of Appeal with the Patents Court on 4 November 2015. In April 2016, the Patents Court ordered that appeal be dismissed.[129]

A more recent decision concerning medical devices which incorporate an ancillary drug substance was that of the CJEU in response to a request for a preliminary ruling under Article 267 TFEU from the *Bundespatentgericht*.[130] The request was made in proceedings brought by *Boston Scientific Ltd* concerning refusal by the *Deutsches Patent- und Markenamt* to issue an SPC in relation to Paclitaxel.

Boston Scientific held a patent which claimed the 'use of taxol for the preparation of a medicament to maintain an expanded vessel luminal area'. They had also obtained a CE certificate of conformity in respect of its medical device, TAXUS™ Express2 Paclitaxel-Eluting Coronary Stent System, which is a Paclitaxel-coated stent. The German Patent Office refused the SPC application, however, on the basis that the 'product' which formed the subject of the SPC application did not have MA. The referring court asked 'whether Article 2 [of the SPC Regulation] must be interpreted as meaning that a prior authorisation procedure, under Directive 93/42, for a medical device incorporating as an integral part a substance, within the meaning of Article 1(4) of that directive, must be treated in the same way, for the purposes of applying that regulation, as an MA procedure for that substance under Directive 2001/83 where that substance has been the subject of an assessment provided for in the first and second paragraphs of section 7.4 of Annex I to Directive 93/42'.

The CJEU in its reasoning stated that the terms 'medicinal product' and 'medical device' are mutually exclusive, and it therefore follows that a product which meets the definition of a 'medicinal product' within the meaning of Directive 2001/83 may not also be classified as a medical device within the meaning of Directive 93/42. In determining which term applies to a product, the principal mode of action of the product should be considered: 'A product which does not achieve its principal mode of action by pharmacological, immunological or metabolic means therefore falls under the definition of a 'medical device'. Conversely, a product which achieves its principal intended action in the human body by such means may be classified as a medicinal product within the meaning of Directive 2001/83.' The CJEU held that Article 2 should be interpreted as meaning that the effect that a previous CE-mark approval for a medical device which comprises an active ingredient as an integral part of it cannot be

---

127. BL O/466/15 Angiotech Pharmaceuticals Inc. and University of British Columbia, 6 October 2015.
128. Paclitaxel.
129. *See* Case Notes on https://www.ipo.gov.uk/p-ipsum/Case/PublicationNumber/EP2226085.
130. Case C-527/17 *Boston Scientific Ltd v. Deutsches Patent- und Markenamt*.

equated to an approval in accordance with the relevant Medical Product directives. The substance which forms an integral part of the medical device can only enjoy SPC protection if it has been granted a separate MA as an active ingredient in a medicinal product. In other words, authorisation for active ingredients under the MDD is not equivalent or comparable to the MA received pursuant to Article 3(b) of the SPC Regulation.

[3] Active Implantable Medical Devices

The AIMDD defines an 'active implantable medical device' as 'any active medical device which is intended to be totally or partially introduced, surgically or medically, into the human body or by medical intervention into a natural orifice, and which is intended to remain after the procedure'. The term 'active medical device' means any medical device relying for its functioning on a source of electrical energy or any source of power other than that directly generated by the human body or gravity. An example of such a device is an implantable cardiac pacemaker.

In January 2010, the German Federal Court held that an EC Design Certificate under the AIMDD was sufficient to meet the requirements of the SPC Regulation, overturning a decision of the German Patent and Trade Mark Office.[131] The SPC in question was for 'Yttrium-90 glass microspheres'. The microspheres would be placed in or near cancerous tissue and would decay on exposure to a neutron beam in patients undergoing radiotherapy treatment. The Federal Court held that the product contained an active ingredient as an integral part of the device and was subject to the same level of scrutiny as under Directive 65/65/EEC (since replaced by the Medicinal Products Directive).

[4] Borderline Products

Borderline products are those where it is not immediately clear whether they fall within the scope of the Medicinal Products Directive of the Medical Device Regulation 2017/745. Guidance from the European Commission states:[132]

> As a general rule, a relevant product is regulated *either* by the MDD *or* the AIMDD or by the [Medicinal Products Directive]. The conformity assessment procedure or the marketing authorization procedure to be followed prior to placing a given product on the market will therefore be governed either by the MDD/AIMDD or by the [Medicinal Products Directive]. The procedures of both Directives do not apply *cumulatively*.

Further, 'for new active substances and for known substances in a non-established purpose, comprehensive data is required to address the requirements of

---

131. Decision 14W (Pat) 12/07 of 26 January 2010 concerning Yttrium-90 Glass Microspheres.
132. MEDDEV 2.1/3 rev 3.

Annex I to Directive 2001/83/EC. The evaluation of such active substances would be performed in accordance with the principles of evaluation of new active substances'.

In *Laboratoires Lyocentre*,[133] the CJEU held that the classification of a product as a medical device in one Member State did not preclude another country from classifying the same product as a medicinal product on the basis of its pharmacological, immunological, or metabolic action. However, a product that was similar to a medicinal product (specifically, an identical substance with the same mode of action) in the same Member State could not, in principle, be marketed as a medical device unless as a result of another characteristic that is specific to that product and relevant for its classification as a medical device.

Given that there is some degree of flexibility concerning the classification (and thus regulation) of borderline products, it might be reasonable to assume that SPCs should potentially be granted for at least some types of medical devices.

[5] Reform

As discussed above, the Commission recognises that there may be a need to amend the existing legislation to allow SPCs to be granted for medical devices. Recent changes to the EU legislative framework governing medical devices further highlight the need for reform. As discussed in Chapter 19, the former framework of three EU Directives concerning medical devices was replaced with two new EU Regulations: In Vitro Diagnostic Medical Devices Regulation and the Medical Devices Regulation. These new Regulations introduced more stringent clinical testing of high-risk medical devices so as to align the clinical investigation requirements for such medical devices with those for medicinal products.[134] Under these circumstances, it may be even more arguable that the current SPC legislation needs to change in order to compensate medtech companies for the delays in bringing medical devices to market caused by regulatory requirements.

§7.09 UK

As detailed in this Chapter, SPCs are a product of EU law. Under the terms of the European Union (Withdrawal) Act 2018, provisions of EU law which were in force as of 1 January 2021 were incorporated into UK law. This included the provisions of EU SPC legislation. By and large, the provisions under the EU SPC system have remained the same with respect to SPCs covering the UK post-Brexit; however, some amendments have been enacted by way of further UK legislation to reflect the new relationship between the UK and the EU following Brexit, including the complexities of the Northern Ireland Protocol. *See* Chapter 1 for more on Brexit.

---

133. Case C-109/12 *Laboratoires Lyocentre v. Lääkealan turvallisuus- ja kehittämiskeskus and Sosiaali- ja terveysalan lupa- ja valvontavirasto*, 3 October 2013.
134. Directive 2001/20/EC, which is to be replaced with the Clinical Trials Regulation.

[A] Procedure for Seeking SPC Protection Post-Brexit

UK SPC applications filed and granted before 1 January 2021 remain valid for the whole of the UK as they would have under EU law pre-Brexit. For UK SPC applications filed before the end of the transition period but which remained pending as of 1 January 2021, they continued to be examined under the provisions of EU law and granted pursuant to the position pre-Brexit, providing coverage over the whole of the UK.

For UK SPC applications filed after the transition period (after 1 January 2021), the application requirements have remained somewhat consistent with the position before Brexit. This is a result of the Patents (Amendment) (EU Exit) Regulations 2019 which imported EU SPC legislation into UK law. UK SPC applicants will therefore need to continue to have a UK patent granted by the UKIPO or the EPO (with a UK designation) and a valid MA granted in the UK by either the UK's Medicines and Healthcare Products Regulatory Agency (MHRA) or the EU's EMA.

Due to the continued alignment of Northern Ireland with EU regulations post-Brexit pursuant to the Northern Ireland Protocol, there is a discrepancy over which MAs are needed to cover Northern Ireland and Great Britain. In summary:

- Northern Ireland only can be covered by EU MAs granted via the EU's centralised procedure at the EMA;
- Great Britain (England, Scotland, and Wales) only can be covered by a Great Britain MA issued by the MHRA;
- the whole of the UK (England, Scotland, Wales, and Northern Ireland) can be covered by a UK MA issued by the MHRA;
- the UK is no longer covered by EU MAs issued by the EMA; and
- EU MAs granted by the EMA before Brexit have been cloned and converted into Great Britain MAs by the MHRA.

The result is that an applicant may require two separate MAs to cover both Great Britain and Northern Ireland. The Supplementary Protection Certificates (Amendment) (EU Exit) Regulations 2020 SI 2020/1471 (SPC Amendment Regulations) was enacted to address the post-Brexit patchwork quilt of MAs available to applicants looking for approval in the UK and Great Britain.

The SPC Amendment Regulations allow for an SPC to be applied for on the basis of the applicant holding an MA allowing the product to be sold anywhere in the UK – namely either a UK MA, a Great Britain MA or an EU MA; so long as the MA relied upon for the UK SPC application is the first authorisation for the territory concerned and is valid to place the product on the market of that territory.

The deadline for filing an application for a UK SPC remains consistent with the EU position, as within six months of either first MA or grant of the basic patent, whichever is later. If the first MA falls later, the deadline for filing an application for a UK SPC post-Brexit is six months from the grant of the earliest MA which covers any territory within the UK. As an EU MA continues to cover Northern Ireland, the grant of an EU MA by the EMA will start the six-month clock for lodging a UK SPC application, as will a Great Britain or UK MA. In other words, the deadline to file an application for a UK

Chapter 7: Supplementary Protection Certificates §7.09[C]

SPC can be triggered by both EMA and MHRA regulatory approval. This means that if the EU MA is the first granted for a medicinal product, the deadline to apply for a UK SPC will be the same as for a European SPC.

One issue with this approach is that, while UK SPCs remain to be UK-wide rights, the territory which is covered by UK SPC protection will correspond with the parts of the UK which are covered by the MA. For example, an EU MA would mean coverage of only Northern Ireland, and a Great Britain MA would only cover Great Britain.

Article 13A of the SPC Amendment Regulations provides a solution to this issue. Under Article 13A, applicants can apply for an extension to a UK SPC to cover the remaining parts of the UK. In order to do so, the applicant must have applied for and been granted an MA covering the 'unprotected' remaining parts of the UK. The applicant should then notify the comptroller of this before the grant of the UK SPC (and within six months of grant of the later MA and before the patent expires), such earlier SPC being the first authorisation for the product to be placed on the market.

The application fees for a UK SPC remain the same as they were pre-Brexit.

[B] Duration

The term of a UK SPC is calculated on the basis of the date of the first MA received, whether in the UK or in the EEA. The result of this is that if Great Britain MAs are slower to reach grant than those granted by the EMA, the term of the UK SPC will be triggered nonetheless by an earlier MA granted in the EEA, despite the fact that the applicant has not received an equivalent grant in the UK therefore losing out on its period of protection in the UK. Great Britain MAs can, however, be accelerated following a positive opinion from the EMA cutting this delay down.

Following Brexit, UK or Great Britain MAs will no longer be considered 'first authorisations' for the purposes of EU SPCs under the SPC Regulations.

[C] Paediatric Extensions

The six-month paediatric extension period for carrying out studies pursuant to a PIP continues to be available for UK SPC holders.

EU law continued to apply to paediatric extension applications filed before the end of the transition period. Following Brexit, the UK Human Medicines Regulations incorporated similar provisions for the UK. As such, applications should be submitted up to two years prior to the UK SPC expiry.

While applicants are still required to complete an agreed PIP, the concerned product needs only to be authorised in the UK and not all EEA Member States.

The scope of a UK paediatric extension will correspond only to the part(s) of the UK for which a valid MA has been granted and for which a PIP has been completed. Article 13B of the SPC Amendment Regulations enables applicants to apply for an extension to a UK paediatric extension to the remaining parts of the UK, however. To do this, applicants must satisfy the conditions for a UK paediatric extension for an MA to cover the remaining part of the UK and file a request by the two-year deadline.

[D] SPC Manufacturing Waiver

The SPC manufacturing waiver as discussed above continues to apply with respect to UK SPCs. This continuation is by virtue of The Intellectual Property (Amendment etc.) (EU Exit) Regulations 2020 SI 2020/1050 which incorporated the manufacturing waiver into UK law. The EU is not considered a 'third country' for the purposes of the UK manufacturing waiver. For products protected by UK SPCs, third parties will be permitted to manufacture within the UK and without consent for export outside of either the UK and the EU, or for stockpiling in the UK for the purpose of placing the product on the market in the UK or EU following expiry of the UK SPC.

The position is not the same in the reverse direction; however, the UK is considered a 'third country' for the purposes of the EU manufacturing waiver. As a result, if a product is not protected by a UK SPC but is protected by an EU SPC, under the EU manufacturing waiver, third parties are able to manufacture in the countries covered by the EU SPC for the purposes of exporting into the UK.

[E] CJEU Interpretation

Following Brexit, the Courts of England and Wales are no longer bound by decisions of the CJEU. The Courts of England and Wales will therefore be free to interpret SPC legislation in a manner which may depart from that of the European Courts.

CHAPTER 8
Paediatrics

Sally Shorthose, Sarah Faircliffe & Pieter Erasmus

§8.01 INTRODUCTION

Following the United States' lead, the EU has introduced legislation aimed at improving the regulation of medicines as regards use in children. In 1997, the European Commission (Commission) organised roundtable discussions regarding paediatric medicines at the European Medicines Agency (EMA). However, it was not until 2006 that the EU adopted the European Regulation on Paediatric Use (Regulation (EC) No. 1901/2006),[1] which came into force on 26 January 2007. Regulation (EC) No. 1901/2006 made wide changes to the regulatory environment governing the development and authorisation of medicines, particularly those for use in children (up to and including seventeen years of age). In order to ensure that medicines are developed and researched to meet the therapeutic needs of children, Regulation 1901/2006 establishes a regime of requirements, rewards, and incentives, alongside horizontal measures.[2]

In assessing the need for such legislation, it was noted[3] that an estimated 50% to 90% of all medicinal products prescribed for the paediatric population[4] had not been

---

1. Regulation (EC) No. 1901/2006 of the European Parliament and of the Council of 12 December 2006 on medicinal products for paediatric use (OJ L378/1, 27.12.2006), as amended by: Regulation (EC) No. 1902/2006, which amended the text relating to decision-making procedures for the Commission; as well as Regulation (EU) 2019/5, which amended the provisions relating to the imposition by the Commission of financial penalties.
2. Such horizontal measures include establishing an expert PDCO to scrutinise company testing plans; a European network of experts; free scientific advice from the EMA; information tools – inventory of paediatric therapeutic needs, database of studies, and enhanced safety monitoring for marketed products.
3. European Commission Staff Working Paper 13880/04 ADD 1 SEC 2004 1144, dated 25 October 2004.
4. Article 2(1) of Regulation (EC) No. 1901/2006 defines the 'paediatric population' as that part of the population aged between birth and eighteen years.

tested in the paediatric population or had not been licensed for paediatric use. The prescribing physician must take responsibility for such off-label[5] prescriptions. The physiological development and pharmacokinetics of the paediatric population are different from that of adults, and indeed they are different at different stages of a child's development. It is therefore usually not possible to adequately extrapolate from adult studies to determine what effect medicines will have on children,[6] leading to uncertainties as to correct dosage. Age-appropriate formulations are often also required. However, in order to explore ways in which regulators can rely on extrapolation of clinical data from adults to children, with the aim of minimising the need for paediatric studies, the EMA has published and updated a reflection paper.[7]

Historically, pharmaceutical companies have been unwilling to conduct clinical studies and develop medicinal products for use in the paediatric population. Conducting paediatric studies is usually more complex and expensive than the equivalent studies in adults, in part because the paediatric patient population tends to be small relative to the adult population. Increased costs of producing paediatric products, together with the more limited demand for the products, can lead to lower commercial returns. Hence the need for legislation to require paediatric studies in order to ensure better information on, and regulation of, medicines used in children.

In the past, ethical concerns have been raised about testing medicinal products in children. However, off-label paediatric prescription is, in effect, a test of an unlicensed medicinal product and paediatric off-label prescriptions may contain prescribing errors, particularly with respect to dosage. The result is that children may be harmed by adverse reactions from over-dosage, or they are not effectively treated because the product dosage is too small.

§8.02 EUROPEAN REGULATIONS RELATING TO PAEDIATRIC STUDIES

[A] Overview of the EU Paediatric Regulation

Section 4 of the preamble of Regulation (EC) No. 1901/2006 sets out the following:

> This Regulation aims to facilitate the development and accessibility of medicinal products for use in the paediatric population, to ensure that medicinal products used to treat the paediatric population are subject to ethical research of high quality and are appropriately authorised for use in the paediatric population, and to improve the information available on the use of medicinal products in the various paediatric populations. These objectives should be achieved without

---

5. Prescriptions are described as 'off-label' when the medicinal product in question is prescribed in a way that is not in accordance with the instructions on the product label – for example, by prescribing a different dosage or a different means of administration to enable the child to take the medicine.
6. In this Chapter, the words 'child' or 'children' are also used to refer to members of the 'paediatric population' and for this purpose the terms may be used interchangeably.
7. Reflection paper on the use of extrapolation in the development of medicines for paediatrics: EMA/189724/2018, 7 October 2018.

subjecting the paediatric population to unnecessary clinical trials and without delaying the authorisation of medicinal products for other age populations.

As discussed in Chapter 2, §2.02[C], Regulation (EC) No. 1901/2006 provides for a system of obligations together with rewards and incentives intended to facilitate the development and accessibility of paediatric medicinal products and to ensure that such products are subject to high-quality ethical research. These overarching aims are to be achieved without subjecting the paediatric population to unnecessary clinical trials and without delaying the authorisation of medicinal products for the adult population.

Regulation (EC) No. 1901/2006 presented a significant shift with respect to European medicinal product development. Pharmaceutical companies are now often required to submit a Paediatric Investigation Plan (PIP) at a relatively early stage of product development, which defines the paediatric studies to be completed before an application for Marketing Authorisation (MA) (or MA variation/extension) can be submitted (*see* detailed discussion in §8.02[C] below). The PIP should be submitted no later than upon completion of the first-phase human pharmacokinetic studies of the new pharmaceutical indication in adults.[8] Upon completion of the studies in the agreed PIP, the company may be able to obtain a 'reward' for the effort and expense of performing the studies (*see* §8.03 below).

In order to handle the various provisions and requirements introduced by the Regulation, the Paediatric Committee (PDCO) was established at the EMA.

[B] PDCO

Article 3(1) of Regulation (EC) No. 1901/2006 required a new scientific committee to be established by 26 July 2007.[9] The PDCO[10] held its first meeting on 4 July 2007 at the EMA.

Article 4 of Regulation (EC) No. 1901/2006 sets out the membership of the PDCO, which comprises:

(a) five members of the Committee for Medicinal Products for Human Use (CHMP), with alternates;
(b) one member appointed by each Member State not represented through the CHMP members, to be experts from the national competent authorities, with alternates;
(c) three members to represent patient associations, with alternates; and
(d) three members to represent health professionals, with alternates.

---

8. Article 16(1) Regulation (EC) No. 1901/2006 (although statistics show that this timescale is often exceeded).
9. The updated PDCO Rules of Procedure can be found at document EMA/3448440/2008, Rev. 3, 11 October 2021.
10. Article 3(1) of Regulation (EC) No. 1901/2006 states that Regulation (EC) No. 726/2004 applies to the PDCO except as otherwise provided for in Regulation (EC) No. 1901/2006.

In 2012, the EMA published a concept paper involving children and young people in the PDCO.[11]

The PDCO's responsibilities are both product-specific and general.[12] The main responsibility of the PDCO is to assess the content of the PIPs submitted for approval. The PDCO enters into a dialogue with the applicant concerning the proposed PIP and issues an opinion (*see* §8.02[C] below). The PDCO also assesses, in due course, whether the applicant has complied with the PIP. In order for the PDCO to determine whether a particular PIP is suitable, external experts are involved. Standard PIPs for use by applicants in order to assist in reaching an agreement on PIPs for specific types or classes of medicines have been developed by the PDCO. Adhering to the principles and key binding elements contained in a standard PIP should facilitate the PIP approval process. One of the other product-specific tasks of the PDCO is the assessment and granting of waivers and overseeing the deferral scheme, as explained in §8.02[D]. The general tasks of the PDCO include supporting a European network for paediatric clinical trials,[13] establishing an inventory of specific paediatric medicinal product needs (reports by different therapeutic areas are available on the EMA's website) and providing advice regarding paediatric clinical trials.

It is important to note that the PDCO is not responsible for granting MAs of medicinal products for paediatric use; this remains the responsibility of the CHMP/Commission or national competent uthority. However, the CHMP may request the PDCO to prepare an opinion as to the quality, safety, and efficacy of the medicinal product for use in the paediatric population where data has been generated pursuant to a PIP.

In accordance with their Work Plan 2022,[14] the PDCO aims to achieve a number of activities, including defining strategies on how to approach PIPs for identified therapeutic areas, identifying how real-world evidence may support paediatric development, etc.

[C]   PIPs

PIPs set out the proposed research and development programme necessary to test the medicine for paediatric use. The requirement for a PIP is intended to benefit the paediatric population and to generate the data required for a MA application or variation/extension pursuant to Article 7 or 8 of Regulation (EC) No. 1901/2006 (or for the specific 'Paediatric Use Marketing Authorisation' (PUMA) discussed under §8.04

---

11. The Concept paper on the involvement of children and young people at the PDCO can be found at document EMA/PDCO/388684/2012, 17 September 2012.
12. The tasks of the PDCO are set out at Articles 6 and 17 of Regulation (EC) No. 1901/2006.
13. Article 44 of Regulation (EC) No. 1901/2006 states that the PDCO shall develop a European network of existing national and European networks, investigators, and centres with expertise in performing paediatric studies with the objective of coordinating studies relating to paediatric medicines, building up the necessary scientific and administrative competencies at the European level, and to avoid unnecessary duplication of paediatric studies and research.
14. The PDCO Work Plan 2022, which can be found at document EMA/PDCO/517591/2021, was published on 21 January 2022.

Chapter 8: Paediatrics §8.02[C]

below). The results of the research programme conducted in accordance with the PIP then determine the paediatric conditions that a particular medicinal product may be authorised to treat (or indeed confirm that the medicine is not suitable for use in children).

The strategy employed by the Regulation in order to require companies to perform paediatric studies in the situations defined in the legislation is to make validity of an MA (or variation/extension) application dependent upon completion of the programme set out in a PIP, which has been pre-agreed with the EMA. The MA application will be automatically rejected if the applicant fails to provide the results of a completed PIP, unless there is an exemption (waiver or deferral – see §8.02[D] below).

Therefore, Article 7 of Regulation (EC) No. 1901/2006 provides that all applications for MA for new medicines (not authorised in the EU before 26 January 2007) must meet the following requirements:

1. An application for Marketing Authorisation under Article 6 of Directive 2001/83/EC in respect of a medicinal product for human use which is not authorised in the Community at the time of entry into force of this Regulation shall be regarded as valid only if it includes, in addition to the particulars and documents referred to in Article 8(3) of the Directive 2001/83/EC, one of the following:
   (a) the results of all studies performed and details of all information collected in compliance with an agreed paediatric investigation plan;
   (b) a decision of the Agency granting a product-specific waiver;
   (c) a decision of the Agency granting a class waiver pursuant to Article 11;
   (d) a decision of the Agency granting a deferral.

   For the purposes of point (a), the decision of the Agency agreeing the paediatric investigation plan concerned shall also be included in the application.
2. The documents submitted pursuant to paragraph 1 shall, cumulatively, cover all subsets of the paediatric population.

Furthermore, Article 8 extends the application of Article 7 to applications for authorisation of new indications, pharmaceutical forms, and routes of administration as follows:

> In the case of authorised medicinal products which are protected either by a supplementary protection certificate under Regulation (EEC) No. 1768/92, or by a patent which qualifies for the granting of the Supplementary Protection Certificate, Article 7 of this Regulation shall apply to applications for authorisation of new indications, including paediatric indications, new pharmaceutical forms and new routes of administration. For the purposes of the first subparagraph, the documents referred to in Article 7(1) shall cover both the existing and the new indications, pharmaceutical forms and routes of administration.

It should be noted that the Article 8 requirements apply only where the authorised product is protected by a Supplementary Protection Certificate (SPC) or a patent which qualifies for one and that the studies required cover both new and existing indications, pharmaceutical forms, and routes of administration. Article 7 applies to all applications for new products (not authorised in the EU *before 26 January 2007*), irrespective of patent status.

The PIP must include an outline of each proposed trial and the rationale behind the paediatric drug development programme. It sets out:

(a) the processes in place to assess safety, quality, and efficacy;
(b) the processes in place to facilitate the use of the medicinal product by making its use easier, safer, and more effective; and
(c) a proposal for the age-appropriate formulation with respect to all of the different subsets of the paediatric population.[15]

The PIP also has to specify the means by which pain, distress, and fear will be minimised in children taking part in the proposed trial.[16] In paediatric studies, innovative study designs that permit smaller sample numbers while obtaining the maximum amount of information, together with reliance on models and simulations, are favoured.

The Commission has published a Guideline (updated in 2014) on the format and content of PIPs.[17] This guideline aims to facilitate the application process; it establishes key elements that should be included in PIPs, introduces increased flexibility into the application process, incorporates new study concepts (such as extrapolation of results and modelling) and clarifies requirements for the compliance check (*see* §8.02[C][2] below).

[1] PIP Approval Procedures

The contents of the PIP must be approved by the PDCO. The PDCO is required to review the PIP application and adopt an opinion within sixty days.[18]

---

15. Article 15 of Regulation (EC) No. 1901/2006 sets out the detailed requirements for the contents of the PIP.
16. All EU paediatric clinical trials are subject to Regulation EU No. 536/2014, which contains the requirements of clinical trials on minors, including the requirement to obtain informed consent from the parents or legal representatives (*see* Chapter 4).
17. Communication from the Commission: Guideline on the format and content of applications for agreement or modification of a paediatric investigation plan and requests for waivers or deferrals and concerning the operation of the compliance check and on criteria for assessing significant studies, Commission Communication (2014/C 338/01).
18. Pursuant to Article 17(1) of Regulation (EC) No. 1901/2006, following receipt of the PIP, the PDCO shall appoint a rapporteur and shall within sixty days adopt an opinion as to whether or not the proposed studies will ensure the generation of the necessary data determining the conditions in which the medicinal product may be used to treat the paediatric population or subsets thereof, and as to whether or not the expected therapeutic benefits justify the studies proposed.

According to Article 16(1) of Regulation (EC) No. 1901/2006, the PIP should be submitted not later than upon completion of the first-phase human pharmacokinetic studies of the new pharmaceutical indication in adults (although, in practice, this timetable is not always adhered to – *see* the discussion at §8.02[C][3] below). From a practical perspective, with regard to the submission of documents to the EMA, it is mandatory for applicants to use the e-Submission Gateway for all paediatric submissions to the EMA, and applicants should follow the revised guidance on paediatric submissions.[19]

Once the PDCO has adopted an opinion, the procedure set out in Article 25 of Regulation (EC) No. 1901/2006 applies. On day sixty of the procedure, the PDCO may request that the applicant propose modifications to the PIP in order for the PIP to be approved. If such a request is made, the procedure will be suspended until such proposed modifications are submitted by the applicant. Such modifications may comprise the inclusion of additional research not contained in the original PIP application. For example, the PDCO may suggest variations to the studies to include different subclasses of the paediatric population or more patients. The applicant may request a clarification meeting if necessary.

Once the PDCO opinion has been finalised, Article 25 of Regulation (EC) No. 1901/2006 sets out as follows:

(1) Within ten days of its receipt, the EMA shall transmit the opinion of the PDCO to the applicant.
(2) Within thirty days following receipt of the opinion of the PDCO, the applicant may submit to the EMA a written request, citing detailed grounds, for a re-examination of the opinion.[20]
(3) Within thirty days following receipt of a request for re-examination pursuant to paragraph 2, the PDCO, having appointed a new rapporteur, shall issue a new opinion confirming or revising its previous opinion. The rapporteur shall be able to question the applicant directly. The applicant may also offer to be questioned. The rapporteur shall inform the PDCO without delay in writing about details of contacts with the applicant. The opinion shall be duly reasoned and a statement of reasons for the conclusion reached shall be annexed to the new opinion, which shall become definitive.
(4) If, within the thirty-day period referred to in paragraph 2, the applicant does not request re-examination, the opinion of the PDCO shall become definitive.

---

19. Guidance on paediatric submissions, found at document EMA/672643/2017 Rev.4, 13 July 2021. Unless pre-submission interaction is required or an expedited review is foreseen (for example, in the context of COVID-19 related submissions), a letter of intent to submit a PIP or a product-specific waiver is no longer required nor processed. Practically, in advance of the targeted submission deadline, applicants must ensure access to e-Submission Gateway and EudraLink. In addition, from 10 October 2021, a Research Product Identifier (RPI) will be required for paediatric procedures and will be a mandatory field in the electronic application form for PIPs, modifications of agreed PIPs, and requests for waivers.
20. *Ibid.*

(5) The EMA shall adopt a decision within a period not exceeding ten days following receipt of the PDCO's definitive opinion. This decision shall be communicated to the applicant in writing and shall annex the definitive opinion of the PDCO.

(6) In the case of a class waiver as referred to in Article 12, the [EMA] shall adopt a decision within ten days following receipt of the opinion of the PDCO as referred to in Article 13(3). This decision shall annex the opinion of the PDCO.

(7) Decisions of the EMA shall be made public after deletion of any information of a commercially confidential nature.

It is important to note that this procedure results in a final, legally binding decision on a PIP being taken by the EMA (rather than by the Commission, as is the case for MA decisions).

Applications for PIP modification at a later stage are possible and frequently requested in practice. Article 22 of Regulation (EC) No. 1901/2006 provides for an agreed plan to be modified where necessary. Such modifications are required where key elements of the PIP are unworkable or no longer appropriate. A request for modification is not necessary if the modification affects only aspects of a study or measures that are not reflected in any agreed key element.[21]

[2] PIP Compliance Check

Upon filing an application requiring the completed PIP, and as a prerequisite for obtaining the rewards, a compliance check is performed to verify that all the measures agreed in the PIP have been properly completed in accordance with the agreed timelines. If at the time of conducting the assessment of the MA, it is determined that the studies carried out are not in compliance with the agreed PIP, then the product is ineligible for rewards and incentives available under Regulation (EC) No. 1901/2006.[22]

The relevant competent authority or the EMA will perform a detailed check on each key element of the agreed PIP against what has actually been submitted to assess compliance with each key element. Minor deviations from key elements that have been requested by the competent authority that authorised the study should not affect compliance and when conditional language such as 'could' or 'such as' is used in the PIP decision, compliance may be confirmed even if these measures were not followed as suggested.[23] However, the compliance check under Article 23 is without prejudice to the possibility that the competent authority will conclude, when conducting the scientific assessment of a valid application, that the studies are in fact not in conformity with the agreed PIP.[24]

---

21. Communication from the Commission, *Supra* n. 17. *See also* Guidance on paediatric submissions, found at document EMA/672643/2017 Rev. 4, 13 July 2021.
22. Article 24 Regulation (EC) No. 1901/2006.
23. Communication from the Commission, *Supra* n. 17.
24. *Ibid.*

During 2014, there was some litigation[25] concerning the compliance check process. In the action before the General Court, Pfizer alleged that the EMA misinterpreted Article 28(3) of Regulation (EC) No. 1901/2006, when it claimed that the compliance statement for Pfizer's product could not be issued until the studies set out in the PIP had been assessed for the purposes of the new prophylaxis indication. In early 2015, this case was removed from the register, and the matter was not decided upon.

[3] Issues Concerning PIPs

One of the first issues to emerge from the legislation once the PDCO began its operations was that of timing of submission of the PIP for agreement. According to Article 16(1) of Regulation (EC) No. 1901/2006, the PIP should be submitted not later than upon completion of the first-phase human pharmacokinetic studies of the new pharmaceutical indication in adults. Many applicants feel that this is too early in product development to require a PIP, and in practice, this timeline is often not adhered to; the EMA, however, emphasises that it is important to respect the timelines in the legislation, even if not mandatory, and notes that if changes to the PIP become necessary during product development, then these can always be implemented via the PIP modification procedure. In practice, PIP modification is common, with typically three to five modifications per PIP applied between first agreement and PIP completion.

Further issues may arise where clinical studies accepted by the PDCO still require approval from the national/local ethics committees. There is a question as to how to obtain approval for the PIP where the ethics committees challenge paediatric study designs/plans permitted and agreed by the PDCO. Owing to the different approaches taken by the EMA and the Food and Drug Administration (FDA), difficulties may also arise in reconciling PIPs with the paediatric development plans required in the US. Ultimately, it is hoped that dialogues between the FDA and EMA may lead to improved coordination of the requirements for paediatric product authorisation applications in Europe and the US.[26]

However, a more recent and potentially far more significant issue to emerge concerns requests made by the PDCO for the applicant to study further or new paediatric indications, which go beyond the indication(s) on which the application giving rise to a PIP is based (for example, as a result of taking into account off-label use). The PDCO appears to be keen to use its discretion in agreeing PIPs to require an applicant to undertake paediatric studies of broad scope. However, if such requests are too extensive or burdensome, this may discourage applications, particularly for line

---

25. Case T-48/14 - Pfizer *v.* European Commission and EMA.
26. For background, see 'Principles of Interactions between EMA and FDA Paediatric Therapeutics' (June 2007) at https://www.ema.europa.eu/en/partners-networks/international-activities/cluster-activities#paediatric-medicinal-products-section and also 'Paediatric Gaucher disease – a strategic collaboration approach from EMA and FDA' (6 July 2017) EMA/237265/2017.

extensions,[27] and as a result, hinder product development in the EU, so it is important to strike the right balance.

In the first piece of litigation involving interpretation of Regulation (EC) No. 1901/2006, PIP applicant Nycomed Danmark brought an action against the EMA,[28] claiming that the decision of the PDCO (of 28 November 2008) to refuse to grant a PIP waiver under Article 11(1)(b) of Regulation (EC) No. 1901/2006, for a medical imaging agent (perflubatane) for taking echocardiographs by ultrasound, should be annulled. In support of its application for a waiver, Nycomed had argued that the ultrasound imaging agent was designed to diagnose coronary artery disease (CAD), which exists only in the adult population. The PDCO rejected the waiver application, arguing that the actual intended use of the product was not only for CAD but also to improve the visibility of blood flow in heart muscle during an ultrasound scan to detect myocardial perfusion defects. Such defects are a sign of a range of underlying diseases and conditions (not only CAD), some of which occur in children. Paediatric studies were therefore required. In appealing the EMA's decision (based on the PDCO's position), Nycomed submitted that the concept of 'disease or condition for which the medicinal product is intended' in Article 11(1)(b) had been incorrectly interpreted and that it is for the applicant to define the scope of the indication for which the MA for the medicinal product concerned is requested; the PDCO does not have the power to go beyond the indication defined by the applicant and require paediatric studies based on an additional potential paediatric use for the product. The EMA argued that it does have such power based on a different interpretation of the legislation.

On 14 December 2011, the General Court of the European Union upheld the EMA's decision to refuse a waiver, supporting the EMA's interpretation of the (broad) scope of the PDCO's discretion in agreeing a PIP (or PIP exemption). It found that the indication(s) applied for are only a starting point for the PDCO's assessment, and that in agreeing a PIP, the PDCO is able to take into account other potential uses of the medicine in children. Thus, in this case, the decision of the PDCO was based on the finding that the product was intended to help detect myocardial perfusion abnormalities, and such abnormalities are not only a characteristic of the adult condition of CAD but also a sign of other diseases or conditions, some of which manifest themselves in the paediatric population. In reaching its finding, the Court noted that if applicants were able to subjectively determine the intended use of the product at issue, the obligations to perform paediatric studies could be easily circumvented. Thus, one of the key objectives of Regulation (EC) No. 1901/2006, to provide suitably adapted medicinal products for the paediatric population, would not be met.

---

27. Article 8 of Regulation (EC) No. 1901/2006 extends the application of the Article 7 requirements to authorisation for new indications, including paediatric indications, new pharmaceutical forms, and new routes of administration.
28. Case T-52/09 *Nycomed Danmark v. EMA*.

[D] PIP Exemptions, Waivers, and Deferrals

[1] Exemptions

Article 9 of Regulation (EC) No. 1901/2006 sets out classes of medicinal products that are exempt from the paediatric study requirements of Articles 7 and 8.[29] The types of products exempted are:

(i) generics;
(ii) 'hybrid' medicinal products;
(iii) biosimilars;
(iv) homeopathic and (traditional) herbal medicinal products; and
(v) medicinal products containing one or more active substances of well-established medicinal use.

In respect of these products, the usual routes for obtaining MAs apply; however, they are exempt from the requirements imposed by Regulation (EC) No. 1901/2006. There is, therefore, no need to agree a PIP or formally obtain a waiver or deferral of the requirement for paediatric studies.

[2] Waivers

Under Article 11 of Regulation (EC) No. 1901/2006, the requirement of Article 7(1)(a) to provide results of all studies performed and details of all information collected in compliance with an agreed PIP in the application for MA can be waived for certain medicinal products or for particular classes of medical products.

A waiver can be granted if a product or class of products:

(a) is likely to be ineffective or unsafe in part or all of the paediatric population;
(b) is intended for a disease or condition that occurs only in adult populations; or
(c) does not represent a significant therapeutic benefit over existing treatments for paediatric patients.

Under Article 12 of Regulation (EC) No. 1901/2006, the PDCO may itself determine that a product-specific waiver should be imposed where the PDCO considers that the product falls within the requirements set out above. Application of the waiver provision can raise difficult questions where a medicinal product which targets a condition that occurs only in adult populations (e.g., breast cancer) may possibly act with the same mode of action on conditions (e.g., other tumours) that do occur in the paediatric population (for an indication of the PDCO's approach, *see* the discussion on the *Nycomed* case in §8.02[C][3] above).

---

29. Medicinal products authorised under Articles 10, 10a, 13–16, or 16a–16i of Directive 2001/83/EC.

The EMA publishes decisions on class waivers.[30] Since publication of the updated list in 2015, there are now fewer conditions which are automatically exempt from the PIP requirements under the class waiver system. MA applications submitted from 28 July 2018 onwards will be subject to the revised list[31] of class waivers.

The Regulation provides that, where a waiver is granted in respect of the whole paediatric population, the product cannot benefit from the SPC or market exclusivity extension rewards discussed in §8.03[A] below.

[3] Deferrals

Under Article 20 of Regulation (EC) No. 1901/2006, at the time of submitting the PIP, applicants may request a deferral of the initiation or completion of some or all of the measures contained in the PIP. Such deferrals may be granted where:

(a) there is justification on scientific and technical grounds;
(b) there is justification on grounds related to public health;
(c) it is appropriate to conduct studies in adults prior to commencing studies in the paediatric population; or
(d) studies in the paediatric population will take longer to conduct than studies in adults.

Pursuant to Article 21(1) of Regulation (EC) No. 1901/2006, any opinion in favour of a deferral is required to specify the time limits for initiating or completing the measures concerned. These time limits are determined on a case-by-case basis. The aim of the deferral provisions is to ensure that the need for a completed PIP before an MA can be applied does not have the adverse consequence of delaying the availability of the authorised product for the adult population. In the case of applications for new medicines, deferrals are often granted.

§8.03 REWARDS FOR PIP COMPLETION

[A] The SPC Extension Reward

For non-orphan medicinal products, applications under Article 7 or 8 of Regulation (EC) No. 1901/2006 that meet the requirements of Article 36 of Regulation (EC) No. 1901/2006 will be granted a six-month extension of the SPC[32] covering the authorised medicinal product. The extension will be granted to the holder of the patent or SPC.

---

30. *See* EMA decision CW/0001/2015 of 23 July 2015 on class waivers, in accordance with Regulation (EC) No. 1901/2006 of the European Parliament and of the Council: EMA/498952/2015.
31. *See* updated list of waived classes of medicines at https://www.ema.europa.eu/en/human-regulatory/research-development/paediatric-medicines/paediatric-investigation-plans/class-waivers.
32. SPCs are granted pursuant to Regulation (EC) No. 469/2009.

SPCs are protective instruments that assist with the financing of research, development, and licensing of medicines by effectively extending patent protection for the authorised product by a maximum of five years. This is in recognition of the fact that typically between eight to twelve years of the patent term may have already expired before the product is licensed. The additional six-month SPC extension is available for medicinal products even if no paediatric indication is authorised as a result of the paediatric studies,[33] as it is designed to reward research activities and not results. Compliance with the agreed PIP is the key element. Regulation (EC) No. 1901/2006 requires an applicant for an MA to submit evidence of compliance with an agreed PIP in the circumstances defined in Articles 7 and 8 (see §8.02[C] above), irrespective of whether such applicant is eligible for the SPC reward. Equally, in circumstances where an agreed PIP is not essential, the company may apply for one with the aim of benefiting from the SPC extension incentive. If all significant studies contained in the agreed PIP were completed before entry into force of Regulation (EC) No. 1901/2006, then they cannot be used as the basis for claiming the SPC extension, orphan market exclusivity extension, or PUMA rewards or incentives.

To obtain the six-month extension, Article 36 requires that:

(a) the Marketing Authorisation application includes results of all paediatric studies, which must have been conducted in accordance with the agreed PIP;
(b) the product be authorised in all Member States;
(c) the product has not been designated as an orphan medicinal product;[34] and
(d) in the case of a new paediatric indication authorised under an Article 8 application, the product shall not have obtained the one-year extension of the period for marketing protection.[35]

The MA must contain a statement indicating compliance with the agreed PIP in order to allow application of this SPC extension provision. In 2018, twenty-four active substances benefitted from the six-month SPC extension.[36]

By way of illustration, a case brought in the Patents Court for England and Wales has challenged a granted paediatric SPC extension.[37] Dr Reddy's sought revocation of Pfizer's six-month SPC extension for Lipitor, arguing that the legislative requirements had not been complied with. Pfizer had previously obtained an agreed PIP, which

---

33. Although Article 36 of Regulation (EC) No. 1901/2006 requires the results of the studies to be reflected in the summary of product characteristics and, where appropriate, in the package leaflet of the medicine concerned.
34. Orphans are designated pursuant to Regulation (EC) No. 141/2000 and a different reward scheme applies – see §8.03[B].
35. On the grounds that the new indication brings significant clinical benefit when compared to existing therapies pursuant to Article 14(11) of Regulation (EC) No. 726/2004 or Article 10(1) sub-paragraph 4 of Directive 2001/83/EC.
36. See 2018 Report to the European Commission on companies and products that have benefitted from any of the rewards and incentives in the Paediatric Regulation and on companies that have failed to comply with any of the obligations in this Regulation (dated 29 October 2019), Doc. Ref. EMA/103569/2019.
37. Dr Reddy's Laboratories v. Warner-Lambert [2012] EWHC 3715 (Pat).

involved completing two studies and initiating (but not completing) a third follow-up study (this third study not being covered by a deferral). The PDCO had concluded that Pfizer had complied with the agreed PIP and a compliance statement had been included in the MAs as required, hence an SPC extension had been granted in a number of Member States. The UK High Court rejected all the grounds for challenge and did not see the need to refer the case to the European Court. In brief, the Court held that the requirement to start but not complete a study was not unlawful, and the relevant question was rather whether or not the requirements of the PIP had been fulfilled (which they had, in this case). Dr Reddy's argument that Pfizer was not entitled to the SPC extension until it included the results of the completed third study in its MA application was also rejected, given that Pfizer had complied with the PIP. In response to Dr Reddy's argument that pursuant to Article 45(3) of Regulation (EC) No. 1901/2006, an SPC extension should only be granted when 'significant studies' contained in the PIP were completed (which, it alleged, was not the case here), the Court held that Article 45(3) is a transitional provision, relating to research performed before the Regulation came into effect, and did not apply in this case.

[1] Zero and Negative-Term SPCs

Regulation (EC) No. 469/2009 sets out the terms for calculating the duration of the available SPC protection. The SPC term is calculated by reference to the time that has elapsed between the date of filing of the patent and the date of the first MA within the EU, less than five years, subject to a maximum term of five years. It is, therefore, theoretically possible for the calculation of the SPC to result in a zero or even a negative term if the time elapsed is less than five years. Extending a zero or short (under six months) negative-term SPC by six months will obviously result in a short (up to six months) positive term, so this SPC extension reward provision has raised the question of the validity of zero or negative-term SPCs. This has generated quite some debate; the possibility of these six-month SPC extensions was not provided for when the original SPC Regulation (EEC No. 1768/92) was adopted, and thus it did not specifically envisage zero or negative-term SPCs.

In the *Merck and Co., Inc.* case (BL O/108/08), Merck made an application for an SPC to the UK Intellectual Property Office (UKIPO) in order to reserve its right to apply for the six-month paediatric extension in relation to its sitagliptin product, a diabetes treatment. The UKIPO had to determine whether an SPC can be granted for zero or less than zero months in order to enable the holder to benefit from the six-month extension. Given the importance of SPCs in relation to competition between original manufacturers and generics, the market protection afforded by even a short SPC term could be very valuable to an applicant.

In the *Merck* decision, the UKIPO hearing officer cites the views expressed by the Commission that 'the extension of the SPC should not apply in case where the SPC duration is "0". In order for an extension to be granted the SPC is a *sine qua non*.[38] However, despite giving serious consideration to this statement, in the UKIPO hearing officer's view, there is no legislation or case law that prevents the concept of a zero- or negative-term SPC. The hearing officer therefore awarded Merck and Co., Inc. an SPC with a negative term.[39]

The Dutch Patent Office also subsequently awarded a negative-term SPC. The Greek Patent Office took the more generous approach of 'rounding up' the negative term, awarding a zero-term SPC. However, such negative- and zero-term SPCs were rejected by the Patent Offices of Germany, Portugal, and Slovenia. The German Federal Patent Court referred a question to the Court of Justice of the European Union (CJEU) as to whether an SPC can be granted 'if the period of time between the filing of the application for the basic patent and the date of the first authorisation for marketing in the Community is shorter than five years?'[40]

On 8 December 2011, the CJEU gave its judgment in the case, confirming the validity of the concept of negative-term SPCs, which can then be extended by six months under the provisions of Regulation (EC) No. 1901/2006. It also ruled out rounding up the term of an SPC (which would otherwise be of negative value) to zero. However, although this question now seems settled, there are still reported to be differences in approach as between the EU Member States' patent offices in relation to interpreting the requirement that the application for the six-month SPC extension must be lodged no later than two years before SPC expiry.[41]

[B] Rewards for Orphan Medicinal Products That Comply with Regulation (EC) No. 1901/2006

Article 37 of Regulation (EC) No. 1901/2006 sets out the rewards with respect to orphan medicinal products for which the MA application includes the results of all studies conducted in compliance with an approved PIP. Where the orphan medicinal product complies with the conditions of Article 37, the ten-year period of market exclusivity granted pursuant to Article 8(1) of Regulation (EC) No. 141/2000 is extended to twelve years. The following conditions must be met:

(a) the application must include the results of all paediatric studies that have been conducted in accordance with the agreed PIP; and
(b) the MA application shall include a statement indicating compliance of the application with the agreed completed PIP.[42]

---

38. The Record of the Second meeting of national 'Supplementary Protection Certificate' (SPC) experts held on 9 October 2006 in Brussels.
39. BL O/108/08 – Merck and Co., Inc., 14 April 2008.
40. *Merck Sharp & Dohme Corp. v. Deutsches Patent- und Markenamt* Case C-125/10 lodged on 9 March 2010, OJ C 161 from 19 June 2010,17; judgment on 8 December 2011.
41. Article 52 Regulation (EC) No. 1901/2006.
42. In accordance with the requirements of Article 28(3) of Regulation (EC) No. 1901/2006.

There is no requirement that the PIP lead to the authorisation of a paediatric indication, provided that the results of the studies are reflected in the summary of product characteristics and, where appropriate, in the package leaflet of the medicine concerned.

The question of whether there is an entitlement to an extension (to twelve years) of the market exclusivity period, in the case of non-patented orphan medicinal products when compliance with an agreed PIP is voluntary, has come before the General Court.[43] Shire brought an action against the Commission to annul the Commission's interpretation of Article 37. The action concerned the medicinal product Xagrid, which as an orphan medicinal product, enjoyed a ten-year period of market exclusivity up to 18 November 2014. Recital 29 of Regulation (EC) No. 1901/2006 states that since orphan medicinal products 'are frequently not patent-protected, the reward of supplementary protection certificate extension cannot be applied; when they are patent-protected, such an extension would provide a double incentive. Therefore, for orphan medicinal products, instead of an extension of the supplementary protection certificate, the ten-year period of orphan market exclusivity should be extended to twelve years if the requirement for data on use in the paediatric population is fully met.' Further, Article 37 of Regulation (EC) No. 1901/2006 states:

> Where an application for a marketing authorisation is submitted in respect of a medicinal product designated as an orphan medicinal product pursuant to Regulation (EC) No 141/2000 and that application includes the results of all studies conducted in compliance with an agreed paediatric investigation plan, and the statement referred to in Article 28(3) of this Regulation is subsequently included in the marketing authorisation granted, the ten-year period referred to in Article 8(1) of Regulation (EC) No 141/2000 shall be extended to twelve years.

On 1 August 2013, the applicant wrote to the Commission outlining its view that, in light of Recital 29 and Article 37 of Regulation (EC) No. 1901/2006, it was possible to conclude that non-patented orphan medicinal products were eligible for an extension of the market exclusivity period from ten to twelve years, where the requirements outlined in Article 37 of Regulation (EC) No. 1901/2006 were complied with. The applicant stated that Xagrid was a non-patented orphan medicinal product in respect of which a PIP had already been approved by the EMA, and when the results of the studies were available, the applicant intended to seek an extension of the MA for Xagrid in order to include a paediatric indication.

The Commission replied to the applicant's letter stating that it did not share this interpretation of Article 37. In its view, this provision did not confer on non-patented orphan medicinal products entitlement to any extension of the market exclusivity period. There was a further exchange of correspondence, which eventually led Shire to bring its action for annulment.

---

43. *Shire Pharmaceutical Contracts v. European Commission*, CaseT-583/13.

The General Court did not comment on the Commission's interpretation; instead, it examined, at the Commission's request, the question of admissibility pursuant to Article 114(1) of the Rules of Procedure. The case was dismissed as inadmissible; the Court found that the Commission letter had only expressed an 'informed opinion' on the application of Article 37, in general and hypothetical terms, so was unable to produce any binding legal effects on Shire, and thus was not a challengeable decision. Although the Court did not have the opportunity to rule on the question before it, the Commission subsequently changed its mind on its interpretation of Article 37, at least in this case. Xagrid did therefore eventually benefit from a twelve-year period of market exclusivity, as noted in the Commission's 'Inventory of Union and Member State Incentives to support research into, and the development and availability of, Orphan Medicinal Products. State of Play 2015':[44]

> Two medicinal products for which a paediatric investigation plan was completed, *TobiPodhaler* and *Xagrid*, currently enjoy extended (12 year) market exclusivity

A third product, Soliris, has also subsequently benefitted from the two-year exclusivity extension.

[C] Free Scientific Advice from EMA

In order to assist applicants with the requirements of Regulation (EC) No. 1901/2006, the Regulation provides free scientific advice concerning paediatric studies to be made available to applicants. Such advice may be applied at any stage of the product's development and may relate to the content of any PIP or to questions concerning quality, safety, or efficacy in respect of paediatric studies. To the extent that such questions also cover the adult population, an appropriate fee may be charged for the advice relating to the adult population.

Requests for scientific advice are made on a voluntary basis, and the EMA is not bound by the advice that has been provided. The scientific advice is provided by the CHMP through the Scientific Advice Working Party.

§8.04 PAEDIATRIC USE MARKETING AUTHORISATION (PUMA)

Article 30 of Regulation (EC) No. 1901/2006 creates a new type of Marketing Authorisation: Paediatric Use Marketing Authorisation (PUMA).[45] A PUMA is a MA granted in respect of a medicinal product which is already authorised (for adult indication), is

---

44. SWD (2015) 13 final, available at: http://ec.europa.eu/health/files/orphanmp/doc/orphan_inv_report_20160126.pdf
45. The PUMA application procedure became available on 26 July 2007.

not protected by an SPC or by a patent which qualifies for the granting of an SPC[46] (e.g., those products whose patent/SPC protection has expired), and which covers only paediatric indications. Where a PUMA is granted, the product will benefit[47] from an eight-year period of data protection and a ten-year period of marketing protection.[48] The product may also retain the existing brand name of the adult drug[49] and therefore benefit from existing brand recognition.

The policy reason behind the creation of the PUMA is to encourage companies to develop new paediatric indications and formulations for off-patent products. Although the incentives are weak relative to the SPC extension, the PUMA is particularly aimed at attracting small- to medium-sized enterprises (SMEs) and generic pharmaceutical companies. There is no requirement for companies to apply for PUMAs, and the provision has not been widely used so far.[50] Acknowledging that the PUMA concept has not proved particularly attractive to companies, the Commission's PIP guideline[51] now specifies that a PIP application intended to support a future PUMA may be limited to certain paediatric subsets and is not required to address all subsets.

Applicants for PUMAs are automatically eligible for the centralised procedure.[52] The application for a PUMA must be accompanied by data generated in accordance with an agreed PIP. The data must include documentation that demonstrates the quality, safety, and efficacy of the medicinal product in the paediatric population, together with specific data that support the strength, form, or route of administration of the product, where applicable.

The EMA has drawn up a list[53] of off-patent medicines, which are priorities for development as medicines for children. EU funding is available for studies into these medicines.

---

46. The eligibility requirements for SPCs are set out in Regulation (EC) No. 469/2009 concerning the creation of a SPC for medicinal products.
47. Under Article 38 of Regulation (EC) No. 1901/2006, if the PUMA is granted in accordance with Articles 5 to 15 of Regulation (EC) No. 726/2004, the data and marketing protection periods referred to in Article 14(11) of Regulation (EC) No. 726/2004 shall apply. Where the PUMA is granted in accordance with the procedures of Directive 2001/83/EC, the data and marketing protection periods referred to in Article 10 of Directive 2001/83/EC apply.
48. Under Article 14(11) of Regulation (EC) No. 726/2004, the ten-year period shall be extended to a maximum of eleven years if, during the first eight years of those ten years, the MA holder obtains an authorisation for one or more new therapeutic indications that, during the scientific evaluation prior to their authorisation, are held to bring a significant clinical benefit in comparison with existing therapies.
49. Article 30(4) Regulation (EC) No. 1901/2006.
50. The first PUMA was not granted until 2011 (midazolam for treatment of prolonged acute convulsive seizures in paediatric patients from three months to eighteen years). A second PUMA was granted in April 2014 (hemangiol for treatment of proliferating infantile haemangioma). During 2018, the CHMP recommended the granting of PUMAs to: Slenyto (melatonin indicated for the treatment of insomnia in children from two years of age with autism spectrum disorder and Smith-Magenis syndrome); and Kigabeq (vigabatrin indicated for the treatment epilepsy).
51. Communication from the Commission, *Supra* n. 17.
52. Pursuant to Article 31 of Regulation (EC) No. 1901/2006, applications may be made in accordance with the procedure laid down in Articles 5 to 15 of Regulation (EC) No. 726/2004.
53. Revised priority list for studies into off-patent paediatric medicinal products Doc.Ref. EMA/PDCO/98717/2012, Rev. 2013/14.

§8.05 POST-APPROVAL OBLIGATIONS[54]

[A] Duty to Place Product on Market

Once a paediatric indication has been authorised, Article 33 of Regulation (EC) No. 1901/2006 provides that the MA holder has a duty to place the product onto the market 'taking into account the paediatric indication' within two years. The relevant deadlines shall be incorporated in the EMA register. Failure to comply will attract penalties, as set out in §8.06.

[B] Pharmacovigilance

Given the concerns regarding conducting clinical trials in the paediatric population, the general pharmacovigilance measures applicable to all authorised medicines (*see* Chapter 10) are of particular importance in the case of medicines authorised for paediatric use.[55] All applications for new paediatric indications, paediatric line extensions, and PUMAs are required to include details of the measures to be taken to ensure the long-term follow-up of efficacy and possible adverse reactions to the use of the medicinal product in the paediatric population. Furthermore, if the EMA considers a medicinal product to be of particular concern, it may require:

(a) a risk minimisation plan to be put into place; or
(b) specific post-marketing studies to be performed and reviewed by the Competent Authority.

[C] Product Discontinuation

Article 35 of Regulation (EC) No. 1901/2006 contains provisions intended to discourage the discontinuation of authorised paediatric medicines. In the event that a MA holder who has benefited from the rewards under Articles 36, 37, or 38 of Regulation (EC) No. 1901/2006 wishes to withdraw the product from the market, the MA holder must give the EMA a minimum of six months' notice of its intention to discontinue marketing. The MA holder is then obliged to either:

(a) transfer the MA; or
(b) allow a third party that has declared its intention to place the medicinal product concerned onto the market, to use the pharmaceutical, preclinical,

---

54. The post-authorisation requirements are set out at Articles 33 to 35 of Regulation (EC) No. 1901/2006.
55. *See* 'Guideline on conduct of pharmacovigilance for medicines used by the paediatric population', EMEA/CHMP/PhVWP/235910/2005- rev.1.

and clinical information contained in the file of the medicinal product to support a new MA application.[56]

[D]   The Paediatric Symbol

Article 32 of Regulation (EC) No. 1901/2006 required the PDCO to select a symbol to be displayed on products authorised for a paediatric indication. Article 32 also required the package leaflet to contain an explanation of the meaning of the symbol.

However, the PDCO, having held discussions concerning the adoption of the paediatric symbol, has stated that it is unable to recommend any symbol to the Commission because the risks of inclusion of such a symbol on product packaging outweigh the potential benefits.[57] The PDCO recognised the likely marketing advantages of the symbol but did not believe that caregivers and patients would go on to read the explanation contained in the package leaflet. Therefore, parents may associate the symbol on a particular medicine with a particular context and misunderstand the meaning of such a symbol in another context, for a different medicinal product, or a different child. Further, because the symbol would be associated with a particular medicinal product having an indication in children, it would be present on all presentations of such product, regardless of the strength, dose, or formulation, and its presence on any presentation, including those not intended to be administered to children, could lead to a risk of the symbol being misunderstood and could ultimately lead to medical errors. Given the PDCO's recommendations, it seems unlikely that any paediatric symbol will ever be adopted.

§8.06   PENALTIES

Member States are required to determine the penalties to be applied in the event that any of the provisions of Regulation (EC) No. 1901/2006 or any of the implementing measures adopted pursuant to the Regulation are infringed.[58] The penalties are required to be effective, proportionate, and dissuasive.

The EMA may ask the Commission to impose financial penalties for such infringement in relation to centrally authorised products.[59] The Commission will publicise the name of the person sanctioned on the EMA website, together with details of the reasons for and amounts of any financial penalties imposed.[60] Commission

---

56. Under Article 35 of Regulation (EC) No. 1901/2006, such examination is conducted on the basis of Article 10c of Directive 2001/83/EC.
57. *See* 'Recommendation of the Paediatric Committee to the European Commission regarding the symbol', EMEA/498247/2007.
58. Article 49(1) Regulation (EC) No. 1901/2006.
59. The maximum amounts, conditions, and methods of such financial penalties are governed by Article 51(2) of Regulation (EC) No. 1901/2006, which states that Articles 5 and 7 of Decision 1999/468/EC shall apply, where the period in Article 5(6) of Decision 1999/468/EC shall be three months.
60. *See* Article 49(4) of Regulation (EC) No. 1901/2006.

Regulation (EU) No. 488/2012 amended the existing 'Penalties Regulation'[61] to include certain of the provisions of Regulation (EC) No. 1901/2006. The Penalties Regulation lays down rules concerning the application of financial penalties to the holders of MAs granted under the centralised procedure, in respect of infringements of specified obligations, in cases where the infringement concerned may have significant public health implications in the Community, or where it has a Community dimension by taking place or having its effects in more than one Member State, or where 'interests of the Community' are involved.

§8.07 TRANSPARENCY

Article 41 of Regulation (EC) No. 1901/2006 provides for all paediatric clinical trials conducted as part of a PIP to be included in the European Clinical Trials Database (EudraCT database).[62] This includes paediatric trials carried out outside the EU. In a shift towards a more transparent regulatory regime, Article 41 also provides for the paediatric clinical trial information contained in EudraCT to be made available to the public, irrespective of whether the trial was completed or prematurely terminated.[63]

Other transparency measures contained in Regulation (EC) No. 1901/2006 include:

(a) the compulsory inclusion of the results of the paediatric studies in the summary of product characteristics and, if appropriate, in the package leaflet of the medicinal product;[64] and
(b) the publication of the decisions of the EMA[65] which are based on the PDCO opinion on the PIP.

§8.08 PAEDIATRIC RESEARCH

Article 40 of Regulation (EC) No. 1901/2006 sets out the following:

(1) Funds for research into medicinal products for the paediatric population shall be provided for in the Community budget in order to support studies relating to medicinal products or active substances not covered by a patent or a Supplementary Protection Certificate.

---

61. Regulation (EC) No. 658/2007 on financial penalties for infringements by MA holders of centrally authorised products.
62. See Chapter. 4, §4.02 for a description of EudraCT.
63. See 'Guidance on the information concerning paediatric clinical trials to be entered into the EU Database on Clinical Trials (EudraCT) and on the information to be made public by the European Medicines Agency (EMEA), in accordance with Art. 41 of Regulation (EC) No. 1901/2006', Commission Communication 2009/C 28/01.
64. Article 28(1) Regulation (EC) No. 1901/2006.
65. Article 25(7) of Regulation (EC) No. 1901/2006 states that decisions of the EMA shall be published once any information of a commercially confidential nature has been deleted.

(2) The Community funding referred to in paragraph 1 shall be delivered through the Community Framework Programmes for Research, Technological Development and Demonstration Activities or any other Community initiatives for the funding of research.

Article 42 of Regulation (EC) No. 1901/2006 contains further provisions requiring the Member States to collect data concerning existing uses of medicinal products in the paediatric population. Such data were required to be communicated to the EMA by 26 January 2009. Based on the data submitted, the PDCO is tasked with the compilation of an inventory of paediatric therapeutic needs, with particular regard to the identification of research priorities, especially with respect to the development of off-patent products. The inventory of paediatric therapeutic needs was intended to be published by 26 January 2010. The Paediatric Working Party (PEG)[66] carried out a similar exercise between 2001 and 2007 which was adopted by the PEG and served as a basis for the inventory of needs to be established by the PDCO. On 10 December 2010, the PDCO adopted a report on the survey of all paediatric uses of medicinal products in Europe.[67] Based on the survey results and the existing list of paediatric needs, the PDCO has produced a series of inventories of paediatric needs in various therapeutic areas.[68] A revised priority list for studies into off-patent paediatric medicinal products was published by the EMA in August 2013;[69] this was intended to be the basis for potential future funding within the Commission's Horizon 2020 programme. This document notes that submitting a PIP before applying for funding is encouraged.

Regulation (EC) 1901/2006 also mandates establishment of a European network of paediatric research.[70] An implementing strategy for The European Network of Paediatric Research at the EMA (Enpr-EMA) was adopted by the EMA Management Board on 15 January 2008.[71] An organisational structure for the Enpr-EMA was agreed by participants from thirty-eight national research networks and clinical trial centres working together with the EMA in May 2010. Application for Enpr-EMA membership was opened to networks fulfilling certain requirements published following a consultation process.[72] Applications closed in July 2010, and a list of applicants was

---

66. The Paediatric Expert Group was a temporary working party of the CHMP established prior to Regulation [EC] No. 1901/2006 coming into force.
67. Report on the survey of all paediatric uses of medicinal products in Europe: Doc. Ref. EMA/794083/2009.
68. Articles 42 to 43 Regulation (EC) No. 1901/2006; for the inventories of paediatric needs *see* www.ema.europa.eu (specifically at https://www.ema.europa.eu/en/human-regulatory/research-development/paediatric-medicines/needs-paediatric-medicines).
69. Revised priority list for studies into off-patent paediatric medicinal products: Doc. Ref. EMA/PDCO/98717/2012, Rev. 2013/14.
70. Pursuant to Article 44 of Regulation (EC) No. 1901/2006.
71. *See* 'The Network of Paediatric Networks at the EMEA Implementing Strategy', EMEA/MB/543523/2007.
72. The recognition criteria for self-assessment are set out in EMA/241053/2010 dated 5 May 2010.

published in January 2011.[73] The aim of the Enpr-EMA is to facilitate high-quality ethical research on paediatric medicines. The Enpr-EMA does not itself conduct clinical trials or provide funding for studies or research.

In 2015, the EMA launched a pilot scheme to provide for meetings with medicines developers, with the aim of stimulating early dialogue on developing their medicines for use in children. Through PIP assessments, the EMA has identified a number of issues which frequently delay paediatric development, but it is hoped that providing such a forum for early discussion will assist developers in optimising their paediatric development plans, thereby speeding up access to their medicines for children.

§8.09 DEVELOPMENTS

The processes put in place under Regulation (EC) No. 1901/2006 place a high administrative burden on both industry and regulators. The number of applications for PIPs or waivers has been high since the outset and has increased in number. The EMA and FDA have an ongoing collaboration[74] to establish a framework for the exchange of ideas relating to scientific, ethical, and other aspects of paediatric drug development. The aim is to allow companies to put into place global development programmes that are compatible with both the EMA and FDA requirements, which will avoid unnecessary trials in the paediatric population. In order to facilitate the collaboration, EMA staff are able to attend the Paediatric Implementation Team meetings of the FDA, and FDA staff may attend the PDCO meetings.

In July 2012, the EMA published its Five-Year Report to the European Commission (General Report on the experience acquired as a result of the application of Regulation (EC) No. 1901/2006).[75] This was followed by a public consultation by the Commission, in September 2012, on the experience acquired as a result of Regulation (EC) No. 1901/2006. In 2013, the Commission published a progress report on Regulation (EC) No. 1901/2006.[76] This notes that whilst there are encouraging signs that paediatric development has become a more integral part of product development in the EU, some improvements in terms of 'fine-tuning' the implementation of the Regulation are required, and it is acknowledged that the PUMA concept has been a 'disappointment'. In June 2015, the EMA launched a one-year pilot project offering free-of-charge 'early paediatric interaction' meetings with medicines developers to stimulate early dialogue on the development of their medicines for use in children. This initiative aims

---

73. The full listing of applicants for Enpr-EMA membership can be found on the EMA website, www.ema.europa.eu, and in particular at https://www.ema.europa.eu/en/partners-networks/networks/european-network-paediatric-research-european-medicines-agency-enpr-ema#membership-section.
74. *See* 'The Principles of Interaction between EMEA and FDA Paediatric Therapeutics' (June 2007) at < www.ema.europa.eu/pdfs/general/direct/pr/interactions.pdf > .
75. Five-year Report to the European Commission. General report on the experience acquired as a result of the application of the Paediatric Regulation. EMA/428172/2012.
76. Better Medicines for Children – from concept to reality – progress report on the Paediatric Regulation (EC) No. 1901/2006 – COM (2013) 443 final.

to encourage discussions on the paediatric needs that could be addressed with a specific medicine well before the submission of a PIP.

In October 2016, the EMA published its Ten-Year Report to the European Commission (General Report on the experience acquired as a result of the application of Regulation (EC) No. 1901/2006), as required in accordance with Article 50(3) of Regulation (EC) No. 1901/2006.[77] This report noted that the Regulation has had a positive impact on paediatric drug development, as shown by the data collected over the first nine years since its inception. It has led to: more[78] medicines for children as well as better and more information for prescribers and patients; better paediatric research and development; more regulatory support for paediatric matters; and paediatrics now being an integral part of medicine development. However, it also shows that little progress has been made in diseases that only affect children or where the disease shows biological differences between adults and children, particularly rare/orphan diseases.

The Commission commissioned the *Study on the economic impact of the Paediatric Regulation, including its rewards and incentives*,[79] which was published in December 2016. The aforesaid study concluded, among other things, that Regulation (EC) No. 1901/2006 has been able to shift the focus to paediatric medicine development. During the period between 2007 and 2015, the proportion of paediatric trials among all clinical trials increased by 2.5 times and over 100 PIPs were completed. The study also concluded that: 'The Regulation is considered as a commendable first step in the right direction but there remain therapeutic areas where significant unmet need continues to exist, such as in the field of paediatric oncology, and hence further steps and more time is needed to achieve the expected impact. It is claimed that therapeutic areas covered by research in children is driven mainly by commercial interest and reflecting the needs of the adults rather than those of children.'

More recently, in August 2020, the Commission published its joint evaluation,[80] which includes certain observations regarding Regulation (EC) No. 1901/2006. *See also* §14.09, which provides further background to this evaluation and describes the main observations in relation to Regulation (EC) No. 596/2009 on orphan medicinal products. From a paediatrics perspective, whilst the impact of Regulation (EC) No. 1901/2006 has been positive, the evaluation has observed, among other things, that 'The Regulation has no effective instrument for channelling R&D into specific therapeutic areas. Development has been boosted mainly in areas where adult development was already planned. It thus looks as if the Regulation works best in areas where the

---

77. Ten-year Report to the European Commission General report on the experience acquired as a result of the application of the Paediatric Regulation. EMA/231225/2015.
78. From 2007 until 2015, 238 new medicines for use in children and 39 new pharmaceutical forms appropriate for children were authorised in the EU.
79. Available at https://ec.europa.eu/health/sites/health/files/files/paediatrics/docs/paediatrics_10_years_economic_study.pdf.
80. Joint evaluation of Regulation (EC) No. 1901/2006 of the European Parliament and of the Council of 12 December 2006 on medicinal products for paediatric use and Regulation (EC) No. 141/2000 of the European Parliament and of the Council of 16 December 1999 on orphan medicinal products, available at https://eur-lex.europa.eu/legal-content/EN/TXT/?uri=CELEX%3A52020SC0163.

needs of adult and paediatric patients overlap. However, major therapeutic advances have mostly failed to materialise for diseases that are rare and/or unique to children, and which often receive equal amounts of support under the orphan legislation.' The evaluation also found that the SPC mechanism in the context of paediatrics has certain limitations and the Regulation burdensome in certain respects. Furthermore, Regulation (EC) No. 1901/2006 has no 'tools' to promote the development in specific therapeutic areas of paediatric medicines, as well as availability and patient access – and that such goals should inform the future amendment of the Regulation.

As part of the EU's Pharmaceutical Strategy for Europe (dated 25 November 2020),[81] Regulation (EC) No. 1901/2006 is being reviewed and updated. Regarding the interface between this Regulation and the Orphan Drug Regulation, a stakeholder consultation has taken place (from May 2021 until the end of July 2021).[82] In its Inception Impact Assessment guiding the initiative to revise the legislation, the Commission identified the following four key issues to be addressed: insufficient development in areas of greatest unmet medical needs for patients; availability and accessibility vary considerably across member states; scientific and technological developments cannot currently be fully exploited; and certain procedures are inefficient and burdensome. This revision will provide an opportunity to address some of the issues arising with the current framework (including those described in this note) and to 'future-proof' the legislation, as well as a chance to evaluate whether a new package of incentives could focus rewards to provide better stimulation of development in areas of currently unmet medical need. The additional goals of improving availability and patient access will also inform the revised legislation. The latest consultation process, which closed in July 2021, explored a range of possible amendments and policy questions. Respondents were asked for views on topics such as what might constitute effective new measures for promoting the development of medicines to address unmet therapeutic needs for children and rare disease patients (for example, assistance with R&D funding; assistance with authorisation procedures, such as priority review of the application from the EMA and expedited approval from the Commission; additional scientific support for the development of medicines from the EMA; or additional post-authorisation incentives that complement or replace the current incentives and rewards). A Commission proposal for revised paediatric medicines legislation is expected towards the end of 2022.

§8.10 UK

[A] Introduction

Generally, the post-Brexit regulation of paediatric medicines in the UK continues to be aligned with the EU regime set out above. As of 1 January 2021, the UK's paediatric

---

81. Available at https://eur-lex.europa.eu/legal-content/EN/TXT/?uri=COM%3A2020%3A761%3AFIN&qid=1606305129757.
82. *See* https://ec.europa.eu/info/law/better-regulation/have-your-say/initiatives/12767-Medicines-for-children-&-rare-diseases-updated-rules/public-consultation_en.

medicines regulatory framework is set out in the retained Regulation (EC) No. 1901/2006 (as of 31 December 2020), as implemented in the UK by the Human Medicines Regulations 2012, as further amended by the Human Medicines Regulations (Amendment etc.) (EU Exit) Regulations 2019 (UK HMRs).

The relevant UK regulator, the Medicines and Healthcare Products Regulatory Agency (MHRA) has in its guidance[83] noted that the UK PIP application process has been simplified and provides for expedited assessment where possible, and by continuing to follow the submission format, content, and terminology of the EU PIP system.

The MHRA shall, for purposes of Great Britain, be taking decisions on UK PIP and waiver opinions, modifications, and compliance statements to support paediatric market authorisation decisions, while acknowledging that Northern Ireland continues to be part of the EU's system for paediatric medicines development including agreement of EU PIPs or waivers. The format and submission procedure[84] for PIP applications to the MHRA remains largely similar to that of the EU, as discussed above. The MHRA has suggested that applicants consider the parallel submission of PIPs to EMA and MHRA for purposes of allowing parallel assessment and alignment of the agreed paediatric plans across jurisdictions.

[B] PIP Submissions

EU PIPs, modifications to EU PIPs, and full product-specific waivers with completed EMA assessments completed before 1 January 2021 were adopted as UK PIPs with effect from 1 January 2021. Re-submission to the MHRA is not necessary where a valid request for an EU PIP or modification or waiver was made to the EMA, but no EMA decision was given before 1 January 2021; such EU PIPs were adopted as UK PIPs provided that the EU PDCO issued a positive opinion before 1 January 2021. Where a valid request for an EU PIP or modification or waiver was made to the EMA, but the PDCO issued a negative opinion, the MHRA treats such application as refused. However, applicants may submit an updated PIP to the MHRA which addresses the reasons for refusal. EU PIPs which become UK PIPs under the abovementioned transitional provisions are referred to as 'adopted' UK PIPs by the MHRA. New UK PIP submissions after 1 January 2021 that have been assessed and agreed by the MHRA are referred to by the MHRA as 'agreed' UK PIPs.

As regards UK PIPs submissions after 1 January 2021, from a practical perspective, the MHRA accepts the submission of such PIP applications via the electronic MHRA Submissions portal. Regulation 50B (3) of the UK HMRs requires that applications for the agreement of a UK PIP be submitted, unless duly justified, 'not later than upon completion of the human pharmaco-kinetic (PK) studies', as specified in section 5.2.3 of Part I of Annex I to the 2001 Directive', unless the MHRA agrees to accept a

---

83. https://www.gov.uk/guidance/procedures-for-uk-paediatric-investigation-plan-pips.
84. *See* UK guidance at https://www.gov.uk/government/publications/format-and-content-of-applications-for-agreement-or-modification-of-a-paediatric-investigation-plan.

later request. Upon the submission of a PIP application to the MHRA, information must be provided on whether or not there is (i) an agreed EU PIP and the opinion and supporting documentation is included; (ii) an ongoing EU PIP assessment, its timeline in the PDCO assessment cycle (i.e., day 30, 60, clock stop, day 90, or 120); and (iii) any current scientific divergence between the submitted PIP application and the EU PIP.

With regard to a PIP submission with an agreed PDCO opinion from 1 January 2021 or ongoing assessment at EMA from 1 January 2021, in principle, the MHRA will likely aim to maintain alignment with a positive PDCO opinion (if one is reached before the MHRA assessment is completed). However, divergence could occur in the UK as the MHRA will likely take decisions for UK PIPs based on national and NHS paediatric public health needs, such as unmet UK paediatric needs (in this regard, *see* further below), paediatric-only development particularly for an innovative product (such as a new drug class, mechanism of action), the incidence of the disease in the UK population, any additional safety or efficacy concerns for the UK population, etc. (collectively, 'UK Criteria').

In relation to a UK PIP with no EU PIP from 1 January 2021 (i.e., if there is no corresponding EU PIP submission or if the PDCO opinion is negative), a full assessment of such UK PIP is required. The applicant must provide information relating to, among others, if there has been a previous negative PDCO PIP opinion, there was a withdrawn EU PIP prior to the adoption of a PDCO opinion, the current UK submission has been updated since the previous negative or withdrawn EU PIP, etc.

As mentioned above, the unmet needs of the UK paediatric population are an important factor that the MHRA will consider in relation to UK PIP application. These will be defined by, inter alia: (i) therapeutic areas identified by UK health bodies as high-priority public health concerns; (ii) product development in conditions identified after consultations with UK experts and patient groups, including those for rare diseases identified under the auspices of the Department of Health and Social Care (DHSC) policy paper – *UK strategy for rare diseases*;[85] (iii) product development in conditions (or paediatric groups) identified as critically important in the Regulation (EC) No. 1901/2006 Ten-Year Report (as briefly highlighted above in §8.09); (iv) products which are intended to be authorised as orphan medicines; and (v) products that fulfil the criteria of promising or innovative new products and are part of an accelerated MHRA submission or assessment pathway.

[C] PIP Modifications

With regard to the modification of an 'adopted' or 'agreed' UK PIP, Regulation 50B (6) of the UK HMRs provides that the applicant may request a modification of an 'agreed' UK PIP if the implementation of such PIP becomes practically unworkable or no longer appropriate in the circumstances. In this regard, the MHRA will assess the proposed changes based on the scientific arguments brought by the applicant. For both 'adopted'

---

85. https://assets.publishing.service.gov.uk/government/uploads/system/uploads/attachment_data/file/260562/UK_Strategy_for_Rare_Diseases.pdf.

and 'agreed' UK PIPs, upon the submission of a PIP modification, it should be confirmed if the application relates to the modification of: (i) an 'adopted' or 'agreed' UK-PIP; (ii) an agreed EU PIP modification; (iii) an ongoing EU PIP modification assessment; and (iv) if there is a significant scientific divergence between the current agreed EU PIP and the agreed UK PIP. Modifications submitted for UK PIPs where there is an EU PIP should also include the most recent PDCO opinion and PIP summary report. For 'agreed' UK PIPs, there will be either a focused assessment in cases where the EU opinion for the initial UK PIP was accepted by the MHRA, or a full modification assessment in cases where the initial UK PIP underwent full assessment.

In relation to requests for a UK PIP modification from 1 January 2021 onwards, in principle, the MHRA will aim to accept a positive (EU) PDCO opinion on modifications in cases where the initial UK PIP was agreed on the basis of an agreed EU PIP. A focused assessment may be needed where the UK Criteria (as mentioned above at §8.10[B] in the context of PIP submissions with an agreed PDCO opinion from 1 January 2021) are met. If the PDCO opinion is negative whilst the UK assessment is ongoing, the applicant has the option to withdraw the UK PIP modification request or continue with the MHRA assessment. Once a PIP has been withdrawn, a new UK PIP modification may be submitted, and it will undergo review using the UK Criteria. If the applicant continues with the MHRA assessment, the applicant may discuss amendments to the proposals before the final MHRA opinion on the proposed modification is agreed. If there is no agreed EMA/PDCO modification opinion, a full UK assessment of modification will be required.

[D] PIP Waivers

The EMA class waivers list (as mentioned above at §8.02[D][2]) was adopted by the UK with effect 1 January 2021. In principle, the MHRA aims to accept a positive EMA opinion on a class waiver request, but where there is no EMA opinion, MHRA will undertake such an assessment for purposes of the UK.

Should there be a negative EMA opinion on whether a class waiver applies, for purposes of the UK, an applicant may submit a full product-specific waiver request which should include the EMA opinion on the class waiver. If there is an EMA opinion on the applicant's subsequent product-specific waiver request, then this should also be made available to the MHRA to determine if a 'focused' or 'full' assessment is required.

Where there has been a 'full' product-specific waiver granted for purposes of the EU before 1 January 2021, such waiver will be adopted as a UK 'full' waiver; no submission to the UK is required.

[E] Compliance Checks

With regard to 'adopted' UK PIPs, regulation 50A (3) of the UK HMRs requires that applicants submit a compliance check application to the MHRA, where one is required for validation of the corresponding UK MA application. A positive (EU) PDCO CC or interim compliance check will be adopted as the UK compliance check outcome unless subsequent modifications have led to divergence between the UK and EU PIPs. The applicant must adhere to the agreed timelines of those measures which would need to be completed after the EU PDCO compliance check to ensure compliance on the date of the UK MA submission. The PDCO compliance outcome documents should also be submitted ahead of, or at the time of the UK MA application via the electronic MHRA Submissions portal.

In relation to 'agreed' UK PIPs, regulation 50A (3) of the UK HMR provides that applicants must submit a compliance check application with the MHRA where one is required for validation of the UK MA application. A UK assessment is required for full or interim compliance check if: (i) there is any scientific divergence between the 'agreed' UK PIP and the EU PIP; (ii) there is no PDCO CC; and (iii) in the case of an interim compliance check (where there are additional key measures completed prior to UK MA submission). The MHRA may adopt the EU PDCO compliance check outcome if: (i) there is a positive PDCO compliance check; (ii) the UK PIP is equivalent to the EU PIP; or (iii) for interim compliance checks (i.e., where there are no additional key measures completed prior to UK MA submission that requires further compliance check assessment). In this regard, applicants are encouraged to request a compliance check ahead of submission of a marketing authorization application where one is required for validation.

[F] Completed Paediatric Studies

Regulations 78A(13) and (14) of the UK HMR provide that UK MA holders who sponsor a study involving the use of the medicinal product (to which the marketing authorization relates) in a paediatric group must submit to the MHRA the results of such study within the period of six months from the day on which such study ended. This requirement applies irrespective of whether or not: (i) the studies are conducted in accordance with an agreed PIP; or (ii) marketing authorization holder intends to apply for a MA for a paediatric indication in relation to the product.

§8.11 GUIDELINES/PUBLICATIONS

- General guidance: https://www.ema.europa.eu/en/human-regulatory/overview/paediatric-medicines-overview
- Questions and answers: PIP Guidance www.ema.europa.eu
- Questions and answers: Submission of Article 46 paediatric studies www.ema.europa.eu
- Guidance on paediatric submissions, EMA/672643/2017 Rev.2, 18 March 2020
- Communication from the Commission: Guideline on the format and content of applications for agreement or modification of a paediatric investigation plan and requests for waivers or deferrals and concerning the operation of the compliance check and on criteria for assessing significant studies (2014/C 338/01).

- Recommendation of the Paediatric Committee to the European Commission regarding the Symbol, EMEA/498247/2007.
- The Network of Paediatric Networks at the EMA Implementing Strategy, EMEA/MB/543523/2007.
- The PDCO Rules of Procedure, EMEA/3448440/2008, Rev. 2, 25 March 2020.
- The Principles of Interactions between EMA and FDA Paediatric Therapeutics, June 2007: www.ema.europa.eu.
- 2018 Report to the European Commission on companies and products that have benefitted from any of the rewards and incentives in the Paediatric Regulation and on companies that have failed to comply with any of the obligations in this Regulation (dated 29 October 2019), Doc. Ref. EMA/103569/2019 (reports on previous years also available).
- Report on the Survey of all paediatric uses of medicinal products in Europe Doc. Ref. EMA/794083/2009.
- Revised priority list for studies into off-patent paediatric medicinal products Doc.Ref. EMA/PDCO/98717/2012, Rev. 2013/14.
- Five-Year Report to the European Commission – General Report on the experience acquired as a result of the application of the Paediatric Regulation Doc. Ref. EMA/428172/2012.
- Better Medicines for Children – from concept to reality – progress report on the Paediatric Regulation (EC) No. 1901/2006 – COM (2013) 443 final.
- Success of the Paediatric Regulation after 5 years (August 2007 – December 2012) EMA/250577/2013.
- Ten-Year Report to the European Commission General report on the experience acquired as a result of the application of the Paediatric Regulation. EMA/231225/2015.
- Study on the economic impact of the Paediatric Regulation, including its rewards and incentives, December 2016, available at https://ec.europa.eu/health/sites/health/files/files/paediatrics/docs/paediatrics_10_years_economic_study.pdf.
- Reflection paper on the use of extrapolation in the development of medicines for paediatrics: EMA/189724/2018, 7 October 2018.
- Concept paper on the involvement of children and young people at the Paediatric Committee (PDCO), EMA/PDCO/388684/2012, 17 September 2012.
- Commission Staff Working Document – Joint evaluation of Regulation (EC) No. 1901/2006 of the European Parliament and of the Council of 12 December 2006 on medicinal products for paediatric use and Regulation (EC) No. 141/2000 of the European Parliament and of the Council of 16 December 1999 on orphan medicinal products: SWD (2020) 163 final (11.8.2020).
- Case T-52/09 *Nycomed Danmark v. EMA*.
- *Merck Sharp & Dohme Corp. v. Deutsches Patent- und Markenamt* Case C-125/10.
- Dr Reddy's Laboratories *v.* Warner-Lambert [2012] EWHC 3715 (Pat).
- *Shire Pharmaceutical Contracts v. European Commission*, CaseT-583/13.

- Case T-48/14 – *Pfizer v. European Commission and EMA*.
- MHRA Guidance: Legal requirements for children's medicines (last updated 31 December 2020): https://www.gov.uk/government/publications/legal-requirements-for-childrens-medicines.
- MHRA Guidance: Procedures for UK Paediatric Investigation Plan (PIPs) (31 December 2020): https://www.gov.uk/guidance/procedures-for-uk-paediatric-investigation-plan-pips.
- MHRA Guidance: Completed Paediatric Studies – submission, processing and assessment (31 December 2020): https://www.gov.uk/guidance/completed-paediatric-studies-submission-processing-and-assessment.

CHAPTER 9
Advertising Medicinal Products for Human Use

Hester Borgers & Edzard Boonen (main chapter, the Netherlands); Marc Martens & Benedicte Mourisse (Belgium); Alexandre Vuchot, Johanna Harelimana & Nour Saab (France); Christian Lindenthal & Wolfgang Ernst (Germany); Mauro Turrini (Italy); Coral Yáñez & Ana María Sánchez-Valdepeñas López (Spain); Gabriel Lidman & Gunnar Hjalt (Sweden); and Sally Shorthose, Sarah Faircliffe & Pieter Erasmus (United Kingdom)[*]

§9.01 INTRODUCTION

Advertising is used extensively in consumer societies, and it affects the choices and decisions that consumers make. Usually, advertising is acceptable if it is in line with legislation and agreed standards of good practice. There are generally agreed minimum standards: advertising must not be misleading or cause serious or widespread offence. Advertising of medicines is subject to the general provisions and codes applicable to the advertising of other types of products.[1]

However, advertising medicines is also subject to tighter controls, as medicines are not considered ordinary commodities, as they have the potential to cause harmful effects if not used appropriately. Furthermore, it is important to ensure that advertising and promotional activities regarding certain medicinal products as such does not unjustly influence or induce healthcare professionals. Therefore, specific requirements for medicines are established at the European level by Directive 2001/83/EC, which apply in addition to the general rules.

---

[*] The authors wish to acknowledge Anne-Charlotte Le Bihan, Nicolas Carbonnelle, Raquel Ballesteros, Ulf Grundmann, Jean-Baptiste Thiénot, and Hanneke Later-Nijland, being contributing authors of the earlier editions of this chapter.
1. For example, Case C-544/13 and C-545/13, *Abcur AB v. Apoteket Farmaci AB and Apoteket AB*, Judgment of 16 July 2015 about the application of Directive 2005/29/EC.

These general and specific rules apply to medicines both for prescription-use and for over-the-counter (OTC) products.[2] Furthermore, it is important to note that with regard to advertising, often, distinction is made whether the advertisements are aimed at the public or aimed at healthcare professionals (prescribers and suppliers of medicines).

Although OTC product advertising may be directed at healthcare professionals, in practice, it is mostly aimed directly at the consumer. This is in contrast to the advertising of medicinal products available by medical prescription[3] and medicinal products that contain psychotropic or narcotic substances,[4] which are prohibited to the general public. Therefore, these products may only be advertised to healthcare professionals.

Member States have implemented the requirements of Directive 2001/83/EC into their national laws differently, and the rules are not completely harmonised across Europe. Recital 43 to Directive 2001/83/EC acknowledges that Member States have adopted further specific measures concerning the advertising of medicinal products, which may have an impact on the functioning of the internal market, as advertising disseminated in one Member State is likely to have effects in other Member States.

The rise in the use of the Internet has resulted in greater availability of information and an increased ability to purchase products across borders. This has led to the referral of questions from national courts to the European Court of Justice (ECJ) to clarify the law in this area.[5]

There is self-regulation of the activities of pharmaceutical companies in relation to the promotion of prescription products to healthcare professionals through their industry associations. Companies are also encouraged to comply with the provisions of the Code of Practice of the International Federation of Pharmaceutical Manufacturers and Associations (IFPMA), where applicable. IFPMA is the global non-governmental organisation that represents the research-based pharmaceutical, biotech, and vaccine sector.

The representative body of the pharmaceutical industry marketing prescription products in Europe is the European Federation of Pharmaceutical Industries and Associations (EFPIA). EFPIA has a Europe-wide Code of Practice, which is described in §9.03[A][1] below. EFPIA is also a member of the IFPMA, and the EFPIA Code of Practice thus also embodies the principles of the abovementioned IFPMA Code. The EFPIA Code is said to constitute the collection of ethical rules agreed by the EFPIA members for the Promotion of Medicinal Products to healthcare practitioners (HCPs) and the interactions with the HCPs), healthcare organisations (HCOs) and patient organisations (POs), with the intent of guaranteeing that these activities are conducted

---

2. OTC products include those supplied under the supervision of a pharmacist, and those on general sale (e.g., sold in supermarkets).
3. Article 88(1)a Directive 2001/83/EC.
4. Article 88(1)b Directive 2001/83/EC.
5. For example, Case C-649/18 *A v. Daniel B and others*, judgment of 1 October 2020 about the application of Article 34 TFEU, Article 85c of Directive 2001/83/EC, and Article 3 of Directive 2000/31/EC and earlier Case No. C-322/01 *Deutscher Apothekerverband eV v. 0800 DocMorris NV, Jacques Waterval*, judgment of 11 December 2003.

Chapter 9: Advertising Medicinal Products for Human Use   §9.01

while respecting the most stringent ethical principles of professionalism and responsibility. The EFPIA Code applies to all types of communication and interaction, both traditional and digital. The EFPIA Code is discussed in more detail later in this chapter.

Furthermore, national self-regulatory codes of conduct often apply in the different Member States.

There is no Europe-wide guidance regarding OTC products. The Global Self-Care Federation (GSCF) (formerly known as WSMI), a global federation of over fifty regional and national member associations and manufacturers and distributors of non-prescription medicines, supports the development of self-medication industry associations around the world. The GSCF has developed a Code of Ethics for members to uphold and recognise as best practice across the self-care industry. From this Code of Ethics, it follows that GSCF encourages member associations to develop voluntary codes of advertising practice and that it supports truthful labelling.

Outside the EU, some countries permit advertising of prescription medicinal products directly to consumers (DTC), with the most notable examples being the United States and New Zealand. There have been proposals to allow DTC advertising within the European Community (Community). The 2001 review of pharmaceutical legislation recommended allowing DTC advertising, but the European Parliament rejected this proposal.

There is a fine line to be drawn between advertising and the provision of information on medicinal products to patients, and from time to time, this topic sparked debate on a European level.

In 1997, the CPMP, now renamed as CHMP (European Medicines Agency's Committee for Medicinal Products for Human Use), proposed that there should be some coordination at a European level for products authorised by the centralised route in the 'event of an important advertising concern with potential public health implications occurring'.[6] The pharmacovigilance working party was promulgated as the appropriate forum to discuss such issues, but as yet, there has not been any implementation of monitoring and enforcement of the rules at a centralised European level. The first public consultation on the topic of information to patients on medicinal products was launched by the European Commission (Commission) in April 2007. During the consultation, seventy-three contributions were received, including responses from patient organisations, consumer and citizen organisations, and pharmaceutical industry organisations. In December 2007, the Commission presented a report to the European Parliament and Council on the current practice with regard to the provision of information, particularly on the Internet, and its risks and benefits for patients. In the report, the Commission expresses that with the increased use of the Internet in recent years, ensuring reliable and good quality information available on websites has become essential. The information that patients can currently find on the Internet sites of some competent authorities includes the summary of product characteristics (SmPC) and public assessment reports. Most information is available in English, with provision of the information in other official languages of the EU is

---

6. CPMP/183/97 Conduct of Pharmacovigilance for Centrally Authorised Products (15 April 1997).

available to a greater or lesser extent. This report found that there were significant inequalities in the provision of information across Member States. Public consultation confirmed that the legislative framework on information to patients should be improved.[7] In December 2008, the Commission presented its legal proposal to amend Directive 2001/83/EC and Regulation No. 726/2004 with a view to improving and harmonising the information available from pharmaceutical companies about their prescription-only medicines (POMs) to patients. An amended proposal was presented by the Commission on 10 February 2012. However, discussions between Member States on the 'information to patients' proposals did not make progress, and the proposal was withdrawn by Commission in May 2014.[8]

This chapter summarises the requirements for both POMs and OTC products at a European level, and it examines, in detail, the systems in place in the United Kingdom (UK), where self-regulation of advertising in both sectors (i.e., POMs and OTC products) is well-established. The national requirements and features in seven other Member States are summarised. Finally, the Commission's legislative proposals are considered in more detail.

§9.02 LEGISLATIVE BASIS

Legislation on the advertising of medicinal products in Europe was first adopted by the Council of the European Communities on 31 March 1992, by Council Directive 92/28/EEC 'on the advertising of medicinal products for human use'. This was replaced by provisions in Council Directive 2001/83/EC in November 2001 and updated by subsequent amendments. Currently, Title VIII 'Advertising' and Title VIIIa 'Information and Advertising' (covering Articles 86–100) of Directive 2001/83/EC govern the content and control of medicines advertising in Member States.

However, the specific requirements of Directive 2001/83/EC must be considered alongside general requirements on advertising; for instance, Recital 42 of Directive 2001/83/EC states that it is without prejudice to the applications of measures adopted pursuant to Council Directive 84/450/EEC relating to misleading advertising.

[A] The General Principles

The general principles of advertising under Directive 2001/83/EC include:

- unlicensed medicinal products (i.e., those that do not have a Marketing Authorisation) must not be advertised;[9]

---

7. Communication from the Commission entitled 'Report on the current practices with regard to the provision of information to patients on medicinal products', adopted and submitted to European Parliament and Council on 20 December 2007.
8. Official Journal of the European Union, C 153, Volume 57, 21 May 2014.
9. Article 87(1) Directive 2001/83/EC; note, however that homeopathic medicinal products are exempted from this provision (Article 100).

- all parts of the advertising of a medicinal product must comply with the particulars listed in the SmPC;[10]
- the advertising of the medicinal product shall encourage the rational use of the medicinal product and shall not be misleading;[11]
- POMs may only be advertised to those persons who are qualified to prescribe or supply them, for example, healthcare professionals such as doctors, dentists, pharmacists, nurses, and hospital administrators who make buying decisions;
- OTC medicines may be advertised to the general public subject to specific rules;[12]

[B] Promotion of OTC Medicines

Medicinal products 'may be advertised to the general public which are intended and designed for use without the intervention of a medical practitioner for diagnostic purposes or for the prescription or monitoring of treatment, with the advice of a pharmacist, if necessary'.[13]

The advertising of a medicinal product to the general public must not contain any material that:

(a) gives the impression that a medical consultation or surgical operation is unnecessary, in particular, offering a diagnosis or suggesting treatment by mail;[14]
(b) suggests that the effects of taking a medicine are guaranteed, are unaccompanied by side effects, or are better than, or equivalent to, those of another treatment or medicinal product;[15]
(c) suggests that the health of the subjects can be enhanced by taking the medicine;[16]
(d) with the exception of vaccination campaigns, suggests that the health of the subject could be affected by not taking the medicine;[17]
(e) is directed exclusively or principally at children;[18]
(f) refers to a recommendation by scientists, health professionals, or persons (neither scientists nor health professionals) who because of their celebrity, could encourage the consumption of medicinal products;[19]

---

10. Article 87(2) Directive 2001/83/EC.
11. Article 87(3) Directive 2001/83/EC.
12. Article 88(2) Directive 2001/83/EC.
13. *Ibid.*
14. Article 90(a) Directive 2001/83/EC.
15. Article 90(b) Directive 2001/83/EC.
16. Article 90(c) Directive 2001/83/EC.
17. Article 90(d) and Article 88(4) Directive 2001/83/EC.
18. Article 90(e) Directive 2001/83/EC.
19. Article 90(f) Directive 2001/83/EC.

(g) suggests that the medicinal product is a foodstuff, cosmetic, or other consumer product;[20]
(h) suggests that the safety or efficacy of the medicinal product is due to the fact that it is natural;[21]
(i) could, by a description or detailed representation of a case history, lead to erroneous self-diagnosis;[22]
(j) refers, in improper, alarming, or misleading terms, to claims of recovery;[23] and
(k) uses, in improper, alarming, or misleading terms, pictorial representations of changes in the human body caused by disease or injury, or of the action of a medicinal product on the human body or parts of the human body.[24]

All advertising of medicinal products available OTC to the general public must be clearly designated as an advertisement, and it must clearly identify the product being advertised as a medicinal product.[25] The advertising must contain minimum information[26] as follows:

(a) the name of the medicinal product, and its common name (International non-proprietary name (INN) or generic name);
(b) information that is necessary for its correct use;
(c) an express, legible invitation to read the instructions on the outside of the packaging or the package leaflet carefully.

The provisions of Directive 2001/83/EC apply to the advertising of homeopathic medicinal products that are subject to the special, simplified registration procedure,[27] with the exception of Article 87(1), which is the requirement to have a Marketing Authorisation (MA).[28] Only the information specified in Article 69(1) of Directive 2001/83/EC 'may be used in advertising' the product. This is the information that is allowed on the labelling and package leaflets of homeopathic medicinal products, and it includes clear mention of the words 'homeopathic medicinal product', the scientific name of the stock or stocks followed by the degree of dilution, name and address of the registration holder and manufacturer (where appropriate), and a warning advising the user to consult a doctor if symptoms persist.

In case of the advertisement for a traditional herbal medicinal product, in addition to the more general requirements as laid down in Articles 86 to 99, any

---

20. Article 90(g) Directive 2001/83/EC.
21. Article 90(h) Directive 2001/83/EC.
22. Article 90(i) Directive 2001/83/EC.
23. Article 90(j) Directive 2001/83/EC.
24. Article 90(k) Directive 2001/83/EC.
25. Article 89(1)(a) Directive 2001/83/EC.
26. Article 89(1)(b) Directive 2001/83/EC.
27. Article 14(1) Directive 2001/83/EC.
28. Article 100 Directive 2001/83/EC.

advertisement shall contain the statement that traditional herbal medicinal product is for use in specified indication(s) exclusively based upon long-standing use.[29]

[C] What Is Advertising?

Following the Directive, advertising should be understood as including any form of door-to-door information, canvassing activity, or inducement designed to promote the prescription, supply, sale, or consumption of medicinal products. This specifically includes:[30]

- the advertising of medicinal products to the general public;
- advertising of medicinal products to persons qualified to prescribe or supply them;
- visits by medical sales representatives to persons qualified to prescribe medicinal products;
- the supply of samples;
- the provision of inducements to prescribe or supply medicinal products by the gift, offer, or promise of any benefit or bonus, whether in money or in kind, except when their intrinsic value is minimal;
- sponsorship of promotional meetings attended by persons qualified to prescribe or supply medicinal products; and
- sponsorship of scientific congresses attended by persons qualified to prescribe or supply medicinal products, and in particular, payment of their travelling and accommodations expenses in connection therewith.

The following items and activities are not considered to be advertising:[31]

(a) The labelling and package leaflet of the product.
(b) Correspondence needed to answer a specific question about a particular medicine.
(c) Factual informative announcements and reference material, such as information about pack changes, adverse-reaction warnings, trade catalogues, and price lists, provided they do not include product claims.
(d) Information relating to human health or disease, provided there is no reference, even indirect, to medicinal products.

[D] Internet Advertising

The Internet has opened up the availability of information to the general public; however, all the rules applicable to advertising and the provision of information to the public apply vis-à-vis to advertising online. Article 90 of Directive 2001/83/EC

---

29. Article 16g(3) Directive 2001/83/EC.
30. Article 86(1) Directive 2001/83/EC.
31. Article 86(2) Directive 2001/83/EC.

(restating Article 5 of Directive 92/98/EC) lists the material that must not be included when advertising medicinal products to the general public, which thus also applies to online information dissemination and advertising. Advertising on the Internet is acceptable provided it complies with the advertising regulations laid down in Directive 2001/83/EC.

[E] Television Advertising

Council Directive 89/552/EEC, as amended by Directive 2010/13/EU, concerns audiovisual media services, and Article 4(1) provides that 'Member States shall remain free to require media service providers under their jurisdiction to comply with more detailed or stricter rules in the fields covered by this Directive provided that such rules are in compliance with Union law.' Preamble 89 states that 'it is also necessary to prohibit all audiovisual commercial communication for medicinal products and medical treatment available only on prescription in the Member State within whose jurisdiction the media service provider falls, which is reaffirmed in article 9(f), 10(3) and 11(4)(b) of this Directive.' Also, teleshopping for medicinal products subject to an MA, as well as teleshopping for medical treatment, is prohibited.[32]

[F] European Case Law on Advertising of Medicinal Products

The Court of Justice of the European Union (CJEU) has clarified the law on advertising of medicinal products in Europe. These cases have been determined with reference to the over-arching principle of the freedom of movement of goods.

In 2003, the court of Frankfurt am Main, Germany, referred questions to the CJEU about whether the national prohibition on sales applied cross-border. It was held that a national prohibition on the sale by mail order of medicinal products, restricted to the Member State concerned, is a measure having an effect equivalent to a quantitative restriction for the purposes of Article 28 of the EC Treaty (freedom of movement of goods). The defences available under Article 30, where Member States can justify national measures that may impede cross-border trade, may be relied on to justify a national prohibition on sale of medicinal products that are subject to prescription, but not those medicinal products that are not subject to prescription. Therefore, Member States can have restrictions in place for prescription products but not for OTC products when advertising and supplying medicinal products across borders.[33]

In another case, the ECJ has held that Directive 2001/83/EC sets out a definitive maximum standard, so Member States cannot impose stricter rules on advertising.[34] The aim of the legislation is to remove barriers to trade between Member States, and any differences between Member States may affect the functioning of the internal

---

32. Article 21 Directive 2010/13/EU
33. Case No. C-322/01 *Deutscher Apothekerverband eV v. 0800 DocMorris NV, Jacques Waterval*, judgment of 11 December 2003.
34. Case No. C-143/06 *Ludwigs-Apotheke München Internationale Apotheke v. Juers Pharma Import-Export GmbH*, judgment of 8 November 2007.

market. Therefore, it is only where Directive 2001/83/EC expressly sets out some circumstances where stricter legislation may be adopted that Member States have the flexibility to do so.

It was not disputed that the national law in Germany allows pharmacists to obtain, in limited quantities, medicinal products that have been lawfully put into circulation in another Member State, but not authorised in Germany, in order to meet an order from an individual. This provision appeared to the CJEU to implement Article 5(1) of Directive 2001/83/EC, and therefore the provisions of Title VIII on advertising are not applicable.

The German Federal Supreme Court ('*Bundesgerichtshof*') requested a preliminary ruling from the ECJ on whether German legislation was compatible with Directive 2001/83/EC. The first question put to the CJEU concerned the relationship of Directive 2001/83/EC to national legislation with regard to advertising. The Court was asked to consider whether Directive 2001/83/EC provides minimum standards only, allowing the Member States of the EU to impose stricter rules on advertising, or whether it, at the same time, sets a definitive maximum standard, limiting regulation by the Member States.[35]

In this ruling, the CJEU further held that Directive 2001/83/EC aims to remove barriers to trade between Member States. Disparities in national legislation on advertising may impair the functioning of the internal market. Directive 2001/83/EC expressly states the cases in which Member States may adopt stricter legislation on advertising. In the absence of such express permission to adopt stricter legislation, Directive 2001/83/EC sets not just a minimum standard but a maximum at the same time. This is in line with a decision rendered two months earlier in which the CJEU decided that the procedures for obtaining an MA laid down in Directive 2001/83/EC are exhaustive, preventing the Member States from implementing additional procedures.[36]

It was held that Articles 87(3), 88(6), and 96(1) of Directive 2001/83/EC prohibit the advertising of a medicinal product by means of a prize draw announced on the Internet, insomuch as it encourages the irrational use of that medicinal product and leads to the direct distribution to the general public and to the presentation of free samples.[37]

In this judgment, the CJEU held that the campaign in question was not in line with Directive 2001/83/EC. First, the testimonials on the website claimed to improve health in general. This is incompatible with the prohibition of Directive 2001/83/EC on any suggestion that the health of the subject could be enhanced by taking the medicine. At the same time, the testimonials attributed effects to the product that in all likelihood had to be considered misleading, as the product did not possess such properties. Second, while prize drawings, in general, are not prohibited under Directive 2001/83/EC, the Court pointed out that any excessive and ill-considered advertising is

---

35. Case No. C-374/05 *Gintec International Import-Export GmbH v. Verband Sozialer Wettbewerb eV*. Judgment of the Court of 8 November 2007.
36. Case No. C-84/06, *The Netherlands v. Antroposana* et al. Judgment of 20 September 2007.
37. Case No. C-374/05 *Gintec International Import-Export GmbH v. Verband Sozialer Wettbewerb eV*. Judgment of the Court of 8 November 2007,

prohibited. Advertising must encourage the rational use of medicine, and offering a medicinal product as a prize does not encourage rational use. Also, according to the Court, offering this product as a prize must be equated with free distribution, which violates the prohibition on direct distribution of medicinal products to the public by the pharmaceutical industry for promotional purposes. The distribution of free samples is limited, under specific conditions, to persons who prescribe medicinal products.[38]

In its judgment of 2 April 2009 in Case C-421/07, the CJEU ruled that Directive 2001/83/EC is to be interpreted as meaning that dissemination by a third party of information about a medicinal product may be regarded as advertising within the meaning of that directive, even though the third party in question is acting on his own initiative and completely independently, de jure and de facto, of the manufacturer and the seller of such a medicinal product.

In that regard, the Court stated that even where the activity is carried out by an independent third party outside any commercial or industrial activity, advertising of medicinal products is liable to harm public health, the safeguarding of which is the essential aim of Directive 2001/83/EC.[39]

The CJEU left it to the national court to determine whether that dissemination constitutes a form of door-to-door information, canvassing activity, or inducement designed to promote the prescription, supply, sale, or consumption of medicinal products.[40]

This question of whether medicinal products which can be marketed in Poland without having an MA granted in Poland (contrary to Article 6(1) of Directive 2001/83) has been brought by the Commission to the CJEU. This marketing of products in Poland was permitted under Article 4(1) and (3a) of the Law on Medicinal Products ('*Prawo farmaceutyczne*'). The basis for this provision was economic (the imported medicinal product price had to be competitive compared with product on the Polish market) rather than the fact that the product was unavailable (which may justify an exception to Article 6(1) of the Law of Medicinal Products).

The Commission sought an order that Poland has failed to fulfil its obligations under Article 6(1) of Directive 2001/83.

In a judgment delivered on 29 March 2012, the CJEU held that Poland has failed to fulfil its obligations under Article 6 of Directive 2001/83/EC by adopting and maintaining in force Article 4(3a) of the Medicinal Products Law which, when read in conjunction with Article 4(3)(2) and Article 4(1) of the same law, allowed the placing on the market of medicinal products from abroad without an MA, if the price of these products was competitive in comparison with the price of the medicinal products which had obtained an MA in Poland and had the same active substance or substances, the same dosage, and the same form.[41]

---

38. Case No. C-374/05 *Gintec International Import-Export GmbH v. Verband Sozialer Wettbewerb eV*. Judgment of the Court of 8 November 2007.
39. Case C-421/07 *Criminal Proceedings against Frede Damgaard*, judgment of 2 April 2009.
40. *Ibid.*
41. Case C-185/10 *European Commission v. Republic of Poland*, judgment of 29 March 2012.

The CJEU further ordered, in a case between a Hungarian company and the Hungarian National Institute of Pharmacy and Nutrition regarding OTC medicines that with regard to the sale of a medicinal product in Hungary which does not have a marketing authorisation in that Member State but does have such an authorisation in another Member State where it is dispensed without medical prescription, that Article 5(1) and Article 6(1) of Directive 2001/83/EC should be interpreted as precluding a medicinal product which can be supplied without medical prescription in one Member State from also being considered a medicinal product which can be supplied without medical prescription in another Member State where, in that other Member State, the medicinal product in question does not have an MA and has not been classified.[42]

The CJEU further delivered a judgment regarding the interpretation of Articles 96(1) and 96(2) of Directive 2001/83/EC regarding the distribution of free samples of medicinal products to pharmacists, where the CJEU ordered that this article must be understood as precluding pharmaceutical companies from distributing free samples of medicinal products to pharmacists, however, that the provision does not preclude distributing free samples of non-prescription medicinal products to pharmacists.[43]

§9.03 SELF-REGULATION IN EUROPE

[A] Advertising of Prescription-Only Products

A feature of advertising of medicinal products is that there is self-regulation of companies through their industry associations at a national level.

As mentioned above, the representative body of the prescription pharmaceutical industry in Europe, EFPIA has drawn up a code of conduct for its members: the EFPIA Code of Practice, covering nearly all aspects of interaction and communication between the industry and HCPs, HCOs, and POs.

[1] The EFPIA HCP Code

EFPIA members are the national industry associations of thirty-six national associations in Europe and thirty-nine leading pharmaceutical companies. The EFPIA Code of Practice reflects the requirements of Directive 2001/83/EC, as amended. The Directive recognises the role of voluntary control of advertising of medicinal products by self-regulatory bodies and recourse to such bodies when complaints arise. The first EFPIA Code came into effect on 1 January 1992, and it has been updated several times in line with changes in the legislation.

The EFPIA Code is applicable to EFPIA 'Member companies', including separate entities belonging to the same multi-national company, subsidiary company, or any other form of enterprise or organisation. Member Companies are responsible for the

---

42. Case C-178/20, *Pharma Expressz Szolgáltató és Kereskedelmi Kft. v. Országos Gyógyszerészeti és Élelmezés-egészségügyi Intézet*, judgment of 8 July 2021.
43. Case C-786/18, *Ratiopharm v. Novartis Consumer Health*, judgment of 11 June 2020.

activities of other parties ('Third Party') they commission, including, for example, contract sales forces, consultancy and advisory boards, market research companies, and advertising agencies.[44]

The EFPIA Code covers any promotional activity and communication directly towards any member of the medical, dental, pharmacy, or nursing profession or any other persons who, in the course of their professional activities, may prescribe, purchase, supply, or administer a medicinal product.[45]

The EFPIA Code contains rules on the Promotion of POM to HCPs, Interaction between Member Companies and HCPs, HCOs, POs, an Disclosure of Transfer of Value from Member Companies to HCPs, HCOs, and POs.

[2] Applicability of the EFPIA Code

The EFPIA Code sets out the minimum standards companies must follow to comply with the European legislation that the member associations must adopt as a minimum into their national codes. Most Member States have a national industry body, which has its own local code, reflecting additional national requirements.[46]

[3] EFPIA Code and Principles for the Use of Digital Channels

The EFPIA Code gives minimum standard guidelines for so-called digital channels available to healthcare professionals, patients, and the public in the EU.[47] These guidelines have sections on compliance, responsibility, pharmacovigilance, and transparency. The annex contains guidance for various digital channels, such as websites, social media, blogs, podcasts, apps, and webinars.

[B] Advertising of OTC Products

The European industry body for OTC products is the Association of the European Self-Medication Industry (AESGP). AESGP does not have a separate code – self-regulation is handled by national organisations. The AESGP considers itself the voice of the manufacturers of OTC medicines, food supplements, and self-care medical devices in Europe, supporting the mission of access to safe and effective self-care. AESGP states that, along with advice from pharmacists, advertising plays a crucial role in supporting self-care, as it provides individuals with information about the availability and applications of their self-care products. AESGP thus promotes responsible and ethical advertising, as this allows the public to make informed decisions about their health, which in turn will reduce the burden on the national healthcare systems.

---

44. EFPIA Code of Practice 2021, p. 13.
45. *Ibid.*
46. EFPIA Code of Practice 2021, p. 15.
47. EFPIA Code of Practice 2021, Annex 3.

Although most advertising of OTC products will be directed at the general public, pharmaceutical companies also advertise these products to healthcare professionals. This is discussed in more detail in relation to the UK under the Proprietary Association of Great Britain (PAGB) Professional Code.

§9.04 IMPLEMENTATION IN BELGIUM

[A] Legal Basis

The Medicines Act of 25 March 1964 (hereinafter the 'Medicines Act') is the main legislation regarding the advertising of medicinal products. In addition, the Royal Decree of 7 April 1995 applies specifically to human use and the Royal Decree of 9 July 1984 to veterinary use.

The Belgian implementation of Directive 2001/83/EC extends beyond the requirements of Directive 2001/83/EC, as the general ban on the provision of gifts or benefits to wholesalers, healthcare professionals, or medical devices suppliers has been extended to all institutions where medicinal products are prescribed, delivered, or administered (e.g., hospitals). Moreover, the same prohibitions apply to medicinal products for veterinary use. The general principles laid down by European law, as described under the general section above, do indeed apply in Belgium.

[B] Sanctions

Failure to comply with the applicable rules on the advertising and promotion of medicinal products can result in administrative or civil actions against the offender. Criminal sanctions include fines and, theoretically, imprisonment.

Different types of administrative and civil sanctions are provided for:

- fines;
- ban on distribution;
- obligation to publish or circulate a retraction; and
- withdrawal of the advertising permit.

These rules are subject to the review of Federal Agency for Medicines and Health Products (FAMHP) review. Some of the breaches are referred to the public prosecutor.

Actions can also be brought before the commercial court by competing companies based on the Fair Trade Practices Act.

[C] Role of the National Competent Authority

The FAMHP exercises an a priori control on advertising directed to consumers (through a visa or notification procedure) and, in principle, an a posteriori control on advertising intended for the professional audience.

Advertising via television or radio requires prior approval by the minister of public health, whereas advertising of OTC medicinal products to the general public by other means is subject to a notification to the minister.
The applications and notifications are filed with the FAMHP.

[D] Self-Regulation

Some industry associations have issued their own rules to ensure compliance with the advertising rules. Complaints may be brought by both legal entities and natural persons before the ethics committee of the industry association (e.g., pharma.be) against its members. The decisions of the committee are binding on the members of the association.

According to Article 10 of the Medicines Act, invitations to scientific seminars as well as the payment of the related costs (including hospitality) of professionals are allowed provided the legal conditions are fulfilled. Should the participation in the scientific seminar have a duration of multiple consecutive days, manufacturers, importers, and medical wholesalers shall, prior to their participation, submit a request for approval for participation to Mdeon. Mdeon is a self-regulatory body created jointly by the national associations of doctors and pharmacists, the pharmaceutical industry, and the medical devices industry.

According to Mdeon's ethical rules, scientific events organised, sponsored, or otherwise directly or indirectly supported, in Belgium or abroad, by manufacturers, importers, or wholesalers of medicinal products and medical devices to which healthcare professionals participate must be organised within a framework that does not bring into disrepute the scientific nature of the event.

The term 'scientific event' includes all activities consisting of the provision of information, training courses, seminars, scientific meetings, and congresses as well as all forms of scientific meetings organised by manufacturers, importers, or medical wholesale suppliers from Belgium or elsewhere.

According to Mdeon's ethical rules, an application must be filed at least fifteen days before the meeting.

Furthermore, self-regulatory bodies can influence the legal landscape concerning the provision of gifts or benefits to healthcare professionals and organisations.

An example of such influence is the coming into effect of the Sunshine Act.[48] According to this law, pharmaceutical (both for human and veterinary medicinal products) and medical device companies are required to annually disclose to FAMHP all direct or indirect advantages, in money or in kind, processed from Belgium or elsewhere to healthcare professionals as well as to organisations active in the healthcare industry. The transfers of value are disclosed annually by means of a legally accredited online platform.

Before the promulgation of the Sunshine Act, this was a deontological initiative of members of certain self-regulatory bodies. Such transfers of value were disclosed on a

---

48. Articles 41 to 48 of Law on diverse provisions on health of 18 December 2016, B.S. 27/12/2016.

platform operated by Mdeon called Betransparent. Because this practice was proven to be very relevant, an official act was promulgated.

According to Article 44, §1 of the Sunshine Act, the tasks of the FAMHP under this Act can be executed by another organisation. Mdeon is accredited as an organisation to execute these tasks of the Sunshine Act, and their Betransparent platform is now legally recognised.[49]

[E] Cases

There have been several cases related to comparative advertising following the launch of generic medicinal products onto the Belgian market in recent years.[50]

The question of whether some sorts of communication (e.g., a catalogue and pricing list,[51] a public health campaign,[52] a financial press release,[53] institutional or corporate advertising that seeks to enhance the image and reputation of a firm without involving product advertising of a medicinal product)[54] qualify as advertisement as defined under the Medicines Act, has also been the subject of legal procedures. Following the case law of the ECJ, the deciding element in these cases is the 'intention to create a promoting effect'.

[F] General Advertising Rules

Advertising of medicinal products is subject to the general advertising requirements notably provided for in Trade Practices and Consumer Protection Act. In practice, case law usually refers to both the Trade Practices and Consumer Protection Act and the Medicines Act, provided the Medicines Act has to be considered, in such context, as a *lex specialis* of the Trade Practices and Consumer Protection Act.

§9.05 IMPLEMENTATION IN FRANCE

[A] Legal Bases

[1] Binding Rules

The provisions governing advertising of medicines and medical devices in France are laid down in the French Public Health Code (PHC).[55]

---

49. Royal Decree of 31 July 2017 concerning the recognition of the organisation referred to in Article 44 §1 of the Law of 18 December 2016 on diverse provisions on health, B.S. 22/08/2017.
50. Brussels, 26 March 2002, *UCB v. Eurogenerics*, Bull. B.M.M., 2004, II, 60–68 and Pres. Comm. Trib. Leuven, 26 March 2002, *UCB v. Dochpharma*, Annuaire Pratique du Commerce et Concurrence, 2002, 170.
51. Criminal court Brussels, 15 January 2016, 2016–2017, T.Gez., 228.
52. President of the commercial court, Brussels, 28 November 2018, AM 2018–2019, 392.
53. Brussels 31 October 2006, Annuaire Pratique du Commerce et Concurrence, 2006, 179.
54. President of the commercial court of Brussels, 17 October 2019, T.Gez, 2021–2022, 326.
55. Articles L. 5122-1 and seq. and R. 5122-1 and seq. of the PHC for medicinal products and Articles L. 5213-1 and seq. and R. 5213-1 and seq. of the PHC for medical devices.

[2] Non-binding Rules

Recommendations for advertising health products are issued by the National Agency for the Safety of Medicines and Health Products (ANSM) and have an interpretative value. Their practical impact is very significant. Recommendations are divided into recommendations for advertising directed at health professionals and recommendations for advertising directed at the general public. There are also specific recommendations for medical devices advertising. These recommendations are available on the ANSM's website.[56]

Although these recommendations are not binding, they are taken into consideration by the courts and by the ANSM responsible for authorising and monitoring of advertising of health products in general and sanctioning non-compliance with advertising recommendations.

The ANSM's decisions on advertising also provide helpful information, as they (i) clarify the guidelines on the standards of health products advertising, and (ii) contribute to building an administrative doctrine.

In addition to its recommendations, the ANSM issued the 'Charter concerning communication and promotion of health products (medicines and medical devices) on the Internet and in the electronic media'[57] regarding advertising on the Internet or on social media. It provides useful guidelines relating to the content that can be published by the pharmaceutical and medical devices industries on their websites, in particular, regarding the promotional aspects. The Charter provides specific recommendations that apply to advertising on the Internet/on social media, in particular:

- the website must be designed in such a way that content intended for the promotion of a health product is explicitly distinct from other non-promotional content. Advertising must therefore be clearly identified making the advertising nature of the message unequivocal to the public.
- each promotional page of a website must display the mandatory information provided for by the PHC for the product category presented and the public for which it is intended.
- access to the promotional pages must be adapted according to its recipients. Therefore, as the PHC imposes restrictions on advertisements aimed at healthcare professionals, the Charter provides that real access restrictions must be put in place by the operators.

---

56. Medicinal products: https://ansm.sante.fr/documents/reference/recommandations-pour-la-publicite-des-medicaments-aupres-des-professionnels-de-sante (advertising directed towards healthcare professionals) https://ansm.sante.fr/documents/reference/recommandations-pour-la-publicite-des-medicaments-aupres-du-grand-public (advertising directed towards the general public)
    Medical Devices: https://ansm.sante.fr/documents/reference/recommandations-pour-la-publicite-des-dm-dmdiv
57. Charte pour la communication et la promotion des produits de santé (médicaments et dispositifs médicaux) sur Internet et le e-media, dated of March 2014: https://ansm.sante.fr/uploads/2021/03/12/f0175469fbeb1ea62b6e648a88b67fde-2.pdf

– before being put online, the promotional pages of a medicine's website must be submitted for authorisation from the ANSM.

The last version of this Charter has been incorporated into the *'Professional Ethical Provisions,'*[58] a set of ethical conduct rules established by the LEEM[59] which applies to its member companies as of 1 January 2015.

Besides, a 'Charter relating to information aiming to promote medicinal products through canvassing or prospecting'[60] has been signed by both the Economic Committee for Health Products (CEPS)[61] and the President of the French Pharmaceutical Companies Association LEEM. The Charter covers all forms of information on any media promoting the prescription, dispensing or use of medicinal products to healthcare professionals. It specifies in particular:

– the duties of the medical sales representatives;
– the quality standards to be met, in particular with respect to the information provided by sales representatives, the training of the sale representatives regarding the documents used for their activity;
– the ethical standards of the representatives towards patients, healthcare professionals, competitors, social security; and
– the monitoring of the representatives' activities.

[B]   Scope of Application

Medicinal products advertising is defined as 'any form of information, including door to door information, canvassing or inducement, that aims at promoting the prescription, supply, sale or consumption'.[62] The following are not considered being promotional:

– information provided, in the framework of their functions, by pharmacists managing hospital pharmacies;
– correspondence that aims at answering a specific question about a particular medicinal product;
– concrete information and all informative documents relating, for example, to a change in the leaflets or packaging, adverse-event warnings in the context of pharmacovigilance, sales catalogues, and price lists provided they include no information on medicinal products;
– any information relating to human health or human diseases, provided that there is no reference, even indirectly, to a medicinal product; and

---

58. *Dispositions déontologiques professionnelles*, applicable to LEEM members, dated of December 2020.
59. LEEM (*Les Entreprises du Médicament*), the French industry association which represents pharmaceutical companies operating in France.
60. *Charte de l'information par démarchage ou prospection visant à la promotion des médicaments*, dated 15 October 2014.
61. *Comité Economique des Produits de Santé* – CEPS.
62. Article L. 5122-1 PHC.

- any informative documents of scientific, technical, or financial nature relating to an establishment or a company that are not intended to promote a medicinal product.[63]

Same definition applies with respect to medical devices advertising covering any form of information designed to promote the prescription, supply, sale, or use of medical devices.[64]

[C] French Legal Requirements

[1] Medicinal Products Advertising

The PHC sets out general and specific requirements for advertising of medicinal products as well as restrictions with regard to advertising directed at the public[65] and advertising directed at healthcare professionals.[66]

Only authorised medicinal products may be promoted, and advertising must be consistent with the provisions of the MA and therapeutic strategies recommended by the National Health Authority.[67]

Advertising medicinal products is prohibited when the product is subject to a risk/benefit reassessment procedure.[68] Medicinal products advertising must be neither misleading nor undermine the protection of public health. It must present the medicinal product in an objective manner and promote its proper use.[69] The information contained in the advertising must be 'accurate, up-to-date, verifiable and sufficiently complete' to allow the recipient to form a personal opinion regarding the therapeutic value of the medicine.[70]

Under the PHC, the 'responsible pharmacist' (*'Pharmacien responsable'*), appointed in every pharmaceutical establishment,[71] oversees the medicinal products advertising activities of that establishment and is therefore liable for any breach of medicinal products advertising regulations.

All advertising for medicinal products, whether directed at the general public or healthcare professionals, must be pre-approved by the ANSM.[72] The approval of the ANSM is named a '*visa*'. The *visa* is deemed granted in the absence of decision by the ANSM within two months of the last day of the session during which the application was filed. A *visa* has a validity period of two years but cannot exceed the validity period of the MA.[73] A copy of each advertisement must be kept for three years and must be

---

63. Article R. 5124-67 PHC.
64. Article L. 5213-1 PHC.
65. Articles L. 5122-6 to L. 5122-8 and R. 5122-3 to R. 5122-7 PHC.
66. Articles L. 5122-9 to L. 5122-10 and R. 5122-8 to R. 5122-17 PHC.
67. Articles L. 5122-2, L. 5122-3 and R. 5122-1 PHC.
68. Article L. 5122-3 PHC.
69. Article L. 5122-2 PHC.
70. Article R. 5122-9 PHC.
71. Articles L. 5124-2 and R. 5122-2 PHC.
72. Article L.5122-8 and L.5122-9 PHC.
73. Articles R. 5122-5 and R. 5122-13 PHC.

provided to the ANSM upon request, together with a list of recipients and information regarding the date and method of distribution.[74]

[a] Medicinal Products Advertising Directed at Healthcare Professionals

Detailed rules for advertising to healthcare professionals are set out in Articles L. 5122-9 to L. 5122-10 and R. 5122-8 to R. 5122-17 of the PHC. These include requirements as to the content of such advertising, for example, the requirement to include the pharmaceutical form of the medicinal product and its adverse reactions.

Whilst previously advertising directed at healthcare professionals did not require pre-approval, since 2012, the ANSM pre-approves all advertising for medicinal products, regardless of its recipients.

[b] Medicinal Products Advertising Directed at the Public

Advertising to the public is limited to medicinal products that are not subject to prescription and that are not reimbursable by the compulsory national health insurance.[75] Besides, the MA must not contain any prohibition or restriction on advertising to the public due to a possible risk to public health, in particular, when the medicinal product is not suitable for use unless a physician is involved in the diagnosis, initiation, or monitoring of the treatment.

Details of the precise requirements in respect of content of such advertising are set out in Articles L. 5122-6 to L. 5122-8 and R. 5122-3 to R. 5122-7 PHC.

[2] Medical Devices Advertising

Specific provisions apply to advertising of medical devices[76] which have been introduced into the PHC by the Law n° 2011-2012 of 29 December 2011 on the reinforcement of the safety of medicinal and health products which led to the Decree n° 2012-743 of 9 May 2012 dedicated to the 'Advertising of Medical Devices'. These rules harmonised the advertising regime for medical devices with the regime applicable to medicinal products. Applicable requirements for advertising medical devices depend on:

- the level of risk for human-health attached to the device;
- whether the device is subject to reimbursement, even partially, by compulsory health insurance schemes; and
- whether advertising is intended for the general public or for healthcare professionals.

---

74. Article R. 5122-2 PHC.
75. Article L. 5122-3 PHC. Pursuant to this same article, this restriction does not apply to vaccines and tobacco-weaning medicinal products which can be advertised, even if they can be prescribed or reimbursed.
76. Article L. 5213-1 and seq. and R. 5213-1 and seq. PHC.

The advertising must present the medical device objectively, particularly in terms of its performance and compliance with essential safety and health requirements as defined by the conformity certificate and promote the proper use of the product. Moreover, advertising must neither be misleading nor present any risk to public health.[77] All information must be accurate, up-to-date, verifiable, and sufficiently complete to enable either (i) the public to understand the intended use of the medical device, or (ii) the healthcare professionals to appreciate the characteristics and performance of the medical device that is presented.[78] There are also detailed rules regarding the precise content of the advertising. For some medical devices, advertising requires prior authorisation by the ANSM.[79]

Furthermore, general advertising provisions of the French Consumer Code apply to advertising of medicinal products and medical devices. The French Consumer Code prohibits any advertising that is false or misleading.[80]

[D] Specific Forms of Advertising

[1] Meetings and Congresses

The ANSM has issued a recommendation relating to congresses and meetings, in particular, regarding the distribution of special editions of scientific articles collections.

[2] Advantages and Gifts

The French so-called *anti-gift* provisions strictly frame the conditions under which companies in the health sector are allowed to provide advantages, in cash or in kind, to healthcare professionals, medical students, or associations of healthcare professionals or medical students, and civil servants who participate in public health or social security policies and/or have authority to rule in health-related matters.[81]

The *anti-gift* regime was significantly amended in 2017,[82] but the implementing texts were only published years after in June 2020.[83] This new regulation has been in force since 1 October 2020.

The principle remains the prohibition of transfers of value from the healthcare industry (companies manufacturing or marketing health products or providing health

---

77. Article L. 5213-2 of PHC.
78. Article R. 5213-3 PHC.
79. Article L. 5213-4 PHC provides that prior authorisation from the ANSM is only required for medical devices that present an important risk to human health and that are listed by a ministerial order (https://www.legifrance.gouv.fr/loda/id/JORFTEXT000026451423/).
80. This is assessed on the basis of the product's nature, composition, substantial quality, origin, properties, conditions of use, results expected from its use, etc. *See* Article L. 121-2 of the Consumer Code.
81. Article L. 1453-4 and seq. PHC.
82. Ordinance n° 2017-49 of 19 January 2017 on advantages offered by persons manufacturing or marketing health products or services.
83. Decree n° 2020-730 of 15 June 2020 relating to the advantages granted by those manufacturing or marketing health products or providing health services.

services) to the abovementioned beneficiaries.[84] Certain transfers of value, limitatively enumerated, are subject to derogations and thus permitted under terms and conditions set out in articles L. 1453-7. and seq. of the PHC. These include, for instance, not only remuneration, compensation, and reimbursement of expenses for research, exploitation of research, scientific activities and consultancy, services or commercial promotion but also hospitality provided to healthcare professionals in the context of scientific or promotional events, as well as donations and gifts intended exclusively to financially support research and scientific activities.

Such permitted transfers of value must all be subject to an agreement that will be submitted for declaration or authorisation, depending on the amounts at stake,[85] to the relevant competent authorities which might be the administrative authority (Regional Health Authority – 'ARS'), or the National Board of the healthcare professional concerned (*Conseil national de l'Ordre*).

Under the declaration procedure:[86]

- the convention must be signed at the time of the submission;
- it be submitted to the competent authority 8 working days before the grant of the advantage (the date of the service or event – not the date of payment); and
- the competent authority has the possibility to make recommendations.

Under the authorisation procedure:[87]

- the convention must only be a draft at the time of the submission;
- the competent authority will have 2 months to grant an authorisation. In case of refusal, the applicant can submit an amended submission within 15 days and the competent authority will have 15 additional days to issue a final decision;
- if the competent authority does not answer nor request additional information or documents, the authorisation will be deemed granted at the end of the two-month period; and
- the decision issued by the competent authority is binding, therefore the transfer of value cannot take place in the absence of an implicit (i.e. no reply within the set time frame) or explicit approval.

The PHC also specifies the mandatory information required for the submission and the specific mentions that the contract framing the transfer of value must include.[88]

The regulatory framework governing transfers of value to healthcare professionals also provides for derogations. Indeed, pursuant to Article L. 1453-6 of the PHC, some categories of advantages in kind or in cash, that are of negligible value and related to the professional practice of the beneficiary, fall out of the scope of the anti-gift

---

84. Article L. 1453-4 and seq. PHC.
85. Order of 7 August 2020 fixing the amounts above which an agreement provided for in Article L. 1453-8 of the PHC is subject to authorisation.
86. Article R. 1543-15 PHC.
87. Article R. 1453-18 PHC.
88. Article R. 1453-14 PHC.

regime.[89] The Order published on 7 August 2020[90] specifies the ceilings under which the advantages are considered to be of negligible value. It sets both the maximum amounts for such benefits and the maximum frequency per calendar year. These advantages could be, for example, unplanned meals or collation, the provision of a book or journal, including subscription to a journal, or office supplies.

Non-compliance with these provisions is subject to criminal sanctions involving fines (up to EUR 750,000 for companies) and imprisonment.

In addition, transparency obligations might apply as any 'advantage' with a value that equals to or exceeds EUR 10, granted by healthcare companies to healthcare actors, shall be disclosed on a public database 'transparence.sante.gouv.fr '.[91] This disclosure requirement is also subject to criminal sanctions.

[3]   Samples of Medicinal Products

Free samples of health products are subject to specific derogations under the anti-gift regime. Indeed, the Order[92] fixing the amounts below the benefits of which are considered to be of negligible value provides that samples of health products are not prohibited advantages when (i) they are provided for health purposes or demonstration, (ii) their value does not exceed EUR 20, and (iii) they are provided within the limit of three per calendar year.

Besides, it is specified that as a derogation the following samples of health products are authorised without a limitation of their amount:

- samples of medicinal products, the supply of which is governed by articles L.5122-10 and R.5122-17 PHC;
- samples and demonstration samples supplied to the healthcare professional for educational or training purposes and that cannot be used for the patient's care; and
- samples and demonstration samples used by the healthcare professional for educational purposes with the patient or given to the patient exclusively for the purpose of testing or adaptation to the product and for temporary use.

Pursuant to Article L. 5122-10 of the PHC, samples of medicinal products may be delivered to healthcare professionals authorised to prescribe or deliver medicinal products in hospital pharmacies only upon their request.[93]

These samples may not contain psychotropic substances or substances subject to narcotics regulations. They have to be identical to the medicinal product concerned

---

89. Article L. 1453-6 PHC.
90. Order of 7 August 2020 fixing the amounts below which benefits in kind or in cash are considered to be of negligible value pursuant to 4° of Article L.1453-6 of the Public Health Code.
91. Article L. 1453-1 PHC.
92. Order of 7 August 2020 fixing the amounts below which benefits in kind or in cash are considered to be of negligible value pursuant to 4° of Article L.1453-6 of the Public Health Code.
93. Article L. 5122-10 PHC.

and be labelled 'free sample'. They may only be supplied in limited quantities, for a restricted period of time and under specified conditions.[94]

The direct supply of samples to the public or to places accessible to the public, such as medical or pharmaceutical congresses, is forbidden.[95]

[E] Sanctions

[1] *Administrative Sanctions*

[a] Administrative Authorities

The ANSM is a public entity placed under the supervision of the Ministry of Health responsible for controlling whether an advertisement is compliant or not. In order to do so, they generally rely on the recommendations they published as to the contents of advertisements of medicinal products and medical devices (that are specific depending on whether they are directed at the public or at healthcare professionals – *see* explanations in the sections below).

The General Directorate for Competition, Consumption and Fraud Enforcement (DGCCRF) is another administrative authority authorised to conduct investigations (in particular, under French Consumers regulations) and report breaches or infringement which could lead to warnings, injunctions (mainly compliance injunctions), or official reports that could be sent to the public prosecutor.[96]

[b] Control of Advertising Directed at the Public

The advertising visa may be suspended or withdrawn by the ANSM, issuing a fully motivated decision, in case of non-compliance with the applicable advertising provisions[97] in particular in the following circumstances:

- the advertising is misleading or affects public health or gives a non-objective presentation of the medicinal product or does not promote its proper use;
- the advertising does not comply with the provisions of the MA; and/or
- the advertising mentions unauthorised therapeutic indications.

The ANSM may also order suspension of advertising which has not obtained an advertising visa (for medicinal products) or approval (for medical devices).

---

94. Article R. 5122-17 PHC.
95. Article L. 5122-10 PHC.
96. Article L. 511-3 Consumer Code.
97. Articles L. 5122-8 and -9 PHC.

[c]   *Control of Advertising Directed at Healthcare Professionals*

Should the advertising be misleading, affect public health, give a non-objective presentation of the medicinal product, not promote its proper use, not comply with the provisions of the MA, or be distributed while the medicinal products' risk/benefit assessment is being re-evaluated following a pharmacovigilance notification, the ANSM may suspend or withdraw the visa. In all cases, the company may present its observations and arguments against the contemplated measures.[98]

When the ANSM withdraws an advertising visa, the CEPS (Economic Committee for Health Products)[99] may impose a financial penalty on the company whose advertising, directed at healthcare professionals, has been prohibited by the ANSM.[100] The fine can go up to 10% of the latest overall pre-tax income made by the company in France in the six months preceding and the six months after the prohibition order. The fine is set with regard to the seriousness of the prohibition order and in relation to the value of sales.[101]

Similar financial penalties may be imposed by CEPS in respect of advertising of medical devices which has been prohibited by the ANSM.[102]

These administrative sanctions are individual decisions that can be subject to an administrative review before its director, and ultimately, that can be appealed before the administrative courts within two months of the ANSM's decision.

[2]   Criminal Sanctions

Breaches of several of the advertising provisions of the PHC amount to criminal offences punishable by various substantial levels of fines and in some cases by imprisonment.[103] Furthermore, a court may prohibit the sale or order seizure and confiscation of the products and destruction of advertising materials.[104]

The provisions of the French Consumer Code also apply to medicinal products advertising. The French Consumer Code prohibits any advertising that is false or misleading.[105] The DGCCRF is authorised to establish breaches of Article L. 121-1 of

---

98. Practice shows that even well-grounded objections formulated by pharmaceutical companies are often disregarded, making it necessary to request the cancellation of the measures before the administrative courts.
99. *Comité Economique des Produits de Santé* – CEPS.
100. Article L. 162-17-4 of the Social Security Code and L. 5122-9 PHC. Practice shows that these financial penalties are often but not always imposed on the company.
101. Practice shows that the penalties imposed are generally less than 10%, varying between 2 and 8%.
102. Article L. 165-8-1 of the Social Security Code; Articles L. 5213-4 and L. 5213-5 of the PHC; Decree N° 2013-950 of 23 October 2013.
103. Articles L. 5422-18 PHC.
104. Article L. 5422-14 PHC.
105. This is assessed with regard to the product's nature, composition, substantial quality, origin, properties, conditions of use, results expected from its use, etc. *See* Article L. 121-2 Consumer Code.

the Consumer Code by means of statements, which are then sent to the public prosecutor.[106]

§9.06 IMPLEMENTATION IN GERMANY

[A] Legal Basis

The provisions concerning pharmaceutical advertising in Germany are laid out in the Advertising of Medicinal Products Act ('Heilmittelwerbegesetz' – HWG). Title VIII and Title VIIIa of Directive 2001/83/EC have been implemented into the Advertising of Medicinal Products Act by the 12th Amendment of the Medicinal Products Act[107] dated 30 July 2004 and by the 14th Amendment of the Medicinal Products Act[108] dated 29 August 2005.

The Advertising of Medicinal Products Act sets out the rules for medicines advertising in general and specific requirements and restrictions for advertising directed at the public, individuals, and for advertising directed at healthcare professionals. It covers advertising in all kinds of media, such as the Internet, printed material, and TV commercials.

The Advertising of Medicinal Products Act is supplemented by the general rules of the German Act against Unfair Competition[109] as well as the German Medicinal Product Act. The latter also contains some provisions effecting the advertisement of medicines and the conduct with healthcare professionals and patient organisations.

Any marketing authorisation holders (MAHs) and any third parties, such as journalists or PR agencies, are responsible ensuring compliance with advertising provisions.[110]

[B] Scope of the Advertising of Medicinal Products Act

The Advertising of Medicinal Products Act applies to:

- medicinal products as defined in section 2 of the German Act on the Implementation of EU Regulations Concerning Medical Devices (Medizinprodukterecht-Durchführungsgesetz – MPDG);
- medical devices as defined in article 2, point 1 of Regulation (EU) 2017/745; and

---

106. Article L. 511-3 Consumer Code.
107. Zwölftes Gesetz zur Änderung des Arzneimittelgesetzes.
108. Vierzehntes Gesetz zur Änderung des Arzneimittelgesetzes.
109. Gesetz gegen den unlauteren Wettbewerb – UWG.
110. Doepner. *Commentary on the Advertising of Medicinal Products Act* ('Heilmittelwerbegesetz'), 1, reference number 13.

- other treatments, if the claim refers to the diagnosis, remedy, or relief of illnesses, medical conditions, bodily harm, or pathological disorders of humans or animals as well as plastic surgery, if the advertising claim refers to a modification of the human body where there was no medical need.

'Other treatments' cover cosmetic products pursuant to Regulation (EG) Nr. 1223/2009 (last modified by Regulation (EU) 2015/1298 and section 2 of the Food, Articles of Daily Use Law and Feed Act).[111,112]

The Advertising of Medicinal Products Act does not provide a legal definition of 'advertising'. Therefore, it is necessary to refer to the definition in Directive 2001/83/EC as stated above (*see* §9.02[C]). Under German law, advertising is generally understood in a very broad manner and captures any commercial act which is intended to promote the sale of goods and services. Thus, most communication by companies is considered advertising.

However, the Advertising of Medicinal Products Act only covers product-related advertising. It does not apply to image campaigns of a company. The medicinal products must be distinguishable and identifiable in order to be considered product advertising. In deciding whether borderline cases fall within the scope of the Advertising of Medicinal Products Act, the overall impression is examined to see whether the company's image is the key message.[113]

The Advertising of Medicinal Products Act does not apply to written correspondence and documents that are not intended for promotional use but are intended to answer questions in relation to a certain medicinal product.[114]

[C]   **National Sanctions**

A breach of the Advertising of Medicinal Products Act is considered a breach of unfair competition law pursuant to section 3a of the Act Against Unfair Competition, and civil proceedings are regularly brought by competitors or associations taking an interest in fair competition. Often, competitors or associations, such as the Association for Social Competition[115, 116] or the Centre for Protection against Unfair Competition,[117, 118] send a warning letter asking for a cease-and-desist declaration. The warning letter can precede an unfair competition law proceeding but is not mandatory. Competitors can also apply for a preliminary injunction at a German court without sending a warning letter. German courts may grant preliminary injunctions without an oral hearing (ex parte injunctions). The associations are interested in preserving fair competition in the

---

111. Lebensmittel-, Bedarfsgegenstände- und Futtermittelgesetzbuch – LFGB.
112. Section 1 paragraph 2 Advertising of Medicinal Products Act.
113. Judgment of the German Federal Court of Justice dated 17 June 1992, GRUR 1992, 873.
114. Section 1 paragraph 5 Advertising of Medicinal Products Act.
115. www.vsw.info, 13 July 2016.
116. Verband Sozialer Wettbewerb e.V. – VSW.
117. www.wettbewerbszentrale.de, 13 July 2016.
118. Wettbewerbszentrale.

Chapter 9: Advertising Medicinal Products for Human Use §9.06[E]

relevant market by reviewing advertising claims themselves or by pursuing complaints from third parties.

There are also criminal law sanctions. A breach of the provisions of the Advertising of Medicinal Products Act can lead to the imposition of fines and/or up to one year of imprisonment.[119] However, there is very little published case law on criminal law sanctions pursuant to the Advertising of Medicinal Products Act.

Section 299b of the German Criminal Code (Strafgesetzbuch – StGB) prohibits granting, offering or promising benefits to members of the medical professions in their capacity as professionals in order to be given preference within national or foreign competition with regard to the prescription or procurement of medicinal products. Conversely, Section 299a prohibits members of the medical profession from receiving or requesting such benefits. Significantly, the provision applies to all members of the medical profession with a state-regulated education, such as physicians, dentists, veterinaries, psychotherapists, as well as paramedical professionals. The acts covered by both provisions shall be punished by a fine or imprisonment for up to three years. Thus, these anti-bribery provisions have to be taken into careful consideration, for instance, in cases where advertising or marketing strategies regarding medicinal products or medical devices encompass the distribution of promotional gifts or similar activities.

[D]   Role of the National Competent Authority

The Advertising of Medicinal Products Act does not set out statutory powers available to the Competent Authority in Germany, the Federal Institute for Drugs and Medical Devices,[120] or any local regulatory authorities. There is no advertising standards unit and therefore no official body reviewing advertising, as in the UK, before the advertising is broadcasted or communicated. Local regulatory authorities can review advertising material once it has been distributed and impose sanctions.

[E]   National Implementation Beyond Requirements of Directive 2001/83/EC

There are provisions in the Advertising of Medicinal Products Act that extend beyond the requirements of Directive 2001/83/EC. Germany has laid out particularly strict provisions in contrast to other Member States.

[1]   Testimonials

Under German law, recommendations of third parties or testimonials are prohibited where advertising claims are addressed to the general public.[121] It was debated

---

119. Sections 14 and 15 Advertising of Medicinal Products Act.
120. Bundesinstitut für Arzneimittel und Medizinprodukte – BfArM.
121. Section 11 paragraph 1 no. 11 Advertising of Medicinal Products Act.

whether this was in line with Community law. It was clarified in the ECJ decision in Gintec[122] (*see* section 2.1 for details of the case) that Member States in their national legislation cannot provide for an absolute and unconditional prohibition of any statement from third parties. However, Article 90(c) of Directive 2001/83/EC requires that there is a prohibition on the use, in the advertising of medicinal products to the general public, of statements from third parties where they give the impression that the use of the medicinal product contributes to the reinforcement of general well-being.

[2] Internet Presentations

Section 10, paragraph 1 of the Advertising of Medicinal Products Act provides that prescription medicinal products may only be advertised where the intended audience is medical professionals, dentists, vets, pharmacists, and persons legally marketing medicinal products. This provision thus prohibits the broad marketing of such regulated medicinal products.

The German Federal Court of Justice has found it necessary to apply and interpret Article 88, paragraph 1, lit. (a) of Regulation 2001/83/EC with regard to section 10, paragraph 1 of the Advertising of Medicinal Products Act in a civil law dispute between two pharmaceutical companies. The German Federal Court of Justice has made a reference for a preliminary ruling, asking the ECJ to interpret the Community law.[123]

The background to the case is that the defendant had put information about medicinal products available by prescription on an Internet website. The information included the product package, the description of indications, and the directions for use. The website was available to all Internet users. The claimant argued that this constituted a breach of section 10, paragraph 1, of the Advertising of Medicinal Products Act. The District Court in Hamburg found that there had been a breach, which was upheld by the Court of Appeal. The German Federal Court of Justice has requested the ECJ's interpretation of the validity of the Act. In response, the ECJ stated that information displayed on the packaging and the notice of use are de facto objectives since regulations prohibit any promotional element in these items and they are compulsory. Therefore, the Court concluded that 'Article 88(1)(a) of Directive 2001/83/EC must be interpreted as meaning that it does not prohibit the dissemination on a website, by a pharmaceutical undertaking, of information relating to medicinal products available on medical prescription only, where that information is accessible on the website only to someone who seeks to obtain it and that dissemination consists solely in the faithful reproduction of the packaging of the medicinal product, [...], and in the literal and complete reproduction of the package leaflet or the summary of the product's characteristics, which have been approved by the authorities with

---

122. Case No. C-374/05 – *'Gintec'* Judgment of the European Court of Justice dated 8 November 2007.
123. Decision dated 16 July 2009, file no I ZR 223/06.

competence in relation to medicinal products.' The Court specifies nevertheless that 'on the other hand, the dissemination, on such a website, of information relating to a medicinal product which has been selected or rewritten by the manufacturer, which can be explained only by an advertising purpose, is prohibited'.[124]

Accordingly, the German Federal Court of Justice ruled that the prohibition of advertising medical products to the general public pursuant to section 10 paragraph 1 does not apply to such information on a website.[125]

[3]   Advertising for Telemedicinal Services

The advertisement for telemedicine services is a hotly debated and litigated topic in Germany. The relevant provision, section 9 of the Advertising of Medicinal Products Act, basically prohibits the advertisement for telehealth services unless, according to generally accepted professional standards, personal medical contact with the person to be treated is not required.

The question of which telemedicinal services can be advertised under that restriction is rather open. In a recent decision, the German Federal Court of Justice reasoned that such standards are not regulations of professional law governing HCPs but rather correspond to the generally recognised professional standards from section 630 (2) of the German Civil Code (BGB), which regulates the obligations arising from a medical treatment contract. According to this, such standards can also only develop over time, for example, from the guidelines of medical societies. In the decided case, a health insurance company had advertised a 'comprehensive primary medical care' including diagnosis, therapy recommendation, and sick note by way of remote treatment, which at present does not yet correspond to general professional standards, according to the German Federal Court of Justice. An advertisement for a general remote treatment is thus excluded, and any advertisements for such services should be closely reviewed.

[4]   Further Requirements

The provisions of the Advertising of Medicinal Products Act go beyond the requirements of Directive 2001/83/EC (medicinal products for human use) – and medical devices (*see* chapter 19 on medical devices) – and the Act has been amended frequently in line with the changing market. It is, therefore, essential to review advertising material on a case-by-case basis. The interpretation of provisions of the Advertising of Medicinal Products Act by the local courts may differ.

---

124. Case No. C-316/09, '*MSD Sharp & Dohme GmbH v/ Merckle GmbH*'. Judgment of the European Court of Justice dated 5 May 2011.
125. Decision dated 19 October 2011, file no I ZR 223/06.

[F] Self-regulation

The German Association of Researching Pharmaceutical Manufacturers (VFA)[126] has founded the Association of Voluntary Self-Regulation for the Pharmaceutical Industry (FSA)[127] which established the FSA codex also regulating the advertising of medicines. This codex only applies to member companies of the VFA and FSA but is binding for them. It is no law and does therefore not need to be observed by non-members. This has also been confirmed by the German Federal Court of Justice.[128] Still, in some instances, courts relied on the more detailed provisions of the FSA codex in order to interpret the more general statutory requirements under the HWG, the UWG and the anti-bribery provisions in the German Criminal Code.

With respect to Medical devices, 'Advertising' covers any form of information designed to promote the prescription, supply, sale, or use of medical devices.

§9.07 IMPLEMENTATION IN ITALY

[A] Legal Basis

Title VIII and Title VIIIa of Directive 2001/83/EC have been implemented into the Italian Legislative decree 24 April 2006 n. 219, as amended (the Decree), Title VIII (Articles 113–128).

[B] Scope of the Decree

The Decree applies to advertisements of medicinal products as defined by Article 1(1) of the Decree. Article 113 of the Decree defines 'advertising of a medicinal product' as follows:

1. Any action of information, research of clients or incitement, aimed at promoting the prescription, supply, sale or consumption of medicinal products. It includes in particular:
   a) the advertising of medicinal products to the public;
   b) the advertising of medicinal products to persons authorised to prescribe or supply them, including the following: (1) visits by medical sales representatives to persons qualified to prescribe or supply medicinal products; (2) the supply of samples of medicinal products; (3) the provision of inducements to prescribe or supply medicinal products by the gift, offer or promise of any benefit or bonus, whether in money or in kind, except when their intrinsic value is minimal; (4) sponsorship of promotional meetings attended by persons qualified to prescribe or supply medicinal products;

---

126. Verband Forschender Arzneimittelhersteller e.V. – VFA.
127. Freiwillige Selbstkontrolle für die Arzneimittelindustrie e.V. – FSA.
128. Bundesgerichtshof – BGH, I ZR 157/08.

(5) sponsorship of scientific congresses attended by persons qualified to prescribe or supply medicinal products and in particular payment of their travelling and accommodation expenses in connection therewith.
2. The following are not covered Title VIII of the Decree on advertising of medicinal product:
   a) The labelling and the accompanying package leaflets, which are subject to the provisions of Title V,
   b) Unsolicited correspondence needed to answer a specific question about a particular medicinal product,
   c) Factual, informative announcements and reference material relating, for example, to pack changes, adverse-reaction warnings as part of general drug precautions, trade catalogues and price lists, provided they include no product claims,
   d) Information relating to human health or diseases, provided that there is no reference, even indirect, to medicinal products.

[C]   Role of the National Competent Authority

The Italian Medicines Agency (AIFA) is the competent authority in case of breaches of the Decree insofar as the violation concerns advertising of medicinal products to healthcare professionals, and the Italian Ministry of Health is the competent authority in case of breaches of the Decree insofar as the violation concern advertising of medicinal products to the public. However, in case of breach of advertising rules in general, other authorities/bodies may come into play (*see* further §9.07[F] below).

In particular, AIFA is responsible for issuing the authorisation for the advertising of medicinal products to healthcare professionals, whilst the Italian Ministry of Health is responsible for issuing the authorisation for the advertising of medicinal products to the public.

In case of both authorisations, a silent consent procedure applies, equal respectively to ten days for AIFA and forty-five days for the Italian Ministry of Health.

Both AIFA and Italian Ministry of Health have issued guidelines concerning practical aspects relevant in case of an advertising authorisation application.

Said Guidelines include, among others, the following.

- AIFA Guideline of 2010 concerning the advertising information and materials which may be disseminated in occasion of scientific congresses before healthcare professionals.
- Ministry of Health Guidelines concerning the advertising, amongst others, of non-prescription medicinal products (so called OTC and SOP) by means of new technologies of 17.02.2010, as subsequently modified on 6.02.2017, which regulate the advertising of non-prescription medicinal products before the general public, amongst others:
    - in Internet webpages, including by means of hyperlinks and banners;

- in MMS, SMS/text messages;
- in Social networks.

In particular, based on these Guidelines, the advertising of non-prescription medicinal products in Social Networks is, in principle, not allowed, although some exceptions apply.

Advertising of non-prescription medicinal products is admitted on Facebook and on YouTube subject to certain specific limitations (for example, in terms of positioning of the promotional information and in terms of interaction allowed with users in relation to said promotional information).

The strict approach adopted by the Italian Ministry of Health is due to the fact that the advertising of medicinal products must be based on texts/materials which remain stable over time, and contents share on Social Networks are, by definition, normally constantly changing due to their interactive nature.

[D] Self-Regulation for Promotion of Prescription-Only Products

Farmindustria (the national association of the originator pharmaceutical industry in Italy) has a Code of Conduct, which implements EFPIA-relevant Code and provides several rules on the promotion of medicinal products (both under prescription and OTC products) and on the relationship between pharmaceutical companies and healthcare professionals. Farmindustria also provides rules on the activities performed by medical sales representatives.

[E] Self-Regulation for Promotion of OTC Products

The Institute of Self-regulation[129] issued a Code of Self-Regulation applicable to all products that also applies to advertising in relation to medicinal products. Although the Code only applies to members, the obligation of members to apply the Code in all contracts with third parties makes it more widely applicable.

[F] General Advertising Rules

Italian legislative decree 6 September 2005, n. 206 (Italian Consumers Code) regulates, among others, the advertising of consumer products in general before consumers, Italian legislative decree 2 August 2007, n. 145 regulates, among others, the advertising of consumer products in general before professionals, and Article 2598 of the Italian Civil Code regulates fair commercial practices between competitors, potentially, also with regard to advertising.

Competence for breach under Italian legislative decree 6 September 2005, n. 206 and Italian legislative decree 2 August 2007, n. 145, the Italian Consumers Code is the

---

129. Istituto di Autodisciplina Publicitaria – IAP.

Italian Antitrust Authority, while competence for unfair competition practices is the Tribunal (civil ordinary jurisdiction).

[G] Regional Control

Guidelines on the promotion of medicinal products to healthcare practitioners have been issued at national level by Conference State-Regions. These guidelines, as implemented at regional level, provides several rules on a number of topics related to the promotional activities of the sales force (e.g., regarding the supply of samples of the products, number of visits to healthcare professionals, gifts and benefits-in-kind, sales force requirements, etc.).

[H] National Sanctions

Italian Legislative decree 24th April 2006, n. 219 provides ad hoc sanctions in case of breach of the specific provisions therein contained, which also includes criminal sanctions such as personal imprisonment.

Other provisions may apply in case of unlawful advertising of medicinal products and lead to either civil, administrative or again criminal sanctions.

Civil sanctions may apply, for example, in cases of advertising contrary to fair trade principles among competitors. Administrative sanctions may apply, for example, in cases of misleading advertising contrary to the Italian Consumers Code (*see* further §9.07 [I] below). Finally, criminal sanctions may apply (i.e., the crime of 'comparaggio')[130] in case of promotional activities intended to pursue unlawful objectives, such as the increasing of prescriptions and/or sales of medicinal products as a result of payment or gifts to healthcare professionals.

[I] Online Sales of Medicinal Products on the Internet

Online sales of under prescription medicinal products on the Internet are currently prohibited in Italy (*see* Article 112 quarter of Italian legislative decree 219/2006).

In particular, the Italian competition authority, which is responsible, *inter alia*, as seen for unlawful commercial practices against costumers and which also collaborates with other authorities, like AIFA, on anti-counterfeiting activities, in the past has blocked access from Italy to websites liable for selling medicinal products under prescription and liable for other violations under Italian laws.

---

130. The crime of 'comparaggio' is similar to the crime of bribery, but it refers specifically to conducts of prescribers or pharmacists who cause the increasing of sales of a certain sanitary product (including medicinal products) versus a payment, promise of payment, or other benefit in kind.

§9.08 IMPLEMENTATION IN THE NETHERLANDS

[A] Legal Basis

Pharmaceutical advertising is subject to various legal regimes. Specific legislation is laid down in Chapter 9 of the Dutch Medicines Act (*in Dutch: Geneesmiddelenwet*), implementing the provisions of Directive 2001/83/EC, as amended, and further specified in relation to inducement in the Policy Rules for Inducements under the Medicines Act 2018. These rules are further explained in the Code of Conduct for Pharmaceutical Advertising (*in Dutch: Gedragscode Geneesmiddelenreclame*), which is a self-regulatory code of the Foundation for the Code for Pharmaceutical Advertising (*in Dutch: Stichting CGR*), which most companies located in the Netherlands are a member of and therefore comply with this code.

Specifically related to medical devices, the Medical Devices Act (MDA) (*in Dutch: Wet medische hulpmiddelen*) contains a criminal law provision regarding the recommendation of unsuitable medical devices and the marketing of unsuitable medical devices (Article 11 MDA). There is also the self-regulatory Code on Public Advertising Medical Self-Care Devices (*in Dutch: Code Publieksreclame Medische Zelfzorg Hulpmiddelen 2019*) from the Inspection Board of the Public Promotion of Health Products ('the Board') (*in Dutch: Keuringsraad KOAG KAG*) on public advertising.

There are also more general rules concerning misleading and comparative advertising that apply to all products (not just medical) in the Dutch Civil Code (*in Dutch: Burgerlijk Wetboek*).[131] These rules are further specified in the self-regulatory Dutch Code of Conduct on Advertising (*in Dutch: Nederlandse Reclame Code*) of the Foundation on Advertising Codes (*in Dutch: Stichting Reclame Code*).

Furthermore, healthcare practitioners may breach laws regulating professional conduct and be subject to disciplinary rules if they break advertising or inducement rules.

[1] The Dutch Medicines Act

Although Directive 2001/83/EC leaves some discretion to Member States to create additional rules with regard to pharmaceutical advertising, the Dutch Medicines Act comprehensively implemented the provisions of Directive 2001/83/EC.

Directive 2001/83/EC does not provide a definition of advertising; instead it lists activities in Article 86 that are considered to qualify as an advertisement. The Dutch Medicines Act however does include such a definition, which is:

> any form of exercising influence with the apparent intention to encourage prescription, supply or use of prescription medicinal products, or giving instruction thereto.[132]

---

131. As laid down in articles 6:194–6:196 of the Dutch Civil Code.
132. Article 1(xx) Medicines Act.

The words 'apparent intention' are meant to distinguish between general and objective information provided by the pharmaceutical industry regarding the pharmaceutical product (instructions for use, leaflet etc.) and information provided with the intention to advertise.

[a] Enforcement

The Dutch Inspectorate for Healthcare ('the Inspectorate') (*in Dutch: Inspectie Gezondheidszorg en Jeugd*) is authorised to enforce the Dutch Medicines Act. It should be noted that there is no involvement of the Dutch Medicines Evaluation Board[133] (MEB) concerning such enforcement, which is the national competent authority responsible for issuing MAs.

Anyone can file a complaint with the Dutch Inspectorate Healthcare and Youth (*in Dutch: Inspectie Gezondheidszorg en Jeugd*) IGJ, which has the discretion to decide whether to follow up on complaints or to refer the complainant party to the relevant Industry Code or, in case relevant, to the Authority Consumer and Market (ACM).

[b] Sanctions

A breach of the Medicines Act is subject to both criminal sanctions following proceedings according to the Dutch Criminal Code and administrative fines imposed by the Inspectorate in accordance with the Policy document regarding the administrative fines of the Minister of Healthcare, Welfare and Sports which entered into force on 17 December 2018.[134]

When a breach of a provision of the Medicines Act can be penalised according to both administrative law and criminal law, the working agreement between the Inspectorate and the Public Prosecution Service is consulted in order to determine whether the breach will be submitted to the Public Prosecution Service.[135]

Although the Inspectorate has complete discretion regarding fines, it is guided by policy rules published by the Minister of Health that lay down categories of fines related to categories of breach of the Medicines Act. The policy rules state that for a first breach of particular stipulations of the Medicines Act, the Inspectorate may issue a warning instead of an administrative fine.[136] However, upon infringement of particular provisions, an administrative fine may be imposed immediately (the Directly Penalizable fines, 'DB'). In such an event, the imposition of an immediate fine does not have to be preceded by a warning. In the policy document, many breaches of advertisement rules are subject to immediate fines by the Inspectorate. However, in practice, the Inspectorate is reserved in exercising this option and often turns to a warning first.

---

133. College ter Beoordeling van Geneesmiddelen – CBG-MEB.
134. Beleidsregels bestuurlijke boete VWS 2019, kenmerk 2018-2207875, 17 December 2018, Stcrt 2018, 72501, as amended from time to time.
135. Article 3 Beleidsregels bestuurlijke boete VWS 2019, kenmerk 2018-2207875, 17 December 2018.
136. Article 2 Beleidsregels bestuurlijke boete VWS 2019.

Breach of the advertisement rules is subject to the highest category of administrative penalties. The amount of the fine actually imposed is dependent on multiple factors.

First, it must be assessed what the standard base amount is. For all advertisement rules, this is set at EUR 150,000.

Second, the type of product which the advertisement relates to must be chosen:

- Prescription drug ('UR'): 100% of the standard amount.
- Over the counter, but sale only in presence of pharmacist ('UA'): 80%.
- Over the counter, also outside of a pharmacy ('AV' or 'UAD'): 60%.

Third, the severity of the offence (extent, duration, reach, and inducement) is taken into account to decide if there are mitigating circumstances, no special circumstances, or aggravating circumstances.

Fourth, each type of article breach is categorised, which shows the severity of the breach. The higher the category, the more severe the breach thus enlarging the fine.

Fifth, accountability is taken into account. The severity of the breach is susceptible to the question of whether the infringer has made efforts to prevent a breach in the first place. If this is considered to be the case, the amount of the fine is reduced by 30%. Sixth, the amount of the fine is reduced for smaller companies or for natural persons.

Finally, account is taken of repeated offences. If this is the second breach, the fine is doubled. Every repeated offence within four years doubles the fine compared to the previous breach, until the maximum provided by law is reached.

Administrative fines can be challenged in administrative proceedings in three instances. Objection can be made with the Minister of Healthcare, Welfare and Sports. If denied, appeal can be lodged with the administrative court. The higher court would be the Council of State, section administrative law.

[c]   Inspections

The Inspectorate has far-reaching powers to conduct investigations, including access to institutes and companies, seizure of information, and interviewing employees. The Inspectorate has made use of these powers in investigating suspected breaches of pharmaceutical advertising. Pharmaceutical companies as well as individual healthcare practitioners and other parties may be investigated. Furthermore, the Inspectorate can decide to file a complaint with the Foundation Code of Conduct for Pharmaceutical Advertising (*in Dutch: Stichting Code Geneesmiddelen Reclame*) (*see* under [5] under [D]) on the basis of the Code of Conduct Pharmaceutical Advertising or to inform the public prosecutor, which may lead to further investigation, with potential criminal charges and enforcement under criminal law. Any decision or penalty brought on the basis of the Code of Conduct Pharmaceutical Advertising is informal and does therefore not exclude the possibility of imposing administrative fines by the Inspectorate or bringing of criminal charges by the public prosecutor.

[d] Cooperation with Other Regulating Institutes

The Inspectorate co-ordinates with other bodies, such as the Advertising Code Committee and the Authority Consumer and Market, to divide complaints and tasks in relation to breaches of advertising legislation and advertisement rules. Complaints relating to breach of advertising rules will be forwarded to the Advertising Code Committee. The Inspectorate also monitors the activities of the bodies involved, including sending inspectors to attend hearings conducted by these bodies. These bodies will refer certain cases to the Inspectorate. Due to the Working Arrangement between the Inspectorate and the Advertising Code Committee, the Inspectorate may also file a complaint with the Advertising Code Committee for a breach of the self-regulatory codes. Furthermore, a complaint regarding violation of the Advertising Code (coming from healthcare professionals or competitors from the pharmaceutical industry) may be filed with the Advertising Code Committee. The Advertising Code Committee will give the other party the opportunity to submit a statement of defence after which the Advertising Code Committee will set a hearing with both parties and render judgment.

[B] Civil Law

Any party can start civil actions, either in interim relief proceedings or full first-instance hearings, to enforce the Dutch Civil Code and its general legislation on advertising in the context of civil relationships. This includes competitors who are disadvantaged by unlawful advertising, although an interim injunction may be denied if that competitor himself breaches the regulations on which its claim is based.[137] Typically, claimants request a civil court:

- to order an injunction to stop unlawful activities;
- to award damages;
- to order public rectification, often on the basis of a proposed text; and/or
- to withdraw unlawful material or products.

Civil judgments may be challenged in the Court of Appeal and on points of law in the Supreme Court. However, a competitor cannot claim violation of the Dutch Medicines Act in civil litigation, since it only serves to protect the interest of public health, not the interests of competitors.[138]

---

137. District Court Rotterdam, 27 March 2014, ECLI:NL:RBROT:2014:2601, *Omega Pharma v. Proctor & Gamble*.
138. Supreme Court 24 March 2006, ECLI:NL:HR:2006:AU7935, *Pfizer v. Cosmetique Active*; Supreme Court 10 November 2006, ECLI:NL:HR:2006:AY9317, *AstraZeneca v Menzis* and recently District Court The Hague 14 December 2021, ECLI:NL:RBDHA:2021:13754, *Boehringer Ingelheim v AstraZeneca*.

[C] Criminal Law

Where health and safety are severely compromised, sanctions on the basis of the Criminal Code may be requested by the public prosecutor. Punitive sanctions will be imposed by the criminal court on the basis of the Criminal Code. This option is hardly ever used in practice, mainly because the public prosecutor has discretion and gives priority to ordinary major crimes.

[D] Self-regulation

The interpretation of provisions and the identification of the type of activities to be considered breaches of the Medicines Act is subject to national judgment. Detailed rules of what would be considered (un)lawful advertising were developed by the industry, and norms were laid down in the self-regulatory industry codes, as mentioned before in this chapter.

In 1998, the Foundation Code of Conduct Pharmaceutical Advertising was established by the pharmaceutical industry, and the Code of Conduct Pharmaceutical Advertising entered into force. This Code contains rules to be observed when advertising medicinal products as well as specific rules relating to the interaction between industry and healthcare practitioners.

Advertising of medicinal products to the general public is only allowed for OTC products and is subject to further and more specific rules set out in the separate OTC Advertising Code (*in Dutch: Code voor de Publieksreclame voor Geneesmiddelen*). This Code was established by the Board for Public Advertising of Medicinal Products or Health Products. The OTC Code forms an integral part of the Code of Conduct Pharmaceutical Advertising.[139] Civil courts also take the decisions taken on the basis of the Code into account when deciding a civil claim, although they are not bound by those decisions and can divert.

[1] Enforcement

The abovementioned Industry Codes are enforced on the basis of contracts between the members of the Foundation and the Foundation itself. Those involved in pharmaceutical advertising are usually members of the Foundation, often via membership of a representative organisation that is a member of the Foundation (e.g., of the innovative industry or generic industry).[140] Members accept the authority of the Foundation and agree to act in accordance with the rules set out in the relevant codes. However, in practice, non-members of the Foundation are for practical purposes subject to the same interpretation of the Medicines Act interpreted in accordance with the code, as the

---

139. Article 5.6.1 Code of Conduct Pharmaceutical Advertising.
140. For instance, all members of Dutch Association Innovative Medicines (*Vereniging Innovatieve Geneesmiddelen*) or Association of the Dutch Generic Industry BOGIN.

courts do use the Code of Conduct Pharmaceutical Advertising for interpretation and inspiration.[141]

Enforcement of the Code of Conduct Pharmaceutical Advertising is carried out by the Advertisement Code Committee and the Appeal Committee, which acts upon complaints of third parties and issues binding decisions. The Inspectorate may appeal a decision. Although anyone can file a complaint, most complaints are lodged by competitors. Companies are under an obligation to cooperate fully with the rulings of the Advertisement Code Committee and Appeal Committee.[142]

If a party does not comply with the binding decision of the Advertisement Code Committee, the complainant can apply to the civil court for relief and request an order for compliance, as the Advertisement Code Committee has no power to enforce a decision. Despite this, the Foundation actively monitors compliance with decisions, and the Foundation informs the Inspectorate of cases of non-compliance, which may be published and picked up by the Inspectorate.

[2] Sanctions

Breach of the Code of Conduct Pharmaceutical Advertising may result in the following penalties:

- admonition;
- an order to stop the breach – for example, by ordering an immediate cessation of activities;
- an order to implement measures to prevent further breaches;
- a public rectification;
- an order to withdraw material;
- publication of the decision of the Advertisement Code Committee, including the penalty; and
- payment of costs of the procedure, including costs of the complainant.

However, as mentioned above, there are no sanctions to enforce these orders, but a consecutive order from a civil court may be enforced by monetary penalties due to the claimant.

[3] Code of Conduct Pharmaceutical Advertising

The Code of Conduct Pharmaceutical Advertising pertains – in the broadest sense – to advertising for and information about medicinal products, verbally, written or assisted by audiovisual methods, by way of exhibitions, congresses, conferences, or in any other way.[143] Advertising aimed at the Dutch audience is subject to Dutch law.[144]

---

141. As mentioned by the Advertising Code Committee in Aventis/Novo Nordisk, JGR 2005/59.
142. Article 2.2 Code of Conduct Pharmaceutical Advertising.
143. Article 1.1 Code of Conduct Pharmaceutical Advertising.
144. Use of Dutch language or message in Dutch media or Dutch websites.

Advertising of unauthorised medicinal products is only allowed to healthcare professionals within an international scientific context and is subject to certain restrictions.[145] Companies must have a dedicated scientific department responsible for providing education and advice and for compliance with the Code of Conduct for Pharmaceutical Advertising.[146]

The Advertising Code contains detailed rules intended to apply to all forms of advertising, most importantly:[147]

- general rules of conduct and general advertising rules;
- specific rules for face-to-face oral promotion (e.g., by sales representatives);
- specific rules for written advertisements aimed at healthcare professionals;
- specific rules for advertising at exhibitions;
- specific rules regarding hospitality; and
- specific rules regarding gifts or other promotions.

Generally,[148] advertising must:

- be truthful;
- not exaggerate the properties;
- not mislead;
- not induce unnecessary use of medicinal products; and
- not compromise good taste and decency.[149]

[a]   Information

As stated in the Introduction, §9.01, provision of information must be allowed, regardless of its source. As the difference between information provision and advertising is not clear-cut, the Code of Conduct Pharmaceutical Advertising includes guidance to distinguish between these categories. Generally, information provided should be complete, neutral, balanced, and in accordance with the SmPC of that particular product.[150] An important category of activities held to qualify as information is 'disease awareness campaigns', which are widely used to inform the public about certain medical conditions and their treatment without referencing specific treatments. If options for treatment are mentioned, a complete overview of all options should be presented, including all pharmaceutical therapies available. The party responsible for providing information should be clearly stated.

---

145. Article 5.2.1.1(b) Code of Conduct Pharmaceutical Advertising.
146. Article 5.9.1 and 5.9.2 Code of Conduct Pharmaceutical Advertising.
147. Chapter V Code of Conduct Pharmaceutical Advertising.
148. *Ibid.*
149. Article 5.2.1.5 Code of Conduct Pharmaceutical Advertising.
150. Article 5.7 Code of Conduct Pharmaceutical Advertising.

[b] Comparative Advertising

Comparative advertising is allowed subject to the claims being correct and capable of substantiation and not damaging to other products. Direct comparison by use of brand names is prohibited.[151] A comparative claim is considered to be capable of substantiation if the claim is supported by two independent scientific studies. In advertisements aimed at the general public, claims such as 'unique' are not allowed.[152] Besides the requirements as laid down in the advertising codes, there are specific requirements on comparative advertising in general in the Dutch Civil Code.[153] If the advertiser is sued on the basis that a claim in a (comparative) advertisement is false, misleading or otherwise not allowed, the burden of proof concerning the facts named in the advertisement rests on the advertiser. The advertiser must offer, within a short period (mostly within weeks in preliminary injunction proceedings in civil court), proof of the correctness and completeness of those facts.[154]

[c] Samples

The supply of limited samples of new medicinal products to healthcare professionals only is allowed, subject to keeping appropriate records for five years.[155]

[d] Internet Advertising

The Advertising Code contains specific rules regulating the use of Internet websites.[156] Important features relate to linking between websites. Often websites contain both information intended for healthcare practitioners as well as information aimed at the general public. It is accepted that restricting access (e.g., by requesting the healthcare administration code) is sufficient to prevent the public from seeing the information aimed at healthcare professionals. Providing an Internet address next to telephone or contact information on the packaging is permitted if it is recognised as an important communication tool.

The Advertising Code Committee has in several consistent decisions confirmed a specific responsibility for sponsors of informative websites, who bear full responsibility for content of websites and compliance with the codes, and a sponsor must actively pursue compliance with the website owner.

---

151. Articles 25 OTC Code.
152. Explanation to Article 25, OTC Code.
153. Articles 6:194 to 6:196 of the Dutch Civil Code.
154. Article 6:195 of the Dutch Civil Code.
155. Article 6.2.4 Code of Conduct Pharmaceutical Advertising.
156. Article 5.8.12 Advertising Code.

[4] OTC Advertising Code

Under the rules of the OTC Code, advertising aimed at consumers for OTC products, medical devices, and healthcare products is subject to prior assessment before release or use in the public domain by the Board of Approval. Typically, public relations material and press statements are considered to be information to journalists unless they are confirmed advertorials. Advertising of OTC products is only allowed for indications that can be diagnosed without intervention of a healthcare professional.

Advertising to the general public must:

- include the (brand) name of the product and the generic name of the active substance;
- include information necessary for appropriate use, including important safety warnings and instruction to read the information leaflet before use; and
- be clearly labelled as to its nature (e.g., 'advertisement, advertorial or company information').[157]

Use of testimonials is allowed, but they may not contain reference to 'before' and 'after' use of the medical product and should accurately reflect the user experience.

Distribution of free samples to the public, refunds, vouchers, or implied buying obligations are not allowed.[158] However, the Appeal Code Committee allowed a refund system financed by a pharmaceutical company but executed by a third party.[159]

It is prohibited to indicate the reimbursement status of a product under health insurance policies.[160]

[5] Inducement

On inducement, the Minister of Public Healthcare, Welfare and Sport has published the Inducement Policy Rules Medicines 2018.[161] Generally, offering financial incentives to healthcare professionals is prohibited. Equally, medical professionals are not allowed to request benefits from the industry.[162] Examples of financial incentives are:

- gifts;
- hospitality;
- sponsoring/financial grants/discounts; and
- fees for services.

---

157. Articles 8.1 and 11 OTC Code.
158. Article 7 under [a] OTC Code.
159. Appeal Code Committee, 17 September 2009, B09.006, *Pfizer v. Eleveld*.
160. Article 12 OTC Code.
161. Beleidsregels gunstbetoon Geneesmiddelenwet 2018, Staatscourant 2018, nr. 11305.These policy rules are in force since 19 February 2018.
162. Article 6.2.3 Code of Conduct Pharmaceutical Advertising.

[a] Gifts

Gifts representing a small monetary value and that are useful in relation to the profession or practice of the recipient are allowed. 'Small value gifts' are considered to have a shop value of up to EUR 50, including VAT (19%) per gift, with a maximum of EUR 150 per year. 'Small value' is a maximum of EUR 150 per therapeutic class,[163] per healthcare practitioner and per MA. Indirect gifts, such as unconditional lease of equipment or rent of facility, are subject to these rules as well.[164]

[b] Hospitality

Offering hospitality, including financial support to attend meetings, is allowed in relation to scientific or promotional gatherings. The latter is referred to as a 'manifestation', for which more restrictive rules apply. In order to qualify as a scientific meeting, the meeting should fall into one of the three categories:[165]

(a) The contents of the meeting have been designated as scientific by either a scientific association or, an independent institution which has been approved by the association of professionals concerned.
(b) The meeting has been organised by a partnership of healthcare practitioners, scientific organisations, or other independent groups of institutions. Two conditions should be complied with:
- The organiser determines – completely independently – the contents of the programme based on the independent needs of the healthcare practitioners; who the speakers will be; what the location will be; the duration of the meeting; and by whom the meeting can be attended.
- In case one of the speakers has ties with the industry or a third party, the objectivity of the presentation should be assessed by the scientific association concerned.
(c) The organisation is in the hands of, or takes place on the instructions of – a pharmaceutical company, and the meeting has been assessed beforehand on its contents, meaning that (1) the objectivity of the presentations should be guaranteed and (2) the programme foresees a need for independent information of healthcare practitioners. Besides, it should be assessed beforehand whether the hospitality is appropriate.

Offering financial support to attend meetings is only acceptable for reasonable costs of healthcare practitioners that are strictly limited to the main objective of the meeting. In addition, the meeting should be at an appropriate location. The following rules apply:

---

163. Therapeutic class entails an ATC main group, being the first level of the Anatomical Therapeutic Chemical classification system of the World Health Organisation (WHO).
164. Article 6.2.2. Code of Conduct Pharmaceutical Advertising.
165. Beleidsregels gunstbetoon Geneesmiddelenwet, under B.2.

(1) Scientific meeting
   (a) The hospitality for such meetings may not surpass the strictly necessary and the costs which are borne by the pharmaceutical company or a third party (or which are not invoiced) may, per healthcare practitioner and per therapeutic class, not exceed EUR 500 at a time, with a maximum of EUR 1,500 per year. For the maximum of EUR 1,500 per year, the amounts which have already been received for other meetings organised by third parties for the same therapeutic class, will be taken into account.[166]
   (b) The medical practitioner bears a minimum of 50% of all reasonable costs for travel, residence, and enrolment, required for the attendance of the meeting, personally.[167]
(2) Manifestations

Whenever a meeting does not meet the conditions as set out above, the meeting qualifies as a manifestation. For manifestations, the hospitality should be appropriate as well.

Furthermore, the costs of hospitality may not exceed EUR 75 per healthcare practitioner, with a maximum of EUR 375 per year per therapeutic class.[168]

Any hospitality that includes a financial compensation must be set out in a written contract in which the details of the hospitality are clearly described.[169]

[c]   Sponsoring and Grants

Sponsoring of healthcare professionals is allowed irrespective of the subject matter as long as this does not interfere with the normal prescription policy and behaviour. The Code of Conduct Pharmaceutical Advertising contains specific rules regarding sponsoring of activities and offering of financial grants.[170] In particular, sponsoring activities should be set out in a written contract, clearly establishing the goals of the sponsoring and the fact that no consideration is agreed upon.

[d]   Services

Healthcare professionals maintain relationships with the pharmaceutical industry and offer a variety of services, notably providing information in relation to treatment of disease, speaking engagements, lecturing, advising, or involvement in clinical investigations. These relationships are widely recognised and considered beneficial for both the industry as well as the medical field, as long as the relationships are transparent.

The terms and conditions on which services are offered by healthcare practitioners should be laid down in a contract in which purpose and services need to be

---

166. Article 6.4.6 Code of Conduct Pharmaceutical Advertising.
167. Ibid.
168. Article 6.4.8. Code of Conduct Pharmaceutical Advertising.
169. Articles 6.4.6(3) and 6.4.8(2) Code of Conduct Pharmaceutical Advertising.
170. Article 6.5 Code of Conduct Pharmaceutical Advertising.

recorded clearly. Financial compensation must be reasonable and realistic, usually expressed as an hourly rate. The reasonableness of the agreed hourly rate may be determined based on the rates that apply for providing healthcare, as laid down in the Explanation to the Code of Conduct Pharmaceutical Advertising.[171]

Furthermore, in the Netherlands, there is a Transparency register. The Code of Conduct Pharmaceutical Advertising contains the provision that healthcare practitioners on the one hand, and pharmaceutical companies (e.g., MAH) on the other hand, should declare information to the Transparency Register concerning all contracts in relation to services provided by the healthcare practitioner, hospitality contracts that include a financial compensation, sponsoring contracts, and support of patient organisations.[172]

[E]   Medical Devices

The Board also adopted a specific code for medical devices with a pharmaceutical appearance but with a mode of action intended for self-medication without the intervention of a doctor (e.g., nose sprays and eye drops). The Board will not review other medical devices, such as diagnostic medical devices or devices used in hospitals.

As of 1 April 2014, the Board started to perform CE-marking checks for medical devices, prior to reviewing the advertising. As of 1 January 2015, these checks were performed for all medical devices on the market which are advertised. The CE-marking check will consist of a check of the legal status of the product as a medical device and the plausibility of the clinical and scientific substantiation of the claims.

In addition, the Code of Conduct Medical Devices applies to the relationships between suppliers of medical devices and healthcare professionals. It contains provisions on gifts, discounts, sponsorship, and payment for services and hospitality. The provisions have been drafted taking account of the provisions of the abovementioned guidance document on financial incentives.

[F]   Healthcare Products

Under European legislation, healthcare products are distinctly different from medicinal products. Therefore, healthcare products may not be presented as having medicinal properties. The Board assesses whether or not unlawful claims are made suggesting medicinal properties for healthcare products.

As the difference between claims justifiable for healthcare products may be subtle, the Board publishes an indicative list of over a thousand claims that are considered to be allowed or not for use in relation to healthcare products. The list contains groups of physical indications (e.g., 'skin') and types of claims (e.g.,

---

171. Explanation of the Code of Conduct Pharmaceutical Advertising, page 22. Updated on 1 July 2020.
172. Article 7.2.1 Code of Conduct Pharmaceutical Advertising

'moisturising'). Claims not listed are subject to new assessment, and if considered acceptable, they will be added to the list.

§9.09 IMPLEMENTATION IN SPAIN

The advertising legislation framework in Spain comes from both regulatory bodies and self-regulation. Spain has seventeen regional governments (and therefore seventeen different Health Authorities) that are empowered to lay their own legislation down. At a national level, the relevant governing bodies are the Directorate General of Basic Services of the National Health System and Pharmacy (DGCBF) of the Spanish Ministry of Health and the Spanish Agency of Medicines and Medical Devices (AEMPS).

[A] Regulatory Aspects

[1] Legal Basis

In Spain, the main principles concerning the advertising of medicinal products are laid down in Articles 78 and 80 of the Consolidated Text of the Law on Guarantees and Rational Use of Medicines and Medical Devices, approved by the Royal Legislative Decree 1/2015 of 24 July (Consolidated Text). This Consolidated Text does not incorporate any mention of the Ministry of Health verifying whether a medicinal product meets the requirements set forth in Article 80.1 in order to be advertised and establishes that non-prescription medicines shall not need a previous administrative authorisation to be advertised, without prejudice of the necessary controls carried out by the competent administrative authority in order to verify whether the publicity complies with the relevant legislation applicable and with the scientific and technical specifications stated in the MA or not (Article 80 (2) and (3)).

As a development to these articles, the advertising of medicines has been the object of the regulation laid down by Royal Decree 1416/1994 (by means of which Directive 92/28/EEC was transposed into Spanish legislation), which is regarded as the main national rule governing the advertising of medicinal products for human use and that has to be interpreted in accordance with the abovementioned Consolidated text. In addition, the Ministry of Health published the '*Guidelines for the advertising of medicinal products for human use to the public*' in June 2019 (2nd edition). There have also been some other regulations at a regional level, interpreting the principles in the legislation and setting their own proceedings for compliance. The rules laid down by the two main Spanish regions, Madrid and Cataluña, are of importance. For Madrid, these include Circular 1/2000 on advertising aimed at persons qualified to prescribe and supply medicinal products, Circular 1/2002 on medical sales representative visits and other medicinal products advertising activities, and the Madrid Clarification Document on Valid Advertising Forms (as of September 2015). For Cataluña, rules include the Guidance for the Advertising of Human-Use Medicinal Products, released in April 2016 (4th edition).

[2] The General Principles as Interpreted by Spanish Authorities

First, medicinal products for which an MA has not been granted must not be advertised. This prohibition applies to:

  (i) medicines that are undergoing the authorisation process, whether nationally in Spain, or using the centralised procedure; and
  (ii) medicines authorised in countries other than Spain.

In light of the above, only medicines that have complied with all the steps needed to obtain an MA in Spain can be advertised.

Second, advertising should encourage the rational use of the medicine by presenting it objectively, accurate, balanced, honest, complete, must not be misleading, and must not exaggerate its properties. In particular:

- Comparative advertising is allowed for medicines with a similar safety and efficacy, and with an equivalent therapeutic effect. This comparison must be scientifically and objectively compared. In any case, this should explicitly cite the scientific studies on which it is based.
- The use of exaggerated claims, hyperlative terms or adjectives that presume that the medicinal product has some special merit, quality, or property that cannot be justified scientifically. (e.g., 'effective', 'safe', and 'quality'), used either in isolation or in combination with other words, unless it is part of text or an additional phrase that justifies the information.
- Adjectives or terms such as 'absolute', 'excellent', 'maximum', 'optimum', 'perfect', 'total', or similar words relating to the quality, effectiveness, purity, or safety of the medicine can be only used if they appear in the SmPC ('*ficha técnica*').
- The term 'new' cannot be used to describe a medicinal device that has been widely available in Spain for more than two years.
- Advertising mottos or slogans may be used if they do not mislead and do not introduce concepts or words that exaggerate product characteristics.
- Adverse reactions information and statements must reflect the available evidence. It cannot be claimed that a medicinal product has no adverse effects, toxicity, or reaction risks.

[3] Advertising Aimed at Persons Qualified to Prescribe or Supply Medicinal Products

Advertising aimed at healthcare professionals must follow the same principles laid down in European legislation, such as advertising in written form, visits of medical sales representatives, supply of samples, incentives, and sponsorship of scientific meetings.

In this framework, one form of advertising is the supply of samples to the healthcare professional. In particular, the supply of samples is only allowed when the following requirements (Article 16 RD 1416/1994) are complied with:

- its formula contains one or several active ingredients that are new in the therapeutic field;
- its pharmaceutical form, dosage, and/or administration are new and represent a therapeutic improvement in respect of the current status of the medical profession; or
- new pharmacological actions with new therapeutic indications have been discovered.

The supply of samples is also subject to quantitative limits and other restrictions: a specific authorisation to manufacture and distribute free samples must be requested to the AEMPS by the healthcare company, only ten samples per healthcare professional and year can be supplied, and so forth.

With regard to advertising in written form, besides the ordinary previous advertising notice (*see* Table 9.1), there is also a requirement to issue a notice of valid advertising form to the relevant Regional Health Authority under Article 15.3 RD 1416/1994, by the owners of scientific or professional publications and audiovisual media, in which advertising of medicines in any written form is likely to be released (editors of journals, books, bulletins, optical or magnetic means, etc.). In addition, the manufacturer of the medicinal product must provide in the written advertising the minimum technical and scientific information to enable the recipients to judge for themselves the therapeutic value of the medicinal product, including information, such as the particulars of the product specification sheet, the prescription and dispensing regimen, and its prescription or pharmaceutical dosage form.

[a]   *Advertising Using the Internet*

The Internet is one of the most relevant platforms for transmitting information to a mass audience; this is why the regulation of advertising of medicinal products focuses increasingly on it.

According to the interpretation delivered by the Madrid and Cataluña governments (*see* Madrid Circular 1/2000, and Cataluña Guidance for the Advertising of Human-Use Medicinal Products, as of April 2016), all web pages must comply with the same requirements as all other forms of advertisement in terms of content and scope of distribution. It must also be clear that the use of the website is restricted to healthcare professionals qualified to prescribe or supply medicines. In order to secure a restricted access to healthcare professionals, any proper technical means must be implemented. According to Article 39.b of the Madrid Circular 1/2000, 'it shall be considered as an effective restriction measure the fulfilment of an online form, in which the user willing to access to the promotional information can state their relevant professional details so as to make out if it is or not a qualified person to prescribe or supply medicinal products'. Finally, the restricted use should always be warned of by means of a specific mention (at least in the Spanish language), such as: 'The information is exclusively aimed to healthcare professionals qualified to prescribe or supply medicinal products, and therefore a specialised training is needed for its proper interpretation.' The disclaimer must be clearly written or audible and emphasised.

The release of any kind of advertising aimed at persons qualified to prescribe or supply medicinal products must be subject to a previous notice to the Regional Health Authority from the Spanish region in which the healthcare company is based under Article 25 RD 1416/1994 (see Table 9.1 below).

[4] Advertising Aimed at the General Public

This kind of advertising also follows the principles laid down in Directive 2001/83/EC. With regard to Internet advertising, the following are highlighted:

- The name of a website cannot include the name of a prescription-use medicine (Madrid document on valid advertising forms) since it can be regarded as a form of promotion aimed at the general public.
- The website must indicate when it was last updated.
- The editorial content must not be mixed up with advertising messages, which must be clearly identified as such.
- The owner of the website is responsible for the links stated.
- The sponsoring of websites of patient associations, users, and persons not qualified to prescribe or supply medicines may be only made on an institutional basis. Any promotional information appearing on these kinds of websites is regarded as advertising aimed at the general public, and thereby it is subject to the applicable legal restrictions.

At this point, it is also important to highlight that, nowadays, there is a specific rule which regulates the sale of non-prescription human use medicinal products by way of telecommunication systems: Royal Decree 870/2013 of 8 November, on distance selling of non-prescription medicinal products for human use. According to its provisions, online selling of non-prescription medicinal products is allowed so far as some requirements are fulfilled:

- Only legally authorised pharmacies are allowed to sell the aforesaid medicinal products through a website.
- It is mandatory to give the competent Regional Authority prior notice of the intention of starting the online selling, at least fifteen days in advance.
- Online sales should be carried out with the intervention of a pharmacist and with previous personal advice, in accordance with provisions established in Articles 19.4 and 86.1 of the Consolidated Text.
- Online sales must comply with current legislation applicable to the medicinal products which are to be sold.
- Online sales of medicinal products must be made directly from the pharmacy, which is responsible for their dispensing, without any intermediary.
- Presents, prices, quizzes, or similar activities in order to promote or related to online sales of medicinal products are banned.

– When the buyer is in the territory of a Member State other than Spain, online sales must comply with both the requirements established in the abovementioned Consolidated Text and any other enforceable requirement stated in the destination Member State.

Since 1 July 2015, the online sales of non-prescription medicinal products are finally possible given that the AEMPS has developed the software application ('*distafarma.es*') so that the autonomous regions may keep a record of the pharmacies that want to sell non-prescription medicinal products on Internet. They will receive a European common logo that certifies the quality of the online sales.

Pharmaceutical companies must also issue a notice listing any promotional/advertising activity carried out in the last year ('Annual Advertising-Activities Index') (Article 21.b RD 1416/1994). This index must cover not only professional-aimed advertising but also any promotional activity aimed at the general public.

[B] Infringements and Remedies under the Law

The breach of legal obligations concerned with advertising of medicinal products is severely punished under Consolidated Text, with fines up to EUR 30,000 for minor infringements, from EUR 30,001 to EUR 90,000 for serious infringements, and from EUR 90,001 to EUR 1 million for very serious infringements. The fine can be higher than 1 million depending on the benefits obtained from infringement (Article 114 of the Consolidated Text).

The quantum of the fines depends on the degree of cooperation, negligence, fraud, collusion, company turnover, non-compliance with previous warnings, number of affected people, harm caused, benefits obtained, and recurrence of infringement.

Table 9.1 Advertising Aimed to the Persons Qualified to Prescribe or Supply Medicinal Products

Public Control	Responsible	Relevant Authority	Relevant Rules
Previous notice of valid advertising form Content of the notification: - Utilisation of an appropriate channel. - Statement declaring that the channel is exclusively targeted to healthcare providers.	**Owners** of publications/ audiovisual media on which advertising of medicines in documental form is likely to be released	The notice must be issued to the **Health Authority of the Spanish region where the editor/ responsible person for the publication is based**	Article 15.3 RD 1416/1994 Proceedings to issue this notice have been respectively set up in Madrid (by means of DGF Circular 1/ 2000, and DGF Document on Valid Advertising Forms, September 2015) and Cataluña (by means of *Guidance on Advertising of Human-Use medicinal products*, April 2016)
Area of dissemination: national or regional			Article 25 RD 1416/1994 Proceedings to issue this notice have been respectively set up in Madrid (by means of DGF Circular 1/2000) and Cataluña (by means of *Guidance on Advertising of Human-Use medicinal products*, April 2016)

Public Control	Responsible	Relevant Authority	Relevant Rules
Previous communication of advertising Content of the notification: - Name of the laboratory - Name of the medicinal product - Channel used - SmPC or package leaflet - Copy of the advertisement - Report from the scientific department of the laboratory	**Holders of the Marketing Authorisation** of the medicinal product object of the advertising or promotional information	The communication form and the related documentation must be submitted before the release to the **Health Authority of the Spanish region where the holder of the Marketing Authorisation is based**	Article 25 RD 1416/1994 Proceedings to issue this notice have been respectively set up in Madrid (by means of *DGF Circular 1/2000*) and Cataluña (by means of *Guidance on Advertising of Human-Use medicinal products*, October 2009)
Annual advertising index Submission of an annual index of all the advertising activity carried out.	**Holders of medicinal products Marketing Authorisations**	**Health Authority of the Spanish region where the holder of the Marketing Authorisation is based**	Article 21.b RD 1416/1994 Proceedings to issue this notice have been respectively set up in Madrid (by means of *DGF Circular 1/2000*) and Cataluña (by means of *Guidance on Advertising of Human-Use medicinal products*, April 2016) Article 21.b RD 1416/1994 Proceedings to issue this notice have been respectively set up in Madrid (by means of *DGF Circular 1/2000*) and Cataluña (by means of *Guidance on Advertising of Human-Use medicinal products*, April 2016)

Public Control	Responsible	Relevant Authority	Relevant Rules
Previous advertising authorisation Requested only **exceptionally** by decision of the Spanish Ministry of Health Content of the request of authorisation: – Name of the laboratory – Name of the medicinal product – Mean used – Package leaflet – Copy of the advertisement – Report from the scientific department of the laboratory	**Holders of the Marketing Authorisation** of the medicinal product object of the advertising or promotional information	Spanish Ministry of Health	Article 26 RD 1416/1994
Previous authorisation for the supplying of free samples	**Applicant or holders of the Marketing Authorisation of the medicinal product object of supplying as sample.**	AEMPS	Article 16(4) RD 1416/1994

Advertising of unauthorised medicinal products, advertising of medicinal products carried out inconsistently with the terms of the authorisation or with the applicable law, and offering of incentives to the general public linked to promotion and advertising of medicinal products have been characterised as serious and very serious offences under Article 111.2 b and c of the Consolidated Text.

The Consolidated Text also provides other measures to be carried out in addition to the imposing of fines, such as cease-and-desist actions and closure of businesses.

[C] Self-regulation

The association for the pharmaceutical industry is called Farmaindustria, and its membership includes the great majority of pharmaceutical companies based in Spain. Due to the special nature of pharmaceutical products and the need to protect the health of citizens, Farmaindustria collaborates with public administration in establishing a regulated and economic framework for the medicines sector.

Farmaindustria has adopted its own ethical codes consistent with those of EFPIA.

[1] Spanish Code of Good Practice for the Pharmaceutical Industry

In 1991, Farmaindustria adopted, as Spanish Code, the European Code of Practice for the Promotion of Medicines approved by EFPIA. According to changes in the European Code, the Spanish Code has been updated several times. The latest available version of the Spanish Coded is dated September 2021.

New variations in the EFPIA legislative framework have led to the approval of a new Farmaindustria Code, which came into force in January 2014: the Spanish Code of Good Practice for the Pharmaceutical Industry (Farmaindustria Code or The Code). This new regulation recasts the Spanish Code of Good Practice for the Promotion of Medicines and Interaction with Healthcare Professionals and its Guide, and the Code of Practice on Relationships between the Pharmaceutical Industry and Patient Organizations.

[a] Promotion of Medicines and Interaction with Healthcare Professionals

The Code is applicable to Farmaindustria member companies or other companies abiding by the Code and takes priority over other self-regulation systems in medicines promotion – except for the two specific rules of Article 19.4 referring to countries where EFPIA member association codes apply. In this case, the applicable codes would be:

(a) for promotion conducted, sponsored, or organised by a company located in Europe, or under its control, the code of the national association of the country where the company is located (if the company is not located in Europe, it should apply the EFPIA code); and

(b) the code of the national association of the country where the promotion is conducted.

Under the Farmaindustria Code, prescription products cannot be promoted to the general public. For that reason, their promotion shall only be aimed to those healthcare professionals qualified to prescribe or supply them. However, there is an exception to this rule, when the promotion has been authorised by the competent healthcare authority, e.g., vaccination campaigns.

The Code defines 'promotion' as 'any activity undertaken, organised, or sponsored by a pharmaceutical company or under its control – subsidiaries, foundations, associations, institutes, agencies, etc. – designed to directly or indirectly promote the prescription, dispensing, sale or consumption of its medicines'.

According to the Farmaindustria Code, a medicinal product cannot be advertised so long as it has not obtained an MA; this ban includes those medicinal products having obtained said authorisation in any other country different from Spain but not in Spain directly. Any information provided must be compatible with the SmPC; the valid means for publicity, characteristics of the different promotional materials and of the publicity itself are established in the Code (it shall be precise, honest, balanced, objective, based on an appropriate scientific evaluation, not misleading, etc.). When a pharmaceutical company funds or sponsors the promotion of a medicinal product, this fact has to be clearly indicated.

The Farmaindustria Code prohibits any offer or supply of gifts, discounts, or premiums to healthcare professionals, in a direct or indirect way, whether in cash or in kind, in order to avoid the encouraging of the prescription or dispensation of prescription medicines, except for writing instruments or instruments for professional use which are not related to prescription of medicines and which value not exceed EUR 10 (Article 10.1).

The Farmaindustria Spanish Code also establishes that, in case of scientific and promotional meetings and events organised or sponsored by pharmaceutical companies, these events must be notified in advance and the failure to notify constitutes an infringement of the Code. The Rules of Procedure of the Control Bodies of the Code (Article 9), which develops the procedure for notification, provides that notification must be sent to the Surveillance Unit (the body responsible for active monitoring of compliance with the Codes) at least ten working days before the scheduled date. However, not all meetings and events must be notified. Pharmaceutical companies must provide prior notification for scientific or promotional meetings or events only when:

- they are organised directly or indirectly, or sponsored wholly or mainly, by the notifying company;
- they include at least an overnight stay; and
- they involve the participation of at least twenty health professionals having their activity in Spain.

About promotion on the Internet, the Code provides that 'Promotional material must include a prominent and clearly legible warning indicating that the information contained on the web page is intended only for healthcare professionals qualified to prescribe or dispense medicines, and specialised training is therefore required for its adequate interpretation.'

According to the code, pharmaceutical companies are responsible for the content spread across the means, supports, and channels of communication online that directly or indirectly they control or finance. For this reason, they must implement guidelines establishing standards of conduct and consequences of its infringement, as well as a procedure for monitoring the content to which they give access, copy temporarily, or link.

[b] *Relationships Between the Pharmaceutical Industry and Patient Organisations*

In order to ensure that relationships between the pharmaceutical industry and patient organisations take place in an ethical and transparent manner, EFPIA adopted in October 2007 the EFPIA Code of Practice on Relationships between the Pharmaceutical Industry and Patient Organizations. After that, on 30 June 2008, Farmaindustria agreed to approve its own Code of Good Practices for the Interrelation between the Pharmaceutical Industry and the Patient Organizations (like the Spanish Code of Good Practice for the Promotion of Medicines and Interaction with Healthcare Professionals, this second Code adopted by Farmaindustria also copies the majority of the articles from the EFPIA Code). As has already been mentioned in §9.09[C][1], this body of rules (the Spanish Code of Good Practice for the Promotion of Medicines and Interaction with Healthcare Professionals and the Code of Good Practices for the Interrelation between the Pharmaceutical Industry and the Patient Organizations) is now consolidated by the new Farmaindustria Code.

This Farmaindustria Code covers any activity carried out, organised, or sponsored by a pharmaceutical company or organisations under its control from which can derive direct or indirect collaboration and support with patient organisations. Collaboration shall be documented in a written agreement that should contain (as a minimum):

- the activities to be carried out;
- the amount of funding;
- the purpose;
- a description of significant indirect support (e.g., the donation of a public relations agency's time and the nature of its involvement); and
- significant non-financial support.

The Farmaindustria Code also requires pharmaceutical companies to have an approval process in place for these agreements prior to their implementation.

As transparency is one of the main objectives pursued by both European and Spanish Codes, each company must make publicly available a list of patient organisations to which it provides financial support or any other type of support. This information should be updated at least annually.

In addition to the aforesaid obligation, it is remarkable how the Farmaindustria Code also establishes a wide regulation of the disclosure of transfers of value from pharmaceutical companies to healthcare professionals and patient organisations (rules on transparency, Article 18), consistent with those stated in the EFPIA Codes.

[2] Spanish Code of Good Practices for the Promotion and Advertising of Non-Prescription Medicinal Products

In the field of medicines advertising targeted to the general public, the Personal Healthcare Association (ANEFP) is the association that includes the pharmaceutical companies that manufacture and market medicines and products for self-care of health, as well as member companies, agencies of advertising, communication, consulting, human resources, etc. They passed their own code of good practices in 2007, and it stands as a guide that sets guidelines for action in the field of promotion and advertising of medicines intended for the self-care of health, and it establishes a mediation procedure for the resolution of conflicts between affiliated companies. The purpose of this code is to guarantee a minimum of legality and veracity in promotion activities, especially for the public, in general.

Since 2013, it is not necessary for this kind of advertising to obtain a previous authorisation from the competent authorities. Therefore, the ANEFP developed that year a 'seal of quality', that acts as a guarantor of quality by analysing *ex ante* if the advertising fulfils the requirements set in the regulation.

In December 2014, the Spanish Ministry of Health, the ANEFP and the Association for Self-Regulation of Commercial Communications (Autocontrol) signed an agreement which establishes mechanisms for the correct evaluation of the advertising of medicinal products aimed at the general public.

[D] Infringements and Remedies under the Farmaindustria Code

The Committee, the Surveillance Unit, and the Jury of Autocontrol (hereinafter the 'Jury') are the bodies responsible for ensuring effective application of the Farmaindustria Code.

The Jury, which is the independent out-of-court body that adjudicates complaints submitted on advertising issues and whose decisions are binding for Autocontrol members, does not belong to the organisation structure of Farmaindustria. Therefore, Farmaindustria and Autocontrol signed an Agreement by means of which resolutions of the Jury should be complied with by every Farmaindustria member company when it is resolving any disputes related to the application of 'the Spanish Codes' (now known as the Farmaindustria Code).

Farmaindustria has established different procedures, such as the Complaint Procedure, which is initiated when a complaint is received from any person with a legitimate interest, from the Surveillance Unit, or even from EFPIA. The complaint and accompanying documentation should be addressed to the Secretary of the Committee. The Secretariat informs the company against which the complaint has been lodged, which can respond within five days. The whole dossier will be provided to the Committee, and a mutually acceptable agreement between the parties will be attempted through mediation. If the Committee achieves an amicable agreement between the parties, the claim presented will be settled, and referral to the Jury is not required. If an agreement cannot be reached, the Committee Secretariat shall refer the dossier to the Jury, which will make a final decision. Both an amicable agreement and the Jury's resolution must be immediately complied with by the parties.

Farmaindustria also has an Investigation Procedure initiated by the Surveillance Unit. During the procedure, companies may be required to provide any information or documentation the Surveillance Unit deems appropriate. In the end, the Surveillance Unit will decide to (i) file the case, (ii) transfer the recommendations that it considers appropriate and file the case, or (iii) initiate an automatic sanctioning procedure before the Committee.

Fines that could be imposed pursuant to Article 22.2 of the Farmaindustria Code are:

- for minor breaches: EUR 6,000 to EUR 120,000;
- for serious breaches: EUR 120,001 to EUR 240,000; and
- for very serious breaches: EUR 240,001 to EUR 360,000.

During 2013-2016, Farmaindustria published eighteen amicable agreements and seven resolutions, increasing considerably the number of resolutions between the years 2017 and 2022 up to a total of thirteen. The majority of these resolutions referred to infringements due to inconsistency between information in the advertisement and the SmPC and the approved indications, the objectivity principle, and the promotional and no promotional nature of articles published by journalists. Almost all complaints are related to minor breaches.

In order to avoid infringements of the Code, companies can submit queries to the Surveillance Unit to obtain advice from the Committee in advance, as the answers to these queries will be binding on both the Surveillance Unit and the Committee.

§9.10 IMPLEMENTATION IN SWEDEN

[A] Legal Basis

The main provisions in Sweden governing the advertising or marketing of medicinal products are laid down in the Medicinal Products Act (2015:315) (the Act), which is complemented by the Medical Products Ordinance (2015:458) (the Ordinance) and Regulation (EC) No. 726/2004. In addition, EC Directives are implemented into binding provisions by the Swedish Medical Products Agency (the MPA).[173] These provisions are published in the MPA's Code of Statutes.[174] Relevant regulations regarding advertising of medicinal products have been published in LVFS 2009:6 (the Code). The Code contains detailed regulations regarding advertising of medicinal products for human use, which are based on Directive 2001/83/EC (the Directive) and Directive 2008/29/EC, whereas the Act contains the general provisions stated in the Directive.[175]

The Act sets out the rules for the advertising of medicinal products in general and specific requirements and restrictions for advertising directed at the public and for advertising directed at healthcare professionals. Moreover, the Act sets out the statutory powers available to the competent authority in Sweden, the MPA. The MPA is authorised to intervene quickly to prevent future use of material breaching applicable rules and regulations regarding advertising of medicines by prohibition and conditional fines for non-compliance.[176] In accordance with the Act, an MAH shall have a function with scientific competence monitoring of the information regarding its medicinal products.[177]

Regulations in the Swedish Marketing Act (SFS 2008:486) (the Marketing Act) are also applicable to the marketing of medicinal products as *lex generalis*. The Marketing Act is applicable in respect of marketing of all types of goods and services, including medicinal products and medical devices. The Marketing Act contains provisions regarding, *inter alia*, generally accepted marketing practices, unfair marketing practices, and misleading marketing practices.[178] When determining whether advertising is compatible with generally accepted marketing practices, it shall be considered whether the advertising observes established standards and case law applicable with respect to the industry, such as the ethical rules provided by the Swedish Association of the Pharmaceutical Industry (LIF) and the Code of Advertising Practice maintained by the International Chamber of Commerce. The Swedish Consumer Agency is the supervising authority with respect to the compliance of the rules in the Marketing Act.

The Swedish Radio and Television Act contains provisions in respect of marketing of medicinal products on television. Advertising of medicinal treatments that are only available by prescription may not be broadcast on television, unless it concerns sponsorship where only the name of the company is presented. Sales programmes for pharmaceutical products or for medical treatments may not be broadcast on television.[179]

---

173. Sw: *Läkemedelsverket*.
174. 'LVFS'.
175. Articles 87.2, 87.3, 89.1.a, 90, 91.1, and 92 of the Directive.
176. Chapter 14, Section 3 of the Act.
177. Chapter 12, Section 2 of the Act.
178. Sections 5, 6, and 8 respectively of the Marketing Act.
179. Chapter 8, Section 14 of the Swedish Radio and Television Act (2010:696).

[B] Scope of the Regulations

The Act provides no explicit definition of advertising or marketing of medicinal products. This was a conscious choice by the legislator. The term 'marketing'[180] used in the Act shall be construed within the meaning of Article 86 of the Directive.[181] The Act thus applies to all marketing activities of medicinal products, as defined by the Directive.

The Act provides general provisions in respect of marketing. More detailed regulations are provided in the Code.

Marketing is defined generally in the Marketing Act, without an explicit reference to medicinal products.[182] There is no doubt, however, that the Marketing Act applies to the marketing of medicinal products, as it applies to the marketing of goods and services in general.

[C] Role of the MPA: The National Competent Authority

The supervising authority with respect to advertising of medicinal products is the MPA. This authority monitors advertising in all types of media, such as daily journals, magazines, radio, Internet, and television (previously monitored by the Swedish Consumer Ombudsman). The supervision of advertising of medicinal products is also done by the Director General of the Swedish Consumer Agency, the Consumer Ombudsman.[183] Before the implementation of the Directive in Sweden (2006), the supervising function was traditionally managed by the industry itself through the Swedish Pharmaceutical Industry's Information Examination Board (IGN) and the Information Practices Committee (NBL). The industry and the MPA assisted these organisations by reporting complaints and concerns about advertising of medicinal products, but the MPA had less-defined powers to intervene in these matters. The industry organisations still have an important function and participate actively in the work of maintaining fair marketing practices within the industry. The MPA monitors how the system of self-reporting is working and has the authority to intervene where companies do not abide by the industry's own regulations and systems.

[1] Complaints to the MPA

Following the changes to the Act in 2006, the MPA has greater powers to sanction transgressions of the advertising-related provisions of the Act, and it has investigated a number of matters, prompted both by third-party complaints and on its own initiative.

---

180. Sw: *marknadsföring*.
181. Proposition to amendment of the Medicinal Products Act, 2005/06:70, p. 193.
182. Section 3 of the Marketing Act.
183. Sw: *Konsumentombudsmannen*.

Chapter 9: Advertising Medicinal Products for Human Use §9.10[D]

Even though the MPA has the statutory powers to enforce the relevant provisions of the Act, the MPA still refers matters to the NBL. Breaches of the Act mainly arise from:

- product claims that are inconsistent with the SmPC;
- lack of clarity that the product advertised is a medicinal product; and
- a lack of information that is useful to the consumer, such as restrictions for use in children or a notice that a doctor needs to be consulted before starting treatment.

[2]   Sanctions

Pursuant to the Act, the MPA is authorised to issue prohibitive injunctions in conjunction with conditional fines for non-compliance with relevant provisions of the Act.[184]

Companies employing unfair marketing practices in breach of the Marketing Act may be prohibited from continuing the practice or starting similar practices by means of prohibitive injunctions in conjunction with conditional fines.[185] The specific rules on, for instance, misleading advertisements and special offers carry sanctions of prohibitive injunctions in conjunction with conditional fines, market disruptions fees between Swedish Krona (SEK) 5,000–5,000,000, and third-party damages.[186]

The IGN and NBL may impose fines on member companies that breach the ethical rules of the LIF. The maximum fine is SEK 500,000.[187]

The Consumer Ombudsman has powers to represent consumer interests and pursue legal action in the Patent and Market Court (PMD) at Stockholm District Court on behalf of consumers in matters concerning, *inter alia*, advertising of medicinal products. Actions before these courts can also be initiated by competitors, consumers, or trade/consumer associations.[188]

The prohibitions on bribery and taking bribes under the Swedish Penal Code must be considered in the context of gifts or other benefits offered to the public as well as private medicinal practitioners, as the level of acceptance concerning benefits is very low in Sweden.[189]

[D]   Self-Regulation

In addition to the statutory rules on marketing and advertisements, the pharmaceutical industry is regulated by a framework of ethical rules operated by the LIF.

---

184. Chapter 14, Section 3 of the Act.
185. Sections 23, 26, and 28 of the Marketing Act.
186. Sections 23, 26, 28, 29, 31, and 37 of the Marketing Act.
187. Section 42.2 of the Statutes of the IGN and the NBL (Appendix 2 of the Ethical Rules).
188. Sections 47–49 of the Marketing Act.
189. Chapter 10, Sections 5a-e of the Swedish Penal Code (1962:700).

[1] The LIF

LIF is the trade association for the research-based pharmaceutical industry in Sweden. LIF has about eighty member companies and thereby represents approximately 80% of the total sales of pharmaceuticals in Sweden.

A system of self-regulation in the pharmaceutical sector has been maintained by LIF since 1969 in order to ensure that the information supplied by pharmaceutical companies follows the ethical rules for the pharmaceutical industry. LIF is a member of EFPIA and IFPMA and is also covered by the regulations of these international organisations.

Questions regarding the Ethical Rules (as defined below) may be referred to LIF's compliance officer who is a professionally trained pharmacist. The compliance officer is the decisive body regarding proper locations for medicinal conferences and is the contact person for IFPMA's Code Compliance Network.[190] Decisions by the compliance officer may be appealed to the NBL.[191]

[2] The Ethical Rules

The regulations operated by LIF are provided in the 'Ethical Rules for the Pharmaceutical Industry' in Sweden (the Ethical Rules), which came into force on 1 October 2007 and were latest revised in June 2022. The rules consist of:

- rules on medicinal product information that, in connection with marketing of medicinal products, is targeted at physicians, dentists, veterinary surgeons, pharmacists, or other personnel within Swedish healthcare or distribution of medicinal products;
- rules on medicinal products information that, in connection with the marketing of medicinal products on the Swedish market, is targeted at the general public;
- rules of cooperation – agreement on cooperation with healthcare;
- rules of cooperation – agreement on cooperation with pharmacies;
- rules on disclosure of transfer of value;
- ethical rules for interaction between pharmaceutical companies and user organisations/interest groups;
- ethical rules for interaction between pharmaceutical companies and politicians;
- rules for non-interventional studies;
- rules for financial support for National Quality Registers within the health service;
- reference to regulations in the Penal code regarding bribes;
- statues of the IGN and the NBL;

---

190. Chapter 1, the Ethical Rules (Background and Purpose) and Section 4.7 of the Statues of the IGN and the NBL (Appendix 2 of the Ethical Rules).
191. Section 36 of the Statues of the IGN and the NBL (Appendix 2 of the Ethical Rules).

– rules of procedure for the IGN and the NBL.

In principle, only member companies of LIF are bound by the Ethical Rules. However, since 1 July 2002, there has been an agreement in place between LIF and the Swedish Association for Small and Medium-sized Companies Active in Research and Development (R&D), which renders the Ethical Rules binding for the members of the latter organisation as well. Formally, there is no obstacle against initiating a matter against pharmaceutical companies that are not members of either of the two associations. Fines may, however, only be imposed on companies that are bound by the Ethical Rules.

The Ethical Rules are divided into two sections: the first section regulates drug information addressed to physicians and other healthcare personnel, and the second section regulates information targeted at the general public. The rules are applicable to any type of media used by the pharmaceutical industry in its marketing activities.

The Ethical Rules are based on both national law and case law, including the provisions regarding information and advertisement of medicinal products contained in domestic and EU pharmaceutical legislation and other enactments or in directives issued by government agencies (e.g., the MPA), and also on non-judicial standards such as the Code of Advertising Practice maintained by the International Chamber of Commerce and the Code of Conduct adopted by the EFTA's Pharmaceutical Industries Association. The regulations are concordant with WHO's ethical rules for marketing drugs and the IFPMA and the EFPIA Codes of Pharmaceutical Marketing Practices.[192]

The responsibility to comply with the rules on information rests with the pharmaceutical company concerned or its representative in Sweden. The representative is also responsible for information administered directly by a foreign principal.[193]

[3] The IGN and the NBL

The IGN and the NBL shall ensure that the pharmaceutical companies follow the Ethical Rules, legal statutory provisions, and general non-statutory criteria for good business practice in the industry.[194] LIF is the governing body of the two agencies.[195] The duties of the IGN and the NBL are performed separately and consist primarily of monitoring the market, assessing cases, as well as pre-examination of vaccine campaigns and information about prescription drugs on web pages available to the general public.

[4] The IGN

The monitoring of the market and the industry's compliance with the Ethical Rules is supervised by the IGN (named IGM before 1 January 2017). The IGN board consists of

---

192. Chapter 1 (Background and Purpose) of the Ethical Rules.
193. Chapter 1, Section 1, Article 28 of the Ethical Rules.
194. Section 3 of the Statutes of the IGN and the NBL (Appendix 2 of the Ethical Rules).
195. Section 1.2 of the Statutes of the IGN and the NBL (Appendix 2 of the Ethical Rules).

a president and two board members. At least one of the members shall have medicinal knowledge, be a licenced physician, hold a clinical speciality, and be clinically experienced. At least one of the members shall be highly educated within the healthcare field, have substantial and broad experience within that field, and also have certain insights into marketing law.

In order for the IGN to be able to monitor the market, the pharmaceutical companies must send new, up-to-date drug information to the IGN, such as publications, advertisements, invitations, mailings, television advertisements, or information on websites. The pharmaceutical companies shall send information regarding marketing activities to IGN.

The IGN may examine marketing activities that the IGN finds questionable in the course of monitoring the market as well as activities which are questioned by a private individual, a company, an association, or LIF's Compliance Officer.[196] IGN handles the examination of marketing activities.

The IGN may also provide general advice before advertising is used, in the form of non-binding decisions.[197]

Assessments of whether information supplied and marketing measures taken by the industry are compatible with the rules and with good business practice, and making decisions in cases taken up for consideration in connection with monitoring the market, are made by both the IGN and the NBL.[198]

Some 4,000 marketing practices are reviewed by the IGN each year, of which the IGN, on its own initiative, makes a deeper review of forty to sixty cases. Upon initiation of such a case, the IGN contacts the company concerned, requesting an explanation. In approximately half of the cases, the explanation received by the IGN is satisfactory or only a minor infringement, with an informal closing of the file. In these instances, the cases are closed without a formal decision or fines being imposed. In the remaining cases, the IGN makes a formal decision, and fines are imposed.

The IGN also receives between twenty and sixty complaints per annum from companies, Country Councils and individuals, such as doctors and nurses. In these cases, a formal decision is always made, even when the complaint is dismissed, so that the decisions can be appealed to the NBL.[199] Consequently, the IGN formally handles approximately 80 to 120 cases per year.

[5] The NBL

The NBL is a committee consisting of a chairperson and eleven members representing legal and medical expertise, and expertise from the industry itself. Moreover, the interests of the general public, generally the consumers, are also represented.[200] The Board of the NBL, *inter alia*, examines issues referred by the IGN and processes appeals

---

196. Sections 5.1 and 18 of the Statutes of the IGN and the NBL (Appendix 2 of the Ethical Rules).
197. Chapter 1, Section 1, Article 31 of the Ethical Rules.
198. Sections 4.3 and 4.4 of the Statutes of the IGN and the NBL.
199. Ministry of Health and Social Affairs, Ministry publications Series 2004:13, 51–52.
200. Sections 11.1-11.5 of the Statutes of the IGN and the NBL (Appendix 2 of the Ethical Rules).

on decisions made by the IGN or LIF'S Compliance Officer. NBL also handles filed complaints from relevant authorities, such as the MPA, and matters concerning information and other marketing activities for products other than pharmaceuticals, such as diagnostic preparations.[201] In addition, the NBL may issue advisory statements explaining what is or should be considered good industry practice in any particular case.[202]

The NBL reviews approximately ten appeals from the IGN per year. Most of these appeals originate from complaints by companies and individuals. In addition, the NBL handles approximately thirty cases per year; most are initiated by the MPA. In the MPA cases, the NBL shares the objections against the advertising at issue in the majority of the cases, and fines are imposed.

[6]   Agreements on Forms of Collaboration with the Healthcare Sector

Pharmaceutical companies and the healthcare sector have collaborated for several years in Sweden, which has provided important developments in healthcare. In November 2013, LIF entered into a joint agreement with the Swedish Association of Local Authorities and Regions (SALAR) (*Sw: Sveriges Kommuner och Landsting, SKL*), Swedish Medtech, and Swedish Labtech. The agreement, which has been incorporated into the LIF Ethical Rules of 2014, has been developed jointly by the parties and consists of rules regarding, *inter alia,* meetings, consultation and assignments, collaborative projects, market research, and donations. The subject of the agreement is to safeguard a continued development of trustful collaboration between the pharmaceutical companies and the healthcare sector. The parties to the agreement are responsible for ensuring that their members have a functioning self-regulatory system for compliance with the agreement. The agreement shall be evaluated by the parties annually in order to adjust it if needed.[203]

Further, in 2012, LIF entered into an agreement with SALAR, Swedish Medtech, and Sweden Bio regarding cooperation concerning financial support to the National Healthcare Quality Registers. The purpose of the agreement is to provide guidelines for the ethical, legal, and financial considerations necessary for a good cooperation between the parties. This agreement has also been incorporated into the Ethical Rules.

LIF has also entered into agreements with trade organisations regarding cooperation with employees at pharmacies. These rules are to be found in previous versions of the Ethical Rules, nevertheless they are still applicable. There are also existing agreements between LIF and the County Council of Stockholm (Sw: *Stockholms läns landsting*), Karolinska Institutet, the Stockholm Association of Doctors (*Sw: Stockholms Läkarförening*), and the Association of Health Professionals (*Sw: Vårdförbundet*) regarding cooperation between the pharmaceutical industry and healthcare professionals/researchers.

---

201. Section 5.2 of the Statues of the IMG and the NBL (Appendix 2 of the Ethical Rules).
202. Section 4.2 of the Statutes of the IGN and the NBL.
203. Chapter 2, Section 1 (Background and Purpose) of the Ethical Rules.

[7] Other Applicable Rules

The LIF Ethical Rules provide regulations regarding disclosure of transfer of value (which are based on the Disclosure Code of the EFPIA), regulations regarding the interaction between pharmaceutical companies and veterinary care personnel, regulations regarding cooperation between pharmaceutical companies and user organisations/interest groups, and regulations regarding interaction between pharmaceutical companies and politicians. These rules are applicable to LIF's member companies as well as the members of the Swedish Association for Small and Medium-sized Companies Active in Research and Development (R&D) (*Sw: Innovativa Mindre Life Science Bolag, IML*) and the Association for Generic Medicinal Products (*Sw: Föreningen för Generiska Läkemedel, FGL*), since they have agreed to apply the Ethical Rules.

In addition, the Ethical Rules of the Swedish Medical Association (*Sw: Sveriges Läkarförbund*) are also relevant in respect of advertising of medicinal products as these rules govern what doctors may and may not do in respect of marketing activities. The rules prohibit medical practitioners from participating in certain forms of marketing. Further, the rules regarding bribes in the Swedish Penal Code (1962:700) (*Sw: brottsbalken*) may be applied to marketing of medicinal products.[204]

§9.11 IMPLEMENTATION IN THE UK

[A] Legal Basis

The advertising of medicines is controlled by a combination of statutory measures (with both criminal and civil sanctions) enforced by the competent authority in the UK, the Medicines and Healthcare Products Regulatory Agency (MHRA), and self-regulation through Codes of Practice for the pharmaceutical industry, administered by trade associations.

The legal basis for the control of advertising is contained in Part 14 of the Human Medicines Regulations 2012 (the Human Medicines Regulations)[205] which came into force on 14 August 2012. The Regulations are the result of the MHRA's consolidation and review of UK medicines legislation. They repeal Part 6 of the Medicines Act 1968, which concerned advertising of medicinal products, and consolidate, with only minor and drafting amendments, the previous subordinate legislation made under the Medicines Act 1968 – the Medicines (Advertising) Regulations of 1994[206] ('The Advertising Regulations'), and the Medicines (Monitoring of Advertising) Regulations of 1994 ('The Monitoring Regulations').[207] In doing so, despite Brexit, the Human Medicines Regulations continue to be based on Titles VIII and VIIIa of the Directive 2001/83/EC on the advertising of medicines for human use. The UK goes further than

---

204. Chapter 10, Sections 5a-5e of the Swedish Penal Code (1962:700).
205. Statutory Instrument 2012/1916.
206. Statutory Instrument 1994/1932.
207. Statutory Instruments 1994/1933.

Directive 2001/83/EC in some requirements, such as the UK policy-based prohibition on advertising medicinal products for the purpose of inducing abortion.

Part 14 of the Human Medicines Regulations contains a variety of prohibitions on advertising, including those relating to unlicensed medicines, prescription medicines, recommendations by scientists, and advertisements aimed at children. In addition, the Regulations set out the information that needs to be included in advertisements and established rules for sampling, the promotion of medicinal products by medical sales representatives, and hospitality at meetings. They also set out the statutory powers available to the MHRA in carrying out its functions, including taking any action where a potential breach has been identified. Finally, the Regulations contain provisions regarding complaints about advertisements and permit ministers to apply to a court for an injunction prohibiting a particular advertisement. The Human Medicines Regulations set out the rules for medicines advertising in general, and specific requirements and restrictions for advertising directed at the public and for advertising directed at healthcare professionals. Any person, MAH, or any third party such as a journalist or public relations (PR) agency is responsible for ensuring that the Regulations are complied with. The advertisements must comply with the requirements set out in the Regulations as regards the form and content of the advertisements, including the requirement that an advertisement must not be misleading.[208] Any person who fails to comply with the provisions of the Regulations is guilty of an offence,[209] with liability for a fine and/or imprisonment. Equivalent provisions under previous legislation[210] have been used to bring criminal prosecutions for misleading advertising and imposing fines on both the company and the employee in the company responsible for the advertisement. The decision and the fines imposed were upheld on appeal.[211]

The case concerned the promotion of Surgam, a medicinal product containing tiaprofenic acid, which was launched in 1982 for the relief of arthritis. The advertisement comparing Surgam to another medicinal product, Indomethacin, was published in the *British Medical Journal* on four different dates. The advertisement claimed that Surgam operated by selectively inhibiting prostaglandins that caused pain, without causing gastric disorder. The company, Roussel, and an employee, Dr Good, who was the officer at Roussel responsible for the advertisement, were prosecuted under section 93 of the Medicines Act of 1968. The company was convicted and fined GBP 5,000 on each of four counts of issuing a false and misleading advertisement, and Dr Good was convicted on four counts of consenting and conniving at the issue of a misleading advertisement relating to a medicinal product.[212] Dr Good was fined GBP 250 on each count or was to serve thirty days of imprisonment in default of paying the fine within thirty days. The Court of Appeal upheld the conviction.[213]

---

208. Regulation 280(3).
209. Regulation 303.
210. Section 93 Medicines Act 1968.
211. *R v. Roussel Laboratories Ltd, R v. Good* (Christopher Saxty) Court of Appeal (Criminal Division) (1989) 88 Cr. App. R. 140; Times 13 June 1988.
212. 19 December 1986 at the Central Criminal Court (Judge Capstick QC).
213. R. Roussel Laboratories and Good (1988) 88 Cr App Rep 140, 153 JP 298, 3 BLMR 128.

[B] Scope of the Regulations

The Regulations apply to advertisements for 'medicinal products' which is defined in Regulation 2 as:

(a) any substance or combination of substances presented as having properties of preventing or treating disease in human beings; or
(b) any substance or combination of substances that may be used by or administered to human beings with a view to—
  (i) restoring, correcting or modifying a physiological function by exerting a pharmacological, immunological or metabolic action, or
  (ii) making a medical diagnosis.

'Advertisement' is widely defined in Regulation 7 as including anything designed to promote the prescription, supply, sale or use of that product. This includes, in particular:

(a) door-to-door canvassing;
(b) visits by medical sales representatives to persons qualified to prescribe or supply medicinal products;
(c) the supply of samples;
(d) the provision of inducements to prescribe or supply medicinal products by the gift, offer or promise of any benefit or bonus, whether in money or in kind, except where the intrinsic value of such inducements is minimal;
(e) the sponsorship of promotional meetings attended by persons qualified to prescribe or supply medicinal products; and
(f) the sponsorship of scientific congresses attended by persons qualified to prescribe or supply medicinal products, including the payment of their travelling and accommodation expenses in that connection.

It does not include:

(a) a medicinal product's package or package leaflet;
(b) reference material and announcements of a factual and informative nature, including:
  (i) material relating to changes to a medicinal product's package or package leaflet,
  (ii) adverse reaction warnings,
  (iii) trade catalogues, and
  (iv) price lists, provided that no product claim is made; or
(c) correspondence, which may be accompanied by material of a non-promotional nature, answering a specific question about a medicinal product.

[C] Regulation by the MHRA

The UK's medicines regulatory authority, the MHRA, is responsible for monitoring and enforcing medicines advertising in the UK. The Advertising Standards and Outreach Unit is responsible for monitoring and operating within the MHRA's Vigilance and Risk Management of Medicines division. It works closely with other divisions of the MHRA, notably the MHRA's enforcement group, which currently deals with serious breaches of the Regulations.

The Advertising Standards Unit encourages the reporting of complaints and concerns about advertising, and it strives to resolve complaints speedily within one month of receiving a complaint.

The Regulations also allow the MHRA to require sight of advertising before it is issued. Circumstances where pre-vetting may be required include:

- where a newly licensed product subject to intensive monitoring, is placed on the market;
- where a product is reclassified product, such as from prescription only to pharmacy; or
- where previous advertising for a product has breached the Regulations.

Within the first criterion above and as a matter of policy, the MHRA has committed to vetting initial advertising for all new active substances.

[1] The Blue Guide

The MHRA provided guidance on advertising of medicines since 1999, when Guidance Note No. 23 was published. This guidance is now in the form of what is called 'The Blue Guide.'[214] The third edition of the Blue Guide was published in August 2012 and was revised in September 2014 and more recently in November 2020.

The Blue Guide provides guidance to be read alongside the Human Medicines Regulations and indicates which other UK legislation may apply (e.g., Trade Descriptions Act of 1968 and supporting regulations such as the Consumer Protection from Unfair Trading Regulations 2008).[215] It also gives practical guidance – for example, 'inexpensive' gifts to persons qualified to prescribe or supply medicinal products are considered to be those that do not cost a company more than GBP 6 (excluding VAT) each and represent a similar value to the recipient.

[2] Advertising Using the Internet

The MHRA has published guidance for consumer websites aimed at companies that do not hold MAs but provide services that may lead to the supply of a POM. The guidance

---

214. *The Blue Guide: Advertising and Promotion of Medicines in the UK*: https://www.gov.uk/government/publications/blue-guide-advertising-and-promoting-medicines.
215. Statutory Instrument No. 1277/2008.

is aimed at all websites for consumers registered in the UK or aimed at the UK audience.[216] The target is therefore mainly online clinics or pharmacies. It is designed to help advertisers promote their services without promoting specific prescription-only medicines. The guidance has now been included in the Blue Guide as Appendix 6.[217]

The guidance:

- allows provision of information on a particular condition or disease;
- allows information about prescription-only medicines, provided it is in the context of all treatment options and relevant disease information;
- suggests that the home page of the Internet site should focus on the medical conditions and the service that the website provides and should not include references to named prescription-only medicines;
- suggests that links may be made to further pages about the medical condition. Further pages about the condition, which the consumer chooses to access, may include information about specific medicines provided this is presented in the context of a fair overview of the treatment options i.e., must be non-promotional;
- only allows indicative prices for a particular medical condition to be provided on the home page without mentioning prescription-only medicines. Prices for available treatments/pack sizes may be provided on pages other than home page, but the website should make it clear that the viewer's preferred option will not be prescribed if it is not suitable. Special offers should not be highlighted;
- allows icons to be used to encourage consumers to undertake a medical consultation but does not allow the use of icons or other features to encourage the purchase of prescription medicines;
- does not allow promotional claims for prescription-only medicines;
- does not allow mention of unlicensed medicines;
- suggests that website addresses that name specific prescription medicines in their URL should be avoided, as they may be considered to promote the medicine to the public;
- specifically provides guidance on the prohibition of the advertising of prescription-only medicine to the public on social media networks. In particular, any mention of the availability of a named prescription-only medicine from a clinic in social media is likely to be considered to be an advertisement which is prohibited, and prescription-only medicines should not be named in posts that are linked to the services being provided; and
- encourages registered pharmacies to display the Internet Pharmacy logo of the General Pharmaceutical Council on their website home page to assure consumers that medicines are supplied by a registered pharmacy.

---

216. These websites include those that use '.co.uk' or quote prices in GBP.
217. Advertising of medicines: Guidance for providers offering medicinal treatment services.

[3] Complaints to the MHRA

Full details of how the MHRA investigates complaints and the actions that may be taken are provided in Chapter 8 of the Blue Guide.

The MHRA reports annually on medicines advertising. In the period between January 2021 and December 2021,[218] the MHRA received 144 (compared to 213 in 2019 and 227 in 2020) complaints about medicines advertising. The MHRA investigated a substantial number (53) of the complaints, while referring the majority (89) to other bodies, such as the Advertising Standards Authority (ASA) and the Prescription Medicines Code of Practice Authority (PMCPA). As in the previous years, a substantial number of complaints received concerned the promotion of prescription-only medicines (which should not be promoted to the general public) by cosmetic clinics, online clinics, and pharmacies. The proportion of complaints that relate to advertising on social media continues to rise and the majority of cases the MHRA investigated related to online treatment service providers (third parties) offering prescription-only medicines and/or unlicensed medicinal products for prescription. The MHRA have continued to strengthen their links with the ASA to ensure they are able to share information about cases and direct complaints to the regulatory body best placed to investigate them. The MHRA have continued to work together on a number of issues, including advertising of vitamin-containing injections, prescription-only medicines for weight loss, and botulinum toxin products for cosmetic use. A joint enforcement notice was issued in January 2021 for advertising on social media of prescription weight loss products, which resulted in a significant reduction in the number of complaints in this area being investigated by MHRA.

There is not much overlap between the MHRA activities and those of the UK self-regulation bodies,[219] although they cooperate through the Medicines Advertising Liaison Group (MALG) which is a forum consisting of bodies involved in the regulation of medicines advertising that meets approximately twice a year to discuss current issues in advertising control. During 2021 discussions by the MALG focused on continued actions taken in response to the COVID-19 pandemic, matters relating to Brexit, and issues of current concern, including advertising for lifestyle-related products and joint enforcement initiatives between the MHRA and ASA.

Large numbers of complaints received from pharmaceutical companies are dealt with by the PMCPA. The MHRA does not conduct a second investigation into any complaint that has also been submitted to a self-regulatory organisation unless there is a serious safety issue.

The MHRA reported the following five important learning points that advertisers should consider when preparing their materials:

---

218. MHRA: Delivering High Standards in Medicines Advertising Regulation. Annual report January–December 2021, published 17 March 2022.
219. These are the ABPI through the Prescription Medicines Code of Practice Authority (PMCPA) for prescription medicines and the PAGB for OTC medicines.

- Indication: in the advertisement, it is important to state the authorised indication of the product at the outset; this ensures that claims are set in a clear context.
- Accurate evidence-based claims to support rational use: claims should be supported by the balance of evidence available and include sufficient objective information to allow the reader to judge the importance of the claim for themselves.
- Key safety messages: safety information to support the safe use of the product should be included.
- Advisory boards: Company advisory boards should be kept to a minimum and must be strictly non-promotional, seeking only to answer legitimate business questions from the involvement of experts in a particular field that cannot be obtained by any other means.
- Materials for the public: promotion of prescription-only medicines is prohibited. Where exceptionally companies issue press releases to announce the launch of an innovative new product, these must be factual, balanced and non-promotional in content.

[D]   Sanctions

The Human Medicines Regulations contain a procedure for a review of MHRA's preliminary decision on whether an advertisement complies with Part 14 of the Human Medicines Regulations. This review is undertaken by the Independent Review Panel. This panel usually consists of a legally qualified chairperson and two other members, one with medical or pharmacy expertise and another representing the interests of the consumer.

The functions of the Independent Review Panel are:

- to consider written representations from pharmaceutical companies as to the conformity of their advertising and promotional material with the regulations;
- to advise MHRA on the conformity of advertising and promotional material with the Regulations before a final decision is made by the MHRA;
- to consider written representations from companies against the preliminary decisions given by the MHRA that the advertising or promotional material is in breach of the Regulations; and
- to advise the MHRA on matters relating to the acceptability of published and unpublished advertising and promotional material under the Regulations.

If the MHRA as advised by the Independent Review Panel considers there to be a public health justification, the MHRA will use more formal procedures, such as issuing notices, enforcement action, and prosecution.

The breach of the provisions of the Regulations is a criminal offence; the penalty if found guilty is a fine and/or imprisonment. Advertising issues are, in the majority of cases, resolved administratively, with prosecution reserved for serious cases, for example, where there is a safety issue or a company is uncooperative or repeatedly offends.

Civil sanctions are also available under the Regulations (e.g., publication of a corrective statement where the MHRA has prohibited publication of an advertisement for breaching the Regulations). Guidance on the format of the corrective statement is given.[220] An example of a corrective statement is included in the annex to this chapter.

The policy of the MHRA is to publish a report of the outcome of investigations into complaints about advertising for licensed medicines to inform stakeholders and the public. It will supplement the actions already taken to alert health professionals and the public to misleading advertising, such as the publication of a corrective statement, where a serious risk to public health is perceived. All complaints are published on the MHRA website.

[E] Self-Regulation

The responsibility for advertising content and its compliance with the legal requirements rests with the MAH. The MAH usually meets this requirement by having an internal system of review and sign-off, usually someone who is medically qualified and another senior member of the company. The medical information departments of pharmaceutical companies are usually responsible for initial review and administration of the sign-off system. Each piece of promotional material or activity is reviewed for compliance with the legislation, the Blue Guide, and the relevant codes of practice; if it does not comply, it should not be signed off. However, marketing departments often push the boundaries, and not every case is clear-cut, which may account for the number of cases that come before the self-regulation bodies for review.

Pharmaceutical companies are regulated by Codes of practice operated by the PMCPA[221] and the PAGB.[222] Companies that are not members may agree to be bound by the Codes. If they do not agree or have been expelled from membership, the MHRA is informed and will actively regulate.

In some instances, the MAH may not be the company promoting the product. In the UK, MAHs can add 'own label suppliers' to their MA by a national variation. This is particularly true for OTC products, where the MAH can supply the same product to many different brand companies. In these cases, any advertising or promotional material must be internally signed off by the MAH (who may not be a member company) before submission (e.g., to the PAGB for pre-vetting by the PAGB member company). Extra time must be allowed for these approvals.

---

220. Clause 8.5 of the Blue Guide.
221. The ABPI Code of Practice for the Pharmaceutical Industry covers prescription medicines and is available on the PMCPA website at: www.pmcpa.org.uk.
222. The PAGB Medicines Advertising Codes cover OTC medicines and are available on the PAGB website at: www.pagb.org.uk.

Where decisions are taken by self-regulatory bodies that have an impact on non-members, these may be subject to judicial review.[223]

[1] The Association of the British Pharmaceutical Industry (ABPI) and PMCPA

The ABPI was formed in 1930 and represents manufacturers of prescription medicines. The ABPI manages the advertising and promotion of prescription products under the Code of Practice for the Pharmaceutical Industry at arm's length through the PMCPA. The ABPI Code of Practice has been revised regularly since its introduction in 1958, and it is drawn up in consultation with the British Medical Association, the Royal Pharmaceutical Society of Great Britain, and the MHRA. It is a condition of membership that companies abide by the Code and accept the jurisdiction of the PMCPA.

The PMCPA administers the Code as well as providing advice, guidance, and training. The Code applies to the promotion of prescription-only medicines to healthcare professionals and to information generally available to the public. Direct-to-consumer advertising of prescription-only medicines is not allowed in the UK. The Code does not apply to the promotion of OTC medicines to members of the health professions when the object of that promotion is to encourage their purchase by members of the public.

Promotion is defined as 'any activity undertaken by a pharmaceutical company or with its authority which promotes the administration, consumption, prescription, purchase, recommendation, sale, supply, sale or use of its medicines'.[224] This includes:

- journal and direct mail advertising;
- the activities of representatives including detail aids and other printed material used by representatives;
- the supply of samples;
- the provision of inducements to prescribe, supply, administer, recommend, buy or sell medicines by the gift, offer or promise of any benefit or bonus, whether in money or in kind;
- the provision of hospitality for promotional purposes;
- the sponsorship of promotional meetings;
- the sponsorship of scientific meetings including payment of travelling and accommodation expenses in connection therewith; and
- all other promotion in whatever form, such as participation in exhibitions, the use of audio or video recordings in any format, broadcast media, non-print media, the Internet, interactive data systems, social media, and the like.

Promotion does not include:

---

223. *R v. Code of Practice Committee of the British Pharmaceutical Industry Ex p. Professional Counselling Aids* (1991) 3 Admin L R 697.
224. Clause 1.17 ABPI Code of Practice for the Pharmaceutical Industry 2021.

- replies made to individual enquiries, including letters published in professional journals, as long as they relate solely to the subject matter of the letter or enquiry, are accurate, do not mislead, and are not promotional in nature;
- factual, accurate, informative announcements, and reference material concerning licensed medicines (e.g., pack changes, warnings of adverse reactions, trade catalogues, and price lists), as long as they contain no product claims;
- price lists relating to unlicensed medicines, provided they include no product claims and make clear that the products are unlicensed;
- information supplied by companies to national public organisations, provided it is factual, accurate, and not misleading (e.g., information sent to the National Institute for Health and Clinical Excellence);
- measures or trade practices relating to prices, margins, or discounts which were in regular use by a significant proportion of the pharmaceutical industry on 1 January 1993;
- summaries of product characteristics;
- European and UK public Assessment Reports;
- risk minimisation material approved by the MHRA;
- authorised package leaflets and labels; and
- general information on human health and disease, provided there is no reference to specific medicines.

The Code requires that a company appoint a senior employee to be responsible for ensuring that the company meets the requirements of the Code.

The 2021 edition of the Code is set out to over sixty-five pages. The layout and formatting of the Code have been updated to categorise the various clauses into colour-coded thematic sections – for example, the first grey section entitled 'Overarching Requirements' comprises clauses 1 to 10, which deal with the scope of the Code, definitions of certain terms, overarching obligations and responsibilities, quality standards, etc. The blue section entitled 'Promotion to Health Professionals and Other Relevant Decision Makers' comprises clauses 11 to 14 and these deal with matters dealing with this subject matter. Other broad categories of topics dealt with include interactions with patient organisations, the public (including patients and journalists), and annual disclosure requirements.

As most of the complainants to the PMCPA are competitor pharmaceutical companies, the complaints often involve information, claims, and comparisons made about the promoted product. There is a requirement under the Code that 'information, claims and comparisons must be accurate, balanced, fair, objective and unambiguous and must be based on an up-to-date evaluation of all the evidence and reflect that evidence clearly'.[225] Companies can get an idea of what is acceptable or not from recent upheld complaints. The PMCPA website publishes completed cases since 2006, ongoing cases, and advertised sanctions (including public reprimands) issued in the past twelve-month period.[226]

---

225. Clause 6.1 ABPI Code of Practice for the Pharmaceutical Industry 2021.
226. www.pmcpa.org.uk/cases/.

The Code applies to the promotional activities of the company's representatives, and there is a requirement for training those representatives.[227] The Medical Representatives Examination must be taken by representatives who, in the course of their work, call on doctors, dentists, or other prescribers and/or promote medicines on the basis, *inter alia*, of their particular therapeutic properties. These representatives of the member pharmaceutical companies must pass the ABPI examination within two years of appointment to their position. If they do not, they cannot continue to work as medical representatives.

There is a separate Generic Sales Representatives Examination also administered by the ABPI, which must be passed by representatives who promote medicines primarily on the basis of price, quality, and availability. These representatives usually call on pharmacists in the course of their work.

Public reprimands are among the sanctions available to the PMCPA. Other sanctions include:[228]

- audit of a company's procedures, which may require submission of material to the PMCPA for pre-vetting for a period of time;
- requiring a company to issue a corrective statement; and/or
- requiring a company to recover promotional items.

Serious breaches may be reported to the ABPI Board of Management for further sanctions.[229] This may include suspending or expelling a company from the ABPI, or in the case of non-members, removing the name of the company from the list of companies that have agreed to abide by the Code and informing the MHRA that responsibility for that company under the Code can no longer be accepted.

[2]   PAGB

The PAGB represents the interests of the OTC industry in the UK, and while there may be some overlap in membership of companies with the ABPI, it is the consumer section of those companies that will be directly involved with the PAGB.

The PAGB has Codes in place covering the advertising of OTC products that are subject to an MA, including: the PAGB Consumer Code (last updated in 2019) and the PAGB Professional Code. The PAGB Codes incorporate provisions concerning registered traditional herbal medicines previously contained in PAGB's Traditional Herbal Medicines Code. The PAGB have further put in place the PAGB Packaging Code for Medicines (last updated in 2021) and the PAGB Medical Devices Consumer Code (published in 2019). The PAGB's Codes reflect the UK legislation and provide an interpretation of the law. In some respects, they go beyond what is legally required,

---

227. This fulfils the requirements of Article 93(1) of Directive 2001/83/EC, as implemented into UK law (pre-Brexit) by Regulation 281(3) of The Human Medicines Regulations 2012, as amended.
228. Clause 11.3 of the Prescription Medicines Code of Practice Authority Constitution and Procedure.
229. Clause 12 of the Prescription Medicines Code of Practice Authority Constitution and Procedure.

such as consideration of taste, decency, and comparisons with other products. PAGB member companies must abide by the Codes.

[a] The PAGB Consumer Code

Under the PAGB Consumer Code, all OTC medicines advertising aimed at consumers must be approved by the PAGB prior to its use or release into the public domain.

The pre-vetting process involves sending the advertising copy (e.g., the storyboard for a TV commercial) along with a copy of the MA and SmPC to the PAGB. The PAGB typically aims to review all copies within two working days of receipt, although for larger items or websites, the review takes approximately five working days. In the case of new products or where new claims are being submitted, a medical and legal opinion may be required. In such cases, the PAGB typically takes five working days to obtain such an opinion on the proposed claims. Where it complies with the PAGB Consumer Code, the advertising copy is returned with a PAGB stamp of approval.

The Code covers many forms of advertising materials, from the wording on hot-air balloons to promotional scripts for use by telephone helplines. Only members of the PAGB can use the pre-approval system.

[b] The PAGB Professional Code

The PAGB Professional Code applies to advertising of OTC medicines to persons qualified to prescribe or supply such medicines and appropriate administrative staff, where the object of the advertising is to influence sales and/or recommendations to the general public. These persons 'qualified to prescribe or supply' are generally healthcare professionals, including doctors, dentists, nurses, pharmacists, pharmacy assistants, midwives, optometrists, chiropodists, and other ancillary health workers. It also includes retail staff who are legally entitled to supply medicinal products to members of the public and buyers.

The PAGB Professional Code applies to advertising materials over which members have editorial control. Advertising is taken to include:

- printed advertising materials, e.g., journals, advertorials, booklets, posters, direct mail materials, retailer house publications;
- envelopes addressed to persons qualified to prescribe or supply;
- electronic media advertising, such as websites, press releases intended for Internet publication, and any other Internet advertising;
- audio and audiovisual advertising, e.g., DVDs;
- promotional aids;
- the supply, offer, or promise of any gift, pecuniary advantage or benefit in kind;
- hospitality at professional, scientific, or promotional meetings/events attended by persons qualified to prescribe or supply;
- sponsorship of professional, scientific, or promotional meetings and events;

- sponsorship of written materials produced by third parties;
- samples and free packs; and
- representations, i.e., any oral communication in order to promote a brand, including the activities of company representatives.

It does not cover:

- photograph of a pack (pack shot), even though the packaging may contain product claims. PAGB has a separate code covering pack design, the 'PAGB Code of Practice for Pack Design for Over-the-Counter Medicines';
- advertisements that do not contain product claims other than on a pack shot;
- informative announcements, including listings in directories of OTC products such as the Chemist & Druggist monthly price list;
- replies made to individual enquiries, including letters published in professional journals, as long as they relate solely to the subject matter of the letter or enquiry, are accurate, do not mislead, and are not promotional in nature;
- publications by wholesalers; and
- press releases and product launches (although these must comply with the Human Medicines Regulations).

The PAGB Professional Code has no requirement for pre-approval of advertising. Instead, it enforces Code provisions through consideration of post-event complaints.

[F] ASA

Although the system of self-regulation works well, advertising may in parallel be subject to scrutiny by the MHRA, as noted earlier, and also the ASA.[230] All advertising in the UK is regulated by the ASA through a system of self-regulation. The ASA considers that its advertising code is among the strictest in the world, and it works closely with statutory regulatory partners such as Trading Standards and Office of Communications (OFCOM). The ASA has established and enforced two main Codes: one for broadcast advertising[231] (BCAP Code); and the other for non-broadcast advertising[232] (CAP Code). The ASA administers the mandatory advertising Codes and monitors compliance. The ASA does not just wait for complaints; it proactively monitors to see that the Codes as well as its rulings are adhered to – for example, by seeing if any necessary changes have been made to advertisements. The principle of both Codes is that advertisements must not mislead, harm, or offend. Therefore, the

---

230. The ASA is the independent body set up by the UK advertising industry to monitor the rules laid down in the advertising Codes; it is funded by a voluntary levy of 0.1% on the cost of buying advertising space and 0.2% on some direct mail. It is independent of the UK government.
231. The UK Code of Broadcast Advertising, or BCAP Code, produced by the Broadcast Committee of Advertising Practice.
232. The UK Code of Non-broadcast Advertising and Direct & Promotional Marketing, or CAP Code, produced by the Committee of Advertising Practice.

Chapter 9: Advertising Medicinal Products for Human Use §9.11[G]

ASA adjudicates generally on advertising in the UK and investigates on the basis of complaints, and this includes advertisements for medicinal products.

The case of Potters Ltd trading as Equazen shows that although an advertisement may meet the requirements of the PAGB Code, it will not necessarily meet those of the ASA CAP Code. This case was investigated on the basis of a single complaint and illustrated that the ASA can intervene in advertisements for medicinal products. The details of the case are given in the Annex to this chapter, and it shows that the ASA Codes have different requirements above and beyond the PAGB Codes.

[G] Association of British Healthcare Industries (ABHI)

The ABHI is the trade association for medical device technology in the UK. It is a condition of ABHI membership that a company adheres to the ethical standards set out in the ABHI Code of Ethical Business Practice (last updated July 2019).

The Code contains guidelines on advertisements and promotions of medical devices addressed solely or primarily to healthcare professionals. These detailed and stringent guidelines apply to advertising in any media (including Internet) that is intended wholly or mainly to influence healthcare professionals or healthcare institutions in their choice of medical devices to be purchased, leased, used, or supplied or in any recommendation that they make to others about such purchase, lease, use, or supply. Examples of such advertising include advertisements in journals, brochures, leaflets, circulars, mailings, catalogues, e-mails, social media sites, and other publications (printed or electronic) which are directed primarily at healthcare professionals or health institutions, printed material used by representatives, posters and other promotional media in public places at healthcare professional events, video recordings intended solely or primarily for release or use at healthcare professional events and online advertisements.

Complaints under the Code may only be made against a company which is an ABHI member or which has agreed to abide by the ABHI Code.

ANNEX: CASE HISTORIES

1. Example of an MHRA Corrective Statement

Case Report: Atrogel Newsletter and Website, April 2009

Schwabe Pharma complained to the MHRA regarding an Atrogel newsletter e-mailed to consumers in April 2009 and a website produced by Bioforce. The complainant was concerned that the newsletter was in breach of the Advertising Regulations because it did not identify that the products were registered as traditional herbal medicines. The complainant was also concerned that the website contained references to clinical studies.

The MHRA upheld the complaint. Bioforce agreed to amend the newsletter and publish a corrective statement. Bioforce also agreed to remove clinical research data from its product website and amend the Herbs for Healthy Living website so it is clearly a separate site.

Date case raised: 17 April 2009.

Date action agreed: 07 July 2009.

Date of publication: 21 August 2009

Corrective Statement from Bioforce

'The MHRA have asked us to provide a corrective statement regarding the above newsletter. The content of the newsletter did not comply with the Medicines (Advertising) Regulations because it did not identify that the products were registered as traditional herbal medicines exclusively based on long-standing use as a traditional remedy. The newsletter did not represent the authorised indications correctly. We are happy to amend the newsletter to clarify the status of the products and apologise for any inconvenience caused. The revised issue can be found below. The Traditional Herbal Medicinal Products Directive was adopted in the UK in October 2005 and provides a means for companies to license herbal products with the MHRA provided that the required standards for product quality and safety can be met, and the indication of the product is established on the basis of its traditional therapeutic use. Advertising and promotion of products that successfully achieve licensed status must comply with the Medicines (Advertising) Regulations 1994 and guidance produced by the MHRA.

Kind regards

J Tan Managing Director'

2. Example of an ASA Complaint

Case Study: Potters Ltd Trading as Equazen, ASA Adjudication 15 October 2008

Chapter 9: Advertising Medicinal Products for Human Use

The advertisement was in the national press in the United Kingdom for 'eye q', a product containing omega-3 and omega-6. The advertisement was headed in chalk written on a blackboard: 'PAY ATTENTION!.' Further text on the blackboard stated 'What will you choose for your child?'.

The advertisement included a pack shot of eye q capsules and eye q chews; both included the text 'Independently tested The Durham Trial Naturally-sourced Omega-3 & Omega-6 oils'. The capsules pack stated '5 years +' and the chews pack stated '3 years +'.

Text in a ticked list stated 'Independently tested* Naturally-sourced omega-3 & omega-6 No aspartame No hydrogenated fats No artificial colours'. The asterisk was linked to small-print text that stated '* Richardson, A.J & Montgomery, P (2005). The Oxford Durham Study: A Randomised, Controlled Trial of Dietary Supplementation with Fatty Acids in Children with Development Co-ordination Disorder. *Pediatrics*, 115, 1360–1366* Sinn, N. & Bryan, J (2007). Effect of supplementation with polyunsaturated fatty acids and micronutrients on Learning and Behaviour problems Associated with Child ADHD. *Journal of Development & Behavioural Pediatrics*, 28, 82–91. For further information please visit www.equazen.com or call the customer service helpline 0870 ....'.

The complainant said that the advertisement was misleading because it implied it could improve school performance for all children, whereas the studies referenced had been conducted on specific groups of children with developmental co-ordination disorder (DCD) and child attention-deficit hyperactivity disorder (ADHD).

The ASA also challenged whether the advertisement – in particular the headline claim, 'PAY ATTENTION!', in combination with 'Independently tested' and references to published studies that had been carried out on children with ADHD – implied that the product could treat the symptoms of ADHD, a serious medical condition, and could therefore discourage essential treatment.

Alleged breaches of the CAP Code

50.3 Marketers should not discourage essential treatment. They should not offer specific advice on, diagnosis of or treatment for serious or prolonged conditions unless it is conducted under the supervision of a doctor or other suitably qualified health professional (e.g., one subject to regulation by a statutory or recognised medical or health professional body). Accurate and responsible general information about such conditions may, however, be offered.

50.21 A well-balanced diet should provide the vitamins and minerals needed each day by a normal, healthy individual. Marketers must not state or imply that a balanced or varied diet cannot provide enough nutrients in general and should not encourage anyone to swap a healthy diet for supplementation. Marketing communications must not imply vitamin or mineral supplements can be used to prevent or treat illness. Marketers may offer vitamin and mineral supplements to certain groups as a safeguard to help maintain good health but they must not, unless the claims are authorised by the Commission, imply that they can be used to elevate mood or enhance normal performance. Claims about higher vitamin or mineral intake for a specific function are permitted if authorised by the Commission. Without well-established proof, no marketing communication should suggest that there is a widespread vitamin or mineral deficiency.

50.1 Medical and scientific claims made about beauty and health-related products should be backed by evidence, where appropriate consisting of trials conducted on people. Where relevant, the rules will also relate to claims for products for animals. Substantiation will be assessed by the ASA on the basis of the available scientific knowledge.

3.1 Before distributing or submitting a marketing communication for publication, marketers must hold documentary evidence to prove all claims, whether direct or implied, that are capable of objective substantiation. Relevant evidence should be sent without delay if requested by the ASA or CAP. The adequacy of evidence will be judged on whether it supports both the detailed claims and the overall impression created by the marketing communication. The full name and geographical business address of marketers should be provided without delay if requested by the ASA or CAP.

7.1 No marketing communication should mislead, or be likely to mislead, by inaccuracy, ambiguity, exaggeration, omission or otherwise.

Assessment

> 1: Upheld. The ASA noted that the claim 'independently tested' was linked via an asterisk to study references, which clarified that the trials had been conducted on children with DCD and those who exhibited learning and behaviour problems associated with child ADHD. The ASA understood that the text had been included in order to clarify to consumers that the studies undertaken had not involved a general population of children and to specify, therefore, that the claims made in relation to eye-q were not targeted at children generally.
>
> The ASA considered, however, that readers were likely to infer from the headline 'PAY ATTENTION!', written in chalk on a schoolroom-type blackboard, in conjunction with the claim 'What will you choose for your child?', that the advertisement was aimed at parents of children in general and that the product could help to improve the attention levels of all children, not any particular group. They acknowledged that the claim 'Independently tested' provided a link to a small-print note clarifying that specific groups of children had participated in the testing, but considered that this information contradicted and rendered ambiguous, rather than clarified, the implication given by the body copy of the advertisement. Although it was appreciated that it was not the message Equazen had intended to convey, the ASA concluded that the ad was likely to mislead about the likely benefit children in general could achieve from the intake of eye-q capsules or chews.
>
> On this point, the advertisement breached CAP Code clauses 3.1 (Substantiation), 7.1 (Truthfulness), 50.1 (Health and beauty products and therapies – general), and 50.21 (Health and beauty products and therapies – vitamins, minerals and other food supplements).

Chapter 9: Advertising Medicinal Products for Human Use

2: Upheld. The ASA understood that the reference to ADHD, a serious medical condition, in the advertisement's small-print note was included to clarify that the testing referred to in the body of the copy had been conducted on a specific group of children and not a general population. The ASA also noted the CAP Code clarified that marketers should not discourage essential treatment or offer specific advice on, diagnosis of, or treatment for a serious or prolonged condition unless it was conducted under the supervision of a suitably qualified health professional. There was concern that the headline claim 'PAY ATTENTION!', in conjunction with the claim 'Independently tested', which clarified that the product had been tested on children with a serious medical condition, indirectly implied a solution for the treatment of ADHD by way of improving the attention capabilities of those children. This was considered problematic for two reasons: eye-q was freely available and not supplied under the supervision of a qualified health professional and, although under the CAP Code marketers could offer vitamin and mineral supplements to certain groups as a safeguard to help maintain good health, they should not imply they could be used to prevent or treat illness.

It was recognised that the intention of Equazen was not to convey that eye-q provided a treatment for ADHD, and the ASA appreciated Equazen's opinion that it would expect sufferers of ADHD and their parents or caregivers to seek medical diagnosis and treatment with an explicitly stated effect on that condition. It was concluded, however, that the ad had indirectly offered a treatment for a serious condition and was therefore in breach of the CAP Code.

On this point, the ad breached CAP Code clause 50.3 (Health and beauty products and therapies – general) and 50.21 (Health and beauty products and therapies – vitamins, minerals and other food supplements).

Action:

The advertisement must not appear again in its current form. Equazen was advised to seek guidance from the CAP Copy Advice team before issuing further ads for eye-q.

CHAPTER 10
Pharmacovigilance

Sally Shorthose, Alexandre Vuchot, Pieter Erasmus, Johanna Harelimana & Nour Saab

§10.01 INTRODUCTION AND BACKGROUND

Pharmacovigilance is the process of collecting the data obtained during clinical trials (pre-authorisation) and monitoring the use of approved medicines to identify previously unrecognised adverse drug reactions (post-authorisation). It includes the ongoing assessment of the medicines' risks and benefits in order to determine what action, if any, is necessary to improve their safe use.

The term *pharmacovigilance* is derived from the Greek *pharmaco* (medicine) and the Latin *vigilantia* (vigilance or watchfulness). The main European guidance document for post-authorisation pharmacovigilance was Volume 9A of the Rules Governing Medicinal Products in the European Union ('Volume 9A'),[1] but these rules were replaced by the Good Pharmacovigilance Practice guidelines (GVP).[2] GVP applies to Marketing Authorisation holders (MAHs), the European Medicines Agency (EMA), and medicines regulatory authorities in EU Member States. The World Health Organization (WHO) definition of pharmacovigilance is 'the science and activities relating to the detection, assessment, understanding and prevention of adverse effects or any other medicine-related problem.'[3] The aims of pharmacovigilance are twofold: to enhance patient care and patient safety in relation to the use of medicines, and to support public health programmes by providing reliable, balanced information for the effective

---

1. Volume 9A – Pharmacovigilance for Medicinal Products for Human Use.
2. GVP was a key deliverable in the 2010 Pharmacovigilance legislation which comprises an introduction and various modules which superseded Volume 9A of the rules governing medicinal products in the EU.
3. *Ibid.*

assessment of the risk-benefit profile of medicines. The EU Pharmacovigilance system is one of the most advanced comprehensive systems in the world.

As a direct result of the thalidomide tragedy,[4] national schemes to collect adverse effects to medicines were founded in the United Kingdom (UK) in 1964 and in Sweden in 1965, and later in other Member States, such as France in 1973.

In the late 1980s, the Council for International Organisation of Medical Sciences (CIOMS)[5] took the lead in preparing guidance to harmonise the requirements for international reporting of drug safety information throughout the world. CIOMS set up working groups comprised of experts selected from the pharmaceutical industry and regulatory authorities to draw up guidance, including a form for the expedited reporting of individual cases,[6] and guidance for drawing up safety information periodically. The form is still used today,[7] and the guidance was used as a basis for the current European guidance.[8] Several definitions used in current European legislation have their origins in CIOMS working groups.

The legal requirement for pharmacovigilance came into force in the EU in 1993[9] and required that the MAH submit 'data on pharmacovigilance and other information relevant to the monitoring of the medicinal product' before the MA could be renewed.

Today, the MA applicant and MAH are subject to pharmacovigilance-related obligations during both pre- and post-authorisation phases, and recent legislation has tightened up the pharmacovigilance obligations significantly; the legislation aims to:

- clarify roles and responsibilities;
- minimise duplication of effort;
- free up resources by rationalising and simplifying PSURs and adverse reaction (ADR) reporting;
- establish a clear legal framework for post-authorisation monitoring.

Pre-authorisation and post-authorisation pharmacovigilance have different legislative bases, leading to different definitions. The difference between pre-authorisation and post-authorisation definitions of pharmacovigilance reflects that less is known about the medicinal product in the pre-authorisation phase and that as such, an adverse event may be related to the underlying medical condition rather than the drug.

One of the key personnel required by an organisation to fulfil its pharmacovigilance obligations is the Qualified Person for Pharmacovigilance (QP PhV) required by

---

4. CIOMS, *International Reporting of Adverse Drug Reactions. Final Report of the CIOMS Working Group* (Geneva, Switzerland: WHO, 1990).
5. CIOMS is an international, non-governmental, non-profit-making, non-political arm of the WHO and UNESCO established in 1949 whose aims include the improvement of the safety of medicinal products.
6. CIOMS I Working Group I devised the CIOMS form for the expedited reporting of individual cases between 1986 and 1989.
7. Corresponds to ICH report E2A Guidance document.
8. CIOMS II Working Group II CIOMS report for aggregated safety information (1989–1991), corresponds to ICH report E2C Guidance document.
9. By the amendment of Article 10 of 65/65/EEC, by Council Directive 93/39/EEC of 14 June 1993.

Directive 2001/83/EC.[10] The QP PhV should not be confused with the QP[11] (*see* Chapter 2 regarding Good Manufacturing Practice) who is responsible for quality aspects of medicinal products, although in some very small organisations it is possible that the same person performs both functions.

During the pre-authorisation stage, an MA applicant must provide, in the application, a detailed description of the intended pharmacovigilance system,[12] and in the post-authorisation stage, the MAH must implement that system. The system put in place will include the staff and processes, so that whenever a patient suffers an adverse reaction after taking one of the company's medicinal products, the details are collected, entered into a database, coded according to the Medical Dictionary for Regulatory Authorities (MedDRA), and reported to EudraVigilance. Until the recent change in legislation, the reports were submitted to competent authorities. Serious reactions have to be reported within fifteen days, and these Individual Case Safety Reports (ICSRs) are entered into the relevant module of the European Union Drug Regulating Authorities Clinical Trials Database (EudraVigilance database).[13] All reactions must be reported periodically in periodic safety update reports (PSURs).

Most pharmaceutical companies have a central pharmacovigilance department, which may or may not be located within the EU. They may have data-input centres in different locations around the world. Some companies have separate databases for pre- and post-authorisation pharmacovigilance. The data obtained pre-authorisation are generally more detailed – for example, they may include information from laboratory testing and other clinical data. It is also not known at the time the data is entered whether the patient was taking the investigational medicinal product (IMP) or a comparator medicinal product or placebo, so the ability to modify the database will be required once the code used to pseudonymise data in the clinical trial is removed (this is termed 'breaking the code'), allowing the company to identify the subjects who took the IMP.

The data on adverse reactions collected during clinical trials are used to write the contra-indications, warnings and precautions, and adverse reaction sections of the summary of product characteristics (SmPC). However, prior to authorisation, as the exposure of the new medicinal product is limited to a small patient population, it is highly unlikely that very rare adverse reactions are picked up during clinical trials.

However, once an MA is granted and the product is placed on the market, it becomes available to a larger number and broader spectrum of patients within a short period of time. Large numbers of adverse reactions are often reported within that initial timeframe; the manner in which such reports are collected depends on the national

---

10. Article 103 of Directive 2001/83/EC requires that 'the marketing authorisation holder shall have permanently and continuously at his disposal an appropriately QP responsible for pharmacovigilance'.
11. Note this is the QP who is responsible for the quality aspects of manufacture of the IMP. *See* Chapter 5.
12. Article (8)(ia) Directive 2001/83/EC of the European Parliament and the Council of 6 November 2001 on the Community code relating to medicinal products for human use, as amended.
13. The two modules are the EudraVigilance Post-Authorisation Module (EVPM) and the EudraVigilance Clinical Trial Module (EVCTM).

systems established in the Member States. There is an increasing tendency for patients themselves to report adverse effects directly to the regulatory authority or to the pharmaceutical company. In some Member States, reporting is mandatory,[14] and in France, for instance, the reporting of hospital admissions resulting from medicine intake is actively sought out.

Accordingly, the first few years in which a new product is marketed are very important for gathering safety information and making frequent reassessments of the risk/benefit ratio. The term risk/benefit balance refers to the evaluation of the positive therapeutic effects of a medicinal product against the risks of such product. In recent years, the collection of post-authorisation data on adverse reactions has led to the withdrawal of some very widely used drugs, for example, the statin product Lipobay (cerivastatin) and COX-2 inhibitors, such as Vioxx (rofecoxib) and Prexige (lumiracoxib).

An example of the European pharmacoviligance system in action is the analysis of the safety of the products used to combat swine flu, which is published by the EMA.[15] The report summarises the data that have been entered into the EudraVigilance database for the different vaccines used in the H1N1 swine flu pandemic and also for Tamiflu. The report includes data on the suspected adverse reports and the total number of people who have been vaccinated or who are estimated to have taken Tamiflu. There are also data on the number of people who have contracted and died of the H1N1 virus. In the first report, after analysis of all the available data, the conclusion reached was that the benefit/risk ratio of the pandemic vaccines and antivirals used for the H1N1 influenza pandemic remained positive. 'The safety profile of the pandemic A (H1N1) 2009 influenza vaccines noted above is reassuring. Most of the adverse events that have been reported after immunisation have not been serious. To date, no unexpected safety concerns have been identified.'[16]

Alongside the consequences for individuals who may suffer an adverse drug reaction, which may be life-threatening or result in a permanent disability, there is an overall cost to society as well. It is estimated that 5% of all EU hospital admissions and 197,000 deaths per year in the EU are due to adverse drug reactions,[17] which has been equated to an estimated total financial cost to society of EUR 79 billion.[18] Given the age of that report, it can be safely assumed that figure is now considerably higher. It is claimed that even small improvements in the pharmacovigilance system can have a major impact on public health and society.[19]

Pharmaceutical companies also face challenges when a medicinal product is withdrawn due to safety concerns after significant investment in pre-clinical and

---

14. Spontaneous reporting became mandatory in France in 1984.
15. For example, EMA/984681/2009, Pandemic pharmacovigilance weekly update.
16. Global Advisory Committee on Vaccine Safety, 16–17 June 2010, Weekly Epidemiological record, 23 July 2010, vol. 85, 30 (pp. 285–292).
17. The Commission document entitled 'Strengthening pharmacovigilance to reduce adverse effects of medicines', 10 December 2008.
18. *Ibid.*
19. One-year report on human medicinal reporting pharmacovigilance tasks of the EMA, EMA/171322/2014.

clinical studies. Withdrawals present challenges in terms of adverse publicity or a negative effect on the stock market price of the company. Moreover, the financial impact may continue as individuals harmed following adverse drug reactions seek compensation through claims under product liability legislation. Therefore, it is important for companies and regulatory authorities to respond quickly to safety signals generated through diligent pharmacovigilance activities, and thus limit the human and financial damage.

As Norway, Iceland, and Liechtenstein (the European Free Trade Association (EFTA) states) have adopted the entire Community legislative framework on medicinal products, the pharmacovigilance obligations discussed in this Chapter also apply to these countries.

Pharmacovigilance also operates in relation to veterinary products.[20] Likewise, there is a procedure for reporting adverse incidences with medical devices, called materiovigilance, both of which are outside the scope of this chapter, but *see* Chapter 19 for a brief analysis of the medical devices sector.

In summary, pharmacovigilance can be understood in the context of this Chapter to consist of gathering reports of adverse reactions to medicinal products and reporting and analysing the data. This chapter describes both the pre-authorisation and post-authorisation pharmacovigilance requirements for human medicinal products, including compliance with those requirements. The final section examines the system of inspection that is in place to ensure compliance with the legal requirements.

§10.02   PRE-AUTHORISATION PHARMACOVIGILANCE

In the clinical trials phase, the gathering of data is proactive. The subjects of clinical trials can be healthy volunteers or patients that are actively asked about their experience. Adverse events and reactions are reported to the pharmaceutical company that has developed the product, along with the side-effects reported by subjects who have been given a placebo which commonly include events such as headache and nausea. Subjects often undergo laboratory testing during the course of the trial, so abnormalities in laboratory tests are also reported. The sponsor (defined below in §10.02[A]) has an obligation to report suspected unexpected serious adverse reactions (SUSARs) to regulatory authorities and ethics committees. The pharmaceutical company for which the sponsor conducts the clinical trials has ownership of all the pharmacovigilance data for its new medicinal product, which is termed an IMP.

---

20. Guideline on veterinary good pharmacovigilance practices (VGVP guideline) superseded previous guidelines on veterinary pharmacovigilance on 28 January 2022.

[A] Legislative Framework

The legislative framework for pre-authorisation pharmacovigilance was contained in Articles 16, 17, and 18 of the Clinical Trials Directive (CTD) 2001/20/EC,[21] which was repealed by the Clinical Trials Regulation (CTR) 536/2014, as further discussed in Chapter 4 (Clinical Trials). The European Regulation 536/2014 on clinical trials on medicinal products for human use,[22] adopted in May 2014, came into application on 31 January 2022 replacing Directive 2001/20/EC.

Articles 40 to 46 of the new Regulation set a legislative framework aiming to harmonise the safety reporting rules applicable in the context of clinical trials throughout the EU.

The major development is the creation of the Clinical Trial Information System (CTIS), a single EU portal for the submission of clinical trial applications and authorisations from all EU member states plus Iceland, Liechtenstein, and Norway, as signatories to the European Economic Area treaty. Articles 80, 81 and 82 specify that the EMA is responsible for the creation of the EU Portal and Database.

The new Regulation also introduces measures simplifying the rules on safety reporting and providing more transparency on clinical trials, strengthening the attractiveness of Europe for clinical trials.

A period of three years applies for a complete and successful transition on 31 January 2025. Until 30 January 2023, sponsors of clinical trials may use CTIS to run a trial under the CTR or choose to continue to operate under the CTD. As of 31 January 2023, it will be mandatory for sponsors of clinical trials to use CTIS to start a clinical trial in the EU/EEA. As of 31 January 2025, clinical trials in progress that were approved under the previous Directive will have to comply with the new Regulation and the information must be switched to CTIS.

The definitions relevant to pharmacovigilance in the CTR are:

- A *Sponsor* is an individual, company, institution, or organisation that takes responsibility for the initiation, management, and for setting up the financing of the clinical trial.[23]
- An *Investigator*[24] is an individual responsible for the conduct of a clinical trial at a clinical trial site. If a trial is conducted by a team of individuals at a trial site, the Investigator is the leader responsible for the team and may be called the principal Investigator.

---

21. Directive 2001/20/EC of the European Parliament and the Council of 4 April 2001 on the approximation of the laws, regulations, and administrative provisions of the Member States relating to the implementation of good clinical practice in the conduct of clinical trials on medicinal products for human use.
22. Regulation (EU) No. 536/2014 of the European Parliament and of the Council of 16 April 2014 on clinical trials on medicinal products for human use, and repealing Directive 2001/20/EC.
23. Article 2(14) of the Clinical Trials Regulation 536/2014.
24. Article 2(15 and 16) of the Clinical Trials Regulation 536/2014.

- An *adverse event* is any untoward medical occurrence in a subject to whom a medicinal product is administered and which does not necessarily have a causal relationship with this treatment.[25]
- A *serious adverse event* is any untoward medical occurrence or effect that at any dose requires inpatient hospitalisation or prolongation of existing hospitalisation, results in persistent or significant disability or incapacity, results in persistent or significant disability or incapacity, results in a congenital anomaly or birth defect, is life-threatening, or results in death.[26] Note that any suspected transmission via a medicinal product of an infectious agent will be automatically classified as a 'serious adverse event'.
- An *unexpected serious adverse reaction* is a serious adverse reaction, the nature, severity, or outcome of which is not consistent with the reference safety information.[27]

The definition of SUSARs arises from a combination of the last two definitions. The definitions are important to identify which adverse reactions require expedited reporting.

Article 41 of the CTR 'Reporting of adverse events and serious adverse events by the investigator to the sponsor' requires 'The investigator shall report serious adverse events to the sponsor without undue delay but not later than within 24 hours of obtaining knowledge of the events, unless, for certain serious adverse events, the protocol provides that no immediate reporting is required'.[28] This 'immediate' report is followed by detailed written reports. Other adverse events and laboratory abnormalities are reported according to the Trial Protocol.[29] The sponsor has an obligation to keep detailed records of all adverse events that are reported by the investigator.[30]

Contrary to the CTD that made no reference to the QP PhV, the CTR makes reference to this individual that may oversee all pharmacovigilance activities, including pre-authorisation activities.[31]

Article 42(2) of the CTR deals with the 'Notification of suspected unexpected serious adverse reactions' to the relevant authorities. It is the responsibility of the sponsor to ensure that all relevant information about the SUSARs that are fatal or life-threatening is recorded and reported as soon as possible, and in any case no later than seven days after the sponsor becomes aware of the case.[32] The report is made to the agency which transfers the information to the competent authorities of the Member

---

25. Article 2(32) of the Clinical Trials Regulation 536/2014.
26. Article 2(33) of the Clinical Trials Regulation 536/2014.
27. Article 2(34) of the Clinical Trials Regulation 536/2014.
28. Article 41(2) of the Clinical Trial Regulation 536/2014.
29. Article 41(1) of the Clinical Trial Regulation 536/2014.
30. Article 41(3) of the Clinical Trial Regulation 536/2014.
31. Article s13 (2, 3, 4), 61, and 62 of the Clinical Trial Regulation 536/2014. Mentioned in detail in 2001/83/EC Articles 41 (3) to 52 and 79, 103,113.
32. Article 42 (2)(a) of the Clinical Trial Regulation 536/2014.

States concerned, and to the ethics committee(s) when relevant.[33] All other SUSARs must be reported as soon as possible, but within a maximum of fifteen days of first knowledge by the sponsor.[34] The time limits are stringent, designed to report problems before they become widespread or more serious. It is for this reason that a SUSAR must be reported even if it is 'suspected' rather than definitely proven. All SUSARs are entered in the EudraVigilance database,[35] which includes details of the trial in the requisite form.[36] This meets the obligation under the CTR that each Member State must record all SUSARs in a European database.[37]

In addition, the sponsor must submit annually through the 'Eudravigilance database' to the agency a safety report for each IMP used in a clinical trial.[38]

The legislation is supplemented by guidance. Volume 10 of 'The Rules Governing Medicinal Products in the European Union' contains guidance documents applying to clinical trials. Number of documents in Volume 10 are being revised and updated to bring them in line with the changes required by the CTR. The relevant part applicable to clinical trials authorised under new Regulation EU No. 536/2014 is now 'Chapter V – Additional documents' that provides guidance on safety reporting through Q&A documents which are updated progressively. In particular, Chapter 7 of 'Questions and Answers Document – Regulation (EU) 536/2014 – Version 6.1 (May 2022)' is dedicated to 'Safety Reporting'. It was drafted by the Clinical Trials Facilitation and Coordination Group of the Heads of Medicines Agency (CTFG) and endorsed by the Expert Group on Clinical Trials of the European Commission (Commission). Module VI of GVP deals with technical aspects relating to adverse reaction/event reporting for pre-authorisation and post-authorisation phases. Furthermore, details on requirements for interventional studies, the inclusion of clinical trials' data in PSURs, and the notification of potential changes to the risk/benefit ratio are described in the different modules of the GVP.

The general provisions of the CTR are without prejudice to the civil and criminal liability of the sponsor or the investigator.[39]

[B] First-in-Man Trials

First-in-man, or Phase I, clinical trials have, in recent times, become subject to regulation by the EMA and the national competent authorities. In the UK, these regulations have been implemented by the UK's competent authority, the Medicines

---

33. Article 44 of the Clinical Trial Regulation 536/2014. Ethics committees will now only be involved in the assessment of the events reported only if it has been provided for in the law of the Member State concerned.
34. Article 42(2)(b) of the Clinical Trial Regulation 536/2014.
35. Article 42(1) of the Clinical Trial Regulation 536/2014.
36. The SUSAR reporting form is included at Appendix 3 from Table 1 in 'Detailed Guidance on the European database of Suspected Unexpected Serious Adverse Reactions' (EudraVigilance – Clinical Trial Model).
37. Article 40 of the Clinical Trial Regulation 536/2014.
38. Article 43(1) Regulation 536/2014.
39. Article 95 Regulation 536/2014.

Chapter 10: Pharmacovigilance   §10.02[C]

and Healthcare Regulatory Authority (MHRA), and have been in force in the UK since 1 May 2004.

The study normally comprises a dose range-finding study in a small number of volunteers, or possibly in patients for higher-risk medicinal products. Prior to the Phase I clinical trial, medicinal products have only been tested in animals (pre-clinical testing), and although there is some information about the potential toxicity of the product, it is the first time that safety information from human subjects is gathered. These trials are usually single escalating doses under close clinical supervision. Safety IMP monitoring must take place, but it is unusual to identify serious adverse reactions during such a trial. A notable exception is the case of TGN1412; *see* below Case Study 1. However, in most normal cases, an IMP will usually progress into clinical trials in patients following the Phase I studies.

[1]   Case Study 1

The case of first human study of the monoclonal antibody TGN1412 in the UK illustrates the risks taken by volunteers (*see* further Chapter 4). Eight healthy male volunteers were recruited and dosed by Parexel Clinical Pharmacology Research Unit of the Northwick Park Hospital on 13 March 2006. On the same day, life-threatening Serious Adverse Events (SAEs) described as 'cytokine release syndrome' were reported in six of the eight subjects. The drug codes were broken by Parexel, and it was confirmed that the six subjects who experienced the SAEs had received the active drug and the two who did not have received a placebo. The investigation concluded that the most likely cause was a biological action of the drug that was not predicted from apparently adequate pre-clinical testing.[40]

[C]   **Clinical Trials in Patients**

Phase II and Phase III trials are designed to prove efficacy and gather safety information about the IMP. The comparator may be a placebo, if it is ethical to do so, or an established therapy. The trials may be multi-centre, and the investigator must report adverse events to the sponsor of the trial. The sponsor determines whether any events are reported expediently as SUSARs. Patients are monitored closely and may be given diaries or questionnaires to record how they are feeling. It may sometimes be difficult to distinguish between the patient's underlying medical condition and adverse reactions related to the IMP. At the time of collecting the data, it is not known whether the patient is taking the IMP or placebo or a comparator product. Very occasionally, in light of a pattern of serious adverse reactions, the sponsor will break the code to see whether reactions are due to the IMP. This may bring the clinical trial to a premature end.

Due to the relatively small number of patients involved in clinical trials, only the most common adverse events will be identified, that is, those occurring in one out of ten or one out of a hundred patients. Rare and very rare adverse events are unlikely to

---

40. MHRA: Investigations into adverse incidents during clinical trials of TGN1412.

be seen until the IMP is authorised as a medicinal product and taken by a much larger population.

[D] The Investigator Brochure

The Investigator Brochure[41] is updated as information on the IMP is accumulated during the course of the clinical trials. It is the reference document used to determine whether a reaction is unexpected, and therefore it is very important in determining which serious adverse reactions should be reported expediently.

[E] Reporting SUSARs

Requirements depend on whether the clinical trial was authorised under the CTD or the CTR. In the case of death and life-threatening events, compliance with the seven-day reporting timeframe can be challenging, even though companies do use databases, either developed in-house or available commercially, that streamline the process of MedDRA coding and electronic reporting. The line listings of the SUSARs that are required annually are prepared using the clinical trials safety database. These line listings must be sent to the competent authorities of the Member States where the clinical trial is being conducted. National ethics committees might be involved in the assessment of the SUSARs when required by the relevant national legislation.

The SUSARs are entered into a clinical trial module of the EudraVigilance database, which is a single overall database for European regulatory authorities. Detailed guidance on the database is available.[42]

§10.03 THE MARKETING AUTHORISATION APPLICATION

The stage between pre-authorisation and post-authorisation is the marketing authorisation application (MAA), where all the pre-clinical and clinical data are collated and summarised, including all the pre-authorisation pharmacovigilance data.

The applicant must submit with its application a signed declaration that it has secured the services of a QP PhV, who will be responsible for pharmacovigilance, and that it has the necessary means for the collection and notification of any adverse reaction occurring either in the Community or in a third country.[43] Also included in Module 1, section 1.8.1 of its application dossier (Common Technical Document), a detailed description of its pharmacovigilance system is given, including:

---

41. *See* further Chapter 5.
42. EudraVigilance – EVWEB User Manual Version 1.6 corr. (14 March 2021); Detailed guidance on the collection, verification, and presentation of adverse event/reaction reports arising from clinical trials on medicinal products for human use (CT-3)(11 June 2011).
43. Article 8(3)(n) of Directive 2001/83/EC of the European Parliament and the Council of 6 November 2001 on the Community code relating to medicinal products for human use, as amended.

- the name and contact details (including out-of-hours contact details) of the QP PhV plus a summary of his or her job description, relevant CV information, and the back-up procedure to be applied in his or her absence;
- the location of the sites where pharmacovigilance activities are undertaken (e.g., where the main databases are located, where ICSRs are collated and reported, where PSURs are prepared and processed);
- high-level organisation charts that provide an overview of the applicant's pharmacovigilance units and that indicate the main reporting relationships with management, plus the position of the QP PhV within the organisation;
- information as to whether the applicant has written procedures in place for key pharmacovigilance activities;
- the main databases used (including their location) plus information about responsibility for their operation;
- whether the system complies with the internationally agreed standards for electronic submission of adverse reaction reports;
- a copy of the registration of the QP PhV with the EudraVigilance system and identification of the process used for electronic reporting to the Competent Authorities;
- details of any subcontracting arrangements that the applicant has entered into in respect of its pharmacovigilance activities; and
- a brief description of the locations of the different types of pharmacovigilance source documents, including archiving arrangements.

Article 8(3)(i) of Directive 2001/83/EC requires an applicant to include with its MAA details of the risk management system that will be introduced in addition to details of its intended pharmacovigilance system. This is called an EU Risk Management Plan (EU-RMP), which is described in more detail in §10.06.

Once a product has been shown in clinical trials to be safe and efficacious, and with a positive risk/benefit ratio, an MA is granted following the submission of an MAA. The MAA must include safety data and a risk management plan (RMP) that set out how the safety of the medicinal product will be monitored once on the market.

[A] Legislative Framework

The legislative framework for pharmacovigilance of medicinal products authorised for human use was originally established by Regulation (EC) No. 726/2004[44] and Directive 2001/83/EC[45] (largely Title IX 'Pharmacovigilance', which contains Articles 101–108). Subsequent legislation on pharmacovigilance, that is, Regulation (EU) No. 1235/2010

---

44. Regulation (EC) No. 726/2004 of 31 March 2004 laying down Community procedures for the authorisation and supervision of medicinal products for human and veterinary use and establishing an EMA.
45. Directive 2001/83/EC of the European Parliament and the Council of 6 November 2001 on the Community code relating to medicinal products for human use, as amended.

amending Regulation (EC) No. 726/2004 and Directive 2010/84/EU amending Directive 2001/83/EC have been published in the official Journal. The Regulation entered into force on 1 January 2011 and has been applied since 2 July 2012. Directive 2010/84/EU has been implemented by Member States since 21 July 2012. This framework imposes obligations directly on Member States through their national competent authorities, the EMA, and on the MAH and offers better promotion and protection of public health through more clearly defined roles and responsibilities for the many stakeholders involved, simplified tasks, decreased duplication of effort, and targeted administrative simplification. The legislation was further amended in October 2012 by Regulation (EU) No. 1027/2012, which applied as of 5 June 2013, and Directive 2012/26/EU, which applied as of 28 October 2013. These further changes are covered below in §10.08 (Summary of Recent Changes).

Directive 2010/84/EU includes the following definitions:

- An *adverse reaction* is a response to a medicinal product that is noxious and unintended. This broader definition was introduced to ensure that adverse reactions will include side-effects after medication errors and uses outside the terms of the MA including misuse and abuse.
- A *serious adverse reaction* is an adverse reaction that results in death, is life-threatening, requires in-patient hospitalisation or prolongation of existing hospitalisation, results in persistent or significant disability or incapacity, or is a congenital anomaly/birth defect.[46]
- An *unexpected adverse reaction* is an adverse reaction, the nature, severity, or outcome of which is not consistent with the SmPC.[47]

The term *adverse event* is not defined for post-authorisation pharmacovigilance. In clinical trials, an adverse event is an untoward medical occurrence not necessarily to have been caused by the medicinal product. Although not defined in the post-authorisation legislation, it is possible to have an adverse event reported at any time. However, it is assumed that if a healthcare professional or consumer takes the trouble to file a report associating an event with a medicinal product, there is a connection. On rare occasions, such as when healthcare professionals are asked to follow up on their patient's initial report, the healthcare professional may believe that there was no connection at all. In this case, the report is an 'adverse event'.

Causality is generally determined by the reporter, that is, the healthcare professional, usually the patient's physician or pharmacist, making the report. The reporter may be asked to indicate his or her assessment of causality on the reporting form by selecting the appropriate choice of causality phrase – that is, whether it was 'not caused', 'unlikely' to be caused, 'possibly' caused, 'probably' caused, or 'definitely' caused by the medicinal product. Pharmacovigilance staff can 'upgrade' the causality assessment, for example, upgrade from 'unlikely' to 'possibly' but not 'downgrade' the healthcare professional's classification.

---

46. Article 1(12) of Directive 2001/83/EC.
47. Article 1(13) of Directive 2001/83/EC.

Important factors in determining causality include the temporal relationship between taking the drug and the occurrence of the adverse reaction, and also whether or not the same reaction occurs on re-challenge (i.e., giving a second dose to validate a theory). However, there are ethical issues in giving a patient the medicinal product again following an adverse reaction, especially as allergic reactions can be more severe on second exposure.

Post-authorisation pharmacovigilance obligations apply to all medicinal products authorised in the EU, irrespective of the procedure by which such products were authorised[48] and regardless of their classification. These pharmacovigilance obligations also apply to homeopathic[49] and herbal products.

[B] The Requirements Set Out in Directive 2001/83/EC

The major guidance document for post-authorisation is GVP.[50] This document specifically relates to human pharmacovigilance prepared by the Commission in close consultation with the EMA, Member States, and interested parties.

The MAH must have 'permanently and continuously at his disposal an appropriately QP responsible for pharmacovigilance'[51] (QP PhV). The exact nature of the qualifications is not specified, but according to GVP, the QP PhV should have documented experience in all aspects of pharmacovigilance; that is, the person should have relevant work experience in pharmacovigilance and should hold relevant qualifications such as postgraduate qualifications in pharmacovigilance. If the person is not medically qualified, he or she must have access to someone who is medically qualified. The role may be satisfactorily fulfilled by a suitably qualified consultant or by an employee of the MAH's company. However, in either case, the requirement for the QP PhV to be 'permanently and continuously at the Marketing Authorisation holder's disposal' should be covered in any contract. Therefore, the QP PhV must be at the MAH's disposal twenty-four hours a day, 365 days a year, and must reside in an EEA/EFTA state.[52] This in effect means that the QP PhV has to be contactable, usually by mobile phone, twenty-four hours a day, seven days a week. Holidays are usually covered by a deputy, but in some instances, companies may expect their QP PhV to be available at any time if an urgent safety concern is raised with one of their medicinal products.

In some Member States, national regulations require a QP PhV to be appointed specifically for the purpose of discharging pharmacovigilance obligations in that state.

---

48. Other than homeopathic products registered through the special, simplified registration procedure set out in Article 14(1) Directive 2001/83/EC.
49. Ibid.
50. The Good Pharmacovigilance Practice guidelines which superseded Volume 9A – Pharmacovigilance for Medicinal Products for Human Use.
51. Module 1 paragraph 1.c.1.1. GVP.
52. Article 104(3) of Directive 2001/83/EC of the European Parliament and the Council of 6 November 2001 on the Community code relating to medicinal products for human use, as amended.

This national QP PhV may also act as the EU-wide QP PhV, provided he or she resides in the relevant Member State.

With the implementation of Directive 2010/84/EU, there has been a change in the legislation such that some of the responsibility previously with the QP PhV moved to the MAH.[53] The QP PhV is still responsible for establishing and maintaining a system which ensures that information about all adverse reactions reported to any company personnel, including medical representatives, is collected and collated and is accessible at least at one point within the Community.

The MAH is responsible for some activities for which the QP PhV was previously responsible:

(a) preparing reports for the competent authorities, including reporting of spontaneous reports received by the company, which may be expediently (no later than fifteen days after any employee of the company first receiving the information) or within a PSUR;
(b) ensuring that any request from a competent authority for information required to evaluate the risk/benefit ratio of a product is answered fully and promptly; and
(c) providing any other information to competent authorities that is relevant to the evaluation of the risk/benefit ratio of a medicinal product, for example, the results of post-authorisation safety studies (PASS).

The 'system' required consists of personnel, communication pathways, and a means of storing and retrieving the data. This usually means that the information that comes into the company is entered into a central database. It is possible for companies to input and store the data on a database outside the Community, but there must be a place within the Community where the data can be accessed and interrogated.

Although it is anticipated that the QP PhV will delegate his or her responsibilities, he or she has overall control and oversight of all pharmacovigilance activities, and this individual is the single point of contact with the competent authorities on a twenty-four-hour basis (as mentioned above). Under the new legislation, the EMA and the national competent authorities require that the name of the QP PhV is submitted to them with relevant contact details. There is an obligation to update this information when personnel changes occur. The QP PhV must also ensure that he or she is available for any competent authority pharmacovigilance inspection, during which the competent authority will assess the MAH's compliance with its pharmacovigilance obligations. Failure to meet the key responsibilities set out in Article 103 of Directive 2001/83/EC may, in some Member States, result in criminal sanctions against the QP PhV.

---

53. Although the date for implementation of Directive 2010/84/EU was 21 July 2012, Member States agreed to bring forward the transposition date to 2 July 2012 in order to be in line with the parallel Regulation (EU/1235/2010) which deals with similar and compatible changes to centralised EU pharmacovigilance provisions.

[C] The Reporting of Adverse Reactions

[1] Reports to the MAH

The MAH must, in relation to all authorised products, irrespective of the regulatory route of approval, report adverse reactions received from healthcare professionals, either spontaneously[54] or through post-authorisation studies, regardless of whether or not the medicinal product was used in accordance with the authorised SmPC and/or any other marketing conditions. Adverse reactions identified in worldwide-published scientific literature should also be reported. Reports must be sent electronically, except during exceptional circumstances.

Although healthcare professionals are asked in some Member States to report directly to the national competent authority of the state where the reaction happened, they also report to pharmaceutical company responsible for marketing the product directly, especially if they are also asking for further information (e.g., about a potential side-effect or if a product has been taken during pregnancy). They may report during face-to-face contact with the company's medical representative or by phone to the Medical Director, the pharmacovigilance staff, or the medical information service. All staff, including those on reception and switchboard, are required to have training in pharmacovigilance, and they must have enough knowledge to route an enquiry appropriately. This is particularly important for 'out-of-hours' enquiries, where the initial contact may be picked up by a security guard. Some companies have dedicated pharmacovigilance telephone numbers that may be diverted to the QP PhV or member of staff who is 'on-call' to cover out-of-hours periods.

There are four pieces of information required before a report of an adverse reaction is considered valid ('the minimum information').[55] The clock for expedited reporting starts once a valid report is received by any member of the company's staff. MAHs are expected to obtain at least the minimum information from the person making the report and to follow up to obtain the fullest details possible, which can be sent after the expedited report. The minimum information is:

- the identity and contact details of the reporting healthcare professional;
- information from which the patient may be identified, taking into account any data protection restrictions;
- at least one suspected active substance/medicinal product; and
- at least one suspected adverse reaction.

In practice, information about a suspected adverse reaction will usually be reported from outside the MAH's company to an employee such as a medical representative, or as an enquiry to the MAH's medical information department. The information obtained from the initial report should be passed to the local drug safety

---

54. Unless the healthcare professional making the spontaneous report has made an explicit statement that a causal relationship between the medicinal product and the adverse reaction has been excluded and the Marketing Authorisation holder agrees with this.
55. Guideline on good pharmacovigilance practices (GVP) Module VI (Rev 2)

officer in the MAH's pharmacovigilance department. All original paperwork must be collected and preserved because it forms part of the documentation of the 'case'. The drug safety officer in the territory where the adverse reaction occurred should then contact the patient's healthcare professional directly for further information. The healthcare professional will usually be requested to complete a form in order to record the further information. If the form is collected in a local language, it must also be translated into English.

The local drug safety officer should then send all of the original paperwork to the MAH's central pharmacovigilance department. This paperwork will include: the initial report, the further information report (if appropriate), and the drug safety officer's opinion as to whether the adverse reaction is unexpected or not (according to whether it is included on the SmPC for the locally authorised product). In the central pharmacovigilance department, the data are inputted into the safety database, and in doing so, the data will be coded according to the MedDRA.

Once the report is coded, it is transmitted electronically into EudraVigilance database. The adverse reaction report is also sent, where appropriate, to the drug safety officers in the other territories where the medicinal product is authorised. This is reported according to local reporting requirements, either electronically or on paper.

Adverse reactions may be reported to the national competent authorities as an ICSR or in a PSUR. If the information about the adverse reaction suggests that it should be classified as a serious adverse reaction, it must be reported as an ICSR in an expedited manner. However, if the information is about a non-serious adverse reaction, it should only be reported as an ICSR in an expedited manner on request. Otherwise, it should be reported as part of the PSUR.

The national competent authorities to whom the MAH should report adverse reaction information include one or more of the following: the national competent authority in the Member State in which the reaction occurred, the national competent authority in the Reference Member State, all national competent authorities, and/or the EMA. Which entity/entities depends on the type of MA held by the MAH in relation to the medicinal product in question, and whether the adverse reaction occurred inside or outside of the EU. GVP provides detailed information about the correct chain of reporting.

[2] Reports from Patients/Consumers

In contrast to the United States (US) where consumer reports are the most common means of collecting safety data, this concept is relatively new in Europe, even in relation to over-the-counter (OTC) medicines. However, there is a growing trend for consumers to contact pharmaceutical companies for information directly, particularly since the introduction of package leaflets or patient information leaflets. Pharmaceutical companies are therefore encouraged to follow up with the consumer, during the course of their enquiry, when the consumer has (or thinks he or she has) suffered an adverse reaction to the medicinal product. With the implementation of Directive

2010/84, it is now a requirement that suspected adverse reports directly from patients be recorded by MAHs.

Reports from patients or consumers usually come to a company via the medical information department, usually by telephone, but also by e-mail or letter. Staff in the medical information department must be trained in pharmacovigilance, so when a patient or consumer makes an enquiry about a side-effect, appropriate questions are asked to find out whether there is a potential adverse reaction behind the enquiry. Obviously, in some instances, it will be apparent that the consumer has suffered an adverse reaction – for example, where the consumer is looking for compensation for unexpected 'side effects'. Equally, if a patient asks about the use of a drug during pregnancy, she should be asked whether a drug has been taken and the stage of pregnancy, and the case should be followed up (*see* Pregnancy Registries in §10.03[9]).

Where information about a suspected serious adverse reaction is received directly from a patient or consumer, provided the minimum information is supplied and the report is supported by medical documentation, the MAH should report the reaction as an ICSR using the expedited reporting procedure.[56] However, if no supporting medical documentation is provided, the MAH should (with the patient's consent) contact the patient's healthcare professional in order to obtain further information. Once the healthcare professional confirms the report, the MAH should report it as a spontaneous report from a healthcare professional (i.e., as an expedited ICSR if classified as serious). It is not always easy to obtain healthcare professional follow-up, and although no fee is payable for this, some doctors will request a fee for completing the adverse event form.

Reports from consumers may be picked up from Internet blogs, which may include personal experiences with adverse reactions. It is difficult to know where to draw the line in how far companies should proactively seek out and follow up on these types of reports.

[3] Reports with Name of Active Substance Only

Where an MAH receives information about an adverse reaction that states only the name of the active substance (i.e., the international non-proprietary name (the 'INN'), for example, paracetamol or ibuprofen), rather than the brand name of the medicinal product, if the active substance is included in any of the products for which the MAH holds an MA, the MAH must assume that the information may relate to that product.

[4] Literature Reports

Where an MAH can reasonably be expected to be aware of an adverse reaction reported in the worldwide scientific literature, there is an obligation to report such adverse reaction. Therefore, GVP recommends that the MAH maintain awareness of possible publications by accessing a widely used systematic literature review and reference

---

56. Note that medically unconfirmed reports should not be reported on an expedited basis.

database at least once per week. Different companies conduct their literature reviews in different ways; larger companies will have an extensive library and may subscribe to leading journals, while others may rely on electronic searches to identify relevant articles using suitable keywords.

Once an adverse reaction such as a case report is identified by the MAH, the information is entered into their internal database, and then reported in the same way as a spontaneous case. A copy of the literature is sent in with the report. It is likely that there will be duplication for products that are marketed by a large number of MAHs, and measures are in place to remove duplicate literature reports. Some countries such as the Netherlands have proposed work-sharing the literature review and paying a share to a commercial company to conduct the searches and report on their behalf. This would seem a sensible approach to take across Europe, certainly for older medicinal products that are known most commonly by their INN. However, for products that are branded, including OTC products, there is still the need to search for reports by brand name. This is something that the brand-owner would probably continue to do itself, particularly when a product is very new to the market, so that the MAH retains as much data about its own product itself. Depending on the detail in the case report, the MAH may follow up with the authors of literature to obtain more information.[57]

[5] Reports from Non-Medical Sources

If an MAH becomes aware of a case report from a non-medical source (such as the lay press), every attempt should be made to obtain the minimum information and to follow up on the case as if it had been reported by a healthcare professional or patient.

[6] Timescales for Expedited Reporting

The MAH must report all serious adverse reactions within fifteen calendar days of receiving information about the event. This is called expedited reporting.[58] The day on which the MAH, or the organisation contracted by the MAH to perform this function, becomes aware of a case that fulfils the minimum information should be considered as 'Day 0.' As stated earlier, because the clock starts as soon as any employee of the MAH/contracted organisation receives the relevant information, all personnel should be aware of, and trained in, the MAH's pharmacovigilance obligations. Follow-up reports must be submitted within fifteen days of the day on which the MAH/contracted organisation receives the relevant additional information.

For cases reported in the worldwide scientific literature, the clock starts on the day on which the MAH/contracted organisation becomes aware of a publication containing the minimum information. The fifteen days can be difficult to meet if there

---

57. Guidance to authors is available, e.g., J.K. Aronson, 'Anecdotes as Evidence', Br Med J 326 (2003): 1346.
58. Guideline on good pharmacovigilance practices (GVP) Module VI (Rev 2).

is delay at any stage, and it is one of the compliance measures that will be examined during pharmacovigilance inspections.

[7] MedDRA

As all adverse reactions are likely to be described very differently by different reporters, it is essential to use a medical dictionary to ensure that all reactions are grouped together. MedDRA is a clinically validated international medical dictionary used by regulatory authorities and the regulated biopharmaceutical industry. MedDRA is the classification dictionary endorsed by the *International Conference on Harmonisation* or ICH. MedDRA is used in the US, the EU, and Japan. Indeed, in the EU and Japan, MedDRA must be used for safety reporting, while in the US, the Food and Drug Administration (FDA) has committed to keeping up-to-date with MedDRA, that is gradually becoming the standard to use for adverse event reporting in the US.

MedDRA is managed by the Maintenance and Support Services Organisation (MSSO). MedDRA is free to regulatory authorities and priced according to revenue for the various industry players. MedDRA is also available in Japanese.

The MSSO updates MedDRA upon requests from subscribers to add new medical concepts or to change existing concepts. The decision as to whether to change/add coding is made by MedDRA's international medical officers, who decide how to map the terminology within the grouping categories according to the general consensus.

The MedDRA dictionary is organised by System Organ Class (SOC), with further subdivisions. The dictionary also includes 'Standardised MedDRA Queries', which are intended to facilitate retrieval of MedDRA-coded data as a first step in investigating drug safety issues in pharmacovigilance and clinical development. Standardised MedDRA Queries (SMQs) are groupings of terms that relate to a defined medical condition or area of interest.

The MSSO releases updated MedDRA versions in March and September of each year. The March release is the main annual release and contains changes to all subdivisions, while the September release typically only contains changes to the lower-level and preferred-term subdivisions.

[8] Electronic Reporting

Electronic reporting of serious adverse reactions to the EMA is mandatory, save in exceptional circumstances,[59] for example, where mechanical, programme, electronic, or communication failures prevent electronic reporting. The EMA has provided the necessary technical tools, particularly to small- and medium-sized enterprises (SMEs), as well as to other interested parties, to enable them to report electronically and to facilitate compliance with the electronic reporting requirements. Local reporting requirements can be discussed with the national competent authorities, but electronic

---

59. *Ibid.*

reporting to the EMA must be maintained irrespective of any local arrangement. Most national competent authorities now prefer electronic reporting.

Systems have been put in place for SMEs to help them comply with the expedited electronic reporting requirements. Like all applicants or MAHs, they need to register with EudraVigilance, but SMEs can use a web application called EVWeb to transmit their ICSRs electronically. The staff operating the system needs to undertake three days of EudraVigilance training. All ICSRs need to code adverse reactions according to MedDRA; however, SMEs may obtain a waiver from paying the MedDRA license fee.

[9] Pregnancy Registries

The MAH should follow up on all reports from healthcare professionals where the embryo or foetus may have been exposed to the MAH's medicinal product. This may be either through maternal exposure or transmission of a medicinal product via semen following paternal exposure. Follow-up should be conducted around the anticipated birth date and data on the pregnancy outcome should be collected, including where the outcome is normal. A suitable alert system must be in place to prompt a follow-up at the correct time. If a 'congenital anomaly or birth defect' is reported, this falls within the definition of a serious adverse reaction and must therefore be reported expediently as an ICSR. Otherwise, all pregnancy outcomes following *in utero* exposure should be reported in the PSUR. The pregnancy registry is usually held in the database in such a way that all data on exposure to a particular drug in pregnancy can be retrieved.

[10] Lack of Efficacy

Reports regarding the lack of efficacy of a medicinal product should usually be reported in the PSUR unless the medicinal product in question is used for the treatment of life-threatening disease or is a vaccine or contraceptive, in which case it should be reported as an ICSR on an expedited basis.

[11] Abuse, Misuse, or Overdose

In the event that an MAH receives information about the abuse, misuse, or overdose of its medicinal products, the MAH should follow up in order to obtain information about the early symptoms, treatment, and outcome. However, this information need not be reported on an expedited basis and should instead form part of the PSUR. The MAH should continuously monitor and evaluate the potential impact of overdose, abuse, and misuse of a medicinal product on its risk/benefit ratio.

[12] Public Health Emergency

After the world experienced several health crises, including infectious diseases such as Influenza, Ebola, and the Zika epidemics and recently, the COVID-19 crisis, it appeared that the EU needs to develop a coordinated EU-level action to strengthen Europe's ability to prevent, detect, and rapidly respond to cross-border health emergencies.[60] Hence, the Health Emergency preparedness and Response Authority (HERA) was created and will work together with Member States to analyse and define threats and strategic approaches, coordinating priorities so that the resources devoted to preparedness and response are as effective as possible in case of potential health crises.

§10.04   PSURs

[A]   Introduction

Reports of all adverse reactions, including serious adverse reactions, which must also be also reported on an expedited basis, should be submitted to the competent authorities in the form of PSURs. Since the implementation of the 2012 regulatory framework, PSURs for centrally authorised products must be submitted to EudraVigilance (*see* §10.05[C] below).[61] PSURs are intended to provide an update for the competent authorities on the worldwide safety experience of a medicinal product at defined time points after authorisation. PSURs must therefore comprise a succinct summary of information together with a critical evaluation of the risk/benefit balance of the medicinal product, taking into account any new or changing information. The evaluation should ascertain whether further investigations need to be carried out and whether changes need to be made to the MA, SmPC, or other product information.

[B]   Contents of the PSUR

Detailed guidance as to the content of a PSUR is set out in GVP. Some of the key features of the PSUR include:

- introduction, giving context to the report (e.g., which active substances are covered, dosage forms, and time periods);
- worldwide authorisation status (i.e., where the medicinal product is authorised, where applications are pending, and where applications have not been approved, where authorisations have been suspended, withdrawn, or revoked);
- update of competent authority or MAH actions taken for safety reasons (e.g., information about 'Dear Doctor' letters);
- update of changes to reference safety information (e.g., variations made to the SmPC);
- estimation of patient exposure;

---

60. Communication of the European Commission (2021) 576 final – Introducing HERA, the European Health Emergency preparedness and Response Authority, the next step towards completing the European Health Union.
61. Guideline on good pharmacovigilance practices (GVP) Module VI (Rev 2).

- presentation of individual case histories showing new or relevant safety information plus MAH analysis of such individual case histories;
- information about all adverse reactions reported in the period covered by the PSUR, organised by body systems using the MedDRA dictionary;
- information about any studies conducted;
- other information including:
    - efficacy-related information;
    - risk management plan;
    - risk/benefit analysis report;
    - overall safety evaluation; and
    - conclusion;
- content of any PSUR Bridging report;[62] and
- content of any PSUR Addendum report.[63]

[C] Periodicity of Submission of PSUR

Articles 24(3) of Regulation 726/2004[64] and 104(6) of Directive 2001/83/EC[65] specify the periodicity for submission of PSURs. The format of PSURs is set out in the Commission implementing Regulation (EU) No. 520/2012.[66] Following grant of an MA, a PSUR must be submitted every six months until the day on which the medicinal product is first placed on the market in the EU. Thereafter, PSURs must continue to be submitted every six months (in line with the initial six-month cycle based on the date of the product's authorisation) for the first two years post-marketing and then every twelve months (in line with the initial cycle) for the next two years post-marketing. At the end of this period, PSURs must be submitted at three-year intervals. However, this periodicity may be varied by a condition in the MA or on a request from a competent authority for the immediate submission of a PSUR.[67]

The PSUR submission schedule specified in the legislation means that the MAH is under an obligation to complete PSURs even though a product has not yet been placed on the Community market. As this means that the product will have had only

---

62. PSUR Bridging reports are brief summaries bridging two or more PSURS, which are intended to assist competent authorities in understanding the overall picture created by all PSURs.
63. PSUR Addendum reports are updates to the most recently completed PSUR. An Addendum report is only created when a competent authority requests a PSUR outside the usual reporting schedule.
64. Regulation (EC) No. 726/2004 of 31 March 2004 laying down Community procedures for the authorisation and supervision of medicinal products for human and veterinary use and establishing an EMA.
65. Directive 2001/83/EC of the European Parliament and the Council of 6 November 2001 on the Community code relating to medicinal products for human use, as amended.
66. Commission Implementing Regulation (EU) No. 520/2012 of 19 June 2012 on the performance of pharmacovigilance activities provided for in Regulation (EC) No. 726/2004 of the European Parliament and of the Council and Directive 2001/83/EC of the European Parliament and of the Council.
67. Article 107c(2) of the Directive 2001/83/EC of the European Parliament and the Council of 6 November 2001 on the Community code relating to medicinal products for human use, as amended.

limited exposure, these post-authorisation/pre-marketing PSURs will have to include adverse reaction data collected from other territories in which the product has been marketed as well as information from any ongoing clinical studies or compassionate use.

An MAH may request a change in the periodicity of PSUR submission under Article 107c(6) of Directive 2001/83/EC,[68] in accordance with the procedure in the GVP Module VII. The request is made to Committee for Medicinal Products for Human Use (CHMP) or the Coordination Group for Mutual Recognition and Decentralised Procedures: Human (CMDh) and will be considered by Pharmacovigilance Risk Assessment Committee (PRAC) and the CHMP if it relates to a product approved by centralised procedure (CP), and CMDh otherwise. An MA applicant may also suggest a different periodicity for PSUR submission in its application, although this must be accompanied by a reasoned request for amendment to the usual cycle. For example, for products authorised through line extensions to existing medicinal products and for newly authorised generic products, it is usual for the MA applicant to request to move to a three-year PSUR cycle immediately post-authorisation. Note, however, that the submission cycle for PSURs cannot be extended beyond three years.

The first PSUR should have a 'data lock point' that falls within six months of grant of the MA for a particular medicinal product. The PSUR must be submitted within sixty days of the data lock point. This allows the MAH to fix a point in time and to collect the data on sales and adverse drug reactions up until that specific date. The final section of the PSUR contains any new relevant information to the risk/benefit ratio received since the data lock point. Subsequent PSURs run in time from the data lock point of the first PSUR to the data lock point of the next one, and so on.

Under the new pharmacovigilance legislation, changes have been made to PSURs to lessen the administrative burden. For example, PSURs have a single assessment for the same active substance or a combination of active substances; routine PSUR reporting is no longer necessary for products with low risk or for old or established products unless concerns arise.

In addition, PSUR reporting has become electronic following the establishment of an EU repository. PSURs are to be sent directly to the EMA.

[D] PSUR Work-Sharing Initiative

The European Risk Management Strategy includes an initiative to increase the effectiveness of PSUR information by sharing the PSUR assessment workload throughout the EU. However, PSUR work-sharing has been difficult to achieve because, for many products, PSUR submission is based on national birth dates. Harmonisation of product birth dates throughout the EU will enable PSUR submissions to be synchronised, which will have advantages for both industry and regulatory authorities.

---

68. Directive 2001/83/EC of the European Parliament and the Council of 6 November 2001 on the Community code relating to medicinal products for human use, as amended.

The Heads of Medicines Agencies have undertaken an initiative in this regard to ensure that medicinal products with the same active substance follow the same PSUR submission scheme in all EU Member States. This is achieved by harmonising 'virtual' birth dates and agreeing with the relevant MAH on harmonised dates for submission of the next PSURs.

Harmonisation of birth dates in the EU was taken forward by a working group formed by representatives from Member States and European trade associations. Harmonised EU birth dates were set by mutual agreement between Member States and the MAHs of innovator products. The agreed dates have been published on the Heads of Medicines Agencies website.[69] It is envisaged that the MAHs for generic products will also adopt the same birth dates for their related products. PSUR submission throughout the EU will then be based on these birth dates.

Initially, the harmonisation scheme focused on chemical synthetic substances that were authorised in the EU after December 1976, and excluded herbal products, homeopathic products, vaccines, or blood products. Work is ongoing to agree on harmonised birth dates for pre-1976 chemical synthetic substances, and it is hoped that eventually vaccines and herbal, homeopathic, and blood products will be included in the scheme.

The advantages of this initiative for the MAH are obvious: the MAH needs to submit only one PSUR for a drug substance authorised nationally in several different Member States. The advantage for the competent authorities is that one authority can take the lead in the assessment, while the other authorities receive a summary of the safety data for all medicinal products containing a particular active ingredient from all the MAHs around the same time.

§10.05 THE PHARMACOVIGILANCE ACTIVITIES OF THE KEY PARTIES

In terms of regulatory authorities, the EMA and national competent authorities are involved in both pre- and post-authorisation activities, but usually the pre- and post-authorisation activities are organised separately within these organisations.

A rapporteur or co-rapporteur Member State for the centralised procedure, and the Reference Member State in an application under the decentralised procedures, is likely to stay involved in post-authorisation pharmacovigilance, for example, for the assessment of the PSURs.

[A] The EMA

The EMA's role in relation to pharmacovigilance extends further than supervision of centrally authorised products. The EMA has a legal responsibility to coordinate pharmacovigilance and monitor the safety of medicines throughout the EU and to

---

69. https://www.hma.eu/about-hma/working-groups/periodic-safety-update-reporting-psur-synchronisation-and-work-sharing.html.

ensure the provision of advice for the safe and effective use of medicines. This is achieved principally though the PRAC.

The EMA takes appropriate action if adverse drug reaction reports suggest changes to the risk/benefit ratio of a medicinal product. The EMA's scientific committee is the CHMP, which tends to implement the recommendations made to it by the PRAC on all matters relating directly or indirectly to pharmacovigilance. This involves providing advice on the safety of medicinal products and on the investigation of adverse reactions in order to enable effective risk identification, assessment, and management, leading to recommendations for synchronised action by the national competent authorities.

The EMA's other key pharmacovigilance obligation was to establish a data-processing network for the exchange of pharmacovigilance information about medicinal products marketed in the EU, which would allow all competent authorities to share such information at the same time.[70] The system that has been put in place to fulfil this requirement is called EudraVigilance.

The EMA is also required to collaborate with the WHO in matters of international pharmacovigilance by promptly submitting appropriate information regarding any measures taken in the EU that may have a bearing on public health protection in countries outside of the EU.[71]

[B] Pharmacovigilance Working Party

The Pharmacovigilance Working Party had its last meeting in July 2012 and was replaced under revised legislation by the PRAC which discusses and advises on all pharmacovigilance referrals (*See* §10.08 [B] below).

[C] Competent Authorities of the Member States

Further to Directive 2001/83/EC, Member States are directly responsible for establishing and operating a pharmacovigilance system for the collection and evaluation of information on the safety of medicinal products, particularly information regarding adverse reactions or information that is relevant to the risk/benefit balance.[72]

Pursuant to GVP, each Member State must have in place a system for receiving and evaluating pharmacovigilance data. Furthermore, as Member States are responsible for conducting pharmacovigilance inspections and otherwise monitoring the MAH's compliance, the system must also allow for regulatory action to be taken as

---

70. Article 107 of Directive 2001/83/EC of the European Parliament and the Council of 6 November 2001 on the Community code relating to medicinal products for human use, as amended.
71. Article 27 of Regulation (EC) No. 726/2004 of 31 March 2004 laying down Community procedures for the authorisation and supervision of medicinal products for human and veterinary use and establishing an EMA.
72. Article 101 of Directive 2001/83/EC.

necessary (which shall include the application of 'effective, proportionate and dissuasive penalties'[73] as appropriate). Member States largely discharge their pharmacovigilance obligations through their competent authorities. Article 67(4) of Regulation (EC) No. 726/2004[74] dictates that public funding shall be made available to national competent authorities in relation to such pharmacovigilance activities (which include the operation of communication networks and the practice of market surveillance), and the national competent authority shall be responsible for controlling and managing such funds.[75]

Member States are required to take 'all appropriate' measures to encourage healthcare professionals, which will include general physicians, hospital physicians, and pharmacists, to voluntarily report suspected adverse reactions[76] to the relevant national competent authority.[77] Although GVP identifies some of the generic features of the system that all Member States should adopt in order to encourage spontaneous reporting, the implementation of this requirement has differed between Member States. For example, in the UK, a 'yellow card' reporting system has been in place for over forty years, with yellow cards being made freely available to healthcare professionals via their professional publications and with details of the scheme, particularly how to make reports, being prominently displayed on the website of the UK's competent authority, the MHRA.

In any event, GVP indicates that all Member States' systems for spontaneous reporting should encourage both healthcare professionals and patients to report suspected adverse reactions, in the latter's case, either directly to the competent authorities or indirectly via patient organisations or healthcare professionals. The reporting process should be straightforward and user-friendly (e.g., being free post, phone, and/or Internet-based) to encourage compliance and should ensure that an acknowledgement message is sent to the case sender. Reports should be collected and validated by the competent authority and entered into a database[78] that will be used to identify potential signals and analyse data in order to clarify risk factors or confirm changes to reporting profiles. Serious adverse reactions – that is, those that result in

---

73. Article 102(f) of Directive 2001/83/EC.
74. Regulation (EC) No. 726/2004 of 31 March 2004 laying down Community procedures for the authorisation and supervision of medicinal products for human and veterinary use and establishing an EMA.
75. Article 105 of Directive 2001/83/EC.
76. Article 102 of Directive 2001/83/EC.
77. As regards reporting obligations, the entity that will fulfil the function of the competent authority in relation to a particular medicinal product will depend on the procedure through which that medicinal product was authorised. Therefore, for medicinal products authorised via national procedures (including mutual recognition and decentralised procedures), the competent authority is the competent authority of the Member State(s) in which an MA is held. For practical reasons, where marketing authorisations are held in multiple Member States, the Member States have agreed that it shall be the reference Member State that will assume the majority of pharmacovigilance obligations. Conversely, where medicinal products are authorised via the centralised procedure, the competent authority is the Commission, although pharmacovigilance responsibilities are split between the pre-authorisation rapporteur and the EMA.
78. EudraVigilance Database Management System (EVDBMS).

death, hospitalisation, or increased length of stay in hospital, and so on – should be handled with the highest priority.

Member States can also impose mandatory obligations on healthcare professionals to report suspected serious or unexpected adverse reactions.[79]

Member States' obligations regarding the pharmacovigilance system also include ensuring that the information collected is communicated to the appropriate persons.[80] This is achieved via the EudraVigilance system, which was established in accordance with Article 101 Directive 2001/83/EC and Article 57(1) Regulation 726/2004/EC and clarification with the 2012 legislation. EudraVigilance is the European computer database of reported adverse reactions and adverse events. Two different EudraVigilance modules[81] were created to address the collection of the different types of adverse reactions reportable within the EU pharmacovigilance framework. EudraVigilance was created by the EMA in December 2001 and is maintained by EMA staff that are responsible for processing adverse reaction information received from the competent authorities and the MAHs. EMA staff are also responsible for ensuring that the information collected is made available for scientific assessment by the various competent authorities in order to enable them to meet their obligation to carry out continuous safety surveillance of medicinal products available in the EU. MAHs may access information in the EudraVigilance database that relates to the medicinal products for which they hold an MA. Healthcare professionals and patients are also to access the EudraVigilance database, with varying access to the levels of information.

The system of communication between the various EU competent authorities is called EudraNet and allows electronic exchange of reports between the EMA and Member States in the EudraVigilance database. This means that the reporter only has to report to one, or at most two, national competent authorities for national and decentralised authorisations; reporting is direct for centralised authorisation. Rules are in place between the competent authorities to ensure that these reports are entered into the EudraVigilance database, thereby minimising duplication.

Once a medicinal product has been on the market for a number of years, generic versions of the product containing the same active ingredient are developed and marketed. This results in a large number of different MAHs for products containing the same active ingredient, all of which may receive reports of adverse events directly from healthcare professionals and consumers. Once a product enters this phase of the lifecycle, the competent authorities are in the best position to oversee the data, as in addition to receiving information directly, they get reports via many different MAHs. The national competent authorities have an obligation to send reports of all serious adverse reactions to all MAHs who have MAs in their territory for products that contain the same active ingredient as any suspected product. There can be a number of suspected products named in a report, as there is a tendency for the report to list all the medication the patient was taking at the time of the adverse reaction, which may

---

79. Article 101 of Directive 2001/83/EC.
80. Article 107a(5) of Directive 2001/83/EC.
81. The two modules are the EudraVigilance Post-Authorisation Module (EVPM) and the EudraVigilance Clinical Trial Module (EVCTM).

include OTC products. The MAH is expected to include these reports when reporting periodically back to national competent authorities in the PSUR. The result is that there is a duplication of effort as a large number of MAHs review the same reports, and report them back to the regulatory authorities who already have the reports in their database.

If, as a result of the evaluation of pharmacovigilance data, and in accordance with the guidelines produced by the Commission, a competent authority considers that an MA should be suspended, revoked, or varied, it shall forthwith inform the EMA, the other Member States in which the MAH has an MA, and the MAH.[82] A competent authority may suspend an MA where urgent action is required to protect public health without prior notification to the EMA, the other Member States, and the MAH, provided that these parties are informed no later than the following working day.[83]

Member States are also obliged to ensure that their national competent authorities cooperate with certain international bodies (such as the WHO and its Collaborating Centre for International Drug Monitoring) and with any other non-EU regulatory bodies with whom the Member State has formal arrangements in place for data exchange. Member States should also actively cooperate with the PRAC. The CHMP, through PRAC, plays an important role in this EU-wide pharmacovigilance activity by closely monitoring reports of potential safety concerns and, when necessary, making recommendations to the Commission regarding changes to an MA or the product's suspension/withdrawal from the market.

In cases where there is an urgent requirement to modify the MA of a medicinal product due to safety concerns, the CHMP can issue an 'Urgent Safety Restriction' to inform healthcare professionals about changes in the use of a medicinal product.[84]

At a national level, Member States should ensure that their pharmacovigilance system facilitates contact between the various national/regional pharmacovigilance centres and healthcare professionals. This can be achieved by, for example, publishing regular bulletins, offering lectures at scientific meetings, and providing information on requests in relation to pharmacovigilance matters.

§10.06 RISK MANAGEMENT AND EU-RMP

[A] Introduction

An EU-RMP is required[85] with applications for any product containing a new active substance, a similar biological medicinal product, or a generic/hybrid medicinal product where a safety concern has been identified with the reference medicinal

---

82. Article 107i(1) of Directive 2001/83/EC of the European Parliament and the Council of 6 November 2001 on the Community code relating to medicinal products for human use, as amended.
83. Article 107i(2) of Directive 2001/83/EC of the European Parliament and the Council of 6 November 2001 on the Community code relating to medicinal products for human use, as amended.
84. See EMA SOP/H/3052.
85. GVP – Module V – Risk – Management systems.

product. It is also required with an application for a paediatric-use Marketing Authorisation (PUMA) or an application involving a significant change in an MA (e.g., new dosage form, new route of administration, new manufacturing process of a biotechnologically derived product, or significant change in indication).

GVP guidance strongly recommends that the applicant enters into discussions with the relevant competent authority at an early stage about whether or not an EU-RMP must be prepared, and if needed what the content should be.

If an EU-RMP is required, it should be included with the application in a stand-alone format[86] to enable circulation to pharmacovigilance and risk management experts for their assessment. Where appropriate, the EU-RMP should be accompanied by other relevant documents, such as study protocols.

The aim of a risk management system is to ensure that the benefits of a particular medicine exceed the risks by the greatest margin as regards both individual patients and the target population as a whole. Obviously, while this may be achieved by either increasing the benefits or reducing the risks, by definition, a risk management system is concerned with the latter.

[B] Content of the EU-RMP

The EU-RMP is made up of Part I, Part II, and nine annexes.

Part I of the EU-RMP consists of the Safety Specification, which is where the MA applicant summarises the safety profile of the medicinal product at the particular point in time of its lifecycle, and a Pharmacovigilance Plan, which is based on the Safety Specification.

The Safety Specification should be a summary of any important identified or potential risks as well as the populations potentially affected by such risks and should highlight any outstanding safety questions that warrant further investigation. Essentially, a Safety Specification should assist the MAH and the competent authorities in identifying the additional specific data that should be collected.

Part II of the EU-RMP is completed where additional risk minimisation activities are necessary. This should contain both the routine and additional activities for each safety concern, as well as the place for efficacy data follow-up.

The annexes are included where applicable:

- Annex 1: Interface between EU-RMP and EudraVigilance;
- Annex 2: Current or proposed SmPC and package leaflet;
- Annex 3: Synopsis of completed and ongoing clinical trials programme;
- Annex 4: Synopsis of completed and ongoing pharmacoepidemiological study programme;
- Annex 5: Protocols for proposed and ongoing studies in the pharmacovigilance plan;
- Annex 6: Newly available study reports;

---

86. In Module 1, Section 1.8.2 of the application dossier (Common Technical Document)

- Annex 7: Other supporting data;
- Annex 8: Details of proposed educational programme, where applicable; and
- Annex 9: Efficacy follow-up plan.

[C] Monitoring of the Risk/Benefit Balance and Identification of Safety Signals

Once a medicinal product is marketed, reports of adverse reactions will follow, either reported directly to the MAH, the EMA, or the national competent authorities. The MAH and EMA/national competent authorities have the responsibility to carry out risk management in a structured and consistent matter.

During all periods of data gathering, it is primarily the company's responsibility to monitor the risk/benefit ratio of its IMP or its medicinal product. One of the key roles of the company's QP PhV is to regularly analyse the data for safety 'signals'. *Signal* is not defined in the legislation or guidance, but it has been defined as an early indicator or warning of a potential problem.[87] A signal is defined by the WHO as 'reported information on a possible causal relationship between an adverse event and a drug, the relationship being unknown or incompletely documented previously'.[88] The number of reports required to establish a signal depends on the quality of the information and the seriousness of the event, but would usually be more than a single report. If the reports are considered to be serious and of high quality, very few (such as between two and five) can be required to establish a signal.

Once a signal has been identified, other data can be examined in order to determine whether there is a relationship between the adverse event and the medicinal product, and the frequency with which it occurs. This may involve analysis of the background frequency of the event in a population not exposed to the drug compared to those exposed, for instance, using the UK's Department of Health-owned General Practice Research Database (GPRD).[89]

[D] Risk Management at the MAH's Initiative

Many MAHs market their products globally and therefore interact with many different regulatory agencies. Receiving a safety signal about such a product is a major concern for pharmaceutical companies, which may lead them to act without waiting for prior agreement of all the regulatory agencies where the medicinal product is authorised.[90]

---

87. *Dictionary of Pharmacovigilance* (Amer Alghabban Pharmaceutical Press, 2004).
88. *Safety of Medicines: A Guide to Detecting and Reporting Adverse Drug Reactions* (Geneva, Switzerland: WHO/EDM/QSM, 2002).
89. The General Practice Research Database has data on patients from the UK, France, Germany, Austria, and the US, and it has collected data since 1987; retrospective studies can be carried out; it is accessed via the MHRA.
90. Case C-120/97 *Upjohn Ltd v. Licensing Authority* established by the Medicines Act 1968 and others 51 BLMR 206 regarding withdrawal of Triazolam (Halcion).

Several lessons in coordination the withdrawal of a product can be learned from the example of Lipobay[91] (cerivastatin). Bayer withdrew Lipobay across Europe and the US in a staggered fashion throughout 2001. The withdrawal led to a global media furore, and while much of the attention was focused on Bayer, the European regulatory agencies were also subject to criticism for their poor communication and lack of coordination processes, which led to delays (see Case Study 2).

It was apparent after these events that the competent authorities of the EU were relatively slow to react where safety concerns for products authorised via the mutual recognition and national systems were concerned. Accordingly, in order to prevent this situation from happening again in Europe, the legislation now provides, 'the holder of a marketing authorisation may not communicate information relating to pharmacovigilance concerns to the general public in relation to its authorised medicinal product without giving prior or simultaneous notification to the competent authority'.[92]

[E] Risk Management at the EMA's Initiative

In 1997, the EMA developed a Crisis Management Plan for centrally authorised products. More recently, the Crisis Management Plan evolved into a 'European Risk Management Strategy.' A follow-on EU Regulatory System Incident Plan was introduced to implement a more global approach to crisis management. After a couple of pilot phases, the procedure is fully established and may be triggered by the EC, the competent authority of a member state or the EMA. The objectives of the EU Regulatory Network Incident Management Plan are:

- Monitoring of incidents and implementing routine measures to remedy situations (proactive incident management).
- To request further analysis under the form of the Preliminary Risk Analysis when additional methods are required.
- In the case of a confirmed crisis, to undertake necessary initiatives to manage and control the situations, with the implementation of urgent and coordinated actions within the EU Regulatory Network (reactive incident management).

In order to meet the above objectives, flexibility, clarity of roles, and a coordinated and focused response needs to be implemented.

The European Risk Management Strategy is aimed at providing a more coherent and proactive approach to the detection, assessment, minimisation, and communication of risks of medicines in Europe, irrespective of their licensing route.

In March 2014, the EMA published its first summary of a risk-management plan for a medicine pursuant to the revised legislation. This is related to the medicine Neuraceq and sets out what is known and what is not known about the medicine's safety and states what measures were to be taken to prevent or minimise consequential risks. The recent changes are designed to increase transparency and public access to

---

91. Known as 'Baycol' in the US.
92. Article 106a Directive 2001/83/EC.

information about medicines. It is expected that the contents of the RMPs will be consulted by stakeholders who may have a professional interest in the information, as well as any member of the public who has an interest, for whatever reason, in the profile of a medicine.

The European Risk Management Strategy has provisions to fund research, and the research priorities for 2009–2010, as recommended by the CHMP Pharmacovigilance Working Party include:

- research into the long-term effects on children and young adults treated with methylphenidate for attention deficiency hyperactivity disorder;
- long-term adverse effects of monoclonal antibodies;
- long-term adverse skeletal effects of biphosphonates;
- use of medicines in pregnancy;
- suicidal behaviour related to certain drug use (e.g., antidepressants, antipsychotics, varenicline, monteluklast); and
- safety aspects of antipsychotics in patients with dementia.

One of the main pillars of the European Risk Management Strategy is the EudraVigilance database, which contains information about authorised medicinal products in the EEA, and serious adverse reaction reports sent electronically by MAHs and national competent authorities. It is therefore important in signal generation. When there is a safety concern, it is also used to identify MAHs, of which there may be hundreds and their contact information. Consequently, EudraVigilance contributes to the protection and promotion of public health in the EEA and provides a powerful tool for the EMA and national competent authorities in monitoring the safety of medicinal products and in minimising potential risks related to suspected adverse reactions.

[1]   Case Study 2: Cerivastatin (Lipobay) Withdrawal

Lipobay was first approved nationally in the UK (as 0.1-mg and 0.3-mg tablets) and approved in other Member States in Europe (Austria, Belgium, Denmark, Finland, France, Germany, Greece, Iceland, Ireland, Italy, Luxembourg, the Netherlands, Portugal, Spain, and Sweden) under the mutual recognition procedure. The drug was first marketed in the UK in April 1997. Bayer later applied for and obtained an MA in the UK for a higher strength (0.8-mg tablet on 30 March 2001), which was launched in April 2001. In the period between the launch and Bayer's voluntary withdrawal, Bayer became aware of a rising incidence of fatal rhabdomyolysis,[93] with eighteen deaths being reported between September 2000 and February 2001. In April 2001, the Spanish competent authority raised concerns about the number of Spanish fatalities and commissioned a study. The results of the Spanish study confirmed those of a similar Bayer study concluded around the same time, holding that the risk of rhabdomyolysis

---

93. Rhabdomyolysis refers to myopathy (muscle weakness) combined with creatine kinase levels of more than ten times the upper limit of the normal range, with decreased renal function or acute renal failure.

was greatly increased when Lipobay was taken concomitantly with gemfibrozil (compared with Lipobay monotherapy). On 26 June 2001, an Urgent Safety Restriction was issued in the EU requiring the EU prescribing information to include a contraindication to prevent the use of Lipobay and gemfibrozil together and restricting the maximum dose to 0.4 mg. In parallel to this change, on 21 June 2001, Bayer voluntarily suspended the marketing and distribution of the recently introduced 0.8-mg tablet in the UK, doing the same in the US on 1 August 2001. On 7 August 2001, Bayer took the decision to withdraw all dosage forms of Lipobay from all markets except Japan,[94] posting a press release to this effect on the Internet the next day. Effectively, the competent authorities and healthcare professionals were essentially informed of Bayer's actions at the same time as the general public. Bayer neither mentioned a complete withdrawal nor did the data of which they were aware justify such a radical course of action. Taken wholly by surprise, the competent authorities and healthcare professionals involved were therefore left scrambling to provide answers to the questions raised by patients and the media.

Formal regulatory action in Europe came after the event, when on 19 September 2001, Portugal notified the EMA of a referral under Article 15a of Directive 75/319/EEC (now Article 36 of Directive 2001/83/EC) regarding all cerivastatin-containing medicinal products approved under the mutual recognition procedure. Portugal asked that a full assessment of the risk/benefit of cerivastatin be carried out because of concerns regarding possible rhabdomyolysis. The CHMP accepted this request, despite the voluntary withdrawal, as there was 'a public health matter to be discussed'. In its opinion of 21 March 2002, the CHMP concluded that the risk/benefit ratio was unfavourable, and that MAs should be withdrawn. This opinion was converted into a Decision by the Commission on 22 August 2002, over a year after the product had been withdrawn.

[F] Risk Management at National Competent Authorities' Initiative

The national competent authorities also monitor the safety information that they receive and historically store the information received from MAHs and healthcare professionals on their own databases. These are now linked to the EudraVigilance database. Some national competent authorities have their own teams of pharmacovigilance assessors who analyse the data, and national competent authorities of Member States can make an Article 31 referral to the EMA for medicines authorised through the mutual recognition and decentralised procedures.[95] While waiting for a decision, the national competent authority can, in exceptional cases, suspend the marketing and prohibits the use of the product in its territory.[96] At the end of the referral, the CHMP opinion will contain a recommendation on whether the MA should be amended,

---

94. Because gemfibrozil was not available in Japan at that time.
95. Article 31 Directive 2001/83/EC: Referral is used when a Member State considers that variation, suspension, or withdrawal of an is necessary for the protection of public health; the Member State refers this to the EMA.
96. Article 31(3) Directive 2001/83/EC as amended.

suspended, or withdrawn. This may be accompanied by a recommendation for changes to the SmPC. It can also contain some conditions for the MA to ensure that the safety of the medicine is monitored appropriately.

See Case Study 3 for an example of the use of this system.

[1]　Case Study 3: Bupropion

Bupropion was referred by Germany under former Article 36 (now Article 31 of the Directive 2001/83/EC, as amended) following reports of serious adverse reactions, including depression, thoughts of suicide, suicide, seizures, cardiovascular effects, and angioedema. It is marketed, among others, under the brand name Zyban and is authorised through the mutual recognition procedure, with the Netherlands acting as the Reference Member State. In its opinion published on 28 November 2002, the Committee for Proprietary Medicinal Products (forerunner to the CHMP) determined that the risk/benefit ratio was still positive but that national competent authorities were required to keep the product under regular review. Zyban is still considered an established treatment to assist with smoking cessation.[97]

§10.07　COMPLIANCE WITH PHARMACOVIGILANCE OBLIGATIONS

All aspects of clinical trials, including pharmacovigilance, are subject to Good Clinical Practice (GCP) inspections, which are covered in further detail in Chapter 4.

Post-authorisation pharmacovigilance obligations are subject to pharmacovigilance inspections. The pharmacovigilance inspections are carried out by competent authorities of the Member States to assess whether MAHs are complying with their pharmacovigilance regulatory obligations.

It is possible for GCP and pharmacovigilance inspectors to examine the same systems and share their information. For logistical reasons, the inspections may be run together, but they are two completely separate processes. Organisations that are not MAHs, but are involved in drug development and hold clinical trial authorisations, are not currently subject to pharmacovigilance inspections but are subject however to GCP inspections.

Regular inspections have been established for many years for GCP as well as Good Manufacturing Practice (GMP) and Good Laboratory Practice (GLP). However, post-authorisation inspections for pharmacovigilance are a relatively recent introduction. The UK competent authority, the MHRA, has taken the lead in these inspections.

The MHRA started conducting post-authorisation pharmacovigilance inspections in the UK on a voluntary basis in 2002; mandatory statutory inspections were introduced in July 2003. The MHRA programme used to require every MAH in the UK to have a regular inspection (three times yearly) of its pharmacovigilance system. In the first five years of the scheme, the MHRA conducted over 300 inspections. However,

---

97. CHMP/EWP/369963/05: Guideline on the development of medicinal products for the treatment of smoking, December 2008.

as the number of MAHs increased, the MHRA developed and adopted a more risk-based approach instead of timetabled regular inspections, therefore focusing on the MAH.

A system of national inspections is in place, and there is now coordination and cooperation between inspectors from different Member States. The EMA coordinates inspections for centrally authorised products with the CHMP and the Pharmacovigilance Working Party and the Inspectors' Working Party. The CHMP can request an inspection of pharmacovigilance while assessing an application, but note that this is usually a GCP inspection, which looks at pharmacovigilance in relation to specific clinical trials. The GCP Inspectors Working Group has issued guidance on coordination and reporting of such inspections.[98, 99] A risk-based approach to inspections is taken, meaning that priority is given to inspections where there are greatest safety concerns. A database is being developed to hold reports of inspections.[100]

The Ad Hoc Pharmacovigilance Inspections Working Group (PhV IWG) was established by the EMA in 2008 with a remit to focus on harmonisation and coordination at the Community level. The PhV IWG published its latest report in March 2014.[101] This report indicates that the CHMP requested nine inspections in 2012, and there were an additional twenty-six national inspections of sites connected with centrally authorised products the same year. In total, about 207 inspections were carried out in the EU/EEA in 2008, showing that the inspections requested by the CHMP are only a small proportion of the total inspections conducted.

[A] Legal Basis for Pharmacovigilance Inspections

The legal basis for the conduct of pharmacovigilance inspections is set out in Article 111 of Directive 2001/83/EC that provides that the competent authority of the Member State concerned shall ensure, by means of repeated inspections, and if necessary unannounced inspections that the legal requirements governing medicinal products are complied with. Moreover, Article 19(1) of Regulation (EC) No. 726/2004 provides that 'the supervisory authorities shall be responsible for verifying on behalf of the Union that the holder of the marketing authorisation for the medicinal product for human use or the manufacturer or importer established within the Union satisfies the requirements laid down in Titles IV and XI of Directive 2001/83/EC'. These Titles refer to Manufacture and Importation and Supervision and Sanctions, respectively. Title XI commences with Article 111 (above). The supervisory authorities for pharmacovigilance shall be responsible for verifying on behalf of the EU that the MAH for the

---

98. Procedure for coordinating pharmacovigilance inspections requested by the CHMP, EMEA/INS/GCP/393141/2005, Procedure no.: INS/PhV/1.
99. Procedure for reporting of pharmacovigilance inspections requested by the CHMP, EMEA/INS/GCP/391114/2005, Procedure no.: INS/PhV/3.
100. Work Plan for ad hoc pharmacovigilance working group (PhV IWG) for 2008 EMEA/INS/PhV/63112/2008, London, 20 April 2009.
101. Annual report of the Pharmacovigilance Inspectors Working Group 2013 (EMA/INS/PhV/732929/2013).

medicinal product satisfies the pharmacovigilance requirements laid down in Titles IX and XI of Directive 2001/83/EC.

More detailed guidelines are provided in the GVP.[102]

The role of the EMA with regard to pharmacovigilance inspections is set out in Regulation (EC) No. 726/2004, and it is also further described in GVP. The EMA is responsible for:

- the coordination of the monitoring of medicinal products that have been authorised within the Union and the provision of advice on the measures necessary to ensure the safe and effective use of these products, in particular, by coordinating the evaluation and implementation of pharmacovigilance obligations and the monitoring of such implementation;[103]
- coordinating as regards medicinal products for human use, the verification of compliance with the principles of GMP, GLP, and GCP, and the verification of compliance with pharmacovigilance obligations.[104]

GVP[105] states that 'In order to determine that marketing authorisation holders comply with pharmacovigilance obligations established within the EU, and to facilitate compliance, competent authorities of the Member States concerned shall conduct, in cooperation with the Agency, pharmacovigilance inspections of marketing authorisation holders or any firms employed to fulfil marketing authorisation holder's pharmacovigilance obligations.' Collaboration between competent authorities allows to maximise coverage and minimise duplication, knowing that the inspections will be routine inspections as well as targeted inspections to MAHs suspected of being non-compliant. Reports provided to MAHs of the outcome of the inspection will be used to improve compliance and may also be used as a basis for enforcement action. The scheduling and conduct of such inspections are driven by routine programmes and risk analysis. The inspection process described in GVP focuses on centrally authorised products but is stated to be generally applicable.

[B] Composition of the Inspection Team

The inspection may be carried out by inspectors in one or more Member States, and inspectors from other Member States may join the 'team'. Generally, the inspection is carried out by pharmacovigilance inspectors from the competent authority in whose territory the MAH's QP PhV is located. If the MAH has an additional facility in another Member State, it will be inspected by the competent authority of the Member State where the facility is located.

---

102. GVP Module I, Pharmacovigilance Systems and their quality systems.
103. Article 57(1)(c) of Regulation (EC) No. 726/2004.
104. Article 57(1)(i) of Regulation (EC) No. 726/2004.
105. GVP Module III 'Pharmacovigilance Inspections'.

Where an inspection is in relation to a specific product, it may involve or be conducted by staff from the rapporteur or co-rapporteur for centralised products, or the RMS for decentralised and MRP products.

The size of an inspection team varies from one to four inspectors and may include occasional observers. For a routine inspection of a small company, one or two inspectors would be on-site for two to three days; for medium-sized companies, two inspectors would be on-site for three to four days; and for large companies, two or three inspectors would likely be on-site for a week.

[C] Timing of Inspections

Routine inspections occur as part of the national competent authorities' obligations, although unlike GMP inspections, there is not a statutory period of time during which an inspection is required to take place. If an MAH has never been inspected, it should be anticipated that a routine inspection will occur in the near future. The focus of a routine inspection is to determine whether the MAH has the personnel, systems, and facilities to meet regulatory requirements. Once inspected, and depending on the outcome, the MAH can anticipate follow-up visits to see whether post-inspection commitments have been met.

Triggers for non-routine inspections can be related or unrelated to specific products' safety concerns or non-compliance with reporting requirements.[106]

Triggers unrelated to specific concerns include:

- the Marketing Authorisation holder has not previously been inspected;
- the Marketing Authorisation holder has placed its first product on the market in the EEA;
- the Marketing Authorisation holder has recently been involved in a merger or takeover process or the Marketing Authorisation holder has significantly changed its pharmacovigilance or related system (e.g., the use of a new database or contracting out of some of the activities).

A non-routine inspection will focus on the reason for the trigger. The concerns that may trigger a non-routine inspection include:

- delays in carrying out obligations or follow-up procedures identified at the time of the grant of the MA;
- delays in expedited (fifteen-day) or periodic reporting (i.e., delay in submission of the PSUR);
- incomplete reporting; submission of poor-quality or incomplete PSURs; inconsistencies between reports and other information sources;
- change in risk/benefit ratio; failure to communicate a change in risk/benefit ratio; previous inspection experience;

---

106. GVP Module III.B. 4.2.

- information received from other authorities; poor follow-up to requests for information from competent authorities; and
- communicating safety concerns to the general public without giving prior or simultaneous notification to the competent authorities or the EMA, and product withdrawal with little or no advance notice to the EEA competent authorities.

[D] Conduct of Pharmacovigilance Inspections

Other than unannounced inspections, the competent authorities will contact the MAH in advance to notify their intention to inspect. The MHRA will indicate to the MAH a date range for the inspection, which is negotiable to a certain extent. Once the MAH and the lead inspector have agreed on the date range, the MAH will be asked to complete and submit a Summary of Pharmacovigilance Systems (SPS). The SPS includes:

- contact details;
- information about the company structure and operating model for pharmacovigilance;[107]
- addresses of sites;
- details of what happens on each site in relation to pharmacovigilance;
- details of the computerised systems used in pharmacovigilance;
- training records;
- archiving;
- quality management system, including lists of standard operating procedures (SOPs), and may require that SOPs and other information are appended.

A deadline is usually set for the return of the SPS, which will be well in advance of the site visit. The SPS provides information to assist both the MAH and the inspectors when preparing for the site visit. This document is used to determine who will be interviewed, and an interview programme may be agreed on in advance to ensure the availability of staff. The inspection plan is then drafted, and logistical issues are addressed, which include the site(s) to be visited, the participants (company divisions/departments, contractors, etc.), and tele- or videoconferencing requirements. Additional documents, such as SOPs, PSURs, and contracts, may be requested prior to inspection.

The QP PhV is the key person at the MAH for the running of the inspection. To assist the MAH, the QP PhV will need a team of staff to obtain and copy documents and to escort the inspectors to wherever on-site they wish to go. A large conference room is usually available at the headquarters for the inspection, and it is where interviews of staff are conducted and where document reviews take place. Inspectors also review

---

107. Which gives background information about the organisation of the company in relation to pharmacovigilance, such as organisational charts.

computer systems in situ, such as medical information databases and pharmacovigilance databases.

At the end of the visit, the inspector will usually hold a meeting and review the main findings orally. The MHRA inspections are graded in one of three ways:

- 'Critical', meaning 'a deficiency in pharmacovigilance systems, practices or processes that adversely affects the rights, safety or well-being of patients or that poses a potential risk to public health or that represents a serious violation of applicable legislation and guidelines'.
- 'Major', meaning 'a deficiency in pharmacovigilance systems, practices or processes that could potentially affect the rights, safety or well-being of patients or that could potentially pose a risk to public health or that represents a serious violation of applicable legislation and guidelines'.
- 'Other', meaning 'a deficiency in pharmacovigilance systems, practices or processes that would not be expected to adversely affect the rights, safety or well-being of patients'.[108]

Once the inspection has been completed, the inspection report is prepared by the lead inspector, usually within thirty days of the site visit, or the last receipt of the requested documents. The inspection report only relates to findings made during the site visit.

The MAH is required to respond to the report within thirty days. In the UK, critical findings are reported routinely to the Pharmacovigilance Inspection Action Group (PIAG), which is a non-statutory and multi-disciplinary group that provides advice to different divisions of the MHRA on any non-compliance found.

[E] Common Findings of Inspections

The MHRA and other competent authorities present common inspection findings periodically to help MAHs improve their pharmacovigilance systems.

There were cases found by inspectors that were system failures or no system in place to report ICSRs or other safety information.

Some common system failures found at inspections are as follows:

(1) QP PhV:
- The QP PhV was not appointed until after the inspection had been announced.
- The roles and responsibilities of the QP PhV were not clearly defined.
- The interim measures for the QP PhV were inadequate (e.g., change of personnel or back-up for absences).
- Company failures existed in notifying the competent authority about details of the QP PhV.

---

108. MHRA website: Good Pharmacovigilance Practice.

- Commonly, the QP PhV does not have an adequate oversight of the pharmacovigilance system, does not have adequate access to medically qualified personnel, and may be lacking in training or experience.
(2) Signal Detection:
    - It is inadequate to look at signal detection only at the time of PSUR production (which can be every six months to up to every three years but was previously up to every five years).
    - Procedures in place did not represent what happened in practice.
    - Documentation relating to signal detection was not produced or retained.
    - Delays were found in reporting significant new safety findings from post-authorisation clinical trials and studies.
(3) Reference Safety Information (Information in SmPC):
    - Delays of up to a year in submitting variations to update the SmPC following identification of a new safety signal.
    - Delays in implementing changes following grant of such a variation in the package leaflet/patient information leaflet.
    - Incorrect version of the SmPC supplied to healthcare professionals.
(4) Processing of the Individual Safety Case Report or ICSRs:
    - Not all information about suspected adverse reaction was accessible at one point in the Community.
    - Lack of healthcare professional follow-up for some cases (e.g., consumer reports and pregnancy outcomes).
    - Late expedited reporting that is, outside the fifteen-day limit.
    - Lack of a quality control check on data entry.
    - Lack of a quality control check on decisions on whether the case needed to be reported on an expedited basis or not.
(5) Literature Searches:
    - Literature searches were inadequate in terms of the sources used.
    - The literature search was inadequate.
    - Local literature was not included.
    - Restrictions were evident in the language of the literature surveyed.
    - Lack of quality control.
(6) Quality Management Systems:
    - Quality management systems were either not in place, or were in place but were insufficiently detailed to ensure consistency.
    - In the worst cases, staff were not aware of the procedure.
    - Training (including refresher training) was found to be lacking or inadequate or was restricted to personnel working in the pharmacovigilance department only.
    - It is anticipated that companies self-regulate to a certain extent, including quality assurance audits, and in some inspections, these were either lacking or not extensive enough or did not include key functions (e.g., signal detection, SmPC updates) in their scope.
    - Inadequacies were present in the retention of records.

(7) PSURs:
- The production of PSURs was found to lack any procedure and was not in the required format or produced to a consistent standard.
- There was no validation of searches, and there was a lack of quality control.
- Some PSURs were incomplete, and there was no mechanism to track submission dates or late submissions.
- There was a lack of oversight by the QP PhV.

(8) Contracts and Agreements:
- Lack of contracts with third parties or contracts still in draft form existed.
- Where contracts exist, they are often lacking detail and are unclear as to the responsibilities of the parties and as to how information is exchanged and reconciled.

(9) IT Systems:
- Disaster recovery and business continuity plans were inadequate.

[F] Sanctions

GVP sets out the sanctions that can be brought for non-compliance. These include:

- education and facilitation – which involves informing the MAH of non-compliance and advising on how it can be remedied;
- inspection – inspection to determine the extent of non-compliance and re-inspection to ensure compliance has been achieved;
- warning – a competent authority may issue a formal warning;
- naming non-compliant MAH – a policy of 'naming and shaming', and making public a list of MAHs found to be seriously or persistently non-compliant will be considered by competent authorities;
- urgent safety restrictions;
- variation of the MA;
- suspension of the MA; and/or
- revocation of the MA.

In addition, the CHMP can impose the following regulatory sanctions: formal caution, which will be considered if the non-compliant MAH has admitted that a criminal offence has occurred; and prosecution in cases of serious or persistent non-compliance. Prosecution may be against the MAH, directors, managers, or the QP PhV.[109]

At the EU level, the Commission has the power under the financial penalties regulation (Regulation 658/2007) to apply financial penalties for the infringement of certain obligations related to centralised MAs. This includes obligations in relation to pharmacovigilance. The current obligations are:

---

109. CHMP Position paper on compliance with pharmacovigilance regulatory obligations, CPMP/PhVWP/1618/01.

- employing an appropriately qualified QP PhV;
- recording and reporting suspected serious adverse reactions;
- reporting suspected, serious unexpected adverse reactions;
- recording in detail all suspected adverse reactions and submitting PSURs;
- communicating information in relation to safety concerns to the general public; and
- collating and assessing specific pharmacovigilance data.

The financial penalties regulation has been amended[110] in light of the new EU pharmacovigilance legislation and the following obligations are covered by the infringement provisions:

- operating a comprehensive pharmacovigilance system including the maintenance of a pharmacovigilance master file;
- submitting a copy of the pharmacovigilance master file to the EMA on request;
- operating a risk management system; and
- performing post-authorisation studies and submitting them for review.

The regulatory authorities largely asked for clarification and for a broadening of the pharmacovigilance activities that would be caught by the financial penalties regulation.

The industry associations considered it was far too early for the financial penalties regulation to apply to the new pharmacovigilance provisions such as the maintenance of the master file. The plea from industry is to wait until there is more experience of the new systems. Also, industry bodies believe that it is incorrect to apply this regulation to Directive 2001/83/EC by cross-reference, as any infringement of this is governed by national laws.

The financial penalties that can be applied to MAHs under the financial penalties regulation are fines not exceeding 5% of the company's EU turnover in the preceding business year where the commission finds that the MAH has committed intentionally or negligently an infringement to its obligations in connection with the MAs listed in Article 1 of Regulation No. 658/2007 concerning financial penalties for infringement of certain obligations in connection with MAs (which includes the provisions that relate to pharmacovigilance). Where the MAH has not terminated the infringement, the commission may impose periodic penalty payments per day not exceeding 2.5% of the MAH's average daily EU turnover in the preceding business year.[111] Smaller fines (not exceeding 0.5% of EU turnover) apply to non-cooperation (e.g., non-compliance, supply of incorrect or misleading information, or non-compliance with a request). Periodic penalty payments per day not exceeding 0.5% of EU turnover may be imposed from the date of notification of the decision until the non-cooperation ceases.[112]

---

110. Regulation 2019/5 of the European Parliament and of the Council of 11 December 2018 amending Regulation No. 726/2004/EC.
111. Article 16 of Regulation No. 658/2007.
112. Article 19 of Regulation No. 658/2007.

In practice, most pharmaceutical companies will hold both centrally authorised and national MAs, and the same QP PhV will have responsibility for these, irrespective of the route of authorisation.

National sanctions, including criminal sanctions, may also apply. In some jurisdictions, the QP PhV can be criminally liable under national laws in situations of serious and persistent non-compliance. Examples of serious non-compliance are failure of the MAH to notify the competent authority about a change in the risk/benefit ratio, deliberate non-compliance, or a failure to improve systems after the identification of non-compliance.

§10.08 SUMMARY OF RECENT CHANGES

The recent legislation on pharmacovigilance comprises Regulation (EU) No. 1235/2010 of the European Parliament and of the Council amending, as regards pharmacovigilance of medicinal products for human use, Regulation (EC) No. 726/2004, laying down Community procedures for the authorisation and supervision of medicinal products for human and veterinary use and establishing an EMA. Regulation (EU) No. 1235/2010 entered into force on 1 January 2011 and has been applicable from 2 July 2012:[113]

- its aim is to reduce the number of ADRs in the EU through the collection of better data on medicines and their safety;
- rapid and robust assessment of issues related to the safety of medicines;
- effective regulatory action to deliver safe and effective use of medicines;
- empowerment of patients through reporting and participation; and
- increased levels of transparency and better communication.

The legislation impacts MA applicants and holders. It aims to:

- make their roles and responsibilities clearer;
- minimise duplication of effort;
- free up resources by rationalising and simplifying reporting on safety issues; and
- establish a clear legal framework for post-authorisation monitoring.

[A] Pharmacovigilance System Master File

The introduction of a pharmacovigilance system master file (PSMF), analogous to a site master file for a manufacturing site, which is open to inspection along with the premises, records, and documents, was intended to reduce the administrative burden on MAHs and competent authorities, by removing the need to submit detailed pharmacovigilance documents with each MAA and variations to update any details and

---

113. Article 4 Regulation (EU) No. 1235/2010.

facilitates the harmonisation and strengthening of pharmacovigilance activities. The specifications are set out in a new guidance document.[114]

Under the GVP rules, MA applicants and MAHs are required to maintain and make available upon request a PSMF. The specifications of the PSMF apply irrespective of the organisation structure of the MAH, including any delegation of activities or their location.

The contents of the PSMF must detail the global availability of safety information for medicinal products; in addition, the information on pharmacovigilance is not confined to local or regional activities. The PSMF's location must be within the EU, along with the residence and location where the QP PhV carried out his or her tasks.

PSMF requirements have applied automatically to medicinal products authorised after 2 July 2012. For those authorised after that date, requirements apply from either the date of renewal of their MA or, whichever is earlier, from 2 July 2015 for centrally authorised medicinal products or 21 July 2015 for others.

[B] Coordination and Inspection: PRAC

The way that competent authorities oversee the pharmacovigilance systems of MAHs has been rationalised, and the EU coordination of inspections has been increased. Pharmacovigilance inspection reports are now examined by the EMA, and Member States are obliged to apply penalties in cases of serious deficiencies.

The PRAC, in place within the EMA, is a committee providing pharmacovigilance assessments and recommendations on the safety of medicines at the European level.

Among other activities, the PRAC issues recommendations on risk management systems, the monitoring of their effectiveness, and the imposition of post-authorisation efficacy studies (PAES).

There is now a more risk-based approach to pharmacovigilance inspections, with better coordination and sharing of information at an EU and global level. Under the Regulatory Cooperation Agreement between the EU and the US FDA, pharmacovigilance inspection reports are shared following the putting in place of confidentiality agreements.

The pharmacovigilance legal framework allows the EU system for medicinal products for human use to be strong, reliable, and rational.

In particular it:

– clarifies roles and responsibilities for the parties concerned, including that of the supervisory authority for pharmacovigilance, which is the competent authority of the Member State in which the pharmacovigilance system master file is located[115] and which shall be responsible for verifying, on behalf of the

---

114. EMA 816573/2011 Rev 2*, GVP – Module II Pharmacovigilance system master file.
115. Article 1(8)(c) Regulation (EU) No. 1235/2010.

EU, that the MAH for the medicinal product meets the requirements laid down by Titles IX and XI of Directive 2001/83/EC.[116] The supervisory authority shall also be entitled, if deemed necessary, to conduct pre-authorisation inspections to verify the accuracy and successful implementation of the pharmacovigilance system described by the applicant in support of his application for authorisation;[117]
- introduced the PRAC, which shall be composed of members appointed by Member States who are competent in the safety of medicines including detection, assessment, minimisation and communication of risk, and in the design of PASS and pharmacovigilance audits, and of members appointed by the Commission, who are independent scientific experts, or representatives of healthcare professionals and patients.[118] The Committee is responsible for the provision of pharmacovigilance assessments, as well as a number of recommendations on the safety of medicines at the EU level;
- introduces the possibility for competent authorities to issue MAs, subject to the conditions set out by Articles 1(8) and 1(9) of Regulation (EU) No. 1235/2010;
- introduces the obligation for MAHs to keep and make available on request a Pharmacovigilance System Master File, that is, a detailed description of the pharmacovigilance system used by the MAH with respect to one or more authorised medicinal products;[119]
- removes the current routine requirement for PSURs for low risk, old and established products;[120]
- introduces specific provisions on the supervision of non-interventional PASS which are applicable, as to centrally authorised medicinal products, only to studies which have commenced after 2 July 2012[121] and, as to nationally authorised medicinal products, only to studies which have commenced after 21 July 2011;[122]
- simplifies adverse reaction reporting and provides a clear legal basis for the reporting of suspected adverse drug reactions, as well as providing a new ADR definition ('a response to a medicinal product which is noxious and unintended')[123] and stating that medication errors resulting in an ADR shall be reported.[124] Following a transitional period, all the information relating to suspected non-serious adverse reactions shall be submitted electronically to the EudraVigilance database;[125]

---

116. Article 1(9)(a) Regulation (EU) No. 1235/2010.
117. *Ibid.*
118. Recital 8 Regulation (EU) No. 1235/2010.
119. Article 1(1)(d) Directive 2010/84/EU.
120. Cf. new Article 107b(3) Directive 2001/83/EC as introduced by Directive 2010/84/EU.
121. Article 3(2) Regulation (EU) No. 1235/2010.
122. Article 2(2) Directive 2010/84/EU.
123. Article 1(1)(a) Directive 2010/84/EU.
124. Cf. Recital 5 Directive 2010/84/EU.
125. *See* new Article 107 Directive 2001/83/EC as introduced by Directive 2010/84/EU.

– strengthens safety, transparency, and communications about medicines, through the establishment of a European medicines safety web portal by the EMA.[126]

These major changes in the pharmacovigilance legislation were followed by further proposals.

On 10 February 2012, the Commission adopted proposals to amend Regulation (EC) No. 726/2004 and Directive 2001/83/EC further in relation to Pharmacovigilance, this is due to recent events, in particular the so-called Mediator case which indicated to the Commission that the pharmacovigilance system could be improved. This conclusion was drawn from a 'stress test' following analysis of the Mediator case.

The Mediator case concerned a drug marketed by Les Laboratoires Servier containing the active ingredient benfluorex which was indicated for diabetes but was also used for weight loss. It was supplied in France for thirty-three years and withdrawn in 2009 after the former French regulatory authority Afssaps (French Agency for the Safety of Health Products) took action when the drug was implicated in causing serious cardiac adverse effects notably to heart valves. The medicinal product was withdrawn from sale in Portugal and Luxembourg at the same time as in France, but it had been withdrawn from the market in Spain and Italy several years earlier. According to the French health ministry, at least 500 people died from heart valve problems after taking benfluorex. The number of serious adverse effects only came to light with the publication of the book '*Mediator 150 mg: How Many Dead?*' by Dr Irene Frachon in 2010. The head of Afssaps resigned in 2011 following an inquiry, and the offices of Afssaps were reported to have been searched in February 2012 in connection with the case. This case brought to light serious flaws in communicating safety concerns between the national authorities in Europe.

The pharmacovigilance amendments are aimed at improving transparency and ensuring that any voluntary action taken by an MAH to withdraw a product from the market is communicated to the EMA (under the regulation) and competent authorities (under the directive) two months in advance. Where the reason for withdrawal of the product is on safety grounds or lack of efficacy that is, the medicinal product is harmful or the risk/benefit ratio is not favourable, the EMA must bring the matter to the attention of Member States and vice versa.

[C] PASS and PAES

A PASS is a study carried out after an MA has been granted for a medicine. Its aim is to assist the EMA to assess the safety and benefit/risk profile of a medicine and to assist with decision-making. The particular aims are to:

– identify, characterise, or quantify a safety hazard;
– confirm the safety profile of a medicine; or
– measure the effectiveness of risk-management measures.

---

126. *See* new Article 26 Regulation (EC) No. 726/2004 as introduced by Regulation 1235/2010.

PASSs can be imposed or voluntary. When imposed, their completion is compulsory. They include studies which are specifically required pursuant to an MA granted under exceptional circumstances or other requests made by PRAC. PRAC will assess the study and include the results in its final report. In the spirit of increased transparency, the EMA publishes the protocols and abstracts of the final study reports on the European Network of Centres for Pharmacoepidemiology and Pharmacovigilance (ENCePP) website.

Alternatively, an MAH may choose to carry out or sponsor a PASS on its own initiative or pursuant to a request in a risk management plan.[127]

A PAES is a study which aims to clarify the benefits of a medicine, including efficacy in everyday medical practice. Guidance regarding the conduct of these studies is provided by the EMA (procedural advice). Additional scientific guidance has been developed by the EMA in cooperation with national competent authorities and other stakeholders.[128]

[D] Specific Conditions Relating to PhV affecting EMA

Additional measures relating to pharmacovigilance can be adopted by the competent authorities. In particular, those authorities may now issue an MA subject to one or more conditions specifically related to pharmacovigilance and lay down deadlines for the fulfilment thereof. These conditions may consist of including additional measures in the risk management system; conducting post-authorisation safety or efficacy studies; complying with stricter obligations on the recording or reporting of suspected adverse reactions. More generally, the competent authority may lay down 'any other conditions or restrictions with regard to the safe and effective use of the medicinal product'. This leaves it a relatively broad margin of discretion.

After the MA has been granted, the competent authority may also impose an obligation on the MAH to conduct post-authorisation safety or efficacy studies. If the same safety concerns apply to more than one medicinal product, the competent authority may, following consultation with the PRAC, encourage the performance of a joint post-authorisation safety study. The MAH is given the opportunity to present written observations in response to the imposition of the obligation, provided he or she so requests within thirty days of receipt of the written notification of the obligation.

[1] PSUR Requirements

An approach to PSURs that is more proportionate to the risks posed by medicinal products has been adopted. In particular, routine reporting is no longer required for certain types of 'lower risk' products. However, in the interests of public health, the

---

127. Further guidance is given in GVP Module VIII – Post-authorisation safety studies.
128. EMA/PDCO/CAT/CMDh/PRAC/CHMP/261500/2015 – Scientific guidance on post-authorisation efficacy studies.

competent authorities may require periodic PSURs for such medicinal products when concerns arise.

[2]   Set-Up of Interconnected Web Portals

Transparency has been improved with the establishment of the European medicines web portal maintained by the EMA. Indeed, the agency's website serves as the European medicines web portal for the transmission of information on medicinal products authorised in the EU and shall make public all relevant information in accordance with Article 26 of Regulation (EC) No. 726/2004, as amended by Regulation (EU) No. 1235/2010. This is linked to national web portals, the objective of which is to facilitate the exchange of, and access to, pharmacovigilance information (such as PSURs and their assessment reports) as well as the reporting through those web portals. The portal allows PSUR reporting to the EMA only, with national competent authorities being able to assess the information via the EMA). Whilst alternative reporting media must remain available, use of the web portal is compulsory as of 2016.

[3]   GVP Guidelines

GVP Guidelines have replaced Euralex Volume 9A. The GVP Guidelines are divided into sixteen modules and apply to all medicinal products, irrespective of the MA granting procedure.

The new pharmacovigilance rules tend towards increasing transparency and closer follow-up on the safety and efficacy of medicinal products marketed in Europe. The level of implication of all stakeholders increases, as well as accessibility to information. Overall, the collection of data and the assessment of pharmacovigilance issues are better coordinated, making the European pharmacovigilance system one of the most elaborate in the world.

Some measures increase the existing tendency of relying on the MAH in particular for innovative products. The competent authorities can now impose post-authorisation studies on MAHs, and only practice will show how frequently, and under which circumstances, this measure will be used.

New web portals dedicated to pharmacovigilance information should ensure a European pharma market in which all stakeholders will be more and better informed on pharmacovigilance issues.

§10.09   UK

[A]   Introduction

Generally, the post-Brexit regulatory regime applicable to pharmacovigilance in the UK continues to be broadly aligned with the EU framework discussed above. As of 1 January 2021, the relevant UK regulatory framework continues to be set out in The

Human Medicines Regulations 2012, as amended by the Human Medicines Regulations (Amendment etc.) (EU Exit) Regulations 2019 (UK HMRs). Pharmacovigilance is addressed primarily in Part 11 read with Schedule 12A of the UK HMRs. The UK HMRs continue to be based on the provisions of, *inter alia*, Directive 2001/83/EC (as of 31 December 2020) and as at the time of updating this chapter, there do not appear to be any substantial planned changes to the UK regime relating to this subject matter.

The MHRA, in its post-Brexit guidance relating to this topic,[129] further continues to reference the same EU guidance[130] for purposes of giving practical effect to the underlying legal provisions relating to the subject matter of this chapter. For the sake of brevity, we do not repeat the EU-based provisions discussed above in the Chapter as they would continue to apply in the UK, but we highlight the main practical local considerations and any specific exceptions and modifications to the EU guidance on good pharmacovigilance practices that apply to UK MAHs and the MHRA.

From a practical perspective, the post-Brexit MHRA guidance[131] provides clarity on the role of the MHRA; the various categories of Good Pharmacovigilance Practice (GPvP) inspections that may be conducted (for example, routine, triggered, pre-authorisation, and service provider inspections); the MHRA's interaction with other regulators in the EU or elsewhere; practical advice to MAHs to prepare for and deal with MHRA GPvP inspections, including the preparation of certain documentation for inspection; details regarding the conduct of GPvP inspections; the grading of inspection outcomes; etc.

During the period from 1 April 2020 to 31 March 2021, the MHRA's GPvP inspectorate conducted thirty-seven inspections of thirty-six MAHs. Five inspections were triggered to assess the resolution of critical findings from previous inspections, sixteen were triggered due to intelligence received, and sixteen were scheduled and conducted in line with the routine national inspection schedule based on an updated risk-based methodology. As part of those routine inspections, five were of MAHs that had never before been inspected by the MHRA (initial inspections), whilst the remaining eleven inspections were routine re-inspections of MAHs. All inspections for this reporting period were conducted remotely due to the impact of the COVID-19 pandemic.[132]

The (EU) GVP referenced above in this Chapter continue to apply in the UK for the most part. The MHRA has published guidance[133] that describes in granular detail the aspects of the EU guidance on GVP that no longer apply to the MHRA and UK MAHs

---

129. Available at https://www.gov.uk/government/collections/good-pharmacovigilance-practice-for-medicines-gpvp.
130. *See,* for example, https://www.ema.europa.eu/en/human-regulatory/post-authorisation/pharmacovigilance/good-pharmacovigilance-practices.
131. Available at https://www.gov.uk/guidance/good-pharmacovigilance-practice-gpvp.
132. *See* at https://www.gov.uk/government/statistics/pharmacovigilance-inspection-metrics-2009-to-present.
133. *See* at https://www.gov.uk/government/publications/exceptions-and-modifications-to-the-eu-guidance-on-good-pharmacovigilance-practices-that-will-apply-to-uk-mahs-and-the-mhra. The exceptions and modifications guidance note is intended to be read alongside the EU GVPs since it only refers to the exceptions and modifications that apply in the UK and is not a full GVP text. The document is based on the EU GVP guidance that applied as of 31 December 2020.

with effect from 1 January 2021 or are to be read subject to modification. The aforesaid modifications are limited primarily to: clarifying the relevance of guidance to products authorised for Northern Ireland or Great Britain only; clarifying references to the MHRA as opposed to EU 'competent authorities'; sections that are no longer applicable to the MHRA and UK MAHs are called out – these are typically the sections that describe the operation of the EU network; specific text is modified to ensure that it adequately describes the practical functioning of pharmacovigilance in the UK, including communication between the MHRA, UK MAHs, patients, healthcare professionals, and other concerned parties; etc.

As mentioned above, the processes and terminology remain, for now at least very similar to those of the EMA and EU, but it should be noted that there are some different requirements for products placed on the market in the UK with respect to Great Britain and Northern Ireland. For products authorised for sale or supply in Northern Ireland, EU pharmacovigilance requirements will continue to apply in addition to UK requirements. For medicines which are authorised nationally in the UK, however, an MAH is required to submit pharmacovigilance data to the MHRA, according to UK requirements, including:

- UK and non-UK Individual Case Safety Reports (ICSRs);
- Periodic Safety Update Reports (PSURs);
- Risk Management Plans (RMPs); and
- Post-Authorisation Safety Studies (PASS) protocols and final study reports, which are assessed in light of all relevant information UK clinical practice in order to provide the best support for patient safety in the UK.

[B] Submission and Receipt of ICSRs

All UK ICSRs (including those for Northern Ireland), whether serious or non-serious, together with serious ICSRs from other countries must be submitted via the new MHRA Gateway and/or ICSR Submissions portal.

Northern Ireland

MAH marketing products in Northern Ireland will also need to comply with EU notification standards into the Eudravigilance database (including serious reports from the UK and other countries and non-serious reports in Northern Ireland). Such cases have to be identified by using the country code 'XI' in the field primary source country for regulatory purposes. There is an option to use either the country code 'XI' or 'GB' as the first two characters of the worldwide case ID and the safety report ID.

For UK cases that relate to Northern Ireland which were initially submitted before 1 January 2021, the worldwide case ID should not be changed, but in line with GVP module VI guidance when sending follow-up reports organisations can change the safety report case ID if needed.

The country code 'GB' is used for all reportable SUSARs occurring in the UK. Although it is possible for organisations to use the country code 'XI' for SUSAR reporting, it will not be a requirement as reporting requirements between Northern Ireland and the rest of UK for clinical trial cases will not differ.

[C] Signal Detection

MAH signal detection systems should already have been set up to ensure compliance with requirements for cumulative signal detection across all available data sources. The MAH will not be obliged to conduct signal detection against the MHRA database, as it will make relevant UK data available for inclusion in those systems. As before, an MAH must notify the MHRA of signals arising from any data source, including standalone signals which the MAH has notified to the EMA or any that have been raised by the EMA.

PRAC signal assessment reports need to be shared with the MHRA once the PRAC recommendation is available.[134]

A new or changed risk comes to light that may necessitate a change to the terms of the MA and an application for variation of the terms of MA, unless the MAH considers that further analysis by the licensing authority is warranted. The MAH may request further analysis by the MHRA in relation to validated signals that cannot be refuted nor confirmed as new or changed risks by the MAH based on their assessment. If a PSUR is due to be submitted within six months of the completion of the MAH's assessment of the signal, the signal should be reported in the PSUR; a separate standalone signal notification is not required unless advised otherwise by the MHRA. If, however, the PSUR includes a signal that corresponds to an important risk,[135] the MHRA should be notified[136] at the time of submission of the PSUR. Refuted signals need only be reported in PSURs.

Where the MAH has been requested to assess a signal by another competent authority, the MHRA may require further analysis using the standalone signal notification form, or, a variation should be submitted or the signal reported in the PSUR as referred to above. In such circumstances, if the signal is included within the PSUR, the MHRA should additionally notify MHRA at the time of PSUR submission.

For products placed on the Northern Ireland market, the MAH must additionally report to the EMA any safety signals that are considered to comprise an 'emerging safety issue'[137] within three working days of learning of the issue.

[D] Risk Management Plans (RMPs)

EU versions of the RMP are still acceptable to the MHRA, except where specific UK-centric information has been requested.

---

134. Signal assessment reports should be submitted to safetyprojects@mhra.gov.uk.
135. *See* GVP Annex 1.
136. Via e-mail at signalmanagement@mhra.gov.uk.
137. *See* GVP-Module IX Signal Management.

[E] Periodic Safety Update Reports (PSURs)

PSURs submitted after 1 January 2021

EU versions of the PSURs are still acceptable to the MHRA, except where specific UK-centric information has been requested, or where there is UK-specific information relevant to the benefit/risk assessment.

While the MHRA may in due course develop different submission requirements and develop a list of UK reference dates for products authorised in Great Britain only, but in the meantime, the EU reference date (EURD) list should be followed for PSUR submissions to the MHRA, and the PSURs should be submitted to the MHRA at the same time as to the EU.

The content and format for all PSURs will remain the same as currently required in the EU, and the expectation is that the same form can be used for both submissions. Where an EU PSUR was submitted prior to 1 January 2021, it will not have to be resubmitted to the MHRA as such, although a copy may be requested.

PSURs for actives/combinations not currently on the EURD list and therefore not subject to the single assessment process should be submitted at least once in six months during the first two years following placing on the market, once a year for the following two years, and every three years after that.

Where the EU assessment results in an amendment to the product information, the MAH must notify the MHRA[138] with a copy of the CMDh Decision or CHMP opinion as soon as available. The MHRA will use this information to avoid unnecessary product divergences but will notify the MAH within fourteen days if it has any further requirements in light of the information submitted. This timescale is dependent on the MAH submitting information in a timely way.

The MHRA has developed a submission portal for PSURs and has set out detailed requirements for submission and the costs of the same.[139]

PSURs for products authorised in the UK will need to be submitted to the MHRA via the submission portal, but where the product is authorised in Northern Ireland, the PSUR will also be submitted to the EMA via the EU PSUR repository. PSURs for products authorised via an EU MA (CAP) which will apply directly in Northern Ireland need only be submitted to the EU PSUR repository.

Information regarding the informal PSUSA follow-up procedure will continue to be submitted to MHRA in the normal way (i.e., via CESP not the MHRA submission portal). Outcomes should be implemented via the same type of variation procedure as in the EU and where the MHRA have additional requirements the MHRA will inform the MAH.

PSURs submitted before 1 January 2021

Where the assessment was concluded but the outcome not implemented before 1 January 2021, the MHRA will take the necessary steps to implement the outcome.

---

138. Via e-mail at safetyprojects@mhra.gov.uk.
139. Register to make submissions to the MHRA - GOV.UK (www.gov.uk).

[F] Post Authorisation Safety Studies (PASS)

PASS protocols and results submitted after 1 January 2021

PASS Protocols

For non-interventional PASS where the study is a condition of the UK MA, the draft protocol shall be submitted to the MHRA prior to the start of the study. Where the MA applies in Northern Ireland, the draft study protocol should also be submitted to the PRAC; unless it relates to a study that is only to be conducted in the UK at the request of the MHRA (in which case the protocol should only be submitted to the MHRA). The MHRA will assess the protocol for any studies which is a condition of a GB MA or a UK MA, where the study is to be conducted in the UK at the request of the MHRA, and will notify the MAH of the outcome within sixty days.

Where the PASS is a condition of the MA, any significant amendments[140] to the draft protocol should also be submitted to the MHRA and where the MA applies in Northern Ireland additionally to the PRAC unless the study is only being conducted in the UK at the request of the MHRA.

There is no specific requirement to submit draft protocols for PASS which is not a condition of the MA but a requirement of the RMP (category 3). The MHRA may request submission of a PASS protocol even where there is no specific requirement to do so, if the MHRA considers that an assessment is required.

PASS Results

Final study reports for non-interventional PASS, whether voluntary or conditions, involving collection of safety data from patients/healthcare professionals shall be submitted to the MHRA no later than twelve months from the end of data collection.

Where the MHRA has made the provision of an interim report, this must be submitted to the MHRA. Interim reports for PASS which are a condition of the MA and all final study report for non-interventional PASS, where the MA applies in Northern Ireland, the study report should also be submitted to the Pharmacovigilance Risk Assessment Committee (PRAC) (unless the study was only conducted in the UK and not at the request of PRAC)

Submission and fees

Imposed PASS that are conditions of the MA (category 1 and 2 studies)

---

140. See Good Vigilance Practice Module VIII for definition.

Protocol and final study reports are to be submitted to PRAC and MHRA as required. The protocol and final study report should be submitted to the MHRA using a Type II (standard) variation procedure (classification C.I.13) with the corresponding fee of GBP 734.

Where the PASS is to be conducted only in the UK, or relates to a product authorised only in Great Britain and the protocol and final study report have not been submitted to the PRAC, the protocol and final study reports should be submitted to the MHRA via a Type II (complex) variation procedure (classification C.I.13) with the corresponding fee of GBP 8,309. Significant amendments to study protocols and interim study reports for categories 1 and 2 PASS should be submitted to the MHRA as post-authorisation measures/commitments via the information update route and will not incur a fee.

Ongoing issues regarding PASS protocols after 1 January 2021

Where the EU PRAC (Pharmacovigilance Risk Assessment Committee) either endorsed a draft study protocol or made a substantial amendment to a draft protocol before 1 January 2021, the MHRA will accept the draft or the amended draft study protocol but may request that further information.

A non-interventional PASS which was proposed or imposed but the draft protocol was not endorsed prior to 1 January 2021, the assessment will be concluded by the PRAC but any information required by the PRAC, together with any information required by the MHRA regarding the protocol, should be submitted directly to the MHRA.

This must happen even if the information was submitted via the EU procedure prior to 1 January 2021.

[G] Safety Referrals

Where a procedure was started but not finished by 1 January 2021, the procedure will follow the usual process but with all information should be submitted to the MHRA. The MHRA will take steps to implement any final decision which was concluded prior to 1 January 2021 but not implemented.

UK products for sale in Northern Ireland will from 1 January 2021 continue to be part of the EU procedure in respect of Northern Ireland and will be subject to the scientific opinion and Commission Decisions or CMDh Decisions.

If the MA is for GB only and the outcome of an EU referral is to be reflected in the MA, the MAH should submit a Type II variation application together with all relevant documentation regarding the referral, which will be assessed by the MHRA, taking into account the EU decision, to determine the necessary updates to the product information.

[H] Major Safety Reviews

A major safety review may be implemented by MHRA to review any medicines or classes of medicines for sale in the UK, to enable MHRA to assess the available data and consider what regulatory action may be needed. The initiation of the review will be publicly announced, together with the reasons for it, the affected products, and the likely timescale. The MAH will also be so notified.

The initial correspondent will be the Qualified Person for Pharmacovigilance (QPPV) but different or additional contacts can be nominated. The MHRA will report the outcome of the review and any remedial actions, such as changes to product information.

A major safety review will incur the following fees for assessment:

- GBP 51,286, where one or two active ingredients, or combinations of active ingredients, are included
- GBP 59,595, where three active ingredients, or combinations of active ingredients, are included
- GBP 67,904, where four active ingredients, or combinations of active ingredients, are included
- GBP 76,213, where five or more active ingredients, or combinations of active ingredients, are included

Where the review relates to two or more authorisations, the fee will be divided by the number of authorisations forming part of the review.

[I] Post-authorisation Measures (PAMs)

Post-authorisation measures and commitments including specific obligations, in place on 1 January 2021 shall remain unaffected. For MAs granted via the reliance route after 1 January 2021 all post-authorisation measures and commitments agreed for the EU MA will also apply. Standalone PAMs should be submitted as a post-authorisation commitment via the MHRA portal using the information update route. The nature of the PAM should be clearly stated in the cover letter. Where data relating to a PAM was submitted before 1 January 2021, a copy of the application should be included in the data submission package for converted EU MAs.

Where your evaluation of data supporting a MEA or LEG recommends that an update to the product information is required, this should be submitted via a Type II variation application.

[J] **Implementation of Outcomes of EU Referrals and Procedures Concerning PSURs, PASS, Signal Assessments and PAMs**

MAH's should continue to monitor the EMA website and implement the outcomes from EU decisions as appropriate, taking particular care to deal with issues that might affect Northern Ireland.

For GB-only MAs, the expectation is that you will follow EU outcomes and make the same changes to the GB-only MA that are made to the corresponding EU MA. In order to do so you will need to submit the corresponding procedure to the MHRA. Where the MHRA assessment results in additional UK-specific requirements, we will contact MAHs directly before or shortly after (within fourteen days) the publication of the EU outcome. However, where necessary data, as outlined above, has not been provided, this may lead to a delay in us contacting you regarding UK specific requests.

[K] **Requirements for MAs Granted via the Unfettered Access route**

Where an MAH holds an MA granted via the unfettered access route, all pharmacovigilance obligations continue to apply and all new information that may impact on the terms of the MA and/or impact on the balance of benefits and risk of the product must be provided to ensure the safety of British patients This information includes information from clinical trials and data on the use of the product outside the terms of the MA.

[L] **Submitting ICSRS**

MHRA reports of all serious suspected adverse reactions that occur in the UK and other countries, and all non-serious suspected adverse reactions that occur in the UK via the MHRA Gateway and/or ICSR submissions portal.

[M] **Provision of Other Pharmacovigilance Data**

PSURs shall be submitted to the MHRA portal. The MHRA will accept copies of the PSUR submitted to the EU in line with the frequency set by the EU.

All other pharmacovigilance data submitted to the EU, including RMPs, PASS protocols, and final study reports etc. should also be submitted to the MHRA, and we will accept copies of the same information submitted to the EU.

§10.10 GUIDELINES/PUBLICATIONS

- Alghabban, Amer. *Dictionary of Pharmacovigilance*. Pharmaceutical Press, 2004. ISBN 9780853695165.
- Annual report of the ad hoc pharmacovigilance inspectors working group 2008, EMEA/INS/PhV/114151/2009.

- CIOMS. 'International Reporting of Adverse Drug Reactions.' Final Report of the CIOMS Working Group. Geneva, Switzerland: WHO, 1990. Corresponds to ICH report E2A Guidance document.
- CIOMS II. Working Group II CIOMS report for aggregated safety information (1989–1991). Corresponds to ICH report E2C Guidance document.
- ENTR/CT4 Revision 1, Detailed guidance on the European database of SUSARs (EudraVigilance – Clinical Trials Module) (April 2004); ENTR/CT3 Revision 2, Detailed guidance on the collection, verification and presentation of adverse reaction reports arising from clinical trials on medicinal products for human use (April 2006).
- *Good Pharmacovigilance Practice Guide*, published by and available from Pharmaceutical Press. ISBN/ISSN 9-78-085369834-0.
- Guideline on the development of medicinal products for the treatment of smoking, CHMP/EWP/369963/05, December 2008.
- MHRA Website: Freedom of Information request 06/099 (8 May 2006), <www.heads.medagencies.org>.
- MHRA: Investigations into adverse incidents during clinical trials of TGN1412.
- Pandemic pharmacovigilance weekly update, EMEA/984681/2009.
- *Safety of Medicines. A Guide to Detecting and Reporting Adverse Drug Reactions*. WHO/EDM/QSM 2002.2. Geneva, Switzerland: WHO, 2002.
- The European Commission. 'Strengthening Pharmacovigilance to Reduce Adverse Effects of Medicines', 10 December 2008.
- The Rules Governing Medicinal Products in the European Union. GVP, Pharmacovigilance for Medicinal Products for Human Use.
- The Rules Governing Medicinal Products in the European Union. Volume 9B, Guidelines on Pharmacovigilance of Veterinary Medicinal Products.
- Exceptions and modifications to the EU guidance on good pharmacovigilance practices that apply to UK MAHs and the MHRA - GOV.UK (www.gov.uk)

CHAPTER 11
Variations to Marketing Authorisations

Alexandre Vuchot, Johanna Harelimana, Nour Saab & Phillipus Putter*

§11.01 REASON FOR VARIATIONS

Throughout the life of a medicinal product, the marketing authorisation holder (MAH) is required to take into account technical and scientific progress and to make any amendments to the marketing authorisation (MA) that may be required. MAHs also have the option of altering or improving the product or the manufacturing process on their own initiative, or adding additional safeguards to the use of the product. All these changes impacting the terms of an MA, that might not only be purely administrative but also more substantive, are called 'variations'. A notification or variation application is needed where any change is proposed either to the product or to an aspect of the manufacturing process (which includes dividing up, packaging, or presentation of the product). Any changes other than to the labelling or the package leaflet must be approved by the competent authority, although the assessment level will vary depending on the Member States' competent authorities concerned as some of them tend to have a more relaxed approach regarding the most straightforward variations.

The system was substantially overhauled in 2008 with the Commission Regulation (EC) 1234/2008 of 24 November 2008 concerning the examination of variations to the terms of MAs for medicinal products for human use and veterinary medicinal products (herein the 'Variations Regulation'). The main purpose was to reflect the practical experience gained under the previous regulations to establish a simpler, clearer, and more flexible legal framework.[1] The basic principle of the current regulatory framework is to ensure that the evaluation procedure is adapted to the level of risk to public or animal health and the impact on the quality, safety, and efficacy of

---

* The authors wish to acknowledge *Tasmina Goraya*, the author of the earlier edition of this chapter.
1. Recital (1) of Regulation (EC) 1234/2008.

the medicinal products concerned, bearing in mind the limited capacity of the EU authorities to cope with the increased regulatory workload. While a risk-based approach was already in place under the previous regulatory framework, additional flexibility was proved to be necessary to fill gaps existing in the previous legislation.

[A] Changes Not Requiring a Variation

Pure labelling and package leaflet changes that are not connected with the summary of product characteristics (SmPC) do not need to go through the procedures of the Variations Regulation. Instead, they need to be submitted to the relevant competent authority. In the absence of objection raised within ninety days, the change can be implemented by the applicant.[2] Such changes would be, for example, a change of the local representative or minor change in the labelling, such as the change of abbreviation for the batch number.

Although these labelling and leaflet changes do not fall under the scope of the European Variations Regulation, they may nevertheless be assessed under national regulations.

However, where a variation leads to the revision of the SmPC, labelling, or packaging leaflet, this revision is considered to be part of that variation.[3]

[B] Variation Legislation

The procedure for variations to MAs is governed by Regulation (EC) 1234/2008 (the 'Variations Regulation'), which replaced Regulation (EC) 1084/2003 and Regulation (EC) 1085/2003 and came into force on 1 January 2010.

The Variations Regulation in its original form applied to MAs granted by the competent authorities of more than one Member State (i.e., in the context of a mutual recognition or decentralised procedure covering several countries) and to those granted centrally by the European Medicines Agency (EMA). After being amended by Regulation (EU) 712/2012,[4] the Variations Regulation also applies to variations to purely national MAs with effect from 4 August 2013.

Another amendment was recently implemented in the context of the public health emergency arising from the COVID-19 pandemic. Regulation (EU) 2021/756 of 24 March 2021 extended the specific derogations provided by Article 21 of the Variations Regulation with respect to human influenza to human coronavirus.[5]

Unless otherwise stated, references to Articles of the Variations Regulation in this Chapter are references to the Variations Regulation as amended by Regulation (EU) 712/2012 and Regulation (EU) 2021/756.

---

2. Directive 2001/83/EC, Article 61(3).
3. Variations Regulation, Article 6.
4. Commission Regulation (EU) No. 712/2012 of 3 August 2012 amending Regulation (EC) No 1234/2008.
5. Commission Delegated Regulation (EU) 2021/756 of 24 March 2021 amending Regulation (EC) No. 1234/2008.

§11.02 CLASSIFICATION OF CHANGES

There are three main types of variations: Types IA, IB, and Type II. Other categories of variations include extensions and urgent safety restrictions.

Since the distinction between Type IA and IB makes a large difference in the procedure that needs to be followed, the European Commission (Commission) adopted Guidelines on the variation categories in December 2009 to facilitate the interpretation and application of the Variations Regulation. Article 4(2) of the Variations Regulation mandates the Commission to update the Guidelines regularly, and new Guidelines were adopted in May 2013 (the 'Variations Guidelines').[6]

The Variations Guidelines provide procedural guidance on the handling of all types of variations to MAs granted under (i) the mutual recognition procedure, (ii) purely national measures, (iii) centralised procedure, and certain special procedures that apply to extensions to MAs, urgent safety restrictions, and the work-sharing procedure. Annex to these Guidelines is divided into four chapters, classifying variations related to:

(1) Administrative changes;
(2) Quality changes;
(3) Safety, Efficacy and Pharmacovigilance changes; and
(4) Specific changes in Plasma Master Files and Vaccine Antigen Master Files.

Annex to the Guidelines provides detailed guidance on how variations are classified, but it does not deal with classification of extensions as they are listed in Annex I of the Variations Regulation.

The Variations Guidelines replace the detailed list set out in the old Regulations. As a result, the Commission has greater flexibility to alter the classifications without having to procure primary legislation by updating the Guidelines pursuant to Article 4(2) of the Variations Regulation.

The requirements and procedures for each type of variation are discussed in more detail in this Chapter.

[A] Types IA and IB

[1] Type IA

Type IA variations are minor changes that have no impact, or only a minimal impact, on the quality, safety, or efficacy of the medicinal product concerned.[7] These do not require prior authorisation, but a 'Do and Tell' procedure applies, under which the change can be implemented before notification.

---

6. https://eur-lex.europa.eu/LexUriServ/LexUriServ.do?uri=OJ:C:2013:223:FULL:EN:PDF OJ C 223, 2.8.2013, pp. 1–79.
7. Variations Regulation, Article 2(2).

The kinds of changes in this category are listed in Annex II (1) of the Variations Regulation. Specifically:

- changes of a purely administrative nature to the identity and contact details of the MAH or the manufacturer or supplier of any starting material, reagent, intermediate, active substance used in the manufacturing process or finished product;
- the deletion of a manufacturing site, including for an active substance, intermediate or finished product, packaging site, manufacturer responsible for batch release, site where batch control takes place;
- minor changes to an approved physiochemical test procedure, where the updated procedure is demonstrated to be at least equivalent to the former test procedure, appropriate validation studies have been performed and the results show that the updated test procedure is at least equivalent to the former;
- changes made to specifications of the active substance or of an excipient in order to comply with an update of the relevant monograph of the European pharmacopoeia or of the national pharmacopoeia of a Member State, where the change is made exclusively to comply with the pharmacopoeia and the specifications for product-specific properties are unchanged;
- changes in the packaging material provided this is not in contact with the finished product and it does not affect the delivery, use, safety, or stability of the medicinal product; and
- tightening of specification limits, where the change is not a consequence of any commitment from previous assessment to review specification limits and does not result from unexpected events arising during manufacture.

Only six categories of variation are listed, a substantial simplification from the former regime that set out forty-six to forty-seven specific changes and their categorisation. The objective was to develop a more principle-based approach to the classification of variations.

In general, the notification must be submitted simultaneously to the relevant authorities within twelve months of the implementation of the variation.

Some Type IA variations require immediate notification after implementation for the continuous supervision of the medicinal product concerned. They are known as 'Type IAIN'. Type IAIN variations are set out in tAnnex to the Variations Guideline. Examples of such variations include (among others) a change of the name and/address of the MAH, a change in the (invented) name of the medicinal product (for centrally authorised products), or a change in components of the flavouring or colouring system of the finished product.

[2] Type IB

Type IB is any minor change that is neither a Type IA or nor a Type II (see §11.02[B]) variation nor an extension.[8] Such minor variations must be notified before implementation, but they do not require a formal approval. A 'Tell, Wait and Do' procedure requires the MAH to wait for thirty days before implementing the change. In the absence of an unfavourable opinion at the end of this period, the notification is deemed accepted. The types of variations that fall within the Type IB category are provided in Annex to the Variations Guidelines. An example of a Type IB variation is an increase or decrease in the scale for a biological/immunological active substance production without a process change (e.g., duplication of line).

[3] Re-classification of Type IA and Type IB Variations

Where one or more of the conditions in Annex for Type IA variations is not met, the variation may be submitted as a Type IB variation unless the change is (i) classified as a Type II variation, (ii) pursuant to a recommendation under Article 5 of the Variations Regulation, or (iii) the MAH considers the changes to have a significant impact on the quality, safety, or efficacy of the medicinal product. The procedure set out in Article 5 of the Variations Regulation is discussed in detail in §11.02[D].

In addition, the competent authorities may reclassify a change that the MAH has identified as Type IB to be a Type II variation during validation of the notification, if in their view, the change may have a significant impact on the quality, safety, or efficacy of the medicinal product concerned.

[B] Type II

[1] Definition

Type II variations are any major change that is not an extension to the MA, and that may have a significant impact on the quality, safety, or efficacy of the medicinal product concerned.[9] Type II variations therefore require more careful regulatory assessment.

[2] Type II Categories

Annex II(2) of the Variations Regulation lists twelve kinds of Type II variations, of which four relate purely to veterinary products. The remainder include:

– addition of a new therapeutic indication or modification of an existing one;

---

8. Variations Regulation Article 2(5).
9. Variations Regulation, Article 2(3).

- significant modification of the SmPC due in particular to new quality, pre-clinical, clinical, or pharmacovigilance findings;
- substantial changes in the manufacturing process, formulation, specifications, or impurity profile of the active substance or finished medicinal product;
- change to the active substance of a seasonal, pre-pandemic, or pandemic vaccine against human influenza.

Furthermore, in point 2 of Annex II of the Variations Regulation the following point (l) is added:

(l) variations related to the replacement or addition of a serotype, strain, antigen or coding sequence or combination of serotypes, strains, antigens or coding sequences for a human coronavirus vaccine.

Any replacement or addition of a serotype, strain, antigen, or coding sequence or combination of serotypes, strains, antigens, or coding sequences for a human coronavirus vaccine is also a Type II variation.[10] In the case of biological medicinal products, all modifications to manufacturing process or site of the active substance are presently classified as Type II variations.

The Variations Guidelines provide in-depth information as to what will amount to a Type II variation.

[3] The International Council on Harmonisation (ICH) Design Space Concept

[a] Introduction

One category of variation in Annex II(2) list adopts the ICH concept of a 'design space', stipulating that any variation that relates to the introduction of a new design space or an extension of an existing approved one will be a Type II variation.[11] The design space for a product covers the combination and interaction of input variables and process parameters that have been demonstrated to provide assurance of quality.

The ICH Q8, Q9, Q10, and Q11 guidelines,[12] all of which had been approved by the EMA, propose the introduction of risk management and quality systems to facilitate the continuous improvement of manufacturing processes over a product's life cycle. This holistic approach is intended to result in quality by design (QbD), so that the current reliance on testing of end products can be reduced. Thus, information as to starting material variables and process variables is assessed as a package whose components' respective impacts on quality can be evaluated. The applicant and

---

10. Variations Regulation, Annex II(2)(l), introduced by Commission Delegated Regulation (EU) 2021/756 of 24 March 2021.
11. Variations Regulation, Annex II(2)(f).
12. *See* http://www.ich.org/products/guidelines/quality/article/quality-guidelines.html. Questions and answers relating to Q8, Q9, and Q10 are also available at http://www.ich.org/products/guidelines/quality/quality-single/article/q8q9q10-questions-answers.html.

regulator should both acquire a more continuous understanding of all aspects of manufacturing processes and controls that ultimately dictate product attributes.

[b] Process Analytical Technology (PAT)

An important component of the concept of QbD is the use of PAT in manufacturing or control processes. PAT is a system for designing, analysing, and controlling manufacturing through measurements of critical quality attributes of raw and in-process materials.
Appropriate monitoring tools incorporated in a process could result in continuous validation of a production process, reducing the requirement for validation testing of multiple batches. This technology is still at a relatively early stage of development. Nevertheless, any application for a variation of an MA relating to a process using PAT should identify that fact in accordance with the principles set out in the EMA PAT team's Reflections Paper of 20 March 2006.[13] The regulators' response in evaluating such an application is likely to be conditioned by the level of product and process knowledge that has been demonstrated.

[c] Quality Risk Management

Similarly, quality risk management systems used in a production process should be identified in any application for a variation with a summary of the methodology applied. This reflects the EMA's preference for a move in the longer term towards less regulatory oversight. Where a given product and manufacturing process have been designed such that parameters are continuously monitored, there is a sound scientific basis for accepting that any identified process change is not likely to have an impact on safety or efficacy.

Further guidance on the QbD concept is available on the EMA's website.[14]

[C] Extensions

A variation will be classified as an extension if it falls within Annex I of the Regulations.[15] Annex I sets out three main categories of extensions:

- changes to the active substance (except for (i) seasonal, pre-pandemic or pandemic vaccine against human influenza vaccine, (ii) replacement of a strain for veterinary vaccine against equine influenza, or (iii) a change of serotype, strain, or antigen for a human corona virus vaccine or (iv) a

---

13. EMEA/INS/277260/2005, available at http://www.ema.europa.eu/docs/en_GB/document_library/Other/2009/10/WC500004890.pdf
14. *See* http://www.ema.europa.eu/ema/index.jsp?curl = pages/regulation/general/process_analytical_technology.jsp&mid = WC0b01ac058006e00e.
15. Variations Regulation, Article 2(4).

veterinary vaccine against avian influenza, foot-and-mouth disease, or bluetongue);
- changes to strength, pharmaceutical form and route of administration (i.e., change of bioavailability, pharmacokinetics, strength/potency, pharmaceutical form, and route of administration); or
- changes specific to veterinary medicines to be administered to food-producing animals (change or addition of target species).

In these cases, the application is evaluated according to the same procedure as the initial MA to which it relates.[16] The extension can be either granted as a new MA or included in the initial MA to which it relates.[17] The Variations Guidelines provide further guidance on submissions of extension applications. In addition, specific guidelines have been introduced in 2003 and set out in a Volume 2C of the European Commission's Notice to Applicants[18] following the difficulties that occurred regarding the classification of extension applications (covered by Annex I) versus variations, particularly regarding the change to pharmaceutical form and strength (the 'Extension Guideline'). These guidelines aim to harmonise the interpretation throughout Europe and to help applicants to decide how a change should be treated

[1] Changes in Pharmaceutical Form

The Extension Guideline specifies that 'pharmaceutical form' is the combination of the form in which the pharmaceutical product is presented by the manufacturer (form of presentation) and the form in which it is administered, including the physical form (form of administration). If the physical form in which the product is supplied by the manufacturer differs from the form in which it is administered to or used by the patient, both elements of information need to be conveyed within the term. In addition, if the product has certain special characteristics that are relevant to its use, that information also needs to be included in the term.

Accordingly, a modified-release tablet is a different form from a prolonged-release tablet; a single-dose preparation is a different form from a multi-dose; and a spray contained in a spray pump is a different form from the same spray contained in a pressurised container. More complex forms such as pre-filled syringes or pressurised preparations may need more information to be provided about the container.

[2] Changes in Strength

Strength is the amount of active substance, and therefore may be expressed as a concentration, either per unit mass or volume, or as a percentage. It is not related to the

---

16. Variations Regulation, Article 19(1).
17. Variations Regulation, Article 19(2).
18. Guideline on the categorisation of Extension Applications (EA) versus Variation Applications (V). See https://ec.europa.eu/health/system/files/2019-08/v2c_ea_v__10_2003_en_0.pdf.

size of container, pack size, or other presentational characteristics, changes to which generally fall within the Type IA or IB variation categories.

[D]   Classification of Unforeseen Variations

The Variations Regulation recognises that not every possible kind of variation can be foreseen and categorised in its annexes, and so a mechanism is set out in Article 5 to enable a classification to be agreed between the EMA and the Member States' competent authorities. Article 5 provides that prior to submission of an unforeseen variation, the MAH may request a recommendation on the classification to:

(a) the EMA where the variation refers to an MA granted under a centralised procedure;
(b) the concerned Member States' (CMS') competent authorities, where the variation relates to a purely national MA; or
(c) the competent authority of the reference Member State (RMS), in other cases.

The recommendation must be delivered within forty-five days following the receipt of the request (which can be extended by a further twenty-five days if consultation with the coordination group of the competent authorities[19] ('Coordination Group') is required) and sent to the MAH, the EMA, and the Coordination Group.

Where a competent authority requests a recommendation on the classification of the variation from the Coordination Group, the recommendation must also be delivered to the competent authorities of all Member States.[20]

§11.03   SUBSTANTIVE REQUIREMENTS OF THE VARIATION APPLICATION

In addition to completion of the necessary forms and payment of fees, Type II variation applications will also require submission of any clinical or non-clinical data necessary to support the variation. The extent of the data depends upon the potential significance of the change's impact on the end product. This is an area under constant review and discussion, as the regulators seek to minimise the administrative burden of MA variations for relatively minor changes.

---

19. Established for the purpose of running the mutual recognition procedure under Article 27(1) Directive 2001/83/EC and Article 31 Directive 2001/82/EC, for human and veterinary medicinal products, respectively.
20. Variations Regulation, Article 5(1a).

[A] Variation Applications for Biological Medicinal Products

[1] Issues Arising in Relation to Biologicals

The PAT and QbD approach was extended in 2007 to include biological medicinal products as well as traditional small molecules. The regulatory issues are more problematic where the product is not a small molecule but an artificially produced version of a natural protein – a vaccine, peptide hormone, or enzyme, for instance. Given proteins comprise chains of amino acids, biological medicinal products can be hundreds of times larger than ordinary chemical molecules and may be thousands of times larger. Further, their biochemical activity may result not from the chemical formula that describes their component atoms, but from the three-dimensional shape of the molecule once it has been made.

There is so far no alternative to manufacturing these products on a commercial scale other than by having living cells synthesise them. Manufacturing processes include microbial cultures, mammalian cell cultures, and propagation of live agents in embryos or animals. Given the dependence of the manufacturing process on biological systems, there will be more variability in biological medicinal products than in small-molecule chemicals. For example, the host cell or organism may produce subtly different forms of the desired molecule through normal genetic mutation. Further, the choice of host cell or organism may affect the form of the biological medicinal product: the synthesis of proteins by bacteria and yeasts varies from mammalian cells.

Consistent process controls are therefore critical to the manufacturing of biological medicinal products. The choice of cell type, the growth conditions, and the extraction mechanism can all lead to variations in the final product that may be difficult or in some cases impossible to measure precisely with current analytical techniques. Incompletely synthesised molecules may end up in the final extract along with traces of the culture medium and random proteins leached from the host cells. Consequently, any process change, no matter how apparently minor, could lead to a significant change in the efficacy or safety of the final product.

[2] Regulatory Guidelines

A series of Guidelines has been issued on how to demonstrate comparability between biological products before and after any change has been made in the manufacturing process. These have been updated since they were originally released. The 'Guideline on similar biological medicinal products containing biotechnology-derived proteins as active substances: quality issues'[21] came into effect in June 2006, but a revised version

---

21. EMEA/CHMP/BWP/49348/2005, see https://www.ema.europa.eu/en/documents/scientific-guideline/guideline-similar-biological-medicinal-products-containing-biotechnology-derived-proteins-active_en.pdf.

of the Guideline took effect on 1 December 2014.[22] The companion Guideline 'on similar biological medicinal products containing biotechnology-derived proteins as active substance: non-clinical and clinical issues' has also been revised and replaced with effect from 1 July 2015.[23]

They address the concern, shared by all regulators worldwide, that any change to the process of production for a biological molecule can have a significant impact on its structure and hence therapeutic effects. Since it may not be possible to characterise a therapeutic protein completely, there is a significant issue as to whether a comparison can be made with sufficient accuracy to enable the regulator to approve the changed process.

[a]   Quality Guidelines

The quality guidelines address requirements regarding manufacturing processes, the biosimilar comparability exercise for quality, the choice of reference medicinal product, analytical methods, physiochemical characterisation, biological purity, and quality attributes for relevant specifications of the biosimilar.

The guidelines focus on the studies that an applicant will need to carry out and provide in support of the application to establish the quality, safety, and efficacy of the altered product. The data required will depend upon the complexity of the molecule concerned – the more complex and the more heterogeneous the end product, the wider the range of analytic techniques that must be deployed to give a reliable demonstration of the acceptability of the change. The variation application must contain characterisation studies to establish the structure and other characteristics and stability data. Although it may not be possible to give an assurance that all differences between the molecules have been identified, the applicant should be able to state that the analytical tools used are as likely to have detected any changes as any other analytical tools that could have been used.

Where a change is not expected to have any impact on the quality criteria of the product, the applicant must provide proof that the in-process control and/or release data found have not been modified as compared to those from the previous process. If, however, there is expected to be an impact on the quality of the product, then a full set of validation data demonstrating characterisation, batch-to-batch consistency, and stability will be required.

[b]   Safety and Efficacy Requirements

If the manufacturing change results in modifying the specification of either the active substance or the finished product, then it may also be necessary to demonstrate safety

---

22. EMA/CHMP/BWP/247713/2012 *see* https://www.ema.europa.eu/en/documents/scientific-guideline/guideline-similar-biological-medicinal-products-containing-biotechnology-derived-proteins-active_en-0.pdf.
23. EMEA/CHMP/BMWP/42832/2005 Rev. 1. *See* http://www.ema.europa.eu/docs/en_GB/document_library/Scientific_guideline/2015/01/WC500180219.pdf.

and efficacy. The particular concern is the potential unpredictable immunogenicity of a substance due to a change. The pre-clinical and clinical studies that might be required will depend upon the degree of knowledge and clinical experience concerning the molecule, the findings in the physico-chemical and biological comparability exercise, and the level of understanding of the molecule's mode of action. This is discussed in the Guideline on non-clinical and clinical issues. The more complex the process and the less understood the molecule's structure and mode of action, the more comprehensive the studies are likely to be required. Further, the product's posology can affect the potential for immunogenicity, and thus it will also be considered.

Non-clinical studies should be designed specifically to detect *differences* in response to the product and not merely the response as such. Both *in vitro* and *in vivo* studies may be required. Pre- and post-change products should be compared concurrently within the same study so that differences in reactivity can more readily be identified. Where an animal model is used, the study will carry more weight if the species is shown by the pre-change product to be a relevant model for man. Given the limited information available from existing analytical techniques, data from emerging technologies, such as genomic or proteomic microarrays, may be considered valuable despite the relative lack of experience in interpreting these new types of data.

Clinical studies that may be required include pharmacokinetic and/or pharmacodynamic studies. Where these studies cannot prove that the change has no impact on the efficacy and safety profile of the drug, additional clinical studies may have to be performed – or the decision not to do so must be justified. Like the non-clinical studies, the additional clinical studies should be designed to demonstrate comparability and not just the characterisation of the clinical pharmacology of the product. Absorption, bioavailability, and elimination characteristics need to be considered. The design of the trial, including selection of patient population, therapeutic indication, and endpoints, should aim to enable the detection of the smallest differences that may be relevant for the target population and should also be measurable with precision.

§11.04 VARIATION APPLICATION PROCEDURE

[A] Forms and Format

For each class of variation, there is a prescribed form that must be used for submission of the variation proposal to the competent authority or the EMA (as the case may be), along with the prescribed fee and any necessary data to obtain approval.

A different procedure applies for each class, subject to the possibilities of grouping applications (*see* §11.04[B]) and invoking the work-sharing procedure (*see* §11.04[C]). The detailed procedures for each case are discussed from §11.04[D] onward, although these are now considerably more similar to each other than they were under the previous system. The Variations Guidelines set out the format and form of documents to be submitted with the variation application.

Manufacturing variation applications should include all necessary information to enable the competent authority to assess the impact of any proposed change. The competent authority is expected to respond to such a request within thirty days, although in exceptional cases, the delay can be extended to ninety days. During this period, the competent authority may require further information about both the particulars supplied and the Qualified Person. The time limit ceases to run pending the applicant's provision of this data ('clock stop').

[B]   Grouping of Applications

The Variations Regulation simplifies the procedure for submitting multiple variations by permitting a single notification or application.[24]

[1]   Grouping of Variations Granted under the Mutual Recognition, Decentralised and Centralised Procedures

Variation applications may be grouped in the following instances where:

- all of the variations concerned are the same Type IA variations, and they affect one or several MAs held by the same holder, they can be submitted as a single notification in accordance with the procedure for Type IA[25] (set out below);
- several variations of the same MA are submitted at the same time, provided that the variations fall within the scope of one of the cases listed in Annex III;[26] Annex sets out fourteen different types of variation where this form of grouping may be permitted;
- the variations to be made to the terms of the same MA do not fall within the cases listed in Annex III, but where (i) the competent authority of the RMS in consultation with the competent authorities of the Member States concerned or, (ii) the EMA (in the case of the centralised procedure) agrees to the grouping of the variations in a single submission.[27]

Where the second and third situations apply, the submission must be made simultaneously to all relevant authorities according to the following procedure:[28]

- the Type IB procedure, if all the variations are minors and at least one of them is of Type IB;
- the Type II procedure, if at least one of the variations is of Type II and providing that none of them are extensions; and

---

24. Variations Regulation, Article 7.
25. Variations Regulation, Article 7(2)(a).
26. Variations Regulation, Article 7(2)(b).
27. Variations Regulation, Article 7(2)(c).
28. Variations Regulation, Article 7(2).

– the extension procedure, if at least one of the variations is an extension, then any other variations can be submitted as part of the same extension application.

In all other circumstances, individual notifications or applications must be submitted.

Further detailed operational guidance on the handling of variations is posted on the EMA website, including guidance entitled 'European Medicines Agency post-authorisation procedural advice for users of the centralised procedure' (Procedure Guidelines), which was last updated on 18 March 2022.[29]

[2] Grouping of Variations to Purely National MAs

The procedure for grouping of variations to purely national MAs is set out in Article 13d of the Variations Regulation, which basically mirrors the same procedure as discussed in §11.04[B][1]. Grouping is permitted if:

– all of the variations concerned are the same Type IA variations, and they affect one or several MAs held by the same holder, they can be submitted as a single notification in accordance with the procedure for Type IA;
– several variations of the same MA are submitted at the same time, provided all the variations fall within the scope of one of the cases listed in Annex III;
– if the competent authority agrees, a single submission can be made if the same variations not covered in (1) or (2) above apply to one or more MAs owned by the same holder.

In all other circumstances, individual notifications or applications must be submitted.

[C] Work-Sharing Procedure

The MAH has the option of applying for a single coordinated assessment of a Type IB or Type II variation or group of variations, affecting several MAs.[30] Provided that none of the variations are classified as an extension, the variations below may be subject to the same work-sharing procedure:

– for MAs granted in accordance with the mutual recognition, decentralised or centralised procedures, where a Type IB, a Type II, or a group of variations

---

29. EMEA-H-19984/03Rev.981 *See* https://www.ema.europa.eu/en/documents/regulatory-procedural-guideline/european-medicines-agency-post-authorisation-procedural-advice-users-centralised-procedure_en.pdf.
30. Variations Regulation, Article 20.

permitted under Article 7(2)(b) or (c) of the Variations Regulation (*see* §11.04[B][1] above) relate to several MAs owned by the same holder;[31] and
- for purely national MAs where a Type IB, a Type II or a group of variations permitted under Article 13d(2)(b) or (c) of the Variations Regulation relate to (i) several MAs owned by the same holder or (ii) one MA owned by the same holder in more than one Member State.

However, the reference authority or the competent authority (in the case of purely national MAs) can refuse to process a submission under the work-sharing procedure where (i) the same changes to different MAs require individual supportive data to be submitted for each medicinal product or (ii) a separate product-specific assessment is required.[32]

If the MAH elects this approach, it must submit to all relevant authorities[33] an application that contains all information required for that class of variation as listed in Annex IV[34] and indicates a preferred reference authority. The Coordination Group will then choose a reference authority. The reference authority may, in practice, be the EMA in the case of MAs granted through the centralised procedure or be a team of two reference authorities if the chosen reference authority has not previously granted an MA for all the medicinal products affected by the application.

The reference authority will then prepare an opinion on the application, including (if necessary) requests for supplementary information from the holder and/or from the other Member States concerned. The opinion is issued within one of the following periods:

- in the case of Type IB or Type II variations, within sixty days of the acknowledgement of receipt of a valid application (which can be reduced on account of urgency or extended to ninety days insofar as it applies to a change to or addition of a therapeutic indication or certain groupings of variations); or
- where the variation falls within Annex V(2) of the Variations Regulation, within sixty days of the acknowledgement of receipt of a valid application. Annex V(2) applies to certain veterinary variations.[35]

Where the reference authority is the EMA, its opinion must be transmitted to the applicant and the Member States together with its assessment report. Where the

---

31. The Coordination Group for Mutual Recognition and Decentralised Procedures – Human has published a best practice guide on work-sharing at: https://www.hma.eu/fileadmin/dateien/Human_Medicines/CMD_h_/procedural_guidance/Variations/CMDh_297_2013_Rev.29_05_2 022_-_BPG_on_Variation_WS_-_Chapter_7.pdf
32. Variations Regulation, Article 20(1).
33. Where the MA is granted under the centralised procedure, the reference authority will be the EMA. In all other cases, the reference authority will be the competent authority of the Member State concerned chosen by the coordination group, taking into account a recommendation of the MAH (Variations Regulation, Article 20(2)).
34. Variations Regulation, Article 20(3).
35. A change or addition of a non-food producing target species; replacement or variation of the active ingredient for veterinary vaccines against avian influenza, foot-and-mouth disease or bluetongue; and the replacement of a strain for veterinary vaccines against equine influenza.

outcome of the assessment is favourable and the variation affects the terms of the Commission decision granting the MA, the EMA's opinion must also be provided to the Commission.[36] The Commission must then amend the decision accordingly.[37] The Member States concerned have sixty days following the receipt of the final opinion of the EMA to approve the opinion and amend the relevant MAs where necessary.[38]

Where the reference authority is a competent authority of a Member State,[39] it must send the opinion to the holder and to all other relevant authorities. In general terms, the relevant authorities must approve the opinion within thirty days from receipt. The relevant MAs are then amended within thirty days following the approval of the opinion.

[D] Products Authorised Through Mutual Recognition[40]

[1] Type IA

Where the product has originally been authorised through the mutual recognition procedure, the RMS and CMSs must be notified simultaneously of any variation. Ordinarily, the notification should be submitted within twelve months after the implementation of the variation, although where continuous supervision of the medicinal product is required, the submission must be done immediately after the implementation. Either way, no notification is needed before implementing the change.[41] The documentation (if any) to be submitted in support of the notice is set out in the Variations Guidelines.

The competent authority of the RMS must within thirty days of receipt of the notification, inform the MAH and the CMSs of the outcome of its review. If the notification is rejected, the MAH must immediately cease to apply the variation. There is no provision for amendment of the variation or appeal; instead, the MAH will simply have to formulate an alternative variation and re-notify it.

If a notification is approved, each competent authority must amend the decision granting the MA within six months of receiving the notification and inform the holder without delay once the decision has been amended.[42]

---

36. Variations Regulation, Article 20(7).
37. Variations Regulation, Article 20 (7(a)).
38. Variations Regulation, Article 20 (7(b)).
39. Variations Regulation, Article 20 (8 (a,b,c)).
40. Best Practice Guides relating to variations granted under the mutual recognition procedure are available on the Heads of Medicines Agencies website at: http://www.hma.eu/96.html (human medicines) and http://www.hma.eu/163.html (veterinary medicines).
41. Variations Regulation, Article 8.
42. Variations Regulation, Article 11 and 23.

[2] Type IB

Where the variation is a Type IB, the submission is more onerous than that of a Type IA variation.[43] Annex IV of the Variations Regulation lists the elements that must be submitted in support of the application, including:

- a list of all the MAs affected;
- a description of all the variations submitted;
- the supporting documentation (if any) stipulated in the Variations Guidelines;
- the relevant fee; and
- if a variation leads to other variations, an explanation of the relation between these variations.

The RMS should additionally receive the list of dispatch dates indicating the Type IB Variation procedure number, the dates on which the applications have been sent to the RMS and the CMS, and confirmation that the relevant fees have been paid as required by national competent authorities.

The RMS will check within seven calendar days whether the proposed changes are Type IB and whether the notification is complete. If the notification is complete, the RMS will acknowledge receipt before the start of the evaluation procedure. If however, the RMS does not consider the variation to be Type IB, it will inform the CMS and the holder immediately. If the CMS does not disagree within a further seven calendar days, the holder will be asked to revise its application and complete it in accordance with the requirements of a Type II application. If the notification is complete, the acknowledgement from the RMS starts a thirty-day clock: unless within that period the RMS has sent the applicant an unfavourable opinion, the variation is deemed accepted by all competent authorities concerned. The CMS and the RMS then have six months to amend the decision granting the MA, and to notify the holder that they have done so.

The RMS is responsible for making the final decision regarding the outcome of the notification according to the 'Variations Guidelines' (point 2.2.2. Type IB variations review for mutual recognition procedure). If the CMSs disagree with the RMS, the RMS must take the final decision on the classification of the proposed variation having taken into account the comments received. The RMS is obliged to notify the MAH of the outcome of the procedure. The RMS must then notify the MAH of the outcome of the procedure within thirty days following the acknowledgement of receipt of a valid notification. If there is an unfavourable outcome, the MAH may amend the notification within thirty days to take due account of the grounds for the non-acceptance of the variation. If the holder does not amend the notification within thirty days as requested, the variation will be deemed rejected by all CMSs.

The receipt of the amended notification starts another thirty-day clock, within which the RMS will inform the holder of final acceptance or rejection of the variation. The CMSs will also be informed of the outcome.

---

43. Variations Regulation, Article 9.

The above procedure does not apply where the variation is submitted as part of a grouping that includes a type II variation or extension.[44]

[3] Type II

For applications for a Type II variation of an MA other than human influenza vaccines, the holder must submit the same list of elements listed in Annex IV as stipulated in Type IB to the RMS and all CMSs. Within sixty days, the RMS shall prepare an assessment report and a decision on the application and communicate it to the other CMSs and the holder.[45] The RMS can reduce the period if the matter is urgent (particularly for safety issues).

Within the report period, the RMS can ask the holder for supplementary information, and the clock is stopped until the information has been provided. In general, the MAH will have a month to supply the supplementary information; however, a longer suspension may be granted where the holder sends a justified request to the RMS.[46]

The evaluation of responses may take up to thirty or sixty days depending on the complexity and the amount of information supplied by the holder. However, once the RMS's report and decision have been finalised and circulated, the CMSs have only thirty days to express any disagreement with the decision. If the CMS does not reject the decision within the thirty-day period, the decision is deemed recognised.[47]

If a decision is recognised by all CMSs, the RMS will inform the holder that the variation has been accepted and inform the CMSs as to whether any amendment is needed to the decision granting the MA.[48] If so, they have to amend the decision granting the MA within two months following the receipt of information regarding the accepted variation.[49]

If the CMSs are unable to agree, then any competent authority can request that the issue causing disagreement to be referred to the coordination group.[50] In general terms, the CMS may disagree with the RMS where there is a potential serious risk to public health or a potential serious risk to human or animal health or the environment (in the case of veterinary medicinal products). The dissenting Member State must then give a detailed submission as to its reasons for dissenting to all Member States concerned, including the applicant, and an arbitration will take place under the procedure of Directive 2001/82/EC.

---

44. Variations Regulation, Article 9(5).
45. This is extendible to ninety days in respect of variations to the indications concerned as listed in Annex V(1), and automatically ninety days for certain variations to veterinary product MAs, listed in Annex V(2).
46. Variations Regulation, Article 10(3).
47. Variations Regulation, Article 10(4).
48. Variations Regulation, Article 11(1 (a,b,c)).
49. Variations Regulation, Article 11(2) and 23(1(a)).
50. Variations Regulation, Article 13.

Chapter 11: Variations to Marketing Authorisations   §11.04[E]

A special, slightly accelerated procedure is set out in Article 12 for variations to MAs for human influenza vaccines. The acceleration reduces the time limit during which the CMSs can respond to the decision.

[E] Centrally Authorised Products[51]

[1] *Advance Notice*

For products authorised centrally, the Procedure Guidelines recommend that the applicant should give the EMA and rapporteur six to twelve months of advance notice of any planned applications for a variation to allow for optimal planning, identification of procedural issues, and handling of overlapping applications. For all Type II variation applications, a Member State competent authority will act as rapporteur, and this will also apply for some Type I variations. The rapporteur will normally be the same one that evaluated the original MA application.

The application must be submitted on the appropriate form, which is different from the one used under the mutual recognition procedure. A separate form is required for each variation unless the multiple variations are the result of a single change. If relying upon this, the fact needs to be clearly explained on the form.

[2] *Type IA and IB Variations*

Type IA variations must be notified within twelve months after implementation of the variation, and the EMA will review the notification within thirty days. There should not need to be any involvement by a rapporteur Member State; however, the Type IA notification will be provided by the EMA to the rapporteur for information.

Type IB variations must be notified before their implementation and should contain all the information and elements required by Annex IV.[52] In this case, a rapporteur will be appointed, which will normally be the one that handled the original MA application. Provided no adverse opinion is received within thirty days, the holder can implement the change. If the notification is rejected, the holder has thirty days to amend it. Where necessary, the MA itself will be updated by the Commission within twelve months, but if approved, the variation can be implemented before this update takes place.

[3] *Type II Variations*

The procedure for Type II variations is similar to the Type IIvariations review for mutual recognition procedure (*see* §11.04, [D], [3]), except that the application must be

---

51. Further regulatory and procedural guidance is available on the EMA's website: http://www.ema.europa.eu/ema/index.jsp?curl=pages/regulation/document_listing/document_listing_000104.jsp&mid=WC0b01ac0580025b88.
52. Variations Regulation, Article15(1).

submitted to the EMA, rapporteur, any co-rapporteur, and all Committee for Medicinal Products for Human Use (CHMP) or Committee for Veterinary Medicinal Products (CVMP) members. In general, a sixty-day evaluation period will apply, which can be reduced having regard to the urgency of the matter (particularly for safety issues) or extended to ninety days for variations listed in Annex V(1) or certain grouping of variations. The application is assessed by the CHMP or CVMP, whose opinion will be decisive. If the holder requires longer than a month to respond to any request for supplementary information, it should send a justified request to the EMA for agreement by the CHMP or CVMP (as the case may be) for additional time that explains why the extra time is needed. For any follow-on request for supplementary information, an additional procedural suspension of up to one month will apply with a maximum of two months' suspension when justified.

On adoption of an opinion by the CHMP or CVMP, the EMA will inform the holder within fifteen days as to whether the opinion is favourable or unfavourable. Where the final opinion is favourable and the variation affects the terms of the Commission decision granting the MA, the EMA will transmit the opinion (together with the grounds for the opinion) to the Commission. The Commission will have two months to amend the MA in nine specific circumstances:[53]

(i) the addition of new therapeutic indications or modifications of existing ones;
(ii) addition of new contraindications;
(iii) a change in posology;
(iv) the addition of a non-food-producing target species or modification of an existing one for veterinary medicinal products;
(v) replacement or addition of a serotype, strain, antigen for a veterinary medicine;
(vi) changes to the active substance of a seasonal, pre-seasonal, or pandemic human influenza vaccine;
(vii) changes to the withdrawal period of a veterinary medicinal product; or
(viii) other Type II variations that are intended to implement changes to the decision granting the MA due to significant public health in the case of medicinal products intended for human use;
(ix) changes to the active substance of a human coronavirus vaccine, including replacement or addition of a serotype, strain, antigen or coding sequence or combination of serotypes, strains, antigens or coding sequences.

For all other variations, the Commission will amend the decision granting the MA within twelve months.

Where the approved Type II variation requires the decision granting the MA to be amended within two months, the variation may only be implemented once the MAH has been informed by the Commission. Where the amendment of the decision granting

---

53. Variations Regulation, Article 23(1a).

Chapter 11: Variations to Marketing Authorisations §11.04[F]

the MA is not required within two months, the variation may be implemented once the EMA has informed the MAH that its opinion is favourable.

Variations related to safety issues must be implemented within a timeframe agreed between the Commission and the holder.

A special accelerated procedure relating to centrally authorised human influenza vaccines has been provided for in Article 18 of the Variations Regulation.

[F] Purely National Procedure

Regulation (EC) 712/2012 introduced Chapter IIa, which applies to variations to purely national MAs from 4 August 2013.

[1] Type IA Variations

The MAH must submit to the competent authority a notification containing the elements listed in Annex IV of the Variations Regulation within twelve months of the implementation of the variation, but the submission must be done immediately after the implementation where continuous supervision of the medicinal product is required.[54] The competent authority must inform the holder within thirty days of receipt of the notification of the outcome of its review.

If the MA requires any amendment to the decision granting the MA, the competent authority will update the MA within six months of informing the holder.[55]

Where Type IA variation is rejected, the competent authority must provide the holder with the grounds for the rejection and the holder must immediately cease to apply any variation that it has already implemented.

[2] Type IB Variations

The MAH must submit to the competent authority a notification containing the elements set out in Annex IV. The competent authority must acknowledge receipt of a valid notification, which will start a thirty-day clock running for reviewing the variations. If the competent authority has not sent the MAH an unfavourable opinion within this thirty-day period, the notification is deemed to be accepted. Where the opinion is favourable, the competent authority will update the MA within six months following the closure of the procedure.

[3] Type II Variations

The MAH must submit to the competent authority an application containing the elements set out in Annex IV. The competent authority will acknowledge receipt of a

---

54. Variations Regulation, Article 13(a).
55. Variations Regulation, Article 23(1)(b).

valid application, which will start a sixty-day clock in which the competent authority will have to conclude its assessment of the application. This period can be reduced depending on the urgency (particularly safety issues) or extended to ninety days for variations listed in Annex V(1) or where certain variations have been grouped.[56]

During this review period, the competent authority may ask the MAH for supplementary information, in which case, the clock will be stopped until such information is provided. In general, this suspension will typically be up to one month. However, if the MAH requires a longer suspension, it should submit a justified request to the competent authority.

Following evaluation, the competent authority will inform the holder of whether the variation has been approved or rejected. If the variation has been approved, the competent authority will amend the MA to reflect the variations within two months (where necessary), provided that all the necessary documentation has been submitted to the competent authority.

The MAH can implement the variation after it has been informed of the acceptance of the variation. Any variations relating to safety issues are implemented within a timeframe agreed between the competent authority and the holder.

This procedure will not apply where the Type II variation is submitted in a grouping that includes an extension.[57]

[G] Urgent Safety Restrictions

There is a special procedure in cases where urgent safety restrictions need to be placed on the product. It applies where interim changes to an MA are required due to new information having a bearing on the safe use of a medicinal product.[58] These changes must be made through a variation to the MA.

If the MAH becomes aware of a concern that he or she considers needs to be communicated immediately to prescribers and users to avoid a risk to human or animal health or to the environment, the MAH can take provisional measures and must inform the competent authorities immediately. If no objection has been raised by the Competent authority within twenty-four hours after receipt of that information, the urgent safety restriction is deemed accepted.[59]

Alternatively, the Commission (for centrally authorised medicinal products) or a competent authority (for nationally authorised medicinal products) can impose restrictions on the holder. In either case, the MAH must submit an application for a variation to take account of the safety restrictions being imposed as soon as possible within fifteen days.

---

56. Variations Regulation, Article 13c(2).
57. Variations Regulation, Article 13c(5).
58. Variations Regulation, Article 2(8).
59. Variations Regulation, Article 22(1).

[H] Human Influenza Vaccines

The Variations Regulation contains special provisions relating to human influenza vaccines in Article 12 (mutual recognition procedure), Article 13f (purely national procedure), and Article 18 (centralised procedure). Article 21 of the Variations Regulation applies to pandemic human influenza and human coronavirus.

The Procedural Guideline governs the annual update of human influenza vaccine applications, required because of the need annually to change the active substance. A special two-step 'fast track' procedure is introduced. The first step deals with the assessment of the administrative and quality data elements (i.e., SmPC, labelling and package leaflet, and the chemical, pharmaceutical, and biological documentation). The second step concerns the assessment of additional data. MAHs of these products are recommended to discuss these annual submissions in advance with the EMA, the RMS, or CMSs.

[I] Human Coronavirus Vaccines

Following the COVID-19 pandemic, the Variations Regulation has been amended to include specific provisions regarding variations pertaining to authorised COVID-19 vaccines.[60]

Indeed, the nature of the SARS-CoV-2 virus made it necessary to address the need to ensure the effectiveness of human coronavirus vaccines against mutations or variants of the virus that may evolve over time. The approach taken by the Commission was in line with the approach used in the past for human influenza vaccines. Article 21 of the Variations Regulation was replaced and extended as it now applies to both pandemic human influenza and pandemic human coronavirus. Article 21 provides that where a pandemic situation with respect to human influenza or human coronavirus is duly recognised, variations pertaining to human coronavirus vaccines might follow an accelerated timetable and could be processed on the basis of less comprehensive data than is normally the case during a pandemic (providing that the benefit-risk balance is proved to be favourable).

§11.05 VARIATIONS TO MAs IN THE UK

[A] Introduction

The UK left the EU on 31 January 2020. One year later, on 1 January 2021, the Medicines and Healthcare products Regulatory Agency (MHRA) adopted its own variation procedure, albeit largely mirrored in EU law. As was the case before Brexit,

---

60. Commission Delegated Regulation (EU) 2021/756 of 24 March 2021 amending Regulation (EC) No. 1234/2008 concerning the examination of variations to the terms of MAs for medicinal products for human use and veterinary medicinal products (available https://eur-lex.europa.eu/legal-content/EN/TXT/?uri = celex%3A32021R0756).

variation procedures vary depending on the responsible competent authority. In the UK, the MHRA (in its capacity as competent authority) is now responsible for national variations. The UK Government is intent on carving out its own regulatory framework governing MA, which will extend to variations as well. In this section, we briefly outline the MHRA's position in respect of variations in the UK after the end of the Brexit transition period.

As outlined in §11.01, the variation procedure was overhauled extensively in 2008 by the introduction of Commission Regulation (EC) 1234/2008 (Variations Regulations), which concerns the examination of variations to MAs for medicinal products. In the UK, the MHRA retained the variation procedures detailed in Chapter IIa of the Variations Regulations.[61] These procedures continue to apply to pending and new variations of national MAs in the UK from 1 January 2021.[62] The legislative authority can now be found in regulation 65C and Schedule 10A to the amended Human Medicines Regulations 2012 (2012 Regulations). The MHRA also states that the variations classification Guidelines[63] will continue to apply unless exempt.[64] These Guidelines outline the various types of variation, including Type IA, Type IAIN, Type IB, Type II, or Extensions.[65] It should be noted, however, that the MHRA may introduce its own variations guidelines in due course, but given the complexity of the regulatory landscape, change is likely to be gradual.

[B] Variation Procedure in the UK

MAs granted in the EU before 1 January 2021 automatically 'convert' to UK MAs pursuant to the Human Medicines Regulations (Amendment etc.) (EU Exit) Regulations 2019 (*see* §5.09). Similarly, UK MA granted for a medicinal product before 1 January 2021 continues to have effect after this date. Any variation to a purely national MA can be presented to the MHRA directly under the reliance route.[66] Where an MAH intends to follow the reliance procedure, such intent must be clearly stated in the application, and relevant supporting evidence, declarations, and other supporting information must be supplied.

---

61. Chapter IIa outlines the procedure for variations to purely national MAs.
62. For further guidance on UK MAs including the application process *see* §5.09.
63. The Guidelines outline the categories of variations, the operation of certain procedures laid down by the Variations Regulations, in addition to the conditions to be met and any required supporting documentation: https://eur-lex.europa.eu/legal-content/EN/TXT/?uri=CELEX:5201 3XC0802(04).
64. Paragraph 3 of Schedule 10A to the 2012 Regulations states that, where a classification is not provided for in Schedule 10A, the MAH may request a recommendation on the classification of a variation from the licensing authority, who must then notify the holder its recommendation within forty-five days of the request.
65. Classification of the three main types of variation, namely Types IA, IB, and II, are discussed in more detail in §11.02. Type IA variations are also known as 'do-and-tell' variations; holders should implement the changes before notifying the MHRA.
66. The reliance route is part of the post-Brexit regime. The MHRA can rely on decisions (including decisions as to variation of MA) of the EC.

Chapter 11: Variations to Marketing Authorisations §11.05[B]

As discussed above, variations are now governed, *inter alia*, by regulation 65C and Schedule 10A to the 2012 Regulations. Regulation 65C states that a UK MAH may apply to vary the authorisation in accordance with Schedule 10A; however, this procedure does not apply to the transfer of an MA from one person to another.[67] The key provisions of Schedule 10A are:

(1) Where an application for variation leads to the revision of the summary of a product's characteristics, labelling or package leaflet, that revision must also be considered by the MHRA as part of the variation.
(2) In cases where several variations are notified or applied for, a separate notification (or application, where appropriate) should be submitted in respect of each variation. This is also known as the 'Grouping of variations'. Some variations are exempt from the grouping requirement.[68]
(3) Where a minor variation of Type IA[69] is made, the holder must submit to the MHRA a notification containing the elements listed in paragraph 9[70] within twelve months. Such notification must be submitted immediately after implementation of the variation.
(4) Minor variations of Type IB[71] require the holder to submit to the MHRA a notification containing the paragraph 9 elements listed above. If the holder does not receive an unfavourable opinion within thirty days, the notification is deemed to be accepted. The MHRA must then either accept or reject the variation or amend the decision granting the UK MA.
(5) Major Type II variations require the holder to submit an application to the MHRA, which must be approved before the 'new' product can be marketed. The MHRA may request further supplementary information before making their decision to accept or reject the variation or amend the decision granting the UK MA of that product. Major variations include adding a new therapeutic indication or updating the current indication.
(6) Applications to extend a UK MA must be assessed by the MHRA in accordance with the procedure applied under Part 5 to the initial authorisation to which it relates. An extension must then either be granted a UK MA in accordance with the same or equivalent procedure as for the granting of the initial UK MA to which it relates or be included in that initial UK MA.

---

67. Regulation 65C(3) of the Human Medicines Regulations 2012.
68. E.g., where one or more of the same minor Type IA variations are notified at the same time; where several variations to the terms of the same UK MA are submitted at the same time; and where one or more of the same variations to the terms of the same UK MA (held by the same holder) are submitted at the same time.
69. Type IA variations are minor changes that have little to no impact on the quality, safety, or efficacy of the medicinal product. *See* §11.02[A][1] for more detail.
70. Including, *inter alia*, a list of the MAs affected by the notification or application, and a description of all the variations submitted.
71. Type IB variations are minor changes that do not fall within the Type 1A or II categories, for example, an increase or decrease in the scale of active substance production without a process change. *See* §11.02[A][2] for more detail.

[C] Northern Ireland

Medicinal products authorised for Northern Ireland remain subject to EU regulatory provisions. Therefore, any variation to an MA for use in Northern Ireland will be managed by the EMA. The MHRA is adamant that requirements for unfettered access (a regime designed to avoid disruption and ensure maximum continuity after the Brexit transition period) will be respected where the MAH is established in Northern Ireland, and the Great Britain authorisation has been obtained as a qualifying Northern Ireland Good.[72]

[D] Summary

The MHRA is clearly intent on providing a robust framework in respect of MA variations. However, at the time of writing (August 2022), the variation procedure in the UK is essentially the same as it was before the end of the Brexit transition period. EU provisions governing variations are complex, and any significant deviation from EU procedure will take time. MAHs should take comfort in the fact that the mechanics of variation remain essentially the same. One of the few 'real' differences is that applications for variation to a purely national (i.e., UK or Great Britain) MA must be submitted directly to the MHRA rather than the EMA.[73]

---

72. 'Qualifying Northern Ireland Goods' are defined as goods that are in free circulation in Northern Ireland (i.e., not under a customs procedure or in an authorised temporary storage facility) before they are moved to Great Britain (i.e., England, Scotland, or Wales).
73. The MHRA updated its guidance on variations to MAs in 2021: https://www.gov.uk/guidance/medicines-apply-for-a-variation-to-your-marketing-authorisation#extensions

CHAPTER 12
Combination Products

Sarah Faircliffe

§12.01 INTRODUCTION

[A] Combination Products

A *combination product* (also referred to as a *fixed-dose combination* or *fixed combination medicinal product*) is a medicinal product comprising a combination of different active substances within a single pharmaceutical form of administration.

Products may sometimes consist of more than one medicinal product or more than one pharmaceutical form of the same medicinal product, presented under a single (invented) name and in a single product package, where the individual products/separate pharmaceutical forms are intended for simultaneous or sequential administration. This kind of product is generally referred to as a 'combination pack',[1] and it is not discussed in this Chapter as it is generally not considered to be a 'combination product' within the scope of the relevant guidance discussed here.

A chemical substance that dissociates *in vivo* into two or more distinct active substances is also regarded as a fixed-combination medicinal product.[2]

The Committee for Medicinal Products for Human Use (CHMP) Guideline on clinical development of fixed-combination medicinal products[3] provides guidance on regulatory considerations which apply to marketing authorisations (MAs) for combination products; the guidance has been developed through different versions over several decades. The current guidance notes that there should be clinical data to support a justification of the pharmacological and medical rationale for the proposed

---

1. CHMP Guideline on clinical development of fixed-combination medicinal products, 23 March 2017, EMA/CHMP/158268/2017, Rev. 2.
2. Ibid.
3. Ibid.

combination product, as well as to establish the evidence base for the relevant contribution of all active substances to the desired therapeutic effect (efficacy and/or safety) and a positive benefit-risk profile for the combination in the targeted indication. The guidance provides examples of potential fixed combination products in terms of which would be acceptable combinations and which would be unacceptable from a regulatory perspective. Combination products that aim at treating patients with unrelated indications and that do not have a therapeutic rationale are discouraged,[4] so, for example, a combination containing an antidepressant and an oral anti conceptive to treat women with depression who do not want to become pregnant would appear not to comply with this guidance.

Fixed combination products are used in a wide range of conditions. They are particularly useful in the management of human immunodeficiency virus/acquired immunodeficiency syndrome (HIV/AIDS), malaria, and tuberculosis,[5] as the combination of active ingredients may be safer, more effective, or more rapidly effective than a single active substance. The combination may also have fewer adverse effects, or it may simplify therapy, relieve the burden of taking numerous pills, and hence improve compliance with the treatment programme.

[B] Combination Products: Requirement for a MA and Regulatory Data Protection

According to the interpretation provided in the European Commission's Notice to Applicants, a 'combination' medicinal product does not fall within the scope of the MAs for the individual substances of the combination medicinal product (where these have previously been separately authorised). Thus, a combination is a 'new and unique' medicinal product requiring a separate MA and Summary of Product Characteristics.[6] Accordingly, a new combination medicinal product will also have an independent period of data exclusivity and market protection from its first authorisation within the Community, since the authorised combination product will not fall within the scope of the global MAs for the previously authorised individual active substances (*see* Chapter 13 regarding the Abridged Procedure for a more detailed discussion of the Global MA concept).[7]

---

4. *Ibid.*
5. WHO Expert Committee on Specifications for Pharmaceutical Preparations, WHO Technical Report Series 929, Annex 5: http://apps.who.int/prequal/info_general/documents/TRS929/WHO_TRS_929_annex5FDCs.pdf.
6. Notice to Applicants of the European Commission, Volume 2A, Procedures for Marketing Authorisation, Chapter 1, Marketing Authorisation, of July 2019, Revision 5.
7. *Ibid*; 'If the medicinal product being assessed contains within the same pharmaceutical form a combination of active substances, it will form a new and unique medicinal product requiring a separate marketing authorisation, regardless whether all of the active substances contained therein were already authorised in a medicinal product or not. In its application for the new combination, the applicant must demonstrate that each active substance has a documented therapeutic contribution within the combination and therefore all compounds are different active substance. The authorisation for this new combination medicinal product is not considered to fall

Chapter 12: Combination Products §12.01[B]

This interpretation was challenged in a case brought by Teva against the EMA,[8] seeking annulment of the EMA's decision refusing to validate the applicants' application for an MA for its generic version of the abacavir/lamivudine combination product on the basis that the product was protected by a ten-year period of regulatory data exclusivity/market protection. Teva contended that the MA holder for the product was not entitled to enjoy a ten-year period of data exclusivity, as the product is a fixed-dose combination combining two active substances which have been supplied and used within the EU as components of a number of different medicinal products for some years. Thus, it was argued that the combination product falls within the same 'global marketing authorisation' as the earlier MAs for its component parts within the meaning of the second subparagraph of Article 6(1) of Directive No. 2001/83 and should not enjoy any further period of data exclusivity/market protection after the expiry of the data exclusivity/market protection relating to these authorisations. However, the applicant decided to discontinue these proceedings before any judgment was given, and so the Notice to Applicants interpretation discussed above has not been held incorrect.

A more recent case in the General Court[9] examined the question of the correct test to establish the 'difference' between two products for regulatory data protection/global MA purposes, when one product has been authorised as a combination product and the other is a monotherapy product containing just one of the compounds identified as an active substance in that combination. The products in question were Fumaderm (containing the substances DMF and MEF, which was authorised by the German regulatory authority, the BfArM, in 1994) and Tecfidera (containing the active substance DMF and authorised through the 'centralised procedure' – *see* Chapter 5 – *Obtaining a Marketing Authorisation* for a discussion of the centralised procedure). The judgment of the General Court of 5 May 2021 held that the Commission was not entitled to conclude that Tecfidera was covered by a different global MA than Fumaderm, which had previously been authorised, without verifying or requesting the European Medicines Agency's CHMP to verify whether, and if necessary, how, the BfArM had assessed the role of MEF within Fumaderm, or without requesting the CHMP to verify the role played by MEF within Fumaderm. This case is currently under appeal and the Advocate General's Opinion delivered on 6th October 2022, recommending that the judgment of the General Court be set aside, although the Court's final decision may or may not follow the Advocate General's reasoning.

For a fuller description of the regulatory data protection accorded to combination products, *see* Chapter 13 on Abridged Procedure.

---

within the scope of the global marketing authorisations of the already authorised medicinal product(s) as described in Article 6(1) of Directive 2001/83/EC'.
8. *Teva Pharma and Teva Pharmaceuticals Europe v. EMA* (Case T-547/12)
9. *Pharmaceutical Works Polpharma v. European Medicines Agency*, Case T-611/18

§12.02 REQUIREMENTS FOR MARKETING APPROVAL OF FIXED-COMBINATION MEDICINAL PRODUCTS

[A] The Application Dossier

Article 10(b) of Directive 2001/83/EC, as amended, provides a specific legal basis for MA applications for fixed combination products, as follows:

> In the case of medicinal products containing active substances used in the composition of authorised medicinal products but not hitherto used in combination for therapeutic purposes, the results of new pre-clinical tests or new clinical trials relating to that combination must be provided in accordance with Article 8(3)(i), but it is not necessary to provide scientific references relating to each individual active substance.

According to Article 10(b) in connection with Annex I Part II.5 of Directive 2001/83/EC, a full dossier comprising the information of Modules 1 to 5 of the 'Common Technical Document', application form must be submitted in relation to the combination product in order to apply for an MA. As explained in the Notice to Applicants,[10] although an application on the basis of Article 10(b) of Directive 2001/83/EC allows the applicant to not provide scientific references relating to each individual active substance (which would not be the case in the context of an application on the basis of Article 8(3) of Directive 2001/83/EC), it is not mandatory to apply for fixed combination MAs on the basis of Article 10(b). In other words, other legal bases (such as 'well-established use' under Article 10a) may be used.

[B] The Application Procedure

Applications for authorisation of combination products will be assessed by regulatory authorities to ensure that quality, safety, and efficacy are established, as for any other product seeking authorisation. Depending on the legal basis chosen by the applicant, it may not be necessary for the applicant to provide scientific references relating to each individual active substance in the application (*see* the discussion of Article 10(b) above).

Guidelines make clear that applicants are required to justify the rationale behind a particular combination of active substances proposed for an intended therapeutic indication. The rationale should also consider the posology, including the dosing frequency, of the components included in the fixed combination. The combined use of the active substances should improve the benefit/risk by either increasing or adding therapeutic efficacy, and/or by improving safety, compared to use of a single active

---

10. Notice to Applicants of the European Commission, Volume 2A, Procedures for Marketing Authorisation, Chapter 1, Marketing Authorisation, of July 2019, section 5.5.

substance.[11] Scientific advice regarding the specific application procedure and specific dossier requirements can be obtained from national competent authorities or the EMA.

In general, the application for MA can either be based on tests and trials performed by the applicant or can be a 'mixed' dossier containing both scientific literature references and data from tests and trials. Any absence of specific fixed-combination data should be justified by the applicant with reference to scientific or regulatory considerations (for example, by making reference to the available information on the individual substances).[12]

In addition, other applicable legislation for the specific active substances has to be considered. For example, Regulation 1394/2007/EC provides specific rules concerning the authorisation, supervision, and pharmacovigilance of advanced therapy medicinal products, such as tissue-engineered products as defined in Directive 2001/83/EC and gene therapy medicinal products or somatic cell therapy medicinal products as defined in Annex I to Directive 2001/83/EC.

[C]   Scientific References, Non-Clinical Tests, and Clinical Trials

The applicant should demonstrate the relevant contribution of all active components to the desired therapeutic effect, as well as the positive risk-benefit for the combination.[13]

Scientific references can consist of scientific literature, for example, relevant scientific publications, or actual data on the individual substances in the combination product. The data may come from the MAs for the individual substances. In this case, permission to access the data can be granted by the MA holder for the individual substance, or the data can be referenced without permission of the respective MA holder once the relevant data exclusivity period for the MA expires. However, additional clinical trials and sometimes also non-clinical tests with the intended combination may be required.

The extent to which scientific references can be used in the application, instead of data from non-clinical tests or clinical trials performed by the applicant, depends, *inter alia*, on whether the components of the combination are already used in combination in practice. If the fixed combination corresponds closely to combinations that are already in widespread (and documented) use, a robust bibliographical data analysis can be provided. If the analysis thoroughly and reliably documents the data, the number of clinical trials to be performed could be reduced.

Should a fixed combination contain one or more new active substances, i.e., not previously authorised in a medicinal product, certain additional development requirements apply.[14]

---

11. CHMP Guideline on clinical development of fixed-combination medicinal products, 23 March 2017, EMA/CHMP/158268/2017, Rev. 2.
12. Notice to Applicants of the European Commission, Volume 2A, Procedures for Marketing Authorisation, Chapter 1, Marketing Authorisation, of July 2019.
13. CHMP Guideline on clinical development of fixed-combination medicinal products, 23 March 2017, EMA/CHMP/158268/2017, Rev.2.
14. *Ibid.*, section 4.4.

Non-clinical or pre-clinical studies are conducted, typically in animals, to obtain additional information on the characteristics of the combination for human use. Non-clinical studies are conducted in a wide range of systems to characterise the properties of the compounds (*in vivo* tests in animals, or *in vitro* tests).

Clinical trials in humans are conducted to allow for collection of safety and efficacy data for the combination product. Clinical trials may vary in size depending on the circumstances of the case.

[D] Necessity for Non-Clinical Tests and Clinical Trials

In the context of combination products, the necessity for tests and trials can be driven by the anticipated interaction of the combination's active components, as well as the extent of the information available from studies of the single components. If the expected systemic exposure to the combination is not sufficiently documented by the existing data to meet the requirements for approval, additional studies will be necessary. Additional studies may also be necessary for certain types or classes of products (*see* section [1] below). If the product contains components that have sufficient existing data, then fewer studies will be needed (*see* section [2] below).

Studies of combination products typically include pharmacodynamic (PD) studies that analyse the action or effects of active substances on living organisms. PD data on the combination may also be gathered to assess whether there are unexpected or undesirable interactions between the active components. Several dose combinations might have to be tested to find the combination that is the safest and most effective.

Pharmacokinetic (PK) studies may also be conducted to determine how the product is absorbed, distributed, metabolised, and eliminated by the body. However, if the PK of the single components are adequately characterised in animals, including the profile for enzyme induction and inhibition and drug-drug interactions, additional non-clinical documentation on PK interactions is generally not needed.[15]

The need for (combination) studies will depend on the type of anticipated interactions between the components and on the range of concentrations and exposures covered in the available studies with the single components.[16] In some cases, the PK interaction (e.g., combination with a metabolism inhibitor) constitutes the rationale for the combination. In this case, such interaction must be documented, and appropriate non-clinical data may be needed.

[1] Situations Where Additional Studies Are Necessary

Additional studies are required if the compounds of the combination target the same organ system or belong to a class of compounds associated with a specific type of toxicity. The toxicological profile of the combination may be studied in non-clinical

---

15. CHMP Guideline on the non-clinical development of fixed combinations of medicinal products, EMA/CHMP/SWP/258498/2005, 24 January 2008.
16. *Ibid.*

studies to support safe human use and identify potential interactions.[17] These studies are also designed to address safety concerns based on the pharmacology or toxicology of the individual components of the product. Depending on the properties of the components of the combination, special studies may be necessary to address immunotoxicity or dependence.[18]

For fixed low (sub-therapeutic) dose combinations that treat hypertension, the CHMP requires that the clinical trials demonstrate that fixed combinations show a statistically significant and clinically better effect than a placebo and a statistically significant increase in effectiveness over substances that are given individually.[19]

If the combination product contains one or more new substances, that is, a substance that has not been authorised individually, different approaches to conduct necessary studies might be considered as additional development requirements apply.[20] In the PK section, a full clinical development of the new active substance is expected, as would be expected for any new active substance, as is a full development of the PD of the new active substance(s), with a special focus on the pharmacological synergism with other active substance(s) in the combination. The potential for potentiating safety concerns should also be evaluated. Extensive trials with the new substance(s), together with additional bridging studies with the combination, may be appropriate. A more extensive non-clinical development programme with the combination, and a limited set of studies with the new active substance alone, may be appropriate.[21]

[2] Situations Where Fewer Studies Are Necessary

[a] Combinations Already in Widespread Use as Free Combination Therapy

If the combination of the compounds is already in widespread use as a free combination therapy (that is, as the combination of the separate compounds, e.g., separate tablets, co-administered), the necessity of conducting additional clinical studies for the fixed combination might be significantly reduced, depending on the specific circumstances. A bibliographic data analysis can be used to provide clinical data and to facilitate the selection of doses for each substance and the proposed dose range of the fixed combination.

When the fixed combination under development includes compounds that are sufficiently documented with regard to their individual combined use in humans, safety studies in animals are, in general, not required. Also, for compounds that belong to the same classes as other compounds in well-established combinations, additional

---

17. Ibid.
18. Ibid.
19. CHMP Guideline on clinical investigation of medicinal products in the treatment of hypertension, 23 June 2016, EMA/CHMP/29947/2013/Rev. 4.
20. CHMP Guideline on clinical development of fixed-combination medicinal products, 23 March 2017, EMA/CHMP/158268/2017, Rev. 2, section 4.4.
21. CHMP Guideline on the non-clinical development of fixed combinations of medicinal products, EMA/CHMP/SWP/258498/2005, 24 January 2008.

non-clinical studies may not be necessary if considerable clinical experience exists and no PK interactions have been identified.[22] However, if the available non-clinical data does not fulfil the recommendations outlined (e.g., in the Guideline on the Non-Clinical Documentation for Mixed Marketing Authorisation Applications),[23] certain testing may be required.[24] In the context of fixed combinations of drugs belonging to different therapeutic classes in the field of cardiovascular treatment and prevention, further guidance with regard to necessary studies is provided in a question-and-answer document issued by the CHMP.[25] It must be noted that due to the heterogeneity of the therapeutic field, different standards might apply in other contexts. Therefore, the question-and-answer document shows some crucial points to be discussed within the scientific and regulatory framework in the specific context, but it is not a general guidance on the necessity of clinical studies for combinations that are already in widespread use.[26]

If a fixed combination of the components is intended to provide for an administration that has the same dose interval, timing, and dose level as the separate monocomponents when administered as a free combination (substitution indication), clinical trial data are necessary to prove that the combination improves therapeutic compliance over the drugs administered separately.[27] In these circumstances, PK and (occasionally) PD data will usually be sufficient for the application. Further, formal bioequivalence studies testing the rate and extent of absorption of each component of the combination, compared to each substance when administered in monotherapy, should be carried out. Depending on the knowledge and experience with the components of the combination, additional safety data might be considered.[28]

Additional studies might be necessary if the components are administered at the same dosing interval but different dose timing than in the free combination treatment (e.g., both components are administered once a day, but one component is taken in the morning, and one is taken in the evening). In this case, it would have to be demonstrated that the change in timing of the administration does not affect the PD effect of any of the components of the fixed combination. Therefore, a non-inferiority PD study is required, which assesses the effect of the fixed combination as compared with both components administered at their usual dose timing. Depending on the knowledge and clinical experience with the components of the combination, the need for additional safety data might be considered.[29]

---

22. *Ibid.*
23. CHMP Guideline on the non-clinical documentation for mixed marketing authorisation applications, CPMP/SWP/799/95, 13 October 2005.
24. CHMP Guideline on the non-clinical development of fixed combinations of medicinal products, EMA/CHMP/SWP/258498/2005, 24 January 2008.
25. CHMP Question and Answer Document on the clinical development of fixed combinations of drugs belonging to different therapeutic classes in the field of cardiovascular treatment and prevention, 23 June 2005.
26. *Ibid.*
27. *Ibid.*
28. *Ibid.*
29. *Ibid.*

Finally, the components of the fixed combination might be administered in different dose intervals compared to the administration in monotherapy; for example, one component generally twice daily and the other component only once a day. In this case, typically, only one component of the fixed combination will be administered at the usual dosing regime, but the dosing regime and timing of the other component is changed when administered as a fixed combination. In these circumstances, the combination has a new dosing regime for one of the components of the fixed combination, involving a change in the dose interval, the dose per intake, and potentially the overall daily dose. Accordingly, data are required that address the PK similarity of the unchanged component (i.e., the component administered in the same dose interval as in the free combination) in comparison with the substance used in monotherapy. Further, the therapeutic equivalence of the component with the modified dosing regime must be demonstrated in clinical studies, as compared with the normal dosing regime given in monotherapy. If the simplification of the dosing regime of the fixed combination requires the administration of a higher dose per drug intake, the clinical safety study also must show that the increase of the dosing regime will not impair the safety profile of the therapeutic regime.[30]

[b] *Combination of Components Already Approved as a Fixed-Combination Product*

If the fixed combination for approval is a generic of an existing fixed combination product, the applicant must establish that the combination has the same qualitative and quantitative composition in active substances as the reference product and the same pharmaceutical form as the reference product. The applicant also must demonstrate bioequivalence with the reference product by appropriate bioavailability studies. Guidelines have been published.[31, 32]

§12.03 CRITERIA FOR APPROVAL OF FIXED-COMBINATION PRODUCTS

[A] The Risk/Benefit Ratio

Applicants must demonstrate that the combination product is safe and effective and that the advantages of the specific combination of active substances outweigh the disadvantages.[33]

Fixed combination medicinal products are advantageous if:

---

30. *Ibid.*
31. CHMP Guideline on the investigation of bioequivalence, 20 January 2010.
32. CHMP Guideline on clinical development of fixed-combination medicinal products, 23 March 2017, EMA/CHMP/158268/2017, Rev. 2.
33. *Ibid.*

- they achieve a level of efficacy similar to the one achievable by each active substance used alone at higher doses, and they are safer than the individual products;
- they achieve a level of efficacy above the one achievable by a single substance, and they are as safe;
- one substance in the combination counteracts a serious or common adverse reaction from another substance in the combination; or
- they simplify therapy by decreasing the number of individual dose units to be taken by the patient.

Disadvantages of fixed combination products may include the inability to adjust the combination to meet the needs of the individual patient, or an increase in adverse reactions.[34]

The EMA Guideline on clinical development of fixed combination products makes clear that the evidence base for establishing the contribution to an overall effect and favourable benefit-risk balance of the fixed-dose combination is expected to support that:

- the population in need of the fixed combination is clearly identified;
- the combination is pharmacologically plausible and based on valid therapeutic principles;
- each component contributes to efficacy and safety and/or enhances PK/PD of (main) active substance(s).

This evidence base can consist of dedicated clinical trials performed with the fixed combination and/or clinical trials with the combined use of the specific monocomponents, literature data, or a combination of both clinical trial and literature data. The clinical requirements to establish the evidence for the therapeutic scenarios in which fixed combinations may be used are described in the Guideline, these therapeutic scenarios being:

- add-on treatment of patients insufficiently responding to an existing therapy with one or more (mono) components;
- substitution in patients adequately controlled with two or more monocomponents used in combination;
- initial combination therapy for patients receiving previously neither of the substances.

Bioequivalence[35] of the combination versus monocomponents taken simultaneously is, in general, required to bridge existing clinical data obtained from the combined use of monocomponents with those from the fixed-dose combination formulation. In case of different dose interval or timing compared to individual monocomponents, additional data may be required. The bioequivalence study may be

---

34. *Ibid.*
35. CHMP Guideline on the investigation of bioequivalence, 20 January 2010.

waived if all clinical data supporting the combined use are obtained with the actual fixed combination formulation.[36]

[B] Relevance of Each Active Substance of the Combination

Each part of the combination must contribute to the claimed indications for the fixed combination medicinal product.[37] The indication must be a well-recognised disease state, syndrome, or pathological entity. If the individual active ingredients are intended to cure different symptoms simultaneously, the applicant must demonstrate that the symptoms regularly occur simultaneously in a clinically relevant intensity and for a relevant period of time. Each individual symptom alone shall not be regarded as an indication for the fixed combination because this symptom may also occur in other diseases, and for treating this symptom alone, the other substances of the combination may be irrelevant.

[C] Relevance of the Specific Dosage Regime

The applicant also has to demonstrate that the dosage of each substance within the fixed combination is safe and effective for a significant population subgroup.

Where substances are intended to simultaneously relieve different symptoms or to prevent different diseases, the doses of each substance should be similar to the doses commonly used for the treatment of each symptom or the prevention of each disease.[38]

For example, to obtain authorisation for a treatment of hypertension, the CHMP requires the applicant to prove that the dosage of each active component independently contributes towards the positive evaluation of the combination.[39]

§12.04 UK

Generally, the post-Brexit regulation of combination products in the UK continues to be aligned with the EU regime discussed above. As of 1 January 2021, the relevant UK regulatory framework continues to be set out in The Human Medicines Regulations 2012, as amended by the Human Medicines Regulations (Amendment etc.) (EU Exit) Regulations 2019 (UK HMRs). The UK HMRs continue to be based on the provisions of Directive 2001/83/EC (as of 31 December 2020), and as at the time of updating this chapter, there do not appear to be any substantial planned changes to the UK regime relating to this subject matter. There are no additional specific requirements regarding

---

36. CHMP Guideline on clinical development of fixed-combination medicinal products, 23 March 2017, EMA/CHMP/158268/2017, Rev. 2.
37. Ibid.
38. Ibid.
39. CHMP Guideline on clinical investigation of medicinal products in the treatment of hypertension, 23 June 2016, EMA/CHMP/29947/2013/Rev. 4.

MAs for fixed-combination products, other than those reflecting Article 10(b) Directive 2001/83/EC.

As regards the requirements for obtaining the appropriate MA for combination products, such requirements are laid down in the guidance applied by the MHRA, which continues to reflect the European Guidance documents.

In relation to the UK requirements regarding number of active ingredients in a combination product and/or the naming of the combination product, a system of 'co-names' was introduced in the late 1980s with the aim of increasing generic prescribing. The initial list consisted of less than twenty names and has increased only slowly. These co-names are part of the British Approved Names system to derive short, distinctive names for substances where the systematic chemical or other scientific names are too complex for convenient general use. British Approved Names were devised or selected by the British Pharmacopoeia Commission and published by the health ministers on the recommendation of the Commission of Human Medicines to provide a list of names of substances or articles referred to in section 100 of the Medicines Act 1968. Examples are co-dyramol (dihydrocodeine tartrate 10 mg and paracetamol 500 mg), co-amilozide (amiloride and hydrochlorothiazide), co-careldopa (levodopa and carbidopa), co-amoxiclav (amoxicillin and clavulanic acid), and co-trimoxazole (sulphamethoxazole and trimethoprim). The co-names were assigned only to combinations of two drug substances. Of these named combinations, pharmacopoeial monographs in the British Pharmacopoeia have been prepared for some but not all combinations. The initiative described met with mixed reactions. Products with the co-prefix caused confusion since some names used similar indicators (e.g., -amol for paracetamol combinations and -zide for hydrochlorothiazide). However, this initiative did not achieve the objective of introducing easily remembered names to be used instead of brand names. It also became clear that a system for indicating dose was required, as almost half the combinations were available in different strengths. The method devised was to give an x/y number of the amounts of the two components respectively in any particular combination – for example, co-zidocapt 12.5/25 (hydrochlorothiazide 12.5 mg, captopril 25 mg) and co-zidocapt 25/50 (hydrochlorothiazide 25 mg, captopril 50 mg). With the replacement of British Approved Names with International non-proprietary names (INNs) in 2005, the practice of naming new fixed combinations with co-names has come to an end, but those that already exist are still used and are listed in the British National Formulary. Even when available in only one fixed combination, the strength of each component is usually indicated on the package labelling. The MHRA has published a general guideline on the naming of medicinal products.

§12.05 GUIDELINES/PUBLICATIONS

- CHMP Guideline on clinical development of fixed-combination medicinal products, 23 March 2017, EMA/CHMP/158268/2017, Rev. 2.
- CHMP Guideline on the non-clinical development of fixed combinations of medicinal products, EMEA/CHMP/SWP/258498/2005, 24 January 2008.

- CHMP Guideline on the non-clinical documentation for mixed MA applications, 13 October 2005, CHMP/SWP/799/95.
- CHMP Question and Answer Document on the clinical development of fixed combinations of drugs belonging to different therapeutic classes in the field of cardiovascular treatment and prevention, 23 June 2005, CHMP/EWP/191583/CHMP. – Guideline on clinical investigation of medicinal products in the treatment of hypertension, 23 June 2016, EMA/CHMP/29947/2013/Rev. 4.
- CPMP Note for Guidance on fixed-combination medicinal products, 17 April 1996, <www.ikev.org/haber/bioav/024095en.pdf>.
- CHMP Guideline on the investigation of bioequivalence, 20 January 2010, CHMP/EWP/QWP/1401/98 Rev.1/Corr.
- Notice to Applicants of the European Commission. Volume 2A, Procedures for Marketing Authorisation, Chapter 1, Marketing Authorisation, of July 2019, <http://ec.europa.eu/health/files/eudralex/vol-2/a/vol2a_chap1_2013-06_en.pdf>.
- WHO Expert Committee on Specifications for Pharmaceutical Preparations, WHO Technical Report Series 929, Annex 5, <http://apps.who.int/prequal/info_general/documents/TRS929/WHO_TRS_929_annex5FDCs.pdf>.
- *Pharmaceutical Works Polpharma v. European Medicines Agency*, Case T-611/18.
- *Teva Pharma and Teva Pharmaceuticals Europe v. EMA* (Case T-547/12).

CHAPTER 13
Abridged Procedure

Pieter Erasmus[*]

§13.01 INTRODUCTION

The safety, efficacy, and a positive risk-benefit balance of each medicinal product is assessed on the basis of the information contained in the Marketing Authorisation (MA) application.

The legal requirements for making an application for an MA are set out in Directive 2001/83/EC of the European Parliament and of the Council of 6 November 2001 on the Community code relating to medicinal products for human use (as amended)[1] and Regulation (EC) No. 726/2004 of the European Parliament and of the Council of 31 March 2004 laying down Union procedures for the authorisation and supervision of medicinal products for human and veterinary use and establishing a European Medicines Agency (as amended).[2] The legal basis for a full application is according to Article 8(3) of Directive 2001/83/EC.

The data contained in an application under Article 8(3) for new innovative medicinal products are typically gathered by performing extensive preclinical and clinical research programmes involving tests and trials on animals and humans. Registration dossiers containing this information are usually referred to as 'stand-alone dossiers' or 'full dossiers'.

However, a growing awareness developed that, for ethical reasons, repetitive testing on animals and patients should be avoided where this would not contribute to the demonstration of safety and efficacy and a positive risk-benefit balance. Directive

---

[*] The author wishes to acknowledge *Hanneke Later-Nijland*, the author of the earlier editions of this chapter.
1. Last amended by Directive (EU) No. 2022/642, entering into force on 20 April 2022 (as at time of update).
2. Last amended by Regulation (EU) No. 2019/5, entering into force partly on 28 January 2019 and partly on 28 January 2022 (as at time of update).

65/65/EEC laid down provisions when an applicant was not required to provide the results of pharmacological and toxicological tests or the results of clinical trials, resulting in what is called the abridged procedure. Under the abridged procedures, applicants are allowed to make use of or refer to data contained in the registration dossier of existing and authorised products, or use publicly available data to show that a medicinal product is safe and effective for therapeutic use.

The other legal bases for applications come under Article 10 of Directive 2001/83/EC; these are:

- according to Article 10, which relates to generic medicinal products and similar biological medicinal products ('biosimilars');
- according to Article 10a, relating to applications which rely on well-established use;
- according to Article 10b, relating to applications for new fixed combination products; and
- according to Article 10c, relating to informed consent.

The application under Article 10b is discussed in detail in Chapter 12 'Combination Products'.

In this Chapter, the principle clauses and definitions in EU law governing abridged procedures are discussed, including references to the legislative history where appropriate. In relation to abridged procedures, the review[3] of the EU law relating to medicinal products resulted in Directive 2004/27/EC, which implemented major changes to Directive 2001/83/EC. However, most of the amendments had already become part of the legislative framework due to precedent-setting judgments by the European Court of Justice (ECJ) that interpreted the scope of the abridged procedure under Directive 2001/83/EC.

§13.02 THREE TYPES OF ABRIDGED PROCEDURES

The abridged procedure enables an applicant to make use of already existing and accessible data with or without the initial MA holder's consent. There are three types of abridged procedures:

(1) *Informed consent:* the abridged procedure contemplated in Article 10c of Directive 2001/83/EC, which is based on informed consent of the initial MA holder to access the registration dossier to obtain an MA for what is effectively the same medicinal product. *See* further §13.02[A] below.

(2) *Bibliographic:* the abridged procedure contemplated in Article 10a of Directive 2001/83/EC, which is based on making use of bibliographic data for substances that have been in well-established use. This is further discussed in §13.02[B] below.

---

3. *See* Chapter 2.

Chapter 13: Abridged Procedure §13.02[A]

(3) *Generic products*: the abridged procedure and hybrid abridged procedure based on reference to an existing registration dossier without consent of the innovator by the applicant for Authorisation of generic or biosimilar products, as provided for in Article 10 of Directive 2001/83/EC. This is further discussed in §13.03 below.

[A] **Abridged Procedure Based on Cross-Reference to Data with Holder's Consent**

Article 10c of Directive 2001/83/EC provides the basis for the informed consent abridged procedure for applications for medicinal products that possess the same qualitative and quantitative composition in terms of active substances and in the same pharmaceutical form as an existing product. This type of abridged procedure allows an applicant to make use of the pharmaceutical, preclinical, and clinical documentation contained in the registration file of a medicinal product for which an MA exists already on the basis of explicit consent by the existing MA holder. For the avoidance of doubt, it is noted that this process does not concern generic medicinal products.[4]

Consent of the MA holder must cover the use of all data contained in the initial registration file. The applicant must prove that the MA holder of the reference product has consented to the use of the dossier at the time of the application. An authenticated letter from the party granting consent is required, and the letter has to name the benefiting party, and clearly specify the medicinal product for which a new MA is sought.[5] In addition, a new letter of access in relation to the Active Substance Master file should be included with the informed consent application, without prejudice to the existing restrictions on access to the manufacturer-restricted part of the Active Substance Master file.

The applicant for an MA for an 'informed consent' product must have continuous access to the registration dossier. The file does not have to be in the possession of the applicant, but the applicant has to have immediate access to the dossier to be able to fulfil any requirements for MA, for example, to update a file or to produce the file for inspection.[6] The informed consent route may be used for commercial reasons for the MA holder to obtain a copy of original MA; for example, Bristol Myers Squibb obtained a copy of the MA corresponding to their product Karvea through an informed consent application for the product 'Irbesartan BMS', both applications used the centralised procedure. Alternatively, different legal entities may enter into a commercial relationship by which a third party wishes to obtain its own MA and the parties typically enter into contracts to cover the arrangement and guarantee necessary access to the registration dossier. Consent may not be withdrawn while the MA application is

---

4. *See* the *Notice to Applicants, Volume 2A Procedures for marketing authorization, Chapter 1 Marketing Authorisation* (Revision 11, July 2019) paragraph 5.6, available at: https://ec.europa.eu/health/sites/health/files/files/eudralex/vol-2/vol2a_chap1_en.pdf.
5. *Ibid.*
6. *Ibid.*

pending. Withdrawal of consent after issuance of the MA will not affect the legitimacy of the MA.[7] Nevertheless, withdrawal of consent may pose a problem to the holder of the MA, forcing revocation of the MA by the MA holder himself. Typically, issues evolving from withdrawal of consent must be dealt with in contractual terms and arrangements between parties giving and receiving consent.

[B] Abridged Procedure Based on Bibliographic Application for Well-Established Use

Pursuant to Article 10a of Directive 2001/83/EC, for active substances that have been well used for over ten years, it is possible to replace results of the preclinical tests and clinical trials in the registration dossier with detailed references to scientific literature demonstrating safety and efficacy. The applicant has to demonstrate that the active substance of the medicinal product for which MA is sought has been in well-established medicinal use within the EU for at least ten years. Although not part of the definition, it is generally accepted that the scientific references replacing preclinical test and clinical trial results must be available in the public domain.

The ECJ ruled in the *'Scotia case'*[8] that application of the bibliographic-abridged procedure should in no way relax the requirements relating to safety and efficacy, as the main objective of the legislation is to protect public health. The abridged procedure is merely intended to free the applicant from the obligation to carry out unnecessary clinical and preclinical tests, and an applicant is not freed from its obligation to show safety and efficacy that would otherwise be shown by submitting the results of preclinical and clinical tests.

[1] Well-Established Medicinal Use

Directive 2001/83/EC does not provide a definition of 'well-established use', but it lists factors to demonstrate that a medicinal product or the constituent has been extensively used with recognised efficacy and an acceptable level of safety.

The following criteria should be taken into account:[9]

- the time period over which a substance has been used;
- quantitative aspects of the use of the substance;
- the degree of scientific interest in the use of the substance;
- the coherence of scientific assessments;
- all aspects of the safety and/or efficacy assessment;
- a review of the relevant literature, taking into account pre- and post-marketing studies and published scientific literature concerning experience in the form of

---

7. *Ibid.*
8. ECJ, 5 October 1995, C-440/93.
9. Annex 1 to Directive 2001/83/EC.

epidemiological studies and, in particular, of comparative epidemiological studies;
- favourable and unfavourable information;
- any missing information and justification for why demonstration of an acceptable level of safety and/or efficacy can be supported even though some studies are lacking; and
- post-marketing experience with other products.

It is important to note that 'medicinal use' is a broad term to mean use as a medicine, not necessarily an authorised medicine.[10]

This type of abridged procedure only applies to an application for MA of medicinal products containing an active substance for the same therapeutic use as for which well-established use is being demonstrated. Unlike the abridged procedure relating to generic medicinal products, this procedure is not open to applications for medicinal products seeking MA for another therapeutic indication or an indication that is not well-established.[11]

[2] Ten Years of Use

Different periods of time may be necessary to establish well-established use. Ten years is the minimum length of time that the medicinal product is used in the EU before an application for well-established use can be made, but longer periods of use may be required, for example, if there has been non-continuous use. The ten-year period starts from the first systematic and documented use of the particular substance as a medicinal product in the EU. This period of use may not coincide with the dossier protection term. Proof of use throughout the ten-year period may come from the documentation provided by the applicant or literature available in the public domain.

Although data concerning use in clinical trials, compassionate use, and named patient supply may be submitted, this cannot replace the requirement to demonstrate a systematic and documented use for that ten-year period in the EU. Where relevant, the prevalence of the condition/disease should be taken into account when demonstrating the extent of use.[12]

Extensive medicinal use which took place in the territory of a new Member State is to be taken into account for the purpose of demonstrating well-established use, regardless of whether such use occurred before the accession of such Member State to the EU.[13]

---

10. *See* the *Notice to Applicants, Volume 2A Procedures for marketing authorization, Chapter 1 Marketing Authorisation* (Revision 11, July 2019) paragraph 5.4, available at: https://ec.europa.eu/health/sites/health/files/files/eudralex/vol-2/vol2a_chap1_en.pdf.
11. *Ibid.*
12. *Ibid.*
13. *Ibid.*

§13.03 ABRIDGED PROCEDURE FOR GENERIC PRODUCTS

Directive 2001/83/EC codified and assembled in a single text the community legislation that had originated with Council Directive 65/65/EEC of 26 January 1965, as amended several times by other Directives. Following the Pharmaceutical Review of 2001, Directive 2004/27/EC introduced new legal definitions to further improve harmonisation throughout the EU. These definitions reflect and codify case law and include:

- the introduction of a definition of a generic product as opposed to the use of the concept of 'essentially similar';
- introduction of a definition of 'reference product';
- introduction of the concept of a global MA;
- a change of the periods of data protection; and
- introduction of marketing protection in addition to data protection.

Articles 10(1) and 10(3) of Directive 2001/83/EC, as amended, provide the legal framework for obtaining marketing approval for generic products by reference to an originator's product registration dossier. The applicant does not have physical access to such dossier, which remains held as confidential information within the files of the competent authority. However, when the applicant has demonstrated that the medicinal product qualifies as generic version of the reference product, the authority responsible for making the assessment of the file of the applicant is referred to and can access to the reference product dossier.

The application form requires the applicant to name 'the reference product' for a generic application and supply the date of first MA within the EU. The chosen reference medicinal product must be a medicinal product authorised in the EU on the basis of a complete dossier in accordance with the provisions of Article 8 of Directive 2001/83/EC. The generic product must have the same qualitative and quantitative composition in active substance(s) as the reference product, the same pharmaceutical form and bioequivalence (where it is appropriate) has to be demonstrated between the generic product and the reference product. An authorised medicinal product can only be a reference product after lapse of a certain period of time, which is referred to as the 'Data exclusivity period.'

[A] Data Protection of a Registration File for Six or Ten Years

The provisions in relation to regulatory data protection or data exclusivity have developed over time. Directive 65/65/EEC originally included in Article 4(8) the particulars required for an MA application:

> 8. Results of: physicochemical, biological or microbiological tests; pharmacological and toxicological tests; clinical trials. However: (a) a list of published references relating to the pharmacological tests, toxicological tests and clinical trials may be substituted for the relevant test results in the case of: (i) a proprietary product with an established use, which has been adequately tested on human

beings so that its effects, including side effects, are already known and are included in the published references; (ii) a new proprietary product, in which the combination of active constituents is identical with that of a known proprietary product with an established use; (iii) a new proprietary product consisting solely of known constituents that have been used in combination in comparable proportions in adequately tested medical products with an established use; ... (b) In the case of a new proprietary product containing known constituents not hitherto used in combination for therapeutic purposes, references to published data may be substituted for the tests of such constituents.

The different Member States interpreted these provisions differently, with some allowing a second applicant to substitute references to the published literature instead of carrying out tests and trials while other Member States considered this insufficient. The Commission then proposed an amendment to Directive 65/65/EEC (these were eventually implemented through Directive 1987/21/EEC), which provided that the second applicant would not be obliged to carry out the tests and trials if a period of time had elapsed since the grant of the original MA. The period of time which was proposed was ten years which would 'enable the partial recovery of the research investment, which might not be protected otherwise, for example by a patent'.

The Commission therefore was looking to balance the interests of the innovative and generic pharmaceutical industries by the introduction of provisions which allowed generic applicants to refer to data contained in the registration dossiers after expiration of a certain protective period.

The provision that became law after Directive 1987/21/EEC introduced the concept of 'essential similarity' (see §13.03[E]), as set out in Article 4(8) of Directive 65/65/EEC (as amended):

Results of:

- physico-chemical, biological or microbiological tests;
- pharmacological and toxicological tests;
- clinical trials. However, and without prejudice to the law relating to the protection of industrial and commercial property:
  (a) The applicant shall not be required to provide the results of pharmacological and toxicological tests or the results of clinical trials if he can demonstrate:
    (i) either that the proprietary medicinal product is essentially similar to a product authorised in the country concerned by the application and that the person responsible for the marketing of the original proprietary medicinal product has consented to the pharmacological, toxicological or clinical references contained in the file on the original proprietary medicinal product being used for the purpose of examining the application in question;
    (ii) or by detailed references to published scientific literature presented in accordance with the second paragraph of Article 1 of Directive 75/318/EEC that the constituent or constituents of the proprietary medicinal product have a well established medicinal use, with recognised efficacy and an acceptable level of safety;
    (iii) or that the proprietary medicinal product is essentially similar to a product which has been authorised within the Community, in accordance with Community provisions in force, for not less than six years

and is marketed in the Member State for which the application is made; this period shall be extended to 10 years in the case of high-technology medicinal products within the meaning of Part A in the Annex to Directive 87/22/EEC or of a medicinal product within the meaning of Part B in the Annex to that Directive for which the procedure laid down in Article 2 thereof has been followed: furthermore, a Member State may also extend this period to 10 years by a single Decision covering all the products marketed on its territory where it considers this necessary in the interest of public health. Member States are at liberty not to apply the abovementioned six year period beyond the date of expiry of a patent protecting the original product. However, where the proprietary medicinal product is intended for a different therapeutic use from that of the other proprietary medicinal products marketed or is to be administered by different routes or in different doses, the results of appropriate pharmacological and toxicological tests and/or of appropriate clinical trials must be provided.

(b) In the case of new proprietary medicinal products containing known constituents not hitherto used in combination for therapeutic purposes, the results of pharmacological and toxicological tests and of clinical trials relating to that combination must be provided, but it shall not be necessary to provide references relating to each individual constituent.

As can be seen, the proposal of a uniform period of data protection of ten years set out in the Commission's report was modified, and Directive 1987/21/EEC amending Directive 65/65/EEC provided that the toxicological, pharmacological, and clinical trials which are necessary to obtain an MA for a medicinal product were not accessible for use by third parties for a minimum period of six years. However, a number of Member States used the discretionary option under the Directive to extend this period of dossier protection to ten years. A mandatory period of ten years was applied to 'high-technology medicinal products', and this period of time was later applied to all MAs which have been authorised through the centralised procedure when introduced under Regulation (EEC) No. 2309/93.

In 2001, the Community code relating to medicinal products for human use was consolidated, and the requirements of Article 4(8) were then set out in Article 8(3)(i) of Directive 2001/83/EC. When Directive 2001/83/EC was updated in October 2005, these provisions were set out in Articles 10(1), which are introduced by 'in derogation of Article 8(3)(i), and without prejudice to the law relating to the protection of industrial and commercial property'.

The period of data exclusivity of six or ten years has applied up until October 2013 for generic applications, after which the 8 + 2 + 1 data exclusivity provisions apply. The six-year countries are Austria, Denmark, Finland, Greece, Iceland, Ireland, Norway, Portugal, and Spain, and six years is the period adopted by the twelve newer Member States during their negotiations for their accession to the EU. The ten-year period of data exclusivity applies in Belgium, France, Germany, Italy, Luxembourg, the Netherlands, Sweden, and the UK. The ten-year period also applies to MAs approved using the centralised procedure.

[B] Data Protection and Marketing Exclusivity, 8 + 2 Years

With the enactment of Directive 2004/27/EC, the period of data protection was harmonised throughout all Member States, and it also introduced an additional term for marketing exclusivity for innovative medicinal products.

The first paragraph of Article 10(1) of Directive 2001/83/EC, as amended by Directive 2004/27/EC, introduced market protection for products authorised by the national competent authorities for applications made after 30 October 2005. The same regime of data exclusivity and market exclusivity is introduced for centrally authorised products on the basis of Article 14(11) of Regulation 2004/726, which applies to applications made after 20 November 2005.

The period is split into an eight-year term and a subsequent two-year term where the generic product cannot be marketed. This concept is generally referred to as the '8 + 2 formula'. The holder of an initial MA is granted eight years (as opposed to six or ten years under previous law) of data protection, during which it will not be possible for generic companies to cross-refer to the registration dossier of this initial product. Therefore, application for generic products based on a reference product cannot be made until after the lapse of the eight years of data protection. It generally takes one year for a generic MA to be granted, but in this case, the generic MA holder cannot place the generic product on the market before a period of two additional years of marketing exclusivity has lapsed for the reference product.

Full harmonisation was reached throughout all Member States in 2015 after lapse of the transitional law period.

[C] Data Protection Rules Applicable Within the EU until 30 October 2015

Due to transitional law, three different terms for registration dossier protection may be applicable in the various Member States. The different terms will co-exist until 31 October 2015, which is the end of the ten-year protection period for those medicinal products authorised on the basis of applications filed before the effective term of the Directive, which was 31 October 2005.[14] During the transitional period, the term of data protection depends on the national legislation applicable in the various Member States and the date of submission of an MA. The terms are as follows:

- Ten years for MAs granted by the following Member States: Belgium, Germany, France, Italy, Luxembourg, the Netherlands, Sweden, UK; this term ended on 31 October 2015.
- Ten years for MAs authorised through the centralised procedure on the basis of Regulation No. 726/2004; this term ended on 20 November 2015.

---

14. The effective term meaning in case of European Directives, the date by which the stipulations of a European Directive must have been implemented in national legislation of the EU Member States.

- Six years for MAs granted by the following Member States: Austria, Denmark, Finland, Ireland, Portugal, Spain, Greece, Poland, Czech Republic, Hungary, Lithuania, Latvia, Slovenia, Slovakia, Malta, Estonia, Cyprus, and also Norway, Liechtenstein, and Iceland, this term has ended on 31 October 2011.
- 8+2 years for all medicinal products authorised through the centralised procedure on the basis of Regulation No. 726/2004, effectively as of 21 November 2005.
- 8+2 years for all medicinal products authorised on the basis of Directive 2001/83/EC after being amended by Directive 2004/27/EC, effectively as of 31 October 2005.

Under the current rules, the reference product is protected against generic competition for ten years after the first MA is received for an active compound in any Member State in the EU (as opposed to six years in some Member States under the earlier rules). Yet, the generic applicant may start the MA approval process eight years after MA was obtained for the reference product.

Under the old rules, that is, applications submitted before 30 October 2005 using national or the mutual recognition procedure or before 20 November 2005 for applications using the centralised procedure, the old regime of regulatory data protection will continue to apply. In the latter case, applications for medicinal products containing new active substances used the centralised procedure increasingly from 2000 up until 20 November 2005, and for these centrally authorised products, the ten-year period of data protection applies in all Member States, including accession Member States.

[D] European Reference Medicinal Product

According to Article 10(1) of Directive 2001/83/EC, a generic application can be submitted in a Member State where the reference product has never been authorised. The applicant must indicate in which Member State the product is or was authorised in accordance with EU law. The competent national authority where the application has been filed can ask the competent authority where the reference product was first authorised for confirmation of grant of authorisation, details of the composition of the medicinal product, and any other data required; for example, the assessment report. These provisions lead to the notion of a European Reference medicinal product. The purpose of this is to give all citizens of the EU access to medicines.

Directive 2004/27/EC introduced a definition of reference product in EU law by amendment of Directive 2001/83/EC. Article 10(2)(a) of Directive 2001/83/EC provides that a product can only qualify as a 'reference medicinal product' if it is a product authorised under Article 6, in accordance with the provisions of Article 8 (i.e., if the MA for the reference product was granted on the basis of a dossier submitted in accordance with Articles 8(3), 10a, 10b, or 10c of Directive 2001/83/EC). Such dossier is often referred to as a 'stand alone' or 'full' dossier, as such dossier will include the result of preclinical and clinical tests. It is therefore possible for generic applications to refer to dossiers based on well-established use, fixed combination dossiers, or informed consent dossiers, since such dossiers contain all relevant information and are therefore considered complete dossiers.

It is not possible for a generic product to base an application for MA on another generic medicinal product, even when the active compounds are completely identical. The reason for that restriction is that the reference (first generic) dossier does not contain all relevant information concerning the medicinal product, as this can be found in part in the registration dossier of the medicinal product initially (innovative) authorised and containing the same active substance.

An important judgment of the ECJ in relation to the scope of use of reference products was given in the *Astra Zeneca* case.[15] In this case, the holder of the MA of the reference product attempted to block the marketing of the generic product by withdrawing the MA for the reference product, while maintaining the MA for its line extension. It was then argued that since the reference product was no longer on the market, the registration dossier of the reference product was no longer available as a source of information for reference by the generic applicant. The ECJ did not agree and ruled that withdrawal of the authorisation for the reference product did not affect the validity of an MA of which the application was submitted at a date when the MA was still in force. Withdrawal of the reference product will not affect the validity and legitimacy of the generic product application for MA. The generic product will have access to the market despite the fact that the reference product may not be marketed anymore.

In October 2014, the ECJ ruled in *Olainfarm*[16] that the holder of an MA for a product that is used as a reference product for the authorisation of a generic product of another manufacturer has the right to a judicial remedy enabling the earlier holder to challenge the decision of the competent authority which granted the MA for the generic product, provided that the holder of the earlier MA was seeking judicial protection of a right conferred on them by Article 10 of Directive 2001/83/EC.[17] This follows from Article 10 of Directive 2001/83/EC, read in conjunction with Article 47 of the Charter of the Fundamental Rights of the European Union. This is, for instance, the case when the holder of the earlier MA is of the opinion that in relation to the generic medicinal product, its own product cannot be regarded as a reference product.

In the *Nivalin*[18] case, the ECJ clarified that a medicinal product, which is not authorised in accordance with Directive 2001/83/EC, but under national legislation only, cannot qualify as a reference product.[19] The ECJ reconfirmed in this case that the abridged procedures were not intended to provide a relaxation of the conditions to prove safety and efficacy of generic medicinal products. Therefore, the ECJ held, in line

---

15. ECJ, 16 October 2003, C-223/01.
16. ECJ, 23 October 2014, C-104/13.
17. *Ibid.*
18. ECJ, 18 June 2009, C-527/07.
19. *Ibid.*

with their argumentation in the *Scotia* case,[20] that in order to be able to grant an MA for a generic medicinal product on the basis of the abridged procedure, what matters is that all the particulars and documents relating to the reference medicinal product remain available to the competent authority concerned by the application for MA. In order to benefit from the abridged procedure, the applicant must show that the reference medicinal product was authorised on the basis of the EU law in force at the time of the application for MA for the generic medicinal product. In *Olainfarm*, the ECJ established that a medicinal product authorised under Article 10a of Directive 2001/83/EC (well-established use within the EU for at least ten years) also fulfilled these requirements, in the sense that a medicinal product authorised on the basis of well-established use could later serve as a reference product for the MA of a generic medicinal product under Article 10 Directive 2001/83/EC.[21]

[1]   Global MA

Directive 2004/27/EC amending Directive 2001/83/EC introduced the concept of a global MA. This concept clarified whether or not medicinal products containing the same active substance but developed in different formulations ('line extensions') could benefit from new and separate periods of data protection.

The term 'line extension' is not a legally defined term, but it is generally and broadly used to refer to all medicinal products containing the same particular active substance, but developed, or at least authorised after the first medicinal product containing the particular active substance had received MA for the first time. For instance, a tablet containing an active substance may be authorised initially, this may be followed by an oral suspension or an injectable form and eventually a cream or ointment may be developed and authorised. All of these further developments of medicinal products containing the same active substance marketed by the same MA holder are usually referred to as line extensions.

Article 6(1) of Directive 2001/83/EC sets out the concept of global MA, which provides that when a medicinal product has been granted an initial MA on the basis of a full registration dossier, any additional strengths, pharmaceutical forms, administration routes, presentations, as well as any variations and extensions shall also be granted MA or be included in the initial MA. All these MAs shall be considered as belonging to the same global MA, in particular for the purpose of the application of the rules relating to registration dossiers for generic products based on reference products.

Each medicinal product containing an active substance for which an earlier development had ever received MA on the basis of a complete dossier may be used to serve as reference product. In other words, each line extension has the same starting point data and marketing protection as the first development. In practice, therefore,

---

20. ECJ, 5 October 1995, C-440/93.
21. ECJ, 23 October 2014, C-104/13.

line extensions only have limited or no protection, depending on the time remaining after the MA of the first medicinal product.

Due to the lack of protection of data gathered and submitted in order to have line extensions authorised, Article 6 of Directive 2001/83/EC provides for a very broad range of reference products that may be used for generic product applications under Article 10(1) Directive 2001/83/EC. It is possible to choose a line extension to serve as a reference product, even though the line extension may have been authorised or placed on the market for less than eight years.

The Notice to Applicants[22] contains several clarifications regarding the applicability of the global MA with respect to combination products. For instance, if the medicinal products being assessed contains – within the same pharmaceutical form – a combination of active substances, it will form a new and unique medicinal product requiring a separate MA, regardless of whether all of the active substances contained therein were already authorised in a medical product or not. The applicant of this combination product will have to demonstrate the therapeutic contribution of each of the active substances within the contribution.

If the medicinal product being assessed contains only one active substance which was part of an authorised combination product, the new medicinal product will form a new and unique medicinal product, requiring a separate MA which does not fall under the scope of the global MA of the already authorised combination product.

[2] *Reference to Products Authorised in the Member States: Cyprus, Lithuania, Malta, Poland, and Slovenia*

On 1 May 2004, Cyprus, the Czech Republic, Estonia, Hungary, Latvia, Lithuania, Malta, Poland, Slovakia, and Slovenia joined the EU. Under the Accession Treaty, new Member States had to comply with EU law by 1 May 2004. However, Cyprus, Lithuania, Malta, Poland, and Slovenia negotiated transitional periods during which MAs for medicinal products granted under national legislation which were (by definition) not compliant with EU law would continue to be valid only in that country but not in the rest of the EU. Existing national MAs in the Czech Republic, Estonia, Hungary, Latvia, and Slovakia had to be upgraded to comply with EU law by 1 May 2004 or withdrawn. As a consequence, national MAs that were not in compliance with European legislation and not covered by the transitional period had to be withdrawn immediately after accession.

Even though such medicinal products may have retained their status as authorised medicinal products, and remained on the market (subject to the conditions set out in the Accession Act of 2003), these products cannot serve as reference products, unless their MA was renewed in accordance with EU legislation.

---

22. See *Notice to Applicants, Volume 2A Procedures for marketing authorization, Chapter 1 Marketing Authorisation* (Revision 11, July 2019) paragraph 2.3, available at: https://ec.europa.eu/health/sites/health/files/files/eudralex/vol-2/vol2a_chap1_en.pdf (last accessed 31 October 2022).

[3]   Similar Biological Medicinal Products

Contrary to the classic chemical medicinal products for which it was relatively easy to analyse the chemical active substance and overall structure and composition, it is or can be quite difficult to characterise a biological medicinal compound. It is therefore not easy to extrapolate the efficacy and safety between a generic biological medicinal product and its reference product. An important feature of a biological medicinal compound is that a small modification can make a huge difference in efficacy and safety. As the difference between generic products and their reference products usually consist of small differences, it becomes evident that, in the situation of biological medicinal products, the ordinary methods of establishing safety and efficacy between the generic and its reference medicinal product are much more complicated. Also, the diversity of biological medicinal products is enormous.

Article 10(4) of Directive 2001/83/EC states that where a biological medicinal product which is similar to a reference biological product does not meet the conditions in the definition of generic medicinal products, owing to, in particular, differences relating to raw materials or differences in manufacturing processes of the similar biological medicinal product and the reference biological medicinal product, the results of appropriate preclinical tests or clinical trials relating to these conditions must be provided. The type and quantity of supplementary data to be provided must comply with the relevant criteria stated in Annex I of Directive 2001/83/EC and related detailed guidelines.

Due to the diversity in the category of biological medicinal products, abridged procedures include additional clinical trials, compared with those submitted for generic applications. However, these clinical trials may be of shorter duration than those conducted by the innovator, for example, by the use of appropriate markers as a surrogate to show a clinical effect.

[E]   Essential Similarity and Generic Medicinal Product

[1]   Development of 'Essentially Similar' and Scope of Abridged Procedure for Generic Medicinal Products up to October/November 2005

Historically, Article 10(1 iii) of Directive 2001/83/EC[23] provided that an applicant did not have to submit the results of toxicological and pharmacological tests or the results of clinical trials if the applicant could demonstrate that the medicinal product was essentially similar to a medicinal product which had been authorised within the EU, in accordance with EU provisions in force for not less than six or ten years, and the product was marketed in the Member State for which the application was made.

---

23. Before the enactment of Directive 2001/83, Directive 65/65, Article 4.8 iii contained an identical clause.

A special procedure for obtaining MA was provided for in the final paragraph of the Directive, often referred to as the 'Proviso'. On the basis of the Proviso, where the medicinal product was intended for a different therapeutic use from that of the other medicinal products marketed or was to be administered by different routes or in different doses, the results of appropriate toxicological and pharmacological tests and/or of appropriate clinical trials had to be provided. This specific procedure was called the hybrid abridged application procedure.

Before discussing the currently applicable legislation allowing abridged application procedures for generic medicinal products, it is important to review the legislative history and case law because these interpretations by the ECJ have been codified and implemented in Directive 2001/83/EC by Directive 2004/27/EC. This case law was decisive for issues in relation to data protection/market exclusivity, the meaning and scope of reference products, and the actual scope of protection of registration dossiers for the first MA of new active substances and line extensions. This case law remains important in understanding and interpreting the current Directive 2001/83/EC as well as Regulation No. 726/2004.

[a]   *Meaning of 'Essential Similarity'*

The concept of 'essential similarity', as instituted by Directive 1987/21/EEC, was fundamental in establishing whether or not a medicinal product would qualify for an application on the basis of the abridged procedure, as well as to the question whether or not a product could serve as reference product. However, it was never defined in EU legislation. Ever since its introduction in 1987,[24] the term 'essentially similar' has been the source of legal debate.

In 1998, the ECJ rendered a landmark decision in the *Generics* case.[25] The *Generics* case concerned the grant of an MA for a generic product for a specific indication of a reference product. The reference product had been marketed for more than ten years for other indications but less than ten years for the indication for which the generic product sought MA. In this case, the Court was asked what 'essentially similar' meant and to what extent applications for MAs could be based on line extensions. The ECJ formulated a number of principles on the basis of which a competent authority would have to establish whether or not a generic medicinal product must be qualified as 'essentially similar' to the reference medicinal product. These principles are:

(a) the generic product must have the same qualitative and quantitative composition in terms of active ingredients;
(b) the generic product must have the same pharmaceutical form;
(c) the generic product must be bioequivalent to the reference product; and

---

24. On the basis of Article 4.8(a)(iii) of Directive 65/65/EEC.
25. ECJ, 3 December 1998, Case 368/96.

(d) in light of scientific knowledge, the generic medicinal product does not differ significantly from the original product as regards safety or efficacy.

The *Generics* case is important not only because it was the first time that the highest Court interpreted 'essential similarity' but also because it showed how the Court balanced the conflicting interests of innovative pharmaceutical companies and generic companies. The ECJ did not give any weight to time and costs invested by innovators in further developing their product and obtaining MA for line extensions (in this case, development of the active substance for new therapeutic indications). The ECJ ruled that all line extensions are eligible to serve as reference products as long as they meet the criteria for essential similarity formulated under (a) -(d), stated above. This decision was the first development into the concept of a global MA, as now captured in Article 6 of Directive 2001/83/EC.

The ECJ's interpretation of 'essential similarity' created doubt about the scope of the hybrid abridged procedure. Under the hybrid application, an applicant is required[26] to submit results of preclinical and clinical tests and trials in cases where the medicinal product is intended for a different therapeutic use from that of the other medicinal products marketed or is to be administered by different routes or in different doses. The ECJ did not determine in *Generics* whether it was necessary for a product to be considered essentially similar in order to be able to rely on the hybrid procedure. Being able to rely on the Proviso was important for the authorisation of new dosage forms because their quantitative composition will, by definition, not be the same. Further, any new pharmaceutical form will be in conflict with the second principle set forth in the *Generics* case, requiring that an essentially similar product have the same pharmaceutical form. The question that remained unanswered was whether or not the data submitted to support an application for a medicinal product on the basis of the Proviso must be accorded a further period of protection of six or ten years so that this data could not be used by third parties to support an application for a product which is generic to the product authorised on the basis of the Proviso.

[b]   Scope of Application of the Hybrid Abridged Procedure

This issue was further considered in 2004 by the ECJ in the *Novartis* case.[27] In this case, the innovative company marketed two medicinal products containing the same active ingredient. The second product was a line extension of the first authorised medicinal product. The MA for the line extension was based on the abridged informed consent procedure. However, due to existing differences in bioavailability and pharmaceutical form, bridging data had to be provided on the basis of applicability of the Proviso, demonstrating that the line extension was as safe and effective as the reference

---

26. Article 4.8 (iii).
27. ECJ, 29 April 2004, C-106/01.

Chapter 13: Abridged Procedure §13.03[E]

product. Only five years after the MA for the line extension was issued, an MA for a generic medicinal product of that line extension was granted. Although all three products contained the same active ingredient, due to the different pharmaceutical form, none of these three products was bioequivalent to each other. Nevertheless, the generic application used the abridged procedure. The generic applicant chose the first authorised product as reference product, referred to data contained in the dossier of the line extension, and submitted additional (often newly generated) data on the basis of application of the Proviso.

Clearly, there was no essential similarity between the generic product and the reference product. The question before the ECJ was whether or not the applicant seeking MA of a generic product on the basis of the abridged procedure was entitled to invoke the Proviso without losing the right to use the abridged procedure. The holder of the MA argued that the Proviso was only applicable if a product was essentially similar. The ECJ did not agree and reasoned that if recourse to the Proviso was only possible in case of essential similarity between the products in question, the Proviso would be largely ineffective in the case of medicinal products to be administered by routes or in doses different from those of other medicinal products on the market. Further, the ECJ referred to the Notice to Applicants, published by the European Commission in 1993, providing guidance on the interpretation of Directive 2001/83/EC and its predecessors, in which it was expressly stated that the Proviso could be applied in situations where the new medicinal product did not satisfy the strict criteria for essential similarity when compared with the reference medicinal product.

The ECJ further ruled that there is no independent period of dossier protection for line extensions, and that the competent authority is entitled to rely on data at its disposal to approve a generic product, even if such data originates from a different MA dossier for a line extension authorised less than ten years ago. As a result, the range of products that could qualify as reference product was considerably broadened.

The ECJ also held that, for example, the applicant for MA for Product C may refer to the pharmacological, toxicological, and clinical documentation relating to a Product B resulting from the development of the reference Product A, even if Products A and B are not essentially similar on account of their different bioavailability.

The Court concluded that new data generated by the initial MA holder for the registration dossier of both the active compound in its initial pharmaceutical form and for the line extension (in this case in a new pharmaceutical form) can be used for the MA of a product which is generic to a line extension.[28] The Court's decision extended the holding in the *Generics* case, which applied to new therapeutic indications for otherwise unaltered medicinal products, to allow applicants to choose any line

---

28. In the words of the Advocate General, 'The proviso operates in circumstances where bridging data are required because of a difference between the new product and the earlier product or products to whose data reference is made. Where product C claims essential similarity to product B which is a variant of product A, no additional data are required. There is therefore no need to proceed under the proviso'.

extensions to serve as reference product, provided that there is no significant difference as regards safety and efficacy in scientific terms.

[c] Essential Similarity and Line Extensions

Another important case, generally referred to as the *APS* case,[29] also related to an application for a medicinal product that was not essentially similar to the reference product which was the medicinal product that was initially authorised (fluoxetine in a capsule form) and had been on the market for over ten years. However, in contrast to the situation in *Novartis,* the new product was essentially similar to the line extension (in a different pharmaceutical form, fluoxetine liquid) which had not been on the market for more than ten years. The UK authority, the Medicines and Healthcare products Regulatory Agency (MHRA) required that the application for the line extension was accompanied by 'bridging data' to show that the line extension was bioequivalent to the first developed product. The applicant disagreed and judicially reviewed the MHRA's decision, and questions were referred to the ECJ by the UK High Court.

The ECJ confirmed that it would be possible to base an application for MA on the abridged procedure where the applicant seeks to demonstrate that the new product is essentially similar to a line extension, when the line extension is a new pharmaceutical form of an already authorised product. The applicant should be able to rely on the data submitted to support the application for the MA for the line extension when the only difference between the original product and the variant is that they have a different pharmaceutical form.

[d] Differences in Active Substance

In the *Generics* case,[30] the ECJ held that a product cannot be 'essentially similar' if such product presents a significant difference in safety and efficacy. The central question in the case before the ECJ in *SmithKline Beecham*[31] was whether or not a product that used a different salt as part of the active substance could be considered essentially similar. In particular, the Court considered whether the safety and efficacy profiles were different, taken the fact that the active substance consisted of a therapeutically active part and an inactive part.[32]

In this case, the active substance of the reference product and the active substance of the medicinal product claiming essential similarity were the same but were in the form of a different salt.

---

29. ECJ, 9 December 2004, C-36/03.
30. ECJ, 3 December 1998, Case 368/96.
31. ECJ, 20 January 2005, C-74/03.
32. *Ibid.*

[e] Safety and Efficacy

The applicant provided pharmacological and toxicological tests to demonstrate that safety and efficacy profiles were similar.[33] During the MA approval process, the competent authority concluded that there were no differences in bioavailability between the two salts.

The holder of the MA of the reference product argued that the medicinal products could not be essentially similar because they contain different, albeit related, active substances. The fact that further pharmacological and toxicological data were necessary in order to demonstrate essential similarity was sufficient to confirm that the active substances are different. Further, the MA holder argued that submission of further particulars in the form of pharmacological and toxicological tests or clinical trials in the context of an abridged procedure is permitted only pursuant to the Proviso, namely where the new product is intended for a different therapeutic indication or is to be administered by different routes or in different doses.

The ECJ agreed with the generic product applicant that additional data may have to be provided to demonstrate essential similarity. Data submitted in the context of the Proviso was designed to compensate for a lack of essential similarity, while data submitted under the application of the abridged procedure was generally intended to prove the existence of essential similarity. The ECJ noted that the applicant was not required to supply the results of pharmacological and toxicological tests or of clinical trials if the applicant could demonstrate that the product was essentially similar to the reference product. The Court concluded that, in support of an application under the abridged procedure, an applicant may, either spontaneously, or at the request of the competent authority of a Member State, supply additional documentation in the form of certain pharmacological and toxicological tests or clinical trials in order to demonstrate that its product is essentially similar to the reference product.

Although the ECJ introduced the term 'active ingredient' as part of the first principle developed in the *Generics* case,[34] it had never been properly interpreted. In this case, the issue of essential similarity was tied to the active principle rather than the pharmaceutical form or therapeutic indications as in the prior cases discussed above. The ECJ clarified that 'active ingredient' relates to the therapeutically active part of a medical product, while the active substance as a whole may differ by virtue of combinations with substances that do not change the safety and efficacy or therapeutic activity. The Court concluded that it does not follow the criterion of essential similarity as earlier established by the Court in the *Generics* case that there must be an exact molecular match between the active ingredients. The ECJ ruled that the abridged procedure was open to applications for MAs in respect of a medicinal product where that product contained the same therapeutic moiety as the reference product but combined with another salt.

---

33. *Ibid.*
34. ECJ, 3 December 1998, Case 368/96.

Taken the considerations on the basis of which the ECJ arrived at this ruling in relation to products containing salts as active ingredients, the ECJ ruling gives a general interpretation of the meaning of 'active ingredient'. A difference that does not present a significant risk to safety and efficacy will not usually prevent two medicinal products from being regarded as essentially similar.

[F]   Abridged Procedures for Generic Medicinal Products after October 2005

[1]   Definition of 'Generic Product' (Instead of 'Essentially Similar')

The requirement of 'essential similarity' is now captured in the definition of a generic product in Article 10(1) of Directive 2001/83. The hybrid abridged procedure (on the basis of the Proviso) is now contained in Article 10(3) Directive 2001/83/EC.

Pursuant to Article 10 of Directive 2001/83/EC, a 'generic medicinal product' shall mean:

> a medicinal product which has the same qualitative and quantitative composition in active substances and the same pharmaceutical form as the reference medicinal product, and whose bioequivalence with the reference medicinal product has been demonstrated by appropriate bioavailability studies. The different salts, esters, ethers, isomers, mixtures of isomers, complexes or derivatives of an active substance shall be considered to be the same active substance, unless they differ significantly in properties with regard to safety and/or efficacy. In such cases, additional information providing proof of the safety and/or efficacy of the various salts, esters or derivatives of an authorised active substance must be supplied by the applicant. The various immediate-release oral pharmaceutical forms shall be considered to be one and the same pharmaceutical form. Bioavailability studies need not be required of the applicant if he can demonstrate that the generic medicinal product meets the relevant criteria as defined in the appropriate detailed guidelines.

Therefore, different salts, esters, ethers, isomers, mixtures of isomers, complexes, or derivatives of an active substance must be considered to be the same active substance, unless they differ significantly in properties with regard to safety and/or efficacy. In those cases, additional information providing proof of the safety and/or efficacy of the various salts, esters, or derivatives of an authorised active substance must be supplied by the applicant.

The various immediate-release oral pharmaceutical forms shall be considered to be one and the same pharmaceutical form. The applicant does not have to conduct bioavailability studies if such applicant can demonstrate that the generic medicinal product meets the relevant criteria, as defined in the appropriate detailed guidelines.

Further information and details on the explanation of the various requirements for generic applications and qualification as a generic medicinal product can be found in Annex 1 to Directive 2001/83/EC and in the Notice to Applicants.[35]

---

35. *See Notice to Applicants, supra* n. 22, paragraph 5.3.

[a] Same Qualitative and Quantitative Composition

The requirement that the generic and reference products have the same qualitative and quantitative composition extends only to the active substance(s) and not to the other ingredients of the product. However, differences in excipient composition or differences in impurities must not lead to significant differences as regards safety and efficacy. The competent authorities will evaluate these differences in light of all scientific knowledge at their disposal.[36] The decision about whether a different form of the active substance is to be regarded as a new active substance should be taken by the competent authorities on a case-by-case basis. This is further discussed in §13.03[F][1][f] below.

[b] Same Pharmaceutical Form

This criterion relating to the same pharmaceutical form contained in the definition of generic medicinal product is evaluated with reference to the standard terms for pharmaceutical dosage forms established by the European Pharmacopoeia. A generic product and a reference product may be considered to have the same pharmaceutical form if they have the same form of administration as defined by the Pharmacopoeia. Furthermore, Article 10(2)(b) of the amended Directive provides that the various immediate-release oral forms, which would include tablets, capsules, oral solutions, and suspensions, shall be considered the same pharmaceutical form for the purposes of Article 10.[37]

According to the ECJ in their *Novartis* judgment,[38] in determining the pharmaceutical form of a medicinal product, account must be taken of the form in which it is presented and the form in which it is administered, including the physical form. In that context, medicinal products which are presented in the form of a solution to be mixed in a drink for administration to the patient are to be treated as all having the same pharmaceutical form, provided that the differences in the form of administration are not significant in scientific terms.

[c] Bioequivalence Demonstrated by Studies

Bioequivalence means that the biological availability of medicinal products is the same. Biological availability relates to the amount of active substance present in the blood at certain times after administration of the medicinal product. In order to demonstrate bioequivalence between a generic medicinal product and its reference product, both products will be administered in clinical trials. Where bioequivalence cannot be demonstrated through bioavailability studies, for example, for locally applied and locally acting drugs, Article 10(3) requires that the results of appropriate

---

36. ECJ, 20 January 2005, C-74/03.
37. *See Notice to Applicants, supra* n. 22, paragraph 5.3.
38. ECJ, 29 April 2004, C-106/01.

preclinical tests or clinical trials be provided in a hybrid application. The need for appropriate bioavailability studies should be addressed in the registration dossier.

[d] Salts, Esters, Ethers, Isomers, Mixtures, Complexes, or Derivations

It is now established in Article 10(2)(b) of Directive 2001/83/EC that different salts, esters, ethers, isomers, mixtures of isomers, complexes, or derivatives of an active substance shall be considered to be the same active substance. However, if there is a significant difference in properties with regard to safety and/or efficacy, additional information providing proof of the safety and/or efficacy of the various salts, esters, ethers, isomers or mixtures thereof, or derivatives of an authorised active substance must be supplied by the applicant.

While there is no further information providing guidance on when additional information is required, the ECJ suggests in the *SmithKline Beecham* case[39] (discussed above) that minor differences that do not affect the therapeutic use do not trigger the need for additional information.

[e] The Hybrid Procedure

If the product for which MA is requested does not entirely fit into the definition of a 'generic medicinal product', as provided in Article 10 (2)(b) or Article 10(3), the applicant must provide additional results of clinical and/or non-clinical research.

This applies in situations where:

- the generic product differs significantly in properties with regard to safety and/or efficacy;
- bioequivalence cannot be demonstrated through bioavailability studies; or
- there are changes in the active substance(s), therapeutic indications, strength, pharmaceutical form or route of administration.

Such applications are generally referred to as hybrid applications, as they are based in part on references to data contained in the registration dossier of the reference product and in part on new data.[40]

In case of hybrid applications, the results of tests and trials submitted must be consistent with the data content standards required in the Annex to Directive 2001/83, as amended.[41]

Some general guidance on the appropriate studies required to show that there is no significant difference in terms of safety and efficacy is given in Annex II to the Notice to Applicants.[42] In any event, this route should not be used as a legal basis for applications for products for which it is possible to demonstrate bioequivalence

---

39. ECJ, 20 January 2005, C-74/03.
40. *See Notice to Applicants, supra* n. 22, paragraph 5.3.2.2.
41. *Ibid.*
42. *Ibid.*

through bioavailability studies, but the applicant failed to submit results of such studies demonstrating bioequivalence.[43]

[f]   New Active Substance

In situations where a medicinal product does not qualify as a generic product, the MA applicant has to determine if such medicinal product has to be qualified as a new active substance for which a full registration dossier would need to be submitted.

Neither Directive 2001/83/EC nor Regulation 2004/726 contains a definition of 'active substance'. The mere fact that a product does not fit into the definition of generic medicinal product in itself does not mean that the product is a new active substance. If that were the case, the hybrid abridged procedure would be effectively meaningless.

The key factor in determining whether or not a medicinal substance would qualify as new active substance is whether or not a significant difference is present in properties with regard to safety and/or efficacy. If additional information concerning changes to the nature of the active substance cannot establish the absence of a significant difference with regard to safety or efficacy, then it may be necessary to submit the results of preclinical tests and clinical trials in accordance with the requirements of Article 10(3).

In the Notice to Applicants,[44] a 'new active substance' is defined very broadly:

A new chemical, biological or radiopharmaceutical active substance includes:

- a chemical, biological or radiopharmaceutical substance not previously authorised in a medicinal product for human use in the European Union;
- an isomer, mixture of isomers, a complex or derivative or salt of a chemical substance previously authorised in a medicinal product for human use in the European Union but differing significantly in properties with regard to safety and/or efficacy from that chemical substance previously authorised;
- a biological substance previously authorised in a medicinal product for human use in the European Union, but differing significantly in properties with regard to safety and/or efficacy which is due to differences in one or a combination of the following: in molecular structure, nature of the source material or manufacturing process;
- a radiopharmaceutical substance which is a radionuclide, or a ligand not previously authorised in a medicinal product for human use in the European Union, or the coupling mechanism to link the molecule and the radionuclide has not been authorised previously in the European Union.

Pursuant to the definition of 'generic medicinal product' under Directive 2001/83/EC, different salts, esters, ethers, isomers, mixtures of isomers, complexes, or derivatives of an active substance are considered generic unless they present a 'significant difference in properties with regard to safety and efficacy'. From the

---

43. Ibid.
44. See Notice to Applicants, supra n. 22, Annex I.

definition above, it appears that the Commission's definition of active substance is broader as it includes the group of isomers, salts, and complexes or derivatives of chemical substances when they are only 'differing in properties with regard to safety and efficacy'.

The judgment in the case of *Sepracor Pharmaceuticals (Ireland) v. Commission*[45] may have provided a legal definition of new active substance, but unfortunately, the action was declared inadmissible.

In this case, *Sepracor Pharmaceuticals (Ireland)* submitted an application for an MA for Lunivia (containing eszopiclone) to the EMA on 23 July 2007 and, in October 2008, received a positive opinion from the Committee for Medicinal Products for Human Use (CHMP) that an MA should be granted, but the CHMP also recommended that it should not be given 'new active substance' status. The CHMP confirmed this opinion in February 2009, and as a result, Sepracor withdrew its application in May 2009, before the Commission decision to grant the MA. The reason given for withdrawal was that this opinion compromised the commercial viability of launching the product in Europe. This was presumably due to the fact that without new active substance status, the product would not receive the 8 + 2 period of data protection. Sepracor brought this action to annul the decision by the Commission that the 'eszopiclone' contained in it was not a new active substance under Article 3(2)(a) of Regulation No. 726/2004. In support of its claims, Sepracor claimed that there was a failure to apply the correct legal criteria for a new active substance, and that the EMA took account of representations made by a third party without informing the applicant of their existence or giving it an opportunity to comment.

In 2013, the CHMP concluded (after re-examination) that teriflunomide, a metabolite of leflunomide, could be considered a new active substance in view of differences between teriflunomide and leflunomide as regards safety. On the same date, new active substance status was granted to Tecfidera (dimethyl fumarate). In view of the scientific evidence, dimethyl fumarate was considered to be different from Fumaderm, which consists of dimethyl fumarate and other active substances. It was clarified that dimethyl fumarate is part of the medicinal product Fumaderm, which was authorised in 1994 in Germany, but it has not been previously authorised as a medicinal product in the EU.

[G] Additional Terms for Protection of Line Extensions

As a consequence of the notion of a global MA (*see* §13.03[D][1]), all line extensions have the same period of data protection and marketing exclusivity as the initially authorised medicinal product.

In order to balance the interests of innovative industry and the generic industry and to stimulate research, development, and innovation, Directive 2004/27/EC

---

45. GC, 4 July 2011, Case T-275/09.

introduced options to extend the period of data protection or marketing exclusivity. Additional terms of marketing exclusivity are eligible for new therapeutic indications for existing medicinal products insofar as they present significant product developments. Generic products, with or without a new therapeutic indication, may not be placed on the market until expiry of the eleventh year. To benefit from the additional year, the new indication must be approved within the first eight years after the initial MA was granted.

An active substance may benefit from one-year additional data protection in three situations:

(1) new therapeutic indication(s) on the basis of Article 10(1) of Directive 2001/83/EC or Article 14(11) of Regulation No. 726/2004;
(2) new therapeutic indication(s) for a well-established substance, on the basis of Article 10(5) the Directive 2001/83/EC;
(3) extension following a change of the supply status of the medicinal product (from prescription-only to over-the-counter sales) on the basis of Article 74(a) of Directive 2001/83/EC.

[1]   Extension for New Therapeutic Indication

The additional year of marketing protection applies to the global MA for the reference medicinal product, meaning that an MA holder can only benefit from the extra year once.

Every application for a new indication must be assessed by the competent authority to determine whether the new therapeutic indication brings a significant clinical benefit in comparison with existing therapies. In the case of products authorised in accordance with the *centralised procedure*, decisions from the Commission authorising new therapeutic indications will contain a clear statement of whether the new indication represents a significant clinical benefit in comparison with existing therapies. In the case of medicinal products authorised through the *decentralised or mutual recognition procedures*, the assessment report by the reference Member State will contain a clear statement of whether the new indication represents a significant clinical benefit in comparison with existing therapies.

The Directive and the Regulation do not provide definitions of the qualitative criteria that must be met to benefit from the additional year of market exclusivity. However, the fundamental elements in Article 10(1) are:

- new therapeutic indication;
- significant clinical benefit;
- existing therapies.

[a] Justification of New 'Therapeutic Indication'

The Commission, in 2007, published guidelines entitled *Guidance on elements required to support the significant clinical benefit in comparison with existing therapies of a new therapeutic indication in order to benefit from an extended (eleven-year) marketing protection period*[46] with the aim to further outline the level of evidence required to support the extended marketing protection period. The guidelines state that a 'new therapeutic indication' may refer to either diagnosis, prevention, or treatment of a disease. The MA should provide a justification for the proposed new indication supported by appropriate scientific information.

In accordance with the abovementioned guidelines,[47] a new indication would normally include the following:

- a new target disease;
- different stages or severity of a disease;
- an extended target population for the same disease, for example, based on a different age range;
- other intrinsic (e.g., renal impairment) or extrinsic (e.g., concomitant product) factors;
- change from the first-line treatment to second-line treatment (or second-line to first-line treatment), or from combination therapy to monotherapy, or from one combination;
- therapy (e.g., in the area of cancer) to another combination;
- change from treatment to prevention or diagnosis of a disease;
- change from treatment to prevention of progression of a disease or to prevention of relapses of a disease;
- change from short-term treatment to long-term maintenance therapy in chronic disease.

[b] Justification of 'Significant Clinical Benefit'

The abovementioned guidelines[48] further require that the claim of significant clinical benefit in comparison to existing therapies has to take into account all existing products at the time of the relevant application. The applicant should also consider non-pharmacological approaches to the diagnosis, prevention, or treatment of the disease in question, as appropriate, such as surgical interventions, radiological techniques, diet, psychotherapy, physical means, and other specific and non-specific therapeutic methods which are considered 'state-of-the art' treatment for the indication in question in the EU. The applicant should provide background information on medicinal products that are not authorised in the EU if they are widely recognised and used by the medical

---

46. Available at https://ec.europa.eu/health/sites/health/files/files/eudralex/vol-2/c/guideline_1 4-11-2007_en.pdf.
47. *Ibid.*, paragraph 3.1.
48. *Ibid.*, paragraph 3.3.

community. The MA should provide scientific data and documentation establishing that the medicinal product for which the extended marketing protection period is sought is of significant clinical benefit in comparison with existing therapies. The justification should generally be supported by results of comparative clinical studies. The choice of the comparator (existing therapy) in clinical trial(s) should be justified by relevant scientific literature, CHMP guidance documents, or scientific advice from competent authorities.

A new treatment could generally offer a significant clinical benefit if it provides a clinically relevant advantage or major contribution to patient care. In general, demonstration of greater efficacy, improved safety profile, and/or more favourable pharmacokinetic properties resulting in demonstrable clinical advantages compared to existing methods may support the notion of significant clinical benefit. The CHMP in case of an application under Regulation (EC) No. 726/2004 or national competent authorities evaluate the claims for significant clinical benefit in comparison to existing therapies on a case-by-case basis.

Since these provisions have come into force, the CHMP reviewed the data and justifications submitted by the applicant, taking into account the provisions of Article 14(11) of Regulation (EC) No. 726/2004, taking into account the provisions of the abovementioned 2007 guidelines. In some cases, the CHMP has considered that the new therapeutic indication brings significant clinical benefit in comparison with existing therapies based on improved efficacy – for example, a variation to the summary of product characteristics (SmPC) for Torisel to add the indication of the treatment of adult patients with relapsed and/or refractory mantel cell lymphoma (MCL) but not in others, for example, Prezista due to lack of proof of superiority over the compared dosage regime. These decisions are available on the EMA website.

[2] *Extension for New Indications for Well-Established Substances*

A non-cumulative data exclusivity period of one year may be granted exclusively to the data concerning the new indications. Every application for a new indication must be assessed by the competent authority to determine whether the new indication for a well-established substance is based on significant preclinical or clinical studies. In the case of products authorised in accordance with Regulation (EC) No. 726/2004, Commission decisions authorising new therapeutic indications for well-established substances will contain a clear statement of whether or not the new indication is based on significant preclinical or clinical studies. In the case of medicinal products authorised through the decentralised or mutual recognition procedures, the assessment report by the reference Member State will contain a clear statement of whether the new indication is based on significant preclinical or clinical studies.

To qualify for the additional year of data protection for new indications for well-established substance, the medicinal product concerned does not have to be initially authorised under the legal basis of the well-established use procedure.

During 2007, the Commission published a guidance document entitled *Guidance on a new therapeutic indication for a well-established substance*[49] with the aim to describe the 'significant pre-clinical or clinical studies' that are necessary to qualify for the additional year of data protection. On the basis of this guidance, applicants for a new therapeutic indication should provide the authority assessing the application with any relevant information to determine whether the application concerns 'a new therapeutic indication' and whether 'significant pre-clinical or clinical studies' have been carried out in relation to this new indication. Further, the significance of the preclinical or clinical studies will be evaluated by the EMA scientific committees or national competent authority on a case-by-case basis. Other important elements in this guidance provide that:[50]

- the applicant should summarise in this report the new preclinical and/or clinical studies carried out in relation to the new indication, and why these should be viewed as significant preclinical or clinical studies;
- the applicant should include any preclinical and/or clinical studies conducted or sponsored by the applicant;
- in principle, when applying for MA for a new indication, it is expected that the applicant has carried out at least one confirmatory clinical trial to compare the new indication to a suitable comparator. This trial would be considered as a significant clinical study;
- exceptionally, other preclinical or clinical studies performed by the applicant could be considered significant if they allowed the use of existing or published data (e.g., clinical trials) to support the MA application in the new indication. Significance of these preclinical or clinical studies will be evaluated by the EMA scientific committees or national competent authority on a case-by-case basis. To be considered significant in this situation, preclinical or clinical studies should have been relevant and necessary to the approval of the MA application in the sought indication; it is the quality (importance of the data in relation to granting of an MA in the new indication), rather than the quantity of the data, which will usually determine the significance of these preclinical or clinical studies.

[3] Change of Supply Status

The supply status of a product is based on whether or not a product may only be obtained with a prescription from a medical doctor (or other persons authorised in a Member State to prescribe medicinal products). Other restrictions on supply may be imposed by national legislation of individual Member States. However, the one-year period of additional market protection is granted only if significant preclinical or

---

49. Available at https://health.ec.europa.eu/system/files/2016-11/10%252520_5_%252520guideline_11-2007_en_0.pdf.
50. *Ibid.*, paragraph 3.

clinical trials were carried out to justify a change in supply status from prescription-only to non-prescription medicinal products.

The legislation does not contain further guidance to interpret the requirement for significant preclinical or clinical trials. The Notice to Applicants[51] provides that the interpretation by competent authorities of the phrase 'significant pre-clinical tests or clinical trials' under Article 74a of Directive 2001/83/EC will be without prejudice to the interpretation of that phrase under Article 10(5), allowing for an additional year of market protection if significant preclinical or clinical studies were carried out in relation to a new indication for well-known substances.

When adopting a decision authorising a change of classification of a medicinal product, the competent authority must assess whether the change is based on significant preclinical tests or clinical trials. In the case of products authorised in accordance with Regulation (EC) No. 726/2004, Commission decisions authorising a change of classification will contain a clear statement of whether the change is based on significant preclinical tests or clinical trials. In the case of medicinal products authorised by the Member States, the decision of each competent authority authorising the change will contain a clear statement of whether the change is based on significant preclinical tests or clinical trials.[52]

§13.04 UK

Generally, the post-Brexit regulation of abridged MA applications in the UK continues to be aligned with the EU regime discussed above. As of 1 January 2021, the relevant UK regulatory framework continues to be set out in The Human Medicines Regulations 2012, as amended by the Human Medicines Regulations (Amendment etc.) (EU Exit) Regulations 2019 (UK HMRs). The UK HMRs continue to be based on the provisions of Directive 2001/83/EC (as of 31 December 2020), and as at the time of updating this Chapter, there do not appear to be any substantial planned changes to the UK regime relating to this subject matter. The MHRA, in its post-Brexit guidance relating to this topic,[53] further continues to reference the same EU guidance[54] for purposes of giving practical effect to the underlying legal provisions relating to abridged MA applications (as referenced in this Chapter in the context of the EU).

The post-Brexit MHRA guidance relating to the legal bases underpinning MAs in the UK confirms, among other things, that:

(1) the *informed consent* abridged procedure contemplated in Article 10c of Directive 2001/83/EC (*see* §13.02[A] above) is provided for in Regulation 56 of the UK HMRs;

---

51. *See Notice to Applicants, supra* n. 22, paragraph 6.4.
52. *Ibid.*
53. Available at https://www.gov.uk/guidance/types-of-application-legal-basis/.
54. *See,* for example, https://ec.europa.eu/health/documents/eudralex/vol-2/index_en.htm.

(2) the *bibliographic (well-established)* abridged procedure contemplated in Article 10a of Directive 2001/83/EC (*see* §13.02[B] above) is provided for in Regulation 54 of the UK HMRs; and
(3) the abridged procedure and hybrid abridged procedure based on reference to an existing registration dossier without consent of the innovator by the applicant (i.e., in respect of generic or biosimilar products) as contemplated in Article 10 of Directive 2001/83/EC (*see* §13.03 above) is provided for as follows:
– for *generic* applications: Regulation 51 of the UK HMRs;
– for *hybrid* applications: Regulation 52 of the UK HMRs; and
– for *similar biological* applications: Regulation 53 of the UK HMRs.

CHAPTER 14
Orphan Medicinal Products

Sarah Faircliffe & Pieter Erasmus

§14.01 INTRODUCTION

Some serious medical conditions are rare and affect only a small number of people. Medicines to treat, diagnose, or prevent such conditions[1] are commonly referred to as 'orphan drugs' (the term used in the EU legislation being 'orphan medicinal product'). It is estimated that between 5,000 and 8,000 rare diseases exist, affecting between 6% and 8% of the population in Europe. The low prevalence of rare conditions can make it very hard for pharmaceutical companies to recoup the costs of developing and bringing to market medicinal products that target such conditions, as low patient numbers pose a number of challenges, not least the lack of potential for large sales volumes. Only around 5% of rare conditions benefit from an authorised treatment. In order to encourage the research and development (R&D) of medicines to diagnose, prevent, or treat orphan conditions, Regulation (EC) No. 141/2000 of the European Parliament and Council of 16 December 1999 on orphan medicinal products[2] establishes a regime of incentives and rewards to encourage investment in the development of orphan medicinal products. Such incentives are available if an application to the European Medicines Agency (EMA) to have the particular medicinal product 'designated' an orphan medicine is successful, the main reward being the benefit of a period of 'market exclusivity' once a designated orphan is granted a Marketing Authorisation (MA).

Various countries have recognised the need to provide incentives to pharmaceutical companies to develop orphan medicinal products. In 1983, the US enacted the

---

1. Under EU legislation, a rare condition is considered to be one that affects no more than 5 in 10,000 people in the EU/EEA.
2. OJ L18/1, 22.1.2000.

Orphan Drug Act, which provides a period of market exclusivity and clinical trial tax incentives to encourage pharmaceutical companies to invest in developing orphan medicinal products. Orphan Drug legislation has since been enacted in Japan (1995), Singapore (1997), Australia (1998), and the EU (2000), plus a range of other countries in more recent years. However, it should be noted that the designation criteria and incentives offered differ between the different schemes.

Orphan medicinal products seeking authorisation in the EU must now use the 'centralised' procedure (*see* Chapter 5). Around 20% of products now authorised via this procedure are designated orphans, which highlights the impact and importance of the orphan legislation.

§14.02 THE EU ORPHAN MEDICINAL PRODUCT REGULATION

Regulation (EC) No. 141/2000 of the European Parliament and Council of 16 December 1999[3] on orphan medicinal products, more commonly known as the Orphan Drugs Regulation (ODR), establishes the criteria and procedure for obtaining orphan status in the EU and the rewards for orphan designated products. The specific objectives of the ODR are to stimulate (R&D) and the placing on the market of designated orphan medicinal products, while ensuring that patients suffering from rare conditions have the same quality of treatment as any other patient. The criteria for designating a product as orphan are described in detail in §14.03[D], but a key feature is the prevalence of the relevant condition, which must affect not more than 5 in 10,000 people in the EU.

Paragraph 2 of Article 3 of the ODR called upon the European Commission (Commission) to adopt an 'implementing' Regulation, which elaborates on the criteria for designation. The implementing regulation, Commission Regulation (EC) No. 847/2000 of the European Parliament and Council,[4] was enacted on 27 April 2000. Regulation (EC) No. 847/2000 sets out the provisions for implementation of the criteria for orphan designation, and it defines the concepts of 'similar medicinal product' and 'clinical superiority'. Together, Regulation (EC) No. 847/2000 and the ODR set out the key EU regulatory framework relating to orphan drugs. Since 2000, these provisions have undergone several relatively minor evolutions, the majority of which are clarifications as to the exact meaning of the terminology and procedures defined in the legislation. Several key guidance documents have been adopted (as referred to in this Chapter), which are updated where necessary (for example, to keep pace with relevant developments in science and technology).

---

3. OJ L18/1, 22.1.2000, as adapted by Regulation (EC) No. 596/2009 of the European Parliament of the Council of 18 June 2009 in respect of the regulatory procedures applicable for the adoption of the Implementing Regulation and decisions.
4. OJ L103/5, 28.4.2000.

§14.03 APPLICATIONS FOR ORPHAN DESIGNATION

In order to apply for designation of a medicinal product as an orphan medicinal product, the sponsor must be established in the Community. The sponsor submits an application for designation to the EMA[5] (*see* §14.03[G] for details of the review procedure). Sponsors must use the EMA's secure online IRIS platform to submit orphan designation applications and to manage pre- and post- designation activities. Information and guidance are available on the EMA website.[6] Either the application can be submitted directly, or the sponsor can request a pre-submission meeting/teleconference. Orphan designation applications are free of charge.

Each application is assigned two coordinators, one from the EMA's Committee for Orphan Medicinal Products (COMP) and one administrator from the EMA secretariat. The COMP reviews the application to determine whether the product meets the requirements for orphan designation. In order to synchronise evaluation of applications for orphan designation with the meetings of the COMP, regular deadlines for submission of applications are fixed and these dates are published on the EMA's website.[7]

In order to qualify for orphan status, the sponsor in question must apply for an orphan designation before submitting a Marketing Authorisation application.[8] More than one sponsor may obtain an orphan medicinal product designation for the same medicinal product intended to diagnose, prevent, or treat the same or a different condition. Each sponsor must submit an application for designation as specified in the guidelines.[9]

This section discusses the specific requirements for applying for orphan status, the evidence required to support such applications, and the approval process.

[A] Pre-application Meeting

Pre-submission meetings are not mandatory, but if sponsors feel they could benefit from a preliminary discussion before the submission of an orphan designation application, they may request a pre-submission meeting/teleconference at least two months prior to their planned submission date. The function of the meeting is to ensure, in advance, that the application meets the EMA's requirements. These meetings usually take the form of a telephone conference, with follow-up calls when necessary.

---

5. Standard Operation Procedure on orphan medicinal product designation and maintenance (SOP/H/3534 – April 2022).
6. www.ema.europa.eu.
7. *Ibid.*
8. ODR, Article 5(1); *see* §14.03[F] for more details.
9. Guideline on the format and content of applications for designation as orphan medicinal products and on the transfer of designations from one sponsor to another, 27.03.2014 (ENTR/6283/00 Rev 5, July 2021); Procedural Advice for Orphan Medicinal Product Designation – Guidance for sponsors (EMA/420706/2019, Rev. 11, September 2021).

[B] Application Contents and Format

In preparing an application for orphan medicinal product designation, sponsors are requested to follow the Commission guideline on the format and content of applications.[10]

The application must be accompanied by the following particulars and documents:

(a) the name or corporate name and permanent address of the Sponsor;
(b) the active ingredients of the medicinal product;
(c) the proposed therapeutic indication; and
(d) justification that the criteria in Article 3(1) are met, and a description of the stage of development, including the indications expected.

In November 2007,[11] the EMA and the US Food and Drug Administration (FDA) adopted a common application form for sponsors seeking orphan designation of medicines in both the EU and the US. The EMA and FDA recognised that the requirement to submit separate applications to the EMA and FDA using different submission formats, in some cases for the same underlying information, placed an additional burden on sponsors. The common application includes sections for the common information required by both agencies and individual sections for each of the EMA and FDA-specific requirements. There are also common procedures for submitting annual reports on the status of development of designated orphans. The EMA now also has special arrangements with Japanese regulators for common review.

Once submitted, the parallel submissions are reviewed independently to ensure that the requirements of their respective jurisdictions are met (and regulators may reach different conclusions on orphan status due to different designation criteria).

Although the common application is not mandatory, the EMA strongly recommends that it is used for all applications. The EMA will thus accept EU applications using the common form, even when the sponsor does not wish to apply for designation in the US/Japan. However, the EMA encourages the sponsor to seek orphan designation from the US and Japan in parallel because the EMA considers that this is in the best interests of the development of orphan drugs.[12] Although sponsors have expressed their desire for a common multi-jurisdiction designation, the ODR does not foresee recognition by the EU of orphan status granted in other regions, and the criteria for orphan designation are not internationally harmonised.

---

10. Guidelines on the format and content of applications for designation as orphan medicinal products and on the transfer of designations from one sponsor to another ENTR/6283/00 (Rev. 5, July 2021).
11. Press release of the Commission, the EMA, and the US FDA, London, 26 November 2007, Doc. Ref. EMEA/557391/2007, 'The European Union and the FDA Working Together to Create Common Application for Orphan Designation for Medicines'.
12. 'Procedural Advice for Orphan Medicinal Product Designation – Guidance for sponsors', EMA/420706/2019, Rev. 11, September 2021.

Chapter 14: Orphan Medicinal Products §14.03[D]

[C] COMP

Applications for orphan designation are reviewed by the COMP (*see* §14.03[G]). The COMP is an EMA scientific committee, created in 2000 under the ODR, and is responsible (among other things) for issuing opinions about whether a particular medicinal product meets the criteria for orphan designation (*see* §14.03[D]) and thus should be granted orphan status. The COMP opinion is given to the Commission, and the Commission makes the final formal decision as to whether orphan designation is granted.

The COMP has taken on an important role both in stimulating the development of orphan medical products and in implementing the orphan drug legislation. In order to conduct its review of designation applications, the COMP utilises a network of nominated experts, which includes clinicians specialising in rare diseases and representatives of patient groups. The COMP was the first of the EMA's scientific committees to include representatives of patient groups as full members. To facilitate transparency, the COMP's opinions are summarised for the public in layperson's language. These summaries are written by the EMA and validated by concerned sponsors and European patient group representatives.

Other responsibilities of the COMP include assisting the Commission with the production of detailed guidelines on orphan medicinal products, advising on the establishment and development of EU policy on orphan medicinal products, and facilitating international communication on orphan drug matters.

[D] Criteria for Orphan Designation

[1] Medicinal Product

If a sponsor seeks to obtain the designation of a medicinal product as an orphan medicinal product, the product must first meet the definition of 'medicinal product' (*see* Chapter 2, §2.02[A]).

Some products may be on the borderline between medicinal products and medical devices (*see* Chapter 2, §2.02[M] and Chapter 19, §19.02). Medical devices and food supplements are not medicinal products and therefore cannot receive orphan designation in the EU, even if they may be used for the treatment of orphan conditions.

[2] Article 3(1) Requirements

If a sponsor seeks to obtain the designation of a medicinal product as an orphan medicinal product, the product must meet the criteria for designation set out in Article

495

3(1) of the ODR. As well as the legislative provisions, a number of guidance documents address the application of the designation criteria.[13]

There is a two-part test for designation; Article 3(1) of the ODR sets out the following:

> a medicinal product shall be designated as an orphan medicinal product if its Sponsor can establish:
>
> (a) that it is intended for the diagnosis, prevention or treatment of a life-threatening or chronically debilitating condition affecting not more than five in 10 thousand persons in the Community when the application is made [known as the 'prevalence criterion'], or that it is intended for the diagnosis, prevention or treatment of a life-threatening, seriously debilitating or serious and chronic condition in the Community and that without incentives it is unlikely that the marketing of the medicinal product in the Community would generate sufficient return to justify the necessary investment; [known as the 'insufficient return on investment criterion'] and
>
> (b) that there exists no satisfactory method of diagnosis, prevention or treatment of the condition in question that has been authorised in the Community or, if such method exists, that the medicinal product will be of significant benefit to those affected by the condition.'

[3]   Article 3(1)(a) Requirements

The designation must be based on either the prevalence criterion or the insufficient return on investment criterion pursuant to Article 3(1)(a). The first of these is by far the most commonly relied upon (the latter being used very rarely; for details, *see* the discussion in §14.03[D][3][b]).

In identifying the relevant orphan condition, the sponsor must take into account the guidance provided[14] and consider the 'medical plausibility' of using the product in question in the proposed orphan indication (*see* §14.03[D][3][c] below for more detail). The designated orphan condition may not be identical to the final therapeutic indication included in the terms of the MA (for example, the authorised indication may relate to a sub-set of patients affected by the orphan condition).

[a]   The Prevalence Criterion

For a medicinal product to be designated as an orphan under the prevalence criterion, it must be intended to diagnose, prevent, or treat a life-threatening or chronically

---

13. *See*, for example, Commission notice on the application of Articles 3, 5, and 7 of Regulation (EC) No. 141/2000 on orphan medicinal products (2016/C 424/03), and other specific guidance referred to in this Chapter.
14. *See* 'Guideline on the format and content of applications for designation as orphan medicinal products and on the transfer of designations from one sponsor to another, 27.03.2014', ENTR/6283/00, Rev.5, July 2021 and other documents referred to therein.

Chapter 14: Orphan Medicinal Products §14.03[D]

debilitating condition. The sponsor needs to establish that the condition affects not more than five in 10,000 persons in the Community at the time the application is made.

For the purposes of the ODR, the prevalence is calculated based on the population of the EU Member States[15] together with Iceland, Liechtenstein, and Norway. The prevalence criterion makes reference only to the incidence within the Community, and therefore if the condition affects a large number of people outside of the Community, but has a low prevalence within the Community (such as is the case for neglected tropical diseases), it may be possible for such conditions to be eligible for orphan designation (as discussed in more detail below).

In preparing an application for orphan medicinal product designation based on prevalence, sponsors should consult the EMA's 'Points to Consider on the Calculation and Reporting of the Prevalence of a Condition for Orphan Designation'.[16] Article 2(1) of Regulation (EC) No. 847/2000 stipulates that for the purpose of establishing prevalence, the sponsor must provide:

(a) documentation that includes appended authoritative references to demonstrate that the disease or conditions for which the medicinal product would be administered affects not more than five in 10,000 persons in the Community at the time at which the application for designation is submitted, where such documentation is available;
(b) data that include details on the condition intended to be treated, and justification of the life-threatening or chronically debilitating nature of the condition, supported by scientific or medical references;
(c) documentation that includes or refers to a review of the relevant scientific literature and information from relevant databases in the Community, where these are available. Where no database in the Community is available, reference may be made to databases in other countries, provided the appropriate extrapolations are made; and
(d) information on a disease or condition where it has been considered within the framework of other Community activities on rare diseases. In the case of diseases or conditions included in projects financially supported by the Community to improve information on rare diseases, a relevant extract must be submitted. In particular, details of the prevalence of the disease or condition must be provided.

---

15. The Member States of the European Union are as follows: Austria, Belgium, Bulgaria, Croatia, Cyprus, Czech Republic, Denmark, Estonia, Finland, France, Germany, Greece, Hungary, Ireland, Italy, Latvia, Lithuania, Luxembourg, Malta, Netherlands, Poland, Portugal, Romania, Slovakia, Slovenia, Spain, and Sweden.
16. COMP/436/01 Rev 1 (June 2019); *see also* 'Guideline on the format and content of applications for designation as orphan medicinal products and on the transfer of designations from one sponsor to another, 27.03.2014', ENTR/6283/00, Rev.5, July 2021.

If a product is for the diagnosis or prevention (rather than treatment) of a condition (e.g., a vaccine), then the prevalence calculation is based on the population to which the product is expected to be administered on an annual basis.[17]

Fulfilling the prevalence criterion is a fairly straightforward task where all of the data demonstrate that the prevalence condition is clearly satisfied.[18] The COMP requires the designation application to include a conclusive statement as to the number of persons affected by the condition in the Community at the time of making the application.[19] However, in some cases, defining orphan population levels is more difficult. Often, because of the rare nature of these conditions, there are few doctors who are educated about the rare disease, and the orphan condition may go undiagnosed for some time or be misdiagnosed. Furthermore, with the advances in new technologies that permit the development of drugs that are specific to a particular patient's genotype or tumour disease, populations are increasingly being categorised by more specifically defined conditions. In circumstances where a sponsor claims that it is medically plausible to use his or her product to treat, prevent, or diagnose only a subset of patients suffering from a particular condition (*see* the discussion in §14.03[D][3][c] below),[20] then the application must report the prevalence of the subsets as well as that of the condition. The difficulties in defining orphan population levels are further compounded by the variation between procedures for identification and maintenance of prevalence data in the different Member States. Orphan population levels may also vary from region to region within the EU, even within a single condition, particularly if it is genetically linked,[21] but it is the overall prevalence within the Community as a whole which is the determining factor.

The question of whether a prevalence of zero (i.e., no cases of the condition to be found in the EU) is sufficient to satisfy the prevalence criterion has been debated. An application for orphan designation of a product containing tecovirimat to treat monkeypox infection was rejected[22] by the Commission, despite the positive opinion of the COMP in favour of granting orphan designation. A parallel application for orphan designation of the same active substance to treat variola infection (also zero prevalence in the EU) was similarly rejected.[23] In its decisions, the Commission explained the reasoning underpinning its finding that the designation criteria had not been met, namely that the sponsor had not established that there were any persons affected by the relevant condition in the EU when the application was made. Prevalence of the condition outside the EU and the risk of its future occurrence in the EU are not relevant

---

17. Commission notice on the application of Articles 3, 5, and 7 of Regulation (EC) No. 141/2000 on orphan medicinal products (2016/C 424/03).
18. For detailed guidance on fulfilling the prevalence criterion, *see* COMP document 'Points to Consider on the Calculation and Reporting of the Prevalence Condition for Orphan Designation', COMP/436/01 Rev 1 (June 2019).
19. *Ibid.*
20. Guidance on medical plausibility of subsets is available: 'Guideline on the format and content of applications for designation as orphan medicinal products and on the transfer of designations from one sponsor to another, 27.03.2014', ENTR/6283/00, Rev.5, July 2021.
21. Some 80% of rare diseases have identified genetic origins, affecting 3%–4% of births.
22. Commission Implementing Decision C(2011)10128 final of 11/1/2012.
23. *Ibid.*

for the purposes of orphan designation, the Commission noted. According to the Commission:

> This criterion of occurrence requires not only that the prevalence is equal to or less than five in 10,000 persons; it also requires that there is affectation by the condition in the EU at the moment when the application is made. This follows from the wording of this provision: *'intended for the diagnosis, prevention or treatment of a life-threatening or chronically debilitating condition affecting not more than five in 10 thousand persons in the Community when the application is made'*. For this criterion to be fulfilled it is thus necessary that there are not more than five persons in 10 thousand persons in the EU affected by the condition. It is therefore not enough for the fulfilment of this criterion that there are no persons affected by the condition. (Italics added)

However, the position on a zero prevalence has now been clarified in the European Commission's Notice on the application of Articles 3, 5, and 7 of the ODR,[24] with the introduction of a more flexible, risk-based approach. This provides that a medicinal product intended to diagnose, prevent, or treat a condition which affects a large number of people in certain non-EU countries, but which has a low prevalence or a prevalence of approximately zero in the EU, may be eligible for designation as an orphan medicinal product with respect to the prevalence criterion, and if all other criteria are met, eligible for the benefits set out in the Regulation. It goes on to specify that where prevalence in the EU is currently approximately zero, account should be taken of the risk that persons in the EU may become affected.

The orphan condition may comprise a broader population than the population defined by the proposed therapeutic indication, and this broader population should thus be the one on which the prevalence estimate is based.[25] In practice, the majority of orphan designation applications concern a condition the prevalence of which falls well below the prevalence threshold. In all cases, but particularly where the population prevalence is less clear or approaching the threshold level, the applicant will need to present and carefully assess evidence of prevalence from all available sources. The evidence should be presented using valid epidemiological designs and statistical methods. The COMP recognises that it will not always be possible to provide data on the actual prevalence of a condition, and the prevalence criterion demonstration may necessarily be based upon estimated data. In such circumstances, the EMA requires evidence that the estimate provides a good approximation.

[b]   The Insufficient Return on Investment Criterion

For designation under the insufficient return on investment criterion, the product must be intended to diagnose, prevent, or treat a life-threatening, seriously debilitating, or

---

24. Commission notice on the application of Articles 3, 5, and 7 of Regulation (EC) No. 141/2000 on orphan medicinal products - (2016/C 424/03).
25. 'Guideline on the format and content of applications for designation as orphan medicinal products and on the transfer of designations from one sponsor to another, 27.03.2014', ENTR/6283/00, Rev.5, July 2021.

serious and chronic condition without taking the prevalence of the condition into consideration. The sponsor must also establish that, without incentives, it is unlikely that the marketing of the medicinal product in the Community would generate sufficient return to justify the necessary investment.

The sponsor must first provide scientific or medical references to support the classification of the condition as life-threatening, seriously debilitating, or serious and chronic in nature. The sponsor must then demonstrate the costs that the sponsor has already incurred or expects to incur in developing the product. All costs and revenue data must be reported in accordance with generally accepted accounting practices, certified by a registered accountant, and accompanied by a signed statement from the sponsor to this effect.[26]

Specifically, Article 2(2) of Regulation (EC) No. 847/2000 stipulates that the sponsor must provide:

(a) data including appropriate details on the condition intended to be treated and a justification of the life-threatening or seriously debilitating or serious and chronic nature of the condition supported by scientific or medical references;
(b) data on all costs incurred by the Sponsor in the course of developing the medicinal product;
(c) details of any tax incentives or other cost recovery provisions received within the Community or in third countries;
(d) a clear explanation of and justification for the method that is used to apportion the development costs between indications where the medicinal product is already authorised for an indication or where the medicinal product is under investigation for one or more indications;
(e) a statement and justification for all development costs that the Sponsor expects to incur after the submission of the application for designation;
(f) a statement of and justification for all production and marketing costs that the Sponsor has incurred in the past and expects to incur during the next ten years that the medicinal product is authorised;
(g) an estimate and justification for the expected revenues from sales of the medicinal product in the Community during the first ten years after Authorisation;
(h) all cost and revenue data shall be determined in accordance with generally accepted accounting practices and shall be certified by a registered accountant in the Community; and
(i) the documentation provided shall include information on the prevalence and incidence in the Community of the condition for which the medicinal product would be administered at the time at which the application for designation is submitted.

---

26. *Ibid.*

There have been very few applications for designation based on this ground.[27] Between April 2000 and April 2005, only two applications were submitted on the basis of insufficient return on investment.[28] One of the applications was withdrawn by the sponsor, and the second application resulted in orphan designation for a booster vaccine for prevention of tuberculosis.[29]

[c]   Medical Plausibility

The Commission Guideline on the format and content of designation applications[30] highlights that all applicants need to address the 'medical plausibility' of using the product in the proposed orphan indication, alongside the designation criteria. Thus the applicant must address the rationale for the use of the product in the proposed orphan indication and, where the orphan indication refers to a subset of a particular broader condition, a justification of the medical plausibility for restricting the product to use in the subset; 'convincing arguments would need to be presented to justify the medial plausibility of any proposed subset and the rational for excluding the larger population'. The COMP must consider the rationale for development of the product in the proposed orphan indication and guard against the so-called salami-slicing of conditions into artificially small sub-sets, which should not be valid for designation purposes.

The Commission Guideline notes the points to take into account when considering the definition of a condition and what constitutes a valid condition as opposed to what would be considered invalid subsets within a condition. The COMP may modify the designated condition applied for, for example, where it considers the 'medically plausible' orphan condition to be broader than the (artificially narrow) one applied for.

In order to support the rationale for the development of the product in the proposed condition, preliminary pre-clinical or some clinical data are generally required.

[4]   Article 3(1)(b) Requirements

Medicinal products that satisfy the requirements of either the prevalence or the insufficient return on investment criterion must also then meet the conditions set out in Article 3(1)(b) of the ODR in order to qualify for designation. Article 3(1)(b) of the ODR requires:

---

27. According to the industry, the criterion's lack of success is due to the difficulty of estimating future investments and returns on that investment a priori, before the therapeutic indications for which the product may be used or the price at which it will be sold are clear.
28. COMP Report to the Commission in relation to Article 10 of Regulation (EC) No. 141/2000 on Orphan Medicinal Products, EMEA/35218/2005.
29. Recombinant modified vaccinia virus Ankara expressing tuberculosis antigen 85A, *see* 'Press Release Committee for Orphan Medicinal Products September 2005 Meeting', EMEA/COMP/299233/2005.
30. 'Guideline on the format and content of applications for designation as orphan medicinal products and on the transfer of designations from one sponsor to another, 27.03.2014', ENTR/6283/00 Rev. 5, July 2021.

that there exists no satisfactory method of diagnosis, prevention or treatment of the condition in question that has been authorised in the Community or, if such method exists that the medicinal product will be of significant benefit to those affected by that condition.

[a] Existing Satisfactory Method

In examining the existence of a 'satisfactory' method, the Implementing Regulation (EC) No. 847/2000 requires the sponsor to provide the details of 'any existing diagnosis, prevention or treatment methods of the condition in question. These may include authorised medicinal products, medical devices or other methods of diagnosis, prevention or treatment that are used in the Community'.[31]

The sponsor must submit justification for (i) why such existing methods are not considered satisfactory; or (ii) the assumption that the medicinal product for which the application is being sought will be of significant benefit to those affected by the condition (the 'significant benefit assumption' – see §14.03[D][4][b] below).[32] The sponsor's justification must make reference to scientific and medical literature or other relevant information.

In considering alternative methods, it is assumed that any authorised medicinal product is to be considered a 'satisfactory' method (as referred to in Article 3(1)(b)) in respect of the authorised indications. This being the case, applicants for orphan designation should seek to show an assumption of significant benefit over any existing authorised medicinal product in accordance with the second part of paragraph Article 3(1)(b) rather than seeking to show that an existing authorised medicinal product is not a satisfactory method.[33] In this context, a medicinal product authorised in one Member State of the EU is generally deemed as being 'authorised in the Community'; it is not necessary for it to have EU authorisation or to be authorised in all Member States.

Commonly used methods of diagnosis, prevention, or treatment that are not subject to MA (e.g., surgery, medical devices) may be considered satisfactory methods if there is scientific evidence as to their value. However, a product prepared in a hospital under a hospital exemption scheme (see Article 3(7) of Directive 2001/83/EC) should not be considered a satisfactory method of diagnosis, prevention or treatment of a condition.[34] The sponsor is required to provide the relevant information, including scientific and medical literature on the existing authorised medicinal product, so that the assessment can be made in light of the evidence provided to demonstrate 'significant benefit' (as discussed below).

---

31. Article 2(3)(a) Commission Regulation (EC) No. 847/2000.
32. For guidance, see 'Guideline on the format and content of applications for designation as orphan medicinal products and on the transfer of designations from one sponsor to another, 27.03.2014', ENTR/6283/00, Rev.5, July 2021.
33. Commission notice on the application of Articles 3, 5, and 7 of Regulation (EC) No. 141/2000 on orphan medicinal products, Section B.4 (2016/C 424/03).
34. Ibid.

In Case T-549/19, *Medac v. Commission*,[35] the General Court held that only products authorised for the same condition may constitute satisfactory methods, the scope of an authorisation being defined by its summary of product characteristics (SmPC). Where a future orphan product is intended for the diagnosis, prevention, or treatment of conditions or categories of patients for which comparative medicinal products are not authorised (according to their respective SmPCs, strictly interpreted), these products cannot be regarded as 'satisfactory' methods.

[b]   Significant Benefit

'Significant benefit' is defined in Article 3(2) of Regulation (EC) No. 847/2000 as 'a clinically relevant advantage (i.e. improved efficacy and/or improved safety) or a major contribution to patient care' that may, for example, be a more convenient method of administration.

Where an existing satisfactory method of treatment for the orphan condition already exists, and thus significant benefit needs to be evaluated (which is the case in the majority of designation applications),[36] the sponsor must compare the proposed orphan medicinal product to those existing (authorised or otherwise) established treatments.[37] Due to the existence of an authorised or established treatment for the condition in question, and low prevalence of the orphan condition, the COMP recognises that it is likely that there will be little or no conclusive clinical experience with the orphan medicinal product that is the subject of the application. The COMP therefore conducts its assessment of significant benefit based on certain assumptions. The assumptions are made at the time of orphan designation and must demonstrate a satisfactory (assumed) significant benefit over existing treatments.

In January 2012, the COMP held a workshop on the 'significant benefit' criterion and its future development.[38] The aim of the workshop was to discuss the assessment of significant benefit by the COMP at the time of orphan designation and MA, and it included discussions on ways to communicate the grounds for significant benefit more explicitly and how to develop a systematic approach to its assessment. The workshop concluded that there was a need to make the main conceptual grounds for significant benefit more explicit, and that a better definition and structure of the scientific justifications for significant benefit, including a review of the level and type of data requirements, was needed. As there are no procedures allowing post-marketing

---

35. *Medac Gesellschaft für klinische Spezialpräparate v. Commission*; Case T-549/19 (2019/C 337/15).
36. Owing to the increasing number of orphan medicines authorised, more and more products need to demonstrate significant benefit. An analysis performed in 2018 on products authorised between 2000 and 2015 showed that demonstration of significant benefit was required in 64% of designations and for 73% of products at the time of MA.
37. For guidance on the justification of significant benefit, *see* 'Guideline on the format and content of applications for designation as orphan medicinal products and on the transfer of designations from one sponsor to another, 27.03.2014', ENTR/6283/00, Rev.5, July 2021.
38. *See* meeting report 'Significant benefit of orphan drugs: concepts and future developments' EMA/326061/2012.

submission of data for significant benefit, strengthening the input on significant benefit at the time of protocol assistance/scientific advice was deemed important and, in addition, there was a need for more comprehensive public information on the assessment of significant benefit (particularly at the time of grant of the MA).

Revised Commission guidance adopted in 2016[39] emphasises that the concept of 'significant benefit' should be strictly interpreted; examples are provided in the Commission Notice so, for instance, 'significant benefit' should not be based on:

- possible increased supply/availability due to shortages of existing authorised products or to existing products being authorised in only one or a limited number of Member States (exceptions may be made if the sponsor has evidence of patient harm);[40]
- enhancement of the pharmaceutical quality of a product in compliance with relevant Committee for Medicinal Products for Human Use (CHMP) guidelines (this is an obligation for all marketing authorisation holders (MAHs));
- a new pharmaceutical form, a new strength, or a new route of administration, unless it brings a major contribution to patient care.

The Commission Notice explains that 'a clinically relevant advantage' may be based on:

- improved efficacy for the entire population suffering from the condition or a particular population subset or a subset that is resistant to the existing treatments; or
- a better safety profile or a better tolerability for the entire population suffering from the condition or for a particular subset.

In both cases, the claim should be based on clinical experience. A 'major contribution to patient care' may be based on:

- ease of self-administration, e.g., if the new treatment allows ambulatory treatment instead of treatment in a hospital only, or if it has a significant impact on convenience of use and reduces treatment burden; or
- significantly improved adherence to treatment due to a change in pharmaceutical form (e.g., modified release formulation), provided there are documented

---

39. Commission notice on the application of Articles 3, 5, and 7 of Regulation (EC) No. 141/2000 on orphan medicinal products (2016/C 424/03).
40. In order to support the aim of EU-wide access to treatment for patients with rare diseases, the Commission has in the past upheld the assumption of significant benefit of a Community Authorisation notwithstanding a national authorisation of an existing satisfactory treatment in a single or limited number of Member States, provided the other criteria for orphan designation were still met. In other words, extending the access of patients to an orphan treatment in terms of widening the territory in which the treatment would be authorised could be regarded as a 'significant benefit'. This possibility has now been restricted by the Commission Notice guidance.

difficulties with the existing form and data showing better clinical outcomes with the new form.

Difficulties should be documented in peer-reviewed publications, patients' registries, or therapeutic guidelines. A better clinical outcome could include better quality of life.

To be regarded as making a major contribution to patient care, the product should at least be equivalent in terms of efficacy, safety, and benefit/risk balance as compared with the authorised medicinal products.

The basis for each assumption should be clearly documented, rather than merely theoretical. The COMP assesses whether or not the assumptions are supported by available data and/or evidence supplied by the sponsor, taking into consideration the existing methods available and the specifics of the condition in question. For example, for certain conditions, ease of self-administration may be an important part of the assessment; but this will not be the case where the patient is hospital bound.

Furthermore, the Commission Notice clarifies that, when an orphan MA is extended to include a new indication within the designated orphan condition, such variation should only be allowed after formal verification that the new indication is of significant benefit compared to existing treatments.

In one of the first European Court judgments[41] regarding Regulation 141/2000, the General Court confirmed that the designation applicant must provide evidence to support the assertion of a significant treatment benefit (where this needs to be established), and the Commission must evaluate whether the new product would achieve a significant benefit when compared to the treatments already available. The Commission has a broad discretion to undertake such a technical evaluation, and the General Court will only overturn such a decision where the Commission has not followed the rules of procedure, has made an error in its assessment of the facts, or has misused its powers.

More recent litigation has further examined the significant benefit criterion and supported a strict approach to its interpretation (particularly at the 'maintenance review' stage; see §14.04[B]). In Case T-329/16 *BMS v. Commission and EMA*, the BMS product Empliciti (elotuzumab) had its orphan designation withdrawn prior to the grant of an MA. The COMP held that BMS was unable to satisfactorily establish the significant benefit of Empliciti over a recently authorised alternative treatment (Kyprolis), despite the very recent approval of Kyprolis (with the consequent challenge of gathering comparative data). BMS challenged this approach and argued for 'a standard of proof that supports the objective of the Regulation', but the General Court confirmed that BMS was obliged to prove significant benefit over all alternative products authorised at the time of grant of the MA.

Case T-733/17 *GMP-Orphan v. European Commission* also involved a challenge to the loss of orphan status as a consequence of the significant benefit assessment during the maintenance review procedure. The COMP held that there was no sufficient

---

41. Case T-74/08 *Now Pharm AG v. European Commission*, 9 September 2010.

demonstration of significant benefit of the orphan-designated Cuprior over an authorised alternative product (which was only authorised in only one Member State). GMP-Orphan's position was that the wider availability of Cuprior represented a significant benefit. The COMP undertook its own investigation and concluded that regulatory mechanisms exist to import the authorised alternative product into other Member States if required. Thus, significant benefit was not established based on availability, since there were in fact no sufficiently significant obstacles regarding access to the alternative product. The General Court agreed with the COMP and held that 'concrete and substantiated evidence and information' are required to support a claim of significant benefit, since the criterion should be strictly applied.

A third General Court case[42] also involved the concept of significant benefit, but specifically addressed the question of whether a new medicinal product can obtain designation if it has the same active substance as an existing orphan designated authorised product held by the same MAH (*see* §14.03[G] for a fuller discussion).

Finally, the General Court has examined the concept of 'significant benefit' in Case T-303/16 *Mylan v. European Commission*,[43] more particularly in relation to the concept of 'clinical superiority' (*see* §14.05[B][2] for a fuller discussion).

[E] Clinical Data at the Designation Stage

For the purpose of orphan designation, and to support the rationale for the development of the product for the proposed condition, some preliminary pre-clinical or clinical data are generally required. In respect of clinical data, the general requirements of the Clinical Trials Regulation[44] apply (*see* Chapter 4). The rare nature of orphan conditions means that there are special considerations for clinical trial design. The low incidence of the condition results in relatively few participants in any trial, which has an impact on the statistical analysis and can impinge on the integrity of the data produced. The sponsor should seek advice from the EMA to ensure that any innovative statistical approaches to clinical trials and novel study designs are acceptable. The EMA can provide free 'protocol assistance' to help the sponsor with the design of appropriate clinical trials (*see* §14.05[A] below).

[F] Timing of Designation Applications

A sponsor may apply to the EMA for designation of a medicinal product as an orphan medicinal product at any stage of the development of the medicinal product. However, the application for orphan designation must be made before the application for MA.[45] If a sponsor applies for designation for a medicinal product for which he has already submitted a Marketing Authorisation application (MAA) in any Member State in the

---

42. Case T-80/16, *Shire Pharmaceuticals Ireland Ltd, v. EMA*, judgment 22 March 2018.
43. Judgment of the General Court of 26 January 2022; currently under appeal.
44. Regulation (EU) 536/2014.
45. Article 5(1) ODR.

Chapter 14: Orphan Medicinal Products §14.03[G]

Community or centrally through the EMA, whether or not such MA has been granted, then the medicinal product is not eligible for designation for an orphan indication that is the same as the proposed therapeutic indication in the MAA; any application for orphan status must be based on a different orphan indication.

In a European Court judgment regarding Regulation 141/2000, the General Court[46] upheld the decisions of the EMA and the Commission that an application for orphan designation was invalid because the applicant already held an MA for the product in the relevant indication. The General Court rejected the applicant's arguments that Articles 5(1) and 2(4)(a) of Regulation 141/2000 were unlawful and made clear that the aim of Regulation 141/2000 is to incentivise companies to develop new treatments for orphan conditions; it is not intended to reward old products unless a new orphan therapeutic indication is developed.

[G] Designation Application Review Procedure and Appeal Process

The COMP is responsible for examining the designation application and adopting an opinion. After validating the application, a summary report on the application is prepared, which is circulated to all COMP members and discussed at the COMP's next plenary meeting. At this stage, the COMP will either adopt an opinion or raise a list of questions to be addressed in writing only or at an oral explanation at the next COMP plenary meeting. The COMP adopts an opinion by day 90 of the procedure. It forwards this to the Commission for adoption of a decision.

If at the end of the procedure, the COMP determines that the application does not satisfy the criteria set out in Article 3(1), the EMA informs the sponsor. Within ninety days of receipt of the COMP's opinion, the sponsor may submit detailed grounds for appeal,[47] which the EMA refers to the COMP for consideration. The EMA then submits the final opinion of the COMP to the Commission. The Commission has thirty days from the receipt of the opinion to issue the final decision as to whether or not orphan status is to be granted. If status is granted, the designated medicinal product is entered into the Community Register of Orphan Medicinal Products.[48]

The question of whether a new medicinal product can obtain designation if it has the same active substance as an existing orphan-designated authorised product held by the same MAH has been addressed by the General Court.[49] The active substance idursulfase was already designated and authorised as an orphan medicinal product, and the MAH submitted a further application for designation for idursulfase-IT: both products were intended as treatments for Hunter syndrome, but it was argued by the sponsor that the second product represented a significant benefit over the first. The

---

46. Case T-264/07 CSL *Behring GmbH v. European Commission* and the EMA, 9 September 2010.
47. Procedural advice on the appeal procedure for orphan medicinal product designation or review of orphan designation criteria at the time of MA; EMA/2677/01 Rev. 3–8 December 2020.
48. For the procedures applicable to orphan designated products, *see* Procedural advice for post-orphan medicinal product designation activities – Guidance for sponsors; EMA/469917/2018, Rev.12, 25 May 2022.
49. Case T-80/16, *Shire Pharmaceuticals Ireland Ltd, v. EMA*, judgment 22 March 2018.

EMA refused to validate the second designation application, on the basis that idursulfase-IT was covered by the original orphan designation and that the active substance idursulfase was already authorised. Historically, the EMA and the Commission had taken the view that companies were only entitled to one period of market exclusivity per active substance per orphan condition.

However, the General Court disagreed with this approach and found that the EMA was not entitled to refuse to validate the designation application. Just because two products contain the same 'active substance' does not necessarily mean that both are the same 'medicinal product'. The Court recognised that significant benefit would need to be established for the designation criteria to be met but noted that validation is a purely administrative step; the sponsor should have the opportunity to demonstrate the significant benefit of its second product during the designation procedure. In the Court's view, it is in the interests of rare disease patients to have access to alternative products offering significant benefit over existing treatments; nothing in the legislation allowed the EMA to refuse to validate the designation application.[50]

[H] Annual Reports

Once a medicinal product has received orphan designation, Article 5.10 of the ODR requires the sponsor to submit to the EMA an annual report on the state of development of the designated medicinal product until an MAA is submitted. Sponsors are no longer required to submit documents but need to complete the relevant fields in the IRIS system (there is an option to upload additional documents if appropriate).[51] The report provides information on the status of the development of the medicine, including a review of ongoing clinical studies, a description of the investigation plan for the coming year, as well as any anticipated or current problems in the process, difficulties in testing and potential changes that may have an impact on the medicine's orphan designation.

The annual reports are specific to the particular designation in question. Therefore, if a particular medicinal product has been granted several designations, a report is required for each designation.

[I] Amendment of a Designation

The designated orphan condition may need to be modified during product development to better reflect the indication that the sponsor intends to request at the time of MA. A change to the designated condition is possible in 'exceptional cases', where the classification of the disease changes.[52] The amendment request will follow the same assessment procedure as for a new designation.

---

50. Case appealed (Case C-359/18 P), but the CJEU agreed with the General Court.
51. *See* Procedural advice for post-orphan medicinal product designation activities - Guidance for sponsors; EMA/469917/2018, Rev.12, 25 May 2022.
52. *See* 'Guideline on the format and content of applications for designation as orphan medicinal products and on the transfer of designations from one sponsor to another, 27.03.2014',

Commission Guidance[53] addresses the question of whether it is possible to grant an orphan MA with a therapeutic indication that differs from the condition that has been accepted in the designation procedure. It provides that if an orphan designation and its continuing benefits are to be maintained, the therapeutic indication applied for and that finally authorised must both fall under the scope of the designated orphan condition. To ensure this, the sponsor may request that the designation decision be amended; this is possible if the new condition differs slightly from that designated previously. If the amended designation is not accepted by the COMP or if the sponsor does not apply to amend the designation, the authorised indication will not be a designated 'orphan indication'.

§14.04 ORPHAN MEDICINAL PRODUCT MA

Designation as an orphan medicinal product does not authorise the marketing of the product. As for any medicinal product, an MA is necessary to ensure that the product has satisfied efficacy, safety, and quality criteria. MAAs for orphan products still need to meet the same standards in respect of quality, safety, and efficacy as all other authorised medicines. However, the procedural options of a conditional approval or, where appropriate, an approval under 'exceptional circumstances', may be available to address the common issue of limited clinical data (*see* Chapter 5).

The MA granted for an orphan medicinal product can only cover orphan-designated therapeutic indications. The sponsors may apply for a separate MA for non-orphan indications. This would be the case where a medicinal product can be used to treat a rare condition, and it can also be used to treat a condition that is not rare and for which the medicinal product is not therefore able to obtain orphan designation. Thus, if a sponsor receives a *new* orphan indication for an approved non-orphan product, a separate orphan MA (under a new proprietary name) that will cover only the orphan indication(s) must be sought.

[A] The Centralised Procedure

Since 20 November 2005, in accordance with Article 3.1 Regulation (EC) No. 726/2004, all MAAs for designated orphan medicinal products are required to be made through the centralised procedure. Under the centralised procedure, a single central application results in an EU-wide MA (*see* Chapter 5, §5.03).

ENTR/6283/00, Rev.5, July 2021 section [H]; also, Procedural advice for post-orphan medicinal product designation activities – Guidance for sponsors; EMA/469917/2018, Rev.12, 25 May 2022.
53. Commission notice on the application of Articles 3, 5, and 7 of Regulation (EC) No. 141/2000 on orphan medicinal products (2016/C 424/03).

[B] Review and Confirmation of Orphan Designation Criteria at the Time of MA ('maintenance review')

Prior to the grant of an MA for the orphan medicinal product, the COMP must review and reconfirm that the orphan designation criteria are still met.[54] The sponsor must submit a report demonstrating that the orphan designation criteria are still maintained by the medicinal product[55] to ensure that there have been no changes that would result in the product no longer being eligible for orphan status at the time the MA is granted. Any changes must be set out in the report, together with any revisions to the information that was provided in support of the application for orphan designation. The COMP may adopt a list of questions and invite the sponsor to an oral hearing. The COMP's review is carried out independently of, but in parallel to, the evaluation of the MAA by the CHMP. If the COMP's view is that the criteria for orphan designation are no longer satisfied, the sponsor may appeal the opinion, but if the appeal is unsuccessful then the product is removed from the Community register of designated products.[56]

The Commission's Notice on the application of Articles 3, 5, and 7 of Regulation (EC) No. 141/2000 on orphan medicinal products[57] tightened up on the assessment of the designation criteria at this 'maintenance review' stage, and in particular, emphasises that any requirement to demonstrate 'significant benefit' must be assessed according to strict standards, with companies normally being required to provide more data than at the time of designation. For example, a claim of significant benefit due to a better safety profile is expected to be better substantiated by data than would have been required at the time of original designation. The COMP's assessment with a view to maintaining the orphan designation will be based on such data. The Notice provides that the significant benefit should include a quantitative element that allows the COMP to measure magnitude of effect as compared with an already authorised product; any advantage of the designated orphan product will be considered in the context of experience with authorised products in the orphan condition, even if comparative clinical studies are not possible. In exceptional cases, if it is not possible to generate a sample big enough to provide sufficient comparative evidence, alternative methods (e.g., indirect comparisons with external data) may be used.

Where two applications for MA for the same condition have been received by the EMA at the same time, they might not remain in parallel during the assessment process. In such cases, it may be difficult for the second product to show significant benefit as compared with the first product due to the limited information available. Thus, the Commission Notice[58] provides that, where the two applications are assessed at the

---

54. For more information, see Procedural advice for post-orphan medicinal product designation activities – Guidance for sponsors; EMA/469917/2018, Rev.12, 25 May 2022 Section 7.
55. The template Sponsor's report may be found on the EMA website: www.ema.europa.eu.
56. Article 5(12) ODR.
57. 2016/C 424/03.
58. *Ibid.*

same time, the sponsor of the second product does not need to show significant benefit as compared with the first product. However, the second sponsor should show data supporting significant benefit as compared with the first product if the notification of MA for it has been published in the Official Journal of the European Union at the time of the re-evaluation of the designation criteria by the COMP. This situation can present a challenge to the sponsor of the second product, but the courts have confirmed the correctness of a strict interpretation of the 'significant benefit' concept at the maintenance review (see the discussion in §14.03[D][4][b] above).

Case T-549/19 *Medac v. Commission*[59] is a case in the General Court which brings into question the interpretation of the designation requirement of no alternative 'satisfactory method' to treat, diagnose, or prevent the orphan condition. In this case, Medac's product 'Trecondi – Treosulfan' was granted an MA, but its orphan status was withdrawn after the maintenance review. Medac challenged the withdrawal, and one of the arguments before the Court concerned the correct interpretation of the concept of 'satisfactory method'; Medac claimed that the COMP's request for data about Trecondi as compared with unauthorised uses of other medicines constituted an incorrect interpretation of the designation criteria. The General Court held that only products authorised for the same condition may constitute satisfactory methods, the scope of an authorisation being defined by its SmPC. Where a future orphan product is intended for the diagnosis, prevention, or treatment of conditions or categories of patients for which comparative medicinal products are not authorised (according to their respective SmPCs, strictly interpreted), these products cannot be regarded as 'satisfactory' methods. The Commission's decision to withdraw Trecondi's orphan status was annulled.

§14.05 MARKET EXCLUSIVITY AND OTHER INCENTIVES

Articles 6 to 9 of the ODR provide various incentives to support research into and development of orphan medicinal products and to increase the availability of such products. Other Community incentives include research funding, grants, and possible tax incentives at the individual Member State level.[60]

[A] Protocol Assistance and Fee Reductions

Protocol assistance is a specific type of scientific advice that the sponsor may request from the EMA[61] after the medicinal product has been designated an orphan drug. Protocol assistance questions are submitted to the Scientific Advice Working Party

---

59. *Medac Gesellschaft für klinische Spezialpräparate v. Commission*; Case T-549/19 (2019/C 337/15).
60. For details of the incentives available in individual Member States, see 'Inventory of Union and Member State Incentives to support research into, and the development and availability of, Orphan Medicinal Products. State of Play 2015'; SWD (2015) 13 final.
61. See EMA Guidance for applicants seeking scientific advice and protocol assistance, EMA/4260/2001, Rev.9, 30 June 2017.

(SAWP), a division of the CHMP. Although not legally binding (on either the sponsor or CHMP), the sponsor has the opportunity to amend its proposed development strategies in accordance with the advice provided, thus helping to smooth the MAA process.

Protocol assistance is limited to queries about future development strategies for the designated orphan drug indication. The advice sought may be in relation to:

(a) the quality of medicinal products: including how the product is manufactured and chemical, pharmaceutical, and biological tests;
(b) non-clinical aspects: the toxicological and pharmacological tests to be carried out; and
(c) clinical aspects: questions relating to conducting studies in human patients or healthy volunteers, including clinical pharmacological trials designed to determine the efficacy and safety of the product for pre- or post-Authorisation activities, including pharmacovigilance plans and risk management programmes.

Protocol assistance extends beyond the pure scientific advice to demonstrate the quality, safety, and efficacy of the medicinal product in accordance with Regulation (EC) No. 726/2004;[62] it may also include information about how to demonstrate significant benefit, and how to demonstrate clinical superiority.

Applicants may request a clarification after receipt of the final advice letter or ask for a follow-up to the initial request for scientific advice or protocol assistance.

Pursuant to Article 5 of the ODR, sponsors of designated orphan medicinal products are eligible to apply for a reduction[63] of all fees payable. Fee reductions are granted out of a special fund from the Commission. The amount of this fund is set annually by the European Parliament.

The percentage fee reduction available can depend on whether the sponsor is a small and medium-sized enterprise (SME) and/or whether paediatric-related assistance is being sought but can amount to a full (100%) reduction on certain fees. Sponsors who wish to receive fee reductions should write a Letter of Intent to the EMA. In order to ensure that the reduction is applied to the fee for protocol assistance requests, sponsors should submit their fee reduction Letter of Intent as early as possible, and at least three weeks before making a protocol assistance request.

[B] Market Exclusivity

Of the various incentives the ODR offers, by far the most important is the award of market exclusivity for the ten years following the grant of an MA. Specifically, where

---

62. Regulation (EC) No. 726/2004 established Community procedures for the authorisation and supervision of medicinal products for human and veterinary use and established a European Agency for the Evaluation of Medicinal Products.
63. EMA Public statement on fee reductions for designated orphan medicinal products and details of fees can be found on the EMA website, www.ema.europa.eu.

Chapter 14: Orphan Medicinal Products §14.05[B]

an MA is granted for a designated orphan medicinal product, the Community and the Member States shall not, for a period of ten years, either accept an application for an MA, grant an MA, or accept an application to extend an existing MA, for the same therapeutic indication in respect of a 'similar medicinal product'[64] (see §14.05[B][1] below). The period of market exclusivity may be further extended by two years if agreed paediatric studies (see Chapter 8) are completed. The period may be reduced to six years if the market exclusivity is no longer justified (see §14.05[C] below) and exclusivity may be 'broken' if certain criteria are met (see §14.05[B][2] below).

The market exclusivity for an orphan medicinal product is independent of the existence of patents (or other intellectual property rights) and can coexist with such rights. If a pharmaceutical company is considering launching a competing medicinal product, it is therefore important to consider the various types of rights that might exist in respect of a particular medicinal product or medical condition. For example, the protection afforded by a patent with respect to a medicinal product may prevent another person from selling the same (infringing) medicinal product; the orphan market exclusivity may prevent competitors from being granted an authorisation to market another similar medicinal product for treatment of the same orphan condition.

The Commission's Notice on the application of Articles 3, 5, and 7 of Regulation (EC) No. 141/2000 on orphan medicinal products[65] clarifies that, where the therapeutic indication approved through the MA procedure is a subset of the designated orphan condition, the MAH will benefit from market exclusivity for the product in question, for that indication. If the same sponsor subsequently applies for MA for a second subset of the condition, the product will not benefit from any additional period of market exclusivity, for that second authorised indication. Furthermore, new subsequent formulations and routes of administration of an orphan medicinal product that has already been authorised fall within the scope of the existing orphan designation (although see the discussion of the *Shire v. EMA* case in §14.03[G] regarding the possibility of distinguishing between different 'medicinal products' for designation purposes').

[1] Meaning of 'Similar Medicinal Product'

Article 3 of the Implementing Regulation (EC) No. 847/2000 defines a 'similar medicinal product' as a medicinal product containing a similar active substance or substances as contained in a currently authorised orphan medicinal product, and that is intended for the same therapeutic indication. 'Active substance' means a substance with physiological or pharmacological activity, and 'similar active substance' means an identical active substance, or an active substance with the same principal molecular structural features (but not necessarily all of the same molecular structural features) and which acts via the same mechanism. A non-similar product is not caught by the ODR's market exclusivity provisions.

---

64. Article 8(1) Regulation (EC) No. 141/2000.
65. 2016/C 424/03.

In 2018, the Implementing Regulation was amended in respect of the 'similarity' concept by Regulation (EU) 2018/781. This was as a result of a consultation on adaptation to technical progress of the similarity concept, in light of the Commission's view that the 'definitions require adaptation...due to major developments in the field of biological medicines including ATMPs [advanced therapies]'. The implementing Regulation now reflects the fact that, in practice, the requirements for demonstrating 'similarity' may differ between product types (chemical/biological/advanced therapies), and the definition of 'similar active substance' has been extended accordingly. So, for advanced therapies for which the principal molecular structural features cannot be fully defined, 'similarity between two active substances shall be assessed on the basis of the biological / functional characteristics'. There is separate guidance on 'molecular structural features' for chemical, biological, and advanced therapy and radiopharmaceutical products.

In September 2008, the Commission published guidance on the general principles and procedure for assessing similarity.[66] This notes that software programs may be used to measure the degree of structural similarity between molecules. It also provides examples of factors that are not considered relevant to concluding whether mechanisms of action are the same (these being differences between substances in terms of mode of administration, pharmacokinetic properties, potencies, or tissue distribution of the target).

[2] 'Breaking' Market Exclusivity

Article 8(3) of the ODR permits derogation from the market exclusivity provided under Article 8(1) in certain circumstances, notwithstanding the similarity of the relevant products.[67] It is therefore possible for an MA to be granted for the same therapeutic indication in a similar medicinal product (the 'second medicinal product') if:

(a) the holder of the MA for the original orphan medicinal product has given his or her consent to the sponsor of the second medical product;
(b) the holder of the MA for the original orphan medicinal product is unable to supply sufficient quantities of the medicinal product; or
(c) the sponsor of the second medical product can establish in the MAA that the second medicinal product, although similar to the orphan medicinal product already authorised, is safer, more effective, or otherwise clinically superior.

---

66. Commission Communication: C(2008) 4077 final, "Guideline on aspects of the application of Art. 8(1) and (3) of Regulation (EC) No. 141/2000: Assessing similarity of medicinal products versus authorised orphan medicinal products benefiting from market exclusivity and applying derogations from that market exclusivity' (OJ 2008/C 242/08).
67. In September 2008, the Commission issued a Guideline as to how to apply the derogations from market exclusivity: C(2008) 4077 final, 'Guideline on aspects of the application of Art. 8(1) and (3) of Regulation (EC) No. 141/2000: Assessing similarity of medicinal products versus authorised orphan medicinal products benefiting from market exclusivity and applying derogations from that market exclusivity' (OJ 2008/C 242/08).

The third of these provisions is the most commonly relied on.

Article 3 of Regulation (EC) No. 847/2000 provides the following definition of 'clinical superiority':

> (d) 'clinically superior' means that a medicinal product is shown to provide a significant therapeutic or diagnostic advantage over and above that provided by an authorised orphan medicinal product in one or more of the following ways:
> (1) greater efficacy than an authorised orphan medicinal product (as assessed by effect on a clinically meaningful endpoint in adequate and well controlled clinical trials). Generally, this would represent the same kind of evidence needed to support a comparative efficacy claim for two different medicinal products. Direct comparative clinical trials are generally necessary, however comparisons based on other endpoints, including surrogate endpoints may be used. In any case, the methodological approach should be justified;
> (2) greater safety in a substantial portion of the target population(s). In some cases direct comparative clinical trials will be necessary; or
> (3) in exceptional cases, where neither greater safety nor greater efficacy has been shown, a demonstration that the medicinal product otherwise makes a major contribution to diagnosis or to patient care.

For applicants who are developing or seeking to develop a product where an issue with respect to similarity to a designated orphan medicinal product might arise, protocol assistance is available on request from the CHMP. If the applicant intends to rely on the derogation of clinical superiority, it is recommended that the applicant seek protocol assistance on the appropriateness of the studies intending to demonstrate such clinical superiority.

A decision to apply the waiver under Article 8(3)(c) ('clinical superiority' basis) is currently being challenged in the European Courts. In Case T-303/16,[68] Mylan was unsuccessful in the General Court in challenging the Commission's decision to allow derogation from the market exclusivity of the orphan product Tobi Podhaler on the grounds of clinical superiority. In its judgment, the Court considered both the concepts of 'significant benefit' and 'clinical superiority', particularly in relation to each other. The judgment is currently under appeal.[69]

[3] Procedure for Assessing Similarity and Derogations

For any MAA, it is necessary for the competent authority to determine whether there are any authorised orphan medicinal products against which a similarity assessment should be undertaken. This ensures that acceptance of the application will not infringe the market exclusivity of an authorised orphan product. In order to assess potential

---

68. *Mylan v. European Commission*; judgment of 26 January 2022.
69. Case C-237/22 P *Mylan v. European Commission*.

similarity, the second applicant must provide information on (non-)similarity and, if applicable, the justification for relying on one of the derogations.

The competent authority for the assessment of similarity and derogations depends on the procedure used to request the MA of the second medicinal product. If the second product's MAA is applied for centrally, the assessing body is the EMA. For national, mutual recognition, or decentralised procedures, the competent authority is the national competent authority(ies) concerned; however, these procedures may only be used where the second medicinal product is not itself an orphan medicinal product. The second applicant is required to provide the following information:[70]

(a) a report on non-similarity containing the comparison of the second medicinal product with authorised orphan medicinal product(s). The report must address the molecular structural features, mechanism of action, and therapeutic indication;
(b) if applicable, the following is also required to support the request for derogation:
   (i) for derogation under Article 8(3)(a): a signed letter from the holder of the authorised orphan product confirming his or her consent;
   (ii) for derogation under Article 8(3)(b): a report describing why the supply of the authorised orphan medicinal product is considered insufficient, and details of why patients' needs are not being met, including qualitative and quantitative reference substantiating these claims;
   (iii) for derogation under Article 8(3)(c): a comparative report justifying the clinical superiority of the second medicinal product, with particular references to the results of clinical studies and scientific literature.

The similarity check needs to be repeated before a product, which has successfully completed the scientific assessment stage of the procedure, actually receives an MA. If issues are identified at this stage, the second applicant is required to submit information on (non) similarity and/or justify the applicability of one of the derogations before the MA is granted. The procedural clock is stopped until such documentation is submitted.

The first case concerning the grant of a market exclusivity derogation to be brought before the General Court was discontinued on the grounds that the action had become devoid of purpose, since the contested measure had been withdrawn.[71]

---

70. For details, *see* Commission Communication: C(2008) 4077 final, "Guideline on aspects of the application of Art. 8(1) and (3) of Regulation (EC) No. 141/2000: Assessing similarity of medicinal products versus authorised orphan medicinal products benefiting from market exclusivity and applying derogations from that market exclusivity', Section 3.
71. *Novartis v. European Commission*: Case T-269/15; Order of the General Court of 15 May 2019.

[4] Impact of a Second Orphan Authorisation Granted under the Derogation Provisions

In the event that a second product, also a designated orphan, meets the criteria for breaking the market exclusivity of a prior authorised orphan and is also successful in obtaining an MA, then this second product will benefit from its own independent ten-year period of market 'exclusivity' (starting on the date of its authorisation and sharing 'exclusivity' with the first product for the remainder of that product's ten-year period but then continuing to benefit from exclusivity for the remainder of the ten years).

[5] Interpretation of the Market Exclusivity Provisions: European Court Judgments

Three judgments from the European General Court have considered possible limitations on the existence or scope of the market exclusivity awarded to authorised orphan products. In the first two cases discussed below, the judgments have tended to uphold the principle that Article 8(1) ODR provides a strong, broad market protection, which reflects the importance placed on having an effective EU orphan drugs policy. The third case discussed below was dismissed as inadmissible, but nonetheless raises an interesting question, which seems to have been settled by the Commission outside of litigation.

[a] Case T-140/12, Teva v. EMA

This case was the first to consider the interpretation of the orphan market exclusivity provisions. It concerned the market exclusivity awarded to two orphan products held by the same MAH (Novartis); the first product (imatinib/Glivec) was authorised as an orphan in November 2001 to treat chronic myeloid leukaemia (CML) (among other indications); market exclusivity for this product thus expired in November 2011. In January 2012, since Glivec's regulatory data protection had also expired, Teva sought to obtain authorisation for a generic version of Glivec by means of an abridged application, and their application covered a number of indications, one of which was CML. However, the EMA refused to validate this application on the grounds that the market exclusivity period running in relation to the second Novartis product (nilotinib/Tasigna) prevented them from doing so. In February 2006, Novartis applied for orphan designation of nilotinib as a treatment for CML and was granted it on the basis that the designation criteria were satisfied. Although imatinib and nilotinib were found to be 'similar' (within the meaning of Article 8(1)) and were both intended to treat CML, Novartis then went on to secure authorisation of nilotinib by waiving its own market exclusivity for imatinib and granting itself consent (in accordance with Article 8(3)) to apply for an MA. Nilotinib was held to meet the 'significant benefit' criterion contained in the orphan designation criteria, in relation to imatinib.

Nilotinib was granted an MA for treatment of CML in November 2007 and thus, as an authorised orphan product, it had the benefit of market exclusivity until November 2017, in accordance with Article 8(1) ODR. When Teva then applied for a generic imatinib authorisation, they faced the problem that because imatinib and nilotinib are 'similar' for the purposes of the application of the market exclusivity provisions, the regulatory authority (the EMA) interpreted Article 8(1) ODR as meaning that they had to refuse to validate the application in so far as it covered the CML indications for which nilotinib is authorised, due to the ongoing nilotinib market exclusivity (even though the imatinib exclusivity had expired).

In an action to annul the rejection of their application, the applicant argued that this was an incorrect interpretation of the legislation and that a similar second-generation product should not benefit from a new market exclusivity period for the same indications as those already authorised for a first orphan product. In other words, since Novartis had already benefitted from a full term (ten years) of market exclusivity for Glivec, it should not be able to rely on the nilotinib exclusivity to, in effect, extend this protection (to around sixteen years, in this case).

In rejecting Teva" arguments, the General Court made a number of points in relation to orphan market exclusivity. The question to be answered was as follows: can an orphan product benefit from market exclusivity where the MA for such product was granted due to reliance on one of the Article 8(3) derogations, namely where the sponsor of the first product (who in this case was also the sponsor of the second product) has consented? The Court found that Tasigna, as a designated orphan, benefits from ten years of market exclusivity in so far as the authorised therapeutic indications are concerned, according to Article 8(1), and that Article 8(3) has no bearing on the conditions under which the authorisation for a 'similar' product may be granted and says nothing about whether an authorisation based on the consent derogation confers market exclusivity on the similar product. If that similar product is an orphan, the ten years of market exclusivity with which it is endowed by virtue of Article 8(1) cannot be curtailed due to the existence of an orphan which was authorised for the same indications and which benefits from market exclusivity for those indications. The Court confirmed that independent designations/MAs granted in accordance with separate procedures trigger separate market exclusivity periods, which may overlap in time. It stated that the Tasigna sponsor cannot be penalised for relying on the consent derogation to obtain his authorisation and that 'equally irrelevant' for the purpose of applying Article 8(3) is the fact that the MAH for the original orphan product and the sponsor of the second product are the same. According to the Court, since nothing in the ODR suggests that the application of Article 8(3) precludes the application of Article 8(1), then the (orphan) Tasigna authorisation in respect of the same indications as for the original orphan product automatically confers ten years of market exclusivity; the fact that the indications for which both products are authorised are similar cannot undermine the market exclusivity enjoyed by each by virtue of Article 8(1). The Court's view was that market exclusivity must be granted in all cases in which an orphan designated product has been authorised, in order to attain the objective of the orphan drug legislation to incentivise development of orphan

Chapter 14: Orphan Medicinal Products §14.05[B]

products. The Court also noted the general principle that the market exclusivity period 'cannot be regarded as equivalent to the data protection periods enjoyed by any product .... as the effects and scope of each of those mechanisms are different'.

Teva appealed[72] the judgment, raising three arguments. First, they claimed that the General Court erred in law in its interpretation of the conditions for the application of the ten-year market exclusivity period, and the interpretation was contrary to the scheme of Article 8 of the ODR. Further, the fact that Article 8 does not address conflicting periods of market exclusivity granted under Articles 8(1) and 8(3) of the ODR shows that the legislature did not envisage such situations. The Court of Appeal upheld the General Court's interpretation, outlining that the grant of a ten-year period of market exclusivity falls in line with the objective to incentivise sponsorship of orphan medicinal products. The Court agreed with the General Court's approach that since the ODR does not contain any provision under which it is possible not to apply the ten-year period of market exclusivity to orphan medicinal products, where a similar medicinal product that has been granted MA under Article 8(3) is an orphan product, it enjoys the market exclusivity provided in Article 8(1) of the ODR.

Teva's second argument was that the General Court erred in law in its interpretation of the term of the market exclusivity period. Teva submitted that the General Court's interpretation will, in practice, lead to the prolongation of the market exclusivity period for Glivec because of the orphan status of the second product, Tasigna, in the same indication. The Court of Appeal rejected this argument, stating that the General Court was right to conclude that the ten-year period of market exclusivity for the second product cannot be curtailed when there is a first orphan medicinal product which has received MA for the same therapeutic indications, and which benefited from market exclusivity for those indications. It agreed with the view of the General Court, the EMA, and the Commission that the marketing exclusivity attaching to the first product, at least formally, will not be extended as a result of the fact that MA has been granted for the second (similar) product.

Finally, Teva submitted that the General Court failed to examine the alternative case put forward, namely that there should be an exception to the market exclusivity granted to a second medicinal product so as to permit the authorisation of a generic version of the first product, once the period of exclusivity for that first product has expired. The Court held that the General Court had considered and rejected these arguments in the judgment under appeal. The appeal was dismissed.

It remains to be seen whether, eventually, the legislation may be changed to specifically address such situations.

[b]   Case T-452/14 Laboratoires CTRS v. European Commission

This case was an action brought by the MAH (CTRS Laboratoires, or CTRS) of an orphan product (Orphacol/cholic acid). CTRS was concerned about the authorisation of a second product (Kolbam) eroding the scope of Orphacol's market exclusivity. A

---

72. Case C-138/15 P.

preceding, separate, General Court action had already been required to consider the separate question of whether Orphacol should be granted an MA (in relation to the legal basis of the application, namely well-established use); this was resolved in favour of CTRS, and an authorisation was granted; as a designated orphan, Orphacol had the benefit of ten years of market exclusivity (in two liver disease indications). A separate product, Kolbam (developed by a different company), contained the same active ingredient, so it could not subsequently be authorised for either of Orphacol's approved indications due to the market exclusivity, but was granted an MA for a further three indications (also in liver disease).

However, CTRS was concerned about references in both the SmPC and the EMA's assessment report of Kolbam to the efficacy and safety of cholic acid in treating the Orphacol therapeutic indications. In their action before the General Court, CTRS argued that these statements were, in effect, claiming that Kolbam is effective for treating the Orphacol therapeutic indications, thereby implying that Kolbam is also authorised for those indications. CTRS submitted that this resulted in the circumvention of the market exclusivity from which Orphacol benefitted, as it could encourage off-label prescribing of Kolbam in the Orphacol indications. The Commission argued that since, formally, the MA for Kolbam was not granted for the Orphacol therapeutic indications, there could be no breach of Orphacol's market exclusivity for those therapeutic indications, but the General Court agreed with CTRS and held that the Commission Decision granting Kolbam's marketing authorisation should be annulled.

The Court made the general point that 'if the effectiveness of Article 8(1)…is to be ensured, the off-label prescribing of a medicinal product for therapeutic indications covered by the market exclusivity attaching to another medicinal product by virtue of that provision should not be facilitated. Such a consideration is particularly compelling given that off-label prescribing is not prohibited, or even regulated, by EU law'. In finding that Orphacol's ten-year period of market exclusivity was being undermined by statements about the efficacy of Kolbam in the Orphacol indications, the judgment confirms and upholds strong market exclusivity protection for orphan medicinal products.

[c]   CaseT-583/13 Shire Pharmaceutical Contracts v. European Commission

This action concerned whether Article 37 of Regulation (EC) No. 1901/2006 (the Paediatric Regulation) confers an entitlement to an extension (to twelve years) of the market exclusivity period, in the case of non-patented orphan medicinal products when compliance with an agreed Paediatric Investigation Plan (PIP) is voluntary.

Shire ('the applicant') brought an action against the European Commission (the 'Commission') to annul the Commission's interpretation of Article 37. The action concerned the medicinal product Xagrid, as an orphan medicinal product, enjoyed a ten-year period of market exclusivity up to 18 November 2014.

Recital 29 of Regulation (EC) No. 1901/2006 states that since orphan medicinal products 'are frequently not patent-protected, the reward of supplementary protection certificate extension cannot be applied; when they are patent-protected, such an extension would provide a double incentive. Therefore, for orphan medicinal products, instead of an extension of the supplementary protection certificate, the ten-year period of orphan market exclusivity should be extended to twelve years if the requirement for data on use in the paediatric population is fully met.' Further, Article 37 of Regulation (EC) No. 1901/2006 states:

> Where an application for a marketing authorisation is submitted in respect of a medicinal product designated as an orphan medicinal product pursuant to Regulation (EC) No 141/2000 and that application includes the results of all studies conducted in compliance with an agreed paediatric investigation plan, and the statement referred to in Article 28(3) of this Regulation is subsequently included in the marketing authorisation granted, the ten-year period referred to in Article 8(1) of Regulation (EC) No 141/2000 shall be extended to twelve years.

On 1 August 2013, the applicant wrote to the Commission outlining its view that, in light of Recital 29 and Article 37 of Regulation (EC) No. 1901/2006, it was possible to conclude that non-patented orphan medicinal products were eligible for an extension of the market exclusivity period from ten to twelve years, where the requirements outlined in Article 37 of Regulation (EC) No. 1901/2006 were complied with. The applicant stated that Xagrid was a non-patented orphan medicinal product in respect of which a PIP had already been approved by the EMA, and when the results of the studies were available, the applicant intended to seek an extension of the MA for Xagrid in order to include a paediatric indication.

The Commission replied to the applicant's letter stating that it did not share this interpretation of Article 37. In its view, this provision did not confer on non-patented orphan medicinal products entitlement to any extension of the market exclusivity period. There was a further exchange of correspondence, which eventually led Shire to bring its action for annulment.

The General Court did not comment on the Commission's interpretation; instead, it examined, at the Commission's request, the question of admissibility pursuant to Article 114(1) of the Rules of Procedure. The case was dismissed as inadmissible; the Court found that the Commission letter had only expressed an 'informed opinion' on the application of Article 37 in general and hypothetical terms, so it was unable to produce any binding legal effects on Shire, and thus was not a challengeable decision. Although the Court did not have the opportunity to rule on the question before it, the Commission subsequently changed its mind on its interpretation of Article 37. Xagrid did therefore eventually benefit from a twelve-year period of market exclusivity, as noted in the Commission's *'Inventory of Union and Member State Incentives to support research into, and the development and availability of, Orphan Medicinal Products. State of Play 2015'*:[73]

> Two medicinal products for which a paediatric investigation plan was completed, *TobiPodhaler* and *Xagrid*, currently enjoy extended (12 year) market exclusivity.

---

73. SWD (2015) 13 final.

[C] Market Exclusivity Review: Possible Reduction of Term

Article 8(2) of the ODR provides that the ten-year period of market exclusivity (*see* §14.05[C]) may be decreased to six years, if at the end of the fifth year, it is established that the orphan medicinal product no longer meets the criteria in Article 3 of the ODR.[74] For example, market exclusivity will be reduced if it is shown on the basis of available evidence that the product is sufficiently profitable, and maintenance of market exclusivity is not justified.

In September 2008, the Commission issued guidelines[75] on the review procedure under Article 8(2) of Regulation (EC) No. 141/2000. The Commission guidance confirmed that reviews under Article 8(2) are not routine. The review process does not arise automatically; rather, it is triggered when a Member State informs the EMA that it has sufficient information that the designation criteria are no longer met with respect to a specific designation of an orphan medicinal product. Member States should only inform the EMA if they have sufficient indications suggesting that the designation criteria are no longer met; in that case, they should submit the necessary information to the EMA by the end of the fourth year of market exclusivity.

In the event that the COMP is required to conduct a review of market exclusivity, the determination of continued eligibility is based on the same set of criteria on which the orphan designation was first granted. The Member State instigating the review should provide the rationale for its doubts and include appropriate data demonstrating why at least one of the original designation criteria is no longer met. The COMP's assessment is undertaken in accordance with the following procedure:

(a) The COMP reviews the initial designation criteria, and if they are still met, the COMP adopts an opinion recommending that the period of market exclusivity not be reduced.
(b) If the criteria are no longer met, the COMP reviews whether any of the other designation criteria of Article 3(1) are met. If other criteria are fulfilled, the COMP adopts an opinion recommending the period not be reduced.
(c) If none of the Article 3(1) criteria is met, the COMP may adopt an opinion recommending reduction of the period of market exclusivity.

Based upon the opinion issued by the COMP, the Commission makes a decision as to whether market exclusivity is to be maintained or reduced. In exceptional circumstances, the Commission may adopt a decision that is not in accordance with the opinion of the COMP. When exercising its discretion, the Commission considers the particular circumstances in light of the key objectives set out in the preamble to the ODR.

---

74. Article 8(2) Regulation (EC) No. 141/2000.
75. C(2008) 4051 final, 'Guideline on aspects of the application of Art. 8(2) of Regulation (EC) No. 141/2000: Review of the period of market exclusivity of orphan medicinal products'.

However, it should be noted that the utility of this provision has been questioned, due to its lack of use in practice. In particular, under the existing rules, orphan status cannot be challenged on the grounds of product profitability if such status was not sought on the basis of the 'insufficient return on investment' criterion. As applications for orphan designations have so far, in all cases but one, been based on the 'prevalence' criterion, it has been practically impossible to trigger a reduction of the market exclusivity period for any orphan product.[76]

§14.06 TRANSFER OF ORPHAN DESIGNATION

Article 5(11) ODR permits sponsors to transfer orphan designation to a new Sponsor. Such transfers may arise for various business or regulatory reasons. For example, transfer may be required by the Competition Commission, or a sale of the part of the business that deals with the orphan medicinal product may necessitate a transfer. An orphan MA applicant must also hold the orphan designation in order for the authorised product to benefit from the ODR's incentives. The sponsor requesting a transfer is required to submit an online application (via the IRIS system) to the EMA. The following documentation needs to be supplied:[77]

(a) the name and address of the transferor and the proposed transferee;
(b) a statement certifying that a complete and up-to-date designation application has been either made available or transferred to the proposed transferee;
(c) proof of the transferee's establishment in the EEA; and
(d) a document stating the date on which the proposed transfer will be implemented, that is, when the proposed transferee can actually take over the responsibility and rights of the designation for the orphan medicinal product

Transfers are free of charge. The EMA will provide an opinion on the transfer within thirty days of the submission of the required documentation, and the opinion will be sent to the sponsor, the transferee, and the Commission. If such transfer is approved by the Commission, the Commission will amend the decision granting orphan designation. The transfer will be accepted from the date of notification of the amended Commission decision.

In acknowledging a potential loophole in the legislation, Commission guidance[78] addresses the transfer of designations between sponsors in order to prevent the

---

76. Commission Staff Working Document – Joint evaluation of Regulation (EC) No. 1901/2006 of the European Parliament and of the Council of 12 December 2006 on medicinal products for paediatric use and Regulation (EC) No. 141/2000 of the European Parliament and of the Council of 16 December 1999 on orphan medicinal products: SWD(2020) 163 final (11.8.2020).
77. *See* Guideline on the format and content of applications for designation as orphan medicinal products and on the transfer of designations from one sponsor to another, 27.03.2014 (ENTR/6283/00 Rev. 5, July 2021); *see also* Checklist for sponsors applying for the transfer of Orphan Medicinal Product (OMP) designation (EMA/41277/2007 Rev. 15, 18 May 2022).
78. Commission notice on the application of Articles 3, 5, and 7 of Regulation (EC) No. 141/2000 on orphan medicinal products (2016/C 424/03).

situation of a company being able to rely on a third party holding a separate designation which will subsequently be transferred to that company, thereby circumventing the restrictions on that company being able to apply for the designation. The guidance says that a sponsor can receive only one orphan designation per condition for any given medicinal product. Moreover, it is not possible to transfer an orphan designation to a sponsor who already has an MA for the same medicinal product and condition. Any additional pharmaceutical form should be granted by varying the existing MA. Where a sponsor applies for a separate MA to establish a distinction between two pharmaceutical forms (to avoid medication errors), the separate authorisation will be subject to the same market exclusivity period.

§14.07 TRANSPARENCY

Due to the potential significance of the market exclusivity granted to an authorised orphan in terms of its impact on the market entry of other products, it is important for the designation process to be transparent. This should enable all potential MA applicants to have good overview of the regulatory landscape as they assess the opportunities for product development and approval. A COMP working party was established to address transparency and communication issues. The EMA publishes summaries of COMP opinions on products that have been granted orphan designation. The summaries aim to explain in clear language the disease and the basis on which the designation was granted. The work of the COMP is made transparent through the publication of minutes, agendas, and summary meeting reports on the EMA website.

In June 2009, the EMA launched a public consultation on its general transparency policy. The aim was to set out the rationale for and the scope of an EMA Transparency Policy, the objectives to be achieved and the prerequisites to be fulfilled, as well as the proposed way forward. In relation to orphan drugs, the key transparency initiatives related to the assessment of the completeness of information outlined in the European Public Assessment Reports for orphan drugs and exploring how best to inform the public of the outcome of the review of the criteria for orphan designation at the time of the MA.

Details of orphan medicines under evaluation are published by the EMA (once the MAA has been validated). The International non-proprietary name (INN)/common name substance type and therapeutic area are disclosed.

§14.08 RESEARCH

Grants are available from both Community and Member State programmes and initiatives that support orphan drug R&D.

In June 2009, the Council published its recommendation on action in the field of rare diseases,[79] which sets out detailed recommendations in relation to the following:

---

79. Council Recommendation of 8 June 2009 on an action in the field of rare diseases (2009/C151/02).

(a) plans and strategies in the field of rare diseases;
(b) adequate definition, codification, and inventorying of rare diseases;
(c) research on rare diseases;
(d) centres of expertise and European reference networks for rare diseases;
(e) gathering the expertise on rare diseases at the European level;
(f) empowerment of patient organisations; and
(g) sustainability.

The Commission responded with an implementation report based upon the Council's recommendation and information provided by Member States.[80] This report noted that actions on rare diseases featured prominently in the new Health Programme and the EU Research and Innovation Programme Horizon 2020. Under the current programme, Horizon Europe (2021–2027), a European Partnership on rare diseases is planned for the 2023/24 Work Programme.

European Reference Networks (ERNs)[81] play an increasingly important role, not only in research but also in sharing information to improve diagnosis and the quality of care, as well as in providing clinical practice guidelines in medical fields where expertise is rare. ERNs link thematic expert centres across the EU and provide sustainable clinical networks to pool medical expertise and rare disease data from patient registries.[82] The EU's European Platform on Rare Disease Registries is a focal point for the hundreds of rare disease registries in the EU, helping with pooling and searching rare disease data.

Most EU Member States now have national plans to support rare disease research and treatment access.

§14.09 FUTURE DEVELOPMENTS

The orphan field has generated considerable interest within the pharmaceutical industry in recent years as it has become apparent that (at least for the more successful orphan products) the ability to command high prices, coupled with valuable market exclusivity, can offer attractive returns. This has led some to criticise the legislation as offering too great an incentive to industry without necessarily ensuring commensurate benefits to patients.

---

80. Implementation report on the Commission Communication on Rare Diseases: Europe's challenges [COM (2008) 679 final] and Council Recommendation of 8 June 2009 on an action in the field of rare diseases (2009/C 151/02), COM (2014) 548 final.
81. Virtual networks involving healthcare providers across Europe that were first established in 2017 and are financed under the EU health programme and other sources. By 2022, twenty-four ERNs were working on a range of issues.
82. Commission Staff Working Document – Joint evaluation of Regulation (EC) No. 1901/2006 of the European Parliament and of the Council of 12 December 2006 on medicinal products for paediatric use and Regulation (EC) No. 141/2000 of the European Parliament and of the Council of 16 December 1999 on orphan medicinal products: SWD (2020) 163 final (11.8.2020).

Over 200 medicines have been granted an EU MA, in over 100 orphan indications, with anti-cancer treatments accounting for around one-third of all designations and authorised products so far. Many of these products target diseases for which there are no alternative treatment options. However, around 95% of rare diseases still have no authorised treatment.

As part of the Commission's new pharmaceutical strategy, a Commission report[83] published in August 2020 evaluated the EU legislation governing medicines for rare diseases and children. It made an extensive assessment of the measurable impact of the orphan legislation, noting the positive outcomes as well as identifying some of the weaknesses and areas for clarification or improvement. The report is part of a wider ongoing review; in 2016, the Council called on the Commission[84] to examine the impact of pharmaceutical incentives (including those for orphan drugs) on the availability and accessibility of medicinal products.

This report considered five evaluation criteria: the effectiveness, efficiency, relevance, coherence, and EU-added value of the ODR (together with a similar assessment of the Paediatric Regulation). With a particular focus on incentives, it concluded that, while various incentives provided by the ODR have spurred the development of new treatments for rare diseases, not all orphan products authorised are the direct results of such incentives.[85] However, it is also noted that all orphan medicines were available on average nine months earlier and to more people across the EU than would have been the case without the legislation, and the average additional protection offered by the market exclusivity reward is calculated at 3.4 years. Less positively, the report concluded that the ODR is becoming less effective in directing research to areas where there are no treatments yet, and product development tends to cluster around certain (more profitable) therapeutic areas such as oncology. Moreover, procedures can be inefficient and burdensome.

The report also identified a number of 'inefficiencies' in the ODR, such as 'indication stacking' – orphan products authorised for two or more orphan indications on the EU market. These indications refer to distinct orphan conditions, and each entitles the product in question to a period of market exclusivity. These periods may run in parallel, with their own start and finish dates. In certain cases, the ten-year market exclusivity incentive can represent overcompensation. The report concluded that consideration should be given to the possibility of the ODR providing differentiated incentives, depending on the type of application for MA or the level of investment in R&D.

---

83. Commission Staff Working Document – Joint evaluation of Regulation (EC) No. 1901/2006 of the European Parliament and of the Council of 12 December 2006 on medicinal products for paediatric use and Regulation (EC) No. 141/2000 of the European Parliament and of the Council of 16 December 1999 on orphan medicinal products: SWD(2020) 163 final (11.8.2020); *see also* European Commission Study to support the evaluation of the EU Orphan Regulation: Final report July 2019.
84. Council conclusions on strengthening the balance in the pharmaceutical systems in the EU and its Member States - https://www.consilium.europa.eu/en/press/press-releases/2016/06/17/epsco-conclusions-balance-pharmaceutical-system/.
85. Of the 131 orphan medicines authorised in the EU since 2000, the Orphan Regulation was estimated to be responsible for at least 8–24 new ones.

Advances in personalised medicine may add another layer of complexity to the current regulatory framework; for example, pharmacogenomics, which investigates how genetic variations influence the activity of medicinal products in patients, is leading to classification of ever-smaller patient 'sub-populations'. In this way, newly identified 'sub-conditions' defined by a particular genetic profile may come to fall within the prevalence criteria of Article 3 of the ODR. In this respect, the Commission's Notice on the application of Articles 3, 5, and 7 of Regulation (EC) No. 141/2000 on orphan medicinal products[86] notes that while there is an increasing shift towards personalised medicine, leading to the stratification of the patient population, 'subsetting' a condition with the use of biomarkers will not be acceptable unless the sponsor provides solid scientific evidence that the activity of the product would not be shown on the larger population.

The Commission's 2020 report notes that the current legislation is less relevant than it might be, due to the evolution of the ODR's objectives over time; today, it is clear that lack of treatment options is a broader problem than in 2000, affecting not only rare diseases but also infectious diseases. Moreover, the market for orphan medicines has become more financially attractive. This changing context calls into question whether the system of rewards and incentives instituted by the ODR remains relevant to current needs. Looking to the future, developments in the pharmaceutical sector, especially in the field of advanced therapies, personalised medicine, and innovative trial design, will have significant implications and challenges for the current ODR framework, perhaps necessitating policy changes in defining orphan conditions and deciding which subset(s) to take into consideration when applying for orphan designation.

The report concludes that the added value of the ODR is somewhat modest. In particular, the Orphan and Paediatric Regulations, both alone and combined, have not provided sufficient incentives to foster the development of medicinal products for children with rare diseases. Access to orphan medicines varies considerably across Member States, although mainly due to factors beyond the ODR's ambit, such as different national pricing and reimbursement systems, companies' strategic decisions on market launch, and the role of healthcare providers. There is no EU-wide legislation that obliges Member States to give any special consideration to medicinal products designated as orphans when making pricing and reimbursement decisions. Each Member State is responsible for determining whether a particular orphan medicinal product will be reimbursed under its national healthcare system, and the Member States have different schemes for dealing with pricing and reimbursement decisions. Problems with EU-wide availability are particularly evident in respect of the smaller Member States where very low patient numbers can discourage companies from placing the product on the market. In 2004, the Commission commissioned a survey from Alcimed, which revealed that of the ten orphan medicines on the market at that

---

86. OJ 2016/C 424/03.

time, all ten were only available in nine of the then twenty-five Member States.[87] Equal patient access throughout the EU is still seen as an issue.

Based on the findings of the August 2020 report, the Commission published consultations regarding proposed amendments to the ODR (and paediatric legislation). A November 2020 Inception Impact Assessment[88] proposed the following options for a redesigned orphan product incentive framework:

(1) market exclusivity to remain the main reward, but with variable duration;
(2) as in (1) above, and changes to the designation criteria will better identify rare diseases;
(3) as in (1) above, and a novel reward for medicines addressing unmet medical needs will be introduced; or
(4) no market exclusivity – a novel reward for medicines addressing unmet medical needs will be introduced.

The Commission's proposals for amended legislation under its new pharmaceutical strategy, included an amended ODR, are expected to be published in autumn/winter 2022.

§14.10 UK

[A] Introduction

Generally, the post-Brexit regulation of orphan medicinal products in the UK continues to be aligned with the EU regime set out above. As of 1 January 2021, the UK's orphan medicinal product regulatory framework is set out in the retained Regulation (EC) No. 141/2000 (as of 31 December 2020), as further implemented in the UK by the Human Medicines Regulations 2012, as further amended by the Human Medicines Regulations (Amendment etc.) (EU Exit) Regulations 2019 (UK HMRs).

The relevant UK regulator, the Medicines and Healthcare Products Regulatory Agency (MHRA), has published guidance[89] relating to the review of applications for orphan designation at the time of an MA or variation application for purposes of Great Britain. As set out in some further detail below, the MHRA is making available incentives (in the form of market exclusivity and full or partial refunds for MA fees) to encourage the development of medicines for rare diseases. A waiver from scientific advice fees is also available for UK-based SMEs.

---

87. Alcimed study on orphan drugs Phase I Overview of the conditions for marketing orphan drugs in Europe.
88. Ref. Ares (2020) 7081640 – 25/11/2020.
89. https://www.gov.uk/guidance/orphan-medicinal-products-in-great-britain.

[B] Application for Orphan Designation in Great Britain

The review of applications from companies for orphan designation at the time of an MAA is within the remit of the MHRA. If a medicinal product has been granted orphan designation in the EU under Regulation (EC) No.141/2000, a Great Britain orphan MAA may be lodged under regulation 50G of the UK HMRs.

A UK-wide orphan MAA may only be considered by the MHRA in the absence of an active EU orphan designation. If a UK-wide orphan MA is granted, and the medicinal product subsequently receives an EU orphan designation, the MAH must submit a variation to change this to a Great Britain orphan MA.

In order to qualify for orphan designation, the medicine must meet the following criteria:

- the medicine must be intended for the treatment, prevention or diagnosis of a disease that is life-threatening or chronically debilitating;
- the prevalence of the indicated condition in Great Britain must not be more than 5 in 10,000, or it must be unlikely that marketing of the medicine would generate sufficient returns to justify the investment needed for its development; and
- there must be no satisfactory method of diagnosis, prevention or treatment of the condition concerned exists in Great Britain, or, if such a method exists, the medicine must be of significant benefit to those affected by the condition. In this regard, 'satisfactory methods' may include authorised medicinal products, medical devices, or other methods of diagnosis, prevention, or treatment which are used in Great Britain.

While the MAA procedure is underway, applications for orphan designation are examined in parallel by the MHRA's advisory committee, being the Commission on Human Medicines (CHM). Unless there are issues with the orphan designation application, the decision on orphan status will be made at the time of the decision on approval of the MA. If the MHRA is of the view that the criteria for orphan designation are not met, there will be an opportunity to appeal the decision to the CHM before the MA is granted.

From a practical perspective, it is mentioned that there are no additional fees to apply for orphan designation. Further, in the UK/Great Britain orphan designation per se is not granted separately from the MA. Therefore, should there be a change in ownership of the MA, upon the successful application of a change of control application, the orphan designation will automatically transfer to the new owner.

[C] Market Exclusivity

Upon the granting of an MA with orphan status, the medicinal product benefits from market exclusivity from similar products in the approved orphan indication for up to ten years. Such market exclusivity period commences from the date of first approval of the product in Great Britain. The remaining market exclusivity periods for EU centrally authorised orphan medicine MAs granted prior to 1 January 2021, which have been converted to Great Britain MAs, will continue to apply. In this regard, it is not necessary for MAHs to submit orphan maintenance reports to the MHRA, but they may be provided as additional information.

Orphan medicines authorised in Great Britain with the results of studies from a PIP included in the product information are eligible for an additional two years of market exclusivity.

The market exclusivity is subject to review. In this regard, regulation 58D of the UK HMRs establishes the possibility for the MHRA to request that the market exclusivity be reduced from ten to six years under certain circumstances where, for example, the orphan criteria are no longer met in relation to the medicinal product in question.

[D]   SMEs

Companies that wish to benefit from the scientific fee waiver must confirm their SME status in accordance with the MHRA's published guidance and must further ensure that they have the relevant documentation in place.

[E]   MA Variation Applications

In the context of MA variation applications in respect of new or extensions to orphan therapeutic indications, MAHs with orphan designations must also lodge the completed *Great Britain Orphan Drug Designation Application Form* with such variation application. The orphan designation criteria will be assessed in parallel to the approval of the new indication. In this regard, a new period of market exclusivity is only granted if the applied therapeutic indication falls within a new orphan condition. In respect of non-orphan indications, a new MAA is required.

[F]   Orphan Register

All medicines that gain an orphan designation from the MHRA are listed on the MHRA's online Orphan Register.[90] Once the period of market exclusivity for an indication expires or is withdrawn, the orphan designation for that indication terminates and is accordingly removed from the Orphan Register. However, the medicine will continue to appear on the Orphan Register if other authorised orphan indications remain within their period of exclusivity.

---

90. https://www.gov.uk/government/publications/orphan-registered-medicinal-products/orphan-register.

§14.11 GUIDELINES/PUBLICATIONS

- Alcimed study on orphan drugs Phase I Overview of the conditions for marketing orphan drugs in Europe. Press Release Committee for Orphan Medicinal Products September 2005 Meeting, EMEA/COMP/299233/2005.
- Commission notice on the application of Articles 3, 5, and 7 of Regulation (EC) No. 141/2000 on orphan medicinal products (2016/C 424/03).
- Guideline on the format and content of applications for designation as orphan medicinal products and on the transfer of designations from one sponsor to another (ENTR/6283/00 Rev 5, July 2021).
- Procedural Advice for Orphan Medicinal Product Designation – Guidance for sponsors (EMA/420706/2018 Rev 11 – 30 September 2021).
- Procedural advice for post-orphan medicinal product designation activities - Guidance for sponsors; EMA/469917/2018, Rev.12 – 25 May 2022.
- COMP Members interaction with sponsors of applications for orphan designations, EMEA/COMP/150409/2006, Rev. 1 – 16 December 2020.
- COMP Report to the Commission in relation to Article 10 of Regulation 141/2000 on orphan medicinal products, EMEA/35218/2005.
- Council Recommendation of 8 June 2009 on an action in the field of rare diseases (2009/C 151/02).
- Significant benefit of orphan drugs: concepts and future developments, EMA/326061/2012.
- EMA Public Statement on fee reductions for designated orphan medicinal products (www.ema.europa.eu).
- Guideline on aspects of the application of Article 8(1) and (3) of Regulation (EC) No. 141/2000: Assessing similarity of medicinal products versus authorised orphan medicinal products benefiting from market exclusivity and applying derogations from that market exclusivity, C (2008) 4077 (2008/C 242/08).
- Guideline on aspects of the application of Article 8(2) of Regulation (EC) No. 141/2000: Review of the period of market exclusivity of orphan medicinal products, C (2008) 4051.
- Points to Consider on the estimation and reporting on the prevalence of a condition for the purposes of orphan designation, COMP/436/01, Rev 1 – June 2019.
- European Medicines Agency Guidance for applicants seeking scientific advice and protocol assistance (EMA/691788/2010 Rev. 7 – September 2014).
- Procedural advice on the appeal procedure for orphan medicinal product designation or review of orphan designation criteria at the time of marketing authorisation; EMA/2677/01 Rev. 3, 8 December 2020.
- Standard Operating Procedure on orphan medicinal product designation and maintenance, SOP/H/3534 – April 2022.
- Procedural advice for post-orphan medicinal product designation activities - Guidance for sponsors; EMA/469917/2018, Rev.12 - 25 May 2022.

- Checklist for sponsors applying for the transfer of Orphan Medicinal Product (OMP designation (EMA/41277/2007 Rev. 15 – 18 May 2022.
- SEC(2006) 832, Commission Staff Working Document on the experience acquired as a result of the application of Regulation (EC) No. 141/2000 on orphan medicinal products and account of the public health benefits obtained.
- Inventory of Union and Member State Incentives to support research into, and the development and availability of, Orphan Medicinal Products. State of Play 2015'; SWD (2015) 13 final, 26.1.2016.
- Council Recommendation of 8 June 2009 on an action in the field of rare diseases (2009/C151/02).
- Implementation report on the Commission Communication on Rare Diseases: Europe's challenges [COM(2008) 679 final] and Council Recommendation of 8 June 2009 on an action in the field of rare diseases (2009/C 151/02), COM(2014) 548 final.)
- Council conclusions on strengthening the balance in the pharmaceutical systems in the EU and its Member States – https://www.consilium.europa.eu/en/press/press-releases/2016/06/17/epsco-conclusions-balance-pharmaceutical-system/
- European Commission Study to support the evaluation of the EU Orphan Regulation: Final report July 2019.
- Commission Staff Working Document – Joint evaluation of Regulation (EC) No. 1901/2006 of the European Parliament and of the Council of 12 December 2006 on medicinal products for paediatric use and Regulation (EC) No. 141/2000 of the European Parliament and of the Council of 16 December 1999 on orphan medicinal products: SWD(2020) 163 final (11.8.2020) European Commission Inception Impact Assessment Ref. Ares(2020) 7081640 – 25/11/2020.
- Case T-74/08 *Now Pharm AG v. European Commission*, 9 September 2010.
- Case T-264/07 CSL *Behring GmbH v. European Commission* and the EMA, 9 September 2010
- Case T-452/14 *Laboratoires CTRS v. European Commission*.
- Case T-140/12 *Teva v. EMA*.
- CaseT-583/13 *Shire Pharmaceutical Contracts v. European Commission*.
- Case T-269/15 *Novartis v. European Commission*.
- Case C-138/15P, *Teva v. EMA*.
- Case T-80/16, *Shire Pharmaceuticals Ireland Ltd, v. EMA*.
- Case T-329/16 *BMS v. Commission and EMA*.
- Case T-733/17 *GMP-Orphan v. European Commission*.
- Case T-549/19 *Medac Gesellschaft für klinische Spezialpräparate v. Commission*; (2019/C 337/15).
- Case T-303/16 *Mylan v. European Commission*; judgment of 26 January 2022; appeal Case C-237/22 P *Mylan v. European Commission*.

- UK Guidance on Orphan Medicinal Products (last updated 22 February 2021) (https://www.gov.uk/guidance/orphan-medicinal-products-in-great-britain).
- Policy paper: UK strategy for rare diseases: 2020 update to the implementation plan for England (Published 26 February 2020) (https://www.gov.uk/government/publications/uk-strategy-for-rare-diseases-2020-update-to-the-implementation-plan-for-england).
- Policy paper: Rare diseases strategy (Published 22 November 2013) (https://www.gov.uk/government/publications/rare-diseases-strategy).

CHAPTER 15
Biopharmaceuticals

Marc Martens, Benedicte Mourisse & Sophie Vo[*]

§15.01 INTRODUCTION

Biological medicinal products, also known as 'biopharmaceuticals', form a specific category of products characterised by the fact that contrary to chemical medicinal products, their active ingredient is a biological substance derived from living cells.

Biologicals are among the best-selling and fastest-growing drugs in the world. The patent expiry for originator biological products has created new opportunities for entry into the market of the so-called biosimilars – given the nature and the characteristics of biological medicinal products, no 'generics' exist as compared to chemical medicines.

The main types of biological medicines are:

- immunological medicinal products;[1]
- medicinal products derived from human blood and human plasma;[2]
- medicinal products developed by means of one of the biotechnological processes listed in the Annex to Regulation No. 726/2004, namely: recombinant DNA technology, controlled expression of genes coding for biologically active proteins in prokaryotes and eukaryotes, including transformed mammalian cells and hybridoma, and monoclonal antibody methods; and
- advanced therapy medicinal products (ATMPs).[3]

---

[*] The authors wish to acknowledge *Nicolas Carbonnelle*, an author of the earlier edition of this chapter.
1. Article 1(4) of Directive 2001/83/EC.
2. Article 1(10) of Directive 2001/83/EC.
3. As defined under Regulation 1394/2007. *See* further Chapter 17.

§15.02 SPECIFIC NATURE OF BIOPHARMACEUTICALS AND CONSEQUENCES

[A] Biological Starting Materials

A biological substance is a substance that is produced by or extracted from a biological source and that needs for its characterisation and the determination of its quality a combination of physico-chemical-biological testing, together with the production process and its control.[4]

Starting materials of biological medicinal products are any substance of biological origin, such as micro-organisms, organs and tissues of either plant or animal origin, cells or fluids (including blood or plasma) of human or animal origin, and biotechnological cell constructs (cell substrates, whether they are recombinant or not, including primary cells).[5]

Most biopharmaceuticals' active substances are proteins – be they biotechnology-derived proteins or monoclonal antibodies. The latter are a large and complex form of biological active substances, of which the mechanism of action is highly complex. Specific regulatory guidelines have been developed with respect to the development of products based on monoclonal antibodies,[6] as well as biosimilar monoclonal antibodies,[7] in order to take into account the specificities of this type of product.

[B] Product Complexity and Variability

In comparison to chemical medicinal products, biological medicinal products are much more complex, as the size of the molecules that form the active substance is generally much bigger for the latter. Also, the administration route is often different: while chemical medicines can often be administered orally, most biopharmaceuticals are administered via injection or infusion because proteins are affected by the digestive system.

Biological material is also characterised by its variability, as a consequence, with a greater difficulty to characterise biological molecules as compared to small chemical molecule medicines. This variability of biopharmaceuticals (which can be seen at scales as small as a single batch of product) is a parameter that needs to be adequately controlled and retained within accepted and predefined limits. It is one of the key elements of the evaluation of biological products.

Where genetically-modified cells are used to produce biopharmaceuticals, it is worth noting that each manufacturer has its own unique cell lines, on the basis of which it develops its manufacturing process, which is in itself unique and proprietary.

---

4. Directive 2001/83/EC, Annex I, Section 3.2.1.1., b), third subparagraph.
5. Directive 2001/83/EC, Annex I, Section 3.2.1.1., b), second subparagraph.
6. EMA/CHMP/BWP/532517/2008.
7. EMA/CHMP/BMWP/403543/2010.

In addition, biological molecules are highly influenced by changes in their manufacturing process – which can count as much as five times the number of steps that the manufacture of a chemical molecule requires. For that reason, it is commonly said that where biologicals are concerned, 'the process is the product'.

[C] Possible Immunogenicity

Another feature of biological medicinal products that is linked to their very nature is that they have the ability to cause immune reactions. As a matter of fact, unlike chemical medicinal products, biopharmaceuticals can be recognised by the immune system. While the immunogenicity is the researched effect in vaccines, in other biopharmaceuticals, it is often regarded as an undesirable effect of the medicine. The underlying difficulty with immunogenicity is that it depends on multiple factors, including factors related to the patient, such as gender, age, disease state, etc.[8]

The current guideline on immunogenicity assessment of biotechnology-derived therapeutic proteins[9] has been revised in order to take into account the experience and knowledge gained in the field of immunogenicity. Before the revision, it was often established that most marketing authorisation applications (MAAs) for biological medicinal products lack a clear strategy to approach immunogenicity. Following this, the revised guideline has addressed this by formulating some specific requirements for the presentation of the immunogenicity.

Some specific aspects of immunogenicity that are exclusively or primarily relevant for monoclonal antibodies are addressed in a separate guideline.[10]

§15.03 MARKET ACCESS FOR INNOVATIVE BIOLOGICALS

[A] MAA Routes

All medicinal products listed in the Annex to Regulation No. 726/2004 must follow the centralised procedure.[11] Among these products, the following biopharmaceuticals are listed:

1. Medicinal products developed by means of one of the following biotechnological processes:
   – recombinant DNA technology,
   – controlled expression of genes coding for biologically active proteins in prokaryotes and eukaryotes including transformed mammalian cells,
   – hybridoma and monoclonal antibody methods.

---

8. *See* Guideline on immunogenicity assessment of biotechnology-derived therapeutic proteins, EMEA/CHMP/BMWP/14327/2006, Rev 1.
9. *Ibid.*
10. Guideline on immunogenicity assessment of monoclonal antibodies intended for in vivo clinical use (EMA/CHMP/BMWP/86289/2010).
11. *See* Chapter 5 in this regard.

1a. Advanced therapy medicinal products as defined in Article 2 of Regulation (EC) No 1394/2007 of the European Parliament and of the Council of 13 November 2007 on advanced therapy medicinal products.

Products that do not fall within these categories may follow other marketing authorisation (MA) routes. This is notably the case for products made of biological substances of which the manufacturing process does not involve biotechnology methods. These products can be authorised at national level, unless they fall within another category of products that must follow the centralised procedure. For example, while vaccines from strains developed by means of recombinant DNA technology, including gene deletion, would have to follow the centralised route, vaccines that are produced without having recourse to any of the technologies listed in the annex would not.

That would be the case of products that contain a new active substance for which the therapeutic indication is the treatment of AIDS, cancer, neurodegenerative disorder, diabetes, auto-immune diseases, and other immune dysfunctions or viral diseases or products designated as orphan medicinal products pursuant to Regulation (EC) No. 141/2000.

§15.04 MA DOSSIER

[A] General Requirements Applicable to All Biological Medicinal Products

In addition to the standard requirements for securing an MA set out in Article 8 of Directive 2001/83/EC (*see* further Chapter 5), Annex I to Directive 2001/83/EC provides for requirements specific to biopharmaceuticals.

[B] Information Concerning the Active Substance

Like for any other medicinal product, the MAA dossier must contain information on the nomenclature of the active substance, including recommended international non-proprietary name (INN), European Pharmacopoeia name if relevant, and chemical name(s).

For biotechnological medicinal products if appropriate, the schematic amino acid sequence and relative molecular mass must be provided.[12] A list must be provided of physicochemical and other relevant properties of the active substance. For biological medicinal products, this list must include biological activity of the active substance.[13]

---

12. Directive 2001/83/EC, Annex I, 3.2.1.1., a), second subparagraph.
13. Directive 2001/83/EC, Annex I, 3.2.1.1., a), third subparagraph.

[C] Manufacturing Process of the Active Substance

As regards the manufacturing process of the active substance, Directive 2001/83/EC imposes a number of specific requirements for biological medicinal products. These requirements add up to the other requirements applicable to any other medicinal products.

The origin and history of the starting materials have to be described and documented in the MAA dossier.[14]

Compliance must be demonstrated by the MA applicant with the specific measures for the prevention of the Transmission of animal Spongiform Encephalopathies (in particular, compliance with the Note for Guidance on Minimising the Risk of Transmitting Animal Spongiform Encephalopathy Agents via Medicinal Products and its updates, published by the Commission in the Official Journal of the European Union, must be demonstrated).[15]

When cell banks are used, the cell characteristics must be shown to have remained unchanged at the passage level used for the production and beyond. Seed materials, cell banks, pools of serum or plasma, and other materials of biological origin and, whenever possible, the materials from which they are derived must be tested for adventitious agents. If the presence of potentially pathogenic adventitious agents is inevitable, the corresponding material must be used only when further processing ensures their elimination and/or inactivation, and this must be validated. Whenever possible, vaccine production must be based on a seed lot system and on established cell banks. For bacterial and viral vaccines, the characteristics of the infectious agent must be demonstrated on the seed. In addition, for live vaccines, the stability of the attenuation characteristics must be demonstrated on the seed; if this proof is not sufficient, the attenuation characteristics must also be demonstrated at the production stage.

For medicinal products derived from human blood or plasma, the origin and the criteria and procedures for collection, transportation, and storage of the starting material must be described and documented in accordance with provisions laid down in Part III of Annex I to Directive 2001/83/EC.

Finally, the MAA dossier must include a description of the manufacturing facilities and equipment.

[D] Description and Composition of the Finished Medicinal Product

For substances that cannot be defined molecularly, the description and composition of the finished biopharmaceutical shall be expressed in units of biological activity.

Where an International Unit of biological activity has been defined by the World Health Organisation (WHO), this unit must be used. In case no International Unit has

---

14. Directive 2001/83/EC, Annex I, 3.2.1.2., c).
15. *Ibid.*

[E] Non-clinical Aspects

As far as non-clinical aspects are concerned, the Directive requires that for biological medicinal products, comparability of material used in non-clinical studies, clinical studies, and the medicinal product for marketing must be assessed.

For biological medicinal products, such as immunological medicinal products and medicinal products derived from human blood or plasma, the requirements may have to be defined on a case-by-case basis. A justification of the testing program carried out must be provided by the applicant.

The following elements must be taken into consideration when establishing the testing program: (i) all tests requiring repeated administration of the product must be designed to take account of the possible induction of, and interference by, antibodies and (ii) examination of reproductive function, of embryo/foetal and perinatal toxicity, of mutagenic potential and of carcinogenic potential must be considered. Where constituents other than the active substance(s) are incriminated, validation of their removal may replace the study.

Detailed guidance can be found on non-clinical aspects of biopharmaceuticals in the International Convention on Harmonisation (ICH) harmonised tripartite guideline on *'Preclinical Safety Evaluation of Biotechnology-Derived Pharmaceuticals'*.[16] The guideline sets out a basic framework for preclinical safety evaluation of products derived from characterised cells through the use of different expression systems, which include bacteria, yeast, insect, plant, and mammalian cells. It may also be applicable to other biotechnology-derived medicinal products, such as those derived from plasma and recombinant DNA protein vaccines. However, the guidance does not extend to cover antibiotics, allergenic extracts, heparin, vitamins, cellular blood components, conventional bacterial or viral vaccines, DNA vaccines, and cellular and gene therapies or tissue-engineered products.[17]

The Preclinical Guideline states that preclinical safety testing should notably take into account Biological Activity and Toxicological Data, the selection of animal models, the number and gender of animals, the dose selection and the selection of the route for administration (which should ideally be the same as that proposed in the clinical phase), and immunogenicity.

---

16. Note for Guidance on preclinical safety evaluation of biotechnology-derived pharmaceuticals, CPMP/ICH/302/95, which came into operation in March 1998. EMA/CHMP/ICH/731268/1998.
17. Paragraph 1.3 EMA/CHMP/ICH/731268/1998.

§15.05 CLINICAL TRIALS

Clinical trials involving biological investigational medicinal products are subject to the same legal requirements as other medicinal products (*See* further Chapter 4 on Clinical Trials). Given the particular nature of biologicals, Directive 2001/20/EC, however, provides for the possibility for the Member States to subject the commencement of clinical trials with medicinal products the active ingredient or active ingredients of which is or are a biological product or biological products of human or animal origin, or contains biological components of human or animal origin, or the manufacturing of which requires such components, to a prior written authorisation.[18]

Furthermore, specific guidance has been developed by the European Medicines Agency (EMA) in respect of the clinical trials involving investigational biopharmaceuticals, such as the *Guideline on the requirements for quality documentation concerning biological investigational medicinal products in clinical trials*.[19]

In general, when evaluating biopharmaceuticals, the approach to be adopted by applicants is more creative and flexible than the approach followed with chemical compounds. Regulatory requirements change rapidly and are sometimes determined by the regulatory authorities on a case-by-case basis. Against that background, obtaining Scientific Advice from the EMA is strongly advised.[20] It is also preferable to obtain this Scientific Advice as early as possible in the development process. It is important to note that the regulatory standards for biologicals accepted by regulatory agencies in other developed countries are not necessarily acceptable to the EMA.

§15.06 PRODUCT-SPECIFIC REQUIREMENTS

[A] Plasma-Derived Medicinal Products

By derogation from the provisions of Module 3 (chemical, pharmaceutical, and biological information), the dossier requirements mentioned in 'Information related to the starting and raw materials' for starting materials made of human blood/plasma may be replaced by a certified Plasma Master File. Notwithstanding this, the collection and testing of human blood and human plasma is subject to Directive 2002/98/EC of the European Parliament and of the Council of 27 January 2003, setting standards of quality and safety for the collection, testing, processing, storage, and distribution of human blood and blood components.[21] This Directive notably requires that the donors of blood and blood components (including plasma) have been duly informed before the donation and that the donation is voluntary and unpaid.

A 'Plasma Master File' consists of stand-alone documentation, which is separate from the dossier for MA and provides all relevant detailed information on the

---

18. Article 9(5) of Directive 2001/20/EC.
19. EMA/CHMP/BWP/534898/2008 rev. 1 corrigendum.
20. Guidance has been issued by the EMA for applicants seeking scientific advice and protocol assistance: EMA/4260/2001 Rev. 13.
21. OJ L 33, 8.2.2003, p. 30.

characteristics of the entire human plasma used as a starting material and/or a raw material for the manufacture of sub/intermediate fractions, constituents of the excipient and active substance(s), which are part of medicinal products or medical devices. The relevant provisions concerning medical devices incorporating stable derivatives of human blood or human plasma are included in Regulation (EU) No. 2017/745 of the European Parliament and of the Council of 5 April 2017 on medical devices, amending Directive 2001/83/EC, Regulation (EC) No. 178/2002 and Regulation (EC) No. 1223/2009 and repealing Council Directives 90/385/EEC and 93/42/EEC.[22]

The evaluation and certification requirements applicable to Plasma Master Files are detailed under section 1.1 of Part III of Annex I to Directive 2001/83/EC. In accordance with that section, the Plasma Master File must include information on the plasma used as starting/raw material, and notably:

- information on the origin of the plasma, more specifically:
    - information on centres or establishments in which blood/plasma collection is carried out,– including inspection and approval, and epidemiological data on blood transmissible infections;
    - information on centres or establishments in which testing of donations and plasma pools is carried out, including inspection and approval status;
    - selection/exclusion criteria for blood/plasma donors;
    - system in place which enables the path taken by each donation to be traced from the blood/plasma collection establishment through to finished products and vice versa.
- Information on the plasma quality and safety, including:
    - compliance with European Pharmacopoeia Monographs;
    - testing of blood/plasma donations and pools for infectious agents, including information on – test methods and, in the case of plasma pools, validation data on the tests used;
    - technical characteristics of bags for blood and plasma collection, including information on anticoagulants solutions used;
    - conditions of storage and transport of plasma;
    - procedures for any inventory hold and/or quarantine period;
    - characterisation of the plasma pool.
- Information on the system in place between the plasma-derived medicinal product manufacturer and/or plasma fractionator/processor on the one hand, and blood/plasma collection and testing centres or establishments on the other hand, which defines the conditions of their interaction and their agreed specifications.

Any Plasma Master File must be updated and re-certified on an annual basis, and any subsequent change to the Plasma Master File must follow the evaluation procedure laid down by Commission Regulation (EC) No. 1085/2003 of 3 June 2003 concerning the examination of variations to the terms of an MA for medicinal products for human

---

22. OJ L 119, 4.5.2016, p. 1–88.

use and veterinary medicinal products falling within the scope of Council Regulation (EEC) No. 2309/93.

§15.07 ATMPS

ATMPs are biological medicinal products manufactured from human and/or animal tissues and cells. This category of products is subject to a specific legal framework that is further outlined in Chapter 17.

§15.08 VACCINES

This category of products is subject to a specific legal framework that is further outlined in Chapter 18.

§15.09 SPECIFIC MARKET SURVEILLANCE MEASURES APPLICABLE TO BIOLOGICAL MEDICINAL PRODUCTS

[A] Pharmacovigilance Requirements

Regulation (EC) No. 1235/2010 amending, as regards pharmacovigilance of medicinal products for human use, Regulation (EC) No. 726/2004 and Regulation (EC) No. 1394/2007, has tightened the provisions on pharmacovigilance. Since the entry into force of that regulation, all biological medicinal products authorised after 1 January 2011 are subject to additional monitoring.

As a consequence, the Summary of Product Characteristics of the product and the package leaflet must include the statement '*This medicinal product is subject to additional monitoring*', preceded by a black symbol.

For more detailed information on the regime of additional monitoring, please refer to Chapter 10 (Pharmacovigilance).

[B] Changes to the Manufacturing Process

When changes are considered to the manufacturing process of a biopharmaceutical, the process is not as straightforward as what applies to chemical medicines. As a matter of fact, any change in the manufacturing process can affect the final product in a significant way. Therefore, comparability must be shown between the product resulting from the amended manufacturing process and the initially authorised product.

Demonstration of comparability of the pre- and post-change product is a sequential process, beginning with quality studies (limited or comprehensive) and supported, as necessary, by non-clinical, clinical, and/or pharmacovigilance studies.

A specific guideline addresses the non-clinical and clinical issues of the comparability of biotechnology-derived medicinal products after a change in the manufacturing process.[23] The guideline gives advice on the non-clinical and clinical requirements of the comparability exercise, comparing post-change product to pre-change product where manufacturing process changes are made by a single manufacturer, including those made by a contract manufacture. The guideline details the non-clinical and/or clinical bridging studies that are required to demonstrate that the manufacturing change has no impact on safety and efficacy.

MAHs must demonstrate that the quality, safety, and efficacy have not been affected by the change. The minimum data required for such a demonstration are physico-chemical and in vitro/in vivo biological testing to characterise the products. However, in some cases, additional preclinical and clinical studies may also be necessary. The guidance explains that the demonstration of comparability is a sequential process, and therefore the extent will vary from manufacturer to manufacturer, and further demonstrations of comparability will only be required where warranted by the data on a case-by-case basis.

In respect of manufacturing process, it must be stressed that early attention must be paid, as regards the scale-up from laboratory-scale production to clinical production. The scale-up can indeed entail serious pitfalls, both from a technical and regulatory perspective. For example, the use of a particular filtration process which would have limited capacity as compared with other filtration processes may need to be carefully considered at an early stage in order to find out alternatives before production on a very large scale.

§15.10 REGULATORY DATA PROTECTION

Under Directive 2001/83/EC, any product being granted an MA enjoys a period of regulatory data protection. The '8 + 2 + 1' rule, as introduced by Directive 2004/27/EC, applies identically to chemical medicines and biopharmaceuticals.

In other words, originators enjoy a ten-year data exclusivity period starting from the date of the initial approval of the reference medicinal product. During the first eight years, no abridged procedure may be initiated (in case of biological products: no biosimilar application). An application may be filed as soon as the first eight years of data exclusivity have expired. At that time, no biosimilar can be put on the market for another two years, but the biosimilar applicant can seek an MA by referring to the data of the reference product (abridged procedure).

The ten-year period may be extended by one additional year if during the first eight years of those ten years, the MAH obtains an authorisation for one or more new therapeutic indications which, during the scientific evaluation prior to their authorisation, are held to bring a significant clinical benefit in comparison with existing therapies.

---

23. EMEA/CHMP/BMWP/101695/2006.

Chapter 15: Biopharmaceuticals   §15.12[A]

The '8 + 2 + 1' rule is without prejudice to other data and/or market exclusivity rules as provided for under the Orphan Drugs (*see* Chapter 14) or Paediatrics regimes (*see* Chapter 8). A biopharmaceutical that would apply and obtain an orphan drug designation and/or a paediatric indication would enjoy the specific market exclusivity and incentives provided for under these specific regimes.

§15.11   THE EMA'S BIOLOGICS WORKING PARTY

An ad hoc working party has been set up within the Committee for Medicinal Products for Human Use (CHMP). It is named the Biologics Working Party (BWP) and is composed of independent experts who have particular expertise and/or regulatory experience of issues related to medicinal products produced by biotechnological means.

The mandate and objectives[24] of the BWP include the provision of support to the CHMP on dossier evaluations. The BWP prepares reports on all MAAs for biopharmaceuticals, and CHMP considers the BWP report prior to issuing its opinion.

The BWP also provides recommendations to the EMA's scientific committees on all matters relating directly or indirectly to quality and safety aspects relating to biological and biotechnological medicines. The BWP also assists the CHMP with the preparation and review of guidelines, international liaison duties, the making of public statements, and the conduct of workshops and training in the field of biological product safety and quality.[25]

§15.12   BIOSIMILARS

[A]   Concept of 'Biosimilar'

A biosimilar is a biological medicinal product that contains a version of the active substance of an already authorised original biological medicinal product (reference medicinal product) in the EEA. In that sense, it is 'similar' to the originator product. The key issue for biosimilars is the comparability of the active substance in the biosimilar product with the active substance of the originator.

As the current Guideline on similar biological medicinal products[26] states, the standard generic approach (demonstration of bioequivalence with a reference medicinal product by appropriate bioavailability studies) which is applicable to most chemically-derived medicinal products is, in principle, not sufficient to demonstrate

---

24. The Mandate, Objectives and Rules of Procedure for the CHMP Biologics Working Party (BWP), EMEA/CHMP/BWP/206296/2004, Rev.1.
25. The general reports of the BWP can be found on the EMA website: https://www.ema.europa.eu/en/committees/working-parties-other-groups/chmp/biologics-working-party/biologics-working-party-documents.
26. CHMP/437/04 Rev 1.

similarity of biological/biotechnology-derived products due to their complexity. Producing an 'exact' copy of a biological medicinal product is impossible to do without access to the original process (e.g., by using the same cell line).

The EU was the first region in the world that regulated biosimilars. This happened in 2003, upon revision of Directive 2001/83/EC. From that moment on, the biosimilar approach was put in place, in which substantially more data is required from the applicant for a biosimilar MA than from an applicant for a generic MA, specifically as regards the comparability of the biosimilar in terms of safety and efficacy. Similarity to the reference medicinal product in terms of quality characteristics, biological activity, safety, and efficacy based on a comprehensive comparability exercise needs to be established.

[B]   Generics Versus Biosimilars

Generics and biosimilars differ in many aspects. While generics are often based on simple, small, and stable molecules that are easy to characterise, biosimilars are made of complex, large, and unstable molecules of which the characterisation is complex.

Generics are manufactured by means of chemical processes that are easy to reproduce, which means that identical copies of the reference product can be manufactured. The pharmaceutical legislation defines generics as a 'medicinal product which has the same qualitative and quantitative composition in active substances and the same pharmaceutical form as the reference medicinal product, and whose bioequivalence with the reference medicinal product has been demonstrated by appropriate bioavailability studies'.[27] A conventional will hence be considered to be therapeutically equivalent to a reference medicinal product once pharmaceutical equivalence and bioequivalence have been established – this entails that the active substance of both products is identical, and both products have comparable pharmacokinetics.

By contrast, biosimilars are based on biological substances which are extremely complex and not easy to reproduce. For these reasons, while the abridged procedure for generics merely requires bioequivalence studies, substantially more data is required to support the MAA for a biosimilar. All these data are to be gathered by means of comparability studies intended to demonstrate the similarity of the biosimilar.

The comparability exercise involves substantial costs for the developers of biosimilars, as the data requirements are very high. While comparability studies are required from originators when they intend to make changes in their manufacturing process, the data requirements in that case are lower. Therefore, the term used in the EU regulatory environment when dealing with the comparability exercise in the context of an MAA for a biosimilar is 'biosimilarity'. The term refers to the comparability between a biosimilar and its reference medicinal product.

---

27. Article 10(2), b) Directive 2001/83/EC.

As the Guideline on similar biological medicinal products[28] states, '[a] biosimilar should be highly similar to the reference medicinal product in physicochemical and biological terms. Any observed differences have to be duly justified with regard to their potential impact on safety and efficacy.' The comparability exercise is a step-wise exercise[29] that is described in further EMA guidelines. The process entails a comprehensive physicochemical and biological characterisation of the active substance.

Quality issues are notably addressed in the following guidelines:

- Similar biological medicinal products containing biotechnology-derived proteins as active substance: Quality issues (CHMP/BWP/247713/2012)
- Step 5 note for guidance on biotechnological/biological products subject to changes in their manufacturing process (CPMP/ICH/5721/03)

These guidelines require the manufacturer of the product that is claimed to be similar to the reference product to evaluate certain data. These are, *inter alia*, the relevant physicochemical and biological characterisation data regarding quality attributes of both products, the results from analysis of relevant samples from the appropriate stages of the manufacturing process (e.g., intermediate, drug substance, and drug product), the need for stability data, including those generated from accelerated or stress conditions, to provide insight into potential product differences in the degradation pathways of the product and, hence, potential differences in product-related substances and product-related impurities, the batches used for demonstration of manufacturing consistency as well as historical data that provide insight into potential 'drift' of quality attributes with respect to safety and efficacy, following either a single or a series of manufacturing process changes.

In short, the manufacturer needs to consider the impact of changes over time to confirm that no unacceptable impact on safety and efficacy profiles has occurred.

In addition to the evaluation of these data, manufacturers are required to consider also:

- critical control points in the manufacturing process that affect product characteristics, e.g., the impact of the process change on the quality of in-process materials, as well as the ability of downstream steps to accommodate material from a changed cell culture process;
- adequacy of the in-process controls including critical control points and in-process testing: In-process controls for the post-change process should be confirmed, modified, or created, as appropriate, to maintain the quality of the product;
- non-clinical or clinical characteristics of the drug product and its therapeutic indications.[30]

---

28. CHMP/437/04, Rev 1, also known as the 'Overarching Guideline'.
29. Overarching Guideline, section 3.3.
30. CPMP/ICH/5721/03.

At any time in the process, in case the biosimilar comparability exercise indicates that there are relevant differences between the intended biosimilar and the reference medicinal product making it unlikely that biosimilarity will eventually be established, the guidelines recommend that a stand-alone development to support a full MAA should be considered.[31]

§15.13 'ME-BETTERS'

In a bid to gain competitive advantage, the developers of biosimilars are looking for similar medicinal products that offer clinical advantages over the originator products. These new drugs are sometimes referred to as 'me-betters'. They not only correspond to the originator drug's therapeutic profile but also improve on it, for example, by optimising dosing regimens or tolerability in function of the existing experience and of the state of the art.

Given the large amount of data required for the abridged application process, in circumstances in which the new medicinal product has advantages over the originator product, it is conceivably easier to demonstrate this superiority in a full MAA. In such circumstances, the applicant needs to weigh the advantages of not having to wait for data exclusivity to expire against the need to produce its own clinical studies and toxicological testing. Notably, if the dosing schedule is to be optimised, then the developer will almost certainly need to conduct Phase II studies, thereby eliminating most of the benefit, in terms of cost of development and time saved, of a biosimilar development.

§15.14 MAA ROUTE

Biosimilars follow a specific abridged procedure. Directive 2001/83/EC was amended by Directive 2004/27/EC to provide for an MAA route specific to biosimilars. Since then, Article 10(4) of Directive 2001/83/EC states:

> Where a biological medicinal product which is similar to a reference biological product does not meet the conditions in the definition of generic medicinal products, owing to, in particular, differences relating to raw materials or differences in manufacturing processes of the biological medicinal product and the reference biological medicinal product, the results of appropriate pre-clinical tests or clinical trials relating to these conditions must be provided. The type and quantity of supplementary data to be provided must comply with the relevant criteria stated in Annex I and the related detailed guidelines. The results of other tests and trials from the reference medicinal product's dossier shall not be provided.

Not all biopharmaceuticals are eligible for the biosimilar route. Eligibility depends on the ability to sufficiently characterise the product and to demonstrate its biosimilarity with the reference medicinal product. While the biosimilar approach will

---

31. Overarching Guideline, section 3.3.

likely be successfully applied to products that are highly purified and can be thoroughly characterised (such as many biotechnology-derived medicinal products), it will not be the case for other types of biological medicinal products, which by their nature, are more difficult to characterise such as biological substances arising from extraction from biological sources and/or those for which little clinical and regulatory experience has been gained.

§15.15 MAA DOSSIER REQUIREMENTS

Part II, 4. of Annex I to Directive 2001/83/EC provides for a specific approach when a biological medicinal product which refers to an original medicinal product having been granted an MA in the Community is submitted for an MA by an independent applicant after the expiry of data protection period.

This approach entails that:

- Information to be supplied will not be limited to Modules 1, 2, and 3 (pharmaceutical, chemical, and biological data), supplemented with bio-equivalence and bio-availability data. The type and amount of additional data (i.e., toxicological and other non-clinical and appropriate clinical data) shall be determined on a case-by-case basis in accordance with relevant scientific guidelines.
- Due to the diversity of biological medicinal products, the need for identified studies foreseen in Modules 4 and 5 will be required by the competent authority, taking into account the specific characteristic of each individual medicinal product.
- In case the originally authorised medicinal product has more than one indication, the efficacy and safety of the medicinal product claimed to be similar has to be justified or, if necessary, demonstrated separately for each of the claimed indications.

The general principles to be applied are addressed in a guideline nicknamed the 'overarching guideline',[32] which addresses the general principles and approach towards biosimilars.

General guidelines supplement the overarching guideline and address the non-clinical and clinical issues[33] and quality issues[34] for similar biological medicinal products containing biotechnology-derived proteins as active substances.

---

32. CHMP/437/04 Rev. 1.
33. EMEA/CHMP/BMWP/42832/2005 Rev. 1.
34. EMA/CHMP/BWP/247713/2012.

Several product-specific guidelines have also been published by the EMA. These address, e.g., non-clinical and clinical development of biosimilars containing recombinant human insulin and insulin analogues,[35] biosimilars containing low-molecular-weight heparins,[36] or the non-clinical and clinical issues relating to biosimilars containing monoclonal antibodies.[37]

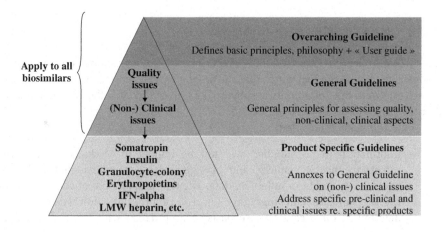

§15.16 STRATEGIC ISSUES AND NEXT STEPS

As at 1 September 2022, eighty-six biosimilars have been authorised by the EMA, although some of these have been withdrawn from the market.[38] The authorised biosimilars include the following:

Medicine Name	Active Substance	Marketing Authorisation Date	Marketing Authorisation Holder/Company Name
Filgrastim Hexal	filgrastim	6-02-2009	Hexal AG
Zarzio	filgrastim	6-02-2009	Sandoz GmbH
Mvasi	bevacizumab	15-01-2018	Amgen Technology (Ireland) UC

---

35. EMEA/CHMP/BMWP/32775/2005 Rev. 1.
36. EMEA/CHMP/BMWP/118264/2007 Rev. 1.
37. EMA/CHMP/BMWP/403543/2010.
38. *See* https://www.ema.europa.eu/en/human-regulatory/overview/biosimilar-medicines-overview.

Chapter 15: Biopharmaceuticals §15.16

Medicine Name	Active Substance	Marketing Authorisation Date	Marketing Authorisation Holder/Company Name
Blitzima	rituximab	13-07-2017	Celltrion Healthcare Hungary Kft.
Alymsys	bevacizumab	26-03-2021	Mabxience Research SL
Oyavas	bevacizumab	26-03-2021	STADA Arzneimittel AG
Inhixa	enoxaparin sodium	15-09-2016	Techdow Pharma Netherlands B.V.
Bemfola	follitropin alfa	26-03-2014	Gedeon Richter Plc.
Accofil	filgrastim	17-09-2014	Accord Healthcare S.L.U.
Sondelbay	teriparatide	24-03-2022	Accord Healthcare S.L.U.
Riximyo	rituximab	15-06-2017	Sandoz GmbH
Flixabi	infliximab	26-05-2016	Samsung Bioepis NL B.V.
Rixathon	rituximab	15-06-2017	Sandoz GmbH
Imraldi	adalimumab	24-08-2017	Samsung Bioepis NL B.V.
Zessly	infliximab	18-05-2018	Sandoz GmbH
Remsima	infliximab	10-09-2013	Celltrion Healthcare Hungary Kft.
Inflectra	infliximab	10-09-2013	Pfizer Europe MA EEIG
Erelzi	etanercept	23-06-2017	Sandoz GmbH
Truxima	rituximab	17-02-2017	Celltrion Healthcare Hungary Kft.
Byooviz	ranibizumab	18-08-2021	Samsung Bioepis NL B.V.
Abevmy	bevacizumab	21-04-2021	Mylan IRE Healthcare Limited
Insulin lispro Sanofi	insulin lispro	19-07-2017	sanofi-aventis groupe

Medicine Name	Active Substance	Marketing Authorisation Date	Marketing Authorisation Holder/Company Name
Herzuma	trastuzumab	9-02-2018	Celltrion Healthcare Hungary Kft.
Stimufend	pegfilgrastim	28-03-2022	Fresenius Kabi Deutschland GmbH
Zirabev	bevacizumab	14-02-2019	Pfizer Europe MA EEIG
Ruxience	rituximab	1-04-2020	Pfizer Europe MA EEIG
Ogivri	trastuzumab	12-12-2018	Viatris Limited
Nepexto	etanercept	20-05-2020	Mylan IRE Healthcare Limited
Yuflyma	adalimumab	11-02-2021	Celltrion Healthcare Hungary Kft.
Hyrimoz	adalimumab	26-07-2018	Sandoz GmbH
Hefiya	adalimumab	26-07-2018	Sandoz GmbH
Idacio	adalimumab	2-04-2019	Fresenius Kabi Deutschland GmbH
Inpremzia	insulin human (rDNA)	25-04-2022	Baxter Holding B.V.
Zercepac	trastuzumab	27-07-2020	Accord Healthcare S.L.U.
Fulphila	pegfilgrastim	20-11-2018	Viatris Limited
Ziextenzo	pegfilgrastim	22-11-2018	Sandoz GmbH
Trazimera	trastuzumab	26-07-2018	Pfizer Europe MA EEIG
Insulin aspart Sanofi	insulin aspart	25-06-2020	sanofi-aventis groupe
Hukyndra	adalimumab	15-11-2021	Stada Arzneimittel AG
Kanjinti	trastuzumab	16-05-2018	Amgen Europe BV
Movymia	teriparatide	11-01-2017	STADA Arzneimittel AG

Chapter 15: Biopharmaceuticals §15.16

Medicine Name	Active Substance	Marketing Authorisation Date	Marketing Authorisation Holder/Company Name
Libmyris	adalimumab	12-11-2021	Stada Arzneimittel AG
Semglee	insulin glargine	23-03-2018	Viatris Limited
Hulio	adalimumab	17-09-2018	Viatris Limited
Grastofil	filgrastim	17-10-2013	Accord Healthcare S.L.U.
Amgevita	adalimumab	21-03-2017	Amgen Europe B.V.
Tevagrastim	filgrastim	15-09-2008	Teva GmbH
Ratiograstim	filgrastim	15-09-2008	Ratiopharm GmbH
Retacrit	epoetin zeta	18-12-2007	Pfizer Europe MA EEIG
Nivestim	filgrastim	7-06-2010	Pfizer Europe MA EEIG
Ontruzant	trastuzumab	15-11-2017	Samsung Bioepis NL B.V.
Pelmeg	pegfilgrastim	20-11-2018	Mundipharma Corporation (Ireland) Limited
Cegfila (previously Pegfilgrastim Mundipharma)	pegfilgrastim	19-12-2019	Mundipharma Corporation (Ireland) Limited
Nyvepria	pegfilgrastim	18-11-2020	Pfizer Europe MA EEIG
Terrosa	teriparatide	4-01-2017	Gedeon Richter Plc.
Amsparity	adalimumab	13-02-2020	Pfizer Europe MA EEIG
Omnitrope	somatropin	12-04-2006	Sandoz GmbH
Abseamed	epoetin alfa	27-08-2007	Medice Arzneimittel Pütter GmbH Co. KG
Abasaglar (previously Abasria)	insulin glargine	9-09-2014	Eli Lilly Nederland B.V.

Medicine Name	Active Substance	Marketing Authorisation Date	Marketing Authorisation Holder/Company Name
Kirsty (previously Kixelle)	insulin aspart	5-02-2021	Mylan Ireland Limited
Aybintio	bevacizumab	19-08-2020	Samsung Bioepis NL B.V.
Onbevzi	bevacizumab	11-01-2021	Samsung Bioepis NL B.V.
Pelgraz	pegfilgrastim	21-09-2018	Accord Healthcare S.L.U.
Grasustek	pegfilgrastim	20-06-2019	Juta Pharma GmbH
Benepali	etanercept	13-01-2016	Samsung Bioepis NL B.V.
Livogiva	teriparatide	27-08-2020	Theramex Ireland Limited
Silapo	epoetin zeta	18-12-2007	Stada Arzneimittel AG
Binocrit	epoetin alfa	28-08-2007	Sandoz GmbH
Epoetin Alfa Hexal	epoetin alfa	27-08-2007	Hexal AG
Ovaleap	follitropin alfa	27-09-2013	Theramex Ireland Limited

While the legal and regulatory framework for these products has been widely harmonised, differences still exist between EU Member States in the perception of biosimilars and, related thereto, in their use. Several factors contribute to this situation.

Among the most important factors, the approach of pharmacovigilance for these products, the labelling requirements, the possibilities of interchangeability and substitution, and the extrapolation of indications are the most commonly cited.

Indeed, biosimilars have an inherent complexity that does not allow them to be compared to generics. Even the name under which a biosimilar is sold can be challenging, as the inherent variability of biologicals can lead to rejecting the use of a same INN for a given biological product and a biosimilar to that product. The WHO's INN Expert Group addressed the issue following requests from regulatory authorities. A working paper issued in 2014 suggests a voluntary system by which an application can be made to the INN Secretariat for a Biological Qualifier (BQ). A BQ is a code formed of four random consonants in two 2-letter blocks separated by a 2-digit checksum, assigned at random to a biological active substance manufactured at a specified site. The scheme would apply to all biological active substances to which INNs are assigned and are applicable retrospectively, if possible. The majority of EU

Member States, however, think that biosimilars should be closely aligned with their reference biological, and that an INN qualifier for biosimilars would be contrary to such alignment. There is concern in that regard that a distinct INN for biosimilars would undermine the trust of healthcare professionals and the public in biosimilars, as stated in the summary record of the Commission's Pharmaceutical Committee's 71st meeting, held on 23 October 2013 in Brussels.[39] The Commission has not changed its thinking ever since.[40]

The related labelling issues also concern the possibility and/or necessity to include information relating to the reference product on the biosimilar label. Industry stakeholders support the view that new guidance for transparent labelling for biosimilars that would replace or supplement EMA's Quality Review of Documents guidance (which does not distinguish between biosimilars, generics, and hybrid products in terms of labelling) would contribute to facilitating physicians and patients' understanding and acceptance of these products.

The question of substitutability or interchangeability between an originator and a biosimilar also raises concern, certainly so when considering the high variability of biological substances and the risk of immunogenicity. In the EU, the decisions on interchangeability and/or substitution rely on national competent authorities and are outside the remit of the EMA/CHMP,[41] which can thus lead to diverging approaches among Member States – notably as to the additional data that may be required from the applicants to demonstrate the possibility of substituting the reference product with the biosimilar. To date, most European countries have not authorised substitution – some countries even adopted measures preventing it. In Germany, since 2011, pharmacists may substitute, within the framework of the *aut idem* substitution, biotechnologically-manufactured products among each other which (a) have been approved with reference to the same reference product and which (b) have been produced by the same manufacturer with the same manufacturing process. It is worth underlining that the only difference between these substitutable products is their trade name; the products are actually identical, so there is no real 'biosimilar substitution' at stake. In France, substitution is authorised by law.[42] Three cumulative conditions must be met for the substitution of biosimilars to be allowed: (i) the substitution must occur when initiating a course of treatment; (ii) the biosimilar must belong to the same group as the prescribed product (i.e., it must belong to a so-called similar biologic group, which will need to be further defined by the ANSM, the French competent authority for medicinal products – to date, no such list has been issued by the ANSM yet); and (iii) only if the prescribing physician has not explicitly prohibited substitution of the prescribed biological by indicating the terms 'non-substitutable' in handwritten characters on the

---

39. https://health.ec.europa.eu/system/files/2016-11/pharm639_summary_0.pdf.
40. Pharmaceutical Committee 21 October 2015, WHO Biological Qualifier: https://health.ec.europa.eu/system/files/2016-11/pharm697_who_biological_qualifier_0.pdf.
41. EMA Procedural advice for users of the Centralised Procedure for Similar Biological Medicinal Products applications, EMA/940451/2011.
42. Changes were made to the French Code for Public Health to that purpose, through Article 47 of an Act of 23 December 2013 on the financing of the French social security system – available on www.legifrance.gouv.fr.

prescription. If these three conditions are all met, then the pharmacist may substitute the originator with the corresponding biosimilar. However, this law is not yet in force, since this will only be possible under the condition that an implementing act that would include further details would be passed by administrative courts. However, this act has not yet been issued, which means that, at the moment, actual implementation of biosimilar substitution in France is not yet possible.

Given these issues, which are being discussed among stakeholders – including regulatory bodies and the industry, interesting developments and evolutions are expected in the field of biological medicinal products.

§15.17   UK

The EU Directive 2001/83/EC on the Community code relating to medicinal products for human use remains in force in the UK under The Human Medicines Regulations 2012 (UK HMR), meaning the regulation of biopharmaceuticals in Great Britain and Northern Ireland remains closely aligned with the EU after the Brexit transition period. The main differences since 1 January 2021 relate to the MHRA's regulation of biosimilar products in Great Britain at a national level in accordance with its own published guidance (UK Biosimilar Guidance).[43] Although the MHRA is also the competent authority for Northern Ireland, due to the Northern Ireland Protocol, it will regulate biosimilars in Northern Ireland in accordance with EU guidance.

A confirmatory pharmacokinetic trial should always be conducted to demonstrate the bioequivalence of the biosimilar to the original biologic as the '*Reference Product*'. However, similar to the EU's reduced emphasis on comparative efficacy trials, the UK Biosimilar Guidance provides that 'in most cases, a comparative efficacy trial may not be necessary if sound scientific rationale supports this approach', the reason being that the efficacy of the Reference Product can usually be extrapolated from the biological events known to be triggered by binding the active substance to comparable targets. Where biosimilar applicants have sufficient comparative analytical and functional data to justify the absence of an efficacy trial, based on the comparable binding properties and functional characteristics of the biosimilar to the Reference Product, justification for the absence of an efficacy trial should be appended to the Common Technical Document of the submitted application. To use non-Great Britain Reference Products in clinical studies, the applicant should submit evidence that the non-Great Britain Reference Product is representative of the Great Britain Reference Product.

Biosimilar products approved before 1 January 2021 continue to be authorised in the UK. Biosimilar applications submitted after 1 January 2021 may only be made with reference to a Reference Product that is:[44]

– authorised for at least eight years in the UK or by conversion from EU MAs; or

---

43. 'Guidance on the licensing of biosimilar products' (published 6 May 2021).
44. Regulation 48 of UK HMR (as amended by The Human Medicines (Amendment etc.) (EU Exit) Regulations 2019).

- where an EU MA was in force on 31 December 2020 (the day the UK exited the EU), but no UK MA is in force because the EU MA was not converted; or
- where an EU MA had ceased to be in force on or before 31 December 2020 but not for reasons to do with efficacy, safety, or quality.

CHAPTER 16
Homeopathic, Herbal, and Traditional Herbal Medicinal Products and Cannabis-Based Medicinal Products

Pieter Erasmus[*]

§16.01 INTRODUCTION

Homeopathic, herbal, and traditional herbal medicinal products, like all other medicinal products, may only be placed on the market in a Member State of the EU when a Marketing Authorisation (MA) or registration has been obtained with the competent authority of the Member State. The authorisation or registration of homeopathic, herbal, and traditional herbal medicinal products is based on Directive 2001/83/EC, as amended.[1]

Based on the recent increase in interest in the medical use of cannabis and cannabinoids (among other uses, such as in the context of foodstuffs, cosmetics, etc.) and with a number of such medicinal products becoming available in Europe,[2] this chapter provides a brief overview of the EU regulatory framework pertaining to cannabis-based medicinal products. Like all other medicinal products, cannabis-based medicinal products may only be placed on the market in a Member State of the EU when an MA or registration has been obtained with the competent authority of the Member State. However, the approaches of the various Member States may differ

---

[*] The author wishes to acknowledge *Hanneke Later-Nijland*, the author of the earlier editions of this chapter.
[1] Directive 2001/83/EC of the European Parliament and of the Council of 6 November 2001 on the Community code relating to medicinal products for human use, Official Journal L 311/67.
[2] See *Developments in the European Cannabis Market* (2019) from page 13, available at https://www.emcdda.europa.eu/publications/emcdda-papers/developments-in-the-european-cannabis-market_en.

significantly with regard to the products permitted as well as the local regulatory frameworks governing cannabis and cannabinoids.

For the authorisation or registration of medicinal products, Directive 2001/83/EC makes a distinction between 'general' medicinal products (*see* Chapter 5), 'homeopathic medicinal products',[3] 'herbal medicinal products',[4] and 'traditional herbal medicinal products'.[5] Directive 2001/83/EC does not make specific reference to cannabis-based medicinal products or similar concepts.

Homeopathic medicinal products are medicinal products that are prepared from substances called homeopathic stocks. Stocks can be plant, animal, human, mineral, and chemical substances recognised by, among others, the European Pharmacopoeia. The manufacturing process of a homeopathic product involves the dilution (reducing the concentration) and succussion (vigorous shaking) of the stock to activate the healing potential. The homeopathic medicinal product could be the stock itself or its dilutions.

Herbal medicinal products are solely derived from plants and plant extracts. Their active ingredient may be one or more herbal substances, such as plants, algae, fungi, or lichens, or one or more herbal preparations or a combination thereof. Though homeopathic medicinal products may also be prepared from plants, the manufacturing process is substantially different. Herbal medicinal products are typically manufactured from roots, leaves, or other parts of the plant in powdered or extracted form.

A herbal medicinal product is considered to be a traditional herbal medicinal product, under Directive 2001/83/EC, as amended, when it fulfils certain conditions in Article 16a of the Directive. These conditions are that the herbal medicinal product is intended and designed for use without the supervision of a medical practitioner; is exclusively for administration in accordance with a specified strength and doses; is an oral, external, and/or inhalation preparation; has been in medicinal use throughout a period of at least thirty years; and the effect or efficacy is plausible on the basis of long-standing use and experience.

Distinctions among the different medicinal products are relevant under the Directive in order to determine which authorisation or registration procedure is applicable. As mentioned above, cannabis-based medicinal products are not specifically referred to in Directive 2001/83/EC.

In Directive 2001/83/EC, as amended, the term 'authorisation' is used to refer to the 'general' MA procedures set out in Chapter I of the Directive and as discussed in Chapter 5 of this book. With the term 'registration', the Directive refers to 'special' authorisation procedures for homeopathic and traditional herbal medicinal products. These special authorisation procedures are named 'simplified registration procedures'.[6] To make a distinction between the simplified registration procedure for

---

3. *See* definition at Article 1(5) of Directive 2001/83/EC.
4. *See* definition at Article 1(30) of Directive 2001/83/EC.
5. *See* definition at Article 1(29) of Directive 2001/83/EC, read with Article 16a(1) of Directive 2001/83/EC.
6. Article 14 of Directive 2001/83/EC, as amended, pertains to the simplified registration procedure for homeopathic medicinal products, while Article 16a of Directive 2001/83/EC, as amended, pertains to the simplified registration procedure for *traditional* herbal medicinal products.

homeopathic medicinal products and the simplified registration procedure for traditional herbal products, the Directive names the simplified registration procedure for traditional herbal medicinal products 'traditional use registration'. The Directive does not contain a separate term for the simplified registration procedure for homeopathic medicinal products. In this chapter, 'simplified registration procedure' is therefore used to refer to the special authorisation procedures for both homeopathic and traditional herbal products. The term 'traditional use registration' is used for the simplified registration procedure solely for traditional herbal medicinal products, and the term 'homeopathic simplified registration procedure' is used for the simplified registration procedure solely for homeopathic medicinal products.

A distinction is made between two groups of homeopathic medicinal products. One group is homeopathic medicinal products that are placed on the market without therapeutic indications, intended for oral or external use, and with a sufficient degree of dilution to guarantee the safety of the product. This group may obtain a registration on the basis of the homeopathic simplified registration procedure as set forth in Articles 14 and 15 of Directive 2001/83/EC, as amended. Under the homeopathic simplified registration procedure, only the quality and safety of the product are assessed. The efficacy of these homeopathic medicinal products is not assessed.

The other group refers to homeopathic medicinal products that do not fulfil the conditions of the homeopathic simplified registration procedure and therefore falls under Article 16 of Directive 2001/83/EC. These homeopathic medicinal products shall follow the general rules for MA set out in Articles 8, 10, 10a, 10b, 10c, and 11 of Directive 2001/83/EC (Title III, Chapter 1), as determined in Article 16 of the Directive, before they can be placed on the market (hereinafter referred to as 'Article 16 authorisation').

One of these general rules regards the bibliographic Marketing Authorisation procedure, also called the well-established use procedure (Article 10a) (hereinafter referred to as the 'bibliographic authorisation procedure'). In principle, every application for an MA must contain the results of tests and trials on the quality, safety, and efficacy of the product. The bibliographic authorisation procedure contains an exception, and it determines that an applicant of a medicinal product that can demonstrate by references to published scientific literature that the medicinal product has a well-established medicinal use within the EU for at least ten years with a recognised efficacy and an acceptable level of safety is not required to provide the results of preclinical tests or the results of clinical trials.

Herbal medicinal products will also need to follow the general rules for MA as set out in Title III, Chapter 1 of Directive 2001/83/EC before they can be placed on the market. The bibliographic authorisation procedure of Article 10a of the Directive may be available.

However, taking into account the particular characteristics of herbal medicinal products, as also applies for homeopathic medicinal products, it may be difficult to satisfy the requirements for obtaining a general MA. Even the requirements of the bibliographic authorisation procedure may not be feasible. Therefore, a herbal medicinal product that satisfies the definition of traditional herbal medicinal product may apply for a simplified registration procedure, the traditional use registration. Under the traditional use registration, the efficacy of traditional herbal medicinal products is not assessed by clinical testing or demonstrated by scientific literature but is solely based on a long-standing use and experience of the product.

This chapter discusses the different authorisation and registration procedures available for homeopathic, herbal, and traditional herbal medicinal products, as well as cannabis-based medicinal products, under Directive 2001/83/EC, as amended. The application procedure and the requirements are set out for each product.

§16.02 HOMEOPATHIC MEDICINAL PRODUCTS

[A] Introduction to Homeopathic Medicinal Products

Those medicinal products that fall under the definition of 'homeopathic medicinal product' as provided in Article 1(5) of Directive 2001/83/EC, as amended, may only be placed on the market within the EU if they are registered in accordance with the homeopathic simplified registration procedure or authorised in accordance with the Article 16 authorisation procedure.

[B] Legal History of Homeopathic Medicinal Products

Until the adoption of Directive 92/73/EEC[7] in 1992, homeopathic medicinal products were explicitly excluded from the scope of European pharmaceutical legislation. There was no requirement to obtain an MA for homeopathic medicinal products at the European level. The available procedures were not suitable for the particular characteristics of homeopathic medicinal products, such as the low level of active principles that they contain and the difficulty of applying conventional statistical methods relating to clinical trials.

However, assessing this type of medicinal product is important for ensuring safe and good-quality homeopathic medicinal products on the market in the EU. Therefore, Directive 92/73/EEC determined that homeopathic medicinal products must be authorised in all European Member States. Specific provisions applicable to homeopathic medicinal products were introduced in Directive 92/73/EEC. The provisions determined that Member States must ensure that homeopathic medicinal products that are manufactured and placed on the market within the EU are either registered in accordance with the homeopathic simplified registration procedure, or those homeopathic medicinal products that do not fulfil the criteria of the homeopathic simplified registration procedure are to obtain an Article 16 authorisation.

---

7. Council Directive 92/73/EEC of the Council of the European Communities, widening the scope of Directives 65/65/EEC and 75/319/EEC on the approximation of provisions laid down by law, Regulation, or administrative action relating to medicinal products and laying down additional provisions on homeopathic medicinal products, Official Journal L 297/8. This Directive is repealed and codified in Directive 2001/83/EC.

Directive 92/73/EC was subsequently included in Directive 2001/83/EC as part of the general codification of EC pharmaceutical legislation.

Revisions of Directive 2001/83/EC in 2003 and 2004 brought some substantive modifications for homeopathic medicinal products. Directive 2003/63/EC[8] provides more clarity for the assessment of applications by setting out specific provisions in Annex I of Directive 2001/83/EC on the proof of quality and safety of homeopathic medicinal products. Directive 2004/27/EC[9] regards the review process of Directive 2001/83/EC (see Chapter 2, §2.01), which led to the insertion of the mutual recognition procedure and decentralised procedure for most medicinal products.

The mutual recognition and decentralised procedures now apply for homeopathic medicinal products entitled to the homeopathic simplified registration procedure. The Article 16 authorisation procedure is not harmonised throughout the EU. Also, Directive 2004/27/EC introduced the possibility of changing the dilution criteria of 1:10,000 part of the mother tincture for the homeopathic simplified registration procedure through a specialist committee (Article 14(1), third paragraph, of Directive 2001/83/EC).[10, 11]

[C] Current Legislative Framework for Homeopathic Medicinal Products

Specific provisions applicable to homeopathic medicinal products are now set out in Chapter 2, Articles 13 through 16, of Directive 2001/83/EC, as amended. Article 13 requires Member States to ensure that homeopathic medicinal products that are manufactured and placed on the market within the EU are either registered in accordance with the homeopathic simplified registration procedure of Articles 14 and 15, alternatively, authorised according to the Article 16 authorisation procedure. Article 14 specifies the conditions under which a homeopathic medicinal product may apply for the homeopathic simplified registration procedure, while Article 15 regards the documents to be included in the application for a homeopathic simplified registration. Article 16 of course deals with the Article 16 authorisation procedure, which determines that homeopathic medicinal products that do not fulfil the requirements of the homeopathic simplified registration procedure shall be authorised and labelled in accordance with the general rules governing MAs in Articles 8, 10, 10a, 10b, 10c, and 11 of Directive 2001/83/EC.

---

8. Directive 2003/63/EC of 25 June 2003 amending Directive 2001/83/EC of the European Parliament and of the Council on the Community code relating to medicinal products for human use, Official Journal L 159/46.
9. Directive 2004/27/EC of the European Parliament and of the Council of 31 March 2004 amending Directive 2001/83/EC on the Community code relating to medicinal products for human use, Official Journal L 136/34.
10. *See also* https://echamp.eu/eu-policy-and-regulation/eu-legislation/homeopathic-medicinal-products.
11. *See also* Chapter 5 – Obtaining a Marketing Authorisation.

[D] Definition of Homeopathic Medicinal Product

A 'homeopathic medicinal product' is defined in Article 1(5) of Directive 2001/83/EC as:

> Any medicinal product is prepared from substances called homeopathic stocks in accordance with a homeopathic manufacturing procedure described by the European Pharmacopoeia or, in the absence thereof, by the pharmacopoeias currently used officially in the Member States. A homeopathic medicinal product may contain a number of principles.

The status of a homeopathic medicinal product is recognised throughout the EU since Member States have adopted and accepted an identical definition.

A homeopathic medicinal product is prepared using substances or products that are recognised as homeopathic stocks by the European Pharmacopoeia or a pharmacopoeia officially used in a Member State. Homeopathic medicinal products may contain large numbers of active homeopathic substances or a combination of active substances of biological, chemical, and herbal origin. The finished medicinal product could be the stock itself or its dilutions.[12]

From a terminology perspective, the *'stock'* essentially refers to the substances, products, or preparations used as starting materials for the production of homoeopathic preparations.[13] *'Starting material'* (also known as 'raw material', 'source material', or 'mother substance') refers to the original raw material used for the production of homeopathic medicines. This material may be obtained from natural sources, for example, botanical, zoological, microbiological, mineral, chemical, animal and human origin, or synthetic procedures. Source materials may undergo preliminary treatment in order to be further processed.[14] The term 'mother tincture' refers to the initial homeopathic preparation made from source material that can be further potentised (also called 'liquid stock'), sometimes used as homeopathic medicines, is regarded as the most concentrated form of a finished homeopathic medicine. Mother tinctures are obtained classically by maceration or percolation (sometimes also by digestion, infusion, decoction, or fermentation) techniques from source materials according to a procedure prescribed by a recognised homeopathic pharmacopoeia.[15]

Therefore, the stock is the starting material for the homeopathic manufacturing process. In the manufacturing process, the stock is diluted and succussed in successive steps purportedly to activate the healing potential, while eliminating side effects of the raw material. Dilution involves the process of reducing the concentration of a solution. Succussion involves the vigorous shaking or banging against a firm object of a diluted homeopathic preparation.

---

12. *Guidance on Module 3 of the Homeopathic Medicinal Products Dossier* (November 2007), published by the Homeopathic Medicinal Product Working Group, to be found at: http://www.hma.eu/uploads/media/HMPWG_dossier_guidance_mod3.pdf.
13. *See* Annex 2: Glossary of *Safety Issues in the Preparation of Homeopathic Medicines* (2009) (World Health Organization), available at https://apps.who.int/iris/handle/10665/44238.
14. *Ibid.*
15. *Ibid.*

This dilution and succussion is called potentisation. The result is a homeopathic medicinal product with a certain potency. A sufficient degree of dilution is important to guarantee the safety of the medicinal product and to determine whether the homeopathic simplified registration procedure or the Article 16 authorisation procedure needs to be followed.

Anthroposophic medicinal products[16] described in an official pharmacopoeia and prepared by a homeopathic method are to be treated, with regard to the registration and marketing, in the same way as homeopathic medicinal products.[17]

[E]   Homeopathic Simplified Registration Procedure

The homeopathic simplified procedure allows the registration of homeopathic medicinal products without requiring particulars and documents on tests and trials on the safety and efficacy of the product. The procedure applies to homeopathic medicinal products produced in accordance with a homeopathic manufacturing procedure that satisfies all of the following criteria:

- they are administered orally or externally;
- they do not contain a specific therapeutic indication; and
- they do not contain more than 1:10,000 part of the mother tincture or 1:100 part of the smallest dose of an active substance that is used in allopathic (traditional) medicine and for which a doctor's prescription is required.[18]

If new scientific evidence so warrants, the European Commission may amend the dilution criteria[19] by the procedure as described in Article 5a of Decision 1999/468/EC.[20] Even though this decision has been repealed by Regulation (EU) No. 182/2011, Article 12 of this regulation stipulates that the effects of Article 5a of the Decision shall be maintained for the purposes of existing basic acts making reference thereto.

[F]   Application Procedure for Homeopathic Simplified Registration

The requirements of the application dossier for a homeopathic simplified registration are set out in Article 15 of Directive 2001/83/EC, as amended. The application for the homeopathic simplified registration procedure may cover a series of medicinal products derived from the same homeopathic stock or stocks. An application shall include the following documents in order to particularly demonstrate the pharmaceutical quality and the batch homogeneity of the products:

---

16. *See* further at https://echamp.eu/eu-policy-and-regulation/eu-legislation/anthroposophic-medicinal-products.
17. Preamble to Directive 2001/83/EC, as amended, paragraph 22.
18. Article 14(1) Directive 2001/83/EC, as amended.
19. Article 14(1), para. 2, Directive 2001/83/EC, as amended.
20. Decision 1999/468/EC of the Council of the European Union of 28 June 1999 describes the procedures for the exercise of implementing powers conferred on the Commission.

- scientific name or other name given in a pharmacopoeia of the homeopathic stock or stocks;
- statement of the various routes of administration, pharmaceutical forms, and degree of dilution;
- dossier describing how the homeopathic stock(s) is/are obtained and controlled and justifying the homeopathic use, on the basis of an adequate bibliography;
- manufacturing and control file and a description of the method of dilution and potentisation;
- manufacturing authorisation;
- copies of any registrations or authorisations obtained for the same medicinal product in other Member States;
- one or more mock-ups of the outer and immediate packaging; and
- data concerning the stability of the medicinal product.

Clinical, pharmaceutical, and therapeutic data do not have to be included in the application. Article 14(2) of Directive 2001/83/EC expressly states that proof of therapeutic efficacy is not required for homeopathic medicinal products registered in accordance with the simplified registration procedure.

Homeopathic medicinal products that fall under the homeopathic simplified registration procedure may be registered on the basis of a national procedure, mutual recognition procedure, or decentralised procedure, as discussed in Chapter 5 of this text. In case of a homeopathic simplified registration, where existing registrations have been obtained for the same homeopathic medicinal product in other Member States, or in view of the granting of a registration in more than one Member State, the criteria and rules of the mutual recognition procedure or the decentralised procedure in Articles 28 and 29(1) to (3) of Directive 2001/83/EC shall apply.[21]

Although detailed procedures and timescales of the application process are different in each Member State, a basic overview of the application process for national, mutual recognition, or decentralised procedures is set out in Chapter 5 of this book. The timescale for the assessment of the application of a homeopathic simplified registration may differ slightly compared to the general MA procedures, as the efficacy with a homeopathic simplified registration is not assessed by the competent authority.

After a registration has been granted and the homeopathic medicinal product is placed on the market, it will need to be reviewed after five years for a re-evaluation of the risk/benefit balance. Once the registration is renewed, it will continue in effect indefinitely. A registration of a homeopathic medicinal product that is not marketed within three years of being approved or that is no longer actually on the market for a period of three consecutive years will lapse unless there are exceptional circumstances for the competent authority to grant an exception.[22]

---

21. Article 13 Directive 2001/83/EC, as amended.
22. Article 14(2) in conjunction with Article 24 of Directive 2001/83/EC, as amended.

[G] Article 16 Authorisation Procedure

Those homeopathic medicinal products that do not comply with the criteria of Article 14 of the homeopathic simplified registration procedure need to be authorised and labelled in accordance with the Article 16 authorisation procedure contemplated in Article 16 of Directive 2001/83/EC, as amended. As a consequence, these products follow the general rules governing the MA procedures of medicinal products set forth in Articles 8 (application), 10 (abridged procedure), 10a (bibliographical Marketing Authorisation), 10b (combination substances), and 10c (subsequent applications) of Directive 2001/83/EC (*see* Chapters 5 and 13).

The bibliographical authorisation procedure provides that an applicant of a medicinal product that has a well-established medicinal use within the EU for at least ten years, with a recognised efficacy and an acceptable level of safety, is not required to provide the results of preclinical tests or the results of clinical trials. The test and trial results are replaced by appropriate scientific literature. However, Member States may introduce specific rules for the preclinical (pharmacological and toxicological) tests and clinical trials of homeopathic medicinal products (other than the rules already set out for the homeopathic simplified registration procedure), intended to establish the safety and efficacy of these medicinal products in accordance with the principles and characteristics of homeopathy as practised in its Member State. These particular rules of the Member States are to be notified to the Commission.[23]

The Article 16 authorisation procedure is not harmonised throughout the EU. Therefore, homeopathic medicinal products that fall under the Article 16 authorisation procedure can only be registered on the basis of a national procedure (*see* Chapter 5).

[H] Applicability of Other Provisions of the Directive to Homeopathic Medicinal Products

Although Chapter 2 of Directive 2001/83/EC, regarding homeopathic medicinal products, does not explicitly set out which additional provisions of Directive 2001/83/EC are also applicable for homeopathic medicinal products, the Directive, at a number of other provisions, specifies that such provision also applies to homeopathic medicinal products. For example, Article 53 of Title IV, regarding manufacture and importation of medicinal products, states that the provisions of this Title shall also apply to homeopathic medicinal products. The same applies to Title VII, wholesale distribution of medicinal products (Article 85); Title VIIIa, information and advertising (Article 100); and Title XI, supervision and sanctions (Article 119).

Title V, labelling and package leaflet (Article 68), also applies to homeopathic medicinal products. In addition, Article 69 of Title V specifically determines that for the homeopathic simplified registration procedure, in addition to the clear mention of the words 'homeopathic medicinal product', the labelling and, where appropriate, the package leaflet shall bear the following, and no other, information:

---

23. Article 16(2) Directive 2001/83/EC, as amended.

- the scientific name of the stock or stocks followed by the degree of dilution;
- name and address of the registration holder and manufacturer;
- method of administration and route;
- expiry date;
- pharmaceutical form;
- contents of the sales presentation;
- special storage precautions;
- special warning;
- manufacturer's batch number;
- registration number;
- the note 'homeopathic medicinal product without approved therapeutic Indications'; and
- a warning advising the user to consult a doctor if the symptoms persist.

Member States may require the use of certain types of labelling in order to show the price of the product and the conditions for refunds by social security bodies.

Title IX, pharmacovigilance, is solely applicable to homeopathic medicinal products under the Article 16 authorisation procedure (Article 16(3) of Directive 2001/83/EC).

§16.03 HERBAL AND TRADITIONAL HERBAL MEDICINAL PRODUCTS

[A] Introduction to Herbal and Traditional Herbal Medicinal Products

Like all other medicinal products, herbal and traditional herbal medicinal products require an MA or registration before they can be placed on the market in the EU. Directive 2001/83/EC also applies to herbal and traditional herbal medicinal products.

Herbal medicinal products may be authorised on the basis of the general MA procedures as set out in Title III, Chapter 1, of Directive 2001/83/EC (*see* Chapter 5). For herbal medicinal products, it may be difficult to obtain the required results of tests and trials on the quality, safety, and efficacy of the product. The bibliographical authorisation procedure in Article 10a of Directive 2001/83/EC, as amended, contains an exception to these requirements of tests and trials. Those herbal medicinal products that have a well-established medicinal use within the EU with a recognised efficacy and an acceptable level of safety demonstrated by scientific literature may be authorised on the basis of the bibliographical authorisation procedure. Under this procedure, the applicant does not have to provide the results of preclinical tests or the results of clinical trials.

Significant numbers of herbal medicinal products, despite their long tradition, however, also do not fulfil the requirements of the bibliographic authorisation procedure, and they are therefore not eligible for a general MA. In order to maintain these products on the market and to overcome difficulties encountered by Member States in applying pharmaceutical legislation to herbal medicinal products and having regard to the particular characteristics of these medicinal products, specific provisions were

Chapter 16: Homeopathic, Herbal and Similar Products §16.03[B]

introduced during the review process of Directive 2001/83/EC (*see* Chapter 2, §2.01). In this regard, Directive 2004/24/EC[24] amending Directive 2001/83/EC introduced the traditional use registration for traditional herbal medicinal products. Particulars and documents on tests and trials on safety and efficacy are not required under the traditional use registration, provided that there is sufficient evidence that the product has been in medicinal use throughout a period of at least thirty years, including at least fifteen years within the EU.

[B] Herbal Medicinal Products

[1] Definition of Herbal Medicinal Products

In Article 1(30) of Directive 2001/83/EC, as amended, a 'herbal medicinal product' is defined as:

> Any medicinal product, exclusively containing as active ingredients one or more herbal substances or one or more herbal preparations, or one or more such herbal substances in combination with one or more such herbal preparations.

More specifically, a herbal medicinal product is: (1) a 'medicinal product', as defined in Article 1(2) of Directive 2001/83/EC; and (2) exclusively containing as active ingredient(s) (term not further defined in the Directive; for case law, *see*, among others, the *MIT* case):[25]

> (a) one or more 'herbal substances', defined in Article 1(31) of Directive 2001/83/EC as:
>
>> All mainly whole, fragmented or cut plants, plant parts, algae, fungi, lichen in an unprocessed, usually dried, form, but sometimes fresh. Certain exudates that have not been subjected to a specific treatment are also considered to be herbal substances. Herbal substances are precisely defined by the plant part used and the botanical name according to the binomial system (genus, species, variety and author).[26]
>
> (b) one or more 'herbal preparations', defined in Article 1(32) of Directive 2001/83/EC as:
>
>> Preparations obtained by subjecting herbal substances to treatments such as extraction, distillation, expression, fractionation, purification, concentration or fermentation. These include comminuted or powdered

---

24. Directive 2004/24/EC of the European Parliament and of the Council of 31 March 2004 amending, as regards traditional herbal medicinal products, Directive 2001/83/EC on the Community code relating to medicinal products for human use, Official Journal L 136/85.
25. European Court of Justice, May 2006, nr. C-431/04, *Jur.* 2006, MIT, I-4089.
26. This definition corresponds with the definition for herbal drug in the European Pharmacopoeia.

herbal substances, tinctures, extracts, essential oils, expressed juices and processed exudates.[27]

(c) a combination of (a) and (b).

[2]   General MA Procedure for Herbal Medicinal Products

Herbal medicinal products must follow the general rules for MA in Title III, Chapter 1, of Directive 2001/83/EC before they can be placed on the market. For most herbal medicinal products, it is difficult to fulfil the requirements for obtaining a general MA. However, one of the general MA procedures, the bibliographic authorisation procedure set out in Article 10a of Title III, Chapter 1, of the Directive, may be attainable for herbal medicinal products. If the applicant can demonstrate by detailed references to published scientific literature that the constituent or the constituents of the herbal medicinal product has or have a well-established medicinal use within the EU for at least ten years, with a recognised efficacy and an acceptable level of safety, then the applicant is not required, under the bibliographic authorisation procedure, to provide the results of preclinical tests or the results of clinical trials.

See Chapter 5 for the general MA procedures and the application process.

[C]   Traditional Herbal Medicinal Products

[1]   Current Legislative Framework for Traditional Herbal Medicinal Products

Specific provisions applicable to traditional herbal medicinal products are set out in Chapter 2a (being Articles 16a through 16i) of Directive 2001/83/EC, as amended by Directive 2004/24/EC. Article 16a sets out the traditional use registration procedure. As regards the structure of Chapter 2a, Articles 16b and 16c regards the application process of the traditional use registration. Article 16d declares the mutual recognition and decentralised procedure applicable to the traditional use registration, while Article 16e regards the conditions for refusal of a traditional use registration. The conditions for the list of herbal substances and preparations are set out in Article 16f. Article 16g states which Articles of Directive 2001/83/EC also apply to the traditional use registration and provides for some additional requirements for the labelling, the user package leaflet, and the advertisement of traditional herbal medicinal products. The establishment and competence of the Committee on Herbal Medicinal Products (HMPC) and the establishment of EU herbal monographs are set out in Article 16h.

---

27. This definition corresponds with the definition for herbal drug preparation in the European Pharmacopoeia.

Chapter 16: Homeopathic, Herbal and Similar Products   §16.03[C]

Last, Article 16i provides for the report of the Commission concerning the application of the provisions of Chapter 2a.

[2]   Definition of Traditional Herbal Medicinal Products

Directive 2001/83/EC, as amended, defines 'traditional herbal medicinal products' in Article 1(29) as: '[a] herbal medicinal product that fulfils the conditions laid down in Article 16a(1).' As sketched above, Article 16a regards the traditional use registration. The conditions of the traditional use registration are set out in §16.03[C][3] below.

[3]   Traditional Use Registration

Article 16a(1) provides for a simplified registration procedure, the traditional use registration, for those herbal medicinal products that satisfy the criteria listed in the Article. These cumulative criteria are:

(a) they have indications exclusively appropriate to traditional herbal medicinal products which, by virtue of their composition and purpose, are intended and designed for use without the supervision of a medical practitioner for diagnostic purposes or for the prescription or monitoring of treatment;[28]
(b) they are exclusively for administration in accordance with a specified strength and posology;
(c) they are an oral, external,[29] and/or inhalation preparation;
(d) the period of traditional use as laid down in Article 16c(1)(c) has elapsed;[30] and
(e) the data on the traditional use of the medicinal product are sufficient; in particular the product proves not to be harmful in the specified conditions of use and the pharmacological effects or efficacy of the medicinal products are plausible on the basis of long-standing use and experience.

The supporting evidence for traditional use must show that the product (or a corresponding product) has been in medicinal use throughout a period of at least thirty years. Reference to a source published thirty years ago is not sufficient, as this solely

---

28. Since at the pre-registration stage, it is not yet known whether a prescription is required, the Directive uses the somewhat long-winded description 'intended and designed for use without the supervision of a medical practitioner' instead of the requirement that it is an over-the-counter drug (non-prescription drug).
29. According to the public statement of the HMPC on the interpretation of the term 'external use' for use in the field of traditional herbal medicinal products, the term 'external' in Article 16a(1) of the Directive shall be interpreted as 'application to the skin', although oral, nasal, rectal, vaginal, ocular, and auricular use may be considered external use as well, provided no safety concerns exist, and local action is intended. Injections are not considered external use within the meaning of the Directive.
30. I.e., the product (or a corresponding product) has been in medicinal use throughout a period of at least thirty years preceding the date of the application, including at least fifteen years within the EU.

proves that the product was in use thirty years ago. It is, however, not necessary that the marketing of the product was based on a specific registration. A reduction in the number or quantity of ingredients of the medicinal product in the thirty-year period is allowed.[31]

The traditional use registration procedure also applies to medicinal products wherein vitamins or minerals are present, provided that the medicinal product otherwise (i.e., except for the word 'exclusively') satisfies the requirements of Article 1(30) of Directive 2001/83/EC, as amended, and that there is well-documented evidence for the safety of the vitamins or minerals that are present.[32]

However, the traditional use registration procedure is only to be used where no MA can be obtained pursuant to the general authorisation procedure in Articles 6 *et seq.* of Directive 2001/83/EC, as amended. The traditional use registration is, in particular, intended for herbal medicinal products that cannot get a general MA because of a lack of sufficient scientific literature demonstrating a well-established medicinal use with recognised efficacy and an acceptable level of safety. In addition, the homeopathic simplified registration procedure of Article 14 of Directive 2001/83/EC applies if a traditional herbal medicinal product is a homeopathic medicinal product as well.[33]

In order to promote harmonisation, Member States may recognise registrations of traditional herbal medicinal products granted by another Member State based on EU herbal monographs or consist of substances, preparations, or combinations thereof contained in the EU List (*see* §16.03[G] and [H] hereafter). Chapter 4 of Title III regarding the mutual recognition procedure and the decentralised procedure shall then apply by analogy to traditional use registrations. For traditional herbal medicinal products that are not based on an EU herbal monograph or the EU List, Member States should take due account of registrations granted by another Member State.[34]

Directive 2004/24/EC, amending Directive 2001/83/EC as regards traditional herbal medicinal products, gave manufacturers a long transition period of seven years to register their traditional herbal medicinal products which were already on the EU market when the Directive 2004/24/EC entered into force on April 2004. A traditional herbal medicinal product which was not registered by 30 April 2011 may not be on the market after 1 May 2011. After this date, manufacturers can however still apply for the traditional use registration procedure.

[4] Application Procedure for Traditional Use Registration

In order to obtain a traditional use registration, the applicant and registration holder must be established in the EU and must submit an application to the competent authority of the concerned Member State.[35]

---

31. Article 16c(1)(3) Directive 2001/83/EC, as amended.
32. Article 16a(2) Directive 2001/83/EC, as amended.
33. Article 16a(3) Directive 2001/83/EC, as amended.
34. Article 16d Directive 2001/83/EC, as amended.
35. Article 16b Directive 2001/83/EC, as amended.

Chapter 16: Homeopathic, Herbal and Similar Products §16.03[C]

Applications should be submitted in the format referred to in the Notice to Applicants, in the relevant volumes of the Rules Governing Medicinal Products in the European Union (*see also* Chapter 2, §2.04[E] and Chapter 5, §5.02[B]).

The application shall contain the particulars and documents referred to in Article 16c of Directive 2001/83/EC, as amended. These particulars and documents include:

- general information on the applicant and manufacturer;
- name of the medicinal product;
- qualitative and quantitative particulars of all the constituents of the medicinal product;
- evaluation of the potential environmental risks;
- description of the manufacturing method;
- therapeutic indications, contra-indications, and adverse reactions;
- posology, pharmaceutical form, method and route of administration, and expected shelf life;
- reasons for any precautionary and safety measures to be taken;
- description of the control methods employed by the manufacturer;
- the summary of the product characteristics (without the clinical particulars specified in Article 11[4] of Directive 2001/83/EC);
- mock-up of the outer and immediate packaging;
- document showing that the manufacturer is authorised to produce medicinal products in its own country;
- results of the pharmaceutical tests;
- in case of combinations of herbal substances with herbal preparations, information relating to the combination as such;
- any authorisation or registration obtained by the applicant in another Member State;
- bibliographic review of safety data together with an expert report; and
- bibliographical or expert evidence of the medicinal use of at least thirty years, including at least fifteen years within the EU.

If the product has been used in the EU for less than fifteen years but is otherwise eligible for the traditional use registration, the Member State concerned shall refer the product to the HMPC. The HMPC shall consider whether or not the other criteria for the traditional use registration are fully complied with. If the HMPC considers it possible, it shall establish an EU herbal monograph, as discussed in §16.03[G] hereafter, which shall be taken into account by the Member State when making its final decision for granting the traditional use registration.[36]

---

36. Article 16c(4) Directive 2001/83/EC, as amended.

Medicinal use that has taken place in the territory of a new Member State is to be taken into account for the purpose of the application, even if it has partly or fully occurred before the accession of that State to the EU.[37]

Annex I of Directive 2001/83/EC, as amended by Directive 2003/63/EC, regarding analytical, pharmacotoxicological, and clinical standards and protocols in respect of the testing of medicinal products, shall apply. Part III of Annex I sets forth the specific details that need to be included in a traditional use application.

A traditional use registration shall be refused if the application does not comply with the criteria for a traditional use registration laid down in Articles 16a and 16b and the application criteria of Article 16c of Directive 2001/83/EC, as amended. It shall also be refused under any of the following circumstances:

- the qualitative and/or quantitative composition is not as declared;
- the indications do not comply with the conditions in Article 16a;
- the product could be harmful under normal conditions of use;
- the data on traditional use are insufficient, especially if pharmacological effects or efficacy are not plausible on the basis of long-standing use and experience; and/or
- the pharmaceutical quality is not satisfactorily demonstrated.[38]

The refusal of a traditional use registration and the reasons will be notified to the applicant, the Commission, and any competent authority that requests it.

[5] Labelling, Package Leaflet, and Advertising of Traditional Herbal Medicinal Products

The general rules for labelling, package leaflet, and advertising in Articles 54 to 65 of Directive 2001/83/EC are applicable to the traditional use registration. In addition, the labelling and user package leaflet for traditional use registrations shall contain a statement to the effect that:

- the product is a traditional herbal medicinal product for use in specified indication(s) exclusively based upon long-standing use; and
- the user should consult a doctor or a qualified healthcare practitioner if the symptoms persist during the use of the medicinal product or if adverse effects not mentioned in the package leaflet occur.

A Member State may require that the labelling and the user package leaflet also state the nature of the tradition in question.[39]

---

37. *Notice to Applicants, Volume 2A, Procedures for Marketing Authorisation, Chapter 1, 'Marketing Authorisation'* (July 2019), available at https://ec.europa.eu/health/sites/health/files/files/eudralex/vol-2/vol2a_chap1_en.pdf.
38. Article 16e(1) Directive 2001/83/EC, as amended.
39. Article 16g(2) Directive 2001/83/EC, as amended.

With regard to advertisements, the general Articles 86 to 99 of Directive 2001/83/EC, as amended, apply, and any advertisement for a traditional herbal medicinal product shall contain the following statement: 'Traditional herbal medicinal product for use in specified indication(s) exclusively based upon long-standing use.'[40]

[6]   Other Applicable Provisions for Traditional Use Registration

Article 16g(1) of Directive 2001/83/EC, as amended, explicitly describes which other provisions of the Directive shall apply by analogy to the traditional use registration. These include: Article 6(1) that provides that no medicinal product may be placed on the market of a Member State unless an MA or registration has been issued; Article 12 regarding the experts with the necessary technical or professional qualifications who have drawn up the documents for an application; Articles 40 to 52 regarding the manufacturing and importation of medicinal products; Articles 76 to 85 concerning the wholesale distribution of medicinal products; Articles 101 to 108 regarding the pharmacovigilance; Articles 111(1) and (3), 112, and 116 to 118 regarding supervision and sanctions; and some of the general provisions in Title XIII of the Directive. Also, Directive 91/356/EEC principles and guidelines of Good Manufacturing Practice for medicinal products for human use apply to the traditional use registration.[41]

[D]   Safety and Efficacy of Herbal and Traditional Herbal Medicinal Products

In principle, every application for an MA must contain the results of tests and trials on the safety and efficacy of the product. However, for certain herbal medicinal products and for traditional herbal medicinal products, there are exceptions.

For herbal medicinal products under the bibliographic authorisation procedure, the particulars relating to the safety and efficacy do not have to be presented when it is demonstrated by detailed references to published scientific literature that the product has a well-established medicinal use as contemplated in Article 10a of Directive 2001/83/EC, and as defined in Part 2 of Annex I to that Directive (as amended by Directive 2003/63/EC).

In respect of traditional use registrations, Directive 2001/83/EC, as amended, allows the registration and marketing of traditional herbal medicinal products without requiring particulars and documents on tests and trials on safety and efficacy. The efficacy of these products is assessed on the basis of a long history of use and experience (at least thirty years, including at least fifteen years in the EU).

The preamble of Directive 2004/24/EC, amending Directive 2001/83/EC as regards traditional herbal medicinal products, determines that the long tradition of a medicinal product makes it possible to reduce the need for clinical trials, insofar as the

---

40. Article 16g(3) Directive 2001/83/EC, as amended.
41. Commission Directive 91/356/EEC laying down the principles and guidelines of Good Manufacturing Practice for medicinal products for human use, Official Journal L 193/30.

efficacy of the medicinal product is plausible on the basis of long-standing use and experience as testified by bibliographic or expert evidence. Preclinical tests do not seem necessary where the medicinal product, on the basis of the information on its traditional use, proves not to be harmful in specified conditions of use. However, even a long tradition does not exclude the possibility that there may be concerns with regard to the product's safety, and therefore the competent authorities should be entitled to ask for all data necessary for assessing the safety.

[E] Manufacturing and Quality of Herbal and Traditional Herbal Medicinal Products

The requirements regarding the manufacturing and quality of conventional medicinal products also apply to herbal medicinal products authorised under both the bibliographic authorisation procedure and the traditional use registration.

The quality aspect of a medicinal product is independent of its traditional use so that no derogation is made with regard to the necessary physicochemical, biological, and microbiological tests. Products shall comply with the quality standards in the relevant European Pharmacopoeia or those in the Pharmacopoeia of a Member State.[42]

The HMPC has published several guidance documents, which can be found on the website of the European Medicines Agency (EMA).[43]

Applications for traditional use registrations are dealt with by national competent authorities (Article 16b(2) Directive 2001/83/EC). Although the guidance documents published by the HMPC provide some guidance for the competent authorities, subtle differences in interpretation may exist between Member States.

[F] HMPC

Directive 2004/24/EC gives the responsibility of herbal medicinal products to a special HMPC.

The HMPC is part of the EMA, which is established by Article 55 of Regulation (EC) No. 726/2004 of 31 March 2004, as amended.[44] The EMA is responsible for coordinating the existing scientific resources put at its disposal by Member States for the evaluation, supervision, and pharmacovigilance of medicinal products. The HMPC was established in Directive 2004/24/EC, replacing the CHMP Working Party on Herbal Medicinal Products.

The HMPC aims to harmonise procedures and provisions concerning herbal medicinal products in EU Member States, and to further integrate herbal medicinal products in the European regulatory framework.

---

42. Consideration (5) of Directive 2004/24/EC.
43. *See* at https://www.ema.europa.eu/en/human-regulatory/herbal-medicinal-products.
44. Regulation (EC) No. 726/2004 of the European Parliament and of the Council of 31 March 2004 laying down Community procedures for the authorisation and supervision of medicinal products for human and veterinary use and establishing an EMA, L 136/1.

The HMPC is responsible for the preparation of a draft 'EU list of herbal substances, preparations and combinations thereof for use in traditional herbal medicinal products', as well as the establishment of EU herbal monographs for herbal medicinal products[45] (see §16.03[G] below). The HMPC also provides EU Member States and European institutions with its scientific opinion on questions relating to herbal medicinal products and the authorisation thereof.[46]

The HMPC is composed of scientific experts in the field of herbal medicinal products.[47] It has one member appointed by each of the EU Member States[48] for a term of three years, which may be renewed, as well as a chair. Each member has an alternate appointed by its Member State for a term of three years, which may be renewed as well. In order to complement its expertise, the HMPC may appoint up to five co-opted members chosen on the basis of their specific scientific competence. Co-opted members are also appointed for a term of three years, which may be renewed, but they do not have alternates. The HMPC currently has thirty members, one chair, and five co-opted members.[49]

[G] EU Herbal Monograph

The HMPC is responsible for establishing EU herbal monographs (previously known as Community herbal monographs).[50] These monographs have relevance for the traditional use registration as well as the general authorisation of herbal medicinal products (they are not limited to traditional herbal medicinal products).[51]

An EU herbal monograph comprises the HMPC's scientific opinion on a given herbal medicinal product, based on its evaluation of available scientific data (well-established use) and/or on the historic use of that product in the EU (traditional use).

In order to promote harmonisation, herbal medicinal products may be registered in all Member States on the basis of a monograph established by the HMPC.[52] This means that Chapter 4 of Title III regarding the mutual recognition procedure and the decentralised procedure shall apply by analogy to traditional use registrations when a EU herbal monograph has been established, and the herbal medicinal product consists

---

45. For both traditional (simplified registration procedure applies) and non-traditional (general authorisation procedure applies) herbal medicinal products, Article 16h(3) of Directive 2001/83/EC, as amended.
46. For instance, an opinion could be given on the adequacy of the evidence of the long-standing use of the (corresponding) product, as is clear from Article 16c(1)c of Directive 2001/83/EC, as amended.
47. Described in Article 16h(2) of Directive 2001/83/EC, as amended, and more detailed in the Rules of Procedure of the HMPC, to be accessed at https://www.ema.europa.eu/en/committees/committee-herbal-medicinal-products-hmpc.
48. As well as a member from each EEA-EFTA state (Iceland and Norway).
49. In addition to that, there are eight observers: one from the Council of Europe as well as observers from Albania, Bosnia, and Herzegovina, Kosovo, Macedonia, Montenegro, Serbia, and Turkey. A list of members can be found on the website of the EMA.
50. The herbal monograph list can be found on the website of the EMA. See at https://www.ema.europa.eu/en/human-regulatory/herbal-products/european-union-monographs-list-entries.
51. Article 16h(3) Directive 2001/83/EC, as amended.
52. Consideration of Directive 2004/24/EC.

of herbal substances, preparations, or combinations thereof contained in the EU List (*see* §16.03[H] hereafter). For other traditional herbal medicinal products, Member States shall, when evaluating an application, take due account of registrations granted by another Member State.[53]

EU herbal monographs are not legally binding, but instead, should be taken into account by competent authorities when examining an application for an herbal medicinal product. When new EU herbal monographs are established, the registration holder shall consider whether it is necessary to modify the registration dossier accordingly and notify the competent authority of the Member State of any such modification.[54]

However, the national competent authorities may have a different position on certain recommendations or statements set out in the monograph. They may therefore request the applicant to provide supplementary information during the national evaluation procedure, in particular, on the safety and the traditional use of the product.

[H] EU List

The EU list (previously known as Community List), which is developed by the HMPC by way of 'list entries', complements traditional-use monographs and solely has relevance for traditional use registrations.

With a view to further facilitate the registration of certain traditional herbal medicinal products in the EU, the EU List is established on the basis of the scientific opinion of the HMPC.[55] Following the provisions of Directive 2001/83/EC,[56] the EU List shall contain, for each herbal substance or preparation, the indication, the specified strength and the posology, the route of administration, and any other information necessary for the safe use of the herbal substance or preparation used as an ingredient of a traditional medicinal product.[57]

In contrast to the EU herbal monographs, the EU List is legally binding to both applicants and competent authorities in the Member States insofar as it regards traditional herbal medicinal products. If an application for a traditional use registration relates to a herbal substance, preparation, or a combination thereof contained in the EU List, an applicant will be required neither to provide information about (previous) authorisations or registrations obtained in other Member States or third countries nor to provide evidence of the safe and traditional use of a medicinal product for which the applicant seeks a traditional use registration on the condition that the applicant demonstrates that the proposed product and related claims in the application comply with the information contained in the EU List. In addition, competent authorities are not allowed to require additional data to assess the safety and the traditional use of the

---

53. Article 16d Directive 2001/83/EC, as amended.
54. Article 16h(3), paragraphs 2 and 3, Directive 2001/83/EC, as amended.
55. *Notice to Applicants, Supra* n.37.
56. Article 16f Directive 2001/83/EC, as amended.
57. The EU List can be found on the website of the EMA. *See* at https://www.ema.europa.eu/en/human-regulatory/herbal-products/european-union-monographs-list-entries.

Chapter 16: Homeopathic, Herbal and Similar Products   §16.04

product.[58] Also, a traditional use registration based on the EU List may not be refused on the ground that the product is harmful under normal conditions of use or the data on traditional use are insufficient.[59]

When a herbal substance, preparation, or a combination thereof ceases to be included in the EU List, registrations pursuant to such List containing this substance shall be revoked unless the particulars and documents referred to in this section are submitted within three months.[60]

Applicants who refer to the EU List still need to demonstrate the quality of the medicinal product they wish to register.

§16.04 CANNABIS-BASED MEDICINAL PRODUCTS

While the medical use of cannabis and cannabinoids can refer to a wide variety of preparations, one important distinction between different forms of cannabis preparations and cannabinoids for medical use is between: those that have an MA for medical use; and those that do not.[61] This text concerns itself with the former – i.e., those cannabis-based medicinal products (that are either plant-derived or synthetic) that have, or are required to have, an MA.

As a starting point, as regards the legal status of cannabis, the Single Convention on Narcotic Drugs, 1961, as amended[62] (hereinafter referred to as the '1961 Convention'),[63] at Schedule I, includes 'Cannabis and Cannabis resin: and Extracts and tinctures 'of Cannabis' as a drug subject to the measures of control provided for in terms of the 1961 Convention, where the following definitions apply:[64]

> 'Cannabis' means the flowering or fruiting tops of the cannabis plant (excluding the seeds and leaves when not accompanied by the tops) from which the resin has not been extracted, by whatever name they may be designated.
>
> 'Cannabis plant' means any plant of the genus *Cannabis*.
>
> 'Cannabis resin' means the separated resin, whether crude or purified, obtained from the cannabis plant.

---

58. Article 16f(2) in conjunction with Art. 16c(1)(b), (c), and (d) of Directive 2001/83/EC, as amended.
59. Article 16f(2) in conjunction with Art. 16e(1)(c) and (d) of Directive 2001/83/EC, as amended.
60. Article 16f(3) Directive 2001/83/EC, as amended.
61. *See Medical Use of Cannabis and Cannabinoids* (December 2018) at pages 7–8, available at http://www.emcdda.europa.eu/system/files/publications/10171/20185584_TD0618186ENN_PDF.pdf.
62. Available at https://www.unodc.org/pdf/convention_1961_en.pdf.
63. The 1961 Convention forms part of the so-called International Drug Control Conventions (United Nations Office on Drugs and Crime), which also includes the Convention on Psychotropic Substances of 1971, as amended, and the United Nations Convention against Illicit Traffic in Narcotic Drugs and Psychotropic Substances of 1988, as amended. *See* at https://www.unodc.org/documents/commissions/CND/Int_Drug_Control_Conventions/Ebook/The_International_Drug_Control_Conventions_E.pdf.
64. *See* Articles 1(b) to 1(d) of the 1961 Convention.

Broadly speaking, under the 1961 Convention, the signatory state parties[65] must, among other things, take such legislative and administrative measures as may be necessary to limit the production/cultivation, manufacture, export, import, distribution of, trade in, use and possession of drugs exclusively to scientific and medical purposes.[66] This, of course, includes cannabis (as defined above). With regard to cannabis specifically, Article 28, read with Article 23 of the 1961 Convention, provides for certain requirements that must be implemented in respect of the cultivation of cannabis; and Article 28(3) provides that the parties must adopt such measures as may be necessary to prevent the misuse of, and illicit traffic in, the leaves of the cannabis plant.[67]

For present purposes, this text is concerned only with the use of cannabis (and its derivatives) for purely medical purposes, in which case the 1961 Convention does not apply.

From an EU medicinal regulatory perspective,[68] where cannabis and/or cannabinoids are intended to constitute a 'human medicinal product', as contemplated in Directive 2001/83/EC,[69] such medicinal product must first obtain MA prior to it being legally sold, supplied, and marketed. As is the case with homeopathic, herbal, and traditional herbal medicinal products, and like all other medicinal products requiring MA, cannabis-based medicinal products may only be placed on the market in a Member State of the EU when an MA has been obtained with the competent authority of the Member State in terms of Directive 2001/83/EC. For further information regarding the various routes in terms of which cannabis-based medicinal products can be authorised, please refer to Chapter 5, which are equally applicable in this case.

To date, except for Acomplia, an inverse agonist at the CB1 receptor, which was withdrawn from the market in 2008, no EU-wide MA has been granted for cannabinoid-containing medicinal products. However, nabiximols (under the trade name Sativex) has received approval in several countries using the decentralised and mutual recognition procedures.[70] To date, a number of cannabinoid-containing medicinal products have been authorised for marketing in a number of EU Member States, including:

---

65. As of February 2018, the 1961 Convention has 186 state parties. The Holy See, the State of Palestine, and all member states of the United Nations are state parties, with the exception of Chad, East Timor, Equatorial Guinea, Kiribati, Nauru, Samoa, South Sudan, Tuvalu, and Vanuatu.
66. *See*, among others, Article 4(c) of the 1961 Convention.
67. Interestingly, Article 28(2) provides that the 1961 Convention does not apply to the cultivation of the cannabis plant exclusively for industrial purposes (fibre and seed) or horticultural purposes. Certain jurisdictions (for example, the UK) continue to prohibit the cultivation of hemp (being a strain of the Cannabis plant) for any purposes, including purely industrial purposes, without the applicable licence from the UK Home Office.
68. *See also* the EMA's *Compilation of terms and definitions for Cannabis-derived medicinal products* (EMA/HMPC/161753, dated 22 September 2021), available at https://www.ema.europa.eu/en/documents/other/compilation-terms-definitions-cannabis-derived-medicinal-products_en.pdf.
69. *See* Article 1 of Directive 2001/83/EC.
70. *See Medical Use of Cannabis and Cannabinoids* (December 2018) at page 18, available at http://www.emcdda.europa.eu/system/files/publications/10171/20185584_TD0618186ENN_PDF.pdf.

Chapter 16: Homeopathic, Herbal and Similar Products   §16.04

Marinol and Syndros;[71] Cesamet and Canemes;[72] Sativex (as mentioned above);[73] and Epidiolex.[74]

Many national pharmaceutical regulatory systems include schemes that permit patients to access unapproved medicines under medical supervision and under specific circumstances (for example, serious conditions and non-responsiveness to conventional treatments). These schemes may be known as early-access programmes, special access programmes, named-patient programmes, managed-access programmes, etc. Such schemes also often provide early access to medicines that are undergoing clinical trials or that have been approved for use in other countries.[75] Under these schemes, access to unapproved medicines (such as unapproved cannabis-based medicinal products) usually requires a prescription by a licensed medical practitioner and approval by the pharmaceutical regulator for the patient to obtain and use the medicine.[76] Many EU Member States have some form of compassionate access programme for unauthorised medicines. In the context of unauthorised cannabis-based medicinal products being accessed via these schemes, the conditions upon which such access is granted depend on the individual EU Member State in question. There is wide variation in how these schemes are implemented at national level, and each country has its own rules and procedures for allowing cannabis preparations to be provided to patients.[77]

The question may arise whether or not certain cannabis-based medicinal products may be subject to the more-simplified authorisation processes contemplated above in the context of homeopathic and herbal medicines, or whether they will be subject to the standard Article 16 authorisation route. As was mentioned above in this chapter, manufacturers of traditional herbal medicines with well-established uses are not usually required to provide evidence of efficacy and safety from clinical trials. Instead, they are required only to demonstrate evidence of product quality and consistency to ensure that consumers receive standardised doses of herbal products that are free from contaminants and adulterants. The justification for this relaxed

---

71. *Ibid.*, page 9. The active ingredient is dronabinol (i.e., synthetic delta-9-THC), indicated for anorexia associated with weight loss in patients with acquired immune deficiency syndrome (AIDS) and nausea and vomiting associated with cancer chemotherapy, usually after previous treatments have failed. *See* http://www.emcdda.europa.eu/system/files/publications/10171/20185584_TD0618186ENN_PDF.pdf.
72. *Medical Use of Cannabis and Cannabinoids, supra* n.70. The active ingredient is nabilone (i.e., a synthetic cannabinoid similar to THC), indicated for the treatment of nausea and vomiting associated with chemotherapy, usually after previous treatments have failed.
73. *Medical Use of Cannabis and Cannabinoids, supra* n.70. The active ingredient is nabiximols and containing approximately equal quantities of THC and CBD from two cannabis extracts. This product is indicated for the treatment of muscle spasticity resulting from multiple sclerosis.
74. *Medical Use of Cannabis and Cannabinoids, supra* n.70. The active ingredient is plant-derived CBD, indicated for the treatment of seizures associated with Lennox-Gastaut syndrome or Dravet syndrome in patients two years of age or older.
75. See *Medical Use of Cannabis and Cannabinoids, supra* n.70, page 18.
76. *Ibid.*
77. *Ibid.*, page 19.

regulatory approach is that herbal medicines have histories of traditional or well-established use, generally in the absence of reports of serious adverse events.[78] Certain critics of herbal medicines are of the view that there may be a lack of evidence to support many of the therapeutic claims made for these traditional herbal medicines; and many herbal medicines may be used in addition to (rather than instead of) conventional medicines and may therefore interact with pharmaceutical medicines in unknown ways, which may pose a risk to patients.[79]

In accordance with the provisions of Article 71(2) of Directive 2001/83/EC, from a general medicines classification perspective, the fact that a medicine contains a substance classified as a narcotic under the 1961 Convention, for example, would be a factor that a Member State should bear in mind if the supply of such medicine is subject to 'special medicine prescription'. The supply of herbal medicines, on the other hand, would generally not be subject to medical prescription. Therefore, in this regard, cannabis-based medicinal products would be difficult to regulate as a (traditional) herbal medicine in the EU while it remains a substance under the 1961 Convention, or while local legislation in many Member States do not permit the medicinal use of cannabis.[80]

§16.05 UK

Generally, the post-Brexit regulation of homeopathic, herbal, and traditional herbal medicines in the UK continues to be aligned with the EU regime discussed above. As of 1 January 2021, the relevant UK regulatory framework continues to be set out in The Human Medicines Regulations 2012, as amended by the Human Medicines Regulations (Amendment etc.) (EU Exit) Regulations 2019 (UK HMRs). The UK HMRs continue to be based on the provisions of Directive 2001/83/EC (as of 31 December 2020), and as at the time of updating this chapter, there do not appear to be any substantial planned changes to the UK regime relating to this subject matter. The post-Brexit MHRA guidance relating to the legal bases underpinning MAs in the UK[81] confirms, among other things, that:

(1) the *traditional herbal registrations* procedure contemplated in Article 16a of Directive 2001/83/EC is provided for in Regulation 127 of the UK HMRs;
(2) the *certificate of homeopathic medicinal products* procedure contemplated in Article 14(1) of Directive 2001/83/EC is provided for in Regulation 103 of the UK HMRs; and
(3) the *national homeopathic products* procedure (called the National Rules Scheme) contemplated in Article 16(2) of Directive 2001/83/EC is provided for in Regulation 50(6)(g) and Schedule 10 of the UK HMRs.

---

78. *Ibid.*
79. *Ibid.*
80. *Ibid.*
81. *See* at https://www.gov.uk/guidance/types-of-application-legal-basis.

With regard to traditional herbal registrations, the post-Brexit MHRA guidance[82] provides practical guidance for such applications (via the MHRA Submissions electronic portal) prior to marketing these products on the UK market, including the various supporting documents required and the affixing of the traditional herbal registration (THR) Certification Mark. Among other things, applicants must demonstrate that the herbal medicinal product has been traditionally used to treat the stated condition (which must be a permitted indication) for a minimum of thirty years. For products intended to be marketed in the whole of the UK or Northern Ireland only, at least fifteen years of the thirty years of use must relate to use in the EU/European Economic Area (EEA). For products intended to be marketed in Great Britain only, the MHRA may be able to accept the fifteen years of traditional evidence from a wider range of countries in addition to the UK and EU/EEA countries. A traditional herbal registration is only granted by the MHRA if the medicine is used for minor health conditions where medical supervision is not required.

In the context of homeopathic medicines, the post-Brexit MHRA guidance[83] sets out information on how to register homeopathic medicinal products through the Simplified Homeopathic Registration Scheme or the UK Homeopathic National Rules Scheme. In essence, under the Simplified Registration Scheme, applicants must submit data on the quality of the product and show that it is dilute enough to guarantee safety. The first dilution to be registered must be at least a 1 in 10,000 dilutions of the starting material. The scheme does not allow indications. To qualify for the Simplified Registration Scheme, the products must be for oral or external use, be sufficiently dilute to guarantee safety, and make no therapeutic claims. Under the National Rules Scheme, there is no restriction on the first dilution to be authorised or the pharmaceutical form. Applicants may claim that the product is used within the UK homeopathic tradition for the relief or treatment of minor symptoms and conditions which do not require the supervision of a doctor. Applicants must further submit data that demonstrates quality, safety, and use within the UK homeopathic tradition, and they must include details of labelling and product literature with such application.

From a UK cannabis-based medicinal products regulatory perspective, in October 2016, the MHRA issued an opinion on the regulatory status of products containing CBD,[84] in which they stated that their current view was that 'products containing cannabidiol (CBD) used for medical purposes are a medicine' and would therefore be required to obtain MA before they could be legally sold. For the classification as a human medicinal product (HMP), the definition of Article 1 of Directive 2001/83/EC (as already described in Chapter 5) is decisive, i.e.:

> Any substance or combination of substances presented as having properties for treating or preventing disease in human beings;
> OR

---

82. Available at https://www.gov.uk/guidance/apply-for-a-traditional-herbal-registration-thr.
83. Available at https://www.gov.uk/guidance/register-a-homeopathic-medicine-or-remedy.
84. MHRA Statement on products containing Cannabidiol (CBD), available at https://www.gov.uk/government/news/mhra-statement-on-products-containing-cannabidiol-cbd.

Any substance or combination of substances which may be used in or administered to human beings either with a view to restoring, correcting or modifying physiological functions by exerting a pharmacological, immunological or metabolic action, or to making a medical diagnosis.

A product is an HMP either because of its pharmacological efficacy or because of its presentation (i.e., labelling and related health claims) (the HMP Test).

In accordance with the first limb of the HMP Test, in the UK regulatory environment, a product is likely[85] to be classified by the MHRA as an HMP because of its labelling and related health claims, where the marketing includes, for example, references to medical conditions, comparison with licensed medicines, references to interference with the normal operation of a physiological function, product names which refer to adverse medical conditions, references to medical and/or clinical research and testing, etc.

A product is an HMP by function under the second limb of the HMP test if it has a pharmacological effect. In the context of HMPs containing CBD/cannabis, for example, it is understood that the pharmacological effect of CBD depends on the dose and form of application. Insofar as CBD is an active ingredient in a number of licensed HMPs (for example, Epidiolex and Arvisol), it is evident that such dosage/application of CBD has a pharmacological effect and is therapeutically effective.

Currently, the MHRA appears primarily concerned with ensuring that CBD products do not make health-related claims in respect of their labelling or other marketing and has not taken blanket action in respect of all CBD products in respect of any possible pharmacological effects. However, there remains the possibility that they may reassess this position, especially given the increasing number of licensed medicines containing CBD as an active pharmaceutical ingredient, by virtue of which it seems difficult to reconcile the position that CBD does not have a general pharmacological effect, and it should, therefore, only be considered a human medicinal product where health-related claims are made for CBD products. Indeed, this is the position that the UK Veterinary Medicines Directorate has taken in respect of CBD products for animals, requiring that all such products obtain animal medicine MAs. The regulatory regime in the UK is therefore in flux and should be followed closely.

---

85. *See* MHRA's *'A Guide to What Is a Medicinal Product'* (March 2020), available at https://assets.publishing.service.gov.uk/government/uploads/system/uploads/attachment_data/file/872742/GN8_FINAL_10_03_2020__combined_.pdf.

CHAPTER 17
Advanced Therapy Medicinal Products

Marc Martens, Benedicte Mourisse & Sophie Vo[*]

§17.01 INTRODUCTION

[A] History

Advanced Therapy Medicinal Products (ATMPs) form a relatively new category of biological medicinal products in the legal landscape. The first reference to ATMPs in the pharmaceutical legislation dates back to 2009, when European Commission Directive 2009/120/EC, amending Directive 2001/83/EC of the European Parliament and of the Council on the Community code relating to medicinal products for human use as regards ATMPs, was adopted. Directive 2009/120/EC modified Part IV of Annex I to Directive 2001/83/EC (hereafter referred to as Part IV) by defining the specific requirements applicable to gene therapy medicinal products and somatic cell therapy medicinal products.

In addition to gene therapies and somatic cell therapies, scientific progress made it necessary to create a third category of ATMP, that is, the tissue-engineered products. In order to regulate this new category of products, a whole new set of rules was adopted in the form of a regulation. Hence, Regulation (EC) No. 1394/2007 of the European Parliament and of the Council of 13 November 2007 on ATMPs and amending Directive 2001/83/EC and Regulation (EC) No. 726/2004 (hereinafter, the ATMP Regulation) is a *lex specialis*, which introduces additional provisions to those laid down in Directive 2001/83/EC.

The scope of the ATMP Regulation is limited to the fundamental regulatory issues, notably the marketing authorisation (MA) procedure for ATMPs and the introduction of incentives for small- and medium-sized enterprises (SMEs). The related

---

[*] The authors wish to acknowledge *Nicolas Carbonnelle*, an author of the earlier edition of this chapter.

guidelines and technical requirements (such as good manufacturing practice (GMP) or good clinical practice (GCP)) are not set out in detail in the ATMP Regulation. These are drafted by the Commission on a progressive basis, following consultation with the European Medicines Agency (EMA), which means that although the ATMP Regulation cannot be described as an 'empty shell', numerous of its requirements are to be found in other legal instruments.

The rules applicable to ATMPs can be analysed in a two-level framework, the first level being from a regulatory level and the second being from a technical level. This first level includes the existing Directives on which the ATMP Regulation is built (see §17.02 hereafter) and includes the ATMP Regulation itself, which describes the specific rules that apply to ATMPs. The technical level contains the technical requirements (such as the type of pre-clinical and clinical data required) and any further technical requirements (e.g., GMP, GCP). The constitutive elements of the technical level are not defined in the ATMP Regulation itself, which gives more flexibility to the ATMP regulatory framework. Such flexibility was required in order to keep pace with the fast-moving evolution of ATMP-related technologies; therefore, the authors of the ATMP Regulation had to find a balance between the possibility for patients to gain rapid access to promising therapies with the appropriate guarantees of safety and quality.[1]

Among the amendments to Directive 2001/83/EC provided for by Article 28 of the ATMP Regulation, a fifth paragraph is added to Article 4 of the Directive which states the following:

> This Directive and all Regulations referred to therein shall not affect the application of national legislation prohibiting or restricting the use of any specific type of human or animal cells, or the sale, supply or use of medicinal products containing, consisting of or derived from these cells, on grounds not dealt with in the aforementioned Community legislation. The Member States shall communicate the national legislation concerned to the Commission.

The preparatory documents of the ATMP Regulation indicate that the aim of this article was to leave the ethical debates surrounding the use of embryonic and umbilical cord blood tissues and cells to the Member States. The final text is indeed ethically neutral on this point.

However, unlike a Directive which requires national implementation, the ATMP Regulation is directly applicable in all Member States. The fact that the European authorities chose to create an 'ethically neutral' framework with the ATMP Regulation thus leaves certain flexibility to each Member State to put restrictions, or merely forbid, the use of certain types of cells or tissues on its territory for ethical reasons.

As a peculiar consequence of this, a Member State may make it impossible for an ATMP to be commercialised on its territory, even though the product has been granted an MA through the centralised procedure (which is, in principle, mandatory for such products, see §17.03[A] hereafter).

---

1. Brévignon-Dodin, Laure & Singh, Pawanbir, 'ATMP in Practice: Towards a New Industry Landscape in Tissue Engineering', *Journal of Commercial Biotechnology* 15, no. I (2009): 60.

Chapter 17: Advanced Therapy Medicinal Products §17.01[B]

[B] Definitions

[1] Gene Therapy Medicinal Products (Section 2.1, Part IV, Annex I to Directive 2001/83/EC)

A 'gene therapy medicinal product' is a biological medicinal product which has the following characteristics:

(a) it is composed of an active substance which contains, or consists of, a recombinant nucleic acid used in, or administered to, human beings with a view to regulating, repairing, replacing, adding, or deleting a genetic sequence;
(b) its therapeutic, prophylactic, or diagnostic effect relates directly to the recombinant nucleic acid sequence it contains, or to the product of genetic expression of this sequence.

The definition of 'gene therapy medicinal products' shall not include vaccines against infectious diseases.

Directive 2001/83/EC indicates that a great diversity of products exist which fall into the definition of 'gene therapy medicinal products', for example: (i) gene therapy medicinal products based on allogeneic (coming from another human being) or xenogeneic cells, (ii) gene therapy medicinal products using autologous human cells (emanating from the patient himself), and (iii) administration of ready-prepared vectors with inserted (prophylactic, diagnostic, or therapeutic) genetic material.

[2] Somatic Cell Therapy Medicinal Products (Section 2.2, Part IV, Annex I to Directive 2001/83/EC)

A 'somatic cell therapy medicinal product' is a biological medicinal product which has the following characteristics:

(a) it contains or consists of cells or tissues that have been subject to substantial manipulation so that the biological characteristics, physiological functions, or structural properties relevant for the intended clinical use have been altered, or of cells or tissues that are not intended to be used for the same essential function(s) in the recipient and the donor;
(b) it is presented as having properties for, or is used in or administered to human beings with a view to treating, preventing, or diagnosing a disease through the pharmacological, immunological, or metabolic action of its cells or tissues.

Annex I of the ATMP Regulation contains a list of manipulations which are not considered substantial manipulations for the purpose of the aforementioned definition.

Those manipulations are cutting, grinding, shaping, centrifugation, soaking in antibiotic or antimicrobial solutions, sterilisation, irradiation, cell separation, concentration or purification, filtering, lyophilisation, freezing, cryopreservation, and vitrification.

Part IV states that somatic cell therapy medicinal products include the following: cells manipulated to modify their immunological, metabolic, or other functional properties in qualitative or quantitative aspects; cells sorted, selected, and manipulated and subsequently undergoing a manufacturing process in order to obtain the finished medicinal product; cells manipulated and combined with non-cellular components (e.g., biological or inert matrixes or medical devices) and exerting the principle intended action in the finished product; autologous cell derivatives expressed in vitro under specific culture conditions, and cells genetically modified or otherwise manipulated to express previously unexpressed homologous or non-homologous functional properties.

The Annex also indicates that the entire manufacturing process, from the collection of the cells from the patient (autologous situation) until the re-injection into the patient, shall be considered one single intervention.

As for the other medicinal products, the following three results of the manufacturing process are identified:

- starting materials: materials from which the active substance is manufactured, that is, organs, tissues, bodily fluids, or cells;
- active substances: manipulated cells, cell lysates, proliferating cells, and cells used in conjunction with inert matrixes and medical devices;
- finished medicinal products: the active substance in the form of its final container for the intended medical use.

[3]   Tissue-Engineered Products (Article 2(b) of the ATMP Regulation)

A 'tissue-engineered product' is a product that:

- contains or consists of engineered cells or tissues; and
- is presented as having properties for, or is used in or administered to human beings with a view to regenerating, repairing, or replacing a human tissue.

A tissue-engineered product may contain cells or tissues of human or animal origin, or both. The cells or tissues may be viable or non-viable. It may also contain additional substances, such as cellular products, bio-molecules, bio-materials, chemical substances, scaffolds, or matrices.

Products which contain or consist exclusively of non-viable human or animal cells and/or tissues, which do not contain any viable cells or tissues and which do not act principally by pharmacological, immunological, or metabolic action, are excluded from this definition.

The ATMP Regulation specifies that cells or tissues shall be considered engineered if they fulfil at least one of the following conditions:

- the cells or tissues have been subject to substantial manipulation, so that the biological characteristics, physiological functions, or structural properties relevant for the intended regeneration, repair, or replacement are achieved. The list of manipulations which are not considered substantial manipulations, annexed to the ATMP Regulation, is also relevant for the purpose of this definition;
- the cells or tissues are not intended to be used for the same essential function or functions in the recipient as in the donor.

[C] Combined ATMPs and the Classification Rules

[1] Combined ATMPs

Article 2(1)(d) of the ATMP Regulation states that a 'combined advanced therapy medicinal product' is an ATMP, providing that it fulfils two conditions:

  (i) it incorporates, as an integral part of the product, one or more medical devices within the meaning of Article 1(2)(a) of Directive 93/42/EEC or, one or more active implantable medical devices within the meaning of Article 1(2)(c) of Directive 90/385/EEC;[2] and
  (ii) its cellular or tissue part must contain viable cells or tissues, or its cellular or tissue part containing non-viable cells or tissues must be liable to act upon the human body with action that can be considered primary to that of the devices referred to.

In the event that the two conditions are fulfilled, a combined ATMP is subject to the same rules as an ATMP. As a consequence, their MA is subject to the centralised procedure.

Moreover, Article 6 of the ATMP Regulation provides that medical devices and active implantable medical devices, which form part of a combined ATMP, have to comply with the essential requirements of Directive 93/42/EEC and Directive 90/385/EEC, respectively. Currently, these provisions concerning medical devices are now included in Regulation (EU) 2017/745. Specific guidelines have been drafted with respect to the evaluation of combined ATMPs.[3]

A public consultation conducted by the Commission has shown[4] that the separate assessment of the medical device and the medicinal product is regarded as an excessive

---

2. The relevant provisions concerning medical devices are now included in the Regulation (EU) 2017/745 of the European Parliament and of the Council of 5 April 2017 on medical devices, amending Directive 2001/83/EC, Regulation (EC) No. 178/2002 and Regulation (EC) No. 1223/2009 and repealing Council Directives 90/385/EEC and 93/42/EEC (OJ L 117 5.5.2017, p. 1.).
3. *See* www.ema.europa.eu/docs/en_GB/document_library/Regulatory_and_procedural_guideline/ 2011/03/WC500102598.pdf.
4. *See Report from the Commission to the European Parliament and the Council in accordance with Article 25 of Regulation (EC) No 1394/2007 of the European Parliament and of the Council on*

burden in the cases where the device is not marketed separately. Stakeholders claim for a single assessment in such cases, where the Committee for Advanced Therapies (CAT) performs the whole evaluation. The consultation also showed that the separate assessment requirement tends to incentivise the use of already approved devices rather than developing new, better-targeted devices because the recourse to an already CE-marked device is perceived by developers as a facilitating factor in the regulatory procedure leading to the market. The issue might thus have an impact on the overall quality and innovative character of the products proposed to the market.

[2] Classification Rules

Additional classification rules creating a hierarchy between the different categories of ATMPs, based on technical aspects of the products, can be found from Article 2(3) until Article 5 of the ATMP Regulation. According to those provisions:

- an ATMP containing both autologous (emanating from the patient himself) and allogeneic (coming from another human being) cells or tissues shall be considered to be for allogeneic use;
- a product which may fall within the definition of a 'tissue-engineered product' and within the definition of a 'somatic cell therapy medicinal product' shall be considered to be a 'tissue-engineered product';
- a product which may fall within the definition of a 'somatic cell therapy medicinal product', a 'tissue-engineered product', and a 'gene therapy medicinal product' shall be considered to be a 'gene therapy medicinal product'.

An optional procedure, laid down in Article 17 of the ATMP Regulation, assists applicants in determining whether a given product based on genes, cells, or tissues meets the scientific criteria which define ATMPs. This procedure has been established by the legislator with a view to addressing any questions which may arise concerning the border with other areas, for example, that of medical devices, and to do so as early as possible. The CAT (*see* below, §17.03[A][2]) delivers scientific recommendations on ATMP classification, following consultation with the Commission, within sixty days after receipt of a request.

Summary reports of the outcomes of the ATMP assessment by the CAT are available on the website of the EMA.[5]

The Commission's report on the application of the ATMP Regulation[6] points out that the classification of products is one of the practical difficulties in the application of the regulation. Among others, the question of whether a manipulation of a living material is to be considered substantial is assessed on a case-by-case basis, and it may

---

advanced therapy medicinal products and amending Directive 2001/83/EC and Regulation (EC) No 726/2004, COM(2014) 188 final, p. 11.
5. *See* https://www.ema.europa.eu/en/human-regulatory/marketing-authorisation/advanced-therapies/advanced-therapy-classification/scientific-recommendations-classification-advanced-therapy-medicinal-products.
6. COM(2014) 188 final, *o.c.*

be difficult to answer. Also, given their characteristics, an increasing number of innovative products are difficult to categorise, as their characteristics allow to potentially classify them as medicines, medical devices, cosmetics, or tissues and cells. More clarity is deemed necessary in that field, not only in order to achieve a level of public health protection as high as possible but also to secure the developers and investors position in that they can anticipate the regulatory framework that will apply to their products at the earliest stage of development. The uncertainties in that respect are reinforced by the diverging approaches of Member States' competent authorities. The role of the CAT, and notably its provision of scientific recommendations (which are free of charge), can help developers and investors find their way in the regulatory landscape. However, the recommendations of the CAT are non-binding and can thus be disregarded and, in addition, the Member States' authorities are, until now, not entitled to seek recommendations from the CAT.

§17.02 RELATIONSHIP BETWEEN THE ATMP REGULATION AND OTHER EUROPEAN LEGISLATION

The ATMP Regulation is built on various Directives or Regulations, those concerning medicinal products for human use,[7] quality and safety standards for human tissues and cells,[8] medical devices[9] and active implantable medical devices,[10] and on the Regulation concerning centralised MA procedures.[11] Reference is made in the ATMP Regulation to all of the aforementioned instruments.

An important interaction exists between the ATMP Regulation and Directive 2004/23/EC, which sets standards of quality and safety for human tissues and cells intended for human applications. ATMPs may be derived and/or produced from such human tissues and cells. A specific set of rules apply to those products, whereby not all phases of the manufacturing process of an ATMP fall within the scope of the ATMP Regulation. This is provided for not only by the Directive itself (Article 2(1)) but also by the ATMP Regulation (Article 3). Pursuant to these provisions, the donation, procurement, and testing of human tissue and cells involved in the manufacture of ATMPs

---

7. Directive 2001/83/EC of the European Parliament and of the Council of 6 November 2001 on the Community code relating to medicinal products for human use, Official Journal L 311, 28 November 2001, 67.
8. Directive 2004/23/EC of the European Parliament and of the Council of 31 March 2004 on setting standards of quality and safety for the donation, procurement, testing, processing, preservation, storage, and distribution of human tissues and cells, Official Journal L 102, 7 Apr. 2004, 48.
9. Regulation (EU) 2017/745 of the European Parliament and of the Council of 5 April 2017 on medical devices, amending Directive 2001/83/EC, Regulation (EC) No. 178/2002 and Regulation (EC) No. 1223/2009 and repealing Council Directives 90/385/EEC and 93/42/EEC, OJ L 117 5.5.2017, p. 1.
10. *Ibid.*
11. Regulation (EC) No. 726/2004 of the European Parliament and of the Council of 31 March 2004 laying down Community procedures for the authorisation and supervision of medicinal products for human and veterinary use and establishing an EMA, Official Journal L 136, 30 April 2004, p. 1.

remain governed by the provisions of Directive 2004/23/EC and its national implementing instruments.

Directive 2004/23 states that Member States are responsible for the designation of a competent authority or authorities responsible for implementing the requirements of the Directive and for accrediting, designating, authorising, or licensing the conditions in which the procurement and testing are carried out. Moreover, Article 6(1) of the Directive adds that 'Member States shall ensure that all tissue establishments where activities of testing, processing, preservation, storage or distribution of human tissues and cells intended for human applications are undertaken have been accredited, designated, authorised or licensed by a competent authority for the purpose of those activities.'

These provisions leave room for manoeuvre for the Member States concerning the regulation of tissue establishments, which results in different approaches being used among the Member States.

In this respect, the harmonisation is growing over time. In particular, Directives 2015/565[12] and 2015/566[13] respectively provide detailed rules on the coding of the human cells and tissues intended for human application and lay down procedures for verifying the equivalent standards of quality and safety of tissues and cells imported from non-European Economic Area (EEA) countries.

One of the important features of Directive 2015/566 is that it strives to the adherence to the principle of voluntary and unpaid donation. To that end, it requires the importing tissue establishments to have in place written agreements with third-country suppliers where activities with the tissues and cells to be imported into the EU are carried out outside of the EU. Where the human tissues and cells to be imported are intended to be used exclusively in manufactured products such as ATMPs, the Directive only applies to the donation, procurement, and testing which takes place outside of the EU as well as to contributing to ensuring traceability from donor to recipient and vice versa.

Exemptions may be put in place by Member States for one-off imports, insofar their national legislation ensures at least that traceability is ensured from donor to recipient and vice versa, and that the imported tissues and cells are not applied to anyone other than their intended recipients. Tissues and cells intended for the industrial manufacturing of medicinal products will most likely not benefit from such exemptions, although the definition of 'one-off import' leaves room for interpretation and tailored regulatory frameworks could be put in place. As a matter of fact, a 'one-off import' is defined as 'the import of any specific type of tissue or cell which is for the personal use of an intended recipient or recipients known to the importing tissue establishment and the third country supplier before the importation occurs. Such an

---

12. Commission Directive (EU) 2015/565 of 8 April 2015 amending Directive 2006/86/EC as regards certain technical requirements for the coding of human tissues and cells, Official Journal, L 93/43, 9 April 2015
13. Commission (EU) 2015/566 of 8 April 2015 implementing Directive 2004/23/EC as regards the procedures for verifying the equivalent standards of quality and safety of imported tissues and cells, Official Journal, L 93/46, 9 April 2015 – hereafter, Directive 2015/566.

import of any specific type of tissue or cell shall normally not occur more than once for any given recipient. Imports from the same third country supplier taking place on a regular or repeated basis shall not be considered to be 'one-off imports'.[14]

The Directive also reinforces the control measures on the importing establishments' suppliers, as the written agreements will have to establish the right of the competent authorities to inspect the activities, including the facilities, of any third-country suppliers during the duration of the written agreement and for a period of two years following its termination.[15]

§17.03 THE MARKET ACCESS FOR ATMPS

The ATMP Regulation makes a distinction between two regimes with respect to market access. The normal route to the market for ATMPs is the centralised procedure (*see* §17.03[A][1]). However, a specific regime, called the 'hospital exemption', has been put in place under specific circumstances (*see* §17.03[B]).

[A] Ordinary Regime

[1] The Procedure

Article 27 of the ATMP Regulation amends the Annex to Regulation 726/2004. It also provides a list of products for which the MA may only be granted through the centralised procedure, and ATMPs are included in that list. As a consequence, the MA for ATMPs must, in principle, follow the centralised procedure.

The MA procedure here is similar to the regular centralised MA procedure as provided for by Regulation 726/2004, with the exception of the intervention of the CAT. Article 8 of the ATMP Regulation provides that the Committee for Medicinal Products for Human Use (hereafter, CHMP) is obliged to consult the CAT on any scientific assessment of ATMPs necessary to draw up the required scientific opinions. The CAT is also consulted in the event that an applicant requests a re-examination of the opinion (*see* details below).

The same principles apply to Combined ATMPs.

[2] The CAT

Articles 20 to 23 of the ATMP Regulation establish a sixth scientific committee within the EMA: the CAT. It met for the first time on 15 January 2009. The key role of the scientific committee is the preparation of a draft opinion on each advanced therapy

---

14. Article 2, c) of Directive 2015/566.
15. Article 7(3) of Directive 2015/566.

medicinal product submitted to the EMA for evaluation as part of a marketing authorisation application (MAA), prior to the adoption of a final opinion by the CHMP. The CHMP retains overall responsibility for scientific evaluation of human medicines at the EMA.

[a] Role and Responsibilities

The CAT is a multidisciplinary committee, gathering experts to assess the quality, safety, and efficacy of ATMPs, and to follow scientific developments in the field. The intervention of this special committee echoes the complex nature of ATMPs.

The main responsibility of the CAT is to prepare a draft opinion on each ATMP application submitted to the EMA,[16] before the CHMP adopts a final opinion on the granting, variation, suspension, or revocation of an MA for the medicine concerned. At the request of the EMA Executive Director or of the European Commission, an opinion is also drawn up on any scientific matter relating to ATMPs.

Other responsibilities of the CAT include the certification of quality and non-clinical data for SMEs developing ATMPs. Certification was designed to help SMEs attract investments and/or obtain revenue for the development of ATMPs.

The CAT also provides (free of charge) scientific recommendations on the classification of ATMPs, as well as scientific advice. The CAT can be involved in any procedure regarding the provision of advice for undertakings on the conduct of efficacy follow-up, pharmacovigilance, and risk management systems of ATMPs. At the request of the CHMP, the CAT also advises on any medicinal product which may require, for the evaluation of its quality, safety, or efficacy, expertise in ATMPs, and provides assistance in the tasks identified in the work programmes of the CHMP working parties.

Finally, the CAT provides scientific assistance in the elaboration of any documents related to the fulfilment of the objectives of the ATMP Regulation and provides, at the request of the Commission, scientific expertise and advice for any Community initiative related to the development of innovative medicines and therapies that requires expertise on ATMPs.

[b] Composition

Article 21 of the ATMP Regulation prescribes the composition of the CAT, which should include: (i) five members of the CHMP, with their alternates, appointed by the CHMP itself; (ii) one member and one alternate appointed by each EU Member State whose national competent authority is not represented among the members and alternates appointed by the CHMP; (iii) two members and two alternates appointed by

---

16. Scientific recommendations are published by CAT on the EMA website. *See* https://www.ema.europa.eu/en/human-regulatory/marketing-authorisation/advanced-therapies/advanced-therapy-classification/scientific-recommendations-classification-advanced-therapy-medicinal-products.

the European Commission to represent clinicians; and (iv) two members and two alternates appointed by the European Commission to represent patients associations.

Members of the CAT are appointed for a renewable term of three years. The Chair and Vice-Chair of the CAT are elected from its members for a term of three years, which may be renewed once. The last election of the Chair and Vice-Chair took place in February 2009.

[B]   Exemptions

Article 28(2) of Regulation 1394/2007 inserted a paragraph 7 into Article 3 of Directive 2001/83/EC. That provision provides an exemption (the so-called hospital exemption) from the scope of the harmonised pharmaceutical legislation where certain very specific, cumulative conditions are met. The hospital exemption is a specific, additional form of exemption from the scope of application of Directive 2001/83/EC. Another example of exemption from the scope of application of such Directive that is also relevant for ATMPs, is the 'specials' exemption, which is applicable to all types of medicinal products that are 'supplied in response to a bona fide unsolicited order, formulated in accordance with the specifications of an authorised health-care professional and for use by an individual patient under his direct personal responsibility'. This is applied on a national competent authority basis.

According to the hospital exemption, ATMPs that are prepared on a non-routine basis according to specific quality standards and used within the same Member State in a hospital under the exclusive professional responsibility of a medical practitioner in order to comply with an individual medical prescription for a custom-made product for an individual patient, do not fall within the scope of European pharmaceutical legislation. Such products are instead subject to national legislation, notably with respect to their manufacture.

The Regulation thus empowers Member States to authorise the use of ATMPs in hospitals for individual patients in the absence of an MA, providing flexibility to address the situation of individual patients. However, a too-large application of this exemption may discourage the application for MAs. This topic has been widely discussed for a while now. On 28 March 2014, the Commission produced a report on the application of this Regulation.[17]

As the report points out, many ATMPs currently fall under the scope of the hospital exemption, and some stakeholders reported their concern that a 'too broad use of the hospital exemption may deter the submission of marketing authorisation applications'. The Commission acknowledges moreover that 'if the hospital exemption became the normal route to market advanced therapies, there would be detrimental consequences for public health', pointing out the fact that products covered by a

---

17. COM(2014) 188 final, *o.c.*

hospital exemption are not covered by the legislation on clinical trials, which ensures the obtention of reliable information about the efficacy and safety profile of a medicinal product, and also the fact that the hospital exemption entails the use of a treatment on a small number of patients, which in its turn undermines the collection of data on efficacy and safety of the treatment. The use of the data generated under a hospital exemption in MAA dossiers constitutes an issue that is currently regulated at Member State level, which creates potentially diverging approaches: Member States may decide to principally accept or refuse the use of such data in MAAs.

Moreover, the hospital exemption regime does not provide for transmission of information between Member States, and this creates a risk that patients are exposed to unsafe or ineffective treatments while appropriate reporting of results would limit such risk.

As at 20 October 2022, approximately sixteen ATMPs are covered by an MA (in addition to seven previous ATMP MAs having been withdrawn or not renewed).[18] It is worth noting that a significant number of developers of ATMPs that were on the market prior to the entry into force of the ATMP Regulation did not apply for an MA. Indeed, a large proportion of those developers applied for a hospital exemption, or for a 'specials' exemption. As a consequence, the number of MAs granted since the entry into force of the ATMP Regulation does not reflect the ATMP market accurately: a number of ATMPs are on the market, but the vast majority of these products is not covered by an MA. The actual number of products present on the EU market is difficult to assess.

From the Commission's report of March 2014, it was anticipated that proposals will be made in order to clarify the conditions under which the hospital exemption is possible and the requirements attached to that exemption, with the objective to better strike a balance between the need to ensure that ATMPs are made available to patients only after their quality, safety, and efficacy have been demonstrated, and the need to facilitate early access for new treatments in case of unmet medical needs. The report also calls, notably, for a clarification of the conditions under which the 'specials' exemption should apply to ATMPs. Following some shortcomings identified in the Commission's report of March 2014, the Commission and EMA published a joint action plan on ATMPs in October 2017, which aims to streamline procedures and better address the specific requirements of ATMP developers.[19] One of the action points is for the Commission to initiate a reflection process with the Member States on the hospital exemption. At the time of updating this Chapter (July 2022), this is still an ongoing action point.

---

18. *See* https://www.ema.europa.eu/en/documents/report/cat-quarterly-highlights-approved-atmps-october-2022_en.pdf.
19. European Commission DG Health and Food Safety and European Medicines Agency Action Plan on ATMPs: https://www.ema.europa.eu/en/documents/other/european-commission-dg-health-food-safety-european-medicines-agency-action-plan-advanced-therapy_en-0.pdf.

§17.04 MAA DOSSIER

[A] Specific Requirements Set Out in Part IV of Annex I to Directive 2001/83/EC

Part IV of Annex I to Directive 2001/83/EC (hereafter referred to as Part IV) stipulates that MAAs for ATMPs must follow the ordinary common technical document (CTD) format requirements (Modules 1, 2, 3, 4, and 5). In addition to the technical requirements for Modules 3, 4, and 5 for all biological medicinal products, sections 3, 4, and 5 of Part IV also describe certain specific requirements for ATMPs. For the main part, these sections explain how the general requirements in Part I of Annex I apply to ATMPs. In addition, where appropriate and taking into account the specificities of ATMPs, they explain the additional requirements specific to ATMPs.

Given the specific nature of ATMPs, Annex I prescribes a risk-based approach for determining the extent of quality, non-clinical, and clinical data to be included in the MAA. The risk-based analysis must comply with the scientific guidelines relating to the quality, safety, and efficacy of medicinal products, as published on the website of the EMA.

Where a risk analysis is performed, it may cover the entire development of the product. The Annex lists a number of risk factors that may be considered, including: the origin of the cells (autologous, allogeneic, xenogeneic); the ability to proliferate and/or differentiate and to initiate an immune response; the level of cell manipulation; the combination of cells with bioactive molecules or structural materials; the nature of the gene therapy medicinal products; the extent of replication competence of viruses or micro-organisms used in vivo; the level of integration of nucleic acids sequences or genes into the genome; the long-term functionality; and the risk of oncogenicity and the mode of administration or use. It further provides that relevant available non-clinical and clinical data, or experience with other related ATMPs, may also be considered in the risk analysis.

Any deviation from the requirements of the Annex must be scientifically justified in Module 2 of the MAA dossier. In this case, the Annex requires that Module 2 should also include a detailed description of the risk analysis, including the methodology followed, any risks identified, and their implications for the development and evaluation programme, and any deviations from the requirements of the Annex resulting from the risk analysis.

Part IV also sets out specific requirements concerning Module 3 (Quality), Module 4 (Non-clinical study reports), and Module 5 (clinical study reports).

While some of the requirements of Part IV are common to all types of ATMPs, others are only relevant to gene therapy medicinal products, somatic cell therapy medicinal products, and tissue-engineered products, the latter two being subject to the same requirements.

Finally, section 3.4 of Part IV sets out specific requirements concerning Module 3 for ATMPs containing devices.

In the Commission's report dated 28 March 2014, it was identified that stakeholders feel that additional flexibility should be applied, as the specific requirements currently laid down to ATMPs do still not take sufficiently into consideration the fact that ATMPs present very different characteristics than those of chemical-based medicinal products. Following this outcome, the EMA issued additional guidance on the application of the risk-based approach for ATMPs that have not been subject to substantial manipulation to explain to developers the possibilities afforded by the risk-based approach (flexibility, reduction of certain requirements for the submission of an MAA depending on specific risks).[20]

[B] Other Requirements Applicable to ATMPs

[1] Summary of Product Characteristics, Labelling, and Package Leaflet

The ATMP Regulation provides derogations to Directive 2001/83 in terms of Summary of Product Characteristics (SmPC), labelling, and package leaflet. These derogations reflect the specific nature of ATMPs. These include the following:

- Annex II of the ATMP Regulation defines the contents of the SmPC for ATMPs;
- Annex III defines the labelling requirements; for example, packaging must bear the unique donation and product code in accordance with Directive 2004/23, and, where the product is intended for autologous use, the statement 'for autologous use only'; and
- Annex IV sets out the information that must be included in the package leaflet, which must be consistent with the SmPC.

[2] GMPs

The ATMP Regulation requires the Commission to draw up guidelines on GMPs specific to ATMPs.[21] In November 2017, the Commission adopted Guidelines on Good Manufacturing Practice (GMP) specific to ATMPs. The guidelines provide a specific GMP framework that is adapted to the specific characteristics of ATMP.[22] These guidelines take into account the input received from the external stakeholders, the CAT, the GMP working group, and the competent national authorities. The guidelines adopt the EU GMP requirements to the specific characteristics of ATMPs and address the novel and complex manufacturing scenarios utilised for these products.

---

20. EMA/CAT/216556/2017; also identified as an action point in the joint action plan on ATMPs in October 2017.
21. Article 5 of the ATMP Regulation.
22. EC, C(2017) 7694 final, EudraLex The Rules Governing Medicinal Products in the European Union (Volume 4) Good Manufacturing Practice Guidelines on Good Manufacturing Practice specific to Advanced Therapy Medicinal Products, 22 November 2017: https://health.ec.europa.eu/system/files/2017-11/2017_11_22_guidelines_gmp_for_atmps_0.pdf.

[3] Post-Authorisation Requirements

The ATMP Regulation lays down requirements regarding the post-authorisation phase, including: follow-up of efficacy and adverse reactions, risk management, and traceability.

[a] Follow-Up of Efficacy and Risk Management

In this respect, Article 14 of the ATMP Regulation provides that, in addition to the requirements for pharmacovigilance laid down in Articles 21 to 29 of Regulation 726/2004, the applicant's MAAs must also set out the measures envisaged to follow-up on the efficacy of, and adverse reactions to, ATMPs. Moreover, where there is a particular cause for concern, the Commission may, on the advice of the EMA, include in the MA a requirement that the MA holder either:

- put in place a risk management system to identify, characterise, prevent, or minimise risks related to ATMPs, including to evaluate the effectiveness of that system; and/or
- carry out, and submit to the EMA, specific post-marketing studies.

In addition, the EMA may also request the MA holder to submit additional reports evaluating the effectiveness of any risk management system and the results of any such studies performed. Any evaluations or studies carried out by the MA holder shall be included in the periodic safety update reports (PSURs) provided for by Regulation 726/2004.

The EMA will supervise the MA holder's compliance with the above requirements and inform the Commission in the event of any breach.

If serious adverse events or reactions occur in relation to a combined ATMP, the EMA will inform the relevant national competent authorities responsible for the implementation of Regulation (EU) 2017/745 of the European Parliament and of the Council of 5 April 2017 on medical devices, amending Directive 2001/83/EC, Regulation (EC) No. 178/2002 and Regulation (EC) No. 1223/2009 and repealing Council Directives 90/385/EEC and 93/42/EEC.

Further guidance on safety and efficacy follow-up and risk management are provided in the guidelines published by the CHMP.[23]

[b] Traceability

Recital 22 of the ATMP Regulation states that it is essential to be able to monitor the safety of ATMPs that a system be put in place that allows complete traceability of both the patient and the product, including its starting materials. Such a system should be

---

23. *See* https://www.ema.europa.eu/en/human-regulatory/overview/advanced-therapy-medicinal-products-overview.

compatible with the traceability requirements laid down in Directive 2004/23 and in Directive 2002/98. It must also respect the provisions laid down in Regulation (EU) 2016/679 of the European Parliament and of the Council of 27 April 2016 on the protection of natural persons with regard to the processing of personal data and on the free movement of such data, and repealing Directive 95/46/EC (General Data Protection Regulation).[24]

In order to meet those objectives, Article 15 of the ATMP Regulation provides that the MA holder for an ATMP must establish and maintain a system to ensure that the individual product and its starting and raw materials, including all substances coming into contact with its constituent cells or tissues, can be traced through the sourcing, manufacturing, packaging, storage, transport, and delivery to the hospital, institution, or private practice where the product is used. Those institutions must also establish and maintain such a traceability system, which must contain sufficient detail to allow linking of each product to the patient who received it, and vice versa.

The traceability system must be complementary to, and compatible with, the requirements established in Directive 2004/23/EC, as regards human cells and tissues other than blood cells, and Directive 2002/98/EC, as regards human blood cells.[25]

The MA holder must keep data for a minimum of thirty years after the expiry date of the product, or longer if required by the Commission as a term of its MA.

The ATMP Regulation also provides that, in case of bankruptcy or liquidation of the MA holder, and in the event that the MA is not transferred to another legal entity, the data must be transferred to the EMA.

However, in the event that the MA is suspended, revoked, or withdrawn, the MA holder still remains subject to the traceability obligations.

§17.05 INCENTIVES FOR SMEs

Recital 23 of the ATMP Regulation provides that as:

> science evolves very rapidly in this field, undertakings developing advanced therapy medicinal products should be enabled to request scientific advice from the Agency, including advice on post-authorisation activities. As an incentive, the fee for that scientific advice should be kept at a minimal level for small and medium-sized enterprises, and should also be reduced for other applicants.

The ATMP Regulation therefore provides for a 90% reduction of fees for scientific advice and the possibility to defer the payment of fees until the MA is granted. Moreover, in the event that the product presents a particular public health interest to the EU, the fee payable by an SME for a MA can be reduced by 50%, and the applicant will not have to pay any fees in the event that the MA is not granted.

Incentives are also provided for non-SMEs. For example, these applicants may be entitled to a 65% reduction of the EMA's fees for scientific advice regarding ATMPs.

---

24. OJ L 119, 4.5.2016, pp. 1–88.
25. Part IV of Annex I to Directive 2001/83/EC, s. 3.1.

As the Commission's report on the application of the ATMP Regulation points out, no incentive exists for post-marketing obligations. While a 50% fee reduction for MA and post-marketing activities had been offered to SMEs and hospitals for a time in cases where there was a public health interest in the concerned ATMP, this fee incentive does not apply anymore. The report suggests that reintroducing such incentives might favourably influence the number of products reaching the market, as the costs incurred for post-marketing obligations can be very significant and even unaffordable for smaller companies in the period preceding profitability of the ATMP.

§17.06　TRANSITIONAL PERIOD

As mentioned above, the ATMP Regulation entered into force on 30 December 2007 and is applicable since 30 December 2008. Transitional provisions were provided for products that had already been authorised under national or Community legislation before 30 December 2008.

In the case of ATMPs other than tissue-engineered products, the transitional period expired on 30 December 2011. All such products should now be compliant with the ATMP Regulation – which does not preclude that these products may be covered by a 'hospital exemption' or a 'specials' exemption (see §17.03[B] above).

Tissue-engineered products were granted a longer transitional period of four years. Compliance with the ATMP Regulation was required by 30 December 2012 for these products.

§17.07　UK

The EU Directive 2001/83/EC, as amended by the ATMP Regulation 1394/2007, remains in force in the UK under the Human Medicines Regulations 2012 (UK HMRs), meaning the regulation of ATMPs in Great Britain, like other biopharmaceuticals, remains closely aligned with the EU after the Brexit transition period.

The MHRA regulates ATMPs in Great Britain according to the same principles that previously applied and in Northern Ireland according to the EMA's centralised procedure. In the UK, the procedure for assessing MAAs for ATMPs is the same as for licensing medicines generally but with additional specific requirements. The current EU requirements regarding data, traceability, exemptions from licensing, packaging, and post-market authorisation have been transposed into the UK HMR via the Human Medicines (Amendment, etc.) (EU Exit) Regulations 2019.

§17.08　CONCLUSION

The EU and the UK are attempting to implement an open market for ATMPs, in which quality standards are consistently applied and adequately monitored.

The cutting-edge sector of healthcare biotechnology will most probably always be a step ahead of the regulations that govern it. However, the ATMP Regulation provides a framework that both ensures the quality and safety of the innovative products currently being developed and favours equal access to those technologies for all European and UK citizens.

In practice, there are currently twenty-one ATMPs that have been granted an MA in the EU through the centralised procedure under the provisions of the ATMP Regulation. While many other products are currently under development, only thirty-six MAAs have been submitted to the EMA between June 2009 and July 2022. A certain number of products, which is difficult to evaluate, is also present on the market under an exemption regime, be it the 'hospital exemption' or the 'specials' exemption. These regimes are not harmonised, hence the existence of diverging approaches among Member States.

On the other hand, the CAT is regularly consulted with respect to ATMP classification. During the same period, it issued 568 scientific recommendations on advanced therapy classification.

These figures do not accurately reflect the level of activity in the healthcare biotechnology sector. It is a common knowledge that most of the research and development of ATMPs is conducted by academia, not-for-profit organisations, and SMEs (they account for 70% of the sponsors for clinical trials on ATMPs, while big pharmaceutical companies account for less than 2% of such sponsorships).

CHAPTER 18
Vaccines

*Marc Martens & Phillipus Putter**

§18.01 INTRODUCTION

[A] General Overview

Vaccines are drugs that are applied to healthy people and cause the generation of defences (antibodies) which act to protect the individual against future contact with infectious agents, preventing infections or diseases.

Vaccines are one of the breakthroughs of biomedical research as they have vital importance in contributing to the reduction of the impact of many infectious diseases. By using vaccines, we have eradicated smallpox;[1] we are eradicating Poliomyelitis in the world, measles is no longer a common problem (common cause of encephalitis and mental disabilities not long ago), there are no cases of diphtheria and other diseases such as pertussis (whooping cough), tetanus, hepatitis B or B meningococcal meningitis are being controlled.

However, despite the fact that the level of harmful effects caused by vaccines is extremely low, since vaccines were introduced first, there have been several examples of undesirable effects on recipients.

One of the examples that can be mentioned occurred in Germany in 1930 when 256 newborn children were vaccinated with an oral bacillus Calmette-Guérin (BCG) vaccine. Nevertheless, 130 of them developed tuberculosis and 77 died over the next

---

* The authors wish to acknowledge *Raquel Ballesteros*, the author of the earlier editions of this chapter.
1. As an interesting fact, the first vaccine was discovered by Edward Jenner in 1796 to fight the smallpox, and it owes its name to milkmaids from that time that were in direct contact with the cowpox, that is much less aggressive than the human one, and by that way they become immunised and did not get the smallpox.

few months since the BCG lot had been contaminated by a virulent strain of Mycobacterium tuberculosis. Another case occurred in the US, where in 1955, an inadequately inactivated poliovirus vaccine was administered to the subjects. This incident led to 51 cases of paralytic poliomyelitis and five deaths. Another 113 cases of paralysis and 5 deaths were caused by contacts of those who received the vaccine. The mass swine influenza campaign, also in the USA in 1976, caused 500 cases of Guillain-Barré syndrome, which led to 25 deaths.

Nevertheless, fortunately in the majority of the cases, serious adverse effects are rarely associated with vaccines despite the desire for antivaccine activism. An example is the hypothetical association between either vaccines containing thimerosal or measles-mumps-rubella (MMR) and autism, where a causal link between those vaccines and autism was not found.

Despite the possible incidents that have occurred to the moment resulting from the use of vaccines, the value that vaccines have for humanity is unquestionable. Vaccines prevent diseases that previously caused major epidemics, deaths, and horrific consequences. Moreover, traditionally the main target for many vaccines has been infants; nowadays, an increasing number of vaccinations are also recommended after infancy. For example, the human papillomavirus (HPV) vaccine is offered to teenage girls, and influenza vaccines are offered annually to all older adults and others to be at high risk of influenza.

[B] Vaccines Working Party

The Committee for Medicinal Products for Human Use (CHMP), aware of the importance of certain scientific fields, establishes every three years working parties related to those issues. They are composed of a group of experts in the matters who are selected from the list of European Experts of the Agency.

Those working parties aim at providing information to the CHMP related to their specific field of expertise and have competencies in some tasks, such as the scientific evaluation of marketing authorisation applications (MAA) or evaluation of scientific guidelines issued by the European Medicines Agency (EMA).

Given the major public health interest in the European Union (EU) about vaccines, the Vaccines Working Party (VWP) was created in 2005[2] as a permanent working party. This working party is comprised of up to twelve experts who belong to other national institutions with expertise in quality, safety, or efficacy aspects of vaccines. When necessary, the working party may avail itself of collaborators with proven expertise in specific scientific or technical fields. Neither the members nor the collaborators shall have any direct interests in the pharmaceutical industry, in order to guarantee their independence.

The mandate and objectives also include the cooperation with other international working parties in vaccine issues, the monitoring of the development of new vaccine

---

2. EMEA/CHMP/VWP/73919/2004: Mandate, objectives and rules of procedure for the CHMP vaccine working party (VWP).

technologies, or being the liaison with interested parties, such as the pharmaceutical industry.

[C] The EU Vaccines Strategy[3]

In the context of the COVID-19 crisis, the European Commission has issued a European Strategy to improve and accelerate the development and production of vaccines against COVID-19 and to create a flexible and robust regulatory framework.[4]

The Strategy imbedded in the Communication of the Commission of 17 June 2020 has the following objectives:

- Ensuring the quality, safety, and efficacy of vaccines.
- Securing timely access to vaccines for Member States and their population while leading the global solidarity effort.
- Ensuring equitable access for all in the EU to an affordable vaccine as early as possible.

The Strategy rests on two pillars:

- Securing sufficient production of vaccines in the EU and thereby sufficient supplies for its Member States through *Advance Purchase Agreements (APAs)* with vaccine producers via the Emergency Support Instrument (ESI 2). Additional financing and other forms of support can be made available on top of such agreements.
- Adapting the EU's regulatory framework to the current urgency and making use of existing regulatory flexibility to accelerate the development, authorisation, and availability of vaccines while maintaining the standards for vaccine quality, safety, and efficacy. This includes an accelerated marketing authorisation (MA), flexibility in relation to labelling and packaging, and a proposal to provide temporary derogations from certain provisions of the GMO legislation to speed up clinical trials of COVID-19 vaccines and medicines containing genetically modified organisms.

§18.02 DEVELOPMENT OF VACCINES

Vaccine development is a long, complex, and expensive process. Since vaccines are biological products made from living organisms, their development cycle differs from pharmaceutical products.

There exists an exploratory phase where the disease is understood, as well as its epidemiological data and proteins (antigens) that should be used to prevent or treat it.

---

3. *See* further Chapter 22 on Pandemics and Epidemics.
4. Communication from the commission to the European parliament, the European council, the council and the European investment bank EU Strategy for COVID-19 vaccines, COM/2020/245.

Subsequently, the safety of those antigens shall be evaluated, and the best possible vaccine will be selected.

During the clinical development, between 10 (Phase I) and 1,000 people (Phase III) participate in the clinical studies, and the first batches of vaccines are produced (clinical batches and industrial lots for the purpose of compliance).

All data collected in these previous phases are sent to the appropriate authorities in order to obtain the authorisation for its commercialisation. Once the MA is granted, the manufacturing process will begin: to produce one batch of vaccine takes up to twenty-two months.

[A] Non-clinical Aspects

[1] Basic Science Phase

The first step in developing a new vaccine is to identify natural or synthetic antigens that might help prevent or treat a disease. As antigens, researchers often include virus-like particles, weakened viruses or bacteria, weakened bacterial toxins, or other substances derived from pathogens, and this phase often lasts two to four years. These antigens shall be characterised and purified.

In addition, vaccine may also be composed of adjuvants[5] aimed at enhancing, accelerating, and prolonging the specific immune response towards the desired response to vaccine antigens. These adjuvants shall also be controlled prior to the preclinical phase. The Guideline on adjuvants in vaccines for human use[6] pretends to address the quality, non-clinical and clinical issues arising from the use of new or established adjuvants in vaccines. It is particularly recommended to evaluate immune-toxicological effects.

---

5. These adjuvants include for instance:
   - Mineral salts, e.g., aluminium hydroxide and aluminium or calcium phosphate gels.
   - Oil emulsions and surfactant-based formulations, e.g., MF59 (microfluidised detergent stabilised oil-in-water emulsion), QS21 (purified saponin), AS02 [SBAS2] (oil-in-water emulsion + MPL + QS-21), Montanide ISA-51 and ISA-720 (stabilised water-in-oil emulsion).
   - Particulate adjuvants, e.g., virosomes (unilamellar liposomal vehicles incorporating influenza haemagglutinin), AS04 ([SBAS4] Al salt with MPL), ISCOMS (structured complex of saponins and lipids), polylactide co-glycolide (PLG).
   - Microbial derivatives (natural and synthetic), e.g., monophosphoryl lipid A (MPL), Detox (MPL + M. Phlei cell wall skeleton), AGP [RC-529] (synthetic acylated monosaccharide), DC_Chol (lipoidal immunostimulators able to self-organise into liposomes), OM-174 (lipid A derivative), CpG motifs (synthetic oligonucleotides containing immunostimulatory CpG motifs), modified LT and CT (genetically modified bacterial toxins to provide non-toxic adjuvant effects).
   - Endogenous human immunomodulators, e.g., hGM-CSF or hIL-12 (cytokines that can be administered as either protein or plasmid encoded), Immudaptin (C3d tandem array).
   - Inert vehicles, such as gold particles.

6. EMEA/CHMP/VEG/134716/2004. This guideline is since 2016 under review, and a new draft guideline has been released in April 2018 by the CHMP (see EMEA/CHMP/VWP/164653/05 Rev. 1).

The quality-related data on the adjuvant shall include information concerning the adjuvant individually, the combination with the antigen, and the final product. This information shall encompass a description, the process of manufacture, the characterisation, the routine testing, and stability-indicating parameters.

The toxicity of the adjuvant shall also be studied for the adjuvant alone and for its combination with the proposed antigen, given that it is important to assess whether the combination exerts a synergistic adverse effect in the animal model compared to the individual components.

Vaccines may also contain other additives, such as excipients or preservatives. The safety of all these additives shall be subject to appropriate preclinical studies case by case, given that the same additive may cause systemic or local reactions or not, depending on the antigen it is combined with.

When new combined vaccines contain antigens that are already known, preclinical toxicity testing may not always be necessary.

[2] Preclinical Testing

Once selected the proposed antigen and any possible additive, it is necessary to test them with animals prior to introducing a candidate vaccine into humans. The selection of the animal species shall be done case by case, and the animal subjects may include mice and monkeys.

The aim of this phase is to check any potential toxicity, pyrogenicity, adverse immunologic effects, or teratogenic/reproductive effects of the candidate vaccine. In addition, this test is important to test the immunogenicity of the proposed vaccine, that is, the ability to provoke an immune response.

Thanks to these studies, researchers may have an idea of the cellular responses they might expect in humans. They may also suggest a safe starting dose for the next phase of research as well as a safe method of administering the vaccine. Researchers may adapt the candidate vaccine during the preclinical phase to try to make it more effective.

In this phase, it is possible to do challenge studies with animals: animals are vaccinated, and then they are infected with the target pathogen. Those studies are excluded from the trials with humans.

The information required for those studies was established in the note for guidance on preclinical pharmacological and toxicological testing of vaccines.[7] This note has been removed by the CHMP Working Party and Vaccine Working party (VWP) in July 2016 who agreed to refer to the World Health Organization (WHO) guideline on non-clinical evaluation of vaccines.[8]

---

7. CPMP/SWP/465/95.
8. *See* Questions and answers on the withdrawal of the CPMP Note for guidance on preclinical pharmacological and toxicological testing of vaccines (CPMP/SWP/465), EMA/CHMP/SWP/242917/2016.

It is important that new combinations produced either by formulation or at the time of reconstitution of antigens or serotypes are studied for appropriate immunogenicity in an animal model, if available, before initiation of human clinical trial.[9]

Given the complexity of obtaining the immune response desired, many candidates' vaccines do not go beyond this stage and will not be tested under clinical trials.

[B] Clinical Trials

As the basic methodological and statistical aspects of the design of clinical trials with vaccines do not differ from the rest of medicinal products, the regulation[10] and the majority of the existing guidelines available for the evaluation of clinical trials (such as those issued by regulatory agencies as the EMA or the International Conference of Harmonization (ICH)) shall apply to clinical trials with vaccines as well.

Nevertheless, during the planning, implementation, and evaluation of the clinical trials, the singular characteristics of the vaccines shall be taken into account. It is of particular importance that usually the vaccines are intended for use by healthy individuals, which requires paying particular attention to the ethical aspects and safety issues (the clinical development of vaccines is built on rigorous ethical principles of informed consent from volunteers, with an emphasis on vaccine safety as well as efficacy). In addition, many such vaccines are administered to infants; it is necessary to carry out particularly effective planning and a conscientious appraisal of a proper risk-benefit analysis. However, the efficacy data is usually obtained after its commercialisation as it is difficult to prove the protective efficacy of the vaccine evaluated on the basis of previous formal studies. The protective efficacy studies are not feasible in all cases (in others, these studies are simply not necessary).

Each vaccine may pass through four stages in its clinical development, which may last several years:

Phase I clinical trials are small-scale trials which are designated to establish the toxicity, reactogenicity, form of administration, proper dosage of a vaccine, as well as to provide preliminary information about the vaccine's capacity to generate immune response and its side effects. The vaccine is administered to a small group of healthy subjects (usually 20 to 50 volunteers, more often no more than 100 volunteers, nevertheless, the number may vary depending on each clinical trial).

In Phase II, vaccines are administered to a higher number of volunteers (usually more than 100). This Phase looks mainly to further assess the evaluation of the vaccine safety and immunogenicity.

Vaccines that progress to Phase III clinical trials are studied on a large scale of many hundreds/thousands to evaluate safety and efficacy in the relevant population for which the vaccine is designed. If the vaccine retains safety and efficacy over a

---

9. WHO guidelines on non-clinical evaluation of vaccines.
10. That is, the Regulation No. 536/2014 of the European Parliament and of the Council on clinical trials on medicinal products for human use, and repealing Directive 2001/20/EC which entered into force on 16 June 2014, and it is applicable since 28 May 2016.

defined period, the manufacturer is able to apply to the regulatory authorities for a licence to market the product for human use.

Phase IV happens after the vaccine has been licensed and introduced into use and consists of studies which are done after the vaccine has been marketed to gather information on its effects in various populations and any rare adverse effect associated with its long-term use.[11]

Organisations such as the EMA, the food and drug administration (FDA), and the WHO have developed guidelines to help to design the clinical development programmes for new vaccines.[12] The FDA and the EMA guidelines are mainly addressed to investigators and/or public or private organisations that might be interested in the development and the onward authorisation of the vaccines, the correct design of the clinical development plan of the product, and ensuring compliance with the regulatory requirements imposed by such organisations. Instead, the WHO guidelines were developed in response to requests from national regulatory authorities for assistance in the evaluation of clinical trials, both during the clinical development of a new vaccine and also during the regulatory review of dossiers submitted in support of applications for MAs. The WHO guidelines also outline the data that should be obtained during the different stages of vaccine development in order to support a marketing approval and establishes international guidance to govern the protection of individual patient while safeguarding public health.

Focusing on the Guideline on clinical evaluation of new vaccines issued by the EMA, the guideline replaced the Note for Guidance on Clinical Evaluation of New Vaccines (CPMP/EWP/463/97) and came into effect on 1 February 2007. The main areas addressed in the guideline are: (a) characterisation of the immune response and related immunogenicity issues; (b) the design and conduct of studies of protective efficacy and vaccine effectiveness; (c) the evaluation of potentially clinically important immune interference; (d) circumstances in which very limited data might be acceptable; and (e) pre-authorisation and post-authorisation safety data. However, the guideline is not addressed to non-clinical studies, except with regard to those that might be relevant to characterisation of the immune response to the antigenic components of vaccines and the clinical development of 'therapeutic vaccines', viral-vector-based gene therapy products, anti-tumour vaccines, and anti-idiotype vaccines (including monoclonal antibodies used as immunogens). The guideline is generally applicable to vaccines which contain one or more immunogenic antigens, whatever the type of antigen(s) included. Since 2016, the guideline has been under review, and a new draft guideline was released in April 2018 by the CHMP (*see further*).[13]

---

11. *See* further §18.05 below.
12. Guideline on clinical evaluation of new vaccines (EMEA/CHMP/VWP/164653/2005); Guidance for Industry: General principles for the development of vaccines to protect against global infectious diseases. FDA, December 2011; and Guidelines on clinical evaluation of vaccines: regulatory expectations. Geneva, World Health Organization 2004.
13. Draft Guideline on clinical evaluation of vaccines, EMEA/CHMP/VWP/164653/05 Rev. 1.

The most important sections of the guideline regarding clinical trials are listed below:

[1] Pharmacokinetic/Pharmacodynamic Studies

As stated in the guideline, pharmacokinetic studies are usually not required for vaccines because they do not provide useful information about the proper doses, unless new delivery systems are employed or the vaccine contains novel adjuvants or excipients. It is noted that pharmacodynamics (the antigenic capacity or immunogenicity) becomes a key aspect in the development of the vaccines while the characterisation of the pharmacokinetic profile has little relevance.

In the development of any new vaccine, adequate data on immunogenicity should be assembled during the clinical development programme. This includes:[14]

(a) General methodological considerations: primary pharmacodynamics studies should be done to investigate an appropriate dose, schedules, and routes of administration during the evaluation of the clinical studies in the case that an appropriate animal disease model is available. Early clinical studies should provide sufficient information on the safety and immunogenicity of the antigenic components in a candidate vaccine in the target population to identify the primary immunisation schedule and optimal dose to be evaluated in subsequent confirmatory studies of safety and immunogenicity and, where feasible and necessary, protective efficacy.

(b) Characterisation of the immune response: the guideline describes the minimum requirements for immunological testing, the need to study the possible effects of the immune response of the vaccine in different types of recipients, and the confirmation of the correlation between the immune response to an antigen and the protective efficacy of the vaccine.

(c) Clinically important differences in immune responses: comparative immunogenicity studies are desirable to be performed in order to study the possible immune responses to: (i) antigen(s) in a candidate vaccine versus similar antigen(s) in licensed comparator(s), (ii) antigens in a candidate vaccine when administered to different populations or at different doses or schedules, (iii) antigens when given separately versus administration as components of a candidate combined vaccine, (iv) antigens in a candidate vaccine when given alone or with other vaccines, and (v) antigens in different formulations or lots of a candidate vaccine.

(d) Analysis and presentation of immunological data: the data must be presented using a standard approach described by the guideline and in detail.

---

14. Section 4.1.1 of the Guideline on clinical evaluation of new vaccines (EMEA/CHMP/VWP/164653/2005).

(e) Essential immunogenicity studies related to dose findings, determination of the primary vaccination schedule, and persistence of immunity and consideration on booster doses must be performed.

[2] Efficacy and Effectiveness

In this section, the guideline refers to pre-authorisations studies whose initial goal is to evaluate the protective efficacy of the vaccine and, in the post-authorisation phase, its effectiveness.

As previously mentioned, demonstration of protective efficacy may not be necessary or feasible for all vaccines. For example, if an immunological correlate of protection against a specific infection has been clinically validated, immunogenicity studies can be considered sufficient (e.g., diphtheria, tetanus). However, when a protective study is going to be performed, the guideline highlights the following points that need to be considered:

(a) The possibility, in some cases, to use a randomised controlled study design to estimate the protective efficacy of a candidate vaccine by comparing it with a licensed vaccine used against the same infection;
(b) The use of secondary attack rate studies when the infection to be prevented is associated with a relatively high incidence of secondary cases;
(c) On the subject of the populations for analysis, the guideline suggests that: (i) the populations of interest should be predetermined and the primary analysis population should be chosen in consonance with the main study objectives, (ii) in studies that contrast disease rates among vaccinated and control groups that do not get any protection, the main purpose would be to show the superiority of the vaccinated group and, (iii) if the study contrasts the relative efficacy of a new vaccine with an authorised vaccine, then the intention would be to prove at least equivalence in terms of safety.
(d) In all the possible scenarios that may arise, the applicant must provide a clear and adequate justification for the primary and secondary endpoints. In turn, the choice of primary endpoint may have a major influence on the selection of the most appropriate study design.
(e) Whatever the chosen endpoint(s), endorsed techniques should be used for diagnosis (e.g., clinically apparent and/or non-apparent infections) or for other evaluation (e.g., histology) and should be predefined in the protocol. Nevertheless, the applicant might be required to use experimental laboratory techniques for establishing infection and progression of infection due to the lack of well-validated methods. On these terms, it is highly important to assess the sensitivity, specificity, and reproducibility of the techniques adopted.
(f) It is crucial that the same techniques for case detection are applied in all treatment groups until the study has been completed. Should the primary

endpoint be clinically apparent disease, the possible range of clinical presentations will determine the mode of case ascertainment. If the endpoint is other than clinically apparent disease, it is vital that subjects are supervised at regular intervals in order to identify clinically non-apparent infections or any variations in other indicators.

[3]   Special Considerations for Vaccine Development

As a final point to highlight in this section, the guideline contains a number of considerations to take into account in certain cases:

(a) immune interference, especially in the case of vaccines with more than one antigen and the administration of multiple vaccines;
(b) cross-reacting immune responses;
(c) the use of different vaccines to prime and boost;
(d) vaccine lots and lot-to-lot consistency studies;
(e) bridging studies; and,
(f) circumstances in which approval might be based on very limited data.

In any case, the guideline points out that it should be read taking into account Directive 2001/83/CE, other applicable guidelines issued by the EMA, the ICH, or the WHO and its own Annex, which includes some specific issues regarding Supplementary Protection Certificate (SPC) requirements related to vaccines.[15]

[4]   Revision of the Guideline of Clinical Evaluation

As mentioned previously, the Guideline on clinical evaluation of new vaccines has been under review since 2016. A draft of new guideline on clinical evaluation of vaccines was released on 26 April 2018.[16] Many requests for scientific advice on vaccine clinical development programmes have pointed to the need to provide updated or additional guidance on some issues. For example, on considerations for conducting vaccine efficacy trials, identification of immune correlates of protection, vaccines intended to be used in heterologous prime-boost regimens, and vaccines to be administered to pregnant women to protect their infants during the first months of life. The draft includes a discussion of factors to consider when planning and interpreting the results of comparative immunogenicity, expands considerations for the design of vaccine efficacy trials, including the selection of appropriate control groups in different circumstances, reconsiders the role of sponsors in the provision of vaccine effectiveness data in the post-licensure period to reflect the fact that most studies are conducted by public health authorities.

---

15. Guideline on clinical evaluation of new vaccines: Annex: SPC requirements (EMEA/CHMP/VWP/382702/2006).
16. Draft Guideline on clinical evaluation of new vaccines (EMEA/CHMP/VWP/164653/05 Rev. 1).

Chapter 18: Vaccines §18.03[A]

§18.03 MAA

The MA is the administrative proceeding by which regulatory authorities allow a company to commercialise a new vaccine. Regulatory authorities ground their decisions in a risk/benefit criterion after having received the MAA, so the demonstration of the efficacy and safety are fundamental issues.

In the MA file, the most relevant characteristics of the new vaccine shall be established in order to provide information to healthcare professionals. This authorisation may be modified, due to new posology or indications, or even suppressed.

Either for the authorisation decision or for the modification, the criterion that shall be taken into consideration by the regulatory authorities would be the risk/benefit one, rather than cost/effectivity, normally considered by public health authorities.

[A] The MA Procedures

In order to obtain an MA for a vaccine, Regulation (EC) No. 726/2004[17] establishes four different procedures:[18]

[1] Centralised

This procedure is obligatory when the antigen of the vaccine is a monoclonal antibody or a recombinant DNA protein vaccine. This procedure is also obligatory for medicinal products for human use containing a new active substance when the therapeutic indication is the treatment of AIDS, cancer, a neurodegenerative disorder, diabetes, auto-immune diseases, or other immune dysfunctions or viral diseases. The COVID-19 mRNA vaccines are also falling under this obligatory proceeding as they are covered by Article 3(1) and point 1 of Annex I of Regulation 726/2004.

This procedure results in a valid authorisation for all the Member States with the same characteristics, files, information pamphlets, and conditioning material.

The EMA[19] is responsible for the authorisation and coordination of the procedure, although the scientific evaluation is carried out by the authorities of the Member States.

[2] National

The older vaccines were usually authorised through this procedure. However, nowadays, it is used principally for the authorisation of generics. Given that the same

---

17. Regulation (EC) No. 726/2004 of the European Parliament and of the Council of 31 March 2004 laying down Community procedures for the authorisation and supervision of medicinal products for human and veterinary use and establishing a European Medicines Agency.
18. Those procedures are analysed in further detail in Chapter 5.
19. European Medicines Agency pre-authorisation procedural advice for users of the centralised procedure of 2 June 2016 (EMA/339324/2007).

vaccine could be analysed under different national authorities, there could be differences in the authorisations, such as period of validity or storage temperature.

[3] Decentralised and Mutual Recognition

These procedures are used when the authorisation is not solicited in all the Member States but in some of them. When a vaccine is already authorised in a Member State, the procedure to use is mutual recognition (MRP). In such a case, the State where the vaccine is already authorised (or leads the review of an application in a MRP) is considered the 'Reference Member State', and the other Member States where the further authorisation is submitted, the 'Concerned Member States'.

When the vaccine is not yet authorised in any Member State, the procedure to use is the decentralised one. In order to avoid discrepancies between regulatory authorities of different Member States, there exists a coordination group[20] of the EMA that strives to reach an agreement, and when it is not possible, there also exists the possibility of arbitration proceedings before the CHMP.

The main consequence of these procedures is that the vaccines may only be authorised in certain countries but not for the whole EU. In such a case, the technical file and specifications will be the same for the countries where it is authorised, but there may be variations in the package leaflet and SmPC (summary of product characteristics).

[B] MAAs

The MAA encompasses the required information in order to obtain an authorisation of commercialisation of a vaccine, according to Article 8 of Directive 2001/83/EC. Independently of the procedure chosen to authorise the vaccine, the structure of the application shall be the same, grounded on modules of information. The documentation required is defined as the Common Technical Document (CTDoc).

The specification of the information required in each module for medicinal products of human use is established in Annex I of Directive 2001/83/EC. Given that, as aforementioned, vaccines are special medicinal products, they shall be subject to special requirements when applying for the authorisation.

[1] Module 1

This section includes the package leaflet and the SmPC and the rest of packaging material. It also includes information about the experts who make the studies reflected in Module 2 (quality, non-clinical, and clinical) and an annex on the environmental risks (genetically modified organisms).

---

20. Coordination Group for Mutual Recognition and Decentralised Procedures – Human (CMDh).

Chapter 18: Vaccines §18.03[B]

[2]   Module 2

It encompasses a critical overview of the quality aspects as well as a critical review and a summary of the clinical and non-clinical parts. The most important documents of this part affect the efficacy, safety, and the assessment of risk and benefit.

[3]   Module 3

The information regarding the process of production of the vaccine is established in this module. It shall include the chemical, pharmaceutical, and biological information. In this point, in addition to requirements stated in module 3,[21] a Vaccine Antigen Master File (VAMF) system shall apply. This file is defined as:

The VAMF is a stand-alone part of the marketing authorisation application dossier (MAA) for a vaccine. One given VAMF contains all relevant information of biological, pharmaceutical and chemical nature for one given vaccine antigen, which is common to several vaccines from the same MA applicant or MAH.[22]

Given that a vaccine may contain more than one antigen, there are as many active substances as vaccine antigens. Consequently, it is necessary for one VAMF for each antigen. The introduction of such a file is aimed at simplification of existing procedures. This file shall include the following information regarding each one of the active substances of the vaccine:[23]

(1) General information, including compliance with the monographs of the European Pharmacopoeia.
(2) Information on its manufacture.
(3) Characterisation.
(4) Quality control.
(5) Reference standards and materials.
(6) Container and closure system.
(7) Stability, including information on cumulative stability in those cases where it is relevant.[24]
(8) Equipment and facilities.
(9) Adventitious agents' safety evaluation.

The EMA, as a first step, shall carry out a scientific and technical evaluation of each VAMF, according to the Guideline on requirements for vaccine antigen master file (VAMF) certification,[25] in a system analogous to the centralised procedure, and a

---

21. Section 1.2, Part III, Annex I, Directive 2001/83/EC.
22. EMEA/CPMP/4548/03/Final/Rev 1 Guideline on requirements for vaccine antigen master file (VAMF) certification.
23. EMEA/CPMP/BWP/3734/03 Guideline on the scientific data requirements for a vaccine antigen master file (VAMF).
24. Section 3.2.2.8, Part I, Annex I Directive 2001/83/EC.
25. EMEA/CPMP/4548/03/Final/Rev 1.

certificate of compliance will be issued if the evaluation is positive. This certificate is valid throughout the EU.

Subsequently,[26] the competent authority that will grant, or has granted, the MA shall take into consideration the certification or re-certification variation of the VAMF on the concerned medicinal product. When the vaccine is tried to be authorised before the centralised procedure, this second step is merely theoretical since the EMA is the competent authority in both cases.

If the VAMF suffers any modification after the vaccine is authorised, it is necessary for a new evaluation carried out by the Agency, according to the procedure stated in Regulation (EC) No. 1234/2008.[27]

There is a large number of guidelines[28] that seek to ensure consistent vaccine production, according to which was valued at toxicological and clinical trials, and they also seek to minimise the risks inherent in biological materials.

Whenever possible, vaccine production shall be based on a system of established cell banks and seed lots. For bacterial and viral vaccines, the characteristics of the infectious agent must be shown in the planting materials. In addition, for live vaccines, the stability of the attenuation characteristics shall be demonstrated in the planting material; if this test is not sufficient, attenuation characteristics shall also be demonstrated at the stage of production.

[4]   Module 4

A Table of Contents shall be provided that lists all of the non-clinical study reports and gives the location of each study report in the CTDoc.

It encompasses non-clinical studies, pharmacology, pharmacokinetic, and toxicology. It consists of pharmacological toxicological data. This includes all data about a medicinal product collected from animals relating to toxicity and the mechanism of action of a medicinal product.

[5]   Module 5

Information about the clinical trials is included in this module. The key issue in the development of a new vaccine is the demonstration of its efficacy, which is defined as the reduction of probability of developing an illness after vaccination with respect to a non-vaccinate. Given the speciality of vaccines, there shall be a special emphasis on vaccine safety and efficacy.

---

26. Guideline on Plasma Master File (PMF) and Vaccine Antigen Master File (VAMF) 'Second Step'.
27. Commission Regulation (EC) No. 1234/2008 of 24 November 2008 concerning the examination of variations to the terms of marketing authorisations for medicinal products for human use and veterinary medicinal products.
28. *Inter alia*: CPMP/BWP/819/01 Questions and Answers on Bovine Spongiform Encephalopathies (BSE) and Vaccines; CPMP/BWP/477/97 Pharmaceutical and Biological Aspects of Combined Vaccines; or EMEA/CPMP/BWP/2758/02 Guideline on pharmaceutical aspects of the product information for human vaccines.

Therefore, in this section, the information regarding the different phases of the clinical trials shall be submitted from initial clinical trials in humans and beyond.

[C] Conditional MA in Emergency Situations

In cases of a pandemic, alternative and fast-track approval of an MA are open for vaccines under Article 14-a of Regulation 726/2004.[29] According to this provision, in order to meet unmet medical needs of patients, an MA may, for life-threatening diseases, be granted prior to the submission of comprehensive clinical data provided that the benefit of the immediate availability on the market of the medicinal product concerned outweighs the risk inherent in the fact that additional data are still required. In emergency situations, an MA for such medicinal products may also be granted where comprehensive preclinical or pharmaceutical data have not been supplied.

The standard timeline for the evaluation of a medicine is a maximum of 210 active days. MAAs for COVID-19 products were treated by EMA in an expedited manner allowing a timeline for evaluation to be reduced to less than 150 working days.

The EMA used the rolling review procedure for most of the medicines for COVID-19. This allowed EMA to begin assessing data as they became available during the development process to expedite the subsequent formal MAA assessment even further.

Substantial support has been provided to the applicants through presubmission guidance.[30]

§18.04 THE OFFICIAL CONTROL AUTHORITY BATCH RELEASE

Once an MA is obtained, each batch of vaccines may still be assessed for quality before release for use. In this sense, Article 114.1 of Directive 2001/83/EC states that:

1. Where it considers it necessary in the interests of public health, a Member State may require the holder of an authorisation for marketing:
   - live vaccines,
   - immunological medicinal products used in the primary immunisation of infants or of other groups at risk,
   - immunological medicinal products used in public health immunisation programmes,
   - new immunological medicinal products or immunological medicinal products manufactured using new or altered kinds of technology or new for a particular manufacturer, during a transitional period normally specified in the marketing authorisation,

   to submit samples from each batch of the bulk and/or the medicinal product for examination by an Official Medicines Control Laboratory or a laboratory that a Member State has designated for that purpose before release on to the market

---

29. *See* further Chapter 6 relating to conditional marketing authorisations in general.
30. *See* in particular: European Medicines Agency pre-authorisation procedural advice for users of the centralised procedure (EMA/821278/2015. Rev. 20 June 2022).

unless, in the case of a batch manufactured in another Member State, the competent authority of that Member State has previously examined the batch in question and declared it to be in conformity with the approved specifications. Member States shall ensure that any such examination is completed within 60 days of the receipt of the samples.

Article 114 of Directive 2001/83 allows, but does not require, a Member State laboratory to test a batch of an immunological medicinal product before it can be marketed. The procedure to be followed within the European Economic Area (EEA), including EU for batch to be tested before it can be marketed is set out in the document 'EU Administrative Procedure for Official Control Authority Batch Release', hereinafter EU Administrative Procedure (revised version in force from 1 July 2022).[31] As described in the EU Administrative Procedure, this 'Official Control Authority Batch Release' (OCABR) consists of analytical controls and document reviews which are additional to the batch release that must be carried out by the manufacturer for a given batch in accordance with Article 51 of the said Directive 2001/83/EC. The competent authorities issue a Batch Release Certificate when the results are satisfactory.

In particular,

(1) The Member State where the vaccine is to be marketed shall inform the MAH that the vaccine is to be subjected to the OCABR;
(2) The MAH shall submit samples of the batch to be released together with production and control protocols to an Official Medicines Control Laboratory (OMCL)[32] within the EU.
(3) Then, the OCABR procedure will consist of:
    (a) a critical evaluation of the manufacturer's production and control protocol; and,
    (b) testing of samples submitted by the manufacturer: this testing usually consists of just one phase (Phase I testing). However, in some cases, it is necessary to perform a Phase II testing. For example, in case of a significant change in the manufacturing process or a change in the manufacturing site, adverse events, marked inconsistencies in the manufacturing process, changes in the manufacturer's test procedures, unexpected variability in the results of quality control tests performed by the

---

31. Please *see also* EU Administrative Procedure for Official Control Authority Batch Release (OCABR) of Centrally Authorised Immunological Medicinal Products for Human Use and Medicinal Products Derived from Human Blood and Plasma (version in force from 1 July 2010) applicable specifically to Centrally Authorised Products when submitted to Official Control Authority Batch Release. Please also bear in mind that there are Products Specific Guidelines for Immunological Products Consisting of Vaccines http://www.edqm.eu/.
32. The OCABR is carried out by Official Medicines Control Laboratories (OMCLs) of the Member States whose activities are coordinated by the European Pharmacopoeia Secretariat within the European Directorate for the Quality of Medicines and Healthcare (EDQM). The European Pharmacopoeia Secretariat also has the responsibility for developing legally binding monographs to ensure appropriate quality control and harmonised quality standards across manufacturers. A list of OMCLs is available from the EDQM, Department of Biological Standardisation, OMCL Networks and HealthCare (DBO), OCABR Section of the Council of Europe, and it is regularly updated (*see* www.edqm.eu).

manufacturer or the OMCL or a critical inspection report from the medicines inspectorate.

The OMCL shall complete the OCABR within sixty days from receipt of the protocol and samples (and the fees, where required).

(4) If a batch is satisfactory for release, the corresponding OMCL shall prepare an OCABR Certificate. The 'European Union Official Control Authority Batch Release Certificate' delivered by a National competent authority is the document used by a Member State to indicate that 'Official Control Authority Batch Release' has taken place.

On the contrary, when a batch does not fulfil the specifications, this information shall be communicated to the MAH and, by a rapid and confidential information exchange mechanism, to specified contact persons in the EU OCABR network (including OMCLs, competent authorities, EMA, the EU Commission, EDQM, and any OCABR network observer approved through a specific network procedure) for use in the context of control of medicines by the relevant authorities.

(5) The MAH must ensure that the competent authorities of the Member States where the batch will be marketed are provided with a copy of the OCABR Certificate and the corresponding 'marketing information form'.[33] A model of 'marketing information form' is presented in Annex IV of the EU Administrative Procedure.

After sending this information, the MAH could market the batch in the Member State where the batch is to be marketed if, within seven working days, the competent authority in that Member State has not raised any objection.

Directive 2001/83/EC establishes that Member States must recognise the OCABR performed in any other Member State; in other words, OCABR carried out by any given Member State must be mutually recognised by all other Member States requiring OCABR for that batch. Nevertheless, Member States can exercise control over the batch as part of its post-marketing surveillance.

As mentioned above, this regulation concerns EU/EEA Member States but is also applied by any other State having signed a formal agreement, which includes recognition of OCABR, with the EU. Currently, Switzerland has done so via a Mutual Recognition Agreement (MRA).

More extensive testing may need to be performed by an OMCL. Examples of events that might trigger Phase II testing include:

- a significant change in the manufacturing process;
- a change in the manufacturing site;
- adverse events;
- marked inconsistencies in the manufacturing process;
- changes in the manufacturer's test procedures;

---

33. Annex IV of the EU Administrative Procedure provides with a model of marketing information form.

- unexpected variability in the results of quality control tests performed by the manufacturer or the OMCL;
- a critical inspection report from the medicines' inspectorate;
- need to monitor, through testing, the consistency of a key quality parameter for a defined period.

§18.05 POST-MARKETING SURVEILLANCE: PHARMACOVIGILANCE

As mentioned before, unlike other medicinal products, vaccines are administered to healthy subjects, the majority of whom are children. For this reason, it is expected that the benefit of the vaccines (that is the protection from the development of the disease) far exceed the risk of adverse reactions after its administration. Therefore, the risk-benefit balance should be very favourable when it comes to the commercialisation of the vaccine.

It is important to remember that the monitoring of the safety of a vaccine takes place throughout its whole 'life': during the first studies in the preclinical phase, in its first applications to humans during clinical trials and once approved during the post-marketing phase. Even before marketing an exhaustive vaccine study has been carried out, nevertheless, the number of subjects who were administered the new vaccine is limited, so it is possible that adverse reactions may occur at the marketing stage, sometimes severe. Moreover, one of the added difficulties of assessing the safety of vaccines is that it cannot be measured directly but can only be inferred from the absence of adverse effects. Clinical trials carried out before the approval of a vaccine do not have sufficient statistical power to detect potential adverse effects. In addition, it is important to mention that during the conduct of clinical trials, certain population groups have been excluded, as in the case of people with chronic diseases, individuals in certain drug treatments, premature infants, or pregnant women. For this reason, it is necessary to monitor vaccines after extended use in the population.

By the time that an MA is granted, the MAH must have its pharmacovigilance in place:

- A risk specification must be finalised that includes a description of possible safety issues related to the intrinsic character of the vaccine and/or the intrinsic character of the individual response.
- A risk management plan (RMP) must be agreed with EU competent authorities. Any specific safety monitoring imposed should be taken into consideration in the RMP. Plans should be in place for the monitoring of vaccine effectiveness.
- Pharmacovigilance systems and procedures to achieve adequate monitoring of safety must be in place. The general considerations for pharmacovigilance and for development of a pharmacovigilance plan are the same as for all other types of medicinal products. However, vaccines are almost always administered to healthy persons. This fact has implications for the continued re-assessment of the overall risk-benefit relationship for the vaccine. Applicants

should consult the separate guidance under development regarding pharmacovigilance for vaccines.[34]

[A] Some Institutions That Ensure Post-Authorisation Safety of Vaccines

With its aim of ensuring effective and reliable use of vaccines in the world and the immunisation policies and recommendations, the WHO, through its Global Advisory Committee on Vaccine Safety (GACVS), uses the best available data, reviews, compiles, and regularly publishes information regarding the safety of all vaccines. GACVS was established in 1999 to respond promptly, efficiently, and with scientific rigour to vaccine safety issues of potential global importance. The Committee provides independent, authoritative, scientific advice to WHO on vaccine safety issues of global or regional concern with the potential to affect in the short- or long-term national immunisation programmes.

In Europe, the European Centre for Disease Prevention and Control (ECDC) was created in 2005 with the duty to identify, assess, and communicate current and emerging threats to human health posed by infectious diseases.[35] Regarding vaccines, Whereas Article 8 of Regulation (EC) 851/2004 establishes that the ECDC 'should support existing activities, such as relevant Community action programmes in the public health sector, with regard to the prevention and control of communicable diseases, epidemiological surveillance, training programmes and early warning and response mechanisms and should foster the exchange of best practices and experience with regard to vaccination programmes'. Likewise, Article 11 of the mentioned Regulation sets out that the Centre shall coordinate data collection, validation, analysis, and dissemination of data at Community level, including vaccination strategies.

We should also highlight the work of one independent institution, the Brighton Collaboration, which reviews and inspects exhaustively all the security issues regarding vaccines. The Brighton Collaboration has developed a multi-disciplinary international work group that, in accordance with the WHO, the ECDC, and the Centres for Disease Control and Prevention (CDC),[36] has established the case definitions for an exhaustive number of adverse events following immunisation (AEFI) with vaccines. This allows to the professionals from all over the world to share and compare the security data of the vaccines with different geographical origins. The complete list of such Brighton Collaboration's definitions is available on https://brightoncollaboration.org/public/what-we-do/setting-standards/case-definitions/available-definitions.

---

34. *See*, for instance, Guideline on clinical evaluation of new vaccines (EMEA/CHMP/VWP/164653/2005, p.18).
35. Article 3 of the Regulation (EC) No. 851/2004 of the European Parliament and of the Council of 21 April 2004 establishing a European Centre for disease prevention and control (Regulation (EC) 851/2004).
36. CDC within the United States Department of Health and Human Services is the national focus for developing and applying disease prevention and control, environmental health, and health promotion, and health education activities designed to improve the health in the United States.

html, and its use is recommended, in particular, by the main organisations involved in the evaluation of safety of vaccines, such as the WHO, FDA, and EMA.

Finally, it is very important to highlight the work accomplished by the CIOMS[37]/WHO Working Group on Vaccine Pharmacovigilance. This working party was created in 2005 with the vision to globally support surveillance of vaccine safety and the evolving need of a harmonised view on terminology and case definitions used in vaccine pharmacovigilance. Specifically, the group was to provide tools for higher excellence of signal detection and investigation of AEFIs and to contribute to the development and dissemination of definitions of AEFIs as developed by the Brighton Collaboration process.[38]

[B] GVP Module for Vaccines

The EMA published, in December 2013, the first GVP considerations chapter titled Guideline on good pharmacovigilance practices (GVP): Product- or population-specific considerations I: Vaccines for prophylaxis against infectious diseases (EMA/488220/2012, hereinafter GVP module for vaccines) as part of the chapters on product- or population-specific considerations of the Good pharmacovigilance practices (GVP),[39] which are currently under development in relation to pregnancy and geriatric population.

According to the Definition and Application of Terms for Vaccine Pharmacovigilance: Report of CIOMS/WHO Working Group on Vaccine Pharmacovigilance (2012), the introduction of the module sets out that vaccine pharmacovigilance is 'the science and activities related to the detection, assessment, understanding and communication of adverse events following immunisation and other vaccine- or immunisation-related issues and to the prevention of untoward effects of the vaccine or immunization'. While the overall objectives and processes of pharmacovigilance are similar for vaccines and other types of medicinal products, the GVP module for vaccines focuses on vaccine-specific aspects and unique challenges that should be considered when designing and implementing pharmacovigilance activities for vaccines. The following aspects should be considered when conducting vaccine pharmacovigilance:[40]

- Vaccines are usually administered to otherwise healthy individuals, often very young or vulnerable; they may be administered to a large fraction of the population, and vaccination is mandatory in some countries; there is, therefore, a high level of safety required for vaccines, and tolerance to risk is usually low;

---

37. Council for International Organizations of Medical Sciences (CIOMS), an international, non-governmental, non-profit organisation established jointly by WHO and UNESCO in 1949.
38. *See* Definition and Application of Terms for Vaccine Pharmacovigilance: Report of CIOMS/WHO Working Group on Vaccine Pharmacovigilance (2012).
39. *See* further Chapter 10 on Pharmacovigilance.
40. Section P.I.A.2. Aspects specific to prophylactic vaccines of the GVP module for vaccines.

- Assessment of causality between adverse events and vaccines may be difficult: several vaccines are often administered concomitantly, it is inevitable that, with high vaccine uptake, incident cases of many natural diseases in given population cohorts will occur in temporal association with vaccination, and considerations of dechallenge and rechallenge are not relevant to many vaccines that are administered only once or have long-term immunological effects;
- Vaccines are complex biological products which may include multiple antigens, live organisms, adjuvants, preservatives, and other excipients, and each of these components may have safety implications; variability and changes in the manufacturing process, new components, and new production, and administration technologies may impact on safety, and this may require specific pharmacovigilance systems;
- Benefit-risk balance for vaccines also depends on factors acting at the population level, including the incidence, geographical distribution, seasonal characteristics, and risk of transmission of the infectious disease in the target population, the proportion of infected persons with a clinical disease, the severity of this disease, vaccine coverage, and community immunity;
- Concerns raised by the public may have an impact on the vaccination programme and should be adequately addressed;
- Effective communication about safety of vaccines and vaccination is difficult: perceptions of harm may persist despite evidence that a serious adverse event is not related to the vaccination, and communicating about vaccine safety to multiple audiences (e.g., healthcare providers, patients, and parents) is complex.

The GVP module for vaccines is divided into three sections:

(1) PIA. in which an introduction to the module is made: it includes some aspects regarding terminology, specific aspects of prophylactic vaccines, changes of the benefit-risk balance, and aspects related to vaccination programmes;
(2) PIB which provides guidance specifically for vaccines in relation to the pharmacovigilance processes described in the Modules of the GVP; and
(3) PIC which provides guidance related to the operation of the EU network: roles and responsibilities of the different stakeholders (vaccinated persons and, in the case of paediatric vaccination, their parents/carers, healthcare professionals, MAHs, competent authorities in the Member States, and the EMA), reporting of reactions and emerging safety issues, the risk management system of a vaccine and its possible updates, signal management, safety communication, and transparency of pharmacovigilance for vaccines within the EU and vaccines intended for markets outside the EU.

[C] Post-Marketing Authorisation Approval Requirements

[1] RMP

At granting an MA for vaccines, some conditions are established in order to control that the requirements fulfilled when it was authorised continue existing, e.g., post-licensure commitments or follow-up measures such as stability studies, trials in populations that have not been studied yet, etc.

At establishing post-MA requirements, the special characteristics of vaccines shall be taken into consideration: they are almost always administered to healthy people; they carry intrinsic risks – vaccine antigens or excipients/adjuvants; or there may be any biological variation or quality defects.

Therefore, it is necessary to establish effective systems to identify, evaluate, and communicate any potential risk, regarding the intrinsic character of the vaccine or of the individual response, and that rapidly distinguish possible cause from likely coincidence.

In this point, it is important to highlight the existence of RMPs agreed with the competent authority, aimed at monitoring the safety of the vaccines. A guideline[41] on good pharmacovigilance practices about Risk Management Systems has been developed by the EMA.

[2] Variation of the Original VAMF Certificate[42]

When any of the characteristics set in a VAMF certificate is modified, the vaccine antigen shall need a new certification of compliance, according to Commission Regulation (EC) No. 1234/2008.

It is necessary to submit a VAMF variation application to the EMA, to the coordinator(s), and to Member States(s). Depending on the level of the variation,[43] the agencies involved shall be different:

- Type 1A variations: only the EMA;
- Type 1B variations: EMA and primary coordinator who was appointed for the application for initial certification;
- Type II variations: As per initial certification.

If the evaluation is positive, the agency delivers a certificate of compliance with the evaluation report attached.

---

41. EMA/838713/2011 Rev. 1 Guideline on good pharmacovigilance practices (GVP) Module V – Risk management systems (Rev. 1).
42. Section 6 of the Guideline on requirements for vaccine antigen master file (VAMF) certification EMEA/CPMP/4548/03/Final/Rev 1.
43. Articles 8 to 10 and 14 to 16 of Commission Regulation (EC) No. 1234/2008 of 24 November 2008 concerning the examination of variations to the terms of marketing authorisations for medicinal products for human use and veterinary medicinal products.

[3] License Renewals

An MA of a vaccine, as well as of the common medicinal products for human use,[44] is valid for five years, and it may be renewed upon application by the MAH at least nine months before its expiry. The renewal assessment must be based on a general re-evaluation of the benefit/risk balance of the vaccine.

When applying for a renewal, the MAH shall submit an update of the RMP in view of re-assessing the overall benefit/risk balance of the medicinal product concerned.

§18.06 VACCINES IN THE UK

[A] Introduction

Vaccines have transformed modern medicine globally. Vaccines are at the sharp end of public health, and as such, their development, trial, and marketing are closely monitored. New vaccines face strict regulatory hurdles, which includes, *inter alia*, proof of safety and efficacy. Exceptions exist, for example, where there is an urgent public need, such as the COVID-19 pandemic.[45] Novel infectious diseases (e.g., swine flu, Zika, Ebola, and COVID-19) require constant innovation due, in part, to the complexities of viral genetics. As with other drugs, developing a novel vaccine is time-consuming, expensive, and complex. Manufacturers often spend years or even decades on researching and developing a new vaccine with no guarantee that it will be successful.

The UK left the EU on 31 January 2020. With respect to vaccine development, MA, and post-marketing surveillance in the UK, the EU regulatory framework is generally followed. In this section, we address the key developments regarding vaccine development, MA, and post-market monitoring in so far as the regulatory framework diverges from EU law.

[B] Development of Vaccines in the UK

The development process was outlined in some detail in §18.02. This includes preclinical research, lead identification, formulation development, and clinical trials. In the UK, this process is collaborative, and manufacturers rarely work in isolation without regulatory input. This is especially true where there is an urgent public need, and where regulatory bodies may be involved from the very early stages of research and development.

---

44. Guideline on the processing of renewals in the centralised procedure (EMEA/CHMP/2990/00 Rev.4). A new draft guideline on the processing of renewals in the centralised procedure has been published on July 2015 (Rev.5) whose deadline for comments was on 14 September 2015.
45. *See* Chapter 22 for a more detailed guide to pandemics and epidemics.

In the UK, manufacturers work closely with the Medicines and Healthcare products Regulatory Agency (MHRA), the Department for Health and Social Care (DHSC),[46] the Joint Committee on Vaccines and Immunisation (JCVI),[47] and NHS England and the UK Health Security Agency (UKHSA).[48] The role of EU regulatory bodies has already been discussed in this chapter, but it is important to note that manufacturers may also collaborate with relevant EU and international regulators, such as the EMA, CHMP, and WHO, which is especially relevant with respect to novel infectious diseases, such as COVID-19.

[C] Pre-approval and MA

Vaccines are subject to the same MA procedures outlined in §5.09. After Brexit, Directive 2001/83/EC was retained by the Human Medicines Regulations 2012, as amended (UK HMRs). The procedure for obtaining MA in the UK remains largely the same as it was before Brexit, however vaccines no longer require approval via the centralised procedure.

In the EU, applicants for vaccine MA need to submit a VAMF.[49] This requirement for a VAMF was retained by Regulation 50(5) of the UK HMRs. However, the MHRA recently issued guidance[50] stating that no VAMF is currently in use in the UK, and that applicants proposing such a submission (which will be subject to the same standards and criteria as apply now) should contact the MHRA for further guidance. In addition to obtaining MA, the MAH must also submit any new vaccine destined for the UK market to a central laboratory for testing. In the UK, this is administered primarily by the National Institute for Biological Standards and Control (NIBSC).[51]

The 2012 Regulations do provide some flexibility. For example, the MHRA can accept an application for the variation[52] of an MA in some circumstances.[53] The MHRA

---

46. DHSC is a ministerial department responsible for developing and delivering policies that aim to protect global and domestic public health, including vaccines.
47. The JCVI is an independent statutory body established by the National Health Service (Standing Advisory Committees) Order 1981 (SI 1981/597). As a Departmental Expert Committee, JCVI advises various UK government departments with respect to vaccines and immunisation. This is not to say that the JCVI merely 'suggests' or 'advises' – the secretary of state must act in accordance with certain JCVI advice (Health Protection (Vaccination) Regulations 2009 (SI 2009/38)).
48. UKHSA was formerly known as Public Health England and is responsible for protecting the public from infectious diseases. Following the COVID-19 pandemic, UKHSA has further reinforced its role in the detection of epidemics. UKHSA is also responsible in part of the roll out of immunisation programmes, in collaboration with the National Health Service (NHS) and DHSC.
49. See §18.03[B][3] for further detail.
50. Guidance on licensing biosimilars, ATMPs, and PMFs (last updated 10 May 2021): https://www.gov.uk/guidance/guidance-on-licensing-biosimilars-atmps-and-pmfs.
51. Pursuant to regulation 60A of the UK HMRs, the MHRA has the power to impose batch testing in respect of a UK Marketing Authorisation for medicinal products including live vaccines and other immunological products.
52. See Chapter 11, which outlines the procedure for variation applications.
53. For example, a seasonal flu vaccine. Although flu vaccines are available every year, due to viral mutation these vaccines must be 'updated' annually.

also administers the Early Access to Medicines Scheme (EAMS), which permits the use of innovative new vaccines before MA has been granted.

[D] Post-marketing Pharmacovigilance

The EU's post-marketing pharmacovigilance protocols are discussed in depth in §18.05. The aim of pharmacovigilance is to ensure, *inter alia*, that any adverse events are identified and reported accurately. The MHRA's *Yellow Card Scheme* also enables healthcare professionals and patients to voluntarily submit reports of adverse reactions.[54]

Part 11 of the UK HMRs sets out the main obligations of MAHs with respect to post-marketing pharmacovigilance in the UK. The main obligations of MAHs are found in Regulations 182 to 188. A non-exhaustive list of key MAH obligations is set out as follows:

(1) MAHs must operate a system of pharmacovigilance, including, for example: maintaining a master file; monitoring the outcome of the measures contained in the RMP; evaluate all scientific information relevant to the product and considering options for minimising and preventing the risk presented by the use of the product.[55]
(2) MAHs must audit its pharmacovigilance system regularly, noting the main findings of each audit and outlining a corrective plan of action. Any note placed on the system can be removed only when the measures outlined in the corrective plan have been fully implemented.[56]
(3) MAHs must record all suspected adverse reactions to the product occurring in the UK which are brought to its attention. It does not matter whether the reaction is reported spontaneously by patients or healthcare professionals, or occurred in the context of a post-marketing study. All reports recorded must be accessible (electronically or physically) at a single point within the UK.[57]
(4) MAHs must electronically submit to the MHRA a report on all serious suspected adverse reactions within fifteen days of knowledge of the reaction.[58] All non-serious suspected adverse reactions must be reported within ninety days of knowledge of the reaction. Regulation 188 contains various other obligations, such as collecting follow-up information and collaborating with the MHRA in the detection of duplicates of suspected adverse reaction reports.

---

54. https://yellowcard.mhra.gov.uk/
55. Regulation 182 of the UK HMRs.
56. Regulation 184 of the UK HMRs.
57. Regulation 187 of the UK HMRs.
58. More specifically, Regulation 188 of the UK HMRs states that the MAH must submit the report 'before the end of the period of 15 days beginning on the day following the day on which the holder gained knowledge of the reaction'.

[E] Summary

In terms of innovation, British soil is fertile, and vaccine development is a prime example. The emergence of COVID-19 in late 2019 served as a catalyst, demonstrating that the regulatory landscape in the UK could be flexible yet robust. This flexibility paid dividends when the UK became the first country to authorise a vaccine for the virus.[59]

Obtaining MA for a vaccine is complex, time-consuming, and expensive. The UK regulatory landscape post-Brexit is largely the same as it was before, although the MHRA is now in charge along with the DHSC, JCVI, and UKHSA. The UK HMRs have been amended several times, notably implementing various EU rules and regulations. Whether the MHRA will diverge from EU law to any meaningful extent remains to be seen. Cross-border collaboration is vital for manufacturers, and any significant change could disrupt the market and stifle innovation.

§18.07 GUIDELINES/PUBLICATIONS

- Commission regulation (EC) No. 1234/2008 of 24 November 2008 concerning the examination of variations to the terms of marketing authorisations for medicinal products for human use and veterinary medicinal products.
- Communication from the Commission to the European Parliament, the European Council, the Council and the European investment bank EU Strategy for COVID-19 vaccines. COM/2020/245 final.
- Communication from the Commission to the Council, the European Parliament, the European Economic and Social Committee and the Committee of the Regions on strengthening coordination on generic preparedness planning for public health emergencies at EU level. COM(2005) 605 final.
- Definition and Application of Terms for Vaccine Pharmacovigilance: Report of CIOMS/WHO Working Group on Vaccine Pharmacovigilance (2012).
- Directive 2001/83/EC of the European Parliament and of the Council of 6 November 2001 on the Community code relating to medicinal products for human use.
- EU Administrative Procedure for Official Control Authority Batch Release (OCABR) of Centrally Authorised Immunological Medicinal Products for Human Use and Medicinal Products Derived from Human Blood and Plasma.
- European Medicines Agency pre-authorisation procedural advice for users of the centralised procedure of 2 June 2016 (EMA/339324/2007).
- Global safety of vaccines: strengthening systems for monitoring, management and the role of GACVS (*Expert Rev. Vaccines* 8(6), 705–716 (2009).

---

59. Although China and Russia granted MA faster, the UK conducted large-scale clinical trials before rolling out the vaccines (Pfizer and BioNTech).

- Guidance for Industry. General principles for the development of vaccines to protect against global infectious diseases. FDA, December 2011.
- Guideline on adjuvants in vaccines for human use (EMEA/CHMP/VEG/134716/2004).
- Guideline on clinical evaluation of new vaccines (EMEA/CHMP/VWP/164653/2005).
- Guideline on clinical evaluation of new vaccines: Annex: SPC requirements (EMEA/CHMP/VWP/382702/2006).
- Guideline on clinical evaluation of vaccines: Regulatory expectations. Geneva, World Health Organization, 2004.
- Guideline on good pharmacovigilance practices (GVP): Product- or population-specific considerations I: Vaccines for prophylaxis against infectious diseases (EMA/488220/2012).
- Guideline on good pharmacovigilance practices (GVP) Module V – Risk management systems (Rev 2). (EMA/838713/2011 Rev. 2).
- Guideline on non-clinical local tolerance testing of medicinal products, (EMA/CHMP/SWP/2145/2000 Rev. 1, Corr. 1*).
- Guideline on pharmaceutical aspects of the product information for human vaccines (EMEA/CPMP/BWP/2758/02).
- Guideline on Plasma Master File (PMF) and Vaccine Antigen Master File (VAMF) 'Second Step'.
- Guideline on requirements for vaccine antigen master file (VAMF) certification (EMEA/CPMP/4548/03/Final/Rev 1).
- Guideline on the scientific data requirements for a vaccine antigen master file (VAMF) (EMEA/CPMP/BWP/3734/03).
- ICH guideline S6 (R1) – pre-clinical safety evaluation of biotechnology-derived pharmaceuticals (EMA/CHMP/ICH/731268/1998).
- Mandate, objectives and rules of procedure for the CHMP vaccine working party (VWP) (EMEA/CHMP/VWP/73919/2004).
- Note for guidance on pre-clinical pharmacological and toxicological testing of vaccines (CPMP/SWP/465/95).
- Regulation No. 536/2014 of the European Parliament and of the Council on clinical trials on medicinal products for human use, and repealing Directive 2001/20/EC which entered into force on 16 June 2014 but will apply no earlier than 28 May 2016.
- Regulation (EC) No. 726/2004 of the European Parliament and of the Council of 31 March 2004 laying down Community procedures for the authorisation and supervision of medicinal products for human and veterinary use and establishing a European Medicines Agency.
- Regulation (EC) No. 851/2004 of the European Parliament and of the Council of 21 April 2004 establishing a European Centre for disease prevention and control.

- The European Vaccine Action Plan 2015–2020 (EVAP). (EUR/RC64/15 Rev.1).
- Work plan for the Vaccines Working Party (VWP) for 2016 (EMA/CHMP/VWP/833298/2015EMA).
- WHO guidelines on non-clinical evaluation of vaccines.

CHAPTER 19
Medical Devices

Kevin Munungu & Sophie Vo

§19.01 INTRODUCTION

Medical devices have become extremely important in the healthcare sector due to their impact on health and the large healthcare expenditure for medical devices. There are approximately 500,000 types of medical devices on the European market, ranging from simple bandages and spectacles to life-maintaining implantable devices, such as cardiac pacemakers, to equipment for screening and diagnosing disease conditions, sophisticated diagnostic imaging, and minimal invasive surgery equipment.[1] According to recent reports, globally, the medical device industry is expected to generate USD 432.6 billion by 2025 worldwide.[2]

One of the many reasons for the growing importance of medical devices is also the increase in occurrence of chronic diseases, such as diabetes mellitus. Diabetes mellitus, often referred to simply as 'diabetes', is a syndrome of disordered metabolism due to a defect in either insulin secretion or insulin action in the body, resulting in abnormally high blood sugar levels.[3] As diabetes mellitus currently cannot be cured, diabetics must continuously control their blood sugar levels. Blood glucose monitoring is usually done with blood glucose systems or blood glucose meters. Diabetics pierce the skin with a small lancet in order to draw blood to test it for sugar levels. Some diabetics also need insulin pumps in order to inject the necessary dosage of insulin. Blood glucose systems, insulin pumps, and lancets are all considered medical devices. Today, there are even blood glucose meters available that can be easily applied

---

1. *Medical Devices*, European Union, https://ec.europa.eu/growth/sectors/medical-devices_en.
2. Brette Blakely et al., 'Ethical and regulatory implications of the COVID-19 pandemic for the medical devices industry and its representatives', https://bmcmedethics.biomedcentral.com/articles/10.1186/s12910-022-00771-2#ref-CR1, accessed on 1 July 2022.
3. *Health Topics: Diabetes: Overview*, WHO, https://www.who.int/health-topics/diabetes#tab=tab_1.

together with smart phones. The test results are shown on the smart phone display and can be locally saved or transmitted to a computer for a personal diary.

The World Health Organization (WHO) projects that the number of diabetics will exceed 366 million by the year 2030 (the previous estimate in the year 2009 was 350 million by the year 2030). In the year 2000, there were an estimated 171 million patients with diabetes mellitus worldwide.[4] In the year 2007, there were already an estimated 246 million people with diabetes mellitus worldwide. In 2004, an estimated 3.4 million people died from consequences of high blood sugar. More than 80% of diabetes deaths occur in low- and middle-income countries. WHO projects that diabetes deaths will double between 2005 and 2030.[5] The prevalence of overweight and obese children and teenagers strongly contributes to the spread of this chronic disease, according to the International Society of Paediatric and Adolescent Diabetes (ISPAD).[6] That means that there will be an increased demand for medical devices, such as blood glucose meters and insulin pumps, in the near future. The top ten countries, in numbers of people with diabetes, are: India, China, USA, Indonesia, Japan, Pakistan, Russia, Brazil, Italy, and Bangladesh.[7]

Against this backdrop, this chapter analyses the regulatory framework applicable to medical devices in the EU and UK. In its original form, the legislative framework for medical devices in the EU comprised of three main directives.[8] These directives covered three main device groups: medical devices, in vitro diagnostic medical devices, and active implantable medical devices. On 5 April 2017, new regulations on medical devices[9] and in-vitro-diagnostics[10] were adopted in the EU. The replacement of the original directives aimed at overcoming regulatory flaws identified by both manufacturers of devices in Europe and European Member States. Among the flaws, it appeared that the interpretation and application of the directives varied substantially between Member States (which undermined the free movement of medical devices within the internal market).[11] In addition, there were few gaps or uncertainties concerning the

---

4. S. Wild et al., *Global Prevalence of Diabetes: Estimates for the Year 2000 and Projections for 2030*, Diabetes Care 27 no. 5 1047, 1051 (May 2004).
5. *Health Topics: Diabetes: Data and Statistics*, WHO, http://www.euro.who.int/en/health-topics/noncommunicable-diseases/diabetes/data-and-statistics.
6. < http://web.ispad.org/sites/default/files/resources/files/ispad_guidelines_2009_-_nutrition.pdf >, 25 July 2016.
7. Wild, *supra* n. 4.
8. Council Directive 93/42/EEC of 14 June 1993 concerning medical devices; Directive 98/79/EC of the European Parliament and of the Council of 27 October 1998 on in vitro diagnostic medical devices; Council Directive 90/385/EEC of 20 June 1990 on the approximation of the laws of the Member States relating to active implantable medical devices.
9. Regulation (EU) 2017/745 of the Parliament and of the Council of 5 April 2017 on medical devices, amending Directive 2001/83/EC, Regulation (EC) No. 178/2002 and Regulation (EC) No. 1223/2009 and repealing Council Directives 90/385/EEC and 93/42/EEC.
10. Regulation (EU) 2017/746 of the European Parliament and of the Council of 5 April 2017 on in vitro diagnostic medical devices and repealing Directive 98/79/EC and Commission Decision 2010/227/EU.
11. Proposal for a Regulation of the European Parliament and of the Council on medical devices, and amending Directive 2001/83/EC, Regulation (EC) No 178/2002, and Regulation (EC) No 1223/2009.

status of certain products, such as devices manufactured by utilising non-viable human tissues or cells.[12]

The new regulations aim to address these flaws and allow rapid and cost-efficient market access for medical devices to the benefit of patients and healthcare professionals.[13]

The Regulation 2017/745 on medical devices entered into force on 26 May 2021, while the Regulation 2017/746 on in vitro diagnostic medical devices entered into force on 26 May 2022. In order to ease the reading of this chapter, we focus on the regulation on medical devices first (§19.02) and then scrutinise the regulation on in vitro diagnostic medical devices (§19.03). We also analyse the rules framing the advertising of medical devices (§19.04). This chapter further includes a brief overview of the medical device regulatory regime currently applicable in Great Britain post-Brexit (§19.05).

§19.02 MEDICAL DEVICES

The principal European legislation for medical devices is Regulation (EU) 2017/745 of 5 April 2017 on medical devices (Medical Devices Regulation (MDR)). The main objectives are to harmonise the medical device laws of the Member States of the EU, and to ensure the safety and protect the health of patients, users, and other persons.[14]

A medical device is a product that is used for medical purposes on humans. e.g., in diagnosis, prevention, monitoring, treatment, or surgery. Medical devices are divided into different classes depending on their intended purpose (§19.02[A]). This division determines the conditions under which these devices may be placed on the market in the EU (§19.02[B]). The Regulation also provides several obligations to economic operators intervening in the supply chain of medical devices (§19.02[C]) as well as various procedures to enable these operators to take any preventive or corrective actions (§19.02[D]).

[A] Notion of Medical Device

[1] Regulatory Definition of a Medical Device

Article 2 of the MDR defined a medical device as follows:

> a medical device is as any instrument, apparatus, appliance, software, implant, reagent, material or other article intended by the manufacturer to be used, alone or in combination, for human beings for one or more of the following specific medical purposes:

---

12. *Ibid.*
13. *Ibid.*
14. Recitals Directive 93/42/EEC; Antonio Dai Pra, *Healthcare Resource Guide: European Union* (15 Oct. 2019), https://2016.export.gov/industry/health/healthcareresourceguide/eg_main_10858 2.asp.

- diagnosis, prevention, monitoring, prediction, prognosis, treatment or alleviation of disease;
- diagnosis, monitoring, treatment, alleviation of, or compensation for, an injury or disability;
- investigation, replacement or modification of the anatomy or of a physiological or pathological process or state;
- providing information by means of in vitro examination of specimens derived from the human body, including organ, blood and tissue donations;

and which does not achieve its principal intended action by pharmacological, immunological or metabolic means, in or on the human body, but which may be assisted in its function by such means.

It results from this definition that a medical device is, first and foremost, a product that is intended by the manufacturer to be used for a medical purpose on human beings. This also include devices intended for the control or support of conception and products specifically intended for the cleaning, disinfection, or sterilisation of active devices.[15] It should be noted that 'implantable devices' have been explicitly included in the definition of 'medical device' by the MDR, which represents a change to the previous approach of regulating them separately.

However, this definition excludes devices intended to be used on animals which implies that these devices do not fall within the scope of the MDR. However, in contrast to the American system, the definition retained in the EU does not include devices that are solely intended to affect the structure or any function of the body without any specific medical purpose.

[2] Classification of Medical Devices

[a] General Principles

Medical devices are divided into four classes, ranging from low risk to high risk: Class I, IIa, IIb, and III.[16] Annex VIII of the MDR classifies medical devices according to their intended purpose.[17]

Class I medical devices with low risk include, for example, swabs, fixation bandages, and orthopaedic support devices. Class IIa applies to medical devices with a moderate risk, such as some invasive products or catheters. Products with a higher risk fall into Class IIb, for example, implants, surgical invasive single-use products, and contraception products. Class III governs high-risk products such as cardiac valves. For the original Directive, the European Commission had issued a set of guidelines on the classification of medical devices that also shows the purpose of medical device

---

15. Article 2(1) MDR.
16. Article 51(1) MDR.
17. Annex VII to MDR.

classification and explains how to carry out the classification.[18] So far, a comparably comprehensive set of guidelines has not been established for the MDR.

[b]   Classification Rules

The classification of a medical device depends on the potential risk that is associated with the technical design and manufacture of the device, as well as where and how on the human body it will be used.

In particular, classification is based on the following criteria:

- whether a medical device is non-invasive or invasive (in the sense that it is intended to be used surgically or inserted into a natural body orifice);
- the duration of its use;
- how much contact it has with blood, body liquids, or tissues that may be reintroduced into the body;
- how much contact it has with injured skin;
- whether it is related to heart, circulatory system, or central nervous system disease diagnosis or function;
- whether it is implantable or not (in the sense that it is introduced into the human body by surgical intervention);
- whether it emits ionising radiation, supplies energy to the human body, or is intended for recording X-rays;
- whether it incorporates a product that if used separately would be considered a medicinal product; and
- finally, whether it is used for contraception or the prevention of the transmission of sexually transmitted diseases.[19]

In addition, if a medical device is intended to be used in combination with another device, the classification rules apply separately to each medical device. Accessories to a medical device are classified in their own right separately from the medical device with which they are used.[20] Software that drives or influences the use of a medical device is automatically classified in the same class as the medical device to which it is related.[21] Medical devices must be classified based on their most critical specified use, and if several rules apply to the same device, the strictest rules resulting in the higher classification apply.[22]

As it pertains to standalone software as medical devices, the MDR provides that software intended to provide information which is used to take decisions with diagnosis or therapeutic purposes is generally classified as Class IIa.[23] The same rule

---

18. *Guidance Document - Classification of Medical Devices - MEDDEV 2.4/1 rev.9,* European Commission, http://ec.europa.eu/DocsRoom/documents/10337/attachments/1/translations.
19. *See* Annex VIII of MDR for a full description of the classification criteria.
20. Annex VIII of MDR, Ch. II, 3.2.
21. Annex VII of MDR, Ch. II, 3.3.
22. Annex VII of MDR, Ch. II, 3.5.
23. Rule 11 of Annex VIII of MDR.

applies for software which is intended to monitor physiological processes, except where specific dangers to the patient's health require a higher classification.

[B] Placing a Medical Device on the Market in the EU

In order to place a medical device on the European market, its manufacturer must demonstrate that it satisfies with the general safety and performance requirements provided in Annex I of the MDR. These requirements relate to the design and manufacture of the medical devices, as well as the information that their manufacturer supplies (§19.02[C][1]). Except for Class I medical devices, notified bodies are in charge of assessing the conformity of the devices with the general safety and performance requirements. For the majority of medical devices, clinical data are sufficient in order to establish their conformity with the general safety and performance requirements (§19.02[C][2]). The obligations pertaining to the placing of a medical device on the market lie on the shoulders of its manufacturer. However, in case the latter does not reside in the EU, it must designate an authorised representation within the EU (§19.02[C][3]).

[1] *General Safety and Performance Requirements for Marketing of Medical Devices*

Annex I of the MDR sets out the general requirements and any specific requirements that are imposed on the device based on its intended purpose. Section 1 of this Annex establishes the general principle applicable to all medical devices as follows:

> 1. Devices shall achieve the performance intended by their manufacturer and shall be designed and manufactured in such a way that, during normal conditions of use, they are suitable for their intended purpose. They shall be safe and effective and shall not compromise the clinical condition or the safety of patients, or the safety and health of users or, where applicable, other persons, provided that any risks which may be associated with their use constitute acceptable risks when weighed against the benefits to the patient and are compatible with a high level of protection of health and safety, taking into account the generally acknowledged state of the art.

The avoidance of risks does constitute an overriding importance. This is clearly reflected in the first chapter of Annex I to the MDR which emphasises the importance of a risk-management system and appropriate risk control measures.

Annex I of the MDR provides requirements with regard to two general aspects: on the one hand, the design and manufacture of the device and, on the other hand, the information supplied with the device.

Chapter 19: Medical Devices §19.02[B]

[a] *General Requirements Regarding the Design and Manufacture of the Medical Device*

The design and construction of all medical devices must be in accordance with the safety principles of Chapter I, taking into account the state of the art at the time of design and construction.[24] Risks involved in design and construction of medical devices must be eliminated or reduced as much as possible, and in case, any residual risks remain, the users of the concerned devices must be properly informed.[25]

According to the MDR, the following aspects – where appropriate – must be taken into account in the design and manufacture of a device:

- the choice of materials and substances used, particularly as regards toxicity and, where relevant, flammability;
- the compatibility between the materials and substances used and biological tissues, cells, and body fluids, taking account of the intended purpose of the device and, where relevant, absorption, distribution, metabolism, and excretion;
- the compatibility between the different parts of a device which consists of more than one implantable part;
- the impact of processes on material properties;
- where appropriate, the results of biophysical or modelling research the validity of which has been demonstrated beforehand;
- the mechanical properties of the materials used, reflecting, where appropriate, matters such as strength, ductility, fracture resistance, wear resistance, and fatigue resistance;
- surface properties; and
- the confirmation that the device meets any defined chemical and/or physical specifications.[26]

As explained above, medical devices and manufacturing processes must be designed to eliminate or reduce as far as possible the risk of infection to patients or users.[27]

[b] *General Requirements Regarding the Information to Be Supplied with the Device*

Medical devices must also be accompanied by information on safety, use, and the identity of the manufacturer, taking into account the likely training and knowledge of potential users of the medical device.[28] More particular essential requirements apply to particular medical devices, for example, devices with a measuring function, devices

---

24. Annex I of MDR, Ch. II.
25. *Ibid.*
26. Annex I of MDR. Ch. II (10.1).
27. Annex I of MDR, Ch.- II (11.1).
28. Annex I of MDR, Ch. III (23).

that produce or are associated with ionising radiation, and devices that are connected to or equipped with an energy source.[29]

In this regard, the MDR provides that each medical device shall enable the identification of the device and its manufacturer and detail any safety and performance information relevant to the user or any other person. However, the Regulation seems relatively flexible as to where these information must appear.[30] The manufacturer of a device may detail these information on the device itself, on the packaging or in the instructions for use. However, if the manufacturer has a website, the information concerning the device must be made available and kept up to date on the website.

Annex I of the MDR further details the information that should be contained on the label of the device, on the packaging which maintains the sterile condition of the device, and in the instructions for use of the device.

[2] Conformity Assessment Procedures

[a] Role of Notified Bodies

The MDR provides for conformity assessment procedures.[31] A manufacturer must follow particular conformity assessment procedures depending on whether the device is a Class I, IIa, IIb, or III device.[32]

Article 52 of the Regulation refers to the applicable Annexes depending on the classification of the device. The different conformity assessment procedures are described in Annexes IX (Conformity assessment based on a quality management system and on assessment of technical documentation), X (Conformity assessment based on type-examination), and XI (Conformity assessment based on product conformity verification).

If the medical device is a Class I device that is not placed on a market in a sterile condition as a reusable medical device and if it does not have a measuring function, the notified body does not have to be involved in the conformity assessment procedure. Class I devices have the lowest risks, so that the European legislator does not require the involvement of a notified body. Manufacturers of these devices must only declare the conformity of their products by issuing the EU declaration of conformity after drawing up a technical documentation. Several annexes of the MDR specify the information that a manufacturer must fill in the EU declaration of conformity[33] and the technical documentation.[34]

In contrast, as far as Class IIa, IIb, or III medical devices are concerned, the manufacturer must lodge an application for assessment of his or her quality system

---

29. Ibid.
30. Annex I of MDR, section 23.1.
31. Article 52 of MDR.
32. Ibid.
33. Article 19 of MDR, read together with Annex IV of MDR.
34. Annexes II and III of MDR.

with a notified body. Fulfilment of essential and other legal requirements is determined by a notified body in a formal conformity assessment procedure.

A notified body is a public or private organisation that has been accredited to validate the compliance of the medical device with the MDR. Notified bodies designate whether a medical device meets the required standards and thereby conforms to the Regulation.[35] The Member States must notify the Commission and other Member States of the bodies that they have designated for carrying out the tasks pertaining to the procedures referred to in the conformity assessment procedures in Article 42 of the MDR and the specific tasks for which the notified bodies have been designated. The Commission then assigns identification numbers to these notified bodies and publishes a list of notified bodies,[36] which is frequently updated.

Lists of notified bodies can be downloaded on the New Approach Notified and Designated Organisations (NANDO) website.[37] As there are multiple notified bodies in most Member States, the applicants can choose between the bodies. Although the notified bodies do not differ in their role, the option to choose between the listed notified bodies leads to a certain competition between the notified bodies, as they may charge different fees for their rendered services.

Notified bodies must be impartial, independent, and must be neither directly involved in the design, construction, marketing, or maintenance of the devices nor represent the parties engaged in these activities.[38]

Notified bodies can be set up under either private or public law, but they do not carry out their designated tasks by way of public power. Only the accreditation is an authoritative act based on public power.

In contrast with approval procedures for marketing medicinal products, the conformity assessment procedure for medical devices does not take place on a national level anymore. Although the approval for marketing the medical device is granted in a Member State by a national notified body, the approval is binding throughout the EU. This means that if a Belgian manufacturer of medical devices has passed a conformity assessment procedure with a notified body in Belgium, he or she may affix the CE mark and distribute the medical device in every Member State of the EU without any additional conformity assessment procedure.

[b]   Supporting Evidence

The conformity assessment procedure for all classes of medical devices involves a clinical evaluation of the device.[39] The objectives of clinical evaluation are: (a) to verify that, under normal conditions of use, a device performs in the way intended by the manufacturer and that it is designed, manufactured, and packaged in a suitable way;

---

35. Annex VII of MDR.
36. Article 43 of MDR.
37. *Nando Information System*, European Commission, https://ec.europa.eu/growth/tools-databases/nando/.
38. Annex VII of MDR (1.2).
39. Article 61 and Annex XIV of MDR.

and (b) to determine any undesirable side effects and assess whether these constitute risks.[40]

The clinical evaluation must follow a defined and methodologically sound procedure which is based on the following criteria:[41]

- a critical evaluation of the relevant scientific literature currently available relating to the safety, performance, design characteristics, and intended purpose of the device, where the following conditions are satisfied:
  it is demonstrated that the device subject to clinical evaluation for the intended purpose is equivalent to the device to which the data relate, and
  the data adequately demonstrate compliance with the relevant general safety and performance requirements;
- a critical evaluation of the results of all available clinical investigations; and
- a consideration of currently available alternative treatment options for that purpose, if any.

The clinical evaluation of a device must be documented and/or fully referenced in a clinical evaluation report which shall support the assessment of the conformity of the device.[42]

Finally, subject to certain exceptions,[43] in the case of implantable devices and class III devices, clinical investigations shall be performed to demonstrate the compliance with general safety and performance requirements. However, a manufacturer of a device is exempted from this obligation if it demonstrates that the following conditions are fulfilled:

- the device the marketing of which is intended is equivalent to an already marketed device manufactured by another manufacturer;
- the two manufacturers have a contract in place that explicitly allows the manufacturer of the second device full access to the technical documentation on an ongoing basis, and;
- the original clinical evaluation has been performed in compliance with the requirements of this Regulation; and
- the manufacturer of the second device provides clear evidence thereof to the notified body.

[c] CE Marking

When the manufacturer has performed the conformity assessment procedure, he or she must affix the CE marking.[44] The CE marking must be used for medical devices and for

---

40. Article 61 s. 1 of MDR.
41. Article 61 (3) of MDR.
42. Annex XIV of MDR, Part A (4).
43. Article 61(4) and (6) of MDR.
44. Article 20(1) of MDR.

in vitro diagnostic medical devices. As the MDR does not apply to in vitro diagnostic medical devices, the Regulation (EU) 2017/746[45] sets out separate provisions regarding CE marking for in vitro medical devices that are similar to the provisions set out by the Directive.

The only exceptions to the rule of CE marking are custom-made devices and devices intended for clinical investigation.[46] Custom-made devices are any devices specifically made in accordance with a duly-qualified medical practitioner's written prescription that gives – under his or her responsibility – specific design characteristics and is intended for the sole use of a particular patient.[47] A medical device intended for clinical investigation means any device intended for use by a duly-qualified medical practitioner when conducting investigations as referred to in section 2.1 of Annex X of the Directive in an adequate human clinical environment.[48]

Custom-made devices and devices intended for clinical investigation must undergo their own type of assessment procedure. Member States must not create any obstacle to custom-made devices if they meet the conditions in Article 52 paragraph 8 in combination with Annex XIII of the Regulation and devices intended for clinical investigation if they meet the conditions in Articles 62 to 80 and Article 82 and in Annex XV of the Regulation.[49] Custom-made devices must be accompanied by a statement referred to in section 1 of Annex XIII of the Directive that must be available to the particular patient identified by name, an acronym, or a numerical code.[50]

The CE marking is issued by the manufacturer, also called self-certification, if the medical device is a Class I device and does not need to be sterilised or is not used to measure a function. These medical devices can be placed on the market purely by self-certification. The manufacturer must draw up a declaration of conformity and affix the CE mark on the medical device.[51]

Products in Class Is, Im, IIa, IIb, or III must have a Certificate of Conformity issued by a notified body. The manufacturer must affix the CE mark on the medical device, which must be accompanied by the identification number of the notified body.[52]

[d] CE Labelling

The CE mark of conformity must always appear in a visible and legible form on a medical device.[53] Also, the instructions for use and the sales packaging must bear the CE mark.[54]

---

45. Regulation (EU) 2017/746, *supra* n. 10.
46. Article 20(1) MDR.
47. Article 2(3) MDR.
48. Article 2(46) MDR.
49. Article 21(1a) of MDR.
50. Article 21(2) of MDR.
51. Article 52(7) of MDR.
52. Article 20(5) of MDR.
53. Article 20(3) of MDR.
54. *Ibid.*

It is prohibited to affix marks or inscriptions that are likely to mislead third parties with regard to the meaning or the graphics of the CE marking. The CE mark can be either a stamp or a label as long as it is permanently affixed to the device.

Violations of the provisions regarding the fitting of a CE mark may be considered by national courts as a violation of unfair competition law. For example, if the CE mark falls below the minimum dimension of 5mm, a competitor can file for a preliminary injunction or initiate a main proceeding against the distributor or manufacturer. The court might then prohibit further distribution of the medical device until the fitting of the CE mark complies with the regulatory framework. Therefore, distributors and manufacturers should pay particular attention to labelling and fitting of the CE marking.

[e] Registration

The MDR contains a number of provisions[55] which provide for an online registration of certain information. This information is made publicly available at the European Data Base on Medical Devices (EUDAMED).[56]

[3] *The Responsibilities of Manufacturers of Medical Devices*

The MDR distinguishes three economic operators that are likely to play a specific role in the supply chain of medical devices: the 'manufacturer', the 'distributor', and the 'importer'. Under certain circumstances, the manufacturer should also have an 'authorised representative'.

The MDR defines these actors as follows:

- The 'manufacturer' is a natural or legal person who manufactures or fully refurbishes a device or has a device designed, manufactured, or fully refurbished, and places that device on the market under its name or trademark.[57]
- The 'importer' is any natural or legal person established within the EU who places a product from a third country on the EU market.[58]
- The 'distributor' is any natural or legal person in the supply chain, other than the manufacturer or the importer, who makes a product available on the market. This third category appears to be a residual category and cover any other economic operator which makes the product available on the market other than the manufacturer or the importer. In other words, in terms of reasoning, one must verify at first whether a specific economic operator is the manufacturer or the importer. In the negative case, the last stage is to verify whether or not this operator should be considered a distributor.

---

55. Articles 28, 29, 30, and 31 of MDR.
56. *Medical Devices: New regulations*, European Commission, https://ec.europa.eu/growth/sectors/medical-devices/new-regulations/eudamed_en.
57. Article 2(30) of MDR.
58. Article 2(33) of MDR.

Since the manufacturer places its device on the market, it bears the corresponding responsibilities detailed above. Article 10(1) of the MDR specified that, when placing their devices on the market or putting them into service, manufacturers shall ensure that they have been designed and manufactured in accordance with the general safety and performance requirements. However, if the manufacturer is located outside the EU, it shall have an authorised representative within the EU market.[59] According to MDR, an 'authorised representative' is a person who has received and accepted a written mandate from a manufacturer, located outside the EU, to act on the manufacturer's behalf in relation to specified tasks with regard to the latter's obligations under the Regulation.[60]

[C] Post-Market Surveillance, Vigilance, and Market Surveillance

The MDR requires the manufacturers to establish certain post-market surveillance procedures. In this respect, 'post-market surveillance' means all activities carried out by manufacturers in cooperation with other economic operators to institute and keep up to date a systematic procedure to proactively collect and review experience gained from devices they place on the market.[61]

Articles 83 to 86 of MDR set up specific requirements for post-market surveillance, especially regarding a post-market surveillance plan,[62] a post-market surveillance report,[63] and – for manufacturers of class IIa, class IIb, and class III devices – the requirement of periodic safety update reports.[64]

It is also mandatory for manufacturers of medical devices to report serious incidents and field safety corrective actions.[65] In this context, a 'serious incident' is defined as any incident that directly or indirectly led, might have led, or might lead to any of the following:

- the death of a patient, user, or other person;
- the temporary or permanent serious deterioration of a patient's, user's or other person's state of health;
- a serious public health threat.[66]

A 'field safety corrective action' means corrective action taken by a manufacturer for technical or medical reasons to prevent or reduce the risk of a serious incident in relation to a device made available on the market.[67]

---

59. Article 11(1) of MDR.
60. MDR, Article 2(32).
61. Article 2(60) of MDR.
62. Article 84 of MDR.
63. Article 85 of MDR.
64. Article 86 of MDR.
65. Article 87 of MDR.
66. Article 2(65) of MDR.
67. Article 2(68) of MDR.

For the reporting in context of Vigilance Measures, the MDR also provides for specific reporting obligations.[68]

The European legislator has also issued guidelines on a Medical Devices Vigilance System.[69] The guidelines describe the European system for the notification and evaluation of incidents and field safety corrective actions involving medical devices. Annex 3 of the guidelines contains several report forms. The forms require reporting of the model and/or catalogue number, the serial number, and/or the lot/batch number. Only information that is considered 'optional' is marked by the addition in brackets of 'if applicable'.

[D] Surveillance Role of Member States and Competent Authorities

With respect to devices that conform to a Member State's harmonised national standards, Member States must presume compliance with the essential requirements of the European Regulatory Framework.

Where a Member State observes that a device, when used for its intended purpose, may compromise the health and/or safety of patients or users, it must take steps to withdraw the device from the market or to restrict or stop the device from being placed on the market or used.[70] A Member State must immediately inform the Commission if it takes any steps of this kind, and it must indicate to the Commission the reasons why it has taken these steps.

The Commission must then consult with the parties. Following the consultation, the Commission may decide that the steps that the Member State has taken are justified or unjustified.

After a device has been placed on the market, Member States retain certain duties to record and evaluate information on any serious incidents that relate to the device. After carrying out an assessment, Member States must inform the Commission and other Member States of any steps taken or contemplated to minimise the recurrence of any reported incident.[71]

In practice, it is the competent authorities of Member States that fulfil the obligations and duties of Member States.

§19.03 IN VITRO DIAGNOSTIC MEDICAL DEVICES

The main European legislation for in vitro diagnostic medical devices is Regulation (EU) 2017/746 of 5 April 2017 on in vitro diagnostic medical devices (IVDR). This

---

68. Article 92 of MDR.
69. *Guidance document - Market surveillance - Guidelines on a Medical Devices Vigilance System - MEDDEV 2.12/1 rev.8*, European Commission, https://ec.europa.eu/docsroom/documents/32305/attachments/1/translations.
70. Article 95 of MDR.
71. Article 96 of MDR.

Regulation provides the rules concerning the placing on the market of in vitro diagnostic medical devices for human use and accessories for such devices in the EU. This Regulation also applies to performance studies concerning such in vitro diagnostic medical devices and accessories conducted in the EU.

This subchapter does not present in detail all the rules applicable to in vitro diagnostic medical devices; especially, considering the large amount of similarities with the rules applicable to medical devices in general. We essentially focus on the definition of an in vitro diagnostic medical device (§19.03[A]) and the rules determining their placing on the market in the EU (§19.03[B]).

[A]   Notion of in Vitro Diagnostic Medical Device

[1]   Regulatory Definition of In Vitro Diagnostic Medical Device

The Regulation 2017/746 definition of a medical device is identical to the definition of 'medical device' under the Regulation 2017/745.[72] This means that an in vitro medical device must first meet the general definition of a medical device. In addition, the product must be in line with the definition of 'in vitro diagnostic medical device'.

'In vitro diagnostic medical device' means any medical device that is a reagent, reagent product, calibrator, control material, kit, instrument apparatus, equipment, or system, whether used alone or in combination, intended by the manufacturer to be used in vitro for the examination of specimens, including blood and tissue donations, derived from the human body, solely or principally for the purpose of providing information:

- concerning a physiological or pathological state;
- concerning a congenital abnormality;
- to determine the safety and compatibility with potential recipients; or
- to monitor therapeutic measures.[73]

The Regulation 2017/746 does not apply to devices manufactured and used only within the same health institution and on the premises of their manufacture or used on premises in the immediate vicinity without having been transferred to another legal entity.[74] Accessories must be reviewed separately. 'Accessory' is not an in vitro diagnostic medical device, but it is intended specifically by its manufacturer to be used with an in vitro diagnostic medical device to enable that device to be used in accordance with its intended purpose or to assist the medical functionality of the in

---

72. Article 1(2) of IVDR.
73. Article 2(2) of IVDR.
74. Article 5(5) of IVDR.

vitro diagnostic medical device specifically and directly in terms of its/their intended purposes.[75]

[2] Classification of In Vitro Diagnostic Medical Devices

In vitro diagnostic medical devices shall be divided into classes A, B, C, and D, taking into account the intended purpose of the devices and their inherent risks. For a better understanding of the IVDR regulations, the new risk classes are summarised in the following table.

The presentation is based on the provisions of Article 47 of the IVDR in connection with its Annex VIII of the IVDR.

Class A	Products with a low risk, e.g., products for general laboratory use, accessories which possess no critical characteristics, buffer solutions, washing solutions, and general culture media and histological stains, intended by the manufacturer to make them suitable for in vitro diagnostic procedures relating to a specific examination.[76]
Class B	Products that do not pose a life-threatening danger, e.g., devices for the detection of pregnancy, fertility testing.[77]
Class C	Products that pose a significant, potentially life-threatening risk, e.g., devices intended to be used in screening, diagnosis, or staging of cancer.[78]
Class D	Products that can be life-threatening for more than one individual, e.g., devices for detection of the presence of, or exposure to, a transmissible agent that causes a life-threatening disease with a high or suspected high risk of propagation.[79]

For the classification of a device as 'in vitro medical device', the intended purpose of the manufacturer is therefore important. Advertising claims can have a serious impact on the classification of the device, as any advertising claim of the manufacturer can be taken into account to assess the intended purpose. Advertising should not be misused to declare and distribute a device simply as 'medical device', although it is clearly suited only for in vitro purposes.

---

75. Article 2(4) of IVDR.
76. Annex VIII of IVDR, Rule 5.
77. Annex VIII of IVDR, Rule 4.
78. Annex VIII of IVDR, Rule 3.
79. Annex VIII of IVDR, Rule 1.

[B] Placing an In Vitro Diagnostic Medical Device on the Market

[1] General Safety and Performance Requirements for Marketing In Vitro Diagnostic Medical Devices

In vitro diagnostic medical devices must meet the applicable essential requirements for marketing set out in Annex I of the IVDR, taking account of the intended purpose of the devices concerned. According to Annex I of the IVDR, an in vitro diagnostic medical device must achieve the performance intended by their manufacturer and shall be designed and manufactured in such a way that, during normal conditions of use, they are suitable for their intended purpose.[80] Before placing the device on the market, the manufacturer must demonstrate that the device is safe and effective and that it does not compromise the clinical condition or the safety of patients, or the safety and health of users or, where applicable, other persons, provided that any risks which may be associated with their use constitute acceptable risks when weighed against the benefits to the patient and are compatible with a high level of protection of health and safety, taking into account the generally acknowledged state of the art.

In addition, the design and manufacture of an in vitro diagnostic medical device must be in such a way that they are suitable for their purposes as specified by the manufacturer, taking account of the generally acknowledged state of the art. In particular, the device must achieve the manufacturer's performance standards for:

- analytical sensitivity;
- diagnostic sensitivity;
- analytical specificity;
- diagnostic specificity;
- accuracy;
- repeatability;
- reproducibility, including control of known relevant interference; and
- limits of detection.[81]

[2] Conformity Assessment Procedures

The conformity assessment procedure for class A devices should be carried out under the sole responsibility of manufacturers, since such devices pose a low risk to patients.[82]

For class B, class C, and class D devices, an appropriate level of involvement of a notified body is compulsory:[83] Classes B and C devices require a conformity

---

80. Annex I of IVDR, Chapter 1, point 1.
81. Annex I of IVDR, Chapters I and II.
82. Article 48(10) of IVDR; *see also* recital 56 of IVDR.
83. *See* Recital 56 of IVDR.

assessment as specified in Chapters I and III of Annex IX, which also requires the involvement of a notified body.[84]

Manufacturers of Class D devices have to comply with a conformity assessment as specified in Chapters I, II, and III of Annex IX of the IVDR.[85]

The main difference between in vitro diagnostic medical devices and other medical devices is that the examination is mainly performed in a reagent. In vitro diagnostic medical devices usually do not come in touch with patients themselves but with specimens derived from the human body. Therefore, the perceivable risk of in vitro medical devices is often different from those medical devices that directly touch the human body.

In vitro medical devices for self-testing are an important exception to this rule. A 'device for self-testing' is defined as any device intended by the manufacturer to be able to be used by laypersons in a home environment.[86] Devices also fall under the provisions of 'device for self-testing' if they are used in hospitals or by a medical practitioner, as long as they are intended for use by laypersons in a home environment.

In vitro diagnostic medical devices for self-testing must be distinguished from so-called point of care tests. Point of care tests are in vitro diagnostic medical devices that are mostly used in hospitals in the emergency or operation room without any specific specimen preparation for single measurements. Their use does not require an exhaustive experience or training in laboratory diagnostics. However, for determining whether the device is a 'device for self-testing', again the intended purpose by the manufacturer is decisive.

In vitro medical devices for self-testing must be designed and manufactured in such a way that they perform appropriately for their intended purpose, taking into account the skills and the means available to users and the influence resulting from variation that can reasonably be anticipated in users' technique and environment. The information and instructions provided by the manufacturer should be easily understood and applied by the user.[87] In particular, the manufacturer must ensure that the device is easy to use by the intended lay user at all stages of the procedure, and that the risk of user error in the handling of the device and in the interpretation of the results is reduced as far as practicable.[88] Where reasonably possible, the in vitro medical devices for self-testing must include user control – that is, a procedure by which the user can verify that, at the time of use, the product will perform as intended and be warned if the device has failed to provide a valid result.[89]

There are further marketing specifications for in vitro medical devices regarding information supplied by the manufacturer. As far as devices for self-testing are concerned, the test results need to be expressed and presented in a way that is readily understood by a layperson. Information must be provided to the user about action to be

---

84. Article 48(7,9) of IVDR.
85. Article 48(3) of IVDR.
86. Article 2(5) of IVDR.
87. Annex I of IVDR, Chapter III.
88. Annex I of IVDR, Chapter II.
89. Annex 1 of IVDR, Chapter II, point 19.3.

taken in case of positive, negative, or indeterminate results, and on the possibility of false positive or false negative results. Specific particulars may be omitted provided that the other information supplied by the manufacturer is sufficient to enable the user to use the device and to understand the results produced by the device. The information provided must include a statement clearly directing that the user should not make any decision of medical relevance without first consulting his or her medical practitioner. The information must also specify that when the device for self-testing is used for monitoring of an existing disease, the patient should only adapt the treatment if he or she has received the appropriate training to do so.[90]

The conformity assessment procedures result in affixing the CE marking. We refer the reader to the relevant sections on subchapter §19.02.

§19.04 HOW TO ADVERTISE MEDICAL DEVICES

In contrast to medicinal products, the European legislator has only provided few advertising rules for medical devices. Article 7 of MDR solely states that 'in the labelling, instructions for use, making available, putting into service and advertising of devices, it shall be prohibited to use text, names, trademarks, pictures, and figurative or other signs that may mislead the user or the patient with regard to the device's intended purpose, safety and performance'. In particular, it is prohibited to mislead the user or patient by:

- ascribing functions and properties to the device which the device does not have;
- creating a false impression regarding treatment or diagnosis, functions or properties which the device does not have;
- failing to inform the user or the patient of a likely risk associated with the use of the device in line with its intended purpose;
- suggesting uses for the device other than those stated to form part of the intended purpose for which the conformity assessment was carried out.[91]

Due to the lack of certainty as to content, each Member State must find its own rules for the advertising of medical devices. Hence, there is no full harmonisation regarding EU law, and there are different national provisions and measures in the Member States. In Belgium, for example, the Royal Decree on medical devices strictly prohibits advertising for devices not bearing the CE marking. However, at fairs, exhibitions, and demonstrations, the presentation of devices which do not bear a CE marking shall be tolerated provided that a visible sign clearly indicates their non-conformity and the impossibility of putting these devices into service before they are brought into conformity by the manufacturer or his or her authorised representative.[92]

---

90. Annex I of IVDR, Chapter III, point 20.4.2.
91. Article 7 of MDR.
92. Royal Decree of 18 March 1999, Article 17.

In some Member States, codes of conduct or codes of practice contain advertising rules. Several national associations have issued codes of conduct or codes of practice that apply to the marketing of medical devices. The Association of British Pharmaceutical Industry (ABPI), which is a trade association for companies in the UK, and the Association of British Healthcare Industries (ABHI) have Codes of Practice that their members must adhere to. The ABHI is the leading and largest industry association for the medical technology sector in the UK.[93] In Spain, most companies that market medical devices belong to the Association of Manufacturers of Medical Devices (FENIN), and the member companies are bound by FENIN's Code of Conduct.[94] In Italy, most companies that market medical devices belong to the Medical Devices Industry Association (Assobiomedica).[95] In Germany, the Association of Diagnostic Industry (Verband der Diagnostica-Industrie e.V. – VDGH) represents most of the German diagnostic industry and has issued a Code of Conduct regarding business practices concerning manufacturers of in vitro diagnostics.[96] This underlines the impact of associations and their codes of conduct or codes of practice on the market.

For further general information on advertising, please refer to Chapter 9.

§19.05 UK

The UK's exit from the EU on 31 January 2020 resulted in a divergence in medical device regulations governing Great Britain, Northern Ireland, and the EU. Because the EU MDR and IVDR came into effect after the Brexit transition period, being on 26 May 2021 and 26 May 2022, respectively, the previous EU Directives 93/42/EEC on Medical Devices (Previous EU MDD), 98/79/EC on in vitro diagnostic medical devices (Previous EU IVDD), and 90/385/EEC on active implantable medical devices (Previous EU AIMDD) remain effective in Great Britain under the UK Medical Devices Regulations 2002 (UK MDR). In comparison, under the Northern Ireland Protocol, the EU MDR and IVDR applies to Northern Ireland as it does to the EU Member States, noting that the EU MDR now covers the regulation of active implantable devices in addition to general medical devices; that is, there is no separate regulation for active implantable medical devices.

Although the Previous MDD and Previous IVDD presently regulate medical devices in Great Britain, the UK Medicines and Healthcare products Regulatory Agency (MHRA) recently completed a consultation process on the future regulation of medical devices in the UK, which will lead to the reform of the medical device regulatory framework in Great Britain. The initial expectation was that the reformed regulatory framework would come into effect during the latter part of 2023. However, recent developments suggest a twelve-month extension to the timeline for the implementation

---

93. www.abhi.org.uk.
94. www.fenin.es.
95. www.assobiomedica.it.
96. www.vdgh.de.

of the reforms, accounting for the extensions to certain Brexit transitional arrangements.[97] This area of regulation is in flux, so relevant Government guidance should be monitored closely.

Despite the divergence between Great Britain and Northern Ireland, the MHRA remains the competent authority for both regions. The remainder of this section of this chapter covers the regulation of medical devices in Great Britain under the UK MDR.

[A]   Definition of Medical Device

Part II of the UK MDR applies to medical devices and their accessories.[98] Accessories are treated as medical devices in their own right.[99]

The UK MDR defines a medical device as

> an instrument, apparatus, appliance, material or other article, whether used alone or in combination, together with any software necessary for its proper application, which –
>
> (a) is intended by the manufacturer to be used for human beings for the purpose of –
>   (i) diagnosis, prevention, monitoring, treatment or alleviation of disease,
>   (ii) diagnosis, monitoring, treatment, alleviation of or compensation for an injury or handicap,
>   (iii) investigation, replacement or modification of the anatomy or of a physiological process, or
>   (iv) control of conception; and
> (b) does not achieve its principal intended action in or on the human body by pharmacological, immunological or metabolic means, even if it is assisted in its function by such means,
>
> and includes devices intended to administer a medicinal product or which incorporate as an integral part a substance which, if used separately, would be a medicinal product and which is liable to act upon the body with action ancillary to that of the device.[100]

It should be noted that 'implantable devices' and 'in vitro diagnostic medical devices' (IVDs) are covered by different Parts of the UK MDR, reflecting the three separate EU Directives (*see* §19.05[D] on IVDs).

[B]   Borderline Products

Like the Commission, the MHRA has also issued guidance on 'borderline products'[101] for the demarcation between medical devices and medicinal products, albeit not as

---

97. *See* https://www.gov.uk/government/publications/implementation-of-the-future-regulation-of-medical-devices-and-extension-of-standstill-period/implementation-of-the-future-regulations.
98. Regulation 6 of UK MDR.
99. *Ibid.*
100. Regulation 2(1) of UK MDR.
101. 'Borderline products: how to tell if your product is a medicine' (published on 6 January 2021).

detailed as the MDCG 2022-5 guidance document. The MHRA's guidance document is similarly, not legally binding, but helpfully provides non-exhaustive lists of issues the MHRA considers when deciding whether a product is a medicine or not.

[C] Classification of Medical Devices

Under the UK MDR, medical devices are divided into four classes, ranging from low risk to high risk: Class I, IIa, IIb, and III.[102] Annex IX of the Previous EU MDD, as adopted by the UK MDR, classifies medical devices according to their intended purpose, the rules of which may result in a lower class for some devices compared to under the EU MDR.

According to Annex IX of the Previous EU MDD, the classification of a medical device depends on the potential risk that is associated with the intended purpose of the device, how long it is intended to be in use for and if the device is invasive, implantable or active, or contains substance, which in its own right is considered to be a medicinal substance. All active implantable medical devices and their accessories are Class III. See §19.05[D] on IVDs.

If a medical device is intended to be used in combination with another device, the classification rules apply separately to each medical device. Accessories to a medical device, except active implantable devices, are classified in their own right separately from the medical device with which they are used.[103] Software that drives or influences the use of a medical device is automatically classified in the same class as the medical device to which it is related.[104] Medical devices must be classified on the basis of their most critical specified use, and if several rules apply to the same device, the strictest rules resulting in the higher classification apply.[105]

[D] In Vitro Diagnostic Medical Devices

The regulation of IVDs is covered by Part IV of the UK MDR. An IVD must first meet the general definition of a 'medical device' under the UK MDR (as cited above in §19.05[A]), as it is:

> any medical device which:
>
> (a) is a reagent, reagent product, calibrator, control material, kit, instrument, apparatus, equipment or system, whether used alone or in combination; and
> (b) is intended by the manufacturer to be used *in vitro* for the examination of specimens, including blood and tissue donations, derived from the human body, solely or principally for the purpose of providing information –
>   (i) concerning a physiological or pathological state,
>   (ii) concerning a congenital abnormality,

---

102. Regulation 7(1) of UK MDR.
103. Annex IX of Previous EU MDD, Chapter II, 2.2.
104. Annex IX of Previous EU MDD, Chapter II, 2.3.
105. Annex IX of Previous EU MDD, Chapter II, 2.5.

(iii) to determine the safety and compatibility of donations, including blood and tissue donations, with potential recipients, or
(iv) to monitor therapeutic measures,

and includes a specimen receptacle but not a product for general laboratory use, unless that product, in view of its characteristics, is specifically intended by its manufacturer to be used for *in vitro* diagnostic examination.[106]

Part IV of the UK MDR does not apply to devices manufactured and used only within the same health institution and on the premises of their manufacture or used on premises in the immediate vicinity without having been transferred to another legal entity.[107]

Like general medical devices, an 'accessory' intended specifically by its manufacturer to be used with an IVD to enable that device to be used in accordance with its intended purpose must be reviewed separately to the device.[108]

Presently, in vitro diagnostic medical devices are grouped into four categories based on their perceived risk for the purposes of conformity assessment routes.[109] For general in vitro diagnostic medical devices, the conformity assessment procedure involves a self-declaration of conformity whereas self-test in vitro diagnostic medical devices may require lodgement with a UK Approved Body for examination of the device before a declaration is made, depending on the risk category of the device. As explained in the EU sections of this chapter, the differences in how general in vitro diagnostic medical devices and self-testing in vitro diagnostic medical devices are regulated is to account for the intended purpose of the device, such as the skills required to use the device (whether it is by a professional or lay person) and the influence on the user resulting from the device.

[E] Software as Medical Devices

The MHRA has issued guidance specifically dealing with software as medical devices, which assists with determining whether software is a 'medical device' that is regulated under the UK MDR in Great Britain.[110] If software is not incorporated into a device and the software is not provided as part of a system or module in a system, consideration must be had as to whether or not such software is a computer program or functional document in of itself. Once satisfied that the software is a computer program or functional document, the key threshold question to consider is if the software is intended to have a medical purpose, which is referrable to the purposes in the definition of 'medical device' under the UK MDR (cited in §19.05[A] above). If the intended purpose of the software is only:

---

106. Regulation 2(1) of UK MDR.
107. Regulation 33 of UK MDR.
108. Regulation 32(1) of UK MDR.
109. Regulation 40 of UK MDR.
110. 'Guidance: Medical device stand-alone software including apps (including IVDMDs)' (v1.08 published in July 2021).

- for patient or professional medical education;
- to monitor fitness/health/wellbeing;
- to store or transmit medical data without change;
- to be used for administrative functions, such as to book appointments, request prescriptions, or have virtual consultations;
- for decision support by providing information to enable a healthcare profession to use their knowledge to make a clinical decision; or
- data or a database for storing data,

then it is unlikely regulated as a medical device under the UK MDR. The intended purpose of the manufacturer may be informed by the device's labelling, instructions for use, and any promotional material.

[F] Placing Medical Devices on the UK Market

To legally place medical devices or put it into service on the Great Britain market, manufacturers and importers must comply with the requirements of the UK MDR and UK General Product Safety Regulations 2005 (GPSR), including in relation to general safety and performance requirements, market and product marking, and registration with the MHRA.[111]

[1] Registration

The Government guidance as at the time of writing[112] provides that to register medical devices with the MHRA, for placement on the Great Britain market, the medical devices must conform with the UK MDR or in the alternative, the EU MDR or EU IVDR until 30 June 2023. Further, until 30 June 2023 (although it has been suggested that this will be extended to July 2024),[113] the CE mark received under the Previous MDD, AIMDD, and IVDD remains acceptable on the Great Britain market to the extent they remain valid in the EU market.

UK-based manufacturers and UK Responsible Persons (appointed by non-UK manufacturers) may register medical devices with the MHRA. For Northern Ireland-based manufacturers, registration with the MHRA for the Northern Ireland market would allow placement on the Great Britain market without additional registration in Great Britain.

After the Brexit transition period ended on 31 December 2020, businesses bringing products from the EU into Great Britain are now likely to be importers, rather than distributors, resulting in additional legal compliance requirements. Where the

---

111. Regulations 7A-10 of UK MDR for general medical devices; regulations 21A-24 of UK MDR for active implantable medical devices; regulations 33A-36 of UK MDR for in vitro diagnostic medical devices.
112. *See* https://www.gov.uk/guidance/regulating-medical-devices-in-the-uk#registrations-in-great-britain (dated 1 January 2022), which is in the process of being updated to reflect the proposed extension of certain timelines.
113. *See* footnote 97 above.

importer is not the UK Responsible Person, they would be required to inform the relevant manufacturer or UK Responsible Person of their intention to import the device, enabling the manufacturer or UK Responsible Person to inform the MHRA of the details of the importer.

Registrations with the MHRA are available via the Public Access Database for Medical Device Registration, not EUDAMED.

[2] Conformity Assessment Procedures

The UK MDR provides for conformity assessment procedures, the route of which depends on the class of the device.[114] The procedures are relatively similar to the EU process, involving the lodgement of an application for assessment of the quality system for Class IIa, IIb, and III (and sterile and measuring Class I) medical devices but with a UK Approved Body instead of EU Notified Bodies.

[3] UKCA Marking

The UK Conformity Assessed (UKCA) marking came into effect on 1 January 2021 for goods newly placed on the market in Great Britain and from July 2024, all devices placed on the Great Britain market must conform with the UKCA marking requirements.[115] Although the MHRA will continue to accept the CE mark that is used in the EU, EEA, and Northern Ireland in Great Britain until July 2024, those devices must have been CE marked under, and fully conform with, the applicable EU legislation.

Once the manufacturer has performed the conformity assessment procedure, the UKCA mark must be affixed to the medical device as required by law.[116]

The only exceptions to the rule of UKCA marking are custom-made devices, devices intended for clinical investigation, in vitro diagnostic medical devices for performance evaluation, and a non-compliance device used in exceptional circumstances (such as humanitarian grounds).[117]

Similar to CE labelling, manufacturers and distributors should pay close regard to the specific requirements for affixing the UKCA marking in a clearly visible, legible, and indelible form, violation of which may constitute non-compliance with UK consumer protection law.[118]

It is likewise prohibited to affix marks or inscriptions that are likely to mislead third parties with regard to the meaning or the graphics of the UKCA marking.

---

114. Regulations 13, 27, and 40 of UK MDR.
115. Regulation 10 UK MDR.
116. Regulations 11, 25, and 37 of UK MDR.
117. Regulations 12, 26, and 39 of UK MDR.
118. Regulations 10, 24, and 36.

[4] Post-Market Surveillance, Vigilance, and Market Surveillance

Similar to the EU MDR and IVDR, the UK MDR requires the manufacturers of medical devices to establish certain post-market surveillance procedures where they continuously monitor the performance of the medical device. Manufacturers must submit vigilance reports to the MHRA when adverse incidents occur in the UK via the Manufacturer's On-line Reporting Environment (MORE) system. However, unlike the EU MDR and IVDR, most of the requirements around post-market surveillance and vigilance for Great Britain are not explicitly set out in the UK MDR but covered in guidance material.

§19.06 HOW TO ADVERTISE MEDICAL DEVICES

In contrast to medicinal products, which are regulated under the UK Human Medicines Regulations 2012 (*see* Chapter 9), the advertising of medical devices in Great Britain is not regulated under specific legislation. It is regulated under general consumer advertising laws, being the Consumer Protection from Unfair Trading Regulations 2008 (UK CPR) and Business Protection from Misleading Marketing Regulations 2008, in combination with self-regulation by industry bodies.

The key consumer law issues worth noting for the advertisement of medical devices are:

- commercial practices which are in all circumstances considered unfair (listed in Schedule 1 of the UK CPR);[119]
- misleading advertising;[120] and
- aggressive advertising.[121]

Relevant industry self-regulatory bodies include:

- Proprietary Association of Great Britain for self-care medical devices;
- Association of British HealthTech Industries for medical devices aimed at healthcare professionals; and
- Advertising Standards Authority, as the UK's independent advertising regulator that administers the non-broadcast Advertising Code (CAP Code) and broadcast Advertising Code (BCAP Code).

The CAP Code and BCAP Code contains specific rules in relation to medicines, medical devices, health-related products, and beauty products, which are outlined in Chapter 9.

---

119. Regulation 3 of UK CPR.
120. Regulations 5 and 6 of UK CPR.
121. Regulation 7 of UK CPR.

CHAPTER 20
Parallel Trade

Christian Lindenthal, Pieter Erasmus & Jonathan Edwards[*]

§20.01 INTRODUCTION TO PARALLEL TRADE

The trade of medicinal products within the Member States of the EU (parallel trade) is facilitated by the fact that differences in price for identical medicinal products exist between the Member States. The parallel trader buys medicinal products that are marketed in Member States at low prices and sells these products in Member States where the same products are marketed at considerably higher prices. The pharmaceutical company marketing its medicinal product with different prices in the respective Member States is thus involuntarily faced with competition in respect of its own products, which are imported by parallel traders from a market at a lower price.

The parallel trade of medicinal products is distinct from the trade of other goods due to the fact that a Marketing Authorisation (MA) is required to put a medicinal product on the market (with few exceptions, for example, import on a named-patient basis). Different kinds of MAs exist, thus different procedures have to be obeyed.

Parallel trade is characterised as *parallel distribution* when it involves medicinal products that are centrally authorised, or as *parallel import* if the products only have national authorisations in the concerned Member States.

For the parallel distribution of centrally authorised medicinal products from one EU Member State to another, the very same medicinal product is already authorised in the Member State of origin and the Member State of destination, and the parallel trader does not need to apply for an MA for the product but only notify the central authority, the European Medicines Agency (EMA) about the intended parallel distribution.

Parallel import of nationally authorised medicinal products requires the parallel trader to obtain an MA for the medicinal product in the Member State of destination, as

---

[*] The authors wish to acknowledge *Hanneke Later-Nijland*, the author of the earlier edition of this Chapter.

the specific parallel imported product has only been authorised for the Member State of origin. The necessary national MA for the parallel imported product can be obtained according to a 'simplified procedure' in the Member State of destination, which is addressed in further detail in §20.03[B] below.

In addition, parallel-traded products must comply with European and national regulations. For example, it is required that relevant information on the medicinal product, such as its application must be provided in the official language of the Member State of destination and that the parallel trader or repackager is indicated on the medicinal product package. The necessary changes in the packaging can infringe trademark rights, if the trademarks owned by the pharmaceutical company marketing the product must be reaffixed on the repacked product by the parallel trader. Also, medicinal products are often covered by patent rights. Therefore, the marketing of a medicinal product covered by patent rights without the consent of the patentee could, in principle, infringe the existing patent rights in the respective Member States of destination.

§20.02 PARALLEL DISTRIBUTION LAW

In general, a medicinal product cannot be put on the market in a Member State without an MA. Therefore, each imported medicinal product must be authorised in the Member State of destination, and it must comply with the applicable laws for medicinal products of that Member State.

The EU MA is valid throughout the EU, and the marketing of a centrally authorised medicinal product requires no additional national authorisation for this product. In addition, the EU MA encompasses all linguistic versions of the labelling and package leaflet for all authorised package sizes. As a consequence, products put on the market in one Member State may, subject to certain requirements, be put on the market under the EU MA in any other part of the EU by a parallel distributor, using the already authorised applicable version for the labelling and package leaflet.

[A] EMA Notice

Regulation 726/2004 requires mandatory notification to the EMA of parallel distribution of centrally authorised products. Specifically, in terms of Article 57(1)(o) of Regulation 726/2004, the EMA is charged with, among other things:

> Checking that the conditions laid down in Union legislation on medicinal products and in the Marketing Authorisations are observed in the case of parallel distribution of medicinal products authorised in accordance with this Regulation.

The notification must be submitted to the EMA, which, since 11 February 2019, must be completed via the EMA's so-called IRIS online platform.[1] Once the applicant

---

1. *See* the EMA's IRIS Regulatory & Scientific Information Management Platform website, https://iris.ema.europa.eu/. In terms of the aforesaid website, IRIS aims to make the handling of

has successfully submitted the application for the parallel distribution notice via the IRIS online platform,[2] the EMA takes approximately sixty days from the time it confirms receipt of the notification application[3] to decide whether or not the proposed a parallel-distributed medicinal product complies with the terms of the EU MA. The status of the application for the parallel distribution notice can be checked by the applicant at any time on the IRIS online platform.

The information that must be provided to the EMA for an initial notification of parallel distribution includes the following:

- A cover letter clearly indicating the name, strength, pharmaceutical form, EU number, and pack-size of the medicinal product in question.
- An editable format of the package leaflet in the language of the Member State of destination in compliance with the latest version of the EU MA.
- A colour scan of all sides of the relabelled and/or repacked outer packaging, as well as the relabelled inner packaging, as they will be marketed in the Member State of destination, clearly showing the braille text label if required according to the MA. It is noted that when submitting the first initial notification for parallel distribution of a centrally authorised product, the parallel distributor will be requested to provide the EMA with images of the finalised product. Mock-ups do not suffice in this regard.

Detailed and updated guidance of all necessary information, including the applicable fees to be paid, are available on the EMA website.[4]

[B] Necessary Licences for Parallel Distributors

A parallel distributor is normally engaged in activities subject to Articles 76 et seq. of Directive 2001/83/EC, addressing the wholesale distribution of medicinal products. Accordingly, a parallel distributor is required to have a valid wholesale distribution licence.

Also, a manufacturing authorisation might be required if the parallel distributor engages in manufacturing activities as defined in Articles 40 et seq. of Directive 2001/83/EC and as interpreted by the European Court of Justice (ECJ). Total and

---

product-related regulatory procedures more efficient and user-friendly. By way of further background, the IRIS platform was initially developed in June 2018 for purposes of orphan designation applications and has since been expanded upon to cover other regulatory and scientific procedures. *See* further the *IRIS Guide to Registration and RPIs* (Version 2.3) for general information regarding IRIS registration process, https://www.ema.europa.eu/en/documents/regulatory-procedural-guideline/iris-guide-registration-rpis_en.pdf.

2. *See* the *IRIS Guide for Parallel Distribution Applicants* (22 April 2021), https://www.ema.europa.eu/en/documents/regulatory-procedural-guideline/iris-guide-parallel-distribution-applicants_en.pdf.
3. *See* Frequently asked questions about parallel distribution on the EMA website, https://www.ema.europa.eu/en/human-regulatory/post-authorisation/parallel-distribution/frequently-asked-questions-about-parallel-distribution.
4. *Ibid.*

partial manufacturing are defined to include dividing up, packaging, and repackaging.[5] A parallel distributor might remove blister packs from the original external packaging and insert the packs into new external packaging. The distributor might also add new user instructions and information in the applicable language, or fix self-stick labels.[6] If the parallel distributor carries out these activities itself, a manufacturing authorisation is required.

A manufacturing authorisation includes authorisation for the wholesale distribution of the medicinal products covered by the authorisation.[7] Therefore, no additional wholesale distribution licence is necessary if a manufacturing authorisation has been obtained for the parallel-distributed product.

[C] Other Requirements

[1] Changes in the Package or Label

Although the centrally authorised medicinal product has a valid MA in all Member States, certain changes to the packaging might be necessary for the parallel distributor to comply with EU law, as interpreted by ECJ case law. The case law of the ECJ requires the repackager and the manufacturer of the original product to be identified on the medicinal product.[8]

As a general note, the EMA advises that only minor changes, which are agreed to by the EMA, are permitted to be introduced by the parallel distributor in the text of the labelling/package.[9]

The EMA requires the following mandatory information on the *outer labelling* of the product: the manufacturer responsible for the batch release (as mentioned in the package leaflet); the words '*parallel distributor/parallel distributed by*' (followed by the name and optionally the address/logo), or the words '*re-packager/repackaged by*' (followed by the name and optionally the address/logo); and the name of the product in Braille, if required in terms of section 16 of the labelling requirements of the Annexes to the EU MA.[10] In addition, some Member States of destination also require specific information regarding, for example, the price of the medicinal product, reimbursement

---

5. *See* Article 40(2) of Directive 2001/83/EC.
6. See, for example, *MPA Pharma v. Rhone-Poulenc Pharma*, Case No. 232/94 [1996] ECR 3671; *Bristol-Myers Squibb v. Paranova*, Joined Cases No. 427/93, 429/93, and 436/93 [1996] ECR 3457; *Eurim-Pharm v. Beiersdorf*, Joined Cases No. 71/94, 72/94, and 73/94 [1996] ECR 3603.
7. *See* Article 77 of Directive 2001/83/EC.
8. See, for example, *Bristol-Myers Squibb v. Paranova, supra* n. 6.
9. *See* under sub-heading '10. What are additional requirements reflecting that the product is distributed in parallel?' under main heading 'Parallel distribution notification check' of the frequently asked questions about parallel distribution on the EMA website, at https://www.ema.europa.eu/en/human-regulatory/post-authorisation/parallel-distribution/frequently-asked-questions-about-parallel-distribution.
10. *Ibid.*

conditions of social security organisations, the legal status for supply to the patient or identification, and authenticity.[11]

The EMA further requires certain information to appear on the *internal package leaflet*, including the following: 're-packager/repackaged by:' (followed by the name and optionally the address/logo); trademark owner identity; internal reference number of the parallel distributor; manufacturer responsible for batch release (same as the manufacturer identified on the outer labelling); etc.[12] As mentioned above, in respect of internal package leaflets, only minor changes are permitted to be introduced by the parallel distributor in the text of the labelling/package leaflet in the following situations and only with the agreement of an EMA assessor: when the composition of the product changes, the parallel distributor must ensure that the composition mentioned in the leaflet/labelling of the parallel-distributed pack corresponds with the actual composition of the pack; and in the context of a parallel distributor having to open a sealed pack for purposes of parallel distribution.[13]

Labelling must appear in the official language or languages of the Member State where the product is placed on the market. Specifically, Title V of Directive 2001/83/EC[14] requires the use of the official language for information relating to, *inter alia*, the name of the product, its active substance, pharmaceutical form and contents, special warnings, method of administration, storage precautions, therapeutic indications, and expiry date. Therefore, the parallel distributor might have to replace the original information with the respective, already authorised, information for the Member State of destination.

Further, the centrally authorised product might have different package sizes that are not used in every Member State. As mentioned above, the distributor may have to change the package of the parallel-distributed product to comply with the specific package size in the Member State of destination.

The potential problems and requirements regarding the necessary changes in view of the abovementioned requirements are discussed below in §20.04[C] in the context of trademarks.[15]

[2] Notice to Local Authorities

After the notification procedure at the EMA has been completed, the parallel distributor of the medicinal product must provide notification to the national competent

---

11. So-called Blue Box Requirements. In this regard, *see Notice to Applicants Guideline on the Packaging Information of Medicinal Products for Human Use Authorised by the Union* (April 2021, Revision 14.6), available at https://ec.europa.eu/health/sites/health/files/files/eudralex/vol-2/2018_packaging_guidelines_en.pdf.
12. *See* under sub-heading '10. What are additional requirements reflecting that the product is distributed in parallel?' under main heading 'Parallel distribution notification check' of the frequently asked questions about parallel distribution on the EMA website: https://www.ema.europa.eu/en/human-regulatory/post-authorisation/parallel-distribution/frequently-asked-questions-about-parallel-distribution.
13. *Ibid.*
14. *See* Article 63 of Directive 2001/83/EC.
15. *See* § 20.04[C].

authority.[16] The information to be provided in this notification regularly will encompass information on the medicinal product, the parallel distributor, and information on the repackaging.

[3] MA Updates

The parallel distributor must ensure that the labelling and the package leaflet are in conformity with the latest annexes to the EU MA for the parallel-distributed product. The labelling and package leaflet must be in strict compliance with the latest terms of the EU MA applicable to the parallel-distributed product and the respective version for the Member State of destination.[17] Additional text on the outer packaging or in the leaflet such as *'procured from within the EU'* or *'imported by'* will not be accepted by the EMA. As mentioned above,[18] only minor changes may be permissible with the agreement or upon request of the EMA. If the composition of a medicinal product changes, the parallel distributor has to ensure that the composition mentioned on the labelling/leaflet corresponds with the actual composition of the pack.

[4] Maintenance Notice

The EMA has to be notified about any changes that occur to medicinal products, e.g., new Annexes, labelling, Member States of destination/origin, or repackagers. The recommended way of this category of notification is via the annual update, a 'DO and TELL' procedure combining all scopes of changes occurring within one year.[19] An alternative is the notification of a change, a 'TELL and DO' procedure by which notices can be submitted at any time.

[5] Quality Control

Should a parallel distributor identify a quality defect of the product when sourcing it, or as a result of subsequent handling in the distribution chain, such parallel distributor

---

16. *See* Article 76 of Directive 2001/83/EC.
17. *See*, among others, under sub-heading '8. What are the post-PD obligations of a parallel distributor?' under main heading 'General' of the frequently asked questions about parallel distribution on the EMA website, available at https://www.ema.europa.eu/en/human-regulatory/post-authorisation/parallel-distribution/frequently-asked-questions-about-parallel-distribution.
18. *See* § 20.02[C].
19. For further guidance regarding annual updates, *see*, among others, under sub-heading '5. What is an annual update?' under the main heading 'Safety updates/bulk changes/annual update' of the frequently asked questions about parallel distribution on the EMA website, available at https://www.ema.europa.eu/en/human-regulatory/post-authorisation/parallel-distribution/frequently-asked-questions-about-parallel-distribution.

is accountable and must report this to the applicable national competent authority as well as the EMA.[20]

A parallel distributor must procure products only from a wholesale distribution authorisation holder in the source state. This supplier is consequently obliged to inform the parallel distributor of any recall activity. If a parallel distributor learns about possible quality defects in the original product, the distributor must have systems in place to confirm whether the affected product was received, trace its utilisation, and initiate recall procedures, if necessary.[21] Also, the parallel distributor must follow the EMA notification procedure and should inform the EMA about possible quality defects.[22]

The parallel distributor making changes to the packaging materials of a parallel-distributed product must have a system for reviewing complaints and for effective recall. A parallel distributor is obliged to inform the competent authority of any defect that might result in a recall of the medicinal product, which will, if necessary, initiate the so-called rapid alert system.[23]

[6] Falsified Medicines

In order to tackle the growing problem of falsified medicines, i.e., medicinal products which contain no or even a different active ingredient than authorised, entering the supply chain, the EU adopted Directive 2011/62/EC (Falsified Medicines Directive - FMD), amending Directive 2001/83/EC. The FMD which had to be transposed by the Member States into their national law by the beginning of 2013 can affect parallel distributors in their capacity as a wholesaler or as a manufacturer of medicinal products.

Wholesalers now have to verify the newly introduced safety features and inform the national competent authority and, where applicable, the MA holder (MAH), of medicinal products they receive or are offered which they identify as falsified or suspect of being falsified.[24] Further, before bringing medicinal products from one Member State into another, wholesalers have to inform the MAH and the EMA about their intention.[25]

Parallel distributors packaging or repackaging medicinal products – and therefore engaging in manufacturing activities – have to apply new safety features if the old ones

---

20. *See*, among others, under sub-heading '4. What are the parallel distributors' responsibilities regarding quality defects?' under the main heading 'Post-Parallel distribution notice guidance' of the frequently asked questions about parallel distribution on the EMA website, available at https://www.ema.europa.eu/en/human-regulatory/post-authorisation/parallel-distribution/frequently-asked-questions-about-parallel-distribution.
21. *Ibid*. *See also* Article 80 of Directive 2001/83/EC.
22. *Ibid*.
23. *Ibid*.
24. *See* Article 80 of Directive 2001/83/EC.
25. *See* Article 76 of Directive 2001/83/EC.

are removed after having verified that the medicinal product concerned is authentic as has not been tampered with.[26]

§20.03 PARALLEL IMPORTATION

Parallel imports of nationally authorised products do not have the same MA in the Member State of origin and the Member State of destination. The respective product does not have an EU-wide authorisation but a national authorisation in the Member State of origin. In most cases, a national authorisation exists in the Member State of destination for a similar product. However, this is an independent authorisation for putting the respective nationally authorised product on the market in the Member State of destination. The parallel importer must therefore obtain a separate MA for the parallel imported product in the Member State of destination.

[A] Parallel Importation Law

Under certain circumstances, a simplified procedure is available to obtain an MA for a parallel-imported medicinal product in the Member State of destination. The simplified procedure is based on the principle of free movement of goods, as established in Articles 34 et seq. of the Treaty on the Functioning of the European Union (TFEU).[27]

The parallel importation of medicinal products is a lawful form of trade within the internal market according to Article 34 TFEU. Derogations from this principle of free movement of goods are only possible with regard to the grounds provided by Article 36 TFEU. The relevant exemptions in view of the parallel trade of medicinal products are the protection of human health and life and the protection of industrial and commercial property.

As stated in Directive 2001/83/EC,[28] the essential aim of any rules governing the production, distribution, and use of medicinal products must be to safeguard public health. However, this objective must be attained by means that will not hinder the development of the pharmaceutical industry or trade in medicinal products within the EU. Consequently, the question arises as to which requirements a parallel importer

---

26. *See* Article 47a of Directive 2001/83/EC.
27. Article 34 TFEU states that *'Quantitative restrictions on imports and all measures having equivalent effect shall be prohibited between Member States'*. Article 36 TFEU provides an exception to the prohibition of quantitative restrictions and measures having equivalent effect between Member States, namely that 'The provisions of Articles 34 and 35 shall not preclude prohibitions or restrictions on imports, exports or goods in transit justified on grounds of public morality, public policy or public security; the protection of health and life of humans, animals and plants; the protection of national treasures possessing artistic, historic or archaeological value; or the protection of industrial and commercial property. Such prohibitions or restrictions shall not, however, constitute a means of arbitrary discrimination or disguised restriction on trade between Member States'.
28. Recitals 1 and 2 of Directive 2001/83/EC.

Chapter 20: Parallel Trade §20.03[B]

must fulfil and, in particular, what kind of documentation the parallel importer must provide to obtain the necessary MA for the parallel imported medicinal product in the Member State of destination.

[B] The Simplified Procedure

The simplified procedure for obtaining an MA for a parallel imported product and its requirements have been developed by the ECJ to promote the free movement of goods within the EU. The Member States must adjust their practice to the case law of the ECJ on parallel importation, which establishes the requirements and prerequisites of the simplified procedure. The simplified procedure is available for medicinal products that are not marketed for the first time in the Member State of destination. Products are considered to be not 'marketed for the first time' if they are identical or essentially similar to products that are already marketed in the Member State of destination.

The parallel importer who buys a product authorised in a Member State is not in possession of all relevant information for obtaining an authorisation in the Member State of destination, as is required for a product that is marketed for the first time in that Member State. Therefore, in general, the importer is not able to provide all necessary information to obtain a 'normal' national MA for that product without the assistance of the manufacturer or the authorities of the Member State of destination. Reliance on assistance from the manufacturer must be avoided, because otherwise the manufacturer (or its licensee) could, of course, impede parallel imports simply by merely refusing to produce the necessary documents.[29] In this regard, the ECJ stated that the national authorities possess legislative and administrative measures to obtain such documents.[30] If the documents to prove conformity with the national requirements can be produced by others, a requirement to authorise the parallel import only if the parallel importer produces said documents violates the free movement of goods according to Articles 34 et seq. of the TFEU.[31]

The development of the case law of the ECJ and the requirements of the simplified procedure are briefly outlined in the following paragraphs.

Officier van Justitie v. De Peijper[32] was an early and fundamental case on parallel imports. The ECJ held that national authorities must not obstruct parallel importations disproportionately if the medicinal product has been granted an MA in the Member State of origin and the imported product is in every respect similar to a medicinal product that has already received an MA in the Member State of destination.[33]

In the *De Peijper* decision, the ECJ was concerned with the question raised during criminal proceedings instituted in The Netherlands against a Dutch trader who was accused of having infringed the Netherlands' Public Health Legislation by supplying pharmacies with medical preparations that were imported from the UK without the

---

29. *Officier van Justitie v. De Peijper*, Case No. 104/75 [1976] ECR 613.
30. Ibid.
31. Ibid.
32. Ibid.
33. Ibid.

consent of the Dutch authorities. The authorities required documents for the 'certification' and thus authorisation of the import, which the parallel importer could not present without the assistance of the manufacturer of the medicinal product or the Dutch authorities. In this case, the product was lawfully marketed in several Member States, including the UK and The Netherlands, was manufactured by the same group of manufacturers, and the imported product from the UK was identical to the product already authorised in The Netherlands. The ECJ held that this legislation, which makes it possible for a manufacturer and its representatives to enjoy a monopoly on the importation and marketing of a product by simply refusing to produce the necessary documents, must be regarded as unnecessarily restrictive and therefore in conflict with the free movement of goods.[34]

In *The Queen v. The Medicines Control Agency, ex parte. Smith & Nephew Pharmaceuticals Ltd.*,[35] the ECJ addressed the issue of necessary prerequisites for obtaining an MA for a parallel imported medicinal product and affirmed the reasoning of the decision in *De Peijper*. The ECJ clarified the requirement of similarity of the medicinal product, which allows for a simplified authorisation procedure for the imported medicinal product. In *The Queen v. The Medicines Control Agency, ex parte. Smith & Nephew Pharmaceuticals Ltd.*, the imported medicinal product was manufactured by different legal entities in the Member State of origin and the Member State of destination, but it was manufactured under a licence granted by the same licensor. The ECJ held that if the product is sufficiently authorised in the Member State of origin and is 'essentially similar' to an already authorised product in the Member State of destination, only limited documentation must be provided to obtain an authorisation for the imported medicinal product. Specifically, the ECJ held that:

> When the competent authority of a Member State concludes that a proprietary medicinal product covered by a Marketing Authorisation in another Member State and a proprietary medicinal product for which it has already issued a Marketing Authorisation are manufactured by independent companies pursuant to agreements concluded with the same licensor and that those two products, although not identical in all respects, have at least been manufactured according to the same formulation, using the same active ingredient, and that they also have the same therapeutic effects, it must treat the imported product as being covered by the latter Marketing Authorisation unless there are countervailing considerations relating to the effective protection of the life and health of humans. If the competent national authority concludes that the proprietary medicinal product to be imported does not satisfy those criteria, a new Marketing Authorisation is required.

In other words, products that are not identical (e.g., due to differences in view of the excipients) might nevertheless be treated as 'essentially similar' under certain criteria, and a simplified authorisation procedure can be used by the parallel importer.

When addressing the question of sufficient similarity and whether or not the parallel importer has a right to obtain an MA in accordance with the simplified

---

34. *Ibid.*
35. *The Queen v. The Medicines Control Agency, ex parte Smith & Nephew Pharmaceuticals Ltd.*, Case No. 201/94 [1996] ECR 5819.

procedure, the ECJ has taken into account whether or not the imported product and the product already authorised in the Member State of destination are manufactured by the same company or companies belonging to the same group. The ECJ also looks at whether or not independent manufacturers contract with the same licensor, creating a common origin of the medicinal products.[36] In a subsequent decision, *Kohlpharma v. Bundesrepublik Deutschland*,[37] the ECJ stated that the absence of such a common origin does not in itself constitute a ground for refusing an MA for a parallel-imported medicinal product. If a common origin with regard to the manufacturers does not exist between the referenced product and the imported product, the parallel importer may demonstrate by means of available and accessible information that the imported product does not differ significantly. In case, the parallel importer does not have access to all necessary information but has made at least a plausible argument that the two medicinal products do not differ significantly, the respective national authority must obtain the necessary information, including information that it can obtain in cooperation with the health authorities in other Member States.[38]

[C] General Requirements for the Simplified Procedure

If the parallel importer is able to show that the imported product does not differ significantly from the referenced product in the Member State of destination for the purpose of assessing safety and efficacy, the competent authorities must decide whether or not to grant an MA based on the fullest information possible, including information that they could obtain by cooperation with the health authorities in other Member States.[39]

Therefore, according to the requirements established by the ECJ for the simplified procedure, the national competent authorities must assess the essential similarity of an imported medicinal product with the referenced authorised medicinal product. If the products are sufficiently similar, the parallel imported medicinal product must be authorised under a simplified procedure.[40]

The ECJ further clarified that the MA of an essentially similar product in the Member State of destination does not have to be valid at the time of importation.[41] The parallel importation with reference to the former MA is still possible if the authorisation in the Member State of destination has expired or has been withdrawn for other reasons than protection of public health and the imported product is sufficiently authorised in the Member State of origin.[42] However, a parallel importer cannot rely on an essentially

---

36. *Officier van Justitie v. De Peijper*, Case No. 104/75 [1976] ECR 613 Case 104/75; *The Queen v. The Medicines Control Agency, supra* n. 35.
37. *Kohlpharma v. Bundesrepublik Deutschland*, Case No. 112/02 [2004] ECR 3369.
38. *Ibid.*
39. *Ibid.*
40. *Ibid.*
41. *Ferring Arzneimittel GmbH v. Eurim-Pharm Arzneimittel GmbH*, Case No. 172/00 [2002] ECR 6891.
42. *Ibid.*

similar product if the MA of the referenced product was revoked or withdrawn to protect human life and health.

The national simplified procedures for obtaining an MA for a parallel imported medicinal product must be in accordance with these general principles established by the ECJ; that is, they must provide a simplified procedure for a parallel importer to obtain an MA. Therefore, the national competent authorities must provide for procedures in which the parallel importer can obtain an MA by establishing a sufficient similarity of the parallel imported medicinal product with the reference product. A table summarising the national procedural differences is provided at the end of the Chapter.

§20.04   INTELLECTUAL PROPERTY LAW

[A]   Introduction

In general, medicinal products are often covered by patent rights and the packaging is labelled with protected trademarks. These Intellectual Property (IP) rights are a potential obstacle for the parallel trade of medicinal products.

ECJ decisions clarify the ability of a patent or trademark holder to prevent the importation of medicinal products. According to the ECJ, only the protection of the 'specific subject matter' and 'essential function' of an IP right can justify a restriction of the free movement of goods according to Article 34 TFEU.[43] According to the case law of the ECJ, once a product is placed on the market within the EU by the right holder, or with the consent of the right holder (e.g., by a licensee or affiliate), the IP rights are exhausted within the EU.[44] The right holder cannot enforce exhausted rights and the free movement of goods prevails.

[B]   Patent Rights and Parallel Trade

Patents provide for the right to prevent third parties from exploiting the patented invention without authorisation. Patents are granted for inventions that are new, involve an inventive step, and are susceptible to industrial application. Patents on a medicinal product may cover the active ingredient, methods of production of the medicinal product, and/or the use of a substance for the preparation of medicament for the treatment of a certain disease. The duration of patent protection is twenty years post-application for the patent. However, due to the lengthy process of obtaining marketing approval for medicinal products, upon launch of a medicinal product there is on average only ten years of protection left. To compensate for this, the protection for a specific medicinal product granted by a patent can be extended by a Supplementary

---

43. *Centrafarm v. Sterling*, Case No. 15/74 [1974] ECR 1147; *Merck v. Primecrown Ltd.*, Joined Cases No. 267/95 and 268/95 [1996] ECR 6285.
44. *See*, e.g., *Zino Davidoff S.A. v. A&G Imports Ltd.*, Joined Cases No. 414/99 through 416/99 [2001] ECR 8691.

Protection Certificate (SPC) for a maximum of five additional years, subject to the specific prerequisites. To facilitate the development and accessibility of medicinal products for use in the paediatric population, a further so-called paediatric extension of the SPC for another six months is available if certain conditions are met. Thus, the maximum possible duration of protection is 25.5 years.

[1]   Exhaustion of Patent Rights

The owner of a patent could, in principle, use the patent rights to prevent third parties from marketing products covered by these rights in the Member State of destination, thereby preventing the parallel trade of its product within the EU.

In view of this conflict with the free movement of goods, the ECJ developed case law on the exhaustion of patent rights, which limits the patent owner's right to enforce the right against trade between Member States. This principle of exhaustion applies unless the protection of the 'specific subject matter' of the patent right justifies the restriction of the free trade between Member States.

In the case *Merck v. Primecrown Ltd.*,[45] the ECJ held that the 'specific subject matter' of a patent right is essentially the exclusive right of the inventor to put the product on the market for the first time. This specific subject matter of the patent right is exhausted if the product is sold with the consent of the patentee in a Member State.[46]

According to ECJ case law, the principle of exhaustion even applies where products were placed on the market in a Member State where patent protection, as granted in the Member State of destination, could not be obtained for the parallel-traded product. The ECJ found it sufficient that the product was marketed in the Member State of origin with the consent of the owner of the patent in the Member State of destination.[47] The ECJ, in *Merck v. Primecrown Ltd.*, held that:

> It is for the holder of the patent to decide, in the light of all the circumstances, under what conditions he will market his product and to decide whether or not to market it in a Member State in which there is no protection under the law for the product in question, but once he makes his choice he must then accept the consequences of that choice as regards free movement of the product within the common market, this being a fundamental principle forming part of the legal and economic circumstances which the holder of the patent must take into account in determining how to exercise his exclusive right.

In other words, the patent right is exhausted, and parallel trade cannot be prohibited, if the product is lawfully marketed in another Member State by the patentee him- or herself, with his or her consent, or by a person economically or legally dependent on the patentee.

---

45. *Merck v. Primecrown Ltd.*, *supra* n. 43.
46. *See*, e.g., *Centrafarm v. Sterling*, *supra* n. 43; *Centrafarm v. Winthorp*, Case No. 16/74 [1974] ECR 1183.
47. *Merck v. Primecrown Ltd.*, *supra* n. 43.

A patent right is not subject to exhaustion if the patentee has not consented to the commercialisation. In *Pharmon v. Hoechst*,[48] the imported medicinal product was manufactured in a Member State of origin by the holder of a compulsory licence granted in respect of a parallel patent held by the same patentee. Therefore, the patentee could not freely determine whether to license the respective patent right in the Member State of origin. In these circumstances, the ECJ found that there was no consent by the patentee, and thus there was no exhaustion of the patent right within the EU.[49]

It should be noted that, according to ECJ case law, consent is not assumed and the IP right can be enforced if conditions or limitations set out in a licensing contract are breached to the extent that the conditions or limitations in question relate directly to essential features of the IP right concerned.[50]

[2] Specific Mechanism

An important exception to the principle of exhaustion is the so-called Specific Mechanism with regard to parallel trade from the Central and Eastern European countries that acceded to the EU during 2004.[51] The Specific Mechanism enables the holder or beneficiary of a patent or an SPC to enforce such rights against parallel trade from certain new Member States under specific circumstances, even if the product was put on the market in these new Member States with his or her consent. To implement this, the respective Acts of Accession provide in Annexes[52] that:

> With regard to [the respective Central and Eastern European countries], the holder or beneficiary, of a patent or supplementary protection certificate for a pharmaceutical product filed in a Member State at a time when such protection could not be obtained in one of the above mentioned new Member States for that product, may rely on the rights granted by that patent or supplementary protection certificate in order to prevent the import and marketing of that product in the Member State or States where the product in question enjoys patent protection or supplementary protection, even if the product was put on the market in that new member State for the first time by him or with his consent.
>
> Any person intending to import or market a pharmaceutical product covered by the above paragraph in a Member State where the product enjoys a patent or supplementary protection shall demonstrate to the competent authorities in the

---

48. *Pharmon v. Hoechst*, Case No. 19/84 [1985] ECR 2281.
49. *Ibid.*
50. *Greenstar-Kanzi v. Jean Hustin*, Case No. 140/10 for a community plant variety right.
51. May 2005: Czech Republic, Estonia, Hungary, Latvia, Lithuania, Poland, Slovak Republic, Slovenia; January 2007: Bulgaria, Romania; July 2013: Croatia.
52. Annex IV to Accession Treaty with regard to the Czech Republic, Estonia, Hungary, Latvia, Lithuania, Poland, Slovak Republic, Slovenia, signed 16 April 2003; Annex V, Ch. 1 to the Accession Treaty with regard to Bulgaria and Romania, signed 25 April 2005; Annex IV of the Accession Treaty with regard to Croatia, signed 9 December 2011. The above text follows the wording from the Accession Treaties with the Czech Republic et al. and Bulgaria et al., the text from the Accession Treaty with Croatia is basically identical safe for some very slight editorial amendments.

Chapter 20: Parallel Trade §20.04[B]

application regarding that import that one month's prior notification has been given to the holder or beneficiary of such protection.

The Specific Mechanism with regard to the abovementioned new Member States was enacted to address various disparities in patent protection between the old and new Member States. One of the obvious disparities is the late introduction of patent protection for pharmaceutical compounds and SPCs. Protection for pharmaceutical compound claims and SPCs became available in the new acceding Member States on the following dates:

Accession State	Patent Protection Introduced	Supplementary Protection Certificates Available From
Czech Republic	1 January 1991	10 May 2000
Slovak Republic	1 January 1991	1 July 2002
Romania	21 January 1992	1 January 2007
Slovenia	4 April 1992	1 May 2004
Croatia	1 January 1993	1 July 2013
Latvia	31 March 1993	20 April 1995
Poland	16 April 1993	1 May 2004
Bulgaria	1 June 1993	1 January 2007
Lithuania	1 February 1994	1 January 2002
Estonia	23 May 1994	1 January 2000
Hungary	1 July 1994	1 May 2004

The Specific Mechanism exception will apply to patents that provide product protection for the active ingredient, if the patent had been filed in the old Member States prior to the above-referenced dates.

However, the wording of the Specific Mechanism is not limited to compound claims, so that under its wording, it can arguably be applied also to other claim categories, such as process or use claims, provided that the claims were not available in the accession country from which the parallel trade shall be sourced at the time of filing in the country of destination. Therefore, the arguments regarding the applicability of the Specific Mechanism need to be assessed on a claim-by-claim basis.

Some of the new Member States (e.g., Hungary and the Baltic States) enacted different kinds of 'transitional protection' or 'pipeline protection' in their legislation, enabling the patentee to obtain product protection at a later stage in the new Member State, although that kind of protection was not available at the date of filing of the parallel patent in the old Member States. Furthermore, in some of the new Member States, an application filed prior to the date when 'ordinary' patent protection entered into force may have already been examined and granted according to the new provisions of the patent law. It should be noted, however, that the wording of the Specific Mechanism addresses only the availability of protection in the accession countries at the time of filing in the destination country.

Finally, the question has been raised if in the case where an SPC is invoked, the decisive date for assessing availability of the protection shall be the filing date of the SPC in the destination country and not the filing date of the underlying basic patent. In its decision in *Pfizer Ireland Pharmaceuticals v. Orifarm GmbH*, the ECJ established that the relevant date is the time when the application for a basic patent was filed.[53] In the same decision, the ECJ further clarified that the Specific Mechanism also applies to the paediatric extension available for SPCs.[54]

As mentioned above, the assessment of whether the Specific Mechanism applies requires a detailed analysis of the exact wording of the patent claims granted in the Member State of destination and the situation at the time of filing in the respective new Member State from which the parallel trade of the medicinal product is intended. Thus, the abovementioned dates are not a strict timeline regarding the applicability of the Specific Mechanism, but the applicability must be evaluated on a case-by-case basis.

The Specific Mechanism requires the parallel trader to demonstrate to the competent authorities that one month's advance notice of the intended parallel trade from one of the abovementioned new Member States has been given to the holder or beneficiary of a patent or SPC. As specified in the table at the end of the Chapter, a number of the local regulatory authorities have specified that it shall also be possible to notify the holder of the MA for the reference product. Whether or not such notice to the MAH is considered correct under the Specific Mechanism has been the subject of a referral by the UK Court of Appeal to the ECJ in the *Merck Canada v. Sigma* case.[55] The ECJ ruled in February 2015 that the notification must be given to the holder, or beneficiary, of the patent or the SPC.

Another question referred to the ECJ in the *Merck Canada* case deals with the consequences of the notified party not reacting to the notification, i.e., with the question of whether it is a requirement for invoking a right under the Specific Mechanism that the patent holder has upon notification demonstrated his intention to exercise this option. In this case, the right holder had originally remained silent after receiving the parallel import notification under paragraph 2 of the Specific Mechanism in June 2009 but initiated infringement proceedings in June 2011 when the defendant had been on the market for almost a year. The ECJ ruled that if such right holder or beneficiary does not indicate the intention to oppose a proposed importation during the one-month waiting period, the person proposing to import the pharmaceutical product in question may legitimately apply to the competent authorities for authorisation to import the product, and where appropriate, import and market it. Thus, the Specific Mechanism denies right holders the possibility of relying on his right under the mechanism with regard to any importation and marketing of the pharmaceutical product carried out before such an intention was indicated.

Finally, a third question is part of the referral, dealing with the issue whether it is sufficient that the applicant for regulatory approval notifies even if the actual import

---

53. *Pfizer Ireland Pharmaceuticals v. Orifarm GmbH*, 21 June 2018, Case No 681/16, margin 57.
54. *Ibid.*, margin 73.
55. *Merck Canada v. Sigma*, 15 February 2015, Case No 539/13.

will later be carried out by a different company within the same group.[56] In other words, the question is who should give the notification. The ECJ ruled here that it is not required that the person intending to import or market the pharmaceutical product in question him- or herself should notify, provided that it is possible from the notification to identify that person clearly.

As described above, the regulatory authorities only investigate whether notification has been made but do not assess the patent protection in this regard. Thus, the assessment as to whether the Specific Mechanism applies, and the legal responsibility for enforcing the rights in accordance with the Specific Mechanism, remains with the holder of a patent or SPC. The above ECJ ruling demonstrates the importance for right holders to take notifications under the Specific Mechanism seriously and to seek advice in order to be able to react quickly.

The national differences with regard to the Specific Mechanism are set out in a table at the end of the Chapter.

[C] Trademark Law and Parallel Trade

The packages of medicinal products bear the manufacturer's distinctive signs, which are usually subject to trademark protection.

Under ECJ case law, the free movement of goods (in terms of Article 34 of the TFEU) must prevail, and IP rights cannot be invoked against the importation of goods unless the specific subject matter of the IP right, here the trademark right, is affected. A trademark right grants the trademark owner the right to put products bearing the trademark into circulation for the first time and to protect the owner from competition with products bearing the trademark illegally.[57] The trademark also serves to create goodwill for the customer. Therefore, the essential function of a trademark is to guarantee the consumer that the product bearing the trademark has been manufactured under the control of the trademark owner, and that there has been no subsequent influence on the product.[58] It derives from this that the trademark owner is, in principle, entitled to prevent the importation of goods that have been repacked, as the repacking interferes with the above-described scope of protection.

As has been described above in this Chapter,[59] certain changes to the packaging might be necessary to comply with the EU law, as complemented by ECJ case law, or other regulatory or pharmaceutical provisions applicable to medicinal products. According to the ECJ case law, trademark protection does not, in general, exclude the entitlement of the parallel trader to repack and trade repacked products within the EU. In *Hoffmann-La Roche v. Centrafarm*[60] and subsequent

---

56. *Ibid.*, margin 50.
57. *Centrafarm v. Sterling, supra* n. 43.
58. *See,* among others, *Centrafarm v. Winthorp, supra* n. 46; *Pfizer v. Eurim-Pharm,* Case No. 1/81 [1981] ECR 2913.
59. *See,* among others, § 20.02[C].
60. *Hoffmann-La Roche v. Centrafarm,* Case No. 102/77 [1978] ECR 1139.

decisions,[61] the ECJ has held that a trademark protection is subject to exemptions; that is, the trademark owner is not entitled to rely on the trademark rights if the trademark protection results in a disguised restriction of the free trade within the EU. A disguised restriction occurs when:

- the use of the trademark right contributes to the artificial portioning of the market between Member States;
- the repackaging cannot adversely affect the original condition of the product;
- the importer had given prior notice of the import to the trademark owner; and
- the repackager is named on the new packaging.[62]

The principles established by the ECJ have not become obsolete after the codification of exhaustion of trademark rights in Article 7 of the Directive 89/104/EEC. Article 7 of Directive 89/104/EEC and its implementations in the national trademark laws must be interpreted in view of the primary legislation and thus also in view of Articles 34 et seq. of the TFEU and its interpretation by the ECJ. Therefore, although the repackaging and reaffixing of the trademark, in principle, might preclude the exhaustion of the trademark right, it also has to be assessed whether the enforcement of the trademark right results in a disguised restriction of free trade.

In subsequent decisions, the ECJ clarified and developed the conditions under which a parallel trader is permitted to change the original packaging of medicinal products. The ECJ established five criteria for assessing whether or not the trademark holder can prohibit the parallel trade of the repacked product. If the five BMS conditions,[63] as explained in the following sections [1] to [5], are all satisfied, the trademark holder cannot invoke its rights against the parallel trade of repackaged medicinal products.

[1] The Repackaging Does Not Affect the Product

The original product is not affected if the repackaging does not involve a risk that the product inside the packaging will be exposed to tampering or a risk that the repacking will affect the original condition. It is for the national courts to decide in each case whether or not this requirement is fulfilled.[64] However, the ECJ clarified that the original product cannot be affected if the outer package is replaced, but the internal packaging is not touched, and it is not affected by making the manufacturer's trademark visible through the new external packaging.[65] Also, the original packing is not affected if the original product is packed in more than one package, and only the outer package is affected by the repacking (e.g., removal of blister packs from the original packaging by the repackager and insertion of the original product in new

---

61. See, e.g., *Centrafarm v. American Home Products Co.*, Case No. 3/78 [1978] ECR 1823; *Pfizer v. Eurim-Pharm*, supra n. 58.
62. *Hoffmann-La Roche v. Centrafarm*, supra n. 60.
63. Named after *Bristol-Myers Squibb and others v. Paranova*, Joined Cases No. 427/93, 429/93, and 436/93 [1996] ECR 3457, where these principles have been established.
64. *MPA Pharma v. Rhone-Poulenc Pharma*, supra n. 6.
65. *Pfizer v. Eurim-Pharm*, supra n. 58.

external packaging).⁶⁶ The ECJ also held that if blister packs are cut or batch numbers reprinted with the authorisation and under supervision of public authorities, it may be assumed that the original product is not affected.⁶⁷

Despite the foregoing principle, the ECJ, however, also acknowledged that the original condition of the product inside the packaging might be indirectly affected where, for example:⁶⁸

- the external or inner packaging of the repackaged product, or a new set of user instructions or information, omits certain important information or gives inaccurate information concerning the nature, composition, effect, use or storage of the product, or
- the packaging of the repackaged product is not such as to give the product adequate protection, or
- an extra article inserted into the packaging by the importer and designed for the ingestion and dosage of the product does not comply with the method of use and the doses envisaged by the manufacturer.

[2] The Repackaging Is Not Likely to Damage Reputation

Where it is established that repackaging of the medicinal product is necessary for further marketing in the Member State of destination, the presentation of the packaging should be assessed only against the condition that it should not be such as to be liable to damage the reputation of the trademark or that of its proprietor.⁶⁹ However, the presentation of the new packaging must not be assessed against the criterion that the adverse effect on the trademark rights should be the minimum possible.⁷⁰

The reputation of the trademark is damaged if the new packaging is of poor quality or untidy.⁷¹ However, a potential damage to the reputation is not limited to cases where the repackaging is defective, of poor quality, or untidy. The repackaged pharmaceutical product could be presented inappropriately, and therefore damage the trademark's reputation, where the carton or label detracts from the image of reliability and quality attaching to such a product.⁷² Whether or not the presentation of the repacked product damages the trademark's reputation is a question of fact that the national court decides based on the circumstances of each case.⁷³

With regard to cases of de-branding or co-branding, the ECJ found in *Boehringer Ingelheim II*⁷⁴ that the fact that a parallel importer does not affix the trademark to the new exterior carton ('de-branding') or applies either his own logo or a house-style or

---

66. *MPA Pharma v. Rhone-Poulenc Pharma*, supra n. 6.
67. *Eurim-Pharm v. Beiersdorf*, supra n. 6.
68. *Bristol-Myers Squibb and others v. Paranova*, supra n. 63, margin 65; *Eurim-Pharm v. Beiersdorf*, supra n. 6, margin 56.
69. *The Wellcome Foundation v. Paranova*, Case No. 276/05, 22 December 2008, margin 30.
70. *Ibid.*, margin 27.
71. *Bristol-Myers Squibb and others v. Paranova*, supra n. 63.
72. *Boehringer v. Swingward II*, Case No. 348/04, decision dated 26 April 2007.
73. *Ibid.*
74. *Boehringer Ingelheim and others v. Swingward and others*, Case No. 348/04, 26 April 2007.

get-up or a get-up used for a number of different products ('co-branding'), or positions the additional label so as wholly or partially to obscure the proprietor's trademark, or fails to state on the additional label that the trademark in question belongs to the proprietor, or prints the name of the parallel importer in capital letters can, in principle, be liable to damage the trademark's reputation. This is again for the national court to decide in each particular case.

[3] Indication of the Original Manufacturer and the Repackager

The indication of who repacked the product and the name of the manufacturer must be clearly shown on the external packaging of the repackaged product. It must be printed in such a way that a person with normal eyesight, exercising a normal degree of attentiveness, understands this information.[75] It is, according to ECJ case law, not required that as 're-packager' the undertaking actually repackaging the product and holding an authorisation to do so is indicated; it is sufficient to indicate the undertaking which holds the MA for the product, on whose instructions the repackaging was carried out, and which assumes liability for the repackaging.[76]

Where the parallel importer has added to the packaging an extra article from a source other than the trademark proprietor, he or she must ensure that the origin of the extra article is indicated in such a way as to dispel any impression that the trademark proprietor is responsible for it.[77]

[4] Notice to the Trademark Owner

According to the case law of the ECJ, the failure to provide proper notice in itself gives rise to possible actions by the trademark holder.[78] The notice needs to come from the parallel importer itself. It is not sufficient that the proprietor is notified by other sources, such as the authority which issues a parallel import license.[79] Upon request of the trademark holder, the parallel trader must also provide a sample of the repackaging, which enables the trademark holder to assess that the repackaging does not damage the reputation of the trademark and that it does not affect the condition of the original product.[80] The proprietor of the trademark must have a reasonable timeframe to review the intended repackaging. A timeframe of fifteen working days might be sufficient, depending on the facts of the case.[81]

---

75. *Bristol-Myers Squibb and others v. Paranova, supra* n. 63.
76. *Orifarm and Paranova v. Merck*, Joined Cases No. 400/09, 207/10.
77. *Bristol-Myers Squibb and others v. Paranova, supra* n. 63, margin 73.
78. *Boehringer v. Swingward II, supra* n. 72.
79. *Ibid.*, margin 20.
80. *Boehringer v. Swingward*, Case No. 143/00 [2002] ECR 3759.
81. *Ibid.*

[5] The Repackaging Is 'Necessary'

The condition is directed only at the fact of repackaging the product – and the choice between a new carton (reboxing) and oversticking (relabelling) – for the purposes of allowing that product to be marketed in the importing State and not at the manner or style in which it has been repackaged.[82] Already because of the compulsory nature of certain information on the packaging and in the patient information leaflet (PIL), some changes to parallel-imported product are regularly required. Therefore, today, the core dispute in relation to this BMS condition rather is whether reboxing is necessary or whether relabelling (including bundling or replenishing) of original packs would be sufficient. At least with regard to bundling, it has to be noted, though, that this option is not available for centrally authorised products as every central MA has detailed and specific requirements regarding the packaging of the medicinal products that are the subject of the authorisation and preclude the bundling of the packages of those medicinal products.[83]

With regard to the necessity of reboxing, the ECJ found that a trademark proprietor cannot oppose a new external packaging where medicinal products purchased by the parallel importer cannot be placed on the market in the Member State of destination in their original packaging by reason of national rules or practices relating to packaging, or where sickness insurance rules make reimbursement of medical expenses depend on a certain packaging or where well-established medical prescription practices are based, *inter alia*, on standard sizes recommended by professional groups and sickness insurance institutions.[84] The trademark proprietor may oppose replacement packaging, though, where the parallel importer is able to reuse the original packaging for the purpose of marketing in the Member State of importation by affixing labels to that packaging.[85]

Then again, where, in accordance with the rules and practices in force in the Member State of destination, the proprietor uses several different sizes of packaging in that State, the finding that one of those sizes is also marketed in the Member State of origin is not enough to justify the conclusion that repackaging is unnecessary. Partitioning of the markets would exist if the importer were able to sell the product in only part of the market.[86] However, the trademark proprietor can object a repackaging in a new outer packaging and a reaffixing of the trademark where (i) the medicinal product can be marketed in the Member State of destination in the same packaging as that in which it is marketed in the Member State of origin and (ii) the importer has not demonstrated that the imported product can only be marketed in a limited part of the Member State of destination's market.[87]

---

82. *Boehringer v. Swingward II*, supra n. 72, margin 38.
83. *Aventis v. Kohlpharma and others*, Case No. 433/00, 19 September 2002, margins 22, 25.
84. *Bristol-Myers Squibb and others v. Paranova*, supra n. 63, margin 53.
85. *Ibid.*, margin 55.
86. *Ferring v. Orifarm*, Case No. 297/15, 10 November 2016, margin 22.
87. *Ibid.*, margin 29.

In addition to those cases, the ECJ also recognised that reboxing is necessary if effective access to the market or a substantial part thereof would be hindered because of the strong resistance from a significant proportion of consumers to relabelled medicinal products.[88] Still, the condition that it be necessary is not fulfilled if repackaging of the product is explicable solely by the parallel importer's attempt to secure a commercial advantage.[89]

[6] Burden of Proof

The parallel trader bears the burden to prove that the repackaging complies with the abovementioned requirements, so that the parallel trade of the repackaged product cannot be challenged on the basis of trademark rights.[90] With regard to the requirements that the repackaging has no effect on the original condition of the product and the repackaged product does not damage the reputation of the trademark and its proprietor, it is sufficient that the parallel trader presents evidence that provides for the reasonable assumption that these requirements are fulfilled. The burden of proof then shifts to the proprietor of the trademark, and the proprietor must prove that the reputation has been damaged.[91] Whether or not the reputation of the trademark owner might be damaged is a factual question that the national courts must decide in view of the specific factual circumstances.[92] The national practice is set out in the table at the end of this Chapter.

[7] Rebranding

The same principles as described above apply to cases of rebranding. Sometimes a trademark owner markets identical products in one Member State under trademark X and in another Member State under trademark Y. When parallel importing from the first to the second Member State, an importer will want to replace trademark X with trademark Y on the repackaged products. According to the ECJ, this is not a case of exhaustion as the originator did not put the original products on the market under trademark Y.[93] Therefore, the replacement of the original trademark by that of the importing Member State needs to be objectively necessary in order to place the products on the market.[94]

---

88. *Merck, Sharp & Dohme v. Paranova*, Case No. 443/99, 23 April 2002, margin 33; *Boehringer v. Swingward, supra* n. 80, margin 54.
89. *Merck, Sharp & Dohme v. Paranova, supra* n. 88, margin 27; *Boehringer v. Swingward, supra* n. 80, margin 48.
90. Ibid.
91. Ibid.
92. Ibid.
93. *Pharmacia & Upjohn SA v. Paranova A/S*, Case No. 379/97 [1999].
94. Ibid.

§20.05 COMPETITION LAW

The consequences of parallel trading (i.e., different prices in different Member States) are significant to pharmaceutical companies, and companies have attempted various measures to prevent or control such activities. In this regard, competition law may be infringed by pharmaceutical companies preventing parallel trade. This might be done by a number of activities, including the imposition of restrictive contractual obligations on distributors; price discrimination in favour of domestic sales or resales such as price-based exclusionary conduct, Sales Quota Systems, or dual pricing schemes; etc. For a more detailed discussion of the interaction between parallel trade and competition law, *see* further at §21.06 of Chapter 21.

An example for non-price-based exclusionary conduct is the misuse of IP rights or regulatory systems as it is described in the AstraZeneca case. In the decision *AstraZeneca AB and AstraZeneca plc v. European Commission*,[95] the General Court examined the exclusionary conduct of AstraZeneca under the aspect of abuse of a dominant position. AstraZeneca had withdrawn the MA for its medication product in Denmark, Norway, and Sweden and had launched a similar follow-up product in the form of tablets instead of capsules there. After an examination of the effects of the deregistration of the original product on the granting of parallel import licences in the concerning countries, the General Court stated that the deregistration of a product can constitute an abuse of a dominant position in a certain market as far as it enables to restrict parallel imports of the concerning product. The ECJ confirmed that withdrawal of MAs for reasons other than the protection of public health does not justify the automatic cessation of parallel imports. The protection of public health can be guaranteed by alternative means, such as collaboration with national authorities of other Member States. Consequently, the TFEU precludes the withdrawal of the MA of a pharmaceutical product from entailing, of itself, the withdrawal of the parallel import licence granted for the medicinal product in question, if there is no risk to human health from maintaining that medicinal product on the market of the Member State of importation.[96]

§20.06 UK

[A] Brexit and Exhaustion of IP Rights

As was mentioned above, parallel trade is the import and export of IP protected goods and occurs when the IP rights in those goods are 'exhausted'. In other words, such products have been placed on the market within a specific territory by, or with the permission of, the rights holder. As was also seen above, the exhaustion of IP rights means that IP rights cannot be used to stop the further distribution or resale of those

---

95. *AstraZeneca AB and AstraZeneca plc v. European Commission*, Case No. T-321/05, decision dated 1 July, 2010.
96. *Ibid.*, margin 842.

goods.[97] Following 1 January 2021, with regard to the exit by the UK from the EU, there were some changes to the exhaustion of IP rights system vis-à-vis the UK.

With regard to parallel exports from the UK to the European Economic Area (EEA), goods placed on the UK market by, or with the consent of, the right holder after the transition period (i.e., until 31 December 2020) may no longer be considered exhausted in the EEA. This means that businesses exporting these IP-protected goods from the UK to the EEA might need the IP right holder's consent.[98]

From a UK perspective, in terms of The Intellectual Property (Exhaustion of Rights) (EU Exit) Regulations 2019 (UK Regulations), the incumbent system of EEA-wide exhaustion was retained. Following the end of the transition period, rights in goods placed on the market in the EEA continue to be exhausted in the UK but, absent any agreement between the UK and the EU, there is no such reciprocity for goods put on the market in the UK. In other words, placing the goods on the market in the UK will not exhaust the IP rights in the EEA.

As regards the exhaustion of patent rights specifically, the UK Regulations essentially provide that the principles of free movement of goods and exhaustion of IP rights under, among others, the TFEU is retained in UK domestic law following the transition period, and the ECJ's case law to date will continue to apply in the UK. Therefore, patented goods put on the market in the EEA will be exhausted in the UK but, as before, parallel imports going in the other direction (i.e., from the UK to EEA) may be stopped as coming from a non-EEA country.

[B] Implementation in the UK

The UK parallel import licensing scheme allows a medicine authorised in an EEA Member State to be marketed in the UK, as long as the imported product has no therapeutic difference from the same, equivalent UK product. No MA is required for the holder of a 'product licence (parallel importing)' (referred to as a PLPI). In order to parallel import a product into the UK, it is required, among other things, that:[99]

- the product is manufactured to good manufacturing practice (GMP) standards;
- a wholesale dealer's licence is in place covering importing, storage and sale for each product; and
- the correct PLPI is in place.

In accordance with the provisions of Regulation 172 of the UK Human Medicines Regulations 2012, the holder of a PLPI is exempted from the general prohibition on placing the medicinal product to which the licence relates on the market; or the sale or supply, or offer for sale or supply, of a medicinal product to which a PLPI relates, provided that the acts are done in accordance with the terms of that licence. For these

---

97. *See* https://www.gov.uk/guidance/exhaustion-of-ip-rights-and-parallel-trade-after-the-transition-period.
98. *Ibid.*
99. *See* further at https://www.gov.uk/guidance/medicines-apply-for-a-parallel-import-licence.

Chapter 20: Parallel Trade §20.06[C]

purposes, a *'parallel import licence'* is defined as a licence that is granted by the licensing authority in compliance with the rules of EU law relating to parallel imports; and it authorises the holder to place on the market a medicinal product imported into the UK from another EEA State.

As EU law continued to apply in relation to the UK until 31 December 2020, during that so-called transition period, the status quo was maintained as much as possible and for that short term was 'business as usual' for parallel trading in the UK. Following the end of the transition period, the scheme for parallel trading into the UK is as described above and remains that way at the time of writing. How the nature of the relationship between the EU and the UK develops in the future will determine whether that scheme remains unchanged.

See further the high-level note at §20.06[A] above regarding Brexit and the exhaustion of IP rights.

[C]   **UK Procedure**

The applicant applies for the PLPI using the appropriate application form[100] and fee to the Licensing Division of the Medicines and Healthcare Products Regulatory Agency (MHRA), via the online MHRA Portal.[101] The MHRA website provides detailed practical guidelines regarding the PLPI application process.[102]

When assessing the application, if any information is missing or changes need to be made, the MHRA, as part of their 'two strikes and out' policy, will correspond with the applicant twice, to address deficiencies with the application. If the applicant fails to address all the questions satisfactorily, a third and final letter sent by the MHRA will be a refusal. In some cases, the MHRA may make an exception, for example, when the package leaflet for the product is undergoing user testing. This will be decided on a case-by-case basis and only in exceptional circumstances.[103]

Along with the completed application form, the following documents are required to be submitted to the MHRA:

- proof of payment form;
- the completed label summary template;
- mock ups of all proposed labelling and the patient information leaflet in English;
- user testing report (if applicable);
- the relevant complete sample with the foreign leaflet intact; and
- an updated company functions list (assembler, batch release, storage, importer, and distributor) (if applicable).

---

100. *See* https://www.gov.uk/guidance/medicines-apply-for-a-parallel-import-licence#submit-your-parallel-import.
101. *Ibid.*
102. *Ibid.*
103. *Ibid.*

Since 1 April 2009, there are three categories of PLPI applications, with different fees payable depending on the complexity of the application:

> Simple: This application process applies when the UK product and the product to be imported from an EU Member State have a common origin (i.e., they are manufactured by companies in the same group of companies or are made under licence from the same licensor).
>
> Standard: This application process applies when the UK and imported products are not of common origin and the application is not 'Complex.'
>
> Complex: This application process applies when the UK and imported products are not of common origin, and:
>> the imported product contains a new excipient;
>>
>> the imported product contains an active ingredient made by a different route from that used in the UK product;
>>
>> the imported product is a controlled-release preparation;
>>
>> the imported product is a sterile product that is sterilised in a different way from the UK product;
>>
>> the imported product is a sterile product in which the container is made from a different material from the container of the UK product;
>>
>> the imported product is an influenza vaccine;
>>
>> the product is a metered-dose inhaler;
>>
>> the product is a powder for inhalation;

For the Standard and Complex categories, companies will be required to submit suitable pharmacovigilance plans with the application. This is because a parallel importing company is required to take on responsibility for pharmacovigilance in specific instances (e.g., when the UK reference product licence has been cancelled, or when there is no common origin between the UK and imported products). The requirements for pharmacovigilance are the same for other products.

[D] Product Repackaging and Potential Trademark Infringement

Generally, as a point of departure, all labels, patient information leaflets, and packaging for parallel import medicines must comply with European guidance.[104] The MHRA grants the PLPI in the name of the product applied for by the applicant. The MHRA does not consider the trademark and whether it infringes the IP rights of third parties. The applicant must ensure that it does not infringe such rights.[105]

It is the competence of the national courts to examine whether or not the repackaging complies with the principles set out by the ECJ. The following principles can be distilled from UK case law on this matter: A trademark proprietor may oppose repackaging of products if:

---

104. *See* https://www.gov.uk/guidance/medicines-packaging-labelling-and-patient-information-leaflets.
105. *See* https://www.gov.uk/guidance/medicines-apply-for-a-parallel-import-licence.

(1) the purpose of the repackaging is solely an attempt of the parallel importer to secure a commercial advantage rather than for reasons of achieving effective market access; and/or
(2) the repackaging damages the legitimate interests of the proprietor. A trademark proprietor may not oppose repackaging where it is a requirement of the State of import's national rules or if there is strong resistance from consumers of the importing state to the sale of products in the original packaging.

[E] Notification of Patent Holders

The application form for the PLPI includes a 'tick box' where the applicant must indicate that the relevant rights holder had been notified of the intention to import the product into the UK, in accordance with the so-called Specific Mechanism. The date must be given (and the form states that this date must be at least thirty days before the date of the application). The MHRA does not check whether this has in fact been done.

The Court of Appeal (see *Merck Canada Inc v. Sigma Pharmaceuticals PLC*)[106] referred to the ECJ various questions concerning the precise procedure under the Specific Mechanism, including:

- to whom notice must be given;
- whether the notifying entity must be the importing entity or can be a member of the same group; and
- whether the notified entity is obliged to respond if it intends to exercise its patent rights to prevent the importation taking place.

In this regard, the ECJ, in its judgment dated 12 February 2015,[107] responded to the above as follows:

- the notification must be given to the 'holder' or 'beneficiary' of the protection conferred by a patent or SPC. The term 'holder' must be understood, according to its generally accepted meaning, as referring to the person identified by the patent as the recipient of the protection conferred by the patent. Similarly, the term 'beneficiary' must be understood, according to its generally accepted meaning, as designating any person who enjoys rights conferred by law on the holder of the patent, *inter alia*, by virtue of a licence agreement. It therefore follows that notification must be given to the holder of the patent or SPC, or to any other person enjoying rights conferred by law by that patent or SPC;[108]
- the Specific Mechanism does not require the person intending to import or market the pharmaceutical product in question to give notification him- or herself, provided that it is possible from the notification to identify that person

---

106. [2013] EWCA Civ 326.
107. See Case C-539/13.
108. *Ibid.*, from paragraph 34.

clearly;[109] and a duly notified holder, or beneficiary, of a patent or SPC who fails to reply and does not demonstrate his intention to rely on the rights provided for in the Specific Mechanism is precluded from retroactively relying on those rights.[110]

---

109. *Ibid.*, from paragraph 44.
110. *Ibid.*, at paragraph 22.

CHAPTER 21
Competition Law in the Pharmaceutical Sector

Morten Nissen, Peter Willis & Alexander Brøchner[*]

§21.01 INTRODUCTION

There are no sector-specific rules in the EU on competition law in the pharmaceutical sector. Competition law applies to this sector as it does to any other industry. Nevertheless, the pharmaceutical sector displays a number of special characteristics which may impact the way in which competition rules are enforced.

This chapter provides a practical overview of the competition rules as applied in the pharmaceutical sector in the EU. It is structured as follows: first, it discusses market definition in the pharmaceutical sector (§21.02); it then turns to the application of Article 101 (§21.03) and 102 (§21.04) of the Treaty on the Functioning of the EU (TFEU). Further, it discusses the treatment of parallel trade (§21.05). Finally, it discusses some Merger Control (§21.06) and State aid (§21.07) issues. A brief thematic overview of the post-Brexit position in the UK is then provided in §21.08.

§21.02 MARKET DEFINITION IN THE PHARMACEUTICAL SECTOR

Market definition is a tool to identify and define the boundaries of competition between firms. It serves to establish the framework within which the competition policy is applied by the European Commission (Commission).[1]

---

[*] The authors wish to acknowledge *José Rivas* and *Silvia Pronk*, the authors of the earlier edition of this chapter.
[1] Commission Notice on the definition of relevant market for the purposes of Community competition law, OJ [1997] C 372/5 (the 'Relevant Market Notice'), paragraph 2. The Relevant Market Notice is currently under revision. The revised version is expected to be adopted in the first quarter of 2023.

Market definition is the first necessary step in any competition law analysis; it determines the scope of the analysis and has a strong influence on the result.

In general terms, the Commission defines product markets as comprising all those products and/or services that are regarded as interchangeable or substitutable by the consumer, by reason of the products' characteristics, their prices, and their intended use.[2] Both demand substitution and, to a lesser extent, supply substitution,[3] are taken into account to establish the competitive constraints on the firms when defining the relevant markets. In determining those constraints, the Commission relies on the views of the customers and competitors of the parties, past evidence of substitution, and empirical evidence. In addition, the Commission pays attention to industry practice when defining relevant markets. This has the advantage of creating standard classifications that are known by all market participants.

The geographic market is also defined. The relevant geographic market 'comprises the area in which the undertakings concerned are involved in the supply and demand of products or services, in which the conditions of competition are sufficiently homogeneous and which can be distinguished from neighbouring areas because the conditions of competition are appreciably different in those areas'.[4]

In practice, to define the relevant market of a pharmaceutical product, the Commission distinguishes between (i) approved medicines, (ii) active substances, and (iii) pipeline products.

[A] Approved Medicines

When defining relevant product markets for approved medicines, the Commission follows the Anatomical Therapeutic Classification (ATC) devised by European Pharmaceutical Marketing Research Association (EphMRA). The ATC classifies approved medicines into four different levels, from the most general one to the most specific. The Commission uses the third level (ATC 3) as a starting point, as this allows the Commission to group medicines in terms of therapeutic indications.[5] Recently, the Commission has been more inclined to look beyond the ATC classification for the purposes of market definition by considering whether drugs are bio-substitutable or similar at molecular level.[6]

The Commission also distinguishes between the market for approved medicines that are available over-the-counter (OTC) and the market for those that are available only through prescription.[7] The Commission usually considers branded and generic medicines to be in the same market.

---

2. Relevant Market Notice, paragraph 7.
3. *Ibid.*, paragraph 20.
4. *Ibid.*, paragraph 8.
5. *Reckitt Benckiser/Boots Healthcare International*, Case COMP/M.4007, decision of 6 January 2006.
6. *See*, for instance, *Actavis/Allergan*, Case COMP/M.7480, decision of 16 Mar. 2015, paragraph 11.
7. *Teva/Cephalon*, Case COMP/M.6258, decision of 13 Oct. 2011, paragraph 10; *Teva/Ratiopharm*, Case COMP/M.5865, decision of 3 Aug. 2010, paragraph 22; *Novartis/Alcon*, Case COMP/M.5778, decision of 9 Aug. 2010, paragraph 12.

Despite a trend towards standardisation at a European level, the geographic markets for approved medicines remain national[8] due to differences in administrative procedures and purchasing and reimbursement policies by national healthcare services. In addition, brand and packaging strategies or distribution systems often differ from one Member State to another.

[B] Active Substances

The Commission considers active substances to be upstream of medicines, as they can be mixed for the manufacturing of medicines. Active substances can be used in-house to produce a pharmaceutical specialty, or they can be traded independently. In the latter case, to the extent that the substances are the object of transactions between producers and buyers of active substances, there is an independent market for active substances. This market is separate from the market for the medicines in which they are used.[9] As active substances are not directly subject to the same national regulations as medicines, the geographic market for active substances is at least EEA-wide,[10] if not worldwide.[11]

[C] Pipeline Products

For future products ('pipeline products'), it is often uncertain which products will actually make it to the market and what their intended use will be. The Commission will usually only define a market for products that have reached Phase III of their clinical tests.[12] Pipeline products that are intended to replace an existing product will be included in the existing medicine market, while completely new products are considered a future (innovation) market to be assessed separately.[13] Indeed, in merger decisions such as the Novartis/GlaxoSmithKline's oncology decision,[14] the Commission was be willing to accept divestitures in early pipeline phase I and/or phase II products in order to protect potential innovation. To the extent that future relevant markets can be identified, these relevant markets will usually be worldwide given that companies typically have worldwide research and development (R&D) strategies.[15]

It is important to note that market definition in antitrust cases may be different from that in merger control. In parallel trade cases, relevant markets may be defined with regard to the reimbursement amounts and the scope for profitable parallel trading, rather than the therapeutic indications of the product.[16]

---

8. *Glaxo/Wellcome*, Case IV/M.555, decision of 28 Feb. 1995.
9. *Ciba-Beigy/Sandoz*, Case IV/M.737, decision of 17 Jul. 1996, paragraph 41.
10. *Monsanto/Pharmacia & Upjohn*, Case IV/M.1835, decision of 30 Mar. 2000, paragraph 43.
11. *Ciba-Beigy/Sandoz*, supra n. 9, paragraph 50.
12. *TEVA/IVAX*, Case COMP/M.3928, decision of 24 Nov. 2005, paragraph 51.
13. *Bristol Myers Squibb/Dupont*, COMP/M.2517, decision of 9 Aug. 2001 paragraph 24.
14. *Novartis /GlaxoSmithKline oncology business*, COMP/M.7275, decision of 28 Jan. 2015.
15. *Astra/Zeneca*, COMP/M.1403, decision of 26 Feb. 1999, paragraph 48.
16. D. Bailey, L. John (eds.); Bellamy & Child, *European Union Law of Competition*, 8th edition (Oxford: OUP, 2018), footnote 197.

§21.03 ARTICLE 101 TFEU

[A] The Application of Article 101(1) TFEU

Article 101(1) TFEU prohibits agreements between undertakings, decisions by associations of undertakings and concerted practices that may affect trade between Member States and that have as their object or effect the prevention, restriction, or distortion of competition within the common market. Article 101(2) TFEU provides that prohibited agreements[17] are automatically legally void and, therefore, cannot be enforced in a court of law. However, such agreements may be exempted if they meet the criteria set out in Article 101(3) TFEU.

In the following sections, the conditions of application of Article 101 TFEU are successively analysed, with particular attention to topics likely to have an impact on the pharmaceutical industry.

[1] The Definition of an Undertaking

For the purposes of Article 101 TFEU, an 'undertaking' is any 'entity engaged in an economic activity, regardless of its legal status and the way in which it is financed'.[18]

Undertakings include privately or publicly financed entities, with or without legal personality, as well as natural persons. It is of no relevance that the entity is not for profit,[19] as long as it exercises an economic activity.

In *Commission v. Italy*,[20] the Court defined economic activity as the offering of goods or services on the market; in addition, the activity 'could, at least in principle, be carried out by a private undertaking in order to make profits'.[21]

Special care should be taken in determining whether pension funds and social security schemes are undertakings. The Court of Justice of the European Union (CJEU) has developed a line of case law that distinguishes entities that run an economic activity from those that only exercise an 'exclusively social objective'. In *Poucet et Pistre*,[22] the CJEU held that an organisation involved in the management of the public social security system is not an undertaking within the meaning of Article 101 TFEU because the organisation fulfils an exclusively social function and performs an activity, based on the principle of national solidarity, which is entirely non-profit-making. The same conclusion was reached in the case of an institution providing compulsory insurance against accidents at work,[23] in a case that involved the direct provider of a

---

17. Unless specified otherwise, the term 'agreement' in this chapter designates agreements between undertakings, decisions by associations of undertakings, and concerted practices.
18. *Höfner and Elser*, Case C-41/90 [1991] ECR I-1979, paragraph 21.
19. *IAZ International Belgium SA v. Commission*, Case 96/82 [1983] ECR 3369.
20. *Commission v. Italian Republic*, Case 118/85 [1987] ECR 2599, paragraph 7.
21. *Pavel Pavlov v. Stichting Pensioenfonds Medische Specialisten*, Joined Cases C-180/98 to C-184/98 [2000] ECR I-6451, paragraph 201.
22. *Christian Poucet v. Assurances Générales de France and Caisse Mutuelle Régionale du Languedoc-Roussillon*, Cases C-159/91 and 160/91 [1993] ECR I-00637.
23. *Cisal di Battistelo Venanziano & Co.*, Case C-218/00 [2002] ECR I-691.

statutory sickness fund,[24] and in the case of the Spanish national social security system, where the CJEU held that, since the supply of medical services by the Spanish social security system is not an economic activity, the procurement of inputs for the performance of such activity does not constitute an economic activity either, even if the purchasing entity is a monopsony.[25]

Sometimes, an organisation engages in economic activities and also pursues non-profit social activities. The entity could be considered an undertaking for one function but not the other. For example, a free public school does not carry out an economic activity in providing educational services for pupils, but the school can be an undertaking when renting out facilities.[26]

Different legal persons that are part of the same corporate group are a single undertaking for the purpose of competition law.[27] Thus, an intra-group agreement is not considered an agreement between independent undertakings and is therefore not subject to Article 101 TFEU.

[2] Definition of Agreements, Concerted Practices, and Decisions of Associations

[a] Agreements

The concept of an agreement has been construed very broadly by the Commission and the EU courts. It does not require any particular form, and for the purposes of Article 101(1)TFEU, it does not matter whether the agreement is a legal contract or whether it is legally binding under national law. For example, a mere gentlemen's agreement has been considered to amount to an agreement.[28] In addition, Article 101(1) TFEU does not require that the agreement be put into effect.

The distinction between unilateral conduct and agreements is sometimes unclear. In *AEG*,[29] the manufacturer, AEG, refused to sell its products to resellers who did not comply with its pricing policies. The Court held that the price conditions originated in the distribution agreement and that the policy of not supplying non-price compliant resellers had at least been tacitly accepted by the existing distributors, thereby making the distributors parties to the agreement with regard to the refusal to sell. In *Ford*,[30] the Court considered whether the decision of Ford to stop supplying right-hand-drive cars to German distributors[31] fell under Article 101 TFEU. The Court reasoned that

---

24. *AOK Bundesverband*, Cases C-264, 306, 354, and 355/01 [2004] ECR I-2493.
25. *FENIN v. Commission*, Case T-319/99 [2003], ECR II-357, paragraph 37, confirmed on appeal in Case C-205/03 P [2006] ECR I-6319.
26. J. Faull & A. Nikpay, *The EU Law of Competition*, 3rd edition. (Oxford, 2014), 191.
27. *Viho Europe BV v. Commission*, Case. C-75/95 P [1996] ECR I-5457.
28. *ACF Chemiefarma NV v. Commission*, Case 42/69 [1970] ECR 661, paragraph 112.
29. *AEG v. Commission*, Case 107/82 [1983] ECR 3151.
30. *Ford Werke AG and Ford of Europe Inc. v. Commission*, Joined Cases 228/82 and 229/82 [1984] ECR 1129.
31. Who, unsurprisingly, exported those cars to the UK.

admission to the Ford distribution network implied acceptance of Ford's policy, and that the policy constituted an agreement within the scope of Article 101 TFEU.

In *Bayer Adalat*,[32] Bayer had introduced a supply quota system (SQS) to discourage parallel trade in pharmaceuticals from France and Spain to the UK. Contrary to the Commission, the General Court did not consider that Bayer's SQS was part of an 'agreement' with distributors. Instead, it considered that Bayer acted unilaterally so that the behaviour would not fall within the application of Article 101 TFEU. The General Court highlighted that the concept of an agreement centres on a '*concurrence of wills*' between parties, which was not demonstrated in the case at hand, notably because of the distributor's insistence to try and undertake parallel trade towards the UK.

In short, the particular facts of each case will be determinative whether an 'agreement' has been entered into or not.

[b]   Concerted Practices

The CJEU has defined a concerted practice as 'co-ordination between undertakings which, without having reached the stage where an agreement, properly so called, has been concluded, knowingly substitutes practical cooperation between them for the risks of competition'.[33] For example, an exchange of commercially sensitive information is a concerted practice covered by Article 101(1) TFEU.

A concerted practice does not need to be put into effect in order to fall within the application of Article 101(1) TFEU. In *T-Mobile Netherlands*,[34] the CJEU held that when there has been collusion between undertakings (e.g., a meeting where commercially sensitive information was exchanged) and those undertakings remain active on the market, it is presumed that the undertakings have used the information for determining their behaviour on the market. In other words, it is for the defendants to reverse the presumption and to prove that their behaviour on the market was determined independently from the information obtained. The CJEU underlined that a single occurrence of collusion can be enough to trigger the application of Article 101(1) TFEU.[35]

[c]   Decisions by Association of Undertakings

While trade associations often perform activities that promote efficiency and competition within a sector, their members might use the association to disseminate

---

32. *Bayer AG v. Commission*, Case T-41/96 [2000] ECR II-3383 and confirmed on appeal, *BAI v. Bayer and Commission*, Case C-2/01 P [2004] ECR I-23.
33. *ICI v. Commission (Dyestuffs)*, Joined Cases 48, 49, 51-7/69 [1972] ECR 619, paragraph 64.
34. *T-Mobile Netherlands and others v. Raad van bestuur van de Nederlandse Mededingingsautoriteit*, Case C-8/08 [2009] ECR-I-4529.
35. *Ibid.*, paragraph 59.

commercially sensitive information[36] or to implement or monitor anti-competitive practices.[37] These activities will generally be qualified as agreements or concerted practices between undertakings, but qualifying the prohibited behaviour as a decision by an association of undertakings may lower the burden of proof for competition authorities and complainants. In addition, the inclusion of decisions by associations in Article 101(1) TFEU permits authorities to directly fine the association.[38]

[3] A Restriction of Competition by Object and/or Effect

Article 101(1) TFEU prohibits agreements that restrict competition by *object* and *effect*.

It is settled case law that the words 'object' and 'effect' must be read disjunctively.[39] Where a restriction of competition by object (i.e., a type of coordination that can be regarded, by its very nature, as being harmful to competition) can be shown, anti-competitive effects need not to be demonstrated. In practice, therefore, competition authorities will first determine whether the agreement can be qualified as a restriction by object. Restrictions by object are typically hardcore restrictions such as price fixing, market sharing, or customer allocation. Where no restriction by object is found, a restrictive effect must be shown, in particular, by examining the actual or potential effects of the agreement on competition. This entails a comparison of the competitive situation resulting from the agreement and the situation that would exist in its absence.[40]

[4] An Appreciable Restriction of Competition: de Minimis

When the restriction of competition only has an insignificant effect on the market, the agreement will fall outside Article 101(1) TFEU.[41] The *de Minimis* Notice[42] provides that agreements do not appreciably restrict competition when (i) the aggregate market share held by *all* the parties does not exceed 10% of the relevant market (in agreements between competitors); or (ii) the market share held by *each* party to the agreement does not exceed 15% of the relevant market (in agreements between non-competitors).[43]

The exemptions set forth in the *de Minimis* Notice do not apply to hardcore restrictions, such as price fixing, output limitation, or sharing of markets and customers, as they always constitute, by their very nature, constitute an appreciable restriction

---

36. See the Commission Decision in *UK Agricultural Tractor Exchange*, Case IV/31.370, decision of 17 Feb. 1992, upheld on appeal.
37. For example, *C Belasco and others v. Commission*, Case 246/86 [1989] ECR 2117.
38. In which case, the association is obliged to call for contribution from its members if it is not solvent: Article 23(4) of Council Regulation No. 1/2003, OJ [2003] L 1/1.
39. *Société Technique Minière v. Maschinenbau Ulm GmbH*, Case 56/65 [1966] ECR 234, 246.
40. *GlaxoSmithKline Services v. Commission*, Case T-168/01 [2006] ECR II-2969, paragraph 162.
41. *Völk v. Vervaecke*, Case 5/69 [1969] ECR 295, 302.
42. Commission Notice on agreements of minor importance which do not appreciably restrict competition under Article 101(1) TFEU (*de Minimis* Notice), OJ [2014] C 291/1.
43. *de Minimis* Notice, paragraph 8.

of competition incompatible with Article 101(1) TFEU.[44] Even if these restrictions have only an insignificant effect on the market, Article 101(1) TFEU will therefore apply.

The accompanying Staff Working Document[45] provides some legal certainty by setting out a 'list of restrictions of competition' that have been treated as restrictions by object in the Commission's decisional practice and the case law of the CJEU.

[5]   An Appreciable Effect on Trade Between Member States

For EU competition law to be applicable, trade between Member States must be affected. The Commission has set out a negative rebuttable presumption (known as the NAAT-rule),[46] stating that agreements will, in principle, not appreciably affect trade between Member States when:

(a) the aggregate market share of the parties in any relevant market within the EU affected by the agreement does not exceed 5%; and
(b) in the case of horizontal agreements, the aggregate annual EU turnover in the products covered by the agreement does not exceed EUR 40 million. In the case of vertical agreements, the aggregate annual EU turnover of the supplier in the products covered must not exceed EUR 40 million.

It should be noted that where EU competition rules do not apply due to lack of effect on trade, (often identical) national competition laws of the Member States may be applicable.

[B]   The Application of Article 101(3) TFEU

Despite the wording of Article 101(2) TFEU, agreements that fall within the prohibition of Article 101(1) TFEU are not automatically void. Significant numbers of agreements have been found to restrict competition but have nevertheless been found to be legal under the exception contained in Article 101(3) TFEU.

Article 101(3) TFEU provides that under certain conditions agreements do not violate competition law. Under Article 2 of Regulation 1/2003,[47] once it has been determined that an agreement is prohibited under Article 101(1) TFEU, the burden of proof shifts from the party alleging the infringement to the defendant. For Article 101(3) TFEU to apply, the defendant must prove that the four cumulative conditions for an exemption set out herein are met.

---

44. *Ibid.*, paragraph 13.
45. Guidance on restrictions of competition 'by object' for the purpose of defining which agreements may benefit from the *De Minimis* Notice of 25 June 2014, C(2014) 4136 final.
46. Guidelines on the effect on trade concept contained in Articles 81 and 82 of the Treaty, OJ [2004] C101/81, paragraph 52.
47. Council Regulation No. 1/2003, OJ [2003] L 1/1.

For a number of types of agreements, the Council and Commission have provided safe harbours from the application of Article 101(1) TFEU in so-called block exemption regulations; when relying on a block exemption, the defendant must prove that the agreement falls within a block exemption.

[1] Individual Exemptions

Article 101(3) TFEU sets out four cumulative conditions for an exemption:

- the agreement must contribute to an improvement in the production or distribution of goods or the promotion of technical or economic progress;
- consumers must get a fair share of the resulting benefit;
- the agreement only imposes on the undertakings restrictions that are essential; and
- the exception will not afford the undertakings the possibility of substantially eliminating competition.

The Commission has interpreted these conditions in its Article 101(3) Guidelines.[48]

[2] Block Exemptions

Typically, block exemptions contain market share thresholds above which the block exemption is not applicable, as well as a list of hardcore restraints that disqualify the entire agreement.

Even where all the requirements of the block exemption are met, the Commission may still decide to withdraw the benefit of the exception if the agreement has certain effects that are incompatible with Article 101(3) TFEU.[49] This, however, is exceptional.

The Block Exemption Regulation on technology transfer (TTBER)[50] and the Block Exemption Regulation on research and development (R&D Block Exemption)[51] are particularly relevant for the pharmaceutical sector. The Block Exemption Regulation on vertical agreements[52] is of particular relevance to distribution agreements, but it is beyond the scope of this chapter.

---

48. Guidelines on the application of Article 81(3) of the Treaty, OJ [2004] C 101/97, paragraph 34.
49. Article 29 of Council Regulation No. 1/2003, OJ [2003] L 1/1.
50. Commission Regulation (EU) No. 316/2014 of 21 Mar. 2014 on the application of Article 101(3) of the TFEU to categories of technology transfer agreements, OJ [2014] L 93/17.
51. Commission Regulation (EU) No. 1217/2010 of 14 Dec. 2010 on the application of Article 101(3) of the TFEU to certain categories of research and development agreements, OJ [2010] L335/36. This Regulation will expire on 31 December 2022. They are, therefore, currently under review following a public consultation.
52. Commission Regulation (EU) 2022/720 of 10 May 2022 on the application of Article 101(3) of the TFEU to categories of vertical agreements and concerted practices (VBER). This Regulation entered into force on 1 June 2022.

[a] The TTBER

The TTBER ensures that Article 101(1) TFEU does not apply to certain intellectual property (IP) licensing agreements. An agreement falls within the exemption if it meets the following three tests:

(1) The agreement is a technology transfer agreement. A 'technology transfer agreement' is defined in Article 1(1)(c) TTBER as:
a technology rights licensing agreement entered into between two undertakings for the purpose of the production of contract products by the licensee and/or its sub-contractor(s);
an assignment of technology rights between two undertakings for the purpose of the production of contract products where part of the risk associated with the exploitation of the technology remains with the assignor.

(2) The market share of the parties does not exceed certain thresholds:[53]
If the parties are competitors,[54] their *combined* market share may not exceed 20%.
If the parties are non-competitors, *each* party's market share may not exceed 30%.

(3) The agreement does not contain any hardcore or excluded restrictions. These restrictions are listed in Article 4 TTBER. For agreements between competitors, the TTBER takes a more restrictive view as to reciprocal agreements than non-reciprocal ones. Examples of hardcore restrictions include fixing (minimum) prices, limitation of the output, or allocation of markets.

Article 5 TTBER contains a series of 'excluded restrictions', such as exclusive licenses or the assignment of rights on severable improvements and 'no-challenge' clauses.[55] These restrictions are not covered by the Block Exemption, but the agreement itself may still be exempted under the TTBER if the restrictions can be severed from the rest of the agreement.

In light of the decisional practice of the Commission, the new guidelines explicitly state that settlement agreements which lead to 'a delayed or otherwise limited ability for the licensee to launch the product on any of the markets concerned, may be prohibited by Article 101(1) TFEU'.[56] In particular, if the agreement entails 'a significant value transfer from the licensor to the licensee, the Commission will be particularly attentive to the risk of market allocation or market sharing'.

---

53. Article 3 TTBER.
54. The term 'competitors' is defined in Article 1(1)(n) TTBER.
55. This is without prejudice to the possibility for the licensor to terminate the agreement if an *exclusive* licensee challenges the validity of the licensed technology rights.
56. Guidelines, at paragraphs 238 et seq.

[b] The R&D Block Exemption

The R&D Block Exemption provides undertakings with the legal security to carry out joint R&D without the fear of breaching EU competition law. It exempts (i) agreements for joint R&D, whether or not combined with an agreement to jointly exploit the results; (ii) paid-for R&D, whether or not combined with an agreement to jointly exploit the results; and (iii) agreements for joint exploitation of the results of jointly performed or paid-for R&D pursuant to a prior agreement between the same parties.[57] Four conditions must be satisfied to benefit from the exemption:[58]

(1) All of the parties must have access to the results of the R&D for further research, development, and exploitation as soon as they become available. This does not apply to research institutes, academic bodies, or undertakings which exclusively supply R&D as a commercial service.
(2) If the agreement only covers the R&D, whether joint or paid-for (i.e., where there is no joint exploitation of the results), each party must be free to independently exploit the results of the R&D and any pre-existing know-how necessary for the exploitation.[59]
(3) Joint exploitation must be limited to the results of the R&D, which are protected by IP rights or constitute know-how; and are indispensable for the manufacture/application of the contract goods/technologies.
(4) The undertakings charged with the manufacture, by way of specialisation in production, must be required to fulfil orders for supplies from the other parties, except where the R&D agreement also provides for joint distribution.

For non-competitors, the agreement will be exempted for the duration of the R&D phase, and if the agreement includes joint exploitation, for seven years from the time the contract product was first commercialised within the internal market. After this period of seven years, the agreement continues to be exempted until the parties' combined market share exceeds 25% on the relevant product and technology markets.[60]

For competitors, the exemption will last for the same duration but only if the combined market share of (i) the parties to a joint R&D agreement, or (ii) the financing party and all parties to a paid-for R&D does not exceed 25% in the relevant product and technology markets.[61]

The R&D Block Exemption will not apply if the agreement contains so-called hardcore restrictions,[62] such as restrictions on passive sales, output limitations, price fixing, limitation of active sales for territories or customers which have not been

---

57. Articles 1(a) and 2 R&D Block Exemption Regulation.
58. Article 3 R&D Block Exemption Regulation.
59. The Block Exemption expressly recognises that parties may charge royalties for their pre-existing know-how, as long as the price is not so high as to effectively impede access to the know-how.
60. Article 4(1) and (3) R&D Block Exemption Regulation.
61. Article 4(2) R&D Block Exemption Regulation.
62. Article 5 R&D Block Exemption Regulation.

allocated to a party by way of specialisation, prevention of parallel imports, requirements to make it difficult for users/resellers to obtain the products from other resellers within the internal market; and restrictions on carrying out R&D in fields unconnected to the agreement, or in connected fields after the joint R&D is completed.

[c]   *The Damages Directive*

The Damages Directive,[63] which has been transposed in the legal systems of the Member States, facilitates the access to evidence/disclosure arising from antitrust investigations.[64]

Moreover, the Damages Directive stipulates that, a final infringement decision of a national competition authority will constitute full proof before civil courts in the same Member State that the infringement occurred. Before courts of other Member States, it will constitute at least prima facie evidence of the infringement.[65] The Damages Directive also provides a clear limitation period for victims of a competition infringement of five years starting from the moment when they had the possibility to discover that they suffered harm from an infringement.[66] The Damages Directive also stipulates that victims are entitled to full compensation for the harm suffered, which covers compensation for actual loss and for loss of profit plus payment of interest from the time the harm occurred until the compensation has been paid.[67] Importantly, any participant in an infringement will be responsible towards the victims for the whole harm caused by the infringement (joint and several liability).[68]

Interestingly, in the ambit of the pharmaceutical sector, it is important to note that there are few 'passing on' risks because national health services (NHS) are often the paying customer in competition law infringements, and pharmaceutical companies will therefore have no basis for arguing that the NHS has passed the loss on to individual consumers.[69] Concretely, this means that NHS will be highly likely to sue and settle in order to obtain damages, in particular, after the implementation of the Damages Directive in all Member States because they are unlikely to have 'passed on' the increased price to consumers.[70]

---

63. Directive 2014/104/EU of the European Parliament and of the Council of 26 November 2014 on certain rules governing action for damages under national law for infringements of the competition law provisions of the Member States and of the European Union (OJ L349/1 of 05/12/2014).
64. Articles 5 to 7 of the Damages Directive.
65. Article 9 of the Damages Directive.
66. Article 10 of the Damages Directive.
67. Article 12 of the Damages Directive.
68. *Ibid.*
69. For passing on risks, *see* Articles 12 and 13 of the Damages Directive.
70. As an example, *see* the settlements of the NHS in the Paroxetine and Gaviscon investigations in the UK.

[C] Selection of Cases/The Pharmaceutical Sector Inquiry

[1] Agreements Between Originators and Generics

On 8 July 2009, the Commission published its Final Report on the Pharmaceutical Sector Inquiry, which was launched in order to examine the reasons for a perceived delay in the introduction of innovative and generic medicines for human consumption. Following the Commission's lead, Italian, Polish, Lithuanian, Romanian, French, and Austrian national competition authorities have also carried out sector inquiries in the pharmaceutical sector. The Commission initiated the sector inquiry in January 2008 with unannounced inspections or 'dawn raids' of several pharmaceutical companies. This was the first time this tool had been used in a sector inquiry and foreshadowed the Commission's aggressive stance throughout the sector inquiry.

The Final Report identifies a number of business strategies and regulatory defects which result in a loss of competition. In particular, the Commission highlighted that certain patent litigation settlements, such as 'pay-for-delay' settlements, including in particular, non-challenge and non-compete clauses, may restrict competition, namely those involving a value transfer from the originator to the generic company.[71]

Since then, the Commission has initiated a number of cases which address the concerns highlighted in the Final Report on the Sector Inquiry and has imposed several fines in this regard.

The Commission has since then followed up the sector inquiry with the report 'Competition Enforcement in the Pharmaceutical Sector (2009–2017)', which provides an overview of the Commission and the national competition authorities' enforcement of competition law in the pharmaceutical sector.

[a] Reverse Payment Patent Settlements

The selection of cases pursued by the Commission indicates that patent settlements envisaging a value transfer from the originator to the generic producer ('reverse payment') in order to delay generic entry are not only capable of breaching Article 101 TFEU but also 'likely to attract the highest degree of antitrust scrutiny'.[72]

The rationale behind such settlements is the attempt by the originator of a branded medicine to avoid the price drop provoked by generic entry upon the expiry of the patents held by the originator and, consequently, the loss of its monopoly profits in the market for that product.

---

71. In the wake of the sector inquiry, the Commission conducted four 'patent settlement monitoring' exercises with a view to obtaining a better understanding of the use of patent settlements and to try to identify the type of settlements which could be harmful for competition. The sixth Monitoring Report, published in December 2015, indicates that, while the total number of patent settlements has significantly increased in recent years, the proportion of potentially problematic settlements has stabilised at around 12%.
72. Third Report on the Monitoring of Patent Settlements at paragraph 14.

In April 2011, the Commission sent a Statement of Objections to Cephalon and Teva concerning the reverse payment settlement concluded by those companies, by which Teva undertook not to market its generic version of Cephalon's modafinil before a given date. In November 2020, the investigation resulted in the Commission fining Cephalon and Teva EUR 60.5 million for delaying entry of cheaper generic medicine, as this agreement eliminated Teva as a competitor and allowed Cephalon to continue charging high prices even if the main patent had long expired.[73]

In a second case, the Commission considered that the conclusion of patent settlement agreements between Servier and five generic manufacturers and the acquisition of a competing technology by Servier breached both Article 101 and Article 102 TFEU. On the one hand, Servier entered into a series of patent settlements with producers of the generic version of perindopril, Servier's bestselling drug. Under those agreements, the generic companies undertook to delay their otherwise imminent market entry in exchange for a share of Servier's monopolist profits or a licence to market the generic product in certain Member States. On the other hand, Servier acquired one of the few sources of patent-free technology with a view to preserving its alleged dominant position in the perindopril market. However, the General Court found that Servier did not possess a dominant position, and consequently annulled the fine imposed for the alleged infringement of Article 102 TFEU.[74] In June 2013,[75] the Commission adopted its first fining decision regarding reverse payment settlements. Lundbeck and fines totalling EUR 146 million were imposed on several generic competitors (Alpharma, Merck KGaA/Generics UK, Arrow and Ranbaxy) for having concluded, upon the expiry of the basic patent on Lundbeck's anti-depressant citalopram, settlement agreements by which Lundbeck made substantial payments to its generic competitors in order to keep them out of the market for the duration of the agreement. Such conduct was considered to constitute an infringement 'by object' of Article 101 TFEU. Lundbeck's appeals against the Commission's decision have been dismissed both by the General Court and by the CJEU.[76]

Some national competition authorities have followed the Commission's steps. Most notably, in February 2016, the UK's Competition and Market Authority (CMA) issued a final infringement decision against GSK and other pharmaceutical companies with respect to the anti-depressant paroxetine.[77] These companies, which were preparing to launch generic versions of the product, agreed with GSK not to enter the market in exchange for significant payments, a conduct which could also amount to an abuse by GSK of its dominant position.[78] Following GSK's appeal against this decision to the Competition Appeal Tribunal (CAT),[79] the CAT referred several questions to the

---

73. *Cephalon*, Case AT/39686.
74. *Servier v. Commission*, Case T-691/14.
75. Lundbeck, Case COMP/39226, Decision of 19 Jun. 2013. *See* the Commission Press Release, IP/13/563 of 19 Jun. 2013: 'Commission fines Lundbeck and other pharma companies for delaying market entry of generic medicines'.
76. *Lundbeck A/S and Lundbeck Ltd*, Case C-591/16P.
77. Paroxetine, Case CE/9531-11.
78. *See* the CMA's press release of 12 Feb. 2016: 'CMA fines pharma companies £45 million.'
79. *GlaxoSmithKline PLC v. Competition and Markets Authority*, Case 1252/1/12/16.

CJEU for clarification. This led to the CJEU, *inter alia*, clarifying that a patent settlement agreement should not automatically be characterised as a restriction by object simply because it involves a value transfer from the originator to the generic, as such agreement may be justified, where a transfer is appropriate and strictly necessary, having regard to the legitimate objectives of the parties to the agreement. This could be the case where the value transfer corresponded to costs incurred because of the litigation.[80]

[b]   Other Agreements Having the Effect of Delaying Generic Market Entry

The Commission has made clear that agreements other than patent settlements having the effect of delaying generic market entry may equally breach Article 101 TFEU.

In December 2013, the Commission fined Janssen-Cilag and Sandoz, the respective subsidiaries of Johnson & Johnson and Novartis, for having put in place a so-called co-promotion agreement for the sale of the painkiller fentanyl contrary to Article 101 TFEU.[81] Under the agreement, Janssen-Cilag agreed to make periodic payments to Sandoz in exchange for Sandoz's commitment not to enter the Dutch market with its generic version of the product. The agreement had the effect of delaying generic entry to the Dutch market for seventeen months, during which time the prices for the medicine were kept at an artificially high level.

[c]   Other Anti-Competitive Agreements

Even though the current enforcement trend concerns agreements between originators and generics, certain cooperation agreements between originators may equally cause concerns.[82] In February 2014, the Italian competition authority fined Hoffmann-La Roche and Novartis for their participation in an agreement aimed at excluding the sale of the cheaper of two medicines (i.e., the product that could be used 'off label'), which could both be used in the treatment of eyesight conditions.[83] By having its sales force actively discourage doctors from prescribing Hoffmann-La Roche's *Avastin* on the ground of its alleged harmfulness, the firms created an artificial product differentiation and channelled demand to Novartis' more expensive product. The economic rationale under this agreement lies in the fact that, since both medicines were licensed by a subsidiary of Hoffmann-La Roche, the latter would make more profit through royalties than by commercialising its own product. Furthermore, this conduct hindered access to treatment for many patients and had an estimated cost of EUR 45 million for the

---

80. Generics (UK) Ltd, Case C-307/18, ECLI:EU:C:2020:52.
81. *Fentanyl*, Case COMP/39685, Decision of 10 Dec. 2013. *See* the Commission Press Release, IP/13/1233 of 10 Dec. 2013: 'Commission fines Johnson & Johnson and Novartis € 16 million for delaying market entry of generic pain-killer fentanyl'.
82. *See*, e.g., M. Nissen & F. Haugsted; *Badmouthing Your Competitor's Products: When Does Denigration Become an Antitrust Issue*, American Bar Association, The Antitrust Source, February 2020, Vol. 19, Issue 4.
83. *Roche-Novartis/Farmaci Avastin e Lucentis*, Case No I760, decision of 27 Feb. 2014

national health system in 2012 alone. The CJEU found that such an agreement between competitors marketing two competing products to communicate certain denigrating information to decision-makers constituted a restriction of competition by object and thus infringed Article 101(1) TFEU.[84] In this finding, the CJEU stressed that by providing misleading information on the safety of pharmaceutical products 'given the characteristics of the medicinal products market, it is likely that the dissemination of such information will encourage doctors to refrain from prescribing that product, thus resulting in the expected reduction in demand for that type of use.[85]

In August 2015, the German regional court in Hannover held that an agreement between Almased Vitalkost, a weight-loss product manufacturer, and pharmacies requiring a minimum resale price maintenance in exchange for a 30% cash discount breached German competition law.[86]

On the question of valid patents and royalties, the CJEU has in relation to the application of Article 101 TFEU in the ambit of patent disputes between pharmaceutical companies found that Article 101 TFEU does not preclude a license agreement to pay royalties following an arbitral award which requires royalties to be paid where the relevant patents had been revoked (i.e., such an agreement does not depend on the validity of the licensed IP right), provided the licensee has the right to terminate the licensing agreement.[87]

§21.04 ARTICLE 102 TFEU

Article 102 TFEU prohibits abusive behaviour by undertakings that have a high level of market power either on their own (single dominance) or as a collection of companies (collective dominance) in one or more relevant markets.

It is not in itself illegal for an undertaking to be in a dominant position and any dominant undertaking is entitled to compete on the merits. However, the unilateral behaviour of a dominant undertaking can significantly restrict competition and constitute an abuse of a dominant position. Under Article 102 TFEU, dominant undertakings have a 'special responsibility'[88] to not allow their conduct to impair genuine undistorted competition in the common market.

In the pharma sector, Article 102 TFEU was in the past mainly applied to intra-brand competition (parallel import cases).[89] More recently, Article 102 TFEU has been applied to inter-brand competition, in particular, between originator and generic companies.

---

84. *F. Hoffmann-La Roche and others*, Case C-179/16.
85. *Ibid.*, Case C-179/16, paragraph 93.
86. Hannover Regional Court, decision of 25 Aug. 2015, case 18 O 91/15.
87. *Genentech Inc.*, Case C-567/14, ECLI:EU:C:2016:526.
88. See, inter alia, *Europemballage and Continental Can v. Commission*, Case 6/72 [1973] ECR 215; *Nederlandsche Banden-Industrie Michelin NV v. Commission*, Case 322/81 [1983] ECR 3461; *Tetra Pak Rausing S.A. v. Commission*, Case T-51/89 [1990] ECR II-309.
89. This section thus deals with the application of Article 102 TFEU outside the context of parallel trade.

[A] Establishing Dominance under Article 102 TFEU

Dominance in EU competition law is defined as a position of economic strength enjoyed by an undertaking, which enables it to prevent effective competition being maintained on a relevant market by affording it the power to behave to an appreciable extent independently of its competitors, its customers, and ultimately of consumers.[90] The extent to which a company can act independently depends on the competitive constraints exerted on the undertaking. In the case of dominant companies, such restraints are typically ineffective.[91]

A crucial factor in assessing the existence of dominance is the company's market share. Dominance is presumed above a 50% market share,[92] although such a presumption is rebuttable. In rare cases, dominance may exist below this market share. An assessment of dominance takes into account the competitive structure of the market, as evidenced by the following factors:[93]

- constraints imposed by the existing suppliers and the market position of actual competitors;
- constraints imposed by the credible threat of future expansion by actual competitors, or entry by potential competitors; and
- constraints imposed by the bargaining strength of the undertaking's customers.

Where these constraints are not sufficient to prevent an undertaking from profitably increasing prices above the competitive level for a significant period of time, typically two years, the undertaking does not face sufficiently effective competitive constraints, and it is considered to possess a dominant position.

For certain pharmaceutical products (e.g., prescription products), retail prices tend to be the outcome of national regulation rather than competitive constraints. Other non-price indicators, such as the relative importance of competitors and purchasers, and the effect that competition has on the volume of prescriptions for a particular product, are also used to determine whether a particular pharmaceutical company has significant market power.

Ownership of an IP right grants a form of monopoly over the specific right but does not automatically characterise the right holder as dominant in a particular product market. Instead, further analysis is required to establish whether and to what extent competing products exist.

---

90. *United Brands Company and United Brands Continental v. Commission*, Case 27/76 [1978] ECR 207; *Hoffmann La Roche & Co. v. Commission*, Case 85/76 [1979] ECR 461.
91. The Commission has in the past considered effective competitive constraints to be absent even where actual or potential competition remained. *See United Brands*, supra n. 90 and *Atlantic Container Line and Others v. Commission*, Case T-395/94 [2002] ECR II-875.
92. *Hoffmann La Roche & Co v. Commission*, supra n. 90.
93. These factors are highlighted by the Commission in its Guidance on the Commission's enforcement priorities in applying Article 82 of the EC Treaty to abusive exclusionary conduct by dominant undertakings OJ [2009] C 45/7.

As detailed earlier, the practice of the Commission is to follow the ATC when determining the scope of the relevant product market for approved medicines in the pharmaceutical sector. In *AstraZeneca*,[94] the Commission departed from this classification, instead basing its finding of dominance on a narrow market definition. The Commission found that during the relevant period, the previous generation of antiulcer products (which had the same therapeutic use and thus fell within the same ATC 3 classification) did not exercise a significant competitive constraint on the new-generation products manufactured by AstraZeneca. The Commission's findings were upheld in their entirety by the CJEU.[95]

The Commission found a clear one-side substitution pattern from the previous generation to the new-generation of products, despite the fact that the new-generation products were considerably more expensive. In defining the product market, the Commission noted that new, therapeutically superior products are generally able to extract higher reimbursable prices than previous-generation products, and that the entry of cheaper previous-generation products had little impact on the price or demand for the new-generation ones.

This type of product market analysis paves the way for narrow market definitions for new-generation pharmaceutical products that are therapeutically superior to the old-generation products. As seen in the *Servier* judgment by the CJEU,[96] where the CJEU overturned the Commission's definition of the relevant market, and consequently the finding of Servier possessing a dominant position, the market definition must be based on a thorough analysis that takes into consideration the overall regulatory, therapeutical, and economic context.

[B] Abuse of a Dominant Position

Where a company is dominant, Article 102 TFEU provides that any abuse by one or more undertakings in a dominant position within the common market or in a substantial part of it is prohibited insofar as it may affect trade between Member States. For a particular behaviour to constitute an abuse, it must be unjustified.

Article 102 TFEU provides a list of abusive behaviour, including:

(a) directly or indirectly imposing unfair purchase or selling prices or other unfair trading conditions (*exploitative abuses*);
(b) limiting production, markets, or technical development to the prejudice of consumers (*exclusionary abuses*);
(c) applying dissimilar conditions to equivalent transactions with other trading parties, thereby placing them at a competitive disadvantage (*discriminatory abuses*); and

---

94. *Generics/Astra Zeneca*, Case COMP/37.507, decision of 5 June 2005 (henceforth *AstraZeneca*).
95. *AstraZeneca v. Commission*, Case C-457/10 P, judgment of 6 December 2012, ECLI:EU:C:2012:770.
96. *Servier v. Commission*, supra n. 74.

Chapter 21: Competition Law in the Pharmaceutical Sector   §21.04[B]

(d) making the conclusion of contracts subject to acceptance by the other parties of supplementary obligations that have no connection with the subject of such contracts (*tying abuses*).

Exclusionary conduct is particularly topical given the Commission's Communication on its enforcement priorities in this area,[97] and the focus on exclusionary conduct in the Commission's Pharmaceutical Sector Inquiry. Exclusionary conduct can result directly from limitations imposed, but it can also result indirectly from other abuses, such as discriminatory trading terms, or tying the sale of distinct products.

[1]   Non-price-Based Exclusionary Conduct

[a]   Misuse of IP Rights

Unilateral behaviour by pharmaceutical companies aimed at delaying market entry by generics is a focus point for the Commission. Such behaviour constitutes exclusionary conduct if the companies are dominant, and they misuse the IP and/or regulatory systems (on a national or European level), thereby excluding competitors from the relevant market. In *AstraZeneca*,[98] the dominant company was found to have misused the regulatory and patent protection system in order to block entry by generic manufacturers and was consequently fined EUR 60 million. According to the Commission's findings, AstraZeneca made fraudulent representations before a number of national patent offices in order to extend the basic protection for a particular product by five years, concealing the date on which it first received marketing authorisation for the product.[99] Further, it allegedly switched the form of the particular medication (from capsules to tablets) in order to hamper market access for capsule-form generics and parallel imports.

In an article discussing the case,[100] Commission representatives highlight that the use of marketing authorisation procedures and regulations may be abusive in specific circumstances where the dominant undertaking clearly intends to foreclose competition, in particular, where the authorities or bodies applying such procedures have little or no discretion. As regards the deregulation of capsules, it was of particular relevance for the case that AstraZeneca deregistered its capsules only in countries where it thought the strategy would block or delay generic entry or parallel imports. The

---

97. Communication from the Commission, *supra* n. 93.
98. *Astra Zeneca*, *supra* n. 94.
99. The Commission made this finding despite accepting that there may have been lack of clarity concerning the interpretation of the relevant special protection certificate Regulation. It determined that the interpretation of the relevant provisions was not decisive for the finding of an abuse in this case. Case law has since clarified the interpretation of the special protection certificate Regulation.
100. Niklas Fagerlund and Søren Bo Rasmussen of Directorate-General Competition, 'AstraZeneca: the first abuse case in the pharmaceutical sector', in *Competition Policy Newsletter*, no. 3 (Autumn 2005): 54–56.

AstraZeneca case was confirmed by the CJEU.[101] The CJEU did, however, clarify that whether or not representations to patent offices can be seen as 'misleading' depends on the circumstances of each case and must be assessed *in concreto*. In other words, not every mistake in a patent application gives rise to liability under Article 102 TFEU.

Following in the Commission's footsteps, national competition authorities are pursuing cases of alleged misuse of IP rights and objectionable lifecycle management. In January 2012, the Italian competition authority fined Pfizer for having abused its dominant position by artificially extending the patent protection of one of its medicines in order to prevent generic entry.

Pfizer filed for a divisional patent and a Supplementary Protection Certificate (SPC) for one of its medicines in order to bring its IP protection in Italy in line with other Member States where SPCs were in force and informed generic producers that it would enforce its SPC if they were to enter the Italian market. As a result, Pfizer managed to delay generic entry for seven additional months after the expiry of the original patent.[102] It could be argued that this decision of the Italian competition authority goes beyond the decision in *AstraZeneca*, to the extent that fraudulent representation to the patent office was not at play. Moreover, the fact that this decision was overturned at first instance but then subsequently upheld by the Italian Council of State shows the difficulties of applying the *AstraZeneca* judgment.

Similarly, in April 2011, the UK's Office of Fair Trading (OFT), the predecessor of the current Competition and Markets Authority (CMA) fined Reckitt Benckiser GBP10.2 million for having withdrawn its original Gaviscon medicine from the NHS prescription channel following the expiry of the product's patent. Since no generic name had yet been assigned to the medicine, the withdrawal of Gaviscon resulted in the increased prescription of Reckitt Benckiser's alternative branded product, which was still patent protected.[103]

[b] Refusal to Supply

IMS Health[104] established, on the basis of previous case law, that failure to grant a license, even if it is the act of a dominant company, cannot in itself constitute an abuse of a dominant position. However, in exceptional circumstances, refusal to provide access to a product or service may amount to abuse of a dominant position. Four conditions must be fulfilled to find an abuse: the refusal must relate to a product or service indispensable to the exercise of a particular activity on a neighbouring market; it excludes effective competition on a neighbouring market;[105] it prevents the

---

101. *AstraZeneca v. Commission*, *supra* n. 95.
102. *Ratiopharm/Pfizer*, Case A431, decision of 11 Jan. 2012.
103. *Reckitt Benckiser*, Case CE/8931/08. *See* the OFT's press release 53/11 of 13 Apr. 2011: 'OFT issues decision in Reckitt Benckiser case'.
104. *IMS Health*, Case C-418/01, paragraphs 34–39 and case law cited therein.
105. Unlike the judgment in IMS Health, the General Court found in *Microsoft*, Case T-201/04 that an abuse could arise where the refusal of such a kind as to exclude any effective competition (as opposed to any competition).

emergence of a new product for which there is a potential consumer demand; and the refusal is not objectively justified.

The same principle applies to the refusal to supply raw materials. In *Commercial Solvents*,[106] Commercial Solvents refused to supply raw materials, as it planned to vertically integrate into the downstream market and to utilise all its raw material internally. The CJEU found that Commercial Solvents abused its dominant position by refusing to supply its customers, thereby effectively excluding them from the market.

[c]   Other Non-price-Based Exclusionary Abuses

The French competition authority has adopted several decisions[107] imposing fines against originators which abused their dominant position through the denigration of the competing generic products in order to hinder their entry into the market to the profit of their own branded or generic products. In December 2014, the Paris Court of Appeal confirmed the findings of the French NCA in the Sanofi-Aventis decision.[108] In March 2015, the Paris Court of Appeals confirmed that the inventor of a brand-name drug sought to impede the development of generics through defamation and loyalty rebates.[109]

In these cases, the originator pursued a marketing campaign aimed at denigrating the generic versions of its branded product, by systematically informing doctors and pharmacists that the generic versions were less efficient and/or harmful and of the possibility of personal liability in prescribing or selling such products, despite them being biologically equivalent, thus precluding that the statements put forward by the dominant company could be based on objective findings or verified assertions. The competition authority observed the abnormally low substitution rate between the branded and the generic product and concluded that such campaigns precluded competition on the merits whilst resulting in higher costs for the national healthcare system.

In 2021 and 2022, the Commission started formal investigations into disparagement claims by dominant originator companies. In March 2021, they opened an investigation into the Teva blockbuster multiple sclerosis drug Copaxone. The investigation covers several possible abuses, but the Commission will, *inter alia,* examine indications that Teva's campaign, primarily directed at healthcare institutions and professionals, may have targeted competing products to create a false perception of health risks associated with their use, even following the approval of these medicines by competent public health authorities.[110] The case concerns – like the French cases – allegations against an originator acting against generic producers.

---

106. *Istituto Chemiterapico Italiano SpA and Commercial Solvents Corporation v. Commission,* Joined Cases 6/73 and 7/73 [1974] ECR 223.
107. *Sanofi-Aventis,* decision 13-D-11 of 14 May 2013; *Schering-Plough,* decision 13-D-21 of 19 Dec. 2013.
108. *Sanofi-Aventis c/ Teva,* case 2013/12370 of 18 Dec. 2014.
109. *Reckitt Benckiser PLC c/Arrow Generiques,* case 2014/03330 of 26 Mar. 2015.
110. See press release in Case AT.40588, dated 4 March 2021: https://ec.europa.eu/commission/presscorner/detail/en/ip_21_1022.

In June 2022, the Commission opened a formal antitrust investigation to assess whether Vifor Pharma has restricted competition by illegally disparaging its closest – and potentially only – competitor in Europe on the market for intravenous iron treatment, Pharmacosmos. Vifor Pharma's conduct appears to be aimed at hindering competition against its blockbuster high-dose intravenous iron treatment medicine, Ferinject.[111] This case concerns a situation where an originator is acting against another originator and may therefore have implications also for the biosimilar field.[112]

[2] Price-based Exclusionary Conduct

[a] Fidelity Rebates and Exclusive Purchase Obligations

The Court in *Hoffmann La Roche*[113] determined that an undertaking that is in a dominant position on the market and ties purchasers – even if it does so at their request – by an obligation or a promise to obtain all or most of their requirements exclusively from the dominant undertaking abuses its dominant position.

The Court further established that the same principle applied if, without tying the purchaser by a formal obligation, the company agreed or unilaterally imposed a system of fidelity rebates (defined as discounts conditional on the customer obtaining all or most of its requirements from the dominant undertaking).

The Court found that fidelity rebates are designed to prevent customers from obtaining their supplies from competing producers. They are also abusive because they produce dissimilar results from equivalent transactions. Two purchasers pay a different price for the same quantity of the same product, depending on whether they have a single source or various sources of supply.

Following a complaint, in December 2015, the Spanish NCA has initiated proceedings against IMS Health for an alleged abuse of dominant position in its contractual relationship with wholesale distributors, which led to IMS Health offering commitments to, *inter alia*, remove provisions in its contracts that said data suppliers must give IMS Health equal or better terms as those afforded to its competitors ('most favoured nation' clauses) as well as provisions, which gave IMS Health a right to terminate agreements if a supplier supplied to third parties or decided to compete with IMS.

---

111. *See* press release in Case 40.577, dated 20 June 2022, https://ec.europa.eu/commission/presscorner/detail/en/ip_22_3882.
112. For a comprehensive analysis of the issue of disparagement, *see*, e.g., M. Nissen & F. Haugsted, Badmouthing Your Competitor's Products: When Does Denigration Become an Antitrust Issue, American Bar Association, The Antitrust Source, February 2020, Vol. 19, Issue 4.
113. *Hoffmann La Roche, supra* n. 90, paras 89–90.

[b] Excessive Pricing

Case law concerning excessive pricing is still not an everyday phenomenon within the sphere of competition law, but throughout recent years, judgments and decisions have been made in a number of important cases in the pharma sector.

In 2014, the Italian NCA initiated an investigation on the price increase of Aspen Pharma's anticancer drug,[114] which was followed by an infringement decision against Aspen. Following this, the Commission opened a formal investigation against Aspen,[115] marking the first of its kind into concerns about excessive pricing practices in the pharmaceutical industry, concerning in excessive pricing. The Commission wanted to investigate indicative information suggesting Aspen had unjustifiably increased prices of up to several hundred percent on a number of niche medicines. To address the Commission's concerns, Aspen proposed several commitments to reduce the prices for its products on all national EEA markets to a level no longer raising competition concerns. Following a market test in 2020 of the proposed commitments and the resulting adjustments, the commitments, including a price reduction of 73%, were made legally binding for Aspen.

In August 2015, the UK CMA issued a statement of objections to Pfizer and Flynn Pharma alleging that each abused their dominant position by charging excessive and unfair prices in the UK for phenytoin sodium capsules, an anti-epilepsy drug. Following Pfizer's sale of its UK distribution rights for the anti-epilepsy drugs to Flynn Pharma, it continued to manufacture the drug which it sold to Flynn at prices which were significantly higher than before the sale of the distribution rights. The CMA found that Pfizer and Flynn abused their dominant positions by charging excessive prices of up to 2,600% to the NHS than those historically charged by Pfizer. The legal test for excessive pricing used by the CMA has since then been upheld by the UK CAT.

In April 2020, the Danish Maritime and Commercial High Court found that CD Pharma had abused its dominant position by charging excessive prices for the drug Syntocinon, by increasing its prices for Syntocinon by approximately 2,000%.[116] The finding that this constituted an excessive price was based on a price-cost comparison.

§21.05 PARALLEL TRADE

The single market requires that products, including pharmaceuticals, are traded throughout the EU free of artificial barriers created by private companies. Despite arguments from pharmaceutical companies that parallel trade reduces the revenues

---

114. Case A480, *see* the AGDCM's press release of 27 Nov. 2014: 'Antitrust's investigation on the price increase for Aspen's anticancer drugs.'
115. Case AT.40394 – Aspen.
116. Case BS-3038-2019, *CD Pharma v. Konkurrencerådet* (the Danish Competition Appeals Tribunal).

available for the funding of R&D, the Commission has found that pharmaceutical companies have infringed competition law by preventing parallel trade.[117]

Two types of conduct have been heavily scrutinised: Sales Quota System (SQS) and dual pricing schemes. Competition authorities have used both Article 101 TFEU and Article 102 TFEU to rule against the use of an SQS, while dual pricing schemes potentially violate Article 101 TFEU only. The CJEU has challenged the hard-line approach of the Commission on parallel trade in a number of cases.[118]

Bayer Adalat[119] concerned parallel import of Bayer's Adalat by French and Spanish wholesalers to the UK, where Adalat was priced 40% higher. Due to the parallel imports, the sales of Bayer's UK subsidiary fell by close to 50%. Bayer sought to limit the impact of parallel trade by implementing an SQS by which the French and Spanish wholesalers would only be supplied with a quantity calculated on the basis of orders made in the preceding year. Bayer alleged stock shortages as the reason for this sudden drop in supply. The Commission, following a complaint by the wholesalers, found that Bayer had entered into an agreement with the wholesalers to prevent exports to the UK, thereby infringing Article 101 TFEU. The Commission imposed a EUR 3 million fine on Bayer. Upon appeal, the CJEU annulled the Commission's Decision on the ground that the Commission wrongfully found that there was an agreement between Bayer and the wholesalers because the latter never agreed (tacitly or otherwise) to limit their parallel trade.[120]

In other words, it was held that Bayer acted unilaterally. Consequently, the CJEU annulled the Commission Decision.

In 2008, the CJEU considered whether a dominant supplier who unilaterally limited supplies to counter parallel trading violated Article 102 TFEU.[121] The CJEU found that a dominant company must be able to 'take steps that are reasonable and in proportion to the need to protect its own commercial interests'.[122] In this respect, the CJEU held that a dominant supplier may legally refuse to supply orders that are 'out of the ordinary'.[123] As the terms 'reasonable and in proportion with' and 'out of the ordinary' have not been clearly defined, dominant pharmaceutical companies should remain cautious when refusing to supply products to distributors.

In 1998, GSK introduced general sales conditions that aimed to set up a dual pricing scheme for pharmaceuticals intended for resale in Spain and those that were used by wholesalers for parallel trading. The Commission found[124] that this constituted an agreement that amounted to an export ban and was therefore restrictive of competition by object. The Commission further found that the agreement did not merit

---

117. N. De Souza, 'Competition in Pharmaceuticals: The Challenges ahead Post AstraZeneca', *Competition Policy Newsletter*, no. 1 (Spring 2007), 39.
118. C. Hatton, A. Bicarregui, & D. Cardwell, "Interesting Times' for Pharmaceutical Companies: European Competition Law and the Pharmaceutical Sector', *European Consumer Law Journal* 2–3 (2009): 381–396.
119. *BAI and Commission v. Bayer*, Case C-2/01 P [2004] ECR I-23.
120. In fact, wholesalers used alternative sourcing methods to continue the parallel trading activity.
121. *Sot. Lélos kai Sia*, Case C-468/06, [2008] ECR I-7139 ('Syfait II').
122. *Ibid.*, paragraph 69.
123. *Ibid.*, paragraph 70.
124. *Glaxo Wellcome*, Case IV/36.957, decision of 8 May 2001.

an exemption under Article 101(3) TFEU. On appeal, the CJEU annulled the Commission decision in part.[125] It considered that while the Commission was right to qualify the agreement as a restriction by object, the Commission failed to properly take into account the arguments of GSK on the specific features of the pharmaceutical sector under Article 101(3) TFEU. However, the CJEU did not itself rule on whether the agreement fulfils the criteria of that paragraph. Further, the European Association of Euro-Pharmaceutical Companies (EAEPC) filed a court action before the General Court against the Commission's decision,[126] claiming that the Commission had to assess the dual-pricing system because it had filed an official complaint which meant that the Commission had a duty to take a position on GSK's set-up. However, the General Court upheld the Commission's refusal to reinvestigate GSK's dual pricing scheme. Therefore, legal uncertainty remains as to whether dual pricing can be a legal strategy to limit parallel trade in the pharmaceutical sector.

A parallel case involving GSK has been investigated by the Greek Competition Authority (the HCC). Following a series of complaints from associations of wholesalers and pharmacists, in 2006, the HCC adopted a decision[127] finding that the refusal by GSK to satisfy all the orders of the complainants, with a view to restraining parallel exports of certain pharmaceutical products, constituted an abuse of GSK's dominant position in the Greek market for those products. GSK appealed the HCC's decision before the Athens Administrative Court of Appeal and the Greek Council of State, which partly annulled the decision and referred the case back to the HCC.[128] However, this appeal led to GSK being fined EUR 4 million for abusing its dominant position by restricting its supply to the country's wholesalers.

In March 2015, the Spanish Competition Authority initiated a formal investigation into Pfizer on the suspicion that, by applying a dual pricing scheme in its contracts with distributors, it hindered imports of its products from other countries. The investigation follows a complaint filed by a distributor in 2005. Although the competition authority had decided that Pfizer's dual-pricing scheme did not infringe competition rules, in December 2014, the Spanish Supreme Court ruled that Pfizer's conduct could restrict parallel imports within the EU, thereby confirming a lower court's ruling which annulled the authority's decision.

§21.06 THE EU MERGER CONTROL REGULATION

The EU Merger Control Regulation[129] (EUMR) provides the Commission with the power to control concentrations between undertakings and, where applicable, to

---

125. *GlaxoSmithKline Services v. Commission*, Joined Cases C-501/06 P, C-513/06 P, C-515/06 P, and C-519/06 P, [2009] ECR I-9291.
126. *EAEPC v. Commission*, Case T-574/14.
127. Case No. 318/V/2006, decision of 1 Sep. 2006.
128. Athens Administrative Court of Appeal, judgments No. 2019/2009, 2100/2009, and 1983/2010; Council of State, judgments No. 1923/2012, 1922/2012, 1921/2012, and 1925/2012.
129. Council Regulation No. 139/2004 of 20 Jan. 2004 on the control of concentrations between undertakings, OJ [2004] L 24/1 (the 'EUMR').

prohibit such concentrations where they would significantly impede effective competition. The EUMR applies if:

(1) there is a merger between two previously independent undertakings or the acquisition of direct or indirect control by one or more parties on a lasting basis,[130] and;
(2) the concentration has an EU dimension. Articles 1(2) and 1(3) EUMR set out the relevant turnover thresholds for this purpose.

The Commission acts as a 'one-stop shop' for merger control in the EU; if a concentration meets the turnover thresholds, it needs to be notified to the EU Commission to the exclusion of any other EEA country. If the EU thresholds are not met, individual notifications may be required at national level depending on national thresholds.

[A] Merger Control Procedure

If the EUMR applies to the merger, the Commission has the exclusive authority to assess whether a merger violates the EUMR, excluding the competence of national authorities.

A concentration with EU Dimension must be approved by the Commission prior to any implementation; to this end, it must be notified to the DG Competition Merger Registry.[131] Formal notification is made by completing a Form CO.[132] The Commission, however, encourages pre-notification talks, and in practice, undertakings often submit a draft Form CO to clear up any problems before the official notification.

Once the notification is filed, there are strict deadlines for assessment and approval. The Commission has twenty-five working days to make its preliminary assessment of the transaction (Phase I) and to decide whether to open an in-depth investigation or to approve the transaction (Phase II). The Commission may also decide that the transaction does not fall within the scope of the EUMR. The Commission may clear a merger at Phase I level with commitments.[133]

If an in-depth investigation is opened, the Commission has ninety working days to conduct its investigation. This period can be prolonged at the parties' request, or where the parties offer commitments. At the end of this period, the Commission must either clear the transaction (possibly subject to conditions) or block the transaction. An appeal to the General Court against the final decision is open to all interested parties.

---

130. *Ibid.*, Article 3, control is defined as the possibility of exercising decisive influence and is not limited to the acquisition of shares but can also be obtained through contractual terms or any other considerations of fact or law.
131. Save in exceptional circumstances, *see* Article 7 EUMR.
132. Annexed to Commission Regulation No. 1269/2013 of 5 December 2013, implementing Council Regulation 139/2004 on the control of concentrations between undertakings, OJ [2004] L 133/1, as amended by Commission Regulation No. 1033/2008 OJ [2008] L 279/3.
133. *See*, as an example, merger decision M.7746 *Teva/Allergan* of 10 Mar. 2016.

[B] Referral of Concentrations That Do Not Meet the Thresholds

Article 22 EUMR allows Member States to refer concentrations to the Commission to be examined if they (1) affect trade between member states and (2) threat to significantly affect competition within the territory of the Member State(s) making the request.

On 26 March 2021, the Commission published new guidance on the application of the referral mechanism set out in Article 22 of the EUMR. The Commission will encourage below-threshold referral cases in appropriate cases. Examples of good candidates include (1) a start-up or recent entrant with significant competitive potential but with low turnover; (2) an important innovator or a company who is conducting potentially important research; (3) a target holding competitively significant assets, such as IP; and (4) a target supplying key input for the downstream market. The new guidance aims at addressing the perceived enforcement gap in relation to 'killer acquisitions' falling below merger thresholds in the EU.

The new guidance explicitly refers to the pharmaceutical and biotech sectors, *inter alia*, together with the digital sector as sectors of interest for the Commission.

In March 2021, the first such case was referred to the Commission by the French Competition Authority (FCA) concerning Illumina's acquisition of Grail, which is developing multi-cancer early detection tests that screen for cancer in asymptomatic patients using DNA sequencing. This was the first time the FCA referred a below-threshold transaction to the Commission. The referral was supported by the competition authorities from Belgium, Greece, the Netherlands, Iceland, and Norway. The Spanish, Austrian, and Slovenian competition authorities decided they did not have the power to refer the transaction to the Commission, as it would not be notifiable in their respective jurisdictions. In April 2021, the Commission accepted the referral and asserted jurisdiction over the acquisition, even though it did not meet the notification thresholds in any member state. In July 2021, the Commission opened an in-depth (phase II) investigation into the transaction, which led Illumina to officially submit commitments in January 2022. The Commission's decision to accept the referral request under Article 22 of the EUMR even where the concentration did not have a European dimension was upheld by the General Court.[134]

[C] Substantive Assessment

A definition of the relevant market is a necessary first step for any assessment of the effect of a concentration on competition.[135] Both relevant product markets and geographical markets[136] must be identified, as summarised in §21.02. Merger control differs from other competition law proceedings in that the competition authority applies an *ex ante* assessment, predicting the future competitive outcome of the

---

134. *Illumina*, Case T-227/21, ECLI:EU:T:2021:672.
135. *French Republic and Société commerciale des potasses et de l'azote (SCPA) and Entreprise minière et chimique (EMC) v. Commission (Kali and Salz)*, Cases C-68/94 and C-30/95 [1998] ECR I-01375, paragraph 143.
136. In some cases, temporal markets may also need to be defined.

concentration. The substantive test applied by the Commission is whether the transaction 'significantly impedes effective competition', particularly as a result of the creation or strengthening of a dominant position. The case law defining a dominant position (discussed in §21.04) is therefore important in merger control proceedings. The Commission has published guidelines on its assessment of horizontal[137] and non-horizontal[138] mergers in order to indicate the possible anti-competitive effects of concentrations.

[1] Horizontal Mergers

In its analysis of the compatibility of horizontal mergers with the common market, the Commission breaks down anti-competitive effects of horizontal mergers into two categories: non-coordinated (unilateral) effects and coordinated effects.

Unilateral effects arise where the merger eliminates an important source of competition, increasing the acquirer's or the merged entity's market power. To assess the likelihood of such effects, the Commission will consider the parties' market share, the concentration level in the affected markets, whether customers can easily switch suppliers, barriers to entry or expansion, and levels of actual and potential competition in the market.[139]

Coordinated effects occur when, as a result of the elimination of a competitor through a merger, the remaining competitors will be better able to coordinate their behaviour without the need for an agreement or concerted practice. A merger in such a market may create a collective dominant position and/or make coordination easier, more stable, or more effective for firms.[140] The CJEU has established three criteria for assessing the likelihood of such coordinated effects.[141] First, the undertakings in question must be able to monitor the terms of cooperation; second, credible deterrence mechanisms must exist through retaliation; and third, it must not be possible for potential entrants or customers to jeopardise such coordination. Typically, these criteria can only be fulfilled where there is a limited number of operators in the market, the products are homogenous, and market conditions are transparent.

[2] Non-horizontal Mergers

Non-horizontal mergers include vertical mergers (where the parties operate at different levels of the supply chain) and conglomerate mergers (where the parties supply different ranges of products). Both types of mergers may raise foreclosure issues,

---

137. Guidelines on the assessment of horizontal mergers under the Council Regulation on the control of concentrations between undertakings (the 'Horizontal Merger Guidelines'), OJ [2004] C 31/5.
138. Guidelines on the assessment of non-horizontal mergers under the Council Regulation on the control of concentrations between undertakings, OJ [2008] C 265/6.
139. Horizontal Merger Guidelines, paragraphs 24 et seq.
140. *Ibid.*, paragraph 39.
141. *Airtours v. Commission*, Case T-342/99 [2002] ECR II-2585, paragraph 62.

Chapter 21: Competition Law in the Pharmaceutical Sector   §21.06[D]

although the Commission has stated that non-horizontal mergers are less likely to impede competition than those that generate unilateral effects.

In vertical mergers, anti-competitive effects can result where the vertically-integrated entity ceases or reduces supply to downstream competitors, so as to foreclose them from the market, or makes it more difficult for them to compete in the market, for instance, by raising their costs. However, these effects are only likely to happen where the merged entity has significant market power in the relevant upstream or downstream markets as well as the ability and incentive to foreclose its competitors.

Conglomerate mergers are between parties that are neither competitors nor suppliers of each other but are active in closely-related markets. Such mergers may raise competition concerns where the merged entity has market power in one market and is able to leverage this market power in the connected market (e.g., by tying or bundling its products). This issue was raised by third parties in the GE/Amersham[142] merger. The relevant markets were the manufacture of diagnostic equipment (GE) and the manufacture of diagnostic pharmaceuticals (Amersham). Both companies held market shares of about 40% in some national markets. Third parties alleged that the merged entity would be able to offer bundled packages. Upon examination, the Commission concluded that although the bundling was possible, competitors were able to respond adequately, and barriers to entry in the market were sufficiently low to prevent any significant impediment to competition.

[D]   Selection of Cases

The following paragraphs aim to provide an overview of the main types of assessment and remedies pursued by the Commission in the pharmaceutical sector, through a case study of two Commission decisions in the sector: *GlaxoWellcome/Smithkline Beecham*[143] and *Novartis/Hexal*.[144]

[1]   GlaxoWellcome/Smithkline Beecham

The merger between Glaxo Wellcome (GW) and Smithkline Beecham (SB) created the (at the time) biggest pharmaceutical company worldwide.[145] The Commission expressed serious concerns regarding a number of different markets in which the merged entity would obtain a dominant position.[146] After a series of undertakings offered by the parties, the Commission cleared the merger.

The Commission followed its usual threefold categorisation of the market as: pharmaceutical specialities, active substances, and pipeline products (future markets).

---

142. *Ge/Amersham*, Case COMP/M3304 of 21 Jan. 2004.
143. *GlaxoWellcome/Smithkline Beecham*, Case COMP/M.1846, decision of 8 May 2000.
144. *Novartis/Hexal*, Case COMP/M.3751, decision of 8 Jul. 2005.
145. *EC Competition Policy Newsletter*, no. 23 (October 2000): 69.
146. At the time of the merger, the 'old' Council Regulation (EEC) No. 4064/89 of 21 Dec. 1989 OJ [1989] L 395/1 was in force. Under Article 2 of that Regulation, the substantive test was whether the concentration would create a dominant position.

With regard to future markets, the Commission first identified the areas where either one or both parties had an existing product on the market and a pipeline product; in a second phase, it identified the areas where none of the parties had a product on the market but both had pipeline products.[147] The Commission defined the geographic market as being at least EU-wide, if not worldwide.[148]

The Commission had serious doubts as to the compatibility of the operation in five markets. To address these issues, the parties proposed to out-license SB's 'Ariflo' but only in the event that competing Phase III pipeline compounds for second treatment failed. The Commission accepted this remedy 'under the very special circumstances of this case'.[149] The parties also proposed to out-license 'Famvir', 'Vectavir' or 'Zovirax', 'Kytrill' and 'Kevtril', and 'Monocid.' In view of these undertakings, the Commission cleared the merger.

[2] Novartis/Hexal[150]

In 2005, Novartis notified its proposed acquisition of Hexal and Eon Labs. The merger referred almost exclusively to generics, as Hexal (and its US sister company Eon Labs) is a generic medicines producer, and Novartis already owned Sandoz, one of the EEA's largest generic producers. The merger confirmed the Commission's practice of considering originator and generic medicines in the same market, as they are fully substitutable from the patient's and the doctor's point of view. In view of this and of the important market position of the parties, commitments were proposed in Poland, Germany, and Denmark, following which the Commission authorised the merger.

§21.07 STATE AID

Articles 107 and 108 TFEU prohibit Member States from implementing any State aid measure before it is notified to the Commission and the Commission approves the aid.[151]

[A] Definition of State Aid under the Treaty

The CJEU looks at the effects of the aid to determine if it is within the scope of the Treaty.[152] The CJEU considers five factors:

(1) Whether the measures confer an advantage upon the beneficiary. If a private investor would have made the same investments, the measure is unlikely to

---

147. *Ibid.*, paragraph 150.
148. *Ibid.*, paragraph 75.
149. *Ibid.*, paragraph 195.
150. *Novartis/Hexal*, Case COMP/M.3751, decision of 27 May 2005.
151. Article 108(3) TFEU.
152. *Italy v. Commission*, Case 173/73 [1974] ECR 709.

be State aid. For example, public authorities may decide to participate in a capital increase. If the investment would be a sound one for a private investor (e.g., the shares are purchased at a market price, a sound dividend is paid, the company has potential to grow, etc.), there would be no 'advantage' conferred to the undertaking. If, however, the capital increase is overvalued, and it is only performed to prevent a company from failing, the undertaking gains an 'advantage'.

(2) Whether the aid is granted by a Member State or through State resources. The aid has to be imputable to the State, and the aid must use State resources.[153]

(3) Whether the measures favour certain undertakings or the production of certain goods. This factor distinguishes between selective measures and measures having a general effect. Only the former are capable of constituting State aid. Selectivity can be established when the measure only applies to a region, an industry, or one or more specific undertakings.

(4) If the aid distorts or threatens to distort competition insofar as it affects trade between Member States. Although the courts do not impose a detailed market investigation showing the distortion of competition, it must be shown that the aid strengthens the position of an undertaking compared with other undertakings competing in intra-EU trade.[154]

(5) The aid must affect trade between Member States. This does not require that the beneficiary export its goods or services to other Member States; a beneficiary may compete with products coming from other Member States.[155] Furthermore, it is sufficient that the aid has the potential to affect trade between Member States.[156]

[B] Exemptions

While State aid is in principle forbidden, Articles 107(2) and 107(3) TFEU list a number of categories of aid that are or may be compatible with the common market. In addition, a Block Exemption Regulation exempts certain forms of aid from the obligation to notify.

In 2008, the Commission adopted the first General Block Exemption Regulation.[157] In 2014, the Regulation was replaced by a new General Block Exemption Regulation[158] (GBER) applicable as of 1st of July 2014 and an implementing

---

153. *France v. Commission*, Case C-482/99 [2002] ECR I-4397.
154. *Philip Morris v. Commission*, Case 730/79 [1980] ECR 2671.
155. *Italy v. Commission*, Case C-66/02 [2005] ECR I-10901.
156. *France v. Commission (FIM)*, Case 102/87 [1988] ECR 4067.
157. Commission Regulation (EC) No. 800/2008 of 6 Aug. 2008 declaring certain categories of aid compatible with the common market in application of Articles 87 and 88 of the Treaty, OJ [2008] L 214/3, as amended by Commission Regulation (EU) No. 1224/2013 of 29 Nov. 2013.
158. Commission Regulation (EU) No. 651/2014 of 17 Jun. 2008 declaring certain categories of aid compatible with the common market in application of Articles 107 and 108 of the Treaty, OJ [2014] L 187/1. The GBER entered into force on 1 July 2014.

Regulation.[159] The Regulation includes a section on research, development, and innovation (R&D&I) aid.

In order to be exempted, the aid measure must satisfy all of the common criteria set out in Chapter I of the GBER. These include aid thresholds and transparency requirements. Article 6 of the GBER specifies that only aid that has an incentive effect shall be exempted.[160] In case of ad hoc aid to a large enterprise, the aid must cause the beneficiary to increase the size, scope, and amount spent on R&D&I and to conduct the R&D&I faster.

The GBER lists five aid categories that are exempted:[161]

(1) Aid for R&D projects:[162] Fundamental research may be 100% State funded, 50% industrial research, and 25% experimental development[163]. These percentages may be increased in case of collaboration or wide dissemination of the results.[164] Feasibility studies may be up to 50% State funded. All the above percentages are increased by 10% where the beneficiaries are medium-sized enterprises and by 20% in the case of small enterprises.

(2) Investment aid for research infrastructures:[165] 'Research infrastructures' are defined as facilities, resources, and related services used by the scientific community to conduct research in their respective fields and covers scientific equipment or any other entity of a unique nature essential to conduct research.[166] Research infrastructures that perform economic activities may be up to 50% State funded.

(3) Aid for innovation clusters:[167] 'Innovation clusters' are defined as structures or organised groups of independent parties designed to stimulate innovative activity through promotion, sharing of facilities, and exchange of knowledge

---

159. Council Regulation (EC) No. 1588/2015 of 13 Jul. 2015 on the application of Articles 107 and 108 of the Treaty on the Functioning of the European Union to certain categories of horizontal State aid, OJ [2015] L 248.
160. For aid granted under schemes and aid to SMEs, the incentive effect is presumed where the beneficiary applies for the aid before the start of the work.
161. The new GBER for the first time exempts aid to innovation clusters, aid for process and organisational innovation, and aid to research infrastructures. It also exempts aid for R&D in the fishery and aquaculture sector (Article 30 of the new GBER). Moreover, it provides for the granting of aid to small, young, and innovative enterprises (Article 22(5) of the new GBER).
162. Article 25 GBER.
163. Experimental research includes clinical trials, from Phase I to Phase III; *see* Commission Decision of 5 Jul. 2005 in N 126/2005 *PT Portela & Ca SA*, paragraphs 30–38; and Commission Decision of 8 May 2012 in SA.33866 (2011/N) *Aiuto di Stato a favore di Ricerca, Sviluppo e Innovazione per il progetto FAIV* (Faster Access to Innovative Vaccines) *di Novartis Vaccines S.r.l.*, paragraphs 79–80.
164. In particular, in case of wide dissemination of the results (through conferences, journals, open access repositories, or through open and free software), in case of collaboration with SMEs or research organisations or in case of cross-border collaboration.
165. Article 26 GBER.
166. Article 2(91) GBER.
167. Article 27 GBER.

and expertise and by contributing effectively to knowledge transfer, networking, and information dissemination.[168] Investment aid and operating aid may be provided to the legal entity operating the innovation cluster for a period of ten years. The aid intensity cannot exceed 50% of the eligible costs.

(4) Innovation aid to small- and medium-sized enterprises (SMEs):[169] SMEs may receive aid up to 50% of the industrial property rights costs, of the costs of various innovation advisory[170] and support[171] services,[172] and of the costs for secondment personnel from a large enterprise or a research organisation for the purpose of working, in a newly created function, on R&D&I.

(5) Aid for process and organisational innovation:[173] SMEs and large enterprises[174] may receive aid of up to 50% and 15% of the eligible costs for process[175] and organisational[176] innovation, respectively.

Where the aid does not fulfil the criteria of the GBER,[177] it must be notified to the Commission, which will then carry out an individual assessment. The R&D&I Framework[178] gives guidance on the way in which the Commission will assess such aid projects. The R&D&I Framework provides for the same categories and basic aid intensities[179] as the GBER.

In addition, the R&D&I Framework provides for a detailed assessment when certain aid measures exceed the limits set in the GBER. In this detailed assessment, the Commission assesses whether the aid measure at hand satisfies the common assessment principles, i.e., the contribution to a well-defined objective, the need for state intervention, the appropriateness of the aid measure, the incentive effect, the proportionality of the aid, the avoidance of undue negative effects on competition and intra-EU trade, and the transparency of the aid.[180]

---

168. Article 2(92) GBER.
169. Article 28 GBER.
170. Among others, management consulting, technological assistance, and protection and exploitation of IP rights.
171. Among others, office space, market research, testing, and certification.
172. In the case of innovation advisory and support services, the aid intensity may reach up to 100% where SMEs receive aid of up to EUR 200,000 within a three-year period.
173. Article 29 GBER.
174. Large enterprises are eligible only if they collaborate with SMEs and the SMEs incur at least 30% of the costs.
175. That is, the implementation of a new or significantly improved production or delivery method.
176. That is, the implementation of a new organisational method in the business practices of the undertaking.
177. For example, where the aid amount exceeds the notification thresholds of Article 4 of the new GBER.
178. Framework for State aid for research and development and innovation, OJ [2014] C 198/1, in force since 1 July 2014.
179. The R&D&I Framework provides for higher aid intensities for individual aid which is strictly limited to the minimum necessary. *See* paragraph 89 of the R&D&I Framework.
180. *See* Section 3 of the R&D&I Framework.

§21.08 UK

[A] Introduction

The UK left the EU on 31 January 2020, and the transition period ended on 31 December 2020. However, the fundamental principles of EU, namely the prohibitions on anti-competitive agreements and abusing a dominant position, based on Articles 101 and 102 of the TFEU, continue to operate much as before in the UK, as they formed the basis for the corresponding prohibitions in UK competition law.[181]

The UK has now replaced the EU's Vertical Block Exemption Regulation (VBER) with the Vertical Agreements Block Exemption Order (VABEO).[182] The VABEO retains a similar structure to the previous VBER, but it aims to modernise the approach. There are some helpful changes in the VABEO which are important to note, although they give rise to minor divergences from the EU approach. There are revised approaches to territorial and customer restrictions, giving more flexibility in relation to appointing distributors and exclusivity. Previously where dual pricing (charging a distributor different prices for products to be sold online and offline) was prohibited, it is now exempted. However, the UK CMA notes that any dual pricing should reflect proportionally the costs and investment incurred in selling the product. A key change is that preventing use of the internet for sales is now considered a hardcore restriction. The VABEO and accompanying guidance also provide more detail on active-versus-passive sales and provide a list of excluded restrictions. Last, the use of wide retail parity clauses will now be considered a hardcore restriction. The VABEO came into force on 1 June 2022. There will be a one-year implementation period to give businesses time to make any relevant changes to their agreements. It is also noteworthy that a leniency application made to the Commission before or after the end of the transition period will not protect a firm from being subject to fines in the UK.

UK-specific legislation comprises the Competition Act 1998 (Chapters I and II), which prohibits anti-competitive agreements and abuse of dominance that may affect trade within the UK and the Enterprise Act 2002. Anti-competitive agreements or conduct of UK businesses that have an effect within the EU are prohibited by Articles 101 and 102 TFEU, in much the same way as agreements or conduct of US and Asian businesses are currently subject to EU competition law where their agreements or conduct affect EU markets. A UK participant in a global cartel will therefore continue to face investigation and fines by the Commission, as well as by the UK and other global authorities. A key difference is that the Commission now has power neither to carry out on-site investigations (dawn raids) in the UK nor to ask the CMA to do so on its behalf. The Commission's powers of investigation are limited to making written requests for information, as it does on a regular basis to businesses based outside of the EU.

Since 1 January 2021, the UK has been subject to commitments on subsidy control set out in its free trade agreements with other countries, including the UK-EU

---

181. Competition Act 1998, Chapter I and Chapter II.
182. Competition Act 1998 (Vertical Agreements Block Exemption) Order 2022 SI No. 516.

Chapter 21: Competition Law in the Pharmaceutical Sector §21.08[A]

Trade and Cooperation Agreement (TCA). The TCA includes a commitment by both parties to maintain effective competition laws to address anti-competitive agreements and abuses of a dominant position, essentially maintaining the status quo of the existing EU and UK competition law rules. A number of changes have already been made to the UK rules including, as outlined below.

On 28 April 2022, the Subsidy Control Bill received Royal Assent, becoming the Subsidy Control Act 2022. It aims to move away from the 'bureaucratic' EU state-aid rules and to adopt an approach based more on self-assessment in accordance with a set of principles. Instead of requiring that all subsidies, except those falling under a block exemption, be notified, as is the EU approach, the UK rules will operate on the basis of an assumption that the subsidy is permitted once certain UK-wide principles are followed; namely, that the subsidy delivers good value for the British taxpayer while being awarded in a timely and effective way. Importantly, more power is being delegated to the devolved governments of Scotland, Wales, and Northern Ireland, who will now be responsible for deciding on issuance of subsidies in their own jurisdiction. The CMA is responsible for advising issuing authorities on the compatibility of certain subsidies with the applicable principles. Unlike the Commission, it has no power to adopt binding decisions in respect of subsidies. A newly established government body, the 'Office for the Internal Market', will also help the CMA to monitor the market and subsidies in the UK, between England, Wales, Scotland, and Northern Ireland. The CAT will have jurisdiction to judicially review decisions to award subsidies.

On 16 March 2021, a multilateral working group, including the Federal Trade Commission (FTC), the US Department of Justice, the Canadian Competition Bureau, the European Commission's Directorate General for Competition, and the CMA, was launched at the initiative of the FTC to analyse the effects of mergers in the pharmaceutical sector. The Commission stated that because of the increasing number of mergers in the pharmaceutical sector, there is a need 'to scrutinise closely to detect those that could lead to higher prices, lower innovation or anticompetitive conduct'.[183] A public consultation was carried out between 11 May 2021 and 25 June 2021 with a view to gathering ideas and views from stakeholders.

The CMA is the main UK national competition authority, with responsibility for investigating suspected infringements of the competition rules and for enforcement. The CMA's antitrust law powers are set out in the Competition Act 1998, and its merger control powers are set out in the Enterprise Act 2002. The CMA also has investigation and enforcement powers in the field of consumer protection, and in the early stages of its investigations, it will often examine both consumer and competition issues before deciding where to focus its attention.

The CMA has been very active in enforcing the Competition Act in the pharmaceuticals sector. It is actively engaged in several excessive pricing (abuse of dominance) cases.

---

183. European Commission Press Release, 'Competition: The European Commission forms a Multilateral Working Group with leading competition authorities to exchange best practices on pharmaceutical mergers', https://ec.europa.eu/commission/presscorner/detail/en/ip_21_1203.

[B] Merger Control

There is no requirement to pre-notify or obtain prior clearance for mergers under UK law, the pre-notification regime being voluntary. However, the CMA has the power to intervene and investigate mergers, including those that have not been notified or that have been completed, or both, and it frequently does so. Where the CMA reaches an adverse competition assessment following a second-phase investigation, it can prohibit an anticipated merger or impose remedial measures for a completed merger, including divestment requirements.

The acquisition of material influence, not just the acquisition of control, is subject to the UK merger control regime. For most sectors, including pharmaceuticals, the thresholds for a transaction qualifying for investigation are the target having a UK turnover of over GBP 70 million or the parties having an overlapping share of supply of 25% or more in the UK (or a substantial part of the UK). The 'share of supply' test is interpreted very flexibly – the CAT recently upheld a CMA decision finding that it had jurisdiction even where one of the parties supplied services only indirectly to UK customers.

In 2018, the UK amended the Enterprise Act to lower the applicable threshold for intervention in mergers or acquisitions in three specified sectors: (1) dual-use goods; (2) quantum technology; and (3) computing hardware. In 2020, these thresholds were again lowered, resulting in the CMA having jurisdiction to investigate a transaction where the target business has a UK turnover of above GBP 1 million, or has a share of supply of 25% or more of relevant goods or services in the UK (or a substantial part of it), even if the transaction does not lead to an increase in the merging parties' share of supply. Three additional categories were added: artificial intelligence, advanced materials, and cryptographic authentication.

The National Security and Investment Act 2021 (NSIA) adds another layer of complication for merging entities. The NSIA came into force on 4 January 2022, after receiving royal assent in April 2021. This regime is focused on reviewing transactions on the grounds of national security, giving the government wide powers to intervene where it has concerns. The regime goes further than just mergers and acquisitions (M&A) transactions and covers certain minority investments, acquisitions of voting rights, and acquisitions of assets, including IP. The regime requires mandatory filings of more substantial investments in businesses involved in seventeen 'sensitive sectors'. They include synthetic biology, which means applying engineering principles to biology to produce components or systems that do not exist in the natural world. The seventeen sensitive sectors also include other activities that may be less directly relevant to pharmaceuticals, including artificial intelligence, computing hardware, data infrastructure, certain supplies to the government. Failure to comply with the requirements of the NSIA may lead to a transaction being void, heavy fines, and/or criminal liability.

The CMA's investigation and enforcement powers in respect of mergers extend to foreign-to-foreign mergers where the parties (and especially the target) supply (or supplies) the UK market and the relevant criteria for investigation are met. The

Chapter 21: Competition Law in the Pharmaceutical Sector   §21.08[C]

definition of 'supply' is broad. For example, in the pharmaceuticals sector, in 2019 the CMA investigated, on its own initiative, the acquisition by Roche Holdings, Inc., a subsidiary of the Swiss-based Roche group, of Spark Therapeutics, Inc., a US biotechnology company active in developing gene therapy treatments. Roche was supplying the relevant UK market, but Spark's relevant products were still in clinical development. The ultimate test in UK merger control is whether the merger is likely to result in a substantial lessening of competition in the UK. The CMA concluded that there would not be a substantial lessening of competition in this case.

Following Brexit, mergers in the UK are subject to possible parallel investigations by the CMA and the Commission, as the 'one stop shop' principle no longer applies.

[C]   Anti-competitive Behaviour

[1]   UK Competition Act 1998 Chapter I: Restrictive Agreements

[a]   Reverse Payment Agreements (Pay-For-Delay)

Under specific circumstances, it is clear that a settlement agreement between a holder of a pharmaceutical patent and a manufacturer of generic medicines can be contrary to UK competition law. In 2016, the CMA adopted its first decision on reverse payment agreements. GSK and various generic medicines manufacturers concluded patent settlement agreements whereby the generics suppliers agreed to refrain from entering the market with their own generic medicines, in return for payments and supply by GSK of specified volumes of generic paroxetine tablets for resale on the UK market. The CMA found that the agreements in question infringed the prohibition of restrictive agreements under Article 101 of the TFEU and its UK equivalent (Chapter I of the Competition Act 1998) and constituted an abuse of GSK's dominant position in the relevant market on the basis of Chapter II of the UK Competition Act.

The CMA's 2016 GSK decision[184] was appealed to the CAT, which made a reference for a preliminary ruling to the CJEU.[185]

The CJEU formulated general principles to be applied to reverse payment agreements, on fundamental issues relating to the application of potential competition, object, effect, definition of the relevant market, and abuse. The court held that reverse payment settlement agreements may be considered 'by object' infringements of competition law, thus breaching antitrust rules by their very nature, without needing proof of the effects that the conduct has had on the market.

Following the CJEU's judgment, the CAT applied the ruling to the facts of the four referred cases in its judgment of 10 May 2021.[186] It reduced the imposed fine from GBP

---

184. *GlaxoSmithKline PLC v. Competition and Markets Authority*, supra n. 79.
185. *Generics (UK) Ltd and Others v. Competition and Markets Authority*, Case C-307/18, 30 January 2020, ECLI:EU:C:2020:52.
186. 1251/1/12/16 *Generics UK Limited v. Competition and Markets Authority*; *GlaxoSmithKline PLC v. Competition and Markets Authority*, supra n. 79; *Xellia Pharmaceuticals APS (2) Alpharma LLC v. Competition and Markets Authority*, Case 1253/1/12/16 (1); *Merck KGaA v.*

37.6 million to GBP 22 million and also reduced several other related fines. The CMA had advocated for a smaller reduction of closer to 10%. However, the CAT held that on the grounds of proportionality, a reduction of closer to 40 was more appropriate.

[b]   Recent and Ongoing CMA Chapter I Investigations

Nortriptyline

In a decision on 4 March 2020, the CMA found that four drug makers, including Lexon, were involved in the exchange of commercially sensitive information – including about prices, volumes, and entry plans – to try to keep the price of nortriptyline high. The companies were collectively fined GBP 3.4 million, with Lexon appealing to the CAT.

On 1 June 2020, the CMA announced that it had secured a legally binding disqualification undertaking from Mr Amit Patel, a former director of Auden Mckenzie (Pharma Division) Limited and Auden Mckenzie Holdings Limited. Mr Patel gave an undertaking not to act as a director of any UK company for five years from 13 July 2020. On 21 August 2020, the CMA secured a legally binding disqualification undertaking from Mr Robin Davies, director of Alissa Healthcare Research Limited. Mr Davies gave an undertaking not to act as a director of any UK company for two years as of 24 November 2020. However, On 10 November 2020, Mr Davies applied to the High Court for permission to act as director and take part in the management of certain companies, and on 17 December 2020, he was granted such permission, subject to strict conditions. The court was influenced by Alissa's status as a pharmaceutical supply company during the pandemic, the fact that Mr Davies was the only executive director and the lack of a suitable replacement for him. On 27 August 2020, the CMA issued proceedings in the High Court of Justice, Business and Property Courts, seeking the disqualification of Mr Pritesh Sonpal, a director of Lexon (UK) Limited. However, given the pending appeal against the CMA's decision before the CAT, the assigned judge made an order transferring the disqualification proceedings to the CAT, so that both could be heard together. On 25 February 2021, the CAT upheld the CMA's findings and dismissed the appeal, while also unanimously determining that the first condition of the disqualification proceedings was fulfilled.[187]

Nitrofurantoin and prochlorperazine

On 7 April 2020, the CMA announced a pause in two investigations, concerning alleged anti-competitive agreements in the supply of prochlorperazine and nitrofurantoin, respectively, to reallocate resources to enable the CMA to focus on urgent work during the COVID-19 pandemic. Each of these investigations was the subject of statements of objections issued in 2019.

Both cases resumed in July 2020. On 25 April 2021, the CMA announced that it needed further time to consider the responses to the statement of objections sent in the

---

Competition and Markets Authority, Case 1255/1/12/16; *Generics UK Limited v. Competition and Markets Authority* [2021] CAT 9, Case 1251-1255/1/12/16.
187. *Lexon (UK) Limited v. Competition and Markets Authority* [2021] CAT 5, Case 1344/1/12/20.

nitrofurantoin investigation. In the prochlorperazine investigation, the CMA announced on 22 January 2021 that it had taken the administrative decision to focus on the overarching agreement rather than individual breaches. The CMA published its infringement decision on 3 February 2022 and fined the parties GBP 35 million for the pay-for-delay agreement. From 2013 to 2017, the prices paid by the NHS for prochlorperazine rose from GBP 6.49 per pack of 50 tablets to GBP 51.68 which amounts to an increase of 700%. The parties have appealed the fine at the CAT and as at the time of writing, the proceedings are ongoing.

[c]   UK Competition Act 1998 Chapter II: Abuse of Dominance

UK Court of Appeal clarifies the legal test to be applied in excessive pricing cases

Phenytoin sodium – Pfizer/Flynn

In December 2016, the CMA imposed a record fine of GBP 84.2 million on Pfizer Limited and GBP 5.2 million on Flynn Pharma Limited for charging excessive prices and abuse of dominance in the market for the manufacture and distribution of phenytoin sodium capsules. The UK CAT quashed the CMA's decision (June 2018) finding that the CMA had misapplied the legal test for excessive pricing, not properly applied the evidence adduced by the companies by not taking sufficient account of the prices of comparable products (phenytoin sodium tablets in particular), and not properly considered the economic value of phenytoin sodium capsules. The CMA appealed the CAT judgment to the Court of Appeal (supported by the Commission) and on 20 March 2020, the Court of Appeal broadly upheld the CAT's ruling.

Pfizer supplied phenytoin sodium, a prescription anti-epilepsy drug, in capsule form under the brand name Epanutin in the UK. In 2012, it transferred to Flynn the marketing authorisation for the capsule form that it continued to manufacture for Flynn, which in turn supplied it to the NHS. Flynn de-branded Epanutin and supplied it as a generic. As a consequence of this de-branding, the capsule form was no longer subject to price regulation. Pfizer increased its manufacturing price to Flynn for capsules by between 783% and 1,615%. Flynn raised its price to the NHS by an eyebrow-raising from 2,387% to 2,656%.

The Court of Appeal considered the application of the legal test for excessive pricing established by the CJEU in its seminal *United Brands* judgment. Here, the court stated that the excessive nature of a price could be determined, *inter alia*, through the application of a two-limb test:[188] (1) the price must be excessive when the difference between the cost of production and the selling price of the product is excessive (the excessive limb); and (2) the price must be unfair either in itself or when compared to competing products (the unfair limb).

---

188. *United Brands Company and United Brands Continental BV v. Commission*, EU:C:1978:22, paragraphs 251 and 252.

However, the Court of Appeal said that this two-limb test is not the only method for assessing excessive pricing, and that the CMA has a margin of manoeuvre or appreciation in deciding which methodology to use and which evidence to rely upon.

On 8 June 2020, the CMA announced the timetable for its investigation in the *Pfizer/Flynn* excessive pricing case, following remittal of issues by the CAT and by the Court of Appeal judgment. The initial re-investigation was carried out between June and October 2020, and in March 2021, the CMA took the decision to continue with the investigation. It adopted a new decision in July 2022, this time imposing a fine of GBP 63 million on Pfizer and a fine of GBP 6.7 million on Flynn. The decision had not been published at the time of writing.

Liothyronine

The CMA investigation relates to suspected unfair and excessive pricing by Advanz Pharma (formerly Concordia International RX (UK) Limited) in the supply of liothyronine tablets, including to the NHS).

The CMA's case, contained in two statements of objections, alleged that Advanz Pharma/Concordia abused its dominant position in breach of the Chapter II prohibition of the Competition Act and Article 102 of the TFEU, by charging excessive and unfair prices to the NHS. The CMA issued a third statement of objections in July 2020, which addressed issues arising from the Court of Appeal's judgment of 10 May 2020 in the phenytoin investigation, discussed above, and stated that the CMA maintained its provisional finding of a breach of competition law. The CMA published an infringement decision on 29 July 2021, Advanz Pharma appealed against the decision, and proceedings are ongoing as at the time of writing.

Liothyronine tablets are primarily used to treat hypothyroidism. Until 2017, Concordia was the only supplier. The CMA found that the price that the NHS paid per pack of this drug rose from around GBP 4.46 before it was de-branded in 2007 to GBP 258.19 by July 2017, an increase of almost 6,000%, while production costs remained broadly stable.

Hydrocortisone

On 12 February 2020, the CMA joined together three separate investigations into alleged excessive and unfair pricing, anti-competitive agreements, and abusive conduct in relation to the supply of hydrocortisone tablets in the UK. The CMA issued statements of objections between December 2016 and February 2019, and on 15 July 2021, the CMA published its infringement decision.[189] It found unfair pricing abuses and anti-competitive agreements in relation to the hydrocortisone tablets and imposed total fines of GBP 260 million.[190] The CMA found that the price increased by over 10,000% compared to the original branded version of the drug. In real terms, this meant that the amount paid by the NHS for a single pack of 10mg tablets rose from 70p in April 2008 to GBP 88.00 by March 2016. For the 20mg strength, prices rose from GBP

---

189. August 2017 (Case 50277-1), Mar. 2017 (Case 50277-2), and Feb. 2019 (Case 50277-3).
190. CMA Decision: Hydrocortisone Tablets – Excessive and Unfair pricing and anti-competitive agreements, Case 50277, 15 Jul. 2021.

Chapter 21: Competition Law in the Pharmaceutical Sector §21.08[C]

1.07 to GBP 102.74 per pack over the same period. This meant that for the investigation period, the NHS had gone from spending approximately GBP 500,000 a year on hydrocortisone tablets in 2008 to over GBP 80 million by 2016. This explains the level of fines imposed on the companies. The companies appealed against the decision and proceedings are ongoing.

Lithium-based medication for the treatment of bipolar disease

On 5 October 2020, the CMA opened an investigation into Essential Pharma's intention to discontinue the supply of Priadel, a lithium-based medication for the treatment of bipolar disorder. The Department of Health and Social Care requested the CMA to impose interim measures on Essential Pharma, preventing it from following through with the discontinuance, until the investigation was concluded. However, Essential Pharma agreed to continue supplying the drug to facilitate continued discussions on pricing. On 24 November 2020, the CMA announced its intention to accept commitments from Essential Pharma and sought input from stakeholders on the suitability of the proposed commitments. On 18 December 2020, following minor modifications, the CMA officially accepted the commitments and closed the investigation.

[d]   Market Definition in Abuse Cases

In its GSK preliminary ruling, the CJEU provided guidance on the key issue of market definition, in the context of abuses of dominance, which will have wider implications for the pharmaceutical industry than patent settlement agreements alone. The guidance from the CJEU is that if the generic medicines are as a matter of fact (to be determined by the national court) in a position to enter the market within a short period with sufficient strength to compete with the originator, they are to be considered being within the relevant market. Indeed, this reasoning has already been applied in the recent *Lundbeck* judgment, where the Court of Justice confirmed that the General Court was correct in upholding the Commission's finding that at the time the agreements were concluded, Lundbeck and the manufacturers of generic medicines were potential competitors.[191]

The court also stated that it is for the national court to determine whether the strategy to conclude settlement agreements with the object or effect of delaying generic entry, has the capacity to restrict competition and, in particular, to have exclusionary effects, going beyond the specific anti-competitive effects of each of the settlement agreements that are part of that strategy.

On 6 November 2020,[192] the UK Supreme Court confirmed the scope of the *res iudicata* principle in EU law, holding that findings of fact made in an EU General Court

---

191. Cases C-586/16 P *Sun Pharmaceutical Industries and Ranbaxy (UK) v. Commission*, C-588/16 P *Generics (UK) v. Commission*, C-591/16 P *Lundbeck v. Commission*, C-601/16 P *Arrow Group and Arrow Generics v. Commission*, C-611/16 P *Xellia Pharmaceuticals and Alpharma v. Commission*, and C-614/16 P *Merck v. Commission*. 2 Case C-307/18 Generics (UK) and Others.
192. Judgment 6 Nov. 2020, *Secretary of State for Health and others v. Servier Laboratories Ltd and others* [2020] UKSC 44.

judgment in the course of a judgment annulling a finding of breach of Article 102 TFEU were not binding on a UK Court assessing the damages payable for a breach of Article 101 TFEU. This resulted from a damages action brought before the English High Court, in which the respective health authorities of England, Wales, Scotland, and Northern Ireland sought to recover compensation for Servier's anti-competitive behaviour.[193] Servier argued that the health authorities had failed to mitigate their loss or had negligently contributed to their loss in that they failed to encourage prescribers to prescribe alternative substitutable blood pressure drugs instead of perindopril.

In that context, Servier sought to rely on findings made by the General Court about the degree of substitutability of other drugs for perindopril. Servier contended that those findings were binding as a matter of EU law, and that it was an abuse of process for the health authorities to dispute them. The High Court rejected both arguments but granted permission to appeal on the EU law point. The Court of Appeal likewise rejected the EU law argument, but Servier obtained permission from the Supreme Court to argue that a reference should be made to the CJEU. The UK Supreme Court held that no reference could be made, while the General Court judgment remained subject to appeal. On the substance, it held that the General Court's findings were not binding in the context in which Servier sought to rely on them (i.e., seeking to borrow findings of fact from an annulling judgment made in the context of abuse of dominance under Article 102 TFEU and to deploy them in the entirely different context of mitigation of loss, which had nothing to do with Article 102 or with the consequences of the annulling judgment).

§21.09 GUIDELINES/PUBLICATIONS

- Antitrust: Commission accepts commitments by Aspen to reduce prices for six off-patent cancer medicines by 73% addressing excessive pricing concerns
- Antitrust: Commission fines Johnson & Johnson and Novartis € 16 million for delaying market entry of generic pain-killer fentanyl (IP/13/1233).
- Antitrust: Commission fines Servier and five generic companies for curbing entry of cheaper versions of cardiovascular medicine (IP/14/799).
- Antitrust: Commission welcomes General Court judgments upholding its Lundbeck decision in first pharma pay-for-delay case
- CMA press release: 'CMA fines pharma companies £45 million.' (12 Feb. 2016).

---

193. In 2014, Servier, a French pharmaceutical company, was found by the Commission to have infringed competition law in relation to the supply of Perindopril, a blood pressure drug. The Commission found that Servier had breached Article 101 TFEU by entering into 'pay for delay' agreements, under which generic companies agreed not to enter the market for supplying Perindopril. The Commission also found that Servier had breached Article 102 TFEU both by entering into those agreements and by acquiring certain technology for the production of Perindopril. On appeal, the General Court upheld the Commission decision in relation to Article 101 TFEU but annulled it in respect of Article 102 TFEU on the basis that the Commission had erred in defining the relevant market, and therefore, in its assessment that Servier was in a dominant position. Both parties have appealed.

Chapter 21: Competition Law in the Pharmaceutical Sector §21.09

- CMA press release: 'The CMA has today issued a statement of objections to the pharmaceutical suppliers Pfizer and Flynn Pharma alleging that they have breached competition law.' (6 Aug. 2015).
- CNMC press release: 'La CNMC incoa un expediente sancionador en el mercado de suministro de información sobre ventas a la industria farmacéutica' (22 Dec. 2015).
- Commission Notice on agreements of minor importance which do not appreciably restrict competition under Art. 101(1) TFEU (*de Minimis*), OJ [2014] C 291/1.
- Commission Notice on the definition of relevant market for the purposes of Community competition law, OJ [1997] C 372/5.
- D. Bailey, L. John (eds.); Bellamy & Child, *European Union Law of Competition*, 8th edition (Oxford: OUP, 2018)
- De Souza, N. 'Competition in Pharmaceuticals: The Challenges ahead Post AstraZeneca.' *Competition Policy Newsletter*, no. 1 (Spring 2007).
- European Commission. *Competition Policy Newsletter*, no. 23 (October, 2000).
- Fagerlund, Niklas & Rasmussen, Soren Bo, 'AstraZeneca: The First Abuse Case in the Pharmaceutical Sector', in *Competition Policy Newsletter*, no. 3 (Autumn 2005).
- Framework for State aid for research and development and innovation, OJ [2014] C 198/1.
- Guidance on restrictions of competition 'by object' for the purpose of defining which agreements may benefit from the De Minimis Notice, of 25 June 2014, C(2014)4136 final.
- Guidance on the Commission's enforcement priorities in applying Art. 82 of the EC Treaty to abusive exclusionary conduct by dominant undertakings OJ [2009] C 45/7.
- Guidelines on the applicability of Article 101 of the Treaty on the Functioning of the European Union to horizontal co-operation agreements (the 'Horizontal Guidelines'), OJ [2011] C 11/1.
- Guidelines on the application of Article 101 of the Treaty on the Functioning of the European Union to technology transfer agreements, OJ [2014]C 89.
- Guidelines on the application of Article 81(3) of the Treaty, OJ [2004] C 101/97.
- Guidelines on the assessment of horizontal mergers under the Council Regulation on the control of concentrations between undertakings (the 'Horizontal Merger Guidelines'), OJ [2004] C 31/5.
- Guidelines on the assessment of non-horizontal mergers under the Council Regulation on the control of concentrations between undertakings, OJ [2008] C 265/6.
- Guidelines on the effect on trade concept contained in Articles 81 and 82 of the Treaty, OJ [2004] C101/81, paragraph 52.

- Hatton, C., A. Bicarregui & D. Cardwell. "Interesting Times' for Pharmaceutical Companies: European Competition Law and the Pharmaceutical Sector.' *European Consumer Law Journal*, 2-3 (2009).
- J. Faull & A. Nikpay. *The EU Law of Competition*. 3rd edition. Oxford, 2014.
- M. Nissen & F. Haugsted; *BadmouthingYour Competitor's Products: When Does Denigration Become an Antitrust Issue*–
- OFT press release: 'OFT issues decision in Reckitt Benckiser case' (53/11).
- OFT press release: 'OFT issues statement of objections to certain pharmaceutical companies' (36/13).
- Third Report on the Monitoring of Patent Settlements (2012).
- Fifth Report on the Monitoring of Patent Settlements (2014).
- Sixth Report on the Monitoring of Patent Settlements (2015).
- Seventh Report on the Monitoring of Patent Settlements (2016).
- Eight Report on the Monitoring of Patent Settlements (2017).
- UK VABEO Guidance: https://www.gov.uk/government/publications/vabeo-guidance.

CHAPTER 22
Pandemics and Epidemics

Hester Borgers, Fenna Douwenga, Edzard Boonen & Phillipus Putter

§22.01 INTRODUCTION

As a result of the challenges faced due to the COVID-19 global health crisis, both the European Commission (Commission) and the European Medicines Agency (EMA), for the purpose of restraining the COVID-19 pandemic, have installed special teams that coordinate the issues arising from the coronavirus outbreak, which we discuss briefly in this chapter.

Also, on a national level, many countries worldwide enacted emergency legislation removing certain regulatory barriers and exempting products from regulatory approval requirements, in order to ensure the continuity of access to medical products as good as possible under the circumstances during this global health crisis. This allowed for easier market access for products indispensable in the fight against the spreading of the virus SARS-CoV-2 and treatment of COVID-19. For example, the emergency legislation made it possible to use unregistered medicines, lowered the threshold for obtaining approval for certain clinical trials, and granted market access to unmarked, yet essential, medical devices. The emergency legislation defined the products that are exempted, provided new requirements for those products, and described from what specific provisions they have been exempted.

The initiatives taken by the EU and the EMA and how was and is dealt with the current global health crisis provide us valuable insights about what flexibilities can be created in the normally quite rigid regulatory framework regarding pharmaceuticals and medical devices.

In addition, this chapter discusses special deviations from the rules on market access for pharmaceutical products (including compassionate use), clinical trials, medical devices, and healthcare personnel. Furthermore, Advance Purchase Agreements and the vaccine strategy set up by the EU are discussed. Thereafter, a brief overview of UK-specific measures put in place is outlined.

§22.02 DEFINITIONS OF PANDEMIC AND EPIDEMIC

In opening remarks at the media briefing of 24 February 2020, the World Health Organization (WHO) Director General stated that the WHO would at that time not refer to the COVID-19 outbreak as a pandemic, and as the WHO stated it did not witness an uncontained global spread of the virus, it deemed the use of the definition pandemic not appropriate.[1] However, only three weeks later, the WHO declared that the COVID-19 health crisis could be characterised as a pandemic, it being the first pandemic ever sparked by a coronavirus.[2] At the moment, the WHO does not include a definition of either epidemic or pandemic on their website, and it is important to keep in mind that the discussion regarding the correct and consistent definition of a pandemic as used by the WHO was also a point of interest during the abovementioned H1N1 pandemic after assessment of the functioning of the International Health Regulations (2005) in relation to that specific pandemic.[3] The WHO does not provide for an official definition of either a pandemic or an epidemic at the moment.

When considering other literature, an epidemic is defined as 'the occurrence in a community or region of cases of an illness, specific health-related behaviour, or other health-related events clearly in excess of normal expectancy'.[4] A pandemic is defined as 'an epidemic occurring over a very wide area, crossing international boundaries and usually affecting a large number of people'.[5] A pandemic is therefore a further escalated epidemic.

In previous years, there have been examples of more localised epidemics, such as the SARS epidemic (2003–2004),[6] the Ebola virus epidemic (2014–2016),[7] and the Zika virus epidemic (2015–2016).[8] An example of a pandemic is the influenza A (H1N1) pandemic in 2009.[9]

In future, should a certain disease affect part of the EU, but not the rest of the world, it is likely to be considered an epidemic. However, dependent on the severity of the disease, the current measures taken against the COVID-19 pandemic may nonetheless then be applied as well, if the outbreak of the disease is severe and causes major threats to the supply of healthcare and public health in general.

---

1. WHO Director-General's opening remarks at the media briefing on COVID-19 (24 February 2020).
2. WHO Director-General's opening remarks at the media briefing on COVID-19 (11 March 2020).
3. Implementation of the International Health Regulations (2005) in relation to the Pandemic (H1N1) 2009 report by the Director General of the World Health Organization, WHO (5 May 2011), A64/10.
4. Miquel Porta, *A dictionary of epidemiology (Oxford University Press 6th edn 2016)*.
5. Ibid.
6. *SARS (Severe Acute Respiratory Syndrome)*, WHO, https://www.who.int/ith/diseases/sars/en/ (last accessed 9 July 2022).
7. *Ebola virus disease*, WHO, https://www.who.int/health-topics/ebola (last accessed 9 July 2022).
8. *Zika virus disease*, WHO, https://www.who.int/emergencies/diseases/zika/en/; *Disease outbreaks*, WHO, https://www.who.int/emergencies/diseases/en/.
9. *Influenza A (H1N1) outbreak*, WHO, https://www.who.int/emergencies/situations/influenza-a-(h1n1)-outbreak.

§22.03 THE COVID-19 EMA TASK FORCE AND STEERING GROUP

At the time of writing, the regulatory activities regarding COVID-19 governed by the EMA are handled by the Emergency Task Force (ETF). Previously, the EMA had two task forces with regard to COVID-19. The COVID-19 EMA pandemic Task Force (COVID-ETF) mainly focussed on the development, authorisation, and safety monitoring of medicinal products with regard to COVID-19, which has now been replaced by the ETF. The ETF took over the activities of the COVID-ETF in 2022 and became permanent in line with Article 15 of Regulation (EU) 2022/123 on a reinforced role for the EMA in crisis preparedness.[10]

The second former task force, the COVID-19 Task Force, focussed on the continuation of the EMA's activities and the coordination of the COVID-ETF, which has now been replaced by the COVID-19 Steering Group.

In 2018, based on Decision no. 1082/2013 of the Commission on serious cross-border threats to health, the EMA drafted its plan for emerging health threats, to 'provide internal general guidance on the EMA activities during a health threat'.[11] The EMA health threat plan sets out the general principles according to which the EMA will take action in case of a health threat to the population. The health threat plan is also partly based on the experience gained from the H1N1 pandemic (2009) and the Ebola epidemic (2014–2016).[12]

Under this health threat plan, the EMA has been granted the mandate to establish expert groups, so-called the EMA Task Forces, mainly to assist the relevant EMA Committees (Committee for Medicinal Products for Human Use (CHMP), Pharmacovigilance Risk Assessment Committee (PRAC), and Paediatric Committee (PDCO)) with regard to possible product development and regulatory actions or to engage in early scientific discussions and product reviews on behalf of the CHMP in case of a health threat.[13]

[A] ETF

As described by EMA, the ETF is an advisory and support body that handles regulatory activities in preparation for and during public-health emergencies. As mentioned above, the ETF took over the activities over the former COVID-ETF in March 2022 and has been established on the basis of Article 15 of Regulation (EU) 2022/123. The ETF consists of various experts, including representatives of EMA's committees and working parties, representatives of EMA, representatives of the Clinical Trials Coordination and Advisory Group (CTAG) and clinical trial experts from the national

---

10. 'EMA's governance during COVID-19 pandemic', EMA, https://www.ema.europa.eu/en/human-regulatory/overview/public-health-threats/coronavirus-disease-covid-19/emas-governance-during-covid-19-pandemic.
11. 'Plan for emerging health threats', EMA (10 December 2018), EMA/863454/2018, p. 5.
12. 'EMA establishes task force to take quick and coordinated regulatory action related to COVID-19 medicines', EMA (9 April 2020), www.the EMA.europa.eu/en/news/the EMA-establishes-task-force-take-quick-coordinated-regulatory-action-related-covid-19-medicines.
13. 'Plan for emerging health threats', EMA (10 December 2018), EMA/863454/2018, p. 6.

competent authorities. The ETF is co-chaired by a representative from EMA and the chair or co-chair of the CHMP.

The tasks of the ETF are laid down in Article 15(2) of Regulation (EU) 2022/123, including (in brief) providing scientific advice, providing advice on the main aspects of clinical trial protocols, providing scientific support all with regard to medicinal products intended to combat the disease causing a public health emergency. Further, the ETF should contribute to the work of the scientific committees of the EMA and provide, together with the scientific committees, working parties, and scientific advisory groups of the EMA, scientific recommendations with regard to the medicinal product which has the potential to address the public health emergency. Last, it is laid down that the ETF should cooperate with, among others, the national competent authorities, Union bodies and agencies and the WHO, on scientific and technical issues that relate to the public health emergency.

[B] The EMA COVID-19 Steering Group

The EMA describes the EMA COVID-19 Steering Group as providing strategic oversight at EMA of the evolving scientific and regulatory challenges created by COVID-19. As mentioned above, the Steering Group was formerly known as the EMA COVID-19 Task Force. It further oversees the response from the EMA and the European medicines regulatory network (EMRN)[14] to COVID-19, while adapting EMA's COVID-19 business continuity plan.[15] The EMA mentions that the Steering Group consists of senior EMA staff.[16]

§22.04 THE COMMISSION'S CORONAVIRUS RESPONSE TEAM

In March 2020, the Commission established a coordinating coronavirus response team, chaired by the President of the European Commission Von der Leyen and further consisting of five Commissioners, covering different topics. According to the Commission, this response team focuses on three 'main pillars'. The first pillar covers 'the medical field, working on prevention and procurement and relief measures and foresight'. The second pillar focuses on 'mobility, from transportation to travel advice, as well as Schengen related questions.' The final pillar sees on the 'economy, looking in-depth at various business sectors, such as tourism or transport and trade as well as

---

14. EMA defines 'the European medicines regulatory network' as 'the system for regulating medicines in Europe is based on a closely coordinated regulatory network of national competent authorities in the Member States of the European Economic Area working together with the European Medicines Agency and the European Commission.' *See* 'European medicines regulatory network', EMA, https://www.ema.europa.eu/en/glossary/european-medicines-regulatory-network.
15. 'European Medicines Regulatory Network COVID-19 Business Continuity Plan', EMA and HMA (10 September 2020), EMA/199630/2020, Rev. 1.
16. 'EMA's governance during COVID-19 pandemic', EMA, https://www.ema.europa.eu/en/human-regulatory/overview/public-health-threats/coronavirus-disease-covid-19/emas-governance-during-covid-19-pandemic.

value chains and macro-economy.' Generalising, the aim of the response team was to coordinate the responses between the Member States during the COVID-19 crisis.[17]

§22.05   AVAILABILITY AND MARKET ACCESS OF MEDICINES

One of the key priorities of the EMRN is maintaining and improving the availability of medicines for the EU as shortages can create a serious impact on human and animal health. The EMRN consist of the twenty-seven national authorities of the EU Member States and those of Iceland, Liechtenstein, and Norway. The EMA and the Heads of Medicines Agencies oversee this priority.[18]

During a pandemic or an epidemic, there is a larger possible risk of shortages and supply disruptions in both human and veterinary medicines as a result of (temporary) lockdowns of manufacturing sites, travel restrictions impacting import and export, affected manufacturing, supply and distribution of medicines, and an increased demand for medicines used to treat patients who suffer from the pandemic or epidemic causing disease.[19]

[A]   EMA Executive Steering Group on Shortages and Safety of Medicinal Products

EMA's Executive Steering Group on Shortages and Safety of Medicinal Products (MSSG) became operational in 2022, replacing the former EU Executive Steering Group on Shortages of Medicines Caused by Major Events. The MSSG is established on the basis of Article 3 of Regulation (EU) 2022/123. The members of the MSSG consist of a representative of the agency, a representative of the Commission, and one representative appointed by each Member State. Furthermore, the MSSG is co-chaired by the representative of the agency and by one of the representatives of the Member States.

The tasks of the MSSG are laid down in Articles 4(3) and 4(4) and Articles 5 to 8 of Regulation (EU) 2022/123. These tasks include advising the Commission on whether a shortage may be recognised as an actual or imminent major event, evaluating the information relating to the public health emergency or the major event, providing recommendations thereon to the Commission and the Member States, establishing a list with the main therapeutic groups of medicinal products that are necessary for emergency care, surgery, and intensive care in order to respond to the public health emergency or major event, monitoring shortages of medicinal products on this lists, and to report and provide recommendations regarding these shortages. On 7 June

---

17. Remarks by President von der Leyen at the joint press conference with Commissioners Lenarčič, Kyriakides, Johansson, Valean, and Gentiloni at the ERCC ECHO on the EU's response to COVID-19 on 2 March 2020.
18. 'European Medicines Agencies Network Strategy to 2025', EMA (3 July 2020), EMA/321483/2020.
19. 'Availability of medicines during COVID-19 pandemic', https://www.ema.europa.eu/en/human-regulatory/overview/public-health-threats/coronavirus-disease-covid-19/availability-medicines-during-covid-19-pandemic.

2022, the EMA published the 'List of Critical Medicines for COVID-19 public health emergency under Regulation (EU) 2022/123' as adopted by the MSSG.[20] Important to note is that all marketing authorisation holders (MAHs) of the medicines included in such a list are obliged to provide EMA regular updates, including information regarding potential and actual shortages, stock information, and supply and demand forecasts.

In addition, an enhanced fast-track monitoring system was launched on 17 April 2020 by the EMA, pharmaceutical companies, and the Member States to help prevent and mitigate supply issues with crucial medicines used for treating COVID-19 patients. The system is similar to the Medicines Shortages Single Point of Contact (SPOC) network already used to exchange information on shortages between the EMA and the national competent authorities. Under the fast-track system, each pharmaceutical company should appoint an Industry Single Point of Contact (i-SPOC) who reports to the EMA all ongoing or anticipated shortages of medicines used for treating COVID-19, irrespective of their authorisation route.[21] In June 2022, the EMA published a general call for action for companies to register their i-SPOC, ensuring that communication on shortages regarding all critical medicines between the EMA and the MAHs would be enhanced.[22]

While carrying out its tasks, the MSSG works in close connection with the EMA's scientific committees, their working parties, and other expert groups, including the ETF. In case, a major event or public health emergency may indeed lead to an actual shortage, the MSSG is supported by the EMA working party SPOC.[23]

[B] EMA Additional Temporary Measures

In May 2021, EMA also introduced further temporary measures in order to alleviate the burden on the EMRN and to ensure that it could focus on the COVID-19-related assessments. At the moment of writing, these measures are still in place until further notice. The additional temporary measures are focussed on 'Initial marketing authorisation procedures' and 'Post-authorisation procedures (extension of indications and line extensions)'. In both cases, the measures ensure priority to COVID-19 related medicines, thus speeding up the process and at the same time relaxing the regulatory framework regarding non-COVID-19 medicines.[24]

---

20. 'List of critical medicines for COVID-19 public health emergency (PHE) under Regulation (EU) 2022/123', EMA (7 June 2022), EMA/285556/2022.
21. 'Launch of enhanced monitoring system for availability of medicines used for treating COVID-19', EMA (21 April 2020), https://www.ema.europa.eu/en/news/launch-enhanced-monitoring-system-availability-medicines-used-treating-covid-19 (last accessed 9 July 2022).
22. Call for companies to register their Industry Single Point of Contact (i-SPOC) on supply and availability, EMA (28 June 2022), https://www.ema.europa.eu/en/news/call-companies-register-their-industry-single-point-contact-i-spoc-supply-availability.
23. 'Executive Steering Group on Shortages and Safety of Medicinal Products (MSSG)', EMA, https://www.ema.europa.eu/en/about-us/what-we-do/crisis-preparedness-management/executive-steering-group-shortages-safety-medicinal-products.
24. 'EMA's governance during COVID-19 pandemic', EMA, https://www.ema.europa.eu/en/human-regulatory/overview/public-health-threats/coronavirus-disease-covid-19/emas-governance-during-covid-19-pandemic.

[C] Guidelines and Guidance from the EC on Avoiding Medicines Shortages

On 8 April 2020, the Commission published 'Guidelines on the optimal and rational supply of medicines to avoid shortages during the COVID-19 outbreak', targeted at Member States and aiming to protect public health and preserve the integrity of the single market.[25] Member States were given the following main topics to take action on:

> *Showing solidarity:* lifting export bans and restrictions, avoiding national stockpiling, avoiding that misinformation leads to improper use and unnecessary stockpiling;
> *Ensuring supply:* increasing and reorganising production, ensuring manufacturing continues at full capacity, implementing regulatory flexibility, monitoring available stocks at national level, ensuring necessary support to the wholesale sector, fully enforcing the green lanes, facilitating air freight and other forms of transport, ensuring fair distribution of supply;
> *Optimal use of medicines in hospitals*: equitable distribution of available medicines, exchanging hospital protocols to treat patients, considering alternative medicines on the basis of hospital protocols and national guidelines, extending the expiry dates of medicines, considering the use of magistral preparations or veterinary medicines, using medicines off label and in clinical trials;
> *Optimisation of sales in community pharmacies to avoid hoarding*: introducing measures to reassure persons reliant on medication, introducing restrictions on sales in community pharmacies, limiting online sales of products at risk, reassuring patients.[26]

The Commission also published two guidance documents, both for human medicines and for veterinary medicines, with regard to regulatory expectations and flexibilities. These guidance documents, which are available at the website of the Commission and updated regularly, cover among others, the topics on research and development, evaluation and marketing authorisation (MA), and post-authorisation, in order to help speed up the medicine and vaccine development and approval for COVID-19.[27]

[D] Recommendation from the EC on Conformity Assessment and Market Surveillance Procedures

In order to address the issues created by the coronavirus crisis in the availability of medical devices and personal protective equipment (PPE) during the COVID-19

---

25. 'Guidelines on the optimal and rational supply of medicines to avoid shortages during the COVID-19 outbreak', European Commission (8 April 2020), 2020/C 116 I/01.
26. *Ibid.*
27. 'Guidance for medicine developers and other stakeholders on COVID-19', EMA, https://www.ema.europa.eu/en/human-regulatory/overview/public-health-threats/coronavirus-disease-covid-19/guidance-medicine-developers-other-stakeholders-covid-19.

pandemic, the Commission published the *Recommendation 2020/403 on 13 March 2020 on conformity assessment and market surveillance procedures within the context of the COVID-19 threat* and a clarifying Q&A on Conformity assessment procedures for protective equipment.[28]

In this Recommendation, the EC gave recommendations on how and when the competent authorities may allow the placing on the market of individual devices without going through the required conformity assessment procedure, including the affixing of CE marking, if the use thereof is in the interest of the protection of health (Article 11(13) of Directive 93/42 (MDD) and Article 59 of Regulation 2017/745 (MDR)). For IVD's, Articles 9(1) and 9(2) of Directive 98/79 (IVDD) (and Article 54 of Regulation - IVDR) provides equally for derogations from CE marking and conformity assessment procedures.

According to the EC, the COVID-19 outbreak is seen as a justified circumstance to deviate from the normal conformity assessment proceedings and apply the aforementioned exceptions to PPE and medical devices.[29]

The objective of this Recommendation was to ensure availability of PPE and medical devices for adequate protection during the pandemic. In this regard, the EC asks all economic operators throughout the supply chain, as well as notified bodies and market surveillance authorities, to deploy all the measures at their disposal to support the efforts aimed at ensuring that the supply matched the increasing demand, without the measures having a detrimental effect on the overall level of health and safety.[30]

In order to allow for easier manufacturing of medical devices, the EC has made sure several standards (such as certain European Standards (EN)) are made available for free.[31]

Furthermore, the Recommendation asks notified bodies to prioritise the assessment of PPE necessary for protection in the context of the COVID-19 pandemic (paragraph 2 Recommendation). Market surveillance authorities should prioritise non-compliant PPE and medical devices that raise serious risks to the health and safety of intended users (paragraph 6 Recommendation).

[E] Compassionate Use

In April 2020, the first, and until the time of writing, the last, compassionate use right during the COVID-19 pandemic was given to the investigational antiviral medicine

---

28. Commission recommendation (EU) 2020/403 of 13 March 2020 on conformity assessment and market surveillance procedures within the context of the COVID-19 threat; Conformity Assessment procedures for protective equipment, European Commission, L 79 I/1; Q&A 'Conformity Assessment procedures for protective equipment' (version 2), European Commission (10 July 2020).
29. 'Guidance on medical devices, active implantable medical devices and in vitro diagnostic medical devices in the COVID-19 context' European Commission (3 April 2020), https://ec.europa.eu/docsroom/documents/40607, p. 3.
30. Commission Recommendation (EU) 2020/403 of 13 March 2020 on conformity assessment and market surveillance procedures within the context of the COVID-19 threat, *see* paragraph 1.
31. Guidance on medical devices, *supra* n. 29, p. 2.

remdesivir of the pharmaceutical company Gilead Sciences. In May 2020, the EMA even recommended to expand the first proposed patient group eligible for *remdesivir*. The EMA also emphasised that the national competent authorities could turn to them with regard to the use of *remdesivir*.[32]

§22.06 CLINICAL TRIALS EFFECTED BY A PANDEMIC OR EPIDEMIC

Planned and ongoing clinical trials may face major challenges as a result of a pandemic or epidemic. Such challenges may include difficulty finding trial staff due to changes in availability of healthcare personnel, restrictions of visits to healthcare facilities, the obligation for participants to self-isolate resulting in decreased oversight by the investigators.[33]

IN addition, more clinical trials may be set up to find potential treatments or vaccines to fight the disease causing the pandemic or epidemic, requiring a faster approach and more international approach than is common in clinical trials due to the gravity and international spread of the situation.

[A] Guidance from the EC and EMA

To assist clinical-trial sponsors on the management of clinical trials and how to deal with the extraordinary situations during the COVID-19 pandemic, the Commission issued 'Guidance on the Management of Clinical Trials during the COVID-19 pandemic'.[34] The Guidance includes most of the current guidance across Member States with the aim of serving as a harmonised EU-level set of recommendations, yet national legislation prevails.[35] Furthermore, it is explicitly noted that the simplified measures proposed in the guidance document will only last during the current public health crisis until the revocation of the Guidance. Important points included in the guidance document are how to deal with the self-isolation or quarantine of trial participants, limited access to hospitals, and reallocation of healthcare professionals. The guidance document further includes chapters on safety reporting, risk assessment, changes to informed consent, changes in the distribution of the investigational medicinal product or in vitro diagnostic and medical devices, changes to monitoring, and changes to auditing.

To complement the abovementioned guidance document, the EMA published a further guideline on the implications of the COVID-19 pandemic on methodological aspects of ongoing clinical trials. This document states that sponsors of clinical trials affected by COVID-19 should ensure the integrity of the trials and the interpretation of

---

32. 'EMA recommends expanding remdesivir compassionate use to patients not on mechanical ventilation', EMA (11 May 2020), www.the EMA.europa.eu/en/news/the EMA-recommends-expanding-remdesivir-compassionate-use-patients-not-mechanical-ventilation.
33. 'Guidance on the management of clinical trials during the COVID-19 (coronavirus) pandemic' (Version 5 d.d. 10 February 2022), European Commission (10 February 2022), p. 4.
34. *Ibid.*
35. *Ibid*, p. 3.

the study results, whilst safeguarding the safety of trial participants as a first priority. The actions included in the guideline include to document deviations from the study protocol explaining the reasons, to conduct risk assessments of the impact of COVID-19 on the trial and to engage early with the regulatory authorities to agree any study changes.[36]

§22.07 POSTPONEMENT OF REGULATIONS (EU) 2017/745 AND 2017/746 ON MEDICAL DEVICES

Another important measure taken due to the COVID-19 pandemic was the extension of the transitional period of the Medical Devices Regulations by one year, thus postponing the date of application until 26 May 2021, in order to avoid shortages as a result of a limited capacity of national competent authorities or notified bodies to implement the new Regulations.[37] For future global health emergencies, this may mean that the European Parliament and the Council of the EU may choose to postpone the application of other legislation as well.

§22.08 VACCINE STRATEGY

In general, during a pandemic or an epidemic, a strategic alliance between countries can be very useful to obtain a better negotiation position or to ensure funding of vaccines and therefore early access. Below two of the initiatives with regard to vaccine strategy during COVID-19 are discussed.

[A] The EU Vaccine Strategy

As a part of the EU's general strategy to battle the COVID-19 pandemic, the EU put in place the EU Vaccine Strategy. The main aim was to protect global health as much as possible and to save a substantial amount of money. The strategy was mainly focussed on two ''pillars', on the one side, securing the production of sufficient vaccines (also through Advanced Purchase Agreements, as discussed below), and on the other side, ensuring that the EU rules would be adapted to the current urgent situation and making use of existing regulatory flexibility, whilst still maintaining the necessary level of quality and safety. The Strategy covers among others selection criteria for vaccine candidates, an accelerated procedure for authorisation from the Commission, and flexibility in relation to labelling and packaging requirements.[38]

---

36. 'Implications of coronavirus disease (COVID-19) on methodological aspects of ongoing clinical trials', EMA (26 June 2020), EMA/158330/2020 Rev. 1.
37. Regulation (EU) 2020/561 of the European Parliament and of the Council of 23 April 2020 amending Regulation (EU) 2017/745 on medical devices.
38. Commission Communication EU Strategy for COVID-19 Vaccines (COM(2020)245).

[B] Advance Purchase Agreements

An important part of the EU Vaccine Strategy is Advance Purchase Agreements. Advance Purchase Agreements are agreements with vaccine manufacturers, where the manufacturer goes into an agreement to supply its vaccine (first) to a specific party (for example, a Member State), whilst the other party to the agreement finances the development or manufacturing of the vaccines. Examples of use of Advance Purchase Agreements can be found during the H1N1 pandemic, when several Member States (individually) made agreements with regard to the influenza vaccine. After the H1N1 pandemic, the Commission concluded that it could be useful in the future to ensure discussion with regard to this topic between the Member States.[39]

The EC, on behalf of the Member States, stated that it would enter into agreements with several specific vaccine manufactures, by financing part of the upfront development costs of vaccines in return for an amount of vaccines as soon as those were available and approved. The relevant funding came from the so-called Emergency Support Instrument, whereas the funding provided by the Member States was considered a down-payment for the vaccines.[40]

[C] Inclusive Vaccine Alliance

Before the launch of the EU Vaccine Strategy, France, Germany, Italy, and the Netherlands joined forces and together formed the so-called Inclusive Vaccine Alliance, entering into negotiations with potential manufacturers of vaccines. The Member States worked together to ensure a swift development of the necessary vaccines, with the aim to provide accessible, available, and affordable vaccines for the whole of the EU. The alliance also pledged to make an amount of vaccines available for low-income countries. The alliance further stated that it would work closely together with the EC, also aiming to include other EU Member States in the initiatives that were the result of their negotiations.[41]

In the abovementioned Strategy from the EC regarding an EU-wide vaccine strategy, reference was made to this more local initiative as an important step towards joint action, laying the groundwork for an EU alliance.[42]

---

39. Michael A. Stoto & Melissa A. Higdon, *The Public Health Response to 2009 H1N1: A Systems Perspective* (Oxford University Press January 2015).
40. 'Coronavirus: Commission unveils EU vaccines strategy, European Commission' (17 June 2020), https://ec.europa.eu/commission/presscorner/detail/en/ip_20_1103.
41. 'France, Germany, Italy and the Netherlands working together to find a vaccine for countries in Europe and beyond', Government of The Netherlands, https://www.government.nl/latest/news/2020/06/03/france-germany-italy-and-the-netherlands-working-together-to-find-a-vaccine-for-countries-in-europe-and-beyond.
42. Commission Communication EU Strategy for COVID-19 Vaccines (COM(2020)245).

§22.09 HEALTHCARE PERSONNEL

During pandemics and epidemics, the strict regulatory framework that normally applies to personnel working in healthcare may be relaxed ensuring that sufficient trained personnel are available. During the COVID-19 pandemic, we have seen several examples of this. Further, some other exceptions regarding healthcare personnel in times of a global health crisis are discussed. Much of the specific examples discussed apply directly to the COVID-19 pandemic.

[A] Exceptions to Work as Healthcare Personnel

Pandemics and epidemics place a huge strain on the national and European healthcare systems. Possible options to expand the healthcare workforce are to loosen the requirements with regard to healthcare personnel, for example, by allowing advanced nursing students or retired health personnel to work as qualified health personnel.

To ensure sufficient healthcare personnel during the COVID-19 crisis, many countries, indeed, requested assistance from former healthcare personnel. As a result, former healthcare personnel returned from their retirement or new profession to assist during the health crisis in multiple countries across Europe. Member States often relaxed the registration requirements, for example, by accepting healthcare personnel back in the workforce where their registration had only been expired for a specific period of time and by only deploying them in case of absolute necessity. Examples of countries that have done this are the Netherlands,[43] the UK,[44] and Italy.[45]

The Directive 2005/36 of the Commission on the recognition of professional qualifications sets out the minimum requirements of professional qualifications in the EU for certain professions and regulates the cross-border recognition between Member States and minimum harmonised training requirements. During the COVID-19 crisis, the EC issued a guidance document on the free movement of healthcare personnel and the minimum harmonisation of training in relation to the COVID-19 measures, also often referring to the aforementioned Directive. The guidance document pointed out that the Directive does not apply to not yet fully qualified persons, so that it is therefore up to the Member States to decide if they want to employ such personnel and under which requirements.[46] The guidance document also suggested that Member States could consider early graduation for students at an advanced level to ensure sufficient healthcare personnel, taking into consideration that the sectoral healthcare personnel is subjected to a minimum level of training as set out in the Directive.

---

43. *Evaluatie Extra handen voor de zorg*, SEOR Erasmus School of Economics, 14 October 2021.
44. 'Clinicians considering a return to the NHS', NHS, https://www.england.nhs.uk/coronavirus/returning-clinicians/.
45. 'Italy asks retired medics to return to work as hospitals reach breaking point', Metro (18 March 2020), https://metro.co.uk/2020/03/18/italy-asks-retired-medics-return-work-hospitals-reach-breaking-point-12418937/.
46. Commission Guidance on free movement of health professionals and minimum harmonisation of training in relation to COVID-19 emergency measures – recommendations regarding Directive 2005/36/EC (2020/C 156/01).

[B] Cross-Border Migration of Healthcare Personnel

During pandemics or epidemics, it is possible that at a certain point in time the pressure on the healthcare systems of specific European countries becomes too large to handle by only deploying national healthcare personnel. In the abovementioned Directive 2005/36/EC, the minimum requirements of professional qualifications in the EU for certain professions are set out and the cross-border recognition between Member States is regulated. With regard to healthcare personnel, the Directive contains several articles concerning the requirements of training and acquired rights of, among others, doctors of medicine and nurses responsible for general care.[47]

As mentioned before, the EC issued a guidance document on the free movement of healthcare personnel. In the guidance document, it is pointed out that Member States could decide to take a more lenient approach with regard to certain aspects of the Directive concerning employing healthcare personnel from different Member States, for example, by dropping certain prior check requirements Member States might have, as these are not mandatory under the Directive. Furthermore, the guidance document also touched upon the subject of employing healthcare personnel from outside the EU/European Free Trade Association (EFTA). In the guidance document, it is suggested that Member States may decide to employ healthcare personnel from outside the EU/EFTA, as they ensure that their qualifications are compliant with the minimum levels as laid down in the Directive, or by employing them in a different function without the required minimum level of training according to the Directive.[48]

In case of pandemics and epidemics, the source of the health crisis is an infectious virus, which can also be contained by restricting (inter)national travel as much as possible. During the COVID-19 pandemic, the EC issued a communication regarding a temporary restriction on non-essential travel in the EU.[49] In this communication, it was stated that this travel ban should apply to all non-essential travel from third countries to the EU, explicitly excluding "travellers with an essential function or need', which included 'healthcare professionals, health researchers, and elderly care professionals'. This again underlined the important position of healthcare personnel, especially during a healthcare crisis.

§22.10 PANDEMICS AND EPIDEMICS IN THE UK

The UK left the EU on 31 January 2020, in the middle of one of the most significant public health emergencies of the last century. The UK Government's response to the

---

47. Directive 2005/36/EC of the European Parliament and of the Council of 7 September 2005 on the recognition of professional qualifications.
48. Commission Guidance on free movement of health professionals and minimum harmonisation of training in relation to COVID-19 emergency measures – recommendations regarding Directive 2005/36/EC (2020/C 156/01).
49. Commission Communication COVID-19: Temporary Restriction on Non-Essential Travel to the EU, (COM/2020/115).

global COVID-19 pandemic was unprecedented, requiring swift amendments to existing legislation, and the introduction of new rules and regulations.

In emergency scenarios such as epidemics and pandemics, government procurement of important materials and equipment is under immense strain. Take, for example, the shortage of PPE in hospitals. Suppliers will also be under pressure (albeit financially incentivised) to supply materials and equipment under significant time pressure. Regulators will also face many hurdles: approving vaccines candidates quickly, while upholding scientific rigour and maintaining public safety. Difficulties notwithstanding, the system works and vaccines continue to save lives. For example, a recent Lancet publication estimates that vaccinations prevented approximately 19.8 million COVID-19 related deaths.[50] In this section, we look at the UK's epidemic and pandemic response procedures in so far as they differ from the EU.

[A] Vaccine Task Force

The role of the EMA's COVID-19 Task Force and Steering Group is discussed further in §22.03 above. The UK adopted a similar approach, by forming the Vaccine Task Force (VTF) in April 2020. The VTF sits under the Department for Business, Energy and Industrial Strategy (BEIS) and the Department of Health and Social Care (DHSC). The task force was established, *inter alia*, to future proof the UK's plans in relation to epidemics and pandemics.

The objectives of the VTF are threefold: (i) securing access to promising COVID-19 vaccines for the UK population as quickly as possible; (ii) making provision for international distribution of vaccines; and (iii) strengthening the UK's onshoring capacity and capability in vaccine development, manufacturing, and supply chain to provide resilience for future pandemics.[51] BEIS published an end of year report in December 2020, wherein the department outlined its future strategy, including: (i) the development of a permanent ecosystem for rapidly developing, manufacturing, and supplying vaccines for future pandemics; (ii) creating a diverse informed infrastructure for surveillance of adverse effects; (iii) flexible capacity for manufacturing and testing vaccines; and (iv) a global funding facility for purchasing and distributing vaccines internationally.[52]

[B] Clinical Trials and MA

The UK was the first country to approve a COVID-19 vaccine that had been subject to a robust clinical trial[53] and, more recently, approved the first bivalent COVID-19

---

50. Watson O.J. et al., *Global impact of the first year of COVID-19 vaccination: a mathematical modelling study*, The Lancet Infectious Diseases (23 June 2022), https://www.thelancet.com/journals/laninf/article/ PIIS1473-3099%2822%2900320-6/fulltext.
51. *See* https://www.gov.uk/government/publications/the-vaccine-taskforce-objectives-and-membership-of-steering-group/vtf-objectives-and-membership-of-the-steering-group.
52. *Ibid.*
53. Although China and Russia approved their respective vaccine candidates, faster, clinical evidence of efficacy and safety were not taken into account to the same extent.

booster.[54] Developing safe and effective vaccines relies heavily on successful preclinical and clinical trials, especially in epidemic and pandemic scenarios where time is of the essence. For a detailed overview of the design of clinical trials for vaccine candidates, including pharmacokinetic and pharmacodynamic studies and the assessments of efficacy and safety, *see* Chapter 18.

On 27 May 2022, the UK (alongside Argentina and Peru) proposed a draft resolution at the World Health Assembly.[55] The draft resolution called on WHO member states to strengthen clinical trials for protection from future pandemics. The proposals will, according to a DHSC press release: encourage specific funding to help developing countries increase their capacity for clinical trials; help to counteract existing public health challenges such as tuberculosis; and facilitate collaboration between research groups on clinical trials to increase transparency and efficiency.[56]

MA of medicinal products (including vaccines) in the UK is discussed in further detail in Chapter 5. Importantly, applications for MA can be fast-tracked if applicants can adduce compelling evidence of public benefit, which includes public health emergencies such as COVID-19. Applications for variation of an MA can also be used by manufacturers in public health emergencies.

[C] Vaccine Development and Strategy

As with other biologics and large molecule medicinal products, developing a new vaccine is a significant undertaking, as further illustrated in Chapter 18. In epidemics and pandemics, the general procedure continues to apply with a few important addenda.

When developing novel vaccines, manufacturers and suppliers often collaborate with regulatory bodies and committees, including the Medicines and Healthcare products Regulatory Agency (MHRA), the Joint Committee on Vaccines and Immunisation (JCVI), the UK Health Security Agency (UKHSA), and DHSC. During public health emergencies, collaboration will likely occur much earlier and may also include cooperation with international and EU organisations, such as the EMA and WHO.

Vaccine development is competitive. Epidemic and pandemic scenarios often necessitate collaboration between different commercial entities, which may raise some interesting questions of competition law. Accordingly, on 8 April 2020, the Commission published a temporary framework for the assessment of antitrust issues in respect

---

54. The first bivalent (i.e., triggering an immune response against two different antigens) COVID-19 booster was developed by Moderna, and it was approved by the MHRA on 15 August 2022. The MHRA's decision was based on clinical data.
55. *See* https://apps.who.int/gb/ebwha/pdf_files/WHA75/A75_ACONF9-en.pdf.
56. *See* https://www.gov.uk/government/news/new-clinical-trials-deal-struck-to-better-protect-world-from-future-pandemics.

of business cooperation during the COVID-19 pandemic.[57] The UK Government followed suit in May 2020, relaxing UK competition rules for certain agreements.[58]

Although obtaining MA is an important step, it does not represent the finish line. Suppliers may face manufacturing and distribution constraints, especially when governments set ambitious immunisation targets. In 2020, the Human Medicines (Coronavirus and Influenza) (Amendment) Regulations 2020 and the Human Medicines (Coronavirus) (Further Amendments) Regulations 2020 were introduced, amending the Human Medicines Regulations 2012 (UK HMRs). These amendments introduced a temporary relaxation of certain rules and regulations governing vaccines. In December 2021, DHSC proposed[59] to extend some of these amendments by way of a statutory instrument, which entered into force on 31 March 2022.[60] Some of the key provisions include:

- Extending the derogations under Regulation 3A of the UK HMRs allowing certain preparations, assembly, reformulation, and re-assembly of COVID-19 vaccines without the need for a manufacturer's licence or MA until 1 April 2024.
- Extending the exemption under Regulation 19 of the UK HMRs, which allows the sharing of stocks of COVID-19 vaccines between immunisation centres. Usually, a wholesale dealer's licence is required. The change will remain in force until 1 April 2024.
- The exemption in Regulation 233 of the UK HMRs has been extended, which means that anyone lawfully conducting a retail pharmacy business can continue to sell, supply, or administer vaccines.
- Regulation 235 of the UK HMRs permitted certain types of registered healthcare professionals to administer vaccines to patients as part of the occupational health scheme of local authorities. This provision is now permanent.

---

57. See https://ec.europa.eu/info/sites/default/files/framework_communication_antitrust_issues_related_to_cooperation_between_competitors_in_covid-19.pdf.
58. Last updated 22 April 2022. See https://www.gov.uk/guidance/competition-law-exclusion-orders-relating-to-coronavirus-covid-19.
59. The outcome of the DHSC consultation can be accessed at the following link: https://www.gov.uk/government/consultations/review-of-temporary-provisions-in-the-human-medicines-regulations-2012-to-support-influenza-and-covid-19-vaccination-campaigns/outcome/review-of-temporary-provisions-in-the-human-medicines-regulations-2012-to-support-influenza-and-covid-19-vaccination-campaigns-consultation-response#consideration-of-responses-to-individual-consultation-questions.
60. The Human Medicines (Coronavirus and Influenza) (Amendment) Regulations 2022 (SI 2022/350) were made on 18 March 2022, coming into force on 31 March 2022.

CHAPTER 23
Data Protection in the Pharmaceutical Sector

Clara Clark Nevola & Emma Drake

§23.01 INTRODUCTION

Most of the regulated activities of pharmaceutical actors described elsewhere in this book involve the collection and processing of personal data. In the UK and the EU, the processing of personal data is regulated by a well-established and fast developing framework of data protection legislation. This Chapter does not aim to provide an exhaustive guide to data protection principles and compliance – fuller, dedicated works are more suited.[1] Instead, we address how the key concepts of data protection law apply to the pharmaceutical sector.

§23.02 LEGAL FRAMEWORK AND PENALTIES

[A] Applicable Laws

Data protection law in the EU is governed by both EU and national legislation. The Regulation (EU) 2016/679 (General Data Protection Regulation (GDPR)) came into force in May 2018 and replaced the previous data protection Directive 95/46/EC, which had led to substantial national divergence on fundamental principles of law. Although the directly-applicable GDPR now harmonises many aspects of data protection law, national law in each Member State plays an important part, as the GDPR allows for certain divergence (through 'derogations') in particular areas. There are numerous such derogations relating to use of health data, particularly use of personal data for

---

1. In the UK, the Information Commissioner's Guide to Data Protection provides a useful introduction (https://www.ico.org.uk/for-organisations/guide-to-data-protection/).

research, meaning that there is significant variation in data protection law across the EU for their research and development activities.

In the UK, since Brexit, the national legislation on data protection has been formed of the 'UK GDPR' (being the GDPR as it forms part of the law of England and Wales, Scotland and Northern Ireland by virtue of section 3 of the European Union (Withdrawal) Act 2018) and the Data Protection Act 2018 (2018 Act). At the time of writing, the UK GDPR has begun a process of legislative reform, with the publication of the Data Protection and Digital Information Bill.[2] This bill will, if passed into law in its current form, make a number of revisions to the obligations of the GDPR, with a stated aim of the legislation being to give 'researchers more flexibility to conduct life-saving scientific research'.[3] Any changes made by any resulting law will be the subject of a future volume – under current law, at the time of writing, the UK GDPR very closely mirrors the provisions of the GDPR. Therefore, in this Chapter, unless otherwise stated, references to the GDPR apply equally to the UK GDPR.

This Chapter sets out the main GDPR provisions of relevance to the pharmaceutical sector and signpost areas in which there is particular variation under national implementation of the GDPR. In addition to this divergence, the use of personal data in the pharmaceutical sector may also be regulated by health specific legislation in each country and self-regulatory codes, such as the various national incarnations of the European Federation of Pharmaceutical Industries & Associations (EFPIA) Code.[4] Any organisation collecting or using personal data in the UK or the EU will need to consider both national health law and national data protection law of the countries in which it is operating, together with the GDPR, in order to comply with relevant laws.

Although not strictly data protection laws, data protection lawyers are typically required to consider the EU's ePrivacy regime, derived at the time of writing from amended Directive 2002/58/EC[3] (ePrivacy Directive), particularly, its restrictions on electronic marketing and cookie compliance. These are touched upon in the final section of this Chapter.

[B] Territorial Scope and Establishment

The scope of the GDPR is territorially limited – although it has substantial extra-territorial effect as compared to many other pieces of national or EU legislation. Many pharmaceutical sector participants outside of the EU and the UK respectively will find

---

2. bills.parliament.uk/bills/3322 will provide access to the most current version of the Bill. If, at the time of reading, this has become law, the result of the proposed legislation will be amendments to both the 2018 Act and UK GDPR, which will be visible at https://legislation.gov.uk/ukpga/2018/12 and https://legislation.gov.uk/eur/2016/679/ respectively.
3. gov.uk/government/news/new-data-laws-to-boost-british-business-protect-consumers-and-seize-the-benefits-of-brexit.
4. At the time of writing, the latest version of the EFPIA Code is the EFPIA Code, Final Consolidated Version 2019, Approved by the General Assembly of 27 June 2018 and available at efpia.eu/media/676434/220718-efpia-code.pdf. This must be adopted by EFPIA's various Member Associations into their National Codes – in practice, particularly on direct marketing to healthcare professionals, there is some variation in how this is adopted.

themselves caught by these laws. Article 3 of the GDPR states that its data protection laws extend to any organisation established in the EU or to organisations established outside of the EU where they either offer goods or services to individuals (described in the language of the GDPR as 'data subjects') in the EU (irrespective of whether payment is required) or monitor the behaviour of data subjects, so far as their behaviour takes place in the EU. The UK GDPR adopts the same language for organisations looking to data subject in the UK. Guidance on the extent of this territorial application has been produced by the European Data Protection Board (EDPB) in its Guidelines 3/2018 on the territorial scope of the GDPR under Article 3.

The term establishment is one that has been given wide definition both by supervisory authorities in these guidelines and before them by the Court of Justice of the European Union (CJEU). Recital 22 of the GDPR says that establishment 'implies the effective and real exercise of activity through stable arrangements'. The CJEU has ruled that the processing 'in the context of activities' of an establishment 'cannot be interpreted restrictively'[5] and includes the carrying out of activities in a Member State that lead to a non-EU operator's activities being profitable, where these two activities are 'inextricably linked'.[6] It has also held that establishment 'extends to any real and effective activity [in a jurisdiction] — even a minimal one'.[7] This could potentially extend the scope of the GDPR to the processing of global pharmaceutical organisations with representative offices or subsidiaries located in the EU or UK carrying out promotion or sales activities in their relevant territories. Sponsors of clinical trials located outside of the EU may find themselves considered established in this way.

Once considered established, all processing carried out in the context of this establishment is caught, whether or not this relates to data subjects in the EU. For example, the GDPR would apply to the processing of personal data by a German study sponsor, even where the study's participants are located outside of the EU.

[C] Material Scope of the GDPR

(1) Broad concept of processing

The fundamental concept of processing is defined in Article 4(2) of the GDPR as:

> any operation or set of operations which is performed on personal data or on sets of personal data, whether or not by automated means, such as collection, recording, organisation, structuring, storage, adaptation or alteration, retrieval, consultation, use, disclosure by transmission, dissemination or otherwise making available, alignment or combination, restriction, erasure or destruction.

This, in practice, is broad enough to cover anything done to personal data, including anonymisation.

---

5. C-131/12 *Google Spain SL, Google Inc v. AEPD, Mario Costeja González* ECLI:EU:C:2014:317, paragraph 53.
6. *Ibid.*, paragraph 56.
7. C-230/14 *Weltimmo s.r.o. v. Nemzeti Adatvédelmi és Információszabadság Hatóság*, ECLI: EU:C:2015:639, paragraph 31.

(2) Manual files and the GDPR

Article 2(1) of the GDPR states that only 'processing of personal data wholly or partly by automated means' and to 'processing other than by automated means of personal data which form part of a filing system' is caught by its obligations. 'Filing system' is then defined in Article 4(6) as a 'structured set of personal data which are accessible according to specific criteria, whether centralised, decentralised or dispersed on a functional or geographical basis;' This definition of a filing system has particular importance where a controller is considering the extent to which its hard copy documentation, such as copies of medical record, HR files, or contemporaneous notes might be considered to contain personal data. Certainly, if the data is to be processed in an automated fashion, is intended to become wholly or partly automated, then this is personal data – so a scan of a scribbled interview note would be considered to contain personal data whereas the original document might not have done.

The position has received attention both by the CJEU and by the UK Court of Appeal. In the case of C-25/17 Tietosuojavaltuutettu intervening parties – Jehovan todistajat – uskonnollinen yhdyskunta,[8] the CJEU held that 'it appears that the requirement that the set of personal data must be "structured according to specific criteria" is simply intended to enable personal data to be easily retrieved'. Whilst this appears to allow for a broad scope, the UK Court of Appeal judged in their second decision in Dawson-Damer & Ors v. Taylor Wessing[9] adjudged that this test – at least in the UK – should be:

First, are the files a 'structured set of personal data'? Secondly, are the data accessible according to specific criteria? Thirdly, are those criteria 'related to individuals'? Fourthly, do the specific criteria enable the data to be easily ... retrieved?[10]

In practice, it appears that the ICO's old 'temp test' still remains useful in this context. In guidance issued in 2011, it suggested a 'rule of thumb' that suggested that controllers consider:

If you employed a temporary administrative assistant (a 'temp'), would they be able to extract specific information about an individual from your manual records without any particular knowledge of your type of work or the documents you hold? The 'temp test' assumes that the temp in question is reasonably competent, requiring only a short induction, explanation and/or operating manual on the particular filing system in question for them to be able to use it.[11]

---

8. C-25/17 *Tietosuojavaltuutettu intervening parties – Jehovan todistajat – uskonnollinen yhdyskunta*, ECLI:EU:C:2018:551.
9. *Dawson-Damer & Ors v. Taylor Wessing* [2020] EWCA Civ 352.
10. ico.org.uk/media/for-organisations/documents/1592/relevant_filing_systems_faqs.pdf.
11. *Ibid.*

(3) Other exclusions

Article 2(2) of the GDPR sets out further exclusions of certain processing from its scope. Most of these relate to the limits of European law. Perhaps of most importance to the pharmaceutical sector, processing carried out by natural persons in the course of a purely personal or household activity. If a company takes a recording of the advice given by a healthcare professional, this will be caught by the GDPR. If, by contrast, an individual patient takes a recording of their consultation so they can relisten at a later date, this would benefit from this 'personal' exemption, provided wider use is not made.

[D]   Supervision, Enforcement, and Penalties

Each EU Member State, and the UK, has a data protection supervisory authority. Supervisory authorities are data protection regulators, bodies charged with providing guidance and information on data protection, monitoring compliance and enforcing data protection law. In the UK, the Information Commissioner's Office (ICO) is the supervisory authority. Representatives of each EU supervisory authority and the EFTA EEA states, together with the European Data Protection Supervisor (EDPS) make up the EDPB. The EDPB replaced a similar body constituted under Article 29 of the previous Directive, the Article 29 Working Party (WP29). The EDPB is charged with providing guidance on data protection intended to contribute to the harmonised application of data protection laws throughout the EU. Though this guidance is not binding, they are indicative of supervisory authority's views and are therefore demonstrate the likely approach of these bodies in taking any enforcement action.

Supervisory authorities have both investigatory and enforcement powers, the extent of which may vary procedurally under national law. Investigatory powers must include those set out in the lengthy Article 58 of the GDPR, including abilities to order the provision of information and obtain access to premises. Enforcement powers are addressed under Articles 83 and 84 of the GDPR, with an obligation on Member States to allow the imposition of substantial financial and non-financial penalties. Article 83(1) requires that supervisory authorities impose 'effective, proportionate and dissuasive' fines. Article 83(5) sets the maximum fine at €20 million or 4% of the total annual worldwide turnover of the organisation in breach.[12] This makes data protection a high-risk area for non-compliance.

§23.03   THE DEFINITION OF PERSONAL DATA

The GDPR defines personal data as: 'any information relating to an identified or identifiable natural person' that allows an individual to be identified 'directly or indirectly, in particular by reference to an identifier such as a name, an identification

---

12. Under the UK GDPR, precise details of penalties under Article 83 are set out in Part 6 of the 2018 Act, with the maximum fine set at GBP 17,500,000 or 4% of the total annual worldwide turnover of the organisation in breach.

number, location data, an online identifier or to one or more factor specific to the physical, physiological, genetic, mental, economic, cultural or social identity of that natural person' (Article 4(1)).[13]

In the case of C-434/16 *Novak v Data Protection Commissioner*,[14] the CJEU explained:

> The use of the expression 'any information' in the definition of the concept of 'personal data', within [EU data protection legislation], reflects the aim of the EU legislature to assign a wide scope to that concept, which is not restricted to information that is sensitive or private, but potentially encompasses all kinds of information, not only objective but also subjective, in the form of opinions and assessments, provided that it 'relates' to the data subject.
>
> As regards the latter condition, it is satisfied where the information, by reason of its content, purpose or effect, is linked to a particular person.

This analysis leaves two questions to be considered: does the data cause a data subject to be either directly or indirectly identifiable, whether used alone or in combination with other data, and whether this data then relates to the data subject.

[A] Identifiable

Identifiability of an individual is broadly interpreted. Recital 26 of the GDPR states that 'to determine whether a natural person is identifiable, account should be taken of all the means reasonably likely to be used'. Identifiability is not limited to direct identifiability – the ability to match the data to a face or a name – but extends to indirectly identifiable individuals for whom data can only be identified in combination with other records either held by the organisation, or that could be readily accessed, such as publicly available information.

[B] Relating

The WP29 provided a helpful outline of how to determine whether this information or data 'relates' to an identifiable individual, identifying three different methods in its Opinion No. 4/2007 on the concept of personal data (WP 136):[15]

(1) Content – the data is evident about an identifiable individual, such as a passport number or medical result. The GDPR's Recitals 26 and 30 emphasise that this includes not only 'obvious' identifies such as name but also pseudonymised data and online identifiers such as IP addresses.
(2) Purpose – if the processing of data is one that will result in the data being associated with a data subject, then it will be considered to relate to the

---

13. This definition is one of the areas that the UK's Data Protection and Digital Information Bill proposes to adapt at the time of writing.
14. C-434/16 *Peter Nowak v. Data Protection Commissioner* ECLI:EU:C:2017:994, pp 34–35.
15. WP136, adopted 20 June 2007.

individual if it will be used to 'evaluate, treat... or influence' an individual in a certain way – such as the review of an individual's actions to assess their performance.[16]

(3) Results – if the outcome of the data processing is one that leads to 'an *impact* on a certain individual's rights and interests', then this would be considered personal data. For example, the diminishing dispensing of certain medicines by a pharmacy may not be personal data, unless it will be assessed and used for the result of taking action against a pharmacist or non-compliant patient.

Personal data can also relate to more than one identifiable individual. For example, guidance from the WP29, explains that drug prescription information could be personal data of both the patient and the prescribing doctor:

> Drug prescription information (e.g. drug identification number, drug name, drug strength, manufacturer, selling price, new or refill, reasons for use, reasons for no substitution order, prescriber's first and last name, phone number, etc.), whether in the form of an individual prescription or in the form of patterns discerned from a number of prescriptions, can be considered as personal data about the physician who prescribes this drug, even if the patient is anonymous. Thus, providing information about prescriptions written by identified or identifiable doctors to producers of prescription drugs constitutes a communication of personal data to third party recipients (...).[17]

[C] Deceased Individuals

References to personal data in this Chapter relate only to personal data of living individuals, as the GDPR does not apply to a deceased person. However, some EU Member States (such as France, Hungary, and Denmark) have national laws regulating the use of a deceased person's data. A local legal analysis should always be carried out when handling information relating to the deceased.

[D] Special Category Personal Data

[1] Generally

Much of the data processed in the pharmaceutical sector will fall within the GDPR's 'special categories of personal data', a type of personal data that has additional protection under EU data protection law. Special category personal data is subject to additional protections, and there are stringent conditions for processing it. Article 9 of the GDPR defines special category personal data (often referred to as sensitive personal data, particularly in the UK) as follows:

---

16. *Ibid.*, p. 10.
17. *Ibid.*, p. 7.

personal data revealing racial or ethnic origin, political opinions, religious or philosophical beliefs, or trade union membership, and the processing of genetic data, biometric data for the purpose of uniquely identifying a natural person, data concerning health or data concerning a natural person's sex life or sexual orientation shall be prohibited.

[2] Data Concerning Health

Data concerning health is defined broadly in Article 4(15) of the GDPR as 'personal data related to the physical or mental health of a natural person, including the provision of health care services, which reveal information about his or her health status'. Recital 35 expands upon this, stating that any information 'past, present or future' which relates to physical or mental health and information about the 'physiological or biomedical state' of the individuals regardless of the source of the information.

The EDPB – and the W29 before it – has elaborated on what data may be considered to 'reveal' health status. Annex A to Letter of WP29 Clarifying Scope of Health Data under the Data Protection Directive,[18] while it predates GDPR, is particularly instructive in setting out how both the nature of the data itself, and the context of the processing, can lead to data 'revealing' health status. It explains that:

personal data are health data where:
1. The data are inherently/clearly medical data
2. The data can be used in itself or in combination with other data to draw a conclusion about the actual health status or health risk of a person
3. Conclusions are drawn about a person's health status or health risk (irrespective of whether these conclusions are accurate or inaccurate, legitimate or illegitimate, or otherwise adequate or inadequate)[19]

The WP29 explained that whilst medical data, namely 'data about the physical or mental health status of a data subject that are generated in a professional, medical context' is clearly health data, the category of 'data concerning health' is a 'much broader term'.[20] As noted by the WP29, a 'wide interpretation' is also required as a result of the judgment in the case of C-101/01 *Lindqvist*, where the CJEU held that the expression 'data concerning health' 'must be given a wide interpretation so as to include information concerning all aspects, both physical and mental, of the health of an individual'.[21]

Examples listed by the WP29 as processing that may reveal ill health include processing relating to broken limbs, the wearing of contact lenses or glasses, information on IQ, on allergies, or membership of patient support groups, weight-loss groups

---

18. WP29 Letter to Paul Timmers, 5 February 2015, and its Annex: ec.europa.eu/justice/article-29/documentation/other-document/files/2015/20150205_letter_art29wp_ec_health_data_after_plenary_en.pdf and ec.europa.eu/justice/article-29/documentation/other-document/files/2015/20150205_letter_art29wp_ec_health_data_after_plenary_annex_en.pdf.
19. *Ibid.*, p. 5.
20. *Ibid.*, p. 2.
21. C-101/01 *Criminal proceedings against Bodil Lindqvist* ECLI:EU:C:2003:596, paragraph 50.

Chapter 23: Data Protection in the Pharmaceutical Sector   §23.03[F]

or other support groups with a health objective, as well as 'data about the purchase of medical products, devices and services, when health status can be inferred from the data, or information about the participation in some selectively performed screening tests'. The definition is also considered to include 'future' health status means that categories of health data also include data revealing 'a person's obesity, high or low blood pressure, hereditary or genetic predisposition, excessive alcohol consumption, tobacco consumption or drug use or any other information where there is a scientifically proven or commonly perceived risk of disease in the future'.[22]

The WP29 also explained that to draw conclusions about health, the data need not of itself necessarily reveal ill health, where the information may be ultimately analysed to determine an individual is healthy – for example, where a survey is completed to provide advice on health, the data collected as part of that survey is health data, regardless of the input the data subject provides.[23]

Finally, on inference, the WP29 explained that some information may only become health data where inferences are drawn as to their impact on a person's health – for example, the number of steps taken by a user will not of itself be health data, but a controller choosing to evaluate this number of steps and assess the individual to be living an unhealthy sedentary lifestyle on that basis would be processing health data.[24]

[E]   Criminal Convictions and Offence Data

In addition to special categories of personal data, personal data relating to criminal convictions and offences also benefits from particular protection under Article 10 of the GDPR and may only be processed 'under the control of official authority or when the processing is authorised by Union or Member State law'. In the UK, the conditions for processing special category data (discussed at §23.06 below) are extended to the processing of criminal offence data, but in other countries, this is often very tightly controlled.

[F]   Pseudonymised Data

Pseudonymised data, often referred to as key coded information in the pharmaceutical sector, is personal data which has been processed 'in such a manner that the personal data can no longer be attributed to a specific data subject without the use of additional information' which is held separately and securely.[25] An obvious example of this includes key coded information created and shared with sponsors in the context of clinical trials.

Pseudonymisation is not a method of anonymisation, and pseudonymous data is still personal data as it enables the identification of individuals (albeit via use of a key

---

22. WP Letter Annex, p. 2.
23. *Ibid.*
24. *Ibid.*, p. 4.
25. Article 4(5).

or combination without another). Pseudonymisation is, however, a useful security technique, and it is good practice to routinely pseudonymise data where possible.

[G]   Anonymised Data

Information stops being personal data, and therefore stops being subject to data protection laws, if it has been appropriately anonymised. Anonymised data is 'information which does not relate to an identified or identifiable natural person or to personal data rendered anonymous in such a manner that the data subject is not or no longer identifiable' (Recital 26 GDPR).

When sharing clinical data sets between organisations in different jurisdictions, the differences and complexities of compliance requirements, particular relating to ensuring valid consent, and further processing of data for secondary purposes, can prove a high or insurmountable hurdle. Anonymising the datasets may relieve this burden by removing the data from the scope of data protection law. Adequate anonymisation is also a requirement for any clinical trial data made publicly available on the European Medicine Agency's (EMA's) portal.[26]

However, the threshold for personal data to be considered anonymous is high. WP29 guidance summarises anonymisation as follows: 'an effective anonymisation solution prevents all parties from singling out an individual in a dataset, from linking two records within a dataset (or between two separate datasets) and from inferring any information in such dataset.'[27]

According to WP29 guidance on anonymisation (WP216),[28] whether data has been successfully anonymised should be assessed under three criteria:

- is it still possible to single out an individual?
- is it still possible to link records relating to an individual?
- can information be inferred concerning an individual?

More detail on each of these tests, and how various anonymisation techniques are considered to meet them, can be found in WP216, where the Working Party warned that no single anonymisation technique will always guarantee that all three tests are met.

There is a particular divergence in the approach taken in the UK and in other European countries on whether a secondary individual-level dataset can be considered to be anonymous rather than pseudonymous if the underlying dataset is retained by the initial controller. In WP216, the Article 29 Working Party stated that:

> it is critical to understand that when a data controller does not delete the original (identifiable) data at event-level, and the data controller hands over part of this dataset (for example after removal or masking of identifiable data), the resulting

---

26. ema.europa.eu/en/human-regulatory/marketing-authorisation/clinical-data-publication.
27. Article 29 Working Party, 'Opinion 05/2014 on Anonymisation Techniques' (WP 216) adopted 10 April 2014.
28. *Ibid.*, pp. 11–12.

Chapter 23: Data Protection in the Pharmaceutical Sector §23.03[G]

dataset is still personal data. Only if the data controller would aggregate the data to a level where the individual events are no longer identifiable, the resulting dataset can be qualified as anonymous.

Although this guidance dates to 2014, it is still the view held by a large number of supervisory authorities in Europe, who consider data de-identified in this manner to be pseudonymous rather than anonymous. Indeed, in the case of *Breyer*,[29] the CJEU held that personal data held confidentially by a third party could be used to identify an individual in a separate controller's dataset, it may in at least some circumstances lead to data held by a separate controller being considered personal data in any event. The court appears to have allowed only a narrow scope for anonymisation methods, admitting only that it was unlikely data would remain identifiable where:

> the identification of the data subject was prohibited by law or practically impossible on account of the fact that it requires a disproportionate effort in terms of time, cost and man-power, so that the risk of identification appears in reality to be insignificant.[30]

In contrast, the UK Information Commissioner's draft pseudonymisation guidance[31] allows more flexibility, stating that:

> The status of data can change depending on who holds it. For example, pseudonymous data which you can still identify using a key or other separate identifiers might no longer be identifiable in the hands of a different organisation who does not have access to that key.[32]

In the UK, the ICO's wider draft anonymisation guidance[33] retains the concept of a 'motivated intruder' test, which recommends that in assessing the means likely to be used to identify information, controller should consider whether a third party would be able to re-identify a dataset if they were motivated to attempt it.[34] The ICO explains that this should not assume that such an individual would need to resort to specialist knowledge or equipment, or criminal acts, to obtain access to personal data, that should considered to be a 'determined person with a particular reason to want to identify individuals'.[35] This is a position that the UK Government is seeking to solidify through its proposed Data Protection and Data Processing Bill. In contrast, in a recent decision against WhatsApp, the EDPB rejected arguments relating to motivation as irrelevant to determining the risk of re-identification, stating that:

> The EDPB highlights that neither the definition nor Recital 26 of the GDPR as such provide any indication that the intention nor the motivation of the controller or of

---

29. C-582/14 *Patrick Breyer v. Bundesrepublik Deutschland*, ECLI:EU:C:2016:779.
30. *Ibid.*
31. ICO's Chapter 3: Pseudonymisation, Draft anonymisation, pseudonymisation and privacy enhancing technologies guidance, February 2022.
32. *Ibid.*, p. 5.
33. ICO's Chapter 2: How do we ensure anonymisation is effective? Draft anonymisation, pseudonymisation and privacy enhancing technologies guidance, October 2021.
34. *Ibid.*, p. 15.
35. *Ibid.*

the third party are relevant factors to be taken into consideration when assessing whether the dataset at hand is to be considered personal data or not.[36]

§23.04 CONTROLLERS AND PROCESSORS

European data protection laws allocate different roles and responsibilities to parties in relation to personal data. Organisations processing personal data may be either a controller or a processor. A controller is a party who 'alone or jointly with others, determines the purposes and means of the processing of personal data'.[37] The controller is predominantly responsible for the processing of the data subject's data in accordance with data protection law and shoulders the majority of the compliance burden of the GDPR. Controllers may act independently or jointly with other controllers. Processors, in contrast, 'process personal data on behalf of the controller'.[38] Processors have some direct obligations under the GDPR, relating predominantly to security, international transfers, and record keeping. They may not use the personal data they process for their own purposes – in addition to breaching mandatory contractual provisions under Article 28 of the GDPR, to do so would render the organisation a controller.

When parties share personal data, it is important to establish whether each party is acting as a controller or a processor, as this will determine the data protection responsibilities of the parties. Parties may have both roles for different purposes, e.g., an organisation can be a processor for data storage purposes and a controller for its own usage analytics purposes.

[A] Assessing the Roles of the Parties

In some scenarios, it is easy to work out whether a party acts as a controller or a processor. In others, it is less straightforward. The EDPB has provided guidance on this point in its Guidelines 07/2020 on the concepts of controllers and processor in the GDPR (Controller Processor Guidelines).[39] These Controller Processor Guidelines set out two methods of determining whether a party is a controller:

(1) 'Control stemming from legal provisions' – a party may be required by law to process personal data. For example, market authorisation holders are legally required to carry out pharmacovigilance and are therefore controllers for adverse event data they receive and share.[40]

---

36. https://edpb.europa.eu/system/files/2021-09/dpc_final_decision_redacted_for_issue_to_edpb_01-09-21_en.pdf, p 38.
37. Article 4(7), GDPR.
38. Article 4(8), GDPR.
39. EDPB 'Guidelines 07/2020 on the concepts of controllers and processor in the GDPR' Version 2.0, Adopted on 7 July 2021.
40. *Ibid.*, p. 11.

(2) 'Control stemming from factual influence' – if the law does not clearly determine responsibility, then responsibility for the processing must be determined after 'an assessment of the factual circumstances surrounding the processing.' This can be obvious from the traditional roles held by the controller, which imply data protection responsibility, or from 'established legal practice'. Examples here would include employers bearing responsibility for their employees or healthcare professionals processing personal data relating to the patients in their care. Where this is not the case, then the parties must determine which of them decides 'the "why" and the "how" of the processing'.[41]

It is common for there to be ambiguity about the level of independence that a party is given, and therefore allocating roles can be challenging in practice. A controller may allow its service provider discretion over how the processing takes place (in other words, it can delegate the 'means' of the processing). The Controller Processor Guidelines explain that a processor can 'never determine the purpose of processing' but that there is 'some margin of manoeuvre' on means for a processor to take certain decisions.[42] The EDPB makes a particular distinction between the delegation of 'essential vs. non-essential means' – the first of these may not be delegated. Essential means are, according, to the EDPB:

> means that are closely linked to the purpose and the scope of the processing, such as the type of personal data which are processed ('which data shall be processed?'), the duration of the processing ('for how long shall they be processed?'), the categories of recipients ('who shall have access to them?') and the categories of data subjects ('whose personal data are being processed?').[43]

It is also possible to have multiple controllers involved in the processing of personal data, acting independently or jointly, and a party can be a controller for some activities and processor for others. A party cannot be both a controller and a processor for the same processing activity.

Last, it is worth noting that some parties may not have a data protection role in relation to the data. In its guidance,[44] the ICO gives the example of a courier service contracted by a hospital to deliver mail containing patients' medical records to other health services. The ICO explains that the courier company will be neither a controller nor a processor as, although it physically holds the data, it is not able to access it or control it: 'the term "holding", as used in the definition of "processing", implies considerably more than simply being in possession of a physical object that contains personal data'.

---

41. *Ibid.*, p. 14.
42. *Ibid.*
43. *Ibid*, p. 15.
44. ICO guidance 'Data controllers and data processors: what the difference is and what the governance implications are' Version 1.0, May 2014.

[B] Joint or Separate Control

Where two parties share data as controllers, they are either acting as independent controllers, each processing data for their own purposes, or as joint controllers. Article 26 of the GDPR provides: 'where two or more controllers jointly determine the purposes and means of processing, they shall be joint controllers.' Joint controllers are required under this provision to document the allocation of data protection responsibilities between themselves in writing and to explain this allocation in a transparent manner to data subject.

The Controller Processor Guidelines address joint control at some length, including specific examples relating to the processing of data in the context of clinical trial. It explains that 'the assessment of joint controllership should be carried out on a factual, rather than a formal, analysis of the actual influence on the purposes and means of the processing' and that in determining joint participation, this 'needs to include the determination of purposes on the one and the determination of means on the other hand'.[45]

CJEU case law has emphasised that the responsibilities and involvement of the two controllers does not need to be equal for there to be joint control, and that indeed there is no need even for the data to be shared from one party to the other, so long as the party not receiving the data is involved in the decision to collect it and benefits from the processing.[46] The CJEU has also pointed out that joint controllership may exist for certain stages of the processing but not others: for example, the controllers may collect personal data jointly but then process it as separate controllers at a later stage.[47]

The Controller Processor Guidelines build upon this case law, explaining that determination of purposes may involve both obviously 'common' and 'converging' decisions.[48] On converging decisions, the EDPB explains that it is important to identify 'whether the processing would not be possible without both parties' participation in the sense that the processing by each party is inseparable, i.e. inextricably linked'.[49]

The EDPB further explains that this joint determination of purpose does not mean that the *same* purpose needs to be pursued, if the entities involved 'pursue purposes which are closely linked or complementary [...] for example, when there is a mutual benefit arising from the same processing operation'.[50]

Joint determination of purposes is interpreted flexibly, as a result of both CJEU case law and the Controller Processor Guidelines. It is sufficient that a joint controller has 'exerted influence' over the means of processing, and 'different joint controllers may therefore define the means of the processing to a different extent, depending on who is effectively in a position to do so'. The EDPB explain that this can particularly

---

45. Controller Processor Guidelines, p. 19.
46. *See* C-210/16 *Unabhängiges Landeszentrum für Datenschutz Schleswig-Holstein v. Wirtschaftsakademie Schleswig-Holstein GmbH*, and C-25/17 *Tietosuojavaltuutettu intervening parties – Jehovan todistajat – uskonnollinen yhdyskunta*.
47. Fashion ID GmbH Case (C-40/17).
48. Controller Processor Guidelines, p.19.
49. *Ibid.*, p. 19.
50. *Ibid.*, p. 20.

arise in the case of 'platforms, standardised tools, or other infrastructure allowing the parties to process the same personal data and which have been set up in a certain way by one of the parties to be used by others that can also decide how to set it up'[51]. The use of such common tools will not always lead to joint control, but controllers will have to demonstrate that 'the processing they carry out is separable and could be performed by one party without intervention from the other' or that the other party acts as a processor.[52]

Importantly, a determination that certain personal data is processed jointly with another controller does not mean that these controllers cannot carry out separate processing of these data as separate controllers. The Controller Processor Guidelines explain:

> If one of these entities decides alone the purposes and means of operations that precede or are subsequent [to the joint processing] in the chain of processing, this entity must be considered as the sole controller of this preceding or subsequent operation.

The European Data Protection Supervisor has also indicated that, in a pharmacovigilance context (*see* Chapter 10), it considers market authorisation holders, sponsors, relevant national regulatory authorities (such as the Medicines and Healthcare products Regulatory Agency in the UK) and the EMEA to be joint controllers with respect to medical safety information collected for and stored in national databases and European Union Drug Regulating Authorities Clinical Trials Database (EudraVigilance).[53]

[C] Data Protection Roles in Clinical Trials

In a clinical trial, the data protection roles of the parties involved must be carefully analysed to ensure data protection responsibilities are allocated correctly on a factual analysis. This is an area where there has been considerable variation between Member States. As the European Data Protection Supervisor has noted:

> there is a complex interplay between the obligations of the controller (responsible for personal data processing), of the person or entity responsible for the research (the 'sponsor' in the context of clinical trials) and the person carrying out the actual investigations, who depending on the circumstances could be a separate controller, joint controller and/or processor.[54]

What is not in question is the trial sponsor role as a controller. The data protection role of the investigating site will, however, differ according to the setup of

---

51. *Ibid.*, p. 21.
52. *Ibid.*, p. 22.
53. Opinion on a Notification for Prior Checking Received from the Data Protection Officer of the European Medicines Agency (EMEA) regarding the EudraVigilance database (7 September 2009).
54. European Data Protection Supervisor, 'A Preliminary Opinion on data protection and scientific research' (6 January 2020).

the clinical trial and the Member State's approach. The alternative analyses set out by are discussed generally below; however, local law advice is essential to analyse the data protection roles in each clinical trial in practice due to the variation in approaches across the EU.

[1] Site as a Processor

The Health Research Authority (HRA), which issues guidance to researchers and ethics review boards in England for national health services (NHS) clinical trials, has advised that the site is a controller for the patient care it provides to the study participants, but that it is a processor acting on behalf of the sponsor where it collects and processes data for a clinical trial case report or for clinical trials research purposes.[55] As the site and its investigators have a high degree of responsibility and decision-making power, this guidance does not necessarily reflect the outcome of a data protection analysis of the roles. However, in England at least, sites should position themselves in this split controller/processor role. The CNIL in France has taken a similar approach, designating sites as processors acting on behalf of the sponsor.[56] The Controller Processor Guidelines give this as a possible analysis in their specific example of clinical trials, stating that:

> In the event that the investigator does not participate to the drafting of the protocol (he just accepts the protocol already elaborated by the sponsor), and the protocol is only designed by the sponsor, the investigator should be considered as a processor and the sponsor as the controller for this clinical trial.[57]

[2] Site as a Controller

The rest of the Controller Processor Guidelines example on clinical trials argues that it is likely that sites and sponsors should be considered joint controllers where there is any collaboration over the study protocol. It explains that in choosing to 'collaborate together to the drafting of the study protocol (i.e. purpose, methodology/design of the study, data to be collected, subject exclusion/inclusion criteria, database reuse (where relevant) etc.)' sites and sponsors 'jointly determine and agree on the same purpose and the essential means of the processing'.

Precedent or subsequent processing by the parties would still result in separate control. The Controller Processor Guidelines emphasise the need to distinguish research from 'the storage and use of the same data for the purposes of patient care, for

---

55. Controllers and personal data in health and care research (19 April 2018), accessed on https://www.hra.nhs.uk/planning-and-improving-research/policies-standards-legislation/data-protection-and-information-governance/gdpr-guidance/what-law-says/data-controllers-and-personal-data-health-and-care-research-context/
56. Méthodologie de référence MR-001, a simplified authorisation procedure. Organisations can seek direct authorisation from the CNIL outside the MR-001 procedure, but this will be more time consuming.
57. Controller Processor Guidelines, p. 23.

which the health care provider [the investigator] remains the controller.' Similarly, in these situations, the sponsor, would generally be considered a separate controller for its subsequent use of the clinical trial data for its own research and development purposes.

The joint controller model has been used in Germany for some time, where the association of German Supervisory Authorities has stated that sponsors and sites/investigators act as joint controllers in a clinical trial.[58] However, prior to the finalisation of the Controller Processor Guidelines, sites were considered separate controllers to sponsors in a number of EU countries, and this analysis may remain the typical approach in some countries despite the sprawling interpretation of joint control.

[3] Role of the CRO

The role of the Contract Research Organisation (CRO) is more clear-cut than that of the site and (if separate) an investigator. The CRO is appointed by the sponsor to organise certain aspects of the clinical trial and will, in almost all circumstances, be appointed as a processor of the sponsor. This industry practice is widely accepted throughout the EU, but the role of the CRO will always depend on their tasks and involvement in the clinical trials and should therefore undergo a case-by-case analysis.

The European CRO Federation industry body (EUCROF) has submitted a code of conduct for data processors working in the clinical research industry for approval. If finally adopted, this may provide greater clarity on the role of various processors in the field.

[4] Other Parties and Data Subjects

The role of other parties involved in the clinical trial must also be analysed. The sponsor is likely to have processors, such as the electronic data capture provider, with whom processor agreements will need to be entered (*see* §23.04[D][1]). The sponsor may also have data sharing relationships with other interested parties or co-sponsors, which are likely to be joint controllers. The HRA in the UK has stated that:

> In the health and care research context it is expected that the sponsor will be a controller. In some cases, another organisation will be delegated significant decision-making responsibilities in relation to the data, for example where a clinical trial unit hosted by one organisation is responsible for designing a study and analysing the data for a separate sponsor. In such cases, a joint controller arrangement may be appropriate.[59]

---

58. Kurzpapier Nr. 16 Gemeinsam für die Verarbeitung Verantwortliche, Article 26 DSGVO (19 March 2019), p. 4.
59. HRA website '*Still got questions?*' (24 May 2018), accessed on https://www.hra.nhs.uk/planning-and-improving-research/policies-standards-legislation/data-protection-and-information-governance/gdpr-guidance/still-got-questions/.

Finally, clinical trials should consider the personal data flows not just of the participant patients but also of the investigators. The controller(s) for processing of the investigators' data are likely to be different to the controller(s) of the sponsor's data – the site and the CROs, in particular, may be processors for participants' data but controllers for investigators' data. These relationships must be analysed prior to the clinical trial and reflected in appropriate contractual agreements.

[D] Controllers and Processors in Contract

The data protection roles and obligations of the parties should be recorded in contractual arrangements. The GDPR sets out certain cases in which such contracts are legally required, with prescriptive information about what should be included. Even where such contracts are not required by the GDPR, they remain advisable for most data sharing to provide commercial certainty and protections to the parties.

[1] Processing Agreements

Where a controller engages a processor, they are legally required to put in place contractual data processing terms. The GDPR is prescriptive on what such terms must include, setting out in Article 28 the mandatory provisions to be included in a data processing agreement. These required clauses are clearly set out in Article 28(2)-(4) and will therefore not be detailed here.

In addition to the GDPR-required clauses, parties are free to contract on other issues such as costs and aspects of liability. Taken by themselves, the Article 28 required clauses are often high level and would not provide substantial contractual certainty on the controls available to the controller, so additional detail should be considered. The Controller Processor Guidelines include suggestions from the EDPB on what they believe ought to be included.

Article 28 also specifies that controllers must only use processors who provide 'sufficient guarantees to implement appropriate technical and organisational measures', which places an obligation on the controller to carry out due diligence before engaging a processor. Inspecting a processor's security capabilities and data protection compliance measures is therefore an essential pre-contracting task for the controller.

[2] Joint Controllers

When two parties are joint controllers, Article 26(1) of the GDPR requires that they 'in a transparent manner determine their respective responsibilities for compliance with the obligations under this Regulation.' In particular, the joint controllers must determine how they will respond to data subject requests and how they will provide the required transparency information.

Unlike Article 28, Article 26 does not require joint controllership arrangements to be in writing or legally binding between the parties. Parties can therefore determine the legal nature and structure of the agreement according to their circumstances. However, the arrangement must clearly identify which party is responsible for each of the GDPR's controller obligations.

Individuals are also explicitly granted the right to bring claims against any of the joint controllers, regardless of the terms of that agreement (Article 26(3) GDPR). Any agreement between the joint controllers will not be able to allocate liability for failure to comply with the GDPR on one party rather than another, as under Article 82(4) GDPR, any party involved in the same processing (whether as joint or separate controllers, or controller and processor) is jointly and severally liable to the data subject. Parties can then recover back from the others any compensation paid to the individuals for which they were not responsible.

In addition to documenting the allocation of responsibility, controllers must also make sure that the 'essence of the agreement' is provided to individuals whose data is processed.[60] This type of information can be included in the data protection notice discussed in §23.08.

§23.05   DATA PROTECTION PRINCIPLES

EU and UK data protection law is based on compliance with 'principles' set out in the GDPR in Article 5. These both set out general obligations and sit as the basis of most of the more specific obligations of the GDPR. Below, this chapter addresses on how these principles impact on the processing of data conducted by pharmaceutical organisations.

§23.06   LAWFULNESS

Article 5(1)(a) of the GDPR requires that personal data be processed 'lawfully, fairly, and in a transparent manner in relation to the data subject'.

Lawful processing, in part, means not using personal data in a manner that is prohibited by law, whether by another Article in the GDPR or by other applicable laws. The GDPR also establishes, in Article 6, that personal data will be lawfully processed only where a controller can demonstrate that it has a lawful basis.

Controllers must identify the relevant lawful basis for the processing at the outset and ensure that this is communicated to data subjects.[61] The ICO advises controllers to 'take care to get it right first time – you should not swap to a different lawful basis at a later date without good reason.'[62]

The available legal grounds under Article 6 are:

(a) consent (Article 6(1)(a));

---

60. GDPR, Article 26(2).
61. GDPR, Articles 13 and 14, discussed at §23.07 Fairness and Transparency below.
62. ico.org.uk/for-organisations/guide-to-data-protection/guide-to-the-general-data-protection-regulation-gdpr/lawful-basis-for-processing/.

(b) contractual necessity (Article 6(1)(b));
(c) legal obligations (Article 6(1)(c));
(d) processing necessary to protect an individual's vital interests (Article 6(1)(d));
(e) processing necessary for the performance of a task in the public interest or in the exercise of a controller's official authority (Article 6(1)(e) – in practice, this limb is limited to public authorities; and
(f) processing necessary 'for the purposes of the legitimate interests pursued by the controller or by a third party, except where such interests are overridden by the interests or fundamental rights and freedoms of the data subject' (Article 6(1)(f)). This ground is not available to public authorities.

Where processing is necessary to perform a contract (such as processing associated with providing payments to a healthcare professional) or to comply with a legal obligation (such as processing necessary to comply with pharmacovigilance rules or employment laws), it will be clear which legal basis should be selected. Absent these options, pharmaceutical companies will usually need to make a choice of legitimate interests or consent. For this reason, we focus on these two grounds of Article 6 in this chapter.

Where the processing involves special category personal data, such as data concerning health, then it is additional necessary to identify an appropriate basis in Article 9 to overcome the general prohibition of processing such data. The available grounds under Article 9(2) are:

- the explicit consent of the data subject (Article 9(2)(a));
- processing is necessary to meet employment law or social security law requirements (e.g., collecting health data to provide maternity or disability rights), as set out in EU or Member State law (Article 9(2)(b));
- processing is necessary to protect the vital interests of an individual where the data subject is unable to give consent (Article 9(2)(c));
- certain processing by political, philosophical or religious non-profits, or trade union where processing relates solely to members and is not disclosed without consent (Article 9(2)(d));
- processing involves personal data 'manifestly made public' by the data subject (Article 9(2)(e));
- processing is necessary for the establishment, exercise, or defence of legal claims or whenever courts are acting in their judicial capacity (Article 9(2)(f));
- processing is necessary for 'reasons of substantial public interest, on the basis of EU or Member State law' (Article 9(2)(g));
- processing is necessary for preventative or occupational medicine, including 'assessment of the working capacity of the employee, medical diagnosis, the provision of health or social care or treatment or the management of health or social care systems and services on the basis of EU or Member State law or pursuant to contract with a health professional' (Article 9(2)(h));

- processing is necessary for reasons of public interest in the area of public health, such as protecting against serious cross-border threats on the basis of EU or Member State law (Article 9(2)(i)); or
- processing is necessary for archiving purposes in the public interest, scientific or historical research purposes, or statistical purposes based on EU or Member State law (Article 9(2)(j)).

For processing of special category data to be legitimate, it must have both an Article 6 legal basis and meet one of these Article 9 conditions. Unlike Article 6, which is self-executing, a number of the provisions in Article 9 require controllers to make reference to national or EU legislation. Where a provision requires that there be a basis in EU or Member State law, controllers must look to that law for such basis, and this may lead to substantial local divergence. This is particularly true of Article 9(2)(j), which allow processing for the purposes of research in the public interests. In this chapter, we focus on the UK's approach to special category data, but now that the UK has left the EU, British controllers should be aware that where they collect special category data from EU countries, they may also need to consider the laws of those countries.

[A] Legitimate Interests

Legitimate interests is perhaps the legal basis most frequently used by bodies in the private sector, with the ICO's online guidance acknowledging that it is 'the most flexible lawful basis for processing.'[63] In C-13/16 *Valsts policijas Rigas regiona parvaldes Kartibas policijas parvalde v Rigas pašvaldibas SIA 'Rigas satiksme'* ('*Rigas*'), the CJEU explained that to rely on legitimate interests, a controller must satisfy:

> three cumulative conditions [...] namely, first, the pursuit of a legitimate interest by the data controller or by the third party or parties to whom the data are disclosed; second, the need to process personal data for the purposes of the legitimate interests pursued; and third, that the fundamental rights and freedoms of the person concerned by the data protection do not take precedence.[64]

[1] Identifying a Legitimate Interest

A very large number of interests may be considered to be legitimate. Some interests are identified as being potentially legitimate in the Recitals of the GDPR, including direct marketing and fraud prevention within Recital 47. Research purposes have separately

---

63. ico.org.uk/for-organisations/guide-to-data-protection/guide-to-the-general-data-protection-regulation-gdpr/lawful-basis-for-processing/legitimate-interests/.
64. C-13/16 *Valsts policijas Rigas regiona parvaldes Kartibas policijas parvalde v Rigas pašvaldibas SIA 'Rigas satiksme'* ECLI:EU:C:2017:336, paragraph 28.

been recognised as being a legitimate interest by the WP29.[65] The ICO's guidance on legitimate interests explains that interests 'may be compelling or trivial' and can be those of the controller, or a third party, and could include 'commercial interests as well as wider societal benefits.'[66]

Determining the relevant legitimate interests for particular processing (or the 'purpose test' in the ICO's parlance) requires a controller to go beyond identifying simply the types of data that it wishes to process but instead requires the identification of the specific reasons why this personal data needs to be processed in this way. Legitimate interests for a pharmaceutical company might include promotion of its medicines, promoting disease awareness, identifying healthcare professionals with whom they want to interact, and the research and development of its future products.

[2] Necessity

According to *Rigas*, controllers must then demonstrate that their intended processing of personal data is necessary to achieve the identified legitimate interests. This is not intended to be read strictly, allowing only truly essential processing. Instead, the ICO's guidance explains that:

> 'Necessary' means that the processing must be a targeted and proportionate way of achieving your purpose. You cannot rely on legitimate interests if there is another reasonable and less intrusive way to achieve the same result.[67]

[3] Balancing These Interests Against the Individual's Rights and Freedoms

The last of the *Rigas* tests, typically referred to as a balancing test or legitimate interests' assessment, is the most challenging of the three. Having identified the legitimate interests, and ensured the proposed processing is necessary for those purposes, controller must then demonstrate that these purposes are not outweighed by the rights and freedoms of others. This is inherently a factual analysis – in *Rigas*, the CJEU emphasised that the outcome of any balancing test 'depends in principle on the specific circumstances of the particular case'[68] The ICO's guidance helpfully summarises:

> In particular, if [a data subject] would not reasonably expect you to use data in that way, or it would cause them unwarranted harm, their interests are likely to override yours. However, your interests do not always have to align with the

---

65. Opinion 06/2014 on the notion of legitimate interests of the data controller under Article 7 of Directive 95/46/EC, WP 217.
66. ico.org.uk/for-organisations/guide-to-data-protection/guide-to-the-general-data-protection-regulation-gdpr/lawful-basis-for-processing/legitimate-interests/.
67. *Ibid.*
68. *Rigas*, paragraph 31.

individual's interests. If there is a conflict, your interests can still prevail as long as there is a clear justification for the impact on the individual.

Similarly, the WP29 said in their Opinion 06/2014 on the notion of legitimate of the data controller under Article 7 of Directive 95/46/EC (WP217):

> Legitimate interests of the controller, when minor and not very compelling may, in general, only override the interests and rights of data subjects in cases where the impact on these rights and interests are even more trivial. On the other hand, important and compelling legitimate interests may in some cases and subject to safeguards and measures justify even significant intrusion into privacy or other significant impact on the interests or rights of the data subjects.[69]

Recital 75 of the GDPR and WP217 both express the need to consider that particular individuals that will be affected. Recital 75 tells us that processing data of 'vulnerable natural persons, in particular of children' carries greater risk, whereas WP217 confirms that 'it is important to assess the effect of actual processing on particular individuals'.[70] The previous processing of data may also be a factor in a balancing test – for example, 'whether the data has already been made publicly available by the data subject or by third parties may be relevant'.[71]

[B] Consent

Consent is likely the best-known lawful basis for processing, but it is often overused, misunderstood, or invalidly sought. Article 4(11) of the GDPR sets out the requirements for consent: it should be 'freely given, specific, informed and unambiguous'. It must also be 'an unambiguous indication of the data subject's wishes by which he or she, by a statement or clear affirmative action, signifies agreement to the processing of personal data relating to him or her'.[72] It must also be capable of being withdrawn at any time, and data subjects must be told this at the moment consent is obtained.[73] Processing carried out prior to consent being withdrawn is still lawful,[74] but an alternative legal basis is required for any further processing after such withdrawal. Controllers should only rely on consent where they are comfortable that processing can be halted if consent is withdrawn or where there is no reasonable alternative lawful basis. Sometimes, reliance on consent cannot be readily avoided: electronic direct marketing and the placement of cookies can often be done only with valid consent, and consent may be necessary for certain uses of special category personal data.

---

69. 'Opinion 06/2014 on the notion of legitimate interests of the data controller under Article 7 of Directive 95/46/EC', WP217, adopted 9 April 2014, p. 30.
70. Ibid., p. 39.
71. Ibid.
72. GDPR, Article 4(11).
73. GDPR, Article 7(3).
74. Ibid.

The EDPB has considered each of the tests for valid consent under Article 4(11) of the GDPR in its Guidelines 05/2020 on consent under Regulation 2016/679 ('*EDPB Consent Guidelines*').[75] Taking each in turn:

[1] Freely Given

The data subject being asked to consent must have a real choice in deciding whether or not to consent. As the EDPB Consent Guidelines explains, if the individual 'feels compelled to consent or will endure negative consequences if they do not consent, then consent will not be valid.'[76] Where there is imbalance of power between the individual and the party asking for consent, it is unlikely that consent will be valid as the individual may feel pressured to consent.

[2] Specific

This requires consent to be sought for specific processing activities, rather than a single consent for multiple processing purposes. Individuals should not be asked to consent as part of a wider acceptance of terms. Recital 33 of the GDPR notes that 'it is often not possible to fully identify the purpose of personal data processing for scientific research purposes at the time of data collection. Therefore, data subjects should be allowed to give their consent to certain areas of scientific research.' In practice, this may provide little assistance. The EDPB Consent Guidelines explains that in the EDPB's view, this 'does not disapply the obligations with regard to the requirement of specific consent' and that 'in principle, scientific research projects can only include personal data on the basis of consent if they have a well-described purpose.'[77]

[3] Informed

Closely linked to the principle of transparency (discussed below), this requires information to be provided to individuals to ensure they have had opportunity to understand what they are consenting to by providing information about the envisaged processing activity. Recital 42 of the GDPR dictates that data subjects must be told at least who is processing their data and why and what data will be processed, as well as their right to withdraw consent.

[C] Confidentiality and Consent

In addition to the data protection regime described in this chapter, patient information will benefit from protections under national laws in the field of medical confidentiality.

---

75. Guidelines 05/2020 on consent under Regulation 2016/679, version 1.0 adopted 4 May 2020 (EDPB Consent Guidelines).
76. *Ibid.*, p.7.
77. *Ibid.*, p.30.

In the UK, the common law duty of confidence protects health data provided by a patient to a medical professional in the context of their care. Where the medical professional wishes to use the medical data for another purpose, they must additionally comply with obligations deriving such laws. Typically, such laws limit the use of the patient's data to the purposes for which they were collected, unless specific legal exceptions apply, or if the person to whom the confidential information has consented. Where consent is sought for the purposes of overcoming patient confidentiality obligations, it will not necessarily be the controller's preferred lawful basis for processing, or a consent that would meet the GDPR validity. At least in the UK, patient consent given to waive confidentiality does not need to be obtained to the same standard as GDPR consent. For example, implied consent is acceptable to overcome the duty of confidence, if it is reasonable to infer that the patient agrees to the sharing of their information, such as for the provision of direct care or local clinical audit.[78]

In England and Wales, specific legislation[79] exists to allow confidentiality to be lifted to allow patient data to be shared without the consent of the patient in situations in which it would be difficult or impractical to obtain consent. In order to benefit from this, the intended recipient of the data will need to make an application (commonly called a 's251 application' after the statutory provision that sets it out) explaining how they intend to use the confidential information and why consent is not feasible. The application is evaluated by the Confidentiality Advisory Group (CAG) who will assess the public interest in the application and whether it can proceed without consent being obtained. Otherwise, as per the GMC's Confidentiality Guidance,

> There may also be circumstances in which disclosing personal information without consent is justified in the public interest for important public benefits, other than to prevent death or serious harm, if there is no reasonably practicable alternative to using personal information.[80]

The GMC goes on to explain that these must be truly 'exceptional' circumstances and that such a disclosure cannot avoid the Section 251 process if the intended disclosure could follow the statutory scheme.[81]

[D] Consent in Clinical Trials

Any clinical trial in the EU requires participants to provide their informed consent. This was initially a requirement of the EU Clinical Trials Directive 2001/20/EC and is replicated in its successor, the Clinical Trial Regulation (Regulation (EU) No. 536/2014). Having obtained participants' consent to take part in a trial to comply with

---

78. *See* GMC, Confidentiality: good practice in handling patient information, January 2017 (GMC Confidentiality Guidance), pp15, 22, and 42.
79. Section 251 of the National Health Service Act 2006 and the Health Service (Control of Patient Information) Regulations 2002.
80. GMC Confidentiality Guidance, p. 18.
81. *Ibid.*, p. 46.

this legislation, the question arises whether this same consent can be relied on as the legal basis for processing their data under the GDPR.

Prior to the GDPR coming into force, with its increased rigour on what constituted valid consent, it was common to rely on consent to comply with both clinical trials legislation and data protection obligation. This approach is no longer straightforward, as the conditions required for valid consent under the GDPR may not be met – in particular, the requirement for consent to be freely given. It is particularly likely that a supervisory authority could conclude that there is an imbalance of power between the sponsor of the trial and the participant, invalidating the consent. The EDPB has given an opinion that this is particularly a risk 'when a participant is not in good health conditions, when participants belong to an economically or socially disadvantaged group or in any situation of institutional hierarchy or dependency'.[82]

In the UK, the HRA has gone further, stating that consent should not be relied on as a legal basis for processing in clinical trials: 'for the purposes of the GDPR, the legal basis for processing data for health and social care research should NOT be consent.'[83]

As a result, relying on consent as a GDPR legal basis for a clinical trial will require careful analysis of the circumstances, and sponsors and investigators should bear in mind that consent obtained for Clinical Trials Regulation (CTR) purposes is distinct from the consent required under GDPR. Reliance on legitimate interests will typically be more appropriate.

[E] Withdrawing Consent

Article 7(3) GDPR gives individuals the right to withdraw their consent at any time. If consent is used as a legal basis for processing the data, and the individual withdraws their consent, there is no longer a lawful basis for processing the data and the processing must stop.

The EDPB Consent Guidelines explain that there is 'no exemption to this requirement for scientific research. If a controller receives a withdrawal request, it must in principle delete the personal data straight away'.[84] If the withdrawal of consent is not possible or would significantly undermine the processing, consent will not be the right legal basis to rely on.

The withdrawal of other types of consent (e.g., informed consent for CTR purposes or consent to waiving confidentiality of medical records) does not affect the GDPR legal basis for processing the data, unless this consent supplied this legal basis.

Therefore, where participants revoke their consent to participate in a clinical trial but the legal basis for processing their data is legitimate interest, their existing data can

---

82. Opinion 3/2019 concerning the Questions and Answers on the interplay between the Clinical Trials Regulation (CTR) and the General Data Protection regulation (GDPR) (Article 70.1.b).
83. hra.nhs.uk/planning-and-improving-research/policies-standards-legislation/data-protection-and-information-governance/gdpr-guidance/what-law-says/consent-research/.
84. EDPB Consent Guidelines, p. 32.

Chapter 23: Data Protection in the Pharmaceutical Sector §23.06[F]

continue to be processed under the GDPR but no further data can be collected after withdrawal as they no longer participate in the trial. By contrast, where the legal basis for processing is consent, and such consent is withdrawn, the processing of their existing data must cease (though the legality of the processing prior to the withdrawal of the consent will not be affected).

If consent is not the appropriate basis, it is important to identify the right basis out of the outset of processing. The EDPB Consent Guidelines makes clear that 'the controller cannot swap from consent to other lawful bases' and that 'if a controller chooses to rely on consent for any part of the processing, they must be prepared to respect that choice and stop that part of the processing if an individual withdraws consent'.[85] If the sponsor has relied on consent as the sole lawful basis of processing and that consent is withdrawn, it is not possible to have a 'back-up' lawful basis to which the sponsor will swap, so that it can continue to process the personal data for the same purpose.

[F] Quality and Safety Monitoring

In order to avoid a scenario where participant consent can be withdrawn, or may not be valid (requiring research using such data to cease), it is preferable and, in most cases, possible to rely on an alternative legal basis under GDPR Articles 6 and 9.

In recent guidance on the interplay between the GDPR and the CTRs, the European Commission[86] and the EDPB[87] distinguished two types of processing relevant to clinical trials: research activities and activities related to quality and safety monitoring.

Under Article 9(2)(i) GDPR, special category personal data can be processed where 'necessary for reasons of public interest in the area of public health such as (...) ensuring high standards of quality and safety of health care and of medical products or medical devices on the basis of Union or Member State law". Where the controller is required by law to monitor the medical safety, the processing can rely on this legal basis.

As is discussed in detail in Chapter 10, in both the UK and the EU, market authorisation holders are required to carry out pharmacovigilance activities both under EU law and under national legislation. Accordingly, pharmacovigilance activities carried out in compliance with these requirements can rely on the Article 9(2)(i) and Article 6(1)(c) ('compliance with a legal obligation to which the controller is subject').

---

85. *Ibid.*, p. 25.
86. European Commission Directorate-General for Health and Food Safety - Question and Answers on the interplay between the Clinical Trials Regulation and the General Data Protection Regulation.
87. Opinion 3/2019 concerning the Questions and Answers on the interplay between the Clinical Trials Regulation (CTR) and the General Data Protection regulation (GDPR) (Clinical Trial Q&A)

[G] Research

The GDPR provides a privileged regime for processing carried out for scientific research purposes, with a number of specific caveats to various obligations. Recital 159 GDPR states that 'the processing of personal data for scientific research purposes should be interpreted in a broad manner including for example technological development and demonstration, fundamental research, applied research and privately funded research' and so should cover the research activities of pharmaceutical companies.

We have touched upon one of the GDPRs research accommodations in §23.06[B][2] above, where Recital 33 purports to allow a broader approach to defining the purposes of consent when it is sought for research purposes. Another of these is Article 9(2)(j), which allows for processing of special category data for the purposes of public interest research, provided this is 'based on' EU or national legislation. Controllers wishing to rely on this ground will also need to implement suitable 'safeguards' for the data as required by Article 89(1). Article 89(1) specifically refers to pseudonymisation (*see* §23.03[F] above) and data minimisation as appropriate safeguards for protecting sensitive personal data used for research purposes. It also envisages national laws specifying additional rules on the handling of data for scientific research purposes. For example, in the UK, the Data Protection Act 2018 sets out a number of specific safeguards that must be followed and provides that the research basis only applies where processing is in the public interest.[88]

For multi-country clinical trials or health research projects, this means that an analysis of local laws is essential in order to rely on Article 9(2)(j).

§23.07 FURTHER PROCESSING

The second data protection principle, under Article 5(1)(b) – one of the fundamental data protection principles, is the principle of purpose limitation, which requires personal data to be 'collected for specified, explicit and legitimate purposes and not further processed in a manner that is incompatible with those purposes' (Article 5(1)(b)). This limits the types of processing that can be carried out on personal data held by the controller, as the controller will need to consider why the data was collected and if the processing they plan on carrying out is in line with that purpose.

For example, using information about hospitalised patients collected for the purposes of patient care to advertise recuperative holidays would be an incompatible use of that data.

[A] Compatible Purposes: Research

Article 6(4) GDPR states that personal data can be used only for a purpose other than that for which it was collected if the subsequent processing is based on the consent of the data subject or on national or EU law. If neither of these applies, the processing for

---

88. Schedule 1, part 1, paragraph 4.

the new purpose can be carried out if the new purpose is compatible with the original one.

Scientific research purposes are specifically identified as a 'compatible purpose' in Article 5(1)(b) of the GDPR. Where a purpose is compatible, Recital 50 specifies that 'no legal basis separate from that which allowed the collection of the personal data is required'. Therefore, if personal data were to be collected for a clinical trial and was later used for a research project, the research purpose would be considered compatible with the original purpose and would not require a separate legal basis.

It is important to note that it is both the EDPB's and ICO's view that where the initial lawful basis is consent, fresh consent must be sought if purposes change, and that compatibility is not usually a feasible option – and so Recital 50 cannot provide a basis for new use of data not covered within the original consent language.[89] This is an area that the UK Government is considering making clear within the UK GDPR as a result of the Data Protection and Digital Identities Bill. This position is particularly problematic for reuse of old study data, where it was typical to rely on consent as the data protection lawful basis prior to the introduction of the GDPR, but language in the consent forms are unlikely to foresee new uses of the data.

Even where recital 50 does apply, this does not exempt the controller from complying with other GDPR requirements, such as the transparency requirement of informing the data subjects, which may make the secondary use of the data complex. In addition, there may be national rules regarding the secondary use of health data. In the UK for example, for research data that is later used for secondary purposes, there is a need to consider the Research Ethics Committee approval that was obtained for the study, which will often specify restrictions on secondary use or data sharing.

[B] Compatible Purposes: Anonymisation

As discussed earlier in this chapter, anonymous data is no longer personal data and therefore is not subject to the GDPR. Therefore, wherever possible a party wanting to use personal data for a purpose other than that for which it was originally collected will want to anonymise the data, in order to avoid the limitations imposed by the purpose limitation principle and the other controller obligations such as the requirement to provide a notice.

However, controllers should note that the very procedure of anonymising data is in itself a separate processing of personal data, which constitutes further processing. In WP216, the WP29 concluded that validly achieved anonymisation could be considered compatible with the original lawful basis. As noted above, this will be of little assistance in most European countries if the anonymisation methods used result in individual level data without deleting the original, as this will not be considered

---

89. EDPB Consent Guidelines, p. 14 and ico.org.uk/for-organisations/guide-to-data-protecti on/guide-to-the-general-data-protection-regulation-gdpr/principles/purpose-limitation/.

anonymous. Nor will this assist if the initial lawful basis was consent, for the reasons set out at §23.06[A] above.

§23.08 FAIRNESS AND TRANSPARENCY

Although we have addressed the requirement ensuring that data is processed lawfully, Article 5(1)(a) also requires that it is processed 'fairly and in a transparent manner'. The GDPR does not expand on what is meant by 'fairly' in this context, but it is discussed in the ICO's online guidance on the GDPR:

> In general, fairness means that you should only handle personal data in ways that people would reasonably expect and not use it in ways that have unjustified adverse effects on them. You need to stop and think not just about how you can use personal data, but also about whether you should.[90]

This is similar to the requirement to carry out a balancing test, discussed above in relation to legitimate interests' assessments. Even if this is not the relevant lawful basis, controllers should consider these principles in relation to all processing they carry out to ensure that fairness is ensured.

One of the best ways to ensure fairness is to tell data subjects how their data will be used. Transparency is both a limb of Article 5(1)(a) and is more precisely addressed in Articles 12-14 of the GDPR. Article 12 sets out a requirement for the controller to provide information to the data subject 'in a concise, transparent, intelligible and easily accessible form, using clear and plain language'. This is generally achieved by way of a data protection notice (sometimes referred to as a privacy notice or privacy policy). The GDPR specifies, in Articles 13 and 14, particular types of information which must be communicated to the individual, but the EDPB has emphasised that the way in which the information is communicated is also important, stating that 'the quality, accessibility and comprehensibility of the information is as important as the actual content of the transparency information'.[91]

For any new processing purposes, the controller will need to consider how to meet their transparency obligations. This involves three main considerations:

(1) Ensuring the information required by GDPR Articles 13 and 14 is included.
(2) Assessing whether the notice will be clear and intelligible to the intended individual. The EDPB recommends the use of examples, definitive language, formatting, and other visual aids to make the text clear.[92] This is of particular importance when processing children's data.

---

90. ico.org.uk/for-organisations/guide-to-data-protection/guide-to-the-general-data-protection-regulation-gdpr/principles/lawfulness-fairness-and-transparency/#fairness.
91. WP260. rev 01, adopted on 11 April 2018.
92. *Ibid.*

(3) Deciding where and when to provide the notice. Articles 13 and 14 provide timing requirements on when information should be provided. The information must be easily accessible to the individual. Controllers must avoid incorporating privacy notices into legal documents such as terms and conditions.

The challenges of ensuring a balance between the precision of the information to be supplied and the clarity to the individual are likely to be made more difficult if the position adopted by the EDPB in collaborating in the Irish Data Protection Commissioner's decision against WhatsApp is upheld (at the time of writing, it is under appeal).[93] In this decision, the Irish DPC and EDPB suggest that notices should set out, *inter alia*:

- the legal basis for the processing by reference to the specific categories of personal data and specified processing operations on those data, including international transfers;
- precisely which laws are relied upon if a notice states that the legal basis is compliance with laws;
- precisely what legitimate interest identified by the controller applies to each processing operation;
- precisely what data is sent to each recipient or category of recipient, with categories to be as specific possible; and
- which adequacy decisions are relied upon and provide details of the specific type of standard contractual clauses relied upon.

None of the items listed above reflect current market practice in the completion of privacy notices in most countries or sectors at the time of writing, but controllers should be aware of the risk that this decision is upheld in its current form and become the expected practice for all.

Where one entity collects information on behalf of another entity, the entity receiving the personal data will still need to ensure they are meeting their transparency obligations. Where a controller does not have a direct relationship with the individuals whose data it processes, the controller will need to ensure that they are providing their notice to individuals via the intermediary.

Organisations transferring personal data to outside the European Economic Area (EEA) (*see* §23.13 below) will also need to inform individuals that they do so, and they are required to make a copy of the transfer mechanism (e.g., a copy of the standard contractual clauses (SCCs) being used or a copy of the Binding corporate rules (BCRs)) available to the individual if requested to do so (Article 13(1)(f)).

There are limited exemptions to the obligation to provide a notice. For research, where data has been obtained indirectly, there is some assistance. Within the GDPR itself, the only exemption to providing a notice where information is collected directly

---

93. edpb.europa.eu/system/files/2021-09/dpc_final_decision_redacted_for_issue_to_edpb_01-09-21_en.pdf.

from the data subjects is where the individual already has all of the relevant information required under Article 13(1). More exemptions are set out in Article 14(5) for indirectly collected data:

(a) The information has already been provided (this is unlikely, given the indirect collection, unless the source has done this on the controller's instruction);
(b) The information would be impossible to provide or would involve a disproportionate effort, especially for archiving or research purposes, or where it would make the achievement of the objectives of the processing impossible or seriously impair them;
(c) The controller is subject to a legal requirement to obtain the data, and this law appropriately prevents notice and provides appropriate safeguards; or
(d) A legally regulated obligation of secrecy prevents the provision of a notice.

§23.09 DATA MINIMISATION, ACCURACY, AND STORAGE LIMITATION

The data minimisation principle, set out in Article 5(1)(c) of the GDPR requires that controllers ensure 'personal data [are] adequate, relevant and limited to what is necessary in relation to the purposes for which they are processed'.[1] The GDPR does not define what is meant by 'adequate, relevant and limited to what is necessary', but the ICO online guidance suggests that:

> adequate – sufficient to properly fulfil your stated purpose;
> relevant – has a rational link to that purpose; and
> limited to what is necessary – you do not hold more than you need for that purpose.[94]

The data minimisation principle prevents an approach of accumulation of data until a purpose is found for it. Instead, data may only be processed for the purposes specifically identified. On the other hand, it is important to still hold sufficient data to carry out processing appropriately. As the ICO guidance acknowledges,

> If the processing you carry out is not helping you to achieve your purpose then the personal data you have is probably inadequate. You should not process personal data if it is insufficient for its intended purpose… Obviously it makes no business sense to have inadequate personal data – but you must be careful not to go too far the other way and collect more than you need.

The principle of accuracy is clearly closely related to the data minimisation principle. Article 5(1)(d) of the GDPR requires that personal data be 'accurate and, where necessary, kept up to date'. Clearly both data subject and controller can suffer from the results of inaccurate data processing – an inaccurate address could lead to sensitive post being sent to an incorrect recipient or failure to collect sufficient

---

94. ico.org.uk/for-organisations/guide-to-data-protection/guide-to-the-general-data-protection-regulation-gdpr/principles/data-minimisation/#how_do_we_decide.

information in an adverse event report could reduce the ability to understand the potential mechanisms at play. This decisions or actions taken on the basis of inaccuracies can cause both financial harm and distress.

As the ICO guidance says, 'it will usually be obvious whether personal data is accurate'.[95] Updating of records should be driven by business need – in some areas, frequent updates will be required, such as records of individuals who have opted out of marketing, others may need no regular review. Steps should be put in place that data is initially captured accurately, and that records of changes made to data are logged and checked where amendments might cause substantial risks to individuals (such as changes to the dosage of a particular drug to be dispensed, or correspondence addresses of patients). Where data is subjective, such as opinion data, it can be important to reflect any challenges received to those opinions, but it may similarly be important to keep a record of decisions made on the basis of the initial subjective data, such as medical treatment on the basis of a medical opinion. The ICO's guidance suggests that it is 'good practice to add a note recording the challenge and the reasons behind it' to any record.

Perhaps the most difficult of data protection principles for practical compliance is that of storage limitation. Article 5(1)(e) of the GDPR requires that data be 'kept in a form that which permits identification of data subjects for no longer than is necessary for the purposes for which the personal data are processed'.

The GDPR itself sets no specific restrictions on retention and does not specifically prohibit indefinite retention. Recital 39 explains, however, that the storage limitation principle 'requires, in particular, ensuring that the period for which the personal data are stored is limited to a strict minimum' and 'time limits should be established by the controller for erasure or for a periodic review'. A number of supervisory authorities across Europe have interpreted this as requiring specific periods to be stated, with a substantial reluctance to accept indefinite periods of retention.

The periods a controller selects for retention of data should be dictated by the purposes of processing. There may be relevant statutory provisions that dictate a maximum or, more often, a minimum retention limit, or that help to settle upon a reasonable period for retention such as maximum limitation periods in litigation. In other cases, a factual assessment will be required into how long the controller needs access to specific datasets used for specific purposes. Consideration should also be given as to whether any of the data could be anonymised, pseudonymised, or given more restricted access within an organisation as it ages.

It is possible that the same data may need to be held by different parts of the business for different lengths of time. For example, in connection with a patient support programme, a communication received from a patient may need to be handled by the communications team for a different period than might be required of any healthcare professional involved in handling the patient or the pharmacovigilance team if it involves an adverse event report. In these circumstances, different periods

---

95. ico.org.uk/for-organisations/guide-to-data-protection/guide-to-the-general-data-protection-regulation-gdpr/principles/accuracy/.

should be set as is appropriate for each purpose and adequate access controls used to control this dissemination.

§23.10 SECURITY AND BREACH REPORTING

Article 5(1)(f) of the GDPR requires the personal data is:

> processed in a manner that ensures appropriate security of the personal data, including protection against unauthorised or unlawful processing and against accidental loss, destruction, or damage, using appropriate technical or organisational measures ('integrity and confidentiality').

Security requirements are more particularly set out in Articles 32–34 of the GDPR. Article 32 requires both controllers and processors to take into account the following, when considering their security measures:

> the state of the art, the costs of implementation and the nature, scope, context and purposes of processing as well as the risk of varying likelihood and severity for the rights and freedoms of natural persons.

Recital 75 of the GDPR explains that these risks are not limited to obvious security risks, but including 'physical, material and non-material damage' such as processing that is discriminatory, deprives data subject of their rights, or that causes then significant social or economic disadvantage. Measures implemented under Article 5(1)(f) and Article 32(2) should address these broader risks. For guidance on particular security measures and how to implement these, controllers and processors should refer to the ICO's guidance[96] and other sources of information security guidance such as the European Union Agency for Cybersecurity[97] and the National Cyber Security Centre.

As well as requiring controllers and processors to implement security measures, the GDPR requires that they report data breaches that result from a breach or failure of these security measures. In the case of processors, they are required to inform their controllers of such breaches under Article 33(2) 'without undue delay'.

Controllers have two types of breach reporting requirements under the GDPR – reporting to the supervisory authority under Article 33 and reporting to the affected individuals under Article 34. It is important to note that it is specifically security breaches that these articles address. There is no obligation to confess other types of infringement, such as a failure to publish a privacy notice or to respond to a rights request on time.

The threshold for reporting to supervisory authorities is easily triggered. Article 33(1) of the GDPR requires controllers to report breaches 'without undue delay and, where feasible, not later than 72 hours after having become aware […] unless the personal data breach is unlikely to result in a risk to the rights and freedoms of natural

---

96. ico.org.uk/for-organisations/guide-to-data-protection/guide-to-the-general-data-protection-regulation-gdpr/security/.
97. enisa.europa.eu/topics/data-protection/security-of-personal-data.

persons'. In contrast, a requirement to inform the affected data subjects where the personal data breach 'is likely to result in a high risk'.

The EDPB has also recently provided guidance on specific scenarios likely to require reporting under each threshold, in its Guidelines 01/2021 on Examples regarding Personal Data Breach Notification.[98] This provides a helpful point of an assessment for a controller that has suffered a breach, to indicate where a report might be avoidable – or absolutely required.

If a breach does not have to be reported, because it is unlikely to pose a risk to data subjects, Article 33(5) of the GDPR still requires that 'the controller document any personal data breaches, comprising the facts relating to the personal data breach, its effects and the remedial action taken'. This is one of many types of document or log that controllers must maintain under the GDPR, as a result of the final data protection principle, accountability.

§23.11 ACCOUNTABILITY

Accountability is a key aspect of data protection compliance, new to data protection legislation with the introduction of the GDPR. It underpins the ability to demonstrate compliance with the other principles discussed in this chapter, and the brevity of its treatment here is due to the fact that it is a general requirement which is dealt with in length and in depth both in EDPB and in national regulator guidance. Organisations in the UK should also note that this is an area that the UK Government proposes to adjust with the Data Protection and Digital Information Bill.

The principle of accountability requires organisations to ensure that data protection compliance is respected within the business, by auditing and documenting compliance.

Some organisations (depending on the type of data processing they carry out) will be required under Article 37 GDPR to appoint a data protection officer (DPO) to oversee data protection governance within the organisation. This is likely to include most organisations with obligations listed in other chapters of this book because this requirement applies to any organisation whose core activities consist of large-scale processing of special category data. Large scale is given a surprisingly restrictive interpretation in guidance from the EDPB.[99]

All organisations are required to carry out Data Protection Impact Assessments (DPIA) for certain types of high-risk processing. A DPIA's purpose is to identify and minimise privacy risks and to document the organisation's assessment and remediation of those risks. Supervisory authorities across the EU and the ICO in the UK have issued 'blacklists' and 'whitelists' indicating the types of processing activities that require a DPIA and those that do not. Even if a processing activity is not on a blacklist, organisations are required to carry out a DPIA for processing activities which fulfil two

---

98. Guidelines 01/2021 on Examples regarding Personal Data Breach Notification, Version 2.0, adopted on 14 December 2021.
99. Guidelines on Data Protection Officers (DPOs), revised and adopted on 5 April 2017, WP 243 rev. 01 (WP243).

or more of the nine criteria identified by the EDPB as posing a high risk to individuals.[100]

Another key compliance document is a record of processing activities, required under Article 30 of the GDPR. This document is a central register for the various purposes of processing an organisation undertakes, the categories of individuals about whom the data is processed, how long the data is kept for and who the data is shared with, as well as security measures in place. Slightly differing obligations apply to controllers and processors.

In addition to these specific compliance documents, Article 25 of the GDPR imposes obligations of data protection by design and default. More precisely, these require controller to put in place specific measures to help ensure that the data protection principles are integrated and embedded within the organisation, and that only the data necessary for each purpose is processed. In practice, these will require organisations of all sizes to consider what additional processes and documentation they need to assist with data protection compliance. These might include policies on handling data subject rights, training materials for staff, screening processes for new projects, and vendors and contracts. Without such procedures, practical compliance is likely to prove impossible. Lawyers cannot make changes to notices, or DPOs make changes to records of processing, if they are not made aware of new processing within the organisation, and new security measures cannot be recommended if privacy and security teams are not properly engaged in the onboarding of new vendors and technologies.

§23.12 DATA SUBJECT RIGHTS

Under the GDPR, individuals have certain rights over their data. None of these are absolute, but exemptions are limited and supervisory authorities interpret them narrowly. These rights are:

- the right to be informed (Articles 13 and 14, discussed above at §23.08);
- the right of access (Article 15)
- the right to rectification (Article 16);
- the right to erasure (Article 17);
- the right to restrict processing (Article 18);
- the right to data portability (Article 20);
- the right to object (Article 21); and
- rights in relation to automated decision-making and profiling (Article 22).

Before these, Article 12 of the GDPR sets out various formalities, including rules addressing how individuals can be identified, the time available to deal with a request to exercise any particular right, the ability to refuse or charge for a request, and how a response should be made.

---

100. Guidelines on Data Protection Impact Assessment (DPIA) and determining whether processing is 'likely to result in a high risk' for the purposes of Regulation 2016/679 (WP 248 rev.01).

Article 12(3) of the GDPR says that the response to a request must be provided to the individual within one month, which can be extended to two months if the request is particularly complex. In these cases, the controller must inform the individual of the delay and provide reasons. It also requires that, where a request has been made electronically, a response shall be made electronically 'where possible, unless otherwise requested by the data subject'.

Article 12(4) obliges controllers to inform data subject if they intend to refuse the request and (if so) to ensure the data subject is made aware of the reasons for refusal and the ability to lodge a complaint with a supervisory authority, or make a court claim. This must happen within a month of the request being made.

Article 12(5) states that the data controller must respond to requests free of charge, unless the request is 'manifestly unfounded or *excessive*' – in these circumstances, the controller may either charge for compliance or simply refuse it.

Article 12(6) of the GDPR says that 'where the controller has reasonable doubts concerning the identity [of the requestor]…the controller may request the provision of additional information necessary to confirm the identity of the data subject'. Article 11, meanwhile, explains that there is no obligation on controllers to collect or retain additional data simply for the purposes of allowing a data subject to exercise rights – for example, a marketing authorisation holder is not required to collect sufficient information ensuring that a patient could readily request a copy of an adverse event report that relates to them, given this is not necessary for the purposes of the relevant legislation.

[A] Access and Portability

Article 15 GDPR gives individuals the right to:

- Find out whether their data is being processed and how it is being used (in effect, a right to receive again a copy of the privacy notice they were due under Articles 13 and 14); and
- Receive access to a copy of the data.

Data subject access requests (sometimes referred to as 'DSARs' or 'SARs') can be time consuming and complex to respond to and are perhaps the most frequently requested right, particularly in the UK. The level of personal data that is considered subject to disclose when these requests are made tends to vary by country, more due to national practice rather than any derogation offered for this under the GDPR. Controllers who receive such requests should allow for time and resources to respond to them, particularly in countries like the UK where the obligation to search and provide data is considered to be particularly broad, and DSARs are often used as a form of discovery exercise in the early stages of employment disputes. The ICO has produced detailed guidance on subject access requests.[101]

Article 15(4) of the GDPR provides an exemption to the obligation to provide a copy of personal data, stating that 'the right to obtain a copy [of personal data] shall not adversely affect the rights and freedoms of others'. National laws also typically include a variety of exemptions. In the UK, for example, Schedule 2 of the Data Protection Act 2018 sets exclusions for legal privilege, confidential references, and a number of other uses of personal data.

The right to portability, set out in Article 20 of the GDPR, is similar to the right of access. In this case, it permits individual to request access in a 'structure, commonly used and machine readable format' to be transmitted to another controller. This is limited to certain circumstances – the processing must be processed by automated means and processed on the basis of consent or contractual necessity. It is perhaps most likely to be used for the purposes of switching service, or allowing the switching of a service. If a pharmaceutical company provides a companion app for patients, it is perhaps in connection with these services that they are most likely to receive such a request. In practice, these requests remain rare.

[B] Right of Rectification

Under Article 16 GDPR, individuals have the right to have their inaccurate data corrected, or completed if it is incomplete. This is closely linked to the principle of accuracy, discussed earlier in this chapter. In most cases, the correction of inaccurate data is straightforward. If the controller disagrees with the data subject's concerns over the accuracy of information, such as over a difference of opinion, it is good practice to take note of this disagreement if the controller has taken this action, in the ICO's view, 'it may difficult to say that it is inaccurate and needs to be rectified.'[102]

[C] Objection

Article 21 of the GDPR allows individuals to object and stop the processing of data where:

- The data is processed on the basis of legitimate interests or official authority, unless the controller can demonstrate that it has 'compelling legitimate grounds' that outweigh those of the data subject, or that it needs to use the data for the establishment, exercise, or defence of legal claims.

---

101. ico.org.uk/for-organisations/guide-to-data-protection/guide-to-the-general-data-protection-regulation-gdpr/right-of-access/
102. ico.org.uk/for-organisations/guide-to-data-protection/guide-to-the-general-data-protection-regulation-gdpr/individual-rights/right-to-rectification/.

- The data is being used for direct marketing.
- The data is used for scientific or historical research, or statistical purposes, unless the processing is necessary for the performance of a task carried out for reasons of public interest.

This right must be 'explicitly brought to the attention of the data subject' in a manner that is 'clearly and separately from any other information.'[103]

[D] Erasure and Restriction

The right to erasure, also called 'the right to be forgotten' is set out in Article 17 GDPR. It allows individuals to request that the controller delete the personal data that it holds about them. This right applies only if:

- the personal data is no longer needed for the purpose for which it is processed;
- the legal basis for the processing is consent, the individual has withdrawn the consent, and the controller has no other legal ground for processing the data.
- the individual has objected to their data being processed, and the controller does not have an overriding legitimate grounds in continuing to process the data;
- the data is processed unlawfully or EU or national law requires its deletion;
- the law requires that data must be erased; or
- the personal data relied upon parental consent under Article 8(1) of the GDPR.

The controller is also required, under Article 19, to inform parties with whom it has shared the data that the individual has asked for their data to be deleted, unless it would be impossible or involve disproportionate effort.

Importantly, although this appears a broad right, there are a number of exemptions which controllers in the pharmaceutical sector can rely on, as the right to erasure does not apply if:

- the controller is required to process the data under EU or national law (relevant for pharmacovigilance and clinical trial records retention);
- the controller is processing the data for reasons of public health or provision of medical care;
- the controller is processing for research purposes and the erasure request would seriously impair the research or make it impossible; or
- the controller needs the personal data for a legal claim (e.g., dispute with participant).

In many pharmaceutical contexts, therefore, the right to erasure will not apply. Additional exemptions may also exist under national laws.

Article 18 of the GDPR gives individuals the right to ask controllers to restrict the use of their personal data, usually in case of a dispute about the legality of the

---

103. GDPR, Article 21(4).

processing or accuracy of the data. It is, in most circumstances, an alternative to the valid erasure of the personal data.

[E] Significant Automated Decisions

Article 22 of the GDPR provides that 'the data subject shall have the right not to be subject to a decision based solely on automated processing, including profiling, which produces legal effects concerning him or her or similarly significantly affects him or her'. This is, unusually, a proactive obligation on the controller much like the individual's right to be informed. Unless the controller can meet a derogation, set out in Article 22(2), such significant automated decisions are not permitted. Such decision-making tools can be used for these significant decisions if they are necessary for entering into or performing a contract with the data subject, are authorised by law, or are based on the data subject's explicit consent. The EDPB has produced detailed guidance on compliance with this right.[104] This is one of the articles that the UK Government wishes to amend in the Data Protection and Digital Information Bill, in particular, to return this to a right to request human review rather than a prohibition.

§23.13 DATA TRANSFERS

In this context, 'transfer' not only means sending or storing personal data outside of the EEA, or UK under the UK GDPR (for example, on non-EEA servers of cloud storage solutions) but also includes any situation in which personal data is made available outside the EEA, for example, by allowing shared access to group company resources to employees of non-EEA offices. Publishing personal data on a website which is intended to be accessed from a third country is also considered to be a transfer of personal data.

Having established whether it has international data transfer flows, an organisation next needs to assess how to ensure such transfers are compliant with data protection laws. International data transfers are permitted only in circumstances listed in Articles 45–49 of the GDPR. The circumstances most likely to apply to companies operating in the pharmaceutical sector are:

> *Adequacy*: the country of the recipient has received an 'adequacy decision' from the European Commission (or, under UK law, a decision given in accordance with the Data Protection Act 2018) confirming that its data protection laws – which must apply to the recipient[105] – provide sufficient safeguards. Transfers to adequate countries can be made without any restrictions.

---

104. WP251 rev 01, revised and adopted on 6 February 2018.
105. In some circumstances, laws of a country may not apply to all possible recipients – for example, Canada's recognised law (PIPEDA) does not apply to all businesses.

SCCs: under Article 46(2)(c), transfers can be made to parties who have entered into clauses approved by the European Commission (or, in the UK, the Information Commissioner), which require the recipient to protect the personal data they receive. New SCCs were released by the European Commission in June 2021, whilst the ICO adopted its own International Data Transfer Agreement and addendum to the EU clauses in early 2022.[106] These clauses are not valid if they have been amended, but parties can add clarifications or additional obligations to them. Transfers to outside the EEA are lawful if the relevant SCCs are entered into by the sender and the recipient. BCRs: Article 47 sets out a mechanism for transferring personal data within a corporate group. Companies wishing to use this procedure will need to draft internal rules on how data will be protected once transferred outside of the EEA. These will then need to be submitted for approval to a data protection supervisory authority in an EU Member State, a process which can take a substantial amount of time. In the UK, any EU authorised BCRS must still be approved by the ICO.

The prior SCCs, issued under the Data Protection Directive, were addressed, alongside the European Commission's Privacy Shield decision, in the *Schrems II* litigation.[107] The CJEU held that the decision underpinning the old SCCs remained valid, but that controllers should not assume that reliance on the SCCs alone is sufficient, and they must 'take measures to compensate for the lack of data protection in a third country by way of appropriate safeguards for the data subject'. In particular, controllers are told that they should assess relevant aspects of the third country's legal system, on a case-by-case basis,[2] but they are not given detailed assistance in the CJEU judgment on the types of measures that should be put in place if they come to the conclusion that reliance on SCCs alone is insufficient.

Data exporters are required to document the transfer impact assessments they are required to carry out and make this available to the competent supervisory authority on request. This assessment must allow the parties to warrant that there is no reason to believe that laws in the third country would prevent compliance with its obligations under the SCCs. Importantly, as well as the laws of the third country, this assessment may also take 'due account' of the 'circumstances' of transfer, including the nature of the data, the purpose of the transfer, the duration of the contract, the number of sub-processors, the methods used to transfer data, and the type of recipient. The completion of these assessments adds an extra level of complexity to any international

---

106. *See* ec.europa.eu/info/law/law-topic/data-protection/international-dimension-data-protection/standard-contractual-clauses-scc_en; and ico.org.uk/for-organisations/guide-to-data-protection/guide-to-the-general-data-protection-regulation-gdpr/international-data-transfer-agreement-and-guidance/ respectively.
107. C-311/18 *Data Protection Commissioner v. Facebook Ireland Limited, Maximillian Schrems* ECLI:EU:C:2020:559.

transfer reliant on SCCs. Organisations seeking to rely on the new SCCs once implemented should ensure that they take account of any relevant guidance on their use.

§23.14 MARKETING TO HEALTHCARE PROFESSIONALS

Chapter 9 focuses on the regulatory issues surrounding advertising medicinal products. In addition to Directive 2001/83/EC and national legislation regulating medical marketing, organisations wishing to market their products or services will also need to consider wider marketing laws.

Direct marketing in the EU must comply with the GDPR, the ePrivacy Directive (Directive 2002/58/EC) and national implementations of the Directive (in the UK, the Privacy and Electronic Communications (EC Directive) Regulations, commonly referred to as PECR).

Direct marketing does not cover all forms of advertising but only that directed to a particular person. The ICO's guidance clarifies that 'indiscriminate blanket marketing does not therefore fall within this definition of direct marketing. For example, leaflets delivered to every house in an area, magazine inserts, or adverts shown to every person who views a website'. Targeted online advertising or advertising emails, letters, or text messages sent to particular individuals or groups fall under the definition of direct marketing.

The sections below address the key privacy issues that organisations should consider when sending marketing to healthcare professionals.

[A] B2B Marketing and B2C Marketing

Privacy laws on marketing differ according to whether the recipient of the marketing is considered to be a corporate entity or an individual.

PECR applies to the sending of unsolicited marketing communications to individual subscribers. Whilst this will include communications sent to private individuals, sole traders, and unlimited liability partnerships, it does not include communications sent to corporate subscribers such as individuals at companies, limited liability partnerships, and some government bodies. Employees of the NHS will be corporate subscribers and marketing to them will therefore fall under business-to-business (B2B) marketing rules. This will also be the case for some locum doctors who chose to operate as limited companies.

Some healthcare professionals, however, will be sole traders or unlimited liability partnerships, such as some locum doctors and partners of GP practices. When marketing to such individuals, organisations should ensure they comply with business-to-consumer (B2C).

[B] Consent

The ePrivacy Directive, and the national legislation across the EU which stems from it, requires that consent is required for certain categories of B2C unsolicited marketing, as shown in the table below. Marketing information which individuals have requested does not require consent, on the basis that individuals have specifically asked to receive it.

Consent to direct marketing must meet GDPR standard. Consent from the individual is required in order to send email or SMS marketing.

Live telephone marketing can be carried out without the need for consent, but only if the marketing organisation has first checked the individual's number against the relevant do-not-call list. In the UK, the do-not-call list is called the Telephone Preference Service (TPS), a free service which individuals can register with to indicate that they do not want to receive marketing calls. Automated calls, however, can only be made with consent, which must specifically cover consent to automated calls.

Postal marketing does not fall under the ePrivacy regime, and therefore, there is more variation at national level. In most EU countries and the UK, postal marketing can be sent without consent.

Article 21(2) of GDPR gives individuals the absolute right to opt out of direct marketing, which applies to all methods direct marketing (both B2B and B2C). Therefore, organisations sending any type of direct marketing communications must provide opt-out mechanisms and ensure that marketing lists are screened against customer opt-out lists.

B2B direct marketing is not regulated by the ePrivacy Directive, so there is much more variation among Member States. In the UK, B2B marketing can be sent without consent but numbers must still be screened against the do-not-call list. This is not the case in all Member States of the EU.

[C] Soft Opt-In

The requirement for consent for direct marketing has a limited exception for an organisation's previous customers. This exemption is often called the 'soft opt-in'. Soft opt-in means that direct electronic marketing can be carried out without consent if all of the three conditions below are satisfied:

(1) the contact details were collected during the course of sale of a product or service to the individual;
(2) the direct marketing materials are in respect only of the organisations *own* similar products or services. Organisations cannot rely on soft opt-in if using contact details obtained by another entity (e.g., subsidiaries or partners); and
(3) the recipient has been given a simple way of refusing the use of their contact details for marketing purposes at the time their details were collected and in all the subsequent communications.

Soft opt-in applies to all B2C direct marketing in the EU and the UK. Its application to B2B marketing is once again not harmonised: some Member States allow all B2B marketing to be done without consent, others require consent but recognise the soft opt-in exemption, while others require explicit consent.

Appendix Guidelines and Publications

Chapter 1 – Brexit

- None

Chapter 2 – Overview of European Pharmaceutical Regulatory Requirements

- 'Evaluation of the Operation of Community Procedures for the Authorisation of Medicinal Products.' Report published by CMS Cameron McKenna and Andersen Consulting. Pharma Review 2001.
- Heaton, C. A. The Chemical Industry. Springer, 1994, 40. ISBN 0751400181.

Chapter 3 – Overview of Intellectual Property Rights

- None.

Chapter 4 – Clinical Trials

- Clinical Trials Information System (CTIS): online modular training programme European Medicines Agency (europa.eu)
- EudraLex - Volume 10 (europa.eu)
- Microsoft Word - CTR QnA v6.1 27-05-2022 (europa.eu)
- https://www.ema.europa.eu/en/documents/other/clinical-trial-information-system-ctis-Sponsor-handbook_.pdf
- Revised guideline on first-in-human clinical trials | European Medicines Agency (europa.eu)

Chapter 5 – Obtaining a Marketing Authorisation

- Vol. 2A of the Rules Governing Medicinal Products in the European Community, Notice to Applicants (Chapter 1, Rev. 11, July 2019).
- Marketing Authorisation, Notice to Applicants. Volume 2B. Common Technical Document (CTDoc). Edition May 2008.

Appendix Guidelines and Publications

- Guide to GMP, published in volume 4 of Eudralex; https://health.ec.europa.eu/medicinal-products/eudralex/eudralex-volume-4_en.
- CHMP Guideline on excipients in the dossier for application for marketing authorisation of a medicinal product Ref. EMA/CHMP/QWP/396951/2006, Rev. 2.
- CHMP Guideline on the Environmental Risk Assessment of Medicinal Products for Human Use, EMEA/CHMP/SWP/4447/00 – Corr 2, January 2015.
- Questions and answers on CHMP Guideline on the Environmental Risk Assessment of Medicinal Products for Human Use (EMA/CHMP/SWP/44609/2010), Rev. 1, June 2016
- Guideline on Similar Biological Medicinal Products, CHMP/437/04, Rev 1 October 2014.
- Guideline on the Acceptability of Names for Human Medicinal Products Processed Through the Centralised Procedure, EMA/CHMP/287710/2014–Rev. 6.
- Guideline on the Definition of a Potential Serious Risk to Public Health in the Context of Articles 29(1) and 29(2) of Directive 2001/83/EC – March 2006 (2006/C133/05).
- List of Standard Terms, published online by the EDQM.
- Procedural advice on publication of information on negative opinions and refusal of Marketing Authorisation Applications for Human Medicinal Products EMA/599941/2012, May 2013.
- Guideline on the readability of the labelling and package leaflet of medicinal product for human use, revision 1 (12 January 2009).
- Operational procedure on Handling of 'Consultation with target patient groups' on Package Leaflets (PL) for Centrally Authorised Products for Human Use Doc. Ref. EMEA/277378/2005, 20 October 2005.
- Commission Notice Handling of duplicate marketing authorisation applications of pharmaceutical products under Article 82(1) of Regulation (EC) No. 726/2004 (2021/C 76/01).
- CHMP procedural advice on the re-examination of CHMP opinions (EMEA/CHMP/50745/2005 Rev.1), February 2009.
- Guidance for companies considering the adaptive pathways approach EMA/527726/2016, 1 August 2016.
- MHRA Guidance: Converting Centrally Authorised Products (CAPs) to UK Marketing Authorisations (MAs), 'grandfathering' and managing lifecycle changes.
- Statutory Guidance: MHRA Fees.
- MHRA Guidance: 150-day assessment for national applications for medicines.

Appendix Guidelines and Publications

Chapter 6 – Conditional Marketing Authorisations

- EMA Guideline on the scientific application and practical arrangements necessary to implement Commission Regulation (EC) No. 507/2006 on conditional Marketing Authorisation for medicinal products for human use falling within the scope of Regulation (EC) 726/2004, EMEA/509951/2006.
- EMA Guideline on procedures for granting of a Marketing Authorisation under exceptional circumstances pursuant to Article 14(8) of Regulation (EC) No. 726/2004 EMEA/357981/2005.
- ICH Topic E3, Note for guidance on structure and content of clinical study reports, CHMP/ICH/137/9.
- http://www.ema.europa.eu/ema/index.jsp?curl=pages/regulation/q_and_a/q_and_a_detail_000133.jsp&mid=WC0b01ac058066e978
- http://www.ema.europa.eu/docs/en_GB/document_library/Scientific_guideline/2016/03/WC500202774.pdf
- https://www.gov.uk/guidance/conditional-marketing-authorisations-exceptional-circumstances-marketing-authorisations-and-national-scientific-advice

Chapter 7 – Supplementary Protection Certificates

- None

Chapter 8 – Paediatrics

- General guidance: https://www.ema.europa.eu/en/human-regulatory/overview/paediatric-medicines-overview
- Questions and answers: PIP Guidance www.ema.europa.eu
- Questions and answers: Submission of Article 46 paediatric studies www.ema.europa.eu
- Guidance on paediatric submissions, EMA/672643/2017 Rev.2, 18 March 2020
- Communication from the Commission: Guideline on the format and content of applications for agreement or modification of a paediatric investigation plan and requests for waivers or deferrals and concerning the operation of the compliance check and on criteria for assessing significant studies (2014/C 338/01).
- Recommendation of the Paediatric Committee to the European Commission regarding the Symbol, EMEA/498247/2007.
- The Network of Paediatric Networks at the EMA Implementing Strategy, EMEA/MB/543523/2007.
- The PDCO Rules of Procedure, EMEA/3448440/2008, Rev. 2, 25 March 2020.
- The Principles of Interactions between EMA and FDA Paediatric Therapeutics, June 2007: www.ema.europa.eu.
- 2018 Report to the European Commission on companies and products that have benefitted from any of the rewards and incentives in the Paediatric

- Regulation and on companies that have failed to comply with any of the obligations in this Regulation (dated 29 October 2019), Doc. Ref. EMA/103569/2019 (reports on previous years also available).
- Report on the Survey of all paediatric uses of medicinal products in Europe Doc. Ref. EMA/794083/2009.
- Revised priority list for studies into off-patent paediatric medicinal products Doc.Ref. EMA/PDCO/98717/2012, Rev. 2013/14.
- Five-Year Report to the European Commission – General Report on the experience acquired as a result of the application of the Paediatric Regulation Doc. Ref. EMA/428172/2012.
- Better Medicines for Children – from concept to reality – progress report on the Paediatric Regulation (EC) No. 1901/2006 – COM (2013) 443 final.
- Success of the Paediatric Regulation after 5 years (August 2007 – December 2012) EMA/250577/2013.
- Ten-Year Report to the European Commission General report on the experience acquired as a result of the application of the Paediatric Regulation. EMA/231225/2015.
- Study on the economic impact of the Paediatric Regulation, including its rewards and incentives, December 2016, available at https://ec.europa.eu/health/sites/health/files/files/paediatrics/docs/paediatrics_10_years_econo mic_study.pdf.
- Reflection paper on the use of extrapolation in the development of medicines for paediatrics: EMA/189724/2018, 7 October 2018.
- Concept paper on the involvement of children and young people at the Paediatric Committee (PDCO), EMA/PDCO/388684/2012, 17 September 2012.
- Commission Staff Working Document – Joint evaluation of Regulation (EC) No. 1901/2006 of the European Parliament and of the Council of 12 December 2006 on medicinal products for paediatric use and Regulation (EC) No. 141/2000 of the European Parliament and of the Council of 16 December 1999 on orphan medicinal products: SWD (2020) 163 final (11.8.2020).
- Case T-52/09 Nycomed Danmark *v.* EMA.
- Merck Sharp & Dohme Corp. *v.* Deutsches Patent- und Markenamt Case C-125/10.
- Dr Reddy's Laboratories *v.* Warner-Lambert [2012] EWHC 3715 (Pat).
- Shire Pharmaceutical Contracts *v.* European Commission, CaseT-583/13.
- Case T-48/14 – Pfizer *v.* European Commission and EMA.
- MHRA Guidance: Legal requirements for children's medicines (last updated 31 December 2020): https://www.gov.uk/government/publications/legal-requi rements-for-childrens-medicines.
- MHRA Guidance: Procedures for UK Paediatric Investigation Plan (PIPs) (31 December 2020): https://www.gov.uk/guidance/procedures-for-uk-paedia tric-investigation-plan-pips.

Appendix Guidelines and Publications

- MHRA Guidance: Completed Paediatric Studies – submission, processing and assessment (31 December 2020): https://www.gov.uk/guidance/completed-paediatric-studies-submission-processing-and-assessment.

Chapter 9 – Advertising Medical Products for Human Use

- MHRA website: Guidance on Advertising for Medicines: http://www.mhra.gov.uk/Howweregulate/Medicines/Advertisingofmedicines/index.htm
- Advertising Standards Authority: www.asa.org.uk/Complaints-and-ASA-action/Adjudications/2008/10/Potters-Ltd/TF_ADJ_ 45161.aspx
- Committee for Advertising Practice: Advertising Codes – Non-Broadcast – Section 12 – Medicines, Medical Devices, Health and Beauty Product: http://www.cap.org.uk/Advertising-Codes/Non-broadcast-HTML/Section-12-Medicines,-medical-devices,-health-and-beauty-products.aspx
- Association of the British Pharmaceutical Institution: The Code of Practice for the Pharmaceutical Industry 2014: http://www.abpi.org.uk/our-work/library/guidelines/Documents/Code%20of%20Practice%202014.pdf

Chapter 10 – Pharmacovigilance

- Alghabban, Amer. Dictionary of Pharmacovigilance. Pharmaceutical Press, 2004. ISBN 9780853695165.
- Annual report of the ad hoc pharmacovigilance inspectors working group 2008, EMEA/INS/PhV/114151/2009.
- CIOMS. 'International Reporting of Adverse Drug Reactions.' Final Report of the CIOMS Working Group. Geneva, Switzerland: WHO, 1990. Corresponds to ICH report E2A Guidance document.
- CIOMS II. Working Group II CIOMS report for aggregated safety information (1989–1991). Corresponds to ICH report E2C Guidance document.
- ENTR/CT4 Revision 1, Detailed guidance on the European database of SUSARs (EudraVigilance – Clinical Trials Module) (April 2004); ENTR/CT3 Revision 2, Detailed guidance on the collection, verification and presentation of adverse reaction reports arising from clinical trials on medicinal products for human use (April 2006).
- Good Pharmacovigilance Practice Guide, published by and available from Pharmaceutical Press. ISBN/ISSN 9-78-085369834-0.
- Guideline on the development of medicinal products for the treatment of smoking, CHMP/EWP/369963/05, December 2008.
- MHRA Website: Freedom of Information request 06/099 (8 May 2006), <www.heads.medagencies.org>.
- MHRA: Investigations into adverse incidents during clinical trials of TGN1412.
- Pandemic pharmacovigilance weekly update, EMEA/984681/2009.
- Safety of Medicines. A Guide to Detecting and Reporting Adverse Drug Reactions. WHO/EDM/QSM 2002.2. Geneva, Switzerland: WHO, 2002.
- The European Commission. 'Strengthening Pharmacovigilance to Reduce Adverse Effects of Medicines', 10 December 2008.

Appendix Guidelines and Publications

- The Rules Governing Medicinal Products in the European Union. GVP, Pharmacovigilance for Medicinal Products for Human Use.
- The Rules Governing Medicinal Products in the European Union. Volume 9B, Guidelines on Pharmacovigilance of Veterinary Medicinal Products.
- Exceptions and modifications to the EU guidance on good pharmacovigilance practices that apply to UK MAHs and the MHRA - GOV.UK (www.gov.uk)

Chapter 11 – Variations of Marketing Authorisations

- None

Chapter 12 – Combination Products

- CHMP Guideline on clinical development of fixed-combination medicinal products, 19 February 2009, www.ema.europa.eu/docs/en_GB/document_library/Scientific_guideline/2009/09/WC500003686.pdf; currently under revision, see CHMP Concept paper on the need to revise the Guideline on the clinical development of fixed dose combinations of medicinal products regarding dossier content requirements, 11 February 2013, and new draft Guideline EMA/CHMP/281825/2015, 23 April 2015 www.ema.europa.eu/docs/en_GB/document_library/Scientific_guideline/2013/03/WC500139482.pdf.
- CHMP Guideline on the non-clinical development of fixed combinations of medicinal products, 24 January 2008 EMEA/CHMP/SWP/258498/2005, http://www.ema.europa.eu/docs/en_GB/document_library/Scientific_guideline/2009/10/WC500003976.pdf.
- CHMP Guideline on the non-clinical documentation for mixed Marketing Authorisation applications, 13 October 2005, CHMP/SWP/799/95 http://www.ema.europa.eu/docs/en_GB/document_library/Scientific_guideline/2009/10/WC500003973.pdf.
- CHMP Question and Answer Document on the clinical development of fixed combinations of drugs belonging to different therapeutic classes in the field of cardiovascular treatment and prevention, 23 June 2005, CHMP/EWP/191583/2005 www.ema.europa.eu/docs/en_GB/document_library/Scientific_guideline/2009/ 09/WC500003319.pdf.
- CPMP Note for Guidance on fixed-combination medicinal products, 17 April 1996, < www.ikev.org/haber/bioav/024095en.pdf >.
- CHMP Guideline on the investigation of bioequivalence, 20 January 2010, CHMP/EWP/QWP/1401/98 Rev.1/Corr. www.ema.europa.eu/docs/en_GB/document_library/Scientific_guideline/2010/01/WC500070039.pdf, which replaced CPMP Note for Guidance on the investigation of bioavailability and bioequivalence, 14 December 2000, < http://www.ema.europa.eu/docs/en_GB/document_library/Scientific_guideline/2009/09/WC500003519.pdf >.
- Notice to Applicants of the European Commission. Volume 2A, Procedures for Marketing Authorisation, Chapter I, Marketing Authorisation, of June 2013, < http://ec.europa.eu/health/files/eudralex/vol-2/a/vol2a_chap1_2013-06_en.pdf >.

Appendix Guidelines and Publications

- WHO Expert Committee on Specifications for Pharmaceutical Preparations, WHO Technical Report Series 929, Annex 5, <http://apps.who.int/ prequal /info_general/documents/TRS929/WHO_TRS_929_annex5FDCs.pdf>.

Chapter 13 – Abridged Procedure

- http://ec.europa.eu/health/files/eudralex/vol-2/a/vol2a_chap1_2013-06_en. pdf.
- Guidance on elements required to support the significant clinical benefit in comparison with existing therapies of a new therapeutic indication in order to benefit from an extended (11-year) marketing protection period', adopted November 2007 http://ec.europa.eu/health/files/eudralex/vol-2/a/vol2a_ chap1_2013-06_en.pdf.

Chapter 14 – Orphan Drugs

- Alcimed study on orphan drugs Phase I Overview of the conditions for marketing orphan drugs in Europe. Press Release Committee for Orphan Medicinal Products September 2005 Meeting, EMEA/COMP/299233/2005.
- Commission notice on the application of Articles 3, 5, and 7 of Regulation (EC) No. 141/2000 on orphan medicinal products (2016/C 424/03).
- Guideline on the format and content of applications for designation as orphan medicinal products and on the transfer of designations from one sponsor to another (ENTR/6283/00 Rev 5, July 2021).
- Procedural Advice for Orphan Medicinal Product Designation – Guidance for sponsors (EMA/420706/2018 Rev 11 – 30 September 2021).
- Procedural advice for post-orphan medicinal product designation activities - Guidance for sponsors; EMA/469917/2018, Rev.12 – 25 May 2022.
- COMP Members interaction with sponsors of applications for orphan designations, EMEA/COMP/150409/2006, Rev. 1 – 16 December 2020.
- COMP Report to the Commission in relation to Article 10 of Regulation 141/2000 on orphan medicinal products, EMEA/35218/2005.
- Council Recommendation of 8 June 2009 on an action in the field of rare diseases (2009/C 151/02).
- Significant benefit of orphan drugs: concepts and future developments, EMA/326061/2012.
- EMA Public Statement on fee reductions for designated orphan medicinal products (www.ema.europa.eu).
- Guideline on aspects of the application of Article 8(1) and (3) of Regulation (EC) No. 141/2000: Assessing similarity of medicinal products versus authorised orphan medicinal products benefiting from market exclusivity and applying derogations from that market exclusivity, C (2008) 4077 (2008/C 242/08).
- Guideline on aspects of the application of Article 8(2) of Regulation (EC) No. 141/2000: Review of the period of market exclusivity of orphan medicinal products, C (2008) 4051.

Appendix Guidelines and Publications

- Points to Consider on the estimation and reporting on the prevalence of a condition for the purposes of orphan designation, COMP/436/01, Rev 1 – June 2019.
- European Medicines Agency Guidance for applicants seeking scientific advice and protocol assistance (EMA/691788/2010 Rev. 7 – September 2014).
- Procedural advice on the appeal procedure for orphan medicinal product designation or review of orphan designation criteria at the time of marketing authorisation; EMA/2677/01 Rev. 3, 8 December 2020.
- Standard Operating Procedure on orphan medicinal product designation and maintenance, SOP/H/3534 – April 2022.
- Procedural advice for post-orphan medicinal product designation activities - Guidance for sponsors; EMA/469917/2018, Rev.12 - 25 May 2022.
- Checklist for sponsors applying for the transfer of Orphan Medicinal Product (OMP designation (EMA/41277/2007 Rev. 15 – 18 May 2022.
- SEC(2006) 832, Commission Staff Working Document on the experience acquired as a result of the application of Regulation (EC) No. 141/2000 on orphan medicinal products and account of the public health benefits obtained.
- Inventory of Union and Member State Incentives to support research into, and the development and availability of, Orphan Medicinal Products. State of Play 2015'; SWD (2015) 13 final, 26.1.2016.
- Council Recommendation of 8 June 2009 on an action in the field of rare diseases (2009/C151/02).
- Implementation report on the Commission Communication on Rare Diseases: Europe's challenges [COM(2008) 679 final] and Council Recommendation of 8 June 2009 on an action in the field of rare diseases (2009/C 151/02), COM(2014) 548 final.)
- Council conclusions on strengthening the balance in the pharmaceutical systems in the EU and its Member States – https://www.consilium.europa.eu/en/press/press-releases/2016/06/17/epsco-conclusions-balance-pharmaceutical-system/
- European Commission Study to support the evaluation of the EU Orphan Regulation: Final report July 2019.
- Commission Staff Working Document – Joint evaluation of Regulation (EC) No. 1901/2006 of the European Parliament and of the Council of 12 December 2006 on medicinal products for paediatric use and Regulation (EC) No. 141/2000 of the European Parliament and of the Council of 16 December 1999 on orphan medicinal products: SWD(2020) 163 final (11.8.2020) European Commission Inception Impact Assessment Ref. Ares(2020) 7081640 – 25/11/2020.
- Case T-74/08 *Now Pharm AG v. European Commission*, 9 September 2010.
- Case T-264/07 CSL *Behring GmbH v. European Commission* and the EMA, 9 September 2010
- Case T-452/14 *Laboratoires CTRS v. European Commission*.
- Case T-140/12 *Teva v. EMA*.

Appendix Guidelines and Publications

- CaseT-583/13 *Shire Pharmaceutical Contracts v. European Commission.*
- Case T-269/15 *Novartis v. European Commission.*
- Case C-138/15P, *Teva v. EMA.*
- Case T-80/16, *Shire Pharmaceuticals Ireland Ltd, v. EMA.*
- Case T-329/16 *BMS v. Commission and EMA.*
- Case T-733/17 *GMP-Orphan v. European Commission.*
- Case T-549/19 *Medac Gesellschaft für klinische Spezialpräparate v. Commission*; (2019/C 337/15).
- Case T-303/16 *Mylan v. European Commission*; judgment of 26 January 2022; appeal Case C-237/22 P *Mylan v. European Commission.*
- UK Guidance on Orphan Medicinal Products (last updated 22 February 2021) (https://www.gov.uk/guidance/orphan-medicinal-products-in-great-britain).
- Policy paper: UK strategy for rare diseases: 2020 update to the implementation plan for England (Published 26 February 2020) (https://www.gov.uk/government/publications/uk-strategy-for-rare-diseases-2020-update-to-the-implementation-plan-for-england).
- Policy paper: Rare diseases strategy (Published 22 November 2013) (https://www.gov.uk/government/publications/rare-diseases-strategy).

Chapter 15 – Biopharmaceuticals

- None.

Chapter 16 – Homeopathic, Herbal and Traditional Herbal Medicinal Products

- None

Chapter 17 – Advanced Therapy and Medicinal Products

- None

Chapter 18 – Vaccines

- Commission Working Document on Community Influenza Pandemic Preparedness and Response Planning. Grounded on COM(2004)201 final.
- Communication from the Commission to the Council, the European Parliament, the European Economic and Social Committee and the Committee of the Regions on strengthening coordination on generic preparedness planning for public health emergencies at EU level. COM(2005) 605 final.
- Definition and Application of Terms for Vaccine Pharmacovigilance: Report of CIOMS/WHO Working Group on Vaccine Pharmacovigilance (2012).
- Directive 2001/83/EC of the European Parliament and of the Council of 6 November 2001 on the Community code relating to medicinal products for human use.
- Draft Guideline on Influenza Vaccines – Non-clinical and clinical module (EMA/CHMP/VWP/457259/2014).

Appendix Guidelines and Publications

- EU Administrative Procedure for Official Control Authority Batch Release (OCABR) of Centrally Authorised Immunological Medicinal Products for Human Use and Medicinal Products Derived from Human Blood and Plasma.
- Global safety of vaccines: strengthening systems for monitoring, management and the role of GACVS (*Expert Rev. Vaccines* 8(6), 705-716 (2009).
- Guidance for Industry. General principles for the development of vaccines to protect against global infectious diseases. FDA, December 2011.
- Guideline on adjuvants in vaccines for human use (EMEA/CHMP/VEG/134716/2004).
- Guideline on clinical evaluation of new vaccines (EMEA/CHMP/VWP/164653/2005).
- Guideline on clinical evaluation of new vaccines: Annex: SPC requirements (EMEA/CHMP/VWP/382702/2006).
- Guideline on clinical evaluation of vaccines: regulatory expectations. Geneva, World Health Organization, 2004.
- Dossier structure and content for pandemic-influenza marketing-authorisation application (EMEA/CPMP/VEG/4717/2003).
- Guideline on good pharmacovigilance practices (GVP): Product- or population-specific considerations I: Vaccines for prophylaxis against infectious diseases (EMA/488220/2012).
- Guideline on good pharmacovigilance practices (GVP) Module V – Risk management systems (Rev 1). (EMA/838713/2011 Rev 1).
- Guideline on Influenza Vaccine – Quality module. EMA/GHMP/BWP/310834/2012.
- Guideline on non-clinical local tolerance testing of medicinal products, (EMA/CHMP/SWP/2145/2000 Rev.1).
- Guideline on pharmaceutical aspects of the product information for human vaccines (EMEA/CPMP/BWP/2758/02).
- Guideline on Plasma Master File (PMF) and Vaccine Antigen Master File (VAMF) 'Second Step'.
- Guideline on requirements for vaccine antigen master file (VAMF) certification (EMEA/CPMP/4548/03/Final/Rev 1).
- Guideline on submission of Marketing Authorisation Applications for pandemic influenza vaccines through the centralised procedure (EMEA/CPMP/4986/03).
- Guideline on the processing of renewals in the centralised procedure (EMEA/CHMP/2990/00 Rev.4).
- Guideline on the scientific data requirements for a vaccine antigen master file (VAMF) (EMEA/CPMP/BWP/3734/03).
- ICH guideline S6 (R1) – preclinical safety evaluation of biotechnology-derived pharmaceuticals (EMA/CHMP/ICH/731268/1998).
- Interim guidance on enhanced safety surveillance for seasonal influenza vaccines in the EU (EMA/PRAC/222346/2014).

- Mandate, objectives and rules of procedure for the CHMP vaccine working party (VWP) (EMEA/CHMP/VWP/73919/2004).
- Note for guidance on non-clinical local tolerance testing of medicinal products, (CPMP/SWP/2145/00).
- Note for guidance on preclinical pharmacological and toxicological testing of vaccines (CPMP/SWP/465/95).
- Pandemic Influenza Risk Management WHO Interim Guidance (WHO/HSE/HEA/HSP/2013.3).
- Pharmaceutical and Biological Aspects of Combined Vaccines (CPMP/BWP/477/97).
- Questions and Answers on Bovine Spongiform Encephalopathies (BSE) and Vaccines. (CPMP/BWP/819/01).
- The European Vaccine Action Plan 2015-2020 (EVAP). (EUR/RC64/15 Rev.1).
- Work plan for the Vaccines Working Party (VWP) (EMA/CHMP/VWP/695450/2014).
- WHO global influenza preparedness plan. The role of WHO and recommendations for national measures before and during pandemics (WHO/CDS/CSR/GIP/2005.5).
- WHO guidelines on nonclinical evaluation of vaccines.

Chapter 19 – Medical Devices

- None

Chapter 20 – Parallel Trade

- None

Chapter 21 – Competition Law in the Pharmaceutical Sector

- Antitrust: Commission accepts commitments by Aspen to reduce prices for six off-patent cancer medicines by 73% addressing excessive pricing concerns
- Antitrust: Commission fines Johnson & Johnson and Novartis € 16 million for delaying market entry of generic pain-killer fentanyl (IP/13/1233).
- Antitrust: Commission fines Servier and five generic companies for curbing entry of cheaper versions of cardiovascular medicine (IP/14/799).
- Antitrust: Commission welcomes General Court judgments upholding its Lundbeck decision in first pharma pay-for-delay case
- CMA press release: 'CMA fines pharma companies £45 million.' (12 Feb. 2016).
- CMA press release: 'The CMA has today issued a statement of objections to the pharmaceutical suppliers Pfizer and Flynn Pharma alleging that they have breached competition law.' (6 Aug. 2015).
- CNMC press release: 'La CNMC incoa un expediente sancionador en el mercado de suministro de información sobre ventas a la industria farmacéutica' (22 Dec. 2015).

Appendix Guidelines and Publications

- Commission Notice on agreements of minor importance which do not appreciably restrict competition under Art. 101(1) TFEU (de Minimis), OJ [2014] C 291/1.
- Commission Notice on the definition of relevant market for the purposes of Community competition law, OJ [1997] C 372/5.
- D. Bailey, L. John (eds.); Bellamy & Child, European Union Law of Competition, 8th edition (Oxford: OUP, 2018)
- De Souza, N. 'Competition in Pharmaceuticals: The Challenges ahead Post AstraZeneca.' Competition Policy Newsletter, no. 1 (Spring 2007).
- European Commission. Competition Policy Newsletter, no. 23 (October, 2000).
- Fagerlund, Niklas & Rasmussen, Soren Bo, 'AstraZeneca: The First Abuse Case in the Pharmaceutical Sector', in Competition Policy Newsletter, no. 3 (Autumn 2005).
- Framework for State aid for research and development and innovation, OJ [2014] C 198/1.
- Guidance on restrictions of competition 'by object' for the purpose of defining which agreements may benefit from the De Minimis Notice, of 25 June 2014, C(2014)4136 final.
- Guidance on the Commission's enforcement priorities in applying Art. 82 of the EC Treaty to abusive exclusionary conduct by dominant undertakings OJ [2009] C 45/7.
- Guidelines on the applicability of Article 101 of the Treaty on the Functioning of the European Union to horizontal co-operation agreements (the 'Horizontal Guidelines'), OJ [2011] C 11/1.
- Guidelines on the application of Article 101 of the Treaty on the Functioning of the European Union to technology transfer agreements, OJ [2014]C 89.
- Guidelines on the application of Article 81(3) of the Treaty, OJ [2004] C 101/97.
- Guidelines on the assessment of horizontal mergers under the Council Regulation on the control of concentrations between undertakings (the 'Horizontal Merger Guidelines'), OJ [2004] C 31/5.
- Guidelines on the assessment of non-horizontal mergers under the Council Regulation on the control of concentrations between undertakings, OJ [2008] C 265/6.
- Guidelines on the effect on trade concept contained in Articles 81 and 82 of the Treaty, OJ [2004] C101/81, paragraph 52.
- Hatton, C., A. Bicarregui & D. Cardwell. "Interesting Times' for Pharmaceutical Companies: European Competition Law and the Pharmaceutical Sector.' European Consumer Law Journal, 2–3 (2009).
- J. Faull & A. Nikpay. The EU Law of Competition. 3rd edition. Oxford, 2014.
- M. Nissen & F. Haugsted; BadmouthingYour Competitor's Products: When Does Denigration Become an Antitrust Issue–
- OFT press release: 'OFT issues decision in Reckitt Benckiser case' (53/11).

- OFT press release: 'OFT issues statement of objections to certain pharmaceutical companies' (36/13).
- Third Report on the Monitoring of Patent Settlements (2012).
- Fifth Report on the Monitoring of Patent Settlements (2014).
- Sixth Report on the Monitoring of Patent Settlements (2015).
- Seventh Report on the Monitoring of Patent Settlements (2016).
- Eight Report on the Monitoring of Patent Settlements (2017).
- UK VABEO Guidance: https://www.gov.uk/government/publications/vabeo-guidance.

Chapter 22 – Pandemics and Epidemics

- None

Chapter 23 – Data Protection in the Pharmaceutical Sector

- None

Table of Cases

Case Name	Case Number	Year	Case Citation	Cited in Chapter
A v. Daniel B and others	C-649/18			9
AB Hässle v. Ratiopharm	C-127/00	2003	ECR I-14781	7
ABBOTT RESPIRATORY/Dosing Regime	G 02/08	2008	Enlarged Board of Appeal's decision	3
Abcur AB v. Apoteket Farmaci AB and Apoteket AB	Case C 544/13 and C-545/13	2015	Judgment of 16 Jul. 2015	9
Abraxis Bioscience LLC v. Comptroller General of Patents	C-443/17			7
ACF Chemiefarma NV v. Commission of the European Communities	42/69	1970	ECR 661	21
Actavis Group PTC EHF and Actavis UK Ltd v. Sanofi	C-443/12			7
Actavis/Allergan	COMP/M.7480	2015	Decision of 16 Mar. 2015	21
AEG v. Commission of the European Communities	107/82 R	1983	ECR 3151	21
Airtour v. Commission	T-342/99	2002	ECR II-2585	21

Table of Cases

Case Name	Case Number	Year	Case Citation	Cited in Chapter
Aiuto di Stato a favore di Ricerca, Sviluppo e Innovazione per il progetto FAIV (Faster Access to Innovative Vaccines) di Novartis Vaccines S.r.l.,	SA.33866 (2011/N)	2012		21
AOK Bundesverband	C-264/01, C-306/01, C-354/01, C-355/01	2004	ECR I-2493	21
Arne Forsgren v. Österreichisches Patentamt	C-631/13			7
Arrow Group and Arrow Generics v. Commission	C-601/16 P	2016		21
Aspen	AT.40394	2021		21
Association Pharmaceutique Belge Europemballage and Continental Can Company Inc v. Commission of the European Communities	IV/32.202 C-6/72	1989 1973	ECR 215	21
Astra Zeneca A/S. Loegemiddelstryrelsen	C-223/01	2003	EUECJ	13
Astra/Zeneca	COMP/ M.1403	1999		21
AstraZeneca / Commission Case	T-321/05	2005	OJ C 29/10/2005	20
AstraZeneca v Commission	C-457/10 P	2021	ECLI:EU:C:2012:770	21
AstraZeneca v. Menzis	ECLI:NL:HR: 2006:ay9317	2006	Dutch Supreme Court 10 November 2006	8

Table of Cases

Case Name	Case Number	Year	Case Citation	Cited in Chapter
Athens Administrative Court of Appeal,	Judgments No. 2019/2009, 2100/2009 and 1983/2010	2009-2010		21
Atlantic Container Line AB and Others v. Commission of the European Communities	T-395/94	1995	ECR II-875	21
Auchinloss and anr v. Agricultural and Veterinary Supplies Limited and ors		1997	RPC 649	3
Aventis v. Novo Nordisk	JGR 2005/59	2005		8
BASF v. Bureau voor de Industriele Eigendom	C-258/99	2001 2002	CJEU RPC 9	7
Bayer AG v. Commission of the European Communities	T-41/96	2000	ECR II-3383	21
BAYER/Nifedipine	T-0570/92	1992		3
Biogen Inc v. SmithKline Beecham Biologicals	181/95	1997	ECR I-357 RPC 833	7
Biogen v. SmithKline Beecham Biologicals SA	C-181/95	1997	ECR I-357	7
BMS v. Commission and EMA	T-329/16			14
Boehringer Ingelheim v. AstraZeneca	ECLI:NL: RBDHA: 2021:13754	2021	District Court The Hague 14 December 2021	8
Boehringer v. Swingward	143/00	2002	ECR 3759	20
Boehringer v. Swingward II	348/04	2007	EUECJ	20
Boston Scientific Ltd v. Deutsches Patent- und Markenamt	C-527/17			7
Bristol Myers Squibb/ Dupont	COMP/ M.2517	2001		21
Bristol-Myers	427/93	1996	ECR 3457	20

Table of Cases

Case Name	Case Number	Year	Case Citation	Cited in Chapter
Bundesverband der Arzneimittel-Importeure eV v. Bayer and Commission of the European Communities	C-2/01 P	2004	ECR I-23	21
CD Pharma vs Konkurrencerådet (the Danish Competition Appeals Tribunal)	BS-3038-2019	2019		21
Centrafarm v. American Home Products Co.	C3/78	1978	ECR 1823	20
Centrafarm v. Sterling	15/74	1974	ECR 1147	20
Centrafarm v. Winthrop	16/74	1974	ECR 1183	20
Cephalon	AT.39686	2020		21
Christian Poucet v.Assurances Ge'ne'rales de France and Caisse Mutuelle Reégionale du Languedoc-Roussillon	C-159/91, 160/91	1993	ECR I-00637	21
Ciba-Beigy/Sandoz	IV/M.737	1996		21
Cisal di Battistello Venanzio & Co v. Istituto nazionale per l'assicurazione contro gli infortuni sul lavoro (INAIL)	C-218/00	2002	ECR I-691	21
CMA Decision: Hydrocortisone Tablets – Excessive and Unfair pricing and anti-competitive agreements	C-50277	2021		21
CMA Hydrocortisone statements	C-50277-1, C-50277-2 and C-50277-3	2017 and 2019		21
Commission of the European Communities v. Italian Republic	118/85	1987	ECR 2599	21
Commission v. Germany	C-290/90	1992	EUECJ	19

Table of Cases

Case Name	Case Number	Year	Case Citation	Cited in Chapter
Corevalve Inc v. Edwards Lifesciences AG and Another		2009	EWHC 6	3
Council of State	Judgments No. 1923/2012, 1922/2012, 1921/2012 and 1925/2012.	2012		21
Criminal proceedings against Bodil Lindqvist	C-101/01			23
Daiichi Sankyo Company v. Comptroller General of Patents, Designs and Trade Marks	Case C-6/11			7
Data Protection Commissioner v. Facebook Ireland Limited, Maximillian Schrems	C-311/18			23
Dawson-Damer & Ors v. Taylor Wessing	[2020] EWCA Civ 352			23
Deutscher Apothekerverband eV v. 0800 DocMorris NV, Jacques Waterval	C-322/01	2003	EU ECJ	9
Dr Reddy's Laboratories v. Warner-Lambert		2012	EWHC 3715	8
DU PONT/Appetite suppressant and Diagnostic Methods	C-T- 81/84 /G01/04	1884		3
DU PONT/Appetite suppressant and G01/04 Diagnostic Methods	C-T- 81/84	1884		3
DUPHAR/Pigs I	C-T-0116/85	1885		3
EAEPC v. Commission	Case T-574/14			21

Table of Cases

Case Name	Case Number	Year	Case Citation	Cited in Chapter
EISAI/Second medical indication	G 05/83	1883		3
Eli Lily and Company v. Human Genome Sciences Inc	C-493/12			7
ERONO/HCG	T-0051/93	1993		3
Eurim-Pharm v. Beiersdorf	71/94, 72/94, 73/94	1996	ECR 3603	20
European Commission v. Republic of Poland	C-185/10	2012		9
F. Hoffmann-La Roche AG v. Accord Healthcare OÜ	Case C-572/15			7
F. Hoffmann-La Roche and others	C-179/19	2018		21
Fashion ID GmbH	C-40/17			23
FENIN v. Commission	T-319/99 (confirmed on appeal in C205/03 P, 2006)	2003	ECR II-357	21
Fentanyl	COMP/39685	2013		21
Ferring Arzneimittel GmbH v. Eurim-Pharm Arzneimittel GmbH	172/00	2002	ECR 6891	20
Ford Werke AG and Ford of Europe Inc v. Commission	228, 229/82	1984	ECR 1129	21
France v. Commission	C-482/99	2002	ECR I-4397	21
France v. Commission (FIM)	102/87	1988	ECR 4067	21
Frede Damgaard: Criminal proceedings against Frede Damgaard R v. Roussel Laboratories Ltd, R v. Good (Christopher Saxty)	C-421/07	2009 1989	EU ECJ Cr. App. R. 140	9

Case Name	Case Number	Year	Case Citation	Cited in Chapter
French Republic and Société commercial des potasses et de l'azote (SCPA) and Entreprise minière et chimique (EMC) v. Commission (Kali and Salz)	C-68/94, C-30/95	1998	ECR I-01375	21
GE/Amersham	COMP/M.3304	2004		21
Genentech Inc. v. Hoechst GmbH	C-567/14			21
Generics (UK) and others v. Commission	C-307/18	2018		21
Generics (UK) Ltd and Others v. Competition and Markets Authority	C-307/18	2020	ECLI:EU:C:2020:52	21
Generics (UK) v. Commission	C-588/16 P	2016		21
Generics UK Limited v. Competition and Markets Authority	1251/1/12/16	2016		21
Generics UK Limited v. Competition and Markets Authority [2021] CAT 9	1251-1255/1/12/16	2021		21
Generics v. Synaptech	C-427/09	2011		7
Generics/AstraZeneca	COMP/37.507	2005	Decision of 5 June 2005	21
Genzyme Biosurgery Corp v. Bureau voor de Industriele Elgendom	BIE 70 (2002)	2002		7
Georgetown University and Others v. Comptroller General of Patents, Designs and Trade Marks	C-422/10			7
Gintec International Import – Export GmbH v. Verband Sozialer Wettbewerb eV	C-374/05	2007	EUECJ	9

Table of Cases

Case Name	Case Number	Year	Case Citation	Cited in Chapter
Glaxo Wellcome	IV/36.957	2001	Decision of 8 May 2001	21
Glaxo/Wellcome	IV/M.555	1995		21
GlaxoSmithKline PLC v. Competition and Markets Authority	Case 1252/1/12/16			21
GlaxoSmithKline Services Unlimited v. Commission of the European Communities	T-168/01	2006	ECR II-2969	21
GlaxoSmithKline Services v. Commission of the European Communities	C-501/06 P, C-513/06 P, C-515/06 P, C-519/06 P	2009	EU ECJ	21
GlaxoWellcome/ Smithkline Beecham	COMP/ M.1846	2000		21
GMP-Orphan v. European Commission	T-733/17			14
Google Spain SL, Google Inc v. AEPD, Mario Costeja González	C-131/12			23
Hannover Reginal Court	Case 18 O 91/15	2015	Decision of 25 August 2015	21
Hoffmann La Roche & Co v. Commission	85/76	1979	ECR 461	21
Hoffmann-La Roche v. Centrafarm	102/77	1978	ECR 1139	20
IAZ International Belgium SA v. Commission	96/82-102/82, 104/82, 105/82, 108/82, 110/82. 96/82	1983	ECR 3369	21
ICI v. Commission (Dyestuffs) T-Mobile Netherlands and others v. Raad van bestuur van de Nederlandse	48/69, 49/69, 51-7/69 C-8/08	1972 2009	ECR 619 EU ECJ	21

Table of Cases

Case Name	Case Number	Year	Case Citation	Cited in Chapter
ICI/Cleaning Plaque	C-T-0144/83	1883		3
Illumina	T-227/21	Pending	ECLI:EU:T:2021:672	21
IMS Health	C-418/01	2004		21
Istituto Chemiterapico Italiano SpA and Commercial Solvents Corporation v. Commission	6/73, 7/73	1974	ECR 223	21
Italy v. Commission	173/73	1974	ECR 709	21
Italy v. Commission	C-66/02	2005	ECR I-10901	21
JCB Service v Commission	C-167/04 P	2006		21
Kingdom of Spain and Italian Republic v. ouncil of the European Union	C-274/11 and C-295/11	2011	CJEU	3
Kingdom of Spain v. Council of the European Union	C-147/13	2015	CJEU	3
Kingdom of Spain v. European Parliament and Council of the European Union	C-146/13	2015	CJEU	3
Klaus Höfner and Fritz Elser v. Macrotron GmbH	C-41/90	1991	ECR I-1979	21
Kohlpharma v. Bundesrepublik Deutschland	112/02	2004	ECR 3369	20
Laboratoires Lyocentre v. Lääkealan turvallisuus- ja kehittämiskeskus	Case C-109/12			7
Lexon (UK) Limited v. Competition and Markets Authority2021] CAT 5.	1344/1/12/20	2021		21
Ludwigs-Apotheke München Internationale Apotheke v. Juers Pharma Import- Export GmbH	C-143/06	2007	EU ECJ	9

Table of Cases

Case Name	Case Number	Year	Case Citation	Cited in Chapter
Lundbeck	AT/39226	2013		21
Lundbeck A/S and Lundbeck Ltd	C-591/16P	2021		21
Lundbeck v. Commission	Case T-472/13	2016		21
Lundbeck v. Commission	C-591/16 P	2016		21
MAI/Trigonelline	T-0143/94	1994		3
Massachusetts Institute of Technology	C-431/04	2006	EUECJ	16
Massachusetts Institute of Technology v. Deutsches Patentamt	C-431/04	2006 2007	RPC 872 IP&T 44	7
Medac Gesellschaft für klinische Spezialpräparate v. Commission	T-549/19			14
Mededingingsautoriteit Commission Decision in UK Agricultural Tractor Exchange SC Belasco and others v. Commission of the European Communities	IV/31.370 246/86	1992 1989	ECR 2117	21
Medeva BV v. Comptroller General of Patents, Designs and Trade Marks	C-322/10			7
Merck & Co Inc v. Deutsches Patent und Markenamt	C-125/10	2011		7, 8
Merck & Co. Inc.	BL O/108/08	2008	UK IPO	8
Merck KGaA v. Competition and Markets Authority	1255/1/12/16	2016		21
Merck Sharp & Dohme Corp v. Clonmel Healthcare Limited	C-149/22			7

Table of Cases

Case Name	Case Number	Year	Case Citation	Cited in Chapter
Merck Sharp & Dohme Corporation v. Comptroller General of Patents, Designs and Trade Marks	C-567/16			7
Merck Sharp Dohme v. Paranova Pharmazeutika Handels GmbH	443/99	2002	ECR 3703	20
Merck v. Primecrown Ltd	267/95, 268/95	1996	ECR 6285	20
Microsoft	T-201/04	2007		21
Ministre de l'Economie v. Millennium Pharmaceuticals	C-252/03	2005	RPC 33	7
Monsanto Co v. Stauffer Chemical Co and Another		1985	RPC 515	3
Monsanto/Pharmacia & Upjohn	IV/M.1835	2000		21
MPA Pharma v. Rhone-Poulenc Pharma	232/94	1996	ECR 3671	20
MSD Sharp & Dohme GmbH v/ Merckle GmbH	C-316/09	2015	Judgment of the European Court of Justice dated 5 May 2011	9
Mylan v. European Commission	T-303/16			14
N V Nederlandsche Banden-Industrie Michelin NV v. Commission of the European Communities	322/81	1983	ECR 3461	21
Neurim Pharmaceuticals (1991) Ltd v. Comptroller-General of Patents	C-130/11			7
Novartis		2003	Gerechtshof Arnhem	9

Table of Cases

Case Name	Case Number	Year	Case Citation	Cited in Chapter
Novartis /GlaxoSmithKline oncology business	COMP/M.7275		Decision of 28 Jan. 2015	21
Novartis AG v. Actavis UK Ltd	C-442/11			7
Novartis AG v. IVAX Pharm UK Ltd	C-T-0116/85	1885	English High Court	3
Novartis Pharmaceuticals UK Limited v. Medimmune Limited and Medical Research Council	[2012] EWHC 181 (Pat)			7
Novartis v. Comptroller General	C-207/03	2005	RPC 33	7
Novartis v. European Commission	Case T-269/15			14
Novartis/Alcon	COMP/M.5778	2010	Decision of 9 Aug. 2010	21
Novartis/Hexal	COMP/M.3751	2005		21
Now Pharm AG v. European Commission	T-74/08			14
Nycomed Danmark v. EMA	T-52/09			8
Officier van Justitie v. De Peijper	104/75	1976	ECR 613	20
Oliver Brüstle v. Greenpeace eV	C-34/10	2011	CJEU	3
Omega Pharma v. Proctor & Gamble	ECLI:NL: RBROT: 2014:2601	2014	District court Rotterdam 27 March 2014	8
Ottung v. Klee & Weilbach A/S and Thomas Schmidt A/S	Case 320/87	1989		21
P Merck v. Commission. 2	C-614/16	2016		21
Paroxetine	CE/9531-11	2016		21
Patrick Breyer v. Bundesrepublik Deutschland	C-582/14			23

Table of Cases

Case Name	Case Number	Year	Case Citation	Cited in Chapter
Pavel Pavlov v. Stichting Pensioenfonds Medische Specialisten	C-180/98 to C-184/98	2000	ECR I-6451	21
Peter Nowak v. Data Protection Commissioner	C-434/16			23
Pfizer v. Cosmetique Active	ECLI:NL: HR:2006: AU7935	2006	Dutch Supreme Court 24 March 2006	8
Pfizer v. Eleveld	B09.006	2009	Commissie Van Beroep Van De Stichting Code Geneesmiddelenreclame	9
Pfizer v. Eleveld	B09.006	2009	Appeal Code Committee 17 September 2009	8
Pfizer v. Eurim-Pharm	C-1/81	1981	ECR 2913	20
Pfizer v. European Commission and EMA	Case T-48/14			8
Pharma Expressz Szolgáltató és Kereskedelmi Kft. v. Országos Gyógyszerészeti és Élelmezés-egészségügyi Intézet	C-178/20	2021		9
Pharmaceutical Works Polpharma v. European Medicines Agency	T-611/18			12
Pharmacia Italia v. Deutsches Patentamt	C-31/03	2005	RPC 640	7
Pharmon v. Hoechst	19/84	1985	ECR 2281	20
Philip Morris v. Commission	730/79	1980	ECR 2671	21
Pioneer Electronics Capital Inc v. Warner Music Manufacturing Europe GmbH	R.P.C. 757	1997		3

Table of Cases

Case Name	Case Number	Year	Case Citation	Cited in Chapter
PT Portela & Ca SA	N 126/2005	2005		21
Queen's University Kingston/Controlling bleeding	T-0893/90	1990		3
R (on the application of Approved Prescription Services Ltd) v. Licensing Authority	C-36/03	2004	EUECJ	13
R (on the application of Generics (UK) Ltd) v. Licensing Authority	C-527/07	2009	EUECJ	13
R (on the application of Novartis Pharmaceuticals UK Ltd) v. Licensing Authority	C-106/01	2004	EUECJ	13
R v. Code of Practice Committee of the British Pharmaceutical Industry Ex p. Professional Counselling Aids		1991	3 Admin L R 697	9
R. v. Licensing Authority and Norgine, ex parte Scotia Pharmaceutical	C-440/93	1995	EUECJ	13
R. v. Licensing Authority ex parte Generics	C-368/96	1998	EUECJ	13
R. v. The Medicines Control Agency, ex parte Smith & Nephew Pharmaceuticals Ltd	201/94	1996	ECR 5819	20
Ratiopharm v. Novartis Consumer Health	C-786/18	2020		9
Ratiopharm/Pfizer	A431	2012	Decision of 11 January 2012	21
Reckitt Benckiser	CE/8931/08	2011		21
Reckitt Benckiser PLC c/Arrow Generiques	C-2014/03330	2015		21
Reckitt Benckiser/Boots Healthcare International	COMP/M.4007	2006	EC 139/2004	21
Roche Products v. Bolar Pharmaceutical	733 F.2d 858	1984		4

Case Name	Case Number	Year	Case Citation	Cited in Chapter
Roche-Novartis/Farmaci Avastin e Lucentis	I760	2014		21
RORER/Dysmenorrhoea	C-T-0081/84	1884		3
Sanofi-Aventis	13-D-11	2013	Decision of 14 May 2013	21
Sanofi-Aventis c/Teva	2013/12370	2014	Decision of 18 December 2014	21
Santen SAS v. Directeur général de l'Institut national de la propriété industrielle	C-673/18			7
Schering-Plough	13-D-21	2013	Decision of 19 December 2013	21
Secretary of State for Health and others v. Servier Laboratories Ltd and others	UKSC 44	2020	Judgment of 6 November 2020	21
Sepracor Pharmaceuticals (Ireland) Ltd v. European Commission Case	C-477/11 P (2012/C 303/10).			5
Sepracor Pharmaceuticals (Ireland) v. Commission	T-275/09			5, 13
Servier v. Commission	Case T-691/14			21
Shire Pharmaceutical Contracts v. European Commission	Case T-583/13			8, 14
Shire Pharmaceuticals Ireland Ltd, v. EMA	T-80/16			14
Smith Kline & French Laboratories v. Evans Medical Ltd		1989	FSR 513	3
SmithKline Beecham plc v. Laegemiddelstyrelson	C-74/03	2005	EUECJ	13

Table of Cases

Case Name	Case Number	Year	Case Citation	Cited in Chapter
Socie'te' Technique Minie're (LTM) v. Maschinenbau Ulm GmbH (MBU)	56/65	1966	ECR 234	21
Sot. Lelos kai Sia EE v. GlaxoSmithKline Anonimi Emporiki Viomikhaniki Etairia Farmakeftikon Proionton "Syfait II"	468/06, C-478/06	2008	EU ECJ	21
Sot.Lélos kai Sia	C-468/06	2008	ECR I-7139 and Syfair II	21
Squibb v. Paranova	429/93, 436/93 A11			20
Sun Pharmaceutical Industries and Ranbaxy (UK) v. Commission	C-586/16 P	2016		21
Synthon v. Merz	C-195/09	2011		7
Tetra Pak Rausing S.A. v. Commission of the European Communities	T-51/89	1990	ECR II-309	21
Teva Pharma and Teva Pharmaceuticals Europe v. EMA	T-547/12			12
Teva UK Ltd & Ors v. Gilead Sciences	C-121/17			7
Teva v. EMA	Case C-138/15			14
Teva/Allergan	M7746	2016	Decision of 10 March 2016	21
Teva/Cephalon	COMP/M.6258	2011	Decision of 13 Oct. 2011	21
TEVA/IVAX	COMP/M.3928	2005		21
Teva/Ratiopharm	COMP/M.5865	2010	Decision of 3 Aug. 2010	21
The Netherlands v. Antroposana et al.	C-84/06	2007		9

Table of Cases

Case Name	Case Number	Year	Case Citation	Cited in Chapter
Tietosuojavaltuutettu intervening parties – Jehovan todistajat – uskonnollinen yhdyskunta	C-25/17			23
Unabhängiges Landeszentrum für Datenschutz Schleswig-Holstein v. Wirtschaftsakademie Schleswig-Holstein GmbH	C-210/16			23
United Brands Company and United Brands Continentaal B V v. Commission of the European Communities	27/76	1978	ECR 207 / EU:C:1978:22	21
University of Queensland and CSL Ltd v. Comptroller General of Patents, Designs and Trade Marks	C-630/10			7
Upjohn Ltd v. Licensing Authority and others	C-120/97	1968	51 BLMR 206	10
Valsts policijas Rigas regiona parvaldes Kartibas policijas parvalde v Rigas pašvaldibas SIA 'Rigas satiksme'	C-13/16			23
Viho Europe BV v. Commission of the European Communities	C-75/95	1996	ECR I-5457	21
Völk v. Vervaecke BBC Brown Boveri/NGK Pasteur-Me'rieux/Merck	5/69 IV/32.368 IV/34.776	1969 1988 1994	ECR 295	21
WARF/Use of embryos	G 2/06	2006		3
Wellcome	IV/39.957/F3	2001	EU ECJ	21

Table of Cases

Case Name	Case Number	Year	Case Citation	Cited in Chapter
Weltimmo s.r.o. v. Nemzeti Adatvédelmi és Információszabadság Hatóság	C-230/14			23
Xellia Pharmaceuticals and Alpharma v. Commission	C-611/16 P	2016		21
Xellia Pharmaceuticals APS (2) Alpharma LLC v. Competition and Markets Authority	1253/1/12/16 (1)	2016		21
Yeda Research and Development Company Ltd and Aventis Holdings Inc v. Comptroller	C-518/10	2011	CJEU	7
Yissum Research & Development Company of the Hebrew University of Jerusalem v. Comptroller General of Patents		2007	CJEU	7
Zino Davidoff S.A. v. A&G Imports Ltd.	C-414/99, C-416/99	2001	ECR 8691	20
	25 W 2146/00	2000	Decision of the Appellate Court Berlin	19
	MD 1994, 34	1994	Decision of the Appellate Court Berlin	19
	6 U 183/96	1996	Judgment of the Appellate Court Frankfurt am Main	19
	6 U 164/98	1996	Judgment of the Appellate Court Frankfurt am Main	19

Case Name	Case Number	Year	Case Citation	Cited in Chapter
	5 U 63/01	2002	Judgment of the Appellate Court Hamburg	19
	M22K 00.4223	2000	Judgment of the Administrative Court in Munich	19

EU Directives

Chapter 1

Directive 2001/83/EC
Directive 2001/95/EC

Chapter 2

Directive 65/65/EEC
Directive 75/318/EEC
Directive 75/319/EEC
Directive 2001/83/EC
Directive 89/342/EE
Directive 89/343/EEC
Directive 89/381/EEC
Directive 92/25/EEC
Directive 92/26/EEC
Directive 92/27/EEC
Directive 92/28/EEC
Directive 92/73/EEC
Directive 2001/82/EC
Directive 2001/83/EC
Directive 2001/20/EC
Directive 90/385/EEC
Directive 93/42/EEC
Directive 98/79/EC
Directive 2004/27/EC
Directive 2004/24/EC
Directive 2003/63/EC
Directive 2003/94/EC

EU Directives

Chapter 3

Directive 98/44/EC
Directive 98/71/EC
Directive 96/9/EC
Directive 2008/95/EC
Directive 2001/83/EC
Directive 2001/29/EC
Directive 2004/27/EC
Directive 2006/114/EC

Chapter 4

Directive 2001/20/EC
Directive 2001/83/EC
Directive 2005/28/EC
Directive 2008/25/EC
Directive 2008/20/EC
Directive 95/46/EC
Directive 2003/94/EC
Directive 91/356/EC
Directive 75/319/EEC
Directive 2001/2/EC
Directive 2002/94
Directive 2003/63/EC
Directive 2004/27/EC

Chapter 5

Directive 2001/83/EC
Directive 97/11/EC
Directive 65/65/EEC
Directive 2002/98/EC
Directive 2003/63/EC
Directive 2003/94/EC
Directive 2004/27/EC
Directive 2004/24/EC
Directive 2004/28/EC
Directive 2003/94/EC
Directive 2001/20/EC
Directive 2001/18/EC
Directive 90/220/EC

Chapter 6

Directive 2001/83/EC

EU Directives

Chapter 7

Directive 65/65/EEC
Directive 90/385/EEC
Directive 93/42/EEC
Directive 98/79/EC
Directive 2001/20/EC
Directive 2001/82/EC
Directive 2001/83/EC

Chapter 8

Directive 2001/83/EC
Directive 20/2001/EC

Chapter 9

Directive 2001/83/EC
Directive 2004/27/EC
Directive 2005/29/EC
Directive 92/28/EEC
Directive 84/450/EEC
Directive 97/7/EC
Directive 89/552/EEC
Directive 2004/24/EC

Chapter 10

Directive 65/65/EEC
Directive 92/28/EEC
Directive 93/39/EEC
Directive 2001/83/EC
Directive 2001/20/EC
Directive 2012/26/EU
Directive 2010/84/EU

Chapter 11

Directive 2001/82/EC
Directive 2001/83/EC

Chapter 12

Directive 2001/83/EC

Chapter 13

Directive 65/65/EEC
Directive 2001/83/EC
Directive 87/21/EEC
Directive 87/22/EEC

EU Directives

Directive 2004/27/EC
Directive 1987/21/EEC
Directive 75/318/EEC

Chapter 15

Directive 2001/83/EC
Directive 2002/98/EC
Directive 2000/70/EC
Directive 93/42/EC
Directive 2003/63/EC
Directive 2001/20/EC
Directive 2004/27/EC
Directive 2000/70/EC
Directive 93/42/EC

Chapter 16

Directive 2001/83/EC
Directive 92/73/EEC
Directive 65/65/EEC
Directive 75/319/EEC
Directive 2003/63/EC
Directive 2004/27/EC
Directive 2004/24/EC
Directive 91/356/EEC

Chapter 17

Directive 2009/120/EC
Directive 2001/83/EC
Directive 90/385/EEC
Directive 93/42/EEC
Directive 95/46
Directive 2004/23/EC
Directive 2002/98/EC
Directive 93/42/EEC
Directive 95/46
Directive 2002/98
Directive 2015/566

Chapter 18

Directive 2001/83/EC
Directive 2001/20/EC

Chapter 19

Directive 93/42/EEC
Directive 90/385/EEC
Directive 98/79/EC
Directive 2000/70/EC
Directive 2001/104/EC
Directive 2001/83/EC

Chapter 20

Directive 2001/83/EC
Directive 2011/62/EC
Directive 89/104/EEC
Directive 2014/104/EU

Chapter 21

Directive 2014/104/EU

Chapter 22

Directive 2005/36/EC

Chapter 23

Directive 95/46/EC
Directive 2002/58/EC
Directive 2001/20/EC

Other Legislation

Chapter 1

European Union (Withdrawal Agreement) Act 2020
The Intellectual Property (Exhaustion of Rights) (EU Exit) Regulations 2019
Supplementary Protection Certificates (Amendment) (EU Exit) Regulations 2020
The Patents (Amendment) (EU Exit) Regulations
General Product Safety Regulations 2005

Chapter 2

The Pure Food and Drug Act 1906
Food, Drug and Cosmetics Act 1938
The Kefauver-Harris Amendment in 1962 to Food, Drug and Cosmetics Act 1938
The Single European Act 1986
The Treaty of Rome
Treaty of Paris
The Treaty on the European Union
The Treaty of Maastricht
The Amsterdam Treaty
The Treaty of Lisbon

Chapter 3

Patents Act 1977
The Patent Cooperation Treaty (PCT)

Chapter 4

The Medicines for Human Use (Clinical Trials) Regulations 2004

Chapter 7

Treaty of Accession of Croatia
Accession Act 1994
Accession Act 2005

Other Legislation

Accession Act 2003
Accession Act 2004
Patents Act 1977

Chapter 9

Medicines Act 1968
Trade Descriptions Act of 1968
ABHI Code of Business Practice
Advertising of Medicinal Products Act
Advertising of Medicinal Products Act 2004
Code of Conduct for Pharmaceutical Advertising (in Dutch: Gedragscode Geneesmiddelenreclame)
Code on Public Advertising Medical Self-Care Devices 2019 (in Dutch: Code Publieksreclame Medische Zelfzorg Hulpmiddelen)
Decree no 2020-730 of 15 June 2020 relating to the advantages granted by those manufacturing or marketing health products or providing health services
Dutch Code of Conduct on Advertising
Dutch Medicines Act
German Medicinal Products Act
Medical Devices Act 2019
Medicinal Products Act 2005
Medicinal Products for Human Use Act 2005
Medicinal Products Act 1992
Policy Rules Medicines 2018 (in Dutch: Beleidsregels gunstbetoon Geneesmiddelenwet)
Swedish Marketing Act (2008)
The Swedish Radio and Television Act 2010
Marketing Act
Fair Trade Practices Act
Trade Practices and Consumer Protection Act
Medicines (Monitoring of Advertising) Regulations of 1994
Medicines (Advertising) Regulations Statutory Instruments 1994 No.1933
Medicines (Advertising) Regulations of 1994
1994 Statutory Instrument 1994 No.1932
The Consumer Protection Act
EC Treaty
Order of 7 August 2020 fixing the amounts above which an agreement provided for in article L. 1453-8 of the PHC is subject to authorisation
Ordinance no 2017-49 of 19 January 2017 on advantages offered by persons manufacturing or marketing health products or services

Chapter 10

Medicines Act 1968

Other Legislation

Chapter 12

German Medicinal Products Act
Dutch Medicines Act
Sweden Medicinal Products Act (1992)
Medicines Act 1968

Chapter 13

Accession Act of 2003

Chapter 14

The United States Orphan Drug Act 1983 amending the Federal Food, Drug, and Cosmetic Act

Chapter 15

Advertising of Medicinal Products Act
Dutch Civil Code
Medicinal Products Act
Second Amendment of the Medical Devices Act
Swedish Marketing Act (2008)
Medicinal Products Act (1992)
Medical Devices Act 1993 (Sweden)
The Medical Devices Act (MDA) (The Netherlands)

Chapter 16

The Human Medicines Regulations 2012

Chapter 18

The Human Medicines Regulations 2012
The National Health Service (Standing Advisory Committees) Order 1981
Health Protection (Vaccination) Regulations 2009

Chapter 19

The Medical Devices Regulations 2002
The General Product Safety Regulations 2005

Chapter 20

Treaty on the Functioning of the European Union (TFEU)
Accession Treaty
Dutch Medicines Act
EC Treaty (Articles 28, 30) Annex V, Chapter 1 of the Protocol of the Accession Treaty for Romania and Bulgaria

Other Legislation

Chapter 21

EC Treaty
Treaty on the Functioning of the European Union (TFEU)
Competition Act 1998 (United Kingdom)
Competition Act 1998 (Vertical Agreements Block Exemption) Order 2022 SI No. 516 (United Kingdom)
Formal Notification Form CO: Annexed to Commission Regulation No 1269/2013 of 5 December 2013, implementing Council Regulation 139/2004 on the control of concentrations between undertakings, OJ [2004] L 133/1, as amended by Commission Regulation No. 1033/2008 OJ [2008] L 279/3.

Chapter 22

The Human Medicines Regulations 2012
The Human Medicines (Coronavirus and Influenza) (Amendment) Regulations 2020
The Human Medicines (Coronavirus) (Further Amendments) Regulations 2020

Chapter 23

European Union (Withdrawal) Act 2018
Data Protection Act 2018
Digital Information Bill
The Privacy and Electronic Communications (EC Directive) Regulations 2003

Indicative List of Reports and Codes of Practice

EFPIA Code on the promotion of prescription-only medicines to, and interactions with, healthcare professionals
Communication from the Commission entitled 'Report on the current practices with regard to the provision of information to patients on medicinal products' adopted and submitted to European Parliament and Council on 20 December 2007
CPMP/183/97 Conduct of Pharmacovigilance for Centrally Authorised Products (15 April 1997)
The Blue Guide: Advertising and Promotion of Medicines in the UK ISBN 0 11 703604 8 The Stationary Office 2005
MHRA: Advertising of medicines: Guidance for consumer websites offering medicinal treatment services. October 2008
MHRA Delivering high standards in Medicines Advertising Regulation. Annual report September 2007–2008
The ABPI Code of Practice for the Pharmaceutical Industry from the Prescription Medicines Code of Practice Authority
The Proprietary Association of Great Britain (PAGB): Medicines Advertising Codes MHRA Delivering high standards in Medicines Advertising Regulation Annual report September 2007–2008
The PAGB Professional Code
PAGB Consumer Code
German Criminal Code

British Code of Advertising, Sales Promotion and Direct Marketing code (the 'CAP Code')
Advertising Code ('Code voor de Publieksreclame voor Geneesmiddelen')
Foundation Code Medicinal Advertising ('Stichting Code Geneesmiddelen- reclame CGR')
Code of Conduct for Medicinal Advertising ('Gedragscode Geneesmidde- lenreclame')
Code of Conduct Medical Devices
The Code of Conduct for the Association of manufacturers of medical devices (FENIN)
German Medical Association's professional code of conduct ('(Muster-)Berufsordnung für die deutschen Ärztinnen und Ärzte')
OTC Advertising Code ('Code voor de Publieksreclame voor Geneesmid- delen')
Beleidsregels gunstbetoon Geneesmiddelenwet, Staatscourant 4 April 2014, nr. 9496
European Data Protection Board (EDPB) Guidelines 3/2018
EDPB 'Guidelines 07/2020 on the concepts of controllers and processor in the GDPR' Version 2.0, Adopted on 7 July 2021.
EDPB Guidelines 05/2020 on consent under Regulation 2016/679, version 1.0 adopted 4 May 2020 (EDPB Consent Guidelines)
ICO guidance 'Data controllers and data processors: what the difference is and what the governance implications are' Version 1.0, May 2014
Opinion 06/2014 on the notion of legitimate interests of the data controller under Article 7 of Directive 95/46/EC, WP 217
EDPB Guidelines 01/2021 on Examples regarding Personal Data Breach Notification, Version 2.0, adopted on 14 December 2021

EU Regulations

Chapter 1

Regulation (EU) No. 536/2014

Chapter 2

Regulation (EU) No. 2015/2424
Regulation (EEC) No. 2309/93
Regulation (EC) No. 1901/2006
Regulation (EC) No. 1902/2006
Regulation (EC) No. 726/2004
Regulation (EC) No. 141/2000
Regulation (EC) No. 726/2004
Regulation (EU) No. 608/2013
Regulation (EC) No. 1084/2003
Regulation (EC) No. 1085/2003
Regulation (EC) No. 847/2000
Regulation (EC) No. 540/95
Regulation (EC) No. 507/2006
Regulation (EC) No. 1383/2003
Regulation (EC) No. 1394/2007
Regulation (EU) No. 2017/745
Regulation (EU) No. 2017/746

Chapter 3

Regulation (EU) No. 1257/2012
Regulation (EU) No. 1260/2012
Regulation (EC) No. 207/2009
Regulation (EC) No. 726/2004
Regulation (EC) No. 6/2002

Chapter 4

Regulation (EC) No. 536/2014
Regulation (EC) No. 1901/2006
Regulation (EC) No. 726/2004
Regulation (EC) No. 1928/2006
Regulation (EC) No. 2984/2006
Regulation (EU) No. 536/2014

Chapter 5

Regulation (EC) No. 726/2004
Regulation (EC) No. 141/2000
Regulation (EEC) No. 2309/93

Chapter 6

Regulation (EC) No. 507/2006
Regulation (EC) No. 726/2004
Regulation (EU) No. 1235/2010

Chapter 7

Regulation (EEC) No. 1768/92
Regulation (EC) No. 469/2009
Regulation (EC) No. 1901/2006
Regulation (EC) No. 1610/96
Regulation (EC) No. 726/2006

Chapter 8

Regulation (EC) No. 1901/2006
Regulation (EEC) No. 1768/92
Regulation (EC) No.726/2004
Regulation (EC) No. 141/2000
Regulation (EU) No. 536/2014
Regulation (EU) No. 488/2012
Regulation (EC) No. 469/2009

Chapter 9

Regulation (EC) No. 726/2004
Regulation (EC) No. 2001/83

Chapter 10

Regulation (EC) No. 726/2004
Regulation (EU) No. 1235/2010
Regulation (EC) No. 1084/2003
Regulation (EC) No. 1085/2003
Regulation (EU) No. 1027/2012

Regulation (EU) No. 520/2012
Regulation (EC) No. 658/2007
Regulation (EU) No. 1235/2010
Regulation (EU) No. 536/2014
Regulation (EU) No. 2019/5

Chapter 11

Regulation (EC) No. 1234/2008
Regulation (EC) No. 1084/2003
Regulation (EC) No. 1085/2003
Regulation (EC) No. 712/2012
Regulation (EU) No. 2021/756

Chapter 12

Regulation (EC) No. 1394/2007

Chapter 13

Regulation (EC) No. 726/2004
Regulation (EEC) No. 2309/93

Chapter 14

Regulation (EC) No. 141/2000
Regulation (EC) No. 847/2000
Regulation (EEC) No. 2309/93
Regulation (EC) No. 726/2004
Regulation (EC) No. 1901/2006

Chapter 15

Regulation (EC) No. 542/95
Regulation (EEC) No. 2309/93
Regulation (EC) No. 141/2000
Regulation (EC) No. 141/2004
Regulation (EC) No. 726/2004
Regulation (EC) No. 1394/2007
Regulation (EC) No. 1235/2010

Chapter 16

Regulation (EC) No. 726/2004
Regulation (EU) No. 182/2011

Chapter 17

Regulation (EC) No. 1394/2007
Regulation (EC) No. 726/2004
Regulation (EC) No. 726/2004

Chapter 18

Regulation (EC) No. 726/2004
Regulation (EC) No. 1234/2008
Regulation (EC) 851/2004
Regulation (EU) No. 536/2014

Chapter 19

Regulation (EC) No. 1882/2003
Regulation (EC) No. 765/2008
Regulation (EEC) No. 339/1993
Regulation (EC) No. 2006/2004
Regulation (EC) No. 178/2002
Regulation (EC) No. 1223/2009
Regulation (EU) No. 2017/745
Regulation (EU) No. 2017/746

Chapter 20

Regulation (EC) No. 726/04

Chapter 21

Regulation (EC) No. 1/2003
Regulation (EC) No. 772/2004
Regulation (EC) No. 139/2004
Regulation (EC) No. 800/2008.
Regulation (EU) No. 316/2014
Regulation (EU) No. 1217/2010
Regulation (EU) No. 330/2010
Regulation (EC) No. 1033/2008
Regulation (EC) No. 1269/2013
Regulation (EEC) No. 4064/89
Regulation (EU) No. 651/2014
Regulation (EU) No. 2022/720
Regulation (EC) No. 1588/2015

Chapter 22

Regulation (EU) No. 2020/561
Regulation (EU) No. 2022/123
Regulation (EU) No. 2017/745
Regulation (EU) No. 2017/746

Chapter 23

Regulation (EU) No. 2016/679
Regulation (EU) No. 536/2014

Index

A

ABHI. *See* Association of British Healthcare Industries (ABHI)
ABPI. *See* Association of British Pharmaceutical Industry (ABPI)
Abridged generic application to biosimilars, application for the, 548
Abridged procedures
  based on bibliographic application for well established use, 464–465
  based on cross-reference to data with holder's consent, 463–464
  for generic medicinal products after October 2005, 480–484
  for generic products, 466–489
Abuse of a dominant position, 679, 700, 702–707
Acquired immunodeficiency syndrome (AIDS), 161, 168, 352, 448, 538, 613
Active implantable medical devices (AIMDD), 23, 237, 242, 589, 591, 632, 650, 652
Active Substance Master File (ASMF), 463
Advance therapy medicinal products (ATMPs), 543, 585–602
Advertising across borders and the Internet, 286, 326–327, 347–348
Advertising self-regulation in Europe, 289–291
Advertising Standards Authority (ASA), 349, 356, 358–361,
AEGSP. *See* Association of the European Self-Medication Industry (AEGSP)
AEMPS. *See* Spanish Agency of Medicines and Medical Devices (AEMPS)
AFSSaPS. *See* French Health Products Safety Agency (AFSSaPS)
Agreement on Trade-Related Aspects of Intellectual Property Rights (TRIPS Agreement), 49, 50, 76
AIDS. *See* Acquired immunodeficiency syndrome (AIDS)
AIMDD. *See* Active implantable medical devices (AIMDD)
Anatomical Therapeutic Classification (ATC), 166, 686
Animal models, 119, 432, 540, 607, 608
Annex II categories, 97, 194, 196, 203, 424, 426, 482, 598
ANSM. *See* National Agency for the Safety of Medicines and Health Products (ANSM)
Application dossier
  requirements of the, 151–159
Application review-COMP, 507–508
Applications for orphan designation, 493–509, 523, 528, 529, 531

Index

Approval to commence a clinical trial, 130–133
ARS. *See* Regional Health Authority (ARS)
Article 16 authorisation procedure, 562, 563, 565, 567, 568
Article 82 of the EC Treaty, 701
ASA. *See* Advertising Standards Authority (ASA)
ASMF. *See* Active Substance Master File (ASMF)
Assessing similarity and derogations, 515–516
Association of British Healthcare Industries (ABHI), 357, 650
Association of the British Pharmaceutical Industry (ABPI), 118, 119, 352–354, 650
Association of the European Self-Medication Industry (AESGP), 290
ATC. *See* Anatomical Therapeutic Classification (ATC)
Authorisations, 147–182
Auxiliary medicinal product (AxMP), 81, 86, 87, 89, 91, 92, 124

B

Bioequivalence demonstrated by studies, 481–482
Biological medicinal products 45, 166, 158, 181, 390, 426, 430–432, 462, 474, 535–540, 543–544, 546–549, 556, 587, 597
Biologics Working Party (BWP), 545
Biopharmaceutical manufacturing process, 543–544
Biopharmaceuticals, 535–557
  Biologics Working Party (BWP), 545
  biosimilars, 545–548
  consequences, 53–537
  market access for innovative biologicals, 537–538
  market surveillance measures, 543–544
  product-specific requirements, 541–543
  regulatory data protection, 544–545
Biosimilars
  abridged application process, 548
  authorisation, 550–554
  concept, 545–546
  Dossier requirements, 538–540
  generics, 546–548
  guidelines, 545
Biotechnology derived products, 18, 544, 546, 549
Bolar provision, 121–122
Brexit, 1–9
Bundesinstitut für Arzneimittel und Medizinprodukte (Germany), 449
BWP. *See* Biologics Working Party (BWP)

C

Cannabidiol (CBD), 583
Cannabis-based medicinal products, 579–583
Case report form (CRF), 106, 107, 113, 114
CAT. *See* Committee for Advanced Therapies (CAT)
CE Labelling, 641–642
CE marking, 323, 640–642, 649, 736
Centralised procedures (CP
  child attention deficit hyperactivity disorder (ADHD), 359–361
  mandatory scope, 160–161, 173
CEPS. *See* Economic Committee for Health Products (CEPS)
CFI. *See* Court of first instance (CFI)
Circular 1/200. *See* Circular 1/2000 on general rules for the application of certain articles of RD 1416/1994 regarding

Index

advertising to professional healthcare professionals.
Classification of unforeseen variations, 429
Clinical superiority, 492, 506, 512, 515, 516
Clinical trials
  conduct of the, 100–104
  directive (CTD), 79, 82, 115, 122, 131, 368, 369, 372, 597
  termination of, 100, 113, 115, 140
CMA. *See* Conditional Marketing Authorisations (CMA)
CMSs. *See* Concerned Member States (CMSs)
Code for non-broadcast advertising (UK), 356, 656
Codes for broadcast advertising (UK), 356, 656
Combination packs, 447
Combination products
  necessity of non-clinical and clinical trials, 452–455
  specific dosage regime, 457
Combinations already approved, 455
Commission decisions, 165, 166, 173, 179, 186, 189, 196, 416, 436, 440, 484, 487, 489, 520, 523, 708, 709, 713
Commission Guideline relating to Medical Device Directions (MEDDEV), 242, 635, 644
Committee for Advanced Therapies (CAT), 26, 30–31, 90, 591, 593–595, 598, 602, 698, 707, 719–724
Committee for Herbal Medicinal Products (HMPC), 26, 29, 33, 570, 573, 576–578
Committee for Medicinal Products for Human Use (previously Committee for Proprietary Medicinal Products (CPMP). *See* Committee for Proprietary Medicinal Products (now the CHMP) (CPMP)
Committee for Medicinal Products for Veterinary Use (CVMP), 26, 28, 33, 440
Committee for Orphan Medicinal Products (COMP), 18, 28–29, 493, 495, 531
Committee for Proprietary Medicinal Products (now the CHMP) (CPMP
  assessment, 164–165, 173, 196consideration, 80, 163, 165, 447
  rapporteur, 163–164
Common technical document (CTDoc), 37, 38, 113, 115, 150, 151, 158–159, 178–181, 372, 450, 556, 597, 614, 616
Community list, 578–579
COMP. *See* Committee for Orphan Medicinal Products (COMP)
Compassionate use, 167, 385, 465, 736–737
Competition law
  agreements, 689–690
  appreciable effect, 692
  associations, 690–691
  block exemptions, 693–696
  Block Exemption Regulation on research and development (R&D Block Exemption), 693, 695–696
  Block Exemption Regulation on technology transfer (TTBER), 693, 694
  concerted practices, 690
  delay generic market entry, 697, 703, 704
  de minimis, 691–692
  dominance, 701–702, 723–725
  EU Merger Control Regulation (EUMR), 709–714

Index

exclusionary conduct, 679, 703–706
individual exemptions, 693
market definition, 685–687
parallel trade, 679, 707–709
pharmaceutical sector, 685–728
pipeline products, 687
reverse payment patent settlements, 697–699
Treaty on the Functioning of the EU (TFEU), 685, 688–709, 714, 715, 718, 721, 724, 726, 727
undertaking, 688–691
Vertical Agreements Block Exemption Order (UK) (VABEO), 718, 728
Vertical Block Exemption Regulation (EU) (VBER), 718
Concerned Member States (CMSs), 15, 33, 39, 90, 92, 93, 95, 151, 168–172, 175, 176, 227, 429, 436–439, 443, 572, 614, 657
Conditional Marketing Authorisations (CMA), 183–200, 698, 704, 707, 718–727
Confidential information, 3, 41, 42, 76–77, 85, 165, 166, 466, 619, 769
Conformity assessment procedures, 242, 638–642, 647–649, 653, 655, 736
Consolidated Text. *See* Consolidated Text of the Law on Guarantees and Rational Use of Medicines and Medical Devices, approved by the Royal Legislative Decree 1/2015, of 24 July.
Contract research organisation (CRO), 80, 107, 108, 116, 125, 144, 761, 762
Co-ordination Group for Mutual Recognition and Decentralised Procedures Human (CMD(H)), 26, 27, 31, 33, 171, 172, 176, 385, 414, 416
Copyright, 41, 42, 74, 75

Coronavirus (COVID-19), 188–189, 422, 426, 440, 443, 729–733, 735, 744
Council for International Organisation of Medical Sciences (CIOMS), 364, 419, 622, 628
Court of first instance (CFI), 61
CP. *See* Centralised procedures (CP)
CPMP. *See* Committee for Proprietary Medicinal Products (now the CHMP)
CRF. *See* Case report form (CRF)
Criteria for orphan designation, 492, 494–506, 510, 524, 529
CRO. *See* Contract research organisation (CRO)
CTDoc. *See* Common technical document (CTDoc)
CTFG. *See* Clinical Trials Facilitation and Coordination Group of the Heads of Medicines Agency (CTFG)
CTIS. *See* Clinical Trials Information System (CTIS)
CTR. *See* Clinical Trials Regulation (CTR)
CVMP. *See* Committee for Medicinal Products for Veterinary Use (CVMP)

D

Database rights, 41, 74–75
Data protection
  accountability, 779–780
  anonymised data, 754–756
  automated decision, 784
  breach reporting, 778–779
  clinical trials, 759–762
  compatible purpose, 772–774
  confidentiality, 768–769
  consent, 767–771, 787
  controller, 756–763
  data concerning health, 752–753
  data minimisation, 776–778

Index

data protection principles, 763
data subject, 780–784
data subject rights, 780–784
data transfer, 784–786
erasure, 783–784
fairness, 774–776
General Data Protection Regulation (GDPR), 747–749
legitimate interest, 765–767
marketing, 786–788
marketing exclusivity, 469, 484, 485
personal data, 749–756
processing agreements, 762
processor, 756–763
pseudonymised data, 753–754
security, 778–779
soft opt-in, 787–788
storage, 776–778
transparency, 774–776
withdrawal of consent, 770–771
DCD. *See* Developmental co-ordination disorder (DCD)
DCP. *See* Decentralised procedures (DCP)
Decentralised procedures (DCP)
application, 172
dispute, 172
Deferrals, 126, 30, 127, 206, 250, 257–258, 260, 275
Derivations, 482
Design rights, 41, 42, 75–76
Developmental co-ordination disorder (DCD), 359, 360
DG. *See* Directorate General (DG)
DGCBF. *See* Directorate General of Basic Services of the National Health System and Pharmacy of the Spanish Ministry of Health
DGCCRF. *See* Trading, Consumer Affairs and Fraud Control (DGCCRF)
Direct to Customer (DTC), 281
Directives, 305–308, 375–376, 567–568, 587–588, 597–598, 696
Directorate General (DG), 23–25, 188, 710
Directorate General (DG) enterprise, 188
Distafarma, 328
DPD. *See* Data protection directive (DPD)
DTC. *See* Direct to Customer (DTC)
Duty to place product on market, 265

E

ECJ. *See* European Court of Justice (ECJ)
eCTDoc. *See* Electronic Common Technical Documents (eCTDoc)
EDMA. *See* European Diagnostic Manufacturer's Association (EDMA)
EDQM. *See* European Directorate for the Quality of Medicines (EDQM)
EFPIA. *See* European Federation of Pharmaceutical Industries and Associations (EFPIA)
Electronic Common Technical Documents (eCTDoc), 38
EMEA. *See* European Medicines Agency (EMEA)
Emergency situations, 96, 187–189, 617
EN. *See* European Standards (EN)
EPARs. *See* European Public Assessment Reports (EPARs)
Epidemic, 729–744
Essential similarity, 467, 474–480, 667
Establishing Dominance under Article 102 TFEU, 701–702
Ethical Committees, 90–93
EudraCT. *See* European Database of clinical trials (EudraCT)
EudraVigilance Clinical Trial Module (EVCTM), 138
EudraVigilance Database Management System (EVDBMS), 388
European Commission, 23–26, 480, 519–521

Index

European Court of Justice (ECJ), 7, 207, 280, 462, 659
European Database of clinical trials (EudraCT), 38, 108, 111, 112, 128, 139, 267
European Directorate for the Quality of Medicines (EDQM), 34, 155, 156, 181, 619
European Federation of Pharmaceutical Industries and Associations (EFPIA
code, 280, 281, 289, 290, 332, 334, 335, 341, 746
European Medicines Agency (EMEA), 5, 19, 32, 64, 81, 145, 147, 184, 238, 247, 281, 363, 422, 434, 449, 461, 491, 541, 576, 586, 604, 628, 629, 657, 729,
European Patent Office (EPO), 8, 43, 45, 46, 48–52, 55, 58, 60, 201, 202, 235, 236, 244
European Public Assessment Reports (EPARs), 27, 166, 196, 524
European reference medicinal product, 470–474
European Standards (EN), 736
European Union (EU)
law, regulations, 14
pharmaceutical legislation, reform of, 14
risk management plan (EU-RMP), 373, 413, 620
treaty, 35
EU-UK Trade and Cooperation Agreement (TCA), 2–4, 719
EVCTM. See EudraVigilance Clinical Trial Module (EVCTM)
EVDBMS. See EudraVigilance Database Management System (EVDBMS)
Exceptional Circumstances, Marketing Authorisation granted in, 185, 197–198
Exhaustion of patent rights, 669–670

Extension for new indications for well-established substances, 487–488
Extension for new therapeutic indication, 485–487

F

Farmaindustria, 332–336
FIM trials. See First-in-man (FIM) trials
First-in-man (FIM) trials, 80, 118–121
Fixed combination medicinal products, criteria for approval of, 450–455
Free scientific advice from EMA, 263
French Health Products Safety Agency (AFSSaPS), 408,
French Public Health Code (PHC), 293, 294, 296, 297, 299, 300, 302
Fulfilment of unmet medical need, 191–192

G

GBER. See General Block Exemption (GBER)
GCP. See Good clinical practice (GCP)
General Block Exemption (GBER), 715–717
General Data Protection Regulation (GDPR), 747–749
General Practice Research Database (GPRD), 392
General Sales List (GSL) products, 21
Generic medicinal products, 15, 16, 160, 293, 344, 462, 463, 465, 471, 472, 474–484, 548
Gene therapy medicinal products, 451, 585, 587, 590, 597
Global Advisory Committee on Vaccine Safety (GACVS), 621, 628
Global Marketing Authorisation, 449
GLP. See Good Laboratory Practice (GLP)

Index

GMP. *See* Good manufacturing practice (GMP)
Good clinical practice (GCP), 33, 38, 81, 100–103, 105–108, 112, 114, 118, 129, 133–136, 141, 396–398, 586
Good clinical practice (GCP) inspections, 105, 107–108, 133–136, 396, 397
Good Laboratory Practice (GLP), 396, 398
Good manufacturing practice (GMP), 5, 33, 86, 103–104, 153, 365, 396, 575, 586, 598, 680
GPRD. *See* General Practice Research Database (GPRD)
Grouping of applications, 433–434
GSL products. *See* General Sales List (GSL) products
Guidance on Advertising of Human-Use medicinal products dated in April 2016, 329, 330
Guideline on good pharmacovigilance practices (GVP) module, 622–623, 629
Guidelines, 37–39, 120–121, 181, 199–200, 275–277, 410, 418–419, 430–432, 458–459, 531–533, 612, 628–630, 726–728, 735, 789–801
Guidelines for the advertising of medicinal products for human use to the public, 324
GVP. *See* Good Pharmacovigilance Practice (GVP)

H

Heads of Agencies for Human Medicines (HMA-h), 32
Heads of Agencies for Veterinary Medicines (HMA-v), 32
Heads of Medicines Agencies (HMA), 32, 171, 370, 386, 733

Herbal and Traditional Herbal Medicinal Products
  manufacturing and quality, 576
  safety and efficacy, 575–576
Herbal medicinal products, 18–19, 559–582
History of EU pharmaceutical legislation, 14, 37, 148, 281, 341, 546, 562, 563, 568, 585, 595
HIV. *See* Human immunodeficiency virus (HIV)
HMA. *See* Heads of Medicines Agencies (HMA)
HMA-h. *See* Heads of Agencies for Human Medicines (HMA-h)
HMA-v. *See* Heads of Agencies for Veterinary Medicines (HMA-v)
HMPC. *See* Committee for Herbal Medicinal Products (HMPC)
Homeopathic medicinal products, 18, 562–568
  current legislative framework, 563
  legal history of, 562–563
  simplified registration procedure, 561–563, 565–567, 572
Horizontal mergers, 712, 727
Human immunodeficiency virus (HIV), 161, 168, 221, 448
Hybrid abridged procedures, 463, 476–478, 480, 483, 490
Hybrid procedure, 476, 482–483

I

IB. *See* Investigator's Brochure (IB)
ICH design space concept, 426–427
ICSR. *See* Individual Case Safety Report (ICSR)
IEC. *See* Independent Ethics Committee (IEC)
IFPMA. *See* International Federation of Pharmaceutical Manufacturers Associations (IFPMA)
Immunogenicity, 432, 537, 540, 555, 607–612

Index

Immunological medicinal products, 21, 535, 540, 617, 618, 628
IMP. *See* Investigational medicinal product (IMP)
Independent Ethics Committee (IEC), 101, 102, 106
Individual case safety report (ICSR), 111, 113, 138, 365, 412
Influenza vaccine, 38, 187, 366, 427, 438-441, 443, 604, 682, 739
Informed consent, 86, 87, 89, 91, 93-96, 98, 101, 102, 106, 117, 124, 132, 133, 143, 462, 463, 471, 476, 489, 608, 737, 769, 77094, 96, 117, 462
INN. *See* International non-proprietary name [for a drug]
Institutional Review Board (IRB), 102, 106
Insufficient return on investment criterion, 496, 499-501, 523
Intellectual property rights, 41-77
International Conference of Drug Regulatory Authorities (ICDRA), 34, 69
International Conference on Harmonisation of the Technical Requirements for Registration, 12-13, 34-35, 88
International Federation of Pharmaceutical Manufacturers Associations (IFPMA), 280, 340, 341
International non-proprietary name [for a drug] (INN), 68-72, 152, 155, 156, 166, 284, 379, 380, 458, 524, 538, 554, 555
International Society of Paediatric and Adolescent Diabetes (ISPAD), 632
Investigational medicinal product (IMP), 88, 103, 104, 106, 109-111, 114, 126, 137, 141, 365, 367, 370-372, 392

Investigator, 104-111, 127, 372
Investigator's Brochure (IB), 86, 88, 92, 106, 111, 126, 127, 129, 423-425, 429, 433-435, 437-439, 441, 444, 445
In vitro diagnostic medical devices (IVDMD), 22, 237, 632, 633, 641, 644-651, 653, 655
  medical devices for self-testing, 648
IRB. *See* Institutional Review Board (IRB)
ISPAD. *See* International Society of Paediatric and Adolescent Diabetes (ISPAD)
Italian Medicines Agency (AIFA), 309, 311

L

LEEM. *See* French Pharmaceutical Companies Association (LEEM)
Line extensions, 113, 265, 385, 471-473, 475-478, 484-489

M

MABEL. *See* Minimal anticipated biological effect (MABEL)
Maintenance and Support Services Organisation (MSSO), 381
Market and data exclusivity, 449, 469
Marketing Authorisation (MA)
  holder (MAH), 377-378, 392-393
  vaccines, 603-630
Market surveillance measures, biological medicinal products
  changes, manufacturing process, 543-544
  pharmacovigilance requirements, 513
Maximum residue limits (MRLs), 28, 38
Me-betters, 548
MEDDEV. *See* Commission Guideline relating to Medical Device Directions (MEDDEV)

MedDRA. *See* Medical Dictionary for Regulatory Authorities (MedDRA)
Medical devices
 advertising, 297–298, 649–650, 656
 borderline products, 651–652
 CE-marking, 323
 classification, 652
 conformity assessment procedure, 638–642, 647–649, 655, 735–736
 definition, 22–23, 633–634, 645–646, 651
 essential requirements for marketing, 647
 information supplied, 636, 648
 in vitro diagnostic devices, 21–22
 labelling, 574–575
 placing on the market, 645
 post-marketing surveillance, 620–625
 registration, 642, 654–655
 software as medical device, 635, 653–654
 UKCA-marking, 655
 vigilance procedure, 643–644, 656
Medical Dictionary for Regulatory Authorities (MedDRA), 365, 372, 378, 381, 382, 384
Medical plausibility, 496, 501
Medicinal products for human use, 279–361
Medicines and Healthcare products Regulatory Authority (MHRA), 129–131, 135–136, 138, 347, 349–350
Merger Control Procedure, 710
Merger Control Regulation, 709–714
MHRA. *See* Medicines and Healthcare products Regulatory Authority (MHRA)
Minimal anticipated biological effect (MABEL), 121
MRLs. *See* Maximum residue limits (MRLs)
MRP. *See* Mutual recognition procedure (MRP)
MSSO. *See* Maintenance and Support Services Organisation (MSSO)
Mutual Recognition Facilitation Group (the forerunner to the CMD(h)), 33
Mutual recognition procedure (MRP)
 application process, 169–170
 dispute procedure, 170

N

National law and interface with EU directives, 15–16
National procedure, 13, 32, 33, 36, 70, 149, 151, 159, 169, 172–173, 175–177, 179, 441, 443, 566, 567, 668
New active substance, 154–155, 160, 166, 180, 242, 243, 347, 390, 451, 453, 470, 475, 481, 483–484, 538, 613
NOAL. *See* No observable adverse effect level (NOAL)
NOEL. *See* No observable effect level (NOEL)
Non-horizontal mergers, 712–713
Non-prescription medicines, 20–21, 289, 309, 310, 324, 327, 328, 335, 489
Non-price based exclusionary conduct, 679, 703–706
No observable adverse effect level (NOAL), 119
No observable effect level (NOEL), 119, 121
Northern Ireland, 5, 8, 179, 180, 199, 243–245, 272, 412–416, 418, 446, 556, 583, 601, 650, 651, 654, 655, 719, 726, 746
Notice to Applicants (NTA), 37, 38, 150, 154, 168, 181, 194, 428, 448–450, 459, 473, 477, 480, 482, 483, 489, 573

Index

Notice to local authorities, 662
NTA. *See* Notice to Applicants (NTA)

O

ODR. *See* Orphan drugs regulation (ODR)
Official Journal of the European Communities, 37
Optional scope (centralised procedure), 160
Orphan designation, transfer of, 523–524
Orphan drugs
  market exclusivity review process, 522–523
  pre application notice and meeting, 493
  regulation (ODR), 492, 494–497, 499, 508, 511, 512, 514, 517–519, 522, 523, 526–528
Orphan drugs regulation (ODR), 492, 494–497, 499, 508, 511, 512, 514, 517–519, 522, 523, 526–528
Orphan medicinal products, 189, 491–533
  marketing authorisation, 189, 491, 493, 520, 521, 531
Orphan medicines (application contents and format), 494
OTC. *See* Over-the-counter (OTC)
Over-the-counter (OTC)
  medicines, 283–285, 289, 290, 292, 352, 355, 378
  products, advertising, 280
Ownership, 43

P

Paediatric Committee (PDCO), 29–30, 249–250
Paediatric investigation plans (PIP), 29, 30, 36, 86, 91, 205, 249, 251, 262, 263, 275, 277, 520, 521

Paediatric medicines
  incentives and rewards, 247, 249, 254, 270, 271, 276
  penalties, 266–267
  post-approval obligations, 265–266
  product discontinuation, 265–266
Paediatric Regulation, 17, 37, 248–249, 270, 276, 520, 526, 527
Paediatric research, 267–270
Paediatric symbol, 266
Paediatric use, 30, 247, 248, 250, 256, 263–265, 268, 276, 391, 532
  Marketing Authorisation (PUMA), 250, 259, 263–265, 269, 391
PAES. *See* Post-authorisation efficacy studies (PAES)
PAGB. *See* Proprietary Association of Great Britain (PAGB)
Pandemics
  advance purchase agreements, 605, 729, 739
  clinical trials, 737–738
  compassionate use, 736–737
  Coronavirus Response Team, 732–733
  COVID-19, 188–189
  definition, 730
  healthcare personnel, 740–741
  Inclusive Vaccine Alliance, 739
  market access, 733–737
  market surveillance, 735–736
  medicine shortages, 733–734
  vaccine development strategy, 743–744
  Vaccine Taskforce (UK), 742
Parallel distributors, licences for, 659–660
Parallel imports
  quality control, 663
  simplified procedure, 665–667
Parallel trade
  patent rights, 668–673
  and trade mark law, 673–678
PASS. *See* Post-authorisation safety studies (PASS)

PAT. *See* Process analytical technology (PAT)
Patent Cooperation Treaty (PCT) application, 43
Patentability and scope of protection, 45–48
Patents
 European, 44–49
 pharmaceutical, 45, 50–56, 209, 721
 unitary patent system, 7, 43, 57–63, 234–243
Pay-for-delay, 697, 721–723, 726, 799
PDCO. *See* Paediatric Committee (PDCO)
Periodic safety update reports (PSURs), 194, 365, 383–386, 409–410, 412, 414–415, 418, 599, 643
Persons placing medical devices on the market, 643
Pharmaceutical patents, 45, 50–56, 209, 721
Pharmaceutical sector inquiry, 697–700, 703
Pharmacodynamic (PD), 79, 81, 121, 123, 432, 452–454, 456, 610–611, 743
Pharmacokinetic (PK), 79, 121, 248, 249, 253, 255, 272, 428, 432, 452–456, 487, 514, 546, 556, 610–611, 616, 743
Pharmacovigilance, 6, 109–111, 137–138, 157, 265, 363–419, 543, 620–625, 627
 Inspection Action Group (PIAG), 401
 inspections, 33, 376, 381, 387, 386–398, 400–401, 406, 418
 PhV IWG, 397
 requirements, 367, 398, 412, 543
 systems, 6, 147, 148, 157, 364–365, 372, 373, 387, 387, 390, 396, 401, 402, 404–408, 410, 620, 623, 627
 working party, 281, 387, 394, 397

PHC. *See* French Public Health Code (PHC)
PIP. *See* Paediatric investigation plans (PIP)
Plasma-derived medicinal products, 116, 541–543
PMCPA. *See* Prescription Medicines Code of Practice Authority (PMCPA)
Post-authorisation pharmacovigilance, 363, 364, 365, 374, 375, 386, 396
Pre-authorisation pharmacovigilance, 367–372
Post-authorisation efficacy studies (PAES), 406, 408–409
Post-authorisation safety of vaccines, 621–622
Prescription Medicines Code of Practice Authority (PMCPA), 349, 351–354
Prescription only products, advertising of, 289–2790
Prevalence criterion, 496–499
Price-based exclusionary conduct, 679, 703–706
Process analytical technology (PAT), 427
Products authorised through mutual recognition, 436–439
Product-specific requirements, biopharmaceuticals, 541–543
Proprietary Association of Great Britain (PAGB)
 Consumer Code, 354, 355
 Medicines Advertising Codes for Traditional Herbal Medicines, 354
 professional code, 291, 354–356
Protection of data storage requirements, 116–118
PSURs. *See* Periodic safety update reports (PSURs)

Q

QbD. *See* Quality by design (QbD)
QP. *See* Qualified person (QP)
Qualified Person PhV, 364, 365, 369. 372, 373, 375–377, 392, 398, 400–406
Qualified person (QP), 88, 100, 103, 104, 154, 157, 326, 365, 372, 373, 375, 433, 740
Quality by design (QbD), 426, 427, 430
Quality risk management, 427

R

Radiopharmaceuticals, 20
RD 1416/1994, 325–331
Reference Member State (RMS), 33, 151, 168–172, 175, 176, 230, 378, 396, 399, 429, 433, 436, 437, 438, 443, 485, 487, 614
Registration of trademarks, 64–67
Regulatory issues with pharmaceutical names, 68–72
Relevance of each active substance of a combination product, 457
Renal cell cancer, 185
Repackaging, 660, 664, 674–678, 682–683
Reporting of adverse reactions, 377–383
Requirements for a CMA, 190–192
Requirements for marketing approval of fixed combination medicinal products, 450–455
Research, development and innovation (R&D&I), 13, 484, 716, 717
Responsible pharmacist, 296
Reverse payment agreements (Pay-For-Delay), 721–722
Risk benefit balance/ratio, 27, 96, 169, 187, 190, 366, 383, 387, 392, 461, 566, 620
RMS. *See* Reference Member State; Reference Member State (RMS)

S

SBPs. *See* Similar biotherapeutic products (SBPs)
Scientific advice working party (SAWP), 263, 511–512
Self-regulation of advertising, 282
Seriously debilitating diseases/life-threatening diseases, 185–187, 382, 617, 646
Significant benefit assumption, 502
Similar biological medicinal products, 158, 181, 390, 430, 431, 462, 474, 545, 547, 549
Similar medicinal products, 56, 492, 513–514, 519, 548
Small and medium enterprises (SMEs), 26, 60, 151, 174, 234, 264, 381, 382, 512, 528, 530, 585, 594, 600–602, 716, 717
SmPC. *See* Summary of product characteristics (SmPC)
SOC. *See* System Organ Class (SOC)
Somatic cell therapy medicinal products, 116, 451, 585, 587–588, 590, 597
SOPs. *See* Standard operating procedures (SOPs)
SPC. *See* Supplementary Protection Certificate; Supplementary Protection Certificate (SPC)
Specific mechanism, 670–673, 683, 684
Sponsor, 104–111, 125–127, 138–139, 322
Standard operating procedures (SOPs), 105, 107, 129, 135, 136, 309, 400
State aid, 685, 714–717, 719, 727
Substantive assessment, 711–713
Summary of product characteristics (SmPC), 27, 36, 38, 71, 88, 129, 150, 153, 156–157, 159, 160, 163, 169–174, 176, 194,

Index

197, 239, 262, 267, 281, 283, 318, 325, 333, 336, 339, 355, 365, 374, 377, 378, 383, 391, 396, 402, 422, 426, 448, 487, 503, 511, 520, 543, 598, 614
Supplementary Protection Certificate (SPC), 3, 8, 17, 42, 56, 121, 201–246, 251, 252, 262, 267, 520, 521, 612, 670, 671, 704
incentives, 7
SUSAR. *See* Suspected unexpected serious adverse event (SUSAR)
Suspected unexpected serious adverse event (SUSAR), 38, 110, 111, 137, 138, 367, 369–372, 412, 419
Swedish Association of the Pharmaceutical Industry, 338–339
Swedish Medical Products Agency, 337
Swedish Pharmaceutical Industries Information Practices Committee, 338
System Organ Class (SOC), 381

T

Technology transfer block exemption (TTBER), 693, 694
Television advertising, 286, 342
TFEU. *See* Treaty on the Functioning of the European Union (TFEU)
Trademarks
  pharmaceutical names, 68–72
  registration, 64–67
Trading, Consumer Affairs and Fraud Control (DGCCRF), 301, 302
Traditional herbal medicinal products
  labelling, package leaflet and advertising, 574–575
  legislative framework, 570–571
Traditional Use Registration Application Procedure, 572–574

Treaty on the Functioning of the European Union (TFEU), 688–707
Trial Amendments and Terminations, 138–141
Trial authorisation, 2, 80, 83, 100, 104, 133, 139, 396
Trial data, 4, 102, 105, 112–118, 126, 174, 189, 754, 761
Trial master file/essential documents, 113–114
TRIPS Agreement, 49, 50, 76
TTBER. *See* Technology transfer block exemption (TTBER)
Type II variation, 416, 417, 425, 426, 429, 434, 435, 438, 439, 440, 442, 445, 624
Types IA and IB variation, 423–425
Type IA_{IN} variation, 424

U

UK GDPR, 746, 647, 773, 784
UK Intellectual Property Office (UKIPO), 6, 53, 64, 210, 224, 231, 239–241, 244, 260, 261
UKIPO. *See* UK Intellectual Property Office (UKIPO)
Unified Patent Court (UPC), 7, 57–63, 202, 234–237
Unitary patent system, 7, 43, 57–63, 234–237
Urgent safety restriction (USR), 390, 395, 403, 423, 442
US Food and Drug Administration (FDA), 6, 11, 180, 255, 269, 276, 381, 406, 494, 609, 622
USR. *See* Urgent safety restriction

V

Vaccines
  developments of, 605–612
  European Medicines Agency (EMA), 608

Index

influenza, 187
marketing authorisation, 421–446
official control authority batch release, 617–620
post-marketing surveillance, 620–625
Vaccines Working Party (VWP), 604–605, 607, 630
Validity (DCP), 171–172, 175
Variations
  application procedures, 432–443
  applications for biological medicinal products, 430–432
  application, substantive requirements, 429–432
  centrally authorised products, 439–441
  change of supply status, 488–489
  changes in pharmaceutical form, 428
  changes in strength, 428–429
  changes in the package/label, 660–661
  changes not requiring a variation, 422
  deviations, 107, 132, 196, 254, 446, 597, 729, 738
  esters, 16, 203, 204, 233, 480, 482, 483
  ethers, 16, 480, 482, 483
  extension guideline, 428
  isomers, 16, 154, 480, 482–484
  legislation, 422
  mixtures, 154, 480, 482, 483
  quality guidelines, 431
  reason for, 421–422
  regulation, 430–432
  safety and efficacy requirements, 431–432
  salts, 16, 207, 233, 240, 478–480, 482–484
  same pharmaceutical form, 428, 481
  urgent safety restrictions (USR), 442

Verband der Diagnostica-Industrie e.V, 650
Vertical Agreements Block Exemption Order (VABEO) (UK), 718
Vertical Block Exemption Regulation (VBER) (EU), 718
Veterinary medicinal products, 415, 28, 33, 38, 154, 228, 238, 239, 292, 419, 421, 438, 440, 543, 628, 794

W

Waivers, 233, 246, 257, 274
Web application of SMEs to register for pharmacovigilance, 382
WHO. *See* World Health Organisation (WHO)
WHO Conference of Drug Regulatory Authorities (ICDRA), 34, 69
Withdrawal of the application, 166
World Health Organisation (WHO), 26, 34, 68, 69, 72, 124, 155, 187, 188, 363, 387, 390, 392, 419, 459, 539, 607, 609, 612, 621, 622, 626, 628, 630, 632, 730, 732, 743
World Intellectual Property Organization (WIPO), 44, 64
World Self-Medication Industry (WSMI), 281. *See also* Extensible mark-up language (XML)
WSMI. *See* World Self-Medication Industry (WSMI)

X

XML. *See* Extensible mark-up language (XML)